U0114602

香港基本法

案例彙編 1997-2010

第一條至第四十二條

李浩然／尹國華——[編著]

自序

編撰本書的目的，是希望令大眾普及對《基本法》的認識。

《基本法》是確保“一國兩制”能夠成功實踐的重要基石。如果把建設特別行政區比喻為建設一棟高樓大廈的話，兩者的關係就好比是，《基本法》本身的條文和起草過程是樓的地基，保證了大樓能夠往上建設。而與《基本法》相關的日常運作，構成了無數案例，這些案例就是在建設上面的樓層。筆者較早前出版的《香港基本法起草過程概覽》集中研究前者，而本書則把焦點放在後者。兩本書實際上是一脈相承的。

本書梳理回歸後首十三年這第一個樓層的發展，包括涉及《基本法》的案例，以及通過司法運作如何充實《基本法》的內容和面貌。

基本法和相關的案例關乎憲政安排，十分複雜。不單涉及實體法，還有不少的法理考慮，包括社會學和歷史學等等。我倆分別從事學術和實務工作，本書希望能夠結合兩者，在給讀者講案例的同時，把法庭的這些理念和分析思考與讀者分享。

《基本法》對香港影響很大，與法治和市民的生活息息相關。回歸以來，已經出現了大量以《基本法》作為基礎進行申請的訴訟。本書努力以深入淺出的方法，把這些案例介紹給讀者。希望讓大家從認識案件，到理解個人權利。這便是本案例書期望能夠達到的目標。

筆者在挑選案例時，選擇與一般市民生活有密切關係，或者是大眾所關心的題目，例如民選立法會議員的案件、政制上的公平，以及對民主的理解問題等等。本書會把法庭如何思考至作出判決的司法過程展現給讀者。

對於案例的選擇，不同人可能會有不同的傾向和考慮。本書並非工具書，所以難免會有遺漏，筆者期望繼續豐富完善。

本書得以面世，全賴多方朋友的支持。包括香港三聯書店和清華大學法學院的各位同仁等等，在此特別致謝。

李浩然、尹國華

目錄

（以《中華人民共和國香港特別行政區基本法》為索引）

第十條	香港特別行政區除懸掛中華人民共和國國旗和國徽外，還可使用香港特別行政區區旗和區徽。 香港特別行政區的區旗是五星花蕊的紫荊花紅旗。 香港特別行政區的區徽，中間是五星花蕊的紫荊花，周圍寫有"中華人民共和國香港特別行政區"和英文"香港"。
第十一條	根據中華人民共和國憲法第三十一條，香港特別行政區的制度和政策，包括社會、經濟制度，有關保障居民的基本權利和自由的制度，行政管理、立法和司法方面的制度，以及有關政策，均以本法的規定為依據。 香港特別行政區立法機關制定的任何法律，均不得同本法相抵觸。

第二章 ｜ 中央和香港特別行政區的關係

第十二條	香港特別行政區是中華人民共和國的一個享有高度自治權的地方行政區域，直轄於中央人民政府。
第十三條	中央人民政府負責管理與香港特別行政區有關的外交事務。 中華人民共和國外交部在香港設立機構處理外交事務。 中央人民政府授權香港特別行政區依照本法自行處理有關的對外事務。
第十四條	中央人民政府負責管理香港特別行政區的防務。 香港特別行政區政府負責維持香港特別行政區的社會治安。 中央人民政府派駐香港特別行政區負責防務的軍隊不干預香港特別行政區的地方事務。香港特別行政區政府在必要時，可向中央人民政府請求駐軍協助維持社會治安和救助災害。 駐軍人員除須遵守全國性的法律外，還須遵守香港特別行政區的法律。 駐軍費用由中央人民政府負擔。
第十五條	中央人民政府依照本法第四章的規定任命香港特別行政區行政長官和行政機關的主要官員。
第十六條	香港特別行政區享有行政管理權，依照本法的有關規定自行處理香港特別行政區的行政事務。
第十七條	香港特別行政區享有立法權。 香港特別行政區的立法機關制定的法律須報全國人民代表大會常務委員會備案。備案不影響該法律的生效。 全國人民代表大會常務委員會在徵詢其所屬的香港特別行政區基本法委員會後，如認為香港特別行政區立法機關制定的任何法律不符合本法關於中央管理的事務及中央和香港特別行政區的關係的條款，可將有關法律發回，但不作修改。經全國人民代表大會常務委員會發回的法律立即失效。該法律的失效，除香港特別行政區的法律另有規定外，無溯及力。

第十八條	在香港特別行政區實行的法律為本法以及本法第八條規定的香港原有法律和香港特別行政區立法機關制定的法律。 全國性法律除列於本法附件三者外，不在香港特別行政區實施。凡列於本法附件三之法律，由香港特別行政區在當地公佈或立法實施。 全國人民代表大會常務委員會在徵詢其所屬的香港特別行政區基本法委員會和香港特別行政區政府的意見後，可對列於本法附件三的法律作出增減，任何列入附件三的法律，限於有關國防、外交和其他按本法規定不屬於香港特別行政區自治範圍的法律。 全國人民代表大會常務委員會決定宣佈戰爭狀態或因香港特別行政區內發生香港特別行政區政府不能控制的危及國家統一或安全的動亂而決定香港特別行政區進入緊急狀態，中央人民政府可發佈命令將有關全國性法律在香港特別行政區實施。
P.059	**Salt & Light Development Inc. 及其他 對 交大銘泰軟體產業有限公司；** **Salt & Light Development Inc. 及其他及博翰專業翻譯有限公司 對 交大銘泰軟體產業有限公司**
第十九條	香港特別行政區享有獨立的司法權和終審權。 香港特別行政區法院除繼續保持香港原有法律制度和原則對法院審判權所作的限制外，對香港特別行政區所有的案件均有審判權。 香港特別行政區法院對國防、外交等國家行為無管轄權。香港特別行政區法院在審理案件中遇有涉及國防、外交等國家行為的事實問題，應取得行政長官就該等問題發出的證明文件，上述文件對法院有約束力。行政長官在發出證明文件前，須取得中央人民政府的證明書。
P.069	**吳嘉玲、吳丹丹 對 入境事務處處長；徐能權 對 入境事務處處長；入境事務處處長 對 張麗華**
第二十條	香港特別行政區可享有全國人民代表大會和全國人民代表大會常務委員會及中央人民政府授予的其他權力。
第二十一條	香港特別行政區居民中的中國公民依法參與國家事務的管理。 根據全國人民代表大會確定的名額和代表產生辦法，由香港特別行政區居民中的中國公民在香港選出香港特別行政區的全國人民代表大會代表，參加最高國家權力機關的工作。
第二十二條	中央人民政府所屬各部門、各省、自治區、直轄市均不得干預香港特別行政區根據本法自行管理的事務。 中央各部門、各省、自治區、直轄市如需在香港特別行政區設立機構，須徵得香港特別行政區政府同意並經中央人民政府批准。 中央各部門、各省、自治區、直轄市在香港特別行政區設立的一切機構及其人員均須遵守香港特別行政區的法律。 中國其他地區的人進入香港特別行政區須辦理批准手續，其中進入香港特別行政區定居的人數由中央人民政府主管部門徵求香港特別行政區政府的意見後確定。 香港特別行政區可在北京設立辦事機構。
P.085	**劉港榕等 17 人 對 入境事務處處長**
P.105	**吳新穩作為吳家豪、吳家煒、吳佳敏的父親及起訴監護人 對 入境事務處處長**
第二十三條	香港特別行政區應自行立法禁止任何叛國、分裂國家、煽動叛亂、顛覆中央人民政府及竊取國家機密的行為，禁止外國的政治性組織或團體在香港特別行政區進行政治活動，禁止香港特別行政區的政治性組織或團體與外國的政治性組織或團體建立聯繫。

第三章 | 居民的基本權利和義務

第二十六條	香港特別行政區永久居民依法享有選舉權和被選舉權。
P.263	**莫泰基 對 香港特區政府政制事務局、選舉管理委員會及選舉署**
第二十七條	香港居民享有言論、新聞、出版的自由，結社、集會、游行、示威的自由，組織和參加工會、罷工的權利和自由。
P.267	**民主黨 對 律政司司長**
P.279	**Brian Alfred Hall 對 律政司司長（代表懲教署署長）**
P.290	**香港特別行政區 對 吳恭劭、利建潤**
P.300	**香港特別行政區 對 Pearce, Matt James**
P.308	**事務律師 對 香港律師會**
P.315	**鄺國熙醫生 對 香港醫務委員會**
P.329	**香港律師會 對 一名事務律師**
P.343	**楊美雲等 8 人 對 香港特別行政區**
P.363	**律政司司長 對 東方報業集團有限公司等**
第二十八條	香港居民的人身自由不受侵犯。 香港居民不受任意或非法逮捕、拘留、監禁。禁止任意或非法搜查居民的身體、剝奪或限制居民的人身自由。禁止對居民施行酷刑、任意或非法剝奪居民的生命。
P.381	**香港特別行政區 對 關健森**
P.386	**Lau Cheong 及 Lau Wong 對 香港特別行政區**
P.406	**李元虹 對 香港特別行政區政府**
P.410	**香港特別行政區 對 蕭逸良**
第二十九條	香港居民的住宅和其他房屋不受侵犯。禁止任意或非法搜查、侵入居民的住宅和其他房屋。
P.415	**香港特別行政區 對 林東**
第三十條	香港居民的通訊自由和通訊秘密受法律的保護。除因公共安全和追查刑事犯罪的需要，由有關機關依照法律程序對通訊進行檢查外，任何部門或個人不得以任何理由侵犯居民的通訊自由和通訊秘密。
P.419	**民主黨 對 律政司司長**
P.421	**香港特別行政區 對 李萬德及陳財成**
P.437	**毛玉萍 對 律政司司長**
第三十一條	香港居民有在香港特別行政區境內遷徙的自由，有移居其他國家和地區的自由。香港居民有旅行和出入境的自由。有效旅行證件的持有人，除非受到法律制止，可自由離開香港特別行政區，無需特別批准。

第三十九條	《公民權利和政治權利國際公約》、《經濟、社會與文化權利的國際公約》和國際勞工公約適用於香港的有關規定繼續有效，通過香港特別行政區的法律予以實施。 香港居民享有的權利和自由，除依法規定外不得限制，此種限制不得與本條第一款規定抵觸。
P.591	**梁國雄、馮家強及盧偉明 對 香港特別行政區**
P.618	**Shum Kwok Sher 對 香港特別行政區**
第四十條	"新界"原居民的合法傳統權益受香港特別行政區的保護。
P.633	**陳華 對 坑口鄉事委員會及其他；謝群生 對 八鄉鄉事委員會、律政司司長**
第四十一條	在香港特別行政區境內的香港居民以外的其他人，依法享有本章規定的香港居民的權利和自由。
P.641	**Chu Woan Chyi 等 5 人及香港法輪大法協會 對 入境事務處處長**
P.666	**Pasa Pananille Dizon 對 香港特別行政區**
第四十二條	香港居民和在香港的其他人有遵守香港特別行政區實行的法律的義務。

下列案件另冊收錄

第四章 ｜ 政治體制

	第一節　行政長官
第四十三條	香港特別行政區行政長官是香港特別行政區的首長，代表香港特別行政區。 香港特別行政區行政長官依照本法的規定對中央人民政府和香港特別行政區負責。
第四十四條	香港特別行政區行政長官由年滿四十周歲，在香港通常居住連續滿二十年並在外國無居留權的香港特別行政區永久性居民中的中國公民擔任。
第四十五條	香港特別行政區行政長官在當地通過選舉或協商產生，由中央人民政府任命。 行政長官的產生辦法根據香港特別行政區的實際情況和循序漸進的原則而規定，最終達至由一個有廣泛代表性的提名委員會按民主程序提名後普選產生的目標。 行政長官產生的具體辦法由附件一《香港特別行政區行政長官的產生辦法》規定。
第四十六條	香港特別行政區行政長官任期五年，可連任一次。
第四十七條	香港特別行政區行政長官必須廉潔奉公、盡忠職守。 行政長官就任時應向香港特別行政區終審法院首席法官申報財產，記錄在案。

第四十八條	香港特別行政區行政長官行使下列職權： （一）領導香港特別行政區政府； （二）負責執行本法和依照本法適用於香港特別行政區的其他法律； （三）簽署立法會通過的法案，公佈法律； 簽署立法會通過的財政預算案，將財政預算、決算報中央人民政府備案； （四）決定政府政策和發佈行政命令； （五）提名並報請中央人民政府任命下列主要官員：各司司長、副司長，各局局長，廉政專員，審計署署長，警務處處長，入境事務處處長，海關關長；建議中央人民政府免除上述官員職務； （六）依照法定程序任免各級法院法官； （七）依照法定程序任免公職人員； （八）執行中央人民政府就本法規定的有關事務發出的指令； （九）代表香港特別行政區政府處理中央授權的對外事務和其他事務； （十）批准向立法會提出有關財政收入或支出的動議； （十一）根據安全和重大公共利益的考慮，決定政府官員或其他負責政府公務的人員是否向立法會或其屬下的委員會作證和提供證據； （十二）赦免或減輕刑事罪犯的刑罰； （十三）處理請願、申訴事項。
第四十九條	香港特別行政區行政長官如認為立法會通過的法案不符合香港特別行政區的整體利益，可在三個月內將法案發回立法會重議，立法會如以不少於全體議員三分之二多數再次通過原案，行政長官必須在一個月內簽署公佈或按本法第五十條的規定處理。
第五十條	香港特別行政區行政長官如拒絕簽署立法會再次通過的法案或立法會拒絕通過政府提出的財政預算案或其他重要法案，經協商仍不能取得一致意見，行政長官可解散立法會。 行政長官在解散立法會前，須徵詢行政會議的意見。行政長官在其一任任期內只能解散立法會一次。
第五十一條	香港特別行政區立法會如拒絕批准政府提出的財政預算案，行政長官可向立法會申請臨時撥款。如果由於立法會已被解散而不能批准撥款，行政長官可在選出新的立法會前的一段時期內，按上一財政年度的開支標準，批准臨時短期撥款。
第五十二條	香港特別行政區行政長官如有下列情況之一者必須辭職： （一）因嚴重疾病或其他原因無力履行職務； （二）因兩次拒絕簽署立法會通過的法案而解散立法會，重選的立法會仍以全體議員三分之二多數通過所爭議的原案，而行政長官仍拒絕簽署； （三）因立法會拒絕通過財政預算案或其他重要法案而解散立法會，重選的立法會繼續拒絕通過所爭議的原案。
第五十三條	香港特別行政區行政長官短期不能履行職務時，由政務司長、財政司長、律政司長依次臨時代理其職務。 行政長官缺位時，應在六個月內依本法第四十五條的規定產生新的行政長官。行政長官缺位期間的職務代理，依照上款規定辦理。
第五十四條	香港特別行政區行政會議是協助行政長官決策的機構。

第五十五條	香港特別行政區行政會議的成員由行政長官從行政機關的主要官員、立法會議員和社會人士中委任，其任免由行政長官決定。行政會議成員的任期應不超過委任他的行政長官的任期。 香港特別行政區行政會議成員由在外國無居留權的香港特別行政區永久性居民中的中國公民擔任。 行政長官認為必要時可邀請有關人士列席會議。
第五十六條	香港特別行政區行政會議由行政長官主持。 行政長官在作出重要決策、向立法會提交法案、制定附屬法規和解散立法會前，須徵詢行政會議的意見，但人事任免、紀律制裁和緊急情況下採取的措施除外。 行政長官如不採納行政會議多數成員的意見，應將具體理由記錄在案。
第五十七條	香港特別行政區設立廉政公署，獨立工作，對行政長官負責。
第五十八條	香港特別行政區設立審計署，獨立工作，對行政長官負責。
	第二節　行政機關
第五十九條	香港特別行政區政府是香港特別行政區行政機關。
第六十條	香港特別行政區政府的首長是香港特別行政區行政長官。 香港特別行政區政府設政務司、財政司、律政司和各局、處、署。
第六十一條	香港特別行政區的主要官員由在香港通常居住連續滿十五年並在外國無居留權的香港特別行政區永久性居民中的中國公民擔任。
第六十二條	香港特別行政區政府行使下列職權： （一）制定並執行政策； （二）管理各項行政事務； （三）辦理本法規定的中央人民政府授權的對外事務； （四）編制並提出財政預算、決算； （五）擬定並提出法案、議案、附屬法規； （六）委派官員列席立法會並代表政府發言。
第六十三條	香港特別行政區律政司主管刑事檢察工作，不受任何干涉。
第六十四條	香港特別行政區政府必須遵守法律，對香港特別行政區立法會負責：執行立法會通過並已生效的法律；定期向立法會作施政報告；答覆立法會議員的質詢；徵稅和公共開支須經立法會批准。
第六十五條	原由行政機關設立諮詢組織的制度繼續保留。
	第三節　立法機關

第六十六條	香港特別行政區立法會是香港特別行政區的立法機關。
第六十七條	香港特別行政區立法會由在外國無居留權的香港特別行政區永久性居民中的中國公民組成。但非中國籍的香港特別行政區永久性居民和在外國有居留權的香港特別行政區永久性居民也可以當選為香港特別行政區立法會議員，其所佔比例不得超過立法會全體議員的百分之二十。
第六十八條	香港特別行政區立法會由選舉產生。 立法會的產生辦法根據香港特別行政區的實際情況和循序漸進的原則而規定，最終達至全部議員由普選產生的目標。 立法會產生的具體辦法和法案、議案的表決程式由附件二《香港特別行政區立法會的產生辦法和表決程式》規定。
第六十九條	香港特別行政區立法會除第一屆任期為兩年外，每屆任期四年。
第七十條	香港特別行政區立法會如經行政長官依本法規定解散，須於三個月內依本法第六十八條的規定，重行選舉產生。
第七十一條	香港特別行政區立法會主席由立法會議員互選產生。 香港特別行政區立法會主席由年滿四十周歲，在香港通常居住連續滿二十年並在外國無居留權的香港特別行政區永久性居民中的中國公民擔任。
第七十二條	香港特別行政區立法會主席行使下列職權： （一）主持會議； （二）決定議程，政府提出的議案須優先列入議程； （三）決定開會時間； （四）在休會期間可召開特別會議； （五）應行政長官的要求召開緊急會議； （六）立法會議事規則所規定的其他職權。
第七十三條	香港特別行政區立法會行使下列職權： （一）根據本法規定並依照法定程序制定、修改和廢除法律； （二）根據政府的提案，審核、通過財政預算； （三）批准稅收和公共開支； （四）聽取行政長官的施政報告並進行辯論； （五）對政府的工作提出質詢； （六）就任何有關公共利益問題進行辯論； （七）同意終審法院法官和高等法院首席法官的任免； （八）接受香港居民申訴並作出處理； （九）如立法會全體議員的四分之一聯合動議，指控行政長官有嚴重違法或瀆職行為而不辭職，經立法會通過進行調查，立法會可委託終審法院首席法官負責組成獨立的調查委員會，並擔任主席。調查委員會負責進行調查，並向立法會提出報告。如該調查委員會認為有足夠證據構成上述指控，立法會以全體議員三分之二多數通過，可提出彈劾案，報請中央人民政府決定。 （十）在行使上述各項職權時，如有需要，可傳召有關人士出席作證和提供證據。

第七十四條	香港特別行政區立法會議員根據本法規定並依照法定程序提出法律草案，凡不涉及公共開支或政治體制或政府運作者，可由立法會議員個別或聯名提出。凡涉及政府政策者，在提出前必須得到行政長官的書面同意。
第七十五條	香港特別行政區立法會舉行會議的法定人數為不少於全體議員的二分之一。 立法會議事規則由立法會自行制定，但不得與本法相抵觸。
第七十六條	香港特別行政區立法會通過的法案，須經行政長官簽署、公佈，方能生效。
第七十七條	香港特別行政區立法會議員在立法會的會議上發言，不受法律追究。
第七十八條	香港特別行政區立法會議員在出席會議時和赴會途中不受逮捕。
第七十九條	香港特別行政區立法會議員如有下列情況之一，由立法會主席宣告其喪失立法會議員的資格： （一）因嚴重疾病或其他情況無力履行職務； （二）未得到立法會主席的同意，連續三個月不出席會議而無合理解釋者； （三）喪失和放棄香港特別行政區永久性居民的身份； （四）接受政府的委任而出任公務人員； （五）破產或經法庭裁定償還債務而不履行； （六）在香港特別行政區區內或區外被判犯有刑事罪行，判處監禁一個月以上，並經立法會出席會議的議員三分之二通過解除其職務； （七）行為不檢或違反誓言而經立法會出席會議的議員三分之二通過譴責。
	第四節　司法機關
第八十條	香港特別行政區各級法院是香港特別行政區的司法機關，行使香港特別行政區的審判權。
第八十一條	香港特別行政區設立終審法院、高等法院、區域法院、裁判署法庭和其他專門法庭。高等法院設上訴法庭和原訟法庭。 原在香港實行的司法體制，除因設立香港特別行政區終審法院而產生變化外，予以保留。
第八十二條	香港特別行政區的終審權屬於香港特別行政區終審法院。終審法院可根據需要邀請其他普通法適用地區的法官參加審判。
第八十三條	香港特別行政區各級法院的組織和職權由法律規定。
第八十四條	香港特別行政區法院依照本法第十八條所規定的適用於香港特別行政區的法律審判案件，其他普通法適用地區的司法判例可作參考。
第八十五條	香港特別行政區法院獨立進行審判，不受任何干涉，司法人員履行審判職責的行為不受法律追究。

第八十六條	原在香港實行的陪審制度的原則予以保留。
第八十七條	香港特別行政區的刑事訴訟和民事訴訟中保留原在香港適用的原則和當事人享有的權利。 任何人在被合法拘捕後，享有盡早接受司法機關公正審判的權利，未經司法機關判罪之前均假定無罪。
第八十八條	香港特別行政區法院的法官，根據當地法官和法律界及其他方面知名人士組成的獨立委員會推薦，由行政長官任命。
第八十九條	香港特別行政區法院的法官只有在無力履行職責或行為不檢的情況下，行政長官才可根據終審法院首席法官任命的不少於三名當地法官組成的審議庭的建議，予以免職。 香港特別行政區終審法院的首席法官只有在無力履行職責或行為不檢的情況下，行政長官才可任命不少於五名當地法官組成的審議庭進行審議，並可根據其建議，依照本法規定的程式，予以免職。
第九十條	香港特別行政區終審法院和高等法院的首席法官，應由在外國無居留權的香港特別行政區永久性居民中的中國公民擔任。 除本法第八十八條和第八十九條規定的程式外，香港特別行政區終審法院的法官和高等法院首席法官的任命或免職，還須由行政長官徵得立法會同意，並報全國人民代表大會常務委員會備案。
第九十一條	香港特別行政區法官以外的其他司法人員原有的任免制度繼續保持。
第九十二條	香港特別行政區的法官和其他司法人員，應根據其本人的司法和專業才能選用，並可從其他普通法適用地區聘用。
第九十三條	香港特別行政區成立前在香港任職的法官和其他司法人員均可留用，其年資予以保留，薪金、津貼、福利待遇和服務條件不低於原來的標準。 對退休或符合規定離職的法官和其他司法人員，包括香港特別行政區成立前已退休或離職者，不論其所屬國籍或居住地點，香港特別行政區政府按不低於原來的標準，向他們或其家屬支付應得的退休金、酬金、津貼和福利費。
第九十四條	香港特別行政區政府可參照原在香港實行的辦法，作出有關當地和外來的律師在香港特別行政區工作和執業的規定。
第九十五條	香港特別行政區可與全國其他地區的司法機關通過協商依法進行司法方面的聯繫和相互提供協助。
第九十六條	在中央人民政府協助或授權下，香港特別行政區政府可與外國就司法互助關係作出適當安排。
	第五節　區域組織

第九十七條	香港特別行政區可設立非政權性的區域組織，接受香港特別行政區政府就有關地區管理和其他事務的諮詢，或負責提供文化、康樂、環境衛生等服務。
第九十八條	區域組織的職權和組成方法由法律規定。
	第六節　公務人員
第九十九條	在香港特別行政區政府各部門任職的公務人員必須是香港特別行政區永久性居民。本法第一百零一條對外籍公務人員另有規定者或法律規定某一職級以下者不在此限。 公務人員必須盡忠職守，對香港特別行政區政府負責。
第一百條	香港特別行政區成立前在香港政府各部門，包括員警部門任職的公務人員均可留用，其年資予以保留，薪金、津貼、福利待遇和服務條件不低於原來的標準。
第一百零一條	香港特別行政區政府可任用原香港公務人員中的或持有香港特別行政區永久性居民身份證的英籍和其他外籍人士擔任政府部門的各級公務人員，但下列各職級的官員必須由在外國無居留權的香港特別行政區永久性居民中的中國公民擔任：各司司長、副司長，各局局長，廉政專員，審計署署長，警務處處長，入境事務處處長，海關關長。 香港特別行政區政府還可聘請英籍和其他外籍人士擔任政府部門的顧問，必要時並可從香港特別行政區以外聘請合格人員擔任政府部門的專門和技術職務。上述外籍人士只能以個人身份受聘，對香港特別行政區政府負責。
第一百零二條	對退休或符合規定離職的公務人員，包括香港特別行政區成立前退休或符合規定離職的公務人員，不論其所屬國籍或居住地點，香港特別行政區政府按不低於原來的標準向他們或其家屬支付應得的退休金、酬金、津貼和福利費。
第一百零三條	公務人員應根據其本人的資格、經驗和才能予以任用和提升，香港原有關於公務人員的招聘、僱用、考核、紀律、培訓和管理的制度，包括負責公務人員的任用、薪金、服務條件的專門機構，除有關給予外籍人員特權待遇的規定外，予以保留。
第一百零四條	香港特別行政區行政長官、主要官員、行政會議成員、立法會議員、各級法院法官和其他司法人員在就職時必須依法宣誓擁護中華人民共和國香港特別行政區基本法，效忠中華人民共和國香港特別行政區。

第五章 | 經濟

	第一節　財政、金融、貿易和工商業
第一百零五條	香港特別行政區依法保護私人和法人財產的取得、使用、處置和繼承的權利，以及依法徵用私人和法人財產時被徵用財產的所有人得到補償的權利。 徵用財產的補償應相當於該財產當時的實際價值，可自由兌換，不得無故遲延支付。 企業所有權和外來投資均受法律保護。

第一百零六條	香港特別行政區保持財政獨立。 香港特別行政區的財政收入全部用於自身需要，不上繳中央人民政府。 中央人民政府不在香港特別行政區徵稅。
第一百零七條	香港特別行政區的財政預算以量入為出為原則，力求收支平衡，避免赤字，並與本地生產總值的增長率相適應。
第一百零八條	香港特別行政區實行獨立的稅收制度。 香港特別行政區參照原在香港實行的低稅政策，自行立法規定稅種、稅率、稅收寬免和其他稅務事項。
第一百零九條	香港特別行政區政府提供適當的經濟和法律環境，以保持香港和國際金融中心地位。
第一百一十條	香港特別行政區的貨幣金融制度由法律規定。 香港特別行政區政府自行制定貨幣金融政策，保障金融企業和金融市場的經營自由，並依法進行管理和監督。
第一百一十一條	港元為香港特別行政區法定貨幣，繼續流通。 港幣的發行權屬於香港特別行政區政府。港幣的發行須有百分之百的準備金。港幣的發行制度和準備金制度，由法律規定。 香港特別行政區政府，在確知港幣的發行基礎健全和發行安排符合保持港幣穩定的目的的條件下，可授權指定銀行根據法定許可權發行或繼續發行港幣。
第一百一十二條	香港特別行政區不實行外匯管制政策。港幣自由兌換。繼續開放外匯、黃金、證券、期貨等市場。 香港特別行政區政府保障資金的流動和進出自由。
第一百一十三條	香港特別行政區的外匯基金，由香港特別行政區政府管理和支配，主要用於調節港元匯價。
第一百一十四條	香港特別行政區保持自由港地位，除法律另有規定外，不徵收關稅。
第一百一十五條	香港特別行政區實行自由貿易政策，保障貨物、無形財產和資本的流動自由。
第一百一十六條	香港特別行政區為單獨的關稅地區。 香港特別行政區可以"中國香港"的名義參加《關稅和貿易總協定》、關於國際紡織品貿易安排等有關國際組織和國際貿易協定，包括優惠貿易安排。 香港特別行政區所取得的和以前取得仍繼續有效的出口配額、關稅優惠和達成的其他類似安排，全由香港特別行政區享有。

第一百一十七條	香港特別行政區根據當時的產地規則，可對產品簽發產地來源證。
第一百一十八條	香港特別行政區政府提供經濟和法律環境，鼓勵各項投資、技術進步並開發新興產業。
第一百一十九條	香港特別行政區政府制定適當政策，促進和協調製造業、商業、旅遊業、房地產業、運輸業、公用事業、服務性行業、漁農業等各行業的發展，並注意環境保護。
	第二節　土地契約
第一百二十條	香港特別行政區成立以前已批出、決定、或續期的超越一九九七年六月三十日年期的所有土地契約和與土地契約有關的一切權利，均按香港特別行政區的法律繼續予以承認和保護。
第一百二十一條	從一九八五年五月二十七日至一九九七年六月三十日期間批出的，或原沒有續期權利而獲得續期的，超出一九九七年六月三十日年期而不超過二零四七年六月三十日的一切土地契約，承租人從一九九七年七月一日起不補地價，但需每年繳納相當於當日該土地應課差餉租值百分之三的租金。此後，隨應課差餉租值的改變而調整租金。
第一百二十二條	原舊批約地段、鄉村屋地、丁屋地和類似的農村土地，如該土地在一九八四年六月三十日的承租人，或在該日以後批出的丁屋地承租人，其父系為一八九八年在香港的原有鄉村居民，只要該土地的承租人仍為該人或其合法父系繼承人，原定租金維持不變。
第一百二十三條	香港特別行政區成立以後滿期而沒有續期權利的土地契約，由香港特別行政區自行制定法律和政策處理。
	第三節　航運
第一百二十四條	香港特別行政區保持原在香港實行的航運經營和管理體制，包括有關海員的管理制度。 香港特別行政區政府自行規定在航運方面的具體職能和責任。
第一百二十五條	香港特別行政區經中央人民政府授權繼續進行船舶登記，並根據香港特別行政區的法律以“中國香港”的名義頒發有關證件。
第一百二十六條	除外國軍用船隻進入香港特別行政區須經中央人民政府特別許可外，其他船舶可根據香港特別行政區法律進出其港口。
第一百二十七條	香港特別行政區的私營航運及與航運有關的企業和私營集裝箱碼頭，可繼續自由經營。
	第四節　民用航空
第一百二十八條	香港特別行政區政府應提供條件和採取措施，以保持香港的國際和區域航空中心的地位。

第一百二十九條	香港特別行政區繼續實行原在香港實行的民用航空管理制度，並按中央人民政府關於飛機國籍標誌和登記標誌的規定，設置自己的飛機登記冊。 外國國家航空器進入香港特別行政區須經中央人民政府特別許可。
第一百三十條	香港特別行政區自行負責民用航空的日常業務和技術管理，包括機場管理，在香港特別行政區飛行情報區內提供空中交通服務，和履行國際民用航空組織的區域性航行規劃程序所規定的其他職責。
第一百三十一條	中央人民政府經同香港特別行政區政府磋商作出安排，為在香港特別行政區註冊並以香港為主要營業地的航空公司和中華人民共和國的其他航空公司，提供香港特別行政區和中華人民共和國其他地區之間的往返航班。
第一百三十二條	凡涉及中華人民共和國其他地區同其他國家和地區的往返並經停香港特別行政區的航班，和涉及香港特別行政區同其他國家和地區的往返並經停中華人民共和國其他地區航班的民用航空運輸協定，由中央人民政府簽訂。 中央人民政府在簽訂本條第一款所指民用航空運輸協定時，應考慮香港特別行政區的特殊情況和經濟利益，並同香港特別行政區政府磋商。 中央人民政府在同外國政府商談有關本條第一款所指航班的安排時，香港特別行政區政府的代表可作為中華人民共和國政府代表團的成員參加。
第一百三十三條	香港特別行政區政府經中央人民政府具體授權可： （一）續簽或修改原有的民用航空運輸協定和協議； （二）談判簽訂新的民用航空運輸協定，為在香港特別行政區注冊並以香港為主要營業地的航空公司提供航線，以及過境和技術停降權利； （三）同沒有簽訂民用航空運輸協定的外國或地區談判簽訂臨時協定。 不涉及往返、經停中國內地而只往返、經停香港的定期航班，均由本條所指的民用航空運輸協定或臨時協議予以規定。
第一百三十四條	中央人民政府授權香港特別行政區政府： （一）同其他當局商談並簽訂有關執行本法第一百三十三條所指民用航空運輸協定和臨時協議的各項安排； （二）對在香港特別行政區注冊並以香港為主要營業地的航空公司簽發執照； （三）依照本法第一百三十三條所指民用航空運輸協定和臨時協議指定航空公司； （四）對外國航空公司除往返、經停中國內地的航班以外的其他航班簽發許可證。
第一百三十五條	香港特別行政區成立前在香港注冊並以香港為主要營業地的航空公司和與民用航空有關的行業，可繼續經營。
第六章 | 教育、科學、文化、體育、宗教、勞工和社會服務	
第一百三十六條	香港特別行政區政府在原有教育制度的基礎上，自行制定有關教育的發展和改進的政策，包括教育體制和管理、教學語言、經費分配、考試制度、學位制度和承認學歷等政策。 社會團體和私人可依法在香港特別行政區興辦各種教育事業。

第一百三十七條	各類院校均可保留其自主性並享有學術自由，可繼續從香港特別行政區以外招聘教職員和選用教材。宗教組織所辦的學校可繼續提供宗教教育，包括開設宗教課程。 學生享有選擇院校和在香港特別行政區以外求學的自由。
第一百三十八條	香港特別行政區政府自行制定發展中西醫藥和促進醫療衛生服務的政策。社會團體和私人可依法提供各種醫療衛生服務。
第一百三十九條	香港特別行政區政府自行制定科學技術政策，以法律保護科學技術的研究成果、專利和發明創造。 香港特別行政區政府自行確定適用於香港的各類科學、技術標準和規格。
第一百四十條	香港特別行政區政府自行制定文化政策，以法律保護作者在文學藝術創作中所獲得的成果和合法權益。
第一百四十一條	香港特別行政區政府不限制宗教信仰自由，不干預宗教組織的內部事務，不限制與香港特別行政區法律沒有抵觸的宗教活動。 宗教組織依法享有財產的取得、使用、處置、繼承以及接受資助的權利。財產方面的原有權益仍予保持和保護。 宗教組織可按原有辦法繼續興辦宗教院校、其他學校、醫院和福利機構以及提供其他社會服務。 香港特別行政區的宗教組織和教徒可與其他地方的宗教組織和教徒保持和發展關係。
第一百四十二條	香港特別行政區政府在保留原有的專業制度的基礎上，自行制定有關評審各種專業的執業資格的辦法。 在香港特別行政區成立前已取得專業和執業資格者，可依據有關規定和專業守則保留原有的資格。 香港特別行政區政府繼續承認在特別行政區成立前已承認的專業和專業團體，所承認的專業團體可自行審核和頒授專業資格。 香港特別行政區政府可根據社會發展需要並諮詢有關方面的意見，承認新的專業和專業團體。
第一百四十三條	香港特別行政區政府自行制定體育政策。民間體育團體可依法繼續存在和發展。
第一百四十四條	香港特別行政區政府保持原在香港實行的對教育、醫療衛生、文化、藝術、康樂、體育、社會福利、社會工作等方面的民間團體機構的資助政策。原在香港各資助機構任職的人員均可根據原有制度繼續受聘。
第一百四十五條	香港特別行政區政府在原有社會福利制度的基礎上，根據經濟條件和社會需要，自行制定其發展、改進的政策。
第一百四十六條	香港特別行政區從事社會服務的志願團體在不抵觸法律的情況下可自行決定其服務方式。
第一百四十七條	香港特別行政區自行制定有關勞工的法律和政策。

第一百四十八條	香港特別行政區的教育、科學、技術、文化、藝術、體育、專業、醫療衛生、勞工、社會福利、社會工作等方面的民間團體和宗教組織同內地相應的團體和組織的關係，應以互不隸屬、互不干涉和互相尊重的原則為基礎。
第一百四十九條	香港特別行政區的教育、科學、技術、文化、藝術、體育、專業、醫療衛生、勞工、社會福利、社會工作等方面的民間團體和宗教組織可同世界各國、各地區及國際的有關團體和組織保持和發展關係，各該團體和組織可根據需要冠用"中國香港"的名義，參與有關活動。

第七章 | 對外事務

第一百五十條	香港特別行政區政府的代表，可作為中華人民共和國政府代表團的成員，參加由中央人民政府進行的同香港特別行政區直接有關的外交談判。
第一百五十一條	香港特別行政區可在經濟、貿易、金融、航運、通訊、旅遊、文化、體育等領域以"中國香港"的名義，單獨地同世界各國、各地區及有關國際組織保持和發展關係，簽訂和履行有關協議。
第一百五十二條	對以國家為單位參加的、同香港特別行政區有關的、適當領域的國際組織和國際會議，香港特別行政區政府可派遣代表作為中華人民共和國代表團的成員或以中央人民政府和上述有關國際組織或國際會議允許的身份參加，並以"中國香港"的名義發表意見。 香港特別行政區可以"中國香港"的名義參加不以國家為單位參加的國際組織和國際會議。 對中華人民共和國已參加而香港也以某種形式參加了的國際組織，中央人民政府將採取必要措施使香港特別行政區以適當形式繼續保持在這些組織中的地位。 對中華人民共和國尚未參加而香港已以某種形式參加的國際組織，中央人民政府將根據需要使香港特別行政區以適當形式繼續參加這些組織。
第一百五十三條	中華人民共和國締結的國際協定，中央人民政府可根據香港特別行政區的情況和需要，在徵詢香港特別行政區政府的意見後，決定是否適用於香港特別行政區。 中華人民共和國尚未參加但已適用於香港的國際協議仍可繼續適用。中央人民政府根據需要授權或協助香港特別行政區政府作出適當安排，使其他有關國際協議適用於香港特別行政區。
第一百五十四條	中央人民政府授權香港特別行政區政府依照法律給持有香港特別行政區永久性居民身份證的中國公民簽發中華人民共和國香港特別行政區護照，給在香港特別行政區的其他合法居留者簽發中華人民共和國香港特別行政區的其他旅行證件。上述護照和證件，前往各國和各地區有效，並載明持有人有返回香港特別行政區的權利。 對世界各國或各地區的人入境、逗留和離境，香港特別行政區政府可實行出入境管制。
第一百五十五條	中央人民政府協助或授權香港特別行政區政府與各國或各地區締結互免簽證協議。
第一百五十六條	香港特別行政區可根據需要在外國設立官方或半官方的經濟和貿易機構，報中央人民政府備案。

第一百五十七條	外國在香港特別行政區設立領事機構或其他官方、半官方機構，須經中央人民政府批准。 已同中華人民共和國建立正式外交關係的國家在香港設立的領事機構和其他官方機構，可予保留。 尚未同中華人民共和國設立正式外交關係的國家在香港設立的領事機構和其他官方機構，可根據情況允許保留或改為半官方機構。 尚未為中華人民共和國承認的國家，只能在香港特別行政區設立民間機構。

第八章 ｜ 本法的解釋和修改

第一百五十八條	本法的解釋權屬於全國人民代表大會常務委員會。 全國人民代表大會常務委員會授權香港特別行政區法院在審理案件時對本法關於香港特別行政區自治範圍內的條款自行解釋。 香港特別行政區法院在審理案件時對本法的其他條款也可解釋。但如香港特別行政區法院在審理案件時需要對本法關於中央人民政府管理的事務或中央和香港特別行政區關係的條款進行解釋，而該條款的解釋又影響到案件的判決，在對該案件作出不可上訴的終局判決前，應由香港特別行政區終審法院請全國人民代表大會常務委員會對有關條款作出解釋。如全國人民代表大會常務委員會作出解釋，香港特別行政區法院在引用該條款時，應以全國人民代表大會常務委員會的解釋為准。但在此以前作出的判決不受影響。 全國人民代表大會常務委員會在對本法進行解釋前，徵詢其所屬的香港特別行政區基本法委員會的意見。
第一百五十九條	本法的修改權屬於全國人民代表大會。 本法的修改提案權屬於全國人民代表大會常務委員會、國務院和香港特別行政區。香港特別行政區的修改議案，須經香港特別行政區的全國人民代表大會代表三分之二多數、香港特別行政區立法會全體議員三分之二多數和香港特別行政區行政長官同意後，交由香港特別行政區出席全國人民代表大會的代表團向全國人民代表大會提出。 本法的修改議案在列入全國人民代表大會的議程前，先由香港特別行政區基本法委員會研究並提出意見。 本法的任何修改，均不得同中華人民共和國對香港既定的基本方針政策相抵觸。

第九章 ｜ 附則

第一百六十條	香港特別行政區成立時，香港原有法律除由全國人民代表大會常務委員會宣佈為同本法抵觸者外，採用為香港特別行政區法律，如以後發現有的法律與本法抵觸，可依照本法規定的程序修改或停止生效。 在香港原有法律下有效的文件、證件、契約和權利義務，在不抵觸本法的前提下繼續有效，受香港特別行政區的承認和保護。

附件一：香港特別行政區行政長官的產生辦法	一、行政長官由一個具有廣泛代表性的選舉委員會根據本法選出，由中央人民政府任命。 二、選舉委員會委員共 800 人，由下列各界人士組成： 工商、金融界　200 人 專業界　200 人 勞工、社會服務、宗教等界　200 人 立法會議員、區域性組織代表、香港地區全國人大代表、香港地區全國政協委員的代表　200 人 選舉委員會每屆任期五年。 三、各個界別的劃分，以及每個界別中何種組織可以產生選舉委員的名額，由香港特別行政區根據民主、開放的原則制定選舉法加以規定。 各界別法定團體根據選舉法規定的分配名額和選舉辦法，自行選出選舉委員會委員。 選舉委員以個人身份投票。 四、不少於一百名的選舉委員可聯合提名行政長官候選人。每名委員只可提出一名候選人。 五、選舉委員會根據提名的名單，經一人一票無記名投票選出行政長官候任人。具體選舉辦法由選舉法規定。 六、第一任行政長官按照《全國人民代表大會關於香港特別行政區第一屆政府和立法會產生辦法的決定》產生。 七、二〇〇七年以後各任行政長官的產生辦法如需修改，須經立法會全體議員三分之二多數通過，行政長官同意，並報全國人民代表大會常務委員會批准。
附件二：香港特別行政區立法會的產生辦法和表決程式	一、立法會的產生辦法 （一）香港特別行政區立法會議員每屆 60 人，第一屆立法會按照《全國人民代表大會關於香港特別行政區第一屆政府和立法會產生辦法的決定》產生。第二屆、第三屆立法會的組成如下： 第二屆 功能團體選舉的議員　30 人 選舉委員會選舉的議員　6 人 分區直接選舉的議員　24 人 第三屆 功能團體選舉的議員　30 人 分區直接選舉的議員　30 人 （二）除第一屆立法會外，上述選舉委員會即本法附件一規定的選舉委員會。上述分區直接選舉的選區劃分、投票辦法，各個功能界別和法定團體的劃分、議員名額的分配、選舉辦法及選舉委員會選舉議員的辦法，由香港特別行政區政府提出並經立法會通過的選舉法加以規定。 二、立法會對法案、議案的表決程序 除本法另有規定外，香港特別行政區立法會對法案和議案的表決採取下列程序： 政府提出的法案，如獲得出席會議的全體議員的過半數票，即為通過。 立法會議員個人提出的議案、法案和對政府法案的修正案均須分別經功能團體選舉產生的議員和分區直接選舉、選舉委員會選舉產生的議員兩部份出席會議議員各過半數通過。 三、二〇〇七年以後立法會的產生辦法和表決程序 二〇〇七年以後，香港特別行政區立法會的產生辦法和法案、議案的表決程序，如需對本附件的規定進行修改，須經立法會全體議員三分之二多數通過，行政長官同意，並報全國人民代表大會常務委員會備案。
附件三：在香港特別行政區實施的全國性法律	下列全國性法律，自一九九七年七月一日起由香港特別行政區在當地公佈或立法實施。 一、《關於中華人民共和國國都、紀年、國歌、國旗的決議》 二、《關於中華人民共和國國慶日的決議》 三、《中央人民政府公佈中華人民共和國國徽的命令》附：國徽圖案、說明、使用辦法 四、《中華人民共和國政府關於領海的聲明》 五、《中華人民共和國國籍法》 六、《中華人民共和國外交特權與豁免條例》

第八條

香港原有法律，即普通法、衡平法、條例、附屬立法和習慣法，除同本法相抵觸或經香港特別行政區的立法機關作出修改者外，予以保留。

案例

回歸後香港原有的普通法律體系是否失效？

P.023 | 香港特別行政區 對 馬維騉等

HKSAR And Ma Wai-Kwan, David, Chan Kok-Wai, Donny And Tam Kim-Yuen

香港特別行政區 對 馬維騉等

CAQL 1/1997

簡略案情

馬維騉等人（答辯人）於 1995 年 8 月被控串謀妨礙司法公正，聆訊在 1997 年 6 月、即香港回歸前開審。在審訊期間，答辯人因應《基本法》提出質疑，經各方一致同意在審訊繼續進行前，先向上訴庭提出以下法律問題並尋求裁定：

（1）香港特別行政區的法律有否包涵普通法的串謀妨礙司法公正罪？

（2）答辯人是否需要對該指控答辯並且進行審訊？

關於第一個質疑，答辯人認為香港主權在 1997 年 7 月 1 日轉移後，普通法並沒有被保留下來。原因是根據《基本法》，香港原本有效的法律，包括普通法法則必須被“採用”才得以延續。然而，全國人民代表大會（或人大常委會和香港特別行政區立法會）並沒有主動和有效地採用這些法律，因此，普通法在 1997 年 7 月 1 日主權變更的同時已經失效。

對於第二個質疑，答辯人認為他們參與審訊的最高法院已經隨著主權於 1997 年 7 月 1 日轉變而終止運作，而香港特別行政區的原訟庭並不是適當地組成的法院，所以對他們的審訊不應繼續。

裁決摘要

上訴庭認為，在解釋《基本法》的時候，必須謹記它的歷史、性質和目的，並以帶目的性的方法去進行。依據《基本法》第 8 條“香港原有法律，即普通法……予以保留”，而《基本法》第 160 條確認“香港特別行政區成立時，香港原有法律除由全國人民代表大會常務委員會宣佈為同本法抵觸者外，採用為香港特別行政區法律……”上訴庭注意到《基本法》其中的一個目的是保證在回歸前已經有效的法律和司法體系得以延續。在細心閱讀第 8 條和第 160 條後，它們並沒有包涵將來需要作出任何行為的要求，反之，它們帶有強制和宣示的意思。由此，上訴庭認為沒有需要在回歸後採取任何延續普通法法規的“採用”行動，沿用的法律包括普通法依然有效。至於答辯人的第二個爭議，上訴庭指出：

> 《基本法》第 81 條列明“…… 原在香港實行的司法體制，除因設立香港特別行政區終審法院而產生變化外，予以保留。”
>
> 《基本法》第 87 條列明“香港特別行政區的刑事訴訟和民事訴訟中保留原在香港適用的原則和當事人享有的權利……”
>
> 《基本法》第 160 條亦確認“…… 在香港原有法律下有效的文件、證件、契約和權利義務，在不抵觸本法的前提下繼續有效，受香港特別行政區的承認和保護。”

由此，上訴庭認為公訴的效力因而得以保留，普通法的串謀妨礙司法公正罪在本港仍然有效，被告人必須繼續對其指控作出回應。

CAQL 1/1997

IN THE HIGH COURT OF THE HONG KONG SPECIAL ADMINISTRATIVE REGION COURT OF APPEAL

Reservation of Question of Law No. 1 of 1997

Between:

HKSAR Applicant

- and -

MA WAI-KWAN, David, CHAN KOK-WAI, Donny and TAM KIM-YUEN Respondents

Coram: The Hon Chan, Chief Judge, Nazareth V-P and Mortimer V-P

Dates of Hearing: 22nd-24th July 1997

Date of Judgment: 29th July 1997

JUDGMENT

Chan, Chief Judge:

Background

The respondents are the three defendants in a criminal trial before the Court of First Instance. They were charged on 11th August 1995 with conspiracy to pervert the course of public justice, contrary to common law. It is alleged that between 12th and 29th June 1995, the three respondents conspired together by offering to pay money to the mother of a Mr Wong who was then charged with robbery before the District Court together with the 3rd respondent and another person. It is further alleged that the purpose of offering money to the lady was to serve as a reward for her son Mr Wong pleading guilty to a lesser offence and maintaining a false version of events which would favour the 3rd respondent and the other person. They were committed for trial in the then High Court after a preliminary inquiry which took several days in December 1996. On 3rd January 1997, Indictment No.1 of 1997 was filed against them. The 3rd respondent also faced an alternative charge of attempting to pervert the course of public justice.

The trial was fixed for hearing on 16th June 1997. The first few days were spent on sorting out prosecution witness statements and other documents. On the fifth day of the trial, the 2nd respondent applied for a permanent stay of the criminal proceedings. This lasted several days. On 27th June 1997, the last working day before 1st July, the trial judge, Deputy Judge Lugar-Mawson, refused to stay the proceedings.

On 3rd July 1997, the tenth day of the trial, the respondents took issue on the Reunification Ordinance, the Basic Law and the preservation of the common law. On 7th July 1997, which was the twelfth day of the trial, the three respondents were, with their consent, arraigned on an amended indictment which was filed on 19th June 1997. They all pleaded not guilty to the first count of conspiracy to pervert the course of public justice. The alternative count against the 3rd respondent was directed by the Court to be put on file, not to be proceeded with without the leave of the Court. The respondents then applied to the Deputy Judge to quash the Amended Indictment. The prosecution opposed this application and applied to reserve certain questions of law for the determination by the Court of Appeal pursuant to section 81 of the Criminal Procedure Ordinance, Cap.221. There was no objection from the respondents. The Deputy Judge made the order.

On 9th July 1997, at a hearing for directions before us, we drew the parties' attention to s.81 of Cap 221 which provides that the questions of law reserved for this Court must be on matters arising from the trial. On the following day, the parties went before the Deputy Judge. His order was amended, apparently with the consent of all parties. This is now before this Court.

Representation of the parties

I should mention that since the questions of law to be determined by this Court involve some important constitutional issues, we requested the Director of Legal Aid to brief leading counsel for the 3rd respondent. However, as it turned out, the Director decided not to do so and was prepared only to instruct junior counsel to hold a watching brief. Pursuant to our directions, counsel for the 2nd respondent filed his skeleton arguments on the questions of law to be decided. Counsel for the 1st respondent indicated that he would adopt those submissions.

On the first day of this hearing, counsel for both the 2nd and 3rd respondents informed us that they had no instructions to act for their clients because of lack of funds. They asked to be released from the case. We gave leave to the solicitors to withdraw but invited both counsel to stay and make submissions on the issues before the Court. They agreed to do so. In the afternoon, Ms Gladys Li, SC, Miss Margaret Ng and Mr Paul Harris appeared before us and offered to assist the Court on the issue of the legality of the Provisional Legislative Council. Counsel for the 2nd and 3rd respondents were willing to be led by this team in view of the importance of the issue involved. We readily extended our invitation to Ms Li, SC, and her team. We are most grateful for their assistance.

The two questions of law

There were initially five questions of law for the determination of this Court stated in the Motion issued by the prosecution and the Order made by the Deputy Judge. I am given to understand that they were framed in order to cover the grounds relied on by the 2nd respondent in his application to quash the Amended Indictment. Having reconsidered the matter, the prosecution decided to pose only two questions for determination. They are:

(1) Is the offence at common law of conspiracy to pervert the course of public justice part of the laws of the Hong Kong Special Administrative Region ("HKSAR")?

(2) Are the accused liable to answer to and to be tried on count 1 of the Indictment No.1 of 1997 ?

Survival of the common law

It is the respondents' contention that the common law has not survived the change of sovereignty on 1st July 1997. Their main submission is that the Basic Law, in particular Article 160, provides that the laws previously in force in Hong Kong which include the common law, rules of equity, ordinances, subordinate legislation and customary law shall be adopted. They argue that it is necessary to have a positive act of adoption either by the National People's Congress (NPC) through its Standing Committee and/or the legislature of the HKSAR. It is submitted that there was no valid adoption of these laws by the NPC or its Standing Committee and that the legality and competence of the

Provisional Legislative Council is in doubt. Furthermore, the NPC Standing Committee had "repealed" the Application of English Law Ordinance (Cap 88) as contravening the Basic Law. As a result, the common law has not survived the change of sovereignty and there is no common law in Hong Kong after 1st July.

Leading counsel for the Government submits that under the Basic Law itself, the common law forms part of the laws of HKSAR. No formal act of adoption of the law previously in force is necessary. A decision is required only to declare which of the laws that are in contravention of the Basic Law are not to be adopted. In any event, the NPC Standing Committee had indeed adopted all the laws previously in force which are not in contravention of the Basic Law. The Reunification Ordinance has not adopted or purported to adopt the common law since that Ordinance was enacted on the basis that the laws previously in force have already been adopted. Counsel submits that the NPC decision not to adopt the Application of English Law Ordinance does not affect the maintenance of the common law in Hong Kong.

The answer to the question whether the common law has survived the change of sovereignty depends on whether the laws previously in force in Hong Kong are automatically adopted upon the establishment of the HKSAR on 1st July 1997 or whether it is necessary to have an overt act of adoption of such laws and if so, whether there has been any valid adoption. This turns on an interpretation of the provisions of the Basic Law.

Interpretation of the Basic Law

Before one attempts to interpret the Basic Law, it is necessary to bear in mind the history, nature and purpose of this document.

On 19th December 1984, the Joint Declaration was signed between the Government of the People's Republic of China (PRC) and the Government of the United Kingdom. By this Joint Declaration, Hong Kong was to be restored to China with effect from 1st July 1997. Under Article 3 of the Joint Declaration, China declared certain basic policies regarding Hong Kong. There was to be established the HKSAR which would enjoy a high degree of autonomy. Under Article 3(12), these basic policies would be stipulated in a Basic Law to be promulgated by the NPC and would remain unchanged for fifty years from 1st July 1997. These policies were further elaborated in Annex I to the Joint Declaration. The Basic Law for the HKSAR was drafted by the Drafting Committee of the Basic Law which consisted of members from China and from Hong Kong. It took many years to complete. It was promulgated on 4th April 1990 and was to take effect from 1st July 1997.

The Basic Law is not only a brainchild of an international treaty, the Joint Declaration. It is also a national law of the PRC and the constitution of the HKSAR. It translates the basic policies enshrined in the Joint Declaration into more practical terms. The essence of these policies is that the current social, economic and legal systems in Hong Kong will remain unchanged for 50 years. The purpose of the Basic Law is to ensure that these basic policies are implemented and that there can be continued stablity (stability) and prosperity for the HKSAR. Continuity after the change of sovereignty is therefore of vital importance.

Mr Fung, SC, for the Government submits that a generous and purposive approach is to be adopted in the interpretation of the Basic Law since it is a constitutional document. See **A.G. of Gambia v. Jobe** [1984]AC 689 and **R. v. Sin Yau-ming** [1992] 1 HKCLR 127. While I agree with this as a general proposition, I would add a few words of caution. The Basic Law is a unique document. It reflects a treaty made between two nations. It deals with the relationship between the Sovereign and an autonomous region which practises a different system. It stipulates the organisations and functions of the different branches of government. It sets out the rights and obligations of the citizens. Hence, it has at least three dimensions: international, domestic and constitutional. It must also be borne in mind that it was not drafted by common law lawyers. It was drafted in the Chinese language with an official English version but the Chinese version takes precedence in case of discrepancies. That being the background and features of the Basic Law, it is obvious that there will be difficulties in the interpretation of its various provisions. (See the discussions in Hong Kong's New Constitutional Order, Yash Ghai, Chapter 5.) In my view, the generous and purposive approach may not be applicable in interpreting every article of the Basic Law. However, in the context of the present case which involves the constitutional aspects of the Basic Law, I agree that this approach is more appropriate.

Relevant provisions in the Basic Law

The provisions

The provisions in the Basic Law which are relevant to the issue of whether the common law has survived the change of sovereignty are as follows:

> "Article 8
>
> The laws previously in force in Hong Kong, that is, the common law, rules of equity, ordinances, subordinate legislation and customary law **shall be maintained**, except for any that contravene this Law, and subject to any amendment by the legislature of the Hong Kong Special Administrative Region.
>
> Article 18
>
> The laws in force in the Hong Kong Special Administrative Region **shall be** this Law, the laws previously in force in Hong Kong as provided for in Article 8 of this Law, and the laws enacted by the legislature of the Region.
>
> Article 19
>
> The Hong Kong Special Administrative Region shall be vested with independent judicial power, including that of final adjudication.
>
> The courts of the Hong Kong Special Administrative Region shall have jurisdiction over all cases in the Region, except that the restrictions on their jurisdiction imposed by the legal system and principles previously in force in Hong Kong **shall be maintained**.
>
> Article 81
>
> The Court of Final Appeal, the High Court, district courts, magistrates' courts and other special courts shall be established in the Hong Kong Special Administrative Region. The High Court shall comprise the Court of Appeal and the Court of First Instance.
>
> The judicial system previously practised in Hong Kong **shall be maintained** except for those changes consequent upon the establishment of the Court of Final Appeal of the Hong Kong Special Administrative Region.
>
> Article 87

> In criminal or civil proceedings in the Hong Kong Special Administrative Region, the principles previously applied in Hong Kong and the rights previously enjoyed by parties to proceedings **shall be maintained**.
>
> Article 160
>
> Upon the establishment of the Hong Kong Special Administrative Region, the laws previously in force in Hong Kong **shall be adopted** as laws of the Region except for those which the Standing Committee of the National People's Congress declares to be in contravention of this Law. If any laws are later discovered to be in contravention of this Law, they shall be amended or cease to have force in accordance with the procedure as prescribed by this Law.
>
> Documents, certificates, contracts, and rights and obligations valid under the laws previously in force in Hong Kong **shall continue** to be valid and be recognized and protected by the Hong Kong Special Administrative Region, provided that they do not contravene this Law. (*my emphases*)

These are the provisions with regard to the laws which are to be in force, the judicial system which are to be in place and the principles relating to legal proceedings which are to be applied in the HKSAR.

Its intention

In my view, the intention of the Basic Law is clear. There is to be no change in our laws and legal system (except those which contravene the Basic Law). These are the very fabric of our society. Continuity is the key to stability. Any disruption will be disastrous. Even one moment of legal vacuum may lead to chaos. Everything relating to the laws and the legal system except those provisions which contravene the Basic Law has to continue to be in force. The existing system must already be in place on 1st July 1997. That must be the intention of the Basic Law.

Its wording

The wording is equally clear. The Basic Law is the constitution of the HKSAR. It is the most important piece of law in the land. It states clearly what the position is as from 1st July 1997. In my view, the word "shall" in these provisions can only be used in the mandatory and declaratory sense. The meaning of these provisions is this. On 1st July 1997 when the HKSAR comes into existence and the Basic Law comes into effect, these **are** to be the laws and legal system in force and the principles applicable in the place. There is no express or implied requirement in any of these provisions that the laws previously in force or the legal system previously in place need to be formally adopted before they can continue to be applicable after the change of sovereignty. On the contrary, the use of the terms "shall be maintained", "shall continue" and "shall be" leaves absolutely no doubt in my mind that there can be no question of any need for an act of adoption. These terms are totally inconsistent with such a requirement.

Article 160

The respondents' argument is based mainly on Article 160 which uses the words "shall be adopted". It is suggested that "shall" in this term is used in the future tense. In my view, that provision cannot be read in isolation but must be considered in the light of the rest of the Basic Law including in particular the articles to which I have referred above. It cannot be construed to have a meaning which is inconsistent with the other articles relating to the adoption of the existing laws and legal system.

In any event, Article 160 even on its own has the same theme as the other provisions. There is a sense of continuity in this article. In the first paragraph of this article, it is provided that any laws which are later to be found to be in contravention of the Basic Law shall be *amended* or *cease to have force*. Laws which have not yet come into force cannot cease to have force. In my view, this paragraph clearly indicates that the laws previously in force in Hong Kong are to be effective on 1st July 1997 without any act of adoption. Paragraph 2 of that article puts the matter beyond argument. It provides that documents, certificates, contracts, rights and obligations valid under the laws previously in force *shall continue* to be valid. How can these continue to be valid if the laws which govern their validity cannot even apply without an act of adoption ? It simply makes no sense that the Basic Law continues the validity of these documents, certificates, contracts, rights and obligations but requires the laws which upholds them to be adopted.

I would also agree that apart from confirming that the laws previously in force are to be the laws of the HKSAR at the time the Region comes into existence, the purpose of Article 160 is to provide for the exclusion of laws which are later found to be in contravention of the Basic Law.

Construing Article 160 either by itself or in conjunction with the other articles, I am firmly of the view that it does not have the effect of requiring the laws previously in force in Hong Kong to be formally adopted in order to be effective after 30 June 1997. In fact, no other article in the Basic Law has such effect.

Joint Declaration

I find support for this view in the provisions in the Joint Declaration which can be used as an aid to the interpretation of the Basic Law. Article 3 provides:

> "Article 3(3)
>
> The Hong Kong Special Administrative Region will be vested with executive, legislative and independent judicial power, including that of final adjudication. The laws currently in force in Hong Kong will remain basically unchanged.
>
> Article 3(12)
>
> The above stated basic policies of the People's Republic of China regarding Hong Kong and the elaboration of them in Annex I to this Joint Declaration will be stipulated, in a Basic Law of the Hong Kong Special Administrative Region of the People's Republic of China, by the National People's Congress of the People's Republic of China, and they will remain unchanged for 50 years."

It is quite clear that the Joint Declaration is a declaration of intent. It evinces the intention of the two Governments and refers to what is to happen in future. Hence the future tense is used. Contrast Annex I to the Joint Declaraion which was to form the basis of the Basic Law. The first paragraph in Section II says:

> "After the establishment of the Hong Kong Special Administrative Region, the laws previously in force in Hong Kong (i.e. the common law, rules of equity, ordinances, subordinate legislation and customary

law) <u>shall be maintained</u>, save for any that contravene the Basic Law and subject to any amendment by the Hong Kong Special Administrative Region legislature. (my emphasis)

The wording is in line with Article 8 of the Basic Law. The inevitable conclusion is that "shall" is not used in the future sense but in the mandatory and declaratory sense.

Chinese text

Mr Fung, SC, for the Government draws our attention to the fact that the Basic Law was enacted in the Chinese language by the PRC and that the Chinese text prevails over the English version in case of discrepancies. When the relevant articles in the Chinese text are considered, there can be no doubt as to what they mean or are intended to mean. The Chinese characters " 採用 *cai yong*" (meaning "adopt") in Article 160 are clearly used in the mandatory and declaratory sense. They do not admit of an interpretation which requires a future act of adoption before the laws previously in force are to be applicable after 1st July 1997. However, I do not think it is necessary to rely on the Chinese text at all. The English text is already quite clear and without ambiguity.

<u>Adoption by NPC Decision</u>

It is submitted on behalf of the respondents that the NPC saw fit to make a Decision on 23rd February 1997 which purported to adopt the laws previously in force. This, it is argued, suggests that it is necessary to have an act of adoption before such laws can become effective after 1st July 1997. In my view, this argument cannot be sustained in the light of the purpose and contents of that Decision.

The Decision on 23rd February 1997 was made for the expressed purpose of exercising the NPC's right under Article 160 of the Basic Law to declare which laws previously in force contravene the Basic Law and are thus excluded from operation after 1st July 1997. The title of the Decision refers to the treatment of laws in *accordance with Article 160* and begins with a recital of the relevant part of that article. The reference to Article 8 in fact reinforces the view that the laws previously in force in Hong Kong will automatically become effective as the laws of the HKSAR except for those that contravene the Basic Law. It also supports the view that Article 160 must be read in conjunction with Article 8.

Under Paragraph 1 of the Decision, the laws previously in force in Hong Kong are adopted as the laws of the HKSAR. Paragraph 2 refers to those laws which are considered as contravening the Basic Law and therefore not to be adopted when the HKSAR comes into existence. It is also significant to note paragraph 4 which refers to the laws "which **have been** adopted".

In my view, this Decision is clear enough. It adopts the laws previously in force in Hong Kong as the laws of the HKSAR when it comes into existence on 1st July 1997. This is strictly speaking not necessary in the light of the clear provisions in the Basic Law. But since it purports to declare invalid those laws which contravene the Basic Law (as it does), it is natural that it also, for the sake of clarity, refers to the laws which are to be adopted on 1st July 1997.

<u>Application of English Law Ordinance</u>

The respondents submit that the Application of English Law Ordinance provided a new basis for the application of the English law and the "repeal" of this Ordinance "throws in doubt the precise scope of the common law to be applied in Hong Kong". I do not agree.

English law which includes the common law has started to apply in Hong Kong since at least 1844 when the previous Supreme Court Ordinance was enacted. That Ordinance was replaced by the Application of English Law Ordinance in 1966. The 1966 Ordinance did not import the English law. Nor did it terminate the application of English law which was applied by virtue of the previous Supreme Court Ordinance and then re-apply the English law all over again. It continued the application of the English law. Its effect was, as its long title indicated, "to declare the extent to which English law is in force in the Colony". It set out clearly the restrictions in the application of English law in Hong Kong and listed those imperial acts which were still in force. The reasons for the non-adoption of this Ordinance by the NPC Standing Committee are obvious. The Basic Law has already adopted the laws previously in force. Further, that Ordinance referred to imperial acts which are either not applicable to the HKSAR any more or have been "localised". In other words, that Ordinance is not only no longer necessary, it also contravenes the Basic Law by its incorporation of imperial acts.

I do not think the non-adoption of the Application of English Law Ordinance has cast any doubt on the continued application of the common law in the HKSAR.

<u>Cut-off date</u>

It is submitted by the respondents that there is an uncertainty in the cut off date of the laws previously in force. They query whether it should be the date of the Joint Declaration in 1984 or the date of the promulgation of the Basic Law in 1990 or 30th June 1997. The relevance of this relates to the common law offence of conspiracy (with which these respondents now face) which was abolished by the Crimes (Amendment) Ordinance 1996.

With respect, this point is beyond argument. The cut off date cannot be the date of the Joint Declaration. It was only a treaty and a declaration of intent. It cannot be the date of the promulgation of the Basic Law since it was then stated to take effect on a future date. The Basic Law came into effect on 1st July 1997. It declares in Article 8 and other provisions that the laws previously in force and the existing legal system are adopted. The only logical and in fact proper conclusion is that 30th June 1997 is the cut off date.

The respondents are alleged to have committed a conspiracy in June 1995 and they were charged in August 1995. That is one year before the enactment of the Crimes (Amendment) Ordinance 1996. It is clear that the charge is not affected by that amendment. (See s.159E(7)).

<u>Survival of the Indictment</u>

The respondents contend that they are not liable to answer to and be tried on the Amended Indictment. The arguments are as follows. The respondents were committed for trial before the resumption of sovereignty. The Indictment was also filed before that date. The Supreme Court before which they appeared had ceased to operate as from 1st July 1997. They should not now be tried before the Court of First Instance of the HKSAR which is not a properly constituted court and the proceedings which were commenced before the resumption of sovereignty cannot be continued. They argue that the reason is because there is no express provision in the Basic Law governing this situation and although there are provisions in the Reunification Ordinance, that Ordinance was not lawfully and validly enacted by a body competent in law to enact it.

The answer to these arguments is simple. There are clear and express provisions in the Basic Law. The laws previously in force are adopted (Articles 8 and 18). The courts of the HKSAR have jurisdiction over all cases in the Region (Article 19). The judicial system except the renaming of the Supreme Court and those changes consequent upon the establishment of the Court of Final Appeal is maintained (Article 81). The principles previously applied and the rights previously enjoyed by parties to criminal and civil proceedings are maintained (Article 87). Under Article 160, documents and rights and obligations valid under the laws previously in force continue to be valid, recognised and protected. Adopting a purposive approach to Article 160, these clearly, in my view, cover indictments, the right of the Government to prosecute offenders and the obligation of an accused person to answer to the allegations made against him.

I have no doubt that by virtue of the above provisions of the Basic Law, the Amended Indictment survives and the pending criminal proceedings against these respondents continue after the change of sovereignty.

The above reasons are sufficient to dispose of the two questions of law reserved for the determination of this Court. The answers to these questions are both clearly in the affirmative.

However, in case I am wrong in my interpretation of the Basic Law, I should deal with the other issues which have been raised in argument. I would also do this out of respect to counsel who have so comprehensively prepared their submissions and because of the public concern which has been generated by this important case. I take note of Ms Li, SC's concern over the risk of an unnecessary ruling, by way of obiter, on important issues such as those raised in the present case.

Hong Kong Reunification Ordinance

In the event that upon its interpretation, the Basic Law does not provide for automatic adoption of the laws previously in force and the legal system in Hong Kong after 1st July 1997, the Government relies on the Hong Kong Reunification Ordinance (Reunification Ordinance) which is an ordinance passed by the Provisional Legislative Council and assented to by the Chief Executive on 1st July 1997.

The long title of the Ordinance sets out what it aims at doing. It reads:

> "An Ordinance to confirm the Bills passed by the Provisional Legislative Council before 1 July 1997, endorse the appointment of judges of the Court of Final Appeal and the Chief Judge of the High Court, assist the interpretation on and after 1 July 1997 of laws previously in force in Hong Kong, *continue those laws and confirm certain other laws, establish the High Court*, the District Court, magistracies and other courts, tribunals and boards, *continue legal proceedings, the criminal justice system, the administration of justice and the course of public justice on and after 1 July 1997*, continue the public service on and after 1 July 1997, assist the construction of certain documents on and after 1 July 1997, transfer the ownership of certain property and rights and provide for the assumption of certain liabilities on and after 1 July 1997, in consequence of the resumption of the exercise of sovereignty over Hong Kong by the People's Republic of China, and for connected purposes." (my emphases)

Adoption of laws

The provisions which relate to the adoption of laws previously in force in Hong Kong are contained in sections 5 and 7 of the Ordinance. Section 5 adds a section to the Interpretation and General Clauses Ordinance, Cap.1. It provides as follows:

> "2A. Laws previously in force
>
> (1) All laws previously in force shall be construed with such modifications, adaptations, limitations and exceptions as may be necessary so as not to contravene the Basic Law and to bring them into conformity with the status of Hong Kong as a Special Administrative Region of the People's Republic of China.
>
> (4) In this section–
>
> 'laws previously in force' means the common law, rules of equity, Ordinances, subsidiary legislation and customary law in force immediately before 1 July 1997 and adopted as laws of the Hong Kong Special Administrative Region."

The definition of "laws previously in force" suggests that all the previous laws have been adopted as the laws of the HKSAR. This is reinforced by section 7 of the Ordinance which provides:

> "7. Maintenance of previous laws
>
> (1) The laws previously in force in Hong Kong, that is the common law, rules of equity, Ordinances, subsidiary legislation and customary law, which *have been adopted* as the laws of the HKSAR, *shall continue* to apply." (*my emphases*)

This section supports the view that the Basic Law has already brought all the laws previously in force in Hong Kong into effect as the laws of the HKSAR on its establishment on 1 July 1997. It also puts all matters beyond doubt by stating that such laws shall continue to apply.

Establishment of courts

As regards the establishment of the High Court, this is provided in section 8 of the Reunification Ordinance. This section provides that section 3 of the Supreme Court Ordinance (Cap.4) is repealed and substituted by a new section 3 which says:

> "3. High Court
>
> (1) There shall be a High Court of the Hong Kong Special Administrative Region consisting of the Court of First Instance and the Court of Appeal.
>
> (2) Subject to the provisions of this Ordinance, the High Court shall be a court of unlimited civil and criminal jurisdiction."

The effect of this section is to state clearly that the previous Supreme Court is now renamed as the High Court and the former High Court is now renamed as the Court of First Instance. The argument put forth by the respondents that the Supreme Court ceases to operate after 1 July 1997 is laid completely at rest.

Continuity of proceedings

With regard to the continuity of legal proceedings, the relevant provisions are sections 10 and 15. They provide that legal proceedings shall not be affected and shall continue after the change of sovereignty.

"10. Continuity of legal proceedings, criminal justice system and administration of justice

(1) Subject to this Ordinance, the continuity of legal proceedings, the criminal justice system, the administration of justice and the course of public justice shall not be affected by the resumption of the exercise of sovereignty over Hong Kong by the People's Republic of China.

15. Pending proceedings

(1) All proceedings, including appeals, pending in any court, statutory tribunal or statutory board or before any magistrate immediately before 1 July 1997 may be continued on and after that date and shall be treated as if they had been pending in the corresponding court, tribunal or board or before the corresponding magistrate of the HKSAR.

(2) Any proceedings pending in any court, statutory tribunal or statutory board or before any magistrate by or against a public officer immediately before 1 July 197 (1997) shall on and after that date be deemed to have been brought by or against, as the case may be, the corresponding public officer in the HKSAR.

(3) Any proceedings brought by, in the name of or against the Queen which are pending in any court, statutory tribunal or statutory board or before any magistrate immediately before 1 July 1997 shall on and after that date be deemed to have brought by, in the name of or against, as the case may be, the HKSAR."

I do not need to refer to other provisions which deal with the saving of judgments (section 11), the rights of audience (section 12), and barristers and solicitors (section 13). Suffice it to say that the position has not changed after 1st July 1997 and all acts done by previous courts and tribunals shall be regarded as continuing to have effect.

It is therefore clear beyond doubt that even if there is any uncertainty in the Basic Law, this has been removed by the provisions in the Reunification Ordinance which I have mentioned above.

The question is whether this Ordinance was lawfully and validly enacted by a body competent in law to enact it. This leads to the legality of the Provisional Legislative Council.

Jurisdiction of the HKSAR Courts

The arguments

Mr Fung, SC, for the Government submits that the HKSAR courts have no jurisdiction to hear and determine the issue of the legality of the Provisional Legislative Council. He argues that the courts must accept the body and the laws made by it.

It is submitted that under Article 19 of the Basic Law, the jurisdiction of the HKSAR courts shall have jurisdiction over all cases in the Region except the restrictions on their jurisdiction imposed by the legal system and principles previously in force in Hong Kong. Hence, the HKSAR courts have no greater power than the courts under British rule. Counsel argues that prior to 1st July 1997, the Hong Kong courts could not have determined the constitutionality of either UK metropolitan or imperial legislation vis-a-vis either the unwritten English Constitution or the Hong Kong Letters Patent. This was because the UK Government was the sovereign of Hong Kong. According to the constitutional hierarchy, the Acts of Parliament and ministerial decisions were not subject to the Hong Kong Letters Patent and therefore the Hong Kong courts had no jurisdiction to query them. The UK legal system was also different from the Hong Kong system. There would be no effective remedy even if the Hong Kong courts are to query the Acts of Parliament or ministerial Decisions. Counsel relies on the case of **Madzimbamuto v. Lardner-Burke** [1969] 2 AC 645, in particular the dictum of Lord Reid:

"If Parliament chose to do any of them (the enactment of a Parliament which has effect over South Rhodesia) the courts could not hold the Act of Parliament invalid."

It is argued that if British Parliament legislates on a topic within its power, the colonial courts are bound by that. Analogies are drawn from the Australian constitution and the Canadian constitution. Counsel submits that the same principles apply to the HKSAR courts.

It is the Government's contention that once the HKSAR courts are satisfied that the Provisional Legislative Council was established, was appointed and is acting under the authority of the Sovereign (the PRC), then the courts have no jurisdiction to question whether it was validly established and are bound to give effect to its enactments. While counsel accepts that the jurisdiction of the HKSAR courts can extend to determining whether the Preparatory Committee was in fact formed by the NPC, they have no power to inquire into the vires of its acts, such as, whether it has acted within its conferred powers or followed the proper procedures or whether it has acted in contravention of the Basic Law. Afterall, counsel argues, the Preparatory Committee is a NPC body and not a HKSAR organisation.

On the other hand, Ms Li, SC, submits that the HKSAR courts have the jurisdiction and the obligation to examine and interpret the Basic Law. Hence, they can examine the Basic Law and the acts of the NPC to determine whether the NPC had properly established the Provisional Legislative Council and whether that body conforms with the Basic Law and the NPC enactments. Counsel further argues that the courts can examine the decisions and acts to see if they are consistent with the basic policies of the PRC as stated in the Joint Declaration. She submits that the analogy with Acts of Parliament is not appropriate.

Jurisdiction of the courts

I would accept for the arguments put forward by Mr Fung, SC, that regional courts have no jurisdiction to query the validity of any legislation or acts passed by the sovereign. There is simply no legal basis to do so. It would be difficult to imagine that the Hong Kong courts could, while still under British rule, challenge the validity of an Act of Parliament passed in U.K. or an act of the Queen in Council which had effect on Hong Kong. However, I cannot find any authority which prohibits the Hong Kong courts to at least examine whether such legislation or imperial act existed, what its scope was and whether what was done in Hong Kong was done in pursuance of such legislation or imperial act. In fact, it is, in my view, the duty of the Hong Kong courts to ensure that the legislation or imperial act is implemented and if there is to be any query about it, the courts should conduct such an enquiry.

Take the example given by counsel. The Queen by Letters Patent appoints Mr X to be a governor of Hong Kong. The Hong Kong courts cannot query the validity of the Letters Patent or why and how she comes to appoint Mr X as the Governor. However, I think that the Hong Kong courts should have the power to examine the Letters Patent and its contents to see whether the Queen has in fact made an appointment and to query whether a particular person turning up at Queen's Pier is the Mr X and whether he acts according to the scope of the Letters Patent which appoints him as Governor.

The PRC is the Sovereign of the HKSAR. Under its Constitution, the NPC is the highest organ of state power. Together with its Standing Committee, they exercise the legislative power of the PRC. It is submitted by Mr Fung, SC, although Ms Li, SC, may have some reservations, that the NPC and its Standing Committee can exercise such power by way of decisions and resolutions. In the absence of arguments to the contrary, I would accept that this is the case. The Decisions and Resolutions relied on have also been admitted without challenge.

In the context of the present case, I would accept that the HKSAR courts cannot challenge the validity of the NPC Decisions or Resolutions or the reasons behind them which set up the Preparatory Committee. Such decisions and resolutions are the acts of the Sovereign and their validity is not open to challenge by the regional courts. I am thus unable to accept Ms Li, SC's argument that the regional courts can examine those decisions and resolutions to see if they are consistent with the Basic Law or other policies. Nor, in my view, can the HKSAR courts examine why the Preparatory Committee set up the Provisional Legislative Council in exercising the authority and powers conferred on its by the NPC to carry out the Sovereign's decisions and resolutions.

However, I take the view that the HKSAR courts do have the jurisdiction to examine the existence (as opposed to the validity) of the acts of the Sovereign or its delegate. In fact, if the matter should ever come to court as in this case, the courts would be failing their duty not to do so. In other words, in the context of this case, I take the view that the HKSAR courts should have the power to examine:

(1) whether there was any NPC decision or resolution setting up or authorising the setting up of the Preparatory Committee,

(2) whether there was any Preparatory Committee decision or resolution setting up the Provisional Legislative Council,

(3) whether the Preparatory Committee had in fact set up the Provisional Legislative Council and whether this Provisional Legislative Council was in fact the body which was set up pursuant to the decisions or resolutions of the NPC and the Preparatory Committee.

Once the courts are satisfied with these, I do not think they can go any further.

Legality of the Provisional Legislative Council

The arguments

The Government's contention is that the Provisional Legislative Council had been validly established under Chinese law. In any event, its establishment was ratified by the NPC.

The Government's first arguments run as follows. On 4th April 1990, the same day as the Basic Law was enacted, a decision was made by the NPC known as "Method for the Formation of the First Government and the First Legislative Council of the HKSAR". This Decision provides for the establishment of a Preparatory Committee in 1996 which was to be responsible for matters relating to the preparation of the establishment of the HKSAR including the first Government and the first Legislative Council in accordance with the Decision. The Decision also makes provisions for the first Legislative Council of the HKSAR and a "through train" so that members of the last Hong Kong Legislative Council who satisfy certain conditions would become members of the first Legislative Council of the HKSAR.

It is contended that because of the political dispute, there was to be no "through train". But there is no provision for a contingency in the Basic Law. Hence, the Preparatory Committee decided on 24th March 1996 to establish this Provisional Legislative Council prescribing the specific and limited tasks of this body with limited powers and a specific term of not more than one year until 30th June 1998. Counsel submits that the Preparatory Committee has the primary obligation imposed by the 1990 NPC Decision to establish the HKSAR Government. The establishment of the Provisional Legislative Council is, in the light of prevailing political reality, plainly incidental to that obligation and in the exercise of power conferred by that Decision of the NPC. Counsel submits that the Provisional Legislative Council does not purport to be the first Legislative Council of the HKSAR. It is just an interim body.

Ms Li, SC, submits that the Provisional Legislative Council is not legal. She argues that the Joint Declaration provides for the Legislative Council of the HKSAR to be constituted by election. This is also stated in Article 68 of the Basic Law. Any Legislative Council must be established in accordance with that article and the method for formation as prescribed in Annex II which provides, amongst other things, that in the first term, the Legislative Council shall be formed in accordance with the decision of the NPC on the method for the formation of the first Government and the first Legislative Council of the HKSAR. It is submitted that the present Provisional Legislative Council, whatever its name, is the de facto first Legislative Council of the HKSAR. It has purported to fulfill the functions of a Legislative Council for the HKSAR and to enact ordinances which are to have the force of law. It must therefore comply with the Joint Declaration, the Basic Law, which include Annex II and the Decision of the NPC by reference. Counsel submits that the Provisional Legislative Council fails to do so.

It is argued that the 1990 NPC Decision does not refer to any Provisional Legislative Council. It mandates the Preparatory Committee to prepare the establishment of the HKSAR and to prescribe the specific method for forming the first Government and the first Legislative Council. But it can do so only in accordance with that Decision. Whilst the NPC left it to the Preparatory Committee to form the first Legislative Council, the Preparatory Committee must comply with criteria set out in paragraph 6 of that Decision. However, the Provisional Legislative Council is admittedly not a Legislative Council which satisfied those criteria. It also contravenes Article 68 of the Basic Law in that it is not constituted by election and not in accordance with the actual situation in the HKSAR or the principle of gradual and orderly progress.

It is further submitted that if the NPC Decision has any legislative effect, this would amount to an amendment to the Basic Law. If it is intended to set up a provisional legislature which does not comply with the provisions of the Basic Law and the 1990 NPC

Decision, it is necessary to amend the Basic Law. However, there is nothing to show that the special procedures as specified in Article 158 have been followed.

It is also argued that nothing in the Decision of the NPC made on 31st August 1994 mandates the Preparatory Committee to form anything other than the first Legislative Council. The Decision of the Preparatory Committee reached on 24th March 1996 on the establishment of the Provisional Legislative Council fails to mention its obligation to prescribe the method for the formation of the first Legislative Council in accordance with the 1990 NPC Decision. In other words, the Preparation Committee did not have powers to do what they did. It is submitted that nothing short of an amendment to the Basic Law can suffice. The NPC "Ratification" in 1997 did not purport to amend the Basic Law.

Events leading to establishment of PLC

To decide on the legality of the Provisional Legislative Council, it is necessary to look into the events which led to its existence. The Joint Declaration sets out the declared basic policies of the PRC regarding Hong Kong. These basic policies are elaborated in Annex I and later incorporated in the Basic Law. One of these policies is that there shall be a Legislative Council. Article 68 of the Basic Law provides that the Legislative Council shall be constituted by election. It further provides for its development and formation in the following terms:

> "The method for forming the Legislative Council shall be specified in the light of the actual situation in the Hong Kong Special Administrative Region and in accordance with the principle of gradual and orderly progress. The ultimate aim is the election of all the members of the Legislative Council by universal suffrage.
>
> The specific method for forming the Legislative Council and its procedures for voting on bills and motions are prescribed in Annex II: 'Method for the Formation of the Legislative Council of the Hong Kong Special Administrative Region and Its Voting Procedures'."

This leads to Annex II which specifies amongst other things that the Legislative Council shall compose of 60 members in each term. The compositions of the Legislative Council in the second and third terms are set out. But this is not specified for the first term. It simply says that it shall be formed:

> "... in accordance with the 'Decision of the National People's Congress on the Method for the Formation of the First Government and the First Legislative Council of the Hong Kong Special Administrative Region'."

It is therefore clear that the method of formation of the Legislative Council in its first term was left to the decision of the NPC. Under Article 62(13) of the PRC Constitution, the NPC has the power to decide on the systems to be instituted in its special administrative regions. On 4th April 1990, the same day as the Basic Law was promulgated, the NPC made such a Decision. The relevant parts of this 1990 NPC Decision are paragraphs 1, 2 and 6. The effect of the Decision is this. The formation of the first Legislative Council must reflect the sovereignty of the State and must be conducive to a smooth transition. A Preparatory Committee is to be established in 1996. This Committee is entrusted with two tasks: first, it is responsible for matters relating to the preparation of the establishment of the HKSAR and second, it is to prescribe the specific method for the forming of the first Government and the first Legislative Council in accordance with the Decision of the NPC. The composition of the first Legislative Council is set out in paragraph 6:20 members to be returned by geographical constituencies through direct elections, 10 members by an election committee and 30 members by functional constituencies. There can be a "through train" for members of the last Hong Kong Legislative Council to become members of the first Legislative Council of the HKSAR provided they satisfy certain conditions: the composition of the last Hong Kong Legislative Council conforms with the Decision and the Basic Law; members uphold the Basic Law; members are willing to pledge allegiance to the HKSAR; members meet the requirements as specified in the Basic Law and the confirmation by the Preparatory Committee.

It is clear that at the time of the promulgation of the Basic Law in April 1990, it was intended that there would be a "through train" for members of the last Hong Kong Legislative Council. The purpose was to ensure continuity and to cause the least possible disruption as a result of the handover.

By 1994, as a result of the political reform proposals made by the last Governor, it was quite clear that the constitution and composition of the last Hong Kong Legislative Council would not be acceptable to the PRC. Consequently, the NPC Standing Committee made another Decision on 31st August 1994. Under that Decision, the Preparatory Committee for the HKSAR "shall be responsible for matters relating to the preparation of the establishment of the HKSAR, and to prescribe the specific method for the formation of the first Legislative Council of the HKSAR and organize the first Legislative Council of the HKSAR in accordance with the 1990 Decision of the NPC". This is not only a confirmation of the 1990 NPC Decision (paragraph 2). It also expressly authorizes the Preparatory Committee to organize the first Legislative Council. The question is: how did it set about doing it?

There has been a lot of political debate on the reasons for the lack of a through train. Ms Li, SC, for the respondents did not concede that the last Legislative Council failed to conform with the 1990 NPC Decision (paragraph 6). I do not propose to make any adjudication on this either. It is not the business of the Court to enter into the political arena and to determine what the real reasons were. In any event, the British Parliament had enacted the Hong Kong Act in 1985 providing that as from 1st July 1997, the Queen shall no longer have sovereignty or jurisdiction over any part of Hong Kong. The result of this is that all the Royal Instructions and Letters Patent would expire on 30th June 1997. That being the case, the Hong Kong Legislative Council which was established thereunder would come to an end upon the cessation of British sovereignty over Hong Kong. Unless members of the last Legislative Council were acceptable by the PRC as the first Legislative Council of the HKSAR, they would simply cease to be Legislative Council members on 30th June 1997.

The result of this unfortunate situation was not only obvious but also potentially disastrous. There would be no Legislative Council on 1st July 1997 unless something is done before then.

Proposals

Mr Fung, SC, for the Government submits that there can only be two possible solutions: to hold an election before 1st July 1997 or to hold it after that date. He says that it is not viable in the absence of Sino-British co-operation to hold elections before 1st July 1997. This is clearly correct. Hong Kong was still under British rule. It would be unrealistic to hold an election for the first Legislative Council in accordance with the Basic Law and the 1990 NPC Decision. The second alternative clearly presents some great difficulties which are almost insurmountable. This would also take time. But the more important thing is that the HKSAR could not afford to have no legislature during the meantime. The Preparatory Committee which was entrusted to set up the first Legislative Council is clearly not a Hong Kong organisation, let alone a legislative body. It could not for example enact electoral laws to carry out an election as soon as possible. There would be no legislature to approve the funding of such election.

Ms Li, SC, submits that it is necessary to amend the Basic Law. However, this may not be possible under its own terms. For one thing, the Basic Law had not then become operative yet. Under Article 159, the power of amendment of the Basic Law is vested in the NPC but the power to propose amendments is vested in three bodies, namely, the NPC Standing Committee, the State Council and the HKSAR. The procedures to be followed to effect an amendment could not then be followed because there was no HKSAR, no Chief Executive and no Legislative Council member to submit a proposal from Hong Kong and for the same reason, there was no Committee for the Basic Law to study the proposal. The NPC could of course amend the Basic Law before it came into effect. But that would be impracticable and politically undesirable.

Role of the court

However, all these proposed solutions (and there may be others) are irrelevant for the present purpose. The Court is not concerned with whether there was any solution or which solution would be better to salvage the unfortunate situation. The Court is to decide whether the particular course of action taken by the Preparatory Committee has any legal basis.

The Preparatory Committee set up an interim body called the Provisional Legislative Council. This may not be politically wise. It may not be popular or acceptable to all. But the Court is not concerned with that. It is the task of the Court to examine whether the NPC had authorised the Preparatory Committee to establish this interim body, whether the Preparatory Committee had done so pursuant to its authority and powers and whether the Provisional Legislative Council is the interim body set up by the Preparatory Committee.

Legality

The NPC is the highest state organ of the PRC which is the Sovereign of the HKSAR. It had made its Decisions in 1990 and 1994 regarding the formation of the HKSAR. It is not disputed that the Preparatory Committee was authorized by the NPC to carry out the tasks which are set out in the 1990 and 1994 NPC Decisions. In my view, it is clearly within the authority and powers of the Preparatory Committee to do acts which are necessary and incidental to the preparation of the establishment of the HKSAR. When it has become clear that there would be no first Legislative Council, the Preparatory Committee decided on 24th March 1996 to set up the Provisional Legislative Council. This was done in December 1996. It is conceded by the Government that the Provisional Legislative Council is <u>not</u> the first Legislative Council of the HKSAR. Nor does it purport to be. It was only set up to do specific acts. The duties of the Provisional Legislative Council include:

(a) to enact laws which are essential for the normal operation of the HKSAR; and to amend and repeal laws where necessary in accordance with the Basic Law;

(b) to examine and approve budgets introduced by the Government;

(c) to approve levying of taxes at public expenditure;

(d) to receive and debate the policy address of the Chief Executive;

(e) to endorse the appointments of the Judges of the Court of Final Appeal and the Chief Judge of the High Court;

(f) the President of the Provisional Legislative Council of the HKSAR to take part in the nomination of six Hong Kong members to the Committee for the Basic Law of the HKSAR under the Standing Committee of the NPC;

(g) to deal with other matters that have to be dealt with by the Provisional Legislative Council of the HKSAR before the formation of the first Legislative Council of the HKSAR.

Further, it is also specified that the laws examined and passed by the Provisional Legislative Council before 1st July 1997 shall only come into force from the day the HKSAR is established. It shall operate until the first Legislative Council of the HKSAR is formed which shall not be later than 30 June 1998.

It is clear that the terms of reference of the Provisional Legislative Council as set out in the 1996 Decision of the Preparatory Committee are necessary and incidental to the initial operation of the first Government of the HKSAR. It was formed to assist the first Government in the absence of the first Legislative Council. Its formation is an interim measure out of necessity. This the Sovereign has undoubtedly the power to do. It was not intended as a breach of the Basic Law. It was done with the intention to implement the provisions of the Basic Law and the NPC Decisions.

Ms Li, SC, argues that the Provisional Legislative Council does not comply with Article 68 of the Basic Law. This may be so. In fact, at one stage, Mr Fung, SC, seems to concede that. But this is not the point. Although the Provisional Legislative Council has purported to act as a legislative body, it does so pursuant to the duties imposed on it by the 1996 Decision of the Preparatory Committee. It is, strictly speaking, not a Legislative Council under Article 68 of the Basic Law. It was not a creation of the Basic Law. It was not meant to be. It is only an interim body formed by the Preparation Committee under the authority and powers of the NPC pursuant to the 1990 and 1994 NPC Decisions. It was never intended to be a Legislative Council of the type and composition as specified in the Basic Law.

The positon is simply this. The NPC did by its 1990 Decision authorise the Preparatory Committee to prepare for the establishment of the HKSAR and specify the method of forming the first Government and first Legislative Council. It did by its 1994 Decision authorise the Preparatory Committee to organise the first Legislative Council. The Preparatory Committee established the Provisional Legislative Council as an interim body to enable the first Government to get going in the absence of the first Legislative Council and to set about forming the first Legislative Council. This is within the ambit of the authority and powers conferred on it under the 1990 and 1994 NPC Decisions.

For these reasons, I am inclined to hold that the Provisional Legislative Council was legally established by the NPC through the Preparatory Committee pursuant to the authority and powers conferred upon it. The NPC being the Sovereign of the HKSAR, the validity of the acts of establishing this interim body cannot be challenged in the HKSAR courts.

Ratification by NPC

The Government also relies on the ratification by the NPC made on 14th March 1997. It was a resolution of the Eighth NPC (not merely the Standing Committee) at its fifth session adopting the working report of the Preparatory Committee which set out the details of its Decision to establish the Provisional Legislative Council. By this adoption, Mr Fung, SC, argues, the NPC has expressly ratified the Preparatory Committee's Decision. It is a ratification by the Sovereign which has the effect of law. Hence, the legality of the Provisional Legislative Council cannot be doubted.

It is argued on behalf of the respondents that this Resolution is not sufficient for the purpose of endorsing or ratifying the Preparatory Committee's decision to set up the Provisional Legislative Council.

The Resolution states that the NPC had examined the working report of the Preparatory Committee and "hereby approves" it. The Chinese text uses words " 批准 pi zhun" which mean that the NPC "permits or allows" the report. This must refer to the acts or actions taken by the Preparatory Committee. However, it is not necessary to rely on the Chinese text because, in my view, the English version of the Resolution to which the report is annexed is quite clear.

The Resolution recites the fact that the Preparatory Committee has adopted in accordance with the Basic Law and other principles a series of decisions, resolutions and proposals including the Decision on the establishment of the Provisional Legislative Council of the HKSAR. It recognizes the election presided by the Preparatory Committee by which the Selection Committee had elected the members of the Provisional Legislative Council. It acknowledges that all these had laid down a foundation for the establishment of the HKSAR and a smooth transition of Hong Kong.

Annexed to the Resolution was the working report of the Preparatory Committee. The report states amongst other things the following:

> "Some doubts have been raised in Hong Kong's public opinion about the power of the Preparatory Committee in making decision on the formation of the Provisional Legislative Council. In fact, Article 2 of the above mentioned Decision of the NPC provides that the Preparatory Committee 'shall be responsible for matters relating to the preparation for the establishment of the HKSAR' . The formation of the Provisional Legislative Council falls within this ambit. It is a power organ established by the NPC. The Preparatory Committee has been authorized to make decisions on matters relating to the establishment of the HKSAR. This authorization covers the power to form the Provisional Legislative Council.
>
> In the light of the actual situation that the legislature must be in place upon the establishment of the HKSAR and in accordance with the above mentioned Decision of the NPC, the plenary session of the Preparatory Committee in March 1996 adopted the Decision to form the Provisional Legislative Council of the HKSAR. In October, it adopted the method on the formation of the Provisional Legislative Council of the HKSAR. The method provides that the Provisional Legislative Council of the HKSAR shall be elected by select ballot by the Selection Committee for the first Government of the HKSAR. The Provisional Legislative Council shall be formed and start working after the appointment of the first Chief Executive of the HKSAR. Its main tasks include enactment of laws which are indispensable to the normal operation of the HKSAR and participation in necessary personnel arrangements. It shall function until the first Legislative Council of the HKSAR is formed but not later than 30th June 1998. The Decision of the Preparatory Committee on the establishment of the Provisional Legislative Council of the HKSAR and the above mentioned method are in compliance with the Decision of the NPC on the method for the formation of the first Government and on the first Legislative Council of HKSAR adopted by the Seventh National People's Congress at its third session on 4th April 1990."

The report not only recognizes the authority and powers of the Preparatory Committee, it also states clearly that the Provisional Legislative Council was in fact formed pursuant to the exercise of such authorization and powers. It regards the formation of the Provisional Legislative Council as necessary and sets out the main tasks of this interim body and its term of office.

In my view, the Ratification is sufficiently clear. It adopts the course of action taken by the Preparation Committee as set out quite fully in its working report. It is clear that the NPC as the highest state organ of the Sovereign of the HKSAR has adopted the setting up of the Provisional Legislative Council and its work before the establishment and formation of the first Legislative Council. The Ratification is a sovereign act which the HKSAR courts cannot challenge.

In view of the conclusions I have reached, it is not necessary to deal with the doctrine of necessity and I do not propose to do so.

Conclusion

For the reasons which I have set out above, I have come to the conclusion that upon a true construction and interpretation of the relevant provisions of the Basic Law, the laws previously in force in Hong Kong including the common law have been adopted and become the laws of HKSAR on 1st July 1997, the judicial system together with the principles applicable to court proceedings have continued, and indictments and pending criminal proceedings have continued to be valid.

The answers to the questions reserved for this Court are that the common law has survived the change of sovereignty and the three respondents are liable to answer to and be tried under the Amended Indictment.

If I am wrong on the interpretation of the relevant provisions of the Basic Law, I am of the view that the provisions of the Reunification Ordinance has made it amply clear that the common law survives, the indictment is still valid and the pending criminal proceedings continue. It is an ordinance which was lawfully and validly passed by the Provisional Legislative Council which was legally established by the Preparatory Committee which is an NPC body and exercises the authority and powers conferred on it by the 1990 and 1994 NPC Decisions. Its establishment was ratified by the NPC on 14th March 1997.

Nazareth V-P:

Introduction

I gratefully adopt the comprehensive statement of the background given in the judgment of my Lord, the Chief Judge.

Upon the two questions of law referred, two principal points arise for decision:

(1) Has the common law survived the resumption of sovereignty by the PRC?

(2) Are the defendants liable to answer to and be tried on indictment No. 1/97?

Whether the common law has survived in HKSAR?

The defendants' submissions were put to us in the skeleton argument of Mr Chandler, who appeared for the 2nd defendant, which was adopted by Mr Egan for the 1st defendant. In substance, the submissions focused and relied primarily upon the words "... shall be adopted as the laws of the Region" in Article 160 of the Basic Law, contending that some additional act extrinsic to the Basic Law was required before the laws previously in force could become the laws of HKSAR on 1st July 1997.

It is not in dispute that the primary source of the law of the Hong Kong Special Administrative Region of the People's Republic of China ("HKSAR") is the Basic Law enacted by the National Congress of the People's Republic of China ("NPC"). The defendants' point to Articles 8, 18, 19, 87 and 160 of the Basic Law. The latter reads as follows:

"Article 160

Upon the establishment of the Hong Kong Special Administrative Region, the laws previously in force in Hong Kong <u>shall be adopted as laws of the Region</u> except for those which the Standing Committee of the National People's Congress declares to be in contravention of this Law. If any laws are later discovered to be in contravention of this Law, they shall be amended or cease to have force in accordance with the procedure as prescribed by this Law.

Documents, certificates, contracts, and rights and obligations valid under the laws previously in force in Hong Kong shall continue to be valid and be recognised and protected by the Hong Kong Special Administrative Region, provided that they do not contravene this Law." (emphasis supplied)

It was argued that significant support for that contention could be derived from the Decision of the Standing Committee of the NPC of 23rd February 1997. Paragraph 1 of that Decision is in the following terms:

"The laws previously in force in Hong Kong which include the common law, rules of equity, ordinances, subordinate legislation and customary law, except for those which contravene the Basic Law, are adopted as the laws of the HKSAR."

Paragraphs 2 and 3 state that Ordinances and subordinate legislation previously in force and set out respectively in Annexes I and II to the Decision are not adopted as the laws of Hong Kong.

Paragraph 4 states:

"such of the laws previously in force in Hong Kong which have been adopted as the laws of the HKSAR shall, as from 1 July 1997, be applied subject to such modifications, adaptations, limitations ..."

If, the argument runs, the Standing Committee of the NPC which exercises many of the legislative powers of the NPC under the constitution of the PRC has seen fit *albeit* in February 1997 to adopt laws previously in force in Hong Kong, then that must be a strong indication of the intention of Article 160 of the Basic Law. However, as will be seen, it is very clear from Articles 8, 18 and 84, that the laws previously in force are by virtue of Article 8 of itself and without any extrinsic act maintained as the laws of HKSAR subject to the reservations in Article 160. Moreover, it has been said the reiteration of the provisions of earlier laws is not unusual in Chinese practice (per Professor Yash Ghai (1997) HKLJ Vol 27 Part 2, 141). In the foregoing light, the decision can be seen to be directed to specifying those laws previously in force in Hong Kong that are not adopted as the laws of the HKSAR.

Similarly, the defendants seek to rely also upon the following paragraph in the preamble to the Hong Kong Reunification Ordinance 1997:

"The National People's Congress, in exercising its powers under Article 160 of the Basic Law on 23 February 1997, resolved which of the laws previously in force in Hong Kong are to be adopted as the valid laws of the Hong Kong Special Administrative Region and the principles on which those laws should be construed and adapted."

They seek also to rely upon a definition of "laws previously in force" inserted into the Interpretation and General Clauses Ordinance by the Hong Kong Reunification Ordinance as meaning the common law etc. in force in Hong Kong immediately before 1 July 1997 and adopted as the laws of the Hong Kong Special Administrative Region. Such reliance suffers from the deficiency identified in relation to the Decision of the Standing Committee of the NPC on 23rd February 1997. Moreover, the Provisional Legislative Council ("PLC") was created by the Preparatory Committee, itself a committee appointed by the NPC. It was appointed some six years and enacted the Reunification Ordinance some seven years after the enactment of the Basic Law. In these circumstances the views (if such they be) expressed in subordinate legislation made some seven years after the enactment of the primary legislation must be of insignificant assistance in construing provisions of the primary legislation.

Returning then to the words of Article 160, although Mr Chandler's skeleton focuses only upon "shall be adopted", it is their association with the earlier words "Upon establishment of the Hong Kong Special Administrative Region" that at first blush suggests a temporal qualification. Upon those words themselves, it could at least be said that as to whether or not an extrinsic act of adoption was required, Article 160 is ambiguous. Even that may be putting it too high. From Article 160 itself, it can be seen that the construction that an extrinsic act is necessary tends to produce anomalous results. Under the last paragraph of Article 160 (itself without any suggestion of anything more being required) rights and obligations under laws previously in force are continued. However that may be, any ambiguity would have to be resolved by reference to the Basic Law as a whole, and beyond that, to its genesis and even to the constitution of the PRC.

Articles 8, 18 and 87 of the Basic Law are as follows:

"Article 8

The laws previously in force in Hong Kong, that is, the common law, rules of equity, ordinances, subordinate legislation and customary law shall be maintained, except for any that contravene this Law, and subject to any amendment by the legislature of the Hong Kong

Special Administrative Region.

Article 18

The laws in force in the Hong Kong Special Administrative Region shall be this Law, the laws previously in force in Hong Kong as provided for in Article 8 of this Law, and the laws enacted by the legislature of the Region.

Article 87

In criminal or civil proceedings in the Hong Kong Special Administrative Region, the principles previously applied in Hong Kong and the rights previously enjoyed by parties to proceedings shall be maintained...."

Articles 19 and 87 may also be said to be relevant.

Plainly, the effect of Article 8 is that the common law continues and that it does so under Article 8 (rather than under Article 160) follows from Article 18. In that light, it can be seen that the real purpose and the effect of Article 160 is to provide for the non-adoption of such of the laws previously in force as the Standing Committee of the NPC declares to be in contravention of the Basic Law.

If Article 160 is to be reconciled with Articles 8, 18 and 84, then upon a common law approach, it would clearly be directory rather than mandatory, thus posing no threat to the survival in the HKSAR of the common law, not to mention the other vital components of Hong Kong law which together are provided for in these articles.

The defendants' contention that an intrinsic act of adoption was necessary to continue the common law must therefore be rejected. That conclusion becomes even clearer in the light of the overwhelming theme of a seamless transition in the Joint Declaration and the Basic Law.

The Chinese text of Article 160

For the HKSAR the Solicitor General relied also upon the Chinese text of the Basic Law, which under the NPC's Decision of 28th June 1990 prevails over the English text. His submissions are on their face plausible, and have not been controverted on behalf of the defendants. It must therefore be accepted that the Chinese text of Article 160 makes it clear that an act of adoption is not necessary. If the English text were ambiguous, this would produce the conclusion mentioned.

Whether the common law offence of conspiracy to pervert the course of justice is part of the law of Hong Kong

There remains to be considered the defendants' ancillary ground that the offence at common law of conspiracy to pervert the course of justice is not part of the law of the HKSAR. The nature of this ground is clearly explained in the judgment of my Lord Mortimer V-P, which I have had the advantage of seeing in draft. I agree with his reasons and conclusion. I would add that 1st July 1997 as the 'cut-off' date is also clear from the implications of the last paragraph of Article 160. It could not have been the intention in 1990 or in 1984, to continue contracts and obligations subsisting in those years with effect from 1st July 1997; it would have been foreseen that a goodly number of these would have long expired before then.

I would, therefore, answer the first question reserved to this Court in the affirmative.

Whether the indictment lapsed on 1st July 1997?

The defendants' challenge to the survival of the indictment was mounted upon the following basis:

(1) that the proceedings commenced and the indictment was filed in the former High Court while the British exercised sovereignty in Hong Kong;

(2) that the former High Court ceased to exist at midnight on 30th June 1997; and

(3) that the defendants are to be tried before the HKSAR Court of First Instance which was established by s.8 of the Reunification Ordinance 1997, which Ordinance is devoid of effect as being the enactment of a legally non-competent body.

The HKSAR's primary response is that the Reunification Ordinance does not enter into it at all; and that Article 160 provides a sufficient answer. It is, of course, the last paragraph of Article 160 that is relied upon.

It is specifically "rights and obligations" that are relied upon. In substance, it is contended that:

(i) the institution of the indictment vested a right in the prosecuting authorities to have it heard and determined in the courts;

(ii) there is a concurrent obligation imposed on the accused to be tried on that indictment, and an obligation to answer to it under s.49 of the Criminal Procedure Ordinance; and

(iii) there is a clear indication in Article 160 of the Basic Law that rights and obligations as before are to continue.

Given the predominant theme of a seamless transition and the purposive approach appropriate to constitutions that is called for (and not only upon that account as will be seen), it seems to me right that the last paragraph of Article 160 should be construed in the manner contended for by the Solicitor General.

That still leaves the question of the creation of the new court to be addressed. For the purpose, Article 81 is invoked. Its first paragraph reads:

> "The Court of Final Appeal, the High Court, district courts, magistrates' courts and other special courts shall be established in the Hong Kong Special Administrative Region. The High Court shall comprise the Court of Appeal and Court of First Instance. "(emphasis supplied)

For reasons similar to those that led me to the conclusion that the words "shall be adopted" in Article 160 do not require an additional act of adoption, it seems to me that the words "shall be established" likewise here do not require any additional act of establishment to legally create the courts mentioned; they stand established by the imperative words of the Basic Law upon the coming into force of that Law.

Likewise, it seems to me, that rules, procedures and the like would for the purpose be sufficiently provided for by the second paragraph of Article 81:

> "The judicial system previously practised in Hong Kong shall be maintained except for those changes consequent upon the establishment of the Court of Final Appeal of the Hong Kong Special Administrative Region."

The first paragraph of Article 87 is also in point:

"In criminal or civil proceedings in the Hong Kong Special Administrative Region, the principles previously applied in Hong Kong and the rights previously enjoyed by parties to proceedings shall be maintained."

For the foregoing reasons, I am satisfied that the indictment did not lapse and that the defendants' challenge to it fails. The second question referred accordingly also falls to be answered in the affirmative.

It is accordingly not necessary to address the HKSAR alternative ground, which is reliance upon the Reunification Ordinance. This contains very detailed and full provision for the continuity of legal proceedings. Understandably, no question has been raised as to the adequacy of those provisions and I can see no reason to suppose that they would not meet all the defendants' points, save the validity of the Ordinance itself. The latter is questioned, as I have said, on the basis of the legal competence of the PLC, the body that enacted it.

It is in this somewhat incidental way that this question of plainly momentous importance to Hong Kong comes to be raised. As I have said, in the light of the conclusions I have already reached, which suffice to dispose of the reference to this Court, it is now not necessary to address that question. In ordinary circumstances I would not have contemplated doing so. But this is no ordinary case. The question having been raised and full submissions received from distinguished senior counsel, it seems to me that it would not be in the public interest to decline to deal with it, for that would be at the same time suppress a potential opportunity for the question to be expeditiously resolved by the Court of Final Appeal and the Standing Committee of the NPC, if it comes to that. That we should deal with the matter was also the unanimous view of counsel, although Ms Li did say that the present circumstances perhaps do not appropriately present all the aspects that have to be examined to resolve the question.

Jurisdiction of HKSAR courts

In his submissions on the HKSAR's primary ground that the HKSAR courts have no jurisdiction to question the legality of the PLC, the Solicitor General began by assimilating the exercise of powers by the NPC (as the supreme organ of the state exercising both legislative and decision-making powers under the PRC constitution) to the exercise of powers previously by the sovereign and the scope for challenge in the previous Hong Kong courts. HKSAR courts, he submitted, had no more jurisdiction to entertain a challenge the legality of a legislature established by the sovereign via the NPC, than the previous Hong Kong courts would have had in respect of a legislature established via an Act of the British Parliament or an amendment of the Letters Patent.

I pause here to note that no instance has been traced by counsel before us of such a challenge in any British colony. Nor for that matter has any direct authority been produced for the proposition that no such challenge may be entertained.

Reverting then to the Solicitor General's submissions, the second paragraph of Article 19 of the Basic Law provides that:

"The courts of the Hong Kong Special Administrative Region shall have jurisdiction over all cases in the Region, except that the restrictions on their jurisdiction imposed by the legal system and principles previously in force in Hong Kong shall be maintained."

This, it is submitted, defines the jurisdiction of the HKSAR courts, and reflects the previous jurisdiction, conferring no greater power.

The establishment of the PLC, it is said, is a matter purely of Chinese national law.

The HKSAR is established under the Basic Law with its national law that of the PRC; and the Basic Law is enacted under Article 31 of the PRC constitution. Both these propositions are obviously right and are not disputed.

No amendment, the submission went on, is necessary to implement the PLC. The method of formation of the legislature was specified in Annex II in the Basic Law; otherwise it was left to the PRC to establish the first government and legislature. This contention, it should be mentioned, was vigorously contested by Ms Li; but it falls to be addressed rather more directly in the context of the next major issue.

Ms Li also strongly opposed the Solicitor General's other submissions. She pointed out that the Basic Law is an interface, in the one country, between the two systems, which results in exceedingly complex questions. The PRC constitution contains some provisions which cannot apply to the HKSAR. The Basic Law, she observes, was passed under Article 31. Is the court, therefore, restricted to Article 31 and precluded from looking further? The answer, Ms Li submitted, must lie in the Basic Law. Specifically, with respect to the HKSAR's submission on the jurisdiction of the HKSAR courts, she pointed out that the basis upon which it proceeds is that there is no distinction between NPC laws and Acts of Parliament (and prerogative orders in council, one may add). She pointed to the judgment of this Court in *Lee Miu-ling and anor v. Attorney General* [1996] 1 HKC 124, which recognised that the Hong Kong courts could examine the compliance of Hong Kong Ordinances with the Letters Patent.

The Solicitor General made it clear that

(a) the HKSAR submission did not for one moment question the competence of Hong Kong courts before 1st July 1997 to determine questions of conformity of Hong Kong statutory law with the Letters Patent; and

(b) similarly, that the HKSAR courts, after 30th June 1997, are clearly empowered to determine questions of constitutionality of SAR made legislation *vis-a-vis* the Basic Law; see, he says, e.g. Article 158 of the Basic Law.

I pause here to note that what on the face of Article 158 appears to be a bare power to interpret the Basic Law, does not seem to import also power to determine the constitutionality of SAR made laws *vis-a-vis* the Basic Law, which seems however to flow from the second paragraph of Article 19.

The Solicitor General contended that *Lee Miu-ling* validates the HKSAR's submission in that it is authority that the Hong Kong courts could determine questions of conformity of Hong Kong statutes with the Letters Patent, but not authority that the appointment of the legislature could be questioned. That does seem to be so. But it leaves unclear the basis upon which such conformity may be questioned given that both the creation of the courts (though perhaps not all their jurisdiction), and of the legislature were acts of the sovereign. In the absence of any authoritative indication of what is the basis of such accepted jurisdiction, it is difficult to see how such limited jurisdiction to question the conformity of legislation can found a challenge to the appointment of the legislature itself, clearly an act of the sovereign in that previous context. Turning to the post 30th June 1997 situation, to the extent that the restrictions on their jurisdiction imposed by the legal system and principles previously in Hong Kong" maintained under the second paragraph of Article 19 of the Basic Law applies, the courts of the HKSAR courts would have the same jurisdiction, i.e. to question conformity of legislation but not the appointment of the legislature. That, it seems to me, must clearly depend upon whether or not the legislature was created by the sovereign, as previously.

Proceeding to the Solicitor General's refinements in reply, he referred to the position of the Hong Kong courts before 1st July 1997 which could not determine the constitutionality of either UK Metropolitan or Imperial legislation vis-a-vis either the unwritten British constitution or the Hong Kong's Letters Patent. Neither, he said, could the Hong Kong courts judicially review metropolitan executive acts upon the following bases:

(a) The doctrine of parliamentary sovereignty.

(b) The principle of constitutional hierarchy whereby Acts of Parliament and ministerial decisions were not subject to the Hong Kong Letters Patent.

(c) The different legal systems under which Parliamentary Acts are enacted and ministerial decisions in the metropolis are made, from that under which the colonial courts operated. English law, though similar, was certainly not the same as Hong Kong law; the British legal system *a fortiori* was not the Hong Kong legal system.

(d) No remedy could properly issue since neither Acts of Parliament or ministerial decisions are subject to Hong Kong jurisdiction.

On the material before this Court, subject to the reservations I have to voice, it seems to me, that those four matters have to be accepted, and likewise the conclusions contended for that the Hong Kong courts could not have entertained any challenge to the Hong Kong Act 1985 or any of the orders in council made thereunder; and that e.g. Hong Kong courts could not have determined the constitutionality of a decision of the Secretary of State applicable to Hong Kong.

In the light of the foregoing, if the Preparatory Committee is a working committee under the NPC and thereby a creature of the sovereign, this Court could not review its constitutionality or the legality of its actions. As to that, given Article 2 of the NPC Decision of 4th April 1990, it is difficult to avoid the conclusion that the Preparatory Committee is a creature of the sovereign, i.e. the NPC. It must follow, in the absence of any other law or principle none having been brought to notice, that this Court cannot inquire into the constitutionality of the PLC.

I would add that I neither need to rely upon nor am I attracted by the additional HKSAR ground that the confirmation of the HKSAR judiciary by the PLC must by the absurdity that would be precipitated by the judiciary thereafter ruling the PLC illegal, precludes or limits the HKSAR courts capability of determining the act of the Preparatory Committee creating the PLC to be illegal or unconstitutional.

Although I am driven to the conclusion I have expressed, I cannot say I have come to accept it without hesitation. Ms Li pointed to a number of matters that could impinge upon it. The analogy between NPC and the British "sovereign" upon further examination may not hold in material respects. There is a written constitution in China, and presumably nothing that corresponds to the Royal Prerogative. Nor has there been a detailed review of the provisions of the PRC constitution according to Ms Li, which it was hinted might bear upon the matter. While, therefore, I find myself unable to resist the conclusion expressed upon the actual submissions made to the Court, I find it necessary to say that even though the foregoing be obiter, it should not be regarded as a concluded view.

That view, however, obviates the necessity to address also the question of the legality of the PLC, but for the reasons already given, I now turn to that matter.

Legality of the Provisional Legislative Council

Ms Li, with Miss Margaret Ng and Mr Paul Harris, presented this aspect of the defendants' case. Her submission was quite simple. The PLC contravenes the Basic Law and the Decision made by the NPC on the same day, in material respects. She was easily able to demonstrate non-conformity by reference to individual provisions in the Basic Law and the Decision. Indeed, the Basic Law does not even mention a Provisional Legislative Council. Therefore, she submitted, the PLC has not been validly constituted. I do not propose here to adumbrate her elaboration of that submission, which I address in this judgment as it arises. The individual provisions that Ms Li said are contravened as follows:

> "Article 68
>
> The Legislative Council of the Hong Kong Special Administrative Region shall be constituted by election.
>
> The method for forming the Legislative Council shall be specified in the light of the actual situation in Hong Kong Special Administrative Region and in accordance with the principle of gradual and orderly progress. The ultimate aim is the election of all the members of the Legislative Council by universal suffrage.
>
> The specific method for forming the Legislative Council and its procedures for voting on bills and motions are prescribed in Annex II: 'Method for the Formation of the Legislative Council of the Hong Kong Special Administrative Region and Its Voting Procedures'.
>
> Article 69
>
> The term of office of the Legislative Council of the Hong Kong Special Administrative Region shall be four years, except the first term which shall be two years."

Annex II, as to such part of it as is relevant, is as follows:

> "I. Method for the Formation of the Legislative Council:
>
> 1. The Legislative Council of the Hong Kong Special Administrative Region shall be composed of 60 members in each term. In the first term, the Legislative Council shall be formed in accordance with the 'Decision of the National People's Congress on the Method for the Formation of the First Government and the First Legislative Council of the Hong Kong Special Administrative Region'. The composition of the Legislative Council in the second and third terms shall be as follows:
>
> ...
>
> 2. Except in the case of the first Legislative Council, ..."

The Decision of the National People's Congress on the method for the formation for the first government and first Legislative

Council of the Hong Kong Special Administrative Region was made, clearly by adoption of resolution, on 4th April 1990, i.e. the same day as the Basic Law was passed. The following of its provisions are relevant:

"1. The first Government and the first Legislative Council of the Hong Kong Special Administrative Region shall be formed in accordance with the principles of state sovereignty and smooth transition.

2. Within the year 1996, the National People's Congress shall establish a Preparatory Committee for the Hong Kong Special Administrative Region, which shall be responsible for matters relating to the preparation of the establishment of the Region and shall prescribe the specific method for forming the first Government and the first Legislative Council in accordance with this Decision. ...

3. ...

4. ...

5. ...

6. The first Legislative Council of the Hong Kong Special Administrative Region shall be composed of 60 members, with 20 members returned by geographical constituencies through direct elections, 10 members returned by an election Committee, and 30 members returned by functional constituencies. If the composition of the last Hong Kong Legislative Council is in conformity with the relevant provisions of this Decision and the Basic Law of the Hong Kong Special Administrative Region, those of its members who uphold the Basic Law of the Hong Kong Special Administrative Region of the People's Republic of China and are willing to pledge allegiance to the Hong Kong Special Administrative Region of the People's Republic of China, and who meet the requirements set forth in the Basic Law of the Region may, upon confirmation of the Preparatory Committee for the Hong Kong Special Administrative Region, become members of the first Legislative Council of the Region.

The term of office of members of the first Legislative Council of the Hong Kong Special Administrative Region shall be two years."

It is helpful in addressing that submission to know the broad nature of the Solicitor General's response. This is that the PLC was in any event validly established under the Basic Law. Little time need be spent upon the several and significant respects in which the PLC does not conform with the Basic Law, and relevant decisions of the NPC or NPCSC, which Ms Li clearly demonstrated. The Solicitor General readily conceded that the Basic Law does not even mention the PLC. More importantly he clarified that the HKSAR case was not that the PLC was the first Legislative Council of the HKSAR, but a provisional legislative body set up by the Preparatory Committee to get what was to be a through train back on track after it had been derailed by the last governor's political reforms. Whatever view one might take of the latter, and whether or not those reforms had been made, the fact was that the 1995 Legislative Council would have lapsed at midnight on 30th June 1997. That was the inevitable result of the end of British sovereignty and the resumption of the exercise of Chinese sovereignty. It was also fully reflected in the Hong Kong Act 1985 of the United Kingdom Parliament.

It was for the PRC to fill the legal vacuum that would ensue. That is not in dispute. On the same day that the NPC enacted the Basic Law, it also passed the Decision providing for establishment of a preparatory committee for the Hong Kong Special Administrative Region in the year 1996, to be responsible for prescribing the specific method for forming the first Legislative Council.

In 1996 the situation was that those provisions were not going to prevent a legal vacuum. Compliance with them required the cooperation of the British. It is not suggested that this would be forthcoming. So elections could not be held before 1st July 1997. There was also no suggestion before us that the elections could be held after that date without an unacceptable legislative vacuum.

By Article 2 of the NPC declaration of 4th April 1990, the Preparatory Committee was responsible for matters relating to the establishment of the SAR including *inter alia* the first Legislative Council in accordance with the Decision. Article 6 specified the detailed composition of the first Legislative Council. This could not be complied with as indicated. Elections could not be held before 1st July 1997; they also could not be held early enough after that day. Some interim arrangements therefore had to be made. It being impossible to form the first Legislative Council under Article 6, the Preparatory Committee decided to form a provisional legislative council under Article 2 to prevent a legal vacuum while the first Legislative Council was being constituted under Article 6.

Although expressed as Decisions of the NPC the Decisions of 4th April 1990 and 8th August 1994 must be regarded as legislation or enactments, given their content and effect. The responsibility placed upon the Preparatory Committee for "matters relating to the preparation of the establishment of the Region" and the direction that it "organise the First Legislative Council" in the two Decisions, must carry with them all such powers as are reasonably necessary to enable the Preparatory Committee to carry out those duties.

If this produced a result that did not accord with the Basic Law, that does not mean the Basic Law itself had to be amended. Reference was made to the PRC constitution, but no such requirement was shown. The detailed provisions for the formation of the first Legislative Council were hived off by the NPC in the contemporaneously made Decision of the 4th April 1990. If any inconsistency arises between the Basic Law and the Decisions in relation to the formation of the first Legislative Council, clearly the latter as the more specific (and later in respect of the 8th August 1994 Decision) must prevail.

The question, therefore, is this: "Was the creation of the PLC sanctioned by the two NPC Decisions?" The question is not whether the PLC conformed to Article 6 of the former, for if the PLC was validly appointed under Article 2 of the 4th April 1990 Decision, or under the 1994 Decision, non-conformity with Article 6 would be irrelevant.

For Hong Kong common law courts, that is not an easy question. It is one that involves interpretation of Chinese law to produce a construction that properly viewed must be made in accordance with Chinese law. However that may be, I cannot see that the Preparatory Committee's establishment of the PLC as other than in accordance with the NPC Decisions, even if the matter is approached upon common law canons of construction. The theme running through the Joint Declaration, the Basic Law enacted to implement the basic policies of the People's Republic of China that the Joint Declaration embodies, and the associated Decisions of the NPC and the Standing Committee of the NPC, was of a smooth transition. A purposive construction is one of the well recognised methods of common law construction, and is clearly called for by the broad policy and principles in terms of which the PRC instruments are formulated and drafted and their constitutional nature.

The inability of the Preparatory Committee to comply with Article 6 of the 4th April Decision did not absolve it from its duty to organise the first Legislative Council. In those circumstances it decided that the appropriate action to take, was to bring the derailed legislative train back on track. This could not be done immediately, for elections take time. If decided that in the interim a provisional body should be constituted to attend to the functions of the Legislative Council that necessarily had to be performed. Not everyone might agree that was the most efficient way of proceeding. But it was done to meet the situation and the object was not to create a provisional legislature but a provisional body with a limited life that had to have legislative powers in order to fill the vacuum while the bringing of the first Legislative Council into being was organised. What was appointed was not the first Legislative Council; it was a body known as the Provisional Legislative Council to act in the interim. What was done was reasonably necessary and within the scope of the duty and concomitant power under the two NPC Decisions. Even upon the common law approach of judicial review that approach could not be faulted as being irrational; plainly it is not.

However, it is said the result of that was to effect a breach of the Basic Law in particular of Article 68, which says that the Legislative Council of the HKSAR shall be constituted by election, and that no amendment was made to the Basic Law. But it is plain from the Basic Law that the special provisions already mentioned were made in respect of the first term and the first Legislative Council. The NPC was entitled to place them in the 4th April Decision. Article 68 not only said that the Legislative Council of the HKSAR shall be constituted by election, it went on to say that:

> "The method for forming the Legislative Council shall be specified in the light of the actual situation in Hong Kong Special Administrative Region and in accordance with the principle of gradual and orderly progress. The ultimate aim is the election of all the members of the Legislative Council by universal suffrage."

For those reasons, in my view, the appointment of the PLC must be regarded as valid under Chinese law and the defendants' challenge to the legality of the PLC rejected.

NPC ratification of the Preparatory Committee's decision to set up the PLC

Yet another ground relied upon by the HKSAR is that the Preparatory Committee's decision to set up the PLC was ratified by the NPC.

On 14th March 1997, the NPC passed a resolution on the working report of the Preparatory Committee. The English translation furnished to us includes the following sentence:

> "The Session hereby approves the Report."

Then, after referring to what the Preparatory Committee had done, the resolution adds this:

> "All these laid down a foundation for the establishment of the HKSAR and the smooth transition of Hong Kong and have facilitated the long-term stability and prosperity of Hong Kong."

In general, it is fair to say that the resolution recognised and approved the work done by the Preparatory Committee.

It is this resolution then that the HKSAR submission contends, constitutes ratification of the Preparatory Committee's establishment of the PLC. It has to be said that it would be regarded as deficient if judged purely upon common law norms. But we are here not dealing with a common law legislature or even a common law jurisdiction; nor in my view could it be right to approach the matter with traditional common law methods and precedents of legislative ratification in mind.

The Preparatory Committee report was annexed to the resolution. It contained the following paragraph:

> "Some doubts have been raised in Hong Kong's public opinion about the power of the Preparatory Committee in making decision on the formation of the Provisional Legislative Council. In fact, Article 2 of the above-mentioned Decision of the NPC provides that the Preparatory Committee 'shall be responsible for matters relating to the preparation for the establishment of the HKSAR' . The formation of the Provisional Legislative Council falls within this ambit. As a power organ established by the NPC, the Preparatory Committee has been authorized to make decisions on matters relating to the establishment of the HKSAR. This authorization covers the power to form the Provisional Legislative Council."

In its resolution the NPC praised the work of the Provisional Committee. In approving the report, the NPC must have approved the action it took. But whether that amounted to ratification, I have found myself ill-equipped to judge. For instance, is a resolution of that sort an accepted form of legislative ratification? Perhaps we should have been assisted by expert evidence. For the reasons that my Lords give, they are satisfied that the resolution constitutes ratification. Having regard to those reasons, I am persuaded that I should not press my reservations to the point of expressing a dissenting view.

The doctrine of necessity

Finally, the last of the HKSAR's layered grounds is referred to as the doctrine of necessity. I do not find it necessary to rely upon it and express no view upon its application to the appointment of the PLC.

Conclusion

To sum up my conclusions, I would answer the two questions in the affirmative.

Upon the submissions made to this Court, in my view:

(i) This Court has no jurisdiction to entertain challenges to the legality of the Provisional Legislative Council, that being a body established by the sovereign.

(ii) The Provisional Legislative Council was validly appointed under the NPC Decisions of 4th April 1990 and 8th August 1994, which have effect as laws in China.

(iii) The appointment of the provisional legislature was ratified by the NPC Resolution of 14th March 1997.

I express no view upon the doctrine of necessity and its application to the appointment of the Provisional Legislative Council.

Mortimer V-P:

I also would answer the two questions referred to this Court in the affirmative.

Representation by counsel

Before I turn to the issues, I also would like to mention the difficulties which arose over the representation of the defendants. The Director of Legal Aid declined the Court's invitation to brief leading counsel for the 3rd defendant and consequently on this reference, he appears in person but with Mr Halley holding a watching brief. The other two defendants declined to brief counsel for this hearing, but Mr Egan for the first and Mr Chandler for the second accepted our invitation to remain to present their submissions for our assistance. A helpful skeleton had been provided by Mr Chandler and that was also relied upon by Mr Egan.

After the short adjournment on the first day, Ms Gladys Li, SC, (Miss Margaret Ng and Mr Paul Harris with her) appeared to offer her services to the Court–it would seem as amicus. For my part, there were serious problems about her locus standi. For obvious reasons it would be difficult for the Court to accept as its amicus counsel who appears without invitation. Fortunately, however, the 1st defendant invited Ms Li to lead Mr Egan to advance submissions limited to the legality of the Provisional Legislative Council (PLC). This she did. Her closely reasoned and attractively presented submissions, I find both helpful and enlightening.

The reference

On 7th July 1997 the three defendants were arraigned before Deputy Judge Lugar–Mawson in the Court of First Instance on count 1 of Indictment No. 1 of 1997. They pleaded not guilty to an offence of conspiracy to pervert the course of justice contrary to common law.

Counsel for the defendants moved to quash count 1 of the Indictment on grounds set out in their motion to quash which have now been argued before us.

Counsel for the Government moved by notice of motion that the issues of law arising should be reserved by the Deputy Judge to this Court under s.81 of the Criminal Procedure Ordinance, Cap. 221. Counsel for the defendants did not oppose. By an amended order, the judge reserved two questions for our determination:

(1) Is the offence at common law of conspiracy to pervert the course of public justice part of the laws of the HKSAR?

(2) Are the accused liable to answer to and to be tried on count 1 of Indictment No. 1 of 1997?

The legislative history

It is useful to briefly set out the legislative history of the establishment of the Hong Kong Special Administrative Region (HKSAR).

On 19th December 1994, by the Joint Declaration, the United Kingdom agreed to restore Hong Kong to the People's Republic of China and the Government of the People's Republic of China decided to resume sovereignty over Hong Kong with effect from 1st July 1997.

By Annex I, the Government of the PRC elaborated its basic policies regarding Hong Kong. By clause 3, it was agreed that

> "The Hong Kong Special Administrative Region will be vested with executive, legislative and independent judicial power, including that of final adjudication. The laws currently in force in Hong Kong will remain basically unchanged".

Under s.2 of that annexure, it was stated

> "... the laws previously in force in Hong Kong ... shall be maintained, save for any that contravene the Basic Law..."

and

> "The legislative power of the Hong Kong Special Administrative Region shall be vested in the legislature of the Hong Kong Special Administrative Region ...".

Also,

> "The laws of the Hong Kong Special Administrative Region shall be the Basic Law, and the laws previously in force in Hong Kong and laws enacted by the Hong Kong Special Administrative Region legislature ...".

The constitution of the PRC provides *inter alia* the following:

> "Article 31
>
> The state may establish special administrative regions when necessary. The systems to be instituted in special administrative regions shall be prescribed by law enacted by the National People's Congress in the light of the specific conditions.
>
> Article 57
>
> The National People's Congress of the People's Republic of China is the highest organ of state power. Its permanent body is the Standing Committee of the National People's Congress.
>
> Article 58
>
> The National People's Congress and its Standing Committee exercise the legislative power of the state.
>
> Article 62
>
> The National People's Congress exercises the following functions and powers:
>
> ...
>
> (13) to decide on the establishment of special administrative regions *and the systems to be instituted there*; " (emphasis supplied)

The Joint Declaration is reflected in the Basic Law with little change. The Basic Law was adopted by the 7th National People's Congress and was promulgated by the President on 4th April 1990.

On the same day by a decision of the National People's Congress ("the NPC"), the Preparatory Committee for the HKSAR was established.

Clauses 2 and 6 of that Decision are in point. The relevant parts read:

"2. Within the year 1996, the National People's Congress shall establish a Preparatory Committee for the Hong Kong Special Administrative Region, which shall be responsible for matters relating to the preparation of the establishment of the Region and shall prescribe the specific method for forming the first Government and the first Legislative Council in accordance with this Decision."

Clause 6 sets out the composition of the first Legislative Council and the conditions to be imposed for those who were to become members of it. Significantly the term of office of members of the first Legislative Council shall be two years–the balance of a 4-year term after the 1995 elections–a through legislative train was intended.

The Basic Law is Chinese law applicable to the HKSAR and is semi- constitutional in nature. It falls for the Hong Kong courts with specified limits to interpret its provisions. The whole tenor of the Basic Law–following the Joint Declaration–is to establish continuity save for those changes necessary upon the Chinese resumption of sovereignty. This principle pervades the whole of the Basic Law and it addresses all aspects of the HKSAR public life. Relevant to our consideration, there are provisions for the continuity of laws, the judiciary, the legal system and the legislature. I now turn to consider the individual questions posed but before I do so, I address one submission by Mr Chandler in which he takes a discrete point, i.e. in any event the offence of common law conspiracy is not applied to the HKSAR by the Basic Law. It is convenient to deal with that issue now.

Section 159E of the Crimes Ordinance, Cap. 200

This engages the true interpretation of the words "the laws previously in force in Hong Kong" which appear, among others, in Articles 8, 18 and 160 of that law. It is those Articles that are mainly relied upon by the Solicitor General in his submissions for the Government. These provisions have been set out by the Chief Judge in his judgment. I do not repeat them here although I will do so later in my judgment.

The Crimes (Amendment) Ordinance 1996 came into force on 2nd August 1996. Section 159E(1) as amended provides:

"Subject to the following provisions of this section, the offence of conspiracy at common law is abolished."

However, sub-section (7) provides that sub-section (1) above does not affect:

"Any proceedings commenced before the time when this part comes into operation."

There is no doubt that the proceedings under count of Indictment 1 of 1997 were valid when commenced and when the trial began. Were the laws which validated those proceedings "laws previously in force in Hong Kong" ?

Three "cut-off" dates for laws previously in force are suggested as possible:

(a) 19th December 1984. The signing of the Joint Declaration.

(b) 4th April 1990. The promulgation of the Basic Law.

(c) 1st July 1997. The coming into force in Hong Kong of the Basic Law.

As the Basic Law was not in force in Hong Kong until 1st July 1997 on the narrow point which arises in this reference, the Basic Law can only refer to those laws previously in force before 1st July 1997. That is the 'cut-off' date.

The words "the laws previously in force in Hong Kong" refer to the law as it was on 30th June 1997 and as it was at the time when the trial of the defendants began. Subject to the other submissions to which I will turn, Articles 8, 18 and 160 do provide for the application to the HKSAR of the law in force on 30th June 1997. On 1st July 1997 these articles validate the offence charged in count 1, the Indictment and those proceedings. That, of course, is subject to consideration of the other issues to which I now turn.

Is the offence at common law of conspiracy to pervert the course of public justice part of the laws of the HKSAR?

Before 1st July 1997 the common law applied to Hong Kong. Arguably, the common law was applied here since Captain Elliot's Declaration in 1841–as was assumed in s.5 of the Supreme Court Ordinance 1844. The purpose of the Application of English Law Ordinance Cap. 88 which came into force in 1966 was–as it said in the preamble– "to declare the extent to which English law is in force in the Colony".

There is no doubt that the common law does not apply to the HKSAR after the change of sovereignty unless it is applied to the HKSAR by Chinese law. This is a self-evident proposition. It is not necessary to consider the provisions of the Hong Kong Act 1985 to the same effect.

The Solicitor General (Mr Andrew Bruce, SC, and Miss Wan with him) appears for the Government. His main submission is that the Basic Law applies the common law to the HKSAR since 1st July 1997. He relies particularly upon Articles 8, 18 and 160. These provide:

"Article 8

The laws previously in force in Hong Kong, that is, the common law, rules of equity, ordinances, subordinate legislation and customary law shall be maintained, except for any that contravene this Law, and subject to any amendment by the legislature of the Hong Kong Special Administrative Region.

Article 18

The laws in force in the Hong Kong Special Administrative Region shall be this Law, the laws previously in force in Hong Kong as provided for in Article 8 of this Law, and the laws enacted by the legislature of the Region.

Article 160

Upon the establishment of the Hong Kong Special Administrative Region, the laws previously in force in Hong Kong shall be adopted as laws of the Region except for those which the Standing Committee of the National People's Congress declares to be in contravention of this Law. If any laws are later discovered to be in contravention of this Law, they shall be amended or cease to have force in accordance with the procedure as prescribed by this Law.

Documents, certificates, contracts, and rights and obligations valid under the laws previously in force in Hong Kong shall continue to be valid and be recognised and protected by the Hong Kong Special Administrative

> Region, provided that they do not contravene this Law."

However, counsel for the defendants submit to the contrary. They contend that the words in Article 8

> "the laws previously in force in Hong Kong ... *shall be maintained* ...",

the words in Article 18

> "the laws in force in the Hong Kong Special Administrative Region shall be this law, the laws previously in force in Hong Kong ...",

and the words in Article 160

> "upon the establishment of the Hong Kong Special Administrative Region, the laws previously in force in Hong Kong *shall be adopted* as laws of the Region ..."

require some positive instrument of acceptance or act of adoption before the provisions take effect. They contend that there has been no such instrument or act of adoption.

The Decision of the Standing Committee of the NPC of the 23rd February 1997, they submit, reinforces the argument. That Decision sets out Article 160 and Article 8 of the Basic Law and by clause 1 adopts the common law as law previously in force in Hong Kong but by Annex I, the Application of English Law Ordinance Cap. 88 is specifically not adopted as a law of the HKSAR.

Additionally, they rely upon the terms of the Reunification Ordinance, pointing out that the Ordinance only preserves those laws which "have been adopted as laws of the HKSAR". See s.5(4) and s.7.

The 23rd February 1997 Decision of the Standing Committee of the NPC and the two sections of the Reunification Ordinance, they submit, reinforces their contention that an act of adoption was necessary. There was no such act and, further, the decision not to adopt the Application of English Law Ordinance, indicates an intention not to adopt the common law. Therefore, the common law has not survived or been applied since the change of sovereignty.

Finally, the defendants submit that no reliance can be placed upon the terms of the Reunification Ordinance because the provisional legislature has not been established according to law and is not competent, therefore, to pass valid legislation for the HKSAR.

Conclusion on the first question

We have heard cogent submissions on how the Court should approach the interpretation of the Basic Law. The Basic Law is made under Article 31 of the Constitution of the People's Republic of China. It is Chinese law applicable to Hong Kong which falls initially to be interpreted by Hong Kong courts used to interpreting laws passed in the common law tradition, applying common law principles. No doubt, from time to time, difficult questions of interpretation will arise, but not, it seems to me, from any inherent difficulty arising between the two traditions. The common law principles of interpretation, as developed in recent years, are sufficiently wide and flexible to purposively interpret the plain language of this semi-constitutional law. The influence of international covenants has modified the common law principles of interpretation.

The Court has the additional assistance of the Joint Declaration if there is real ambiguity. What is more, although there is an official English translation, the Standing Committee of the NPC decided on 28th June 1990 that "in case of discrepancy between the two texts in the implication of any words used, the Chinese text shall prevail".

The general principle was stated in *AG of the Gambia v Jobe* [1984] AC 689 at 700 where Lord Diplock said:

> "A constitution and in particular that part of it which protects and entrenches fundamental rights and freedoms to which all persons in the state are to be entitled, is to be given a generous and purposive construction."

The words of Lord Wilberforce in Minister of Home *Affairs v Fisher* [1980] AC 319 at 328 are also of value:

> "These antecedents... call for a generous interpretation avoiding what has been called 'the austerity of tabulated legalism,'suitable to give to individuals the full measure of the fundamental rights and freedoms referred to. ... Respect must be paid to the language which has been used and to the traditions and usages which have given meaning to that language. It is quite consistent with this, and with the recognition that rules of interpretation may apply, to take as a point of departure for the process of interpretation a recognition of the character and origin of the instrument, and to be guided by the principles of giving full recognition and effect to those fundamental rights and freedoms with a statement of which the Constitution commences."

However, in my judgment, the language in the Basic Law is so clear that the first question can be answered without falling back on these principles of interpretation.

The Solicitor General submits that the decision of the NPC not to adopt the Application of English Laws Ordinance Cap. 88 is of no significance as the Ordinance was in any event purely declaratory. The common law has been applied in Hong Kong probably since 1841, certainly since 1844. Further, no formal act or instrument of adoption was required. The language of the Basic Law in Articles 8, 18 and 160 is imperative and clear. The Basic Law adopts the common law save where excepted as being in contravention of it in the Standing Committee of the NPC's Decision of 23rd February 1997.

I agree with these submissions. Indeed, on the first question I do not find the contrary to be arguable. My answer to the first question, therefore, is in the affirmative. The common law previously applied in Hong Kong was adopted into the law of the SAR on 1st July 1997 by the Basic Law.

Are the accused liable to answer to and be tried count 1 of Indictment No. 1 of 1997?

It does not follow, of course, because the common law is applied, as we have decided under the first question posed, that is sufficient to validate the continuance of the proceedings and indictments that have been started before the change of sovereignty. The defendants submit that the indictment lapsed with the end of British sovereignty and its legal effect is not preserved either by the Basic Law or under the Reunification Ordinance. The defendants were committed for trial, the proceedings were instituted and the indictment was filed in the High Court under British sovereignty. At midnight on 30th June

1997 when the PRC resumed sovereignty. the Supreme Court (of which the former High Court was part) ceased to exist. It is contended that even if the common law has been applied by the Basic Law it contains no provision which has either preserved the indictment or given the HKSAR courts the power to try the defendants either for offences committed or on proceedings commenced before the change.

Further, the Reunification Ordinance which purports to provide for the continuity of legal proceedings and associated matters in Parts 4 and 5 is not effective because the Ordinance was passed by the provisional legislature which is not legally constituted as the legislature of the SAR.

The Solicitor General submits that Article 160 of the Basic Law is a sufficient answer and on its true construction provides for the validity of the indictment and the continuation of the criminal proceedings. He says this does not depend upon the Reunification Ordinance which is only declaratory of the provisions of this Article. He relies in particular upon the second paragraph of Article 160 which provides:

> "Documents, certificates, contracts, and rights and obligations valid under the laws previously in force in Hong Kong shall continue to be valid and be recognised and protected by the Hong Kong Special Administrative Region, provided that they do not contravene this Law."

Conclusion on the second question

I am satisfied that for the reasons I have given that the words "the laws previously in force in Hong Kong" apply to laws relevant to this criminal trial which were in force on 30th June 1997. The question is, therefore, whether the words "documents" and "rights and obligations" are sufficient to apply to and preserve the validity of the indictment and the criminal trial dependent upon it. Mr Chandler submits that these words must be construed *eiusdem generis* with the words "certificates" and "contracts" and may on their true meaning be relevant to civil rights and obligations and documents supporting those rights but not to criminal proceedings. He could have added that as the construction contended for by the Solicitor General has penal consequences the Court ought to lean against such a construction.

Undoubtedly, it is unusual for important transitional provisions dealing with the validity of trials continuing over the resumption of sovereignty should be so generally expressed. But then the Basic Law is enacted in broad terms and general principles.

I pose the question: in the absence of any other valid provision is this sufficient and appropriate to preserve the proceedings referred to us?

Bearing in mind the principles to which I have referred when considering the interpretation of the Basic Law on the first question and the overwhelming intention of the Basic Law–and the Joint Declaration which was its genesis–to provide for the continuity of the legal system and the law, I believe a strongly purposive construction of the Basic Law is justified and required by those principles. Not without some initial hesitation but nevertheless in the end without doubt, I would decide, first, that the word "documents" is sufficient to apply to and preserve the validity of the indictment upon which the criminal trial is founded. Secondly, the words "rights and obligations" are appropriate and sufficient to continue the right of the Government to prosecute the case and the obligation of the defendants to appear.

On this question, as the other, the Reunification Ordinance is clear. I turn now to consider the question whether the Reunification Ordinance has legal effect, in other words, whether it has been validly passed by a competent legislature.

Is the Provisional Legislative Council established by law?

This question is addressed because it is submitted by the defendants that the Reunification Ordinance is devoid of legal effect as it was not passed by a competent legislature.

I have already outlined the legislative history of the Basic Law and the establishment of the Preparatory Committee by the 4th April 1990 Decision of the NPC. The proposed composition and conditions for membership of the first Legislative Council are to be found in Annex II of the Basic Law and the above Decision. Annex II clause 1 provides:

> "The Legislative Council of the Hong Kong Special Administrative Region shall be composed of 60 members in each term. In the first term, the Legislative Council shall be formed in accordance with the 'Decision of the National People's Congress on the Method for the Formation of the First Government and the First Legislative Council of the Hong Kong Special Administrative Region'."

The relevant parts of the 4th April 1990 Decision, clause 1, 2 and 6 have already been set out in earlier judgments in full and I do not repeat them. The intention was to achieve a legislative through train by providing that members of the last colonial legislature who could meet the conditions should be considered as members of the First Legislative Council under the HKSAR.

During 1994, the new electoral arrangements for the 1995 election to the last colonial Legislative Council were introduced. It is no part of this Court's task to express a view on those arrangements. The view of the Government of the PRC was clear. The electoral arrangements unilaterally decided upon by the British Government were in breach of the Joint Declaration, the Basic Law and the Decision of the NPC of the 4th April 1990. The wholesale changes which would be required in order to comply with the provisions of Annex II of the Basic Law and the Decision of the 4th April 1990 to establish the first Legislative Council under the HKSAR and the Basic Law were not reasonably possible.

It was in these circumstances that on 31st August 1994 the Standing Committee of the NPC, having set out the background, decided

> "The Session hereby decides that the Preparatory Committee for the HKSAR shall be responsible for matters relating to the preparation of the establishment of the HKSAR, prescribe the specific method for the formation of the First Legislative Council of the HKSAR and organise the First Legislative Council of the HKSAR in accordance with the Decision of the NPC on the Method for the Formation of the First Government and the First Legislative Council of the HKSAR."

In our system we would describe this as an enabling provision.

For its part the Preparatory Committee–acting in accordance with Article 2 of the 4th April 1990 Decision–decided on 24th March 1996 to form the Provisional Legislative Council. The Decision provided the means of doing so, its powers and finally and significantly by clause 7:

> "The Provisional Legislative Council of the HKSAR shall

operate until the First Legislative Council of the HKSAR is formed, which shall be not later than 30 June 1998."

Further details for the formation of the PLC were laid down by the Preparatory Committee on 5th October 1996. On 1st February 1997 the Preparatory Committee decided *inter alia* that

"the Provisional Legislative Council shall start functioning before 30 June 1997. The Provisional Legislative Council shall, ... formulate standing orders and voting procedures, examine and pass bills etc. upon the establishment of the HKSAR, the Provisional Legislative Council shall confirm bills which have been passed and submit them for the signing of the Chief Executive before promulgation and implementation so as to complete the legislative process."

Finally, the Preparatory Committee reported to the NPC. The report contains these passages:

"Some doubts have been raised in Hong Kong's public opinion about the power of the Preparatory Committee in making decision on the formation of the Provisional Legislative Council. In fact, Article 2 of the above-mentioned Decision of the NPC provides that the Preparatory Committee 'shall be responsible for matters relating to the preparation for the establishment of the HKSAR'. The formation of the Provisional Legislative Council falls within this ambit. As a power organ established by the NPC, the Preparatory Committee has been authorized to make decisions on matters relating to the establishment of the HKSAR.

This authorization covers the power to form the Provisional Legislative Council.

In the light of the actual situation that a legislature must be in place upon the establishment of the HKSAR and in accordance with the above-mentioned Decision of the NPC, the plenary session of the Preparatory Committee in March 1966 adopted the Decision to form the Provisional Legislative Council of the HKSAR."

On 14th March 1997 the NPC by resolution approved that report.

With that legislative background, I turn to the submissions of counsel.

Ms Gladys Li, SC, made submissions on this issue for the 1st defendant which the other defendants adopted. The thrust of her argument is as follows and I hope I do no injustice to it:

(1) As can be seen from the preamble to the Basic Law and Article 158 the precise limit of the jurisdiction of the Hong Kong courts may cause difficulty. Further, the statement of principles applicable to Hong Kong indicate that certain articles of the constitution of the PRC do not apply to the HKSAR. See for example Articles 123 and 129.

(2) The courts of the HKSAR may therefore consider whether the NPC or its standing committee has made a decision which has legislative effect and to what effect.

(3) Consequently, in this reference this Court may inquire whether the PLC has been established by law; and secondly, whether the PLC conforms with the law of the HKSAR – the Basic Law.

(4) Article 158 of the Basic Law gives wide powers of interpretation to this Court–its decisions being appealable. Note the words

" ... if the courts of the Region ... need to interpret the provisions of this Law concerning affairs which are the responsibility of the Central People's Government, or concerning the relationship between the Central Authorities and the Region, and if such interpretation will affect the judgment on the cases, the courts of the Region shall before making their final judgments which are not appealable, seek an interpretation of the relevant provisions from the Standing Committee of the National People's Congress to the Court of Final Appeal in the Region."

(5) Therefore, this Court can determine whether the PLC conforms with the Basic Law although it may not make the ultimate determination. What is more, it is the duty of this Court to do so.

(6) That the PLC does not conform with the Basic Law, it is not legally constituted and the enactments passed by it–the Reunification Ordinance for the purposes of this case–are of no effect. She relies upon the following reasons:

(a) That in spite of the Government's contentions, the PLC is the first Legislative Council of the HKSAR and does not conform with the provisions for the establishment of it.

(b) It does not conform with the general principle that "the legislature shall be constituted by election" in the Joint Declaration and the Basic Law. It was not formed by the method laid down in Article 68, Annex II and clause 6 of the 4th April 1990 Decision of the NPC.

(c) That in forming the PLC, the Preparatory Committee did not even pay lip service to clause 6 when making its Decision of the 31st August 1994 and was not acting within the powers conferred upon it.

(d) Finally, that if the legality of the PLC depends upon the "approval" of the Preparatory Committee on 14th March 1997, then this is obviously not sufficient to 'ratify'that which had been done contrary to the Basic Law so as to legitimise the PLC.

(7) In order to establish a valid PLC an amendment to the Basic Law was necessary and this was not done.

In answer to this, the Solicitor General's primary submission is that this Court is a regional court and it is out with its jurisdiction to inquire into the legality of laws enacted by the sovereign power. The NPC is the "highest organ of state power" (see Article 57 of the Constitution) and with its Standing Committee is entrusted to "exercise the legislative power of the state" (Article 59). The legality or validity of laws made by these bodies is not open to challenge in the Hong Kong courts. For my part, I regard that as a self-evident proposition. I did not understand Ms Li, SC, to suggest otherwise at any rate for the purpose of this reference.

However, it is open to the Hong Kong courts to enquire whether laws have been enacted by the NPC or its Standing Committee and to consider the effect of such laws. It is open to the Hong Kong courts to examine whether a body such as the PLC has been established under and in accordance with those valid laws.

Sometimes, the court may need for this the assistance of experts. In this reference there has been no suggestion or challenge that the text of the decisions and resolutions of the NPC and the Standing Committee put before us are not laws which were enacted by them. As to the effect of these laws, the presumption is that things are lawfully and properly done unless the contrary is demonstrated. For reasons which I will give, I am firmly of the opinion that the contrary has not been demonstrated before us. It is open to us, therefore, to accept those decisions at their face value.

Earlier, I have traced the legislative history of the PLC. The Preparatory Committee was empowered to take the necessary steps in accordance with the NPC Decision of the 4th April 1990 and the Basic Law to prepare for the establishment of the HKSAR. At that time, this included the establishment of the first Legislative Council.

It is not our task to examine whether the electoral changes which came into being before the 1995 election made it impossible to establish the first legislature in accordance with that Decision and the Basic Law. It is certainly arguably so. This was the clear perception of those responsible for implementing the Basic Law after the resumption of sovereignty; that is, the perception that the legislative through train had been derailed and that it could not be put back on the tracks before 1st July 1997.

It was in those circumstances that the Preparatory Committee exercising its powers to make arrangements for the establishment of the HKSAR set up the PLC with its limited functions and powers to fulfil the role of the legislative arm of government until replaced by an elected legislature—the first Legislative Council under the Basic Law—not later than 30th June 1998.

Any lingering question as to the lawful exercise of the Preparatory Committee's powers in establishing the PLC was, in my judgment, removed on the 14th March 1997 when the NPC resolved to approve a Preparatory Committee's report which among other things detailed the way in which the provisional legislature had been established. Ms Li submits that this resolution amounted to narrative without ratification. Without any evidence to the contrary, the resolution must be accepted as meaning what it says—that the legislature approved that which the Preparatory Committee had done in the exercise of the powers granted to it.

The PLC and the Basic Law

This leaves Ms Gladys Li's submission that the PLC is established in breach of the Basic Law and that on this ground it must be held to be incompetent as the Legislative Council of the HKSAR. This is founded upon the premise that the provisional legislature is the first Legislative Council under the Basic Law and does not comply with Article 68, Annex II and the 4th April 1990 Decision of the NPC.

But this premise is not correct. The 31st August 1994 Decision of the Standing Committee of the NPC states the Standing Committee's view that the 1994 electoral arrangements in Hong Kong are in contravention of the Joint Declaration, the Basic Law and the Decision of the NPC. Consequently, in that Decision the Standing Committee gave the Preparatory Committee the responsibility of prescribing the specific method for the formation of the first Legislative Council. Clearly, elections could not be held by the Preparatory Committee before the 1st July 1997. It appears from their decisions that the route they chose was to establish the PLC as an interim body until the first legislature could be established under, and in accordance with, the Basic Law.

This is clear from the Decision of the Preparatory Committee of 24th March 1996 to set up the PLC. By clause 7, to which I have already referred, it decided that the PLC should operate until the first Legislative Council of the HKSAR was formed not later than 30th June 1998.

Where there are separate provisions dealing with the same subject matter, the principles of interpretation require that the provisions are interpreted to be consistent with one another if the language will bear such meaning. Failing this, the later provision takes precedence. Here, however, for my part, there is no difficulty. Article 68 indicates that the method for forming the Legislative Council was not set in stone. The second paragraph provides:

> "The method for forming the Legislative Council shall be specified in the light of the actual situation in the Hong Kong Special Administrative Region and in accordance with the principle of gradual and orderly progress. The ultimate aim is the election of all the members of the Legislative Council by universal suffrage."

I am unable to accept that the provisions for the establishment of the PLC are in breach of the Basic Law. Nor am I of the opinion that any amendment to the Basic Law was required even if such had been practical or possible.

It was necessary to have a Legislative Council in place on the 1st July 1997. It was not possible to hold elections for a council which complied with the Basic Law before that date. The Preparatory Committee in accordance with its mandate provided the PLC as an interim body until the necessary arrangements could be made for the establishment of the first Legislative Council under the Basic Law. Far from breaching the Basic Law, therefore, the formation of the PLC was consistent with efforts to comply with the law by making arrangements for the establishment of the first Legislative Council under its provisions before 30th June 1998. The establishment of the PLC was outside the Basic Law and collateral with it. It was part of the arrangements and method for establishing the first Legislative Council.

Conclusion

For these reasons I would hold that from 1st July 1997 the common law is adopted in the HKSAR by the provisions of the Basic Law. I would also hold that the validity and legal effect of proceedings commenced under an indictment before the 1st July 1997 are preserved by the Basic Law after that date.

Finally, I would hold that the Reunification Ordinance—which is in part to the same effect—is part of the laws of the HKSAR having been validly enacted by the PLC which is a competent legislature established under the laws enacted by the NPC and its Standing Committee.

In these circumstances, I do not find it necessary to address the arguments put before us on the doctrine of necessity.

For these reasons I answer both questions referred to us in the affirmative.

Chief Judge, High Court (P Chan)

Vice President (G P Nazareth)

Vice President (Barry Mortimer)

Mr Daniel Fung, SC, Mr A A Bruce, SC and Miss A Wan for the HKSAR

Ms Gladys Li, SC, Ms Margaret Ng, Mr Paul Harris leading
Mr Kevin Egan and Mr Dean Tang (instructed by
Messrs Chung & Kwan for D1) and Mr J P Chandler
(instructed by Messrs Peter W K Lo & Co for D2)
Mr John Halley assigned by D L A to hold a watching brief for D3

第九條

香港特別行政區的行政機關、立法機關和司法機關，除使用中文外，還可使用英文，英文也是正式語文。

案例

是否有絕對的權利要求採用中文或英文進行審訊？

周順鏞 對 破產管理署署長

HCB 1319/1999；CACV 155/2005

簡略案情

上訴人（下稱“周先生”）因一彭姓人士（下稱“彭先生”）對他未能支付約 31 萬元債務為理由，向高等法院提出呈請，要求宣佈彭先生破產。最後，法庭對彭先生作出破產令，同時委任破產管理署署長（“管理署”）為彭先生產業的受託人進行破產程序。周先生是彭先生的唯一債權人。

及後，周先生致函管理署要求該署根據《破產條例》第 19（2）條，對彭先生進行公開訊問。當時管理署正在調查彭先生過去的兩宗可疑轉讓。稍後，管理署致函周先生，因為缺乏經費，所以會延遲對彭先生作公開訊問。後來，周先生再要求管理署公開訊問彭先生，但管理署重申產業金額不足以支付訊問的費用，故周先生需提供資金，否則公開訊問不能進行，然而，周先生拒絕提供資金支持管理署對彭先生進行公開訊問。在往後的接觸中，管理署向周先生明確表示不會補貼公開訊問的費用，如果他堅持要公開訊問彭先生而又拒絕支付費用，管理署只能向法庭提交報告，交由法庭裁定。期間，管理署亦要求周先生羅列出他希望查詢彭先生的問題。然而，周先生對這些要求一律拒絕。最後，在聽罷各方的陳詞，法庭頒令除非周先生向該署繳付港元 19,400.00 作為支付公開訊問的開支，否則該署無需申請公開訊問彭先生。周先生不服該判決，提出上訴。他其中的一個上訴理由是部份文件沒有中譯本，而聆訊時更採用英文，歧視他不懂英文，違反自然公義。

裁決摘要

上訴庭重申《基本法》第 9 條確立“香港特別行政區的行政機關、立法機關和司法機關，除使用中文外，還可使用英文，英文也是正式語文。”而且，根據《法定語文條例》第 5 條，法官可以對在他席前進行的程序中決定選用哪種語言。對於周先生指出聆訊時採用英文對他不公的上訴理由，上訴庭參考了 *Re Cheng Kai Nam [2002] HKLRD 39* 一案，並支持原訟庭法官在該案中的分析，在任何法律程序，中文和英文享有相同地位，而採用何種法定語文是主審法官的決定，參與訴訟的任何一方都沒有憲法權利要求法官必須採用他要求的法定語言來進行法律程序，只要有翻譯員協助便足夠。因此，上訴法庭認為，周先生指原審法官在法庭上用英語聆訊是歧視他不懂英文、而備有翻譯的幫助不足夠，這一指控不成立。該法官的處理方法，沒有違反《基本法》或《人權法》的規定，更沒有違反自然公義原則。在對周先生其他上訴理由綜合考慮後，上訴法庭撤銷了原訟費命令。

CACV 155/2005

香港特別行政區
高等法院上訴法庭
民事司法管轄權
民事上訴

民事上訴案件 2005 年第 155 號
（原高等法院破產案件 1999 年第 1319 號）

有關彭順興（破產人）的事宜

上訴人　周順鏞
　　　　對
答辯人　破產管理署署長

主審法官：高等法院上訴法庭法官楊振權
高等法院上訴法庭法官袁家寧

聆訊日期：2006 年 3 月 9 日

判案書日期：2006 年 3 月 24 日

判案書

由上訴法庭法官楊振權頒發上訴法庭判案書：

背景

1. 1999 年 5 月 28 日，周順鏞先生以彭順興先生未能支付欠款約 31 萬元為理由，向高等法院提出呈請，申請彭先生破產，該筆款項是彭先生在區域法院一宗人身損害案件被判定要支付給周先生的賠償金額，連同利息及訟費。周先生提出呈請時有支付所需之呈請人按金 12,150 元。

2. 1999 年 8 月 25 日，法庭對彭先生作出破產令，而周先生是彭先生的唯一債權人。

3. 1999 年 11 月 2 日，周先生致函破產管理署，（‘管理署’）要求該署根據《破產條例》第 19(2) 條，對彭先生進行公開訊問。當時管理署正調查彭先生曾作出過的兩宗可疑轉讓。該兩宗可疑轉讓涉及華達旅遊貿易公司的權益，轉讓人分別是彭先生的女兒彭勃珍女士和親戚許有海先生，他們每人獲彭先生分配了華達旅遊貿易公司 50% 的權益。

4. 2000 年 1 月 10 日管理署書面通知周先生，指出上述可疑資產轉讓的表面證據成立，會有法律程序跟進；而周先生要求公開訊問彭先生一事，管理署亦會作出安排。

5. 2000 年 4 月 25 日，管理署致函周先生，除了就上述可疑轉讓的調查，再向周先生作出書面交代外，亦同時知會周先生會延遲對彭先生公開訊問，原因是缺乏經費。管理署表示要探討彭先生的家人是否願意代他清還債務和要等候彭先生和許先生的回應，才能作出最終決定。

6. 2001 年 3 月 8 日，管理署回應周先生查詢時，再表示缺乏經費向彭女士和許先生興訟，故希望能和他們庭外和解。

7. 2002 年 10 月 9 日，管理署知會周先生要周先生提供所需資金，否則不會向許先生興訟。

8. 2002 年 11 月 1 日，周先生再要求管理署公開訊問彭先生，但管理署重申產業金額不足以支付訊問的費用，故周先生需提供資金，否則公開訊問不能進行。但周先生拒絕提供資金支持管理署對彭先生進行公開訊問及對許先生興訟。

9. 2003 年 1 月 29 日，管理署向周先生明確表示不會補貼公開訊問的費用。2003 年 2 月 14 日管理署再向周先生提出，如果他堅持要公開訊問彭先生而又拒絕支付費用，則管理署會向法庭提交報告，由法庭裁定是否要對彭先生進行公開訊問。

10. 2005 年 1 月 28 日，周先生再次要求管理署安排公開訊問彭先生。

11. 2005 年 2 月 7 日，管理署向周先生指提出公開訊問涉及的刊登憲報和速記員費用約 19,400 元，如周先生不想提供費用，管理署會向法庭申請指示，原因是破產人的產業，包括周先生曾支付的按金，所餘無幾，不足以支付有關費用。管理署亦要求周先生列出他建議向彭先生查詢的問題，但周先生拒絕支付費用，亦沒有列出希望向彭先生查詢的問題。

12. 2005 年 2 月 22 日，管理署再去信周先生，請他重新考慮會否提供公開訊問彭先生所需費用及列出他希望查詢彭先生的問題。管理署強調如周先生拒絕管理署的要求，但同時堅持管理署必須申請公開訊問，則管理署會向法庭尋求免卻公開訊問彭先生的指示亦會向他追討有關訟費。

13. 2005 年 2 月 23 日，周先生全盤拒絕管理署的請求。

14. 2005 年 2 月 25 日，管理署作為彭先生的受託人，發出傳票，要求法庭作出指示，如周先生拒絕提供所需費用，則管理署無須應周先生根據《破產條例》第 19（2）條發出的通知，向法庭申請第 19（1）所定的公開訊問。

15. 在發出上述傳票時，法庭在同時作出指示，下令有關傳票及報告，需送達給周先生，而周先生需在指定時限內，提交誓章，回應管理署的報告。

16. 2005 年 3 月 31 日，周先生提交回應誓章，逐點駁斥管理署的報告。

17. 有關傳票排期在 2005 年 4 月 29 日由原案法院原訟法庭法官關淑馨審理。

18. 2005 年 4 月 16 日，周先生向法庭提交陳詞概略，首次提出他沒有合法身份作為訴訟的一方的說法，周先生指管理署不應向他發出傳票，更沒有理由要他支付申請的訟費。

19. 周先生指出針對彭先生的破產令發出後，他已不是呈請人，而只是債權人，故管理署不應將他牽涉入有關申請內。

20. 周先生亦指出自巳（己）亦已是在高等法院破產案件編號 2004 年第 5334 號被判定為破產人，故根據《破產條例》第 12(1) 條及 14(1) 條，在未得法庭批准前，管理署不得向他進行任何法律程序。

21. 關法官不接納周先生的論點。

22. 2005 年 5 月 9 日，關法官頒下判決書，作出以下指示：

> "如周先生在作出本命令的 14 天內，不向該署繳付 HK$19,400.00，以支付公開訊問的開支，該署無需申請公開訊問破產人"。

23. 關法官同時判定周先生要支付有關訟費，數額則在雙方有爭議時，交由聆案官評定。

24. 周先生不服關法官的判決，現提出上訴。

關法官判決重點

25. 關法官指出《破產條例》第 97（1）條訂明，當破產案中出現問題時，不論問題是法律或事實問題，法庭為了達至公正，有全權就有關問題作出裁決，而在裁決前，為求達到實質上及程序上的公允，法庭亦應給予會受裁決影響的人士機會，提出支持或反對的理由和證據，因此將有關申請的傳票發給會受裁決影響的人士 一 周先生，令他成為法律程序的一方，是正確的做法。

26. 關法官亦指出，在發出傳票前，管理署已將情況向周先生詳細解釋，包括為何要向法庭尋求指示及所涉及的訟費和支付訟費的責任，但周先生對管理署的警告置若妄聞。

27. 關法官裁定雖然周先生曾被判定為破產人，但針對他的破產命令己（已）應他的申請，在 2005 年 1 月 10 日獲得暫緩執行，因此《破產條例》第 12（1）條不適用，而對周先生作出破產呈請後，法庭亦沒有下令擱置對他進行的訴訟或法律程序，因此第 14（1）條也不適用。

28. 關法官裁定管理署不一定要對一名破產者進行公開訊問，特別是當產業資金不足時，管理署更不應浪費資源。因此管理署並無職責應周先生的要求，對彭先生進行公開訊問，原因是除非周先生願意支付訊問程序的費用，管理署會就有關產業招致開支。關法官強調周先生是不應要求管理署就有關產業招致任何無謂開支。

29. 關法官裁定倘若周先生不同意支付管理署所要求的費用，她便會指示管理署無需申請公開訊問，原因是公開訊問不會有任何實質成效。

30. 關法官指出管理署就有關的可疑轉讓已作出深入調查而周先生亦拒絕在舉行訊問 7 天前向管理署提供他希望查詢彭先生的問題，令人質疑他堅持的公開訊問是否會有任何實質成效。

31. 關法官亦否定周先生指管理署犯有任何行政失當或疏忽職守的行為。

周先生的上訴理由

32. 周先生提出多項上訴理由。

33. 周先生指關法官內庭聆訊的法律程序不公平，有違自然公義。他強調自已（己）身為債權人，不具資格成為指示請求法律程序的一方，原因是指示結果不會影響債權人。

34. 周先生強調關法官指示有關傳票及報告，需送達給周先生，‘拖他落水’前沒有聽取他的意見或陳詞，亦沒有給予他解釋誤會或律師辯護的機會，違反自然公義。

35. 周先生指管理署發出的傳票，不符合《破產（表格）規則》表格 131。原因是傳票不包括向任何債權人發出通知。因此關法官在 2005 年 2 月 25 日將周先生牽涉入案件內的命令不合法。

36. 周先生更指部份文件沒有中譯本，而聆訊時更採用英文，歧視他不識英文。

37. 在事件是非曲直上，周先生指出他成功要求法庭駁回管理署「無須公開訊問」的申請，因為法庭命令只要他在 14 天內支付有關開支，管理署便要申請公開訊問彭先生。因此他才是有關爭議的得勝一方，而關法官卻判罰‘勝方’支付訟費。

38. 周先生指出雖然他是受‘公開訊問’影響人之一，但不表示他必須成為管理署根據《破產條例》要求法庭就‘公開訊問’作出指示的法律程序一方。

39. 周先生強調要求管理署公開訊問彭先生是他作為債權人的權利，而向法庭要求指引則是管理署長的職責，故當他行使上述權利時，不應導致他面對任何不利判決，包括具懲罰性的訟費命令，否則令人不敢行使法律賦予的權利，違反《基本法》和《人權法》保障的“法律面前人人平等”的原則。

40. 周先生亦指出債權人只可參與‘公開訊問’，無權替代管理署署長向法庭提出申請或發表意見。周先生重申事發時，自已亦面對破產故不能動用資產支付公開訊問的費用。最後，周先生指關法官要求他支付的 19,400 元過高，原因是刊登憲報只費 355 元，而兩小時的數碼錄音謄本亦只費 1,500 元，他支付了的按金結餘足以支付有關費用。

討論

41. 就應否公開訊問彭先生一事，周先生和管理署的立場不一致。經詳細調查後，管理署認定公開訊問彭先生不會有任何實質成效，加上產業金額不足支付訊問的費用，而周先生又拒絕負責費用，管理署決定不公開訊問彭先生是合理的決定，亦是有基礎支持的決定。

42. 周先生拒絕接納管理署的決定，堅持必須對彭先生進行公開訊問，但同時拒絕支付有關費用。管理署署長要求法庭作出指示以保障各方權益絕對是正確、合法、合理的申請。

43. 作為彭先生的唯一債權人，周先生對應否公開訊問彭先生的決定有權關注。他一直以來表現的態度亦顯示他重視有關決定。他亦必是認為公開訊問彭先生可能會導致對他有利的成果，否則他不會堅持要管理署公開訊問彭先生。

44. 在上述情況下，法庭命令將管理署的申請和報告，送達給周先生及要求周先生提交誓章回應管理署的報告，絕對是合情合理的命令。

45. 當然周先生可以認同管理署的立場，並將其立場通知管理署和法庭，則法庭可能不需要周先生出席有關聆訊或採納較簡易程序作出指示決定，但周先生郤（卻）提出回應誓章，逐點駁斥管理署的報告，顯示他反對管理署的立場和堅持要公開訊問彭先生的決心。

46. 雖然開庭前不久，周先生首次提出他沒有合法身份作為訴訟的一方，但他仍堅持自己的立場，更強稱管理署有不可推卸的法定職責，對破產人進行公開訊問。他明顯是有利用聆訊的機會，向法庭陳述及道出其立場，並就管理署的作為作出多項投訴。周先生指被強行‘拖落水’的說法，絕對不成立。

47. 事實上爭議的重點並非是周先生應否出席有關指示聆訊，爭議重點是管理署應否對彭先生進行公開訊問及有關費用應由誰負責。

48. 在上述爭議問題，雙方都應法庭要求，出席聆訊，亦有就自己的立場向法庭陳述。法庭亦是經過正當法律程序，才作出決定，並有就決定列出詳細理由。

49. 周先生指是無辜牽涉入有關傳票及有關聆訊的法律程序不公平，違反自然公義是本末倒置的說法。

50. 關法官是為了符合自然公義的原則，才會在作出決定前，給機會被決定影響的一方，即周先生向法庭陳述，道出其立場和論據。

51. 關法官不但有法定權力就破產案中出現的爭議作出裁決，亦有固有司法管轄權就有關聆訊，作出合理的安排。

52. 周先生指關法官在 2005 年 2 月 25 日作出的命令不合法及違反自然公義的說法，不正確。本庭不接納該說法。

53. 香港《基本法》第九條訂明："香港特別行政區的行政機關，立法機關和司法機關，除了使用中文外，還可使用英文，英文也是正式語文。"

54. 香港法例第 5 章《法庭語文條例》第 5 款亦訂明：

> "（1）法官、裁判官或其他司法人員可在於他席前進行的程序中或於他席前進行的程序的任何部份中兼用兩種法定語文或採用其中一種，視乎他認為何者適當而定。
>
> （2）法官、裁判官或其他司法人員根據第（1）款作出的決定是最終決定。"

55. 在 *Re Cheng Kar Nam* [2002] HKLRD 39 案，法庭亦裁定在任何法律程序中文和英文享有相同地位，而採用那（哪）一種法定語文是主審法官的決定，參與訴訟的任何一方都沒有憲法權利要求法官必須採用他要求的法定語言之一進行法律程序，只要有翻譯員協助便足夠。

56. 周先生指關法官在法庭上用英語聆訊是歧視他不識英文，而有翻譯的幫助不足夠。周先生的指控不成立。關法官的處理方法，沒有違反《基本法》或《人權法》的規定，更沒有違反自然公義原則。

57.《破產條例》第 19 款規定如下：

> "（1）凡已作出破產令，破產管理署署長可在破產人的破產解除前的任何時間，向法院申請對該破產人進行公開訊問。
>
> （2）除非法院另有命令，否則如破產人的債權人中的一名債權人在已獲債權人（包括作出通知的債權人）當中佔不少於債權價值四分之一的債權人的贊同下，按照規則通知破產管理署署長，請求他根據第（1）款提出申請，破產管理署署長須如此提出申請。
>
> （3）凡破產人的債權人中的一名債權人在沒有獲得第（2）款所規定的債權人贊同下如此作出請求，則破產管理署署長須根據第（1）款提出申請，但儘管有第（4）款的規定，法院可拒絕對該破產人作出進行公開訊問的指示。"

58. 雖然上述條例沒有訂立法庭作出的命令，可包括要請求管理署署長向法院申請對破產人公開訊問的債權人支付公開訊問所需之費用，但本庭同意關法官的裁定，即《破產規則》第 158A 條賦予法庭權力，為了避免有關產業招致任何開支，下令要求公開訊問的債權人支付訊問的費用，否則管理署署長無須進行公開訊問。

59. 有關條例，包括《破產規則》第 158A 條明顯賦予法庭極大的酌情權就處理破產案件作出適當和合理的命令。雖然關法官明顯認為公開訊問不會導致有用成果，但她給予周先生選擇權，並無不妥。

60. 關法官在聆聽過雙方的陳述及考慮過管理署署長提交的報告，將有關公開的訊問的費用定為 19,400 元，決定全屬酌情權的決定，本庭亦不會更改。

61. 本庭唯一要考慮的問題是關法官下令周先生支付訟費的決定是否正確。《破產條例》第 19（2）條賦予不少於四份之一的債權人絕對權力要求管理署署長向法庭提出公開訊問破產人的申請。在接獲上述要求後，除非法院另有命令，管理署署長亦必須提出公開訊問破產人的申請。

62. 很多時，債權人不一定能掌握全部有關資料，令他們能客觀地決定公開訊問會否導致任何實質成效。無論如何，債權人主觀上希望能盡一切努力，以求從破產人身上取回欠債或部份欠債是可以理解的。在本案有資料顯示彭先生有作過可疑轉讓，周先生要求公開訊問他亦是可以理解的。

63. 在獲得債權人通知要他向法庭申請公開訊問破產人後，除非法庭另有命令，管理署署長亦必須按債權人的要求行事。

64. 在本案，周先生是唯一債權人，亦因此有絕對權力要求管理署向法庭申請公開訊問彭先生。如管理署署長希望能免卻上述法庭責任，他必須先得到法院批准。

65. 為了能知悉正反雙方的立場以作出正確決定，當管理署署長申請免卻公開訊問彭先生時，法庭要求周先生出席和列出其立場及論據是合理正確的做法，亦是符合自然公義原則。

66. 但在上述情況下，周先生只是應法庭邀請出席聆訊及道出其立場及論據，協助法庭作出判決，法庭不應視周先生為聆訊中敵對一方。

67. 在本案，周先生處理問題的方法不一定是全部合理，可能他應對管理署採取更合作的態度。他亦應明白如果沒有所需經費，法庭是很有可能行使酌情權作出指示不須舉行公開訊問。但管理署署長的申請所導致的聆訊是不能避免的。周先生出席聆訊的目的亦只是將其立場及論據向法庭申述，以協助法庭作出決定。

68. 雖然法庭不接納周先生的立場和他提出的論據，本庭認為法庭亦不應下令周先生支付聆訊的訟費。

69. 本庭認同周先生的立場指上述做法可能會阻嚇債權人，令他們不敢行使法律賦予他們的權力，亦有可能被人認為管理署署長或法庭以訟費懲罰一些管理署認為不合作的債權人。

70. 雖然訟費命令是行使酌情權後所作出的，但本庭認為關法官要周先生支付聆訊訟費的命令前，可能沒有考慮以上因素，所以本庭撤銷上述訟費命令，改判不作任何訟費命令。

71. 考慮到案件的背景及有關申請的性質，本庭亦不就上訴作任何訟費命令，上述訟費判令是暫准命令，會在本判案書頒下後 14 天作實。

高等法院上訴法庭法官（楊振權）

高等法院上訴法庭法官（袁家寧）

上訴人：無律師代表，親自應訊。

答辯人：由破產管理署杜淦堃大律師代表。

Re Cheng Kai Nam, Gary

Cheng Kai Nam, Gary 申請司法覆核

HCAL 3568/2001

簡略案情

申請人被檢控並需要在區域法院接受審訊。他是以廣東話作為母語，但被安排審理他的案件的法官只懂英語而不懂廣東話。針對審訊編排官這個安排，申請人向原訟庭申請司法覆核。依據《基本法》第 9 條，即"香港特別行政區的⋯⋯司法機關，除使用中文外，還可使用英文，英文也是正式語文。"申請人認為他享有憲法權利，選擇以他的母語廣東話作供，同時有權要求安排懂廣東話的法官審理案件，以便直接理解他的證供。申請人更認為中文應是基本的官方語文，英語只是擔任輔助的角色。

裁決摘要

法官指出，如果申請人的論據成立，根據《基本法》第 9 條，在行政和立法機關內亦存在與會者必須能直接理解其他與會者發言的憲法權利。但是，法院認定這種情況是不可能的。原因是根據《基本法》第 67 條："⋯⋯非中國籍的香港特別行政區永久性居民和在外國有居留權的香港特別行政區永久性居民，也可以當選為香港特別行政區立法會議員⋯⋯"然而，《基本法》並沒有要求這些議員必須能同時以中文和英文交流。因此，法庭不同意申請人擁有要求懂廣東話的法官進行審訊的憲法權利，並且《法定語文條例》第 5(1) 條的規定"法官⋯⋯可在於他席前進行的程序中⋯⋯兼用兩種法定語文或採用其中一種，視乎他認為何者適當而定。"並沒有違反《基本法》。

法官再指出申請人擁有公平審訊的基本權利是被記載在《香港人權法案》第 11 條中，但根據該條關於語言方面的權利，申請人亦只有給予免費傳譯的保障。據此，該司法覆核批准申請被駁回。

HCAL 3568/2001

IN THE HIGH COURT OF THE

HONG KONG SPECIAL ADMINISTRATIVE REGION

COURT OF FIRST INSTANCE

CONSTITUTIONAL AND ADMINISTRATIVE LAW LIST
NO. 3568 OF 2001

CHENG KAI NAM, GARY Applicant

In the Matter of an Application by CHENG KAI NAM, GARY for leave to apply for Judicial Review (Order 53, rule 3)

Before: Hon. Hartmann J in Court

Dates of Hearing: 30 November and 1 December 2001

Date of Handing Down Judgment: 3 December 2001

JUDGMENT

Introduction

1. The applicant in this matter seeks leave to apply for judicial review. The application has been brought as a matter of urgency because it concerns a criminal trial which is due to commence in the District Court this morning, the applicant being the accused in that trial.

2. The trial has been set down for hearing before a monolingual judge, that is, a judge who does not speak Cantonese. The Official Languages Ordinance, Chapter 5, provides for two official languages in our courts. In this regard, sections 3(1) and (2) of the ordinance reads:

> "(1) The English and Chinese languages are declared to be the official languages of Hong Kong for the purposes of communication between the Government or any public officer and members of the public and for court proceedings.
>
> (2) The official languages possess equal status and, subject to the provisions of this Ordinance, enjoy equality of use for the purposes set out in subsection (1)."

3. Assuming that Chinese means, in Hong Kong, the language of the majority, namely Cantonese, as opposed to the other languages and/or dialects that fall under the description of 'Chinese', it means that our courts allow for two official languages in the spoken form: English and Cantonese.

4. The applicant's native tongue is Cantonese. He is conversant in English. However, at his trial, if he chooses to testify, he will do so in Cantonese. That being so, he wishes his testimony to be considered by a judge who also speaks Cantonese and not by a judge who must receive his testimony through an interpreter.

5. Why is that? As I comprehend it, it is the applicant's contention that language is more than a mechanical means of conveying meaning: language gives colour, subtlety and texture to that meaning. Interpretation, no matter how competent, cannot hope to capture the full dimensions of that colour, subtlety and texture. That being so, all interpretation is an exercise in diminishment.

6. I am told that at the applicant's trial the prosecution case will rely heavily on the evidence of one witness, a past associate of the applicant. Mr Lee, who appeared on behalf of the applicant, said that in substance the trial could end up being one man's word against another's. That being so, he said, credibility will be a matter of material concern and in the assessment of credibility the judge will have to look to the demeanour of the witnesses, one of those witnesses, if he elects to testify, being the applicant himself. But if the judge is not himself a Cantonese speaker, said Mr Lee, if he must rely on an interpreter, how will he be able accurately and fully to assess that demeanour? His ability to do so will be materially diminished by the interpretation because that interpretation, no matter how competent, will not be able to capture what I have earlier described as the colour, subtlety and texture of the language spoken by the witnesses. The applicant, as I understand the complaint, is concerned that this may tell to his disadvantage.

7. In an attempt to have his matter listed before a bilingual judge, that is, one who speaks both Cantonese and English, two applications were made by the applicant's legal representatives to the listing judge in the District Court, Judge Fung. The first application was made on 26 October, the second was made on 29 November, the day before the institution of these judicial review proceedings. In respect of both applications, the listing judge considered it appropriate that the applicant's trial should continue to be listed for hearing before a monolingual judge.

8. Although no respondent has been cited by name in the notice of application for leave to apply for judicial review, it is these two decisions which are challenged. More particularly, the following orders are sought:

(1) an order of *certiorari* to quash the two decisions of the listing judge;

(2) a declaration that the applicant is entitled to have his case heard by a judge who speaks Cantonese; and

(3) an order of prohibition restraining the District Court from proceeding with the applicant's trial pending the resolution of these judicial review proceedings unless that trial is set for hearing before a judge who speaks Cantonese.

9. The decisions of the listing judge are challenged on two bases. First, that the applicant enjoys a constitutional right to have his case determined by a judge who speaks Cantonese, the language which, if he testifies, he will speak at trial. Second, that the listing judge acted unlawfully when he refused the two applications in that his decisions were *Wednesbury* unreasonable.

10. Before moving to these two bases of challenge, it is to be remembered that the matter now before the Court is one in which leave only is being sought. That being so, the test to be applied is whether the material advanced in the application discloses matters which on further consideration might demonstrate an arguable case for the grant of the relief sought. If so, then leave must be granted and the trial scheduled to commence this morning in the District Court will have to be adjourned.

The constitutional issue

11. Despite the wording of section 3 of our domestic statute, the Official Languages Ordinance, that English and Chinese share 'equal status' in our courts, Mr Lee has submitted that since the resumption of sovereignty a new constitutional order has come into existence, one which recognizes the supremacy of the Chinese language over that of English. To this end, Mr Lee has referred to the wording of the Joint Declaration (JD reference 51) which reads:

"In addition to Chinese, English may also be used in organs of government and in the courts in the Hong Kong Special Administrative Region."

12. More importantly, Mr Lee has also made reference to Article 9 of the Basic Law, the syntax of its wording echoing the Joint Declaration. Article 9 reads:

"In addition to the Chinese language, English may also be used as an official language by the executive authorities, legislature and judiciary of the Hong Kong Special Administrative Region."

13. Article 9, said Mr Lee, makes it plain that Chinese is to be the primary official language of Hong Kong and of its judiciary. English, however, 'may also be used', an equally clear statement of its secondary role. As he expressed it, English is only a 'permitted' language.

14. From this basis, Mr Lee has submitted that a constitutional right to use Chinese in the courts of Hong Kong would be undermined if the right did not comprise two essential elements; first, the right to speak Cantonese and, second, the right to be understood by the courts in Cantonese without the intervention of an interpreter. I regret to say that while I have no difficulty in accepting the first essential element proposed by Mr Lee, I can find no basis whatsoever for accepting the second.

15. If Mr Lee is correct in his purposive interpretation of Article 9, it means that a person who uses Cantonese in our courts is entitled as a constitutional right to be understood *directly* in that language by the judge assigned to hear his matter. That may, if one accepts Mr Lee's submissions as to the ease with which alternate or deputy judges can be appointed, be capable of practical manifestation. But Article 9 also refers to the use of Chinese as an official language in our executive branches of government and the legislature. In respect of the legislature it must therefore follow that a member who, as a constitutional right, uses Chinese (Cantonese) is entitled, also as constitutional right, to be understood *directly* in that language by the other members to whom he speaks. That cannot be right. Article 67 of the Basic Law, for example, allows specifically for permanent residents of Hong Kong who are not of Chinese nationality to be elected as members of the Legislative Council. There is nothing, implied or otherwise, in the relevant articles, or in the Basic Law read as a whole, to suggest that those persons who are not of Chinese nationality must nevertheless speak a Chinese language.

16. As to the manner in which Article 9 is worded, instruments of constitution regularly speak to matters which define national or regional identity. In this regard, the Basic Law is no different. The Basic Law, while upholding the territorial integrity of the People's Republic of China, recognizes that Hong Kong has a special history. The Preamble to the Basic Law makes specific reference to this history and to Hong Kong's other 'realities' such as its capitalist system of commerce and its system of law. In this regard, paragraph 2 of the Preamble reads:

"Upholding national unity and territorial integrity, maintaining the prosperity and stability of Hong Kong, and taking account of its history and realities, the People's Republic of China has decided that upon China's resumption of the exercise of sovereignty over Hong Kong, a Hong Kong Special Administrative Region will be established in accordance with the provisions of Article 31 of the Constitution of the People's Republic of China, and that under the principle of 'one country, two systems', the socialist system and policies will not be practiced in Hong Kong. ..."

17. Accordingly, as a work of constitutional architecture, the Basic Law is built upon the foundations of Hong Kong's special history. Part of that history is its adoption of the common law, the root language of which is English. The common law was the law of Hong Kong upon the resumption of sovereignty and Article 81 of the Basic Law enshrines that system.

18. The Basic Law not only enshrines the common law but, in order to give continuing effect to that enshrinement, allows for the recruitment of judges from other common law jurisdictions, there being suggestion that those judges should speak a Chinese tongue. In this regard, Article 92 reads:

"Judges and other members of the judiciary of the Hong Kong Special Administrative Region shall be chosen on the basis of their judicial and professional qualities and may be recruited from other common law jurisdiction."

19. Accordingly, when Article 9 of the Basic Law is read in its broader context, even giving to it the most purposive interpretation, I can find no basis for making the quantum leap that Mr Lee would have me make, namely, to hold that the right to use the Chinese language in a court of law in Hong Kong, implies the right to be understood directly in that language by the court. In my judgment, the constitutional right of a person to use the Chinese language in a court of law in Hong Kong means no more than the right of that person to employ that language, that is, to utilize it, for the purpose of forwarding or protecting his interests. That right to employ or utilize the language does not imply a reciprocal obligation on the part of the court to speak and read that language. It is sufficient if processes, such as the employment of interpreters or translators, exist to facilitate the court comprehending what is said or written.

20. In the course of his submissions, Mr Lee referred to the authority of *R. v. Beaulac* 173 D.L.R. (4th) 193 in which the Supreme Court of Canada considered the broad question of the interpretation of language rights under the Canadian Charter of Rights and Freedoms. In so doing, the court affirmed that language rights are a particular kind of right, distinct from the principles of fundamental justice, having a different origin and purpose. I concur.

21. If language rights are distinct from the principles of fundamental justice, it is not therefore a denial of the applicant's fundamental right to a fair trial to be denied a judge who speaks the official language that the applicant chooses to employ. The applicant's fundamental right to a fair trial is contained in Article 11 of the Bill of Rights. In respect of language, that article says only that in the determination of any criminal charge against him, a person shall be entitled to have the free assistance of an interpreter if he cannot understand or speak the language of the court. That is the minimum guarantee given.

22. Language rights, being distinct from a person's fundamental rights to a fair trial, can only be understood by having regard to their origin and purpose. As such, in my view, little is to be gained in looking at the manner in which language rights are protected in other constitutions. We must look to the Basic Law and why it is that English is preserved as an official language for our courts.

23. Mr Lee asked the rhetorical question: 'Can you imagine the reaction of an Italian tried in Rome by a judge who does not speak Italian?' But Hong Kong is not Rome. Its history is very different.

As a consequence, language rights in our courts of law are different too. In passing, I stop only to observe that Hong Kong is not the only common law jurisdiction which preserves English as an official language of the courts even though the majority of the people are not native English speakers. On a day-to-day basis in those courts interpretation services must be used for those who speak the majority tongue.

24. As to the manner in which either or both of our official languages may be used in our courts of law, I am satisfied that section 5 of the Official Languages Ordinance is applicable and is in no way contrary to the provisions of the Basic Law. Sections 5(1) and (2) read:

> "(1) A judge, magistrate or other judicial officer may use either or both of the official languages in any proceedings or a part of any proceedings before him as he thinks fit.
>
> (2) The decision of a judge, magistrate or other judicial officer under section (1) is final."

Section 5 continues by saying:

> "(3) Notwithstanding subsection (1), a party to or a witness in any proceedings or a part of any proceedings may–
>
> (a) use either or both of the official languages; and
>
> (b) address the court or testify in any language."
>
> (4) Notwithstanding subsection (1), a legal representative in any proceedings or a part of any proceedings may use either or both of the official languages."

The final subsection of section 5 reads:

> "(5) The Chief Justice may make rules and issue practice directions to regulate the use of the official languages in the courts."

25. I have not been informed of any such rules or practice directions applicable to criminal trials in the District Court.

26. Section 5 makes it plain that even though a judge before whom proceedings take place may determine to use *one* official language, his decision does not prohibit the parties to the proceedings or their legal representatives employing the *other* official language. No doubt, in the interests of efficient case judgment and, when applicable, in the general interests of justice, a judge who does not speak Cantonese may determine from time to time that a case is better heard by a judge who does speak Cantonese. But that, of course, will be a matter for the judge to determine, his decision being final.

The challenge to the listing judge's exercise of discretion

27. In these judicial review proceedings, the applicant seeks to challenge two decisions made by the listing judge in the District Court. The first decision was made on 26 October of this year. In the applicant's papers it is described as a decision refusing to list the applicant's trial before a bilingual judge so that a meaningful application could be made to that judge for the trial to be conducted in Cantonese. The second decision under challenge was made on 29 November and is described as a decision refusing to list the applicant's trial before a bilingual judge so that the applicant's evidence could be understood in Cantonese without the intervention of an interpreter.

28. As I understand it, both decisions are said to be *Wednesbury* unreasonable in that the listing judge in exercising his discretion, took into account irrelevant matters or failed to take into account matters that were relevant.

29. Assuming that the listing judge was exercising an administrative function subject to judicial review, what then was the nature of the discretion he was exercising?

30. The listing judge in the District Court has finite resources. I have received no evidence on the matter but it would be entirely artificial of me not to recognize that his essential function is to ensure that trials are listed before appropriate judges with the minimum of delay. The listing judge has a public duty to ensure that all of his judges are able to share in the case load. A variety of factors will influence the listing judge in deciding in any particular case when a matter is to be listed and who is appropriate to try the matter. The spectrum of factors will range from the purely domestic, matters of availability and the like, to the more complex, for example, matters of expertise in particular areas of criminal jurisprudence.

31. As I understand it, there are no rules or practice directions which set priorities for the listing judge. He therefore employs a broad discretion to ensure, in the public interest, that all his judges – bilingual and monolingual – are able to hear trials and that matters are listed as expeditiously as justice allows.

32. It must be remembered that it is not for individual litigants in civil matters or accused in criminal matters to dictate to the listing judge which judge (or category of judge) will hear their case and when.

33. As I have earlier indicated, I am satisfied that the applicant has no constitutional right to demand that his trial be listed before a judge who speaks Cantonese. That being so, it is manifest that the applicant stands in no different position from an accused who, for example, wants his trial heard at a particular time. In each case, the listing judge has a duty to hear the request and to weigh the matters placed before him in support of the request along with the other matters which dictate the exercise of his discretion. Provided he does that and makes a rational decision in good faith I fail to see how the exercise of his discretion can be challenged.

34. The applicant may consider that the decisions of the listing judge were unfair. But that is not enough. What must be alleged is some form of illegality, impropriety or irrationality and, as Godfrey J (as he then was) said in *Re Right Centre Co. Ltd* [1990] 1 HKLR 250, these are steep hurdles.

35. It was Mr Lee's submission that the matters taken into account by the listing judge in refusing to list the applicant's trial before a bilingual judge were irrelevant. They were irrelevant because it was not for him to determine whether the trial should or should not be heard in Cantonese. That was a matter for the trial judge. His function was only to facilitate a situation in which a meaningful application could be made to the trial judge for the trial to be conducted in Cantonese. In short, as I understand the submission, his function was limited to finding a bilingual judge who could consider the applicant's request and, if granted, proceed immediately to use Cantonese in the trial. In my opinion, that cannot be right.

36. The listing judge, of course, fulfils a 'preparatory' role in that he seeks a suitable venue and time for the hearing of a trial. To that extent he facilitates a process by which an accused can be brought before a trial judge so that, once before him, the accused can make whichever applications he deems fit. But because an

accused seeks a bilingual judge it does not mean that the listing judge is obliged to use his best endeavour to find him one. That, with respect, would be to reduce the role of the listing judge to beckoning to the dictates of an accused. As I have said, the listing judge has many matters to weigh in the balance.

37. In the present case, the listing judge was aware of the fact that, pursuant to section 5 of the Official Languages Ordinance, the determination of the language to be used by the judge at trial was a matter for that judge and not him. As he said in giving his first decision:

> "Section 5 stipulates that the judge may use either or both the official languages as he thinks fit and his decision in relation to the proceedings before him is final. My function as the Criminal Listing Judge as opposed to the trial judge is preparatory, that is to make it feasible for an application for use of Chinese to be made to the trial judge."

38. In my judgment, it was entirely rational for the listing judge, in considering both of the applicant's applications, to carry out what was in effect a preliminary assessment of the various factors which the trial judge himself may later take into account in making a determination pursuant to section 5. In effect, as I see it, leaving aside matters such as the availability of other judges to hear the matter (scheduled for 10 days), the listing judge was saying simply: This matter has already been set down before a monolingual judge. It seems to me that, viewing the case in the round, it could, without inconvenience or injustice to the accused, be determined by that monolingual judge. I will therefore leave the trial listed before him in the knowledge that the will make the final determination. If he decides that it should be heard in Cantonese then it will be adjourned and returned to me for relisting.

39. Mr Lee has complained that such a decision merely compounds delay, that the applicant wishes his trial, once scheduled for hearing, to proceed on the scheduled date. But that is a complaint as to the wisdom of the decision and that is not a matter for this Court.

40. In my judgment, it is clear that the listing judge, in considering the applications before him, carried out what I will call a 'filtering process' or, as I have said, made a 'preliminary assessment' of matters relevant to the appropriate language for trial in order to determine whether the applicant's listing should remain as scheduled or be moved to another judge, perhaps at the cost of delay. Such exercises are employed every day in our courts to better ensure the administration of justice. That being so, I fail to see how it can be argued that the listing judge took into account matters that were materially irrelevant or failed to consider matters that were materially relevant.

41. The applicant's Notice of Application contains a complaint that, in making his first decision, the listing judge took into account a fact which was a mistaken fact, namely, that the case had already been fixed some six months ahead and it would be difficult to 're-juggle it' without causing disruption to other accused. Apparently, the matter had not been fixed six months previously; it had been fixed at a materially later date. But if that was a mistake, I do not believe it can be argued that it was a material mistake sufficient to quash the judge's decision. The essence of the decision was that the matter had already been set down and it would be difficult now to reschedule it without causing difficulties for (of) other accused persons.

The length of this judgment

42. I have written this judgment in the knowledge that in leave applications it is, as a general rule, undesirable to consider the merits in depth. Lord Diplock in *Inland Revenue Commissioners v. National Federation of Self-Employed and Small Businesses Ltd* [1982] AC 617 (at page 644) spoke of 'a quick perusal' of the material available in order to determine whether it discloses what, on further consideration, might turn out to be an arguable case. Recently, in *Yu Pik Ying and Another v. Director of Immigration*, Civil Appeal No.603 or (of) 2000, Rogers JA commented:

> "In my view, the application for leave to bring judicial review proceedings should be a short procedure. As the cases indicate it should not involve lengthy applications. Indeed, the more the details of the case are considered, at the application stage, the more undesirable the lengthening of the proceedings becomes. The merits of the application should be considered at the hearing of judicial review, if leave be granted. It is indeed undesirable that the merits are considered in depth until the case is fully prepared since even the expression of preliminary views can have undesirable effects. It is for this reason that in my view the application stage should be more of a weeding out process, stopping those applications doomed to failure."

43. In the present case, however, reasonably lengthy and complex arguments needed to be analysed to understand what lay at their core. Were they, despite the clothing of constitutional importance and the excitement of public interest, applications that were doomed to failure?

Conclusion

44. Employing the test stated earlier in this judgment, in my judgment, it cannot be argued that the applicant has a constitutional right to be tried by a judge who speaks whichever of the two official languages the applicant will use at his trial. He has no such right. The applicant's constitutional right is to use, that is, to utilize or employ Cantonese at his trial and, if necessary, to have himself understood by means of interpretation or translation.

45. The applicant does, of course, have a constitutional right to a fair hearing. His concerns over demeanour are legitimate concerns. Those concerns, however, have been anticipated by the Court of Appeal which has enunciated guiding principles for his protection.

46. As to the complaint that, in refusing the applicant's applications for re-listing before a bilingual judge, the listing judge acted in a manner that was *Wednesbury* unreasonable, in my judgment that matter too is not capable of argument.

47. Accordingly, the application for leave to apply for judicial review is refused.

48. As to costs, I have not had an opportunity to hear from the parties. Indeed, no respondent is cited in the Notice of Application. I also bear in mind that this application has been made *ex parte* albeit on notice. I will therefore order that costs be reserved with liberty to apply to set the matter down for argument.

Judge of the Court of First Instance, High Court (M. J. Hartmann)

Mr Martin Lee, S.C., instructed by Messrs C.L. Chow and Law, for the Applicant

Mr Daniel Marash, S.C., instructed by Department of Justice

第十八條

在香港特別行政區實行的法律為本法以及本法第八條規定的香港原有法律和香港特別行政區立法機關制定的法律。

全國性法律除列於本法附件三者外，不在香港特別行政區實施。凡列於本法附件三之法律，由香港特別行政區在當地公佈或立法實施。

全國人民代表大會常務委員會在徵詢其所屬的香港特別行政區基本法委員會和香港特別行政區政府的意見後，可對列於本法附件三的法律作出增減，任何列入附件三的法律，限於有關國防、外交和其他按本法規定不屬於香港特別行政區自治範圍的法律。

全國人民代表大會常務委員會決定宣佈戰爭狀態或因香港特別行政區內發生香港特別行政區政府不能控制的危及國家統一或安全的動亂而決定香港特別行政區進入緊急狀態，中央人民政府可發佈命令將有關全國性法律在香港特別行政區實施。

案例

中國大陸的法律能否視為本地法？

P.059 Salt & Light Development Inc. 及其他 對 交大銘泰軟體產業有限公司

Salt & Light Development Inc. 及其他及博翰專業翻譯有限公司 對 交大銘泰軟體產業有限公司

Salt & Light Development Inc. Exclusive Investments Limited v. Sjtu Sunway Software Industry Limited

Salt & Light Development Inc. 及其他 對 交大銘泰軟體產業有限公司

HCA 2939/2004 ; HCA 2992/2004

Salt & Light Development Inc. Exclusive Investments Limited Beauhorse Professional Translation Limited v. Sjtu Sunway Software Industry Limited

Salt & Light Development Inc. 及其他及博翰專業翻譯有限公司 對 交大銘泰軟體產業有限公司

HCA 2992/2004

簡略案情

本案件是關於一間公司的股權買賣。原告同意將一間在深圳有業務的公司（下稱“T 公司”）的所有股權賣給被告。但這個買賣並沒有完成，據被告稱不成交的原因是原告虛假聲稱或者虛假保證，即 T 公司正在向深圳市工商行政管理局（“SABIC”）申請營業執照，並同時在跟其他相關的國家部門申請牌照和批核。但事實上，T 公司從來沒有提交這些申請。被告還進一步認為原告已經違反了繼續保持所有必須的牌照有效的保證。訴訟過程中，被告企圖根據《高等法院規則》第 26 號命令，向原告施行質詢書，要求原告確認，在 T 公司被 SABIC 強制停業後，T 公司有否再向 SABIC 申請復業。原告反對這申請，但被告強調這關係到原告有否滿足買賣中的陳述或者保證。最後，聆案官下令原告答覆此質詢，原告遂向原訟庭法官提出上訴。

裁決摘要

法官認同聆案官的決定，認為該質詢書有助減少案件的一些枝節。但原告認為他有權拒絕提供相關答案，理由是，若原告沒有取得相關政府執照與繳交法定稅項和收費的話，可能會被深圳市當局起訴，所以原告可以根據《證據條例》第 65（1）（a）條，即原告有權為了避免 "自我導致入罪" 的原因，拒絕回答任何問題。雖然該權利只適用香港法律所指的刑事罪行，但原告認為香港特別行政區是中華人民共和國的一部份，在避免“自我導致入罪”特權的問題上，中國法應被視為本地法而不是外國法，所以，本案符合第 65（1）（a）條的要求。可是，法官拒絕接納原告的理由，並認為中國大陸法律是外在的法律，不是本地法。裁定原告不享有第 65（1）（a）條的特權。法院進而解釋依據《基本法》第 18 條和第 84 條，認為除卻非常特定的條件下，國家刑事法律不能應用在香港。在《基本法》的框架下，香港既是中國的一部份，但同時擁有獨立的法律體制，這就是“一國兩制”的基礎。而且，香港跟內地沒有刑事交互強制執行的協議，所以第 65（1）（a）條對原告沒有幫助。最後，法官駁回上訴並下令原告對質詢書提供答案。

HCA 2939/2004

IN THE HIGH COURT OF THE

HONG KONG SPECIAL ADMINISTRATIVE REGION

COURT OF FIRST INSTANCE

ACTION NO. 2939 OF 2004

Between:

SALT & LIGHT DEVELOPMENT INC.	1st Plaintiff
EXCLUSIVE INVESTMENTS LIMITED	2nd Plaintiff
- and -	
SJTU SUNWAY SOFTWARE INDUSTRY LIMITED	Defendant

AND

HCA 2992/2004

IN THE HIGH COURT OF THE

HONG KONG SPECIAL ADMINISTRATIVE REGION

COURT OF FIRST INSTANCE
ACTION NO. 2992 OF 2004

BETWEEN

SALT & LIGHT DEVELOPMENT INC.	1st Plaintiff
EXCLUSIVE INVESTMENTS LIMITED	2nd Plaintiff
BEAUHORSE PROFESSIONAL TRANSLATION LIMITED	3rd Plaintiff
- and -	
SJTU SUNWAY SOFTWARE INDUSTRY LIMITED	Defendant

Before: Mr Recorder McCoy, SC, in Chambers

Date of Hearing: 6 April 2006

Date of Judgment: 13 April 2006

JUDGMENT

1. In these 2 appeals from a decision of Master Kwan ordering that 6 interrogatories be answered by a named director of the Plaintiffs, the parties have sensibly agreed that the outcome of the appeal in HCA 2939/04 must be identical to that in the conjoined appeal HCA 2992/04. In those circumstances it was further agreed that HCA 2939/04 would be exclusively considered, the interrogatories being identical in both actions.

Background: Factual Context

2. By a Deed dated 23 August 2004 Salt & Light Development Inc. (1st Plaintiff) and Exclusive Investments Limited (2nd Plaintiff) agreed to sell and Sjtu Sunway Software Industry Limited (Defendant) agreed to purchase 100,000 shares, as to 90,000 shares thereof held by the 1st Plaintiff and 10,000 shares held by the 2nd Plaintiff, in the capital of Beauhorse Professional Translation Limited ("Beauhorse"), being the entire issued share capital of Beauhorse. Beauhorse was incorporated in Hong Kong in 1990 and was in business in Hong Kong and in Shenzen, China. It is what occurred in China that is the sole focus of this litigation.

3. Before me the parties agreed that a crucial issue, if not the decisive one at the trial would be the construction of the Deed and a Disclosure Letter of the same date. The Disclosure Letter, was formally adopted by the parties as an integral part of the Deed. That Letter was created by the Plaintiffs "for the purpose of limiting the scope of the indemnities, representations, warranties and undertakings contained in the Deed including its Schedules".

4. It suffices for present purpose to note Clause 7 Schedule 3 of the Deed:

> "7. Government Licences, Approvals, Permits, etc.
>
> The company [Beauhorse] has at all relevant times maintained in force all such government licences, registrations, approvals, permits, qualifications and other authorisations as may be required by it for the purpose of carrying on its business as at the date hereof. The Company has complied in all respects with the terms and conditions of such licences, registrations, approvals, permits, qualifications and authorisations."

5. The other relevant provision is paragraph 10.2 of the Disclosure Letter which provides:

> "The Company [Beauhorse] has started its business operation in the PRC while it is still in the process of applications for necessary licences and approvals. The Company is thus facing administrative actions and/or prosecution in the PRC, as evidenced in the following documents."

6. There follows a reference to 2 documents, both dated 22 April 2004, from the Shenzen Administrative Bureau of Industry and Commerce ("SABIC"), referring to its investigation of Beauhorse for unlawfully carrying on a business without a business licence.

7. The Defendant's case is that by the Deed and Disclosure Letter the Plaintiffs falsely represented and falsely warranted the position, as Beauhorse had never submitted any application for the necessary licences or approvals before the Plaintiffs entered into the Deed. In addition, it is argued that Beauhorse was not just in default for having no business licence, but it also, for example, had not submitted any application for tax registration, filed any audited accounts and tax returns to the PRC authorities, nor paid any business tax or social security funds, as required by Chinese law.

8. The Plaintiffs' case is the denial of any breach, in the alternative if there was a breach that the Defendant had waived it and further that the Defendant was in any event estopped from alleging misrepresentation and/or breach of warranty. The Plaintiffs have sued for non-performance on the basis that the Defendant's rescission was baseless.

9. The original completion date was 22 October 2004, however the Defendant requested that the completion date be extended to 23 December 2004. Upon that date the Defendant did not complete. The Plaintiffs' action followed and the Defendant initially pleaded misrepresentation as its sole defence but by an Amended Defence introduced 9 months later a specific plea of breach of the contractual warranties was added. The Defendant has without an order required the Plaintiffs to answer 6 interrogatories, to which the Plaintiffs continue to resist: O26 r3.

Interrogatories: The Key Provision

10. The key provision to O26 RHC dealing with interrogatories is O26r1(1) which establishes that only interrogatories

"... which are necessary either –

(a) for disposing fairly of the cause or matter; or

(b) for saving costs"

shall be allowed. This overarching provision applies to both forms of interrogatories, those without an order and also ordered interrogatories: see O26 r1(5).

11. In *Baronness Dunn v. Li Kwok Po David* [1994] 2 HKC 597, 600F Barnett J in relation to O26 r1(1)(b) decided, correctly in my respectful judgment, that it was not for the interrogator to have to establish that irrespective of the content of the forthcoming answer that costs must be saved. In rejecting that submission be tellingly stated:

> "An answer favourable to the interrogator would have to be a foregone conclusion. It would require a degree of prescience that would put the proprietors of Happy Valley and Shatin out of business. I am quite satisfied that what was intended and what has been achieved by the amendments to O26 r1 is that the party seeking to interrogate must show that the interrogatory is necessary 'if costs are to be saved'. Put another way, 'if any saving of costs is to be achieved'".

12. In *Lee Nui Foon v. Ocean Park Corporation* (No 2) [1995] 2 HKC 395 Cheung J (as he then was) helpfully summarized the general principles applicable to interrogatories. Cheung J at p 398 highlighted that the litigation value of interrogatories is maximized when directed to precise points on which either an admission or information is sought. That is the case here.

13. Both Hunter J in *Cocoa Merchants Ltd. v. Ferryview Holdings Inc.* [1987] HKLR 577, 580 and Cheung J in *Lau Tak Wah Andy v. Hang Seng Bank Ltd.* [2001] 2 HKC 548, 552 quoted with approval the remarks of Lord Esher MR in *Marriott v. Chamberlain* (1886) 17 QBD 154, 163 that:

> "The right to interrogate is not confined to the facts directly in issue, but extends to any fact the existence or non-existence of which is relevant to the existence or non-existence of the facts directly in issue."

14. To this should be added that the relevance of an interrogatory is to be judged not only by reference to the case of the party putting forward the question, but also from the perspective of the case of the opponent. An interrogatory which is relevant to weakening the opponent's own case is indistinguishable in principle from one seeking to affirmatively advance the interrogator's own case: see *Plymouth Mutual Co-operative and Industrial Society Limited v. Trader's Publishing Association Limited* [1906] 1 KB 403, 417 (CA).

15. This comports with the approach of Lord Finlay LC in *Blair v. Haycock Cadle Co.* (1917) 34 TLR 39 (HL) that if the answer to an interrogatory might form a step in establishing liability it was sufficient justification for its invocation. Therefore whether a conclusive or definitive response to an issue might emerge from answers to interrogatories, was not a criterion in evaluating their validity.

> "It was enough that they should have some bearing on the question and that they might form a step in establishing liability."

16. Lord Haldane at p 40 was to the effect that while an answer to one interrogatory might appear to produce a result insubstantial in itself, yet a series of answers might well produce a valuable coherent significance, that would show they were "necessary".

17. While the prospect of minor incremental advances being established by the answers may suffice, the less an interrogatory appears to be targeted to the core issues in the proceedings the more likely a Court will be to exercise an adverse discretion to its employment. Otherwise the civil justice system would be wrongly encouraging "unnecessary" interrogatories in breach of O26 r1, "as a source of ammunition to be routinely discharged as part of an interlocutory bombardment pending the main battle": per Sir Thomas Bingham MR in *Hall v. Sevalco Ltd.* [1996] PIQR 344, 349 (CA).

18. In my judgment the correct test to apply, when the opposition to interrogatories is, as here, that the answer to them already exists in the pleadings, witness statements etc, is the approach of Colman J in *Det Danske Hedeselskabet v. KDM International Plc* [1994] 2 Lloyd's LR 534, 537:

> "Fifthly; requests for information ascertainable by cross-examination at the trial are inappropriate unless the party questioning can establish that it is essential for the proper preparation of his case that such information is made available to him before trial, in the sense that if the matter is left until cross-examination at the trial that party will, or probably will be irremediably prejudiced in his conduct of the trial or the trial may be unduly interrupted or otherwise disorganized by the late emergence of the information."

19. This approach was itself approved by the English Court of Appeal in *Hall v. Selvaco Ltd.* as being applicable in all civil proceedings. Although the interrogatories in that case were not allowed, this was principally because they were premature, having been served on the same day as a request for further and better particulars and before the exchange of witness statements. That timing is wrong in principle and could be justified only in an exceptional situation.

The 6 Interrogatories

20. Interrogatory 1 asks when did Beauhorse commence business in the PRC. It is opposed by the Plaintiffs on the basis that 2 documents emanating from SABIC record that Beauhorse has "since February 2004" operated in Shenzen (Shenzhen) and that it followed that the Defendant could not establish that it was necessary for disposing fairly of the action or necessary for saving costs for the Plaintiffs to answer it. Mr. Cheung for the Defendant however emphasizes that there is nothing in the pleadings or witness statements from the Plaintiffs on this issue. He submits it is a deliberate omission. The sole basis for the date being somehow definitive is that it is recited by a third party in these 2 documents.

21. It is quite unclear whether the date referred to by SABIC is its own conclusion after an investigation or whether it is based on an admission by Beauhorse or indeed otherwise. The Plaintiffs do not argue that the date is not an issue–they oppose the interrogatory on the basis that the date has already been established and it would follow that it is not "necessary" to answer it. The Defendant's pleadings directly put in issue, in para 9(2)(b) of the Amended Defence and Counterclaim, statements by or on behalf of Beauhorse to SABIC as being untrue or misleading and designed to reduce its liability and administrative penalty. This interrogatory must be answered by the Plaintiffs.

22. Interrogatory 2 asks what were all the licences etc said to have been obtained and maintained by Beauhorse under Clause 7 Schedule 3 of the Deed.

23. The Plaintiffs in opposing this refer to an extract from the Defendant's own witness statement that records that a Plaintiffs' representative had admitted on an unstated day in September 2004 that no application for any "business licence" had ever been submitted by then. This could only explain or answer part of the interrogatory, even if that position is maintained at trial. The Earl of Selborne LC said in *Lyell v. Kennedy* (1883) 8 App Cas 217, 228:

> "The defendant, therefore, must answer the interrogatories relevant to that portion of the Plaintiffs' case. It is no sufficient objection that the Plaintiff may have, and to some extent (on his own shewing) has, other means of proving the facts inquired after. Admissions of the facts by the defendant might simplify the proof and materially diminish the expense of the trial."

24. However the Plaintiffs' opposition to answering is principally in reliance upon para 4 (1A)(b) of the Amended Reply which states in relation to the Disclosure Letter:

> "Beauhorse did not have approvals or licences from business registration, tax, labour or social security authorities in the PRC for carrying on business in the PRC."

It is said this is a complete answer, already provided by the Plaintiffs.

25. Beauhorse has said what it did not have. But it has not said what it did have – which is what it is asked. The Amended Reply negatives a number of specific approvals or licences. It is not stated there that Beauhorse had absolutely no licences etc. whatsoever, in terms of the generality of Clause 7 Schedule 3. If that is the position it should say so, without the possible invocation of special pleading. This is the whole point of interrogatories–to obtain crisp, clearly defined hard–edged trial issues, so that possible lurking ambiguities and potentialities in relation to material matters, which could otherwise become mischievous diversions at trial, are closed down well in advance. Interrogatory 2 requires a precise positive reply as to what licences etc. Beauhorse had; a list of what it had not, may not amount, in sum, to the same thing.

26. Interrogatories 3, 4 and 5 can be dealt with together as they ask in turn whether (and if so, when) Beauhorse has ever applied in the PRC for: a business licence, tax registration, business tax, Enterprise Income Tax, ever withheld and remitted in respect of its employees Individual Income Tax and whether it maintained Social Insurance Fund accounts. In my judgment these must be answered. They align with the objective of Interrogatory 2 by approaching it from a different direction.

27. The subject matter of these interrogatories is fundamental to the Defendant's case and substantially important to the Plaintiffs' own case, which avers that there was no non-compliance.

28. If this issue remains or becomes a live issue at trial (based on the true construction and effect of the Deed and the Disclosure Letter) the Defendant will need to scurry round at very short notice and seek to obtain witnesses from China, with all the inherent associated expense and the real risk of dislocating the trial. It is to obviate that very prospect and in recognition of the underlying importance of the issues, that justifies the interrogatories sought by the Defendant here.

29. The interrogatories do not exceed the legitimate requirements of this litigation. A clear litigious purpose for the fair and efficient conduct of the trial is made out. Necessity is a stringent test but its resonance depends on all the circumstances. It involves a fact–sensitive analysis. In this regard I apply the words of Sir Thomas Bingham MR in *Hall v. Sevalco Ltd.* at 349 emphasising:

> "... the modern, cards face–up on the table, approach to civil litigation, which favoured maximum disclosure of relevant facts and evidence at an early stage of the litigation."

Interrogatory 6: Introduction

30. For the Plaintiffs it was argued that Interrogatory 6 (which asks whether Beauhorse had applied, since 10 September 2004, to SABIC, to recommence its business) should be disallowed, on the basis that it was a 'fishing interrogatory' (as characterized in the Hong Kong Civil Practice 2006 at 26/4/9), as the Defendant had no evidential basis to raise the alleged application to be based on any fact or event.

31. In the course of argument Mr. Johnny Fee for the Plaintiffs accepted that events which postdated the Deed and the Disclosure Letter (both dated 23 August 2004) had obvious litigation relevance, as the original completion date under the contract was 22 October 2004 and the extended completion date was 23 December 2004. It was on 10 September 2004 that SABIC directed Beauhorse to cease business. Mr. Kam Cheung for the Defendant emphasised that in the Deed, the Plaintiffs had expressly warranted, that they had "maintained in force" all necessary licences etc.

32. The Defendant's case was that there had been a consummate failure as at the date of the Deed to comply with the warranty and that the Plaintiffs should answer on oath whether they had either attempted to or had succeeded in, quietly rectifying the position by making 'good title', as it were, before the date of the extended settlement. In my judgment this interrogatory is necessary as an answer would likely eliminate one significant dangling issue, namely the status of compliance by the Plaintiffs with the warranty not just at the time of the Deed but at any time prior to the original completion date or the extended date. It is justified on both limbs of O26 r1(a) and (b). Mr. Cheung rightly emphasised the high litigation value here of having an unequivocal statement prior to trial as to whether in fact all necessary licences etc. were ever sought and moreover ever obtained.

Interrogatory 6: Claim to the privilege against self–incrimination

33. However, Mr. Fee in relation to this interrogatory also invoked on the Plaintiffs behalf the privilege against self-incrimination. It was common ground that the Plaintiffs were at risk of prosecution in Shenzen [*sic*], China for a range of possible offences arising out of the alleged omission to obtain, before the date of the extended settlement, various Government licences and also for default in relation to statutory taxes and fees. This submission requires close examination, as it raises some novel issues under Hong Kong law.

34. A claim to interrogatories, just as much to discovery, is defeated if the privilege against self-incrimination is available: O24 r5, *Taranaki Co-operative Dairy Company Limited v. Rowe* [1970] NZLR 895 (CA).

35. That privilege is not a matter of procedure or of evidence. It is not adjectival. It is a substantive right.

36. On analysis the issues to be resolved have turned out to be:

(1) Can a company claim the privilege against self-incrimination under civil law in Hong Kong?

(2) Can a claim to the privilege against self-incrimination in civil law be based on a risk of proceedings under foreign law?

(3) Is a claim based on a risk of proceedings under the criminal law of China, a claim under foreign law?

(4) Does a Judge have an overriding discretion to exclude a compelled answer or document in civil proceedings based on a risk of proceedings under foreign law?

(5) How should the discretion be exercised in the present case?

Self-incrimination in civil law: United Kingdom statute

37. By s14 Civil Evidence Act 1968 [UK] a party to civil proceedings is not compelled to give answers or documents which will tend to criminate or tend to expose to proceedings for a penalty the person or his spouse under the law of any part of the United Kingdom – which includes the law of Scotland, with its Roman-Dutch (as opposed to common law), roots. But that section also therefore provides that potential criminal liability outside the United Kingdom is no valid basis for a claim to the privilege, within it.

38. S14(1)(a) "shall apply only as regards criminal offences under the law of any part of the United Kingdom and penalties provided for by such law".

Self-incrimination in civil law: Hong Kong statute

39. Section 65 Evidence Ord Cap 8 in its present format was added in 1969, and as the endnote to the section shows, was a response to the United Kingdom statutory initiative a year earlier. It contains 5 subsections.

40. It is only necessary to set out the terms of s65(1) to show that it is identical to the United Kingdom provision save that "under the law of any part of the United Kingdom" is substituted with "under the law of Hong Kong":

"65. Privilege against incrimination of self or spouse

(1) The right of a person in any legal proceedings other than criminal proceedings to refuse to answer any question or produce any document or thing if to do so would tend to expose that person to proceedings for an offence or for the recovery of a penalty–

(a) shall apply only as regards criminal offences under the law of Hong Kong and penalties provided for by such law; and

(b) shall include a like right to refuse to answer any question or produce any document or thing if to do so would tend to expose the husband or wife of that person to proceedings for any such criminal offence or for the recovery of any such penalty."

41. The section speaks of a "person" having the right to refuse to incriminate him/herself and spouse. "Person" can be generally apt in law to include both humans and artificial juristic entities; see the expansive definition of "person" in s3 Interpretation and General Clause Ord Cap 1. S65(1)(a) is explicit that in civil proceedings the "person" may invoke the privilege which generates the right, "only as regards criminal offences under the law of Hong Kong and penalties provided for by such law".

42. This is express statutory direction that in civil proceedings in Hong Kong, only a risk of incrimination under Hong Kong law, is available to provide the right not to be compelled to answer. Lord Diplock stated that this conclusion was declaratory of the common law position immediately prior to the enactment of s14 Civil Evidence Act 1968. See *Rio Tinto Zinc Corporation v. Westinghouse Electric Corporation*, [1978] AC 547, 637. See also *Attorney General for Gibraltar v. May* [1999] 1 WLR 998, 1003G (CA).

Self-incrimination in criminal law: Hong Kong statute

43. Some 34 years after s65 dealing with the civil law was created, s65A was enacted in 2003, providing for the statutory right in criminal law and extending it to spouses too. Since 1991 though Article 11(2)(g) Hong Kong Bill of Rights Ord Cap 383, had, consistently with Article 14(3)(g) of the International Covenant on Civil and Political Rights, affirmed the privilege against self-incrimination that "[i]n the determination of any criminal charges against him" a person was "not to be compelled to testify against himself or to confess guilt."

44. Section 65A Evidence Ord Cap 8 provides:

"65A. Privilege against incrimination of self or spouse in criminal proceedings

The right of a person in criminal proceedings to refuse to answer any question or produce any document or thing if to do so would tend to expose that person to proceedings for an offence or for the recovery of a penalty or for a forfeiture shall include a like right to refuse to answer any question or produce any document or thing if to do so would tend to expose the husband or wife of that person to any such proceedings."

45. In contrast to the replicated United Kingdom model adopted for civil proceedings, this section has no counterpart there. It is one of a number of amendments to criminal law in Hong Kong designed to specially elevate marriage as a formal status from which special rights or privileges flow. See Evidence (Miscellaneous Amendments) Ord 23 of 2003. The trend and momentum of criminal law reform in other common law jurisdictions has been actively in the opposite direction, to downplay matrimony and equalize it with civil unions, formal and informal. Uxorial privilege against self-incrimination has however been recognised at common law for almost 200 years: *R v. All Saints, Worcester (Inhabitants)* (1817) 6 M&S 194, 199–201, *Stapleton v. Crofts* (1852) 18 QB 367, 368; *Riddle v. The King* (1911) 12 CLR 622, 627–629 (HCA) per Griffith CJ.

Does s65 Evidence Ord Cap 8 apply to a corporate person?

46. This important question needs to be answered, as the Defendant submitted that the language affirming the privilege against self-incrimination, a "right" as the section itself calls it, does not extend to corporate persons. Therefore it would follow the Plaintiff companies could not claim the privilege against self-incrimination.

47. It was submitted on behalf of the Defendant that whatever the common law position was, it is to be noted that s65(1)(b) Evidence Ord states that in relation to the "person" asserting the privilege against self-incrimination, that "...the husband or wife of that

person" shall also be similarly protected.

48. Marriage vows do not apply to companies and on a literal reading the privilege would be therefore confined to the warm-blooded. But in my judgment that would be too austere a conclusion in the context of such a fundamental right. It was argued that this choice of legislative language necessarily coloured the intention of s65(1)(a) as being deliberately restricted to individuals. I cannot safely conclude that the possible infelicity of language in s65(1)(b) was actually intended to explicitly abrogate the right in relation to corporate persons; which I also find to have existed prior to its enactment. "Fundamental rights cannot be overridden by general or ambiguous words": *R v. Secretary of State for the Home Department ex parte Simms* [2000] 2 AC 115, 121 per Lord Hoffman. A deeply embedded right cannot be extirpated so easily. As Gibbs CJ said in *Hammond v. The Commonwealth* (1983) 152 CLR 281, 291 (HCA):

> "It would be necessary to find a clear expression of intention before one could conclude that the legislature intended to override so important a privilege as that against self-incrimination."

49. On a purposive construction, that gives full weight to the nature of the underlying constitutional right at stake, the expression "...husband or wife of that person..." must be read to embrace the coexistence of corporate and human forms to mean "husband or wife (where applicable), of that person". I reject the submission based on the language of the section, because I conclude that the weight of common law, both before and after s65(1) came into existence, supports the conclusion that the privilege did and does apply to corporate entities.

Does the privilege against self incrimination apply at common law to companies?

50. The common law has not given a single answer to the applicability of the privilege against self-incrimination to a corporate person. A narrow majority in the High Court of Australia in *Environment Protection Authority v. Caltex Refining Co. Pty Limited* (1993) 178 CLR 477 (HCA) (Mason CJ, Brennan, Toohey and McHugh JJ; Deane, Dawson and Gaudron JJ dissenting) has expressly rejected its availability. The United States Supreme Court has for a hundred years repeatedly reached the same conclusion: *Hale v. Henke* (1906) 201 US 43, *Braswell v. United States* (1988) 487 US 99. But the English Court of Appeal in *Triplex Safety Glass Co. Ltd. v. Lancegaye Safety Glass* (1934) Ltd. [1939] 2 KB 395 (CA), the New Zealand Court of Appeal in *New Zealand Apple and Pear Marketing Board v. Master & Sons Ltd.* [1986] 1 NZLR 191 (CA), the Alberta Court of Appeal in: *Webster v. Solloway, Mills & Co.* [1931] 1 DLR 831, the Supreme Court of Canada in *Klein v. Bell* [1955] 2 DLR 513 and the Court of Appeal of the Isle of Man *In The Matter of Atrium Trading Ltd.* (2003–2005) Manx LR 91 have all upheld it.

51. In *Triplex* Du Parcq LJ giving the judgment of the English Court of Appeal at 409 said:

> "It is true that a company cannot suffer all the pains to which a real person is subject. It can, however, in certain cases be convicted and punished, with grave consequences to its reputation and to its members, and we can see no ground for depriving a juristic person of those safe-guards which the law of England accords even to the least deserving of natural persons. It would not be in accordance with principle that any person capable of committing, and incurring the penalties of, a crime should be compelled by process of law to admit a criminal offence."

This decision has been assumed to be correct and acted upon in a number of judgments of the House of Lords, although curiously the actual point never appears to have been specifically decided. See: *Rio Tinto Zinc Corporation v. Westinghouse Electric Corporation* [1978] AC 547; *British Steel Corporation v. Granada Television Ltd.* [1981] AC 1096, at 1178; *Rank Film Distributors Ltd. v. Video Information Centre* [1982] AC 380.

52. In my judgment a dictum in the joint dissenting judgment of Deane, Dawson and Gaudron JJ in the *Caltex Refining* case at p 532 is very much in point:

> "In the end, it is based upon the deep-seated belief that those who allege the commission of a crime should prove it themselves and should not be able to compel the accused to provide proof against himself. To make an exception in the case of a corporation may trouble the conscience less because a corporation 'has no body to be kicked or soul to be damned'. But that is hardly a sufficient justification for the exception having regard to the underlying principle and the purpose which it serves both of which apply to corporations."

Self incrimination at common law re foreign criminal offences

53. In *Brannigan v. Davison* [1997] AC 238 (PC), it was held that the common law privilege against self-incrimination did not apply where the person was at risk under a law of a different country of criminal or penal sanctions in relation to prior conduct or to the actual giving of evidence. In reaching this conclusion, Lord Nicholls of Birkenhead who delivered the judgment applied the decision of Lord Cranworth VC in *King of Two Sicilies v. Willcox* (1851) 1 Sim NS 301, who had similarly rejected the privilege under a claim based on foreign law.

54. The objections to extending the privilege to foreign law are closely considered by Lord Nicholls at 249F–250B, who concluded:

> "If the privilege were applicable when the risk of prosecution is under the law of another country, the privilege would have the effect of according primacy to foreign law in all cases."

55. Section 65A does not, at least on its face, restrict the privilege to offences committed in Hong Kong; compare the express restriction in s65. However, in *R v. Au Yeung Chi Kwan* [1993] 2 HKC 134 (CA), particularly relied upon by Mr. Fee, the Court of Appeal had endorsed a ruling in a criminal trial that a prosecution witness need not answer whether he had been guilty of various crimes in China.

56. The facts of the case relate to the armed robbery of the King Fook Jewellery Shop in Jordan Road in 1990, by 4 men, each of whom was armed with a gun. In the course of fleeing from the scene with a large quantity of watches and gold ornaments, one of the robbers callously shot dead an off duty immigration officer who was gallantly pursuing the robbers. At the trial of the organizers of the robbery, a number of their accomplices from China gave evidence. One of the accomplices gave evidence for the prosecution and was cross-examined. He admitted his involvement in the King Fook robbery. He also implicated the accused. He was cross-examined and in an effort to have the jury understand his true character and antecedents he was asked whether he had committed any offences in China. The witness himself objected to answering the question. Defence counsel

asked the Judge to direct the witness to answer.

"Mr. Young: Well my Lord with respect, it can't incriminate him if it happened in China.

Court: It can when he gets back to China"

[See *R v. Au Yeung Chi Kwan* [1993] 2 HKC 134, 145C]

57. The Judge, Hooper J, then directed that the witness did not have to answer the question. On appeal the Court of Appeal rejected a ground based on the ruling, noting at 147C "it would be unrealistic and unfair ... that because the judge might not have had exact knowledge of the penal consequences of criminal law in China he should have required the witness to answer". No other Hong Kong decision in criminal or civil law appears to have had to deal with a claim to self-incrimination based on a legal system outside Hong Kong itself. Section 65A Evidence Ord was not in force at the time of *Au Yeung Chi Kwan*, which was therefore a decision at common law. It was the decision of the Privy Council 4 years later in *Brannigan v. Davison* [1997] AC 258 that the common law did not allow the privilege against self-incrimination to be based upon a risk under foreign law.

58. Power JA was, in my judgment, not purporting to lay down an absolute point of principle that in Hong Kong the privilege against self-incrimination could be based on foreign law. Rather the Court of Appeal was endorsing the trial Judge's exercise of his residual discretion to not require the witness to answer on the facts of the case. Seen this way, not only is the decision in *Au Yeung Chi Kwan* not inconsistent with *Brannigan v. Davison*, but is actually a prescient example of how the residual trial discretion remains available and operates in criminal law. I conclude that a similar residual discretion also exists in civil law.

59. The very factors Lord Nicholls of Birkenhead relied upon in *Brannigan v. Davison* (involving a Commission of Inquiry) for excluding the privilege in relation to foreign law might apply with equal vigour in criminal trials. The validity of a claim to the privilege on the basis, say, that a witness might be in peril of the criminal law of Sao Tomé and Principe (the smallest and least populous country in Africa) could only be adjudicated upon with great difficulty. The ascertainment of the law of that country would be needed. An adjournment of unknown length may probably be required. In the context of any criminal trial, but particularly one before a jury, the scenario is wholly destructive of the integrity and fluency of the criminal justice process. But I do not have to resolve any issue in relation to criminal law in this civil proceeding.

Is the criminal law of China "the law of Hong Kong" under s65 Evidence Ord?

60. But for the Plaintiffs it was submitted that (1) offences under Mainland China law should also be included within the expression "the law of Hong Kong" found in s65(1)(a) Evidence Ord, or alternatively (2) that the Court should in any event retain a supplementary discretion despite s65(1)(a) to decline to compel an answer in relation to foreign offences, including offences under Chinese law.

61. The Plaintiffs would superficially have support in what Lord Nicholls said in *Brannigan v. Davison* at 250C-D:

"Second, the contrast being drawn between foreign and domestic law is the contrast between the laws of two different countries. Special considerations may apply in countries with a federal structure, as in Australia and the United States, or in countries with a unitary structure but having different laws applicable in different parts of the country, as in the United Kingdom".

62. But the contrast drawn between foreign and domestic law is not a contrast always between two different countries. Lord Nicholls did not have the unique position of Hong Kong and China in mind in delivering that dictum, which I respectfully distinguish. In Hong Kong a vivid contrast exists between its law and the law in the other parts of the constituent areas comprising the same country – the People's Republic of China. By s2 of the Interpretation and General Clauses Ord Cap 1 "People's Republic of China" is defined as "includes Taiwan, the Hong Kong Special Administrative Region and Macau".

63. It is the Plaintiffs' case that the Hong Kong SAR, being in law part of the country of the People's Republic of China, it follows that Mainland Chinese Law should not be seen, for the purpose of the privilege against self-incrimination, as "foreign law" but as "domestic law".

64. I reject the submission that Mainland Chinese criminal law is "domestic law" for this or any purpose in Hong Kong. In a non-pejorative, technical sense only, the criminal law of Mainland China is for the Hong Kong SAR external law and is therefore given either the appellation "foreign law" or "non-domestic law" – being in either event, not "the law of Hong Kong" within s65(1)(a) Evidence Ord.

65. A combination of Articles 18 and 84 of the Basic Law at a minimum, make it unarguable, that the criminal law of Mainland China, ("National Law" as it is properly described in the Basic Law), may be applied in Hong Kong, outside the very special pre-conditions set out there in Article 18.

66. Mr. Fee's submission would structurally and functionally subvert the separate constitutional model of the HKSAR. Hong Kong is an inalienable constituent part of China, but it enjoys under the Basic Law a separateness that critically includes a legal system operating under the Rule of Law. The paradox which supplies the covalent unifying power between China and the Hong Kong SAR, is that Hong Kong is a part of China yet apart from it, with its own laws – one country: two legal systems.

67. There may be some eventual reciprocity in the enforcement of certain civil law matters, but no such mutuality or convergence exists in criminal law.

Discretion to exclude for incrimination under foreign law

68. In *Brannigan v. Davison* Lord Nicholls of Birkenhead at 251B-D considered that the unqualified inapplicability of the privilege to foreign law was in itself a potentially unsatisfactory principle, as it would by definition deny a court tasked with that circumstance any discretion, regardless of the nature of the crime, under the foreign law and regardless of the likely practical consequences for the witness under that law.

69. In short, the graphic example of a witness or party in civil proceedings refusing to give a relevant answer or to produce a relevant document on the basis that it would incriminate him or his wife for murder contrary to the penal law of any legal system outside Hong Kong, is plainly that type of circumstance. There, the Court would have, in my judgment, the jurisdiction in civil law to exercise a discretion to excuse a witness from giving self-incriminating evidence.

70. In *Arab Monetary Fund v. Hashim* [1989] 1 WLR 565, Morritt J

held first that there was no privilege against self-incrimination in relation to possible criminal offences under foreign laws because of the explicit language of s14 Civil Evidence Act 1968.

71. At 573H–574C Morritt J secondly held that no discretion resided in a Judge to exclude any relevant evidence in civil law on the basis that the compelled answer or document would place the witness in peril of a foreign criminal law. But Morritt J thirdly concluded that the general discretion involved in an equitable remedy (there an interlocutory injunction) was available, so that the foreign incrimination aspect did become a relevant factoring the discretion after all.

72. I respectfully disagree with the second conclusion, but respectfully agree with the first, and third: so in the result the outcome but not the reasoning is shared. I accept the Plaintiffs'submission that in a civil proceeding the Court has a residual discretion to take into account any incrimination under non-domestic law. Of course there is no discretion in relation to Hong Kong law. It is an absolute. But it does not follow that the other extreme also exists, so that no possibility of protection against compelled incrimination disclosure would exist. While at the interlocutory stages or at trial of a civil action, a judge does not normally have any discretion as to the admission of relevant and admissible evidence, the issue in relation to self-incrimination is outside that very normalcy. The consequences of a forced answer could be literally life-threatening. The privilege protects personal freedom and human dignity. It is "deep rooted" in Hong Kong law: *Lam Chi Ming v. The Queen* [1991] 2 AC 212, 22 per Lord Griffiths. It protects "the individual against the affront to dignity and privacy inherent in a practice which enables the prosecution to force the person charged to supply the evidence out of his or her own mouth": *R v. Amway Corporation* (1989) 56 DLR (4th) 309, 323 (SCC) per Sopinka J.

73. In civil law the orthodox capacity for excluding relevant probative evidence is very limited, yet it is wide enough to permit a claim to self-incrimination even under foreign law to be evaluated as a factor in the exercise of a judicial discretion. Lord Nicholls stated in *Branningan v. Davison* at p 251 D that a civil court had "inherent power to conduct its process in a fair and reasonable manner".

74. This special approach within civil law was adopted in *Credit Suisse Fides Trust SA v. Cuoghi* [1998] QB 818 (CA) per Millett LJ at 830 B, per Lord Bingham CJ at 833D–F, with whom Potter LJ at 830 G concurred. These authorities post–date the decision in *Arab Monetary Fund v. Hashim* [1989] 1 WLR 565 and I propose to apply them. Lord Bingham CJ held, directly inconsistent with the second conclusion of Morritt J in *Arab Monetary Fund*:

> "Mr. Cuoghi was not entitled to claim the statutory right not to incriminate himself provided by section 14 of the Civil Evidence Act 1968. This right is, however, one widely respected among civilized nations irrespective of statute, and the judge was in my view fully entitled to indicate that he would exercise his discretion..."

75. In *Beckkett Pte Ltd v. Deutsche Bank AG* [2005] 3 SLR 555 (CA), the Singapore Court of Appeal considered an application for leave by Beckkett Pte Ltd. to be released from the implied undertaking to use documents obtained via discovery from Deutsche Bank AG, for the purpose of obtaining an injunction in Indonesia. There was a significant risk that the Bank might be prosecuted in Indonesia if leave to use the documents were given. The Court of Appeal refused to sanction the use of the documents.

76. Chao Hick Tin JA at paragraphs [35]–[36], after referring to *Arab Monetary Fund v. Hashim* [1989] 1 WLR 565 (Morritt J) and *Credit Suisse Fides Trust SA v. Cuoghi* [1998] QB 818 (CA) concluded that a residual discretion existed to take into account the possibility of a foreign prosecution and the risks of self-incrimination. See also: *Re Casterbridge Properties* [2002] BPIR 428 at [33] per Burton J in the English Chancery Division to the same effect.

The Privilege against Self-incrimination of a Company does not extend to its Directors

77. As the Plaintiffs which alone claim the privilege are corporate a further consideration for the purposes of the exercise of the discretion arises. It is whether the foreign law self-incrimination of a company necessarily extends to also protect the directors of the company, which may themselves be both corporate or human, as the personages through which the Plaintiffs materially exist and operate.

78. In my judgment the privilege against self-incrimination claimed by a company is not descendible–it is personal to the company-incrimination of the self is privileged, incrimination of the company by the director(s), protects the company but not the directors. As the company has a separate legal personality it is that separate personality alone that is protected. It is a distinct legal person and it is that juristic person's privilege only. The principle in *Salomon v. A Salomon & Co. Ltd.* [1897] AC 22 must work both ways.

> "If people choose to conduct their affairs through the medium of corporations, they are taking advantage of the fact that in law those corporations are separate legal entities, whose property and actions are in law not the property or actions of their incorporators or controlling shareholders cannot, for all purposes beneficial to them, insist on the separate identify of such corporations but then be heard to say the contrary when discovery is sought against such corporations"
>
> *Tate Access Inc. v. Boswell* [1991] Ch at 531F–H per Sir Nicholas Browne–Wilkinson V–C.

79. The position is consistent too with the view of Lord Diplock in *Rio Tinto Zinc Corporation v. Westinghouse Electric Corporation* [1978] AC 547, 637G–638A, so while a company may claim privilege in the same way as an individual, the privilege is that of the company and does to extend to the office holders. See also to this effect *Sociedaide Nacional de Combustiveis de Angola UEE v. Lundquist* [1991] 2 QB 310, 336 C (CA) per Beldam LJ. See also: *Rochfort v. Trade Practices Commission* (1982) 153 CLR 134, 145 (HCA) per Mason J (as he then was).

80. It follows that in exercising the discretion that I have found to exist, the separate circumstances of the directors are not included. But if this conclusion is not correct, the Plaintiffs still would not have the discretion exercised in their favour. SABIC dealt with Beauhorse, for its omission to obtain a business licence under sections 31 and 32 of the Administrative Penalty Law [PRC] (中華人民共和國行政處罰法), by the imposition of a modest RMB5,000 administrative penalty. No reason has been advanced why any sanctions against the directors of the Plaintiffs in relation to this or other such offences would be disproportionate from that relativity, in their nature or severity.

81. In *British Steel Corporation v. Granada Television Ltd.* [1981] AC 1096, 1174 Lord Wilberforce ruled that discovery is a remedy

which (being equitable) is discretionary. Therefore a balancing exercise must be performed. This applies too to interrogatories. In *Bank of Valletta Plc v. National Crime Authority* (1999) 165 ALR 60, 62 the Full Federal Court of Australia (Wilcox, Whitlam and Lehane JJ) stated that since *Brannigan v. Davison* the trend of authority:

> "is that it is not a sufficient answer to a requirement that a person give evidence or produce documents to say that to do so will or may constitute a breach of a foreign law; nonetheless a court will weigh the effect of compliance on the person in determining whether or not to insist upon it."

82. A corporate person cannot suffer imprisonment. The alleged offences for which the privilege has been unsuccessfully claimed are typical of the lesser regulatory classification of criminal offences against the minor fiscal interests of the State, in contradistinction to serious crimes against the breathing person that exist in all legal systems. Because s65 has deliberately contracted the privilege it is not for the Court to therapeutically widen it by an excessive allocation of discretionary power.

83. In my judgment the Court retains a very limited discretionary power not to compel disclosure only in circumstances where the offence is one that would expose an individual to a lengthy sentence of imprisonment or worse, under a foreign law. But I do not need to rule on the outer limits. The decision of Hoffman J in *Arab Monetary Fund v. Hashim* (No. 2) [1990] 1 All ER 673 supports the existence of only a very narrow discretion.

84. In circumstances necessarily exposing a person to lengthy imprisonment a Hong Kong civil court would understandably baulk at the consequences of compelled testimony or documents. But the present case does not begin to engage that type of scenario and is only very ordinary. I would not begin to exercise my discretion in the Plaintiffs' favour. The Defendant has an entitlement under Hong Kong civil law, in these proceedings, to learn the nature and extent of any non-compliance by the Plaintiffs, which is of the essence of this action.

85. The Order of Master Kwan is affirmed with only a necessary variation to the date for compliance. The Plaintiffs will answer within 28 days from the date of the sealed Order herein being served upon them: O26 r2(1)(a). The appeal is dismissed with costs to the Defendant in any event.

Recorder of the Court of First Instance of the High Court (Gerard McCoy)

Mr. Johnny Fee, of Messrs. Fairbairn Catley Low & Kong, for the Plaintiffs/Appellants

Mr. Kam Cheung, instructed by Messrs Mason Ching & Associates, for the Defendant/Respondent

---

第十九條

香港特別行政區享有獨立的司法權和終審權。

香港特別行政區法院除繼續保持香港原有法律制度和原則對法院審判權所作的限制外，對香港特別行政區所有的案件均有審判權。

香港特別行政區法院對國防、外交等國家行為無管轄權。香港特別行政區法院在審理案件中遇有涉及國防、外交等國家行為的事實問題，應取得行政長官就該等問題發出的證明檔，上述檔對法院有約束力。行政長官在發出證明檔前，須取得中央人民政府的證明書。

案例

特區法院是否有權審核全國人大或其常委會的立法行為？

P.069 | 吳嘉玲、吳丹丹 對 入境事務處處長；徐權能 對 入境事務處處長；入境事務處處長 對 張麗華

吳嘉玲、吳丹丹 對 入境事務處處長
徐權能 對 入境事務處處長
入境事務處處長 對 張麗華

HCAL 68/1997；HCAL 70/1997；HCAL 71/1997；HCAL 73/1997；CACV 203/1997；CACV 216, 217 & 218/1997；FACV 14, 15 & 16/1998

簡略案情

申請人均是內地出生的中國籍人士。他們有些是以非法方式進入香港，有些則以有效旅遊證件進入香港，然而其中部份人卻違反居留限期，逾期居港。但是，他們一律堅稱，因為其父母是香港永久性居民，根據《基本法》第 24（2）條第 3 款擁有居留權。但入境處處長拒絕接受他們的理據。

原訟庭和上訴庭皆認為根據《基本法》第 22（4）條制定的《入境（修訂）（第 3 號）條例》是合法和有效的，因此，他們必須獲得以單程證形式簽發的出境批准，才可享有居留權。對此，申請人上訴至終審法院。

裁決摘要

在申請人的上訴過程中關於法院的司法解釋權限問題，終審法院同時考慮了《基本法》第 19 條。

法院認為根據《基本法》第 19（1）條，香港特區享有獨立的司法權和終審權。而《基本法》第 80 條，賦予特區各級法院行使特區的審判權。因此，在行使《基本法》所賦予的司法權時，特區的法院有責任執行及解釋《基本法》。必然地，特區法院其中一個職能是監察和審視立法機關所制定的法例或行政機關的行為是否符合《基本法》的要求，如發現有違反《基本法》的情況出現，則法院有權裁定有關法例或行為無效。這是法院按《基本法》執行憲法上的職務，以憲法制衡政府的行政及議會立法。根據《中國憲法》第 57 及 58 條，全國人民代表大會是最高國家權力機關，其常設機關是全國人民代表大會常務委員會，二者行使國家立法權，是主權國行使主權的行為。《基本法》是全國人民代表大會根據《中國憲法》第 31 條而制定的，因此它既是全國性法律，又是特區的憲法。由此可見，特區法院的審查權是源自全國性法律。所以，終審法院認為特區法院具有司法管轄權去審核全國人民代表大會或其常務委員會的立法行為（下稱“該行為”）是否符合《基本法》的規定，以及倘若發現其違反《基本法》時，有權宣佈此等行為無效。

根據《基本法》，特區法院在高度自治的原則下享有獨立的司法權。法院認為這反映了《聯合聲明》所宣示和具體說明的，落實維持香港五十年不變的基本方針政策。《基本法》第 159(4) 條訂明《基本法》的任何修改均不得抵觸既定的基本方針政策。因此，法院必須具有上述的司法管轄權去審核該行為，以確保符合《基本法》。

其次，《基本法》第 19（2）條規定：

> 香港特別行政區法院除繼續保持香港原有法律制度和原則對法院審判權所作的限制外，對香港特別行政區所有的案件均有審判權。

關於在馬維騉一案，終審法院認為上訴庭錯誤判斷，以為基於《基本法》第 19(2) 條及在 1997 年 7 月 1 日前，香港法院不能質疑英國國會通過的法例是否違憲，即是否違反英國的不成文憲法或香港作為殖民地的憲法文件《英皇制誥》，所以在 1997 年 7 月 1 日後，香港法院同樣不能質疑全國人民代表大會的立法行為。終審法院認為把舊制度與新制度相提並論是有所誤解。1997 年 7 月 1 日前，香港是英國殖民地，根據普通法，英國國會擁有最高權力為香港立法而香港法院不能質疑這項權力。但在新制度下，情況截然不同。《基本法》第 19（2）條規定“原有法律制度和原則”對憲法賦予法院的司法管轄權有所限制。但這條款不能把在舊制度下純粹與英國國會法例有關的限制引進新的制度內。

[Chinese Translation — 中譯本]

FACV14/1998

香港特別行政區
終審法院

終院民事上訴 1998 年第 14 號
（原本案件編號：高院民事上訴 1997 年第 216 號）

上訴人　吳嘉玲
　　　　吳丹丹
（兩人皆屬未成年人士，由父親及起訴監護人吳錫年代表）
　　　　對
答辯人　入境事務處處長

FACV15/1998

香港特別行政區
終審法院

終院民事上訴 1998 年第 15 號
（原本案件編號：高院民事上訴 1997 年第 217 號）

上訴人　徐權能
　　　　對
答辯人　入境事務處處長

FACV16/1998

香港特別行政區
終審法院

終院民事上訴 1998 年第 16 號
（原本案件編號：高院民事上訴 1997 年第 203 號）

上訴人　入境事務處處長
　　　　對
答辯人　張麗華
（屬未成年人士，由父親及起訴監護人張妙祥代表）

主審法官：終審法院首席法官李國能
終審法院常任法官烈顯倫
終審法院常任法官沈澄
終審法院常任法官包致金
終審法院非常任法官梅師賢爵士

聆訊日期：1999 年 1 月 6、7、8、11 及 12 日

宣判日期：1999 年 1 月 29 日

判決

終審法院首席法官李國能宣讀判詞：

這是本法院作出的一致判決。

一直以來，香港居民與中國其他地區的居民都有家庭聯繫。自從內地實行門戶開放政策後，香港與中國的關係變得息息相關，家庭聯繫更形廣泛密切。1997 年 7 月 1 日，在中華人民共和國恢復對香港行使主權時，許多在內地出生的中國公民的父母，至少其中一人是擁有香港居留權的香港永久性居民。

在本上訴案中，我等所處理的是他們作為香港永久性居民的身份及在港之居留權問題。有關《基本法》的正確解釋問題亦首次在本法院審理。此等問題對於有關人士的將來，以及憲制法律體系在新制度下的發展極為重要。

有關名稱

為方便起見，我等將會使用以下簡稱：中華人民共和國稱為中國；全國人民代表大會常務委員會稱為“人大常委會”；香港特別行政區稱為特區或香港。

本判決書中提及的“條款”是指《基本法》內的條款。雖然《基本法》的文本並沒有把每條條款內的小段編號，但按照一般做法把小段編號可方便引述。舉例說，第 24 條第二小段將稱為第 24（2）條。

首兩宗上訴案的上訴人及第三宗上訴案的答辯人均為司法覆核程序中的申請人，以下稱為“申請人”。

香港特別行政區入境事務處處長以下稱為“入境處處長”。他是首兩宗上訴案的答辯人，亦是第三宗上訴案的上訴人。

憲制架構

《中華人民共和國憲法》第 31 條規定：

> “國家在必要時得設立特別行政區。在特別行政區內實行的制度按照具體情況由全國人民代表大會以法律規定。”

全國人民代表大會是最高國家權力機關，它的常設機關是常務委員會（《中國憲法》第 57 條）。全國人民代表大會及它的常務委員會行使國家立法權（第 58 條）。

《中華人民共和國香港特別行政區基本法》乃根據第 31 條制定，並由全國人民代表大會通過，於 1990 年 4 月 4 日予以公佈。當香港特別行政區於 1997 年 7 月 1 日成立，即中國恢復對香港行使主權時，《基本法》即成為特區的憲法。

《基本法》的序言說明特區是根據第 31 條成立的：

> “……並按照‘一個國家，兩種制度’的方針，不在香港實行社會主義的制度和政策。國家對香港的基本方針政策，已由中國政府在中英聯合聲明中予以闡明。”

第一章述明總則，載有十一條條文。第 1 條規定香港特別行政區是中華人民共和國不可分離的部份。第 2 條規定全國人民代表大會授權香港特別行政區依照《基本法》的規定實行高度自治，享有行政管理權、立法權、獨立的司法權和終審權。第 5 條規定特區不實行“社會主義制度和政策”，保持原有的資本主義制度和生活方式，五十年不變。

中英政府於 1984 年 12 月 19 日簽訂了關於香港問題的《聯合聲明》，以處理恢復行使主權的事宜。《聯合聲明》自 1985 年 5 月 27 日，即互換批准書之日起生效。中國政府於《聯合聲明》第三

段宣示其對香港的基本方針政策，並謂這些基本方針政策將在《基本法》加以規定，並維持五十年不變。有關方針政策並於《聯合聲明》附件一加以具體說明。

《基本法》

《基本法》第 24（1）條規定，香港特別行政區居民包括永久性居民和非永久性居民。

關於第24（2）條及24（3）條的釋義乃本上訴核心所在。第24（2）條規定，永久性居民為該條文所列出的六個類別的人士，即：

"（1）在香港特別行政區成立以前或以後在香港出生的中國公民；

（2）在香港特別行政區成立以前或以後在香港通常居住連續七年以上的中國公民；

（3）第（1）、（2）兩項所列居民在香港以外所生的中國籍子女；

（4）在香港特別行政區成立以前或以後持有效旅行證件進入香港、在香港通常居住連續七年以上並以香港為永久居住地的非中國籍的人；

（5）在香港特別行政區成立以前或以後第（4）項所列居民在香港所生的未滿二十一周歲的子女；

（6）第（1）至（5）項所列居民以外在香港特別行政區成立以前只在香港有居留權的人。"

我等需要處理的是第三類別的人士，以下稱為第 24（2）條第三類別人士。

第 24（3）條規定，永久性居民在香港享有居留權和有資格依照特區法律取得載明其居留權的永久性居民身份證。

第 24（4）條規定，非永久性居民為有資格依照特區法律取得香港居民身份證，但沒有居留權的人士。

第三章的標題為"居民的基本權利和義務"，而第 24 條是該章內的第一條條文。在第 24（1）及（2）條界定了永久性和非永久性居民的身份後，第三章就永久性居民的基本權利和義務，包括居留權訂定條文。此等權利和義務體現了憲法對各種自由的保障，而自由乃香港文明社會的要素。值得留意的是，只有永久性居民才可依法享有選舉權和被選舉權（第 26 條）。

第三章第 39 條是憲法在保障個人權利方面的重要條款。第 39（1）條規定："《公民權利和政治權利國際公約》……適用於香港的有關規定繼續有效，通過香港特別行政區的法律予以實施。"第 39（2）條規定，香港居民享有的權利和自由，除依法規定外不得限制，此種限制不得與第 39（1）條規定抵觸。

《基本法》第二章的標題為："中央和香港特別行政區的關係"。第 22（4）條規定：

"中國其他地區的人進入香港特別行政區須辦理批准手續，其中進入香港特別行政區定居的人數由中央人民政府主管部門徵求香港特別行政區政府的意見後確定。"

第八章的標題為："本法的解釋和修改"。第 158 條是關於解釋問題，該條文規定：

"本法的解釋權屬於全國人民代表大會常務委員會。

全國人民代表大會常務委員會授權香港特別行政區法院在審理案件時對本法關於香港特別行政區自治範圍內的條款自行解釋。

香港特別行政區法院在審理案件時對本法的其他條款也可解釋。但如香港特別行政區法院在審理案件時需要對本法關於中央人民政府管理的事務或中央和香港特別行政區關係的條款進行解釋，而該條款的解釋又影響到案件的判決，在對該案件作出不可上訴的終局判決前，應由香港特別行政區終審法院請全國人民代表大會常務委員會對有關條款作出解釋。如全國人民代表大會常務委員會作出解釋，香港特別行政區法院在引用該條款時，應以全國人民代表大會常務委員會的解釋為準。但在此以前作出的判決不受影響。

全國人民代表大會常務委員會在對本法進行解釋前，徵詢其所屬的香港特別行政區基本法委員會的意見。"

《聯合聲明》

《基本法》第 24 條內有關永久性居民的定義乃源自《聯合聲明》附件一第十四部。該附件具體說明中國的基本方針政策。第十四部規定，列於該部內的各類人士有居留權並有資格按照香港法律獲得載明此項權利的永久性居民身份證。關於其後列於《基本法》第 24（2）條的首三類人士，第十四部界定為：

"在香港特別行政區成立以前或以後在當地出生或通常居住連續七年以上的中國公民及其在香港以外所生的中國籍子女。"

第十四部又包括以下條文：

"對中國其他地區的人進入香港特別行政區將按現在實行的辦法管理。"

香港法例

就香港而言，"居留權"一詞是在《聯合聲明》中才初次使用。在《聯合聲明》簽訂後，自 1987 年起《入境條例》（香港法例第 115 章）第 2A 條便載有香港永久性居民所享有的居留權的定義：

"具有以下權利 —

（a）在香港入境；

（b）不會被施加任何逗留在香港的條件，而任何向他施加的逗留條件，均屬無效；

（c）不得向他發出遞解離境令；及

（d）不得向他發出遣送離境令。"

附表 1 列出屬香港永久性居民之各類人士。香港永久性居民可獲發永久性居民身份證，而永久性居民身份證之定義則為：載有"持有人擁有香港居留權"字句的身份證（見《人事登記條例》（香港法例第 177 章）第 1A 條）。

人民入境（修訂）（第 2 號）條例

在 1997 年 7 月 1 日前，《入境條例》附表 1 並沒有採用《基本法》第 24（2）條所界定的類別來訂明何類人士屬香港永久性居民。1997 年 7 月 1 日，臨時立法會制定《人民入境（修訂）（第 2 號）條例》（以下簡稱"第 2 號條例"），並以新制定的附表 1 取代舊附表 1。新附表 1 第 2 段規定：

"2. 香港特別行政區永久性居民

任何人如屬以下任何一項，即為香港特別行政區永久性居民—

(a) 在香港特別行政區成立以前或以後在香港出生的中國公民，而在其出生時或其後任何時間，其父親或母親已在香港定居或已享有香港居留權。

(b) 在香港特別行政區成立以前或以後通常居於香港連續 7 年或以上的中國公民。

(c) (a) 或 (b) 項的香港特別行政區永久性居民在香港以外所生的中國籍子女，而在該子女出生時，其父親或母親已享有香港居留權。

(d) ……

(e) ……

(f) ……"

關於該類憑藉血緣成為永久性居民的人士，"第 2 號條例" 第 2 (c) 段規定其父親或母親在其出生時須已享有香港居留權。有關此項要求是否符合憲法的爭論，本法院將會在另一個上訴案中審理。附表 1 第 1 (2) 段界定父母與子女的關係如下：

"在以下的情況下，視為有父母與子女的關係存在—

(a) 任何女子與其婚生或非婚生子女之間的關係，為母親與子女的關係；

(b) 任何男子與其婚生子女之間的關係，為父親與子女的關係；如子女屬非婚生子女，只有當該子女其後因父母結婚而獲確立婚生地位，該男子與該子女之間才存在有父親與子女的關係；

(c) 只有父親或母親與其在香港根據法院命令領養的子女之間的關係，方為父親或母親與領養子女的關係，而該法院命令是指香港法院根據《領養條例》(第 290 章) 作出的命令。"

由此可見，就非婚生子女而言，上述定義對母親和父親的處理並不一樣。任何女子與其非婚生子女之間，被視為有 "父母與子女的關係" 存在；然而，任何父親與其非婚生子女之間，則只有當該子女其後因父母結婚而獲確立婚生地位，才被視為有 "父母與子女的關係" 存在。

1997 年入境 (修訂) (第 3 號) 條例

1997 年 7 月 10 日，臨時立法會制定《入境 (修訂) (第 3 號) 條例》(以下簡稱 "第 3 號條例")。該條例當作自 1997 年 7 月 1 日起實施 (第 1 (2) 條)，並引進一項計劃處理附表 1 第 2 (c) 段所指的該類憑藉血緣成為永久性居民的人士。根據此項計劃，任何人依據第 2 (c) 段所獲得的永久性居民的身份，<u>只可</u>藉其持有以下文件確立——

"(a) 發予他的有效旅行證件，和同樣是發予他並且附貼於該旅行證件上的有效居留權證明書；

(b) 發予他的有效特區護照；或

(c) 發予他的有效永久性居民身份證。"

(見第 2AA (1) 條)。任何持有有效的特區護照或有效的永久性居民身份證的人士，其居留權早已確立。誠如前述，有效的永久性居民身份證的定義是載有 "持有人擁有香港居留權" 字句的身份證。此外，申請領取護照的條件之一是申請人須持有永久性居民身份證 (見《香港特別行政區護照條例》(香港法例第 539 章) 第 3 (2) 條)。因此，雖然法例列出了三種文件，然而，只有 (a) 項是與要求憑藉血緣取得永久性居民身份的人士有關。此類人士<u>只可</u>藉持有有效旅行證件及附貼於該旅行證件上的有效居留權證明書才能確立其身份。以下將簡稱該等文件為 "旅行證件" 及 "居留權證明書"。而提述該等文件時應視為提述有效文件。"第 3 號條例" 載有居留權證明書的法定表格，該表格列明：

"本證明書持有人在香港特別行政區的居留權已確立。本證明書必須附貼於本證明書持有人的有效旅行證件上，方為有效。"

此段陳述強調居留權證明書本身不能單獨使用，必須附貼於旅行證件方為有效。

第 2AA (2) 條規定：

"(2) 任何人憑藉其作為附表 1 第 2 (c) 段所指的香港特別行政區永久性居民而享有的香港居留權，只在按照第 (1) 款確立了他作為該類永久性居民的身份時方可行使，而據此當其作為該類永久性居民的身份並無如此確立時，他就本條例而言須視作並不享有香港居留權。"

所以，若某人並非持有附貼居留權證明書的旅行證件，則視作<u>**並不享有**</u>香港居留權。

居留權證明書的申請可向入境處處長提出，並須按處長以憲報公告指明的方式提出 (見第 2AB (1) 及 (2) 條)。第 2AB (4) 條明確規定此類公告不是附屬法例。此條文的作用是使該公告不須受立法局根據《釋義及通則條例》(香港法例第 1 章) 第 34 條所提出的修訂所限制。若申請人能提出處長所指明的證明，令處長信納申請人屬附表 1 第 2 (c) 段所指的永久性居民，則處長須發出證明書 (第 2AB (6) 條)。若處長不信納申請人屬附表 1 第 2 (c) 段所指的永久性居民，則須拒絕該申請，並將理由通知申請人，以及告知申請人向入境事務審裁處上訴的權利。

第 2AD 條是關於上訴的問題。審裁處須 "就其所裁斷的事實" 裁定上訴人是否屬附表 1 第 2 (c) 段所指的憑藉血緣成為永久性居民的人士。審裁處作出的決定為最終決定。除非經過審裁處作出決定，以及在審裁處作出決定之前，任何人不得申請司法覆核 (第 2AE 條)。

申請人不得在他留在香港的任何時間內提出上訴 (第 2AD (3) 條)。若入境處處長已向他發出遣送離境令，他不得以其享有居留權為理由，就該命令向審裁處上訴。為了強化上述計劃：即他只可藉持有附貼居留權證明書的旅行證件確立其身份，"第 3 號條例" 引入第 53D (3) 條，該條文規定，除非上訴人的身份已按照第 2AA (1) 條所訂明的方式確立，否則審裁處不得以上訴人憑藉附表 1 第 2 (c) 段所指的身份而享有居留權為理由，就該遣送離境令的上訴判上訴人得直。

"第 3 號條例" 訂立了一些新的刑事罪行，包括為報酬而申請居留權證明書、為取得證明書作出虛假陳述、偽造證明書、使用及管有偽造的或經改動的證明書等罪行。然而，追溯條文並不適用於新的罪行，這些罪行只在立例後才生效。

公告

該份於 1997 年 7 月 16 日在憲報刊登、日期為 1997 年 7 月 11 日的公告 (以下稱為 "該公告")，公佈入境處處長已訂立列於 "該公告" 內之條文。關於在申請居留權證明書時居住在中國內地的人士，"該公告" 指明其申請必須 "通過當地的公安廳出入境管理處提出" (甲 (i) 段)。此外，"該公告" 又述明，上述人士根據中國內地現行法律向公安廳出入境管理處所遞交的到香港定居的‘前往港澳通行證’申請書，可視為居留權證明書的申請書（見乙段）。就申請居留權證明書而言，在以下情況下，任何人士如在緊接進入香港境內之前通常居於內地，則被視為在其逗留在香港的期間是居住在內地：（i）若他未獲准許而在香港入境，後又未獲入境處處長授權的情況下在香港逗留，或（ii）同樣，若他獲准許在香港入境，並在如此入境後受逗留條件所規限（丙段）。"該公告"（丁段）又列明申請書須載有何類陳述和資料。若申請人居住在中國以外地方，其申請則須通過當地中國大使館或領事館或以郵遞方式向入境處處長提出，而若居住在台灣或澳門，則規定以郵遞方式提出（甲（ii）及（iii）段）。

"該公告"提及與申請出境通行證有關的內地法律。內地法律有管制措施規管中國公民往來香港。現行的內地法律是於1985年11月22日公佈的《公民出境入境管理法》第17條，以及於1986年12月25日公布的《中國公民因私事往來香港地區或者澳門地區的暫行管理辦法》。中國公民出境須取得出境批准。公安廳出入境管理處是負責發出通行證之機關。一般所指的單程證是為前來定居人士而發，而單程證的簽發受定額制度規限。《暫行管理辦法》第5條規定：

> "內地公民因私事前往香港、澳門定居，實行定額審批的辦法，以利於維護和保持香港和澳門的經濟繁榮和社會穩定。"

一般所指的雙程證，則是發給非為定居而來港的人士。

根據代表入境處處長作出並送交法院的誓章證詞所載，內地機關已實行單程證定額制度多年，而定額數目亦時有改變。現時定額為每天150名。據該誓章證詞所載，情況如下：

> "……內地居民前來定居的合法途徑，仍然是必須取得單程證。公安部出入境管理廳在各省、市或縣的有關辦事處或部門負責決定是否批准發出單程證。入境事務處並無參與涉及輪候單程證之事宜，亦無參與分配或批准發出單程證之事宜，該等事宜是由公安部出入境管理廳單方面負責，而且情況一向如此。關於每天的單程證定額數目，雖然內地機關會徵詢香港機關的意見，然而最終決定仍然是由內地機關作出。換言之，問題並不僅是根據香港法律某人是否有權在香港入境或居留，而是有意在香港入境或居留的內地居民也必須符合關於在中國離境適用的內地法律。"

上述誓章證詞對有關機關的描述與"該公告"之描述略有不同。本法院將會採用"該公告"之描述，以下稱之為"內地出入境管理處"。此誓章證詞又指出，截至1997年年中為止已約有66,000名在二十歲以下的人士提出單程證申請，聲稱屬第24（2）條第三類別以內的人士。

我等注意到內地法律規定中國公民必須得到出境批准方可出境；而與本上訴有關的是上述關於中國公民從內地前來香港（即中國的另一部份）的內地法律。

"第3號條例"計劃的實行

就內地居民聲稱根據《入境條例》新附表1第2（c）段憑藉血緣而擁有永久性居民身份一事，本法院現闡述有關計劃之運作：

（1）內地居民須要通過其在中國內地所居地的"內地出入境管理處"向入境處處長申請居留權證明書。向"內地出入境管理處"所遞交的單程證申請書，可視為居留權的申請書。

（2）經確定其身份、國籍及其父母的婚姻是否有效後，"內地出入境管理處"便會將其申請書送交入境處處長處理。若入境處處長接納其申請，則會發出居留權證明書，而證明書亦會送交內地出入境管理處。

（3）他要受單程證定額制度所規限。內地機關負責實行該定額制度，並決定是否發出單程證。在"內地出入境管理處"批准發出單程證給他時，即會將其居留權證明書附貼於該單程證上。這單程證便是"第3號條例"引入的計劃所預計的有效旅行證件。

（4）他的身份只可藉其持有附貼居留權證明書的單程證確立。若沒有該單程證，則須視作不享有居留權。即使入境處處長信納他憑藉血緣取得永久性居民身份並已發出居留權證明書（證明書會送交"內地出入境管理處"），情況也是如此。按照此計劃，單靠該證明書並不足以確立其身份，其身份只可藉持有附貼該證明書的單程證才能確立。

（5）他不可來香港提出申請，而必須向其所居地的"內地出入境管理處"提出。就此計劃的運作而言，若他身處香港，則視為在其逗留在香港的期間是居住在中國內地。他不得藉提出證據以證明其身份來抗拒根據《入境條例》發出的遣送離境令。他只可藉持有附貼居留權證明書的單程證才能確立其身份。

申請人

各申請人的案情可作簡單陳述如下：

吳嘉玲小姐及吳丹丹小姐（終院民事上訴1998年第14號）

她們兩人是姊妹，是內地出生的中國籍人士。她倆分別於1987年及1989年出生，當時她們的父親已是在香港通常居住連續七年以上的中國公民。他在1976年來港，而兩名申請人則於1997年7月1日沒有通過入境管制站而進入本港。1997年7月4日她們向入境處報到，堅稱根據《基本法》第24（2）條第三類別擁有居留權，但她們的權利未獲入境處處長承認。入境處將她們拘捕，其後批准他們領取擔保書外出。

徐權能先生（終院民事上訴1998年第15號）

他是內地出生的中國籍人士，在1978年出生時，他父親已是在香港通常居住連續七年以上的中國公民，並早於1962年來港，而申請人則於1997年7月1日沒有通過入境管制站而進入本港。1997年7月3日，他向入境處報到，並堅稱根據《基本法》第24（2）條第三類別擁有居留權，但他的權利未獲入境處處長承認。入境處將他拘捕，其後批准他領取擔保書外出。

張麗華小姐（終院民事上訴1998年第16號）

她是內地出生的中國籍人士，在1989年出生時，她父親已是在香港通常居住連續七年以上的中國公民，並早於1967年來港。她不是父母所婚生的，其母親在她出生後的第二天便不幸去世。1994年12月，張小姐持雙程證來港。1995年1月，她的雙程證有效期屆滿，之後一直逾期居留。1997年7月15日，她向入境處報到，並堅稱根據《基本法》第24（2）條第三類別擁有居留權。但她的權利未獲入境處處長承認。入境處將她拘捕，她被拘留4日後，於1997年7月19日獲批准領取擔保書外出。

申請人之立場

兩名吳氏姊妹及徐先生均在1997年7月1日抵港，而張小姐則於此日之前抵步（埗）。除了徐先生外，她們均為未成年人，但他們的實際年齡對本案並不重要。我等明瞭現時大約有1,000至1,500名於1997年7月10日之前抵港的人士聲稱他們均屬《基本法》第24（2）條第三類別所述之永久性居民。

就吳氏姊妹及徐先生而言，入境處處長承認他們均屬《基本法》第 24（2）條第三類別所述之永久性居民，在他們出生時他們的父母其中一人（即父親）屬《基本法》第 24（2）條第二類別所述之永久性居民，而他們是這些居民"在香港以外所生的中國籍子女"，他們的父親則是在香港通常居住連續七年以上的中國公民。

至於張小姐，入境處處長則以她是非婚生為理由，稱她不屬《基本法》第 24（2）條所述之永久性居民。但若非持有此論點，則入境處處長會承認張小姐屬《基本法》第 24（2）條第三類別所述之永久性居民。她亦是在香港以外出生之中國籍人士，而她出生時，其父親屬第 24（2）條第二類別所述之永久性居民。

他們的父親已分別在港居留一段頗長時間。徐先生的父親早於 1962 年來港。張小姐的父親於 1967 年抵港，而吳氏姊妹的父親則於 1976 年到港。雖然第 24（2）條第二類別所述的永久性居民必須為在香港通常居住連續七年以上的中國公民，但我等應該留意到本案所涉及的申請人的父親在香港居住已遠遠超過七年，並且早已成為我們社會的一分子。

申請人堅稱他們屬第 24（2）條所述之永久性居民，故享有第 24（3）條所賦予之居留權。張小姐堅稱她雖屬非婚生，但這不應影響她的永久性居民的身份。

入境處處長的立場

入境處處長所持的立場為申請人受"第 3 號條例"引進的計劃所限制。根據這項計劃，憑藉血緣而享有之永久性居民身份只能以附貼有居港權證明書的單程通行證予以確立。上述申請人無一持有這種通行證，更遑論是附貼有此種居港權證明書的通行證。根據"第 3 號條例"第 2AA（2）條，他們須視作不享有居留權。根據這項計劃，他們不能在香港逗留，必須返回內地向"內地出入境管理處"申請居權證，而向該管理處提出之單程證申請可視為居權證申請。有關人士只能持有附貼有這種居權證的單程證才可確立其永久性居民身份，而在此身份獲確立前，他須視作不享有居留權。

儘管入境處處長信納申請人（張小姐除外）屬第 24（2）條第三類別所述之永久性居民，亦同時承認若張小姐不是非婚生子女，她也屬第 24（2）條第三類別所述之永久性居民，但他們也因上述理由而不享有居留權。此外，儘管申請人在 1997 年 7 月 10 日計劃實施之前已抵（抵）港，情況亦是一樣。入境處處長堅稱，由於在 1997 年 7 月 10 日制定之"第 3 號條例"當作自 1997 年 7 月 1 日起實施，故申請人仍受該項計劃所限制。

透過司法覆核提出異議

各申請人提出司法覆核，要求法院作出多項宣告及命令，以推翻入境處處長的決定。這些均屬例案。

原訟庭法官之判決

原訟庭法官（祈彥輝）只在非婚生子女問題上裁定張小姐勝訴，在其他事項上則裁定各申請人均敗訴，並撤銷他們的司法覆核申請。（見 [1997]《HKLRD》1081 及 [1997]3《HKC》64）。

上訴法庭之判決

各申請人向上訴法庭提出上訴。就張小姐一案而言，入境處處長就非婚生子女問題之判決提出上訴，而張小姐則就司法覆核之判決交相上訴。

由高等法院首席法官陳兆愷、上訴法庭副庭長黎守律及副庭長馬天敏組成之上訴法庭維持原訟庭法官之判決。他們聆聽上訴後，分兩部份作出判決。第一部份處理"第 2 號條例"及"第 3 號條例"所產生的問題（見 [1998]1《HKC》617），而第二部份則處理臨時立法會的合法性問題（見 [1998]1《HKLRD》772 及 [1998]2《HKC》382）。關於第一部份的問題，上訴法庭維持原訟庭法官就"第 2 號條例"判張小姐勝訴之判決，以及維持就"第 3 號條例"的合法性問題判入境處處長勝訴之判決。至於追溯條文方面，上訴法庭則以多數裁定此條文有效，但卻不適用於 1997 年 7 月 1 日前抵港之人士。至於第二部份之問題，上訴法庭裁定法庭受較早前該庭在香港特別行政區訴馬維騉一案的判決所約束（見 [1997]《HKLRD》761 及 [1997] 2《HKC》315（1997 年 7 月））。上訴法庭在該案裁定臨時立法會乃獲合法授權而成立。

上訴法庭作出判決後，徐先生獲發單程證，並以此證離開及再次進入本港。但本案的關鍵並非在此。就本上訴而言，處理徐先生的案件時，應把他當作仍在提出司法覆核申請時的階段，並無持有單程證般處理。

上訴法庭批准申請人向本法院上訴。關於張小姐一案方面，入境處處長就非婚生子女問題之判決提出上訴，而張小姐則交相上訴。至於其他案件，則屬各申請人提出之上訴。

祈彥輝法官及上訴法庭用心撰寫的判詞，特別是高等法院首席法官陳兆愷的判詞，對我等幫助很大。

所爭議之問題

在本上訴案中所爭議之問題如下：－

（1）終審法院在審理這些案件時是否有司法管轄權解釋《基本法》的有關條款，或是否必須根據《基本法》第 158 條請全國人民代表大會常務委會對有關條款作出解釋（"提交人大解釋問題"）。

（2）引進居權證計劃的"第 3 號條例"是否違憲，以及倘若違憲，則"第 3 號條例"在那方面違憲（'第 3 號條例'是否違憲問題"）。

（3）"第 3 號條例"第 1（2）條這項賦予追溯力的條文將該條例當作自 1997 年 7 月 1 日起實施是否符合憲法（"追溯效力問題"）。

（4）"第 2 號條例"引進的附表 1 第 1（2）（b）段是否違憲。該項條文的後果是，如果一名子女屬非婚生，則只有因父母其後結婚而獲確立婚生地位後，父親與該子女之間才可視為有"父母與子女的關係"存在，並僅以此情況為限（"非婚生子女問題"）。

（5）臨時立法會是否一個合法組成的機構（"臨時立法會問題"）。倘若臨立會不是一個合法組成的機構，則由其制定之"第 3 號條例"亦順理成章是違憲的。

法律代表

在本法院以及下屬法院進行訴訟時，申請人均由法律援助署以公帑延聘律師出任他們的法律代表。本案在下屬法院審理時，申請人是由資深大律師張健利代表，而有關臨時立法會問題則由資深大律師戴啟思代表。至於入境處的法律代表則為資深大律師馬道立。他們以及由他們領導的法律代表團對本法院提供了相當大的幫助，我等在此謹表謝意。

憲法賦予法院的司法管轄權

在處理上述受爭議的問題前，我等首先說明憲法賦予香港特別行政區法院的司法管轄權，然後再為解釋《基本法》制定恰當的處理方法；這兩點均至為重要。

香港特區享有獨立的司法權和終審權（《基本法》第19（1）條），而特區各級法院是特區的司法機關，行使特區的審判權（《基本法》第80條）。

在行使《基本法》所賦予的司法權時，特區的法院有責任執行及解釋《基本法》。毫無疑問，香港法院有權審核特區立法機關所制定的法例或行政機關之行為是否符合《基本法》，倘若發現有抵觸《基本法》的情況出現，則法院有權裁定有關法例或行為無效。法院行使這方面的司法管轄權乃責無旁貸，沒有酌情餘地。因此，若確實有抵觸之情況，則法院最低限度必須就該抵觸部份，裁定某法例或某行政行為無效。雖然這點未受質疑，但我等應藉此機會毫不含糊地予以闡明。行使這方面的司法管轄權時，法院是按《基本法》執行憲法上的職務，以憲法制衡政府的行政及立法機構，確保它們依《基本法》行事。

一直引起爭議的問題是，特區法院是否具有司法管轄權去審核全國人民代表大會或其常務委員會的立法行為（以下簡稱為"行為"）是否符合《基本法》，以及倘若發現其抵觸《基本法》時，特區法院是否具有司法管轄權去宣佈此等行為無效。依我等之見，特區法院確實有此司法管轄權，而且有責任在發現有抵觸時，宣佈此等行為無效。關於這點，我等應藉此機會毫不含糊地予以闡明。

根據《中國憲法》（第57及58條），全國人民代表大會是最高國家權力機關，其常設機關是常務委員會，二者行使國家立法權，故此其行為乃屬主權國行使主權的行為。特區法院審核上述二者之行為是否符合《基本法》的司法管轄權是源自主權國，因為全國人民代表大會是根據《中國憲法》第31條而制定特區的《基本法》的。《基本法》既是全國性法律，又是特區的憲法。

與其他憲法一樣，《基本法》既分配權力，也界定權限，並且訂明各項基本權利及自由。與其他憲法一樣，任何抵觸《基本法》的法律均屬無效並須作廢。根據《基本法》，特區法院在《基本法》賦予特區高度自治的原則下享有獨立的司法權。當涉及是否有抵觸《基本法》及法律是否有效的問題出現時，這些問題均由特區法院裁定。因此，全國人民代表大會或其常務委員會的行為是否抵觸《基本法》這問題由特區法院裁定，但當然特區法院所作的決定亦必須受《基本法》的條款限制。

鑑於制定《基本法》是為了按照《聯合聲明》所宣示和具體說明的內容，落實維持香港五十年不變的中國對香港的基本方針政策，上述論點便更具說服力。《基本法》第159（4）條訂明《基本法》的任何修改均不得抵觸既定的基本方針政策。為了行使司法管轄權去執行及解釋《基本法》，法院必須具有上述的司法管轄權去審核全國人民代表大會及其常務委員會的行為，以確保這些行為符合《基本法》。

香港特別行政區訴馬維騉一案是涉及普通法在新制度下的繼續存在以及臨時立法會的合法性問題。上訴法庭（由高等法院首席法官陳兆愷、上訴法庭副庭長黎守律及馬天敏組成）接納政府的陳詞，裁定由於全國人民代表大會的行為是主權行為，因此特區法院並不擁有司法管轄權去質疑這些行為的合法性。上訴法庭並裁定特區法院的司法管轄權只局限於審核是否存在主權國或其代表的行為（而非行為的合法性）。我等認為上訴法庭就特區法院的司法管轄權所作出的這項結論是錯誤的，上文所述的立場才是正確的。

上訴法庭基於《基本法》第19（2）條作出其結論。第19（2）條規定：

> "香港特別行政區法院除繼續保持香港原有法律制度和原則對法院審判權所作的限制外，對香港特別行政區所有的案件均有審判權。"

政府在該案所陳述的論據為1997年7月1日前，香港法院也不能質疑英國國會通過的法例是否違憲，即是否違反英國的不成文憲法或香港作為殖民地的憲法文件《英皇制誥》。因此，這是《基本法》第19（2）條所設想的"原有法律制度和原則"對香港法院審判權所作的一種限制。所以政府辯稱在1997年7月1日後，這限制同樣適用於全國人民代表大會的行為。上訴法庭接納了政府的論據。

把舊制度與此相提並論是對問題有所誤解。1997年7月1日前，香港是英國殖民地。根據普通法，英國國會擁有最高權力為香港立法而香港法院不能質疑這項權力。

基於已申述的理由，在新制度下，情況截然不同。《基本法》第19（2）條規定"原有法律制度和原則"對憲法賦予法院的司法管轄權有所限制。但這條款不能把在舊制度下純粹與英國國會法例有關的限制引進新的制度內。

我等應指出代表入境處處長的資深大律師馬先生在本法院聆訊本案時已不再堅持政府較早前在香港特別行政區訴馬維騉一案所持的立場。他實際上同意特區法院擁有我等所述之司法管轄權去審核全國人民代表大會及其常務委員會的行為是否符合《基本法》，並且同意該案在這方面的判決與我等所闡述之立場有抵觸之處，實屬錯誤。

我等亦應指出高院首席法官陳兆愷在本案就臨時立法會問題作出判決時表示，他在香港特別行政區訴馬維騉一案就特區法院司法管轄權所發表的意見只是針對該案的情況而言，不可理解為全國人民代表大會通過的法律及其行為凌駕《基本法》；他又表示他在該案把特區法院與殖民地時代法院相提並論可能不大恰當，並謂可能在某些適當的案件中，特區法院有司法管轄權去審核影響特區的全國人民代表大會的行為及其通過的法律。

對法院的司法管轄權所作出的任何限制必須以《基本法》為依據。如上文所述，《基本法》第19（2）條提及繼續保持香港原有法律制度和原則對法院審判權所作的限制。第19（3）條便提供了一個例子。第19（3）條規定：－

> "香港特別行政區法院對國防、外交等國家行為無管轄權。……"

《基本法》第158條亦規限終審法院不得在該條款所指的情況下，對《基本法》"關於中央人民政府管理的事務或中央和香港特別行政區關係"的條款進行解釋，且終審法院有責任請全國人民代表大會常務委員會對有關條款作出解釋。稍後討論到有關"提交人大解釋的問題"時，我等會再處理《基本法》第158條的問題。

有關解釋《基本法》的處理方法

首先我等必須認識及了解這份文件的特性。《基本法》是為貫徹獨一無二的"一國兩制"原則而制定的憲法性文件，具有不可輕易修改的地位。制定憲法性文件時，一般都會採用涵義廣泛和概括性的語言。憲法是一份具有靈活性的文件，旨在配合時代轉變和適應環境的需要。

解釋《基本法》這樣的憲法時，法院均會採用考慮立法目的這種取向，而這方法亦已被廣泛接納。法院之所以有必要以這種取向來解釋憲法，是因為憲法只陳述一般原則及表明目的，而不會流於講究細節和界定詞義，故必然有不詳盡及含糊不清之處。在解決這些疑難時，法院必須根據憲法本身及憲法以外的其他有關資料確定憲法所宣示的原則及目的，並把這些原則和目的加以貫徹落實。因此，在確定文件的真正含義時，法院必須考慮文件的目的和有關條款，同時也須按文件的背景來考慮文本的字句，而文件的背景對解釋憲法性文件尤為重要。

關於目的方面，制定《基本法》的目的是按照《聯合聲明》所闡述及具體說明的中國對香港的基本方針政策，在"一國兩制"的原則下成立與中華人民共和國不可分離的香港特別行政區，並實行高度自治。在確定《基本法》某項條款的目的時，法院可考慮該條款的性質，或《基本法》的其他條款，或參照包括《聯合聲明》在內的其他有關外來資料。

有關文本所使用的字句，法院必須避免採用只從字面上的意義，或從技術層面，或狹義的角度，或以生搬硬套的處理方法詮釋文意。法院必須考慮文本的背景。《基本法》某項條款的文意可從《基本法》本身及包括《聯合聲明》在內的其他有關外來資料中找到。法院也可藉用語傳統及文字慣用法去了解所用的文字的意思。

《基本法》第三章一開始便界定包括永久性居民及非永久性居民在內的香港居民類別的定義，接著訂明香港居民的權利和義務，其中包括永久性居民享有居留權。界定了香港居民類別的定義後，《基本法》第三章接著列明受憲法保障的各項自由；這些自由是兩制中香港制度的重心所在。為了令香港居民充分享有上述憲法所保障的各項基本權利及自由，法院在解釋第三章內有關那些受保障的權利及自由的條文時，應該採納寬鬆的解釋。

然而，法院在解釋有關界定香港居民定義的條款，特別是關於永久性居民類別的條款時（有別於解釋該等居民的權利自由等憲法保障），則只應參照任何可確定的目的及背景來考慮這些條款的字句。背景包括《基本法》的其他條款。適用於香港並根據第 39 條繼續有效的《公民權利和政治權利國際公約》（"國際人權公約"）的有關條文，以及任何從該公約歸納出來的有關原則，尤其有助於解釋這些條款的字句。

上文所列關於在解釋《基本法》時法院所應採納的原則，實非詳盡無遺，亦不可能一一盡列。憲法文件的詮釋跟其他文件的詮釋一樣，主要是針對具體問題。一旦出現詮釋問題時，法院便會處理這些問題所帶來的疑難，並在有需要時訂立一些原則加以解決。

我等現轉而處理所爭議的問題。

提交人大解釋問題

《基本法》第 158 條已在本判決書的較前部份原文照錄。第 158（1）條規定《基本法》的解釋權，屬於全國人民代表大會常務委員會。第 158（2）條規定"人大常委會""授權"特區法院"在審理案件時對本法關於香港特別行政區自治範圍內的條款自行解釋"。顯而易見，這包含了憲法上的授權，而雙方大律師也接納這論點。我等認為，"自行"二字強調了特區的高度自治及其法院的獨立性。

但特區法院的司法管轄權並非局限於解釋這類條款。因為，第 158（3）條規定特區法院在審理案件時對《基本法》的"其他條款也可解釋"。

然而對終審法院來說，這項司法管轄權存在一種規限。如果特區法院：

> "在審理案件時需要對本法關於中央人民政府管理的事務或中央和香港特別行政區關係的條款進行解釋，而該條款的解釋又影響到案件的判決，在對該案件作出不可上訴的終局判決前，應由香港特別行政區終審法院請全國人民代表大會常務委員會對有關條款作出解釋。"

由於只有終審法院才能對案件作出不可上訴的終局判決，所以這條款規限了終審法院的司法管轄權。當符合上述指定的條件時，終審法院便有責任請"人大常委會"解釋有關的條款。

第 158（3）條接著規定當"人大常委會"對該等條款作出解釋，"香港特別行政區法院在引用該條款時，應以"人大常委會"的解釋為準。但在此以前作出的判決不受影響。"

第 158（4）條規定"人大常委會"有責任在決定如何解釋有關條款前，先徵詢其所屬的《基本法》委員會的意見。《基本法》委員會是全國人民代表大會在 1990 年 4 月 4 日會議通過設立的。當日的議決是《基本法》委員會為"人大常委會"下設的工作委員會，由十二名成員組成；由"人大常委會"任命內地和香港人士各六名，其中包括法律界人士。香港委員須由香港特別行政區行政長官，立法會主席和終審法院首席法官聯合提名。

根據《基本法》第 158 條，香港法院是在"審理案件"時才有權解釋《基本法》條款。言下之意即是當法院並非在審理案件時，便沒有這項權力。這情況反映出我們的制度內一套確立已久的原則：法院的職責是審判裁決，而非提供參考意見。特區法院有以下的解釋權。《基本法》第 158 條提及：

（a）屬特區自治範圍內的條款，及

（b）《基本法》的其他條款。在這些其他條款內，有兩種屬範圍之外的類別，即涉及（i）中央人民政府管理的事務，或涉及（ii）中央和香港特別行政區關係的條款。我等將（i）或（ii）條款簡稱為"範圍之外的條款"。

根據第 158 條，終審法院以下的各級法院，均有權解釋（a）及（b）項內的條款，包括"範圍之外的條款"。終審法院有權解釋（a）項內的條款，及（b）項內的其他條款，但不包括"範圍之外的條款"。

因此，終審法院以下的各級法院，有權解釋所有的《基本法》條款，不受任何限制。唯一受限制的是終審法院的司法管轄權。第 158（2）條的措辭強調特區的各級法院均有權"自行"解釋在特區自治範圍內的《基本法》條款。

以終審法院來說，當符合以下兩項條件時，便有責任將有關條款提交"人大常委會"解釋：

（1）第一，當有關的《基本法》條款（a）關乎中央人民政府管理的事務，或（b）關乎中央和特區的關係，即為"範圍之外的條款"。以下簡稱此條件為"類別條件"。

（2）第二，當終審法院在審理案件時，有需要解釋這些條款（即"範圍之外的條款"），而這些條款的解釋將會影響案件的判決。以下簡稱此條件為"有需要條件"。

我等認為在審理案件時，唯獨終審法院才可決定某條款是否已符合上述兩項條件；也只有終審法院，而非全國人民代表大會，才可決定該條款是否已符合"類別條件"，即是否屬於"範圍之外的條款"。代表申請人的大律師及代表入境處處長的大律師也接納這個論點。

如果該條款不符合"類別條件"，事情就會告一段落。就算本法院需要解釋該有關條款，而該項解釋又會影響案件的判決，該條款也會因為不屬於"範圍之外的條款"而不能符合"有需要條件"。

如果該條款符合"類別條件"，也只可由終審法院決定有關案件是否符合"有需要條件"。

如果終審法院認為該"範圍之外的條款"已符合上述兩項條件，

便必須請“人大常委會”解釋有關之條款。我等強調提交“人大常委會”解釋的是某些特定的“範圍之外的條款”而非一般性的解釋。

誠如前述，入境處處長接納，若張小姐不是因為非婚生子女這點，她與其他申請人一樣都屬《基本法》第 24（2）條第三類別的永久性居民。第 24（3）條規定永久性居民有居留權。根據“第 3 號條例”引進的居權證計劃，申請人除非擁有內地簽發的單程證，而單程證上又附貼了由入境處處長簽發的居留權證明書，否則並不享有居留權。入境處處長請求法院裁定“第 3 號條例”是符合憲法的，原因是《基本法》第 24 條受第 22（4）條規限。第 22（4）條規定中國其他地區的人士若要進入特區，必須辦理批准手續。這條款還進一步規定進入特區定居的人數，要由中央人民政府主管部門徵求特區政府的意見後確定。入境處處長的論點是由於申請人是第 22（4）條所述的來自中國其他地區的人士，一定要先得到內地當局批准才可進入特區，而這規定也成為居權證計劃的憲法基礎，即申請人必須獲得以單程證形式簽發的出境批准，才可享有居留權。

代表入境處處長的資深大律師馬先生指出第 22（4）條是在《基本法》的第二章內，而第二章的標題是“中央和香港特別行政區的關係”。他認為第 22（4）條是“範圍之外的條款”，原因是這條款符合《基本法》第 158 條所述兩種“範圍之外的類別”。他認為出境批准是關乎中央人民政府管理的事務，而人民由內地進入特區則關乎中央和香港特區的關係。根據入境處處長的論點，本法院在審理本案時，必須解釋第 22（4）條。所以，他認為這條款符合了“類別條件”及“有需要條件”。

資深大律師馬先生清楚指出入境處處長並非要求法院根據《基本法》第 158 條，將這條款提交“人大常委會”解釋，但他一定要作出這些陳詞，令本法院能夠考慮應否將該條款提交“人大常委會”。我等覺得代表入境處處長的資深大律師馬先生作出這些陳詞是恰當的，因為這是關乎法院在憲法上的司法管轄權。

雖然資深大律師馬先生同時依賴該兩種“範圍之外的類別”，但以目前處理的問題來說，我等會純粹基於第 22（4）條涉及中央政府與特區的關係而假設第 22（4）條為一項“範圍之外的條款”。

我等面對的問題關鍵在於法院在考慮該條款是否符合“類別條件”時，應該採用何種考慮原則。

資深大律師馬先生認為當（a）法院在解釋 X 條款時（以本案來說，即《基本法》第 24 條），而該條款屬關於特區自治範圍內的條款，因而並非“範圍之外的條款”，但法院發覺（b）屬關於範圍之外的 Y 條款（以本案來說，即第 22（4）條）是否與解釋 X 條款有關是一個可爭論的問題，則在這情況下，法院應根據第 158 條，將這條款提交“人大常委會”。

我等現在要考慮的是應否根據第 158 條將該條款提交“人大常委會”。現階段本法院需要處理的是，有關論點是否一個可爭論的問題，而非就解釋的問題作出決定。如果該條款須要提交“人大常委會”，便會由“人大常委會”處理；如果不須提交的話，便會由本法院處理。任何論點如果是顯而易見的歪理，當然便沒有爭論餘地。如果本法院在現階段決定這論點是不可爭論的話，提交的問題便告一段落。如果法院決定這論點是可爭論的話，便會進一步考慮是否符合“類別條件”及“有需要條件”。就本案來說，一項“範圍之外的條款”（第 22（4）條）是否與解釋一項“非範圍之外的條款”（第 24 條）有關是一個可爭論的問題。

在決定應採用何種考慮原則來決定該條款是否符合“類別條件”時，法院須要採用“立法目的”這一原則。《基本法》第 158 條其中一個重要的目的是“人大常委會”授權香港法院，包括終審法院，“自行”解釋《基本法》中屬“範圍之外的條款”以外的各章節，特別是關於屬特區自治範圍內的條款。這是特區高度自治的必不可少的部份。

從上述的觀點出發，讓我等討論應採用何種考慮原則。X 條款（這裏指第 24 條）是關於特區自治範圍內的條款，在作出解釋時，必須考慮其背景，這自然包括《基本法》的其他條款，而這些條款可能在某幾方面與解釋 X 條款有關。例如這些條款可能透過增減修訂等形式來規限 X 條款，或潤飾 X 條款的意思，又或提供指標來解釋 X 條款。根據資深大律師馬先生的論點，當一項“範圍之外的條款”（這裏指第 22（4）條）如上述般與 X 條款有關，便須提交“人大常委會”。提交的主題不是要求解釋 X 條款，因它並非“範圍之外的條款”；馬先生的論點似是：提交的主題是請“人大常委會”解釋該“範圍之外的條款”，而該項解釋只限於涉及 X 條款的解釋。這樣的提交，會收回了本法院對解釋《基本法》中關於屬特區自治範圍內的條款（X 條款）的司法管轄權。我等認為這樣做會嚴重削弱特區的自治，而且是不對的。

我等認為，在考慮該條款是否符合“類別條件”時，應採用代表申請人的資深大律師張先生提出的考慮原則 — 實質上，法院審理案件時最主要需要解釋的是哪條條款？如果答案是一條“範圍之外的條款”，本法院必須將之提交“人大常委會”。如果最主要需要解釋的並非“範圍之外的條款”，便不須提交。在這情況下，即使一條“範圍之外的條款”可以**爭辯地**說成與“非範圍之外的條款”的解釋有關，甚至規限了“非範圍之外的條款”時，法院仍無須將問題提交“人大常委會”。

這考慮原則落實了《基本法》第 158 條的兩項主要目的，就是賦予“人大常委會”有權解釋《基本法》，尤其是“範圍之外的條款”，並同時授權特區法院解釋“非範圍之外的條款”，特別是屬自治範圍內的條款，特區法院更可“自行”解釋。

我等覺得相當重要的是：《基本法》第 158 條規定只在解釋“範圍之外的條款”時，才須提交“人大常委會”。當多條條款（包括“範圍之外的條款”）與解決案中涉及的一般性解釋問題有關時，第 158 條並沒有規定法院須請“人大常委會”作一般性的解釋。

法院在採用這考慮原則來審理此案時，實質上最主要需要解釋的是第 24 條，即關於永久性居民的居留權及該項權利內容的規定，而申請人上訴要求行使的權利，正是源自這條款。在這情形下，本法院覺得無須把這條款提交“人大常委會”解釋，儘管第 22（4）條是否與解釋第 24 條有關是一個可爭論的問題。

“第 3 號條例”是否違憲

關於這項爭論，問題的關鍵在於《基本法》第 22（4）條是否規限了第 24（3）條所訂的居留權。原訟庭法官裁定後者是受前者規限。他認為這可能是削弱特區高度自治的一個例子，但這是第 22（4）條所認可的。上訴法庭的兩位副庭長黎守律及馬天敏都同意原訟庭法官的取向。高等法院首席法官陳兆愷也裁定這兩條條款是互有關連，然而他認為第 22（4）條限制了仍在內地的人士去行使這居港權利。如果恰當地解釋《基本法》後，本法院的意見跟原訟庭及上訴法庭的法官意見不同的話 — 該兩條條款並無關連，而第 24 條也不受第 22（4）條影響，則在這情形下，“第 3 號條例”要求永久性居民要先持有單程證才可享有居留權便缺乏憲法上的依據。代表入境處處長的資深大律師馬先生也接納這個論點。至於要求永久性居民持有居權證來核實其聲稱，則是另一回事。

本法院必須強調，若張小姐不是受非婚生的問題所影響，入境處處長便會接納她和本案其他申請人一樣都屬第 24（2）條第三類別所述的永久性居民。本法院現在並非要處理永久性居民類別的定義，而是要處理第 24（3）條所述的人士的居留權問題，而該等人士毫無疑問屬永久性居民。

第 24（3）條規定：永久性居民在特區“享有居留權”。《入境條例》（2A 條）界定了永久性居民享有的權利，即有權入境，不會被施加任何逗留條件，不受任何遞解離境令或遣送離境令的約束。法例界定的居留權，類似普通法的居留權概念。普通法內的居留權曾被描述為“……進入［該司法管轄區］的權利，不受任何障礙或阻礙，任由（居留權擁有人）喜歡何時入境及［隨己意］在境內逗留多久”（見 1972 年英國上訴案例：*Director of Public Prosecutions v. Bhagwan* [1972]《AC》60，見第74頁B行。）因此，進入司法管轄區的權利，或根據法例所界定的入境權利，正是居留權的要素。

本法院在前文界定了永久性居民類別後，已斷定在解釋保障他們權利的憲法條款時，應採用寬鬆的取向。誠如代表申請人的資深大律師張先生所指出，居留權實為一核心權利。事實上，入境權是居留權之要素，如沒有居留權和入境權，申請人便難以享有其他獲憲法保障的權利和自由，特別是選舉權和參選權。在採用寬鬆的取向時，本法院認為，對於任何指第 22（4）條削弱了核心權利的論點均應非常仔細研究。

第 24（3）條賦予永久性居民不受限制的居留權。如果第 22（4）條規限了第 24（3）條這個論點是正確的話，那些毫無疑問擁有永久性居民身份卻仍在內地居住的人士，其居留權利便毫無保障。特區的憲法一方面賦予他們在特區內符合憲法的居留權，但另一方面，卻令這權利受國內機關的酌情權所限制，而這酌情控制權是在特區政府的權力範圍外。單程證所作出的控制，和配額數目及配額分配的決定有關。再者，根據這項論點，這種情況會導致兩類同樣擁有永久性居民身份的人士在憲法上有不同的居留權利，即對於仍在國內居住的人士來說，儘管他們是符合第 24（2）條第三類別的永久性居民，但他們的權利受到第 22（4）條規限；但同樣類別的永久性居民，如在內地以外的地方居住，其居留權則不受此規限。

我等不能接納這個論點。在解釋居留權條款時，定要採用一種寬鬆的取向。我等考慮到第 24 條與第 22（4）條的用詞時，認為第 22（4）條內所指的“中國其他地區的人”包括進入特區定居的人，但不包括《基本法》已賦予其在特區擁有居留權的特區永久性居民。按對言詞的一般理解，根據《基本法》而擁有永久性居民身份的人士不能稱之為“中國其他地區的人”。他們是中國這地區（香港）的永久性居民。將他們形容為是為了定居而進入特區的人也是不正確的。他們進入特區並非為了定居。他們本身為永久性居民，擁有進入特區及在特區隨意逗留的權利。

我等認為，按照第 22（4）條的正確解釋，即使全面履行該條款時亦不會侵犯第 24 條所列的居留權。第 22（4）條並不適用於特區的永久性居民，只適用於內地絕大部份沒有特區居留權的人士，儘管他們居住的地方與特區同屬一國，他們也不能未經批准便進入特區。“批准”應該是指內地機關的批准，這個假設是正確的。再者，這條例規定進入特區定居的人數，由中央人民政府主管部門徵求特區政府的意見後確定。

我等的結論符合《基本法》設立特區的目的，就是在“一國兩制”的原則下實行高度自治。批准在國內的非特區永久性居民的人士進入特區，及決定進入特區定居者的人數都是內地機關的責任。特區政府在不同的制度下行使高度自治，並有責任去接收根據憲法擁有居留權的永久性居民。我等認為，第 22（4）條並沒有容許特區的自治權受到削弱。

代表入境處處長的資深大律師馬先生指出第 24 條是受到第 22（4）條的規限，並援引《聯合聲明》附件一第十四部份以支持這個論點。《聯合聲明》具體說明了中國的基本方針政策。附件一第十四部份列出了永久性居民的類別，亦即現今在《基本法》第 24（2）條的類別。這第十四部份繼而規定中國其他地區的人在進入特區時，“將按現在實行的辦法管理”。資深大律師馬先生所倚賴的“實行的辦法”，在 1984-1985《聯合聲明》發表的當時，就是指內地居民獲得離境批准後才可進入香港的規定。第十四部份訂定這“實行的辦法”須沿用下去，然而，並無跡象顯示，這個部份的原意是要這“實行的辦法”適用於永久性居民，從而規限了他們擁有的居留權，而這居留權早已在這部份有所訂明。因此，我等並不認為《聯合聲明》在這方面能提供任何協助。

資深大律師馬先生除了基於第 22（4）條作出基本陳詞外，亦同時提出另一論點（儘管他只是輕輕帶過）。他指出鑑於內地的法律規定居民來港須有出境批准，故第 24（3）條的解釋便受一項隱含限制的約束，即基於合理的原則，必須遵守關於出境須經批准才可來港的國內法律。如果一條內地的法例可提供憲法基礎去規限《基本法》賦予的一項憲法權利這一論點是正確的話，這便會帶來深遠的影響。

我等認為這論點絕不能成立，原訟庭法官與上訴法庭駁回這點，實屬正確。《基本法》第 18（2）條規定全國性法律除列於《基本法》附件三者外，不在特區實施；而列於附件三之全國性法律，由特區在當地公佈或立法實施。第 18（3）條規定“人大常委會”在徵詢其所屬的《基本法》委員會和特區政府的意見後，可對列於附件三的法律作出增減。但第 18（3）條跟著規限了“人大常委會”的權力，規定任何列入附件三的法律，“限於有關國防、外交和其他按本法規定不屬於香港特別行政區自治範圍的法律”。這條款限制了引用內地的法律，這點在履行“一國兩制”的原則上是非常重要的。如果資深大律師馬先生的論點是正確的話，這便會提供一偏徑，讓內地的法律得以在香港施行。我等認為這論點是毫無基礎可言的。

內地的法律規定內地居民要有出境批准才可進入香港，這法律當然可以全面在國內執行，但卻不能作為一項憲法的基礎來規限《基本法》所賦予的權利。

因此，“第 3 號條例”規定居於內地的特區永久性居民，要先持有單程證才可享有憲法賦予的居留權，這點是違憲的。

然而，這並非表示“第 3 號條例”所引進的整個居權證計劃是違憲。大家必須把享有居留權的永久性居民和**聲稱**是永久性居民的人士區別清楚。所以，立法當局引進一項計劃來核實某些人士**聲稱**擁有永久性居民的身份是合理的做法。我等認為在居權證計劃中，必須持有單程證的規定是違憲的，除此之外，計劃的其他部份都是符合憲法的，不能稱之為逾越核實範疇。因此，該計劃規定聲請人須向入境處處長申請及領取居權證，並且只能在持有居權證後才能確立其永久性居民的身份都是符合憲法。再者，居權證計劃訂明這些人士必須留在內地申請居權證，及在被入境處處長拒發居權證而提出上訴時，也必須留在內地，這方面也是符合憲法。永久性居民因為擁有居留權而有權入境，但**聲稱**擁有這身份的人其身份必須首先獲得核實。

我等裁定因居權證計劃（持有單程證的規定除外）的目的在於核實聲稱人身份，所以是符合憲法的，同時我等亦顧及到入境處處長必須合法地，以公正合理的態度來執行居權證計劃，而且在落實計劃時還有一些制衡的保護措施。

首先，以法例釋義來說，在這核實計劃運作時，法院會對若干條款定下要求，引進合理標準。例如入境處處長可透過憲報公告形式，具體說明該如何申請居權證（第 2AB（2）（a）條），但在行使這項權力時，入境處處長所作出的說明必須是**合理的**，而法庭亦只會作如是詮釋。其次，如果入境處處長不合法地拖延作出接納或拒絕申請的決定，有關申請人雖然身處內地，仍可向特區法院要求作出公法上的補救。再者，如果入境處處長決定拒絕該項居權證的申請，申請人有法定的上訴權，可向入境事務審裁處提出上訴。這項上訴權利是一種全面的保障。入境處處長有法定責任提供拒絕該項申請的理由，申請人在 90 天內可提出上訴。根據法例，審裁處的決定為最終的判決，但審裁處有責任“就其所裁斷的事實”來決定有關人士是否可憑藉血緣成為永久性居民，如答案是肯定的話，則要裁定上訴得直。

分割（違憲部份）

我等經考慮後，認為“第 3 號條例”內的違憲部份，可適當地與符合憲法的部份分割開。分割的準則在於符合憲法的部份是否可清晰地與違憲部份區別出來，從而使符合憲法的部份仍保持完整。我等認為這是可行的。以下乃違憲的部份，應予刪除。在提及法院反對的部份時，我等採用《入境條例》的條款編號，除非另有所指才屬例外。

（1）第 2A（1）條

增加了的文字，即“在不抵觸第 2AA（2）條的條文下”，現予刪除。經刪除後，第 2A（1）條的內容如下：

“（1）香港永久性居民享有香港居留權，換言之，具有以下權利——

(a) 在香港入境；

(b) ……

(c) ……

(d) ……”

（2）第 2AA（1）（a）條

經刪除後，該條款的內容如下：

“（1）任何人作為附表 1 第 2（c）段所指的香港特別行政區永久性居民的身份，只可藉其持有以下文件確立—

(a) 發予他的有效居留權證明書”

除了以上所列之內容外，（a）段的其他文字予以刪除。

（3）第 53D（3）（a）條

第53D（3）條由“第3號條例”第7條增補，刪除後，第53D（3）（a）條的內容如下：

“（a）發予他的有效居留權證明書。”

除了以上所列之內容外，（a）段的其他文字予以刪除。

（4）《入境規例》之附表一

“第 3 號條例”第 10 條於附表一內加入表格 12，即居留權證明書表格。現將表格內的第二句刪除，即

“本證明書必須附貼於本證明書持有人的有效旅行證件上，方為有效。”

經刪除後，只留下第一句，即

“本證明書持有人在香港特別行政區的居留權已確立。”

我等以下稱“第 3 號條例”及其引入的居權證計劃經刪除後的部份為“分割後的第 3 號條例”及“分割後的居權證計劃”。

關於入境處處長的公告，雖然並非附屬法例，但根據我等較早前對“第 3 號條例”的合憲性作出的結論，也可以將我等反對的部份予以刪除。據了解，因為“第 3 號條例”規定申請人須持有單程證，所以便牽涉“內地出入境管理處”，而我等已裁定須持有單程證的規定是違憲的。我等並不知道在“分割後的居權證計劃”下，入境處處長是否願意請“內地出入境管理處”作為入境處在內地的代理機關，方便內地居民申請居權證；本法院也不知道“內地出入境管理處”會否願意牽涉在內。因此，我等將“該公告”內的 A（i）及 B 段剔除。這令到公告內就有關內地居民應向誰申請居權證這方面缺乏交代。入境處處長必須以公告形式，具體說明新的安排。本法院並不反對要向內地的某一單位提出申請這種安排，只要該單位是以香港入境處的代理機構身份運作，方便內地居民申請居權證便行。至於“內地出入境管理處”是不是一個合適的機構提供這項服務，便應由入境處處長及“內地出入境管理處”去考慮。

有關追溯力的問題

“第 3 號條例”在 1997 年 7 月 10 日制訂，但根據第 1（2）條，該條例被視為於 1997 年 7 月 1 日起生效。問題在於這條賦予追溯力的條文（“追溯條文”）是否符合憲法。若不符合的話，第 1（2）條便要從該條例中刪除。

原訟庭法官和上訴法庭副庭長馬天敏都認為該條文是有效的，並影響 (i)1997 年 7 月 1 日之前到港人士以及 (ii) 在 1997 年 7 月 1 日或之後及在 7 月 10 日之前到港人士。上訴法庭副庭長黎守律認為該條文有效但不影響上述第 (i) 類人士。而高等法院首席法官陳兆愷則認為該條文無效，因此均不影響第（i）及第（ii）類人士。可是，他們考慮這個問題時，都是基於他們認為《基本法》第 24 條受第 22（4）條規限所作出的結論，但我等對《基本法》的解釋持有不同的結論，故此我等以不同基礎來考慮這個問題。我等所要考慮的是，到底“分割後的第 3 號條例”中這條“追溯條文”是否違憲。

1997 年 7 月 10 日“第 3 號條例”制定之前，任何憑藉血緣成為永久性居民的人士，如已抵達香港，便擁有憲法賦予的居留權。事實上，他們都已行使了這個權利，不能被遣返內地。“分割後的第 3 號條例”引進一個計劃。根據這個計劃，他們只可藉持有居留權證明書，才能確立他們永久性居民的身份；否則，他們便視作不享有居留權。在 1997 年 7 月 10 日前，他們當然不可能持有居留權證明書。若這條“追溯條文”是符合憲法，他們便會被視為不享有居留權。這樣便會剝奪他們根據《基本法》已享有的、具憲法性的居留權。我等認為，這條“追溯條文”乃屬違憲。代表入境處處長的資深大律師馬先生以“第 3 號條例”有部份違憲為基礎接納這點，這與他在陳詞中聲稱“第 3 號條例”並無違憲的說法有所不同。

我等接著考慮代表申請人的資深大律師張先生所提出的另一個理據，以支持他認為這條“追溯條文”是違憲的陳詞。

在 1997 年 7 月 10 日之前，永久性居民（例如那些獲入境處處長接納為屬於第 24（2）條中第三類別的申請人）享有憲法所賦予的居留權，並因此有權入境及逗留。但是，倘若“第 3 號條例”中的“追溯條文”是符合憲法的話，追溯力便會導致他們觸犯了刑事罪行。根據“分割後的計劃”，他們必須持有居留權證明書，否則，其身份便會被視作未獲確立，而他們便須被視作不享有居留權；這樣，他們便無權入境或逗留，若入境或逗留便會觸犯刑事罪行，違反《入境條例》第 38 條，因該條文禁止未獲批准的人

士入境或逗留，違反者便是觸犯了刑事罪行。

資深大律師張先生爭辯說，這條導致他們觸犯該等刑事罪行的"追溯條文"是違憲的，因為它與"國際人權公約"第15（1）條相抵觸。

"國際人權公約"適用於香港的有關規定，憑藉第39條而繼續有效。"國際人權公約"第15（1）條規定：

> "任何人之行為或不行為，於發生當時依香港法律及國際法均不成罪者，不為罪。……"

"國際人權公約"第15（1）條和香港法例第383章《人權法案條例》中人權法案的第12（1）條完全相同。既然"國際人權公約"第15（1）條適用於香港，引述此條公約是恰當的。

高等法院首席法官陳兆愷認為此條"追溯條文"與"國際人權公約"第15（1）條互相抵觸，也違反憲法。可是，原訟庭法官與上訴法庭副庭長黎守律及馬天敏對"國際人權公約"第15（1）條的理解則為：該條款禁止根據具追溯力的條文向任何人士提出檢控並將他們定罪，但不會令該"追溯條文"失效。

"國際人權公約"第15（1）條所用的文字是："任何人……不為罪。"正如資深大律師張先生指出，在詮釋這一句時，必須緊記"國際人權公約"是國際性公約，其對象是不同法制的國家，包括一些不一定以立法作為刑法來源的國家。有鑑於此，我等認為，根據第39條而適用的"國際人權公約"第15（1）條確實令到該"追溯條文"違反憲法。在我們的法制下，禁止憑具追溯力條文對觸犯刑事罪行的人士定罪這個做法確實會打擊該"追溯條文"的有效性。這個觀點得到Van Dijk及Van Hoof的支持：見《歐洲人權公約 — 理論和實踐》（譯名）*Theory and Practice of the European Convention on Human Rights*（第三版）第485-486頁有關該歐洲人權公約中等同的條文。

倘若我等的判決一如原訟庭及上訴法庭的判決，這便會對有關人士造成不公平的民事後果。他們可被說成是犯了刑事罪；雖然他們不能受到檢控或定罪，但亦可能因此受到不利的待遇，例如，在誹謗法方面以及在各種不同情況下，能否在法律上被認定為"合適及適當"的人選。但若依我等所作的結論，他們便不會面對上述可能產生的後果。

因此，我等從"第3號條例"中刪除該"追溯條文"，亦即第1（2）條。

非婚生子女的問題

根據"第2號條例"引入《入境條例》的附表1內的第1（2）（b）段規定，如子女屬非婚生子女，只有當該子女其後因父母結婚而獲確立婚生地位才存在父親與子女的關係。問題在於究竟這條文在憲法上是否有效。這段規定應與第1（2）（a）段中的母親與子女的關係作一對比；在該條文內，非婚生子女並沒有受到歧視，他們與婚生子女受同等的待遇。

這宗例案的申請人張小姐是一名非婚生子女。她的父母從沒有結婚，母親在她出生後第二天便不幸去世。假若第1（2）（b）段是符合憲法的話，她與父親之間便會被視作不存在"父母與子女的關係"。結果，由於她不屬於"父親或母親是永久性居民"的類別，便不能符合附表1第2（c）段中憑藉血緣成為永久性居民的資格。在其他各方面，入境處處長都接納她是符合資格的。

問題在於經正確解釋第24（2）條第三類別後，非婚生子女是否屬於這個類別。如果是的話，附表1第1（2）（b）段把這類子女摒諸這類別之外便屬違憲。

我等在此要處理的是如何解釋一條界定永久性居民類別的條文。在解釋這條文時，必須考慮其背景，包括《基本法》內其他條文，其中第39條規定"國際人權公約"適用於香港的有關規定繼續有效。背景中有兩項相關的原則。其一，《基本法》和"國際人權公約"都奉行平等原則，反對任何歧視。見《基本法》第25條和"國際人權公約"第3及26條。在這方面，顯而易見，香港本地的法例跟隨著近年的明顯趨勢，通常都把非婚生子女與婚生子女同等看待。其二，"國際人權公約"第23（1）條認定家庭是社會之自然及基本的團體單位，應該受到社會和國家的保護。

在解釋有關條文時，緊記這些原則是很重要的。我等必須指出，若入境處處長的論點正確，則婚生與非婚生子女便會得到不平等的待遇，而非婚生子女的母親和非婚生子女的父親也受到不平等的待遇。再者，由於第24（2）條的永久性居民類別並沒有包括配偶在內，故該條款令他們不能闔家團聚。依入境處處長的論點，父親的非婚生子女不會因為與父親的血緣關係而得到永久性居民的身份；這樣對促進某程度的家庭相聚沒有任何幫助。

當緊記這些原則時，並考慮到第24（2）條第三類別的文字，我等認為這個類別明顯包括婚生及非婚生的子女。第三類別所界定的是在第一和第二類別列明的"[永久性]居民……所生的……子女"。不論是婚生還是非婚生，這些都是該等居民所生的子女。非婚生子女與婚生子女兩者沒有分別，同樣是該等居民所生的。我等認為這就是該條文顯而易見的意思。因此，附表1第1（2）（b）段把父親的非婚生子女（其後因父母結婚而成為婚生子女者除外）摒諸這類別之外是違反憲法的。

資深大律師馬先生向我等指出，"國際人權公約"適用於香港的有關規定乃受英國在1976年5月簽署及確認"國際人權公約"時作出的保留條款所限制。關於香港方面，這些保留條款包括有權繼續引用入境方面的法例來監管進入香港、逗留及離開香港的人士。而且，接受"國際人權公約"的條件是該公約並不影響針對無權進入及逗留在香港的人士的法例。但是，依我等之見，這並不會阻止本法院在解釋有關永久性居民類別的憲法條文時，考慮"國際人權公約"的原則，而這些原則是構成條文背景的一部份。

代表入境處處長的資深大律師馬先生基於中國和英國政府在中英聯合聯絡小組（下稱"聯合聯絡小組"）達成的一項協議而提出其論點。我等沒有該協議的任何記錄。有關這項協議，入境處處長所倚賴的證據來自一本該處在1997年4月印制有關香港居留權的小冊子。這本小冊子內有一段文字，其意思與現在已成為法例的附表1第1（2）（b）段相同，就是對一名父親而言，他的子女不包括非婚生子女，除非他與該子女的母親其後結婚，否則該子女不能成為婚生子女。小冊子述明它是"根據現行的入境條例和常規及基於中、英雙方在[聯合聯絡小組]中的共同看法"而編訂的。

資深大律師馬先生以《維也納條約法公約》第31條為依據提出其論點。這公約的第31（1）條規定："條約應依照其用語按上下文並參照條約的目的及宗旨所具有的通常意義善意解釋"。第31（3）（a）條規定：

> "在考慮上下文之餘，還應一併考慮：
>
> (a)締約國其後所訂關於條約的解釋或適用的任何協議。"

《聯合聲明》附件一第十四部份聲明，現屬於第24（2）條第三類別所指的人士應有居留權。資深大律師馬先生辯稱，在"聯合聯絡小組"達成的協議是其後達成的協議。基於《維也納公約》第31條的規定，在解釋《聯合聲明》這一部份時應依據"聯合聯絡小組"其後達成的協議來解釋，而解釋《基本法》時亦應採用同樣方法。

“聯合聯絡小組”的成立是基於《聯合聲明》附件二：“為了進行聯絡、磋商及交換情況的需要……”。其職能包括就《聯合聲明》的實施進行磋商（附件二第3（a）段）。它是聯絡機構而非權力機構（附件二第6段）。即使其職能包括由兩國政府在其後就有關《聯合聲明》的解釋或其條文的適用訂立協議，而且該協議屬《維也納公約》第31（3）（a）條的範圍，但依我等之見，該協議對本法院須要解釋的問題並無影響。

首先，達成該協議的基礎並不清楚。該協議可能是為了尋求一個實際的解決方法而達成，與解釋條文或其適用的問題無關。由於小冊子沒有區分母親的非婚生子女及婚生子女（第1（2）（a）段亦沒有如此區別），故此該協議是否以解釋條文或其適用為基礎實令人疑惑。倘若協議是基於解釋條文或其適用而達成，則父親與子女的關係便有別於母親與子女的關係，而要為這個區別找到一個合理的基礎並不容易。

其次，即使該協議是基於解釋條文或其適用而達成，第31（3）（a）條只規定須將其納入考慮之列。不過，經考慮後本法院可以作出不同的結論。我等認為本法院所作的結論明顯是正確的。

因此，我等裁定附表1第1（2）（b）段乃屬違憲。原訟庭法官和上訴法庭這樣裁定實屬正確。經分割後，第1（2）（b）段應為：

> “（2）在以下的情況下，視為有父母與子女的關係存在——
>
> （b）任何男子與其婚生或……非婚生子女之間的關係，為父親與子女的關係……”

除這些字句外，條文中其他字句予以刪除。

臨時立法會的問題

資深大律師戴啟思先生為申請人爭辯這個問題時提出，臨時立法會（下稱“臨立會”）並不是《基本法》內所訂明的立法機關，亦不是一個合法組成的機構。任何經“臨立會”通過的法例必先符合普通法的“必需原則”方為有效。他認為“第3號條例”的“追溯條文”並不符合這個原則，因此亦屬無效。代表入境處處長的資深大律師馬先生認為“臨立會”是一個合法組成的機構。他同意“臨立會”並不是《基本法》內訂明的特區立法機關。但當時的情況是，在1997年7月1日之前的立法機關在該日之後便不再延續，套用一般的說法，就是沒有“直通車”。資深大律師馬先生認為，在這情況下“臨立會”是依據全國人民代表大會在1990年4月4日的決定而成立，亦符合該項決定及《基本法》。

有關的決定眾所周知。

在1990年4月4日正式通過的《基本法》規定特區的立法會須由選舉產生（第68（1）條）。第68（2）條規定它的產生方法須根據特區的情況及循序漸進的原則，最終達至全部議員由普選產生這個目標（第68（2）條）。第68（3）條訂明立法會產生的具體方法和法案、議案的表決程序由附件二“香港特別行政區立法會的產生辦法和表決程序”規定。第69條規定立法會除第一屆任期為兩年外，每屆任期均為四年。《基本法》附件二對第二屆和第三屆立法會的產生辦法有所規定。至於第一屆，附件二規定立法會須按照“全國人民代表大會關於香港特別行政區第一屆政府和第一屆立法會產生辦法的決定”產生。

該項決定與《基本法》同時在1990年4月4日經全國人民代表大會通過（下稱“1990年決定”）。第一段述明特區第一屆政府和立法會須“根據體現國家主權、平穩過渡的原則產生”。

第2段規定：

> “在1996年內，全國人民代表大會設立香港特別行政區籌備委員會，負責籌備成立香港特別行政區，根據本決定規定第一屆政府和立法會的具體產生辦法。……”

第6段規定第一屆立法會由60名議員組成，其中20名議員由分區直接選舉產生，10名議員由選舉委員會選舉產生，30名議員由功能團體選舉產生。該段進而規定，如1997年7月1日前的立法局的組成符合該決定和《基本法》的有關規定，其議員擁護《基本法》、願效忠中華人民共和國香港特別行政區，並符合《基本法》規定之條件者，經籌備委員會確認，即可成為第一屆立法會議員。第6段的最後部份規定第一屆立法會議員的任期為兩年。

顯然，從《基本法》及在《基本法》內提及的“1990年決定”來看，當時預期立法局會乘直通車過渡。

為進行1995年選舉，香港的選舉法例有所改變。中國政府不接受這些改變，堅稱這些改變抵觸《基本法》。中國和英國政府在這個問題上的政治爭議人所共知，而結果是沒有直通車。

1994年8月31日，“人大常委會”決定立法局不會有直通車，而籌備委員會須負責籌備成立特區的有關事宜，並須根據“1990年決定”規定第一屆立法會的具體產生方法及組織第一屆立法會。

1996年3月24日，籌備委員會決定成立臨時立法會。“臨立會”是經由負責推選特區第一屆政府的推選委員會選舉產生，並運作至特區第一屆立法會成立時為止，即不應遲過1998年6月30日。臨立會的指定職責，包括制定對特區的“日常運作必不可少”的法例，以及處理除指定在特區第一屆立法會成立之前規定須由臨時立法會處理之外的其他事宜。1996年10日5日，籌備委員會採納了其訂明的方法成立“臨立會”。1997年2月1日，籌委會決定“臨立會”應在1997年6月30日前開始運作，及須在特區成立時確認那些已經通過的條例草案。

《基本法》第160條規定香港特區成立時，香港原有法律除由“人大常委會”宣佈為同《基本法》有抵觸者外，採用為特區法律。1997年2月23日，“人大常委會”議決不採用若干項法例，包括1995年度立法局的選舉法例。

1997年3月14日，全國人民代表大會議決接納籌委會的工作報告，這份報告提及籌委會根據“1990年決定”成立“臨立會”。

1997年5月23日，籌委會採用指定的方式來組成特區第一屆立法會。立法會的選舉須在1998年6月30日前完成，而特區須依據該辦法制訂有關選舉立法會的條例。結果，“臨立會”制訂了這些條例。選舉在1998年5月進行。首屆立法會在1998年7月就職。

《基本法》規定第一屆立法會須按照“1990年決定”來成立。該決定授權籌委會籌備成立特區並根據該決定去規定第一屆政府和立法會的具體產生辦法。我等認為，由籌委會籌組“臨立會”是在“1990年決定”的範圍內，所以也符合《基本法》。該決定第二段所賦予籌備委員會的權力範圍廣濶，足以令籌委會有權成立臨立會。

作出“1990年決定”時，預期會有直通車。因此，第一屆立法會的任期為兩年。但是，“1990年決定”的第6段第二部份規定只有在符合若干條件後，才會有直通車。在沒有直通車的情況下，籌委會成立的“臨立會”職能有限，而運作的時間亦有限。“臨立會”只是一暫時性的機構，是填補根據《基本法》及“1990年決定”第6段的第一部份成立第一屆立法會之前出現的立法真空。“臨立會”並不是根據《基本法》及該決定第6段的第一部份所產生的第一屆立法會，代表入境處處長的資深大律師馬先生也同意這點。成立“臨立會”的目的完全為了使第一屆立法會得以產生。因此，“臨立會”的成立與《基本法》是相符的。“臨立會”制訂的選舉法符合籌委會在 1997 年 5 月就第一屆立法會的產生所作出的決定。這些選舉法使第一屆立法會可在 1998 年 7 月前依據該決定產生。

考慮到我等作出的結論，即“臨立會”是符合“1990 年決定”的合法組成機構，亦與《基本法》相符，故我等無須回應資深大律師戴啟思先生基於“必須原則”所提出的論點。

法庭判令

三宗上訴（終院民事上訴 1998 年第 ***14、15 及 16*** *號）*

有關這三宗上訴案，我等就每宗案件作出宣告並頒令如下：

A（1）我等宣告以下部份的《入境條例及規例》乃屬無效，並從該條例或規例中刪除：

（a）第 2A（1）條的“在不抵觸第 2AA（2）條的條文下”這句。

（b）第 2AA（1）（a）條的條文，以下字句除外：

“（1）任何人作為附表 1 第 2（c）段所指的香港特別行政區永久性居民的身份，只可藉其持有以下文件確立——

（a）發予他的有效居留權證明書。”

（c）第 53D（3）（a）條的條文，以下字句除外：

“（a）發予他的有效居留權證明書。”

（d）《入境規例》附表 1 內的居留權證明書表格 12 內第二句句子，即：

“本證明書必須附貼於本證明書持有人的有效旅行證件上，方為有效。”

（2） 我等宣告在 1997 年 7 月 16 日刊登於憲報，日期為 1997 年 7 月 11 日（1997 年憲報第 (E)21 號）的公告內的第 A（1）段及第 B 段為無效，並從“該公告”中刪除。

（3） 我等宣告“第 3 號條例”第 1（2）條為無效，並從該條例中刪除。

（4） 關於訟費問題，我等不作判令。各申請人的訟費（包括終院民事上訴 1998 年第 16 號入境處處長的上訴中的申請人的訟費）按《法律援助條例及規例》評定。

吳嘉玲小姐及吳丹丹小姐（終院民事上訴 1998 年第 14 號）

有關本上訴案，我等頒令如下：

B（1）判令兩名申請人上訴得直。

（2）判令撤銷入境處處長以下的決定：

（a）約在 1997 年 7 月 4 日扣留申請人的決定，

（b）約在 1997 年 7 月 4 日規定申請人須受擔保約束的決定，

（c）約在 1997 年 8 月 7 日拒絕讓申請人入境的決定。

（3）我等宣告兩名申請人乃屬《基本法》第 24（2）條第三類別的香港特別行政區永久性居民，她們自 1997 年 7 月 1 日開始便擁有這身份；故此，她們享有居留權。

徐權能先生（終院民事上訴 1998 年第 15 號）

資深大律師張先生告知我等現無須撤銷入境處處長的決定，因為處長已同意徐先生有居留權。有關本上訴案，我等頒令如下：

C（1）判令申請人上訴得直。

（2）我等宣告申請人乃屬《基本法》第 24（2）條第三類別的香港特別行政區永久性居民，他自 1997 年 7 月 1 日開始便擁有這身份；故此，他享有居留權。

張麗華小姐（終院民事上訴 1998 年第 16 號）

D（1）我等宣告《入境條例》附表 1 的第 1（2）（b）段中以下字句予以保留，其他字句乃屬無效並從該段中刪除：

“（2）在以下情況下，視為有父母與子女的關係存在—

（b）任何男子與其婚生或⋯⋯非婚生子女之間的關係，為父親與子女的關係⋯⋯”

（2）判令撤銷入境處處長以下的決定：

（a）約在 1997 年 7 月 15 日有關申請人不能享有《基本法》第 24（3）條所指的居港權的決定，

（b）約在 1997 年 7 月 15 日羈留扣押申請人的決定，

（c）約在 1997 年 7 月 19 日規定申請人須受擔保約束的決定，

（d）約在 1997 年 8 月 9 日決定申請人必先按照《入境條例》第 1B 部份指定的模式，確立她在該條例附表 1 第 2（c）段中永久性居民的身份，才有權行使居港權。

（3）我等宣告申請人乃屬《基本法》第 24（2）條第三類別的香港特別行政區永久性居民，她在 1997 年 7 月 1 日開始便擁有這身份，故此她享有居留權。

首席法官常任法官（李國能）

常任法官（烈顯倫）

常任法官（沈澄）

常任法官（包致金）

非常任法官（梅師賢爵士）

資深大律師張健利先生、資深大律師戴啟思先生及大律師郭瑞熙先生（由賈偉林劉天均律師行延聘並由法律援助署署長委派）代表終院民事上訴案 1998 年第 14 和 15 宗的上訴人及終院民事上訴案 1998 年第 16 宗的答辯人

資深大律師馬道立先生及大律師霍兆剛先生（由律政司延聘）代表終院民事上訴案 1998 年第 14 和 15 宗的答辯人及終院民事上訴案 1998 年第 16 宗的上訴人

LAW32/99

第二十二條

中央人民政府所屬各部門、各省、自治區、直轄市均不得干預香港特別行政區根據本法自行管理的事務。

中央各部門、各省、自治區、直轄市如需在香港特別行政區設立機構，須徵得香港特別行政區政府同意並經中央人民政府批准。

中央各部門、各省、自治區、直轄市在香港特別行政區設立的一切機構及其人員均須遵守香港特別行政區的法律。

中國其他地區的人進入香港特別行政區須辦理批准手續，其中進入香港特別行政區定居的人數由中央人民政府主管部門徵求香港特別行政區政府的意見後確定。

香港特別行政區可在北京設立辦事機構。

案例

何謂中國其他地區的人？

P.085 | 劉港榕等 17 人 對 入境事務處處長

在中國大陸出生的無戶籍、非港人婚生子女可否申請居留權？

P.105 | 吳新穩作為吳家豪、吳家煒、吳佳敏的父親及起訴監護人 對 入境事務處處長

Lau Kong Yung And Others v. The Director Of Immigration

劉港榕等 17 人 對 入境事務處處長

HCAL 20/1999；HCAL 21/1999； CACV 108/1999；CACV 109/1999；FAC 10/1999；FACV 11/1999

簡略案情

申請人與另外 16 人反對入境處處長向他們發出的遣送離境令。他們認為根據《基本法》第 24 條第 2 款第 3 項，他們擁有香港居留權。這 17 人中，有些是以非法途徑進入香港，有些則是持雙程證進入，而其中一位是從外國回國途中停留。17 人中有 5 位在他們出生時，其父母至少一方已擁有香港永久性居民身份，其他 12 人則是在其出生后，父母其中一方才拿到香港永久性居民身份。他們全在 1999 年 1 月 29 號前進入香港，即終審法院下達*吳嘉玲、吳丹丹等 對 入境事務處處長* FACV 14, 15 & 16/1998 案的判決書前。該案連同終審法院在*陳錦雅等 對 入境事務處處長*案件的判決，確認《人民入境（修訂）（第 2 號）條例》，《入境（修訂）（第 3 號）條例》部份違憲而無效。原訟庭拒絕申請人的司法覆核和人身保護令申請，但上訴庭卻推翻原審法官的裁決。及後，人大常委會在 1999 年 6 月 26 號接受並頒佈對《基本法》第 22 條第 4 款和第 24 條第 2 款第 3 項的解釋。

該解釋關於《基本法》第 22 條第 4 款的部份訂明：

> 《中華人民共和國香港特別行政區基本法》第二十二條第四款關於“中國其他地區的人進入香港特別行政區，須辦理批准手續”的規定是指各省、自治區、直轄市的人，包括香港永久性居民在內地所生的中國籍子女，不論以何種事由要求進入香港特別行政區，均須依照國家有關法律行政法規的規定，向其所在地區的有關機構申請辦理批准手續，並須持有有關機構制發的有效証件，方能進入香港特別行政區。各省、自治區、直轄市的人，包括香港永久性居民在國內所生的中國籍子女，進入香港特別行政區，如未按國家有關法律，行政法規的規定辦理相應的批准手續，是不合法的。

裁決摘要

終審法院在本案中確認全國人大常委會有權對《基本法》作出解釋，而且該解釋對香港的法院有約束力。由此，終審法院在上述兩個案件對《基本法》第 22 條第 4 款和第 24 條第 2 款第 3 項的解釋，被完全推翻。終審法院最後以大比數批准執行對申請人的遣送離境令。

FACV Nos 10 and 11 of 1999

IN THE COURT OF FINAL APPEAL OF THE HONG KONG SPECIAL ADMINISTRATIVE REGION

FINAL APPEAL NOS 10 AND 11 OF 1999 (CIVIL)
(ON APPEAL FROM CACV NOS 108 AND 109 OF 1999)

Between:

LAU KONG YUNG (an infant suing by his father and next friend LAU YI TO) and 16 others — Respondents

- and -

THE DIRECTOR OF IMMIGRATION — Appellant

Court: Chief Justice Li, Mr Justice Litton PJ, Mr Justice Ching PJ, Mr Justice Bokhary PJ and Sir Anthony Mason NPJ

Date of Hearing: 25, 26, 27 and 28 October 1999

Date of Judgment: 3 December 1999

JUDGMENT

Chief Justice Li:

In February 1999, the Director of Immigration made removal orders under sec 19(1)(b) of the Immigration Ordinance against the 17 respondents. They applied to challenge the removal orders by judicial review and habeas corpus. That challenge failed before Yeung J, [1999] 2 HKLRD 58, but succeeded before the Court of Appeal [1999] 2 HKLRD 516 (Chief Judge, Nazareth and Mortimer VPP). The Director appeals to the Court.

The central question in this appeal relates to "the Interpretation by the Standing Committee of the National People's Congress of Articles 22(4) and 24(2)(3) of the Basic Law of the Hong Kong Special Administrative Region of the People's Republic of China" ("the Interpretation"). The Interpretation was adopted on 26 June 1999, after the Court of Appeal's judgment on 11 June 1999.

Terminology

I shall refer to the Director of Immigration, the appellant, as "the Director" and the 17 respondents to the appeal, who were the applicants on the challenge, as "the applicants". The Immigration Ordinance will be called "the Ordinance". I shall refer to the following in full or in abbreviation as follows: The People's Republic of China as "PRC"; the National People's Congress of the PRC as "NPC"; the Standing Committee of that Congress as "the Standing Committee" or as "NPCSC" ; the Hong Kong Special Administrative Region of the People's Republic of China as "the Region" or "Hong Kong" or "HKSAR".

The applicants

The 17 applicants are Chinese nationals born on the Mainland. They claim the right of abode in Hong Kong by descent on the basis that at least one parent is a permanent resident of Hong Kong. 5 applicants (the 1st, 6th, 10th, 12th and 14th applicants) were born after one of their parents became a permanent resident ("the 5 applicants"). The remaining 12 applicants were born before one of their parents became a permanent resident ("the 12 applicants").

15. applicants (that is the applicants except the 12th and 14th applicants) came from the Mainland on two way permits. The 14th applicant went from the Mainland to Singapore to study in 1994 and came to Hong Kong in July 1997 as a visitor. All applicants had overstayed in Hong Kong in breach of the conditions of stay imposed by the Director except the 12th applicant who had come illegally in the first instance.

All 17 applicants had arrived in Hong Kong before 29 January 1999. Apart from 2 applicants (the 6th and 16th applicants), they allege that they had claimed the right of abode before that date. 29 January 1999 is a significant date because, on that day, the Court delivered its unanimous judgments in *Ng Ka Ling & others v. Director of Immigration* (1999) 2 HKCFAR 4 (also reported at [1999] 1 HKLRD 315 and [1999] 1 HKC 291) ("*Ng Ka Ling*") and *Chan Kam Nga & Others v. Director of Immigration* (1999) 2 HKCFAR 82 (also reported in [1999] 1 HKLRD 304 and [1999] 1 HKC 347) ("*Chan Kam Nga*"). I shall come to these judgments in a moment.

Director's position following outcome of this appeal

At the outset, I should record that in the event of his appeal succeeding and the removal orders being restored, the Director has undertaken to the Court that he will not detain or remove from Hong Kong the 17 applicants pending:

(a) consideration by the Director of whether to revoke the removal orders issued against these 17 applicants; and

(b) the institution of legal proceedings by any of the 17 applicants who may wish to challenge the Director's decision not to revoke the removal order issued against that particular applicant within 28 days of such decision.

The power to revoke is contained in sec 46 of the Interpretation and General Clauses Ordinance, Cap. 1.

Further, Mr Geoffrey Ma SC, for the Director, has informed the Court that in the event of his failing on the appeal so that the removal orders remain quashed, the Director will give consideration to the making of fresh removal orders against the 17 applicants.

So, the position is that whatever the result of the appeal as concerns the removal orders, the Director will consider the question of removal again.

The scheme introduced in July 1997: the original scheme

On 1 July 1997, the Basic Law came into effect. Article 24(2) sets out the six categories of persons who shall be permanent residents who under Article 24(3) shall have the right of abode in Hong Kong. The first three categories are:

> "(1) Chinese citizens born in Hong Kong before or after the establishment of the Hong Kong Special Administrative Region;
>
> (2) Chinese citizens who have ordinarily resided in Hong Kong for a continuous period of not less than seven years before or after the establishment of the Hong Kong Special Administrative Region;
>
> (3) Persons of Chinese nationality born outside Hong Kong of those residents listed in categories (1) and (2);"

On that day, the legislature, then the Provisional Legislative Council, enacted the Immigration (Amendment) (No. 2) Ordinance ("the No. 2 Ordinance"). This Ordinance replaced Schedule 1 to the Immigration Ordinance, Cap. 115 with a new schedule to set out the categories of persons who are permanent residents. In prescribing for the permanent residents by descent in Article 24(2)(3) of the Basic Law, the new Schedule 1 in para. 2(c) ("para. 2(c) of Schedule 1") stipulated the requirement that "the parent had the right of abode in Hong Kong at the time of the birth of the person". I shall refer to this requirement as "the time of birth limitation".

On 10 July 1997, the legislature enacted the Immigration (Amendment) (No.3) Ordinance ("the No.3 Ordinance") to introduce a scheme to deal with the permanent residents by descent under the category in para. 2(c) of Schedule 1 ("the original scheme"). Pursuant to his power under the No.3 Ordinance, the Director specified by notice dated 11 July and gazetted on 16 July 1997 the manner in which applications under the scheme should be made ("the Notice"). That scheme is fully set out in the judgment of the Court delivered on 29 January 1999 in *Ng Ka Ling* and I shall not burden this judgment by setting it out again. In that judgment, the operation of the original scheme in relation to a Mainland resident claiming the status of permanent resident by descent under para. 2(c) of Schedule 1 was set out in these terms (at 21):

"(1) He has to apply to the Director for a certificate of entitlement through the Mainland Exit-Entry Administration in the district where he is residing in the Mainland. His application to the Mainland Exit-Entry Administration for a one way permit may be regarded as an application for a certificate of entitlement.

(2) After confirming the person's identity, nationality and the validity of his parents' marriage, the Mainland Exit-Entry Administration will send his application to the Director for processing. If the Director is satisfied, he will issue a certificate of entitlement. This will be sent to the Mainland Exit-Entry Administration.

(3) He is subject to the quota for one way permits determined and operated by the Mainland authorities. Upon the grant of the one way permit by the Mainland Exit-Entry Administration, his certificate of entitlement will be affixed by them to that permit. The one way permit is the valid travel document for him contemplated by the scheme introduced by the No. 3 Ordinance.

(4) His status can only be established by his holding the one way permit affixed with the certificate of entitlement. Without this, he shall be regarded as not enjoying the right of abode. This is so notwithstanding that the Director is satisfied of his status as a permanent resident by descent and has issued the certificate of entitlement (which would be sent to the Mainland Exit-Entry Administration). Under the scheme, that certificate alone is insufficient to establish his status. It can only be established by holding a one way permit affixed with the certificate.

(5) He cannot come to Hong Kong to make his application. It must be made to the Mainland Exit-Entry Administration in the district in the Mainland where he is residing. If he is physically in Hong Kong, he is treated as residing in the Mainland during his stay in Hong Kong for the purposes of the scheme's operation. He cannot resist a removal order made under the Immigration Ordinance (Cap. 115) by producing evidence to establish his status. He can only establish that status by holding a one way permit affixed with a certificate of entitlement."

The original scheme also provided that, apart from holding (a) the one way permit affixed with the certificate of entitlement, a person's status as a permanent resident by descent under para. 2(c) of Schedule 1 could be established by his holding of (b) a valid HKSAR passport or (c) a valid permanent identity card. But as pointed out in Ng Ka Ling (at 18A–C), any person holding (b) or (c) would already have established his right of abode. So the relevant provision for a person claiming permanent resident status by descent is (a).

The Court's judgments on the challenge to the scheme

In its judgments in *Ng Ka Ling* and *Chan Kam Nga* delivered on 29 January 1999, the Court dealt with a constitutional challenge to the No. 2 and No. 3 Ordinances. For the purposes of this appeal, two aspects of that challenge are relevant, namely, the challenge to the time of birth limitation and the challenge to the original scheme.

As to the former, the Court held in *Chan Kam Nga* that the date of birth limitation in para. 2(c) of Schedule 1 was unconstitutional. The Court so held as a matter of interpretation of Article 24(2)(3) of the Basic Law. According to the judgment, Chinese nationals born on the Mainland even before one parent had acquired the right of abode would be within the category of permanent residents by descent in para. 2(c) of Schedule 1.

As to the challenge to the original scheme, the Court held in *Ng Ka Ling* that the No. 3 Ordinance was unconstitutional to the extent that it requires permanent residents of the Region residing on the Mainland to hold the one way permit before they can enjoy the constitutional right of abode. Accordingly, the Court declared that the relevant provisions in the No. 3 Ordinance and the relevant paras in the Director's Notice as set out in its judgment (at 45J–46G) were null and void.

In *Ng Ka Ling*, the Court rejected the argument that Article 22(4) qualifies the right of abode in Article 24(3). Article 22(4) provides:

"For entry into the Hong Kong Special Administrative Region, people from other parts of China must apply for approval. Among them, the number of persons who enter the Region for the purpose of settlement shall be determined by the competent authorities of the Central People's Government after consulting the government of the Region."

The Court held that the right of abode is a core constitutional right and reasoned (at 35A–D):

"... A generous approach has to be applied to interpreting the right of abode provision. Considering the language of art. 24 and art. 22(4), in our view, "people from other parts of China", including among them persons entering for settlement referred to in art. 22(4), do not include permanent residents of the Region upon whom the Basic Law confers the right of abode in the Region. Persons with permanent resident status under the Basic Law are not, as a matter of ordinary language, people from other parts of China. They are permanent residents of this part of China. Nor is it correct to describe them as persons entering for the purpose of settlement. Their status is that of permanent residents of the Region. They do not enter the Region for the purpose of settlement. They are permanent residents with the right to enter the Region and to remain as long as they wish.

In our view, full effect can be given to art. 22(4), according to its true interpretation, without any encroachment on the right of abode in art. 24. Article 22(4) does not apply to permanent residents of the Region. What it does apply to is the overwhelming part of the population on the Mainland who have no right of abode in the Region. They cannot enter the Region without approval notwithstanding they live in the country of which the Region forms part. ...."

The Court in *Ng Ka Ling* did not strike down the entire original scheme as unconstitutional. The Court made this clear (at 36F–H):

"However, it does not follow that the entire scheme introduced by the No 3 Ordinance is unconstitutional. One must distinguish between a permanent resident who enjoys the right of abode on the one hand and a person claiming to be a permanent resident on the other hand. It is reasonable for the legislature to introduce a scheme which provides for verification of a person's *claim* to be a permanent resident. In our view, the scheme, apart from the requirement of the one way permit, is constitutional as it cannot be said to go beyond verification. Therefore, the scheme is constitutional in requiring a claimant to apply for and obtain a certificate of entitlement from the Director and providing that his status as permanent resident can *only* be established by his holding such a certificate. Further, the provisions of the scheme whereby he must stay in the Mainland whilst applying for such a certificate and whilst appealing against any refusal of the Director to issue a certificate are also constitutional. He has a right to land as part of his right of abode as a permanent resident. But his *claim* to that status must first be verified."

In holding the original scheme apart from the one way permit requirement to be constitutional, the Court stated that it took into account "that the Director must operate it lawfully in a fair and reasonable manner and that there are safeguards to which its operation is subject" which the Court then described as follows (at 36I–37C):

"First, as a matter of statutory construction, the courts would import the requirement of reasonableness into a number of provisions for operating such verification scheme. For example, the Director may specify the manner in which an application for a certificate of entitlement shall be made by notice in the Gazette (s.2AB(2)(a)). But that power is to be construed as what he may reasonably specify. Secondly, if there is unlawful delay by the Director in coming to a decision whether to accept or reject an application, the person concerned, although in the Mainland, can invoke public law remedies in our courts. Thirdly, if the Director decides to refuse the application for a certificate, there is a statutory right of appeal to the Immigration Tribunal. This appeal safeguard is a full one. The Director is under a statutory duty to give reasons for his refusal. There is a period of 90 days within which to appeal. The Tribunal, whose decision the statute provides to be final, is under a duty to determine "on the facts of the case as it finds them" whether the person concerned is a permanent resident by descent and to allow the appeal where it determines that he is."

The Court struck out paras A(i) and B of the Notice. These paragraphs specified the manner in which an application for a certificate of entitlement was to be made. Para. A(i) stated that an application by a person residing in the Mainland of China at the time of application must be made "through the Exit–Entry Administration of the Public Security Bureau in the district where he is residing". Paragraph B stated that an application by such a person for an exit permit to Hong Kong and Macau made to the Exit–Entry Administration of the Public Security Bureau under the laws in force in the Mainland of China for settlement in Hong Kong may be regarded as an application for a certificate of entitlement. In striking out these paragraphs, the Court said (at 38F–I):

"As far as the Director's Notice is concerned, although it is not subsidiary legislation, we can excise the parts which are objectionable following our conclusion on the issue of the constitutionality of the No 3 Ordinance. As we understand the position, the justification for involving the Mainland Exit–Entry Administration is the requirement under the scheme in the No 3 Ordinance for the one way permit which we have held to be unconstitutional. We do not know whether the Director wishes to involve them and whether they are willing to be involved as agent of the Immigration Department on the Mainland to facilitate applications for certificates of entitlement under the scheme as severed. We therefore strike out paras. A(i) and B of the Notice. This leaves a gap in the Notice as to whom an application for a certificate of entitlement should be made by a Mainland resident. The Director would have to specify a new arrangement for them by notice. It is unobjectionable if it has to be made to an entity on the Mainland provided that it functions as an agent of Hong Kong's Immigration Department to facilitate applications for certificates of entitlement. Whether the Mainland Exit–Entry Administration is an appropriate entity for this purpose is for the Director and that administration to consider."

The position after the judgments: the modified scheme

As stated above, the Court delivered its judgments in *Ng Ka Ling* and *Chan Kam Nga* on 29 January 1999. As a result of *Chan Kam Nga*, the time of birth limitation had gone. The effect of the Court's judgment in *Ng Ka Ling* on the original scheme was succinctly summarised by the Chief Judge in the Court of Appeal's judgment in this appeal as follows (at 525J–526D):

"(1) it is reasonable for the legislature to introduce a scheme which provides for the verification of a person's claim to be a permanent resident;

(2) the scheme introduced by the No. 3 Ordinance, apart from the requirement of one-way permits, is constitutional as it cannot be said to go beyond verification. It is constitutional:

(a) in requiring a claimant to apply for and obtain a certificate of entitlement from the Director, and

(b) in providing that his status as permanent resident can only be established by his holding such a certificate;

(3) The provisions of the scheme whereby a person

must stay in the Mainland whilst applying for such a certificate and whilst appealing against any refusal of the Director to issue a certificate are also constitutional;

(4) The Director must operate the scheme lawfully in a fair and reasonable manner. There must be safeguards to which its operation is subject and the requirement of reasonableness must be imported into a number of provisions for operating such a verification scheme."

I shall for convenience use the phrase "the modified scheme" to refer to the scheme that existed after the Court's judgment declaring as null and void the relevant provisions in the No. 3 Ordinance and the Notice.

After the Court's judgment, the modified scheme was unworkable in relation to claimants resident on the Mainland. This was because the Court had declared null and void paras A(i) and B of the Notice. Thus, there was a gap. The Director needed time to work out a new arrangement to fill this gap. This involved discussions with the Mainland authorities. In the present case, the judge held that the task involved was complicated and extremely difficult and that the Government must be given a reasonable time which had not expired. No challenge to this finding was made on appeal. The Court of Appeal agreed with it.

It was common ground in this Court and the courts below and accepted by those courts that, in the meanwhile, the Director could not process any application for a certificate of entitlement by claimants resident on the Mainland.

So, when the Director came to consider the making of the removal orders in question, the position was that the modified scheme prevailed but it was unworkable and the Director could not process applications by claimants residing in the Mainland. Persons ordinarily resident in the Mainland but physically present in Hong Kong without the authority of the Director or subject to conditions of stay are to be regarded under the Notice as residing in the Mainland. That part of the Notice was held to be constitutional and therefore formed part of the modified scheme.

The removal orders

The removal orders against the 17 applicants were made by the Director on various dates in February 1999. I shall take the removal order and the related documentation from the case of the 1st applicant Lau Kong Yung as a typical example.

The removal order was in these terms:

<u>REMOVAL ORDER</u>

Whereas it appears to me that

<u>Master LAU Kong-yung</u>

... is contravening or has contravened a condition of stay in respect of him: ...

in exercise of the powers conferred by section 19(1)(b) of the Immigration Ordinance (Chapter 115), I hereby make a removal order requiring the said person to leave Hong Kong.

The order was signed by Mr MAK Kwai Yun, Assistant Director of Immigration ("Mr Mak"). He was exercising delegated authority from the Director.

Section 19(1)(b)(ii) provides:

"(1) A removal order may be made against a person requiring him to leave Hong Kong –

(b) by the Director if it appears to him that that person –

(ii) has ... landed in Hong Kong unlawfully or is contravening or has contravened a condition of stay in respect of him;"

Paragraph 1 of an internal memorandum to Mr Mak from an immigration official stated:

"This is a case for consideration of issue/non-issue of removal order, and/or strong or powerful humanitarian grounds or other circumstances which would justify remaining in the Hong Kong Special Administrative Region. The case file is attached for your perusal. I am satisfied that the status of this person as a permanent resident under paragraph 2(c) of Schedule 1 to the Immigration Ordinance cannot be established in accordance with section 2AA(1) of the Ordinance."

Section 2AA(1) of the Ordinance, with the omission of the parts declared null and void by the Court in *Ng Ka Ling*, provided:

"2AA.Establishing status of permanent resident under paragraph 2(c) of Schedule 1

(1) A person's status as a permanent resident of the Hong Kong Special Administrative Region under paragraph 2(c) of Schedule 1 can only be established by his holding of

(a) a valid certificate of entitlement issued to him;

(b) a valid HKSAR passport issued to him; or

(c) a valid permanent identity card issued to him."

Paragraph 2 of the memorandum set out the name of the applicant and the file reference and stated: "I believe that the person entered Hong Kong on or about 10 September 1997 from the Mainland of China".

Paragraphs 3 and 4 read:

"3. I am of the view that there are no known powerful or strong humanitarian grounds or other exceptional circumstances which could justify recommendation for remaining in the Hong Kong Special Administrative Region.

4. I recommend this person's removal under section 19(1)(b) and detention pending removal under section 32(3A) of the Immigration Ordinance. I further recommend that this person be removed to the Mainland of China under section 25(4)."

After Mr Mak made his decision, he appended the following minute on the internal memorandum:

"I have considered the circumstances in respect of the one person named above and hereby order the removal of the person under section 19(1)(b) of the Immigration Ordinance. I have signed the removal order in respect of this person and I also authorise his detention under section 32(3A) pending removal. I further direct that this person be removed to the Mainland of China."

The removal order together with a "Summary of facts and reasons for removal" was then served on the 1st applicant who was later released on his recognizance. The summary had three paragraphs. The first set out the applicant's details. The second stated the reasons for removal:

> "Master LAU has contravened his condition of stay by overstaying in the Hong Kong Special Administrative Region since 2 December 1997 and his status as a permanent resident of the Hong Kong Special Administrative Region under paragraph 2(c) of Schedule 1 to the Immigration Ordinance cannot be established in accordance with section 2AA(1) of the same Ordinance."

The third paragraph contained a summary of facts. In the case of the 1st applicant, it was in these terms:

> "Master LAU arrived at the Hong Kong Special Administrative Region on 10 September 1997, travelling on his Two-way Chinese Exit Permit, and was permitted to remain until 1 December 1997. He did not depart and had overstayed since 2 December 1997. On 1 February 1999, he surrendered to the Immigration Department for regularization of stay and was referred to the Victoria Immigration Centre for enquiries on 2 February 1999. He is currently detained at Pui Chi Boys' Home.
>
> Though Master LAU was born in the Mainland of China to his Hong Kong permanent resident father, Mr LAU Yi-to, his status as a permanent resident of the Hong Kong Special Administrative Region under paragraph 2(c) of Schedule 1 to the Immigration Ordinance cannot be established in accordance with section 2AA(1) of the same Ordinance.
>
> He has no close relatives in the Mainland of China. His parents and brother are in the Hong Kong Special Administrative Region."

In making the removal orders, Mr Mak was plainly satisfied that none of the applicants held a certificate of entitlement (or a HKSAR passport or a permanent identity card).

But the question of whether he had considered humanitarian grounds or other exceptional circumstances had not been raised as an issue in the proceedings and there was no evidence directed to this issue.

Both Mr Mak and the immigration official who wrote the internal memorandum to him in most of the 17 cases and authorized the recommendation in the other cases filed affidavits. But they were directed to a different issue, namely, whether the statement of facts in the summary in 15 of the 17 cases (i) meant that the Immigration Department had accepted their status as permanent residents by descent or (ii) was merely setting out the applicant's claim. The Judge found as a fact that the statement simply set out the claim. That finding was not challenged on appeal. In the other two cases, the wording in the summary made clear that it was setting out the claim.

The documentation may tend to suggest that the question of humanitarian grounds or other exceptional circumstances was considered. The internal memorandum referred to the lack of "powerful or strong humanitarian grounds or other exceptional circumstances which could justify recommendation for remaining in the HKSAR". And Mr Mak's minute enclosed on the memorandum stated that he had considered the circumstances in respect of the applicant concerned.

Although the summary of facts and reasons for removal touched on the whereabouts of the applicant's family, they did not refer to the absence of humanitarian grounds or other exceptional circumstances, these being discretionary grounds. But nothing can be read into this. The summary was expressed to be served under para. 8(1)(b) of the Third Schedule to the Immigration Regulations. This provision obliges the Director to serve such a summary after notice of appeal against a removal order has been given. In these cases, a summary was served, notwithstanding that no notice of appeal appears to have been filed. In any event, an appeal to the Immigration Tribunal cannot be brought on discretionary grounds. Sec. 53D of the Ordinance. In these circumstances, the summary in these cases should not be regarded as dealing with the question whether such grounds existed.

The question whether the Director in making the removal orders considered discretionary grounds such as humanitarian grounds or other exceptional circumstances was not an issue in this Court or the lower courts. And no evidence was directed at this question. In these circumstances, although the documentation may tend to suggest that they were considered, it would not be right for the Court of Final Appeal to make a finding on this question for the first time.

One thing however is clear. In February 1999, in the context of the scheme as modified by the Court's judgments, the applicants were concentrating on maintaining their claim to the right of abode to the Director as a matter of right. They were not putting a case to him for the exercise of discretion under any statutory provision, section 19 or otherwise. This point was emphasised by Mr Ma SC for the Director:

> "The Director was not required to consider any other basis since it was clear that all these applicants were only claiming permanent resident status to enable them to exercise the right of abode by reason of Article 24(2)(3). No other matters were put before the Director (see para. 7 of the Director's submissions in reply)."

Mr Ma SC also maintains that the evidence shows that the Director did consider the position of the applicants from a humanitarian point of view. I have already concluded that no such finding of fact should be made by the Court.

It should be noted that a claimant cannot lodge an appeal to the Tribunal against the refusal by the Director to issue a certificate of entitlement while he is in Hong Kong (see s.2AD(3)). And the lodging of an appeal confers no right to remain in Hong Kong (see s.2AD(9)). Although a claimant can appeal against the making of a removal order on the ground that he has the right of abode, the Tribunal cannot allow an appeal on this ground unless the claimant's status has been established in the manner prescribed by sec. 2AA(1), that is by holding a certificate of entitlement (or a HKSAR passport or a permanent identity card). These aspects of the original scheme survived the challenge and were part of the modified scheme. See *Ng Ka Ling* at 18J–19C and 36H.

The events leading to the Interpretation

On 26 June 1999, the Standing Committee of the National People's Congress adopted the Interpretation. Before its adoption, Mr Qiao Xiaoyang, Deputy Director of the Legislative Affairs Commission of the Standing Committee ("Mr Qiao"), made a speech to it on 22 June 1999 explaining the Interpretation which was then in draft form.

Mr Qiao's speech set out the events leading to the Interpretation. On 20 May 1999, the Chief Executive of the HKSAR under Articles 43 and 48(2) of the Basic Law submitted a report to the State Council "seeking the assistance of the Central People's Government in resolving the problems encountered in the implementation of the relevant provisions of the Basic Law". The report set out the circumstances. It noted that the Court's interpretation of Articles 22(4) and 24(2)(3) differed from the HKSAR Government's understanding of the relevant provisions. It stated that Hong Kong's prosperity and stability would be seriously affected, citing the recent survey conducted by the HKSAR Government that at least an addition of 1.67 million persons in the Mainland would qualify as a result of the Court's judgments; about 690,000 in the first generation and 980,000 in the second generation after the first generation have ordinarily resided for 7 years. The report requested the State Council "to seek an interpretation of Articles 22(4) and 24(2)(3) in accordance with the stipulations of the Constitution of the PRC and the Basic Law".

According to Mr Qiao's speech, having considered the Chief Executive's Report, the State Council submitted to the NPCSC the Motion regarding the request for an interpretation of Articles 22(4) and 24(2)(3) of the Basic Law.

Mr Qiao's speech stated that the Council of Chairmen of the NPCSC examined the Motion and considered that the issue raised concerned the interpretation of relevant provisions by the Court and that the provisions are within those referred to in Article 158(3). Mr Qiao stated:

> "Before making its judgment, [the Court] had not sought an interpretation of the NPCSC in compliance with the requirement of Article 158(3). Moreover, the interpretation of [the Court] is not consistent with the legislative intent. In accordance with ... Article 67(4) of the Constitution of the PRC .... and Article 158(1) of the Basic Law ... and in order to ensure the proper implementation of the Basic Law, it is imperative and appropriate for the NPCSC to make an interpretation of the relevant provisions of the Basic Law. In view of this, the Council of Chairmen has put forth *The Interpretation by the NPCSC of Articles 22(4) and 24(2)(3) of the Basic Law of the HKSAR of the PRC (Draft)* and has consulted the Committee for the Basic Law of the HKSAR under NPCSC".

Mr Qiao then explained the contents of that draft.

The Interpretation

The Interpretation by the NPCSC on 26 June 1999 was gazetted in Hong Kong. An English translation was also published in the gazette for information.

The Interpretation was headed: The Interpretation by the NPCSC of Articles 22(4) and 24(2)(3) of the Basic Law.

The Preamble stated that the Standing Committee had examined the State Council's Motion regarding the request for an interpretation of Articles 22(4) and 24(2)(3) of the Basic Law which was submitted upon the report furnished by the Chief Executive of the HKSAR under the relevant provisions of Articles 43 and 48(2) of the Basic Law. The Preamble went on to say that the issue raised in the Motion related to the interpretation of the relevant provisions of the Basic Law by the Court. Those provisions concerned affairs which are the responsibility of the Central People's Government and concerned the relationship between the Central Authorities and the HKSAR. The Preamble, after stating that before making its judgment, the Court had not sought an interpretation of the NPCSC in compliance with the requirement of Article 158(3) of the Basic Law, continued: "Moreover the interpretation of the Court of Final Appeal is not consistent with the legislative intent." The concluding part of the Preamble recited that, having consulted the Basic Law Committee under the NPCSC, the NPCSC has decided to make, under the provisions of Article 67(4) of the Constitution of the People's Republic of China and Article 158(1) of the Basic Law an interpretation of the provisions of Articles 22(4) and 24(2)(3) of the Basic Law.

I shall set out in full the rest of the Interpretation which followed, using the abbreviations "HKSAR" and "PRC":

> "1. The provisions of Article 22(4) of the Basic Law of the [HKSAR] of the [PRC] regarding "For entry into the [HKSAR], people from other parts of China must apply for approval" mean as follows: People from all provinces, autonomous regions, or municipalities directly under the Central Government, including those persons of Chinese nationality born outside Hong Kong of Hong Kong permanent residents, who wish to enter the [HKSAR] for whatever reason, must apply to the relevant authorities of their residential districts for approval in accordance with the relevant national laws and administrative regulations, and must hold valid documents issued by the relevant authorities before they can enter the [HKSAR]. It is unlawful for people from all provinces, autonomous regions, or municipalities directly under the Central Government, including persons of Chinese nationality born outside Hong Kong of Hong Kong permanent residents, to enter the [HKSAR] without complying with the appropriate approval procedure prescribed by the relevant national laws and administrative regulations.
>
> 2. It is stipulated in the first three categories of Article 24(2) of the Basic Law of the [HKSAR] of the [PRC] that the "permanent residents of the HKSAR shall be:
>
> > (1) Chinese citizens born in Hong Kong before or after the establishment of the [HKSAR];
> >
> > (2) Chinese citizens who have ordinarily resided in Hong Kong for a continuous period of not less than seven years before or after the establishment of the [HKSAR];
> >
> > (3) Persons of Chinese nationality born outside Hong Kong of those residents listed in categories (1) and (2);".
>
> The provisions of category (3) regarding the "persons of Chinese nationality born outside Hong Kong of those residents listed in categories (1) and (2)" mean both parents of such persons, whether born before or after the establishment of the [HKSAR], or either of such parents must have fulfilled the condition prescribed by category (1) or (2) of Article 24(2) of the Basic Law of the [HKSAR] of the [PRC] at the time of their birth. The legislative intent as stated by this Interpretation, together with the legislative intent of all other categories of Article 24(2) of the Basic Law of the [HKSAR] of the [PRC], have been reflected in the "Opinions on the Implementation of Article 24(2) of the Basic Law of the [HKSAR] of the

[PRC]" adopted at the Fourth Plenary Meeting of the Preparatory Committee for the [HKSAR] of the National People's Congress on 10 August 1996.

As from the promulgation of this Interpretation, the courts of the [HKSAR], when referring to the relevant provisions of the Basic Law of the [HKSAR] of the [PRC], shall adhere to this Interpretation. This Interpretation does not affect the right of abode in the [HKSAR] which has been acquired under the judgment of the Court of Final Appeal on the relevant cases dated 29 January 1999 by the parties concerned in the relevant legal proceedings. Other than that, the question whether any other person fulfils the conditions prescribed by Article 24(2)(3) of the Basic Law of the [HKSAR] of the [PRC] shall be determined by reference to this Interpretation."

The issues on the Interpretation

The central question in this appeal relates to the Interpretation. Three issues on the Interpretation arise from the submissions made to the Court. First, the power of the NPCSC to make the Interpretation. Secondly, the effect of the Interpretation. And thirdly, the date from which the Interpretation is applicable.

Mr Geoffrey Ma SC, for the Director, submits that the Court should not deal with the question of the effect of the last paragraph of the Interpretation which excluded "the parties concerned in the relevant legal proceedings" from the operation of the Interpretation. Mr Denis Chang SC for the 17 applicants, who maintains that the last paragraph has no interpretative effect in that it was not an interpretation of any article of the Basic Law, did not urge us to resolve this question. It is not necessary to deal with it on this appeal.

Article 67 (4) of the Chinese Constitution

Article 67 (4) of the Chinese Constitution provides:

"The Standing Committee of the National People's Congress exercises the following functions and powers:

(4) to interpret laws;"

Article 158 of the Basic Law

Article 158 of the Basic Law provides:

"The power of interpretation of this Law shall be vested in the Standing Committee of the National People's Congress.

The Standing Committee of the National People's Congress shall authorize the courts of the Hong Kong Special Administrative Region to interpret on their own, in adjudicating cases, the provisions of this Law which are within the limits of the autonomy of the Region.

The courts of the Hong Kong Special Administrative Region may also interpret other provisions of this Law in adjudicating cases. However, if the courts of the Region, in adjudicating cases, need to interpret the provisions of this Law concerning affairs which are the responsibility of the Central People's Government, or concerning the relationship between the Central Authorities and the Region, and if such interpretation will affect the judgments on the cases, the courts of the Region shall, before making their final judgments which are not appealable, seek an interpretation of the relevant provisions from the Standing Committee of the National People's Congress through the Court of Final Appeal of the Region. When the Standing Committee makes an interpretation of the provisions concerned, the courts of the Region, in applying those provisions, shall follow the interpretation of the Standing Committee. However, judgments previously rendered shall not be affected.

The Standing Committee of the National People's Congress shall consult its Committee for the Basic Law of the Hong Kong Special Administrative Region before giving an interpretation of this Law."

The power of the Standing Committee

Article 67(4) of the Chinese Constitution confers on the Standing Committee the function and power to interpret laws. This power includes the Basic Law which is a national law. The Basic Law itself provides in Article 158(1) that the power of interpretation of this Law shall be vested in the Standing Committee.

Article 158(2) contains the authorization by the Standing Committee to the courts of the Region to interpret on their own in adjudicating cases the provisions of this Law which are within the limits of the Region's autonomy. Article 158(3) provides that the Region's courts may also interpret other provisions of this Law in adjudicating cases, that is provisions other than those which are within the limits of the Region's autonomy. But Article 158(3) proceeds to provide that if the courts in the Region in adjudicating cases need to interpret provisions which I shall refer to as "the excluded provisions" (the expression used in *Ng Ka Ling*), namely, the provisions concerning affairs which are the responsibility of the Central People's Government or concerning the relationship between the Central Authorities and the Region, then the courts shall before rendering judgments which are not appealable, seek an interpretation of the relevant provisions from the Standing Committee through the Court of Final Appeal. Thus, where the conditions provided for are satisfied, the Court of Final Appeal is under a *duty* to seek an interpretation of the excluded provisions from the Standing Committee. It is convenient to refer to this as a "judicial reference". Article 158(3) goes on to provide that when the Standing Committee makes an interpretation of the provisions concerned, the courts of the Region, in applying those provisions, shall follow the Standing Committee's interpretation. However, judgments previously rendered shall not be affected. Article 158(4) provides that the Standing Committee shall consult its Committee for the Basic Law before giving an interpretation.

Mr Denis Chang SC submits that the Standing Committee had no power to make the Interpretation because under Article 158, properly interpreted, the Standing Committee cannot interpret the Basic Law except upon a judicial reference by the Court which would relate only to the excluded provisions. Mr Chang argues that Article 158 imposes a constitutional restraint on the Standing Committee's power and that this accords with the high degree of autonomy accorded to the Region by the Basic Law adopted by the National People's Congress which included the power of final adjudication. See Basic Law Articles 2 and 19.

This argument cannot be accepted. It is clear that the Standing Committee has the power to make the Interpretation. This power originates from Article 67(4) of the Chinese Constitution and is contained in Article 158(1) of the Basic Law itself. The power of interpretation of the Basic Law conferred by Article 158(1) is in general and unqualified terms.

That power and its exercise is not restricted or qualified in any way by Articles 158(2) and 158(3). By Article 158(2), the Region's courts are authorized to interpret on their own in adjudicating cases the provisions within the limits of the Region's autonomy. The words "on their own" underline the absence of a duty to refer the provisions in question to the Standing Committee for interpretation in contrast to the mandatory requirement relating to the excluded provisions provided for in Article 158(3). That provision enables the courts to interpret provisions other than those within the limits of the Region's autonomy but, where the conditions provided for are satisfied, obliges the Court of Final Appeal not to interpret the excluded provisions and to seek an interpretation from the Standing Committee. So, there is no question of Article 158(3) restricting the Standing Committee's general power in Article 158(1). That provision is directed to limiting the Court's power by requiring a judicial reference of the excluded provisions in the circumstances prescribed.

In any event, the entire scheme of Article 158 is inconsistent with the argument that restrictions are to be implied from Articles 158(2) and 158(3) on the general power of interpretation conferred by Article 158(1). The authority given by Article 158(2) to the courts of the Region stems from the general power of interpretation vested in the Standing Committee. Article 158(3) extends that authority but subject to a qualification requiring a judicial reference. The reference results in the making by the Standing Committee of an interpretation which proceeds from the general power vested in it by Article 158(1). Mr Chang SC's submission, if it were accepted, would deny to the Standing Committee power to interpret provisions in the Basic Law other than the excluded provisions. Such a limited power of interpretation would be inconsistent with the general power conferred by Article 158(1).

Mr Chang SC relies on the different wording of the equivalent article (then numbered 169) to Article 158 in the draft Basic Law (April 1988). It reads:

> "The power of interpretation of this Law is vested in the Standing Committee of the National People's Congress.
>
> When the Standing Committee of the National People's Congress makes an interpretation of a provision of this Law, the courts of the Hong Kong Special Administrative Region, in applying that provision, shall follow the interpretation of the Standing Committee. However, judgments previously rendered shall not be affected.
>
> The courts of the Hong Kong Special Administrative Region may interpret the provisions of this Law in adjudicating cases before them. If a case involves an interpretation of the provisions of this Law concerning defence, foreign affairs and other affairs which are the responsibility of the Central People's Government, the courts of the Region, before making their final judgment on the case, shall seek an interpretation of the relevant provisions from the Standing Committee of the National People's Congress.
>
> The Standing Committee of the National People's Congress shall consult its Committee for the Basic Law of the Hong Kong Special Administrative Region before giving an interpretation of this Law."

This draft article does not assist. We do not know why it was that the text of Article 158 was adopted in preference to the draft and, in any case, the draft would not lead to a different interpretation of Article 158 from that reached on the wording of that Article.

Accordingly, the Standing Committee has the power to make the Interpretation under Article 158(1). The Interpretation is binding on the courts of the HKSAR.

This conclusion on the power of the Standing Committee to interpret under Article 158(1) derives some support from Professor Yash Ghai in his work: "Hong Kong's New Constitutional Order" (2nd ed. 1999) p. 198. He expressed the view that the power of the Standing Committee to interpret is a general power. It is "plenary in that it covers all the provisions of the Basic Law; this power may be exercised in the absence of litigation."

In *Ng Ka Ling*, the Court discussed the conditions, referred to as the classification condition and the necessity condition, that have to be satisfied before a judicial reference should be made by the Court under Article 158(3) to the Standing Committee for an interpretation of the excluded provisions (at 30H–33H). In relation to the classification condition, the Court adopted (at 33C–E) the test: As a matter of substance what predominantly is the provision that has to be interpreted in the adjudication of the case ("the predominant test"). Applying that test, the Court did not make a judicial reference in *Ng Ka Ling*. The Preamble to the Interpretation expressed the view that before judgment the Court had not sought an interpretation of the relevant provisions of the Standing Committee "in compliance with the requirement of Article 158(3)". As this view proceeds upon an interpretation of Article 158(3) which differs from that applied by the Court in *Ng Ka Ling*, the Court may need to re-visit the classification and necessity conditions and the predominant test in an appropriate case.

THE EFFECT OF THE INTERPRETATION

Clause 1

Mr Chang SC points out that Clause 1 only interprets the first sentence of Article 22(4) of the Basic Law. He submits that Clause 1 properly read does not have the effect of linking Article 22(4) and Article 24 and therefore does not render constitutional the relevant provisions in the No. 3 Ordinance requiring the holding of the one way permit in addition to the certificate of entitlement before the right of abode could be enjoyed.

We are concerned with the position of permanent residents by descent under Article 24(2)(3) of the Basic Law. The Interpretation clearly states that they are included in "people from other parts of China who must apply for approval". The phrase "including those persons of Chinese nationality born outside Hong Kong of Hong Kong permanent residents" is used twice and plainly refers to the permanent residents by descent. The words "who wish to enter [HKSAR] for whatever reason" are wide and mean what they say.

The Interpretation provides that such permanent residents by descent wishing to enter Hong Kong for whatever reason must apply to the Mainland authorities for approval and must hold valid documents issued by the relevant authorities before entry. The necessity for such approval is reinforced by the statement that it would be unlawful for such permanent residents to enter HKSAR without complying with the prescribed appropriate approval procedure. That procedure required exit approval and the valid document is the one way permit issued for those coming for settlement under a quota system. (See *Ng Ka Ling* (at 19I–20J)). Mr Qiao in his speech explaining this part (clause 1) of the draft Interpretation referred specifically to permanent residents by descent being subjected to a quota system. He said:

> "In particular, regarding the arrangement for children

born in the Mainland by Hong Kong permanent residents to come to settle in Hong Kong, special quotas are taken from the daily quotas for Mainland residents coming to Hong Kong for settlement. The relevant Mainland authorities together with the relevant HKSAR authority would examine and verify the credentials of the applicants and then issue relevant documents in batches to the persons concerned who only then may come to settle in Hong Kong. The legislative intent of Basic Law 22(4) is to affirm the long-standing system for exit-entry administration between the Mainland and Hong Kong. .... This legislative intent is solely meant to ensure that Mainland residents come to Hong Kong in an orderly manner and is consistent with the general interest of Hong Kong."

The effect of the Interpretation is that as a matter of the Basic Law, permanent residents by descent must obtain exit approval from the Mainland authorities and must hold the one way permit before entry into the HKSAR. The Interpretation therefore clearly links Article 22(4) and Article 24.

Further, the Interpretation has, in my view, the effect that permanent residents by descent are within the second sentence of Article 22(4). What gave rise to the Interpretation was *Ng Ka Ling* where the Court held in a passage (at 35A–B) already quoted in this judgment that ".... in our view "people from other parts of China", including among them persons entering for settlement referred to in Article 22(4), do not include permanent residents of the Region upon whom the Basic Law confers the right of abode in the Region".

Considered in the light of that judgment, the effect of the Interpretation in interpreting "people from other parts of China" (with among them persons coming for settlement) to include permanent residents by descent, is that permanent residents by descent are within the second sentence. They are therefore subjected to the quota system.

Clause 2

Mr Chang SC accepts that if the Standing Committee has the power to make the Interpretation, then it is effective to render the time of birth limitation constitutional. The effect of the Interpretation is that Article 24(2)(3) means that the person concerned must have at least one parent who was a permanent resident within Article 24(2)(1) or 24(2)(2) at the time of birth of the person concerned.

The applicable date

The Interpretation, being an interpretation of the relevant provisions, dates from 1 July 1997 when the Basic Law came into effect. It declared what the law has always been. Compare the common law declaratory theory of judicial decisions, see *Kleinwort Benson Ltd v. Lincoln City Council* [1998] 3 WLR 1095 at 1117–1119 and 1148.

As noted above in the earlier section headed *"The issues on the Interpretation"*, I leave aside in this appeal, as requested by Mr Ma SC for the Director, the question of the persons who should not be affected by the Interpretation ("the unaffected persons question").

Summary of views on Interpretation

In summary:

(1) The Standing Committee has the power to make the Interpretation under Article 158(1).

(2) It is a valid and binding Interpretation of Article 22(4) and Article 24(2)(3) which the courts in the HKSAR are under a duty to follow.

(3) The effect of the Interpretation is:

 (a) Under Article 22(4), persons from all provinces, autonomous regions or municipalities directly under the Central Government including those persons within Article 24(2)(3), who wish to enter the HKSAR for whatever reason, must apply to the relevant authorities of their residential districts for approval in accordance with the relevant national laws and administrative regulations and must hold valid documents issued by the relevant authorities before they can enter the HKSAR.

 (b) To qualify as a permanent resident under Article 24(2)(3), it is necessary that both parents or either parent of the person concerned must be a permanent resident within Article 24(2)(1) or Article 24(2)(2) at the time of birth of the person concerned.

(4) The Interpretation has effect from 1 July 1997.

The resulting position

As a result of the Interpretation, the original scheme is and has since 1 July 1997 been constitutional.

The time of birth limitation in the No. 2 Ordinance is and has since 1 July 1997 been constitutional.

The provisions in the No. 3 Ordinance and the Notice declared by the Court to be unconstitutional (as set out in the two declarations set out in A(1) and A(2) of *Ng Ka Ling* at 46A–F) are and have since 1 July 1997 been constitutional.

In *Ng Ka Ling* the Court also declared section 1(2) of the No. 3 Ordinance unconstitutional. (See the declaration in A(3) of *Ng Ka Ling* at 46F–G.) Section 1(2) had deemed the No. 3 Ordinance, although enacted on 10 July 1997, to have come into effect on 1 July 1997. In my view, this is not affected by the Interpretation. In *Ng Ka Ling*, the Court in holding this retrospective provision to be unconstitutional relied on two grounds.

First, on the modified scheme, the No. 3 Ordinance took away the constitutional right of abode which a permanent resident by descent, who had arrived in Hong Kong on or after 1 July and before 10 July 1997, was already enjoying under the *Basic Law* (at 39C–E). This ground is affected by the Interpretation. This is because the effect of the Interpretation was that Article 22(4) qualified Article 24(2)(3) and with that qualification, unless the requirement of Mainland approval in Article 22(4) was satisfied, the person concerned could not enjoy the right of abode.

The second ground relied on by the Court was that the retrospective provision rendered the persons concerned guilty of criminal offences and was unconstitutional as contrary to article 15(1) of the International Covenant on Civil and Political Rights as applied to Hong Kong by virtue of Article 39 of the *Basic Law* (at 39F–40F). This ground is not affected by the Interpretation. On the basis of this ground, the retrospective provision in section 1(2) of the No. 3 Ordinance remains invalid.

The new Schedule 1 and the new Notice

Following the Interpretation, on 16 July 1999, the Legislative Council passed a resolution under sec. 59A of the Immigration Ordinance to amend Schedule 1. The relevant amendment for this appeal is that para. 2(c) was repealed and substituted by:

"(c) A person of Chinese nationality born outside Hong Kong before or after the establishment of the Hong Kong Special Administrative Region to a parent who, at the time of birth of that person, was a Chinese citizen falling within category (a) or (b)."

I shall refer to this as the new para. 2(c) of Schedule 1. It contains the time of birth limitation as did the former para. 2(c).

On 16 July 1999, the Director gazetted a new Notice to replace the Notice ("the new Notice"). The new Notice is similar in substance to the former Notice. Para. A(i) is in the same terms. A Mainland resident shall apply for a certificate of entitlement through the Exit-Entry Administration of the Public Security Bureau in the district where he is residing. Para. B is similar in effect although the wording is different. It reads:

"Where a person is at the time of application residing in the Mainland of China, an application for settlement in Hong Kong made to the offices or departments of the Exit-Entry Administration of the Public Security Bureau under the laws in force in the Mainland of China, whether before or after the gazetting of this notice, may be regarded as an application for a Certificate of Entitlement or certified duplicate."

The former Notice is similar: "... an application for an exit permit to Hong Kong and Macau made to the Exit-Entry Administration of the Public Security Bureau under the laws in force in the Mainland of China for settlement in Hong Kong, ... may be regarded as an application for a Certificate of Entitlement. ...".

The operation of the original scheme

As a result of the Interpretation, the original scheme is and has since the enactment of the No. 3 Ordinance been constitutional. We now have the new para. 2(c) of Schedule 1 and the new Notice. *Ng Ka Ling* fully set out the original scheme with the relevant statutory provisions. In the earlier section headed: "*The scheme introduced in July 1997: the original scheme*", I quoted the passage in *Ng Ka Ling* (at 21) on the operation of the original scheme as it affects a Mainland resident claiming the status of permanent resident by descent.

The following features of the original scheme should be highlighted. First, a Mainland resident claiming the status of permanent resident by descent can only establish his status by holding a valid one way permit (i.e. the valid travel document as far as he is concerned) affixed with a certificate of entitlement. Sec. 2AA(1). (Any person holding a valid HKSAR passport or a permanent identity card, the other two documents mentioned in that provision would already have established his right of abode.) Without it he shall be regarded as not enjoying the right of abode. Sec. 2AA(2).

Secondly, in accordance with para. A(i) of the new Notice (and formerly the Notice), a Mainland resident must apply for a certificate of entitlement through the Exit-Entry Administration of the Public Security Bureau in the district where he is residing. He cannot come to Hong Kong to make the application. If he is physically in Hong Kong, he is treated as residing in the Mainland during his stay in Hong Kong. See para. C of the new Notice (and formerly the Notice). Whilst he can appeal to the Immigration Tribunal against the Director's refusal to issue a certificate of entitlement, he cannot appeal at any time when he is in Hong Kong. Sec. 2AD(3).

Thirdly, he cannot appeal to the Immigration Tribunal against the making of a removal order on the ground that he has the right of abode. As pointed out in *Ng Ka Ling* (at 19B-C):

"To bolster the scheme that he can only establish his status by holding a travel document affixed with a certificate of entitlement, s.53D(3) introduced by the No 3 Ordinance provides that the tribunal shall not allow an appeal against a removal order on the ground that the appellant enjoys the right of abode by virtue of the status in para.2(c) of Schedule 1 unless his status has been established in the manner prescribed by s.2AA(1)."

The policy reasons for such a scheme laid down by the legislature include the discouragement of illegal entry into Hong Kong and of illegal stay here in contravention of conditions of stay as well as the prevention as a matter of fairness of queue jumping ahead of the Mainland residents who have applied but have remained in the Mainland.

The making of removal orders

I should make some observations on the Director's power to make removal orders under section 19(1)(b)(ii), in the context of the original scheme, against claimants to the status of permanent resident by descent who are physically in Hong Kong but are treated as resident on the Mainland.

Under that provision,: "a removal order may be made against a person requiring him to leave Hong Kong ... by the Director if it appears to him that that person ... has ... landed in Hong Kong unlawfully or is contravening or has contravened a condition of stay in respect of him."

So, where a Mainland resident claiming the status came to Hong Kong illegally or remains here in contravention of a condition of stay, the Director "may" make a removal order against him. The Director has a discretion. But that discretion has to be exercised in the context of the statutory scheme (that is, the original scheme). That scheme requires that the person concerned can only establish his status by holding a one way permit affixed with the certificate of entitlement and that he must apply for the certificate of entitlement in the Mainland through the Mainland authorities and cannot remain in Hong Kong in the meanwhile.

In the context of the original scheme, in considering the making of a removal order against a Mainland resident claiming the status, the Director, apart from being satisfied that the Mainland resident has landed in Hong Kong unlawfully or is contravening or has contravened a condition of stay, need only be satisfied in the usual case that he does not hold a one way permit affixed with a certificate of entitlement (or a valid HKSAR passport or a valid permanent identity card) as required by section 2AA(1).

Two further points should be made. First, an illegal immigrant, whether he entered illegally or has contravened a condition of stay, does not have, as a general rule, a right to a hearing, conducted fairly and in accordance with the rules of natural justice, before a removal order is made against him. See the Court of Appeal's decisions in *R v. Director of Immigration, Ex parte Chan Heung-mui* [1993] *3 HKPLR 533* and *Attorney-General v. Ng Yuen-shiu* [1981] HKLR 352. In the latter case, on appeal to the Privy Council, their Lordships assumed this to be correct [1983] 2 AC 629 at 636B. A person claiming to be a permanent resident by descent who landed unlawfully or is contravening or has contravened a condition of stay is in a similar position in this regard.

Secondly, in relation to such a person the Director has no duty to consider humanitarian grounds in considering the making of a removal order against him. But he can take such grounds into account if he thinks it appropriate in the case in question. This is consistent with the position under section 13. This provides that the Director may authorize a person who landed unlawfully to remain subject to such conditions of stay as he thinks fit. It has been observed that the Director is under no duty to take humanitarian grounds into account. See the observations of Litton JA (as he then was) in *R v. Director of Immigration, Ex parte Chan Heung Mui* at 543. Indeed, the Privy Council agreed in *Nguyen Tuan Cuong v. Director of Immigration* [1997] 1 WLR 68 at 75 with what Litton JA stated (at 545) in *Ex parte Chan Heung Mui* in relation to section 13:

> "Section 13 of the Ordinance imposes no statutory duty of any kind upon the director, beyond the broad duty falling upon him to administer the scheme of immigration control embodied in the Ordinance fairly and properly."

Further, if what is suggested is that the Director should consider the exercise of some other statutory discretion (apart from sections 13 and 19) to enable such a claimant to stay in Hong Kong temporarily or permanently, the position would be similar to that under sections 13 and 19 as regards humanitarian grounds.

In the present case, as I have already noted under the earlier section headed "the removal orders", the applicants were not putting a case to the Director for the exercise of any discretion under section 19 or any other provision. They were concentrating on maintaining their claim to the right of abode as a matter of right.

The removal orders against the 17 applicants

The Judge upheld the removal orders. But they were quashed by the Court of Appeal. The question before us is whether the removal orders (i) should be restored or (ii) should remain quashed.

The lower courts considered the matter on the basis that when the Director made the removal orders in question in February 1999, (i) the scheme was the modified scheme albeit unworkable at that time and (ii) the time of birth limitation had gone. However, the Court must now approach the problem from a different perspective after the Interpretation. Having regard to the conclusions reached on the Interpretation, since 1 July 1997 the time of birth limitation has been constitutional and the scheme that has prevailed since then and prevailed in February 1999 was the original scheme. But the Director did not consider the making of removal orders in such context. He considered them in the context of (i) and (ii) above. Necessarily so, since that was after the Court's judgments and well before the Interpretation.

In *R v. Hull University Visitor, Ex parte Page* [1993] AC 682 at 702 B – C, Lord Browne-Wilkinson stated the test on judicial review for error of law thus:

> "... in general any error of law made by an administrative tribunal or inferior court in reaching its decision can be quashed for error of law."

But "what must be shown is a relevant error of law, i.e., an error in the actual making of the decision which affected the decision itself" (at 702D–E).

That the error must be a relevant error in the above sense was put by Lord Diplock in *Secretary of State for Education and Science v. Tameside Metropolitan Borough Council* [1977] AC 1064H –1065B in these terms. After pointing out that the discretion in question was vested in the Secretary of State and that it is not for any court of law to substitute its own opinion for his, he continued:

> "but it is for a court of law to determine whether it has been established that in reaching his decision unfavourable to the council he had directed himself properly in law and had in consequence taken into consideration the matters which upon the true construction of the Act he ought to have considered and excluded from his consideration matters that were irrelevant to what he had to consider: see *Associated Provincial Picture Houses Ltd. v. Wednesbury Corporation* [1948] 1 K.B. 223, per Lord Greene M.R., at p. 229. ...."

The Director considered the exercise of his power to make removal orders in the context of (i) the absence of the time of birth limitation and (ii) the modified scheme, on the basis that in law that was the position at that time. That was an error. Understandably so, since he was taking the legal position after the Court's judgments but the correct legal position resulting from the Interpretation involved a valid original scheme and a valid time of birth limitation. The critical question is whether that error of law was a relevant error.

I should first dispose of the error in law as regards the time of birth limitation. In my view, that error was not a relevant error. If no error were made, the time of birth limitation was valid and the claim to permanent resident status of a number of applicants (that is, the 12 applicants referred to in the earlier section headed "*the applicants*") could not get off the ground.

But was the error regarding the scheme that prevailed a relevant error for judicial review purposes ? The power of the Director in question here is the power to make a removal order. First, this power was the same whether the context was the original scheme or the modified scheme. The two schemes have the common feature that a claimant could only establish his status as a permanent resident by descent by holding one of the documents prescribed in section 2AA(1). Leaving aside the HKSAR passport or the permanent identity card document and concentrating on the relevant document as far as such a claimant is concerned, the difference between them was that whereas the original scheme required a claimant resident on the Mainland to hold (i) the one way permit affixed with (ii) a certificate of entitlement, the modified scheme required only (ii).

Secondly, as regards the proper exercise of the power, I have held that under the original scheme, the Director in the usual case need only ask whether the claimant holds one of the documents required by section 2AA(1), apart from being satisfied as to the precedent condition in section 19(1)(b)(ii) itself. He has no duty to consider humanitarian grounds, although he can do so. The position under the modified scheme was similar.

So, as far as the power and its proper exercise are concerned, there is no difference between the modified scheme and the original scheme. In these circumstances, the error made was not a relevant error.

The point can be made on behalf of the applicants that if when the removal orders were made, it was known that the original scheme was valid, they would have had the opportunity of putting forward humanitarian grounds. But this point cannot avail them on the present challenge to the removal orders. First, the conduct of the Director in making the decisions in question could not be impugned by reference to the possible loss of this opportunity.

Secondly, in any event, he is under no duty and hence not bound to take humanitarian considerations into account. Assuming the applicants would have put forward humanitarian grounds, any failure by the Director would not have availed them since the Director was not bound to consider them. Lord Diplock in the passage quoted above referred to the matters which upon the construction of the statute he ought to have considered and excluded matters irrelevant to what he had to consider. So, for impugning a decision one is concerned with what the decision maker is bound to consider. See also *Minister for Aboriginal Affairs v. Peko-Wallsend Limited* (1986) 162 CLR 24 at 39.

As there was no relevant error of law, the removal orders should be restored.

The Court of Appeal's judgments

The Court of Appeal quashed the removal orders. It held that in February 1999 the Director had exercised his power to remove unlawfully by simply asking whether the applicants held one of the documents required by section 2AA(1). It considered the matter in the context that at the time the removal orders were made, the modified scheme prevailed but was unworkable and applications for certificate of entitlement could not be processed. In that extraordinary situation where there was no workable modified scheme, it held that the Director should have taken into account wider considerations both for and against the applicants.

If the modified scheme had been a workable scheme at the time, the position as regards the making of removal orders would have been similar to that under the original scheme. Even in the extraordinary situation where the modified scheme was not workable, I have considerable doubts whether the Court of Appeal was right in holding that he should have had regard to wider considerations. As the scenario involving an unworkable modified scheme is now a matter in the past, it is best to leave the judgments of the Court of Appeal to one side. I wish however to make clear that I should not be taken as approving those judgments and their reasoning.

Orders

Accordingly, the appeal by the Director is allowed. The order of the judge in the judicial review proceedings is restored and the applicants' applications for judicial review are dismissed. The order of the judge in the habeas corpus proceedings is restored and the writs of habeas corpus issued in respect of the applicants are discharged.

As to costs, as suggested by Mr Ma SC for the Director, there should be no order as to costs save that the 17 applicants' (that is, the respondents') costs be taxed in accordance with Legal Aid Regulations.

Pursuant to the undertakings given to the Court set out in the earlier section headed "Director's position following outcome of this appeal", the Director will be considering whether to revoke the removal orders. There are special circumstances relating to the 17 applicants. They arrived before the Court's judgments on 29 January 1999 and except for two of them, they allegedly made their claims before then. Further, they may be able to rely on events subsequent to the making of the removal orders. The Director will no doubt consider these 17 applicants with such sympathy as they deserve, bearing in mind their special circumstances.

Mr Justice Litton PJ:

I agree with the Chief Justice's judgment, and likewise with Mr Justice Ching PJ's. I also agree with Sir Anthony Mason NPJ's observations on the Interpretation.

The Court of Appeal held that the removal orders made in February 1999 in respect of the 17 applicants were unlawful: Not because the Director did not have the lawful authority to do so under s.19(1)(b)(ii) of the Immigration Ordinance nor because the circumstances specified in that section did not apply, but because the decision-making process was flawed. He had, according to the Court of Appeal, failed to take into account relevant matters and this vitiated the entire decision-making process, resulting in that court reversing the trial judge (Mr Justice Yeung) and quashing the removal orders.

The application for relief under Order 53 r.3

To consider whether the Court of Appeal had erred, it is necessary to go back to the beginning: To the application for leave to apply for judicial review made under Order 53 r.3 of the Rules of the High Court. It is a long and rambling document consisting of, originally, 41 paragraphs: It has since been amended to add considerably more paragraphs. In so far as it is possible to identify in that document the grounds on which, ultimately, the Court of Appeal based its decision to quash the removal orders, it is, as stated in the application, "Wednesbury unreasonableness": the second of the three grounds stated by Lord Diplock in his classic speech in the House of Lords in *Council of Civil Service Unions v. Minister for the Civil Service* [1985] 1 AC 374 at 410. This was a shorthand way of expressing Lord Greene MR's well-known proposition in *Associated Provincial Picture Houses Ltd. v. Wednesbury Corporation* [1948] 1 KB 223 at 229 to this effect:

> "... a person entrusted with a discretion must, so to speak, direct himself properly in law. He must call his own attention to the matters which he is bound to consider. He must exclude from his consideration matters which are irrelevant to what he has to consider. If he does not obey those rules, he may truly be said, as is often said, to be acting 'unreasonably' . Similarly, there may be something so absurd that no sensible person could ever dream that it lay within the powers of the authority. Warrington L.J. in *Short v. Poole Corporation* [1926] Ch. 66 at 90 gave the example of the red-haired teacher, dismissed because she had red hair. That is unreasonable in one sense. In another sense it is taking into consideration extraneous matters. It is so unreasonable that it might almost be described as being done in bad faith; and, in fact, all these things run into one another."

The threshold for the court's intervention under this ground, as the courts have repeatedly said, is necessarily high. Where a departmental head of government is entrusted by the legislature with administrative responsibilities it is not for the courts to say how those responsibilities should be discharged. It is only where the administrator has acted beyond the range of responses reasonably open to him under the statutory scheme that the court's power of intervention under s.21I of the High Court Ordinance, Cap. 4, can properly be invoked.

The situations adumbrated in Lord Greene MR's judgment, as quoted above, range over a wide spectrum. Since 1947 when the *Wednesbury Corporation* case was decided the proposition has been refined. It is impossible to set out all the cases decided on Wednesbury principles since that time. At one end of the spectrum is a case like *R. v. Secretary of State for Foreign and Commonwealth Affairs ex parte World Development Movement Ltd* [1995] 1 WLR 386 [The Pergau dam case] where the Divisional Court in acceding to the application for judicial review found that the Minister, when he purported to exercise power conferred by statute, had taken into account considerations outside the scope of the statute. The case turned on the proper construction of s.1(1) of the Overseas Development and Cooperation Act 1980 of the United Kingdom which authorised the Secretary of State to give overseas assistance for the purpose of promoting development of an overseas territory or the welfare of its people: The project to be funded, the Pergau dam hydro-electric project in Malaysia, was not economically sound: That was conceded: But the Secretary of State contended that there were wider political and economic considerations to be taken into account in deciding to give financial assistance to Malaysia, including the fulfilment of an undertaking given by the former Prime Minister a few years before. The Divisional Court held that the Secretary of State had gone outside the statutory purpose: That of promoting development overseas. The case falls more comfortably into the category of "illegality" rather than that of "Wednesbury unreasonableness" so-called.

At the other end of the spectrum are those instances, often asserted but seldom with success, of administrators whose decisions in themselves are said to be "Wednesbury unreasonable": Lord Diplock in *Council of Civil Service Unions* at 410 spoke of them as decisions "so outrageous in its defiance of logic or of accepted moral standards that no sensible person who had applied his mind to the question to be decided could have arrived at it." In more homely language Henry LJ in *R. v. Lord Chancellor, ex p. Maxwell* [1996] 4 AER 751 at 756a referred to these decisions which warrant interference as ones which "jump off the page at you". None of the three judgments in the Court of Appeal referred in terms to "*Wednesbury* unreasonableness", but the applicants in their printed case seek to justify that court's decision on that ground. They say that in the circumstance where there was, in February 1999, no operable scheme whereby an application could have been made for a certificate of entitlement, it was "*Wednesbury* unreasonable" to rely on the absence of the certificate to decide on removal. If, by this, the applicants meant that, in the circumstances prevailing (in what Nazareth V-P in his judgment called "the interregnum"), it was "outrageous" to have overstayers and illegal migrants removed, they failed in the Court of Appeal. The Court of Appeal did not quash the removal orders on this ground. What, then, was the basis upon which that court did quash the removal orders? One would look in vain to the application lodged under Order 53 r.3 for an answer.

The Director's power of removal

No administrator ever exercises power in a vacuum. It is always done in the context of a statutory scheme, a legislative framework. As the Chief Justice has remarked in his judgment, the policy reasons laid down by the legislature in enacting Immigration (Amendment) Ordinances No. 2 and 3 included the discouragement of illegal entry into Hong Kong and of illegal stay here in contravention of conditions of stay, as well as the prevention of queue-jumping ahead of Mainland residents who have applied for certificates of entitlement but have not broken the law.

What the Director had in February 1999, underpinning his exercise of power under s.19(1)(b)(ii), was an incomplete statutory scheme. He was faced with applicants claiming to be permanent residents; but they were in fact Mainland residents with no certificates of entitlement and were illegally in Hong Kong. The scheme introduced by the No. 3 Ordinance was incomplete only to this extent: We had in *Ng Ka Ling v. Director of Immigration* (1999) 2 HKCFAR 4 declared as unconstitutional the provisions in that Ordinance in so far as they required permanent residents of the Hong Kong SAR to hold one-way permits issued by the Mainland authorities before they could enjoy the right of abode. We were at pains to emphasize that the provisions in Ordinance No. 3 for *verification of* a person's claim to be a permanent resident remained intact. There were provisions in Part 1B of the Immigration Ordinance, governing the exercise of the Director's functions and duties relating to persons claiming to be permanent residents by descent under paragraph 2(c) of Schedule 1, which survived the constitutional challenge in *Ng Ka Ling*. Section 2AA(1), as excised by this Court's judgment, reads:

"2AA **Establishing statutes of permanent resident under paragraph 2(c) of Schedule 1**

(1) A person's status as a permanent resident of the Hong Kong Special Administrative Region under para 2(c) of Schedule 1 can only be established by his holding of:

(a) a valid certificate of entitlement issued to him

This was not a provision the Director could ignore. The statutory requirement that the status as a permanent resident could only be established by holding a certificate of entitlement is wholly incompatible with what the applicants claim in their application for judicial review: A declaration that they are permanent residents with the right of abode and entitled not to have removal orders made against them.

Whilst it is true that in February 1999 there was no procedure in place whereby a person claiming a right of abode under Part 1B could in fact have made an application for a certificate of entitlement, this did not mean that the Director's exercise of lawful power under s.19(1)(b)(ii) was at large. Whether there was a full scheme in place or not, the applicants had no right to remain in Hong Kong. In the exercise of his power of removal the Director had obviously to bear in mind the policy of the legislature under Part 1B: the scheme for the orderly entry of permanent residents and the discouragement of illegal entry and stay. The fact that part of the machinery had broken down did not mean that the power of removal was not governed by statute. The absence of a workable scheme in February 1999 meant simply that, at that time, residents in the Mainland claiming the status of permanent residents were unable to put forward their claim: This did not amount per se to the deprivation of a core right guaranteed by the Basic Law.

It is of some significance to note that, in their applications for relief under Order 53 r3 of the Rules of the High Court, the applicants had sought an order of *mandamus* requiring the Director to "specify by a notice in the Gazette the manner in which a person who is not overseas or not in Macau or Taiwan and who claims to be a permanent resident under paragraph 2(c) of Schedule 1 Immigration Ordinance might apply under section 2AB(1) for a certificate of entitlement...". This is directed to the absence of a workable scheme following *Ng Ka Ling*: not to the legality of the exercise of power under s.19(1)(b)(ii). It failed in limine and was not pursued on appeal. It must be assumed therefore that, in the Court of Appeal, the applicants were no longer maintaining that the Director was under the duty as alleged.

The Court of Appeal

It is not easy to extract from the three judgments of the Court of Appeal the *ratio decidendi* for the decision to quash the removal orders.

All three judges concluded that the power of removal under s.19(1)(b)(ii) was a discretionary power: Rightly so: Section 19(1) says "A removal order may be made against a person requiring him to leave Hong Kong ... etc": This means that the Director has a discretion not to order removal even if the conditions in subsection (b)(ii) are satisfied. This is right as far as it goes. But in the context of the removal of a person falling within Part 1B of the Immigration Ordinance the Director must have regard to the overall objective of the statutory scheme. As mentioned earlier, the provisions of s.2AA(2) remained in place after this Court's judgment in *Ng Ka Ling*.

Likewise s.2AB(5) which says:

> "(5) For the removal of doubt, it is hereby declared that the making of an application under subsection (1) does not give the applicant the right of abode or right to land or remain in Hong Kong pending the decision of the Director on the application."

The intention of the legislature could not have been clearer. It was not for the Director to frustrate that intention.

Mr Justice Chan CJHC in considering the Director's exercise of discretionary power to remove under s.19(1)(b)(ii) said that the Director might have to take into account "policy matters such as the number of possible applications" and whether the applicants had come illegally or had remained in breach of conditions of stay and the "integrity of the statutory scheme". And he added:

> "If the Director decides to allow every such applicant to remain in Hong Kong pending verification of his claim, this may encourage other people, whether they are genuine applicants or not, to come to Hong Kong by every possible means, whether legal or illegal. In that case, the whole certificate of entitlement scheme will break down. This would also defeat the purpose of an orderly settlement in Hong Kong of persons residing in the Mainland who fall within the third category of Article 24(2)."
>
> All of this seems to argue strongly for a decision to remove.

The applicants had not put forward any ground for remaining in Hong Kong other than a right to remain. Once it was clear that they had no such right, since they did not have certificates of entitlement issued to them, what possible grounds remained for impeaching the Director's decision? The Chief Judge in his judgment spoke of "the nature" of the applicants' claims, the "quality of the supporting material" and the Director's failure to consider such material: But this is to say, in effect, that the Director had a duty to consider the material. What material? And more importantly, wherein lies that duty? The Chief Judge seems to have found the duty in the Basic Law itself: In parts of his judgment he spoke of the Director's duty "to implement the Basic Law".

This is a misapprehension of the constitutional position. The Basic Law is the constitutional framework for the Hong Kong SAR. All statutes passed by the legislature must be consistent with that framework. By its very nature, the definition of functions and responsibilities in the Basic Law is stated in broad and general terms. Administrators function within the confines of their particular statutes. Hence, the question as to the factors which an administrator is bound to take into account in exercising a statutory power is determined generally by construing the statute which conferred the power. It would be a rare case indeed where, in administrative law terms, there is such a gap in the statutory framework that the exercise of power has to be judged, not by construing the relevant statute, but by the Basic Law itself. The present is not such a case. In this regard the Chief Judge erred.

Nazareth V-P appears to have taken a slightly different approach to that of the Chief Judge. He did not identify the source of the Director's duty but said nevertheless that there was a duty "to have regard to all relevant matters": This, the learned Vice-President said, should result in at least *some* persons not being removed: That is, those cases where the applicants'status could be "readily verified without the sort of effort or delay that would be unreasonable in the circumstances". The learned Vice-President added:

> "If the claim can be easily determined in a matter of days, it is difficult to see how removal before that is accomplished could be right. Conversely, if the claim is going to take months, it is equally not difficult to see why removal of such a person, whose entitlement to permanent resident status is not verified but only claimed, should not be reasonable."

The learned Vice-President did not explain how, faced with hundreds or perhaps thousands of "applications", the Director and his staff might distinguish between those which could be "easily determined in a matter of days" from those which required months of effort, without a fairly sophisticated system in place. This was, in effect, to impose upon the Director an administrative framework of the court's making: Until such system was in place, no removal order could lawfully be made in respect of persons coming within Part 1B of the Ordinance. Nowhere in the Immigration Ordinance can such a fetter on the exercise of power under s.19(1)(b)(ii) be found, expressly or by implication.

This point needs emphasis: In proceedings for judicial review, the ground of failure to take into account a relevant consideration can only be made out if the decision-maker has failed to take into account a consideration which he is bound to take into account in making that decision: see Mason J in *Minister for Aboriginal Affairs v. Peko-Wallsend Ltd* (1986) 162 CLR 24 at 39. What factors he is bound to take into account is determined by construing the statute conferring the power. If an administrator misconstrues a statute and asks himself the wrong question, or fails to ask himself the right question, the Court can properly intervene and quash his decision on the ground of illegality. But that question must be clearly identified: A vague statement pointing to "all relevant matters" is not enough.

When counsel asks: "Is the Director entitled to throw the applications into the waste-paper basket?", that is simply using a figure of speech. It obscures the reality on the ground. The Director is faced with a situation of mass applications, not simply a handful of envelopes where his officers have the time and leisure to examine the individual contents. It requires the setting up of procedures so that his officers can handle them effectively. If the Director, as the person ultimately responsible for administering the statutory scheme under the Immigration Ordinance, has a duty to consider humanitarian grounds, then he will have to establish internal guidelines for his officers. The expression "strong humanitarian grounds" has been used repeatedly in the course of argument: But where in the legal framework within which the Director operates does one find a duty to consider strong humanitarian grounds? And is there a distinction between strong humanitarian grounds and humanitarian grounds simpliciter? The Chief Judge found such a duty in the Basic Law: A finding which is unsound. Nazareth V-P never sought to identify the source of that duty.

Mortimer V-P appears to have adopted a similar approach to that of the Chief Judge. He said that, in the absence of a complete scheme for dealing with applications for certificates of entitlement, the Director "must at least consider the evidence which that person seeks to put before him in support of the claim. Failure to do so renders the decision unlawful.... *The authority for such an enquiry by the Director rests within Article 24 [of the Basic Law] itself"*. [Emphasis added]. For reasons which I have earlier put forward this approach is unsound.

Discipline of law

The limited role of the Court in exercising its supervisory responsibilities under s.21I of the High Court Ordinance must constantly be borne in mind. A crucial aspect of the rule of law in Hong Kong is that administrators exercise their functions and duties within the law. To do so, the law must be clear. Where a statute in express terms requires a decision-maker to take into account certain factors and an applicant can show that he has failed to do so, that is one ground for judicial review. *Certiorari* may issue, depending on the importance of the factor omitted: It may be so insignificant that the failure to take it into account could not have materially affected the decision. Otherwise, the decision may properly be impugned. But where the conditions governing the exercise of power are satisfied, to seek to impeach the decision nevertheless is a very different matter. It brings the decision-maker within the area of an *abuse of power*: The power is undoubtedly there, but it has been *improperly exercised*. If the court is to intervene, it can only do so on clearly stated grounds. That is why Order 53 r.3(2)(a) of the Rules of the High Court governing judicial review proceedings is stated in mandatory terms: An application for leave must be made by filing a notice in Form 86A containing a statement of the *grounds* upon which it is sought. This makes for good administration under the rule of law. If the decision-making process is vitiated by the administrator's failure to take some factor or another into account, those factors must be clearly identified, so that the next time round the decision-maker would not offend again. These are basic propositions, but failure to bear them firmly in mind led the Court of Appeal into error.

The Court of Appeal was persuaded to quash the removal orders because a number of factors relevant to the decision-making process were not considered by the Director. But these were put in vague and general terms in the three judgments. They bear little relationship to the grounds stated in the formal application lodged by the applicants purportedly in compliance with Order 53 r.3. The application itself, containing the "grounds" on which relief was sought, as amended, numbers well over 50 paragraphs. Paragraphs 37 and 41 have been augmented and subdivided into separate paragraphs by amendment. Even in its unamended form the application should have alerted the judge dealing with ex parte leave to the possibility that there was something flawed in the process. No system of administrative law can operate in the amorphous way seen in this case. Grounds for quashing the exercise of administrative power by the court if well-founded should be capable of being stated clearly and succinctly, in a few numbered paragraphs. I would emphasize the word *few*. Once leave to apply for judicial review is granted, amendment of the grounds should rarely occur. All too often applications are made for amendment after leave to issue proceedings has been granted, as if Order 53 r.3 were simply the portals to a playground of infinite possibilities where the administrators could then be made to leap through more and more hoops of fire. It is up to the judges of the High Court to stop this kind of extravaganza.

What has happened in this case is simply this: The discipline of law and of legal procedures broke down in the lower courts. The proceedings in the Court of Appeal became an academic discourse.

It is to be hoped that nothing similar will be seen again in this Court.

Conclusion

In my judgment the Court of Appeal has clearly erred in reversing Yeung J. I agree with the orders proposed by the Chief Justice.

Mr Justice Ching PJ:

I have had the advantage of reading the judgment of the Chief Justice in draft form. I, too, would uphold this appeal for the reasons set out by the Chief Justice and I would only add the following brief comments.

I am in no doubt but that the Standing Committee of the National People's Congress had power to make the interpretation which it did on 26 June 1999. It was the exercise of the power vested in it by Article 67(4) of the Chinese Constitution. That power is repeated in the first paragraph of Article 158 of the Basic Law with express reference to that law. Nowhere is there any provision by which it divested itself of that power or by which it assigned that power to this or any other Court. Instead, the second paragraph of the Article authorised the Courts of Hong Kong in adjudicating cases 'to interpret on their own ... the provisions of this law which are within the limits of the autonomy of the region.' The authorisation is therefore limited in scope. The third paragraph of the Article then requires the Courts in Hong Kong, when adjudicating cases where it is necessary to interpret the provisions of the Basic Law concerning affairs which are the responsibility of the Central People's Government or concerning the relationship between the Central Authorities and Hong Kong, to seek an interpretation of the relevant provisions before making a final judgment which is not appealable. This paragraph does not purport to bestow any power upon the Standing Committee. That would have been unnecessary since the relevant power was already vested in it. Instead, the Article placed a duty upon the Courts in Hong Kong to seek an interpretation when the circumstances so required.

I am equally in no doubt that the Interpretation took effect as from 1 July 1997. In making it, the Standing Committee did not purport to act, and has never purported to act, as a Court. Nor did it purport to be amending the law. It was doing exactly what it said it was doing, namely interpreting the law. That must mean that they were explaining what the law is and has been since the Basic Law came into effect.

I am in agreement with the Chief Justice that the Interpretation means that as from 1 July 1997, so far as relevant to the arguments put forward to us, that persons from the Mainland seeking to settle in Hong Kong need both a one-way exit permit and a certificate of entitlement which are to be applied for in the Mainland. The difference between that and what was laid down by this Court is the requirement for the one-way permit. In the period between our judgment (29 January 1999) and the Interpretation (26 June 1999) there was no system in place by which application could be made for a certificate of entitlement.

As a matter of law the position is clear. The respondents had either entered Hong Kong illegally or had stayed in Hong Kong in breach of the conditions upon which they were permitted to enter. They had no legal claim to stay. Whatever scheme for an application for a certificate of entitlement was or was not in place, they had no legal claim to remain in Hong Kong. The Director was therefore justified, as a matter of law, in making the removal orders under section 19(1)(b) of the Immigration Ordinance, Cap. 115. This would have been so whether the orders had been made before our judgment, after our judgment up to the Interpretation or after the Interpretation. The respondents, in these circumstances can only rely upon an exercise of discretion by the Director in their favour. They cannot succeed on that basis. First, given that such a discretion exists, no appeal was made to the Director to exercise it in their favour. It is for a person seeking an indulgence to persuade the relevant authority to give it to him. It is not for the authority to embark upon an enquiry as to whether or not or, if so, how he should exercise it. Secondly, there is clear authority, cited by the Chief Justice, that although the discretion may exist the Director is not bound to exercise it. Thirdly, even if it be shown that the Director ought to have exercised his discretion and in so doing refused or neglected to take into consideration the changes in the law between 29 January 1999 and 26 June 1999 that would have made no difference.

I would uphold the appeal but, at the request of the appellant make no order as to costs save that the respondents' costs be taxed under the Legal Aid Regulations. I agree with the orders proposed by the Chief Justice.

Mr Justice Bokhary PJ:

As to the Standing Committee of the National People's Congress's Interpretation of 26 June 1999 ("the Interpretation"), I agree – and confine myself to saying that I agree – that it has the effect in law stated by the Chief Justice and Sir Anthony Mason NPJ.

Turning to the Court of Appeal's judgment in the present case, I say at once that I fully recognize the great care which the learned judges of that court took in deciding what ought to be done in the situation facing them. But there is now no need to pronounce on whether they were right or wrong in law on the basis of the understanding of the position prevailing at the time of their judgment.

What now matters is as follows. The removal orders made by the Director of Immigration in the present case were made between the time of this Court's judgments of 29 January 1999 in *Ng Ka Ling v. Director of Immigration* (1999) 2 HKCFAR 4 and *Chan Kam Nga v. Director of Immigration* (1999) 2 HKCFAR 82 and the time of the Interpretation five months later. That being so, it was not possible for the Director, when making the removal orders, to "understand correctly the law that regulates his decision-making power [so as to] give effect to it". The words which I have just quoted are those used by Lord Diplock in *CCSU v. Minister for Civil Service* [1985] AC 374 at p.410F when identifying the first duty of an administrative decision-maker. Accordingly the removal orders in question have been vitiated by the operation of classic judicial review principles fundamental to the preservation of the rule of law.

It is true that the position under the Interpretation is less favourable to the applicants than was the position as it was understood to be at the time when the removal orders were made. But that places no real impediment in the applicants' path. If they had proceeded on the basis of what the Interpretation says, they would undoubtedly have applied to the Director on humanitarian grounds to exercise his discretion not to make removal orders against them.

It would be sufficient for the applicants' purposes in the present appeal if humanity was a consideration which the Director had to take into account. As it happens, it is even more. Humanity is the application. To ignore it would be exactly the same as throwing the applications into the wastepaper basket unread. The Director would not have been entitled to do that. And in fairness to him, I feel bound to make it clear that I cannot imagine that he would have dreamt of doing anything of the kind. For that would have been a wholesale abandonment of his undoubted duty to exercise his statutory powers fairly and properly.

I cannot improve on how Prof. Jeffrey Jowell QC puts it in his recent article "Of Vires and Vacuums: The Constitutional Context of Judicial Review" [1999] PL Autumn 448. He powerfully points out (at p.460) that "the powers intended by a legislative scheme ...must not be construed in a vacuum", that it is necessary "to identify the underlying principles which should govern the decision in question" and that:

> "To this end the general notions of fairness that may reside in the common law may prove helpful, but it is more helpful still to engage openly with the necessary qualities of a modern constitutional democracy."

That approach is, as I see it, by far the most likely one to secure the general public's understanding of, and support for, the rule of law as a practical concept in people's daily lives. The reality is as John Austin portrayed it (in "Lectures on Jurisprudence or the Philosophy of Positive Law", ed. Robert Campbell, 5th ed. (1885), vol. 1, p. 485) when he said that: "The conduct of nineteen men out of twenty, in nineteen cases out of twenty, is rather guided by a surmise as to the law, than by a knowledge of it." And that surmise must surely be based essentially on their appreciation of the qualities of the society in which they live.

In Hong Kong where we aspire to be humane as well as orderly, it is plain that the Director would have been duty-bound at least to read the applications to see if they or any one or more of them disclosed a strong and obvious case for a favourable exercise on humanitarian grounds of his discretion. By a "strong" case, I mean one which stands out even among so many other cases deserving sympathy. By an "obvious" case, I mean one where the material facts are clear or easily verifiable.

It is true that even where an administrative decision has been vitiated by a failure on the part of the decision-maker to understand correctly the law regulating his decision-making power, the courts may nevertheless in certain circumstances decline to quash that decision. Thus they may so decline if it can be seen that the same decision would inevitably have been made even upon a correct understanding and application of the relevant law. This "inevitability" test was endorsed by the Privy Council in *Nguyen Tuan Cuong v. Director of Immigration* [1997] 1 WLR 68 at p.77B. In my view, it cannot be said that the removal orders were inevitable. For no open-minded person would attempt to say for certain what the result would have been if humanitarian applications had been made and considered.

I would dismiss these appeals by the Director. For in my judgment, these removal orders should remain quashed. That is how I see the law. That would leave the Director in a position to consider–with the benefit of legal advice in the context of the up–to–date situation and untrammeled by previous removal orders – whether or not to make fresh removal orders. Perhaps he would not make any. But if my view of the law does not prevail and the removal orders are restored, then I can only emphatically express the hope that the applicants' cases for revocation will receive the sympathetic consideration called for by their special circumstances.

Sir Anthony Mason NPJ:

I agree with the reasons for judgment of the Chief Justice. In the light of the importance of the cases and the novelty of the issues, it is appropriate that I state in my own words the basis of my thinking on some issues. The comments which follow are not intended to qualify in any way my agreement with the Chief Justice's reasons.

The power to make an Interpretation and its binding effect

The Basic Law is the constitution of the Hong Kong Special Administrative Region of the People's Republic of China established under the principle of "one country, two systems". It is a national law of the PRC, being an enactment of the National People's Congress made in the exercise of legislative powers conferred upon the NPC by the PRC Constitution.

Article 8 of the Basic Law preserves the common law in Hong Kong, Article 80 vests the judicial power in the courts of the Region and Article 81 maintains the judicial system previously practised in Hong Kong except for changes consequent upon the establishment of the Court of Final Appeal of the HKSAR. Article 81 is followed by Article 82 which vests the power of final adjudication in the Region in the Court of Final Appeal. By these and other provisions, the Basic Law maintains the common law and a common law judicial system in the Region. This conjunction of a common law system under a national law within the larger framework of Chinese constitutional law is a fundamental aspect of the principle of "one country, two systems" which is recited in the Preamble to the Basic Law.

As is the case with constitutional divisions of power, a link between the courts of the Region and the institutions of the People's Republic of China is required. In a nation–wide common law system, the link would normally be between the regional courts and the national constitutional court or the national supreme court. Here, however, there are not only two different systems, but also two different legal systems. In the context of "one country, two systems", Article 158 of the Basic Law provides a very different link. That is because the Article, in conformity with Article 67(4) of the PRC Constitution, vests the general power of interpretation of the Basic Law, not in the People's Supreme Court or the national courts, but in the NPC Standing Committee.

Consistently with that vesting of the general power of interpretation in the Standing Committee, the Standing Committee authorizes the courts of the Region to interpret "on their own, in adjudicating cases" the provisions of the Basic Law which are within the limits of the autonomy of the Region. The expression "on their own" stands in contrast to the mandatory reference requirement under Article 158(3) which applies to the Court of Final Appeal in relation to what the Chief Justice calls "the excluded provisions".

The expression "in adjudicating cases" is of particular significance. In the common law world, these words would be surplusage. Interpretation of a law, even of a constitution, is the business of the courts, being an incident of the adjudication of cases. In the People's Republic of China, however, under Article 67(4), the Standing Committee of the NPC exercises, as well as other functions and powers, the power "to interpret laws", because the PRC Constitution does not provide for a separation of powers that is the same as or similar to the common law doctrine of the separation of powers. Article 57 of the PRC Constitution provides that the NPC is the highest organ of state power and the NPCSC is its permanent body.

The Standing Committee's power to interpret laws is necessarily exercised from time to time otherwise than in the adjudication of cases. So the expression "in adjudicating cases" makes it clear that the power of interpretation enjoyed by the courts of the Region is limited in that way and differs from the general and free–standing power of interpretation enjoyed by the Standing Committee under Article 67(4) of the PRC Constitution and Article 158(1) of the Basic Law.

This conclusion may seem strange to a common lawyer but, in my view, it follows inevitably from a consideration of the text and structure of Article 158, viewed in the light of the context of the Basic Law and its character as the constitution for the HKSAR embodied in a national law enacted by the PRC.

This conclusion on the power of the Standing Committee to interpret under Article 158(1), as the Chief Justice points out, gains some support from Professor Yash Ghai's work: "Hong Kong's New Constitutional Order" (2nd ed 1999) p.198. There the author concluded that the Standing Committee has a general power to interpret the Basic Law. The power is "plenary in that it covers all the provisions of the Basic Law; this power may be exercised in the absence of litigation."

In argument, it was submitted that the last two sentences of Art. 158(3) support a different conclusion, namely that the Standing Committee's power of interpretation is confined to matters referred to it by the Court of Final Appeal. The argument is that the last two sentences are confined to an interpretation given on such a reference and that is significant because the penultimate sentence requires the courts of the Region to follow that interpretation and the last sentence states that "judgments previously rendered shall not be affected". The absence of similar provisions in relation to an interpretation by the Standing Committee otherwise than on a reference, so the argument runs, suggests the absence of such a power, that being a conclusion which, speaking generally, might appeal to a common lawyer.

In my view, the suggested conclusion does not follow from the matters on which it is based. The general power of interpretation of the Basic Law vested in the Standing Committee by Article 158(1) is plainly a power to give an authoritative interpretation of the Basic Law binding on all institutions in the Region. There was no occasion to spell out the obvious in the Basic Law. Nonetheless it may have seemed desirable to make specific provision for what was to happen when an interpretation is to be given on a reference, in order to make clear beyond any doubt, the effect the Interpretation would have when it was returned to the Court of Final Appeal on the reference, and to ensure that it was the interpretation of the Standing Committee rather than the Court's judgment applying the interpretation that would have authoritative force. The penultimate sentence, it will be noted, is directed to "the courts of the Region" not simply to the Court of

Final Appeal.

As to the effect of a free-standing interpretation by the Standing Committee, that is, an interpretation given otherwise than on a reference, judgments previously given are protected by the vesting of judicial power in the courts of the Region and the vesting of the power of final adjudication in the Court of Final Appeal. Under the common law, a final judgment would not be re-opened as between the parties to the litigation in which the judgment was delivered by reason of the subsequent adoption of a new interpretation of the relevant legal instrument.

I conclude the discussion of this point by observing that, although the Interpretation is made by the Standing Committee, the permanent body of the NPC, which is the highest organ of state of power and exercises legislative power, the Interpretation is not *simply* legislation, as an amendment to the Basic Law would be. It is expressed to be an Interpretation and to state "the legislative intent" of the Basic Law in a way that differs from the view taken by the Court in *Ng Ka Ling*. It satisfies the requirements of Article 158(1) so that it is an "interpretation" within the meaning of that provision with the consequences that attach to such an interpretation.

The actual effect of the interpretation

On this question, there is no occasion for me to add to the reasoning of the Chief Justice except to emphasize the point that, although Clause 1 is expressed to be an interpretation of Article 22(4), not of Article 24, the Clause is clearly linked to Article 24, the very purpose of the Interpretation being to displace the construction placed on the two Articles in *Ng Ka Ling*.

The form in which the Interpretation is expressed is no doubt a reflection of the Standing Committee's view, expressed in the preamble to the Interpretation, that the Court of Final Appeal in *Ng Ka Ling* should have referred the interpretation of Article 22(4), an "excluded provision", to the Standing Committee under the mandatory requirement of article 158(3) of the Basic Law. In *Ng Ka Ling*, this Court saw the critical question as one which involved the interpretation or inter-action of Articles 22(4) and 24(2) and applied the "predominant test". The Standing Committee, however, has simply focussed on the interpretation of the excluded provision, Article 22(4), and has issued the Interpretation of that provision which necessarily impacts upon, and has consequences for, Article 24(2). What this means for the mandatory reference requirement is not a matter which arises for consideration in this case.

The challenge to the Director's decisions

The effect of the Interpretation in speaking to the meaning of the Basic Law, as it has operated from the time of its commencement, has the consequence that the Director misapprehended, through no fault of his own, the law, that is, the legislative scheme. But that misapprehension was not an error of law which affected his decisions to make orders for removal. The validation of the entire legislative scheme by the Interpretation did not affect the legality or the relevance of the grounds on which the orders were made.

Had the applicants and the Director appreciated that the legislative scheme was valid in its entirety, the applicants might well have asked the Director to refuse, on discretionary grounds, to make removal orders. If the Director were under an enforceable duty to take account of discretionary considerations, then it might be said that he failed to take account of considerations relevant to the making of his decisions with the consequence that they were vitiated.

However, as the Chief Justice has pointed out, there is no enforceable duty imposed by the Ordinance to take account of discretionary considerations. The Director can have regard to them, if he so chooses, but he is at liberty to disregard them. The fact that there is no enforceable duty to take account of them means that disregarding them cannot constitute an error of law: *Minister for Aboriginal Affairs v. Peko-Wallsend Limited* (1986) 162 CLR 24 at 39.

It follows that the Director made no error of law in failing to take account of discretionary considerations, assuming that there was such a failure on his part, a question which has been left unresolved. In this respect, it should be noted that the Director was not asked to take account of such matters, the applicants then being concerned to establish their claimed right of abode.

In the events which happened the Director made no relevant error of law and as relevant error on the part of the decision-maker that affects his decision is the foundation of relief by way of judicial review, the applicants' case must fail.

The applicants sought to overcome this obstacle by drawing upon the speeches in *Kleinwort Benson Ltd v. Lincoln City Council* [1998] 3 WLR 1095 to support the proposition that a change in the law, operating retrospectively, cannot alter historical facts. So much may be accepted. In that case, an alteration in the law, as it was then understood to be, brought about by judicial decision, did not convert a payment, which was not made under mistake of law when the payment was made, into a payment made under a mistake of law. That was because it was the payer's mind at the time of payment that was relevant. There is, however, no parallel between such a case and making of an administrative decision the validity of which depends upon the application to it of the applicable law, even if it is a law whose true import is ascertained or declared after the making of the decision.

In the final analysis the most that can be said is that the applicants, as a result of the Standing Committee's Interpretation, have lost a possible opportunity of advancing a case based on discretionary considerations, which they might have advanced had the effect of the Interpretation been known before the removal orders came to be made. Although the applicants could not reasonably be expected at that time to act on the possibility that such an interpretation would issue – an expectation that would be attributed to them in the case of an interpretation issued by an appellate court in a common law system – for reasons already stated that circumstance does not give rise to relief for error of law on the arguments presented on the applicants' behalf.

Even if the loss of a relevant opportunity were to be seen as amounting to an injustice, brought about by a change in the law operating with effect from 1 July 1997, that loss does not fall within an established ground for relief. Under the common law as it presently stands, loss of an opportunity to advance a case attracts relief when it proceeds from a denial of natural justice on the part of the decision-maker but there was no denial of natural justice by the decision-maker here. Furthermore, there is no legal basis in this case for attributing to the Director the loss of such an opportunity.

The undertaking, offered by Mr Ma SC on behalf of the Director, to consider revocation of the removal orders addresses this problem among others and will enable the Director to take account of discretionary considerations, if he is so minded.

Chief Justice Li:

The Court is unanimous in its conclusions on the Interpretation. These have been summarised in my judgment in the section headed "Summary of views on Interpretation".

The Court, by majority (Mr Justice Bokhary PJ dissenting), allows the appeal by the Director. By such majority: (1) The order of the judge in the judicial review proceedings is restored and the applicants' applications for judicial review are dismissed. (2) The order of the judge in the habeas corpus proceedings is restored and the writs of habeas corpus issued in respect of the applicants are discharged. (3) There should be no order as to costs save that the applicants' (that is, the respondents') costs be taxed in accordance with Legal Aid Regulations.

With these orders, the Director's undertakings to the Court are effective. These have been set out in my judgment in the section headed "*Director's position following outcome of this appeal*".

Chief Justice (Andrew Li)

Permanent Judge (Henry Litton)

Permanent Judge (Charles Ching)

Permanent Judge (Kemal Bokhary)

Non-Permanent Judge (Anthony Mason)

Mr Geoffrey Ma SC and Mr Joseph Fok SC (instructed by the Department of Justice) for the Appellant

Mr Denis Chang SC, Ms Gladys Li SC and Ms Margaret Ng (instructed by M/s Pam Baker and Company and assigned by the Director of Legal Aid) for the Respondents

---

吳新穩作為吳家豪、吳家煒、吳佳敏的父親及起訴監護人 對 入境事務處處長

HCAL 22/2000

簡略案情

申請人吳新穩先生，以起訴監護人身份代表其三名子女，家豪、家煒和佳敏向法庭提出司法覆核許可申請，要求法庭推翻入境事務處處長要遣送家豪、家煒和佳敏回內地的決定。資料顯示，申請人與林女士在內地同居，並且分別於 1994 年、1995 年和 1997 年在內地誕下家豪、家煒和佳敏。三名子女於 2000 年 1 月非法進入香港，並且在 2000 年 1 月 29 日，由申請人陪同下向入境事務處自首，要求留在香港居留，但處長拒絕他們的申請，並決定將他們遣送離開香港。事實上，申請人於 1983 年在香港與另一名女士結婚，而該婚姻到目前仍屬有效。據申請人稱，林女士身體不佳，不能適當地照顧三名子女。他並指出其三名子女在內地因未有戶籍，所以不能以香港永久性居民在內地出生的非婚生子女身份申請到香港，令他們長期不能夠根據《基本法》行使他們聲稱擁有的香港永久性居民身份。

裁決摘要

原訟庭法官確認全國人大常委會對《基本法》第 22 條第 4 款所作的解釋在香港法院有約束力，因此，就算根據《基本法》第 24 條第 2 項第 3 款申請人的三名子女擁有香港居留權。要行使該居留權，他們必須在內地申請和獲得有關當局發出的單程證才能合法到香港行使居留權。而且，根據入境事務處處長向內地公安局的出入境管理署的查詢，非婚生子女可以加入其母親的戶籍，並能以香港永久性居民在內地出生的非婚生子女身份，申請到香港定居。因此，法官認為入境處處長的決定是合符情理的，法院並沒有理由干預其決定。據此，該申請被撤銷。

HCAL 22/2000

香港特別行政區
高等法院
原訟法庭

憲法及行政訴訟 2000 年第 22 號

申請人	吳新穩為吳家豪、吳家煒、 吳佳敏的父親及起訴監護人
	及
答辯人	入境事務處處長

主審法官：高等法院原訟法庭法官楊振權

聆訊日期：2000 年 12 月 5 日

判案書日期：2000 年 12 月 5 日

判案書

申請人吳新穩先生以起訴監護人身份代表其三名子女，家豪、家煒和佳敏向法庭提出司法覆核許可申請，要求法庭推翻入境事務處處長要遣送家豪、家煒和佳敏回國內的決定，令他們能留在香港與申請人團聚。

家豪、家煒和佳敏分別在 1994 年、1995 年和 1997 年在國內出生，他們的生母是林永花女士。

家豪、家煒和佳敏於 2000 年 1 月非法進入香港，並且在 2000 年 1 月 29 日由申請人陪同下向入境事務處自首，要求留在香港居留，但處長拒絕他們的申請並決定將他們遣送離開香港。

資料顯示申請人與林永花女士在國內同居，並且誕下該三名非婚生子女。事實上，申請人在 1983 年在香港與唐彩霞女士結婚，該婚姻到目前仍屬有效。申請人指稱林永花女士身體不佳故不能適當地照顧三名子女。他並指出三名子女在國內未有戶藉，所以不能以香港永久性居民在國內出生的非婚生子女的身份申請到香港，令他們長期不能夠根據基本法行使他們聲稱擁有的香港永久性居民身份。

首先本席須指出申請人的三名子女都是非法入境的人士，是沒有權留在香港，亦沒有合理的期望可以獲准在香港長期居留。全國人民代表大會常務委員會在 1999 年 6 月 26 日就基本法第二十二條第四款作出解釋，該解釋照錄如下：

> 「《中華人民共和國香港特別行政區基本法》第二十二條第四款關於"中國其他地區的人進入香港特別行政區，須辦理批准手續"的規定是指各省、自治區、直轄市的人，包括香港永久性居民在內地所生的中國藉子女，不論以何種事由要求進入香港特別行政區，均須依照國家有關法律行政法規的規定，向其所在地區的有關機構申請辦理批准手續，並須持有有關機構製發的有效証件方能進入香港特別行政區。各省、自治區、直轄市的人，包括香港永久性居民在國內所生的中國藉子女，進入香港特別行政區，如未按國家有關法律，行政法規的規定辦理相應的批准手續，是不合法的。」

人大常委會就基本法第二十二條第四款所作的解釋是清晰明確的，而有關的解釋對香港各級的法院有約束力，本席亦必須依循。這一點亦已得到香港終審法院在*劉港榕及另外十六人對入境事務處處長* [1999] 3 HKLRD 778 一案獲得認同。

申請人聲稱家豪、家煒和佳敏是非婚生子女，根據基本法第二十四條第二項第三款擁有香港居留權。即使申請人的聲稱獲得確認，要行使該居留權，申請人的三名子女必須在國內申請和獲得有關當局發出的單程証才能合法到香港行使居留權。

入境事務處處長亦曾向國內公安局的出入境管理署查詢，所獲的答覆是，從 1999 年 8 月 3 日起，非婚生子女可以加入其母親的戶籍，亦能以香港永久性居民在國內出生的非婚生子女身份，申請到香港定居。

本席必須指出背景與家豪、家煒和佳敏相同的人士數目衆多，他們要到香港行使居留權，都必須在國內輪候辦理有關手續，並且獲發單程証之後才能到香港行使居留權。如該等人士是非法入境者或逾期居留人士而又無須返回國內申請便可留在香港，必會引起其他人士爭相效法，對香港社會造成衝激，對其他合法輪候的人士亦是非常不公平。

處長秉公辦理，是合情合理的，申請人絕不應有任何投訴。當然在個別特殊情況下，處長可以行使酌情權，以人道的理據容許一名無合法居留的人士留在香港，但是是否行使酌情權或是否考慮行使有關酌情權，是由處長全權決定，其它的權力機構，包括法庭亦無權強制或指導處長應該如何行使法例賦予他的酌情權。

在本案，處長亦考慮過申請人的家庭情況，包括林永花女士的健康情況。處長認定並無足夠的人道理據，批准家豪、家煒和佳敏在未獲得單程証及在非法入境的情況之下，繼續在香港居留。處長的決定是合理和合法的。處長在作出有關決定的過程中，亦未犯有任何程序上的錯誤，所以無任何理據容許本席干預處長的決定。不論法庭怎樣同情申請人家庭的情況，包括子女們在國內非婚生子女的身份所引起的不便，本席亦須受法律的規限，亦無權推翻處長之決定。

本席必須依循人大常委會就基本法有關條款的解釋和終審法院就有關問題所作的裁決，所以本席亦可說是愛莫能助。申請人在本案未能夠提出任何可以爭拗的論點，支持他的申請，所以他的申請需要被撤消。

高等法院原訟法庭法官（楊振權）

出席：吳新穩為吳家豪、吳家煒、
吳佳敏的父親及起訴監護人（申請人）（無律師代表）
黃惠冲，高級政府律師，代表答辯人

第二十四條

香港特別行政區居民，簡稱香港居民，包括永久性居民和非永久性居民。

香港特別行政區永久性居民為：

（一）在香港特別行政區成立以前或以後在香港出生的中國公民；

（二）在香港特別行政區成立以前或以後在香港通常居住連續七年以上的中國公民；

（三）第（一）、（二）兩項所列居民在香港以外所生的中國籍子女；

（四）在香港特別行政區成立以前或以後持有效旅行證件進入香港、在香港通常居住連續七年以上並以香港為永久居住地的非中國籍的人；

（五）在香港特別行政區成立以前或以後第（四）項所列居民在香港所生的未滿二十一周歲的子女；

（六）第（一）至（五）項所列居民以外在香港特別行政區成立以前只在香港有居留權的人；

以上居民在香港特別行政區享有居留權和有資格依照香港特別行政區法律取得載明其居留權的永久性居民身份證。

香港特別行政區非永久性居民為：有資格依照香港特別行政區法律取得香港居民身份證，但沒有居留權的人。

案例

何謂“通常居住地”？

P.110 | 入境事務處處長 對 劉芳

P.117 | 王家衍 對 入境事務處處長

何謂“永久居住地”

P.122 | Gutierrez Josephine B. 對 人事登記處處長及人事登記審裁處

Gutierrez Joseph James, 未成年人經由他母親及起訴監護人 Gutierrez Josephine Balando 對 人事登記處處長及人事登記審裁處

子女是否必須是婚生子女？

P.136 | 吳嘉玲、吳丹丹 對 入境事務處處長；徐權能 對 入境事務處處長；入境事務處處長 對 張麗華

The Director Of Immigration v. Lau Fong

入境事務處處長 對 劉芳

HCAL 128/1999；CACV 287/2000；FACV 10/2003；FAMV 14/2003

簡略案情

答辯人於 1966 年在遼寧省大連市出生。據資料顯示，答辯人於 1993 年 1 月 9 日首次進入香港，當時她是過境前往孟加拉，並持有中華人民共和國護照。她於 1993 年 1 月 12 日在孟加拉與一名梁姓香港永久性居民結婚。答辯人於 1993 年 1 月 16 日使用孟加拉護照（護照上的名字是 Uasha Chakma）進入香港。基於她已成為一名香港永久性居民的妻子，她獲准逗留在香港直至 1993 年 4 月 16 日。然而，她逾期居留，並於 1993 年 5 月到醫院產女時被拘捕。1993 年 9 月 8 日，答辯人在警誡下表示，1991 年年底左右，她在深圳與一名已婚男子發展一段感情並於 1992 年 8 月左右發現懷孕。但她因為不想非婚生子，於是在男友的安排下飛往孟加拉與其梁姓朋友假結婚。

1995 年 12 月 23 日，答辯人持有一張單程證再次進入香港，並准許逗留至 1996 年 12 月 23 日。該證的發出日期為 1995 年 11 月 21 日。答辯人然後以該單程證為證明文件，取得一張香港身份證。其後，她被准許延長逗留至 2005 年 6 月 8 日。調查發現，1996 年 2 月 6 日一名入境事務主任接見答辯人時表示，她的丈夫是香港永久性居民，她是以妻子的身份申請單程證，並說他們於 1990 年 4 月在內地結婚。這明顯跟她較早時給予入境處的資料和有關的出入境記錄不符。1996 年，入境事務處處長（“處長”）求助於北京公安局，結果，內地出入境機關於 1999 年 6 月 28 日通知處長，答辯人的單程證是藉欺詐手段取得的，並要求取消其身份並遣返內地。然而，在得知該單程證是以欺詐手段取得後，答辯人仍然成功於 1999 年 9 月 3 日進入香港並有權逗留至 2005 年 6 月。

答辯人於 1999 年 9 月 5 日離開香港。但當答辯人企圖於 1999 年 10 月 4 日持香港身份證進入香港時，遭入境事務處根據《入境條例》第 115 章（“該條例”）第 11（1）條拒絕。她獲通知會被根據該條例第 18 條遣返內地，並且按照該條例第 32 條，被羈留以等候遣送。處長認為答辯人逗留香港的批准已於她 9 月份離港時失效，而且答辯人的單程證乃藉欺詐手段取得的，她的身份證因此屬無效，而其非永久性居民身份亦應予撤銷。對處長的決定，答辯人提請司法覆核。在原訟庭答辯人的申請被拒絕，但上訴庭推翻原訟庭的裁決並且撤銷了處長的相關決定。處長遂向終審法院提請上訴。

裁決摘要

《基本法》第 24 條確認“香港特別行政區非永久性居民為：有資格依照香港特別行政區法律取得香港居民身份證，但沒有居留權的人”。而根據《基本法》第 31 條，香港居民享有“旅行和出入境的自由”。而終審法院另一案例 *Gurung Kesh Bahadur 對 入境事務處處長* [2002]2 HKLRD 775，亦清楚指出《入境條例》第 11（10）條已於《基本法》實施時失去對香港居民的效力。因此，除非處長根據《人事登記條例》第 177 章附例第 19（3）條取消答辯人的身份證，否則該身份證仍然有效，即答辯人可以此根據《基本法》出入香港，處長無權加以阻止。終審法院認為處長不能以簡易的判斷來否決憲法賦予答辯人出入香港的權利。結果，處長的上訴被駁回。

FACV No. 10 of 2003

IN THE COURT OF FINAL APPEAL OF THE HONG KONG SPECIAL ADMINISTRATIVE REGION

FINAL APPEAL NO. 10 OF 2003 (CIVIL)
(ON APPEAL FROM CACV NO. 287 OF 2000)

Between:

THE DIRECTOR OF IMMIGRATION — Appellant

- and -

LAU FONG — Respondent

Court: Chief Justice Li, Mr Justice Bokhary PJ, Mr Justice Chan PJ, Mr Justice Ribeiro PJ and Sir Anthony Mason NPJ

Dates of Hearing: 8 and 9 March 2004

Date of Judgment: 26 March 2004

JUDGMENT

Chief Justice Li:
1. I agree with the judgment of Sir Anthony Mason NPJ.

Mr Justice Bokhary PJ:
2. I agree with the judgment of Sir Anthony Mason NPJ.

Mr Justice Chan PJ:
3. I agree with the judgment of Sir Anthony Mason NPJ.

Mr Justice Ribeiro PJ:
4. I agree with the judgment of Sir Anthony Mason NPJ.

Sir Anthony Mason NPJ:

Introduction

5. This is an appeal pursuant to leave granted by the Appeal Committee from a judgment of the Court of Appeal (Rogers VP, Woo JA and Sakhrani J) allowing the respondent's appeal from a judgment of the Court of First Instance (Hartmann J). Hartmann J dismissed the respondent's application for judicial review of decisions of the appellant, the Director of Immigration ("the Director"). The Director's decisions were (i) to refuse the respondent permission to land in Hong Kong; (ii) to remove her from Hong Kong; and (iii) to detain her pending removal.

6. The appeal raises important questions of constitutional and immigration law. In *Gurung Kesh Bahadur v. Director of Immigration* (2002) 5 HKCFAR 480 ("*Gurung*"), this Court decided that when a non-permanent resident returns to Hong Kong during the currency of a previous permission to remain, he or she is entitled to be re-admitted by virtue of art.31 of the Basic Law (the freedom to travel) and that s.11(10) of the Immigration Ordinance, Cap. 115 ("the Ordinance") does not apply. The principal issue in the appeal is whether the same conclusion follows if an immigration officer concludes that the previous permission to remain and the status of non-permanent resident was obtained by fraud or deception. In such a case, does an immigration officer have power under s.11(1) of the Ordinance to refuse permission to enter Hong Kong, to remove the person from Hong Kong under s.18(1) of the Ordinance and to detain him under s.32 pending removal?

7. If an immigration officer has such powers, other questions arise, including questions as to the burden and standard of proof and standards of review applicable in a challenge by way of judicial review to the exercise of these powers.

The facts

8. On 23 December 1995 the respondent, a Chinese national, born on 23 July 1966, in Dalian City, Liaoning Province, was granted permission to land in Hong Kong under s.11(1) of the Ordinance and permission to remain until 23 December 1996 under s.11(2) of the Ordinance. She had a one-way Exit Permit issued to her on 21 November 1995 by the Bureau of Exit Entry Administration of the Public Security Bureau of the People's Republic of China.

9. On 8 January 1996 the respondent applied for and obtained a Hong Kong identity card under the Registration of Persons Ordinance, Cap. 177 ("the ROP Ordinance"). She produced her one-way Permit in support of her application. She also applied for and received on 9 January 1996 a document of identity which she used on the many occasions she travelled to and from Hong Kong. This document was due to expire on 9 January 2003 but was renewed on 8 June 1998 because all its pages had been filled by stamping.

10. The respondent's permission to stay in Hong Kong was extended from time to time. On 3 September 1999, she was given permission to land and remain in Hong Kong until 8 June 2005.

11. On 6 February 1996 she was interviewed by an immigration officer. She was asked about the circumstances in which she applied for the one-way Permit. She stated that she applied as the wife of Leung Wai Ming, a Hong Kong permanent resident, whom she had married in the Mainland in April 1990.

12. The respondent's account that she had married Leung Wai Ming in the Mainland in April 1990 and had come to Hong Kong to be with him was in conflict with her earlier statements and with travel records, as appears below.

13. She first entered Hong Kong on 9 January 1993 when she was in transit to Bangladesh. She was then carrying a passport of the People's Republic of China. On arrival in Bangladesh she married Leung Wai Ming on 12 January 1993. She obtained a Bangladeshi passport in the name of Uasha Chakma, a woman ostensibly born in Bangladesh.

14. On 16 January 1993 the respondent entered Hong Kong, using her Bangladeshi passport. On the basis that she was married to a Hong Kong permanent resident, she was permitted to remain in Hong Kong until 16 April 1993. She overstayed and was arrested in May 1993 when she went into hospital where she gave birth to a daughter, Tin Wai, on 23 May 1993. Leung Wai Ming denied he was the father.

15. On 8 September 1993 the respondent, under caution, stated in an interview that, about late 1991, she commenced a relationship in Shenzen (Shenzhen) with Ng Kam Chuen, a Hong Kong permanent resident who was married. In or about August 1992 she discovered she was pregnant with Ng's child. As she did not wish to give birth to an illegitimate child in the Mainland, Ng arranged for her to fly to Bangladesh where she met his friend Leung Wai Ming who, for payment, entered into a sham marriage with her. The purpose was to reinforce her claim to be a citizen of Bangladesh which was supported by the Bangladeshi passport.

16. Not only was this account inconsistent with her later account on 6 February 1996 that she had married Leung Wai Ming in China in April 1990, a check of his travel records revealed that he had not left Hong Kong between October 1989 and 16 May 1990.

17. Further, the respondent, at her interview on 6 February 1996, acknowledged that she had not been in contact with Leung Wai Ming after her repatriation to the Mainland on 29 January 1995. She did not know his whereabouts. They were subsequently divorced. Indeed, it seems that they met only to obtain a divorce.

18. In September 1996, the Director sought the assistance of the Ministry of Public Security in Beijing. The Chinese Bureau of Exit Entry Administration replied on 28 June 1999, confirming that the one-way Permit had been obtained by fraud. The Bureau asked the Director to annul her registration and repatriate her to the Mainland as soon as possible. Enclosed with the letter was a letter from the Public Security Bureau of Dalian City stating that a marriage certificate relating to the respondent and Leung Wai Ming was issued on 11 April 1992.

19. It seems that the Director was aware that the Chinese Bureau of Exit Entry Administration had confirmed that the one-way Permit had been obtained by fraud when, on 3 September 1999, the respondent was given permission to land and remain in Hong Kong until 8 June 2005. Nothing turns on this circumstance.

20. On 5 September 1999 the respondent departed from Hong Kong for the Mainland. The Immigration Department was unable to make contact with her.

21. Subsequently when the respondent attempted to enter Hong Kong via Lo Wu on 4 October 1999, she was stopped by immigration officers. She was refused permission to land under s.11(1) of the Ordinance. She was informed that she would be removed to the Mainland under s.18 of the Ordinance. She was detained under s.32 pending removal.

22. The decision to refuse permission to land in Hong Kong was taken by Mr Lam Kin Yee, Senior Immigration Officer at Lo Wu Control Point, on the recommendation of Mr Wong Lok Wah, an Immigration Officer, who had examined the respondent under s.4(1) of the Ordinance. The grounds of the decision were:

(a) there was a written confirmation from the Mainland authorities that the respondent's one-way Permit for her settlement in Hong Kong was obtained by fraudulent means in November 1995 and that her residence status in Hong Kong should be revoked;

(b) that her permission to stay in Hong Kong had expired on her departure from Hong Kong on 5 September 1999 pursuant to s.11(10); and

(c) that her permission to land and remain in Hong Kong as well as her identity card and the two documents of identity were vitiated by her fraudulently obtained one-way Permit on the strength of which she had entered Hong Kong for settlement.

23. The identity of the officer who made the decisions to authorise the respondent's detention and her removal under s.18 is not entirely clear. That is immaterial because the two decisions were consequential upon the decision to refuse the respondent permission to land.

24. The respondent commenced proceedings for judicial review of the decisions referred to in paras 21 and 22 on 6 October 1999. The next day Stock J granted leave to apply and the respondent was released after entering into a recognizance pursuant to s.36 of the Ordinance.

25. The respondent also sought a review by the Chief Executive in Council under s.53 of the Ordinance. The Chief Executive in Council affirmed the decision to remove the respondent.

The Judgment of Hartman J

26. Hartmann J delivered judgment on 29 June 2000. He applied s.11(10) of the Ordinance and held that the respondent's permission to remain in Hong Kong expired immediately after her departure. Hartmann J's judgment was delivered before this Court delivered judgment in *Gurung*, so he did not have the advantage of this Court's decision that, since the coming into operation of the Basic Law, s.11(10) does not apply to residents, whether permanent or non-permanent, who are exercising the right to travel.

27. Hartmann J went on to hold that the respondent had to seek a new permission, when she attempted to return, as she enjoyed no subsisting right to reside in Hong Kong, and that the Director's exercise of discretion to refuse her permission was not *Wednesbury* unreasonable. The judge held also that the Director was under no obligation to proceed in accordance with the rules of natural justice to ensure a fair hearing. The applications to quash the order refusing permission to land and the removal order were dismissed with costs.

The Court of Appeal

28. The Court of Appeal held that the respondent should have been treated as a person who had been permitted to remain in Hong Kong and was therefore a non-permanent resident. The Court concluded that, following *Gurung*, s.11(10) did not apply and the procedure of s.11(6) or s.19 of the Ordinance should have been followed. The consequence was that the decisions could not stand. The appeal was allowed and orders were made quashing the decision under s.11 refusing permission to land, the decision authorising detention pending removal and the decision to remove the respondent from Hong Kong.

The arguments of the parties in this appeal

29. On the art.31 issue the Director contends:

(1) the freedom to travel under art.31 of the Basic Law is conferred on "Hong Kong residents" only, whether they be permanent or non-permanent residents;

(2) non-permanent residents are defined by art.24 of the Basic Law as persons who "are qualified to obtain Hong Kong identity cards in accordance with the laws of the Region" ;

(3) the respondent was not so "qualified" because she obtained a one-way Permit by fraud, that Permit was the basis of her obtaining entry to Hong Kong and a limit on stay and that limit on stay was the basis of her obtaining an identity card;

(4) the consequence is that the respondent was not a non-permanent resident, that art.31 had no application and that ss 7, 11(10) and 18 of the Ordinance applied.

Implicit in the Director's argument is the proposition that an identity card is not itself evidence that the holder has the status of a non-permanent resident. The respondent submits, however, that an identity card is prima facie evidence that the holder has the status of a non-permanent resident.

30. The respondent's case is:

(1) that, in order to comply with the requirements of arts 35 and 39 of the Basic Law and art.14.1 of the International Covenant on Civil and Political Rights ("the ICCPR") as applied to Hong Kong by art.10 of the Hong Kong Bill of Rights Ordinance, Cap. 383, a person impeaching another person's resident status must prove his case to an appropriate standard before a court or tribunal amenable to judicial review which adjudicates on the facts and complies with the requirements of procedural fairness;

(2) that a Hong Kong identity card is prima facie evidence of the holder's status as a non-permanent resident;

(3) that the Director bears the onus of establishing unlawful entry and the invalidity of the permission to stay;

(4) that the Director must prove his case at least to what is called "the flexible civil standard", that is, "on the balance of probabilities having regard to the seriousness of the matters that have to be proved and the general assumption that a person has acted legally not illegally" (see *R v. Home Secretary, Ex parte Rahman* [1998] QB 136 at 173C–D, per Hobhouse LJ;

(5) that the procedure under ss 4(1), 7, 11(1), 18 and 32 of the Ordinance was inapplicable in the present case; and

(6) that the Government and the Director should have acted under ss 11(6) and 19 which entail appropriate procedures whereby the respondent could challenge the decisions made.

Non-permanent resident status

31. Article 24 defines the non-permanent residents of the Hong Kong Special Administrative Region. They

> "shall be persons who are qualified to obtain Hong Kong identity cards in accordance with the laws of the Region but have no right of abode."

Although art.31 of the Basic Law confers on non-permanent residents certain rights and freedoms, including "freedom to travel and to enter or leave the Region", their status as non-permanent residents rests on their having qualifications prescribed by the laws of Hong Kong.

32. For these qualifications it is necessary to turn to the ROP Ordinance and Regulations. Every person in Hong Kong is required to be registered under that Ordinance, unless exempted or excluded by the s.3(1). The respondent was not exempted or excluded. Application for registration is to be made in the manner prescribed by regulations made under s.7 (s.3(2)).

33. Regulation 3(1) of the ROP Regulations requires every person who is not exempted or excluded to obtain an identity card. An applicant for registration or for an identity card is required to furnish detailed particulars, including

> "(xi) any –
>
> (A) travel document bearing an endorsement to the effect that he is authorized under the Immigration Ordinance ... to remain in Hong Kong; or
>
> (B) document issued under that Ordinance authorizing him to remain in Hong Kong, held by him;
>
> (xia) (where the applicant does not have a right of abode in Hong Kong) the conditions of stay (including a limit of stay) imposed in relation to him under section 11 of the Immigration Ordinance ..."

The Regulation requires the applicant to "acknowledge the correctness of the particulars by signing" in the place provided in the form (reg.4(1)(b)).

34. A person who, in furnishing particulars under reg.4, makes a statement or furnishes particulars which he knows is or are false in a material particular commits an offence punishable by fine or imprisonment for 2 years (reg.19(2C)). Where a registration officer believes on reasonable grounds

> "(a) that an identity card has been obtained as the result of the commission of an offence specified in" reg.19(2C); or
>
> "(b) that a person is in possession of an identity card in respect of which an offence under" reg.19(2C) "has been committed"

he may declare the identity card to be invalid and order it to be surrendered (reg.19(3)).

35. In this respect, reg.19(3) is significant. It provides for a declaration of invalidity of an identity card where its issue has been induced by fraudulent particulars. Until such a declaration is made, the card is valid and effective for all purposes.

36. Registration under the ROP Ordinance imposes legal obligations in connection with the identity card. A registered person is required to use the names entered on the identity card and to furnish the number of the card to the satisfaction of a public officer requiring such number (s.5(1)).

The legal significance of an identity card

37. In the light of its very nature, the procedures under which it is brought into existence and the purposes which it serves, an identity card amounts to official recognition and confirmation that the holder is a resident of Hong Kong, has satisfied the qualifications for registration and, in the case of a non-permanent resident, that he has the status of a non-permanent resident of Hong Kong, subject to the holder having, at any given time, unexpired permission to remain in Hong Kong.

38. It has to be recognised that an identity card is valid until declared invalid and that it is an official document which, subject to the qualification just mentioned, recognises and confirms that the holder is a resident of Hong Kong, thereby indicating that he has satisfied the qualifications for registration and, in the case of a non-permanent resident, that he has the status of a non-permanent resident of Hong Kong. The recognition of an identity card as such an official document is not inconsistent with the provisions of regs 21 and 22 of the ROP Regulations assuming that these provisions are capable of applying outside as well as within legal proceedings and proceedings before the Immigration Tribunal.

39. The Director's case is that art.24 defines the class of non-permanent residents by reference to their qualifications to obtain Hong Kong identity cards not by reference to their holding such cards. There can be no argument about that. The point of the definition is to include in the class of non-permanent residents those who do not yet hold identity cards but are qualified to obtain them in accordance with the laws of Hong Kong. But it

does not follow that the holding of a non-permanent identity card, subject to the holder having, at any given time, unexpired permission to remain in Hong Kong, is of no effect simply because facts of the kind referred to in reg.19(2C) and (3) exist or may exist. Article 31 links the status of a non-permanent resident to the laws of Hong Kong and, under those laws, the respondent was recognised as having the relevant qualifications until appropriate steps were taken under those laws to establish that she lacked those qualifications.

The Ordinance

40. The Director's case is that s.7(1) applied to the respondent. The sub-section provides

> "A person may not land in Hong Kong without the permission of an immigration officer or immigration assistant ..."

The sub-section sets out certain exceptions which have no application to the respondent. Although the respondent had, at the time of her re-entry into Hong Kong, an unexpired permission to remain in Hong Kong, the Director argues that this permission had expired earlier on her departure from Hong Kong, pursuant to the operation of s.11(10). Whether s.11(10) applied to the respondent depended upon her status as a non-permanent resident. *Gurung* decided that s.11(10) does not apply to such a resident with an unexpired permission to remain when the resident seeks to re-enter Hong Kong in the exercise of the freedom to travel under art.31 of the Basic Law.

41. The question then is whether the respondent's status as a non-permanent resident could be determined on the procedure which was adopted by the Director, by means of examination under s.4(1), the application of ss 7(1), 11(10), 18 and detention pursuant to s.26. There are elements in this procedure which indicate a legislative intent that the procedure cannot apply to a case where the question in issue is whether a person, having an unexpired permission to remain in Hong Kong and claiming the status of a non-permanent resident supported by the holding of an identity card, no longer enjoys that status because, in the view of officers of the Department, the permission and the issue of the card were induced or affected by fraud or deception.

42. In the Ordinance, there are strong indications of such a legislative intent. First, the provisions for examination under s.4(1)(a) and refusal of permission to land under s.11(1) prescribe no procedure which complies with the requirements of procedural fairness. There is nothing which requires an immigration officer to give notice to the individual, outlining the case against the individual and affording an opportunity to the individual to answer that case. The absence of provisions of this kind strongly suggests that the procedure was intended to apply only in simple, straightforward cases, not in important cases where an issue of resident status is involved. This impression is re-inforced by s.27 which confers powers to detain a person being examined under s.4(1)(a) but limits the period of detention to a maximum of 48 hours, that is, for not more than 24 hours pending the examination and for not more than a further 24 hours pending a decision to give or refuse him permission to land. In cases where an issue of resident status is involved, as here, the issue will often be complex and require the making of inquiries and obtaining evidence from other jurisdictions. Resolution within a timeframe of 48 hours would often be practically impossible.

43. Secondly, the procedure under ss 4(1)(a), 7(1), 11(10), 18 and 26 contrasts with the procedure prescribed by s.19 where an order for removal is made under that section. Section 19(5) requires the Director to cause written notice to be served as soon as practicable on the person against whom it is made informing him–

(a) of the ground on which the order is made; and

(b) that if he wishes to appeal he must do so by giving to an immigration officer or immigration assistant written notice of his grounds of appeal and the facts upon which he relies within 24 hours of receiving the notice of the order.

An appeal may be brought to the Immigration Tribunal established under s.53F against a removal order under s.19 on the ground that the person

> "had at the date when the removal order was made the permission of the Director of Immigration to remain in Hong Kong."

The s.19 procedure not only provides safeguards which are absent in the procedure followed by the Director but it also provides for a determination of the relevant issue by a quasi-judicial tribunal on the facts.

44. The Ordinance enables a decision refusing permission to land to be made under s.7(1) by an immigration officer and a decision under s.18 to be made by an immigration officer or chief immigration assistant. Although it is to be expected as a matter of good administration, difficult decisions, such as those taken in the present case, would be made by senior immigration officers, the point remains that the legislature provided for different procedures culminating in removal from Hong Kong. One procedure, culminating in a s.18 removal, which allows lower level decision-making is appropriate for simple, straightforward cases. The other, culminating in a s.19 removal, requires high level decision-making, with substantial safeguards, as is appropriate to the determination of cases involving a claim to status, whether it be permanent or non-permanent resident status.

45. It follows, as a matter of interpretation of the Ordinance and the ROP Ordinance and Regulations, that the procedure adopted by the Director was not authorised by the Ordinance. It would be surprising if it were otherwise. Had the respondent not sought to exercise her constitutional freedom to travel under the Basic Law flowing from the non-permanent status she enjoyed by virtue of her permission to remain in Hong Kong and her identity card, the Director would plainly not have been able to resort to ss 4(1)(a), 11 and 18. He would have been compelled to resort to s.19 with its attendant safeguards.

46. In the circumstances, the actions of the Director amounted to an interference with the exercise by the respondent of her constitutional freedom to travel, on the basis of an administrative decision that her permission to remain in Hong Kong had been procured by fraud, a decision taken under a procedure which did not incorporate the safeguards appropriate to the determination of the important issue of status under the Basic Law. In the absence of a determination of that issue according to the appropriate procedure, preventing the respondent from entering Hong Kong was an interference with her constitutional freedom to travel under the Basic Law.

Conclusion

47. For these reasons the appeal should be dismissed with costs, with an order for legal aid taxation of the respondent's costs.

Chief Justice Li:

48. The Court unanimously dismisses the appeal with costs, with an order for legal aid taxation of the respondent's costs.

Chief Justice (Andrew Li)

Permanent Judge (Kemal Bokhary)

Permanent Judge (Patrick Chan)

Permanent Judge (R.A.V. Ribeiro)

Non-Permanent Judge (Sir Anthony Mason)

Mr David Pannick, QC and Mr William Marshall, SC (instructed by the Department of Justice) for the appellant

Mr Philip Dykes, SC and Mr Hectar Pun (instructed by Messrs Yip & Partners and assigned by the Legal Aid Department) for the respondent

---

王家衍 對 入境事務處處長

HCAL1660/2001；CACV 1937/2001

簡略案情

上訴人王家衍於 1974 年 2 月 2 日在福建出生。1990 年 11 月 12 日，上訴人持“前往港澳通行證”編號 0252136（“該單程證”）從內地來港。該單程證註明持有人名為“萬家演”，出生日期為 1973 年 2 月 16 日，住址為陝西。申請人以此身份獲准逗留至 1991 年 11 月 12 日，並一再獲准延期逗留至 1998 年 11 月 12 日。其後，上訴人易名為王家演。後來，入境事務處於 1996 年 5 月 6 日接獲內地出入境管理局來函，指出該單程證是通過非法手段取得的，要求將申請人遣返內地。1997 年 11 月 4 日，入境事務處接獲上訴人以“王家演”為名的核實永久性居民身份證資格申請書，聲稱在 1990 年 11 月 12 日至 1997 年期間通常居於香港連續 7 年，屬《入境條例》附表 1 第 2（b）段所指的香港永久性居民。翌年 2 月 17 日，入境事務處就上訴人涉嫌管有和行使以非法手段取得的單程證一事扣查申請人。然而，上訴人拒絕回答任何問題，並要求安排返回內地。入境事務處遂於同日將申請人遣返內地。

自 1999 年 4 月，上訴人多次持內地簽發的護照或往來港澳通行證訪港，該等證件均註明持有人為“王家衍”，出生日期為 1974 年 2 月 2 日，出生地點為福建。2001 年 6 月 4 日，上訴人根據《入境事務條例》附表 1 第 2（c）段，向入境事務處提交核實永久居民身份證資格申請書及居留權證明書申請書。對於上訴人的申請，入境處處長一律予以拒絕。上訴人其後向原訟庭提出的司法覆核亦被駁回。2001 年 8 月，針對原訟庭的判決，上訴人上訴至上訴庭。2003 年 2 月 26 日，入境事務處接獲內地出入境管理局提交關於上訴人的個人背景資料，據稱上訴人在 1988 年利用假戶口遷移證，將戶口假遷移至陝西省，再將姓名改為萬家演，出生日期改為 1973 年 2 月 16 日，並假冒其父為萬清白（蔡清白）、其母為陳蕊，以承繼財產為由，申請赴港定居，並於 1990 年 11 月通過上述手段騙取該單程證赴港定居。由此，入境事務處助理處長遂向申請人發出遣送離境令。上訴人不服，並向入境事務審裁處和人事登記審裁處提出上訴。該上訴同時被駁回。

據上訴人聲稱，該單程證是由其祖父的朋友代辦，是真確的，所以，他以此在香港逗留是合法的。再者，上訴人認為他一直居住在香港，是入境事務處的失職而導致他遲了加入爭取居港權的行列，招致上訴人失去了*吳嘉玲*一案判決所指的受惠人的條件，沒有成為 1999 年 6 月 26 日所宣佈的寬免政策的受惠人。

裁決摘要

上訴庭接納*江秀美（譯音）對入境事務處處長*（*Kong Sau Mei v. Director Of Immigration* [1999] 1 HKC 174）一案的判決，同意如果有關人士持一護照入境，但入境事務處處長其後有理由相信該護照屬非法取得，則該人士屬非法入境，而入境事務處處長可作出遣送離境令。該案的法官認為，入境事務處人員准許有關人士入境是因當時他們並無理由懷疑該人士所持護照是以非法手段獲得的。入境處准許該人士入境後才發覺該非法行為，顯然當時給予的入境許可是因詐騙而獲得，因此應視作無效並被取消。在這情況下，就算該非法獲得的護照並非由入境人士親自以非法手段獲得，而該獲照又是真確且有效的護照，入境事務處處長也有權力及合理地發出遣送離境令。而根據*律政司對入境事務審裁處和陳鴻昌（譯音）*（*AG v. Immigration Tribunal and Chen Huan Qiong*（No. 2）HCMP 2182/1995）一案，有關人士對他是否知道該旅遊證件是偽造的，與他是否合法或非法入境一事無關重要。據此，上訴庭認定上訴人所憑藉以進入香港的該單程證是以非法手段獲得，就算申請人並不知情並且入境事務處也因不懷疑該單程證的合法性而准許上訴人於 1990 年 11 月 12 日進入香港，並不表示上訴人是合法地進入香港，他其實是非法入境者，而且他在該非法入境後留在香港的期間，均不能被視為通常居住於香港，所以上訴人不能符合《入境條例》附表 1 第 2（b）段的規定。

關於上訴人強調他因入境事務處的疏忽而沒能受惠於特區政府的寬免政策，上訴庭認為是強詞奪理，不合邏輯。事實上，上訴人是在 1974 年或 1973 年出生。他父母分別在 1989 年 10 月 11 日後（即於 1982 年 10 月 11 日來港 7 年後）及於 2000 年 10 月 25 日後（即於 1993 年 10 月 25 日來港 7 年後）才成為香港永久性居民。很明顯，申請人在內地出生時，其父或母並非“通常居於香港連續 7 年或以上的中國公民”，因此申請人的情況並不符合《入境條例》附表 1 第 2（c）段的規定，也沒有符合*吳小彤*案所述的任何條件。

據此，該上訴被駁回，上訴人需支付入境事務處處長的訟費。

CACV 1937/2001

香港特別行政區
高等法院上訴法庭
民事司法管轄權
民事上訴

案件編號：民事上訴案件 2001 年第 1937 號
（原高院憲法及行政訴訟 2001 年第 1660 號）

申請人　王家衍
對
答辯人　入境事務處處長

主審法官：高等法院上訴法庭副庭長胡國興
高等法院原訟法庭法官張舉能

聆訊日期：2005 年 1 月 21 日

判案書日期：2005 年 1 月 25 日

判案書

由高等法院上訴法庭副庭長胡國興頒發上訴法庭判案書：

序言

1. 這是一宗有關居留權司法覆核申請的上訴。

2. 2001 年 8 月 7 日，申請人王家衍（又名王家演）申請許可，針對入境事務處處長的決定擬提出司法覆核，該決定拒絕了申請人要求入境處簽發香港永久性居民身份證的申請。

3. 2001 月 8 月 8 日，高等法院原訟法庭法官鍾安德拒絕批予司法覆核許可。

4. 2001 年 8 月 13 日，申請人針對鍾法官的命令向本庭提出上訴。

5. 上訴原定於 2002 年 8 月 28 日聆訊。當天本庭把聆訊押後，讓入境處可就本案作出進一步調查。及後，本上訴的聆訊再押後了一次，原因是為了等候申請人就入境事務處處長的決定向人事登記審裁處提出的上訴的結果。

6. 2004 年 7 月 8 日，人事登記審裁處就申請人應否獲發永久性居民身份證作出裁決，認為入境事務處處長的決定正確，駁回申請人的上訴。

有關事實

7. 代表答辯人的署理高級政府律師何展鵬在本案的背景方面備就了一個時序表，其中所列事項，除第（16）項外，雙方都全無爭議，如下：

（1）02.02.1974　申請人在福建出生。

（2）11.10.1982　申請人聲稱的父親王家福先生持前往港澳通行證來港。

（3）12.11.1990　申請人持前往港澳通行證編號 0252136（“該單程證”）從國內來港；該單程證註明持有人為“萬家演”，出生日期為 1973 年 2 月 16 日，住址為陝西。申請人以此身份獲准逗留至 12.11.1991，其後一再獲准延期逗留至 12.11.1998。

（4）20.02.1991　申請人易名“王家演”，然後以此姓名申領香港身份證及簽證身份書。

（5）25.12.1993　申請人聲稱的母親許明灣女士持單程證來港。

（6）06.05.1996　入境事務處接獲國內出入境管理局來函，指出該單程證是通過非法手段取得的，要求將申請人遣返內地。

（7）04.11.1997　入境事務處接獲“王家演”的核實永久性居民身份證資格申請書，聲稱在 1990 年 11 月 12 日至 1997 年期間通常居於香港連續七年，屬《入境條例》附表 1 第 2（b）段所指的香港永久性居民。

（8）17.02.1998　入境事務處就申請人涉嫌管有和行使以非法手段取得的單程證一事將申請人扣查。申請人拒絕回答任何問題，並要求安排返回國內。入境事務處遂於同日將申請人遣返內地。

（9）15.04.1999　自當天起，申請人多次持內地簽發的護照或往來港澳通行證訪港，該等證件均註明持有人為“王家衍”，出生日期為 1974 年 2 月 2 日，出生地點為福建。

（10）04.06.2001　入境事務處接獲申請人提交的核實永久居民身份證資格申請書；這是申請人首次根據《入境事務條例》附表一第 2（c）段聲稱在香港擁有居留權。入境事務處其後又接獲申請人的居留權證明書申請書。

（11）07.08.2001　申請人提出本案的司法覆核許可申請。

（12）08.08.2001　原訟法庭鍾安德法官拒絕給予申請人司法覆核許可。

（13）13.08.2001　申請人提出本上訴。

（14）25.04.2002　申請人與入境事務處人員會面，期間表示他的姓名是王家衍，別名王家演，1974 年 2 月 2 日生於福建，但拒絕就過去曾以另一身份來港一事作出解釋，亦不回答有關該單程證的問題。

（15）28.08.2002　上訴法庭押後聆訊，以便答辯人就申請人在 1990 年 11 月 12 日至 1998 年 2 月 17 日期間身在香港一事提供進一步資料。

（16）26.02.2003　內地出入境管理局向入境事務處提供申請人的個人背景資料，並指出申請人在 1988 年利用假戶口遷移證將戶口假遷移至陝西省，將姓名改為萬家演，出生日期改為 1973 年 2 月 16 日，並假冒其父為萬清白（蔡清白）、其母為陳蕊，以承繼財產為由申請赴港定居，於 1990 年 11 月通過上述手段騙取該單程證赴港定居。

（17）02.04.2003　入境事務處助理處長向申請人發出遣送離境令。

（18）10.04.2003　申請人就遣送離境令向入境事務審裁處提出上訴。

（19）24.04.2003　入境事務審裁處根據《入境條例》第 53C 條決定無須進行聆訊而將申請人的上訴駁回。

（20）19.06.2003 申請人申請永久性居民身份證，於同日遭拒絕。申請人於同日向人事登記審裁處提出上訴。

（21）31.10.2003 上訴法庭指示，本上訴應在人事登記審裁處上訴案審結後才恢復進行聆訊。

（22）08.07.2004 人事登記審裁處經聆訊後駁回申請人的上訴。

上訴理由

8. 申請人在 2001 年 8 月 13 日的上訴通知書中列出他的上訴理由，如下：

"本人王家衍，父親王家福、母親許明灣是香港永久性居民。根據 1999 年 1 月 29 日終審法庭的判決，香港永久居民在內〔地所生〕子女擁有居港權。本人符合以上條文，本人有居留權，根〔據〕基本法 24 條例法律平等。本人要求平等對待。"

9. 在申請人 2005 年 1 月 7 日傳真給法庭的信中，他詳細列出該單程證的申請過程。簡言之，該單程證是他祖父的朋友一位劉先生替他辦理手續而取得的。接到該單程證時，申請人方知其上所載持證人的姓氏、出生日期及地點皆有錯誤，但劉先生的答覆是有誤無妨，將來在香港可予以更正。故此申請人持該單程證來港。他對劉先生如何辦手續及為何該單程證的持證人資料與他自己的不同並不知情，但他肯定該單程證是真的單程證，是有效的證件。正因如此，香港入境處也根據該單程證准許他入境，並發給他香港身份證，又給他辦理延期至 1998 年 11 月 12 日，所以該單程證已生效。而且，從 1990 年 11 月 12 日他以該單程證來港定居，並獲得居留延期至 1998 年 11 月 12 日，這超過 7 年期間他是在香港合法居留，因此他具備永久性居民的資格。

10. 有關政府宣布的寬免政策一事，申請人說，入境處說 1996 年 5 月 6 日開始找不到申請人，而申請人一直在香港，也正因入境處如此失職，使申請人遲了加入爭取居港權的行列，招致申請人失去了*吳嘉玲*案判決所指的受惠人的條件，沒有成為 1999 年 6 月 26 日所宣布的寬免政策的受惠人。

11. 申請人主要的上訴理由可簡述如下：

（1）該單程證是有效而非偽造的證件，他持之進入香港，並不是非法入境。

（2）自 1990 年 11 月 12 日他入境之日起計，直至 1998 年 11 月 12 日止，申請人連續在香港合法居留，共超過 7 年，故此他已具備永久性居民的資格。

（3）申請人應受惠於終審法院*吳嘉玲*案判決，應成為香港政府 1999 年 6 月 26 日所宣布的寬免政策的受惠人。

12. 本庭在下文逐一處理這三個問題。

通常居港連續 7 年

13. 香港法例第 115 章《入境條例》附表 1 第 2 段規定：

"任何人如屬以下一項，即為香港特別行政區永久性居民——

（a）⋯。

（b）香港特別行政區成立以前或以後通常居於香港連續 7 年或以上的中國居民。

（c）中國公民在香港特別行政區成立以前或以後在香港以外所生的中國籍子女，而在該子女出生時，該中國公民是符合（a）或（b）項規定的人。"

14. 雙方不爭議的事實是申請人從 1990 年 11 月 12 日起至 1998 年 2 月 17 日止在香港連續居住了 7 年。雙方所爭議的是申請人是否在該期間"通常居於"香港。在這一問題上，國家出入境管理局 2003 年 2 月 26 日至香港特區入境事務處信件的內容至為重要。有關的內容摘錄如下：

"王家衍，男，1974 年 2 月 2 日出生，家庭住址是福建省晋江市羅山莆山村；其父親王家福，1945 年 1 月出生；母親許明灣，1953 年 5 月 29 日出生；妹妹王錮鎰，1978 年 5 月 25 日出生；妹妹王燕泥，1976 年 1 月 15 日出生。其父王家福于（於）1982 年 9 月 18 日獲發第 0824272 號單程證赴港定居；其母親許明灣、妹妹王錮鎰于（於）1993 年 11 月 18 日獲發第 0360373、0360374 號前往港澳通行赴港定居。

目前，王家衍的內地戶口仍在福建，其于（於）1999 年 12 月 28 日以探望母親許明灣為由申請赴港探親，並獲發第 4110011 號往來港澳通行證，2001 年 7 月 17 日再次持該證赴港探親。

為達到赴香港定居的目的，1988 年，王家衍伙同他人利用假戶口遷移證將戶口假遷移至陝西省榆林市，將其姓名改為萬家演，出生日期改為 1973 年 2 月 16 日，並假冒其父為萬清白（蔡清白）、其母為陳蕊，以繼承財產為由，申請赴港定居，1990 年 11 月通過上述弄虛作假手段騙取了第 0252136 號前往港澳通行證赴港定居。"

15. 《入境條例》第 2（4）（a）（i）條規定，非法入境後留在香港的期間均不被視為通常居於香港。在*江秀美*（譯音）*對入境事務處處長*[1] 一案，如有關人士持一護照入境，但入境事務處處長其後有理由相信該護照屬非法取得，則該人士屬非法入境，而入境事務處處長可作出遣送離境令。在該案，祁彥輝法官指出，入境事務處人員准許有關人士入境是因當時他們並無理由懷疑該人士所持護照可能是以非法手段獲得。入境處准許該人士入境後發覺該非法行為，明顯證實入境許可是因入境處人員被詐騙而獲得，因此應被取消。在這情況下，就算該非法獲得的護照並非由入境人士親自以非法手段獲得，而該獲照又是真而有效的護照，但入境事務處處長也有權力及合理地發出遣送離境令。

16. 在本案，入境處處長有權信納出入境管理局 2003 年 2 月 26 日信內載的資料，以及可接納出入境管理局的結論，斷定該單程證是非法取得的證件。至於出入境管理局如何達致該結論，則屬內地當局事務。這法律原則在多宗案例已確立。參閱*李富山*（譯音）*對入境事務處處長*[2]，*徐小惠*（譯音）*對入境事務處處長*[3]，及*馮雪芳*（譯音）*對入境事務處處長*[4] 等案。

17. *在律政司對入境事務審裁處和陳鴻昌*（譯音）[5] 一案，楊振權法官援引英國的兩個案例，指出案例清楚顯示，有關人士是否知道他的旅遊證件是偽造的對他是否合法或非法入境一事無關。

18. 上述各案例皆適用於本案。因為申請人所憑藉以進入香港的該單程證是以非法或弄虛作假手段在國內獲得，就算申請人並不知情，香港入境事務處也因不懷疑獲發該單程證的合法性而准許申請人於 1990 年 11 月 12 日進入香港，但這並不表示申請人是合法地進入香港，他其實是非法入境，因此他在該非法入境後留在香港的期間均不被視為通常居住於香港，所以申請人不能符合《入境條例》附表 1 第 2（b）段的規定。申請人不是"通常"居於香港連續 7 年或以上的中國居民，故並不能成為香港特區永久性居民。

寬免政策的受惠人

19. 就申請香港特別行政區居留權的問題，1999 年 1 月 29 日終審法院判決了*吳嘉玲及其他人士對入境事務處處長*[6]和*陳錦雅及其他人士對入境事務處處長*[7]兩案。在*吳嘉玲*案，終審法院裁定《基本法》第 24 條第 2 款第（3）項並不受第 22 條第 4 款〔須以國內機關簽發的單程證（“單程證”）來港〕規限，香港永久性居民在香港以外所生的中國籍子女申請居留權者不須先取得單程證才可獲取居留權。在*陳錦雅*案，終審法院裁定永久性居民在香港以外所生的中國籍子女，不論他們是在父母之中最少一人取得永久性居民身份之前或之後出生，均屬《基本法》第 24 條第 2 款第（3）項所述的人士，享有居留權。

20. 1999 年 6 月 26 日全國人民代表大會常務委員會對居留權問題作出解釋（“人大常委會解釋”），取代了終審法院上述的裁決，該等裁決不再適用。2002 年 1 月 10 日，終審法院在*吳小彤及其他人士對入境事務處處長*[8]一案清楚闡述和解釋了*吳嘉玲*和*陳錦雅*兩案及人大常委會解釋的關係和效果，對居留權的問題作出了決定性的結論。

21. *吳小彤*案和人大常委會的解釋對本庭均有約束力，本庭必須遵守。根據該案例及該解釋，永久性居民在香港以外所生的中國籍子女，只有符合下列三項其中一項條件的才可獲法庭頒發濟助：

（1）申請人在 1997 年 7 月 1 日之前已抵達香港，而且申請人在出生時其父母之中最少一人已經是永久性居民。符合這條件者有權在香港申請或繼續申請獲取居留權，無須領取單程證；或

（2）〔有合法理期望者〕申請人曾收到（a）法律援助署在 1998 年 12 月 7 日至 1999 年 1 月 29 日間發出的有關公函，述明申請人不必參與當時的訴訟程序或展開新訴訟程序，或（b）保安局局長在 1998 年 4 月 24 日發出的有關信件，內容大意是入境事務處會依循法院的判決處理居留權的申請。對於符合這條件者，入境事務處處長應考慮行使《入境條例》第 11 條、第 13 條和第 19（1）條賦予他的酌情決定權，在決定前不把申請人遣送離開香港；或

（3）〔政府寬免政策受惠者〕（a）申請人在 1997 年 7 月 1 日至 1999 年 1 月 29 日期間在香港，和（b）在該期間他在香港時向入境事務處提出居留權的聲稱，和（c）入境事務處存有該聲稱的記錄或聲稱由其他香港政府官員在執行職務時轉交予入境事務處。如果有文件可以明確（i）辨認出申請人是永久性居民的子女；（ii）提供有關申請人的資料，如出生日期和地點；和（iii）要求申請人來香港以便定居或要求給予申請人居留權，入境事務處處長應視之為居留權的聲稱。對於符合條件者，入境事務處處長應按照*吳嘉玲*和*陳錦雅*兩案的上述裁決考慮申請人的申請。

22. 若申請人不能符合上述條件的任何一項，申請人就沒有居留權；即使在他出生時其父或其母已經是永久性居民，他必須先向國內機關取得單程證，才可以在香港行使永久性居民的居留權。

本案案情

23. 申請人是在 1974 年或 1973 年出生。他父母分別在 1989 年 10 月 11 日後（即於 1982 年 10 月 11 日來港 7 年後）及於 2000 年 10 月 25 日後（即於 1993 年 10 月 25 日來港 7 年後）才成為香港永久性居民。事實很明顯，申請人在國內出生時，其父或母並非“通常居於香港連續 7 年或以上的中國公民”，因此申請人的情況並不符合《入境條例》附表 1 第 2（c）段的規定，也不符合*吳小彤*案所述的第（1）項條件。

24. 本案也沒有任何事實可支持申請人符合*吳小彤*案所述的第（2）項條件。

25. 既然申請人承認他遲了加入爭取居港權的行列（見上文第 10 段），所以在事實方面，他並沒有成為寬免政策的受惠者，不可能符合*吳小彤*案所述的第（3）項條件。

26. 至於申請人的論點，稱他自 1990 年 11 月 12 日起一直留在香港，由於入境處失職而找不到他，使他遲了加入爭取居港權的行列，以致失去成為寬免政策的受惠人，這是強詞奪理，完全不合邏輯。

27. 事實很明顯，申請人清楚明白該單程證上載持證人的姓名、出生日期及地點均與他自己的不同，他居留於香港的合法性必然存疑，但他自己並不去爭取，卻推說是入境處遲了去尋找他而招致他失去成為寬免政策受惠人的權利，本庭認為這說法是全無理據支持的。

28. 申請人在他呈交本庭日期為 2005 年 1 月 21 日的書面陳詞中強調，該單程證是真的證件，不論以甚麼理由發出，都是有效的證件，是有法律地位的，入境事務處及國內部門都無權以任何藉口推翻其法律地位。本庭認為，基於本案的證據，這論據是不能成立的。原因很簡單，證據清楚顯示該單程證的持證人是萬家演而不是申請人，申請人不能李代桃僵，利用該單程證入境香港，這涉及非法的欺騙行為，是香港法律所不容的。

結論

29. 基於上述各項理由，本庭認為入境處處長及人事登記審裁處的各項決定及裁決，在法律上均無犯錯，而本案案情也沒有任何合理可爭辯之處，促使本庭認為法庭該受理申請人的司法覆核申請，因此本庭駁回上訴，並作出暫准訟費令，申請人須支付入境事務處處長本上訴的訟費。

高等法院上訴法庭副庭長（胡國興）

高等法院原訟法庭法官（張舉能）

申請人：無律師代表。

答辯人：由律政司署理高級政府律師何展鵬代表。

註：

1. *Kong Sau Mei v. Director of Immigration* [1999] 1 HKC 174, at 183-184.

2. *Li Fu Shan v. Director of Immigration*, HCAL 813/2001 (7 Nov 2002, Hartmann J, unreported), paras 78 to 81.

3. *Tsui Siu Wai v. Director of Immigration*, HCMP 1665/1994 (6 Dec 1994, Chan J (as he then was)unreported), p 21.

4. *Fung Suet Fong v. Director of Immigration*, HCAL 108/2002 (10 Jan 2004, Chung J, paras 46 to 49).

5. *AG v. Immigration Tribunal and Chen Huan Qiong* (No. 2), HCMP 2182/1995 (5 Dec 1995, Yeung J (as he then was)unreported)pp12-13.

6. (1999) 2 HKCFAR 4 (29 Jan 1999)

7. (1999) 2 HKCFAR 82 (29 Jan 1999)

8. *Ng Siu Tung & Ors v. Director of Immigration* (2002) 5 HKCFAR 1 (10 Jan 2002)

Gutierrez Josephine B. v. Commissioner Of Registration & Registration of Persons Tribunal

Gutierrez Josephine B. 對 人事登記處處長及人事登記審裁處

Gutierrez Joseph James, a minor By Gutierrez Josephine B., also know as Gutierrez Josephine Balando, his mother and next friend v. Commissioner of Registration & Registration Of Persons Tribunal

Gutierrez Joseph James, 未成年人經由他母親及起訴監護人 Gutierrez Josephine Balando 對 人事登記處處長及人事登記審裁處

HCAL 136/2010；HCAL 137/2010

簡略案情

申請人為菲律賓國籍母子兩人。母親從 1991 年開始一直被批准在香港做家庭傭工，期間一共轉換過八個僱主，並且於 1996 年在香港跟一位美國人誕下其第五名兒子，即現在的兒子申請人，但她跟該男子已經失去聯繫。在 2006 年 12 月，兩位申請人根據《入境條例》附表一、第 2（f）條要求入境處核實他們的永久居民身份但被拒。而他們於 2008 年向人事登記處申請永久居民身份證的要求亦不被接納，他們遂向人事登記審裁處提出上訴。可是，審裁處最後認定他們並不能證明他們以香港作為永久居住地，而拒絕他們的上訴。申請人遂向原訟庭提起司法覆核申請，要求推翻人事登記處和人事登記審裁處的決定。母親認為審裁處忽略了她已經在香港生活了 19 年，完全融入了本地的環境，在菲律賓已經沒有家庭，大部份兒女都在香港生活。而且，她所有資產也在香港，社交圈子亦主要是本地的教會並打算在香港終老，因此她已經把香港作為永久居住地。至於兒子，由出生開始 15 年裏一直以香港為家，他的生活建立在香港也紮根在香港，而這個也是他唯一的家。

裁決摘要

法院同意審裁處對永久性問題的看法，除了主觀的意願外，申請人也必須客觀地證明他們已經採取了充足的行動去把香港作為他們一直永久的唯一居住地，而非是有限的一段時間。但把香港作為通常居住地的行動和行為不一定能反映把香港作為永久居住地的決心。因此，單單跟原居地聯繫的割離不足以證明這永久性的要求。他們應該有實質的行動去證明他們能解決在香港長久生計的現實問題。作為母親的申請人顯然不能滿足這個要求，所以答辯人拒絕她的申請的決定，並非明顯地不合理，因此，並沒有理由對該決定作出干預。

至於兒子的情況，法庭認為未成年兒童的一般居住地是跟他的監護人居住地一致的原則既持久又有效，適用於本案，而且，並沒有證據顯示他或者其母親曾經做過甚麼額外的行動去滿足該永久性的要求。

法庭進一步考慮《基本法》第 24 條（2）（4）條，對於兒子認為他因為已經連續在香港居住 7 年而應該擁有永久居留權的論據，法庭同意 *Commissioner of Registration v. Registration of Persons Tribunal* HCAL 39/2005 一案的分析，認為在申請前 7 年中他曾離開香港 3 次，延續性已經被破壞，所以並不滿足連續 7 年的要求。

最後，他們的覆核申請被拒絕。

HCAL 136/2010

IN THE HIGH COURT OF THE

HONG KONG SPECIAL ADMINISTRATIVE REGION

COURT OF FIRST INSTANCE

CONSTITUTIONAL AND ADMINISTRATIVE LAW LIST
NO. 136 OF 2010

Between:

GUTIERREZ JOSEPHINE B. **Applicant**

- and -

COMMISSIONER OF REGISTRATION 1st Respondents

REGISTRATION OF PERSONS TRIBUNAL 2nd Respondent

HCAL 137/2010

IN THE HIGH COURT OF THE

HONG KONG SPECIAL ADMINISTRATIVE REGION

COURT OF FIRST INSTANCE

CONSTITUTIONAL AND ADMINISTRATIVE LAW LIST
NO. 137 OF 2010

Between:

GUTIERREZ JOSEPH JAMES, a minor **Applicant**

By GUTIERREZ JOSEPHINE B., also known as GUTIERREZ JOSEPHINE BALANDO, his mother and next friend

- and -

COMMISSIONER OF REGISTRATION 1st Respondents

REGISTRATION OF PERSONS TRIBUNAL 2nd Respondent

(Heard together)

Before: Hon Lam J in Court

Date of Hearing: 26 October 2011

Date of Judgment: 10 November 2011

JUDGMENT

1. These Applicants are mother and child and they apply by judicial review to challenge the refusals of the Commissioner to issue permanent identity cards to them. Their appeals to the Registration of Persons Tribunal were dismissed on 31 May 2010. The mother is a Philippine national and she has been working in Hong Kong as a foreign domestic helper since 1991. Her application involves a challenge to the constitutionality of Section 2(4)(a)(vi) of the Immigration Ordinance ["the Impugned Provision"]. For reasons explained below, the validity of her claims also has bearing on the application of the child. The child was born in Hong Kong on 1 December 1996 and he is now almost 15 years old.

2. In the test case of *Valiejos Evangeline B v Commissioner of Registration* HCAL 124 of 2010, this court ruled in the judgment of 30 September 2011 that the Impugned Provision is inconsistent with Article 24(2)(4) of the Basic Law. For all intents and purposes, that judgment disposed of this issue in the present proceedings.

3. The remaining issues in respect of the mother's case are,

(a) Whether the Tribunal was correct in concluding that the mother did not satisfy the ordinary residence requirement;

(b) Whether the Tribunal was correct in concluding that the mother did not satisfy the permanence requirement.

4. The same issues are pertinent to the child's case because the Tribunal held at para.73 of its Decision that,

> "... the Tribunal accepted the principle that an infant of tender age was not capable of forming an intention on his place of permanent residence and whether his residence amounted to ordinary residence should be viewed against his mother's residence because she lived with him at all material time."

5. Ms Li SC challenged this approach to be wrong in law.

6. Another issue arising in the child's case (but not in the mother's case) is the finding of the Tribunal at para.79 of the Decision,

> "Apparently, when the [child] left Hong Kong on 31 March 2004, his prior stay in Hong Kong could not be treated as a period continuous to the period when he stayed in Hong Kong on the strength of a new visitor visa. The latest visitor visa granted to the [child] prior to the date of submitting the VEPIC application was 17 April 2004. So in any event, the [child] could not satisfy the requirement of ordinary residence in Hong Kong for at least 7 continuous years prior to his VEPIC application."

This has to be understood in light of the Tribunal's reference to the movement records of the child at para.77 and to the effect of Section 11(10) of the Immigration Ordinance at para.78.

7. Ms Li also challenged this finding as wrong in law.

8. The backgrounds in respect of the mother and child are set out in the Agreed Facts adopted by the parties before the Tribunal. I annex the Agreed Facts to this judgment. The relevant VEPIC applications were filed on behalf of the mother on 21 December 2006 and on behalf of the son on 20 December 2006 respectively. Insofar as there are other facts or evidence relevant to each remaining issue, I will refer to the same in my discussion on each issue.

The role of the court

9. Before I embark on the consideration of the grounds of challenge raised by Ms Li, it is necessary to set out clearly the role of the court in the exercise of its judicial review jurisdiction concerning decisions of the Commissioner and/or the Director of Immigration in immigration matters. These public officials are given the primary duty in assessing whether an applicant satisfies the requirement of the law in applications relating to verification for eligibility to permanent identity card.

10. In *Ng Ka Ling* at p.36 to 37, the Court of Final Appeal held that a scheme for the verification of a person's claim to be permanent resident by the Director is constitutional. The following dicta also confirmed that the primary decision maker in the process of verification is the Director, not the court,

> "In holding the scheme ... to be constitutional as it is

directed towards verification, we have taken into account that the Director must operate it lawfully in a fair and reasonable manner and that there are safeguards to which its operation is subject."

11. This is reiterated in *Prem Singh*[2] by Ribeiro PJ at paras. 56 to 58. At para.58, His Lordship said,

"Accordingly, a non–Chinese person claiming the right to permanent resident status and hence a right of abode, must apply to the Director for his claim to be verified. In accordance with BL art.24(2)(4), the Director is entitled to seek evidence which would establish that the applicant satisfies the entry, seven year and permanence requirements ..."

12. In making decisions in the verification process, the Director (and Tribunal in hearing appeals) bears primary responsibility as in the case of the Secretary for Security in processing a claim under the United Nations Convention Against Torture. Thus, in this respect, the observation by Chief Justice Li as to the role of the court in the latter context in *Secretary for Security v Prabakar* (2004) 7 HKCFAR 187 at para.45 is equally apposite in the present context,

"It is for the [Director] to make such a determination. The courts should not usurp that official's responsibility. But having regard to the gravity of what is at stake, the courts will on judicial review subject the Secretary's determination to rigorous examination and anxious scrutiny to ensure that the required standards of fairness have been met. ... If the courts decide that they have not been met, the determination will be held to have been made unlawfully."

13. In the recent judgment in *TK v Michael Jenkins* HCAL 126 of 2010, 21 October 2011, this court discussed the role of the court in a judicial review in the context of a CAT claim at paras.26 to 29. I have referred counsel to this judgment at the hearing on 26 October and neither Ms Li nor Lord Pannick QC contended that a different approach should be adopted in the present context.

14. Hence, though it is ultimately for the court to decide what is the law pertaining to the ordinary residence and the permanence requirements, the primary decision maker who makes the relevant finding of facts and applies the facts to the law is the Director (and on appeal, the Tribunal). In respect of matters which fall within the primary remit of the Director, the court would only intervene on traditional judicial review grounds though examining the primary decisions with anxious scrutiny given the fundamental nature of the right being involved.

15. As explained in *TK v Michael Jenkins*, under this approach, insofar as the application of the relevant legal principle involves value judgments, the court would not disturb such value judgments on the part of the primary decision maker unless it is shown to be unreasonable on the enhanced *Wednesbury* standard. To the same effect is the judgment of Moses LJ in *R (Davies) v Revenue and Customs Commissioners* [2010] STC 860 at para.15 cited by Lord Pannick.

The mother's failure to satisfy the permanence requirement

16. The Tribunal referred to the judgment of Ribeiro PJ in *Prem Singh* as to the law on the permanence requirement. It summarized the relevant test at para.44 of the Decision,

"The permanence requirement therefore includes both a subjective and an objective element. The appellants had to prove that during the relevant period up to the time of submitting the VEPIC application they had satisfied the permanence requirement by proving that (a) they intended to reside permanently in the HKSAR and (b) they had taken action with a view to residing permanently in the HKSAR and nowhere else."

17. The Tribunal also referred to Paragraph 3(1)(a) of the Schedule to the Immigration Ordinance and took the matters set out in that provision into account in assessing whether the mother satisfied the permanence requirement.

18. After referring to the evidence and the facts, the tribunal examined various specific matters,

(a) The Tribunal paid special regard to the answers given by the mother to the Director and came to the conclusion that she maintained a strong tie and connection with the Philippines (para.57);

(b) The Tribunal explained how it weighed the evidence as regards the religious activities of the mother and said, "... Such activities might throw some light on her quality of life during her leisure time; it did not support her claim of 'ordinarily resident' in Hong Kong conclusively" (para.58);

(c) The Tribunal rejected the mother's reliance on her taking out a Lifetime Protection Plus policy with the HSBC in respect of the permanence requirement because the policy was taken out in about July 2008, one and half year after she filed her application (para.59);

(d) After reiterating the test for the permanence requirement (paras.60 and 61), the Tribunal concluded at para.62,

"Having carefully considered the evidence submitted by both sides, in particular, the Agreed Facts A, the First Affidavit, the exhibits annexed with the Summary of Case and the 3 affirmations filed by the Respondent, the Tribunal could not conclude that the [mother] had taken any steps with a view to residing permanently in Hong Kong or that the [mother's] presence in Hong Kong amounted to 'ordinarily resident' here and her presence in Hong Kong was voluntarily and for settled purpose. ..."

19. The main attack advanced by Ms Li in her oral submissions at the hearing was that the Tribunal failed to make the relevant finding of facts and to give adequate reasons for its conclusions. Counsel submitted that it is impossible to discern how the Tribunal had applied the facts to the *Shah* test[3], in particular the Tribunal did not address why it concluded that the mother did not adopt Hong Kong as her abode voluntarily and for settled purpose.

20. In respect of the conclusion of the Tribunal on the permanence requirement, Ms Li submitted that the Tribunal failed to take the following relevant matters into account or failed to attach sufficient weight to them. Ms Li also submitted that the Tribunal's determination in this regard is irrational and/or biased.

"(1) She has been in Hong Kong for almost 19 years and has taken Hong Kong as her place of permanent residence and has completely integrated into the local society;

(2) She does not have a "home" in the Philippines. Her husband and she have been separated since 1992 and he is now living with another woman in the

Philippines with whom he has two children;

(3) Her children from her marriage with her husband in the Philippines are all grown up and having their own lives. Two of her other children Ceasar and Marc John are currently working in Hong Kong as FDHs;

(4) Her mother is in the Philippines and is being supported by her other children;

(5) She does not own any land or property in the Philippines. All of her assets are located in Hong Kong. In particular, she has taken out a Lifetime Protection Plus policy with the HSBC that requires instalment payments up to the age of 65;

(6) Her future lies in Hong Kong. She plans to continue to live and work in Hong Kong to save for her old age, and to support Master Gutierrez until he is old enough to stand on his own;

(7) She enjoys a cordial relationship with her current employers' family. Her employers are kind, understanding and supportive to her. They treat her and her son as part of their family;

(8) Her son has developed a close bond with her employer's son Zachary, who is seven years old, and who often introduces her son to his friends as "brother". Her employer's family also welcome Marc and Ceasar to visit;

(9) She has developed her social circle in Hong Kong. She is an active member of the Kowloon Filipino Baptist Church. She was baptized into the Baptist faith in February 2003 and worships there every Sunday. She also takes part in the choir during services and is involved in sharing the gospel of Christ with new people in the church. Over the years, her involvement in the Church has grown, and she has participated in many activities, fundraising events and ongoing training and education organized by the Church."

21. Ms Li also referred to the de-registration of the mother as a voter in the Philippines. At para.52 of the Decision, the Tribunal alluded to this. It cannot have any relevance to this application because she only did so after she filed her VEPIC application.

22. This court invited parties to focus on the permanence requirement at the oral hearing because if the mother failed to persuade this court to intervene the Tribunal's decision on that requirement her application for judicial review cannot succeed.

23. Despite that, in view of Ms Li's submissions, I will say a few words on the ordinary residence aspect. To be fair to the Tribunal, it did refer to the *Shah* test extensively at para.32 of the Decision. However, the Tribunal also referred to the submissions of the parties on the Australian case of *Clarke v Clarke* [1964] VR 773. At para.37 of the Decision, the Tribunal appears to accept the approach of Smith J in that case to be persuasive.

24. The way in which the Tribunal dealt with the issue of ordinary residence indicated that it placed substantial weight on the connection maintained by the mother with her home country. In so doing, the Tribunal was obviously influenced by the dicta in *Clarke* relied upon by counsel for the Commissioner (cited at para.35 of the Decision).

25. Unfortunately, it seems that neither party referred the Tribunal to the observations of Lord Scarman in *Ex p Shah* at p.342 E to H including His Lordship's remarks on *Clarke*[4]. Though His Lordship said that the case was correctly decided on its facts, insofar as the approach adopted in it was inconsistent with the principles of law set out in the earlier authorities His Lordship would have rejected the same.

26. Bearing in mind the different context in which the issue arose in *Clarke* and the caution of Lord Scarman, I do not think it is helpful for reference to be made to that case in the present context. Though I have not heard submissions from Lord Pannick in this regard (and no reference was made to this aspect of the decision of the Tribunal in the skeleton submissions), it is difficult to escape from the impression that the Tribunal had been led astray by its reliance on *Clarke* from applying the *Shah* test properly.

27. Coming back to the permanence requirement, the Tribunal correctly directed itself to the test laid down in *Prem Singh*. The Tribunal was correct in identifying that there are both subjective and objective aspects in the test. Given that the requirement must be satisfied before the filing of the application according to *Fateh Muhammad* [5], the Tribunal was correct in rejecting any reliance on the insurance policy.

28. At para.62 of the Decision, the Tribunal specifically stated it was not satisfied that the mother had taken any steps with a view to residing permanently in Hong Kong. As submitted by Lord Pannick, this referred to the objective aspect of the test. In this connection, it is perhaps helpful to recap what Ribeiro PJ said at paras.64 and 66 of *Prem Singh*[6],

> "64. The permanence requirement makes it necessary for the applicant to satisfy the Director both that he intends to establish his permanent home in Hong Kong and that ***he has taken concrete steps to do so***. This means that the applicant must show that his residence here is intended to be more than ordinary residence and that he intends and ***has taken action to make Hong Kong, and Hong Kong alone, his place of permanent residence***. The nature of the permanence requirement may be illuminated by contrasting the 'taking of Hong Kong as a person's place of permanent residence' with merely ordinary residence in Hong Kong." (my emphasis)

> "66. The permanence requirement in BL art.24(2)(4) ***demands more*** in at least two respects. The intention must be to reside, and the steps taken by the applicant must be with a ***view to residing, in Hong Kong permanently or indefinitely, rather than for a limited period***. Such intention and conduct must also be ***addressed to Hong Kong alone*** as the applicant's only place of permanent residence. ..." (my emphasis)

29. The following propositions can be derived,

(a) As submitted by Lord Pannick, the contrast made between the permanence requirement and the ordinary residence requirement shows that, in general, actions or conducts which are referable to ordinary residence are not *per se* sufficient in meeting the permanence requirement. Otherwise, His Lordship would not describe the permanence requirement as demanding more;

(b) Having said so, it does not mean that actions or conducts referable to ordinary residence would not be relevant at all. I can readily envisage that there are cases where the concrete step relied upon by an applicant has to be considered in light of other actions or conducts for the purpose of assessing the intention of the applicant behind such step;

(c) But there has to be some objective concrete steps taken by an applicant for the purpose of making Hong Kong his or her only permanent residence;

(d) Such steps must be addressed to the taking up of Hong Kong, and Hong Kong only, as permanent residence. Thus, steps taken to sever one's link with his or her country of origin are not enough.

30. There is a distinction between severing link with one's country of origin and the making of Hong Kong as one's permanent residence. Before one can make a place his or her only permanent residence, he or she must take some concrete steps turning such aspiration into a realistic proposition in terms of long term livelihood at that place. This can either be achieved by one's independent means or the sponsorship of other persons.

31. If an applicant can produce evidence of such concrete step, then the evidence as to the severance of link with the country of origin would be relevant in making good a case of taking Hong Kong as the only place of permanent residence. But an applicant cannot rely on the latter without the proof of the former.

32. Paragraph 3(1) of Schedule I to the Immigration Ordinance requires an applicant to furnish certain information to the Director when he or she makes an application for verification of eligibility. In the judgment of 30 September 2011 in HCAL 124 of 2010, this court observed at para.115 that whilst the information provided is relevant it may not be determinative. Neither Ms Li nor Lord Pannick argued against that proposition at the hearing on 26th October.

33. I have considered the list of matters Ms Li relied upon in conjunction with the Affidavit of the mother filed in ROPT No.175 of 2008 on 7 April 2010. Applying the enhanced *Wednesbury* test, I am unable to say that the conclusion of the Tribunal is irrational or unreasonable. Nor do I see how the Tribunal can be criticized for failing to take relevant matters into account. As Lord Pannick submitted, most of the matters referred to in that list were matters referable to the ordinary residence of the mother. The only exception is the insurance policy, which for good reason, the Tribunal ruled to be irrelevant for the purpose of this VEPIC application[7]. As regards other matters on the list, none of them can really be regarded as concrete step towards taking Hong Kong as the only permanent residence of the mother.

34. Some of the matters in the list deal with the mother's link with the Philippines. As explained above, those matters cannot be a substitute for evidence as to concrete steps taken towards making Hong Kong as her permanent residence. The other matters in the list deal with the mother's (and her son's) social connections in Hong Kong. But such social connections lack the requisite quality: they cannot be regarded as steps turning an aspiration to have Hong Kong as her permanent residence into a realistic proposition in terms of long term livelihood.

35. This is self-evident from the list. The only item I need to comment on is her relationship with her current employer's family. The mother's own affidavit stated that she worked for this employer for nearly two years since 2008. In other words, when she submitted her application for verification on 21 December 2006, she was working for another employer. That previous employment, according to the Agreed Facts, was terminated on 26 April 2008. She signed a FDH employment contract with the new employer on 25 April 2008 and permission was granted by the Director for her to work for this new employer on 26 June 2008. Thus, her relationship with the family of this new employer cannot assist her in the present application.

36. In any event, unlike the successful applicant in HCAL 124 of 2010, there is no evidence to suggest that the employer would sponsor her livelihood in Hong Kong in support of her application for permanent residence.

37. Turning to Ms Li's contention as to inadequacy of reasons, I have referred to the legal requirement as to the Tribunal's duty to give reasons in my judgment in the *Domingo* case, HCAL 127 & 128 of 2010, 3 November 2011, paras.16 and 17 and the judgment in *TK v Michael Jenkins* HCAL 126 of 2010, 21 October 2011, paras.88 to 90.

38. Further, the adequacy of reasons has to be considered against the arguments advanced before the Tribunal. In the written submissions placed before the Tribunal, counsel for the mother relied on the same matters (now relied upon by Ms Li) to contend that she had satisfied the permanence requirement. The Tribunal applied the correct test and asked itself the right question: whether the mother had taken any steps with a view to residing permanently in Hong Kong. It answered in the negative. Though it had not set out the list of the matters item by item, it is clear from a fair reading of the Decision that it very much had such list in mind when it made the determination. The fact that it chose to refer to some more pertinent items only cannot reasonably justify an inference that it had neglected other items which, as explained above, are of no real assistance to the case of the mother.

39. Given the self-evident irrelevance of the other items, I am of the view that the Tribunal has given adequate reasons for its decision in holding that the mother did not satisfy the permanence requirement.

40. Therefore the challenge by the mother fails.

Permanence requirement in respect of the son

41. The Tribunal accepted the submission of the Commissioner based on *In re P (GE) (an infant)* [1965] 1 Ch 568 and applied it in Para.73 of its Decision.

42. That case concerned a wardship application. In modern parlance, it is a child abduction case. The child in question was brought by his parents into England in 1957. After living in England for several years, the father separated with the mother. The child lived with the mother though arrangement was made so that he saw his father regularly. Without the consent or prior notice to the mother, the father took the child to Israel in November 1962. The mother commenced wardship proceedings in the English court. At first instance, the judge held that the court had no jurisdiction because the child was not physically present in England and he was an alien. On appeal, the Court of Appeal held that the English court had jurisdiction over a child ordinarily resident within England though he was neither a British subject nor physically present when the proceedings were taken out.

43. The three members of the Court of Appeal reached the conclusion that the child was ordinarily resident in England on different bases. The Tribunal alluded to the judgment of Lord Denning MR which provided support for its approach.

44. More recent authorities can be found in the context of cases decided under the Hague Convention on Child Abduction. In *Re B*

[1993] 1 FLR 993, Waite J held at p.995,

> "The habitual residence of the young children of parents who are living together is the same as the habitual residence of the parents themselves and neither parent can change it without the express or tacit consent of the other or an order of the court."

45. This is a rule based on common sense. As a matter of law, the parents of a child have the power to determine where a child should live and at the same time have the duty of taking care of and maintaining the child. Conversely, a child usually has no independent means to provide for himself and cannot determine for himself where he would reside contrary to the wishes of his parents. Thus, there have been cases decided under the Convention where the court sent a child back to his country of habitual residence even though the child objected. It is therefore impossible to apply the concept of ordinary residence to a child without having regard to the position of the parents. Under the *Shah* test, in assessing whether a child is staying at a place voluntarily and for a settled purpose, one must have regard to the situation of his parents.

46. I see no reason why these considerations should not be applied in the context of Article 24(2)(4). By the same token, as a matter of common sense, the same consideration applies in the context of the permanence requirement. This is implicitly recognized in Paragraph 3(1)(b) of Schedule 1 to the Immigration Ordinance.

47. The rule has since been applied in many cases, including cases in Hong Kong, see for example *N v O* [1999]1 HKLRD 68. I referred this case to the parties at the hearing. In my experience in hearing Convention applications, the court in that context always applied the approach that the habitual residence of a child depends upon the intention of his or her primary carer. There are cases where the habitual residence of a child was held to be different from that of the primary carer, but that still depends on the intention of the primary carer. I discussed those cases in my judgment in *LCHY v CWF* [2003] 3 HKC 508 at paras.29 to 38. I did not refer parties to that judgment as I did not recollect its potential relevance before the hearing.

48. I have considered whether I should invite further submissions on that case. In view of what I shall say below, I decide that it is not necessary and I should not delay in giving judgment in view of the general public importance of other issues decided in these cases.

49. The reason for taking this course is that, as I have indicated at the hearing, the crucial issue in these cases is the permanence requirement. As regards the approach in assessing whether a child satisfies this requirement, as submitted by Ms Li, a child of tender age would not have the ability to satisfy the objective aspect in terms of taking concrete steps to make Hong Kong his permanent residence. He must depend on his parents. Thus, in a case like the present where the mother (being the sole carer of the child) cannot satisfy this aspect of the permanence requirement, it is unlikely that her child could satisfy the same.

50. Ms Li submitted it is wrong to adopt this approach as if it is a rule of law applicable in all cases and one must have regard to the facts of the case. I agree it is necessary to have regard to the individual facts of the case. But I do not think the Tribunal adopted such an inflexible approach. The Tribunal carefully said at para.73 that the intent for permanent residence and the ordinary residence for a child "should be viewed against his mother's residence because she lived with him at all material time". Then at para.74 the Tribunal referred to the lack of association with the child's father. The Tribunal said, "It was therefore sensible to take the [son's] ordinary residence and permanence issues as his mother's." At para.75, the Tribunal referred to the evidence before it, thus having regard to the facts of these cases.

51. In her skeleton submissions, at Ms Li referred to the following matters to contend that the son had satisfied the permanence requirement. These are the same matters as set out in counsel's submissions placed before the Tribunal.

> "(1) The root of Master Gutierrez is in Hong Kong. He was born in Hong Kong and grows up here. He does not have a home in the Philippines or anywhere else. Hong Kong is his home and he wants to live here and be taken care of by Madam Gutierrez who works here;
>
> (2) He has completely integrated into the local society. All of his friends are in Hong Kong. The employer's son treats him like brother. He speaks, reads and writes fluent English. He also speaks some Mandarin and Cantonese. He was baptized at the Kowloon Filipina Baptist Church in July 2008;
>
> (3) He feels like an "alien" in the Philippines. He only speaks very little Tagalog. He does not have any friends there. No one would become his caretaker in the Philippines;
>
> (4) Although Master Gutierrez holds a Philippine passport, whenever he visits the Philippines, he is required to pay airport tax like a foreigner;
>
> (5) His half-brothers Ceasar and Marc John, to whom he is particularly close, are currently working in Hong Kong as FDHs. Ceasar came to Hong Kong about 14 months ago while Marc has been here more than four and a half years already. Both Ceasar and Marc John are working in Discovery Bay. They go to church together on Sundays;
>
> (6) In Master Gutierrez's spare time, he goes swimming and plays tennis in the Residents Club. In 2006, He took a swimming course in Discovery Bay. He also participated in the tree-planting activities Madam Gutierrez referred to in her affidavit in support of his appeal. He also enjoys participating in various activities in Hong Kong such as football, rugby and enrolling in interest course such as "Basics of Flying";
>
> (7) He is sometimes taught by Madam Gutierrez, Ceasar and Marc John and is also receiving free mathematics and piano lessons from a retired teacher and a friend of Madam Gutierrez."

52. It is clear from these submissions that the son did not and could not assert that he had independent means from the mother to satisfy the objective element in the permanence requirement. Nor is there any suggestion that the mother intended to leave the son in the care of somebody's else (and that such person was willing to take up such responsibility and had the means to do so).

53. Given this court's conclusion on the necessary ingredient in the permanence requirement in the mother's case, none of the matters relied upon in respect of son's case establishes that requisite concrete step had been taken by the son or by the mother on his behalf. On this ground alone, the son's challenge to the decision of the Tribunal fails.

The gaps in the son's continuous presence in Hong Kong [8]

54. Not being a Chinese citizen, and none of his parents satisfied the criteria in Article 24(2)(4), the son cannot acquire Hong Kong permanent resident status by birth in Hong Kong pursuant to Article 24(2)(1) and (2)(5). He therefore has to rely on Article 24(2)(4).

55. After his birth on 1 December 1996, the son was granted permission to remain in Hong Kong on visitor condition on 12 December 1996. He got a Philippine passport on 26 March 1997. He left Hong Kong for the Philippines on 30 August 1997.

56. Focusing on the seven years immediately prior to his application for verification on 20 December 2006 (viz. starting from 20 December 1999), there were three occasions when the son was away from Hong Kong. The details were set out at para.77 of the Decision. On each occasion, upon his return, he was given permission to enter and remain in Hong Kong on visitor condition.

57. At paras.78 to 80, the Tribunal considered the implication of such absence in the light of Section 11(10) of the Immigration Ordinance. That sub-section provides,

> "Any permission given to a person to land or remain in Hong Kong shall, if in force on the day that person departs from Hong Kong, expire immediately after his departure."

58. At para.79 of the Decision, the Tribunal analysed the effect of this provision in relation to the son's departure and return to Hong Kong in 2004 as follows,

> "... when the [son] left Hong Kong on 31 March 2004, his prior stay in Hong Kong could not be treated as a period continuous to the period when he stayed in Hong Kong on the strength of a new visitor visa ...."

59. This should be read together with the earlier reference by the Tribunal at para.34 of the Decision to the judgment of Appeal Committee in *Sun Jie v Registration of Persons Tribunal* FAMV 20 of 2006.

60. With the break in the continuity in 2004, the Tribunal held that the son's continuous ordinary residence in Hong Kong immediately before his verification application could only have commenced from 31 March 2004. Thus he could not meet the seven year requirement.

61. Plainly, in so holding, the Tribunal accepted the argument at para.29 of the written submissions of the Commissioner. The relevant analysis [*sic*] are as follows,

> "(1) Ordinary residence entails presence m a place a person can lawfully remain. If he cannot lawfully reside in a place by reason of his having no permission to stay, he cannot be treated as ordinarily resident there. Thus where a person who has been ordinarily resident in Hong Kong leaves and by his departure from Hong Kong the remaining period of his permission to stay expired by operation of s.11 (10) of the Ordinance, the period of absence from Hong Kong cannot be treated as ordinary residence: see Sun Jie v Registration of Persons Tribunal, FAMV 20/2006 (*unrep.*, 28 September 2006) §4, CACV 320/2004 (*unrep.*, 13 December 2005) §§8–11; applied in Commissioner of Registration v Registration of Persons Tribunal, HCAL 39/2005 (unrep., 25 January 2007) §§31–41.
>
> (2) In the present case, the Son has been permitted to remain in Hong Kong as a visitor subject to time limitation. Section 11(10) of the Ordinance provides that:–
>
> *"Any permission given to a person to land or remain in Hong Kong shall, if in force on the day that person departs from Hong Kong, expire immediately after his departure."*
>
> In other words, every time the Son departed from Hong Kong, his permission to remain expired immediately. Thereafter he had no right to remain in Hong Kong until he presented for arrival clearance and was granted afresh permission to remain on visitor condition upon fulfilment of relevant immigration requirements. The subsequent permission was not a continuation of the previous permission to remain (which had already expired), but was fresh permission based on the Son having satisfied the relevant immigration requirements at the time of arrival in Hong Kong. Thus his periods of absence could not amount to residence, still less ordinary residence, in Hong Kong.
>
> (3) Section 2(6) of the Ordinance (175 Skel §52) has no application. It presupposes that a person is ordinarily resident in Hong Kong, such that his temporary physical absence may in some circumstances still be regarded as ordinary residence. But that very premise is absent here, for according to Sun Jie, the Son's period of absence from Hong Kong (when he had no permission to remain here) cannot be regarded as ordinary residence.
>
> (4) The Son's periods of absence from Hong Kong cannot be regarded as *de minimis:* see Prem Singh §§75–76."

62. *Sun Jie v Registration of Persons Tribunal* concerns an applicant who came from the Mainland and worked in Hong Kong for 6 odd years. Upon the end of his employment, his limit of stay also expired. He therefore left Hong Kong at the end of 1999. But he continued to keep a rented flat here. He returned to Hong Kong as a visitor in March 2000, stayed for 2 days and then went to the Republic of Nauru. He somehow got a Nauru passport and returned to Hong Kong on 1 April 2000. Upon arrival, he was allowed to enter and remain as a visitor until 2 May 2000. Before the expiry of that period, he got married with a Hong Kong resident and applied to change of his status from visitor to a dependent of his wife. Pending the processing of that application, he was granted extensions of stay. The application for change of status was refused. After that he applied for verification in February 2001. That application was rejected on the ground that his departure at the end of 1999 broke the continuity of his ordinary residence in Hong Kong.

63. In the Court of Appeal (CACV 320 of 2004, 22 December 2005), Rogers VP referred to five propositions put forward by counsel which His Lordship accepted as correct. For present purposes, it is only necessary to refer to the following propositions,

> "(b) Where a person who is ordinarily resident in Hong Kong leaves Hong Kong temporarily he may be treated as still remaining ordinarily resident so long as such absence is during a valid limit of stay which has not expired.

(c) Where a person who has been ordinarily resident in Hong Kong leaves because his permission to stay ends the period of absence from Hong Kong cannot be treated as ordinary residence.

(d) The provisions of section 2(6) of the [Immigration Ordinance] must be read with the foregoing propositions in mind, thus the 'circumstances of the person' which the subsection makes relevant will include the question of whether the person was entitled to be in Hong Kong during that period of absence.

(e) The common law concept of ordinary residence is not a purely subjective matter. It is also necessary to see what has happened as a matter of objective fact during the period and this includes whether a person would be entitled to remain."

64. At para.9, His Lordship had the following observations,

"Although I have no doubt that these propositions are correct, it seems to me that this case is governed by one very simple proposition namely that it is impossible for somebody to be ordinarily resident in a place when he cannot be resident there."

65. Mr Sun sought leave to appeal and his application was rejected by the Appeal Committee of the Court of Final Appeal. In the Determination, Chan PJ said,

"3. The main ground of appeal is that the Court of Appeal had misinterpreted the term 'ordinary residence' in the Immigration Ordinance, Cap.115 ... in holding that absence from Hong Kong for a period during which the applicant did not have permission to stay in Hong Kong had broken the continuity of his ordinary residence for the purpose of acquiring permanent residence in Hong Kong. It is submitted that this interpretation prevents the applicant, a law abiding non-resident, from accumulating the requisite period of residence and leaves him at the mercy of the Immigration Officer.

4. We do not think this is reasonably arguable ground of appeal. The applicant was given permission to remain and hence to acquire ordinary residence in Hong Kong on the basis of his employment. When his employment was terminated, he no longer had any permission to remain and his ordinary residence also came to an end. In order to succeed, the applicant has to show that he falls within s.2(6) of the Ordinance. It is clear that he does not. His absence was not a merely temporary hiatus in a continuous period of ordinary residence. This is because when he returned, he was permitted to remain on a completely different basis which the Registration of Persons has found to be false. There was no continuity between his residence here as an employee and his presence as a visitor permitted to remain as a result of his false representations."

66.The false representation was his false claims to the Immigration officers in 2000 that he had never entered Hong Kong before April 2000, see para.4 of the judgment of the Court of Appeal.

67. In *Commissioner of Registration v Registration of Persons Tribunal* HCAL 39 of 2005, 25 Jan 2007, Reyes J applied *Sun Jie* in the context of a person who tried to advance a case of continuous ordinary residence based on his different periods of stay in Hong Kong under visitor visa notwithstanding breaks in between. His Lordship considered the implication of reading *Sun Jie* with Section 11(10) of the Immigration Ordinance. At para.34, Reyes J said,

"It follows that ... during any period of absence from Hong Kong, his limit of stay having expired upon departure from the HKSAR, Mr Bruce would have had no lawful permission to enter or reside here."

68. The son is in the same position. During the three occasions when he left Hong Kong, his previous permission to stay expired. Thus, for those periods when he was outside Hong Kong, he did not have any lawful right to remain in Hong Kong. When he came back on each occasion, the Director would give him a fresh permission to enter and to remain for a limited period, which were extended from time to time till his next departure. But the Director was not under any legal duty to give him such permission. Thus, there were breaks in the continuity of his presence in Hong Kong.

69. Ms Li sought to meet this analysis by reference to the following,

(a) The decision of the Court of Final Appeal in *Gurung Bahadur v Director of Immigration* (2002) HKCFAR 480;

(b) Section 2(6) of the Immigration Ordinance;

(c) Two dicta of Lord Scarman in *Ex p Shah*[9].

70. *Gurung Bahadur v Director of Immigration* (2002) HKCFAR 480 concerned a Nepali who had changed his status from a visitor to a dependant of his wife, a Hong Kong permanent resident. He was given a limit of stay and at the time of the incident, the limit had not yet expired. He left Hong Kong in October 1997 and returned on 4 November 1997. The Director refused to permit him to enter and made a removal order against him. He applied for judicial review on the basis of his right as a non-permanent resident under Article 31 of the Basic Law: the freedom to travel and to enter or leave Hong Kong.

71. His challenge succeeded. However, it is important to understand that he was able to assert the right under Article 31 to prevail over the effect of Section 11(10) of the Immigration Ordinance because of his status as dependant with an unexpired limit of stay. This is obvious from the following paragraphs in the judgment of Li CJ in the Court of Final Appeal,

"40. Section 11(10) itself is not unconstitutional. It is its application to a non-permanent resident, ***whose permitted limit of stay has not expired***, which is inconsistent with his rights under art.31 of the Basic Law. Section 11(10) continues validly to apply to persons who are not non-permanent residents with an unexpired limit of stay, for example, to visitors.

41. As with any person, including a permanent resident who enjoys the right of abode, a non-permanent resident ***with an unexpired permitted limit of stay*** may be examined by immigration officials under s.4 of the Ordinance. But he does not require permission to land under s.7 because ***the previous permission with the unexpired limit of stay remains effective***. As pointed out by Mr Pannick, such a non-permanent resident in effect would enjoy an important element of the right of abode. See ss.2A(1)(a) and 7(1). But this is only one of the elements of the right of abode and is enjoyed by such a

non-permanent resident ***during and only during the unexpired permitted limit of stay***. There is nothing surprising in this result. It follows from his rights to travel and to enter guaranteed by art.31. These rights in the new order were created by the Basic Law.

42. It must be emphasized that this judgment only concerns a non-permanent resident in a position like the respondent, ***whose permitted limit of stay has not expired***. A person whose limit of stay has expired would cease to be a non-permanent resident and would be in a very different position. ..."

72. Thus, the case does not assist a person whose limit of stay expired upon his departure from Hong Kong. That would be the position of a visitor. As observed by the Chief Justice, a visitor is not a non-permanent resident and in respect of him Section 11(10) applies in full force. The situation of a visitor is governed by *Sun Jie*.

73. Though multiple journey visas were issued to the son, his status remains that of a visitor. On each occasion when he returned to Hong Kong a fresh permission to land and remain in Hong Kong as visitor for a limited period was granted by the Director. There was no application for the change of his status from that of a visitor to a dependant. Therefore, Section 11(10) applies to him and he is caught by *Sun Jie*.

74. Ms Li's reliance on Section 2(6) of the Immigration Ordinance and *Ex p Shah* cannot take the argument further because they had been duly considered by the Court of Appeal in *Sun Jie*. In that case, counsel for Mr Sun relied heavily on *Ex p Shah* (as shown in the judgment at first instance[10] and para.7 of the judgment of Rogers VP). At para.10 of the judgment of the Court of Appeal, Rogers VP explained why *Ex p Shah* could not help Mr Sun,

"As explained in the *Shah* case ordinary residence has to be understood in its natural meaning. As is acknowledged in the reported cases, a person who is ordinarily resident in a particular place is, of course, at liberty to travel and move from place to place. Such a person will remain ordinarily resident in his place of ordinary residence even when he is away. ... Despite all that, ordinary residence must entail presence in that place and if a person cannot lawfully be in that place he cannot reside there, still less can he be ordinarily resident there."

And at para.11, after referring to the facts of the case,

"... A person cannot be in any better position to claim to be ordinarily resident because he is not physically in a place where, if he were present, his residence would not be treated as being ordinary residence."

75. Section 2(6) was dealt with at proposition (d) set out at para.8 of the judgment of the Court of Appeal. In other words, during a period of absence where a person has no right to be in Hong Kong (and as such his return to Hong Kong would have to be subject to a fresh permission from the Director to enter and remain), for the purpose of that section the person cannot be regarded as temporarily absent. This was also the reason why the Appeal Committee held that there was a break in the continuity of residence in the case of Mr Sun, see para.4 of the Determination.

76. I am bound by the decision of the Court of Appeal and the Determination of the Appeal Committee in *Sun Jie*. And I do not think *Sun Jie* is in any way inconsistent with *Ex p Shah*. In *Ex p Shah* the House of Lords dealt with students holding student visas, permitting them to stay in the UK for the course of his study. Thus, the students were in a similar position as Mr Gurung Bahadur. Lord Scarman did not address the issue of gaps of absence during which a person has no permission to remain. Had His Lordship been asked to consider this issue, what he said at p.348D by way of rider indicates that he would probably give the same answer as the Court of Appeal and the Appeal Committee in *Sun Jie*. The rider is,

"... unless it be that of one who has no right to be here, in which event presence in the UK is unlawful ..."

77. Therefore, the Tribunal is correct in holding that the son did not have seven year continuous ordinary residence in Hong Kong immediately before his application on 20 December 2006.

78. In the circumstances, the son's challenge must also fail on this alternative ground.

Results

79. Both applications for judicial review are dismissed with costs, such costs are to be taxed if not agreed.

Judge of the Court of First Instance, High Court (M H Lam)

Ms Gladys Li, SC, Mr Kwok Sui Hay and Ms Jocelyn S.L. Leung, instructed by Messrs Barnes & Daly (D.L.A.), for the Applicants

Mr Lord Pannick, QC, Mr Anderson Chow, SC and Ms Eva Sit, instructed by Department of Justice, for the 1st Respondent

---

Footnotes:

1 (1999) 2 HKCFAR 4

2 (2003) 6 HKCFAR 26

3 The test for ordinary residence as laid down in *Ex p Shah* [1983] 2 AC 309.

4 His Lordship referred to a different report of the same case: *Clarke v Insurance Office of Australia* [1965] 1 LL Rep 308.

5 (2001) 4 HKCFAR 278

6 (2003) 6 HKCFAR 26

7 In so saying, I should not be taken as deciding that the taking out of an insurance policy would be sufficient as a concrete step to satisfy the permanence requirement. Whether that is sufficient must be assessed against all the facts of a particular case and the primary decision makers are the Director and the Tribunal. All I said here is that in this case the Tribunal correctly excluded the policy from consideration in view of the date of the relevant VEPIC application.

8 The gap point was only argued in the context of the son's case. However, there appears to be gaps in the mother's case as well: in 2003 and 2005 when she changed employers she, according to the movement records, left Hong Kong during those gaps. Since I have not heard submissions on this point in respect of those gaps, I would just put down a marker here.

9 [1983] 2 AC 309 at p.342D and p.348D to E.

10 HCAL 186 of 2002, 16 August 2004

Annex I

Appellant: Ms. GUTIERREZ Josephine B

Agreed Facts

The Appellant's Personal and Family Background

1. Ms. GUTTIERREZ Josephine B also known as GUTIERREZ Josephine Balando ("**Ms GUTIERREZ**") was born in the Philippines on 23 September 1963.
2. Ms GUTIERREZ is a Philippine national.
3. She married Mr. GUTIERREZ Marcial B. ("**Mr. GUTIERREZ**") in the Philippines in 1977 but they have since separated.
4. Ms GUTIERREZ has four children born of Mr. GUTIERREZ, all of whom reside in the Philippines, namely:–
   (i) Michael Ceasar B. GUTIERREZ, the first child, was born in the Philippines on 15 January 1980, aged 31;
   (ii) Marc Jonh B. GUTIERREZ, the second child, was born in the Philippines on 19 April 1983, aged 26;
   (iii) Marvin B. GUTIERREZ, the third child, was born in the Philippines on 9 April 1986, aged 23; and
   (iv) Marcial B. GUTIERREZ JR., the fourth child, was born in the Philippines on 27 August 1987, aged 22.
5. Ms GUTIERREZ has a fifth child, Joseph James GUTIERREZ("Joseph"), who was born out of the wedlock in Hong Kong on 1 December 1996. Joseph is now 13 years old and resides in Hong Kong with Ms GUTIERREZ.

The Appellant's Employment History in Hong Kong

First Employment

6. On 22 March 1991, Ms GUTIERREZ signed an employment contract to work as a foreign domestic helper ("**FDH**") in Hong Kong for Ms SIU Mun Yee ("**Ms SIU**").
7. On 18 April 1991, Hong Kong Immigration Department "**ImmD**") received Ms GUTIERREZ's application for a Hong Kong entry visa to work as an FDH for Ms SIU.
8. On 6 June 1991, Ms GUTIERREZ's FDH visa application was approved and she was issued with a visa for employment with Ms SIU for twelve months.
9. In about July 1991, Ms GUTIERREZ arrived in Hong Kong to take up her employment with Ms SIU. Her permission to remain to work for Ms SIU as an FDH was subsequently extended upon application until 23 July 1993 or two weeks after termination of contract, whichever was earlier.
10. In August 1991, Ms GUTIERREZ registered for and was issued a Hong Kong Identity Card ("**HKIC**") no. XXXXXXX(X). A replacement HKIC no. XXXXXXX(X) was issued to her on 28 October 1991 upon reporting loss.
11. Ms GUTIERREZ's employment contract with Ms SIU was terminated on 6 September 1992.
12. On 15 September 1992, Ms GUTIERREZ applied to ImmD for extension of stay to enable her to settle her labour case against Ms SIU.
13. On 1 October 1992, Ms GUTIERREZ's condition as an FDH in Hong Kong was varied. She was granted permission to remain on visitor condition until 17 November 1992 to facilitate her attending a conciliation meeting arranged by the Labour Department.

Second Employment

14. On 2 November 1992, Ms GUTIERREZ applied to ImmD for change of employer ("**C/E**") to work for Mr. John HORWOOD ("**Mr. HORWOOD**").
15. On 2 November 1992, Ms GUTIERREZ was granted extension of stay on visitor condition until 8 December 1992.
16. On 11 November 1992, Ms GUTIERREZ signed an employment contract with Mr. HORWOOD to work as an FDH in Hong Kong.
17. On 29 January 1993, Ms GUTIERREZ was granted extension of stay on visitor condition until 19 February 1993 to facilitate the finalization of the formalities of the C/E application.
18. On 16 February 1993, Ms GUTIERREZ's C/E application was approved, and she was granted permission to take up her employment as an FDH in Hong Kong for Mr. HORWOOD until 16 February 1994 or two weeks after termination of contract, whichever was earlier.
19. Ms GUTIERREZ's employment with Mr. HORWOOD was terminated on 12 October 1993.
20. On 12 October 1993, Ms GUTIERREZ's condition of stay in Hong Kong was varied. She was granted permission to remain on visitor condition until 19 October 1993 to facilitate her departure arrangements.

Third Employment

21. On 18 October 1993, Ms GUTIERREZ applied to ImmD for C/E to work for Mr. Christopher ROCK ("**Mr. ROCK**"). She was granted extension of stay on visitor condition until 18 December 1993.
22. On 6 December 1993, Ms GUTIERREZ signed an employment contract with Mr. ROCK to work as an FDH in Hong Kong.
23. On 11 December 1993, Ms GUTIERREZ's C/E application was approved, she was granted permission to take up employment as an FDH in Hong Kong for Mr. ROCK until 11 December 1994 or two weeks after termination of contract, whichever was earlier.
24. On 16 December 1994, Ms GUTIERREZ was granted extension of stay to continue her employment as an FDH in Hong Kong with Mr. ROCK until 11 December 1995 or two weeks after the termination of contract, whichever was earlier.
25. On 31 January 1995, Ms GUTIERREZ's employment with Mr. ROCK was terminated.

Fourth Employment

26. On 24 February 1995, Ms GUTIERREZ's condition of stay in Hong Kong was varied. She was granted permission to remain on visitor condition until 7 March 1995 to facilitate settlement of her labour case against Mr. ROCK.

27. After her labour case was settled on 28 February 1995, Ms GUTIERREZ applied for C/E to work for Mr. YUE James Kuo Wei ("**Mr. YUE**"). On 7 March 1995, Ms GUTIERREZ was granted an extension of stay on visitor condition until 7 April 1995 to process the C/E application.

28. On 4 April 1995, Ms GUTIERREZ withdrew the C/E application to work for Mr. YUE and applied to work for Mr. LUI Shui Hing Peter ("**Mr. LUI**") instead. She was granted extension of stay on the same day on visitor condition until 18 April 1995 to process the C/E application.

29. On 8 April 1995, Ms GUTIERREZ signed an employment contract with Mr. LUI to work as an FDH in Hong Kong.

30. On 19 April 1995, Ms GUTIERREZ was granted permission to work as an FDH in Hong Kong for Mr. LUI until 12 March 1996 or two weeks after termination of contract, whichever was earlier.

31. On 5 March 1996, Ms GUTIERREZ was granted an extension of stay to continue her employment as an FDH in Hong Kong for Mr. LUI until 19 April 1997 or two weeks after termination of contract, whichever was earlier.

32. On 23 April 1996, Ms GUTIERREZ's employment with Mr. LUI was terminated.

Permission to Remain in Hong Kong on Visitor Condition

33. On 6 May 1996, Ms GUTIERREZ applied to ImmD for an extension of stay in order to look for a new employer in Hong Kong.

34. On 22 May 1996, Ms GUTIERREZ's application was refused and she was reminded that her permission to remain in Hong Kong only lasted up to 7 May 1996, but her voluntary departure on or before 29 May 1996 would be facilitated.

35. On 31 May 1996, Ms GUTIERREZ applied to ImmD for an extension of stay in order to file a labour claim against Mr. LUI.

36. On 3 June 1996, Ms GUTIERREZ was granted an extension of stay on visitor condition until 2 July 1996 which upon applications was further extended until 12 August 1996 to facilitate settlement of her labour case.

37. On 12 August 1996, Ms GUTIERREZ applied for extension of stay for the reasons that she had her passport taken from her as she was indebted to finance companies and that she wanted to look for a new employer. The application was refused and she was reminded that her permission to remain in Hong Kong only lasted up to 12 August 1996.

38. On 19 August 1996, Ms GUTIERREZ applied for extension of stay in order to process her C/E application to work for Mr. FUNG Chi Sing Tonly ("**Mr. Fung**"), and she was called up to attend ImmD for an interview with required documents on 5 September 1996.

39. On 5 September 1996, Ms GUTIERREZ was unable to produce the specified documents from Mr. FUNG as required and her application was therefore cancelled. Ms GUTIERREZ was granted extension of stay on visitor condition until 12 September 1996 and was required to leave Hong Kong on or before that day.

40. Since September 1996, Ms GUTIERREZ submitted applications for extension of stay for various reasons including application for C/E in Hong Kong, objection lodged to the Chief Secretary under section 53 of the Ordinance against ImmD's refusal to her C/E application, arrangement of someone to take her son (Joseph) back to the Philippines, and to pursue her labour claim against Mr. LUI; she was granted permissions to remain in Hong Kong on visitor condition until the latest 28 June 1997.

Fifth Employment

41. On 3 June 1997, Ms GUTIERREZ was informed that ImmD was prepared to reverse its previous decision and approve her application for C/E. On 19 June 1997, Ms GUTIERREZ was granted permission to remain in Hong Kong to work as an FDH for Mr. Howard Lee SELLARS Jr. ("**Mr. SELLARS**") until 19 June 1998 or two weeks after the termination of contract, whichever was earlier.

42. By subsequent contract renewals and extensions of stay, Ms GUTIERREZ was granted permission to work as an FDH for Mr. SELLARS until 19 June 2003 or two weeks after termination of contract, whichever was earlier.

43. Ms GUTIERREZ was released by Mr. SELLARS on 10 June 2003.

Sixth Employment

44. On 3 June 2003, Ms GUTIERREZ signed an employment contract with Mr. Peter Michael CHADWICK ("**Mr. CHADWICK**") to work as an FDH in Hong Kong.

45. On 4 July 2003, Ms GUTIERREZ was granted permission to remain in Hong Kong as an FDH to work for Mr. CHADWICK until 4 July 2005 or two weeks after termination of contract, whichever was earlier.

46. By replacement of HKIC on 18 March 2004, Ms GUTIERREZ was issued with a SMART HKIC no. XXXXXXX(X).

47. On 4 July 2005, Ms GUTIERREZ was released from contract by Mr. CHADWICK.

Seventh Employment

48. On 28 June 2005, Ms GUTIERREZ signed an employment contract with Mr. Jason WILLINGHAM ("**Mr. WILLINGHAM**") to work as an FDH in Hong Kong.

49. On 28 July 2005, Ms GUTIERREZ was granted permission to remain in Hong Kong as an FDH to work for Mr. WILLINGHAM until 28 July 2006 or two weeks after termination of contract, whichever was earlier.

50. On 1 August 2005, Ms GUTIERREZ departed Hong Kong. On 12 August 2005, Ms GUTIERREZ entered Hong Kong on the strength of a re-entry visa and was permitted to remain in Hong Kong as an FDH to work for Mr. WILLINGHAM until 28 July 2007 or two weeks after termination of contract, whichever was earlier.

51. Upon subsequent contract renewal and extension of stay, Ms GUTIERREZ was granted permission to remain in Hong Kong as an FDH to work for Mr. WILLINGHAM until 28 July 2008 or two weeks after termination of contract, whichever was earlier.

52. Ms GUTIERREZ's employment with Mr. WILLINGHAM was terminated on 26 April 2008.

Eighth Employment

53. On 25 April 2008, Ms GUTIERREZ signed an employment contract with Mr. Randal Arthur LEONARD ("**Mr. LEONARD**") to work as an FDH in Hong Kong.

54. On 26 June 2008, Ms GUTIERREZ was granted permission to remain in Hong Kong as an FDH to work for Mr. LEONARD until 26 June 2009 or two weeks after termination of contract, whichever was earlier.

The Appellant's Reported Connection in Hong Kong and the Philippines

55. During Ms GUTIERREZ's employment as an FDH in Hong Kong, she has been staying in her employers' respective residence.

56. Ms GUTIERREZ's widowed mother, aged 70, resides in the Philippines.

57. Ms GUTIERREZ's fifth child, Joseph, who was born in Hong Kong on 1 December 1996, was all along given permission to remain on visitor condition during his presence in Hong Kong, and has been staying with Ms GUTIERREZ at her employers' respective residences.

Application for Verification of Eligibility for Permanent Identity Card ("VEPIC")

58. On 21 December 2006, ImmD received the VEPIC application from Ms GUTIERREZ. She laid claim to the permanent resident status of the Hong Kong Special Administrative Region (**"HKSAR"**) under paragraph 2(f) of schedule 1 to the Immigration Ordinance, Chapter 115 (**"the Schedule" and "the Ordinance"** respectively).

59. By a letter of 4 June 2007, ImmD informed Ms GUTIERREZ that her VEPIC application was refused on the ground that–

(i) paragraph 2(f) of the Schedule was not applicable to her as she was born in the Philippines and is a Philippine citizen at birth;

(ii) she was unable to fulfill the residence requirement for permanent resident status of the HKSAR under paragraph 2(d) of the Schedule; and

(iii) she was not eligible for permanent resident status of the HKSAR under other provisions of the Schedule.

Application for Hong Kong permanent identity card ("HKPIC")

60. On 24 September 2008, Ms GUTIERREZ applied for registration of a HKPIC. On the same day, the HKPIC application was refused because there was insufficient evidence to show that Ms GUTIERREZ had the right of abode in Hong Kong.

Appeal to the Registration of Persons ("ROP") Tribunal

61. On 3 October 2008, The ROP Tribunal received from Ms GUTIERREZ's Solicitors an appeal lodged by Ms GUTIERREZ against the decision of the Commissioner not to issue a HKPIC to her on 24 September 2008.

Dated the 9th day of April 2010.

(Signed)	(Signed)
Messrs Barnes & Daly Solicitors for the Appellant	(SUEN Sze Yick) Government Counsel Department of Justice Solicitors for the Commissioner of Registration

Annex II

Appellant: Master GUTIERREZ Joseph James

Agreed Facts

The Appellant's Personal and Family Background

1. Master GUTIERREZ Joseph James (**"Master GUTIERREZ"**) was born in Hong Kong on 1 December 1996.
2. Master GUTIERREZ is a Philippine national.
3. His mother, Ms GUTIERREZ Josephine Balando (**"Ms GUTIERREZ"**), is a Philippine national. She has been working as a foreign domestic helper in Hong Kong since 23 July 1991.
4. When Master GUTIERREZ was born on 1 December 1996, Ms GUTIERREZ was remaining in Hong Kong on visitor status.
5. Master GUTIERREZ's father is said to be a U.S. citizen. Ms GUTIERREZ was not married to him and she had no contact with him.

Remaining in Hong Kong on Visitor Condition

6. On 12 December 1996, Master GUTIERREZ was granted permission to remain on visitor condition until 16 December 1996.
7. With subsequent extensions of stay granted from December 1996 to June 1997, Master GUTIERREZ's permission to stay in Hong Kong on visitor status was extended until 30 August 1997.
8. Master GUTIERREZ was issued with a Philippine passport on 26 March 1997.
9. On 30 August 1997, Master GUTIERREZ left Hong Kong for the Philippines.
10. On 10 January 1998, Master GUTIERREZ arrived in Hong Kong and was permitted to remain in Hong Kong on visitor condition until 13 February 1998.
11. With subsequent extensions of stay granted in February 1998, Master GUTIERREZ's permission to stay in Hong Kong on visitor condition was extended until 13 March 1998.
12. On 3 April 1998, Master GUTIERREZ was granted permission to stay in Hong Kong on visitor condition until 19 June 1998 which was coterminous with Ms GUTIERREZ's stay as FDH in Hong Kong.
13. With an extension of stay granted on 6 July 1998, Master GUTIERREZ's permission to stay in Hong Kong on visitor condition was extended until 19 June 1999.
14. Apart from several absences from Hong Kong without permission to stay, Master GUTIERREZ was granted permission to stay in Hong Kong on visitor status until 11 May 2007 upon subsequent applications for extension of stay or arrivals in Hong Kong.

The Appellant's Application for Verification of Eligibility for Permanent Identity Card ("VEPIC")

15. On 20 December 2006, ImmD received the VEPIC application from Master GUTIERREZ. Master GUTIERREZ laid claim to the permanent resident status of the Hong Kong Special Administrative Region (**"HKSAR"**) under paragraph 2(f) of Schedule 1 to the Immigration Ordinance, Chapter 115 (**"the Schedule"**).
16. By a letter of 25 September 2008, ImmD informed the Solicitors that the VEPIC application of Master GUTIERREZ was refused.

The Appellant's Application for Hong Kong permanent identity card ("HKPIC")

17. On 16 October 2008, Master GUTIERREZ applied for registration of a juvenile HKPIC under the guardianship of Ms GUTIERREZ. On the same day, the HKPIC application was refused because there was insufficient evidence to show that Master GUTIERREZ had the right of abode in Hong Kong.

The Appellant's Appeal to the Registration of Persons ("ROP") Tribunal

18. On 17 October 2008, the ROP Tribunal received from the Solicitors an appeal lodged by Ms GUTIERREZ against the decision of the Commissioner not to issue a HKPIC to Master GUTIERREZ.

Dated the 9th day of April 2010

(Signed)	(Signed)
Messrs Barnes & Daly Solicitors for the Appellant	(SUEN Sze Yick) Government Counsel Department of Justice Solicitors for the Commissioner of Registration

吳嘉玲、吳丹丹 對 入境事務處處長
徐權能 對 入境事務處處長
入境事務處處長 對 張麗華

HCAL68/1997；HCAL70/1997；HCAL71/1997；HCAL73/1997；CACV203/1997；CACV216/1997；CACV217/1997；CACV218/1997；FACV14/1998；FACV15/1998；FACV16/1998（判決書參考 P.071）

簡略案情

申請人吳嘉玲和吳丹丹兩人是姊妹，是內地出生的中國籍人士。她倆分別於 1987 年及 1989 年出生，當時她們的父親已是在香港通常居住連續 7 年以上的中國公民。他在 1976 年來港，而兩名申請人則於 1997 年 7 月 1 日沒有通過入境管制站進入本港。1997 年 7 月 4 日她們向入境處報到，堅稱根據《基本法》第 24（2）條第 3 款擁有居留權，但她們的權利未獲入境處處長承認。

申請人徐權能先生是內地出生的中國籍人士，在 1978 年出生時，他父親已是在香港通常居住連續 7 年以上的中國公民，並早於 1962 年來港，而申請人則於 1997 年 7 月 1 日沒有通過入境管制站而進入本港。1997 年 7 月 3 日，他向入境處報到，亦堅稱根據《基本法》第 24（2）條第 3 款擁有居留權，但他的權利未獲入境處處長承認。

申請人張麗華小姐是內地出生的中國籍人士，在 1989 年出生時，她父親已是在香港通常居住連續 7 年以上的中國公民，並早於 1967 年來港。出世時父母未正式註冊結婚，其母親在她出生後的第二天便不幸去世。1994 年 12 月，張小姐持雙程證來港。1995 年 1 月，她的雙程證有效期屆滿，之後一直逾期居留。1997 年 7 月 15 日，她向入境處報到，並堅稱根據《基本法》第 24（2）條第 3 款擁有居留權。但她的權利未獲入境處處長承認。

入境處處長認為張麗華小姐並非婚生子女，所以不被包括在《基本法》第 24（2）條第 3 款中。而且，根據臨時立法會通過的《入境（修訂）（第 3 號）條例》，依靠《基本法》第 24（2）條第 3 款獲得的永久性居民身份只可持有有效旅行證件及附貼於該旅行證件上的有效居留權證明書，才能確立其身份。否則，根據《入境（修訂）（第 3 號）條例》第 2AA（2）條，他們須視作不享有居留權，須返回內地向“內地出入境管理處”申請居權證，單程證申請可視為居權證申請。

裁決摘要

原訟庭和上訴庭皆認為張麗華小姐應包括在《基本法》第 24（2）條第 3 款中，但根據《基本法》第 22（4）條制定的《入境（修訂）（第 3 號）條例》各申請人的居留請求不被接納。對於上訴庭的判決，各方均提出上訴。

終審法院並不接納入境處處長的主張申請人必須獲得以單程證形式簽發的出境批准，才可享有居留權。法院認為《基本法》第 24（3）條規定：永久性居民在特區"享有居留權"。而《入境條例》2A 條亦界定了永久性居民享有的權利，即有權入境，不會被施加任何逗留條件，不受任何遞解離境令或遣送離境令的約束。根據普通法概念，居留權被描述為"……進入（該司法管轄區）的權利，不受任何障礙或阻礙，任由（居留權擁有人）喜歡何時入境及（隨己意）在境內逗留多久"。因此，《基本法》第 22（4）條並不適用於特區的永久性居民，只適用於內地絕大部份沒有特區居留權的人士。所以，《入境（修訂）（第 3 號）條例》規定居於內地的特區永久性居民，要先持有單程證才可享有憲法賦予的居留權是違憲的。另外，法院基於平等原則、"國際人權公約"第 23（1）條認定，家庭是社會之自然及基本的團體單位，應該受到社會和國家的保護和對《基本法》第 24（2）條第 3 款的一般理解，裁定非婚生子女也應該包括在內。

呂尚君及顏秀英 對 入境事務處處長

HCAL 109/1997

簡略案情

申請人呂尚君及顏秀英不滿入境事務處對其兒子呂俊鳴發出遣送離境令，向法院申請許可要求司法覆核。第一申請人呂尚君於 1979 年 1 月從內地來港定居，現在是香港永久性居民。第二申請人顏秀英女士於 1973 年在內地與一董姓男子結婚，為他誕下 2 男 1 女。董先生去世後，顏女士於 1986 年與呂先生在內地成婚。顏女士與先夫董先生所誕下的三名子女遂改姓呂，分別是呂俊暉，呂俊玲及呂俊鳴。於 1991 年 4 月顏女士經泉州公安局批准與兩名子女，即呂俊暉及呂俊玲來港定居。據當時內地規定同一時間最多只可申請兩名子女隨行，於是呂俊鳴便得一人留下在鄉中與顏女士之生母居住。但因顏母年事已高，且在鄉間並無其他親戚，呂先生及顏女士需要經常回鄉探視呂俊鳴。呂先生及顏女士雖已向內地申請呂俊鳴到港定居，但遲遲未得要領。於是呂俊鳴便於 1997 年初持雙程證來港。在雙程證過期後仍然留在香港並沒有返回內地。1997 年 6 月底呂俊鳴被入境事務處截獲，1997 年 11 月 28 日入境事務處頒發遣送離境令。呂先生及顏女士不服，向法庭申請許可要求司法覆核。呂俊鳴當年 23 歲。

裁決摘要

代表申請人的律師指出《基本法》並無就“子女”一詞作出解釋或訂出定義，因此認為第 24（3）條應包括繼子繼女，但這說法被當時的高等法院首席法官陳兆愷否定。法庭認為第 24（1）及（2）條是有關居民本身的地位，第 24（3）條是有關這些居民的子女的地位。第 24（3）條的重點在他們“所生”的子女，而不是他們在“香港以外”的子女。再者，呂俊鳴既非第一申請人在香港所生，不能滿足第 24（1）條的要求，而第二申請人在港居留亦未滿 7 年，不符合第 24（2）條的條件，因此法庭認定呂俊鳴的情況不符合基本法第 24（3）條，第二申請人只能於在港居住滿 7 年後才可申請呂俊鳴來港。

HCAL109/97

香港特別行政區
原訟法庭

高院行政申訴 1997 年第 109 號

申請人　呂尚君及顏秀英
　　　　訴
答辯人　入境事務處

審理法官：高等法院首席法官陳兆愷

聆訊日期：一九九八年一月二十七日

宣判日期：一九九八年二月二十七日

判案書

申請人呂尚君及顏秀英不滿入境事務處就他們的兒子呂俊鳴於 1997 年 11 月 28 日所發出的遣送離境令，向法院申請許可要求司法覆核。

第一申請人呂尚君於 1979 年 1 月從國內來港定居，現在是香港永久居民。於 1986 年初，呂先生與第二申請人顏秀英女士在國內結婚。顏女士生於國內，父親姓陶，在顏女士 4 個月大的時候把她送給一對姓顏的夫婦，以後為顏姓夫婦撫養。顏女士於 1973 年在國內與一董姓男子結婚，為他生下 2 男 1 女。於 1982 年，顏女士的養父養母及丈夫均先後病逝。於 1986 年，經朋友介紹，她與呂先生在國內成婚。顏女士與已去世的丈夫董先生所誕下的三名子女遂改姓呂，就是呂俊暉，呂俊玲及呂俊鳴。於 1991 年 4 月顏女士經泉州公安局批准與兩名子女，即呂俊暉及呂俊玲來港定居。但據當時國內規定同一時間最多只可申請兩名子女隨行，於是呂俊鳴便得一人留下在鄉中與顏女士之生母陶女士居住。但由於陶女士年事已高，而且在鄉中並無其他親戚，呂俊鳴便沒有人照顧。於是呂先生及顏女士需要經常回鄉探視。呂俊鳴現年 23 歲。據顏女士稱，她在香港辦理領取身份証時已有表示在鄉中尚有一名兒子，因此顏女士及兩名已申請來港定居的子女的身份証號碼是順次序的，而且更預留一個號碼給尚未來港之呂俊鳴。呂先生及顏女士已向國內申請呂俊鳴到港定居，但遲遲未得要領。於是呂俊鳴便於 1997 年初持雙程証來港。在雙程証過期後仍然留在香港並沒有返回國內。於 1997 年 6 月底呂俊鳴被入境事務處截獲，入境事務處於 1997 年 11 月 28 日頒發遣送離境令。呂先生及顏女士不服，向本法庭申請許可要求司法覆核。

無可否認呂先生是香港永久居民，不過顏女士因為只是於 1991 年 4 月才來港定居，到現時為止尚未成為香港永久居民。基本法第 24 條規定：

> ※ 香港特別行政區永久性居民為：
>
> （1）在香港特別行政區成立以前或以後在香港出生的中國公民；
>
> （2）在香港特別行政區成立以前或以後在香港通常居住年連續 7 年以上的中國公民；
>
> （3）第 1、2 兩項所列居民在香港以外所生的中國籍子女；
>
> （4）……

臨時立法會於較早前修訂人民入境條例，就基本法第 24（3）條規定若干條件以甄別誰可根據第 24（3）條申請成為香港永久居民。若干在港的永久居民的子女曾就有關「人民入境修訂條例（1997 年）」是否違反基本法與特區政府訴訟。經訴訟後原訟法庭裁定此修訂法例並無抵觸基本法。就該裁決特區政府及有關訴訟人士已向上訴庭進行上訴。期間有多名本港居民的子女因為可能受到該裁決所影響亦提出訴訟。入境事務處認為如果這些新的案件是同類的，那麼在等候上訴期間，這些從國內來的子女可以留下香港等候上訴裁決。不過入境事務處認為呂俊鳴及若干其他案件與正在等候上訴的案件類別不同，因此決定頒發遣送離境令。入境事務處認為案件不同的理由就是呂俊鳴並不符合第 24（3）條的條款，無論上訴的案件結果如何亦與呂俊鳴案件無關。

代表申請人的郭大律師在陳詞中指出：基本法並無就子女　詞作出解釋或訂出定義，因此子女可包括繼子繼女。就基本法第 24（3）條，大律師認為可作以下解釋，就是只要符合四個條件，便可成為香港永久居民：第一，第一申請人呂先生必須是根據第 24（1）或（2）條是香港永久居民；第二，呂俊鳴是中國籍；第三，他是在香港以外出生的；第四，呂俊鳴是呂先生的子女，這包括是呂先生的繼子。大律師謂在目前的階段，只要法庭認為他的陳詞是可爭辯的話，便應批准申請人進行司法覆核。

我認為申請人就基本法第 24（3）條的解釋是斷章取義，而且有違基本法賦予香港永久性居民地位的精神。這條款不能像申請人那樣分段解釋。第 24（1）及（2）條是有關居民本身的地位，第 24（3）條是有關這些居民的子女的地位。條款的重點在他們「所生」的子女，而不是他們在「香港以外」的子女。因為如果這些子女是在香港出生，他們已包括在第 24（1）條內，無須依靠第 24（3）條父母的？庇下。「所生」二字是配合主詞「居民」的動詞。我認為第 24（3）條所指的是第 1、2 項香港永久性居民所生的中國籍子女。在英文版本中亦有寫明：

> ※Article 24
>
> (3) Persons of Chinese nationality born outside Hong Kong of those residents listed in categories (1) and (2);

因此基本法第 24（3）條非常清楚，如要符合此條款，呂俊鳴必須是呂尚君的親生兒子。

根據呂先生和顏女士所提出的事實，我對他們深表同情。尤其是顏女士經歷不少變故，呂先生亦刻盡丈夫及繼父的義務及責任。不過很明顯呂俊鳴不是呂先生所親生。至於顏女士，因為在港居留並未滿 7 年，不符合第 24（2）條，因此她的申請對呂俊鳴亦無幫助。

我認為呂俊鳴的情況很明顯不符合基本法第 24（3）條。無論上訴案件如何判決，呂俊鳴亦不會受益。因此入境事務處所頒發的遣送離境令是有合理的依據。呂先生及顏女士要求申請許可進行司法覆核並無理由，不予批准。顏女士須於在港居住 7 年之後才可申請呂俊鳴來港。

高等法院首席法官（陳兆愷）

申請人：由郭瑞熙（賈偉林，劉天均律師行）代表

答辯人：由吳能明（首席政府律師）代表

談雅然、陳偉華 對 入境事務處處長
謝曉怡 對 入境事務處處長

HCAL 13/1998；HCAL14/1998；CACV 301/1999；FACV 20/2000；FACV21/2000

簡略案情

上訴人談雅然、陳偉華及謝曉怡（“上訴人”）均屬內地出生未成年的中國公民。他們根據內地法律被領養，而且，在他們被領養時，或事實上在他們出生時，領養父母雙方或一方已成為香港永久性居民。與訟各方同意各上訴人乃根據內地法律所接受的領養，屬香港法例第 290 章《領養條例》第 17 條所述的海外領養，因此，該等領養與該條例下的有效領養令具相同效力，即：

> ……幼年人真正父母所具有的關於幼年人的權利及義務均告終絕，領養子女在與領養人的關係中，須完全處於屬領養人在婚姻中所生的子女的地位……其與真正父母之間的家庭關係將完全及永久終止；就所有事項而言，領養父母的地位須猶如真正父母一樣。

上訴人堅稱他們屬第 24 條第 2 款第 (3) 項所指的永久性居民，並享有居留權。處長對此提出爭議。案件初審時原訟法庭法官判決上訴人勝訴，入境事務處處長提出上訴。上訴法庭裁定入境事務處處長上訴得直。

裁決摘要

終審法院在審理上訴人的上訴時指出全國人大常委會在 1999 年 6 月 26 日對《基本法》第 24 條第 2 款第 3 項所作出的解釋（“該解釋”）並沒有考慮領養子女的問題。法院在考慮了*吳嘉玲及其他人士對入境事務處處長*（1999）2 HKCFAR 4 和*入境處處長對莊豐源*（2001）4 HKCFAR 211 的案件後，認為本案所牽涉的領養問題並不滿足“類別條件”的要求，所以，終審法院無須根據《基本法》第 158 條第 3 款向全國人大常委會提請司法解釋。至於在考慮《基本法》第 24 條第 2 款第 3 項關於領養子女的問題時，法院亦考慮了《國際人權公約》第 23（1）條即“家庭為社會之自然基本團體單位，應受社會及國家之保護。”此公約之相關適用條文根據《基本法》第 39 條規定繼續有效。法院明白在解釋第 24 條第 2 款第 3 項時，若把其解釋為涵蓋領養子女，便能促進家庭團聚；反之，則會令家庭分裂，與《國際人權公約》第 23（1）背道而馳。但根據該解釋，第 24 條第 2 款第 3 項所強調的是出生時的狀況，包括時間和地點。在這基礎上，不能否認的事實是在上訴人出生的時刻，他們跟領養父母是一點關係也沒有的，所以，領養子女並不包括在《基本法》第 24 條第 2 款第 3 項內。最後，終審法院以大比數駁回了上訴人的上訴。

〔中譯本 – 司法機構法庭語文組譯〕

〔Chinese Translation – Prepared by Court Language Section, Judiciary〕

FACV 20 & 21/2000

香港特別行政區
終審法院

終院民事上訴 2000 年第 20 及 21 號
（原本案件編號：高院民事上訴 1999 年第 301 號）

上訴人　談雅然
（屬未成年人士，由母親及起訴監護人文月桂代表）
陳偉華
（屬未成年人士，由父親及起訴監護人曾向才代表）
對
答辯人　入境事務處處長

及

上訴人　謝曉怡
（屬未成年人士，由父親及起訴監護人謝家樹代表）
對
答辯人　入境事務處處長

主審法官：終審法院首席法官李國能
終審法院常任法官包致金
終審法院常任法官陳兆愷
終審法院常任法官李義
終審法院非常任法官梅師賢爵士

聆訊日期：2001 年 5 月 14、15 及 16 日

判案書日期：2001 年 7 月 20 日

判案書

終審法院首席法官李國能、終審法院常任法官陳兆愷、終審法院常任法官李義及終審法院非常任法官梅師賢爵士：

《基本法》第二十四條訂明屬於香港特別行政區（“香港特區”或“特區”或“香港”）永久性居民的六個類別人士，並賦予他們在特區的居留權。第二十四條第二款所列的首三個類別人士為：

> “（一）在香港特別行政區成立以前或以後在香港出生的中國公民；
>
> （二）在香港特別行政區成立以前或以後在香港通常居住連續七年以上的中國公民；
>
> （三）第（一）、（二）兩項所列居民在香港以外所生的中國籍子女；”

本上訴的問題是：第二十四條第二款第（三）項是否包括領養子女，是否包括在香港以外出生而被香港永久性居民領養的中國公民？

案件事實

有關領養子女為上訴人談雅然、陳偉華及謝曉怡（“上訴人”）。他們均屬未成年人士，是控告答辯人入境事務處處長（“處長”）的司法覆核程序中的申請人。就本案所要討論的問題而言，案件的詳細事實並不重要，主要的事實可簡列如下：

（1）上訴人是在內地出生的中國公民。

（2）他們乃根據內地法律被領養的。

（3）在他們被領養時，事實上在他們出生時，領養父母雙方或一方已成為香港永久性居民。

在內地領養的效力

上訴人按照內地法律被領養，此等領養在香港的效力並沒有受到爭議。各方同意：

（1）各上訴人根據內地法律所接受的領養，屬香港法例第 290 章《領養條例》第 17 條所述的海外領養，因此，該等領養與該條例下的有效領養令具相同效力。

（2）該條例下的有關領養令效力如下：

> “……幼年人真正父母所具有的關於幼年人的權利及義務均告終絕，領養子女在與領養人的關係中，須完全處於屬領養人在婚姻中所生的子女的地位……其與真正父母之間的家庭關係將完全及永久終止；就所有事項而言，領養父母的地位須猶如真正父母一樣。”

見 *J v. C*〔1970〕AC 668 一案第 719 頁 D-F 及《領養條例》第 13 條。這項陳述與《1958 英國領養法》有關，而各方均接受無論該法與上述條例之間有任何分歧，有關陳述仍適用於本案。

原審法官與上訴法庭

上訴人堅稱他們屬第二十四條第二款第（三）項所指的永久性居民，並享有居留權。處長對此提出爭議。案件初審時由當時的原訟法庭法官祁彥輝審理，結果上訴人勝訴：〔1999〕2 HKLRD 505，〔1999〕3 HKC 148。其後上訴法庭（上訴法庭副庭長梅賢玉、當時是上訴法庭法官的梁紹中及羅傑志）裁定處長勝訴，判決處長上訴得直：〔2000〕2 HKLRD 161。

莊豐源

在與本判案書同日宣告的*入境處處長對莊豐源*（“*莊豐源*”）一案的判案書中，法庭考慮了《基本法》第二十四條第二款第（一）項的正確解釋。在該判案書中，法庭列出近期事件的始末，包括 1999 年 6 月 26 日通過的《全國人民代表大會（“人大”）常務委員會（“常委會”）關於《基本法》第二十二條第四款和第二十四條第二款第（三）項的解釋》（“該解釋”）。法庭並考慮了多項與本上訴有關的問題，包括解釋《基本法》時的處理方法，以及關於第一百五十八條第三款的爭議，即某條款（在該案為第二十四條第二款第（一）項）是否屬於第一百五十八條第三款所指的“範圍之外的條款”。

我等認為無須在本判案書重覆*莊豐源*一案中就相同問題所述的內容。因此，我等只會提述該判案書的有關段節。

案中爭議

本上訴出現的爭論點為：

（1）“該解釋”有否就有關領養子女方面的問題，解釋第二十四條第二款第（三）項（“第一爭論點”）？

（2）如果沒有的話，第二十四條第二款第（三）項是否屬於

法院有責任向常委會作出司法提請，要求常委會解釋的“範圍之外的條款”（“第二爭論點”）？

（3）如果不是的話，法院應該如何就領養子女的問題來正確解釋第二十四條第二款第（三）項（“第三爭論點”）？

第一爭論點

正如*劉港榕對入境處處長*（1999）2 HKCFAR 300（“*劉港榕*”）一案的裁決及*莊豐源*一案的討論（見第6節）所述：（1）根據中國憲法第六十七條第（四）項及《基本法》第一百五十八條，常委會有權解釋《基本法》。（2）根據第一百五十八條第二款及第一百五十八條第三款，香港法院獲授權在審理案件時對《基本法》進行解釋。（3）但香港法院所獲授予的解釋《基本法》的權力：（a）須符合第一百五十八條第三款就“範圍之外的條款”施加於本院，即終審法院的司法管轄權的限制；“範圍之外的條款”必須透過司法提請轉交常委會進行解釋（“範圍之外的條款”即“關於中央人民政府管理的事務或中央和特區關係”的條款）；及（b）須受到常委會根據第一百五十八條所作的解釋的約束。（4）如常委會曾對《基本法》作出解釋，無論有關解釋是根據第一百五十八條第一款作出或根據第一百五十八條第三款的司法提請作出，香港法院均有責任依循。

正如*莊豐源*一案所述（見第5節），根據“該解釋”：（1）第二十二條第四款的條款的意思，是指中國其他地區的人，包括香港永久性居民在香港以外所生的中國籍子女，不論以何種事由要求進入香港特區，均須取得內地機關批准方能進入香港特區；及（2）第二十四條第二款第（三）項的條款的意思，是指如要符合資格成為該規定所述的永久性居民，在有關人士出生時，其父母雙方或一方須是第二十四條第二款第（一）項或第二十四條第二款第（二）項所述的永久性居民。這項關於有關人士出生時其父母身份的規定，以下稱為“出生時間的規定”。

現時的問題是，“該解釋”有否就有關領養子女的問題，對第二十四條第二款第（三）項作出解釋。如有的話，香港法院有責任依循。

代表處長的資深大律師霍兆剛先生同意，常委會當時並沒有接獲有關解決領養子女問題的請求，“該解釋”也沒有處理這個問題。可是，他陳詞指該解釋既已將第二十四條第二款第（三）項解釋為包含“出生時間的規定”，便已經以暗示的方式處理了領養子女的問題。

這項陳詞不能接受。我等認為，“該解釋”完全沒有以暗示方式提及第二十四條第二款第（三）項內有關領養子女地位的問題。因此，常委會並沒有就有關領養子女的問題，對第二十四條第二款第（三）項作出解釋。

可是，本院受“該解釋”的約束，而“該解釋”把第二十四條第二款第（三）項解釋為包含“出生時間的規定”。現在要考慮的是，第二十四條第二款第（三）項是否屬“範圍之外的條款”。如果不是的話，本院在對該條款定出關於領養子女的正確解釋時，便要考慮這項規定可有甚麼幫助（如有的話）。

第二爭論點

正如在*吳嘉玲及其他人士對入境事務處處長*（1999）2 HKCFAR 4（“*吳嘉玲*”）一案的裁決及*莊豐源*一案的討論（見第7節）所述，如情況符合類別條件及有需要條件，本院必須根據第一百五十八條第三款向常委會作出司法提請。本案情況符合有需要條件。本院在審理本案時需要對第二十四條第二款第（三）項作出解釋，而有關解釋又影響到本案的判決。問題是本案情況是否符合類別條件。第二十四條第二款第（三）項是否屬“範圍之外的條款”？

代表處長的資深大律師霍兆剛先生的陳詞與*莊豐源*一案的相類，其內容如下：

（1）決定某項條款是否屬“範圍之外的條款”時的“相關考慮因素是，實施該項《基本法》有關條款（不論是按所提出的兩種或多於兩種的解釋的任何一種）會否對（i）中央人民政府管理的事務或（ii）中央和特區關係產生實質（意指實在而非重大）影響”。

（2）按此驗證標準，第二十四條第二款第（三）項屬“範圍之外的條款”。本案的爭論點與第二十四條第二款第（三）項的解釋有關，並涉及在香港以外（包括內地）出生而被香港永久性居民領養的中國居民進入香港的問題。正如喬曉陽副主任在其說明“該解釋”草案的演辭所述（見*莊豐源*一案第5節），第二十四條第二款第（三）項與第二十二條第四款是密不可分的。根據該條款，中國其他地區的人，包括在內地出生而被香港永久性居民領養的中國居民，均須取得內地機關批准方能進入香港。在此情況下，本院現在解釋的第二十四條第二款第（三）項，其實是一條實施起來，會對（i）中央人民政府管理的事務或（ii）中央和特區關係產生實質影響的條款。

在*莊豐源*一案中（見第7.3節），本院的結論是，“該解釋”的序言不能理解為常委會已清楚表示第二十四條第二款第（三）項本身屬“範圍之外的條款”，本院並作出以下裁決（見第7.4節）：參照第一百五十八條第三款的背景及目的來解釋該條款所用字句時，採用處長所建議的驗證標準以決定某條款是否屬“範圍之外的條款”，這是沒有理據的。該條款也不能解釋為訂明以事實來決定實施某條款所產生的實質影響，藉此作為分類的驗證標準。

正如本院在*莊豐源*一案所述（見第7.4節），第一百五十八條第三款集中述及有關條款時，規定本院須考慮條款的特性。第二十四條第二款第（三）項的特性是，它是用來界定其中一類享有居留權的永久性居民，即第二十四條第二款第（一）項及第二十四條第二款第（二）項所列的永久性居民在香港以外所生的中國籍子女。考慮到條款的特性，有關條款並不涉及中央人民政府管理的事務或中央和特區關係。這是一項關於特區自治範圍內的條款而並非“範圍之外的條款”。因此，本院無須向常委會作出司法提請。

第三爭論點

考慮過第一及第二爭論點所得的結論後，接著要考慮的就是第二十四條第二款第（三）項關於領養子女的正確解釋。

由於常委會沒有對第二十四條第二款第（三）項作出關於領養子女的解釋，因此，香港法院在缺乏這種具約束力的解釋的情況下，便引用普通法以解釋《基本法》。這問題已在*莊豐源*一案中討論過（見第6.1及6.2節）。該案各方同意應引用普通法，本案亦然。在*吳嘉玲*一案及*莊豐源*一案（見第6.3節），本院已討論過普通法對解釋《基本法》的處理方法，本案也應採用同樣的處理方法。

基本上，法院的職責是詮釋《基本法》文本使用的文字，以確定那些文字所表達的立法原意。有關條款的文字，必須參照其背景及目的來考慮。法院必須避免只從字面上的意義，或從技術層面，或狹義的角度，或以生搬硬套的處理方法詮釋文字的含義，也不能賦予其所不能包含的意思。法院參照了有關條款的背景及目的來詮釋文本字句，一旦斷定文本字句確是含義清晰後，便須落實這些字句的清晰含義。含義清晰即所用文字沒有歧義，就是在合理情況下不能得出另一對立的解釋。

目的

正如在*莊豐源*一案所述（見第 8.2 節），連同第二十四條第三款一併考慮後，第二十四條第二款的目的是賦予被界定為香港特區永久性居民的人士居留權。某些人士會包括在內，那些不包括在內的會被排除於外。在這種意義上，第二十四條第二款的目的可說是要界定香港特區永久性居民的範圍，從而限制香港特區的人口。

背景

本院在解釋第二十四條第二款第（三）項時，不但要參照其目的，還必須參照其背景。關於背景部份，上訴人依據（1）《公民權利和政治權利國際公約》（"國際人權公約"）—— 該公約已通過載有《香港人權法案》（"人權法案"）的香港法例第 383 章《香港人權法案條例》收納入香港法律；及（2）本土法在《基本法》制定前的狀況。

國際人權公約和人權法案

《基本法》第三十九條規定：

> "〔國際人權公約〕、《經濟、社會與文化權利的國際公約》和國際勞工公約適用於香港的有關規定繼續有效，通過香港特別行政區的法律予以實施。
>
> 香港居民享有的權利和自由，除依法規定外不得限制，此種限制不得與本條第一款規定抵觸。"

一如前述，國際人權公約是通過人權法案在香港實施。第十九（一）條收納了國際人權公約的第二十三（一）條，條文如下：

> "家庭為社會之自然基本團體單位，應受社會及國家之保護。"

下稱"人權法案第十九（一）條"。

代表談雅然和陳偉華兩名上訴人的資深大律師李志喜女士的陳詞為代表上訴人謝曉怡的大律師司徒栢先生採納。她陳詞說，領養是一個使人受惠的制度。（處長對此並無爭議。）她呈述：在決定如何解釋該條款時，必須對人權法案第十九（一）條予以相當的重視。她亦援引了《經濟、社會與文化權利的國際公約》的第十條及第十一條，以及《兒童權利公約》的第二十條及第二十一條。不過，她同意此等條文，就其論據而言，不能為人權法案第十九（一）條提供重要的增補。資深大律師李女士申述：在解釋第二十四條第二款第（三）項時，若把其解釋為涵蓋領養子女，便能促進家庭團聚，符合人權法案第十九（一）條；而相反的解釋則會令家庭分裂，與該條的要旨相違。她指出於*吳嘉玲*一案（第 41 頁），本院採納此處理方法，裁定非婚生子女屬第二十四條第二款第（三）項之內的，故此沒有就此問題提請常委會解釋該條款。資深大律師李女士甚而更呈述，促進家庭團聚以符合人權法案第十九（一）條既然是這麼重要，除非第二十四條第二款第（三）項明言把領養子女摒諸於該條款外，否則，法院應把其詮釋為包括領養子女在內。

另一方面，代表處長的資深大律師霍先生呈述：雖然人權法案第十九（一）條屬本案背景之一部份，但有關領養子女方面，此條款卻說不上對於解釋第二十四條第二款第（三）項有何幫助。他提出了兩個理由以支持其陳詞。第一，倘若在不能合法逗留，以及沒有法例規定內地兒童可以領養為目的而獲得入境權的情況下，家庭生活未能在香港得以牢固地建立，即使政府禁止在香港特區以外的地方領養的子女入境，這也不等於違反了國際人權公約所規定政府須負的責任。參閱 *AS v. Canada*, Communication No. 68/1980（31 March 1981）UNHRC；*X and Y v. The United Kingdom*, Application No. 7229/75（15.12.77）EHRC。儘管這論據很可能是對的，但正如資深大律師李女士所呈述，上訴人一方於本案並沒有提出政府是違反了人權法案第十九（一）條。故此，針對違反責任一事而作出此論據對處長的陳詞實在沒有幫助。

處長的陳詞指出，對法院這次的解釋工作來說，人權法案第十九（一）條沒有多大用處，陳詞所據的第二個理由是：適用於香港的國際人權公約乃受限於就出入境事宜而作出的一項保留條文。這條*適用於香港的*國際人權公約，亦即是受限於該保留條文的國際人權公約，根據《基本法》第三十九條繼續有效，並須通過香港特區的法律予以實施。當這國際人權公約於香港初次引用時，香港還是聯合王國的屬土，聯合王國訂定了如下所述的保留條文（"該保留條文"）：

> "聯合王國政府保留權利，不時按其需要，繼續實施有關管制進入聯合王國、居留及離開聯合王國的出入境法例。因此，聯合王國政府對公約……的接納，是受聯合王國對當時無權進入及在聯合王國居留人士實施的法例所約束。聯合王國亦就其每一屬土，保留同樣的權利。"

此保留條文反映於《香港人權法案條例》第 11 條（"第 11 條"）。此條規定：

> "對於無權進入及停留於香港的人來說，本條例不影響管限這些人進入、逗留於及離開香港的出入境法例，亦不影響這些法例的適用。"

該保留條文及第 11 條的影響是：國際人權公約和人權法案不適用於那些涉及無權進入及停留於香港的人的出入境法例，亦不會對此等法例有任何影響。

代表處長的資深大律師霍先生呈述：由於本案關注的，是屬於該保留條文及第 11 條的範圍內的出入境事宜，故此，在這次的解釋過程中，不能考慮人權法案第十九（一）條。

我等不能接納此陳詞。在本案，我等要關注的是，按照第二十四條第二款第（三）項的正確解釋，領養子女是否屬永久性居民並享有居留權。我等無須關注那些涉及並不享有此種權利的人的出入境法例。由於該保留條文及第 11 條的效力是：國際人權公約和人權法案不適用於那些涉及沒有居港權的人的出入境法例，故並不影響本案所討論的問題。因此，要在領養子女這方面正確解釋第二十四條第二款第（三）項，人權法案第十九（一）條合理地成為了背景的一部份。

本土法

資深大律師李女士就兩方面依據在《基本法》制定以前有關本土法的狀況。第一是出入境方面。第二是領養子女方面。

有關出入境的法律，資深大律師李女士向本院介紹 1997 年 7 月 1 日以前，在不同時間適用於香港，錯綜複雜的香港和聯合王國的出入境法例，藉此帶出一點：在有關獲得某些出入境權利的問題上，領養子女的身份是獲得確認的。至於如何從這些錯縱複雜的出入境法例中理出一個頭緒來，本院認為無須在此判案書討論。一如*莊豐源*一案（第 8.2 節）所指，1997 年以前的出入境法例有其本身的歷史背景，此等法例乃源自（聯合王國政府）意識到有大量移民從英聯邦國家湧入聯合王國的危機。無論如何，即使以往的出入境法例與現在的解釋工作有關，領養子女的身份在該等法例中獲得確認這事實，亦難以對我等有任何幫助。上訴人一方可以藉此爭辯，說第二十四條第二款第（三）項應解釋為涵蓋領養子女。但另一方面，答辯人一方亦一樣可爭辯：由於以往的出入境法例具明文確認，故此，《基本法》第二十四條第二款第（三）項既然沒有明文提及領養子女，這便應視為一個重要的指標，顯示該條款不能解釋為包括他們在內。援引以往的出入境法例最終對本案是起不到任何作用的。

相反，上訴人依據關乎領養子女地位的本土法狀況作為背景的一部份，該本土法狀況對本案有著明顯的幫助。領養在社會上被視為一種使人受惠的制度。一如前述，按照《領養條例》發出的有效領養令的效力是（這包括本條例所界定的本港領養和海外領養）：對於被領養的子女而言，"領養父母就各方面來說須猶如真正父母一樣。"參閱前文援引的 *J v.C.* 第 719 頁 D-F。這點大家也沒有異議。故此，本院不需要深究《領養條例》的條文和案例法。

總括而言，人權法案第十九（一）條及本土法中有關領養子女方面的條文，屬於背景的一部份，都對本案有幫助。因此，它們對於本院在處理第二十四條第二款第（三）項的解釋時，應可提供所需的資料。當本院解釋有關條款時，必須考慮兩項原則：第一，家庭作為社會之自然基本團體單位，應受到保護；第二，領養子女跟親生子女在領養父母的家庭是同樣重要的一分子。

參照第二十四條第二款第（三）項的目的及背景後，對此條款所作的解釋

如前述，本院應在解釋第二十四條第二款第（三）項的文本字句前，先參照該條款的目的和背景。第二十四條第二款第（三）項的條文如下：

> "第(一)、(二)兩項所列居民在香港以外所生的中國籍子女。"

經過常委會解釋後，該條款包含"出生時間的規定"，即是，有關人士出生時，其父母雙方或一方必須是符合第二十四條第二款第（一）項或第（二）項規定的永久性居民。

有關人士要成為第二十四條第二款第（三）項所述的永久性居民，必須符合三個規定。第一，有關人士必須為中國公民。第二，有關人士必須在香港以外出生。第三，有關人士出生時，其父母至少一方必須是符合第二十四條第二款第（一）項或第二十四條第二款第（二）項規定的永久性居民。

本上訴的爭論點關乎第三項規定內父母與子女的關係的性質。這當然包括親生父母與子女的關係。爭論點在於由領養所產生的領養父母與被領養子女的關係是否屬於該項規定的涵蓋範圍內。

資深大律師李女士呈述：該條款的"生"字，表示若要成為此項所指的永久性居民，父母與子女的關係和父母的身份乃其中一項必要的條件。本院得悉有關目的和背景，尤其是家庭應受保護，以及領養子女跟親生子女在家庭是同樣重要的一分子這兩項原則，便應把第二十四條第二款第（三）項解釋為不單包括親生子女，還包括領養子女。一如前述，資深大律師李女士甚而提出，除非有明文規定把領養子女摒諸於該條款外，否則，應把該條款解釋為包括他們在內 —— 儘管她根本無須提出如此陳述。至於把"出生時間的規定"引用於領養子女一事，大律師同意領養父母是考慮的因素。她的主要論據是：領養的時間才是有關日期，即是，領養父母其中一方在當時必須是符合第二十四條第二款第（一）項或第二十四條第二款第（二）項規定的永久性居民。她還提出另一交替論據：出生時間是有關日期，即是，領養父母其中一方在有關人士出生時必須為永久性居民。（根據案情，上訴人等符合上述任何一個論據的要求。）由於本院現須決定如何解釋該條款，資深大律師李女士因此提出：用不同字眼重新擬定該條款，欲藉此更佳地反映結果，並非一個有效的做法。她認為應該由本院解釋而得出這結果。

倘若第二十四條第二款第（三）項的文字語意含糊，即是能夠合理地得出另一對立的解釋，那麼，根據本院必須考慮人權法案第十九（一）條所規定的家庭有受保護的權利，以及親生子女跟領養子女在家庭內是同樣重要的一分子這兩項原則，本院便必須傾向於接受領養子女是包括在有關條款的涵蓋範圍內的這個解釋，因為這解釋有助達致一定程度的家庭團聚。雖然，一如在吳嘉玲一案（第 41E 頁）所指出，依照第二十四條第二款的永久性居民分類，並不能達致整個家庭的團聚，因為，舉例來說，配偶是不在此列的，但倘若從該條款的文本字句，可得出一個有助達致一定程度的家庭團聚的解釋，本院便應傾向於這解釋。

可是，參照第二十四條第二款第（三）項的目的及背景後，該條款的文字，當中出現"……所生"一片語，是否語意含糊？顯而易見，這段文字指的只是親生子女，根本不可能把它們解釋作包括領養子女。如果裁定它們有相反的意思，便要把"生"字解釋作只是關乎出生地點，即是香港以外，而把"所生"中的"所"這字眼當作是實際上無意義的。

"出生時間的規定"支持了這個解釋。該規定是：有關人士出生時，其父母任何一方須是符合第二十四條第二款第（一）項或第二十四條第二款第（二）項規定的永久性居民。這規定著眼於出生的時間，顯示出父母的關係是指親生父母與子女的關係，而不包括領養父母與領養子女的關係。若根據上訴人主要的論據，即引用領養的時間而非出生的時間來考慮，這將會是以一個實質上不同的規定來取代原先的規定。若根據上訴人的交替論據，以有關人士的出生時間來作考慮，但卻以領養父母的身份作為著眼點，這並不恰當，因為在當時，有關人士與領養父母根本沒有任何關係，唯一存在的關係是他與親生父母的關係。

在 *Lui Sheung Kwan & Another v. Director of Immigration*〔1998〕1 HKLRD 265 一案，有關人士的父親是永久性居民，但母親卻還未成為永久性居民。該名母親在上一段婚姻所生的一名子女，即是該名父親的繼子女，聲稱自己是符合第二十四條第二款第（三）項規定的永久性居民。當時的高等法院首席法官陳兆愷裁定：由於該名子女並非其繼父"所生"，故此他並不符合該條款的規定。鑑於領養子女跟繼子女的身份有所不同，上訴人認為無需要質疑該案的決定。此項關於繼子女的決定是正確的，亦符合本判決書內就領養子女所作之結論。

《入境條例》附表 1 第 1 段（2）（c）

香港法例第 115 章《入境條例》附表 1 列出香港特區永久性居民的各項類別。附表 1 第 1 段（2）（c）規定："在以下的情況下，視為有父母與子女的關係存在：（c）只有父親或母親與其在香港根據法院命令領養的子女之間的關係，方為父親或母親與領養子女的關係，而該法院命令是指法院根據《領養條例》作出的命令。"

故此，就附表 1 的目的而言，第 1 段（2）（c）只確認在香港辦理的領養。經考慮本判案書所作之結論，即領養子女並不符合第二十四條第二款第（三）項的規定，第 1 段（2）（c）超出了《基本法》所規定的範圍。本院沒有機會聽取雙方就第 1 段（2）（c）的法律效力而呈述的全面論據，雙方亦沒有就此事發表任何意見。

結果

故此，本院駁回上訴，不作任何訟費命令，但判令上訴人的訟費須按照《法律援助條例》及《法律援助規例》評定。

終審法院常任法官包致金：

本席認為，《基本法》第二十四條第二款第（三）項包括了領養子女。故此，本席判決上訴得直，恢復原訟法庭在判定領養兒童勝訴時所作的聲明和命令。

雖然本席最終作出的結論跟本院其他法官所作的結論相反，但本席對於他們就第一和第二爭論點所表達的意見完全贊同；對他們就第三爭論點所述的意見亦差不多全部同意。本席跟其他法官分歧之處在於結尾部份。本席認為第二十四條第二項第（三）款的字眼可理解為包括領養子女，這與其他法官不同。

本席有此理解的原因如下：倘若第二十四條第二款第（三）項只是指第（一）、（二）兩項所列居民所生的中國籍子女，那麼這個理解未必能成立。但事實上，第二十四條第二款第（三）項指的是這些居民在香港以外所生的中國籍子女。故此，"生"一字可解釋為只關乎出生地點，而"所"一字可解釋作純粹意味著父母與子女的關係。領養父母與領養子女的關係無疑是父母與子女的關係。

如果，正如本席所認為，該條款是可以這樣解釋的話，本席便毫不懷疑這就是第二十四條第二款第（三）項應被賦予的解釋。因為這解釋促進家庭團聚，而家庭團聚在我們社會的各個層面，包括憲法的層面，都受到珍視的。

關於領養父母至少一方於何時必須擁有香港永久性居民的身份，才可使領養子女符合第二十四條第二款第（三）項的規定這一點，若認為領養父母至少一方，於有關領養在法律上生效時已擁有該身份便被視為足夠的話，本席須表達一些意見。在領養的情況下，這時間畢竟就是父母與子女的關係開始存在的時間。但本席最終認為有需要把第二十四條第二款第（三）項解釋為：領養父母至少一方必須於最終領養的子女出生時，以及有關領養在法律上生效時，擁有永久性居民的身份。本席認為這雙重規定是由於親生子女與領養子女均同樣地包括在該條款內，故此有必要統一處理。事實上，本上訴的所有領養子女都符合這雙重規定。

最後，本席處理代表入境事務處處長的大律師所提出領養有被濫用之虞這問題。根據本席理解，大家所恐懼的，是有人並非真的為了使有關兒童成為新家庭的成員而辦理領養，目的只是把該名兒童帶進香港，其親生家庭則仍留居別處。這並非本案任何一名兒童的情況。本席不排除在將來的案件中，有人提出這論據：此等只會破壞、不會促進家庭團聚的虛假領養，絕對不屬第二十四條第二款第（三）項所涵蓋的範圍。

終審法院首席法官李國能：

本院以多數裁決（常任法官包致金持不同意見）駁回上訴，不作任何訟費命令，但判令上訴人的訟費須按照《法律援助條例》及《法律援助規例》評定。

終審法院首席法官（李國能）

常任法官（包致金）

常任法官（陳兆愷）

常任法官（李義）

非常任法官（梅師賢）

資深大律師李志喜女士及大律師吳靄儀女士（由彭思帝理律師行延聘並由法律援助署委派）代表 FACV 20/2000 一案的上訴人

大律師司徒栢先生（由周振文、洪珀姿律師事務所延聘並由法律援助署委派）代表 FACV 21/2000 一案的上訴人

資深大律師霍兆剛先生及大律師翟紹唐先生（由律政司延聘）代表答辯人

Chan Kam Nga And 80 Others v. Director Of Immigration

陳錦雅及其他 80 人 對 入境事務處處長

HCAL 104/1997；CACV 40/1998；FACV 13/1998

簡略案情

上訴人由其父親作為監護人代表訴訟，並在本案中代表其餘 80 位情況跟她類同的訴訟人，其中有 12 位是成年人士。各上訴人的基本情況大致相同，即他們都是在內地出生的中國公民，在他們出生時其父母都不是香港的永久性居民，但是在此之後，其父母中至少一方在香港連續居住 7 年以上獲得了永久性居民的身份。這些上訴人部份持雙程證入境，部份為非法入境者。面對入境事務處處長的遣返令，他們同時以《基本法》第 24 條（2）第 2 和第 3 款來反對，並申請作為香港永久性居民，繼續留在香港。入境事務處認為依據《人民入境（修訂）（第 2 號）條例》中的相關規定，各原告並不符合作為香港永久性居民的條件，因為他們父母在他們出生時並未獲得香港永久性居民的身份。所以，法庭面對的問題是《基本法》第 24 條（2）第 3 款只適用於該子女出生時其中一方父母已經是香港永久居民。

裁決摘要

原訟庭法官接受上訴人的論據，但上訴庭卻認為《基本法》第 24 條的焦點是父母的身份，所以，出生的時間尤為重要，因此推翻了原審的裁決。然而，終審法院卻認為，以平常性解釋方法（“Natural Interpretation”），上訴人對《基本法》第 24 條的理解是對的。因為，在一般情況下，只會查問申請人的生父母是否香港永久性居民，並不會詢問他出生時其父母是否已經是香港永久性居民。終審法院亦認為用目的性解釋方法（“Purposive Interpretation”），其結果也應一樣。《基本法》第 31 條確認《公民權利和政治權利國際公約》第 23（1）條，在香港的效力，即家庭是社會之自然及基本的團體單位，應該受到社會和國家的保護。在此情形下，不應局限子女出生時其父母的身份，所以《人民入境（修訂）（第 2 號）條例》企圖只容許子女在出生時，父母一方已是香港永久性居民才擁有永久性居民身份的要求，是違反《基本法》第 24 條的。因此，法庭宣告各上訴人均擁有香港永久性居民身份。

FACV No. 13 of 1998

IN THE COURT OF FINAL APPEAL OF THE HONG KONG SPECIAL ADMINISTRATIVE REGION

FINAL APPEAL NO. 13 OF 1998 (CIVIL)
(ON APPEAL FROM CACV No. 40 OF 1998)

Between:

CHAN KAM NGA
(an infant suing by his father and next friend
CHAN KWING WOON) and 80 OTHERS — Appellants

- and -

DIRECTOR OF IMMIGRATION — Respondent

Court: Chief Justice Li, Mr Justice Litton PJ, Mr Justice Ching PJ, Mr Justice Bokhary PJ and Sir Anthony Mason NPJ

Date of Hearing: 12 January 1999

Date of Judgment: 29 January 1999

JUDGMENT

Chief Justice Li:
I agree with Mr Justice Bokhary PJ's judgment.

Mr Justice Litton PJ:
I agree with Mr Justice Bokhary PJ's judgment.

Mr Justice Ching PJ:
I agree with Mr Justice Bokhary PJ's judgment.

Mr Justice Bokhary PJ:
Of these 81 appellants, 69 are minors suing by their next friends while 12 are adults suing in the normal way. All 81 came to Hong Kong from the Mainland. Some came here on two way exit permits, were permitted to remain for limited periods, and then overstayed. Others were brought here as unauthorized entrants. The 46th, 48th and 58th appellants arrived here after 1 July 1997. The other 78 arrived here before that date. Anyway all 81 are here now. They all face orders made by the Director of Immigration ("the Director") for their removal to the Mainland. And they all resist such removal by asserting the right of abode here. This raises a number of questions. But the present appeal concerns only one of these questions: can a child become a Hong Kong permanent resident under category (3) of Article 24 of the Basic Law by virtue of a parent's Hong Kong permanent resident status under category (2) of that article not only if such status of the parent's had been acquired *before* the child's birth but even if it had not been acquired until *after* the child's birth?

How this question is answered will affect not only these 81 appellants but many other persons now and in the future. The appellants submit that it should be answered "yes". But the Director submits that it should be answered "no". By his judgment of 26 January 1998, Keith J answered it "yes" in the appellants' favour. But by their judgment dated 20 May 1998, the Court of Appeal (Chan CJHC, Nazareth VP and Mortimer VP) reversed the judge and answered it "no" in the Director's favour. The question is now before this Court. And I approach it with a keen sense of its wide implications.

The right of abode

It is natural that Article 24 is the first article in that chapter of our constitution, the Basic Law, which contains our fundamental rights and duties. For it is the article which says who has the right of abode in Hong Kong. And the right of abode in a place is the fundamental right without which the full array of fundamental rights available in that place cannot be accessed. This is because the right of abode in a place is the right, in the eyes of its law, to call that place home: coming and going at will; staying as long as you like.

Conferred on permanent residents

In Hong Kong this key right is conferred on permanent residents. Throughout the world constitutions extend their overarching protection to all persons within the jurisdiction, but reserve the fullest measure of rights to citizens. Our constitution follows this global pattern: doing so by reference to permanent residents rather than citizens. Article 24 lays down six categories of permanent residents. And it confers on all of them, whichever category they come within, the right of abode here along with all the other rights enjoyable here (subject only to the Chinese citizenship qualification necessary for certain official posts).

The six categories of persons who constitute the permanent residents of Hong Kong are defined by the second paragraph of Article 24 as:

"(1) Chinese citizens born in Hong Kong before or after the establishment of the Hong Kong Special Administrative Region;

(2) Chinese citizens who have ordinarily resided in Hong Kong for a continuous period of not less than seven years before or after the establishment of the Hong Kong Special Administrative Region;

(3) Persons of Chinese nationality born outside Hong Kong of those residents listed in categories (1) and (2);

(4) Persons not of Chinese nationality who have entered Hong Kong with valid travel documents, have ordinarily resided in Hong Kong for a continuous period of not less than seven years and have taken Hong Kong as their place of permanent residence before or after the establishment of the Hong Kong Special Administrative Region;

(5) Persons under 21 years of age born in Hong Kong of those residents listed in category (4) before or after the establishment of the Hong Kong Special Administrative Region; and

(6) Persons other than those residents listed in categories (1) to (5), who, before the establishment of the Hong Kong Special Administrative Region, had the right of abode in Hong Kong only."

The crucial facts

Looked at in the context of categories (2) and (3) of Article 24, the following crucial facts common to all of these 81 appellants are to be noted:

(1) All of them are of Chinese nationality.

(2) They were all born outside Hong Kong (namely in the Mainland).

(3) Each of them has a father who is a Hong Kong permanent

resident by virtue of category (2) i.e. through being a Chinese citizen and having been ordinarily resident in Hong Kong for a continuous period of not less than seven years. (It may be mentioned in passing, although it cannot affect the result of this case one way or the other, that the mothers of 25 of these appellants also happen to be Hong Kong permanent residents by virtue of category (2).)

(4) No parent of any appellant had become a Hong Kong permanent resident until after that appellant's birth: because no such parent had been ordinarily resident in Hong Kong for a continuous period of seven years until after his or her appellant child's birth.

So this appeal turns on whether that fourth fact operates to take these appellants and other persons like them out of category (3).

The rival contentions

For the appellants it is contended that the child of a Hong Kong permanent resident is a person born of a Hong Kong permanent resident whether that parent became a Hong Kong permanent resident *before or after* that child's birth. For the Director it is contended that the child of a Hong Kong permanent resident is not a person born of a Hong Kong permanent resident unless that parent had become a Hong Kong permanent resident *before* that child's birth.

The natural construction

In the Court of Appeal the Chief Judge of the High Court said that "The focus is certainly on birth". Nazareth VP said that: "The criterion 'born ... of' a permanent resident, immediately and naturally goes to the time of birth". And Mortimer VP said that the words of Article 24 "focus upon parentage, the status of the parents, the place of birth and the birth itself". As it seems to me, however, the word "born" had to be used in category (3) because the category covers persons born outside Hong Kong. Whatever else the words "born ... of" do or do not cover, they must cover a birth child. Each of these 81 appellants is the birth child of the parent on whose Hong Kong permanent resident status he or she relies.

Simply as a matter of giving words their natural meaning, I am of the view that the construction for which the appellants contend is correct.

Let me explain why I am of that view. Take any parent and birth child. Asked if the child is a person born of the parent, one is bound to answer "yes". Now take the same parent and child, adding the fact that the parent is a Hong Kong permanent resident. Asked if the child is a person born of a Hong Kong permanent resident, one would surely still answer "yes". One would not pause to enquire when the parent became a Hong Kong permanent resident. As a matter of ordinary language, that is irrelevant to the question of whether the child is a person born of a Hong Kong permanent resident.

And the purposive one too

That natural meaning gives effect to an obvious purpose of Article 24. That article, in conferring upon a child the right of abode in Hong Kong through a parent who has that right, serves the purpose of enabling that child to be with that parent here, thereby securing the unity of the family. If such a purpose needs reinforcement then it is to be found in article 19(1) of the Bill of Rights which provides – word for word as article 23(1) of the International Covenant on Civil and Political Rights ("the ICCPR") does – that: "The family is the natural and fundamental group unit of society and is entitled to protection by society and the State". And Article 39 of the Basic Law provides that the "provisions of [the ICCPR] as applied to Hong Kong shall remain in force". For this humane purpose it matters not whether the parent's right of abode here had been acquired before the child's birth or afterwards.

In *Minister of Home Affairs v. Fisher* [1980] AC 319 the Privy Council was concerned with the Bermuda Constitution. Delivering their Lordships' advice, Lord Wilberforce pointed out (at p.330 B–E) that international instruments, including the ICCPR, could not be disregarded as influences upon the legislative policy behind the Bermuda Constitution even though those instruments had no legal force in Bermuda. They were matters which must have been present to the mind of the draftsman. In our case the position is much stronger. For as we have seen, Article 39 of the Basic Law gives article 23(1) of the ICCPR constitutional force in Hong Kong.

Typical population growth

In rejecting the construction of Article 24 contended for by the appellants, the Chief Judge of the High Court said:

> "According to that construction, if an elderly person becomes a permanent resident in Hong Kong after a continuous period of seven years, then all of his children in Mainland China would automatically become permanent residents by virtue of Article 24(3). It would follow that each one of the children of each of his children would be entitled to apply for permanent resident status under the same Article. This 'family tree' would grow to a number which is difficult to imagine. In my view, this cannot be the intention of the Basic Law. It is clearly not the intention of the drafters of the Basic Law that thousands of persons born in Mainland China would one day become permanent residents of the HKSAR just as one person in say his late 70s has managed to become a Hong Kong permanent resident by staying here for a continuous period of 7 years many years down the road."

What that example does not do is spell out how long it would be before there came the "one day" when thousands of the elderly person's descendants born in the Mainland would become Hong Kong permanent residents. Category (3) does not cover the grandchildren of persons covered by categories (1) or (2): grandchildren are not "born of" their grandparents. Mainland–born grandchildren would not come within category (3) unless and until at least one of their own parents had ordinarily resided in Hong Kong for a continuous period of at least seven years. And this seven–year period would apply to each succeeding generation born in the Mainland.

In any event, it is open to question whether Mainland–born descendants are the ones who would most add to Hong Kong's population. If the children of the elderly person given in the example settled in Hong Kong, their children would probably be born here, as would succeeding generations. But the growth of Hong Kong's population through generation after generation of persons born and brought up here would be typical of population growth throughout the world.

I do not propose to give examples, extreme or otherwise, of situations which acceptance of the Director's construction could bring about. It is enough simply to note that such construction, if accepted, is bound to result in many instances of siblings some of whom do not have the right of abode in Hong Kong and some of whom do. This would be because some would have been born before a parent achieved seven years' ordinary and continuous residence here, and some would have been born after that.

Two arguments advanced on behalf of the Director remain to be considered.

The Sino–British Joint Liaison Group argument

Of these the first concerns the Sino–British Joint Liaison Group. How this argument is put on behalf of the Director may be taken from the Director's printed case which deals with it in two paragraphs which read:

> "Insofar as there is any ambiguity or doubt as to the true construction of BL24(3), the interpretation given to it by paragraph 2(c) of Schedule 1 to the No. 2 Ordinance in fact also reflects the agreement of the Joint Liaison Group set up under the Joint Declaration and there is a presumption that legislation is intended to give effect to the terms of an international agreement.
>
> Furthermore, as a matter of law, any subsequent agreement between the parties to an international treaty regarding its interpretation or as to the application of its provisions is required to be taken into account in construing it: see Article 31(3) of the Vienna Convention. This rule applies whether or not there is any ambiguity."

The first part of this argument can be disposed of on the simple basis that the wording of Article 24 and its obvious purpose leaves no ambiguity or doubt as to the correctness of the appellants' construction. The second part of the argument is answered by what the judgment of the Court delivered today by the Chief Justice in FACV Nos 14, 15 and 16 of 1998 says in regard to the Sino–British Joint Liaison Group and the Vienna Convention. Taking into account the matters put forward by the Director does not dictate acceptance of the Director's construction.

I would take this opportunity to make it clear that on all points, whether as to these or other matters, what I say in this judgment is of course to be read subject to what the whole Court, speaking with one voice, says in that judgment.

The lacuna argument

The second of these two arguments of the Director's is the one summarized thus in a single paragraph of the Director's printed case:

> "Alternatively, the Director submits that insofar as BL24(3) is silent on the question whether at the time of birth, one of the parents has to be a Hong Kong permanent resident (as defined in BL24(1) and (2)), this lacuna can be (and has been) filled by the legislature."

This argument can be disposed of even more shortly. Article 24's silence on the time of birth does not leave a lacuna in that regard. The natural interpretation, which gives effect to the purpose of Article 24, simply disregards the time of birth.

Unconstitutional addition

The Immigration (Amendment) (No. 2) Ordinance 1997 was passed on 1 July 1997. By s.5 this amendment Ordinance repealed Schedule 1 of the Immigration Ordinance, Cap. 115, and replaced it with a new Schedule 1, paragraph 2(c) which is similar in substance to category (3) of Article 24 save that it includes these words which are not to be found in category (3): "if the parent had the right of abode at the time of the birth of the person." I will refer to these words as "the additional words".

Mr Geoffrey Ma SC for the Director conceded in the course of the argument that the use of the "right of abode" concept in the additional words would be unconstitutional even if the introduction of the "time of birth" limitation by way of the additional words were constitutional. Mr Ma's concession was made – and rightly made – for these reasons. There was a time when there was no such thing as the right of abode in Hong Kong. Instead there was the right to land and remain here. And even after there came into existence such a thing as the right of abode here, a person did not acquire that right simply by being a Chinese citizen who was born here or who had ordinarily resided here for a continuous period of not less than seven years.

Of course if the only vice in the additional words lay in their use of the "right of abode" formula, that vice could be removed very easily. All that would be needed is a legislative amendment abandoning that formula and replacing it with a reference to Chinese citizenship coupled with either birth in Hong Kong or not less than seven years' ordinary and continuous residence here.

But that is not the only vice in the additional words. The "time of birth" limitation would be unconstitutional if the Director's construction of Article 24 is wrong and the appellants' construction thereof is right. For the reasons which I have given, I am of the view that the Director's construction is indeed wrong and that the appellants' construction is indeed right. And there is no getting around this by way of legislative amendment.

Result

Taking that view and on that basis, Keith J made a declaration to the effect that the additional words contravene Article 24 of the Basic Law. The Court of Appeal set aside that declaration. In my view, they were wrong to do so. The additional words do indeed contravene Article 24 of the Basic Law. Such contravention results not only from the legislatively curable vice of using the "right of abode" formula. Also and more fundamentally, it results from the legislatively incurable introduction of the "time of birth" limitation. They are therefore irremediably unconstitutional and null and void.

I would allow this appeal. But since, for the reasons which appear above, a declaration in the terms made by the judge may be open to misunderstanding, I would not simply restore his declaration. Instead I would declare as follows:

(1) Each appellant can become a Hong Kong permanent resident under category (3) of Article 24 of the Basic Law by virtue of a parent's Hong Kong permanent resident status under category (2)of that article whether such status of the parent's was acquired before or after the appellant's birth.

(2) The words "if the parent had the right of abode at the time of the birth of the person" in paragraph 2(c) Schedule 1 of the Immigration Ordinance, Cap. 115 (which schedule was introduced by the Immigration (Amendment) (No. 2) Ordinance 1997) contravene Article 24 of the Basic Law and are therefore unconstitutional and null and void.

That covers the constitutional challenge in the present case. It is not necessary or appropriate to make any declaration in the present case about any other part of Schedule 1. Paragraph 2(a) thereof, it is to be noted, follows the wording of category (1) of Article 24 and then adds this qualification: "if his father or mother was settled or had the right of abode in Hong Kong at the time of the birth of the person or at any later time". The absence in the present case of any declaration that that qualification is unconstitutional is not to be taken as any indication that the same is constitutional.

As to costs, I would order that (i) each side bears its own costs here and below and that (ii) there be legal aid taxation of the appellants' costs here and below.

Sir Anthony Mason NPJ:

I agree with Mr Justice Bokhary PJ's judgment.

Chief Justice Li:

The Court being unanimous, the appeal is allowed to make the declarations and the orders as to costs set out under the heading "Result" in Mr Justice Bokhary PJ's judgment.

Chief Justice (Andrew Li)

Permanent Judge (Henry Litton)

Permanent Judge (Charles Ching)

Permanent Judge (Kemal Bokhary)

Non-Permanent Judge (Sir Anthony Mason)

Ms Gladys Li SC and Ms Margaret Ng (instructed by Messrs Pam Baker & Co.) for the appellants

Mr Geoffrey Ma SC and Mr Joseph Fok (instructed by the Department of Justice) for the respondent

---

入境事務處處長 對 莊豐源

HCAL 67/1999；CACV 61/2000；FACV 26/2000

簡略案情

答辯人是一名中國公民，屬未成年人士，由祖父及起訴監護人莊曜誠代表。答辯人在 1997 年 9 月 29 日於香港出生，亦即是在香港特區成立以後出生，當時，他的父母只是持雙程證來港的中國公民，在答辯人出生及以後的時間，父母任何一方都沒有在香港定居或享有居留權。答辯人聲稱他屬《基本法》第 24 條第 2 款第 1 項所指的永久性居民，並享有居留權。雖然入境事務處處長（"處長"）接納答辯人是在特區成立後於香港出生的中國公民，但否決其聲稱。處長認為香港法例第 115 章《入境條例》附表 1 第 2（a）段（"第 2（a）段"）規定"在香港出生的中國公民若要成為永久性居民，則在其出生時或其後任何時間，其父母的任何一方必須已在香港定居或已享有香港居留權。"（註）而按《基本法》第 24 條第 2 款第 1 項的正確解釋，該條款並不賦予非法入境、逾期居留或在香港臨時居留的人在香港所生的中國公民居留權。故此，處長認為第 2（a）段與《基本法》相符。又因答辯人的父母在其出生時或其後任何時間，均沒有在香港定居或享有香港居留權，所以他不符《基本法》第 24 條第 2 款第 1 項的規定。

但原審法官批准答辯人司法覆核的申請，並裁定第 2（a）段有關父母的規定與《基本法》第 24 條第 2 款第 1 項相抵觸，同時宣告答辯人為香港特區的永久性居民，享有香港特區居留權。上訴法庭維持原審法官的命令，駁回處長的上訴。

裁決摘要

在考慮了不同的學術意見後，終審法院認為《基本法》第 24 條第 2 款第 1 項並不滿足終審法院在*吳嘉玲及其他人士對入境事務處處長*一案中所闡述的"類別條件"，即有關的《基本法》條款不關乎中央人民政府管理的事務，亦不關乎中央和特區的關係，因此無需根據《基本法》第 158 條第 3 款就《基本法》第 24 條第 2 款第 1 項的解釋向全國人大常委會作出司法提請。終審法院亦認為在體現"一國兩制"前提下，應該以普通法的原則去解釋《基本法》，即"對所用字句，以及賦予這些字句含義的用語傳統及慣用方法必須加以尊重。"

終審法院最後認定在全國人大常委會沒有作出具約束力的解釋下，法院必須按照普通法處理法律釋義。參照了有關條款的背景及目的來詮釋文本字句，一旦斷定文本字句確是含義清晰後，便須落實這些字句的清晰含義。法院不會基於任何外來資料而偏離這些字句的清晰含義，賦予其所不能包含的意思。《基本法》第 24 條第 2 款第 1 項的含義清晰，沒有任何歧義。其意思是指在 1997 年 7 月 1 日之前或之後在香港出生的中國公民，皆擁有香港特別行政區永久性居民身份。因此，終審法院駁回處長的上訴。

註：該條例已於 2000 年修改，現版本：「2（a）. 在香港特別行政區成立以前或以後在香港出生的中國公民。（由 2002 年第 84 號法律公告代替）」

[中譯本－司法機構法庭語文組譯]

[Chinese Translation－Prepared by

Court Language Section, Judiciary]

FACV No. 26 of 2000

香港特別行政區
終審法院

終院民事上訴 2000 年第 26 號
（原本案件編號：高院民事上訴 2000 年第 61 號）

申請人　入境事務處處長
　　　　對
答辯人　莊豐源
（屬未成年人士，由祖父及起訴監護人莊曜誠代表）

審理法官：終審法院首席法官李國能
　　　　　終審法院常任法官包致金
　　　　　終審法院常任法官陳兆愷
　　　　　終審法院常任法官李義
　　　　　終審法院非常任法官梅師賢爵士

聆訊日期：2001 年 3 月 5 日至 7 日

宣判日期：2001 年 7 月 20 日

判案書

終審法院首席法官李國能：

這是本院的一致判決。

本席於此首先將本判案書的各節列出，以便參照。

1. 引言

《基本法》第二十四條訂明了屬香港特別行政區（“香港特區”或“特區”或“香港”）永久性居民的幾個類別，並賦予他們在特區的居留權。該等人士中，其中一個類別為“在[香港特區]成立以前或以後在香港出生的中國公民。”（見第二十四條第二款第（一）項）

答辯人莊豐源是一名中國公民，他在 1997 年 9 月 29 日於香港出生，亦即是在香港特區 1997 年 7 月 1 日成立以後出生。故此，答辯人聲稱他屬第二十四條第二款第（一）項所指的永久性居民，並享有居留權。

上訴人入境事務處處長（“處長”）接納答辯人是一名在 1997 年 9 月 29 日於香港出生的中國公民，但否決其聲稱。處長堅稱：

（1）香港法例第 115 章《入境條例》附表 1 第 2（a）段（下稱第“2（a）段”）規定在香港出生的中國公民若要成為永久性居民，則在其出生時或其後任何時間，其父母的任何一方必須已在香港定居或已享有香港居留權。答辯人的父母在 1997 年 9 月即他出生時或其後任何時間，均沒有在香港定居或享有香港居留權。

（2）按第二十四條第二款第（一）項的正確解釋，其含義必然是該條款並不賦予非法入境、逾期居留或在香港臨時居留的人在香港所生的中國公民居留權。故此，第 2(a) 段與《基本法》相符。

答辯人承認他未能符合第 2（a）段關於父母的規定。

1997 年 7 月 1 日至 1999 年 7 月 16 日期間，第 2（a）段規定任何人如屬以下類別，即為香港特區永久性居民：

> “在香港特別行政區成立以前或以後在香港出生的中國公民，而在其出生時或其後任何時間，其父親或母親已在香港定居或已享有香港居留權。”

附表 1 的第 1(5) 段規定任何人如屬以下情況，即為在香港定居：（a）他是通常居於香港及（b）他在香港並不受任何逗留期限的限制。

立法會於 1999 年 7 月 16 日根據《入境條例》第 59A 條議決將第 2（a）段修訂如下：

> “任何人如屬以下任何一項，即為〔香港特區〕永久性居民——”
>
> （a）在香港出生的中國公民，而——
>
> （i）其出生日期在 1987 年 7 月 1 日之前；或
>
> （ii）其出生日期在 1987 年 7 月 1 日當日或之後，且在其出生之時或其後任何時間，其父或母已在香港定居或已享有香港居留權。”

作出修訂的理由是在 1987 年 7 月 1 日之前，居留權的概念在香港入境條例中並不存在。該修訂的效力是，在 1987 年 7 月 1 日之前出生的人士，不受關於父母規定的規限，而在當日之後出生的人士則受此規限。第 2（a）段在修訂前適用於答辯人。但無論如何，由於他在 1987 年 7 月 1 日之後出生，他的情況在第 2（a）段修訂後維持不變。

2. 原審法官及上訴法庭

原審法官（當時為原訟法庭法官司徒敬）判答辯人勝訴：[2000] 1 HKC 359。他裁定第 2（a）段有關父母的規定與《基本法》第二十四條第二款第（一）項相抵觸。他批准答辯人司法覆核的申請，並宣告答辯人為香港特區的永久性居民，享有香港特區居留權。上訴法庭（上訴法庭副庭長梅賢玉和當時是上訴法庭法官的梁紹中和羅傑志）維持原審法官的命令，駁回處長的上訴：[2000] 3 HKLRD 661。處長現向本院提出上訴。

3. 案件事實

雙方對案件事實並無爭議。答辯人的父母都是中國公民，在內地結婚。答辯人為中國公民，他是在父母持雙程證從內地來香港探訪時，於 1997 年 9 月 29 日在香港出生。當時，其父母是合法逗留在香港，但是其父或母在其出生時或其後任何時間，均沒有（i）在香港定居或 (ii) 已享有香港居留權。其父母獲准延期逗留至 1997 年 11 月 24 日。此後他們逾期居留，遭截獲並被送回內地。答辯人獲准延期逗留，等候本訴訟的結果。

4. 案中爭議

下屬法院所解決的爭議是，按照第二十四條第二款第（一）項的正確解釋，第 2（a）段中有關父母的規定是否和該條文相抵觸。（"第二十四條第二款第（一）項的爭議"）

在本上訴中，處長提出另一爭議。處長接受全國人民代表大會常務委員會沒有就第二十四條第二款第（一）項作過對香港特區法院具約束力的解釋。全國人民代表大會下稱"全國人大"，而其常務委員會下稱"全國人大常委會"或"常委會"。處長認為根據《基本法》第一百五十八條第三款，本院有責任請常委會對第二十四條第二款第（一）項作出解釋。

第一百五十八條規定：

> "本法的解釋權屬於 [常委會]。
>
> [常委會] 授權 [香港特區] 法院在審理案件時對本法關於 [香港特區] 自治範圍內的條款自行解釋。
>
> [香港特區] 法院在審理案件時對本法的其他條款也可解釋。但如 [香港特區] 法院在審理案件時需要對本法關於中央人民政府管理的事務或中央和 [香港特區] 關係的條款進行解釋，而該條款的解釋又影響到案件的判決，在對該案件作出不可上訴的終局判決前，應由 [香港特區] 終審法院請 [常委會] 對有關條款作出解釋。如 [常委會] 作出解釋，[香港特區] 法院在引用該條款時，應以 [常委會] 的解釋為準。但在此以前作出的判決不受影響。
>
> [常委會] 在對本法進行解釋前，徵詢其所屬的 [香港特區] 基本法委員會的意見。"

"關於中央人民政府管理的事務或中央和特區關係"的條款下稱"範圍之外的條款"，而本院根據第一百五十八條第三款有責任作出的提請下稱"司法提請"。處長認為第二十四條第二款第（一）項是"範圍之外的條款"。這個問題沒有在下屬法院出現，因為第一百五十八條第三款規定須由本院而非下屬法院作出司法提請。這個新的爭議下稱"第一百五十八條第三款的爭議"。

只有在本院裁定無須就第一百五十八條第三款的爭議作出司法提請時，本院才需考慮第二十四條第二款第（一）項的爭議。

5. 歷史

我等現在對近期和本案相關的事情作一簡單回顧。

在*吳嘉玲及其他人士對入境事務處處長*一案中（1999）2 HKCFAR 4（"*吳嘉玲*"），本院須考慮的其中一個問題是：第二十二條第四款是否涵蓋特區的永久性居民（該條款規定中國其他地區的人進入香港特區須辦理批准手續）。在該案中，代表處長的大律師雖然沒有要求司法提請，但認為第二十二條第四款屬"範圍之外的條款"，至於是否須要作出司法提請，則留待本院自行決定。本院裁定，如果某條款符合了兩項條件，本院便有責任將之提交常委會，而該條款是否符合了這兩項條件，則須由本院在審理案件時決定：（1）類別條件，即該條款是屬於"範圍之外的條款"；及（2）有需要條件，即本院在審理有關案件時，需要解釋"該範圍之外的條款"，而該解釋會影響到該案的判決（第 30 頁 I－第 31 頁 B）。本院裁定在驗證該條款是否符合類別條件時，應考慮實質上，最主要需要解釋的是哪條條款。本院假設第二十二條第四款屬"範圍之外的條款"，並裁定第二十四條是屬於特區自治範圍內的條款。本院認為第二十四條是最主要的條款，裁定無須作出司法提請。本院繼而裁定第二十二條第四款不適用於特區的永久性居民。此外，本院判定按照第二十四條第二款第（三）項的正確解釋，非婚生子女屬此條款所指的範圍內。

吳嘉玲一案之判決於 1999 年 1 月 29 日宣讀，同日本院亦就*陳錦雅及其他人士對入境事務處處長*一案（1999）HKCFAR 82（"*陳錦雅*"）作出判決。本院對第二十四條第二款第（三）項的意思作出如下解釋：在香港以外出生的子女，如果其父或母在其出生之前或之後取得第二十四條第二款第（一）項或第二十四條第二款第（二）項所指的永久性居民身份，則該子女可成為第二十四條第二款第（三）項所指的永久性居民。

在*吳嘉玲*一案及*陳錦雅*一案中，特區政府的陳詞均沒有稱第二十四條第二款第（三）項屬"範圍之外的條款"。

1999 年 5 月 20 日，香港特區行政長官向國務院提交了報告（"行政長官報告"）要求協助。該報告說明了有關情況，並稱基於本院的判決，更多人士獲准來港會對香港的繁榮穩定造成嚴重和不利的影響。該報告稱本院的解釋和特區政府對"那些條款的措辭、目的和立法原意"的理解不同。該報告並要求國務院請常委會根據真正的立法原意，對第二十二條第四款和第二十四條第二款第（三）項作出立法解釋。該報告表明香港特區政府會實施本院對非婚生子女作出的裁定，不會就此問題提請對第二十四條第二款第（三）項作出解釋。

1999 年 6 月 26 日，常委會通過"全國人大常委會關於《⋯⋯基本法》第二十二條第四款和第二十四條第二款第（三）項的解釋"（"該解釋"）。根據"該解釋"，（1）第二十二條第四款是指中國其他地區的人，包括香港永久性居民在內地所生的中國籍子女，不論以何種事由要求進入香港特區，均須向內地的機關申請辦理批准手續，方能進入香港特區。（2）第二十四條第二款第（三）項是指該項所述的永久性居民的資格是，有關人士的父母雙方或一方，在該人士出生時，必須屬第二十四條第二款第（一）項或第二十四條第二款第（二）項所指的永久性居民。"該解釋"亦表明：

> "本解釋所闡明的立法原意以及《⋯⋯基本法》第二十四條第二款其他各項的立法原意，已體現在 1996 年 8 月 10 日 [全國人大][香港特區] 籌備委員會第四次全體會議通過的《關於實施 <⋯⋯基本法 > 第二十四條第二款的意見》

中。”

“該解釋”未獲通過前，常委會法制工作委員會副主任喬曉陽先生（“喬先生”）在其講話中陳述了事情的背景。他表示國務院研究了行政長官的報告，並提出了關於提請解釋第二十二條第四款和第二十四條第二款第（三）項的議案。他指出常委會委員長會議已審議了該議案，並在徵詢了基本法委員會的意見後提出了關於第二十二條第四款和第二十四條第二款第（三）項的解釋草案。他繼而對該草案作出說明。

1999 年 12 月 3 日，*在劉港榕對入境事務處處長*一案中（1999）2 HKCFAR 300（“*劉港榕*”），本院裁定常委會有權根據第一百五十八條第一款作出“該解釋”，而其對第二十二條第四款和第二十四條第二款第（三）項所作的解釋是有效和具約束力的，香港特區法院必須以其為準。本院裁定有關第二十二條第四款和第二十四條第二款第（三）項的解釋之效力正如前述。本院在作出上述裁定時，承認“該解釋”和本院較早前在判決中所裁定的不同。（見第 326 頁 G- 第 327 頁 B）。

正如前述，“該解釋”引用了籌備委員會《關於實施第二十四條第二款的意見》。該委員會依據全國人大於 1990 年 4 月 4 日（《基本法》通過的當天）通過的《關於香港特區第一屆政府和立法會產生辦法的決定》而在 1996 年成立。該決定述明籌委會“負責籌備成立特區的有關事宜，根據本決定規定第一屆政府和立法會的具體產生辦法”，以及規定該委員會由內地和不少於 50% 的香港委員組成。

1996 年 8 月 10 日，籌委會對實施第二十四條第二款發表意見。“該意見”的開頭部份說：

“《……基本法》第二十四條第二款對 [香港特區] 永久性居民的問題作出了規定。為了實施上述規定，特提出以下意見，以備 [香港特區] 制定實施細則時參照。”

第一段是關於第二十四條第二款第（一）項，該段說明：

“基本法 [第二十四條第二款] 第（一）項規定的在香港出生的中國公民，是指父母雙方或一方合法定居在香港期間所生的子女，不包括非法入境、逾期居留或在香港臨時居留的人在香港期間所生的子女。”

籌委會工作報告於 1997 年 3 月 14 日獲全國人大議決接納，報告述明委員會已提出了上述意見。

6. 有關解釋《基本法》的處理方法

我等接著考慮的是，香港法院在《基本法》釋義的問題上，應採取何種處理方法。須考慮的問題如下：（1）普通法是否適用；（2）常委會所作解釋的效力；（3）普通法對法律釋義的處理方法。

6.1 普通法是否適用

代表特區政府的處長立場非常清晰。其立場是本院如同下屬法院一樣，在解釋《基本法》時，必須引用在香港發展的普通法，這符合《基本法》所維護的“一國兩制”原則。答辯人持相同的立場。

處長並沒有主張香港法院在解釋《基本法》時，應引用內地制度的原則。該制度有別於香港以普通法為基礎的制度。在該制度下，常委會的立法解釋可以闡明或補充法律。處長在本訴訟中援引了廉希聖教授於 1999 年 8 月 10 日提出的意見，廉教授（在第 17 段中）說：

“就立法解釋的性質而言，全國人大常委會一方面可以對法律文字、法律用語作出闡釋；另一方面可以通過‘進一步明確界限’和‘補充規定’，使法律的界限更清楚，內容更具體，更便於操作。”

另見陳弘毅教授：The Interpretation of the Basic Law (2000) HKLJ Vol. 30 Part 3 411-3 及陳弘毅教授：An Introduction to the Legal System of the People's Republic of China (1998) 95-6。

常委會根據《中國憲法》第六十七條第（四）項及《基本法》第一百五十八條有權解釋《基本法》。正如下文論述，根據第一百五十八條第二款及第一百五十八條第三款，香港法院獲常委會授權，在審理案件時，除受制於第一百五十八條第三款對本院就“範圍之外的條款”行使管轄權的規限，以及受常委會根據第一百五十八條作出的解釋的約束外，可對《基本法》作出解釋。與訟雙方的共同立場是香港法院在行使其獲授予的解釋權時，必須引用普通法，這是符合《基本法》中有關普通法可在香港特區延續的規定。見第八條及第十八條第一款。《基本法》也規定香港特區法院依照適用於特區的法律包括普通法審判案件，其他普通法適用地區的司法判例可作參考。見第十九條第一款、第八十四條及第八十七條第一款。基本上，《基本法》為香港特區以普通法為基礎的不同司法制度訂定了條文。全國性法律除列於附件三者外，不在香港特區實施。附件三限於有關國防、外交和其他按《基本法》規定不屬於特區自治範圍的法律。見第十八條第三款。

6.2 常委會所作解釋的效力

然而，若常委會依據《中國憲法》第六十七條第（四）項及《基本法》第一百五十八條所授的權力對《基本法》作出解釋，香港法院便有責任依循。本院在*劉港榕*一案亦作如此裁定，並表示常委會根據第一百五十八條第一款的規定對《基本法》作出解釋的權力是源自《中國憲法》，而這項權力是“全面而不受限制的”（第 323 頁 B）。尤其是，常委會這項權力的適用範圍擴及《基本法》的每一項條款，而並非限於第一百五十八條第三款所指的“範圍之外的條款”。

同樣，若常委會根據第一百五十八條第三款的規定，應本院所作的司法提請對某項“範圍之外的條款”作出解釋，香港法院在引用有關條款時，亦應以常委會的解釋為準，但在此之前作出之判決則不受影響。這在第一百五十八條第三款有明文規定。

常委會對《基本法》作出解釋的權力是源自《中國憲法》及《基本法》。常委會對《基本法》作出解釋時是在一種與香港制度迥異的制度下行使職責。如前所述，在內地制度下，常委會作出的立法解釋可闡明或補充法律。若常委會對《基本法》某項條款作出解釋，不論是根據第一百五十八條第一款（涉及任何條款），或根據第一百五十八條第三款（涉及“範圍之外的條款”），香港法院均須以其解釋為準。因此，常委會解釋《基本法》的權力在特區是完全獲得承認及尊重的。正如本院在*劉港榕*一案所裁定，實施“一國兩制”原則的《基本法》的效力就是如此。一國之內存在兩制，常委會在不同制度下依照第一百五十八條的規定作出的解釋在特區是具有約束力的，並且是特區制度的一部份。

如前所述，處長接納，常委會並沒有就第二十四條第二款第（一）項作出對香港法院具約束力的解釋。他接納，“該解釋”內關於“以及第二十四條第二款其他各項的立法原意……已體現”在《關於實施基本法第二十四條第二款的意見》這項陳述，並不構成一項對第二十四條第二款第（一）項具約束力的解釋。若有此具約束力的解釋，香港法院便有責任依循。

6.3 普通法對法律釋義的處理方法

香港法院根據《基本法》行使獨立司法權。見第二條及第八十條。香港特區法院行使獨立司法權時的其中一項基本職能是解釋法律，其中包括《基本法》，但此項職能受制於第一百五十八條第三款對本院就"範圍之外的條款"行使管轄權的規限，以及受常委會根據第一百五十八條而作出的解釋的約束。除受上述事宜規限外，解釋法律便屬法院的事務，此乃特區法院獲授予獨立司法權的必然結果。這項由三權分立論產生出來的原則乃普通法的基本原則，並藉《基本法》在香港繼續保存下來。

法院根據普通法解釋《基本法》時的任務是詮釋法律文本所用的字句，以確定*這些字句所表達的立法原意*。法院的工作並非僅是確定立法者的原意。法院的職責是要確定*所用字句的含義*，並使*這些字句所表達的立法原意*得以落實。法例的文本才是法律。法律既應明確，又應為市民所能確定，這是人眾認為重要的。

法院不會把有關條款的字句獨立考慮，而會參照條款的背景及目的。見*吳嘉玲*案第 28–29 頁。法律釋義這項工作需要法院找出有關條款所用字句的含義，而在這過程中需要考慮該條款的背景及目的。這是一種客觀的探究過程。法院必須避免只從字面上的意義，或從技術層面，或狹義的角度，或以生搬硬套的處理方法詮釋文字的含義，也不能賦予其所不能包含的意思。正如法院在關於解釋憲法的 *Minister of Home Affairs v. Fisher* 一案中指出 [1980] AC 319，329E，"對所用字句，以及賦予這些字句含義的用語傳統及慣用方法必須加以尊重。"

正如本院在*吳嘉玲*一案（第 29 頁 A–C）裁定，法院在解釋第三章內有關那些為兩制中香港制度的重心所在，並受憲法保障的自由的條款時，應該採納寬鬆的解釋。然而，法院在解釋有關界定永久性居民類別的條款時，則只應參照任何可確定的目的及背景來考慮這些條款的字句。

為協助解釋有關條款，法院會考慮《基本法》的內容，包括《基本法》內除有關條款外的其他條款及其序言。這些均屬有助於解釋的內在資料。

有助於瞭解《基本法》或《基本法》某些條款的背景或目的的外來資料，一般均可用來協助解釋《基本法》。這些可供考慮的外來資料包括《聯合聲明》，以及於 1990 年 4 月 4 日通過《基本法》之前不久，即於 1990 年 3 月 28 日提交全國人大審議的《關於基本法（草稿）的解釋》。審議上述解釋時以及簽署《聯合聲明》時，本地法例的狀況很多時也會用作解釋《基本法》的輔助資料。雖然《基本法》於 1997 年 7 月 1 日才實施，但由於《基本法》的背景及目的是在 1990 年制定《基本法》時確立，故一般來說，與解釋《基本法》相關的外來資料是制定前資料，即制定《基本法》之前或同時期存在的資料。

就本案而言，除了與背景及目的有關的制定前資料外，本院無須在此探究其他外來資料會有甚麼幫助（即使有的話）；特別是制定後資料能否給予協助的問題。就本案而言，本院只須說明：在常委會*沒有*作出具約束力的解釋，而法院必須按照普通法處理法律釋義的情況下，若法院在借助內在資料及適當的外來資料去確定有關條款的背景及目的，並參照該背景及目的後作出詮釋，斷定文字的含義清晰，則外來資料，不論其性質，也不論其屬制定前或制定後資料，均不能對解釋產生影響。含義清晰即所用文字沒有歧義，就是在合理情況下不能得出另一對立的解釋。

法院參照了有關條款的背景及目的來詮釋文本字句，一旦斷定文本字句確是含義清晰後，便須落實這些字句的清晰含義。法院不會基於任何外來資料而偏離這些字句的清晰含義，賦予其所不能包含的意思。

如法院需考慮採用外來資料，而這些資料並不是與背景及目的有關的制定前資料，法院便應依循普通法原則審慎處理有關事宜。一般而言，普通法的處理方法是不會把所有外來資料先收入考慮之列，然後再衡量資料的分量。法院應要求考慮制定後資料時尤須審慎。這是因為如前所述，在包括三權分立的普通法制度下，法例一經制定，解釋法律便屬法院的事務。解釋《基本法》亦然。不過，如前所述，法院在這方面的權力是受制於第一百五十八條第三款對本院就"範圍之外的條款"行使管轄權的規限，以及受常委會根據第一百五十八條作出的解釋的約束。

7. 第一百五十八條第三款的爭議

正如本院在*吳嘉玲*一案裁定，若某條款符合類別及有需要這兩項條件，本院便須按第一百五十八條第三款的規定作出司法提請。在本案，處長及答辯人均同意有關條款符合有需要條件。本院在審理本案時需要解釋第二十四條第二款第（一）項，而這項解釋將影響本案的判決。本案的爭議是有關條款是否符合類別條件。

7.1 雙方陳詞

代表答辯人的資深大律師李志喜女士陳詞說，第二十四條第二款第（一）項訂明了享有居留權的永久性居民的其中一個類別。因此，這項條款屬關於香港特區自治範圍內的條款而非"範圍之外的條款"。

代表處長的資深大律師霍兆剛先生在陳詞時提出下述理據，爭辯說第二十四條第二款第（一）項屬"範圍之外的條款"：

> (1) 決定某項條款是否屬"範圍之外的條款"時的"相關考慮因素是，實施該項《基本法》有關條款（不論是按所提出的兩種或多於兩種的解釋的任何一種）會否對 (i) 中央人民政府管理的事務或 (ii) 中央和特區關係產生實質（意指實在而非重大）影響"。
>
> (2) 按此驗證標準，第二十四條第二款第（一）項屬"範圍之外的條款"。非法入境者、逾期居留者或在香港臨時居留的人，若非因為非法入境、逾期居留或在香港臨時居留，他們在香港所生的中國公民子女便會在內地出生，並受出境須經批准和父母其中一人須為永久性居民的規定限制。他們離開內地進入香港，對內地的出入境管制及治安（這屬中央人民政府管理的事務），以及對從內地前往香港的出入境事務（這關乎中央和特區關係）產生實質影響。

處長試圖從該解釋的序言有關第二十四條第二款第（三）項的內容中，找出支持論據，證明第二十四條第二款第（一）項屬"範圍之外的條款"。

資深大律師霍先生同意，按他提議的以實質影響為基礎的標準來驗證，關於出生時間及非婚生兩項問題，單單第二十四條第二款第（三）項本身（即使不涉及第二十二條第四款）已屬"範圍之外的條款"。

7.2 入境處搜集的數字

處長表示，事實證明該條款符合他所提議的以實質（即實在）影響為基礎的驗證標準，他並倚賴一些由入境處搜集並已呈交本院審視的數字作為根據。從這些數字來看，若處長就第二十四條第二款第（一）項提出的建議不獲接納，則由 1997 年 7 月 1 日至 2001 年 1 月 31 日的 43 個月內，共有 1991 名在香港出生的中國公民，將會有資格成為上述條款所指的永久性居民。這些人士的母親如不是非法入境者、便是持雙程證者或短暫逾期居留人士，而他們的父親如不是在香港臨時居留，便是本身並非香港居民。這類兒童每月約有 46 人，每年約 555 人。

按這些數字分析，處長承認沒有迹象顯示，處長被判敗訴會導致大批人士立即從內地湧入香港。

依我等之見，實可進一步說，按過去這 43 個月的數字分析，也不能說處長被判敗訴會令香港承擔任何重大風險。

即使處長的提議獲認同，上述 1991 名中國公民的數字也應與在這段期間於香港出生並有資格成為永久性居民的中國公民的人數互相對比。這批中國公民總數達 22,850 人，他們的母親雖然是非法入境者或持雙程證者或短暫逾期居留人士，但由於他們的父親如不是已在港定居，便是香港永久性居民，故他們亦有資格成為永久性居民。

7.3 "該解釋"的序言

處長並非說"該解釋"包含了對涉及"範圍之外的條款"之第一百五十八條第三款的解釋。然而，處長提出第二十四條第二款第（一）項屬"範圍之外的條款"這項意見時，試圖從"該解釋"的序言有關第二十四條第二款第（三）項的內容中找尋支持論據。"該解釋"的原文為中文，英文譯本由香港特區政府律政司擬備，並說明譯文供參考之用，不具立法效力。

該序言述明常委會審議了國務院應行政長官提交的報告而提出的關於提請解釋第二十二條第四款和第二十四條第二款第（三）項的議案。該序言續說：

> "鑑於議案中提出的問題涉及……終審法院 1999 年 1 月 29 日的判決對……《基本法》有關條款的解釋，該有關條款涉及中央管理的事務和中央與［香港特區］的關係，終審法院在判決前沒有依照……《基本法》第一百五十八條第三款的規定請……［常委會］作出解釋，而終審法院的解釋又不符合立法原意，經徵詢……［常委會］［香港特區］基本法委員會的意見……［常委會］決定，根據《中華人民共和國憲法》第六十七條第（四）項和……《基本法》第一百五十八條第一款的規定，對……《基本法》第二十二條第四款和第二十四條第二款第（三）項的規定，作如下解釋"

基本法委員會（該會根據第一百五十八條第四款成立）香港委員陳弘毅教授認為，"該解釋"沒有明示或暗示第二十四條第二款第（三）項屬"範圍之外的條款"。（見 2001 年 1 月 23 日南華早報）。他撰文表示：

> "常委會在其於 1999 年 6 月發布的解釋文本中，根本沒有明言該會認為第二十二條第四款及第二十四條第二款第（三）項這兩項條款，是涉及中央政府與特區關係的。
>
> 事實上，常委會在"該解釋"的中文本（也是唯一的真確本）刻意以條款一詞，讓這問題懸而不決。條款一詞譯成英文可以是"provision"（單數）或"provisions"（眾數），而英譯本中條款一詞為眾數純粹是譯者本人對中文本的主觀詮釋。
>
> 負責草擬"該解釋"的官員喬曉陽向常委會解釋時強調，"第二十二條第四款與第二十四條第二款第（三）項是密不可分的"（原文為中文，由筆者翻譯）。按本人理解，喬曉陽發言的這部份是為了說明常委會對兩項條款都作出解釋是有理據的，即使嚴格來說，只有前者涉及中央政府和特區關係。
>
> 常委會根本沒有明確表示第二十四條第二款第（三）項是一項涉及中央政府和特區關係的《基本法》條款，而"該解釋"的中文本或喬先生的發言均沒有作出這暗示。"

另一方面，基本法委員會內地委員吳建璠教授則持不同看法。他認為，"該解釋"指出第二十二條第四款及第二十四條第二款第（三）項均屬"範圍之外的條款"，理應提請人大對兩者都作解釋。他並表示他持相同看法，即兩項條款均"屬範圍之外的條款"。吳教授撰文論述"該解釋"的內容如下：

> "全國人大常務委員會（在 6 月 26 日）的《解釋》指出，基本法［第二十二條第四款］和［第二十四條第二款第（三）項］都是涉及中央管理的事務和中央與特區關係的條款，特區終審法院在 1 月 29 日判決前未按基本法［第一百五十八條第三款］的規定請全國人大常務委員會作出解釋。"

見吳教授於 1999 年 8 月 25 日《中國法律》第 54 頁所載的文章。

處長以吳教授的看法為依據，而答辯人則以陳教授的看法為依據。鑑於觀點各有不同，"該解釋"的序言便不能理解為常委會已清楚表示第二十四條第二款第（三）項本身屬"範圍之外的條款"。法院必須參照常委會所要審議的議案這背景來理解該序言。該議案要求就第二十二條第四款和第二十四條第二款第（三）項的兩項條款作出解釋，而喬先生認為該兩項條款是密不可分的。（在本案的辯論中所用的是喬先生發言的英譯本，譯本摘錄自香港大學出版社出版的"Hong Kong Constitutional Debate: Conflict over Interpretation"一書（2000 年版）第 481 至 486 頁）。常委會應請求作解釋的條款，並非只是第二十四條第二款第（三）項單獨一條，而不涉及第二十二條第四款。若參照背景來理解，序言中關於應提請哪些條款這點所表達的意見，不可能理解為只有第二十四條第二款第（三）項單獨一條須要常委會作出解釋，因為情況並非如此。

7.4 第二十四條第二款第（一）項是否屬"範圍之外的條款"？

如前所述，根據第一百五十八條第二款及第一百五十八條第三款的規定，香港法院獲常委會授權在審理案件時對《基本法》作出解釋。法院獲授予的解釋權是受制於第一百五十八條第三款對本院就"範圍之外的條款"行使管轄權的規限，以及受常委會根據第一百五十八條作出的解釋的約束。

第一百五十八條第三款說明"範圍之外的條款"時，把焦點集中在有關條款而沒有提及其實施的影響。依我等之見，第一百五十八條第三款不可能解釋為，訂明以事實來決定實施某條款所產生的實質影響，藉此作為驗證該條款是否屬"範圍之外的條款"的標準。參照第一百五十八條第三款的背景及目的來解釋該條款所用字句時，採用這樣的驗證標準是沒有理據的。

再者，答辯人提出的實質影響驗證標準意味著《基本法》的大部份條款，即使不是全部條款，均有可能屬"範圍之外的條款"；而某項條款是否屬這類條款則取決於事實。代表處長的資深大律師霍先生接納此說法是正確的。我等無法從第一百五十八條第三款看出有任何迹象，顯示這項條款的施行是取決於事實調查，即調查實施某項條款所帶來的影響。

第一百五十八條第三款集中述及有關條款時，規定本院須考慮條款的特性。所考慮的問題是，該條款是否具有涉及中央人民政府管理的事務或中央和特區關係的特性。第二十四條第二款第（一）項訂明在 1997 年 7 月 1 日之前或之後在香港出生的中國公民這類別人士為永久性居民。這項條款的特性是，它是用來界定其中一類享有居留權的永久性居民。考慮到條款的特性，我等認為第二十四條第二款第（一）項並不涉及中央人民政府管理的事務或中央和特區關係。這是一項關於特區自治範圍內的條款而並非"範圍之外的條款"。因此，本院無須向常委會作出司法提請。

7.5 其他論點

本院在*吳嘉玲*一案曾先討論類別條件然後探討有需要條件。陳弘毅教授爭辯說，正確的處理方法是先考慮有需要條件。見陳教授在"Hong Kong's Constitutional Debate：Conflict over Interpretation"一書第 113 頁題為"The Court of Final Appeal's Ruling in the Illegal Immigrant Children Case：A Critical Commentary on the Application of Article 158 of the Basic Law"的文章。這論點可予鄭重考慮，但本案並不涉及這爭議，故無須作出判決。在本案，雙方均同意有關條款符合有需要條件，而本院在本判案書中，考慮類別條件之前已處理了這個問題。

本院在*吳嘉玲*一案裁定，主要詮釋驗證標準是決定某項條款是否符合類別條件的標準。確立這標準的背景是，當時的情況涉及兩項條款，其一為"範圍之外的條款"，另一為自治範圍內的條款，於是涉及兩者關係的問題便出現了。正如雙方所接納，本院在此要處理的情況並非如此，而本案亦不適合重新審視主要詮釋此驗證標準，但遇上合適案件時，重新審視這問題也許亦屬恰當。

關於本院向常委會作出司法提請時所應採用的程序，處長作出下述陳詞。首先，本院須決定呈送常委會的提請文件的內容。提請文件應包含足夠資料，包括與訟各方的陳詞。其次，本院應讓與訟各方均有機會就提請文件的內容陳詞。此外，處長亦接納提請文件呈送常委會後，應在法庭公開發表。處長建議的程序看來亦屬恰當，但本院無須對此作出裁定。而且，雙方也沒有就這問題在本院進行全面辯論。

8. 第二十四條第二款第（一）項的爭議

8.1 雙方陳詞

第二十四條第二款訂明下述為香港特區的永久性居民：—

"（一）在香港特別行政區成立以前或以後在香港出生的中國公民；

（二）在香港特別行政區成立以前或以後在香港通常居住連續七年以上的中國公民；

（三）第（一）、（二）兩項所列居民在香港以外所生的中國籍子女；

（四）在香港特別行政區成立以前或以後持有效旅行證件進入香港、在香港通常居住連續七年以上並以香港為永久居住地的非中國籍的人；

（五）在香港特別行政區成立以前或以後第（四）項所列居民在香港所生的未滿二十一周歲的子女；

（六）第（一）至（五）項所列居民以外在香港特別行政區成立以前只在香港有居留權的人。"

雙方均同意，"該解釋"沒有包含任何對第二十四條第二款第（一）項作出的，並對香港法院有約束力的解釋，故本院應採用普通法的處理方法解釋該條款。答辯人的理據很簡單。第二十四條第二款第（一）項的含義一如該條款所述，不多也不少，就是指 1997 年 7 月 1 日之前或之後在香港出生的中國公民。處長的理據是，藉兩種獨立途徑之其中一種，本院應解釋第二十四條第二款第（一）項的含義必然是不包括在香港的非法入境、逾期居留或在香港臨時居留的人所生的中國公民。該兩種途徑為：（1）參照該條款的背景及目的對其作出解釋。（2）對該條款作出解釋時，考慮"該解釋"內有關"第二十四條第二款其他各項的立法原意……已體現"在籌備委員《關於實施第二十四條第二款的意見》這項陳述。

8.2 參照第二十四條第二款第（一）項的目的及背景後，對此條款所作的解釋

第二十四條第二款界定誰是香港特區永久性居民，而第二十四條第三款則賦予他們居留權。因此，連同第二十四條第三款一併考慮後，可見第二十四條第二款的目的是賦予被界定為香港特區永久性居民的人士居留權。根據該定義，某些人士會包括在內，那些不包括在內的會被排除於外。在這種意義上，第二十四條第二款的目的可說是要界定香港特區永久性居民的範圍，從而限制特區的人口。

第二十四條第二款第（一）項的背景特別包括兩項本院應審視的事宜。第一是第二十四條第二款的其他類別，第二是聯合王國及中華人民共和國於 1984 年 12 月簽署的《聯合聲明》，以及當中涉及出入境法律方面的背景。

若以第二十四條第二款的其他各項作為部份背景來考慮時，便會注意到有一點很重要。當永久性居民身份的資格是取決於有關人士的父母任何一方的身份時，條款使用"所生"這字眼來清楚說明。因此，第二十四條第二款第（三）項界定該類別人士為第（一）、（二）兩項所列居民在香港以外所生的中國籍子女。同樣，第二十四條第二款第（五）項界定該類別人士為在 1997 年 7 月 1 日"之前或之後第（四）項所列居民在香港所生未滿二十一周歲的子女"。與此截然不同的是，第二十四條第二款第（一）項界定該類別人士時提及出生地點，即香港，而沒有文字訂明與父母有關的規定。這樣的差異實在重要。

《聯合聲明》附件一內載中華人民共和國政府關於對香港的基本方針的具體說明，而《基本法》的制定是為確保這些基本方針能得以實施。附件一第十四部列出在香港特區享有居留權的各類別人士。有關條款為：—

"在 [香港特區] 成立以前或以後在當地出生或通常居住連續七年以上的中國公民及其在香港以外所生的中國籍子女。"

第二十四條第二款第（一）、（二）及（三）項以相同字眼描述以上條款所述的各類人士。

處長依據 1984 年香港的出入境法律的狀況作為《聯合聲明》附件一的部份背景，並以此作為考慮第二十四條第二款第（一）項的背景之一。當時，任何人均不能單憑在香港出生而依法取得在香港的出入境權利，而在 1983 年之前，這些權利可藉此而取得；在香港出生的英籍人士獲賦予出入境權利。見原訟法庭司徒敬法官的判詞 [2001] 1 HKC 第 367-8 頁，第 374-5 頁。處長因此爭辯說，若實施附件一的第二十四條第二款第（一）項的目的，是單憑在香港出生便獲賦予永久性居民的身份，這便與之前的情況不相符。

依我等之見，任何人在 1983 年後皆不能單憑在香港出生而取得在香港的出入境權利這點，不能作為正確解釋第二十四條第二款第（一）項的依據。正如原訟法庭司徒敬法官所指出（第 375 頁），這是因為英國國籍法及對香港出入境法例的相應修訂均有其本身的歷史背景。當時聯合王國意識到有大量移民從英聯邦國家進入聯合王國的危機，為了要處理這危機所帶來的問題，便改變以 jus soli 決定公民身份的政策。（jus soli 的英文意思是"土地的權利"，亦即以出生地決定兒童的公民身份的原則）。因此不應因這歷史背景而假定《基本法》亦追隨這種政策轉變。

處長指出，與答辯人情況相同的人士，若非其父母在其出生時在港探訪，他會在父母一向居住的內地出生；而他亦須符合父母其中一人在其出生時為第二十四條第（一）或第（二）項所指的永久性居民的規定，才可根據第（三）項憑籍血源而取得永久性居民身份的資格。即使符合該項規定，他仍須取得第二十二條第四款所指的出境批准。這的確是那些與答辯人情況相同而在內地出生的人士所會遇到的結果，也是第二十四條第二款第（三）項的規定有別於第二十四條第二款第（一）項的規定之必然結果。然而不能因此說，既然不同類別各有不同的規定，第二十四條第二款第（一）項便應視為含糊的條款。

參照第二十四條第二款第（一）項的背景及目的來考慮這項條款所用的文字後，可見其含義清楚明確，就是在 1997 年 7 月 1 日之前或之後在香港出生的中國公民享有永久性居民的身份。這項條款的含義沒有含糊不清之處，亦即在合理情況下不能得出另一對立的解釋。

8.3 "該解釋"及"籌委會的意見"

處長的依據是，"該解釋"述明第二十四條第二款其他各項的立法原意已體現在籌委會《關於實施第二十四條第二款的意見》中（"有關陳述"）。如前所述，他接納這並非常委會對第二十四條第二款第（一）項作出的具約束力的解釋。他的論據是，普通法處理法律釋義時有足夠的靈活性可讓本院對此項陳述加以考慮，並接納處長所建議的解釋，判他勝訴。他並非將"該解釋的有關陳述"擱置一旁，而以"籌委會的意見"作為其建議的根據。

本院有責任在常委會沒有作出具約束力的解釋的情況下，按照普通法來處理法律釋義，而按普通法原則，經正確詮釋第二十四條第（二）款第（一）項後，"有關陳述"不能影響其清晰的含義。

如前所論，根據普通法的處理方法，本院的任務是要參照第二十四條第二款第（一）項的背景及目的對其所用字句作出詮釋，以確定*這些字句所表達的立法原意*。如前文斷定，第二十四條第二款第（一）項的含義清晰，沒有任何歧義。其意思是指在 1997 年 7 月 1 日之前或之後在香港出生的中國公民。依循普通法的原則，本院無法基於"有關陳述"而偏離本院認為是第二十四條第二款第（一）項的清晰含義，而以有關字句所不能包含的意思代之。

9. 結果

因此，本院駁回處長的上訴，不作任何訟費命令，但判令答辯人的訟費須按照《法律援助條例》及《法律援助規例》予以評定。

首席法官（李國能）

常任法官（包致金）

常任法官（陳兆愷）

常任法官（李義）

非常任法官（梅師賢）

資深大律師霍兆剛先生及翟紹棠先生（由律政司延聘）代表上訴人

資深大律師李志喜女士及郭瑞熙先生（由賈偉林、江令名律師行延聘並由法律援助署委派）代表答辯人

Fateh Muhammad v. Commissioner Of Registration & Registration Of Persons Tribunal

Fateh Muhammad 對 人事登記處處長及人事登記審裁處

HCAL 40/1999；CACV 272/1999；FACV 24/2000

簡略案情

上訴人在 1962 年 10 月利用巴基斯坦護照首次進入香港並申請到香港身份證。除了於 1967 年因結婚離港一個月，1976 年因二度婚姻離港三個月以及 1985 年因其父去世離港六個月外，上訴人一直在香港生活和工作。1993 年 2 月，上訴人被指控犯有兩項罪行，最後被判處監禁至 1997 年 2 月 27 日。在其刑滿前幾天，保安局長決定將其驅逐出境。1998 年 5 月 13 日上訴人向人事登記處處長（“處長”）申請核實其永久性居民身份，1998 年 6 月 17 日，該申請被拒絕。1998 年 6 月 29 日，上訴人再次向處長書面提交申請，要求獲得香港永久性居民身份證，1998 年 7 月 2 日，處長再拒絕了這一申請。同年 8 月，上訴人向人事登記審裁處（“審裁處”）對處長的拒絕決定提起上訴。1999 年 1 月 14 日，審裁處開庭聽取了當事人意見，並於 29 日支持上訴人的上訴請求。及後，處長上訴到高等法院，對審裁處的決定申請司法覆核。原訟庭於 1999 年 6 月 24 日裁定上訴人並不是香港永久性居民且不具有居港權，同時撤銷了審裁處的決定。上訴人對此不服並向上訴庭提出上訴。2000 年 4 月 19 日，上訴法庭駁回其上訴。

裁決摘要

上訴人認為他在香港居住超過 7 年，根據《基本法》第 24 條第 2 款第 4 項，擁有居留權。終審法院同意在事實上，上訴人確是在香港居住了超過 7 年，但他因為觸犯刑事罪行而被判監禁，而他出獄至上訴時仍沒能達到連續居住 7 年的要求。終審法院認為《入境條例》第 2（4）（b）條並未違反《基本法》，它所針對的是實質的監禁而並非短暫的、可忽略的離開或拘留。在這問題上，終審法院認為一個實質的監禁不能作為第 24 條第 2 款第 4 項所說的通常居住。至於《入境條例》附表 1 第 1（4）（b）條規定申請人在提交申請前必須緊接著連續居港 7 年，並沒有歧視非中國人的成份，亦不違反《公民權利和政治權利國際公約》中第 26 條以及《基本法》中第 25 與第 39 條。這種情況在全球不同的政治地域也很常見。因此，終審法院認定上訴人並不滿足《基本法》第 24 條第 2 款第 4 項的要求並駁回了其上訴。

FACV No. 24 of 2000

IN THE COURT OF FINAL APPEAL OF THE HONG KONG SPECIAL ADMINISTRATIVE REGION

FINAL APPEAL NO. 24 OF 2000 (CIVIL)
(ON APPEAL FROM CACV NO. 272 OF 1999)

Between:

FATEH MUHAMMAD	Appellant
- and -	
COMMISSIONER OF REGISTRATION	1st Respondent
REGISTRATION OF PERSONS TRIBUNAL	2nd Respondent

Court: Chief Justice Li, Mr Justice Bokhary PJ, Mr Justice Chan PJ, Mr Justice Nazareth NPJ and Sir Anthony Mason NPJ

Date of Hearing: 21-23 May 2001

Date of Judgment: 20 July 2001

JUDGMENT

Chief Justice Li:
I agree with the judgment of Mr Justice Bokhary PJ.

Mr Justice Bokhary PJ:
Introduction

The issue in this case is whether the appellant, Mr Fateh Muhammad, has Hong Kong permanent resident status and therefore the right of abode here. If he does not, then it may well be that he will acquire such status and right in future. But that depends on what may happen in future. This appeal is concerned with Mr Muhammad's present position.

Apart from temporary absences abroad, Mr Muhammad has lived in Hong Kong ever since the 1960s. Nothing turns on those absences. On 13 May 1998 he applied to the 1st respondent, the Commissioner of Registration, for verification of his eligibility for a Hong Kong permanent identity card. Such a card signifies official recognition of the holder's Hong Kong permanent resident status with the right of abode here. On 17 June 1998 the Commissioner refused such verification. On 29 June 1998 Mr Muhammad made a formal application by which he asked the Commissioner to issue him a Hong Kong permanent identity card. On 2 July 1998 the Commissioner refused to do so.

Mr Muhammad then appealed to the 2nd respondent, the Registration of Persons Tribunal, against such refusal. His notice of appeal was filed on 4 August 1998. That appeal was heard by the Tribunal on 14 January 1999. And it was allowed by the Tribunal on 29 January 1999.

The matter then went to court. It did so by way of judicial review proceedings brought in the High Court by the Commissioner against the Tribunal and Mr Muhammad. Those proceedings were heard by Keith JA sitting as an additional judge. On 24 June 1999 Keith JA handed down his judgment. He made: (i) a declaration that Mr Muhammad was not a Hong Kong permanent resident and did not have the right of abode here; and (ii) an order of *certiorari* quashing the determination by which the Tribunal had allowed Mr Muhammad's appeal against the Commissioner's refusal to issue him a Hong Kong permanent identity card. Mr Muhammad appealed to the Court of Appeal against Keith JA's judgment. On 19 April 2000 the Court of Appeal (Mayo VP and, as they then were, Rogers and Ribeiro JJA) handed down its judgment, dismissing Mr Muhammad's appeal against Keith JA's judgment.

Mr Muhammad now appeals to this Court from the Court of Appeal's judgment. He appeared before us by leading and junior counsel. So did the Commissioner. The Tribunal did not appear before us, it being a nominal respondent to the present appeal.

Whether Mr Muhammad has the right of abode in Hong Kong turns on the interpretation of art. 24 of the Basic Law. This article confers the right of abode in Hong Kong on those persons whom it defines as the permanent residents of Hong Kong. In its second paragraph, it defines them as:

> "(1) Chinese citizens born in Hong Kong before or after the establishment of the Hong Kong Special Administrative Region;
>
> (2) Chinese citizens who have ordinarily resided in Hong Kong for a continuous period of not less than seven years before or after the establishment of the Hong Kong Special Administrative Region;
>
> (3) Persons of Chinese nationality born outside Hong Kong of those residents listed in categories (1) and (2);
>
> (4) Persons not of Chinese nationality who have entered Hong Kong with valid travel documents, have ordinarily resided in Hong Kong for a continuous period of not less than seven years and have taken Hong Kong as their place of permanent residence before or after the establishment of the Hong Kong Special Administrative Region;
>
> (5) Persons under 21 years of age born in Hong Kong of those residents listed in category (4) before or after the establishment of the Hong Kong Special Administrative Region; and
>
> (6) Persons other than those residents listed in categories (l) to (5), who, before the establishment of the Hong Kong Special Administrative Region, had the right of abode in Hong Kong only."

It is Mr Muhammad's contention that he comes within category (4). The courts below held that he does not. To understand their reasoning, it is necessary to be aware of these facts. Although Mr Muhammad has lived in Hong Kong for much more than seven years, his time in Hong Kong unfortunately includes his imprisonment here from 27 April 1994 to 27 February 1997 serving a sentence for conspiracy to utter forged banknotes and conspiracy to deliver counterfeit banknotes. And of course seven years have not yet elapsed from the time of his release from prison to even the present time let alone have elapsed from the time of such release to the time of any application made by him for Hong Kong permanent resident status.

In the circumstances outlined above, the courts below held against Mr Muhammad on the basis of their view of the law, the effect of which view may be summarised as follows. First, they held that the ordinary residence required by art. 24 does not include time spent serving a prison sentence. Secondly, they held that the seven continuous years required under art. 24(2)(4) must come immediately before the time when an application for Hong Kong permanent resident status is made in reliance on those seven continuous years. Thirdly and accordingly, they held that the legislature was acting constitutionally when it passed legislation under which (a) imprisonment or detention does not count as ordinary residence and (b) the seven years' ordinary and continuous residence relied upon in an application for Hong Kong permanent resident status made in reliance upon art. 24(2) (4) must come immediately before the time when the application is made.

There is another point which the courts below chose not to decide because it was possible to dispose of the matter on their view of the "imprisonment" and "immediately before" points. Until I have dealt with those two points, I will say nothing more about the other point beyond identifying it as the "limit of stay" point.

Imprisonment or detention

Section 2(4) (b) of the Immigration Ordinance, Cap. 115, provides that "a person shall not be treated as ordinarily resident in Hong Kong ... during any period ... of imprisonment or detention pursuant to the sentence or order of any court". This provision has been in the statute book since 1971. In challenging its constitutionality, Mr Philip Dykes SC for Mr Muhammad says that what it catches includes even: detention pending a trial which results in acquittal or the dropping of charges; detention due to mental illness; detention as a debtor; detention pending extradition which eventually fails; detention of an eventually acquitted person due to a refusal by a magistrate of bail which is then granted by a judge; and one day's imprisonment.

As to the last item in that list of Mr Dykes's, I would not like to think that such pointless deprivations of liberty are part of the Hong Kong legal scene. In any event, I would not preclude an argument, whether on the *de minimis* principle by which the law ignores trifles or on some other basis, that a term of imprisonment of that short duration would not defeat an abode claimant. The view might well be taken that such a short period of imprisonment does not interrupt the continuity of residence for the purpose of art. 24(2) (4) of the Basic Law and, accordingly, of s.2(4) (b) of the Immigration Ordinance.

Turning to the other items in Mr Dykes's list, I would exclude them from s.2(4) (b) 's ambit on this simple basis. In a provision like s.2(4) (b) "detention" and "order" must, in my view, be read as being of the same nature as "imprisonment" and "sentence" respectively. Accordingly the only kind of detention covered by s.2(4) (b) is detention in a training centre or in a detention centre. (The word "order" in s.2(4) (b) is needed because, although s.4 of the Training Centres Ordinance, Cap. 280, speaks of a "sentence of detention", s.4 of the Detention Centres Ordinance, Cap. 239, speaks of a "detention order".)

The expression "ordinarily resident" is to be given its natural and ordinary meaning. What that meaning is depends on the context in which the expression appears. The courts have often had to grapple with the expression's natural and ordinary meaning in legislation eg. as in *Levene v. Inland Revenue Commissioners* [1928] AC 217 and *Inland Revenue Commissioners v. Lysaght* [1928] AC 234 (where liability to tax was concerned) and as in Reg v. Barnet LBC, ex parte Shah [1983] 2 AC 309 (where entitlement to educational allowance was concerned). Although residence and its nature can be highly relevant to the common law concept of domicil, it was pointed out by Lord Carson in *Gout v. Cimitian* [1922] 1 AC 105 at p.110 that the expression "ordinarily resident" (found in that case in an Order in Council) could not be interpreted by the considerations which apply when determining domicil, and must be given its usual and ordinary meaning.

No single judicial pronouncement or combination of such pronouncements in regard to the meaning of the expression "ordinarily resident" can be conclusive for the purposes of every context in which that expression appears. But as a starting point at least, Viscount Sumner's observation in *Lysaght's* case at p.243 that "the converse to 'ordinarily' is 'extraordinarily' " is, I think, of wide utility. Serving a term of imprisonment, at least when it is not of trivial duration, is something out of the ordinary. Of course it does not mean that a person in prison in any given jurisdiction is never to be regarded as ordinarily resident in that jurisdiction for any purpose. Certainly I would not be disposed to hold, for example, that the fact of being in prison somewhere would of itself render a person not ordinarily resident there when his being so would render him liable to tax.

The present context is a different and somewhat special one. For the question to which it gives rise is this. Does being in prison or a training or detention centre in Hong Kong pursuant to a criminal conviction which has never been quashed and a sentence or order which has never been set aside constitute ordinary residence here when seven years' ordinary and continuous residence here is a qualification prescribed by the Basic Law for attaining a valuable status and right, namely Hong Kong permanent resident status and the right of abode here? In such a context, there is a very strong case for saying that residence while serving a substantial term of imprisonment or detention in a training or detention centre is not ordinary residence. So in my judgment: (i) the answer to the question posed above is "no" ; (ii) art. 24 of the Basic Law is to be construed accordingly; and (iii) s.2(4) (b) of the Immigration Ordinance (construed in the way explained above) is therefore constitutional.

I turn now to the "immediately before" point.

Immediately before

Even in pre-handover days, the categories of Hong Kong permanent residents were identified in Schedule 1 to the Immigration Ordinance. When it became necessary to replace it with a new schedule which complied with art. 24 of the Basic Law and implemented its provisions in detail, an amendment ordinance, namely the Immigration (Amendment) (No. 2) Ordinance 1997, was passed replacing the old Schedule 1 with a new one. That new one is the current one. My references to Schedule 1 will be to it, and my references to paragraphs will be to its paragraphs.

Paragraph 2(d) sets out this category of Hong Kong permanent resident:

> "A person not of Chinese nationality who has entered Hong Kong with a valid travel document, has ordinarily resided in Hong Kong for a continuous period of not less than 7 years and has taken Hong Kong as his place of permanent residence before or after the establishment of the Hong Kong Special Administrative Region."

That simply tracks the language art. 24(2) (4) of the Basic Law. But it is preceded by para. 1(4) (b) which provides that for a person under para. 2(d), the seven years must come "immediately before" the date when he applies to the Director of Immigration for Hong Kong permanent resident status.

Article 24(2) (4) of the Basic Law confers the right of abode on non-citizens in certain circumstances. I think that it may even be fairly said that it concedes that right to them in those circumstances. In the context of setting out the categories of persons who shall have the right of abode in Hong Kong, it is scarcely realistic to suppose that it was intended to confer that right on persons whose seven years' ordinary and continuous residence ended long before they took, or ends long before they take, Hong Kong as their home. It would be surprising indeed if the right of abode were to be conferred upon persons who ordinarily resided in Hong Kong without taking Hong Kong as their home and thereafter severed all connections with Hong Kong.

So unless its wording simply cannot support such a reading, a purposive construction of art. 24(2) (4) drives the Court to say that the seven continuous years required by art. 24(2) (4) must come immediately before the time when an application for Hong Kong permanent resident status is made in reliance on those seven continuous years. In my view, the wording of art. 24(2) (4) supports such a reading. Such support is to be found generally in the tenor of the provision and particularly in the implicit link between the twin requirements of seven years' ordinary and continuous residence and of having taken Hong Kong as one's place of permanent residence. In my judgment, the seven continuous years required by art. 24(2) (4) of the Basic Law must come immediately before the time when an application for Hong Kong permanent resident status is made in reliance on those seven continuous years.

On the constitutionality or otherwise of para. 1(4) (b), there remains Mr Dykes's argument that it is unconstitutional as being discriminatory against non-Chinese citizens, contrary to art. 26 of the International Covenant on Civil and Political Rights as enshrined in arts 25 and 39 of the Basic Law. I am able to deal with this argument quite shortly. Once it is held, as I have held, that para. 1(4) (b) merely provides explicitly what art. 24(2) (4) provides implicitly, there is simply no room left for challenging its constitutionality by reference to any other provision contained in or incorporated by the Basic Law. I would just add that different treatment of citizens and non-citizens in regard to the right of abode is a common if not invariable feature of the laws of countries throughout the world, including those with constitutions which prohibit discrimination. That difference of treatment flows inevitably from the fact of the political boundaries which are drawn across the globe. The "immediately before" requirement is not racist. It applies regardless of race, and there are rational and cogent grounds for it.

In my judgment, for the reasons given above, para. 1(4) (b) of Schedule 1 to the Immigration Ordinance is constitutional.

Common law principles

On the "imprisonment or detention" and "immediately before" points, the Commissioner succeeds on common law principles without having to rely on his alternative arguments based on what the Standing Committee of the National People's Congress's 26 June 1999 Interpretation said about certain statements made in the Preparatory Committee's 10 August 1996 Opinions. Since I arrive on common law principles at conclusions which are the same as the ones which the Commissioner says can also be derived from that other source, it is unnecessary to address those alternative arguments.

Mr Muhammad does not yet have the right of abode

The view which I have formed on the true construction of art. 24(2) (4) of the Basic Law and on the constitutionality of s.2(4) (b) of the Immigration Ordinance and para. 1(4) (b) of Schedule 1 to that Ordinance is sufficient to dispose of the matter as it now stands. Mr Muhammad does not yet have Hong Kong permanent resident status and therefore does not yet have the right of abode here. This is because he has not yet achieved the necessary period of seven years' ordinary and continuous residence in Hong Kong immediately before applying for Hong Kong permanent resident status.

Mr Muhammad is being permitted to live in Hong Kong and may well acquire Hong Kong permanent resident status and therefore the right of abode here before too long. This is because on 26 February 1999 the deportation order which had been made against him on 24 February 1997 was rescinded and is therefore to be ignored for all purposes. Hence it would appear that he has been ordinarily and continuously resident in Hong Kong ever since his release from prison on 27 February 1997. On that footing, if he continues to be ordinarily resident here, he will achieve the requisite residence in three years'time from now.

Limit of stay

The "limit of stay" provisions contained in paras 1 and 3 of Schedule 1 to the Immigration Ordinance would then arise.

Paragraph 3 (1) (c) provides that a person seeking to establish Hong Kong permanent resident status under para. 2(d) (which tracks art. 24(2) (4) of the Basic Law) is required to be settled in Hong Kong at the time of his declaration that he has taken Hong Kong as his place of permanent residence. This brings one back to para. 1(5) which reads:

> "A person is settled in Hong Kong if –
>
> (a) he is ordinarily resident in Hong Kong; and
>
> (b) he is not subject to any limit of stay in Hong Kong."

Item (a) poses no problem. It is subsumed by the requirements of art. 24(2) (4) of the Basic Law as I have construed those requirements.

Keith JA had misgivings over para. 1(5) (b) 's constitutionality. In the Court of Appeal, one member was silent on para. 1(5) (b), another drew attention to Keith JA's misgivings and yet another thought that para. 1(5) (b) was constitutional.

On the material before us, there is no reason to assume that the Director of Immigration would refuse to exercise his discretion in favour of lifting any limit on Mr Muhammad's stay once he has achieved seven years' continuous and ordinary residence in Hong Kong and then applies to the Director for Hong Kong permanent resident status. But is it constitutional to make such an applicant's Hong Kong permanent resident status dependent on a successful exercise of administrative discretion or, failing that, a successful administrative appeal or, failing even that, a successful judicial review challenge? This is a serious question to be determined on some future occasion on which it may arise.

Result

Keith JA made no order as to costs other than an order for legal aid taxation of Mr Muhammad's own costs. But in addition to ordering legal aid taxation of Mr Muhammad's own costs, the Court of Appeal ordered costs in favour of the Commissioner. Mr Joseph Fok SC, who appeared for the Commissioner here and below, informed us that he had not asked the Court of Appeal for costs in favour of the Commissioner. Mr Fok also informed us that even if the Commissioner were successful before us, he would not seek costs here and would be agreeable to our setting aside the costs order made in his favour by the Court of Appeal. Mr Fok's approach is a sensible one to adopt in the circumstances.

In the result, I would set aside the order for costs made by the Court of Appeal in the Commissioner's favour, but otherwise dismiss this appeal, and make no order as to the costs before us other than an order for legal aid taxation of Mr Muhammad's own costs.

Mr Justice Chan PJ:

I agree with the judgment of Mr Justice Bokhary PJ.

Mr Justice Nazareth NPJ:

I agree with the judgment of Mr Justice Bokhary PJ.

Sir Anthony Mason NPJ:

I agree with the judgment of Mr Justice Bokhary PJ.

Chief Justice Li:

The Court unanimously sets aside the order for costs made by the Court of Appeal in the Commissioner's favour, but otherwise dismisses this appeal, and makes no order as to the costs before us other than an order for legal aid taxation of Mr Muhammad's own costs.

Chief Justice (Andrew Li)

Permanent Judge (Kemal Bokhary)

Permanent Judge (Patrick Chan)

Non-Permanent Judge (G. P. Nazareth)

Non-Permanent Judge (Sir Anthony Mason)

Mr Philip Dykes SC and Mr Maurice K.F. Ng (instructed by Messrs Barnes & Daly and assigned by the Legal Aid Department) for the appellant

Mr Joseph Fok SC and Mr Jat Sew-tong (instructed by the Department of Justice) for the 1st respondent

The 2nd respondent absent

Maura Juliet A. Raquiza v. The Director Of Immigration

Maura Juliet A. Raquiza 對 入境事務處處長

HCAL 20/2006；CACV 272/2006

簡略案情

申請人是菲律賓人，1988 年 8 月 26 日開始在港從事家庭傭工，其逗留許可被多次延長至 1992 年 2 月 27 日。因其僱傭合約於 1992 年 1 月 7 日被終止，她只被批准以遊客身份逗留至同年 1 月 28 日。其間，她於 1 月 23 日簽了新的僱傭合約，並且於 26 日離港回菲等待新合約的處理。她在 1992 年 6 月返港工作，後因續約而獲准延長逗留至 1997 年 7 月 15 日。在 1996 年 10 月 15 日，申請人與一香港永久性居民結婚。由 1997 年 4 月 14 日起她便以家屬身份在香港居住。不幸地，其丈夫於 1997 年 12 月搬離他們的居所並於 1999 年 1 月申請離婚。然而，申請人與其丈夫似乎於同年 5 月達成了協定，其丈夫會取消離婚申請並承擔延續申請人家屬簽證的申請。事實上，申請人的家屬簽證最後被延至 2003 年 3 月 15 日。

在該婚姻破裂後，申請人於 2001 年 5 月 16 日基於已經以家屬簽證在港居留 3 年以上為由，申請無條件逗留。因為申請人沒有應處長的要求出席會面，該申請於翌年 8 月被認定為放棄。申請人在其逗留許可屆滿前（即 2003 年 3 月 15 日前），經一家律師所幫助，以不同理由再作出申請。首先，她以其丈夫作承擔人，其後她又以她本人作承擔人提出申請。正當這些申請被覆核期間，申請人丈夫又表示願意作為該申請的承擔人。因此，申請人與其丈夫於 2003 年 6 月 9 日被入境處分別接見。會談中申請人丈夫表達了與申請人復合的意願，同時亦願意繼續支持申請人在香港居住。可是，申請人於同日則表示她想離婚和不再需要家屬簽證。申請人確認入境處主任曾向她指出如果她離婚，她將需要離開香港，然而，申請人表示她只希望能延長一個月時間好讓她能處理強積金和離婚事宜。最後，按照她的意願，她被批准延長逗留至同年 7 月 9 日。往後的延期申請一律被處方拒絕。

裁決摘要

在原訟庭審訊時，申請人認為她根據《基本法》第 24 條，應享有居港權；而且，她亦認為入境處處長有責任提醒她應有的憲法權利。關於第一個爭論，原訟庭法官認為申請人在回歸前並沒有在香港連續居留滿 7 年，原因是她於 1992 年 1 月曾離開香港超過 4 個月，這不是一個可以忽略的短暫時間，而且離港原因是由於申請人的逗留期限已滿，沒有權利繼續留港。至於申請人在回歸前作為家庭傭工的時間可以被計算為連續居住 7 年的論點，原訟庭亦根據上訴庭案例 *Huang Bingzhi v. Immigration Tribunal* HCAL 1718/2000 予以否定，並認為相關的入境條例並無追溯效力的問題。所以，原訟庭法官認為申請人逗留時間應從她申請家屬簽證時開始計算，不幸的是，該簽證只延續至 2003 年 6 月，距離 7 年的要求還差數月，因此，申訴人並不符合《基本法》第 24 條的要求。

至於申請人的第二個論點認為入境處處長沒有履行其提醒的責任，原訟庭法官認定本案的案情跟 *Somporn Yoothip v. Secretary For Security & Another* HCAL122/2004 一案截然不同。本案中申請人沒有如該案的當事人般作出積極申請，而且，入境處亦曾提醒申請人離婚的後果。因此，該論點亦被法官否定。申請人不滿該判決，但上訴庭支持原訟庭法官的結論並駁回申請人的上訴。

CACV 272/2006

In The High Court of the

Hong Kong Special Administrative Region

Court of Appeal

Civil Appeal No. 272 of 2006
(on appeal from HCAL NO. 20 of 2006)

Between:

MAURA JULIET A. RAQUIZA — Applicant

- and -

THE DIRECTOR OF IMMIGRATION — Respondent

Before: Hon Rogers VP, Le Pichon JA and Sakhrani J in Court

Date of Hearing: 27 July 2007

Date of Handing Down Judgment: 3 August 2007

JUDGMENT

Hon Rogers VP:

1. This was an appeal from a judgment of Chu J given on 11 July 2006. The matter before the judge was an application for judicial review. An order for certiorari was sought to quash the decision of the Director of Immigration given on 4 May 2004 whereby the Director refused to grant an extension of stay. The judge dismissed the application. At the conclusion of the hearing of this appeal judgment was reserved.

Background

2. On this appeal there was no dispute as to the facts found by the judge. In brief, the applicant is a Philippine National who first came to Hong Kong on 26 August 1988 to work as a foreign domestic helper. For that purpose she had an employment visa. Her permission to stay in Hong Kong was extended at various times until 27 February 1992. However, because her contract of employment was terminated in January of that year, her permission to stay was curtailed and she was permitted to remain in Hong Kong as a visitor until 28 January 1992. In the intervening time she had signed a new contract of employment on 23 January 1992. Having done that, she left Hong Kong on 26 January. She then waited in the Philippines whilst the new employment contract was processed.

3. It was not until 5 June 1992 that the applicant returned to Hong Kong, taking up her new employment as a foreign domestic helper. Thereafter, as her contracts were renewed, her permission to stay was extended and the final permission to remain in Hong Kong as a foreign domestic helper was extended until 15 July 1997.

4. On 15 October 1996 the applicant married a Hong Kong permanent resident. That marriage, unfortunately, did not last long. The husband moved out of the matrimonial home in December 1997 and in January 1999 he petitioned for divorce. It would seem that in May 1999 the applicant and her husband had reached some agreement whereby the divorce petition would be withdrawn and the husband would sponsor the applicant's application for renewal of her dependent visa.

5. In the meantime, on 14 April 1997 the applicant had been allowed to change her immigration status to take up residence in Hong Kong as the dependent of her husband. The initial permission to remain on that basis was until 15 March 1998. On 20 March 1998 that permission was extended until 15 March 2000 and on 27 March 2000 her dependent visa was extended until 15 March 2003.

6. After the breakup of the marriage, the applicant applied on 16 May 2001 for unconditional stay on the basis of having resided in Hong Kong as a dependent for more than three years. That application was treated as abandoned in August of the following year because the applicant did not attend the interviews requested by the Director.

7. Just before the permission to remain until 15 March 2003 expired the applicant sought assistance from a firm of solicitors. With the solicitors' help further applications were made on alternative bases. The first was that the application was made with the support of her husband as her sponsor and the other on her own sponsorship.

8. Whilst those applications were in the process of being reviewed the husband was apparently re-contacted. He indicated his willingness to support the application and on 9 June 2003 the applicant and her husband attended the Immigration Department and were interviewed separately. The husband indicated he would like to reunite with the applicant and would continue to support her stay in Hong Kong, but on the same day, the applicant wrote a letter indicating that she wanted to file for divorce and did not want a dependent visa. She requested an extension of one month to enable her to make arrangements in relation to her MPF and to file for divorce.

9. The judge recorded that the applicant regretted that move soon afterwards but that it did reflect her feelings at the time, which were prompted by the fact that she felt that she had been insulted by her husband. The applicant was granted an extension until 9 July 2003 as requested in her letter of 9 June. Further extensions were requested and duly refused.

The judgment below

10. The applicant relied on Article 24(4) of the Basic Law as giving her a right to remain in Hong Kong as a permanent resident. The relevant provisions read:

> "The permanent residents of the Hong Kong Special Administrative Region shall be:
>
> ...
>
> (4) Persons not of Chinese nationality who have entered Hong Kong with valid travel documents, have ordinarily resided in Hong Kong for a continuous period of not less than seven years and have taken Hong Kong as their place of permanent residence before or after the establishment of the Hong Kong Special Administrative Region"

11. The judge then went on to consider section 2(4) of the Immigration Ordinance Cap. 115 ("the Ordinance"). Section 2(4) (a) (iv) reads as follows:

> "(4) For the purposes of this Ordinance, a person shall not be treated as ordinarily resident in Hong Kong–
>
> (a) during any period in which he remains in Hong Kong–

...

(vi) while employed as a domestic helper who is from outside Hong Kong"

12. On the two issues that were argued, the judge held that, in the first place, the applicant's residence in Hong Kong was broken between 27 January and 4 June 1992 when she was not in Hong Kong and did not have permission to remain in Hong Kong. On that basis she was not resident and could not have been resident in Hong Kong. Hence there was no continuous period of residence, still less ordinary residence, commencing from August 1988.

13. On the second issue argued, namely as to whether the period when the applicant was a foreign domestic helper prior to 1 July 1997, when the provisions of section 2(4) (a) (iv) came into force, could be taken into account. The judge held that the wording of the Ordinance was clear that the period had to be excluded when calculating the period of ordinary residence and that that construction was confirmed by comparison with the previous version of section 2(4) (a) prior to the amendment.

14. The judge rejected the argument that the statute should not be interpreted retrospectively so as to impair an existing right because prior to the 1997 amendment, under Schedule 1 of the Immigration Ordinance, a non-Chinese National could not acquire permanent residence even though he had continuously ordinarily resided in Hong Kong for seven years or more. Hence there was no question of impairment of any existing or accrued right.

15. As the judge pointed out, her finding in respect of the construction issue rendered unnecessary the further argument that it was the duty of the Director to inform or alert the applicant as to her rights as having been ordinarily resident in Hong Kong for a continuous period of seven years or more. The judge, however, went on to consider that matter and held that the Director did not have a duty, either generally or in the context of the particular case, as contended for by the applicant.

This appeal

16. On this appeal Mr Dykes SC, who appeared on behalf of the applicant in this court but not in the court below, sought to argue on a construction of the Ordinance that it should not be given retrospective effect. Two subsidiary points were also argued but were only relevant should he succeed on the first point. Those points were that the judge had been wrong to hold that the period of ordinary residence had been broken in 1992 and had also been wrong in failing to hold that the Director had a duty to advise the applicant as to her rights as to being a permanent resident.

17. It became clear in the course of argument that Mr Dykes' main point verged on arguing that section 2(4) (a) (iv) was invalid in view of Article 24(4) of the Basic Law. That was a point which had not been taken either in the application for judicial review, the court below or in the notice of appeal. Furthermore, in the opening paragraph of the skeleton for this appeal it had been said that "Underlying broader constitutional issues do not arise in this case." The footnote specifically said that the skeleton argument assumed the constitutionality of section 2(4) without conceding the point.

18. When the matter was pointed out by the court, application was made for the notice of appeal to be amended and for there to be an adjournment to allow the Director to prepare the case to meet this challenge. That application was refused. In the first place the argument appeared to be hypothetical in that the only argument put as to invalidity was in respect of persons of Chinese race who had come to Hong Kong as foreign domestic helpers from countries other than China. Whether or not there were any such persons who would now be affected is simply not known. Perhaps more importantly, however, the step of striking down legislation as being unconstitutional is a grave step which should only be taken on mature consideration with the court being given all the assistance possible. In the present circumstances it appeared to be highly undesirable to allow such a point to be taken belatedly with an adjournment being required in this court. It might be added that no amendment to the notice of appeal had been presented to the court.

19. The main argument in this court, therefore, turned on the question as to the construction of section 2(4) (a) (iv) because, on any footing, the applicant would have to take into account a period when she was a foreign domestic helper prior to 1997 in order to have a period of seven years prior to June 2003 when she was resident in Hong Kong. In my view the provisions of the Ordinance are clear. A period when an applicant is a foreign domestic helper cannot be taken into account as being a period of ordinary residence whether that occurred before or after the coming into force of the subsection on 1 July 1997.

20. As the judge held there is no question of any retroactive effect of the Ordinance since prior to 1 July 1997 the applicant could not have become a permanent resident in view of the fact that she could not have brought herself within the provisions of the then existing Schedule 1 of the Ordinance.

21. In those circumstances the subsidiary points which were argued do not have any bearing. It suffices to say that, on any footing, any period of ordinary residence must have ceased between 27 January and 4 June 1992 since quite apart from the fact that the applicant was not in Hong Kong she had no right or permission to be in Hong Kong at that stage. Hence it would have been impossible for her to have been ordinarily resident. Furthermore, since the applicant had no rights of which she could be advised, any argument as to an obligation on the part of the Director to give advice as to her rights cannot arise.

22. In those circumstances, I consider this appeal must be dismissed with an order *nisi* of costs in favour of the Director.

Hon Le Pichon JA:

23. I agree.

Hon Sakhrani J:

24. I also agree.

Vice-President (Anthony Rogers)

Justice of Appeal (Doreen Le Pichon)

Judge of the Court of First Instance (Arjan H Sakhrani)

Mr Philip Dykes SC, instructed by Messrs Littlewoods, for the Applicant/Appellant

Mr Anderson Chow SC, instructed by Department of Justice, for the Respondent/Respondent

---

Lau Kong Yung And Others v. The Director Of Immigration

劉港榕等17人 對 入境事務處處長

HCAL 20/1999；CACV 108/1999；CACV 109/1999；FACA 109/1999；FACA 10/1999；FACA 11/1999（判決書參考 P.086）

簡略案情

申請人劉港榕與另外 16 人反對入境處處長向他們發出的遣送離境令。他們認為根據《基本法》第 24 條第 2 款第 3 項，他們擁有香港居留權。這 17 人中，有些是以非法途徑進入香港，有些則是持雙程證進入，而其中一個是從外國回國途中停留。17 人中有 5 人在他們出生時其父母至少一方已擁有香港永久性居民身份，其他則是在其出生後父母其中一方才拿到香港永久性居民身份的。他們全在 1999 年 1 月 29 日前進入香港，即終審法院下達*吳嘉玲、吳丹丹等對入境事務處處長* FACV 14、15 & 16/1998 案的判決書前。該案連同終審法院在*陳錦雅等對入境事務處處長*案件的判決，確認 1997 年的《入境（修訂）（第 2 號）條例》規定第 24 條第 2 款中的第三類別永久性居民只能在父或母於其出生時已有居留權才能成為永久性居民，是違反憲法，及《入境（修訂）（第 3 號）條例》部份違憲而無效。

原訟庭拒絕申請人的司法覆核和人身保護令申請，但上訴庭卻推翻原審法官的裁決。及後，人大常委會在 1999 年 6 月 26 日接受並頒佈對《基本法》第 22 條第 4 款和第 24 條第 2 款第 3 項的解釋。

該解釋關於《基本法》第 24 條第 3 款的部份訂明：

> 《中華人民共和國香港特別行政區基本法》第 24 條第 2 款前 3 項規定："香港特區永久性居民為：（一）在香港特別行政區成立以前或以後在香港出生的中國公民；（二）在香港特別行政區成立以前或以後在香港通常居住連續七年以上的中國公民；（三）第（一）、（二）兩項所列居民在香港以外所生的中國籍子女"。其中第（三）項關於"第（一）、（二）兩項所列居民在香港以外所生的中國籍子女"的規定，是指無論本人是在香港特別行政區成立以前或以後出生，在其出生時，其父母雙方或一方須是符合《中華人民共和國香港特別行政區基本法》第 24 條第 2 款第（一）項或第（二）項規定條件的人。本解釋所闡明的立法原意以及《中華人民共和國香港特別行政區基本法》第 24 條第 2 款其他各項的立法原意，已體現在 1996 年 8 月 10 日全國人民代表大會香港特別行政區籌備委員會第四次全體會議通過的《關於實施〈中華人民共和國香港特別行政區基本法〉第二十四條第二款的意見》中。"

裁決摘要

終審法院在本案中確認全國人大常委會有權對《基本法》作出解釋而且該解釋對香港的法院有約束力。據此，終審法院最後以大比數批准執行對申請人的遣送離境令。

陳偉文等106人 對 入境事務處處長

HCAL 20，23，27，28，29，30，31，32，33，34，39，40，41，42，44，49，50，52，53，55，56，58，60，61，62，64，72，73，74，75，76，79，80，81，83，84，85，86，87，88，90，94，98，102，103，104，105，106，107，108，110，112，118，119，120，121，123，125，126，127，128，129，130，131，132，134，137，138，139，140，141，144，145，147，148，149，151，152，153，156，157，163，164，166，167，170，172，173，175，177，178，179，181，182，183，185，186，189，190，192，193，194，195/2000

簡略案情

本案共涉及 106 宗司法覆核案件及同等數目申請人，其中三名申請人在開審前致函法庭，表示放棄申請。由於各申請人之背景相似，他們的申請所引發之法律爭議亦相同，所以法庭決定一併處理他們的申請。這些申請人中，除了數名是持中華人民共和國護照外，其餘都是持雙程證以訪客身份抵港（部份申請人是在 1999 年 1 月 29 日終審法院作出有關判決後，或在 1999 年 6 月 26 日人大常委會作出有關解釋後才首次抵港）。逗留期滿後，申請人都拒絕離開香港，並聲稱根據香港終審法院在 1999 年 1 月 29 日就 *陳錦雅 對 入境事務處處長* [1999]1 HKLRD 304 一案作出的判決，擁有香港居留權。

申請人均聲稱其父親或母親現在是香港永久性居民，他們亦同意當他們出生時，雙親都未成為香港永久性居民。他們的父親或母親是在他們出生後，才成為香港永久性居民。申請人都聲稱是香港特區永久性居民，擁有香港居留權。入境事務處處長拒絕核實他們的身份，亦不批准他們在香港居留的要求，並下令他們必須離開香港。由此他們向法庭提出司法覆核申請，要求法庭推翻處長的決定，同時要求法庭核實他們香港永久性居民的身份，並頒令他們擁有香港居留權。

裁決摘要

原審法官認為全國人大常委會 對 《基本法》第 22 及 24 條所作之解釋，實際上已否定了終審法院在 *陳錦雅 對 入境事務處處長* [1999] 1 HKLRD 304 一案作出的判決。事實上，終審法院在*劉港榕及其餘 16 人 對 入境事務處處長* [1999] 3 HKLRD 778 一案中已清楚確認人大釋法對香港法院的約束力與影響。

至於全國人大常委會在 1999 年 6 月 26 日解釋《基本法》之消息公布後，香港特區行政長官在新聞發佈會作出的優惠政策與及後的相關行政安排，法院認為是負責任及合理的，並不接納申請人主張要用廣義的角度去解釋該優惠政策和相關行政安排。因此，所有申請人的覆核申請全被駁回。

HCAL 20、23、27、28、29、30、31、32、33、34、39、40、41、42、44、49、50、52、53、55、56、58、60、61、62、64、72、73、74、75、76、79、80、81、83、84、85、86、87、88、90、94、98、102、103、104、105、106、107、108、110、112、118、119、120、121、123、125、126、127、128、129、130、131、132、134、137、138、139、140、141、144、145、147、148、149、151、152、153、156、157、163、164、166、167、170、172、173、175、177、178、179、181、182、183、185、186、189、190、192、193、194、195/2000

香港特別行政區
高等法院
原訟法庭

憲法及行政訴訟 2000 年第 20 號

申請人　陳偉文

憲法及行政訴訟 2000 年第 23 號

申請人　莊江海

憲法及行政訴訟 2000 年第 27 號

申請人　李麗君

憲法及行政訴訟 2000 年第 28 號

申請人　卓金都

憲法及行政訴訟 2000 年第 29 號

申請人　卓棟梁

憲法及行政訴訟 2000 年第 30 號

申請人　陳金珠

憲法及行政訴訟 2000 年第 31 號

申請人　吳麗萍

憲法及行政訴訟 2000 年第 32 號

申請人　林麗娜

憲法及行政訴訟 2000 年第 33 號

申請人　鄭煌輝

憲法及行政訴訟 2000 年第 34 號

申請人　林榕楠

憲法及行政訴訟 2000 年第 39 號

申請人　高麗森

憲法及行政訴訟 2000 年第 40 號

申請人　李躍再

憲法及行政訴訟 2000 年第 41 號

申請人　龔琼瑤

憲法及行政訴訟 2000 年第 42 號

申請人　陳玉容

憲法及行政訴訟 2000 年第 44 號

申請人　陳主程

憲法及行政訴訟 2000 年第 49 號

申請人　許明香

憲法及行政訴訟 2000 年第 50 號

申請人　林榕梅

憲法及行政訴訟 2000 年第 52 號

申請人　蔡茂惕

憲法及行政訴訟 2000 年第 53 號

申請人　程愛農

憲法及行政訴訟 2000 年第 55 號

申請人　傅環

憲法及行政訴訟 2000 年第 56 號

申請人　林金鑫

憲法及行政訴訟 2000 年第 58 號

申請人　劉榮凱

憲法及行政訴訟 2000 年第 60 號

申請人　盧秀密

憲法及行政訴訟 2000 年第 61 號

申請人　吳衍霖

憲法及行政訴訟 2000 年第 62 號

申請人　盧章奕

憲法及行政訴訟 2000 年第 64 號

申請人　盧冰冰

憲法及行政訴訟 2000 年第 72 號

申請人　洪瑞蓮

憲法及行政訴訟 2000 年第 73 號

申請人　盧俊杰

憲法及行政訴訟 2000 年第 74 號

申請人　王雪霞

憲法及行政訴訟 2000 年第 75 號

申請人　陳秀柔

憲法及行政訴訟 2000 年第 76 號

申請人　許美英

憲法及行政訴訟 2000 年第 79 號

申請人　蔡娟娟

憲法及行政訴訟 2000 年第 80 號

申請人　陳淥泓

憲法及行政訴訟 2000 年第 81 號

申請人　蔡端端

憲法及行政訴訟 2000 年第 83 號

申請人　施錦雅

憲法及行政訴訟 2000 年第 84 號

申請人　李俊杰

憲法及行政訴訟 2000 年第 85 號

申請人　蔡友聰

憲法及行政訴訟 2000 年第 86 號

申請人　陳志雄

憲法及行政訴訟 2000 年第 87 號

申請人　陳冰雲

憲法及行政訴訟 2000 年第 88 號

申請人　吳清種

憲法及行政訴訟 2000 年第 90 號

申請人　吳稟治

憲法及行政訴訟 2000 年第 94 號

申請人　程明權

憲法及行政訴訟 2000 年第 98 號

申請人　黃清雅

憲法及行政訴訟 2000 年第 102 號

申請人　郭凱旋

憲法及行政訴訟 2000 年第 103 號

申請人　郭貴容

憲法及行政訴訟 2000 年第 104 號

申請人　王韓杰

憲法及行政訴訟 2000 年第 105 號

申請人　黃鴻媚

憲法及行政訴訟 2000 年第 106 號

申請人　吳育新

憲法及行政訴訟 2000 年第 107 號

申請人　蔡水泳

憲法及行政訴訟 2000 年第 108 號

申請人　蔡金鈕

憲法及行政訴訟 2000 年第 110 號

申請人　張燕婷

憲法及行政訴訟 2000 年第 112 號

申請人　黃麗婷

憲法及行政訴訟 2000 年第 118 號

申請人　潘金女

憲法及行政訴訟 2000 年第 119 號

申請人　施育紅

憲法及行政訴訟 2000 年第 120 號

申請人　李燕霞

憲法及行政訴訟 2000 年第 121 號

申請人　李惠霞

憲法及行政訴訟 2000 年第 123 號

申請人　莊景明為莊佳溶的父親及起訴監護人

憲法及行政訴訟 2000 年第 125 號

申請人　池秀欽

憲法及行政訴訟 2000 年第 126 號

申請人　陳榮安

憲法及行政訴訟 2000 年第 127 號

申請人　施天祥

憲法及行政訴訟 2000 年第 128 號

申請人　吳天增

憲法及行政訴訟 2000 年第 129 號

申請人　施西文

憲法及行政訴訟 2000 年第 130 號

申請人　王育儒

憲法及行政訴訟 2000 年第 131 號

申請人　陳麗容

憲法及行政訴訟 2000 年第 132 號

申請人　陳益群

憲法及行政訴訟 2000 年第 134 號

申請人　施麗婷

憲法及行政訴訟 2000 年第 137 號

申請人　王鴛鴦

憲法及行政訴訟 2000 年第 138 號

申請人　郭文英

憲法及行政訴訟 2000 年第 139 號

申請人　許容川

憲法及行政訴訟 2000 年第 140 號

申請人　蘇宗敏

憲法及行政訴訟 2000 年第 141 號

申請人　肖永立

憲法及行政訴訟 2000 年第 144 號

申請人　林哲峰

憲法及行政訴訟 2000 年第 145 號

申請人　黃巧敏

憲法及行政訴訟 2000 年第 147 號

申請人　李明瑜

憲法及行政訴訟 2000 年第 148 號

申請人　許珊龍

憲法及行政訴訟 2000 年第 149 號

申請人　林學武

憲法及行政訴訟 2000 年第 151 號

申請人　蔡婷婷

憲法及行政訴訟 2000 年第 152 號

申請人　留麗娟

憲法及行政訴訟 2000 年第 153 號

申請人　王白雲

憲法及行政訴訟 2000 年第 156 號

申請人　庄榮榮

憲法及行政訴訟 2000 年第 157 號

申請人　施芳娜

憲法及行政訴訟 2000 年第 163 號

申請人　李俊甫

憲法及行政訴訟 2000 年第 164 號

申請人　蔡雙燕

憲法及行政訴訟 2000 年第 166 號

申請人　施玉炎

憲法及行政訴訟 2000 年第 167 號

申請人　鄒宗星

憲法及行政訴訟 2000 年第 170 號

申請人　張麗娟

憲法及行政訴訟 2000 年第 172 號

申請人　吳榮習

憲法及行政訴訟 2000 年第 173 號

申請人　黃美如

憲法及行政訴訟 2000 年第 175 號

申請人　蔡樹芽

憲法及行政訴訟 2000 年第 177 號

申請人　張紅霞

憲法及行政訴訟 2000 年第 178 號

申請人　張紅春

憲法及行政訴訟 2000 年第 179 號

申請人　吳育仁

憲法及行政訴訟 2000 年第 181 號

申請人　王麗真

憲法及行政訴訟 2000 年第 182 號

申請人　吳麗娜

憲法及行政訴訟 2000 年第 183 號

申請人　吳文謙

憲法及行政訴訟 2000 年第 185 號

申請人　柯金池

憲法及行政訴訟 2000 年第 186 號

申請人　許建民

憲法及行政訴訟 2000 年第 189 號

申請人　洪金炳

憲法及行政訴訟 2000 年第 190 號

申請人　吳新量

憲法及行政訴訟 2000 年第 192 號

申請人　許雲清

憲法及行政訴訟 2000 年第 193 號

申請人　吳玲玲

憲法及行政訴訟 2000 年第 194 號

申請人　蘇文博

憲法及行政訴訟 2000 年第 195 號

申請人　施紅旗
及
答辯人　入境事務處處長

主審法官：高等法院原訟法庭法官楊振權
聆訊日期：2000 年 6 月 29，30 日及 7 月 3 日
判案書日期：2000 年 7 月 11 日

判案書

為了方便處理，在本判案書，憲法及行政訴訟 2000 年 ABC 號申請人 XXX 會寫成 ABC/2000 XXX。餘此類推。

本案共涉及 106 宗司法覆核案件及同等數目申請人。其中三名申請人── 78/2000 李燕燕、99/2000 許清鵬及 180/2000 庄清育在開審前致函法庭，表示放棄申請。因此法庭已下令將他們的申請撤銷，亦不作任何訟費命令。

餘下申請人都聲稱是香港特區永久性居民，擁有香港居留權。他們要求入境事務處處長（以下簡稱處長）核實他們的身份，並批准他們在香港居留。

處長拒絕申請人的要求，並下令他們必須離開香港。

申請人不滿處長的決定，故向法庭提出司法覆核申請，要求法庭

推翻處長的決定。他們亦要求法庭核實他們香港永久性居民的身份，頒令他們擁有香港居留權。

40/2000 李躍再、41/2000 龔琼瑤、42/2000 陳玉容、44/2000 陳主程、50/2000 林榕梅、52/2000 蔡茂惕、53/2000 程愛農、56/2000 林金鑫、58/2000 劉榮凱、60/2000 盧秀密、61/2000 吳衍霖、62/2000 盧章奕及 64/2000 盧冰冰在較早時已獲法庭發出許可，進行司法覆核申請。其餘申請人則向法庭申請許可，以便進行司法覆核申請。

由於各申請人之背景相似。他們的申請所引發之法律爭議亦相同，所以法庭決定將他們的申請一併處理。

17 名申請人，包括 34/2000 林榕楠、39/2000 高麗森、50/2000 林榕梅、55/2000 傅環、75/2000 陳秀柔、84/2000 李俊杰、90/2000 吳熹治、94/2000 程明權、120/2000 李燕霞、121/2000 李惠霞、127/2000 施天祥、129/2000 施西文、130/2000 王育儒、163/2000 李俊甫、177/2000 張紅霞、178/2000 張紅春及 192/2000 許雲清由陳黃林律師事務所轉聘黃錦娟大律師代表。

其餘申請人無律師代表，他們親自向法庭作出陳述。

申請人聲稱其父親或母親現在是香港永久性居民。但他們亦同意當他們出生時，雙親都未成為香港永久性居民。他們的父親或母親是在他們出生後，才成為香港永久性居民。

唯一例外是 76/2000 許美英。她在 1970 年 3 月 11 日出生。她聲稱已逝世的母親施禮智女士在 1963 年已成為香港永久性居民。

許美英在其誓詞附錄兩分文件副本，即其母親之身份証及回港証。身份証發出日期是 1963 年 3 月而回港証發出日期是 1966 年 12 月 5 日。

當然持有身份証或回港証並不表示持有人在証件發出時已擁有香港永久性居民身份。

在香港特別行政區成立以前，一名並非在香港出生的中國公民須在香港通常居住連續七年以上，才能成為香港永久性居民。

許美英未能提出任何資料顯示其母親在她出生時，即 1970 年 3 月 11 日已經在香港通常居住連續七年以上。

許美英未能確立出生時，其母親已經是香港永久性居民，所以她的情況和其他申請人一樣，都屬於出生時，父或母都未成為香港永久性居民。

105/2000 黃鴻媚在 1996 年 11 月 11 日獲得菲律賓永久居留權。她以中國護照多次進出香港。

根據香港法例第 115 章《入境條例》第 2AB 條，任何人士以香港永久性居民在香港以外所生的中國籍子女之身份，希望成為香港永久性居民，必先確立身份而居留權證明書是唯一認可確立身份的方法。申請居留權證明書有下列方式：

（一）如果申請人在申請時居住在中國大陸，要通過當地的公安廳出入境管理處提出。

（二）如果申請人在申請時居住在中國以外地方，要通過當地中國大使館或領事館或以郵遞方式直接向入境事務處處長提出。

（三）如果申請人在申請時居住在台灣或澳門地區，以郵遞方式直接向入境事務處處長提出。

由此可見，國籍或居留權可能影響申請居權証的方式，但和申請人是否是香港特區永久性居民，全無關係。

105/2000 黃鴻媚聲稱擁有香港永久性居民身份，她須申請居權証以確立該身份。如在申請她時居住在菲律賓，她須通過菲律賓中國大使館或領事館或以郵遞方式直接向入境事務處處長提出。

但在本申請，本席只需考慮 105/2000 黃鴻媚是否根據《基本法》第 24 條第 2 款第（3）項擁有香港居留權。她是否擁有菲律賓永久居留權對事件實在是不關痛癢。她的申請和其他申請人的申請相同，不用另行處理。

179/2000 吳育仁在其申請書內指出他在 1979 年 5 月 29 日已獲當時的香港人民入境事務處簽發一張可供其無限制居留用之入境許可証，但他沒有根據入境許可証行使權力，進入香港。他聲稱事後曾以該証向內地公安機關申請來港與父親團聚，未獲批准。他亦曾多次向入境事務處諮詢，都未獲任何解釋或答覆。

事實上，有關之入境許可証上訂明"本証必須於 1979 年 6 月 28 日或該日之前呈示方為有效"。由於証件未有在有效期內行使，故已失效多時。

179/2000 吳育仁不能以上述入境許可証強化其申請，他的情況亦和其他申請人無異。

申請人中，除了數名是持中華人民共和國護照外，其餘都是持雙程証以訪客身份抵港，獲入境處批准短暫在港停留，採訪親友或旅遊。期滿後，申請人都拒絕離開香港，並聲稱根據香港終審法院在 1999 年 1 月 29 日陳錦雅對入境事務處處長 [1999] 1 HKLRD 304 一案所頒下之判令，擁有香港永久居留權。

申請人中，部份是首次到香港，亦有部份曾經多次持雙程証或護照以訪客身份抵港，逗留期滿後，離開香港。

《中華人民共和國香港特別行政區基本法》（以下簡稱《基本法》）第 24 條列出六類人士為香港特別行政區之永久性居民，享有居留權。和本案有關之頭三類香港永久性居民為：

"（一）　在香港特別行政區成立以前或以後在香港出生的中國公民；

（二）　在香港特別行政區成立以前或以後在香港通常居住連續七年以上的中國公民；

（三）　第（一）、（二）兩項所列居民在香港以外所生的中國籍子女；"

在陳錦雅一案，香港終審法院要對《基本法》第 24 條第 2 款第（3）項作出解釋。

1999 年 1 月 29 日，終審法院頒下判令，一致裁定香港特別行政區永久性居民在香港以外所生的中國籍子女，不論其父親或母親之香港永久性居民身份是在其出生前或出生後才確立，都屬香港永久性居民。

根據終審法院上述判令，如申請人聲稱屬實，他們都因為父親或母親現在是香港永久性居民而成為香港永久性居民，擁有香港居留權，雖然他們的父或母在他們出生時仍未成為香港永久性居民。

在同一天香港終審法院在*吳嘉玲、徐權能、張麗華* [1999] 2 HCFAR 4 三宗合併案件中亦頒下判令，一致裁定香港永久性居民在國內所生的中國籍子女，要進入香港定居，並不受《基本法》第 22 條第 4 款的規限，故無須在國內向中央政府辦理批准手續，亦無須受中央政府定下進入香港定居人數的數額所限制。

終審法院裁定有關條例規定在國內居住的香港永久性居民必須持有國內發出的旅遊證件（即單程証）才能享有香港居留權的限制屬違憲及無效。

終審法院上述裁決在社會上引起軒然大波，備受各界關注，個中詳情，無須細表。

但香港特區政府不認同終審法院就《基本法》第22條第4款和第24條第2款第（3）項所作之解釋，認為該解釋有違《基本法》之立法原意。香港特區政府行政長官行使其憲法權力，透過國務院，請求全國人民代表大會常務委員會，根據《基本法》第158條對《基本法》第22條第4款和第24條第2款第（3）項重新作出解釋。

全國人大常委會特別工作委員會副主任喬曉陽先生在1999年6月22日向常委會發言時指出：

> "終審法院在判決前（指陳錦雅及吳嘉玲，徐權能、張麗娟等案件）沒有按照《基本法》第158條第3款的規定提請全國人大常委會進行解釋，而終審法院的解釋又不符合立法原意。根據《人華人民共和國憲法》第67條第(4)項……和《基本法》第158條第1款……的規定，為了保證《基本法》的正確 實施，由全國人大常委會就《基本法》有關條款進行解釋，是必要和適當的。為此，委員長會議提出了《全國人民代表大會常務委員會關於《中華人民共和國香港特別行政區基本法》第22條第4款和第24條第2款第(3)項的解釋（草案）》，並徵詢了全國人大常委會香港特別行政區基本法委員會的意見。"

全國人大常委會在1999年6月26日就《基本法》第22條第4款和第24條第2款第（3）項作出解釋。有關解釋已在香港憲報詳細刊登。解釋之重要部份照錄如下：

> "一.《中華人民共和國香港特別行政區基本法》第二十二條第四款關於"中國其他地區的人進入香港特別行政區須辦理批准手續"的規定，是指各省、自治區、直轄市的人，包括香港永久性居民在內地所生的中國籍子女，不論以何種事由要求進入香港特別行政區，均須依照國家有關法律、行政法規的規定，向其所在地區的有關機關申請辦理批准手續，並須持有有關機關製發的有效證件方能進入香港特別行政區。各省、自治區、直轄市的人，包括香港永久性居民在內地所生的中國籍子女，進入香港特別行政區，如未按國家有關法律、行政法規的規定辦理相應的批准手續，是不合法的。
>
> 二.《中華人民共和國香港特別行政區基本法》第二十四條第二款前三項規定："香港特區永久性居民為：
>
> （一）在香港特別行政區成立以前或以後在香港出生的中國公民；
>
> （二）在香港特別行政區成立以前或以後在香港通常居住連續七年以上的中國公民；
>
> （三）第（一）、（二）兩項所列居民在香港以外所生的中國籍子女"。
>
> 其中第（三）項關於'第（一）、（二）兩項所列居民在香港以外所生的中國籍子女'的規定，是指無論本人是在香港特別行政區成立以前或以後出生，在其出生時，其父母雙方或一方須是符合《中華人民共和國香港特別行政區基本法》第二十四條第二款第（一）項或第（二）項規定條件的人。本解釋所闡明的立法原意以及《中華人民共和國香港特別行政區基本法》第二十四條第二款其他各項的立法原意，已體現在1996年8月10日全國人民代表大會香港特別行政區籌備委員會第四次全體會議通過的《關於實施〈中華人民共和國香港特別行政區基本法〉第二十四條第二款的意見》中。
>
> 本解釋公布之後，香港特別行政區法院在引用《中華人民共和國香港特別行政區基本法》有關條款時，應以本解釋為準。本解釋不影響香港特別行政區終審法院長1999年1月29日對有關案件判決的有關訴訟當事人所獲得的香港特別行政區居留權。此外，其他任何人是否符合《中華人民共和國香港特別行政區基本法》第二十四條第二款第（三）項規定的條件，均須 以本解釋為準。"

香港特區政府要求人大解釋基本法之決定及人大所作出之解釋，在本港造成極大震盪，輿論譁然，聚訟紛紜。

有人認為事件中顯示中央政府干預香港特區自治範圍內之事務，有違一國兩制精神；亦有人認為香港政府"輸打贏要"，案件經終審法院裁定其敗訴後，求助人大常委會，要求重新解釋《基本法》有關條款，目的是推翻終審法院之判決。

他們指出該做法不但嚴重影響香港之法治精神及司法獨立，更是向中央政府雙手奉上香港自治範圍內之自主權。結果是終審法院之裁決被人大常委會之解 釋 所取代，對終審法院之威望亦有影響。事件亦造成社會嚴重分化，令市民對國內移居香港之新移民產生歧視。

但亦有人持不同意見，指出終審法院1999年1月29日之裁定對香港整體造成一個不能承受之重担及壓力。有關問題必須解決，而解 決之最佳方法，是由人大常委會，根據《基本法》第158條重新解釋《基本法》第22及24條。

該等人士指出《基本法》是中華人民共和國法律之一部份；是中華人民共和國第七屆全國人民代表大會第三次會議於1990年4月4日通過，並頒令會在1997年7月1日後在香港特別行政區實施之法律。

根據中華人民共和國憲法第67（4）條，全國人民代表大會常務委員會行使之職權，包括"解釋法律"。

因此解釋《基本法》是人大常委會職權之一。在事件中，人大常委會是應特區政府之要求，解釋《基本法》，目的是要解決特區政府面對而本身不能解決之難題。

在新的憲制規則下，該做法合法、合情、合理，亦是正常法律程序之一部份，絕不影響特區之法治精神及司法獨立。

人大常委會根據第158條就《基本法》有關條款作出之解釋，亦不會影響終審法院已作出之判決，故談不上推翻終審法院之裁決，該做法亦無損終審法院之威望。

更有人認為否定人大常委會解釋《基本法》的人士，是「井底之蛙」。他們的見解抱殘守缺，屬管窺蠡測，是基於不了解大陸法下之「立法解釋權」所導致。

事件引起眾議成林。對各種不同意見，本席不置可否，亦不會再作評論。但本席須指出，整件事件一波三折，對各申請人和背景相同人士確實造成極大困擾及不安，令他們無所適從。

終審法院在1999年1月29日之判決，令有關人士誤認香港居留權就算不是囊中之物，亦是在步武之間，唾手可得；亦鼓勵部份人士非法抵港或逾期留港，以求盡早行使其居留權。但人大常委會對《基本法》第 22 及 24 條所作之解釋，實際上是否定了終審法院之裁決。唾手可得之居留權轉瞬間變成了鏡花水月，望而不可得；多年渴望和父母團聚之願望，亦變了泡影。

本席理解他們面對之困境及失望。

但《基本法》第 158 條開宗明義，清楚列明："本法的解釋權屬於全國人民代表大會常務委員會"及"如全國人民代表大會常務委員會作出解釋，香港特別行政區法院在引用該條款時，應以全國人民代表大會常務委員會的解釋為準。"

人大常委會對《基本法》所作解釋之合法性、有效性和該等解釋對香港特區各級法院的約束性亦獲得終審法院之確認。

終審法院在*劉港榕及其餘 16 人對入境事務處處長* [1999] 3 HKLRD 778 一案中表明其對人大常委會解釋《基本法》之觀點。該觀點在判案書中第 802 頁撮要如下：

"(1) 常委會有權根據第 158 條第 1 款作出'有關解釋'

(2)'有關解釋'是對《基本法》第 22 條第 4 款和第 24 條第 2 款第 (3) 項作出的有效和有約束力的解釋，香港特區法院有責任依循。

(3)'有關解釋'的效力是：

(甲) 根據第 22 條第 4 款，各省、自治區、直轄市的人，包括第 24 條第 2 款第 (3) 項所指的人，不論以何種事由要求進入香港特區，均須依照國家有關法律、行政法規的規定，向其所在地區的有關機關申請辦理批準手續，並須持有有關機關製發的有效證件方能進入香港特區。

(乙) 有關人士要成為第 24 條第 2 款第 (3) 項所指的永久性居民，在其出生時，其父母雙方或一方必須是第 24 條第 2 款第 (1) 項或第 24 條第 2 款第 (2) 項所指的永久性居民。

(4)'有關解釋'由 1997 年 7 月 1 日起生效。"

終審法院非常任法官梅師賢爵士在判案書 820 頁開始詳細分析在一國兩制的憲制基礎下，人大常委會根據《基本法》158 條解釋《基本法》之法理依據。梅師賢爵士的分析如下

"正如在憲制方面三權分立一般，特區法院與中華人民共和國的機構之間須建立聯繫。在一個全國性的普通法體制中，這個聯繫通常是地區法院與全國憲法法院或全國最高法院之間的聯繫。然而，現在不但有兩種不同的制度，而且有兩種不同的法律體制。在'一個國家，兩種制度'的前提下，《基本法》第一百五十八條為一種迥然不同的聯繫作出了規定。該條依照中國憲法第六十七條第四款的規定，訂明《基本法》的全面解釋權屬於全國人民代表大會常務委員會，而不屬於最高人民法院或全國性法院。

同樣地，人大常委會獲得該全面解釋權後，授權特區法院'在審理案件時'對《基本法》關於香港特別行政區自治範圍內的條款'自行'解釋。'自行'一詞與第一百五十八條第三款訂明應由終審法院請全國人大常委會對首席法官稱為'範圍之外的條款'這一強制性規定形成強烈對比。

'在審理案件時'這個短語尤其重要。這句話在普通法適用地區是多餘的。對法律的解釋，甚至對憲法的解釋，都是法院在審理案件時要處理的事情。但是，因為中國憲法並無作出與普通法三權分立論相同或相似的三權分立規定，所以，在中華人民共和國，全國人大常委會除行使其他職權外，還根據憲法第六十七條第四款行使'解釋法律'的職權。中國憲法第五十七條規定，中華人民共和國全國人民代表大會是最高國家權力機關，它的常設機關是全國人民代表大會常務委員會。

全國人大常委會在審理案件這情況以外還必然會不時行使其解釋法律的職權。'在審理案件時'這個短語清楚表明，特區法院享有的解釋權是局限於審理案件時，與全國人大常委會根據中國憲法第六十七條第四款和《基本法》第一百五十八條第一款享有的全面、自立的解釋權有所不同。

普通法地區的律師可能會對這個結論感到奇怪，但依本席看，從《基本法》的文意和它既是由中國制定的全國性法律，也是香港特區憲法這個特徵的角度去考慮第一百五十八條的文句和結構，此乃必然之結論。

正如終審法院首席法官所指，關於全國人大常委會根據第一百五十八條第一款享有解釋權這個結論，從佳日思教授的著作中 Hong Kong's New Constitutional Order（1999 年第二版）第 198 頁得到一些支持。作者在書中總結說，全國人大常委會擁有對《基本法》的全面解釋權。該項權力是'全面的，包括《基本法》所有條文。這項權力可在沒有訴訟的情況下行使。'

答辯人爭辯說，第一百五十八條第三款的最後兩句支持一個不同的結論，即全國人大常委會的解釋權局限於解釋由終審法院提交給它的事宜。答辯人的論據是，最後兩句局限於對由終審法院提交的事宜所作出的解釋，而這一點是重要的，因為倒數第二句規定特區法院應以該解釋為準，而最後一句則說'在此以前作出的判決不受影響'。答辯人的論據續稱，《基本法》並無就全國人大常委會對不經終審法院提交的事宜作出解釋訂定相關條文，說明了全國人大常委會沒有這方面的權力。一般來說，如此結論對普通法地區的律師或具吸引力。

本席認為，答辯人的結論並非其前提之必然結果。第一百五十八條第一款規定屬於全國人大常委會的對《基本法》的全面解釋權，顯然是一項對《基本法》作出權威解釋的權力，而且解釋對特區內所有機構均有約束力。實無須多此一舉，在《基本法》中將明顯不過的事情也一一訂明。然而，如果《基本法》能就全國人大常委會在應終審法院請求作出解釋時將出現的情況作出明文規定，從而清楚闡明解釋發還終審法院後的效果，以及確保全國人大常委會的解釋而不是終審法院引用解釋時所作的判決才具權威性，或不失為可取的做法。值得注意的是，倒數第二句不僅是對終審法院，而是對'香港特別行政區法院'而言的。

至於一個人大常委會自立的解釋，即對不經終審法院提交的事宜所作出的解釋的效果問題，以前的判決將因特區法院享有審判權和終審法院享有終審權而受到保障。根據普通法，終局判決不會因事後對有關法律文件採用了新的解釋，而在各方之間重開已經判決的訴訟。

本席欲藉下述所見結束這一點之論述。雖然'有關解釋'是由行使國家立法權的最高國家權力機關全國人大的常設機關全國人大常委會作出的，但它不像《基本法》的修正案一般僅僅是法規。解釋中說明全國人大常委會決定對《基本法》有關條文作出解釋，並表示要是闡明與本院在吳嘉玲案中的觀點不同的'立法原意'。它符合了第一百五十八條第一款的有關規定，屬於該條所指的'解釋'，產生了隨

解釋而來的效果。”

根據終審法院之裁定，人大常委會對《基本法》有最終解釋權是無庸置疑的。其解釋對香港特區各級法院之約束性可以用「絕對」二字一以貫之。

根據全國人大常委會就《基本法》第 24 條第 2 款第 3 項之解釋，任何人士憑藉香港永久性居民在香港以外所生的中國籍子女之身份而成為香港特區永久性居民，都必須證實他們在出生時，其父親或母親已享有香港居留權。

在本訴訟，申請人在出生時，其父親或母親都未享有香港居留權。他們的父母都是在申請人出生後，才成為香港永久性居民。

在該情況下，申請人究竟能以甚麼論據支持他們的申請？他們要求法庭核實其香港永久性居民身份，頒令他們擁有香港居留權，理據何在？實在令人十分費解。

由於大部份申請人都沒有律師代表，為了公平起見，法庭須從各個角度，探索上述問題，以求做到大公無私、無偏無頗。

申請人都聲稱終審法院於 1999 年 1 月 29 日在*陳錦雅*一案所作之裁決，對他們適用，令他們擁有居港權。

無可否認，終審法院曾裁定香港特區永久性居民在香港以外所生的中國籍子女，不論其父親或母親之永久性居民身份是在其出生前或出生後才確立，都擁有香港居留權。

但終審法院上述之裁定，已被全國人大常委會之有關解釋推反。該解釋明確指明任何人士在出生時，如其父或母未成為香港永久性居民，都不是《基本法》第 24 條第 2 款第 3 項所指的永久性居民，亦不擁有香港居留權。

全國人大常委之有關解釋是根據基本法第 158 條作出。

《基本法》第 158 條列明：

> “本法的解釋權屬於全國人民代表大會常務委員會。
>
> 全國人民代表大會常務委員會授權香港特別行政區法院在審理案件時對本法關於香港特別行政區自治範圍內的條款自行解釋。
>
> 香港特別行政區法院在審理案件時對本法的其他條款也可解釋。但如香港特別行政區法院在審理案件時需要對本法關於中央人民政府管理的事務或中央和香港特別行政區關係的條款進行解釋，而該條款的解釋又影響到案件的判決，在對該案件作出不可上訴的終局判決前，應由香港特別行政區終審法院請全國人民代表大會常務委員會對有關條款作出解釋。如全國人民代表大會常務委員會作出解釋，香港特別行政區法院在引用該條款時，應以全國人民代表大會常務委員會的解釋為準。但在此以前作出的判決不受影響。
>
> 全國人民代表大會常務委員會在對本法進行解釋前，徵詢其所屬的香港特別行政區基本法委員會的意見。”

《基本法》第 158 條的用詞是清澈明確的。在考慮申請人是否擁有香港永久性居民身份時，本席須受全國人大常委會就《基本法》第 24 條第 2 款第（3）項所作解釋之規限，並須以該解釋為準。

《基本法》第 158 條列明，在全國人大常委會就某項條文解釋前，特區法院已作出的判決不受影響。

全國人大常委會在 1999 年 6 月 26 日作出之公布，除了就《基本法》第 22 條第 4 款和第 24 條第 2 款第（3）項作出解釋外，亦解釋了《基本法》第 158 條內所指“但在此以前作出的判決不受影響”的確實意思。

人大常委會之用詞如下：

> “本解釋公布之後，香港特別行政區法院在引用《基本法》有關條款時，應以本解釋為準。本解釋不影響香港特別行政區終審法院 1999 年 1 月 29 日對有關案件判決的有關訴訟當事人所獲得的香港特別行政區居留權。此外，其他任何人是否符合《基本法》第 24 條第 2 款第（3）項規定的條件，均須以本解釋為準。”

人大常委會認定“作出判決，不受影響”只適用於“終審法院 1999 年 1 月 29 日，對有關案件判決的有關訴訟當事人所獲得的香港特別行政區居留權。”

從人大常委之用詞，包括“有關案件判決”，“有關訴訟當事人”顯示，不受人大解釋所影響的人士，只局限於個別案件中直接參與該案件的當事人或經雙方協議或經法庭下令須受該判決約束的人士，並不包括和該案件當事人情況相同的其他人士。

根據上述觀點，不受全國人大常委會在 1999 年 6 月 26 日作出之解釋所影響的人士只是局限於*陳錦雅*、*吳嘉玲*、*徐權能*、*張麗華*等案件中直接參與訴訟的當事人，或其他因雙方協議或法庭命令而受該 等案件判決約束的人士而並不包括本訴訟之任何一名申請人。因為他們都不是“有關案件”的“有關訴訟當事人”。

申請人不能因其情況和上述數宗案件當事人之情況相同，而強稱不受人大常委會有關解釋之影響。

如申請人之聲稱被接納，因為他們的情況和該數宗案件有關當事人之情況相同，他們都可以根據終審法院在 1999 年 1 月 29 日作出之裁決而獲得香港居留權。那麼，所有香港永久性居民在國內出生的子女，只要他們在 1999 年 6 月 26 日前出生，都擁有香港居留權，不論他們出生時，其父或母是否已成為成香港永久性居居（民）。

在該情況下，人大常委所作之解釋便變成毫無作用，更不能解決終審法院在 1999 年 1 月 29 日所作之判決所引發及令香港特區須面對之困難情況。

如解釋全無作用，人大常委為何仍然接受特區政府之要求，作出極具爭議之行動去解釋《基本法》內之有關條款？

無論如何，人大常委之解釋的內容是明確的。該解釋只是“不影響終審法院 1999 年 1 月 29 日，對有關案件判決的有關訴訟當事人所獲得的香港特別行政區居留權。……其他任何人士……均須以本解釋為準。”

從這角度觀之，申請人提出之基本論點是站不著腳的。該論點和《基本法》立法者的立法目的明顯有抵觸。

在其司法覆核申請書內，有律師代表的申請人強稱終審法院在 1999 年 1 月 29 日作出有關判決前抵港之人士，其居港權在終審法院作出判決當天已被確定。他們列出以下數點理由支持該說法。

（一）基於該判決有先例之約束力：

終審法院所作之判決，不單對案件當事人有約束力，其判定之法律原則及作出判定過程中之法律推理對所有人士都有約束力；

（二）有關判決是在一宗公法案件中作出，屬一種公告式之濟助。該公告正式宣布一公共機構應履行之職責。該公共機構應在任何情況下都執行該職責，而非局限於個別案件之直接當事人，否則公法案件之判決會失去其應有之義意。因此特區政府理應將法庭判定之法律原則，不單應用在涉及案件之當事人，亦應將有關法律原則應用在其他境況相同之人士身上。

（三）*陳錦雅*一案屬「測試案件」。其判決應對和案件當事人境況相同之其他人士亦有效。理由是當「測試案件」正在法庭審理時，其他同類案件不能同時提出訴訟，否則構成濫用司法程序。而當法庭作出判決後，其他同類案件亦不能再次重新訴訟。

（四）當某個法庭之判決已令某些人士獲得一些既得權益時，就算該判決事後被推翻，該等人士已獲得之既得權益不應受影響，否則法律會喪失其明確性。

在普通法制下，案件判決之「既判力」（Res judicata）祇對參與案件的當事人或經雙方協議或經法庭下令須受該判決約束的人士適用，對其他人士絕無約束力。

當然，如法院在一宗公法訴訟中作出某項裁決；在有關裁決未被有效更改前，所有公共機構必需以法院之判決執行其職責。但如有關裁決已被上級法庭、或立法機關或其他方式有效地更改，公共機構當然不需，亦不能根據已被更改之裁決，執行其職責，否則公共機構之行為實屬違法。

終審法院在 1999 年 1 月 29 日之判決，實質上已被人大常委會在 1999 年 6 月 26 日所作之解釋更改。處長在處理各申請人之申請時，必須以人大常委之解釋為準。

雖然*陳錦雅*一案屬「測試案件」，但並不表示案件之裁決對所有背景和案件當事人相同的人士都適用。「測試案件」之裁決亦只適用於事前明確表示或默示會受「測試案件」裁決所規限的人士。

在本訴訟之申請人從沒有和處長達成任何協議；雙方亦無共識表示會受陳錦雅一案之裁決所約束。申請人不能依賴陳錦雅一案，辯稱可從該案之裁決得益。

由始至終，申請人都不能因*陳錦雅*一案之裁決而獲任何「既得權益」。上述司法覆核申請書內提出之論點，都不能成立。

該等論點，亦和人大常委之解釋明顯有抵觸。根據《基本法》第八條，該等論點，就算成立，亦不能實施。

代表 17 名申請人的黃錦娟大律師明確向法庭表示，不會就上述任何一點，向法庭作出任何陳述，支持其申請。

在本訴訟，黃錦娟大律師只提出一項理據支持申請。

人大常委在 1999 年 6 月 26 日解釋《基本法》之消息公布後，香港特區行政長官董建華先生在新聞發布會作出公布，公布內有關之部份如下：

"我們在接到全國人大常委會的解釋之後，我們立即召開了行政會議，而作出了以下的決定：

第一，下星期我們將於立法會提交決議修改入境條例的附表，以規定：

（甲）在香港以外所生的港人子女，只有在其出生時，其父或母已獲得永久居民身份，才能擁有居留權；

（乙）非婚生港人子女可以申請居留權。

第二，根據終審法院的判決不受人大常委的解釋所影響的原則下，我們將容許由一九九七年七月一日至一九九九年一月二十九日在港並曾向當局聲稱擁有居留權的人士，以終審法院的判決核實他們永久居民的身份。據統計，這類人士大概有三千七百人。

第三，其他人士只可在符合人大常委會解釋的情況下，才可向當局申請居留權……"

黃錦娟大律師指出她代表的申請人，在 1997 年 7 月 1 日至 1999 年 1 月 29 日期間都曾在香港，並曾向當局聲稱擁有居留權，所以處長應以終審法院在 1999 年 1 月 29 日之判決，來核實他們永久居民的身份。

黃錦娟大律師指出，其當事人向當局聲稱擁有居留權之方式有多種，包括本人或透過父母或其他人士親身或以書信形式向入境事務處作出居留權之查詢，申請延期留港等。

除了直接接觸入境事務處外，部份申請人亦曾向法律援助處申請法援，以便向入境事務處爭取居港權。亦有部份申請人長時間及多次在國內向有關機關申請單程証來港。黃錦娟大律師聲稱上述事件已構成向有關當局聲稱擁有居留權，因此根據上述公布，他們都應受惠於終審法院的判決。

黃錦娟大律師亦辯稱，申請人不但能以口頭或書面向當局聲稱擁有居留權，更能透過行為作出。該等行為包括非法入境、雙程証到期後，拒絕離境等。

黃錦娟大律師認為處長定下額外條件；包括聲稱擁有居留權須向入境處作出；入境處要有聲稱之記錄及作出聲稱時，申請人須身在香港等而要求申請人符合該等條件才能受惠於特首在 1999 年 6 月 26 日作出之公布是不合理的。

任何政府部門或官員就政府作出之政策向公眾作出公布後，受有關政策影響之人士都有一個合理期望，政府會執行有關政策（見 *Ng Yuen Shui v. Attorney General* [1981] HKLR 352 一案）。

在本案聲稱根據《基本法》第 24 條第 2 款第（3）項擁有香港永久居留權人士亦有一個合理期望，特區政府會執行特首在 1999 年 6 月 26 日公布之政策。如特區政府未有確實執行該政策，受影響人士有權向法庭爭取公法之濟助。

法庭有權裁定一個政策聲明之確實意思，但如果政策聲明用詞不完全清楚，模棱兩可，則法庭必須尊重作出決策者就政策之解釋，除非其解釋是荒謬的，是極不合理的（見 R. v. Ministry of Defence Ex Parte Walker [1999] 1 WLR 1209 一案）。

法庭不應以解釋法例之嚴謹演譯方法處理政策＝聲明之內容而須根據事件之背景，以合情合理之態度，決定決策者執行政策之方針，是否和已公布之政策吻合。

有關政府部門亦有權採取合理之方式和程序執行既定政策。除非採用之方式及程序是全不合理的，是任何合理的行政機構都不會採用的，否則法庭無權干預。

保安局局長葉劉淑儀及助理入境事務處處長麥桂炘在 HCAL No. 81/1999 一案中所作之誓章及誓言詳細列出特首在 1999 年 6 月 26 日作出之政策公布時之背景及政府執行該政策所持之立場及採用之程序。

保安局局長之誓章之有關部份詳列如下：

13. 經過人大常委會的解釋後，政府決定制訂政策，辨出以下類別的人：其永久性居民聲請會依據終審法院判決中聲明的法律裁定，而非依據其後人大常委會的解釋所聲明的法律裁定的。

14. 首先，*吳嘉玲及陳錦雅*訴訟中被指名的申請人，顯然不受人大常委會解釋所影響的。就此點而言，請參閱律政司的楊匡怡所作的非宗教式誓詞。誓詞內載有選出*吳嘉玲*訴訴中一起聆訊的四宗測試案件的背景，和選出黎詩雅作為*陳錦雅*訴訟中其他 80 名申請人的測試申請人的背景。基於該份誓詞所載的事實及事項，本人獲政府的法律顧問告知並確信，就終審法院在終院民事上訴 1998 年第 14 至 16 號和終院民事上訴 1998 年第 13 號頒令對某些人士的身份作出終局宣判而言，只有終院民事上訴 1998 年 14 至 16 號中指名的訴訟當事人（即吳嘉玲小姐、吳丹丹小姐、徐權能先生及張麗華小姐）獲宣布為香港特別行政區的永久性居民。在終院民事上訴 1998 年第 13 號中，終審法院則只就裁定該 81 名申請人要求成為永久性居民的聲請時會依據的法律理據作出聲明。

15. 可是政府留意到，除*吳嘉玲及陳錦雅*的訴訟中被個別指名的申請人以外，該等判決擬涵蓋的尚有其他人士的聲請。如楊匡怡的誓詞內的解釋所言，政府曾經以明確協議方式承諾在某些其他人士聽候*吳嘉玲及陳錦雅*的訴訟結果期間不將他們遣送離境。此等其他聲請包括：(a)以*張麗華*該組案件為代表的司法覆核法律程序;(b)受下述（i）及（ii）項協議所涵蓋的其他案件，即（i）代表入境事務處處長的律政司與賈偉林、劉天均律師行之間的協議及（ii）入境事務處處長和法律援助署署長之間的協議；（c）經貝嘉蓮律師行向入境事務處處長發出通知並獲接納為入境事務處處長給予的承諾所涵蓋的 109 宗其他案件中的 79 宗；及（d）聲請人於 1999 年 1 月 29 日或之前根據《基本法》第 24（2）（3）條向入境事務處處長提出居留權聲請的其他個別案件。

16. 政府因此決定該等人士不應受人大常委會的解釋所影響，而他們聲稱擁有的永久性居民身份應根據終審法院於 1999 年 1 月 29 日宣布的判決予以核實。

17. 政府亦考慮到是否有其他人士亦應以同樣方式處理。政府認為要界定何人應以上述方式處理，最公平最合理的做法是以該人是否身在香港為準，以及該人是否曾向入境事務處處長作出居留權聲請以求確立永久性居民地位而入境事務處是存有該項聲請的紀錄的。就此點而言，若干從內地來的人士在三段期間內身在香港，並於身在香港時向入境事務處處長作出居留權聲請而處長是存有該項聲請的紀錄的，該三段期間為（A）1997 年 7 月 1 日至 10 日，（B）1997 年 7 月 11 日至 1999 年 1 月 29 日，及（C）1999 年 1 月 30 日至人大常委會的解釋的日期。

18. 有關（A）類，終審法院於 1999 年 1 月 29 日裁定，因為於 1997 年 7 月 11 日制訂的《1997 年入境（修訂）（第 3 號）條例》並無追溯效力，故此在 1997 年 7 月 1 日至 7 月 10 日期間內身在香港的人不受居留權證明書計劃所影響。政府因此認為儘管人大常委會的解釋或會影響該等人士，如他們在 1997 年 7 月 1 日至 7 月 10 日期間身在香港並在 1999 年 1 月 29 日之前已向入境事務處處長作出居留權聲請，則無須返回內地等候核實身份。只要他們符合終審法院判決所指的居留權條件，儘管有人大常委會的解釋，他們仍會獲得上述身份。

19. （B）類包括 1997 年 7 月 11 日至 1999 年 1 月 29 日期間前往入境事務處提出居留權聲請的人士。政府認為（B）類人士的處理，所依據的法律應與終審法院案件所裁定適用於訴訟人的法律相同。理由是，假如該等人士自行提起法律程序，他們自己本會成為終審法院的訴訟當事人，或本會成為默示協議（以承諾不遣送離境方式）的標的人士，而獲得與*吳嘉玲及陳錦雅*案中申請人相同的處理方式。

20. 政府認為（C）類人士的處理方式，不應以終審法院案件中所宣布的法律為基礎。理由是，該等人士在終審法院的判決宣布之前不在香港，或身在香港而並未在終審法院的判決宣布之前向入境事務處處長提出居留權聲請，因此並無合理理據可讓他們聲稱自己屬於上述判決所涉訴訟的訴訟當事人。

21. 經於 1999 年 6 月 26 日考慮及討論人大常委會作出的解釋後，行政長官會同行政會議作出上文第 4 段所提述的特惠決定。同日，行政長官發表公告解釋特惠決定，說明何人會獲按照終審法院所宣布的法律而非按照人大常委會的解釋處理。現提交作編號“ILSYR-7”的證物為行政長官發表上述公告的新聞發布會的講話謄本，以及作編號“ILSYR-8”的證物為公布該特惠決定的政府新聞處新聞稿。從該等公開陳述可見，特惠決定是以處長的紀錄為基礎。處長的紀錄顯示（A）類及（B）類約有 3,700 人。當時該等紀錄顯示這批人中有 964 人的居留權聲請已獲處長核實。居留權已獲確立的人亦已獲通知有關事實。政府準備透過特惠決定惠及的其他人士合共 2,700 人左右。當中，（a）約有 900 人身在香港而無需在申請獲得處理和知道申請結果之前先返回內地，另有（b）其餘 1,800 人已返回內地。對於已返回內地的（b）組人士，入境事務處處長其後與內地有關當局達成協議，在他們的居留權獲得確立時會安排他們來港。

22. 有關特惠決定的其他細節，保安局在其一份日期為 1999 年 6 月 28 日的文件中向立法會內務委員會加以闡明。該文件的真確副本現予提交作編號“ILSYR-9”證物。

23. 從上文及本人提交作證物的資料所見，任何人如要被納入特惠決定，必須先符合兩項要素，即是在 1997 年 7 月 1 日至 1999 年 1 月 29 日這段相關期間內身在香港，同時曾經提出居留權聲請而入境事務處處長存有該聲請的紀錄。第二項要求顯然可從特惠決定被解作惠及某個估計數目的指定人士這一事實獲得支持。有關聲請須為入境事務處處長存有紀錄的這個要素，是妥善執行特惠決定所必需 的。特惠決定是人大常委會的解釋第 4 段中的例外情況，該段述明除“香港特別行政區終審法院 1999 年 1 月 29 日對有關案件判決的有關訴訟當事人所獲得的香港特別行政區居留權”以外，任何其他人是否符合資格取得永久性居民地位，均須以人大常委會的解釋為準。政府認為特惠決定的涵義和範圍，屬於政府以行政方式釐訂的事宜。如特惠決定並不限於入境事務處處長已存有其居留權聲請紀錄的人，則入境事務處處長在斷定某聲請人在 1997 年 7 月 1 日至 1999 年 1 月 29 日期間內是否身在香港並曾提出居留權聲請時，並無清楚、客觀或無可爭論的準則可以依憑。

麥桂炘生生誓詞之有關部份亦詳列如下：

"7. 為決定某人是否曾向處長提出居留權聲請，政府的政策是：聲稱有居留權必須依照某些原則，以便處長能夠辨別出曾向處長提出居留權聲請而處長存有該等紀錄的人士。

8. 即使在特惠決定作出之前，處長已採用同樣要素去核實及批准於 1997 年 7 月 1 日至 10 日身在香港的人所提出的居留權聲請，而他們須 是終審法院在吳嘉玲案中所裁定不受《1997 年入境（修訂）（第 3 號）條例》所制訂的居留權證明書計劃所影響的人。根據入境事務處紀錄，截至 1999 年 6 月 26 日，共有 964 人的居留權聲請經處長核實和確立。保安局局長在她於 1999 年 6 月 28 日向立法會內務委員會提交的文件（"立法會文件"）中第 11 段引述 964 這個數字。該文件的副本由保安局局長在她的誓章中提交作證物。

9. 在這 964 宗個案，下述各類是處長存有紀錄的居留權聲請而又獲接受為處長存有紀錄的居留權聲請。

9.1 *吳嘉玲及陳錦雅*的訴訟中指名的訴訟當事人。

9.2 受處長或代處長所作出協議涵蓋的在聽候吳嘉玲及陳錦雅的訴訟結果期間不被遣送離境的人士。就此點而言，請參閱律政司的楊匡怡所作的非宗教式誓詞。本人曾讀過該份誓詞的草稿連同其證物，誓詞內載有各項有關協議的描述，而有關同期的通信文件亦提交作為證物。

9.3 以等候*吳嘉玲及陳錦雅*的訴訟結果為理由申請延期逗留或不遣送離開香港的人士。

(a) 以等候*吳嘉玲及陳錦雅*的訴訟結果為理由向訪港華人辦事處申請延期逗留的人士，或於調查組或遣送離境組面晤時以此為理由要求不遣送離開香港的人士，而該等人士獲接受為已向處長遞交居留權聲請者。

(b) 現提交作編號"MKY-1"的證物為以上述理由要求延期逗留的申請書範例一份，以及面晤中獲面見者提出該理由而調查組或遣送離境組作出有關紀錄的面晤報告範例各份。

9.4 向入境事務處自首的人或被拘捕的人，而該人在自首或被拘捕時作出居留權聲請者。

(a) 向入境事務處調查組人員自首或被入境事務處調查組人員拘捕的非法入境者及逾期逗留者如曾明確聲請居留權會獲接受為已向處長提出居留權聲請。現提交作編號"MKY-2"的證物為載有在自首或被拘捕時作出居留權聲請的面晤報告範例各份。

(b) 這些人士會被勸告自動離開香港。如果他們不同意自動離開香港，他們的個案會轉介遣送離境組以發出遣送離境令。在遣送離境令向部份這些人士送達後，他們向入境事務審裁處提出上訴。他們在上訴通知書所持的一項上訴理由是他們擁有香港居留權。現提交作編號"MKY-3"的證物為有關的上訴通知書範例各份。已向部份這些人士送達的遣送離境令，因聽候吳喜玲及陳錦雅的訴訟結果不予執行，而該等人士獲擔保外出。

(c) 此外，向入境事務主任自首或被入境事務主任拘捕而名列法律援助署署長在 1998 年 12 月 7 日之前致入境事務處處長信件名單上的人，獲接受為已向處長提出而處長存有紀錄的居留權聲請。同樣情況適用於 同法律援助署署長在 1998 年 12 月 7 日後向他們發出的信件的人。現提交作編號"MKY-4"的證物為此等由法律援助署署長發出的信件副本。

9.5 被警察拘捕並轉介入境事務處的人，而他們是在與入境事務主任面晤時作出居留權聲請者。

(a) 被警察拘捕並轉介入境事務處出入境審核組的非法入境者及逾期逗留者如曾明確作出居留權聲請會獲接受為曾向處長提出而處長存有紀錄的居留權聲請者。編號"MKY-2"的證物為該等面晤報告的範例各份。

(b) 如同上文第 9.4 段所述組別人士，這些人士亦被勸告自動離開香港。如果他們不自動離開香港，他們的個案會轉介遣送離境組以發出遣送離境令。已向部份這些人士送達的遣送離境令，因聽候吳嘉玲的訴訟結果不予執行，而該等人士獲擔保外出。

9.6 聲稱根據《入境條例》（第 115 章）附表 1 第 2（c）段擁有居留權而申請核實其申領永久性身份證資格的人。

(a) 任何人如身在香港期間藉著將有關標準表格（ROP145）投入居留權組的投遞箱或藉著郵遞向居留權組提出上述申請，而處長信納該人在提出申請時是身在香港的，該人獲接受為曾向處長提出而處長存有紀錄的居留權聲請者。

(b) 現提交作編號"MKY-5"的證物為上述已填妥表格範例一份。

9.7 親自於法院提起司法覆核法律程序聲稱擁有居留權的人士。

(a) 不屬於吳嘉玲及陳錦雅的訴訟中訴訟當事人而已提起司法覆核法律程序聲稱擁有居留權的人士，獲接受為曾向處長提出而處長存有紀錄的居留權聲請者。

(b) 現提交作編號"MKY-6"的證物為此等司法覆核申請書一份。

9.8 獲批予法律援助以聲請居留權的人士。

(a) 獲批予法律援助以提起法律程序宣稱居港權的人士，獲處長接受為曾向處長提出而處長存有紀錄的居留權聲請者。該等人士獲處長承諾在他們聽候吳嘉玲及陳錦雅的訴訟結果期間不予遣送離境。

(b) 由 1997 年 7 月至 1997 年 9 月，處長獲提供已獲批予法律援助以提起法律程序聲請居留權的人士名單。處長同意在該等人士聽候吳嘉玲及陳錦雅的訴訟結果期間不將他們遣送離境。現提交作編號"MKY-7"的證物為上述向處長更新有關人士身份資料的名單範例。

9.9 經法律援助署根據一項1997年10月14日明訂協議轉介入境事務處的人士。

(a) 在1997年10月14日，處長和法律援助署署長之間達成一項協議，憑此處長不會將那些會成功獲得法律援助以爭取居留權但為節省公帑而不獲批予法律援助的人士遣送離境。由1997年9月22日起，法律援助署署長停止向有關居留權聲請的法律援助新申請人再發給法律援助證明書，理由是獲批予法律援助的申請人當中選出的四宗測試案件已涵蓋了有關的法律問題。應法律援助署署長所請求，在1997年10月14日，對於其申請獲法律援助署署長認為會成功獲得法律援助的人，處長承諾不予執行向他們發出的遣送離境令。處長會獲書面通知該等個案的最新名單。

(b) 現提交作編號"MKY-8"的證物為部門之間載有該協議的往來便箋。

(c) 會成功獲得法律援助的個案名單不時轉介予處長。處長接受名列法律援助署署長所轉介的名單上的人是曾向處長提出居留權聲請的人。按照該協議，法律援助署署長曾就422宗會成功獲得法律援助的個案向處長發出通知。

在以上各分段所述各類別的人士中，非法入境者及逾期逗留者會被勸告離開香港。如果他們不同意自動離開香港，他們會在遣送離境令發出後或在考慮向他們發出遣送離境令時獲准擔保外出。如有關人士仍在逗留香港期限之內，在他們定期申請時或可獲延長其逗留期限。"

從上述之誓章及誓詞顯示，政府採取之立場是負責任及合理的。該立場不但符合有關政策之聲明，亦是一個合理解決當時政府面對問題之方法。

本席不同意黃錦娟大律師之陳述，要以一個廣義的角度去解釋特首之政策聲明。該建議和政策聲明之全文不吻合，抵觸公布政策時之整體社會環境，亦會導致有關政策無法合理執行，做成混亂。

處長經過詳細考慮各申請人之背景，認定他們並不符合特首作出之政策聲明及根據該聲明而定下之條件。該做法合情合理。

本席無基礎干預其決定。

處長裁定各申請人都不能受惠於特首在1999年6月26日作出之承諾。該決定是合理及正確的。

當然，申請人中有部份更是在1999年1月29日終審法院作出有關判決後或在1999年6月26日人大常委會作出有關解釋後才首次抵港，他們更不能因特首所作之承諾而受惠。

但基於本席在上文所作之決定，故無須分別處理在1999年1月29日或在1999年6月26日後才首次到港之申請人。

本席理解各申請人之心態。一方面他們懊悔未有當機立斷，在適當時候採取某些行動，以致錯失良機，未能取得香港居留權。另一方面，眼看小部份背景和他們相同的個別人士，機緣巧合或誤打誤撞而獲得香港居留權。因而令申請人感到法律面前，不是人人平等。

但他們須明白，亦須接受，在執行一些嶄新政策或條例時，由於有關人士缺乏經驗；或因資料不全而對事件認知不足；或因處理事件態度不夠認真或無先例可援等等因素，會導致一些混亂、誤會，甚至錯誤等情況出現。很多時候，特別是在民主、開放社會，該等情況可能會令小部份人士獲得一些不應擁有之權益。但這點並不表示背境和該小部份人士相同的所有人士都應獲得該等權益，更不表示不賦于他們該等權益，便會構成不公平，不公正。

任何民主、法治社會，當塵埃落定、混亂情況過後，所有政策及規例都須依法執行。任何借題發揮，瞞天過海，混水摸魚，掩人耳目之行徑都不會得逞。否則，法治、民主、公正都屬空談。

差不多所有申請人都聲稱希望能到香港和年老雙親團聚。他們的願望，本席當然理解。但申請人全部都是成年人士，他們很多都已結婚及育有子女。如他們要來香港定居和父母團聚，則表示他們要和國內之配偶子女分離，他們童年時所受之苦況，會在子女身上重演。

再者，申請人亦不一定要來香港定居，才能和父母團聚。團聚必有其他方法可達到。

無論如何，根據《基本法》第24條第2款第（3）項之正確解釋，全部申請人都不擁有，亦從未擁有過香港永久性居留權。他們出生時，其父或母未成為香港永久性居民，他們都不是香港永久性居民。

終審法院在*陳錦雅*一案之判決，令小部份背景和申請人相同的人士獲得香港居留權，但該判決只對直接參與訴訟之有關當事人有效。其他背景相同之人士，包括本案之所有申請人都不能受益。

申請人亦因為不符合有關條件，故未能因特區政府作出之特惠安排而得益。

人大常委會已經對《基本法》第22條第4款及第24條第2款第（3）項作出解釋。本席在處理各申請人之申請 時，亦必需以該解釋為準，否則本席並非依法執行職務，亦有違本席在香港特區政府成立時所作之「司法誓言」。

再者人大常委之有關解釋亦明確表明香港永久性居民在內地所生的中國籍子女，不論以何種事由要求進入香港，均須在國內向所在地區的有關機關申請辦理批准手續，並須持有有關機關製發的有效證件才能進入香港。

終審法院在*劉港榕*一案亦確認上述程序。

就算申請人根據《基本法》第24條第2款第（3）項擁有香港永久性居民身份，他們亦必需在國內辦理有關手續，獲發有效証件後才能進入香港。

本席已經詳細考慮過案件整體情況及其引發之有關法律觀點。申請人之司法覆核申請並無合理之論點支持。

已獲許可的申請人之司法覆核許可須被駁回。

未獲許可的申請人，因其申請並無可爭拗之論點支持，亦無其他問題要再作考慮，所以其司法覆核許可之申請亦須駁回。

由於案件性質特殊，本席就訟費不作任何命令。

有關訟費之命令是一臨時命令。該命令會在本判案書頒下之日起計14天內作實。

高等法院原訟法庭法官（楊振權）

黃錦娟大律師（由陳黃林律師事務所延聘）代表案件34/2000，

39/2000，50/2000，55/2000，75/2000，84/2000，90/2000，94/2000，120/2000，121/2000，127/2000，129/2000，130/2000，163/2000，177/2000，178/2000，192/2000 的申請人

其餘申請人：無律師代表

申請人：79/2000 蔡娟娟及 128/2000 吳天增，缺席

黃惠冲，李天恩（政府律師）代表答辯人

吳小彤及其他人士 對 入境事務處處長
李淑芬 對 入境事務處處長
冼海珠及其他人士 對 入境事務處處長

HCAL 81/1999；HCAL 2/2000；HCAL 70/2000；CACV 415/2000；CACV 416/2000；CACV 417/2000；FACV 1/2001；FACV 2/2001；FACV 3/2001

簡略案情

本案牽涉的上訴人基本可以分為兩大類：（1）他們出生時父母起碼一方已擁有香港永久性居民身份，以此可以受惠於終審法院*吳嘉玲*一案，根據《基本法》第 24 條第 2 款第 3 項擁有居港權；（2）他們父母是在他們出生後才成為香港永久性居民，他們只能受惠於終審法院*陳錦雅*一案而擁有居港權。各申請人請求終審法院確認他們可以根據《基本法》第 24 條第 2 款第 3 項擁有居港權；除在全國人大常委會對《基本法》第 22 條和第 24 條作出的解釋（下稱"該解釋"）公佈後才進入香港的上訴人外，其餘皆受特區寬免政策所涵蓋（即特區容許於 1997 年 7 月 1 日至 1999 年 1 月 29 日期間抵港，並已就居留權作出聲稱的人士，以*吳嘉玲*及*陳錦雅*兩案判決核實他們聲稱擁有的永久性居民身份），然而他們是不受該解釋影響的，亦即他們無須依靠該寬免，也有權獲得當局以*吳嘉玲*及*陳錦雅*兩案的判決來核實他們的永久性居民身份。各申請人提出的司法覆核申請被原訟法庭駁回。其後，上訴法庭又維持上述決定。最後，各申請人獲許可，並向終審法院提出上訴。於*吳嘉玲*及*陳錦雅*兩案等待判決期間，申請人雖然認為自己的情況與該兩宗案件的當事人相同，但他們並沒有參與該訴訟或展開新的訴訟程序。

根據上訴人的主要論據，他們認為：

根據《基本法》第 158 條第 3 款"在此以前作出的判決不受影響"的原則，該解釋不應該影響各申請人擁有*吳嘉玲*及*陳錦雅*兩案判決所產生的權利。（"此前作出的判決"）

即使上訴人受該解釋影響，但由於政府作出的公開聲明和陳述，以及*吳嘉玲*及*陳錦雅*兩案的處理過程，為他們帶來了一個合理的期望，就是會得到如該兩案的當事人一樣的看待，從而獲得永久性居民身份的核實。（"合理期望"）

在 1997 年 7 月 1 日之前抵港的上訴人，即第 1 期，不受《基本法》第 22 條第 4 款或該解釋規限。而在 1997 年 7 月 1 日至 10 日抵港的申請人，即第 2 期，不受該解釋或已被裁定為沒有追溯效力的《第

3 號條例》所影響。（“第 1 期及第 2 期爭議”）

於 1999 年 1 月 29 日之前抵港的上訴人有一合理期望，就是他們只要符合該寬免政策所規定的條款，便會受到如*吳嘉玲*及*陳錦雅*兩案當事人所得判決一樣的看待。（“寬免政策”）。

裁決摘要

對於“此前作出的判決”論據，終審法院認為判決既可以是法院作出的對個別案件的判決，也可以是法院對某一論點的決定理由。然而，終審法院認為該解釋明確地說明“本解釋不影響香港特別行政區終審法院 1999 年 1 月 29 日對有關案件判決的有關訴訟當事人所獲得的香港特別行政區居留權”（後加強調）。所以，拒絕接納將判決解釋為一般法律原則的決定，認為此乃忽視了《基本法》第 158 條第 3 款最後一句所表達的普通法下的終結性原則。

至於上訴人提出的“合理期望”，在沒有法律上或政策上的理由導致法則無法施行，人們或會對實質的後果或利益有合理期望。如果有關機構沒有使到該期望成真，從而導致對個人造成不公，這種不公等同濫用權力，以致法院可合情合理地進行干預。終審法院認為該期望必須建立在具體的陳述下，既清晰而又不模棱兩可，使上訴人對實質的後果或利益有合理期望。最後，法院除了認為那些曾從法律援助處收到通知，建議他們不用馬上展開訴訟和一名曾從保安局局長收到相關信件的上訴人，滿足了這具體陳述要點，而有可能有合理期望，從而入境處處長有必要重新考慮他們的訴求外，其他上訴人在此論據下，一律得不到救濟。

在“第 1 期及第 2 期爭議”的問題上，法院接納終審法院在審理*劉港榕*一案時並沒有特別處理《基本法》第 22 條第 4 款及第 24 條第 2 款第 3 項兩者的關係，對在 1997 年 7 月 1 日之前已抵達香港的人士造成影響。終審法院再認為，《基本法》第 22 條第 4 款的文字意思是清晰的，在回歸之前已來港的人士並不受此條款的規限。他們有權得到身份核實並行使居港權而無須先取得單程證。他們的身份並不受《基本法》的任何條款影響。由於《第 3 號條例》沒有追溯效力，因此沒有任何香港法例對他們有影響。至於第 2 期的人士，他們是在 1997 年 7 月 1 日之後進入香港特區。由於他們是中國其他地區的人士，當他們想進入香港特區時，便受第 22 條第 4 款的影響，他們需要先取得內地的批准。因此，在這爭議下，只有那些屬於第 1 期並且在出生時，父母任何一方已是香港永久性居民的上訴人，才能擁有居留權。

最後，關於“寬免政策”的論據，終審法院認為根據該政策決定，上訴人如要受惠於*吳嘉玲*和*陳錦雅*兩案的判決，則必須在 1997 年 7 月 1 日至 1999 年 1 月 29 日期間身處香港，並必須在此期間向入境事務處提出居留權的聲稱。該聲稱必須（1）向入境事務處作出；（2）在此寬免期間作出；以及（3）於申請人身處香港時作出。而入境事務處處長規定居留權的聲稱必須在入境事務處存有記錄，此舉並沒有錯誤執行該政策決定，然而，對於某些上訴人個案，入境事務處處長對政策決定中所指的聲稱作出的解釋過於狹隘，偏離了合理的做法。任何文件如能明確（1）指出某人為香港永久性居民，並且另一人為其子女；（2）提供某些資料，例如該子女的出生日期或地點；以及（3）要求該子女來港以便定居或享有其居留權，則理應被理解為是作出了居留權的聲稱。若拒絕接納符合以上準則的文件，則等同錯誤執行該政策決定。因此，這些受影響的上訴人，理應受惠於此政策而得到居留權。

〔中譯本 - 司法機構法庭語文組譯〕

〔Chinese Translation - Prepared by Court Language Section, Judiciary〕

FACV 1-3/2001

香港特別行政區
終審法院

終院民事上訴 2001 年第 1-3 號
（原本案件編號：高院民事上訴 2000 年第 415-417 號）

FACV 1/2001

上訴人　吳小彤及其他人士
對
答辯人　入境事務處處長

FACV 2/2001

上訴人　李淑芬
對
答辯人　入境事務處處長

FACV 3/2001

上訴人　冼海珠及其他人士
對
答辯人　入境事務處處長

主審法官：終審法院首席法官李國能
終審法院常任法官包致金
終審法院常任法官陳兆愷
終審法院常任法官李義
終審法院非常任法官梅師賢爵士

聆訊日期：2001 年 5 月 28，29，30，31 日; 6 月 1，19，20，21 日，以及 9 月 6 日及 7 日

判決日期：2002 年 1 月 10 日

判案書

首席法官李國能、常任法官陳兆愷、常任法官李義及非常任法官梅師賢爵士：

1. 考慮到本判案書的篇幅，我等現將正文分為以下段落，以便參閱：

分段	標題
2	引言
3	背景
13	本上訴案的當事人
21	上訴的主要爭議點
25-39	“在此以前作出的判決”的爭議
40-152	“合理期望”的爭議
40	申請人在合理期望方面的理據基礎
43	*吳嘉玲案及陳錦雅案*
47	*吳嘉玲案及陳錦雅案*的法院決定
54	隨著兩案終審決定而來的事件
58	政府高級官員作出的一般聲明
	（1）1999 年 1 月 29 日以前
65	（2）1999 年 1 月 29 日以後
66	政府機構作出的具體陳述
	（1）由入境事務處 / 保安局局長作出的
67	（2）由法律援助署作出的
78	“例案”
81	在*吳嘉玲*案和*陳錦雅*案的“例案性質”的背景下考慮該等陳述
82	一般陳述
84	具體陳述
87	實質合理期望法則
100	申請人有關實質合理期望的論據
101	有鑑於該等陳述，期望的合理性之考慮
112	根據入境事務處處長指稱體現期望會違反法律的論據，考慮期望的合理性
123	根據《入境條例》第 11 條、第 13 條及第 19（1）條賦予入境事務處處長法定酌情決定權的範圍
134	入境事務處處長的法定權力應用在本案事實上
140	遣送離境令的法律效力及不撤銷遣送離境令的決定
145	個別情況的合理期望
152-163	“濫用程序”的爭議
164-178	“第 1 期及第 2 期”的爭議
166	第 1 期
171	第 2 期
174	第 1 期及第 2 期爭議： 裁定個別情況
179-277	“寬免政策”的爭議
179	寬免政策的事實基礎
189	該政策決定的性質
190	該政策決定
193	適用的原則
200	入境事務處處長對該政策的解釋

引言

2. 在當前的上訴案中，上訴人（"申請人"）（部份申請人是有關訴訟的"代表申請人"）請求本院就多個類別人士所提出的香港居留權聲稱作出裁定。雖然這些類別的人士並非 *Ng Ka Ling & others v. The Director of Immigration*（*吳嘉玲及其他人士對入境事務處處長案*）（（1999）2 HKCFAR 4），以及 *Chan Kam Nga & others v. The Director of Immigration*（*陳錦雅及其他人士對入境事務處處長案*）（（1999）2 HKCFAR 82）的真正當事人，但是他們聲稱有權因該等決定而受惠。儘管全國人民代表大會常務委員會（"常委會"或"人大常委會"）已於 1999 年 6 月 26 日公布《基本法》第二十二條第四款及第二十四條第二款第（三）項的解釋，而該解釋亦已取代本院在該兩項決定中就該兩條條款所作的解釋，但各申請人仍然提出居港權的聲稱。此外，各申請人又請求本院頒令撤銷入境事務處處長根據《入境條例》（第 115 章）第 19 條所發出的遣送離境令及其他多項決定。申請人就此提出五項不同的理由，而這些理由涉及《基本法》的解釋和適用性、合理期望法則、濫用程序，以及在常委會公布該解釋當天香港特別行政區（"香港特區"或"特區"）政府宣布的政策所帶來的影響等問題。

背景

3. 《基本法》第二十四條第二款第（三）項規定，在香港特區成立以前或以後在香港出生及為永久性居民的中國公民在香港以外所生的中國籍子女，以及在香港通常居住連續七年以上及為永久性居民的中國公民在香港以外所生的中國籍子女皆獲賦予永久性居民身份，並享有居留權。《1997 年人民入境（修訂）（第 2 號）條例》（"《第 2 號條例》"）於 1997 年 7 月 1 日制定。該條例作出的規定包括：祇有是在其父母之中最少一人已成為香港永久性居民之後出生的人士才符合第二十四條第二款第（三）項的資格（"出生時間限制"）。在 1997 年 7 月 10 日制定（但其原意是在 1997 年 7 月 1 日起生效）的《人民入境（修訂）（第 3 號）條例》（"《第 3 號條例》"）亦訂下計劃用以核實根據上述《基本法》條款所聲稱的永久性居民身份。

4. 1997 年 7 月初，多名父或母為香港永久性居民但卻不符合上述條例的規定，亦未能遵從上述計劃規定的內地出生兒童，根據第二十四條第二款第（三）項聲稱享有永久性居民身份。他們在入境事務處處長駁回其聲稱及向他們發出遣送離境令後，展開司法覆核程序，質疑該等條例。其後，申請法律援助以便參與該等訴訟程序或展開類似訴訟程序的人數迅速增加。為數眾多的法律援助申請，以及可能引致的大量訴訟，備受關注，更促使政府高級官員就這些訴訟事宜公開回應，表明政府的立場。他們所傳達的回應是：政府將會服從法庭的決定。此外，法律援助署署長亦去信若干申請法律援助的人士述明他們不必展開訴訟程序。

5. 該等訴訟的主要爭議點集中於第二十四條第二款第（三）項的確切涵義和範圍，以及該條款與第二十二條第四款的關係。為了減少案件數目和訴訟費用起見，有關方面挑選了數宗適宜交由法庭就各共同爭議點作出裁定的個案。這些個案雖被視為"例案"或"代表案件"，但事實上，法庭並無頒令指示該等案件的申請人擔當"代表當事人"來代表那些並未參與訴訟或沒有展開新訴訟的人士。同時，席前並無證據顯示當中有任何個案的當事人是已經藉著協議同意服從該等"例案"或"代表案件"的裁決，或同意受該裁決約束的（獲法律援助署指派的律師事務所與代表選出個案者相同的個案或許例外）。最後，該等"例案"或"代表案件"提交終審法院處理。在該等案件聽候最終裁定期間，入境事務處並沒有就某些永久性居民身份的聲稱作出決定，而法律援助署亦暫緩處理有關申請。

6. 1999 年 1 月 29 日，本院就第一宗案件，即*吳嘉玲*案作出多項裁定，其中包括：第二十四條第二款第（三）項不受第二十二條第四款規限，因此第二十四條第二款第（三）項所述，並在內地居住的人士不須以內地機關簽發的單程證來港行使他們作為永久性居民的居留權。據此，本院裁定在《第 3 號條例》中，規定有關人士必須持有單程證一點不符合第二十四條第二款第（三）項的條款，亦即違反憲法。同時，本院也裁定《第 3 號條例》中具有追溯效力的條文亦屬違反憲法。

7. 同日，本院在第二宗案件，即*陳錦雅*案裁定：第二十四條第二款第（三）項適用於香港永久性居民在香港以外所生的中國籍子女，不論他們是在父母之中最少一人取得永久性居民身份之前或之後出生，情況都是一樣。據此，本院又裁定：《第 2 號條例》的其中一部份，即其用意是摒除那些是在父母之中最少一人取得永久性居民身份之前已出生的中國公民的條文，亦屬違反憲法。

8. 在本院發下上述兩案的決定後，政府隨即發表公開聲明，表示會服從法院的決定，並會執行該等決定。然而，政府其後考慮到該做法可能會導致為數極多的人士從內地來港定居，因此改變主意並採取一項不同的政策。

9. 1999 年 6 月 26 日，人大常委會應香港特區政府透過國務院提出的請求，依據《基本法》第一百五十八條第一款所賦予的權力，就第二十二條第四款及第二十四條第二款第（三）項作出解釋（"**該解釋**"）。根據**該解釋**，第二十四條第二款第（三）項受第二十二條第四款規限。因此，第二十四條第二款第（三）項所述的人士，必須向內地機關申請辦理批准手續，才可進入香港特區。**該解釋**又闡明：任何人士要符合第二十四條第二款第（三）

項的資格，其父母之中最少一人必須在其出生時已經是香港永久性居民。就這兩方面而言，**該解釋**實際上已取代了本院在吳嘉玲及陳錦雅兩案的決定中就《基本法》的有關條文所作的解釋。可是，**該解釋**又闡明："本解釋不影響香港特別行政區終審法院1999年1月29日對有關案件判決的有關訴訟當事人所獲得的香港特別行政區居留權"。此外，不受**該解釋**影響的，還有本院在吳嘉玲案的部份決定，亦即《第3號條例》的追溯效力條文違反憲法此一裁定。

10. 其後，本院於1999年12月，就第三宗案件，即*Lau Kong Yung & others v. The Director of Immigration*（*劉港榕及其他人士對入境事務處處長案*）（(1992) 2 HKCFAR 300）裁定：**該解釋**是第二十二條第四款及第二十四條第二款第（三）項的有效和有約束力解釋，自此以後香港特區法院有責任遵從**該解釋**。

11. **該解釋**於1999年6月公布。同日，政府公開宣布一項一般人所說的"寬免政策"（但正如下級法院指出，如此描述該項政策並不適當），其大意為政府將"容許於1997年7月1日至1999年1月29日期間抵港，並已就居留權作出聲稱的人士（以該兩項判決）核實他們聲稱擁有的永久性居民身份"。政府又於同日就寬免政策作出其他聲明，詳情在下文再行評析。

12. 於*吳嘉玲*及*陳錦雅*兩案等待判決期間，當前上訴案的申請人（可能還有不少其他人士）認為自己的情況與該兩宗案件的當事人相同。但他們並沒有參與該訴訟或展開新的訴訟程序。該等人士現宣稱，他們聲稱擁有的永久性居民身份也應該根據該兩項判決獲得核實，又或他們是該寬免政策所涵蓋的人士。

本上訴案的當事人

13. 當前的上訴案是因下列三宗司法覆核申請而引起的：高院憲法及行政訴訟1999年第81號（HCAL 81 of 1999），案中共有5,073名申請人（原有5,308名）；高院憲法及行政訴訟2000年第70號（HCAL 70 of 2000），案中共有39名申請人（原有43名），以及高院憲法及行政訴訟2000年第2號（HCAL 2 of 2000），案中祇有一名申請人。上述申請人俱為在內地出生的中國公民，而且其父母之中最少一人是香港特區的永久性居民。各申請人遂聲稱他們是第二十四條第二款第（三）項所述的永久性居民，並指稱他們的聲稱應以*吳嘉玲*及*陳錦雅*兩案的判決予以核實，即不受**該解釋**影響。現時，大部份申請人仍然留港，而另一些申請人則已返回內地。

14. 有關申請人分為甲、乙兩類：甲類申請人是指那些在其父母之中一人已成為香港永久性居民後才出生的人士；而乙類申請人是指那些在其父及母都未在香港通常居住滿七年之前已出生的人士。屬於甲類的申請人，除非能因吳嘉玲案的判決而受惠，否則便會受到第二十二條第四款的限制，即需領取單程證才可進入香港。至於屬於乙類的申請人，除非他們因上述兩項判決而受惠，否則，他們不單好像甲類申請人一樣受到第二十二條第四款的影響，而且還會受到第二十四條第二款第（三）項的"出生時間限制"影響，又因為他們是在其父或母成為香港永久性居民以前出生的，故此他們根本就不能符合該條款的資格。高院憲法及行政訴訟1999年第81號的絕大部份（4,639名）申請人，高院憲法及行政訴訟2000年第70號的全部申請人，以及高院憲法及行政訴訟2000年第2號的李女士，均屬乙類申請人。

15. 當前案件的申請人是於不同時間和在不同情況下來到香港的。大部份申請人是持雙程證抵港後而逾期逗留的，有一些人是在返回內地之後，再次來港及逾期逗留的，其餘的申請人則是並未持有任何許可證而非法來港，又或他們是沒有經由正常的入境管制站而進入本港的。在某些情況而言，抵港日期是重要的考慮因素（詳見下文）。正因如此，我等現按個別申請人的抵港時間，將他們撥入五段特定時期，這五段時期分別是：

（1）第1期——於1997年7月1日前抵港，並逗留至1997年7月1日或以後的人士，亦即在《基本法》生效前抵港的人士。

（2）第2期——在1997年7月1日至1997年7月10日期間抵港的人士（1997年7月10日亦即制定和在憲報刊登《第3號條例》的日期）。

（3）第3期——在1997年7月11日至1999年1月29日期間抵港的人士（1999年1月29日是終審法院發下該兩項判決的日期）。

（4）第4期——在1999年1月30日至1999年6月26日期間抵港的人士（1999年6月26日是公布**該解釋**的日期，也是政府宣布寬免政策的日期）。

（5）第5期——於1999年6月26日以後抵港或自1997年7月1日開始並沒有來港的人士。

16. 由於有關高院憲法及行政訴訟的申請人為數眾多，各方當事人在1999年第81號案選出19名代表申請人，以及在2000年第70號案選出7名代表申請人，而2000年第2號案的申請人則是單獨提出申請的。在第一宗訴訟中，19名代表申請人的詳情如下：

（1）第1名代表申請人吳小彤女士——已被接納為寬免政策所涵蓋的人士，現不再謀求濟助；

（2）第2名代表申請人吳金枝女士及第9名代表申請人林麗品女士——已退出代表申請人之列，因為與她們聲稱有關的事實備受爭議，致令二人不宜擔當代表；

（3）第5名代表申請人譚小明先生——根據一眾申請人的書面陳詞：他已在終審法院作出有關判決之後獲發單程證。但就根據寬免政策提出的聲稱而言，他仍是代表申請人；

（4）第7名代表申請人劉港榕先生——其永久性居民身份已獲核實，而他亦已獲發單程證，但仍然保留代表申請人的身份，以協助其他與其狀況相若的人士；

（5）第16名代表申請人鄺健婷女士——根據一眾申請人的書面陳詞，她是在法院作出有關原訟判決之後獲發單程證的，但由於她屬乙類申請人，故仍未被視為永久性居民；以及

（6）第18名代表申請人鄧錦青先生——他於1999年7月合法來港並依時離去，當局並沒有向他發出遣送離境令。

17. 案中絕大部份的申請人俱面對入境事務處處長向他們發出的遣送離境令。在這些申請人中，有一部份人申請撤銷遣送離境令被拒，又有一部份人申請給予永久性居民身份被拒，亦有一部份人聲稱可受惠於寬免政策而被拒。

18. 在各高院憲法及行政訴訟中，代表申請人所質疑的各項決定如下：

（a）以1999年第81號案的第3，4，6，8，第10名至第15名，第17名及第19名代表申請人，

2000 年第 70 號案的第 1 名至第 7 名代表申請人，以及 2000 年第 2 號案的申請人而言，他們所質疑的是根據《入境條例》第 19（1）（b）（ii）條發出的遣送離境令；

（b）以 1999 年第 81 號案的代表申請人而言，入境事務處處長曾於過往對他們發出遣送離境令，他們現時所質疑的就是不予撤銷上述離境令的決定；以及

（c）就 1999 年第 81 號案，2000 年第 70 號案的各代表申請人，以及 2000 年第 2 號案的申請人而言，他們所質疑的是裁定他們不是寬免政策所涵蓋的人士的決定。

19. 在上述各項決定中，入境事務處處長均認定有關申請人須予遣送離境，以及認定他們無權繼續留港。

20. 各申請人除謀求本院撤銷上述各項決定外，還請求本院作出宣告：他們是第二十四條第二款第（三）項所述的人士；他們是寬免政策所涵蓋的人士（於第 4 期及第 5 期抵港者除外），以及他們是不受**該解釋**影響的人士，亦即他們有權獲得當局以吳嘉玲及陳錦雅兩案的判決來核實他們的永久性居民身份。各申請人提出的司法覆核申請在原訟法庭遭原訟法庭法官司徒敬駁回。其後，（由上訴法庭副庭長梅賢玉、上訴法庭法官梁紹中及上訴法庭法官祁彥輝組成的）上訴法庭又維持上述決定。最後，各申請人獲給予許可，並向本院提出上訴。

上訴的主要爭議點

21. 儘管各申請人皆聲稱不受**該解釋**影響，然而，案中並不存在質疑該解釋的問題。訴訟各方均同意常委會對《基本法》第二十二條第四款及第二十四條第二款第（三）項所作的解釋從 1997 年 7 月 1 日起便成為法律，對法院有約束力。本院在劉港榕案作出的判決亦已表明此意。此外，訴訟各方亦同意**該解釋**並不包括任何對第一百五十八條的解釋。

22. 案中的主要爭議點見於各申請人提出的 5 項上訴理由。按各申請人提出有關爭論點的先後次序，該等上訴理由順序為：

（1）按第一百五十八條第三款“在此以前作出的判決不受影響”一句的真確解釋，各申請人擁有吳嘉玲及陳錦雅兩案判決所產生的權利，不應受**該解釋**影響。（是項爭議，下稱“在此以前作出的判決”。）

（2）即使申請人被裁定為受**該解釋**影響的人士，但由於政府向他們所作的公開聲明和陳述，以及吳嘉玲及陳錦雅兩案訴訟的方式，為他們帶來了一個合理的期望，就是會得到如該兩案的當事人一樣的看待，而他們聲稱擁有的永久性居民身份會根據該兩項判決獲得核實。這期望應予以體現。（是項爭議，下稱“合理期望”。）

（3）即使前兩項理由不能成立，鑑於本案的所有情況和申請人所受到的嚴重不公，入境事務處處長如對申請人執行該等遣送離境令，會造成不公及濫用程序，法院應下令暫緩執行該等遣送離境令，以防程序遭濫用。（是項爭議，下稱“濫用程序”。）

（4）在 1997 年 7 月 1 日之前抵港的申請人，不受《基本法》第二十二條第四款或**該解釋**規限，而在 1997 年 7 月 1 日至 10 日抵港的申請人不受**該解釋**或已被裁定為沒有追溯效力的《第 3 號條例》所影響。（是項爭議，下稱“第 1 期及第 2 期”。）

（5）於 1999 年 1 月 29 日之前抵港的申請人有一合理期望，就是他們只要符合該寬免政策所規定的條款，便會受到如*吳嘉玲*及*陳錦雅*兩案當事人所得判決一樣的看待。（是項爭議，下稱“寬免政策”。）

23. 各申請人的論據如下：假如第（1）項理由成立，全部申請人，不論是屬於甲類或乙類的人士，也不論是何時抵港，皆應獲判勝訴。假如第（2）項或第（3）項理由成立，情況亦是一樣。第（4）項理由祇是對甲類申請人有所幫助，而乙類申請人則必須證明他們不受**該解釋**（就第二十四條第二款第（三）項作出的解釋）所影響才可利用這項理由。最後一項理由則適用於在第 1、2 及第 3 期抵港的申請人，不論是屬於甲類還是乙類，情況都是一樣。

24. 我等現評析第一項上訴理由。

“在此以前作出的判決”的爭議

25. 御用大律師 Robertson 先生，聯同資深大律師李志喜女士，以及大律師郭瑞熙先生代表各申請人提出：

（1）第一百五十八條第三款明確地包含“在此以前作出的判決不受影響”原則，是項原則對人大常委會根據第一百五十八條第一款所作的獨立解釋，亦具相同效力；

（2）“不受影響”一語應按其固有及通常的涵義來理解，即應理解為“不受損害或質疑”的意思；

（3）“判決”一詞意指判決的法律原則（ratio decidendi）或“決定的理由”或“裁定，包括已宣告的權利”；以及

（4）上述原則適用於當前案件，故能保障本院已於*吳嘉玲*及*陳錦雅*兩案所宣告的所有有關人士的居留權；即在本院頒下有關判決之時該等能夠確立他們是《基本法》第二十四條第二款第（三）項所述人士的居留權。

26. 訴訟各方對各申請人所提出的首兩項陳詞並無爭議。各方均同意“在此以前作出的判決不受影響”的原則適用於常委會根據第一百五十八條第一款所作的獨立解釋。入境事務處處長亦承認是項原則是意味著在此以前作出的判決維持不變，不會受損。

27. 無論如何，常委會因應按第一百五十八條第三款所訂定的司法提請而作出的解釋就是行使第一百五十八條第一款歸於常委會的一般解釋權所作出的解釋。故此，制定保障使按第一百五十八條第三款的司法提請所作出的解釋不予適用於在此以前作出的判決，其實就是對隨著按第一百五十八條第一款作出的解釋而來的後果，即在此以前作出的判決不受影響一點，予以明確的承認。（詳見*劉港榕案*（第 346 頁））

28. 如說有關解釋是按第一百五十八條第三款所述的提請作出的，在此以前作出的判決才不受影響；但如有關解釋是獨立的解釋，則在此以前作出的判決便受影響，這種說法就未免不合情理了。再者，將有關保障理解為俱適用於這兩個情況，既符合將審判權歸屬於特區各級法院的規定（見第八十條），亦與將終審權歸屬於終審法院的做法（見第八十二條）協調一致。要是終審法院的判決不能免受根據第一百五十八條第一款所作的解釋影響，這便會在某程度上削弱本院的終審權。即使一項這樣作出的解釋取代了某一在此以前作出的判決，情況如同該項在 1999 年 6 月 26 日作出的解釋取代了吳嘉玲及陳錦雅兩案的判決一樣，以及闡明有關法律自 1997 年 7 月 1 日起開始適用，以訴訟各方當事人而言，該項在此以前作出的判決仍不受影響，這始終都是他們的權利的

最終裁定。

29. 必須注意的是：**該解釋**最後一段倒數第二句顯示“在此以前作出的判決不受影響”的原則是適用於根據第一百五十八條第一款作出的獨立解釋的。**該解釋**是在這個基礎上作出。這句子是：

> “本解釋不影響香港特別行政區終審法院 1999 年 1 月 29 日對有關案件判決的有關訴訟當事人所獲得的香港特別行政區居留權”。

30. 我等並不是說當前的問題可從上文引述的句子或是從**該解釋**的最後一段找到答案。當前的問題取決於第一百五十八條本身的真確解釋。雖然**該解釋**並不是對該條文作出的解釋，但是，**該解釋**認為（我等亦認為）“在此以前作出的判決”此一原則也是適用於根據第一百五十八條第一款所作的獨立解釋的。

31. 入境事務處處長的主要論據是：他接納“不受影響”一語是“不會受損”的意思，但是，他卻就申請人對“在此以前作出的判決”所作的廣義解釋，提出爭議。入境事務處處長稱：第一百五十八條第三款的“判決”一詞，應按照該詞在普通法下的意思來理解。“判決”表示法院就裁定訴訟，以及就確認或否定該訴訟的當事人的權利所宣布的正式命令（包括所作出的宣告）。嚴格來說，“判決”一詞的確切涵義有別於法官就其決定所述的理由（見 *R v. Ireland* 案（（1970）44 ALJR 263）；*Moller v. Roy* 案（（1975）49 ALJR 311 第 312–313 頁），以及 Lord Simon of Glaisdale 在 *F.A & A.B. Ltd v. Lupton* 案（〔1972〕AC 634，第 658 頁 H））所作的評析。然而，“判決”一詞除用以表示法官的決定外，通常還可用以表示決定的理由。

32. 御用大律師 Robertson 先生陳詞謂：第一百五十八條第三款的“判決”一詞是指“判決的法律原則”或決定的理由或“裁定，包括已宣告的權利”，而他就是要求本院採取這個有利於各申請人的廣義。在這方面，Robertson 先生的論據面對一項根本性的難題。以普通法的法學理論而言，判決的法律原則或決定的理由對有關訴訟的局外人，並無約束力。判決的法律原則及決定理由的重要性在於其作為先例的價值，亦即法院會在日後將有關原則及理由應用於涉及該先前訴訟的局外人的其他案件。

33. 不過，御用大律師 Robertson 先生否認倚據“在此以前作出的判決”的先例價值。他這樣做是正確的。第一百五十八條第三款倒數第二句訂明，香港特別行政區法院在引用該條款時，“應以全國人民代表大會常務委員會的解釋為準”。是項規定的作用就是要毀滅已被常委會解釋所取代的判決的先例價值。

34. 由上述分析看來，要是我等接納申請人的論據，兩個令人詫異的後果便會出現：首先，就是將有關決定的法律原則及邏輯思維從先例的範疇轉移至具約束力判決的境界，且將該判決的約束力引伸至適用於有關訴訟的局外人。其次，將如此引伸而來的約束力給予有關法律原則或邏輯思維，亦會破壞第一百五十八條第三款倒數第二句所預定的作用，而此條款之目的就是：必須依循常委會的解釋，而非以被**該解釋**所取代的判決為準。

35. 儘管本院在吳嘉玲及陳錦雅兩案所宣告的權利僅適用於該兩宗案件各原告人，但當前的申請人仍謀求將“所宣告的權利”等同“判決”一般論處。如此一來，申請人便是將有關判決所宣告的權利，視為對與該兩宗案件各原告人屬同一類別的全部人士盡皆適用。申請人要求將有關判決如此看待的理據，是基於他們對決定的法律原則和理由所提出的論據，我等已在上文表示拒絕接納。

36. 以第一百五十八條第三款的內容而論，即要保存以前判決，使其免受追溯至《基本法》實施日期開始採用的解釋所影響一點而論，“判決”應嚴格地按照其確切涵義來理解。誠然，正如代表申請人的御用大律師指出，第一百五十八條第三款的最後部份確無“在各方當事人之間”的字句，可是，這樣的字句是不必要的。由具管轄權的法院作出的判決，如獲維持有效，便是最終裁定並徹底解決該訴訟各方當事人的權利事宜，而該判決所裁定的亦衹是該訴訟各方當事人的權利。有關判決對該訴訟的各方當事人具約束力（這也包括在該訴訟中獲法庭頒令由某一方代表當事人所代表的同類人士），但對該訴訟的局外人則不具約束力。根據先例法則，某一案件的判決可用以強制其他相若案件得出類似的結果。但有關判決在該訴訟的局外人之間，並無約束力，即使是在該訴訟當事人的一方與另一不是該訴訟當事人的一方之間，有關判決亦無約束力。

37. 於此情況下，第一百五十八條第三款最後一句所表達的是普通法下的終結性原則。根據這個原則，一項不可上訴的終局判決，或是沒有任何一方提出上訴的最後判決，就各方面而言，都是裁定了各方當事人的權利。這樣的判決不能因為有關法律其後有所改變而予以重新審議。亦衹是因為有這樣的判決，該訴訟的各方當事人的權利才不會改變。一個法庭的判決是不會因為其後法律有所改變而受影響的。

38. 必須注意的是本院在上述兩案的決定中所給予的濟助的形式，在*吳嘉玲*案，本院宣告：《入境條例》（第115章）的某些部份，《入境規例》（第 115 章，附屬法例）的某些部份，該份日期為 1997 年 7 月 11 日的通知，以及《第 3 號條例》第 1（2）條皆屬無效。本院並撤銷入境事務處處長的某些決定，以及宣告該案的各原告人自 1997 年 7 月 1 日開始已是《基本法》第二十四條第二款第三類別的香港特區永久性居民，並因此而享有居留權。本院就該案所宣告的權利的受益人是局限於該等法律程序的原告人。而他們並不是代表當事人。故此，本院所宣告的權利不會令任何其他人受益。同樣理由，本院在*陳錦雅*案所宣告的衹是該案“每一名上訴人”所享有的權利，該權利不會擴展惠及他人。儘管*吳嘉玲*及*陳錦雅*兩案被視為“代表案件”，但是，聆訊該兩宗案件的法庭俱無諭令各原告人擔當代表當事人。

39. 雖然各申請人謀求在書面陳詞中提出其他考慮因素（特別是*吳嘉玲*及*陳錦雅*兩案的“例案”性質）來支持他們的論據，可是，代表各申請人的御用大律師 Robertson 先生否認倚據這些考慮因素來支持有關第一百五十八條的論據。這些考慮因素所關乎的是我等接著要評析的“合理期望”爭議。

“合理期望”的爭議

申請人在合理期望方面的理據基礎

40. 大律師陳詞謂各申請人有合理期望，期望會被當作吳嘉玲及陳錦雅兩案的當事人一樣看待，並期望入境事務處處長會在他們的個案中貫徹執行上述兩案的判決。大律師訴稱，引致當前上訴案各申請人存有合理期望的是該兩宗案件的“例案性質”，以及：

（1）政府高級官員在本院作出該兩項判決之前或之後作出的公開聲明；

（2）入境事務處處長及法律援助署署長對若干申請人作出的陳述；以及

（3）各有關法官及大律師在導致本院作出該兩項判決的訴訟過程中所作出的陳述及所採取的程序。

大律師陳詞謂，就是因為上述事項的累積影響才會令到各申請人產生該合理期望的。

41. 故此，我等需要審視這些聲明及陳述以便（1）確定向各申請人傳達的是甚麼訊息；（2）決定究竟該等聲明及陳述是否能夠引起任何合理期望；又如能引起合理期望；則（3）該合理期望為何。

42. 在評析這些問題之前，我等宜先看看兩案訴訟的來龍去脈，因為在訴訟過程中所發生的事情對政府及政府機關作出的聲明，以及對這些意欲宣稱擁有居留權的人士對事件的理解，是有直接影響的。

吳嘉玲案及陳錦雅案

43. 1997 年 7 月初，多名聲稱人展開 5 宗訴訟，以謀求獲得許可來申請司法覆核入境事務處處長對他們發出的遣送離境令。同時，為數甚多的人士亦獲得法律援助來提出訴訟，而且他們的案件亦已展開。

44. 處理該首 5 宗訴訟初審程序的是原訟法庭法官祁彥輝。他理解到這一大批有可能需要聆訊的案件會帶來多項問題。將案件逐一處理不但花費時間和大量金錢，而且情況還會難以控制。故此，他促請這些當事人就該等案件所面對的共同爭議點，選出合適的案件作為“代表案件”交由法庭審理，意思是當法庭就這些“代表案件”所涉及的法律爭議點作出決定後，一些不是該等案件當事人的其他人士對該決定或會感到興趣。結果，這些當事人達成協議，選出 4 宗（共涉及 5 名申請人的）案件，這就是 *Cheung Lai Wah（張麗華）*案（亦即其後終審法院所稱的*吳嘉玲*案）的由來。當時有案件已經在法院席前候審的當事人，以及在當時仍未展開訴訟的人士或某一類別的人士，都沒有請求法庭頒令或向法庭申請要求頒令指定*張麗華*案的申請人作為代表當事人來代表他們，令法庭日後作出的判決不論是對他們有利或不利，都會對他們有約束力。事實上，法庭也沒有作出過這樣的命令。原訟法庭法官祁彥輝結果頒令：在法庭就代表案件作出裁定之前，暫緩處理該首 5 宗訴訟及其餘 3 宗案件。另一方面，法庭亦發出禁制令，禁制入境事務處處長將這些其他訴訟的申請人遣送離港；而入境事務處處長也承諾在該等代表案件審理有結果之前不會遣返*張麗華*案的真正當事人，以及那些獲批法律援助，但在代表案件有結果之前未有展開訴訟的人士。

45. 法庭在 1997 年 9 月份聆訊該等案件，並於 1997 年 10 月 9 日判決各申請人敗訴。各申請人遂提出上訴。入境事務處處長同意延展早前作出的承諾，同意在上訴期間不遣返該承諾所涵蓋的人士。

46. 1997 年 11 月 12 日，另一案件（涉及的申請人共 81 名）又告展開。該案的申請人協商選出其中一人為“代表申請人”。這宗訴訟（稱*陳錦雅*案）所關乎的是第二十四條第二款第（三）項的“出生時間限制”爭議。同樣，法庭並無在該案中諭令此代表申請人代表其他當時並非在法庭席前候審的任何人士或任何類別的人士。事實上，當時也無任何人士採取任何行動請求法庭作出這樣的命令。另一方面，入境事務處處長也同意，在該案有結果之前，不會遣返該案的各方當事人，以及那些已經獲批法律援助，而且也是由同一律師事務所代表的申請人。

吳嘉玲案及陳錦雅案的法院決定

47. 下級法院在過去一年半對這兩宗案件所作的各項決定影響到入境事務處及法律援助署的態度，也影響到他們處理居留權聲稱及法律援助申請的手法。

48. 1997 年 10 月 9 日，原訟法庭法官祁彥輝在張麗華案（後稱*吳嘉玲*案）裁定：第二十二條第四款適用於根據第二十四條第二款第（三）項聲稱擁有永久性居民身份的內地居民；以及《第 3 號條例》引進的核實計劃，即永久性居民身份的申請必須在內地提出的規定，以及必須是持有附錄於居留權證明書的有效旅遊證件（即單程證）的人士才能確立其永久性居民身份的規定，都是符合《基本法》。此外，原訟法庭法官祁彥輝亦裁定《第 3 號條例》的追溯性條文有效。

49. 1998 年 1 月 26 日，原訟法庭法官祁彥輝在*陳錦雅*案裁定：《第 2 號條例》所規定的出生時間限制抵觸第二十四條第二款第（三）項，因此香港永久性居民在香港以外所生的中國籍子女，不論在他們出生之時其父母是否已取得永久性居民身份，均享有香港的居留權。

50. 1998 年 4 月 2 日，上訴法庭在*張麗華*案（後稱*吳嘉玲*案）一致支持原訟法庭法官祁彥輝的決定，亦即認同第二十四條第二款第（三）項是受制於第二十二條第四款的。然而，過半數法官（即高等法院首席法官陳兆愷及上訴法庭副庭長黎守律）裁定：對該等在 1997 年 7 月 1 日《基本法》生效之前已經抵港的人士而言，《第 3 號條例》的追溯性條款無效。與此同時，另一組合的過半數法官（上訴法庭副庭長黎守律及馬大敏）又裁定：對該等在 1997 年 7 月 1 日至 7 月 10 日期間抵港的人士而言，《第 3 號條例》的追溯性條文有效。

51. 1998 年 5 月 20 日，上訴法庭在*陳錦雅*案推翻原訟法庭法官祁彥輝的決定，並裁定：第二十四條第二款第（三）項是有出生時間限制的。故此，衹（只）有那些在出生時其父或母已成為香港永久性居民的人士才可根據第二十四條第二款第（三）項聲稱擁有永久性居民身份。

52. 1999 年 1 月 29 日，本院在*吳嘉玲*案推翻原訟法庭法官祁彥輝及上訴法庭的決定，並裁定：第二十四條第二款第（三）項不受第二十二條第四款規限，因此根據第二十四條第二款第（三）項聲稱擁有永久性居民身份的人士無須向內地機關申請辦理批准手續，而《第 3 號條例》所引進的核實身份計劃所訂定必須將單程證附錄於居留權證明書的條文亦屬無效。另一方面，本院也裁定：在該核實身份計劃中，規定有關永久性居民身份的申請必須在內地提出的條文是有效的，而《第 3 號條例》關於追溯效力的條文則屬無效。

53. 同日，本院在*陳錦雅*案中裁定：《第 2 號條例》的出生時間限制與第二十四條第二款第（三）項不符，故該出生時間的限制並無效力。

隨著兩案終審判決而來的事件

54. 在本院作出該兩項判決之後，政府隨即發表公開聲明，表示會執行本院的決定。政府並就此目的成立一專責小組，且開始與內地機關商議訂定核實居留權聲稱的新程序。有關方面又進行研究以估計能夠根據本院的解釋而符合第二十四條第二款第（三）項的資格的人數，以及評估因此而對社會服務造成的需求和為本港帶來的財政負擔。根據政府調查的結果顯示，符合資格的第一代內地人士共 692,000 名，而第二代的合資格內地人士則為 983,000 名。

55. 案中各申請人批評上述調查，指進行的方法並不可靠，而數字亦極度誇大。他們訴稱：扣除了非婚生子女、第二代人士，以及那些不會來港定居的人士後，受本院決定影響的人士衹（只）是 365,000 名，又假如接納政府早前於 1995 年進行調查所得的數字（各申請人建議我等可採納這個數字），則符合資格的人士只有約 129,800 名。當然，確實的人數是始終無從得知的。

56. 調查方法及數字準確性的爭議更加突顯此事的不明確因素，亦顯示了政府在試圖執行本院決定時將會遇到的困難。政府認為這是一個香港特區不能應付的問題，故在諮詢行政會議和立法會後，決定提請人大常委會就第二十二條第四款及第二十四條第二款第（三）項作出解釋以取代*陳錦雅*案的決定，以及*吳嘉玲*案的部份決定，亦即第二十四條第二款第（三）項不受第二十二條第四款規限，因此根據第二十四條第二款第（三）項聲稱擁有居留權的人士不須向內地機關申請辦理批准手續此一部份的決定

57. 1999 年 6 月 26 日，人大常委會公布**該解釋**。

政府高級官員作出的一般聲明

（1）1999 年 1 月 29 日以前

58. 政府高級官員，包括行政長官、政務司司長及入境事務處處長作出之有關聲明，主要是在 1997 年 7 月至 10 月期間作出的。大批在內地出生而獲給予法律援助的申請人就他們擁有永久性居民身份的聲稱作出追討，並且質疑入境法例是否合乎憲法。為平息社群在主權移交初期的顧慮，政府官員希望向公眾人士清楚交待政府的立場。

59. 載於聲明內的陳述可概述如下：

（1）政府會執行入境法例，而不能確立其居留權身份的人士會被遣返；（政府發言人在 1997 年 7 月 3 日的陳述；入境事務處處長在 1997 年 7 月 13 日的陳述）；

（2）政府會堅守法治精神，而公眾可以向法院控訴政府；（行政長官在 1997 年 7 月 12 日的陳述）；

（3）政府會竭盡所能按照法律就案件作出抗辯；（入境事務處處長在 1997 年 7 月 13 日的陳述；行政長官在 1997 年 7 月 31 日及 10 月 22 日的陳述）；

（4）倘若敗訴，政府"將根據判決修訂法例"；（"東方日報"在 1997 年 7 月 13 日就有關入境事務處處長的陳述作出的報導）；以及

（5）政府的做法會以法院的最終決定為依歸；亦會服從法院的裁定；（行政長官在 1997 年 7 月 23 日、7 月 31 日及 10 月 22 日的陳述）；

60. 上文第（5）段所提述的三項聲明中的首項聲明，是行政長官在 7 月 23 日一次傳媒採訪中作出的。他回應提問時說：

"我們的社區甚為著重法治，所以這些法律挑戰自然是可以預計的。我們會依循法院的最終決定去做……"

61. 7 月 31 日，行政長官在香港澳洲商會發表演說時作出第二項聲明。他說：

"我們預計，有關香港人在內地所生子女的問題，很快會引起另一場法律挑戰。香港的法院已一一應付這些挑戰，將來亦會繼續應付各種挑戰……。這亦證明了香港特區政府會在法庭內據理力爭，並會遵從法院的裁決。"

62. 第三項聲明是行政長官在 1997 年 10 月 22 日在倫敦查塔姆樓（Chatham House）發表演說時作出的。他在提及法律挑戰和法治精神之後說：

"不論在過去或將來，政府都會在法院遭到挑戰。現在以至將來，香港的法院都是應付這些挑戰的場地。這點很重要。政府會在法庭內據理力爭，並會遵從法院的裁決。"

63. 除上文提到的公開聲明外，本院也應提述另外兩項聲明。1997 年 7 月 13 日，當行政長官被問及會否提請人大常委會解釋《入境條例》，以澄清該條例是否抵觸《基本法》時，他回答表示政府已作全面考慮，並認為無需在事前要求人大常委會作出裁定。這回答只不過是傳遞一項信息：政府很有信心其立場是正確的。

64. 1997 年 7 月 23 日，議員在立法會會議上詢問負責有關法律援助署事宜的政務司司長，大量法律援助申請為法律援助署的財政所帶來的影響、法律援助署不待法院就首宗同類性質案件作出裁定便處理其他申請的原因，以及現行安排會否增加法院的工作量。政務司司長回答謂：

"至今為止，有 73 宗個案獲給予法律援助。可是，雙方當事人在法院同意下將會挑選數宗案件作為例案，以便取得法院就法律要點作出的裁定。因此，對於所有獲法律援助者而言，*政府無須為每一名人士展開獨立的訴訟程序*。因為訴訟費用取決於挑選了多少宗案件、案件的複雜程度，以及這些案件將會產生多少宗上訴，所以現階段很難估計訴訟將會所費若干。法律援助署將密切監管在這些案件中的使費。

根據《法律援助條例》（第 91 章），所有法律援助申請都必須從速處理。延誤處理一項申請或會危害合資格申請人的利益。數宗例案預計不會令法院不勝負荷。"（加以斜體以作強調）

政府聲明無需為每名獲法律援助的人士展開獨立的訴訟程序，是為了表示政府的財政負擔將會有限。作出聲明的目的，並非要引導其他不論是否有申請法律援助的人士不去展開訴訟程序。正如東方日報及明報翌日的報導反映，這的確是報界所理解的意思。合理的讀者在閱讀報章的報導後亦會得出同一理解。

（2）1999 年 1 月 29 日以後

65. 在終審法院作出決定後，社會人士自然對於政府將會採取的做法感到焦慮。兩宗判決作出後，高級官員曾發表多項公開聲明。這些聲明可概述如下：

（1）政府尊重法院的裁定，並會服從及落實該等裁定；（保安局局長在 1999 年 1 月 29 日的聲明；行政長官在 1999 年 1 月 30 日的聲明；署理行政長官在 1999 年 1 月 30 日及 1999 年 2 月 5 日的聲明；保安局局長在 1999 年 1 月 30 日的聲明；行政會議召集人在 1999 年 2 月 1 日的聲明；政府發言人在 1999 年 2 月 2 日的聲明）；

（2）政府會與內地機關討論將會採取的步驟；（保安局局長在 1999 年 1 月 29 及 30 日的聲明；行政會議召集人在 1999 年 2 月 1 日的聲明）；

（3）政府會評估判決對社會上各類服務所帶來的影響；（保安局局長在 1999 年 1 月 29 日的聲明；行政長官在 1999 年 1 月 30 日的聲明；署理行政長官在 1999 年 1 月 30 日的聲明；行政會議召集人在 1999 年 2 月 1 日的聲明；署理行政長官在 1999 年 2 月 2 日的聲明）；以及

（4）政府已根據終審法院的判決接受及處理申請（民事法律專員在 1999 年 5 月 19 日的聲明）。

政府機構作出的具體陳述

（1）由入境事務處 / 保安局局長作出的

66. 申請人指稱政府所作出的具體陳述致令他們產生合理期望。該等陳述以書面形式見於入境事務處或其他政府官員，例如行政長官及保安局局長，就有關申請人對居留權的查詢所作的回覆。除提述當時適用的法律外，入境事務處給予若干申請人的標準回覆中（個別個案中使用了少許不同的字眼），均載有下列一段說話：

"高等法院在 1998 年 1 月 26 日決定，如若在香港以外所生的子女是在他們的父母成為香港永久性居民前出生，而他們的父或母事後取得香港永久性居民身份，則這些子女也擁有居留權。特區政府已就該決定提出上訴。由於事件仍在訴訟期間，所以入境事務處暫時未能對屬於這類人士的申請作出決定。"

申請人指稱這項回覆等同引導他們要待至法院就案件作出最後決定之後才採取行動提出聲稱。申請人陳詞指出，要是他們曾採取行動，他們的狀況便會與*吳嘉玲*案及*陳錦雅*案的當事人一樣。保安局局長因應第 13 名代表申請人的查詢函件而作出日期為 1998 年 4 月 24 日的回覆，當中的信息更加明顯：

"上訴法庭將於 5 月 1 日聆訊案件。待整個訴訟的法律程序完畢後，入境事務處將依循法院的最後判決處理居留權證明書的申請。"

（2）由法律援助署作出的

67. 法律援助署在法律程序中作為訴訟一方的代表律師，當然獨立於政府，但作為負責落實《法律援助條例》各項條文的機構，法律援助署顯然是以政府部門的職能行事。法律援助署向各宗案件中已獲給予或正尋求法律援助的人士所作的陳述，是否可以歸因於政府？這是本上訴案的爭議點。我們認為應給予這問題肯定的答案。從下文可以見到，法律援助署在該等訟案中在各方面均聯同入境事務處行事。法律援助署就"例案"作為先例的影響作出聲明，並且為了把訴訟的數量保持在合理範圍內及為了節省訟費，嘗試勸阻申請法律援助的人士展開或參與訴訟程序。在這幾個方面，法律援助署在照顧聲稱人的利益的同時，亦照顧政府的利益。

68. 由 1997 年 7 月初開始，法律援助署便已接受了大量法律援助申請，並協助本身為內地出生子女而父母是香港永久性居民的申請人提起訴訟程序、要求法院撤銷所有針對他們而作出的遣送離境令及 / 或協助他們作出擁有永久性居民身份的聲稱。7 月份有 1,300 宗這類申請。部份獲給予法律援助的申請人獲指派予賈偉林、劉天均律師行。法律援助署、獲指派的律師及大律師與代表入境事務處的律政司意識到所涉及的聲稱人數字龐大，以及事實上案件的訟訴將耗費公帑。他們進行商議，探討利用數宗例案去尋求法院就該等聲稱人及其他聲稱人的共同爭議點作出裁決的可能性。這也是法院在 1997 年 7 月 21 日的指示聆訊中表達的用意。結果，*張麗華*（其後稱為*吳嘉玲*）等案給挑選為"代表案件"。據 1997 年 7 月 15、20 及 29 日的報章報導，法律援助署的高級官員當時聲言法院在該等代表案件的決定會成為同類案件的先例，而且不是所有已獲給予法律援助的案件都須要交由法院聆訊。

69. 由於資深大律師的法律意見是，各申請人的聲稱不會成功，因此，法律援助署在 7 月下旬或 8 月初取消給予*陳錦雅*案案件類別的聲稱人的法律援助證書。上訴後來在司法常務官席前遭駁回，而法律援助署亦拒絕屬於這類別聲稱人的法律援助申請或勸阻其作出申請。

70. 1997 年 8 月初，因為入境事務處處長當時只願意承諾不遣送已獲給予法律援助的人士離境，所以法律援助署須要篩選所有申請。申請人須提供支持文件，使其法律援助申請得到處理。法律援助署因而可以對申請書所提理據作出初步評估。至 1997 年 9 月 1 日，法律援助署總共接獲 1,461 宗申請，其中 901 宗獲給予法律援助，411 宗則被拒絕。餘下申請仍在處理中。至近 1997 年 9 月尾，法律援助署已停止再給予法律援助證書。停止給予證書的理由是待決案件已涵蓋所有法律上的爭議點，而新的個案並無涉及新的爭議點。然而，根據法律援助署的紀錄，這些申請人曾申請法律援助，以及申請在處理中。每名申請人都獲發一張粉紅色的咭紙。

71. 由於政策改變，故法律援助署在 1997 年 10 月中與入境事務處處長取得協議作出安排，由入境事務處處長承諾不遣送已提出（但未獲給予）法律援助申請，以及法律援助署認為其個案是有理據的人士離境。這些人士與在此以前已獲給予法律援助的人士並無不同。他們並獲指派律師替他們繼續提出聲稱。自此以後，法律援助署不時向入境事務處處長呈交有理據的申請人名册，並要求入境事務處處長在針對名册内任何一名申請人發出遣送離境令前，通知法律援助署。至 1999 年 1 月 11 日為止，這類人士共有 422 名。

72. 1997 年 11 月，超逾 70 名屬於*陳錦雅*案類別的人士自費延聘貝嘉蓮律師行展開訴訟程序，就出生時間限制的爭議點尋求答案。他們獲得法院批給司法覆核申請的許可後，也獲給予法律援助。同時，入境事務處處長同意不將這些申請人遣送離境，等待案件聆訊的結果。屬於這類別的申請人總共有 109 名，但只有 79 人能夠符合入境事務處處長訂明的條件，並因此而受惠於入境處處長的承諾。*陳錦雅*案中的申請人人數最終是 81 名。

73. 至於法律援助申請仍待處理的申請人，法律援助署已通知入境事務處處長有關該等申請，並要求入境處處長在針對這些申請人發出任何遣送離境令前，通知法律援助署。

74. 1998 年 12 月，剛在終審法院聆訊*吳嘉玲*案及*陳錦雅*案前，聲稱擁有居留權而申請法律援助的人士數目再度颷升。1998 年 12 月 7 日，法律援助署引入登記制度。按該制度，法律援助署只是審查緊急的個案，包括申請人被拘禁或有遣送離境之虞的個案。至於其他個案，法律援助署只登記申請人能夠提供個人詳情及支持文件的個案，並向每一名申請人發出公函回覆。除無關旨要的字眼變動外，公函回覆中述明：

"關於你的法律援助申請，請注意下列事項：

（1）延長逗留期間……

……

（2）居留權

由於你的法律援助申請與終審法院正在聆訊的法律事宜有關，因此，你無需在現階段就個別個案提出訴訟。"

我們稱這些回覆為"法律援助署覆函"。

75. 1999 年 2 月，終審法院作出判決後，法律援助署以白咭或紙條來確認申請人曾申請法律援助。這些白咭或紙條替代了法律援助署覆函。

76. 1998 年 12 月 7 日至 1999 年 1 月 29 日期間，法律援助署曾向超過 1,000 名尋求法律援助的人士發出法律援助署覆函，並在約一年後，即 1999 年 12 月，將這些人士的名册送交入境事務處。法律援助署要求入境事務處處長以這些申請人屬於寬免政策所述類別來作出考慮。入境事務處處長拒絕要求，只同意根據寬免政策的條款核實屬於寬免政策類別的個案。

77. 申請人訴稱，法律援助署暫緩處理他們的法律援助申請及 / 或向他們陳述無需提出獨立法律程序，這做法是向申請人表達了他們的個案會使他們得到如*吳嘉玲*案及*陳錦雅*案的當事人一樣的看待。而且，他們會因該兩項判決受惠。據申請人說，這項陳述的重要性在於它引導他們不採取行動，而且正就是這行動才會令致他們得到《基本法》第一百五十八條所給予在此以前作出的判決的保障。

"例案"

78. 申請人陳詞指出，*吳嘉玲*案及*陳錦雅*案的訴訟所採取的程序，以及法官和政府官員在訴訟過程中所作的陳述及聲明，再加上前文提到的一般和具體陳述，種種皆令致申請人產生合理期望：即他們會得到如該兩案的當事人一樣的看待。各方當事人、法律援助署及法院均視*吳嘉玲*案和*陳錦雅*案為“例案”。這點從下列情況可見一斑：

（1）按原訟法庭法官祁彥輝的建議，數宗案件給挑選為代表案件，而其他案件則暫時擱置，等候代表案件的結果；

（2）包括法律援助署在內的政府官員在公開聲明中描述這些案件為“例案”；

（3）對於要就相同或相類似的法律爭議點而提起新案的聲稱人，法律援助署不給予其法律援助證書；

（4）祁彥輝法官在他的判決中提述代表案件為“屬例案性質的”案件，並且沒有頒下訟費命令；以及

（5）其他法官在判決中也提到他們的決定有可能對許多其他聲稱人造成的影響。

申請人指稱此等事實導致他們相信，法院就這些“例案”作出的裁定會解決所有居留權準聲稱人的相同爭議點。

79. 祁彥輝法官是為了“把訟費維持在最低水平，但同時確保法院已就全部有關法律爭議作出決定”的目的，在案件管理的背景下提出建議和作出指示的。他不是說聲稱擁有居留權的人士會得到如法院席前的訴訟人一樣的看待。他所說的話亦非針對某人應否展開訴訟程序的問題。

80. 在*吳嘉玲*案及*陳錦雅*案中，爭議中問題屬公法的範疇。這兩宗案件普遍被認為是“例案”。人們可以假設，在例案中所宣告的原則（這些原則構成法律問題的答案）會適用於相同狀況的人士。結果是，政府及政府機構在其他案件中會執行法院的決定，以及如有需要的話，其他法庭會按先例法則執行法院的決定。至於有關例案的一般性原則，見 *R v. Hertfordshire County Council, Ex parte Cheung* 一案（The Times, 4 April 1986, 第12頁）。另 見 *R v. Secretary of State for the Home Department, Ex parte Bajram Zeqiri* 一案（〔2001〕EWCA Civ 342, 第43段）。案件現正在英國上議院進行上訴，結果待決。

在吳嘉玲案和陳錦雅案的“例案性質”的背景下考慮該等陳述

81. 申請人賴以支持其合理期望的事情大致分為兩大類：（1）政府及政府機構對公眾所作的一般陳述；以及（2）入境事務處及法律援助署作為政府機構向若干申請人作出的具體陳述。陳述是在*吳嘉玲*案及*陳錦雅*案的訴訟之前及訴訟期間作出的，並與申請人聲稱擁有居留權及其向法院追討該權利有關。因此，必須以訴訟的“例案性質”為背景來考慮這些陳述。

一般陳述

82. 我等認為，除了東方日報在 1997 年 7 月 13 日所報導的有關入境事務處處長的聲明，以及行政長官在 1997 年 7 月 23 日、7 月 31 日及 10 月 22 日所作的三項聲明外，在訴訟程序進行前或進行期間直至本院頒下判決為止，由政府作出的或代表政府作出的一般聲明都沒有重大意義，可擱在一旁。對於在法院頒下判決後作出的一般聲明，道理一樣。該些聲明只不過是一個負責任的政府會說的話，即政府尊重法治。一般聲明不能夠產生申請人所堅稱會產生的那種合理期望。

83. 入境事務處處長在 7 月 13 日及其前後作出的聲明與行政長官所作的三項聲明，則屬不同類別。訴訟雙方均同意全部四項聲明在香港受到公眾相當大的關注。雖然行政長官是（在查塔姆樓及澳洲商會發表演説時）向國際及海外人士作出其中兩項聲明的，但以當時的情況而言，這兩項聲明必定在香港引起公眾相當大的關注。而這些聲明所產生的效果，就與入境事務處處長的聲明及行政長官在 1997 年 7 月 23 日向傳媒發表的聲明的效果一樣。四項聲明全都明確承認該兩宗案件的例案性質所帶來的後果。換句話說，考慮到聲明作出的背景情況，聲明等同政府作出陳述，會服從法院審理的最終結果及會執行法院的決定，並會在其他相類情況中採用這決定。作出聲明者或許無意使人按聲明行事，但這不是旨要所在。重點是：聲明的涵義為何？

具體陳述

84. 法律援助署向個別法律援助申請人發出法律援助署覆函（見第 74 段）。覆函內所載具體陳述進一步作出聲明，即覆函受文者無需再展開訴訟程序或參與訴訟程序。換言之，覆函的陳述指出申請人無需採取某項行動。若採取該項行動的話，結果會令致申請人受到《基本法》第一百五十八條所給予“在此以前作出的判決”的保障。政府較早前聲明會服從例案的審理結果，這便起了引導作用。

85. 隨著高等法院作出決定後，入境事務處致居留權申請人士的標準回覆（見第 66 段）中所載聲明，只不過述明以下一點：就是由於訴訟仍然未決，所以入境事務處暫時未能就居留權申請作出決定。信函沒載有會落實法院的決定的陳述。

86. 可是，保安局局長致第 13 名代表申請人（見第 66 段），日期為 1998 年 4 月 24 日的回覆函件，其內載有陳述清楚指出，入境事務處“會依循法院的最後判決來處理居留權證明書的申請”。因為該項陳述沒有聲明受文者無需展開或參與訴訟程序，所以不及法律援助署覆函所載的陳述有力。但回覆函件確實載有聲明清楚顯示，入境事務處會根據法院的最後判決來處理居留權證明書的申請。

實質合理期望法則

87. 在認真處理各方當事人就案件這方面所提出的論據前，我等會約略述明在合理期望的背景下，特別是政府或公共機構改變了先前令人產生合理期望的政策這一情況，針對重大不公而提出司法覆核近年的發展情況，這樣對要處理的論據會有幫助。

88. 在英格蘭普通法內，“合理期望”這個理念有一段相對地短暫但不斷變化的歷史。上訴法院 Lord Denning MR 首先在 *Schmidt & another v. Secretary of State for Home Affairs* 案（〔1969〕2 Ch 149 第 170–171 頁）引入這理念。引入理念初期的目的是為了擴大可能受到行政決定影響的權利和法律權益的範圍，以便援引自然公正規則。有些情形是負責行政的決策者有責任在程序上公平對待有可能受決策影響的人士。已有一段時間，這理念給用來擴大這種情形所及的範圍。所以，倘若公共官員就將來的行為作出承諾及陳述，而令人產生合理期望，認為該等承諾及陳述會得到兑現，決策者便有責任在作出損害該等人士利益的決定前，給予該等受到聲明影響的人士表達其意見的機會。

89. 法院會否命令或准許該項實質合理期望受到保護，這問題最終自然會出現。起初，這論點極具爭議性。爭議初期，對於企圖以重大不公為理由，要求對基於政策理由在行政上否認有合理期望的決定作出覆核，英國上訴法院斷然拒絶（見 *R v. Secretary of State for Home Department & another, Ex parte Hargreaves* 案（〔1997〕1 WLR 906 第 921 頁，第 924–925 頁））。上訴法院裁定，司法覆核只限於涉及 *Wednesbury* 不合理原則的案件。

90. 然而，自此以後上訴法院在一連串的判決中決定，針對重大不公而申請司法覆核的範圍並非那麼局限，而且當官員的行為令人產生有實際利益的合理期望，但基於政府政策而作出的行政決定使期望落空時，法院便可基於範圍更廣的理由覆核該決定，其中最大的理由是重大不公及濫用權力（見 *R v. North and East Devon Health Authority, Ex parte Coughlan* 案（〔2000〕2 WLR 622）；*R v. Secretary of State for Education and Employment, Ex parte Begbie* 案（〔2000〕1 WLR 1115）；*R v. Secretary of State for the Home Department, Ex parte Bajram Zeqiri* 案；及 *R v. The London Borough of Newham and Manik Bibi and Ataya Al-Nashed* 案（〔2001〕EWCA Civ 607））。

91. 上議院的大法官沒有仔細審視實質合理期望這一法則。大法官 Lord Steyn 及大法官 Lord Hobhouse of Woodborough 在 *Secretary of State for Home Department, Ex parte Hindley* 案（〔2001〕1 AC 410 第 491 頁及第 421 頁）中，曾在發言中提述 Lord Woolf MR 在 *Coughlan* 案中所解釋的法則（大法官 Lord Hobhouse 更形容 Lord Woolf MR 的判詞為"有重大價值的"）。按我等的解讀，*Hindley* 案中言論沒有令人對法則產生疑問。我等同意，正如大律師在本案中向我等提出的論據一樣，該法則是香港行政法的一部份，而因此是法院行使其固有的司法管轄權進行監督工作的整個過程中一項重要因素。行使管轄權是要確保，第一，機構合法行使法定的權力而沒有濫用的情況；以及第二，就程序上的和實質的利益而言，法定權力的行使在行政上是公平的（見 *Coughlan* 案（第 875-876 頁））。

92. 該項法則承認，如沒有任何法律上或政策上的首要理由令致法則無法施行，則以下情形可能會產生：人們或會對實質的後果或利益有合理期望，而有關機構沒有使到期望成真，在特定的情況下，導致對個人造成不公。這種不公等同濫用權力，以致法院可合情合理地進行干預。一般來說，是在政府或公共機構或政府或公共機構的代表許下諾言，作出陳述，制定、採取或宣布其做法或政策時，結果產生合理期望的。舉例，見 *Attorney-General of Hong Kong v. Ng Yuen Shiu* 案（〔1983〕2 AC 629）及 *R v. Secretary of State for the Home Department, Ex parte Ruddock & others* 案（〔1987〕1 WLR 1482））。

93. 人們明白到，對於按法例和憲法的規定為執行政府政策而作出的決定可以進行司法覆核，但是最終政府或有關政府機構必須可自由更改政策。（見 *R v. Secretary of State for the Home Department, Ex parte Asif Mahmood Khan* 案（〔1984〕1 WLR 1337 第 1347 頁）；及 *Coughlan* 案（第 647 頁））。同樣，雖然受到法院的司法覆核規限，政府或有關機構還是有權修改或放棄其承諾的（*Coughlan* 案（第 647 頁））。但是，決策者不會因採納新政策而無需考慮合理期望。

94. 由於適用於針對重大不公而申請司法覆核的有關法律原則，隨著最近四宗案例不斷演變，所以在此提述 *Bibi* 一案。提述 *Bibi* 案是因為案中所載的，是這方面的法律發展至今的概述，亦因為申請人是基於案中所述法律觀點提出論據。第一，如決策者曾作出諾言或陳述，令人對決策者會遵守諾言或陳述產生合理期望，法律規定，只要是在決策者的法定權力或其他權力範圍以內，決策者便須在作出決定的過程中，恰當地考慮該合理期望。要強調的是，在本案中這限制的適用至為重要。這點將會在稍後顯現出來。要是決策者不考慮該期望，他就是濫用權力或不合法地行事（*Bibi* 案（第 39 段及第 51 段））。

95. 第二，除非有法律上承認的理由不去體現合理期望，否則合理期望應予體現。要是公共官員的行為引致產生合理期望，那麼為公平起見，決策者應該明示不體現合理期望的原因，以便當決策者的決定遭到質疑時，法院可以驗證該等原因（*Bibi* 案（第 59 段））。

96. 第三，即使決定牽涉以政治考慮來作出政治抉擇，決策者也必須以訴訟當事人的合理期望為本作出抉擇（*Bibi* 案（第 64 段））。

97. 第四，如若決策者不遵從上文第三項所述的規定，他的決定將會因為他沒有作出有關考慮而變得無效。不考慮合理期望構成濫用權力。濫用權力一經確立，法院便可要求決策者行使酌情決定權考慮該合理期望（*Bibi* 案（第 41 段））。

98. 我等會在上文第四項法律論點加上"通常"一詞作為限定性的說明。這樣做的原因，是因為法院只有在行政決定因決策者沒有作出有關考慮而受到極大影響的情況下，才會行使司法管轄權覆核該決定。（見 *Lau Kong Yung* 案第 331 頁 C-D，引用 *R v. Hull University Visitor, Ex parte Page* 案（〔1993〕AC 682 第 702 頁 B-C）；*Nguyen Tuan Cuong & others v. The Director of Immigration & others* 案（〔1997〕1 WLR 68 第 77 頁 B）；及 *R v. Cambridge Health Authority, Ex parte B* 案（〔1995〕1 WLR 898 第 907 頁 B-C））。法院只有在極不尋常的案件裏才會信納該決定並不因為決策者沒有作出有關考慮而受到影響（見 *Grandsen & Co. Ltd. & another v. Secretary of State for the Environment & another* 案（（1985）54 P & CR 86 第 94 頁））。法院一旦信納即使決策者曾作出有關考慮後果也是一樣，就不會撤銷該決定。入境事務處處長非常倚賴這法律觀點。引用這觀點又會引起另一重要的爭議點，這留待稍後討論。

99. 在 *Bibi* 案中，房屋當局許諾各申請人及其他人，在 18 個月內為其提供法律上有保證的房屋住所。案中英國上訴法院裁定房屋當局沒有考慮到當局的諾言令致申請人產生合理期望，故房屋當局是非法行事。法院繼而宣告房屋當局有責任基於申請人有合理期望的原故，考慮申請人要求合適房屋的申請。該期望就是房屋當局會向他們提供保證租賃的合適住所。法院以這形式作出宣告，從而避免自作主張，並將實際的決定權交回房屋當局手上。藉此，法院符合了三權分立的法則及立法意圖，把作出決定的權力留給獲有關法例賦權的機構。

申請人有關實質合理期望的論據

100. 申請人陳詞指出，在已發出遣送離境令的個案中，入境事務處處長根據法律有責任考慮申請人的合理期望，但在發出遣送離境令時沒有按法律這樣做，因此，該等命令應予以撤銷。陳詞續謂法院應行使有關酌情決定權，或者是，法院應該讓入境事務處處長根據法律行使酌情決定權。代表申請人的御用大律師 Robertson 先生同意，假若申請人成功確立其要求濟助的理據，則入境事務處處長行使酌情決定權便是恰當的做法。

有鑑於該等陳述，期望的合理性之考慮

101. 申請人根據上文所述原則確立其要求濟助的理據前，必須首先確立在他們而言，的確存在有合理期望。雖然"合理期望"這一理念有點不精確，但期望必須是合理的：就是，鑑於官員所作的被指稱令人產生期望的行為，該期望是合理的。這點早已獲得明確確立（見大法官 Lord Fraser of Tullybelton 在 *Attorney-General of Hong Kong v. Ng Yuen Shiu* 案（〔1983〕2 AC 629 第 636 頁）所言）。在這方面，期望是否合理至少部份取決於有關公共機構的行為及機構所承擔的事情。而期望是否合理及合理的程度，亦必須取決於申請人*有權*期望甚麼。須要合理的意思是，司法決定"除了必須建基於申請人*事實上*期望的事情外，在顧及有關政策和原則的情況下，也必須建基於申請人*有權*期望的事情"。（Mark Elliot 在 The Cambridge Journal 301 所載的文章"The Human Rights Act 1998 and The Standard of Substantive Review"〔2001〕內，特別是第 319 頁中，提供了啟發性的討論）。因此，要是期望中的利益不是法律上所能授予的，該期望便不是合理期望。正如上文所述，這是本案的關鍵問題。

102. 在*吳嘉玲*案及*陳錦雅*案兩宗訴訟中以"例案"性質為背景而作出的陳述，構成申請人在本上訴案中所倚賴的行為。該等陳述並不須要是明示的。隱含陳述在適當情況下也會產生合理期望（見 *R v. Gaming Board of Great Britain, Ex parte Kingsley* 案（〔1996〕COD 241 第 242 頁））。

103. 然而，入境事務處處長在陳詞中指出，在合理期望能夠被確立前，陳述必須是既清晰又不模棱兩可的。各下級法院均接納這項陳詞，亦有大量案例典據支持這說法（見 *R v. Inland Revenue Commissioners, Ex parte MFK Underwriting Agents Ltd. & others* 案（〔1990〕1 WLR 1545 第 1569–1570 頁）；*R v. Jockey Club, Ex parte RAM Racecourses Ltd.* 案（〔1993〕2 All ER 225 第 236 頁）；*R v. Devon County Council, Ex parte Baker & another* 案（〔1995〕1 All ER 73 第 88 頁）（*Coughlan*（第 651 頁）援引是案，並且明顯表示贊同）；*R v. Commissioners of Inland Revenue, Ex parte Unilever plc* 案（〔1996〕COD 421 第 423 頁）（案中"沒有限制而又並不模棱兩可的陳述之規定"被形容為"基要的"）；及 *The Hong Kong and China Gas Co. v. The Director of Lands* 案（〔1997〕HKLRD 1291 第 1296–1297 頁）等案）。申請人的陳詞謂，如陳述有模棱兩可之處就必須用最有利於申請人的方式來解釋該項陳述。有鑑於上述案例的主流，我等必須拒絕接納申請人的陳詞。

104. 雖然概括而言，賴以支持合理期望的陳述必定是既清晰又不模棱兩可的，但我等接納這說法之餘也承認在某些案件裏，陳述是可以合理地有相互排斥的解釋。這樣，正確的處理方法不但不是只採納對提出合理期望的人士最有利的解釋，而且是在不違反引用 *Wednesbury* 不合理的測試原則的前題（提）下，接納公共機構所採用的解釋。大法官 *Lord Slynn of Hadley* 在 *R v. Ministry of Defence, Ex parte Walker* 一案（〔2000〕1 WLR 806），在提述政府補償計劃中的"軍事活動"一詞時說（第 813 頁）：

> "假若本席的看法是這詞彙的涵義含糊不清以致可以有不同意思，本席就不會認為部長的解釋是'異常至不能被歸於合理性的一類'（見大法官 Lord Mustill 在 *Reg v. Monopolies and Mergers Commission, Ex parte South Yorkshire Transport Ltd* 案（〔1993〕1 WLR 23 第 32 頁 H）中所言）。"

如案中陳述關乎政府政策，法院便應採取這處理方法。一般來說，政府從合乎理性的角度按其有關政策的聲明行事就不會產生不公。許多時候，有關政策的聲明是以廣義的措詞表達出來，詳情細節則留待日後釐定。要是說因為該等聲明的表達方式過於廣泛及不精確，所以它便永遠不會產生合理期望，這種說法就未免太狹隘。可是，要是寬廣的政策之詳情後來獲得辨明或確定，而且詳情反映了之前所宣布的寬廣政策是合乎理性的發展，則法院也應照顧到這點。

105. 我等已解釋過，本案中的陳述劃歸為三大類。第一類是入境事務處處長及行政長官向普羅大眾發表的四項一般聲明（見第 83 段），即政府會服從法院的決定。該項陳述的涵義是，政府將接受及執行香港特區法院最終就有關法律作出的宣告。換句話說，陳述等同政府作出既清晰又不模棱兩可的聲明，會把歸於這類別的人士當作訴訟當事人一樣看待。人大常委員會有可能會根據第一百五十八條第一款作出解釋，而解釋結果令致香港特區法院的決定受到影響。對於這點，陳述沒有作任何保留或限制。陳述從來沒有注意到這可能性。下級法院眾位法官得出的結論是，陳述的涵義並不包含政府會把歸於有關類別的人士當作訴訟當事人一樣看待。恕我等對此不表同意。

106. 第二類是載於致法律援助申請人的法律援助署覆函內的陳述。法律援助署在函中不單聲明政府將接受及執行香港特區法院最終就有關法律作出的宣告，更述明申請人不必參與當時的訴訟程序或展開新的訴訟程序。這項有關政府未來的行為的陳述對申請人起了引導作用，使他們不去採取被稱為不必採取的行動。法律援助署欲藉著該覆函引導覆函受文人不採取行動，而該行動是會將他們置於"在此以前作出的判決"的保障範圍之內的。這陳述也是既清晰又不模棱兩可的。因為陳述以明示方式邀請受文人倚賴政府所宣布的政策而不提出訴訟程序，所以它較第一項陳述更強而有力。

107. 保安局局長致第 13 名代表申請人日期為 1998 年 4 月 24 日的信函屬於一個不同類別。一方面是入境事務處處長及行政長官所作的一般陳述，另一方面是法律援助署覆函，而上述類別處於兩者之間。毫無疑問，1998 年 4 月 24 日的信函比較一般陳述有力，因為它是具名的，並且述明會如何處理該名聲稱有居留權的申請人的申請。可是，信函沒載有關於參與或展開訴訟程序的聲明，所以不及法律援助署覆函有力。一般陳述與具體陳述之間的區分極為重要，原因在下文會顯露出來。

108. 雖然我等剛解釋過，期望的強烈程度因應某類令人產生期望的陳述而有所不同，但全部三類陳述所產生的期望並無不同，即期望政府會把屬於這些類別的人士當作*吳嘉玲*案及*陳錦雅*案的訴訟當事人一樣看待。因第二及第三類陳述所產生的期望而有權受惠的這一類別人士，比較因一般陳述而有權受惠的另一類別人士，數目少了許多。這分別對本上訴案的結果很重要。這點會在下文顯現出來。

109. 就有權因期望而受惠的人士而言，主張有合理期望者是否必須證明其倚賴該期望或遭受損害才可以因陳述而受惠？有主張謂倘若政府已公布周知打算如何行使權力，而權力的行使影響著社會上相當大部份的人士，則不論申請人是否曾特地倚賴政府的說話，政府也不能食言（見大法官 Lord Justice Sedley 在 *Begbie* 案中（第 1133 頁）所述"影響普羅大眾"的權力；另見 *Bibi* 案（第 28–32 頁））。也有主張說倚賴政府的說話"雖然大多數時候都可能有關，但不是必要的"（見 *Bibi* 案（第 28 段））。另一方面，有意見認為"要是法院裁斷合理期望落空時存有不公，那麼只會在十分例外的情況下（而不是在一般情況下）當事人才是沒有因倚賴所說的話而遭受損害"（見大法官 Peter Gibson 在 *Begbie* 案（第 1124 頁）中所言）。

110. 合理期望是否必須建基於因倚賴所說的話而遭受損害，尤其是該基礎關乎大批不明類別及受一般陳述針對的人士？我等認為無需探討這重要的問題。因為在本案中所作出的陳述是用來引導某些受陳述者去倚賴該些陳述，而且我等可以假設這些陳述無論如何都達致了該效果，所以是否須要證明曾倚賴該些陳述，並不成為本案中的爭議點。

111. 入境事務處處長提出論據指出，因一般及具體陳述而產生的期望都因為違反法律而變得不合理。除受到這考慮的限制外，在上文所描述的期望是合理的。作出陳述的背景是*吳嘉玲*案及*陳錦雅*案兩宗訴訟的"例案"性質。這些陳述既清晰又不模棱兩可，而且直接令人產生期望。此外，具體陳述是在用以引導受陳述者倚賴該些陳述的情況下作出的。

根據入境事務處處長指稱體現期望會違反法律的論據，考慮期望的合理性

112. 入境事務處處長陳詞指出，申請人的期望並不合理。他亦指出他不能切實體現該期望，因為這樣做會違反法律。如體現期望會牽涉到決策者違法行事，法院便不會令合理期望獲得體現，這是基本原則（見 *Attorney-General of Hong Kong v. Ng Yuen Shiu* 案（第 638 頁）；*Coughlan* 案（第 647，651 及 656 頁）；*Begbie* 案（第 1125 及 1132 頁））。與這原則一致的是，決策者不能夠為體現期望而行使法定酌情決定權"以致破壞立法的目的"（見大法官 Sedley 在 *Begbie* 案，（第 1132 頁）所言）。

113. 申請人不可能在本院就*吳嘉玲*案及*陳錦雅*案作出決定之後，立即確立其聲稱所擁有的居留權，原因是本院在*吳嘉玲*案中剔除根據《第 3 號條例》第 2AB（2）（a）條在憲報公告的甲（i）款及乙款。該公告指明申請居留權證明書的方法。甲（i）款述明在申請時居住在內地的人士必須"通過當地的公安廳出入境管理處"提出申請。乙款述明當有關人士根據內地實施的法律向當地的公安廳出入境管理處所遞交的到香港定居的'前往港澳通行證'申請書，可視為香港居留權證明書的申請書。在*吳嘉玲*案中，本院提到將公告內的兩款剔除（（1999）2 HKCFAR 第 38 頁）時表示：

> "這令到公告內就有關內地居民應向誰申請居權證這方面缺乏交代。入境處處長必須以公告形式，具體說明新的安排。"

114. 在*劉港榕*案中，終審法院首席法官李國能以下述方式形容當時的情況（（1999）2 HKCFAR 第 314 頁）：

> "為方便起見，該項經本院在判決中宣告即使《第 3 號條例》及公告中的有關條文無效後仍然存在的計劃，本席將稱之為'經修正的計劃'。
>
> 本院作出判決後，對居於內地的聲稱人而言，'經修正的計劃'是不可行的，因為本院已宣告公告內的甲（i）款及乙款無效，故此居權證計劃便出現「罅隙」。入境處處長需要時間作出新安排以填補這個「罅隙」。這便需要與內地機關進行磋商。本案原審法官裁定這項任務既複雜又艱巨，必須給予政府一段合理時間，而該段期限尚未屆滿。在上訴時這方面的裁決並沒有受到質疑，上訴法庭亦同意這點。
>
> 本案在本院及下級法院聆訊時，雙方及各級法院都同意在這段期間入境處處長不可能處理居於內地的聲稱人的居權證申請。"

115. 因此，在人大常委會於 1999 年 6 月 26 日公布**該解釋**前，因為入境處處長尚未填補計劃內的「罅隙」，所以入境事務處不可能根據經修正的計劃體現申請人的期望。但由於入境處處長有權根據《第 3 號條例》第 2AB（2）（a）條以公告形式填補該「罅隙」，故在該階段體現申請人的期望並不違反法律。

116. 然而，入境處處長陳詞說，**該解釋**一經公布後，情況便起了變化。情況的改變就是，在吳嘉玲案中被法院宣告違反憲法的《第 3 號條例》條文及公告（第 1（2）條具追溯力的條文除外），被視為由 1997 年 7 月 1 日起生效。同樣地，本院必須接納，由本院在吳嘉玲案中裁定為無效的《第 2 號條例》中有關出生時間的限制，也同樣生效。該解釋公布以後，入境處處長便無權發出居留權證明書予沒有單程證的申請人。

117. 在**該解釋**公布後，立法會於 1999 年 7 月 16 日根據《入境條例》第 59A 條通過決議，對附表 1 作出修訂。該修訂廢除第 2（c）段而代之以下述條文：

> "（c）中國公民在香港特別行政區成立以前或以後在香港以外所生的中國籍子女，而在該子女出生時，該中國公民是符合（a）或（b）項規定的人。"

新條文載有曾被視為無效的條文上所載的出生時間限制。同日，入境事務處處長根據第 2AB（2）（a）條在憲報刊登新公告取代先前的公告。新公告的內容與先前的相若。

118. 因應**該解釋**而作出的這些轉變，加強了條例中有關居留權證明書的條文。根據這些條文，入境事務處處長不得核實申請人居留權的享有權，亦不能給予他們如吳嘉玲案及陳錦雅案的訴訟人一樣的看待。

119. 入境事務處處長辯稱，申請人不能有合理的期望以為他們會得到如該兩案當事人一樣的看待，是因為**該解釋**及居留權證明書計劃的生效日期分別追溯至 1997 年 7 月 1 日及 7 月 10 日。因此，根據入境事務處處長的論據，申請人的期望與現時有效的法律不符或與該法律有抵觸之處。另一種說法基本上論據相同，就是不可能有合理期望，以為有關法律不會改變。（參看案例 *R v. Secretary of State for Social Security, Ex parte McEntire* 案，大法官 Popplewell，判決於 1992 年 3 月 23 日頒下，未經彙編。）

120. 由於事件發生在 1999 年 6 月 26 日該解釋公布之前，因此，在涉及一般陳述的事上，除了在是否有須要證明倚賴陳述會蒙受損害這點上有保留外，申請人是有期望的，這期望相當於合理期望，入境事務處處長是可以根據《入境條例》第 2AB（2）（a）條訂明公告，使他們的期望在法律上得以體現。該期望是當局會按本院在吳嘉玲案及陳錦雅案判決中所訂立的原則給予申請人相應的看待。但我等關注的是 1999 年 6 月 26 日以後有效的法律，就是入境事務處處長行使其權力時的法律。他的做法就是申請人不滿之處。

121. 在研究 1999 年 6 月 26 日之後的法律前，必須更精密地確定申請人的期望包含甚麼。正如大法官 Lord Scarman 在 *In re Findlay* 案中（〔1985〕1 AC 318 第 338 頁）提出一個極具意義的問題，"他們的合理期望是甚麼？"（在原文中強調）。申請人依據本院在該兩案決定中所述的原則，聲稱：

（1）他們無須先取得內地機關簽發單程證便可根據《基本法》第二十四條第二款第（三）項的規定確立居留權 —*吳嘉玲*案；以及

（2）即使他們在出生時，父母任何一方還未在香港特區取得永久性居民身份，他們也會被視為符合《基本法》第二十四條第二款第（三）項的資格 —*陳錦雅*案。

我等認為，這樣的聲稱能準確地表述申請人的期望。

122. 申請人的期望一經如此表述後 — 事實上也必須如此表述，若要符合兩案決定中所述的原則，便顯然與現時有效的法律及**該解釋**公布以來有效的法律不符。申請人的期望若表述如上，在法律上他們的期望便不能得到體現。

根據《入境條例》第 11 條、第 13 條及第 19（1）條賦予入境事務處處長法定酌情決定權的範圍

123. 這結論沒有解決申請人的案件。申請人進一步呈述，雖然入境事務處處長不能充分體現他們所聲稱的合理期望，但他可以在某種情（程）度上滿足他們的期望，容許他們進入香港及在港居留。他們的論據認為處長可以如此而行，他可以根據《入境條例》若干條文所賦予他的權力行使其酌情決定權 — 即第 11 條（入境准許）、第 13 條（留下准許）及第 19（1）條（下令或拒絕下令遣送離境的權力）。按這理據，處長可恰當地作出對申請人有利的酌情決定，容許申請人進入香港及在港居住，這樣既可有限度地滿足申請人的期望，就是進入香港及在港居住，同時又沒有與法律相違。

124. 申請人亦依據《人事登記條例》（第 177 章）及有關的規例作出爭辯。他們辯稱，根據該條例及有關規例，獲准無條件限制進入香港及在港居住的申請人可獲發給永久性居民身份證，從而根據《入境條例》第 2AA 條確立其永久性居民身份。這論據在於入境事務處處長須行使《入境條例》，特別是第 11 條、第 13 條及第 19（1）條所賦予的酌情決定權，對申請人作出有利的決定。

125. 第 11 條授權入境事務處給予准許進入香港，並視乎情況附加逗留期限及逗留條件予以規限。第 11（5）及（5A）條賦予入境事務處權力撤銷及更改逗留條件，以及更改逗留期限。更改逗留期限的權力，是在逗留期限屆滿後，方可行使的。（參看案例 *Sae-Ang Paisarn v. Director of Immigration*（〔1989〕1 HKLR 205））。第 13 條賦權入境事務處處長批准非法進入香港的人士留在香港，並附加他認為適當的逗留條件予以規限。第 19（1）（b）條規定，在不同的情況下，"規定某人離開香港的遣送離境令可由〔入境事務處處長〕發出"。其中一種情況是"如入境事務處處長覺得"該人：

> "（ii）已非法〔進入〕香港，或正違反或已違反向他施加的逗留條件。"

126. 申請人呈述，他們原來的期望就是得到如*吳嘉玲*案及*陳錦雅*案訴訟當事人一樣的看待，而該三條條文所賦予的酌情決定權範圍廣泛，足可容許入境事務處處長考慮令申請人產生原來期望的各種情況，並讓處長可以合法地體現隨著他們原來期望而會產生的附帶後果。然而，代表入境事務處處長的資深大律師馬道立先生呈述，無論個別的酌情決定權的範圍如何，也不會擴展至批准已由內地來港聲稱擁有居留權，但在法律上不能享有該權利的人士留港。從另一方面來看這論據，就是沒有"不去引用第 1B 部"的酌情決定權。資深大律師馬道立先生亦辯稱，無論個別的酌情決定權的範圍如何，入境事務處處長也有酌情決定權去決定他應考慮甚麼，他沒有可強制性職責去考慮令申請人產生期望的各種情況。

127. 雙方並非建議第 19（1）條的"可"字不是解作"許可"，而是有其他意思，但入境事務處處長的論據是這酌情決定權的範圍，如第 11 條及第 13 條所賦予的酌情決定權一樣，是受到第 1B 部關於附表 1 第 2（c）段所指的永久性居民的條文所限制。根據這論據，第 1B 部的條文構成一全面性的準則，規限那些聲稱根據附表 1 第 2（c）段為永久性居民的人士進入香港及在港居住的權利。因此，入境事務處處長的理據是：他必須行使有關的酌情決定權，包括行使下令遣送離境的權力，使第 1B 部的立法計劃得以體現。

128. 這論據過於側重第 1B 部的立法計劃。這計劃規限那些聲稱根據附表 1 第 2（c）段擁有永久性居民身份，從而根據第 1A 部享有居留權的人士所聲稱享有的權利。但第 1B 部的計劃本意並不是規限或專意規限該等人士以非永久性居民身份在港逗留。該等權利在於入境事務處處長是否行使其法定的權力。故此，大律師也得代入境事務處處長承認，對不能成功地根據附表 1 第 2（c）段取得永久性居民身份的聲稱人，入境事務處處長是可以合法地以人道為理由，拒絕下令遣送他離境。（參看案例*劉港榕*；*R v. The Director of Immigration, Ex parte Chan Heung-mui & others*（（1993）3 HKPLR 533 第 543 頁 et seq））。在劉港榕案中，本院裁定，即使申請人符合第 19（1）（b）（ii）條的條件，入境事務處處長雖然不一定須要考慮人道理由，但也可根據第 19（1）條的規定有酌情決定權不發遣送離境令。

129. 入境事務處處長辯稱，類似的原則也可應用在任何其他可能使他行使其酌情決定權，作出對申請人有利的決定的考慮因素上。換句話說，要是他選擇如此而行，所有這些因素，如人道理由一樣，都是他可以考慮的，但他不一定要考慮這些因素。這個論據不能成立，因為若某些情況帶來合理期望，普通法本身便對決策制定者委以責任，要以良好的行政運作為原則及以公平行事為己任去考慮該等合理期望，只要作出考慮這做法和考慮的範圍不抵觸法定條文及不破壞立法的目的便可（參看 *Bibi* 案，第 51 段）。

130. 雖然該等酌情決定權並沒有明文條件約束，但其範圍必須加以確定。要確定其範圍，須參照常委會所解釋的《基本法》，該條例的目的及其政策，以及第 19（1）條條文的主要精神，就是要落實該條例所訂定的立法計劃。從這方面去考慮第 11 條、第 13 條及第 19（1）條所賦予的酌情決定權，入境事務處處長是可以在特殊的情況下容許個別人士留港，儘管該等人士非法入境及未能根據《基本法》第二十四條按照《入境條例》的規定確立居留權。然而，當行使該三項酌情決定權時，入境事務處處長不可破壞用以界定及限制居留權享有權的憲法及法定計劃，以及違背第 19（1）條的主要精神，這點是清晰明確的。

131. 在考慮酌情決定權的範圍時，我等的做法與英國上訴法院在 *Begbie* 案中的做法一致。英國工黨在大選中獲勝重新執政後，工黨政府便制定《1997 年教育（學校）法令》，廢除一直以來用公帑去資助私立學校個別學生的教育經費制度。這改變與工黨的選舉政綱及工黨政府所公布的教育政策一致。然而，政府亦曾向受惠於該計劃的學生家長聲明，政府會採取步驟以免學生的教育受到影響。為此，法令訂明，教育資助會繼續，直至學生完成目前的教育階段為止。舉例說，當學生由小學升讀中學後，便不會受到資助。不過，這規限卻有例外情況，法例賦予負責有關事務的大臣有酌情決定權，在個別情況下向完成目前教育階段升讀下一教育階段的學生繼續給予教育資助。

132. 該案的申請人申請司法覆核，他們的論據是有關的政策聲明給他們帶來合理期望，讓他們以為當他們完成目前教育階段升讀下一教育階段時仍然會得到教育資助。他們辯稱，這種做法與法令沒有抵觸，負責有關事務的大臣可行使他的酌情決定權使他們的期望得以實現。該項申請遭法院駁回。法院重申是項原則：任何合理期望若與法定的條文有抵觸時必須放棄。法院裁定，在行使酌情決定權決定例外情況時，不可偏離法規的主要目的及作用。

133. 英國上訴法院大法官 Peter Gibson 稱

> "…… 爭論一定是由 1997 年法令開始。任何期望必須受制於法規條款，而負責有關事務的大臣須要根據法規行事，這是理據的共同基礎。第 2（1）條規限學校提供資助學位的能力至第（2）款所規定的情況。第（2）款規定持有資助學位正接受小學教育的學生，當完成小學教育最後一年的課程後，便得停止持有該資助學位，除非負責有關事務的大臣根據第（b）段行使酌情決定權則作別論。該段條文明顯地是要照顧一些特殊情況，當考慮過某個別學生的特殊情況認為合理的話，負責有關事務的大臣會以特殊個案處理。如 Havers 先生呈述，若 Teed 女士所收到的信件當中的承諾能得以實踐，所有在"一條龍"學校中就讀的學生也會因此而獲准保留其資助學位，直至完成其中學教育為止。負責有關事務的大臣必須秉公行事，若准許學生 Heather 保留其資助學位，所有其他有同樣情況的學生也必須得到相同的對待。要強使負責有關事務的大臣向所有如 Heather 情況一樣的學生實踐 Teed 信中的承諾，很明顯不是該條文所能預料的，亦有違第 2（2）（b）條的原意。"（第 1125 頁）

大法官 Laws 述稱

> "本席同意本上訴案須予駁回，簡潔直截（接）的理由是若 Beloff 先生的論據成立，我等便得要求負責有關事務的大臣作出與《1997 年教育（學校）法令》第 2 條背道而馳的行為。"（第 1129 頁）

大法官 Sedley 稱

> "…… 行使酌情決定權時，不得破壞立法的目的。在本案而言，不可單是為了有效地提供資助學位給所有那些不能由法規保留資助學位的學生而行使該酌情決定權，因為此舉顯然是蔑視國會的用意。本席同意大法官 Peter Gibson 及大法官 Laws 的論述，本案的決定是基於此原則而作出的。"（第 1132 頁）

入境事務處處長的法定權力應用在本案事實上

134. 行使有關的法定權力時，不可破壞整體的法定計劃，這結論一經作出後，入境事務處處長便不能合法地容許該四項一般陳述的受陳述者（人數可能超過 600,000 名）（見第 83 段）進入香港及在港居留，因為此舉是要行使第 11 條、第 13 條及第 19（1）條所賦予的特殊權力，這會對整個立法計劃造成破壞。入境事務處處長在行使其權力時，須要公正不阿；在處理一般陳述的受陳述者即居留權聲稱人時，必須公平對待。在這大羣不明類別的人士當中，他不能憑藉甚麼去恰當地分別誰應得到有利的對待。原來聲稱的期望在法律上現已不能得到體現，它是行使酌情決定權時的主要考慮因素，這個期望是一般類別所有人士的共同期望。

135. 結果是入境事務處處長不能合法地行使他的酌情決定權，對一般類別的聲稱人作出有利的決定。

136. 無論如何，即使根據相反的結論，如入境事務處處長可合法地行使其酌情決定權對這類聲稱人作出有利的決定，他也有權去決定入境政策凌駕於這類聲稱人的期望之上。他們的期望只是因政府或官員代表政府作出的一般陳述而起，而入境政策是**該解釋**所認可之法例的基礎，其法律效力自不可推翻。

137. 那些以個別人士身份收到法律援助署覆函的申請人，以及收到保安局局長信件的第 13 名代表申請人，他們以收到具體陳述為理由，堅稱他們有合理的期望。這些申請人的情況不同。由於他們曾收到政府當局發給他們的信件，信內載有所指的陳述，因此，他們可被界定為可區別及可確定的類別。入境事務處處長行使有關的酌情決定權，作出對他們有利的決定，不會破壞整體的法定政策。雖然，有相當數目的人或許會因此而受惠，但相對於有關的聲稱人或準聲稱人而言，他們只佔小部份。他們會構成一明確類別，或可得到特殊的酌情決定權對待。

138. 這一類收到具體陳述的申請人是否可以獲得特殊對待？我等認為答案應該是肯定的。雖然這類申請人原來的合理期望再也不能得到體現，但這期望包括隨着取得居留權後而產生的附帶後果，就是可進入香港及在港居住，入境事務處處長可根據第 11 條、第 13 條及第 19（1）條行使其酌情決定權，作出對這類申請人有利的決定，使他們的合理期望部份得以體現，這種做法是在入境事務處處長的權力範圍之內。從這方面來考慮，他們的期望也沒有抵觸法律。把這類收到具體陳述的人士的合理期望規限如上，入境事務處處長便得根據第 11 條、第 13 條及第 19（1）條，在行使其酌情決定權時，對上述規限了的合理期望加以考慮。這類申請人的原來合理期望因不能落實而引起重大不公，處長可行使其權力，作出對這類申請人有利的決定，稍為減輕他們的不公平情況。

139. 這論點有英國案例 *Coughlan* 支持。在該案件中，政府曾承諾會為有關人士在馬頓健康院（Mardon House）提供終生住宿。案中的其中一項申訴，是當政府改變政策後，有關部長未能為有關人士另外提供可以說是相當於馬頓健康院的地方住宿（參看第 657 頁 C-D）。上訴法院裁定，沒有作出有關安排造成不公情況，相當於衛生部門濫用權力。未能提供另外住宿關乎有關部長是否作出公平的決定。

遣送離境令的法律效力及不撤銷遣送離境令的決定

140. 按照較早前所述，在作出行政決定時，未有顧及該決定會違反以前的承諾或陳述而作出該決定，以及作出行政決定時違反了以前的承諾或陳述，而該承諾或陳述給人合理的期望，以為該承諾或陳述會得到實現，則該行政決定足以構成濫用權力，不能生效（*Bibi* 案，第 39 段），除非能證明即使考慮過該期望，實質上也不會影響該決定，則作別論。入境事務處處長辯稱本案正是如此，因為各方面的政策考慮都支持遣送離境，其理據是不容推翻的。

141. 入境事務處處長有責任去證明，就算他考慮了該合理期望，同樣後果也會如以上所述，無可避免。法庭只會在特殊的情況下才採用此途徑，因為原則上，應該是由受法規託付責任的官員去作出決定，此舉與三權分立的法則相符，而三權分立是香港奉行的普通法體制的主要元素。在本案而言，這已是一個充分的理由去支持為何不依循入境事務處處長所建議的特殊做法。不單如此，我等的結論是：偏離申請人基於具體陳述而產生的期望會造成非常重大的不公平情況（具體陳述載於法律援助署覆函及第 13 名代表申請人收到保安局局長的信件內）。如我等曾經論述，前者明文勸喻受文人無須採取同一的訴訟行動，若他們採取了該行動，便會被列入為"在此以前作出的判決"的保護範圍內。後者則述明入境事務處處長會依循法院的最後判決處理居留權證明書的申請。容許這些具體陳述的受陳述者在港居留看來不會對政策造成重大影響，而且會大大減輕發生在他們身上的不公平情況。在上述種種情況下，我等沒有理據去裁定，假使入境事務處處長曾經考慮過申請人因具體陳述而產生期望，其決定也必然會是一樣。

142. 屬於具體陳述類別的申請人，他們的遣送離境令須予以撤銷，入境事務處處長須重新行使其酌情決定權。在重新行使其酌情決定權時，他須就這類人士的合理期望，考慮是否須要行使其酌情決定權惠及他們，容許他們在港居留。為此，屬"具體陳述"類別的申請人，他們的遣送離境令須予以撤銷，並可得到法庭作出宣告：入境事務處處長須就本判決及就《入境條例》第 11 條、第 13 條及第 19（1）條所賦予的酌情決定權，考慮這類別的申請人的情況。政府向他們作出的陳述，使他們產生合理期望，但又未有依陳述行事，因此有特別需要去紓緩對他們造成不公平的情況。

143. 要注意的是，若入境事務處處長在重新考慮這類人士的某個個案時，決定行使他的酌情決定權，並對該申請人作出有利的決定及容許他在港居留，這只是對原來的合理期望未能體現造成不公的部份濟助。准許他在港居留顯然不等於視他如吳嘉玲案及陳錦雅案的當事人一樣處理他的居留權申請。此舉非入境事務處處長所能做到的。相反，這只是入境事務處處長在法律許可而又不破壞基本的法定計劃的情況下，對合理期望落空造成不公的紓緩方法。

144. 因此而獲准在港逗留的居留權聲稱人，他們最終可能根據別的條文聲稱享有居留權，例如，當他們在香港特區通常居住連續七年後，便可根據《基本法》第二十四條第二款第（二）項作出是項聲稱。然而，這是根據不同的法律程序取得居留權，不是我等在本案中所要考慮的。

個別情況的合理期望

145. 因應我等在以上所述，我等現考慮交由法院審理的個別情況。

146. *第 8 名代表申請人—— 劉邦先生——* 他聲稱是保安局局長發給覆函日期為 1998 年 7 月 10 日的受文人。該覆函是回應一家庭關注組織的請願書。由於該申請人屬於一般陳述類別，因此不能享有濟助。

147. *第 11 名代表申請人—— 陳其悅先生——* 他是超過 1,000 名申請人的代表。這些人收到法律援助署覆函通知他們，鑑於法院待決的案件，他們不必展開任何訴訟。這些回覆構成具體陳述，使他們產生合理期望，以為他們會得到如*吳嘉玲*案及*陳錦雅*案的訴訟當事人一樣的看待。就這類別的申請人，他們的遣送離境令應予以撤銷，而入境事務處處長須就本判決及《入境條例》第 11 條、第 13 條及第 19（1）條所賦予的酌情決定權，重新考慮他們的情況。

148. *第 12 名代表申請人—— 黃玉香女士——* 她所代表的申請人，是依據入境事務處的標準信件中的具體陳述而聲稱有合理期望（參看第 66 段）。這些信件告訴他們，由於案件正待上訴，因此不能作出任何決定。這些信件沒有帶來任何合理期望，因此她不能享有濟助。

149. *第 13 名代表申請人—— 袁智威先生 ——* 他代表的申請人聲稱因入境事務處的信件而產生合理期望。這些信件的內容與入境事務處標準信件的內容相若（參看第 66 段），表示案件正待上訴，因此不能作出任何決定。這些信件沒有給予任何合理期望。由於他是這類信件的受文人，因此不能享有濟助。然而，他亦是保安局局長發給信件日期為 1998 年 4 月 24 日的受文人。保安局局長在該信中表示，入境事務處在處理居留權證明書的申請上會依循法院的判決。這是具體的陳述，帶給他合理期望，使他有權享有如第 11 名代表申請人一樣的濟助。

150. *第 15 名代表申請人—— 葉蔭華女士——* 她所代表的申請人是依據政府官員所作的一般陳述，聲稱該陳述給他們合理期望。由於她屬一般陳述類別，因此不能享有濟助。

151. *終院民事上訴 2001 年第 3 號案中的第 3 名代表申請人—— 周燕平女士——* 她所代表的申請人，是依據政府官員所作的一般陳述。她表示，當她在內地時，她獲詳盡告知該陳述。由於她屬一般陳述類別，因此不能享有濟助。

"濫用程序"的爭議

152. 申請人在其書面陳詞時以濫用權力為其依據的理由。代表申請人的御用大律師 Robertson 先生在口頭辯稱時，把這理由推展成為濫用程序的論據。這論據在下級法院沒有加以論述。這項新的呈述基礎毫不清晰。按我等理解，這論據的說法如下。

153. 入境事務處處長拒絕遵照例案程序，該程序已在原訟法庭得到祁彥輝法官的認同及採納，在上訴法庭及在本院審理*吳嘉玲*案及*陳錦雅*案時亦被接納，因此，處長的做法相當於濫用程序。例案程序涉及選取一些案件作為"代表案件"，並把其他案件押後以等候代表案件的結果。

154. 申請人呈述，要不是入境事務處處長的陳述，表示會依從被選取作為代表案件的審訊結果，法庭也不會採用例案程序。申請人繼而呈述，入境事務處處長命令把那些應得到如例案訴訟人一樣的看待的人遣送離境，這決定是與原訟法庭法官祁彥輝所採用的例案程序及把其他案件押後的做法不符。因此，他們的論據認為此舉相當於濫用程序，應予以補救，使入境事務處處長遵守其陳述或制止入境事務處處長執行針對申請人的遣送離境令。要入境事務處處長遵守其陳述這補救方法出現困難，此點在合理期望的爭議上已加以論述。

155. 濫用程序的典型例子是展開或進行民事或刑事訴訟程序以達到不當的目的，如在合法的訴訟目的及範圍以外取得附帶利益。（案例 *Hunter v. Chief Constable of the West Midlands Police & others*（〔1982〕AC 529），這宗民事訴訟被剔除，是因為展開訴訟是用以對具司法管轄權的刑事法庭的決定作出附帶攻擊。）

156. 一般的補救方法是擱置訴訟程序，理由是有關的訴訟已構成濫用法庭程序。然而，濫用程序可以不同形式出現，因此，所採用的可能是擱置訴訟程序以外的其他補救方法。在 *R v. Horseferry Road Magistrates' Court, Ex parte Bennett*（〔1994〕1 AC 42）案中，法官 Lord Griffiths（第 61 頁）援引案例 *Chu Piu-wing v. Attorney-General*（〔1984〕HKLR 411），並且明顯地認同（當時的）上訴法院副院長麥慕年於第 417-418 頁的論述：

> "必須促使政府官員履行他們在完全明白交易會帶來甚麼後果的情況下所作的承諾，這做法明顯是要顧全公眾利益。"

該案的證人因拒絕遵守傳召出庭令而被判犯了藐視法庭罪，上訴法院判決，針對判罪的上訴得直，理由是廉政公署曾向證人保證他不需要出庭作證。

157. 另一案例是 *R v. Croydon Justices, Ex parte Dean* 案（〔1993〕QB 769），該案的判罪亦被撤銷，理由是警方曾向被控人保證不會就某項控罪檢控他，卻又違反承諾而檢控他，這便是濫用程序。

158. 又在 *R v. Bloomfield* 案中（〔1997〕1 Cr App R 135），法庭基於濫用程序為理由撤銷判罪。控方在該案開審時表示不會提出證據指控被告人。為了控方著想，審訊遂押後，"目的是為避免控方尷尬"（參看第 143 頁）。其後控方改變初衷。被告人以濫用程序為理由申請擱置檢控，遭主審法官拒絕，被告人其後認罪。上訴法庭裁定，容許控方撤銷原來的決定而不向法官提供任何理由解釋當初在主審法官面前所作的決定有何不妥，此舉有損司法聲譽。

159. 上述三個案例，都是大法官 Lord Woolf 用以說明他在 *Attorney-General of Trinidad and Tobago & another v. Phillip & others* 案中（〔1995〕1 AC 396 第 417 頁）的闡述：

> "普通法現已發展了一個強大的保障，保護那些若被檢控便會遭受嚴重不公的人免被檢控。"

如上述案例顯示，在這情況下，法庭不單會把檢控擱置，當檢控成功時，還會把判罪撤銷。在這方面，上述案例顯示，法庭不單會將案件擱置，以防程序被濫用，倘若獲得勝訴一方涉及濫用程序，法庭還會褫奪其在該判決中所取得的利益。然而，本案中並沒有人提出*吳嘉玲*及*陳錦雅*兩案的判決涉及濫用程序或是濫用程序的結果。申請人以該等判決為依據。

160. 上述所提及的案例完全不能支持申請人所提出的濫用程序理念。他們所指的濫用程序是由政府的決定引起的，這些決定都是政府在本院審結有關訴訟後才作出的：其一是尋求**該解釋**；其二是不依陳述行事，這些陳述導致採用例案程序；其三是發出遣送離境令。

161. 發出遣送離境令並非法庭程序中的一部份，而是入境事務處處長在行使法定的權力時所作的命令。即使該命令是受制於法庭行使其監管權時作出的覆核，但仍不會使發出命令此舉成為法庭程序的一環。發出及執行遣送離境令屬於行政程序，完全與法庭程序無關。

162. 因此，在濫用程序方面，上訴法院副院長麥慕年所闡明的意見，以公眾利益原則要求官員遵守他們所作的承諾，在本案並不適用。

163. 基於上述理由，這論據不能成立。

"第 1 期及第 2 期"的爭議

164. 這爭議只適用在 1997 年 7 月 1 日之前，以及在 1997 年 7 月 1 日至 10 日期間抵港的申請人。這些日期的重要性在於 1997 年 7 月 1 日之前《基本法》還未生效，而《第 3 號條例》是在 1997 年 7 月 10 日制訂，雖然其本意是從 1997 年 7 月 1 日起生效。申請人旦述，第二十二條第四款經**該解釋**詮釋後，規定有關人士須取得內地批准才可進入香港，因此於 1997 年 7 月 1 日之前進入香港的人士便不受第二十二條第四款及人大常委會就該條款而作出的解釋規限。就這論點，申請人從上訴法庭在*張麗華*案（〔1998〕1 HKC 617）中的多數決定取得支持。至於在 1997 年 7 月 1 日至 10 日期間進入香港的人士，申請人是依據本院在吳嘉玲案裁決《第 3 號條例》沒有追溯效力的判決。這判決不受該解釋影響。*參看劉港榕案*。

165. 如何回應申請人的論據，其答案取決於參照**該解釋**後，《基本法》第二十二條第四款所具的法律效力。該條款規定：

> "中國其他地區的人進入香港特別行政區須辦理批准手續，其中進入香港特別行政區定居的人數由中央人民政府主管部門徵求香港特別行政區政府的意見後確定。"

第 1 期

166. 這條款是《基本法》中的一部份，在 1997 年 7 月 1 日才開始生效。它規定內地居民須取得內地部門批准才可進入香港特別行政區而*非進入香港*。由於這規定只是由 1997 年 7 月 1 日才開始適用，因此，第二十二條第四款的效力是預期性從該日開始的。根據**該解釋**，所有想進入香港特區的中國其他地區的人士，無論其來港目的是為了甚麼，包括為了定居，都受**該解釋**影響。這規定是一般性適用的，並不單是與第二十四條第二款第（三）項有關連。因此，這規限並非只適用於想根據第二十四條第二款第（三）項進入香港特區行使居留權的人士。

167. 在 1997 年 7 月 1 日之前已進入香港的人士，無論他們是非法或以其他方法來港，並繼續逗留至 1997 年 7 月 1 日之後，當他們在該日之前進入香港時，不能說他們是進入*香港特區*，當時並沒有香港特區，而《基本法》第二十二條第四款當時還未生效。

168. *在劉港榕案*判詞中，終審法院首席法官於第 327F 頁述稱，第二十四條第二款第（三）項一經受第二十二條第四款規限後，除非照第二十二條第四款的規定取得內地批准，否則任何人都不能享有居留權。常任法官沈澄亦認為"把第二十二條第四款及第二十四條第二款第（三）項連在一起，意思是要那些想來港定居的內地人士不僅須要取得單程證，而且也須取得居留權證明書，這些都要在內地申請"。*參看*第 341F 頁。但上訴法庭法官祁彥輝述稱，本院在審理劉港榕案時並沒有特別處理第二十二條第四款及第二十四條第二款第（三）項兩者的關係對在 1997 年 7 月 1 日之前已抵達香港的人士所造成的影響。祁彥輝法官的說法是正確的。

169. 我等認為，第二十二條第四款的文字意思是清晰的，在回歸之前已來港的人士並不受此條款的規限。當 1997 年 7 月 1 日第二十四條第二款第（三）項生效時，第 1 期的申請人已在香港。若他們能在當時按該條款確立他們的永久性居民身份，在沒有《基本法》其他條款或任何有效的本地法例對他們的身份造成不利影響的情況下，他們有權得到身份核實並行使居港權而無須先取得單程證。他們的身份並不受《基本法》的任何條款影響。由於《第 3 號條例》沒有追溯效力，因此沒有任何香港法例對他們有影響。

170. 雖然此論據對甲類申請人士有幫助，但乙類申請人士由於受到出生時間限制，因此仍然受**該解釋**對第二十四條第二款第（三）項的詮釋影響。換句話說，因為他們在 1997 年 7 月 1 日之前已進入香港，第二十二條第四款對他們並不適用。但根據**該解釋**對第二十四條第二款第（三）項的詮釋，他們並不符合第二十四條第二款第（三）項所述的資格，因此，他們的聲稱仍然不能成立。

第 2 期

171. 但在 1997 年 7 月 1 日至 10 日期間抵港的人士，他們的情況並不相同。他們在 1997 年 7 月 1 日之後進入香港特區。由於他們是中國其他地區的人士，當他們想進入香港特區時，便受第二十二條第四款的影響，因此，他們須要取得內地批准才可進入香港。無可否認，他們在進入香港時可依據第二十四條第二款第（三）項，但他們仍然受第二十二條第四款的規限，因該條款與第二十四條第二款第（三）項同時生效。正如上訴法庭副庭長馬天敏在*張麗華*案中述稱（第 667 頁）：

> "在 1997 年 7 月 1 日午夜過後，根據第二十四條第三款的規定，這些申請人的身份都藉血緣關係成為永久性居民。但第二十二條第四款亦同時生效。永久性居民如要行使其居留權及在港定居，只能透過申請 —— 其必然的含意是獲得 —— 准許，而單程證就是准許的證明。"

172. 未獲內地批准而在 1997 年 7 月 1 日至 10 日期間進入香港特區的人士，不能因第二十四條第二款第（三）項受惠。換句話說，他們不能一方面因第二十四條第二款第（三）項受惠而同時又不接受第二十二條第四款的規限。

173. 基於上述理由，在第 2 期期間抵港的甲類及乙類申請人士都不能以此理由獲判勝訴。

第 1 期及第 2 期爭議：裁定個別情況。

174. 因應我等在上文所述，本院必須審理個別情況。

175. *第 3 名代表申請人 —— 羅寶麗女士* —— 她是甲類申請人，在第 1 期來港。她代表另外 32 名有情況相同的申請人。他們據此理由獲判勝訴。

176. *第 4 名代表申請人 —— 朱春敏女士* —— 她是乙類申請人，在第 1 期來港。她代表另外 413 名有情況相同的申請人。由於受出生時間限制影響，他們因此不能以此理由得直。

177. *第 5 名代表申請人 —— 譚小明先生* —— 他是甲類申請人，在第 2 期來港。他代表另一位在第 2 期來港的申請人。他們不能以此理由得直。

178. *終院民事上訴 2001 年第 3 號案中的第 5 名代表申請人 —— 林智樂先生* —— 他是乙類申請人。雖然他是在第 1 期的時間內首次來港，但他返回內地，然後於第 5 期再次來港。無論他被視為第 1 期或第 5 期來港人士（入境事務處處長對此點有爭議），他都受出生時間限制影響，因此，他還是不能以此理由得直。

"寬免政策"的爭議

寬免政策的事實基礎

179. 要了解寬免政策的性質及範圍，必須研究有關的政策決定，該政策決定如何作出及其背後的理據。保安局局長在其誓章中陳述政策決定作出時的情況。申請人沒有就她的誓章內容對她提出盤問。

180. 1999年6月26日，行政會議開會討論在政府的政策上該如何實施**該解釋**。行政會議所關注的問題是甚麼人不會受**該解釋**影響。在**該解釋**的最後一段中，所指的是"有關訴訟當事人"。從行政長官其後的宣布看來，行政會議已清楚明白第一百五十八條第三款所訂明的原則，這原則是在此以前作出的判決不受影響。

181. 大家都清楚知道，*吳嘉玲*案及*陳錦雅*案的具名申請人不會受影響，因這是對他們有利的判決，他們是這些決定的直接受益人。除了他們之外，還有那些在訴訟期間得到入境事務處處長承諾的人士。處長承諾不會把他們遣送離港以待訴訟程序的結果。這些人士包括：

(a) 就*張麗華*（後以*吳嘉玲*案稱之）案中的爭議而提出司法覆核程序及等候代表案件審訊結果的當事人；

(b) 受協議涵蓋的人士，這協議是代表入境事務處處長的律政司與代表這類人士的律師之間，以及入境事務處處長與法律援助署之間所作關於這類人士的協議：入境事務處處長承諾，在等候代表案件審訊結果期間，不會把這類人士遣送離港。

(c) 由*陳錦雅*案的律師向入境事務處處長具報，以及同意受入境事務處處長作出類似承諾涵蓋的人士。

182. 對（a）類別的人士來說並沒有甚麼問題，因他們已向入境事務處處長展開訴訟程序，他們的案件本可如*張麗華*案一樣進行至審結為止。（b）類及（c）類的人士被政府視為訴訟的"間接"當事人，意指倘若他們不是得到入境事務處處長的承諾，他們便會參與待決的訴訟程序或展開新的訴訟程序以爭取他們的居留權，結果也會與代表案件的具名當事人一樣處於相同的情況。

183. 政府亦認為那些在1999年1月29日或之前向入境事務處處長聲稱擁有居留權的人士也應因終審法院的判決而受惠。據保安局局長所述，政府在考慮應否依據該兩案的判決給予其他人相同的看待時，認為最公平及最合理的方法去處理這個問題，是考慮（a）該人是否身處香港，以及（b）該人是否已向入境事務處處長聲稱擁有居留權以尋求確立他的身份，而入境事務處處長對該聲稱存有記錄。接納這類在1999年1月29日或之前向入境事務處處長聲稱擁有居留權的人士的背後理據是：因終審法院已裁定《第3號條例》沒有追溯效力，那些在1997年7月1日至7月10日期間來港的人士應包括在這類別之內。那些在1997年7月11日至1999年1月29日期間來港的人士也應包括在這個類別之內，因為倘若他們為自己提出訴訟程序，要不是按自己的權利進行訴訟，便是受承諾所涵蓋，他們便會成為終審法院審理案件的當事人。

184. 為此，行政長官會同行政會議作出政策決定，內容如下：

(a) 在1997年7月1日至1999年1月29日期間在港並在這段期間向入境事務處處長聲稱擁有居留權的人士，當局應按照1999年1月29日終審法院的判決核實其身份，若符合資格，應給予永久性居民身份；以及

(b) 在1999年1月30日至6月26日期間在港並向入境事務處處長聲稱擁有居留權的人士，不應因"在此以前作出的判決"不受**該解釋**影響的原則而受惠。

185. 1999年6月26日下午，行政長官舉行記者會，會中宣布人大常委會就有關條文的解釋及行政會議的決定如下：

"第二，根據終審法院的判決不受人大常委會的解釋所影響的原則下，我們將容許由1997年7月1日至1999年1月29日在港並曾向當局聲稱擁有居留權的人士，以終審法院的判決核實他們永久居民的身份。據統計，這類人士大概有3,700人。

第三，那些在1999年1月29日之後來港的人士，或者我用另外的說法，第三，其他人士只可在符合人大常委會解釋的情況下，才可向當局申請居留權。"

186. 同日差不多在同一時間，政府亦發表新聞公報，宣布行政會議的決定，該新聞公報詳述有關的政策決定，內容如下：

"全國人民代表大會常務委員會（人大常委會）就《基本法》有關居留權條文的解釋，將不影響法院在此以前作出的裁決這項原則，將會惠及約3,700名人士。

政府發言人今日（星期六）解釋：「受惠的人士必須於1997年7月1日至1999年1月29日期間在港，並曾於這段期間向入境事務處處長聲稱擁有居留權。」

有兩類人士屬於此類別。

發言人表示：「第1類為於1997年7月1日至7月10日期間在港及曾聲稱擁有居留權的人士。」

「終審法院裁定他們不受居留權證明書計劃涵蓋，因為於1997年7月11日頒布的《入境條例》（修訂）（第3號）並無追溯力。」

「只要他們符合終審法院有關居留權的裁決的資格，則雖然人大常委會已就《基本法》條文作出解釋，但他們仍將可享有及保留其居留權。」

另一類受惠者為於1997年7月11日至1999年1月29日期間在港，並曾向入境事務處聲稱擁有居留權的人士。

他說：「此類別包括於1999年1月29日終審法院作出裁決的兩個測試個案共86名訴訟人，以及在相關司法程序中所涉及的有關人士。」

「換言之，在1997年7月1日至1999年1月29日期間在港，並已向入境事務處處長聲稱擁有居留權的內地人士，將可能視為與訴訟有關人士，該等人士為數約3,700人。」

部份該等聲稱擁有居留權人士其申請已獲核實或在最後核實階段。超過900人並已享有或即將享有居留權。

發言人說：「我們會根據終審法院的裁決，處理其餘（約2,700名）聲稱享有居留權人士的申請。」

「該等人士當中約900人現正在港，他們無須在當局處理及決定其申請之前離港。」

「至於已返回內地的其餘約1,800名人士，我們將作出適當安排以便處理他們的申請。」

發言人指出，在1999年1月30日至6月26日期間來港並聲稱擁有居留權的人士，當局將按人大常委會的解釋處理他們的申請。"

187. 這新聞公報在某程度上反映了行政會議在政策決定背後的想法。然而，無論是政策決定本身、行政長官的宣布、或是新聞公報的內容，都沒有提及入境事務處處長應存有聲稱居留權的紀錄的規定。

188. 有人提出一點，是關於行政長官作出的宣布和在同日發表的新聞公報這兩者的翻譯本的準確程度。稍後我等會談論要向哪個部門提出居留權聲稱才是適當，才可以成為該政策決定所指的人士，到那時候我等會處理這點。

該政策決定的性質

189. 我等考慮該政策決定的含意之前必須注意幾點：第一，這個決定的目的是使一批數量有限制的人士能夠受惠於上述兩個判決。這些人曾經，或者本來會控告政府以爭取他們聲稱擁有的居留權。選擇 1999 年 1 月 29 日為截止日是因為這是發下上述訴訟的終審判決的日期。第二，有些人由於聽到各種陳述叫他們等候法庭的決定，而沒有展開訴訟程序或參與當時的訴訟程序。可以理解到該政策決定的作用是在某種程度上回應這些人明顯懷有的怨憤和由於合理期望落空而受到的挫折。第三，必須把行政長官的宣布和當時同時發表的新聞公報合起來一併視為關於行政長官會同行政會議制定的政策決定的公開聲明。該政策決定產生的不是一種權利而是一個期望，期望該政策決定會實施。不可以把行政長官的宣布從當時同時發表的新聞公報和作為兩者的基礎的政策決定脫離，而孤立地衡量。第四，新聞公報裏詳細列出可以因該政策決定而受惠的估計人數和人數的分類。這表示政府在制定該政策決定時，對於如何把該政策決定實施於相關的居留權聲稱人類別的看法。

該政策決定

190. 要理解該政策決定，必須理解它本身特有的背景，包括訴訟的來龍去脈，引起**該解釋**的各事件，該決定背後的目的和理由，和希望聲稱擁有香港永久性居民身份的內地居民在法律上的處境。第一，《第 3 號條例》制定之後，法律規定內地居民只可以在內地申請居留權證明書，這點在*吳嘉玲*案中得到本院支持，內地居民在香港時不可申請。第二，在香港的內地居民如果是非法入境或逾期逗留可被遣送離境，除非入境事務處處長決定不把他遣送離境。如果他作出居留權聲稱而入境事務處處長不同意停止遣送離境，該內地居民便必須採取訴訟程序以堅持他的權利要求。在此情況下，入境事務處處長通常不會把他遣送離境，直至案件解決為止。第三，在*吳嘉玲*及*陳錦雅*兩案訴訟進行期間，入境事務處處長拒絕給予一個包括每個曾到法律援助署求助的人的概括性的承諾，而只願意承諾那些獲給予法律援助的人士和那些曾申請法律援助而法律援助署認為其個案有理據的人士不會被遣送離境。

191. 行政長官的宣布和新聞公報在措辭上有些分別。行政長官僅僅描述該政策決定的大綱，新聞公報則提供多些細節，把籠統的政策變成較為具體的準則。根據這些準則可以對個別情況或各個類別的情況作出決定。該政策決定，宣布和新聞公報都是差不多同時作出或發表的，所以應該合起來一併考慮。

192. 在此背景下衡量，我等認為該政策決定的含意是頗清晰的。如果某人

（1）在 1997 年 7 月 1 日至 1999 年 1 月 29 日期間在香港；以及

（2）曾在此期間向入境事務處提出居留權的聲稱

就可以受惠於上述終審法院的兩個判決。

適用的原則

193. 各申請人關於寬免政策爭議的論據是：行政長官已作出一個公開宣布列出任何申請人要符合那些條件才可以被視為處於和*吳嘉玲*及*陳錦雅*兩案的真正當事人相同的情況。因為這個公開宣布，各申請人有一個合理期望，就是如果他們符合這些條件就會得到和上述兩案的真正當事人相同的對待，以及會受惠於上述終審法院的兩個判決，而他們的居留權聲稱亦會根據該兩個判決核實。按照他們的論據，使這個合理期望落空就是對各申請人不公，也是濫用權力。他們指稱入境事務處處長使這個期望落空，因為他誤解了在公開宣布中表明的政策陳述而且加入額外的條件。各申請人陳詞說：這種做法相當於犯了法律上的錯誤，或者是，入境事務處處長在執行該政策決定時不合理性地行事。據各申請人所說，在本案中的原訟庭及上訴庭的法官錯誤理解這個合理期望的內容是甚麼，也誤以為政府的宣布只相當於對該政策的一個概略的陳述而要由入境事務處加上必要的細節以執行該政策。

194. 各申請人的論據主要是基於一個假設，就是該政策決定只包括行政長官的宣布。我等已解釋過，行政長官的宣布是不可以孤立地衡量的。寬免政策是行政會議的政策決定。這政策由公開宣布和新聞公報闡明。政府當然可以自由制定其政策，但該政策決定的含意是甚麼，則要由法庭確定（*R v. Ministry of Defence, Ex parte Walker* 案〔2000〕1 WLR 806 第 810 頁 D）。但法庭不會理會政策是好是壞，除非可以證明這個政策是如此不合理性，是任何一個合理的政府都不會採用的，*Walker* 案（第 812 頁 D）。因此，是要由法庭判斷政府執行該政策時有沒有誤解或錯誤執行該政策，*Walker* 案（第 810 頁 D, 817 頁 E）。

195. 如果一個政策的含意清晰，而政府對之有誤解，這個誤解便相當於一個法律上的錯誤。如果含意不清晰，或者這個政策的含意容許多過一個解釋，而政府採用了某一特定的解釋，那便要由法庭判斷究竟採用這個解釋是不是「異常至不能歸於合理性的一類」。請看 *R v. Monopolies and Mergers Commission & another, Ex parte South Yorkshire Transport Ltd.& another* 案（〔1993〕1 WLR 23, 32H），大法官 Lord Mustill 所說；大法官 Lord Slynn of Hadley 在 *Walker* 案（第 813 頁 A）引用。

196. 同樣的理性測試準則對政策的執行一樣適用。解釋一個政策就是確定這個政策是甚麼或者這個政策的含意是甚麼。執行一個政策就是作出某個決定，把經確定後的政策實施到一切相關的情況裏。這裏有一個預設假定，就是受委託執行政策的人對政策的解釋是正確的。有些情況裏，制定政策的人同樣是執行政策的人。因為這個原因，當某個決定受質疑，有時候攻擊這個決定的理由是作出這個決定的人既誤解了也錯誤執行了政策。如果檢查對政策的解釋是否正確時是用理性為測試準則，但質疑這個政策的執行方法卻用不同的測試準則，這樣就會令人覺得不合情理。

197. 應用這個測試準則的結果是：一個由於誤解政策而作出的決定，倘這誤解是法律上的錯誤或是不合理性的，這個決定會被撤銷；一個由於錯誤執行政策而作出的決定，倘這錯誤是不合理性的，這個決定也會被撤銷。跟著政府便要按照政策陳述的含意的正確解釋重新作出決定。

198. 在本案中，各申請人唯一可以得到的合理期望是期望該政策決定 — 無論是甚麼也好，都會按照法庭的解釋 —— 對他們施行（根據大法官 Lord Hoffmann 在 *Walker* 案所說，第 816 頁 B）。在本案裏，除了該政策之外，政府並沒有對各申請人作出任何許諾。各申請人的期望是：如果他們在 1997 年 7 月 1 日至 1999 年 1 月 29 日期間在香港，並且在此期間向入境事務處提出居留權的聲稱，他們的居留權聲稱便會根據終審法院的兩個判決核實。

199. 跟著產生的問題是：入境事務處處長有沒有誤解或錯誤執行該政策決定？

入境事務處處長對該政策的解釋

200. 為了執行該政策決定，入境事務處規定任何人如果聲稱為該政策的受惠人都必須符合某些準則。這些準則是：（1）此人在

1997 年 7 月 1 日至 1999 年 1 月 29 日期間必須曾身處香港；（2）在此期間，此人曾向入境事務處作出居留權的聲稱；（3）作出聲稱的時候，他本人身處香港；以及（4）入境事務處處長有這個聲稱的紀錄。

201. 根據這些準則，入境事務處處長接受除了*吳嘉玲及陳錦雅*兩案的具名當事人之外，以下各類別的人士也是該政策決定所指的人士：

（1）被某個協議和承諾涵蓋的，在等待上述案件的結果期間不會被遣送離境的人士；

（2）以希望等待上述案件的結果為理由申請延期逗留或申請不被遣送離境的人士；

（3）向入境事務處自首或被捕，以及以擁有香港居留權為理由拒絕被遣送離境的非法入境者和逾期逗留人士；

（4）被警方拘捕，被轉交予入境事務處及在被會見時作出居留權聲稱的人士；

（5）曾經申請核實是否合資格根據《入境條例》附表 1 第 2（c）段領取永久性居民身份證，以及本人身處香港的人士；

（6）不是*吳嘉玲及陳錦雅*兩案的當事人但曾經親自展開訴訟程序的人士；

（7）在 1997 年 7 月至 1997 年 9 月期間曾獲給予法律援助以採取訴訟程序聲稱擁有居留權，及獲入境事務處處長承諾不把他們遣送離境的人士；以及

（8）根據一個在 1997 年 10 月 14 日達成的明訂協議，由法律援助署轉介到入境事務處的人士；根據該協議，入境事務處處長同意不把他們遣送離境，原因是法律援助署認為他們的個案有理據，但為了節省公帑而沒有給他們法律援助。

202. 各申請人不滿入境事務處處長加入額外的準則，規定聲稱只可以是向入境事務處作出的，以及作出聲稱的時候申請人必須身處香港。他們認為這都是錯的。這些申訴是關於入境事務處處長對該政策決定的解釋。各申請人也指稱：入境事務處處長規定聲稱必須在入境事務處存有紀錄，這規定是錯的；他決定甚麼是構成，甚麼不是構成一個居留權的聲稱，這決定也是錯的。這個論據是針對入境事務處處長對個別申請人施行該政策時的做法。

可以向誰作出聲稱

203. 行政長官主持的新聞界答問會的錄音謄本的中文版說：不受**該解釋**影響的人士是那些曾“向當局”聲稱擁有居留權的人士，但英文版沒有這幾個字。各申請人陳詞說：這可以理解為該政策決定容許他們向入境事務處之外的政府機構作出聲稱。可是，同時發表的新聞公報就明確得多。中文版和英文版都表明該決定的預定受益人是那些曾接觸入境事務處或曾向入境事務處提出聲稱的人。

204. 各申請人也指稱：保安局局長在一個電台訪問中曾說接觸法律援助署也會被認為是足以構成居留權的聲稱。錄音謄本顯示她當時說：

> “他（聲稱人）在 1997 年 7 月 1 日至（1999 年）1 月 29 日期間一定要在香港，無論他現在是不是還在這裏。第二個條件是他一定要曾經在這段期間接觸入境事務處或法律援助署聲稱擁有居留權，而入境事務處或法律援助署有這個紀錄。”

205. 保安局局長在其誓章裏解釋她在那訪問中提到法律援助署的時候，她的意思是指那些獲給予法律援助和由賈偉林、劉天均律師行代表的人士，以及那些曾申請法律援助而法律援助署認為其個案有理據的人士；這兩類人士都已經得到入境事務處處長承諾在等待訴訟的結果期間不會把他們遣送離港。本院沒有理由不接納保安局局長關於這兩點的解釋。沒有證據證明把一個關於該政策（但可能是錯誤）的陳述當作一個有約束力的許諾是合理的做法。請看 *Begbie* 案，初審時大法官 Maurice Kay 於 1999 年 7 月 12 日頒下的判決中所說，謄本第 7 頁。

206. 當參照該政策決定的來龍去脈來考慮該政策決定時，很明顯行政會議的目的是只讓下列人士受惠於該政策，就是曾向入境事務處提出居留權聲稱的人士，或其聲稱已由其他政府機構在執行職務期間轉交予入境事務處的人士。

作出聲稱時身處香港

207. 各申請人陳詞說：有關規定並非要求申請人在作出聲稱的時候必須本人身處香港，而只是要求他必須在 1997 年 7 月 1 日至 1999 年 1 月 29 日期間在香港及在此期間提出聲稱。換言之，這兩個規定是分開的。另一方面，入境事務處處長爭辯說：如果正確理解該政策，便可知該政策的含意是申請人必須於相關的期間內在身處香港的時候曾作出聲稱。

208. 行政長官會同行政會議作出的政策決定裏和行政長官的宣布裏都沒有清清楚楚說明這規定。可是，新聞公報的第二段相當明確的把會受惠於該政策的人士限制為“在港，並曾於這段期間向處長聲稱擁有居留權”的人士。新聞公報的第九段也是如此。依我等之見：規定申請人必須本人身處香港時曾作出居留權的聲稱才符合該政策決定的資格，把該政策決定說明或闡述為包括這個規定是對該政策決定的合理性的解釋，也是合理性地執行該政策決定的做法。制定《第 3 號條例》之後，內地居民 —— 包括全部申請人 —— 只可以在內地申請居留權證明書。內地居民沒有其他方法可以用來聲稱擁有居留權。1997 年 7 月 1 日至 1999 年 1 月 29 日期間，入境事務處面對一個難題。這個難題是由一批內地居民非法來港或持雙程證來港，但拒絕返回內地而引致的。他們都趁在香港的時候以各種方法作出居留權的聲稱。該政策決定明顯是以那些已採取訴訟程序或很可能會採取訴訟程序控告入境事務處處長的人士為對象，目的是把他們當作特殊情況處理。制定該政策決定的目的明顯不是要惠及以下人士，就是那些在 1997 年 7 月 1 日至 1999 年 1 月 29 日期間恰好在香港，卻選擇在不是身處香港的時候向入境事務處作出聲稱的人士，無論他們在這段期間內在港有多少時間及來港的目的是甚麼，他們都不是受惠對象。

要有紀錄之規定

209. 不論是該政策決定，或行政長官的宣布，或新聞公報都沒有提到入境事務處處長必須有聲稱的紀錄這個規定。各申請人陳詞說：入境事務處處長加入這個額外的條件是錯的，特別是有證據顯示入境事務處的紀錄遠遠未臻完備。

210. 如果沒有某種形式的紀錄以核實某人是否該政策所指的人士，要執行該政策決定或任何政策也好，就算可行，也會是極端困難。正如入境事務處助理處長麥先生在其誓章所說，“如果該寬免政策決定的範圍不是限定為那些入境事務處處長有其居留權聲稱紀錄的人士，那麼入境事務處處長就沒有清晰、客觀、或不會引起爭論的基礎可以用來決定究竟某聲稱人在 1997 年 7 月 1 日至 1999 年 1 月 29 日期間是否身處香港並曾聲稱擁有居留權。”

211. 有幾個申請人寫的信入境事務處沒有紀錄，法庭接納這點。但這是個別情況裏的證據上的問題。沒有任何證據顯示入境事務

處的紀錄系統是如此不可靠以致在執行該政策決定時會引起任何嚴重問題。規定要有紀錄，這是執行該政策決定的合理和合理性的做法。

甚麼構成一個聲稱

212. 根據該政策決定，要符合資格是要作出居留權的聲稱；作出居留權的聲稱則沒有特定方法或形式。據助理處長所說，入境事務處採取的準則是"爭取居留權的聲稱必須具有某種形式以使入境事務處處長能夠識別那些曾提出居留權聲稱的人士，並以入境事務處處長存有這些聲稱的紀錄為準"。入境事務處處長規定：要構成一個聲稱，必須以書面或是一些可使入境事務處會有紀錄的方式作出。換言之，聲稱不是一定要用書面形式，但入境事務處一定要有這個聲稱的紀錄。我等認為這個規定不是對該政策決定的誤解，也不是錯誤執行該政策決定的做法。

213. 各申請人反對把這個規定實施於某些個別情況的做法。在經修訂的司法覆核申請書裏，各申請人指稱某幾種行為都足以構成一個聲稱。各申請人不滿入境事務處處長實施該政策時以下幾點做法：（1）入境事務處處長拒絕接納某幾種行為，認為就該政策決定而言這幾種行為不構成一個聲稱，該做法是錯的；（2）有證據顯示有些聲稱人曾接觸入境事務處及想提出居留權的聲稱，但他們被入境事務處職員拒之於門外，而入境事務處沒有這些聲稱的紀錄；（3）入境事務處處長曾接納用某些形式作出的聲稱，但拒絕其他用類似形式作出的聲稱，這構成對某些申請人不公平對待；以及（4）入境事務處處長對呈交給他的聲稱信採用的解釋過於狹隘。

214. 甚麼構成一個聲稱？這問題關係到很多由這些代表申請人所代表的申請人，所以有必要考慮每一種他們指稱曾經作出的聲稱，以及考慮入境事務處處長拒絕任何一種的決定是否不合理性。

（1）在香港逗留 / 在香港逾期逗留

215. 各申請人爭論說：單憑身處香港或在香港逾期逗留（入境事務處處長對此必定有紀錄），申請人就可以被認為是宣稱擁有在這裏的居留權。這不可能是對的。除了宣稱擁有居留權外，還可以有很多其他理由在香港逗留或在香港逾期逗留。就算某人是第二十四條第二款第（三）項所指的人士，他也必須根據《第 3 號條例》確立其永久性居民身份才可以行使其居留權。如果他是非法入境者或逾期逗留人士，他身處香港或繼續在香港逗留便屬違反入境法例，可被警方拘捕及被遣送離境。如果他擁有任何權利，卻不站出來向入境事務處宣稱他擁有這權利，便不能期望會被承認為居留權聲稱人。入境事務處處長拒絕這種聲稱，認為這不是該政策決定所指的聲稱，他是對的。

（2）申請單程證 / 居留權證明書

216. 申請人指稱：在寬免政策期間向內地公安局申請單程證或居留權證明書也應被視為作出聲稱，因為申請是向入境事務處的代理作出的。這論據是不可接受的。這種申請是根據《第 3 號條例》作出的。該政策決定及其背後的理由都不是針對這種聲稱。在多數情況下，這種向公安局作出的申請都是申請人在內地時作出的，而不是當他們本人身處香港時作出。

（3）接觸法律援助署

217. 我等知悉，從 1997 年 7 月初開始便有大批人士接觸法律援助署求助。他們有些獲給予法律援助以展開訴訟程序或參與當時的訴訟程序。入境事務處處長承諾在等待*吳嘉玲*及*陳錦雅*兩案的結果期間不把他們遣送離境。有其他人也曾申請法律援助，他們的個案被認為有理據，但為了節省公帑而沒有獲給予法律援助。法律援助署告知入境事務處處長這些人申請法律援助。根據這兩個部門在 1997 年 10 月達成的一個協議，這些人得到承諾不會被遣送離境。入境事務處處長接受這兩個類別的人士為該政策決定所指的人士。

218. 上述人士之外，我等尚要考慮三類人士，他們也曾接觸法律援助署：（1）一些指稱法律援助署把他們拒之門外，沒有給他們登記，也不准他們作出申請的人；（2）一些曾申請法律援助，後來被轉介到入境事務處的人。轉介時附帶一個要求，就是如果入境事務處處長決定把他們之中任何人遣送離境，應通知法律援助署；以及（3）一些在 1998 年 12 月 8 日至 1999 年 1 月 29 日期間到法律援助處登記了他們的申請，和收到法律援助處覆函的人。覆函中說他們在等待上訴至終審法院的案件的結果期間無需採取任何行動。

219. 證據顯示，法律援助署的慣常做法是接受申請及考慮每宗申請的理據以決定是否給予法律援助。那些被"拒之門外"的人很可能只是查詢一般性的事情，而職員已告知他們當時法庭的判決。如果他們不單是作出查詢，而是認真地提出聲稱，就必會堅持申請法律援助以繼續爭取他們聲稱擁有的權利。法律援助署通常會接受及考慮他們的申請，即使考慮之後決定拒絕所請。還有一些人曾獲給予法律援助，但後來法律援助署聽取法律意見後取消他們的法律援助證書。可是，*陳錦雅*案的初審判決公布之後，如果他們重新申請，他們的申請是會被重新考慮的。無論如何，這些人和法律援助署的這種接觸不可以被視為聲稱，因為這不是向入境事務處作出的聲稱，入境事務處亦沒有紀錄。

220. 至於那些曾經申請法律援助但被轉交予入境事務處的人士，轉交的時候附帶一封信要求入境事務處如要發出遣送離境令便通知法律援助署，我等不清楚法律援助署是否認為這些個案是沒有理據的個案。可是，無論這類人士的個案是否有理據，這些申請人都是有意透過法庭爭取香港居留權，而希望得到法律援助署幫助。如果他們不是有意控告政府便不會申請法律援助。他們採取的步驟和法律援助署代他們採取的步驟是提出聲稱的步驟。既然入境事務處已獲知他們的姓名，入境事務處處長應該有他們的聲稱紀錄。這個類別的人士理應被視為已向入境事務處提出聲稱。可是，這個類別的人士可能沒有代表申請人。

221. 至於那些在 1998 年 12 月 8 日至 1999 年 1 月 29 日期間已在法律援助署登記的人士，他們要提出居留權聲稱的意願也是足夠清楚的。可是，法律援助署沒有處理他們的法律援助申請，卻以法律援助署覆函回覆他們，告訴他們無需採取任何行動，因為終審法院不久便會聆訊和裁定相同的爭議。不幸的是法律援助署沒有在寬免政策期滿之前把他們的姓名，約一千個，轉交予入境事務處。考慮到在那不足兩個月的時間內有這麼多的申請人，這點是可以理解的。這份名單在約一年後，即 1999 年 12 月，才轉交到入境事務處。換言之，這些人有意透過法律援助署提出居留權的聲稱，但他們的聲稱沒有得到處理，入境事務處在相關時間也沒有他們的聲稱的任何紀錄。因此，這些聲稱不是該政策決定所指的聲稱。但是，正如我等較早時在合理期望的爭議部份所說，他們收到的法律援助署覆函可以被視為構成一個具體陳述，由此產生一個合理期望，就是他們會得到如*吳嘉玲*及*陳錦雅*兩案當事人同樣的對待。

（4）申請延期逗留

222. 各申請人爭論說：申請延期逗留應被視為向入境事務處作出居留權的聲稱。關於這點，他們還指稱：入境事務處處事不公平，因為該處把某些延期逗留申請視為構成一個聲稱，但拒絕其他用類似形式作出的聲稱。1999 年 6 月 26 日之後處理的申請便遭受如此對待。

223. 一個持雙程證來港的內地居民，無論是來旅遊、探親，或為了其他目的，通常都會獲准逗留至某一日期。如果他申請延期逗留，他需要提供理由。某些延期逗留申請被入境事務處視為構成該政策決定所指的居留權聲稱。在這些申請裏提供的理由不是宣稱擁有香港居留權或永久性居民身份就是請求留港等待終審法院在吳嘉玲及陳錦雅兩案裏的判決。他們等待兩案的判決，理由明顯是想得到和兩案當事人相同的對待。也有一些非法入境者或逾期逗留人士在被會見時說出同樣的理由以拒絕遣送離境。在所有這些個案中，入境事務處都已接受這種宣稱和請求為構成該政策決定所指的聲稱。

224. 如果某人在他的延期逗留申請裏或被入境事務處職員會見時沒有表示他聲稱擁有居留權，又沒有表示他想等待該兩案的判決，而倚賴其他理由，入境事務處處長有權認為他的申請或他在會見報告裏的陳述並不構成該政策決定所指的聲稱。這裏沒有不公平對待或不同對待這回事。如果某人想繼續留在香港，他要說出留港的真正理由及要表示他是宣稱擁有居留權。他是沒有理由不應該或不可以在他的申請或會見裏表達這個意思。

225. 大律師表示有些情況裏，想延期逗留或拒絕遣送離境的申請人“被施以壓力”，以致在他們的申請書或會見報告裏寫下入境事務處職員促使他們寫出標準化的答案，答案裏沒有宣稱或聲稱擁有居留權。這是在個別情況裏要處理的證據上的問題。

（5）接觸入境事務處

226. 有人指稱：有些申請人親自前往或者由其雙親或親戚代表前往入境事務處作出居留權的聲稱。有些甚至帶同支持其聲稱的文件前往。但他們被阻止或勸止作出聲稱。入境事務處職員都給他們千篇一律的答覆，就是他們應該返回內地，向當地的有關當局申請單程證或居留權證明書。大律師陳詞說：把他們當作只是查詢事情，入境事務處處長又以沒有他們的聲稱紀錄為理由拒絕他們，這樣做是錯的。

227. 要了解上述申訴必須了解當時的情況。據入境事務處職員所說，到入境事務處的辦事櫃枱或透過電話作出的查詢每年遠超過一百萬宗。要將這些查詢全部記錄在案是強人所難。入境事務處職員千篇一律的答覆實際是說明法律規定甚麼，或者據他們理解，法律規定甚麼。如果某人真的想作出居留權的聲稱而不是作出一般性的查詢，他應該不會被這樣的答覆嚇阻。證據顯示如果有人到入境事務處希望作出聲稱並帶備有關文件，他會被請去見一個高級職員。那個職員會和他會面，會面情況會有紀錄。入境事務處處長拒絕那些僅僅作出查詢的人士，因為根據該政策決定，他們並不符合資格，他這樣做不應受批評。

（6）寫信給入境事務處或其他政府部門

228. 有些申請人寫給入境事務處或其他政府機構的信件被認為不足以構成該政策決定所指的聲稱而遭拒絕。大律師陳詞說：入境事務處處長對其中有些信件的解釋過於狹隘。

229. 這些信件分為兩類：第一、寫給入境事務處的；第二、寫給其他政府官員或機構的，如行政長官、律政司司長及保安局局長。第二類的信件必然會轉交予入境事務處以作出較詳細的答覆而不是標準化的答覆。把這些信件視為打算寫給入境事務處的信件是合理的。這些信件之中有些為了各種原因被認為不足以構成聲稱而遭拒絕。我等考慮的只限於一個問題，就是寫這些信件是否應被視為作出居留權的聲稱。

230. 要決定這個問題，必須考慮 1997 年 7 月至 1999 年 1 月尾這段期間發生的事。當時在香港很多內地居民正在聲稱擁有香港居留權，這消息已經廣為報導。這些人有很多申請法律援助以透過法庭爭取他們聲稱擁有的權利。政府官員曾經就這些情況作出公開聲明。不同級別的法庭對某些代表案件作出多個判決。入境事務處擠滿內地申請人，有些宣稱擁有居留權，有些申請延期逗留，有些拒絕遣送離境。他們很多都沒有受過良好教育。差不多所有人都用中文書寫。他們有些因等待來港等了很久而感到沮喪。他們對法庭的多個判決的理解不會是全面的，也不會是準確的。信件的措辭客氣，甚至帶道歉語氣。

231. 在這種情況下，我等認為合理性的做法應該是判斷某位申請人是否實質上已作出聲稱。只要信息清楚及可以合理地被理解為構成一個給予香港居留權的請求，這就足夠構成一個聲稱。在這種情況下，把非法律專業人士所寫的信件當作正式的法律文件般嚴格分析是錯的。

232. 我等認為：任何信件如能明確（1）指出某人為香港永久性居民及另一人為其子女；（2）提供某些資料，如該子女的出生日期或地點；以及（3）要求該子女來港定居或享有其居留權，則理應被理解為實質上作出了居留權的聲稱。不必一定要用如“聲稱”，“要求”，“宣稱”或“權利”這些詞語，也不必一定要提及《基本法》或其具體條文，雖然提及《基本法》或其具體條文是表示聲稱擁有某種權利。如果信件附有支持文件則聲稱會顯得更有力。

對各代表申請人執行該政策

233. 有一點雙方沒有爭議，就是第 4 期和第 5 期內抵港的申請人都不是在該政策決定的範圍內。把該政策的準則及把我等在以上談論的用以衡量入境事務處處長執行該政策時作出的決定的合理性程度的原則應用於各代表申請人，我等的意見如下。

234. *第 1 名代表申請人——吳小彤女士*——入境事務處處長接受她為該政策決定所指的人士。她不尋求任何濟助。

235. *第 2 名代表申請人 ——吳金枝女士* ——正如我等較早時所說，因為她的個案裏有一些關於事實的爭議，她不是合適的代表。

236. *第 3 名代表申請人 ——羅寶麗女士*——她為甲類申請人，於第 1 期抵港。有些申請人的父母曾到入境事務處作出居留權的聲稱，而入境事務處沒有這些聲稱的紀錄。羅女士被選為這些申請人的代表。羅女士倚賴兩件事情，就是在 1997 年 7 月 4 日和 1999 年 1 月 7 日她父親曾到入境事務處。這種形式不構成該政策決定所指的作出聲稱。

237. 羅女士以她的個人身份也倚賴一件事情（在 1998 年 5 月），當時她父親曾接觸法律援助署求助。這不構成一個入境事務處處長有紀錄的聲稱。

238. 根據該政策決定，羅女士並不符合資格。但她以第 1 期甲類申請人身份在第 1 期及第 2 期的爭議上獲判勝訴。

239. *第 4 名代表申請人——朱春敏女士*——她為乙類申請人，於第 1 期抵港。她被選為那些指稱單以逾期逗留人士的身份身處香港就構成居留權聲稱的申請人的代表。有人說入境事務處處長從他的紀錄會得知此事。僅是逾期逗留不構成該政策決定所指的聲稱。

240. 朱女士以她的個人身份也倚賴以下事情——她曾接觸入境事務處和法律援助署提出聲稱。她接觸這兩個部門不是在寬免政策期內發生的。

241. 根據該政策決定，朱女士並不符合資格。

242. *第 5 名代表申請人——譚小明先生*—— 他為甲類申請人，於第 2 期抵港。上訴法庭作出判決後他取得單程證，但在四個爭議上他被選為代表。

（1）有些申請人的書面聲稱遭拒絕，理由是作出聲稱的時候他們不在香港。譚先生是其中一人。該政策決定其中一個條件是某人在作出聲稱時必須身處香港。這種聲稱不符合這個條件。

（2）有些人曾提出書面聲稱而入境事務處處長是有紀錄的，但他以這種聲稱不構成一個聲稱為理由而拒絕這些聲稱。譚先生是這些人的代表。他倚賴他母親代他寫給入境事務處（1997 年 7 月 25 日）和行政長官（1997 年 10 月 1 日）的兩封信。每封信都指出他是一個香港永久性居民的兒子及請求給予他居留權。這兩封信構成一個入境事務處有紀錄的聲稱。

（3）他也是那些在寬免政策期間曾向內地公安局申請居留權證明書或單程證的申請人的代表。這種申請不構成該政策決定所指的聲稱。

（4）有些申請人曾親自或由其親戚代表到入境事務處，帶同有關的文件證據，宣稱擁有居留權，但入境事務處處長沒有這些人曾到該處的紀錄。他是這些申請人的代表。他在 1997 年 7 月 12 日和他的家人曾到入境事務處及獲告知他必須回內地申請。這不構成該政策決定所指的聲稱。

243. 雖然他送往入境事務處的兩封信構成一個入境事務處處長有紀錄的聲稱，但呈交該兩封信的時候他不是本人身處香港。他沒有符合該政策決定所有的條件。他已經獲發給單程證，所以他不是以個人身份根據該政策決定作出聲稱。

244. *第 6 名代表申請人——李宏龍先生*——他為乙類申請人，於第 3 期抵港。（但其後他離境又回來）。在兩個爭議上他被選為代表。

（1）有些申請人曾向法律援助署作出申請以提出聲稱，但入境事務處處長沒有這些紀錄。他是這些人的代表。他的家人（在 1997 年 7 月 31 日）代表他申請法律援助以提出訴訟程序維護他的權利。他的申請在 1997 年 8 月 9 日遭拒絕，那時正是法律援助署接受了大律師意見，認為乙類申請人沒有任何理據的時候。他沒有繼續採取任何行動。這不構成該政策決定所指的聲稱。

（2）有些申請人曾帶同有關的文件證據到入境事務處宣稱擁有居留權，但入境事務處處長沒有紀錄。他是這些人的代表。他在 1997 年 7 月 31 日和他的家人前往入境事務處，但獲告知他的做法不能接受亦沒有方法處理。入境事務處沒有他們到該處的紀錄。這不構成該政策決定所指的聲稱。

245. 根據該政策決定，他並不符合資格。

246. *第 7 名代表申請人——劉港榕先生*——他為甲類申請人，於第 3 期抵港。訴訟程序展開之後，他已獲發給單程證，但他為了其他申請人的利益，在四件事情上仍保留代表申請人的身份。

（1）有些申請人曾寫書面聲稱給入境事務處處長，而入境事務處處長有這些聲稱的紀錄，但他拒絕這些聲稱，理由是它們不構成聲稱。劉先生是這些人的代表，他曾幾次寫信給入境事務處，這是在 1999 年 1 月 2 日、6 日、17 日、22 日和 25 日。他在這些信中聲稱雙親是香港永久性居民而他是他們的兒子，並請求得到居留權。他亦隨信附上各種文件。他被通知在內地提交申請。入境事務處處長認為這些信只構成一個查詢。我等認為這些信已包含我等談論過的必要的內容。每一封都足夠構成一個聲稱。

（2）有些申請人曾寫書面聲稱給入境事務處，而入境事務處有這些聲稱的紀錄，但入境事務處處長指稱他不知道作出聲稱時這些人是在香港，所以他拒絕這些聲稱。劉先生也是這些人的代表。我等認為這是每個個別情況裏證據上的問題。如果某個申請人可以證明在他的信送往入境事務處時他是身處香港，而他信中包含我等談論過的必要的內容，他便是該政策決定所指的人士，無需入境事務處處長知道此人事實上是身處香港。但是我等不必處理劉先生的個案，因為他已獲發給單程證。

（3）有些申請人指稱曾經打電話給入境事務處，但入境事務處沒有紀錄。劉先生也是這些人的代表。電話查詢不構成一個聲稱。這些人不是該政策決定涵蓋的人士。

（4）有些申請人曾帶備有關的文件證據到入境事務處宣稱擁有居留權，但入境事務處沒有這些人曾到該處的紀錄。劉先生是這些人的代表。他在 1998 年 12 月和父母到入境事務處，但被告知他要回內地申請。入境事務處沒有他曾到該處的紀錄。他父親曾申請更改自己的身份證資料，在申請表裏表明他想為他的兒子查詢取得居留權證明書的手續。這行為只是查詢，不獲接納為聲稱。這類入境事務處處長沒有紀錄的查詢不構成該政策決定所指的聲稱。

247. *第 8 名代表申請人——劉邦先生*——他為乙類申請人，於第 3 期抵港。他在三個爭議方面被選為代表。

（1）有些申請人在寬免政策期間曾向法律援助署申請，但入境事務處處長沒有這些申請的紀錄。劉先生是這些人的代表。他在 1998 年 7 月 27 日申請法律援助。入境事務處處長到 1999 年 7 月才知道他這個申請。這不構成一個聲稱，因為這不是在寬免政策期間向入境事務處處長提出或轉交予入境事務處處長的聲稱。

（2）有些申請人曾向入境事務處處長作出書面聲稱，入境事務處處長是有紀錄的，但他拒絕這些聲稱，理由是它們不構成聲稱。劉先生也是這些人的代表。劉先生沒有提供他寫給入境事務處處長的信的任何詳細資料。但是他也倚賴由一個家庭關注組織在 1998 年 4 月 19 日呈交給行政長官的一封請願書。他指稱該請願書中有多名香港永久性居民子女（包括劉先生在內）的詳細資料。當有人呈交請願書給行政長官，而書中寫清楚相關的詳細資料，這請願書便應該會轉交予入境事務處。事實上，這請願書是有轉交予保安局局長。其後，尚有信件寄往保安局及入境事務處處長繼續跟進，信件日期為 1998 年 6 月 29 日及 1998 年 10 月 26 日。用這種形式作出聲稱應被視為是曾向入境事務處作出聲稱。如果這些信件或請願書包含必要的詳細資料，它們便夠明確構成一個聲稱，雖然它們的本意是涵蓋多名申請人。但是，就算該請願書及接續由該家庭關注組織發出的信件可以構成一個聲稱，當呈交這些書信時劉先生不是身處香港。

（3）有些申請人曾帶有關的文件證據到入境事務處宣稱擁有居留權，但入境事務處沒有他們曾到該處的紀錄。劉先生是這些人的代表。他在 1998 年 7 月曾兩次到入境事務處，但入境事務處沒有他曾到過該處的紀錄。這不構成一個聲稱。

248. 根據該政策決定，劉先生並不符合資格。

249. *第 9 名代表申請人——林麗品女士*——她為乙類申請人，於第 3 期抵港。林女士的個案所涉及的事實有爭議之處，以致她被視為不適合作為代表人，但她卻被選為代表在寬免政策期曾經到過法律援助署的那些申請人。法律援助署告知林女士她不能申請加入當時已在法庭開展了的訴訟為當事人，並且無需申請法律援助及只需等候那些待法庭作出判決的案件的結果。入境事務處並無林女士曾經到過法律援助署的紀錄，在此情況下，她的個案並不構成在該政策決定下的一項聲稱。

250. *第 10 名代表申請人——劉桂芳女士*——她為乙類申請人，於第 3 期抵港。她代表在寬免政策期曾嘗試在內地向公安局申請居留權證明書或申請單程證的那些申請人。看來她是在 1996 年 5 月向內地的有關當局提出申請的，但她收到當局的通知指她並不符合資格。劉女士這類的申請並不構成一項聲稱。

251. 根據該政策決定，劉女士並不符合資格。

252. *第 11 名代表申請人——陳其悅先生*——為乙類申請人，於第 3 期抵港。他所代表的申請人超過 1,000 名。這些申請人曾於 1998 年 12 月至 1999 年 1 月期間到過法律援助署，並獲發給法律援助署覆函，告知他們鑑於已有案件等待法庭的判決，他們無需提出任何訴訟。這些申請並不構成一項入境事務處處長存有紀錄的聲稱，因為入境事務處並沒有於該寬免政策期間收到該等申請的通知。

253. 雖然根據該政策決定陳先生並不符合資格，但因為他收到了法律援助署覆函，所以他屬於聲稱有合理期望的具體陳述的受陳述者的類別。

254. *第 12 名代表申請人——黃玉香女士*——她為乙類申請人，於第 4 期抵港。雖然她並沒有根據該政策決定提出聲稱，但她被選為代表曾經以書面方式向入境事務處處長聲稱有居留權的那些申請人。雖然入境事務處存有這些書面聲稱的紀錄，但這些聲稱卻不被接納為符合規定的聲稱。黃女士的父親曾多次致函行政長官及入境事務處（1998 年 4 月 3 日、9 月 23 日、10 月 15 日及 11 月 16 日）。倘若她的信件中載有我等已論及的主要元素，那麼這些信件應被視為符合該政策決定所規定的聲稱。

255. *第 13 名代表申請人——袁智威先生*——他為乙類申請人，於第 4 期抵港。雖然他不屬於該政策決定的類別，但他被選為代表曾經以書面方式向入境事務處處長作出聲稱的那些申請人。雖然入境事務處存有這些書面聲稱的紀錄，但這些聲稱卻不被接納為符合規定的聲稱。袁先生的父親曾多次致函行政長官、律政司司長、保安局局長及入境事務處（1997 年 5 月 25 日、6 月 1 日、7 月 14 日及 21 日、9 月 21 日及 28 日、10 月 19 日、11 月 17 日，以及 1998 年 4 月 6 日及 7 日）。倘若這些信件載有我等已論及的主要元素，那麼它們應足以構成符合該政策決定所規定的聲稱。

256. 因為他是第 4 期的申請人，所以他並沒有根據該政策決定而作出任何聲稱。但他有收到保安局局長所發出日期為 1998 年 4 月 24 日的公函，換言之，他屬於以合理期望為依據申索濟助的具體陳述的受陳述者的類別。

257. *第 14 名代表申請人——施永霖先生*——他為甲類申請人，於第 4 期抵港。雖然他不屬於該政策決定的類別，但是他被選為關乎以下兩項事宜的代表人：

（1）他代表曾經向公安局申請單程證或居留權證明書的那些申請人。他於 1997 年 5 月提出申請，並於 1997 年 5 月 29 日收到人民入境事務處的回覆，請求他提供有關文件及邀請他的母親到人民入境事務處。他於 1997 年 6 月將一份表格送交存檔。然而，向公安局提出申請並不能構成根據該政策決定而提出的一項聲稱。

（2）他亦以他一名親戚（於 1998 年 10 月）所打給入境事務處的一個查詢電話作為他的聲稱，但入境事務處卻沒有這個電話的紀錄。這個情況並不屬於該政策決定的類別。

258. 他以個人身份，以一封由他的律師於 1998 年 6 月 30 日寫給入境事務處的信件作為他的聲稱。入境事務處於 1998 年 10 月 12 日回覆他的律師，指他於 1983 年 1 月 1 日之前出生，因而並不符合擁有永久性居民身份的資格。入境處處長認為他律師這封信只不過是要求取得入境證，當中並沒有任何聲言聲稱享有居留權。倘若他的信件載有有關的主要元素，它應被視為一項聲稱。然而，看來他當時並不是身處香港。

259. *第 15 名代表申請人——葉蔭華女士*——她為乙類申請人，於第 4 期抵港。她不屬於該政策決定的類別，並沒有根據該政策而提出任何聲稱。

260. *第 16 名代表申請人——鄺健婷女士*——她為乙類申請人，於第 4 期抵港。她不屬於該政策的類別。她所依據唯一與聲稱有關聯的事宜是，當她在內地時，她於 1998 年 7 月 4 日向公安局申請單程證，但根據該政策決定，這項申請並不構成一項聲稱。

261. *第 17 名代表申請人——黃漢倫女士*——她為乙類申請人，於第 5 期抵港。她不屬於該政策決定的類別。她以她於 1996 年 11 月 22 日向內地公安局申請單程證作為她的聲稱，但這項申請並不構成一項聲稱。她亦以她父親曾經多次致函行政長官及其他駐港的中國機構，如新華社（1997 年 7 月 18 日、1997 年 12 月 18 日及 1999 年 1 月 28 日）作為她的聲稱。但入境事務處認為這些信件只不過是請求援助或只是請願信而已，並不構成一項聲稱。就算這些信件載有我等已論及的主要元素，這些信件都不是她身處香港時所寫的。

262. *第 18 名代表申請人——鄧鋿青先生*——他為甲類申請人，於第 5 期抵港。他不屬於該政策決定的類別。他所依據唯一與聲稱有關聯的事宜是，他於 1998 年 11 月向內地的公安局申請居留權證明書，但根據該政策決定這項申請並不構成一項聲稱。

263. *第 19 名代表申請人——洪金轉先生*——他為乙類申請人，於第 5 期抵港。他不屬於該政策決定的類別。他所依據唯一與聲稱有關聯的事宜是，他"於 1997 年"曾就單程證作出過查詢，而所得到答覆是：不可能辦得到。這並不是該政策決定中的一項聲稱。

264. *李淑芬女士*（高院憲法及行政訴訟 2000 年第 2 號）——她為乙類申請人，於第 3 期抵港。因為她的病況，司徒敬法官認為她的個案中有特殊情況，必須盡快審理，所以法庭容許她的個案與其他的案件一同聆訊裁決。

265. 她於 1998 年 2 月 19 日以雙程證抵港。1998 年 3 月 5 日，她申請延期留港，但只獲批准多留數天，之後她便逾期逗留。1998 年 9 月 18 日，在父親陪同下，她到入境事務處提出申請，要求入境事務處核實她可獲發永久性身份證的資格。入境事務處拒絕她的申請，並要求她於一個星期內返回內地。但其後她因精神病況入院接受治療。1998 年 12 月 4 日，她父親寫了一封信給入境事務處，但他這封信卻不被接納為構成向入境事務處申請居留權的聲稱，因為信中只是請求當局以人道理由容許李女士在香港定居。有意見認為該信只是父親為女兒請願而寫的，因為當時上訴法庭已作出對她不利的決定，他知道當中並沒有有效理由可以提出來申請居留權。我等認為，這封信能否構成一項聲稱，並非視乎他是否已知道上訴法庭所作出的決定，尤其是當時該決定適值在上訴期間正受到質疑。同樣，該信是否一項聲稱，亦非取決於他對有關法律情況的理解。我等認為，入境事務處不將該信視為包含了我等已論及的所有主要元素，以及不將該信視為構成一項聲稱，是不合理性的做法。無論如何，她於 1998 年 9 月提出核實她可獲發身份證的資格的申請亦足以構成一項聲稱，而這項聲稱入境事務處是存有紀錄的。根據該政策決定她符合享有居留權的資格。

266. *終院民事上訴 2001 年第 3 號案中的第 1 名代表申請人冼海珠女士* —— 她為乙類申請人，於第 3 期抵港（但她後來離港並於第 5 期再次來港）。就關乎訴訟中的兩項事宜，她被選為代表人。

（1）她代表曾經向入境事務處作出口頭聲稱的那些申請人。但入境事務處並無存有這些口頭聲稱的紀錄。她和她的兄弟於 1998 年 2 月初到入境事務處，該處的職員問她是否有資格申請居留權，並告知他們她需要在內地提出申請。不過入境事務處並沒有她這項聲稱的紀錄。根據該政策決定，在入境事務處並無存有紀錄的口頭聲稱不能構成一項聲稱。

（2）她亦代表曾經向內地機關申請單程證的申請人。這些申請並不符合構成聲稱的規定。

267. 根據該政策決定，她並不符合資格。

268. *終院民事上訴 2001 年第 3 號案中的第 2 名代表申請人 —— 陳仲秀先生* —— 他為乙類申請人，於第 3 期抵港（他後來離港並於第 5 期再次來港）。他以以下的口頭聲稱作為他的聲稱：他和母親於 1997 年 9 月到入境事務處。不過入境事務處並無存有該次到訪的紀錄。根據該政策決定，這並不是一項聲稱。他亦以他於 1997 年 10 月向內地公安局所提出的申請作為他的聲稱。但是當局通知他，他並不符合資格。根據該政策決定，這項申請亦不是一項聲稱。

269. 根據該政策決定，他並不符合資格。

270. *終院民事上訴 2001 年第 3 號案中的第 3 名代表申請人 —— 周燕平女士* —— 她為乙類申請人，於第 5 期抵港。根據該政策決定，她並不符合資格。不過她的個案卻被選為一個例子，來說明有些申請人在接受會見時所遭遇的看待。她指稱當她接受會見時（在該寬免政策期之外），她被迫將入境事務處職員所提供的標準答案寫在會見報告上。倘若這點是有關聯的，我等認為這是個別個案中需要處理的證據事宜。

271. *終院民事上訴 2001 年第 3 號案中的第 4 名代表申請人 —— 鍾志光先生* —— 他為乙類申請人，於第 3 期抵港（他後來離港並於第 5 期再次來港）。他以曾經向入境事務處作出口頭聲稱作為他的聲稱。他曾經和母親及姊妹到入境事務處向該處職員說他想申請居留權。該處職員對他說該處並沒有這樣的程序，他需在內地申請。但是入境事務處並無存有他所說的聲稱的紀錄。他的口頭聲稱並不構成一項聲稱。

272. 根據該政策決定，他並不符合資格。

273. *終院民事上訴 2001 年第 3 號案中的第 5 名代表申請人 —— 林智樂先生* —— 他為乙類申請人，於第 1 期抵港（他後來離港並於第 5 期再次來港）。他亦以曾經於 1997 年 7 月底及 1997 年 10 月向入境事務處提出口頭聲稱作為他的聲稱。但是入境事務處處長並無存有這些口頭聲稱的紀錄。他亦指稱（但為入境事務處所否認）當他接受會見時，該處職員給他一套答案著他從中作出選擇。倘若這是一項有關聯的事宜，我等認為這是個別個案中需要處理的證據事宜。

274. 根據該政策決定，他並不符合資格。

275. *終院民事上訴 2001 年第 3 號案中的第 6 名代表申請人 —— 冼小燕女士* —— 她為乙類申請人，曾經多次來港，其中兩次是在實施寬免政策的期間。她亦以曾經和母親到過入境事務處要求取得表格申請遷居香港作為她的聲稱，但是入境事務處並無這項聲稱的紀錄。

276. 根據該政策決定，她並不符合資格。

277. *終院民事上訴 2001 年第 3 號案中的第 7 名代表申請人 —— 邱寶珍女士* —— 她為乙類申請人，於第 4 期抵港。她並沒有作出任何有權根據該政策決定而受惠的聲稱。

結論

278. 基於上文所闡述的理由，我等就本上訴案中所涉及的五項爭議得出以下的結論。

（1）"在此以前作出的判決"的爭議

279. 按《基本法》第一百五十八條第三款"在此以前作出的判決不受影響"的真確解釋，*吳嘉玲*及*陳錦雅*兩案的判決只對該兩案的真正當事人具約束力。由於本上訴案的申請人並非該兩案的當事人，故除非他們於本上訴案中就其他爭議點獲判勝訴，否則他們是受到該解釋影響的，此外也不能因該兩項判決而受惠。

（2）"合理期望"的爭議

280. 入境事務處處長於 1997 年 7 月 13 日發表的聲明和行政長官於 1997 年 7 月 23，31 日和 10 月 22 日發表的聲明，大意為政府會服從法院的決定，並且會執行該等決定。以當時的事態發展和*吳嘉玲*及*陳錦雅*兩案的例案性質來考慮，以上聲明相當於對公眾表示，政府會把與該兩案當事人處於同一狀況的人士當作該案當事人一樣看待。

281. 法律援助署於 1998 年 12 月 7 日至 1999 年 1 月 29 日期間回覆法律援助申請人的公函中（下稱"法律援助署覆函"），述明他們不必參與當時的訴訟程序或展開新的訴訟程序。這項陳述相當於向那些申請人表示，政府會執行法院在*吳嘉玲*及*陳錦雅*兩案所作的決定，同時也對那些申請人起了引導作用，使他們不採取上述行動，但若他們採取上述行動，便會與那些待決案件的當事人處於同一狀況，並置於"在此以前作出的判決"之保護範圍內，那些申請人亦因此都會因該兩項判決而受惠。

282. 保安局局長寄給第 13 名代表申請人，日期為 1998 年 4 月 24 日的信，內容大意為入境事務處會依循法院的判決處理居留權證明書的申請。這項陳述相當於向該名代表表示，他的個案將會以處理*吳嘉玲*案和*陳錦雅*案中當事人的同一方式處理。

283. 由於人大常委會作出了**該解釋**，而事情亦隨之出現變化，對那些因應此等陳述而產生合理期望的人士，入境事務處處長受法律規限，不能充分體現他們原本的合理期望。

284. 雖然**該解釋**帶來了變化，但入境事務處處長根據香港法例第 115 章《入境條例》第 11 條、第 13 條和第 19（1）條，仍有酌情決定權，可准許不符合《入境條例》第 1B 部規定的人士進入香港和在香港居住。但是，處長不能對一批屬於不明類別的人士合法行使酌情決定權，因為這樣做會損害整個法定計劃。即使他可以這樣行使酌情權，入境政策既是**該解釋**所認可之入境條例的基礎，其效力自不可推翻，所以處長也有權裁定，無論這些人士有甚麼期望，政策的效力也會凌駕於他們的期望之上。因此聽了入境事務處處長及行政長官作出以上一般陳述的受陳述者不能以這理由獲判勝訴。

285. 至於那些收到"法律援助署覆函"的受陳述者和收到保安局局長日期為 1998 年 4 月 24 日來信的第 13 名代表申請人，入境事務處處長可根據《入境條例》第 11 條、第 13 條和第 19（1）條行使酌情決定權，把他們視作特殊個案處理。此舉不會損害**該解釋**所認可的法定計劃。鑑於入境事務處處長對這些申請人發出遣送離境令時，沒有考慮到他們的合理期望，或根據這些條文在何種程度上可以合法地回應他們的期望，故遣送離境令須予以撤銷。這些申請人有權要求入境事務處處長根據《入境條例》第 11

條、第 13 條和第 19（1）條，重新行使酌情決定權，使他們因處長未能體現他們的合理期望而蒙受的重大不公能得到恰當的考慮。

（3）"濫用程序"的爭議

286. 發出和執行遣送離境令並不是法院程序的一部份。這只是入境事務處處長行使其法定權力。對本上訴案的申請人發出遣送離境令及執行這些命令並不構成濫用法庭程序。

（4）"第 1 期及第 2 期"的爭議

287. 那些屬於甲類（即在其父母之中最少一人已成為香港永久性居民後出生）而又在 1997 年 7 月 1 日前（即在《基本法》條文，特別是第二十二條第四款生效前）抵港的申請人，有權要求他們根據第二十四條第二款第（三）項所取得的永久性居民身份，在香港予以核實而無須領取單程證。他們的身份一經確立，他們就有權在香港行使居留權。

288. 那些屬於乙類（即在其父或母成為香港永久性居民前出生）而又在 1997 年 7 月 1 日前抵港的申請人，受**該解釋**對第二十四條第二款第（三）項中"出生時間限制"的詮釋的影響。他們不屬第二十四條第二款第（三）項所指人士的類別，除非他們在本上訴案中就其他爭議點獲判勝訴，否則不能因*陳錦雅*一案的判決而受惠。

289. 在第 2 期（即在 1997 年 7 月 1 日至 7 月 10 日期間）抵港的申請人，無論屬甲類或乙類，均受**該解釋**對第二十二條第四款作出的詮釋所規限。**該解釋**規定他們在來港定居前，必須先取得單程證。除非他們在本上訴案中就其他爭議點獲判勝訴，否則不能因*吳嘉玲*一案的判決而受惠。

（5）"寬免政策"的爭議

290. 行政長官在 1999 年 6 月 26 日宣布的政策決定是行政長官會同行政會議對哪些人不受**該解釋**影響作出的決定。在考慮該政策決定時，必須同時參照*吳嘉玲*和*陳錦雅*兩案訴訟的來龍去脈；引起**該解釋**的事件；該政策決定背後的目的和理由，以及來港人士作出居留權聲稱的背景。

291. 根據該政策決定，申請人如要受惠於*吳嘉玲*和*陳錦雅*兩案的判決，則必須在 1997 年 7 月 1 日至 1999 年 1 月 29 日期間身處香港，並必須在此期間向入境事務處提出居留權的聲稱。該聲稱必須（1）向入境事務處作出；（2）在此寬免期間作出；以及（3）於申請人身處香港時作出。當參照該政策決定的來龍去脈來考慮該政策決定時，很明顯行政會議的目的只讓下列人士因該政策而受惠。就是已向入境事務處提出居留權聲稱的人士，或其聲稱已由其他政府官員在執行職務期間轉交予入境事務處的人士。入境事務處處長對此政策決定並無誤解。

292. 入境事務處處長規定居留權的聲稱必須是在入境事務處存有紀錄的，此舉並沒有錯誤執行該政策決定。

293. 然而，考慮到來港人士作出聲稱的背景和情況，對於某些個案，入境事務處處長對政策決定中所指的聲稱作出的解釋過於狹隘，偏離了合理的做法。任何文件如能明確（1）指出某人為香港永久性居民，並且另一人為其子女；（2）提供某些資料，例如該子女的出生日期或地點；以及（3）要求該子女來港以便定居或享有其居留權，則理應被理解為是作出了居留權的聲稱。若拒絕接納符合以上準則的文件，則等同錯誤執行該政策決定。

濟助

294. 基於以上的結論，我等現作出命令如下：

295. *高院憲法及行政訴訟 1999 年第 81 號案中的第 3 名代表申請人——羅寶麗女士*（以第 1 期甲類申請人身份在"第 1 期及第 2 期"的爭議上獲判勝訴）

（1）上訴得直；

（2）撤銷對她作出的遣送離境令；

（3）宣告她為第二十四條第二款第（三）項所指的永久性居民，在香港享有居留權。

296. *高院憲法及行政訴訟 1999 年第 81 號案中的第 11 名代表申請人——陳其悅先生*（在"合理期望"的爭議上獲判勝訴）

（1）上訴得直；

（2）撤銷對他作出的遣送離境令；

（3）指示入境事務處處長按照本判決，考慮行使《入境條例》第 11 條、第 13 條和第 19（1）條賦予他的酌情決定權。

297. *高院憲法及行政訴訟 1999 年第 81 號案中的第 13 名代表申請人——袁智威先生*（在"合理期望"的爭議上獲判勝訴）

（1）上訴得直；

（2）撤銷對他作出的遣送離境令；

（3）指示入境事務處處長按照本判決，考慮行使《入境條例》第 11 條、第 13 條和第 19（1）條賦予他的酌情決定權。

298. *高院憲法及行政訴訟 2000 年第 2 號案中的李淑芬女士*（在"寬免政策"的爭議上獲判勝訴）

（1）上訴得直；

（2）宣告她為該政策決定所指的人士。

299. 至於其他代表申請人的上訴，則予以駁回。

300. 我等並指示訴訟各方須按照本判決，就本院對每位代表申請人及其代表的每位人士之上訴應作出的正式命令，一起進行商議並擬備該等命令的草稿，呈予本院批准。訴訟各方如未能達成協議，則應向本院作出書面陳詞，如有需要時，可就上述書面陳詞向本院申請指示如何擬備。

301. 關於本上訴案的訟費，我等不作任何命令，各申請人本身的訟費則須按《法律援助規例》評定。

終審法院常任法官包致金：

I. 目錄

302. 按以下的分題，本席的判詞分為十一個部份：—

II. 引言

303. 本案有超過 5,000 名上訴人向本院提出上訴。他們全部都是從內地來港的。他們援引香港的憲法《基本法》為上訴的依據，聲稱擁有香港永久性居民的身份，因而在港有居留權。不過他們的情況有很多不同之處，而這些差異對大律師代表他們所提出的其中一些論據有重要的影響。

III. 在此以前的判決不受影響

304. 然而，就他們所提出的第一項論據而言，毫無疑問，他們的處境都是一樣的。基於稍後會提到的明顯理由，本席稱此為“在此以前的判決不受影響”的論據。代表大部份上訴人的御用大律師 Geoffrey Robertson 先生能言善辯地呈述此項論據，其論據為代表其餘上訴人的資深大律師李志喜女士所認同。不過代表答辯人入境事務處處長的資深大律師馬道立先生則極力反對此論據。在未列述及闡釋此論據前，本席必須引述《基本法》中的某些條文，並說明本港憲法的一些發展過程。

305. Yash Ghai 教授於他的著作《Hong Kong's New Constitutional Order》，第 2 版（1999），第 195 頁，形容《基本法》第一百五十八條為一條“很複雜的條文，條文本身為解釋有關法律帶來了一些棘手的問題”。本席現將第一百五十八條的全文列出，內容如下：

> “本法的解釋權屬於全國人民代表大會常務委員會。
>
> 全國人民代表大會常務委員會授權香港特別行政區法院在審理案件時對本法關於香港特別行政區自治範圍內的條款自行解釋。
>
> 香港特別行政區法院在審理案件時對本法的其他條款也可解釋。但如香港特別行政區法院在審理案件時需要對本法關於中央人民政府管理的事務或中央和香港特別行政區關係的條款進行解釋，而該條款的解釋又影響到案件的判決，在對該案件作出不可上訴的終局判決前，應由香港特別行政區終審法院請全國人民代表大會常務委員會對有關條款作出解釋。如全國人民代表大會常務委員會作出解釋，香港特別行政區法院在引用該條款時，應以全國人民代表大會常務委員會的解釋為準。但在此以前作出的判決不受影響。
>
> 全國人民代表大會常務委員會在對本法進行解釋前，徵詢其所屬的香港特別行政區基本法委員會的意見。”

306. 為了正確地應用第一百五十八條第三款倒數第二句句子的法律效力，必須在某程度上將該款的最後一句句子的解釋縮窄。問題是：在甚麼程度？

307. 1999 年 1 月 29 日，本院頒下 *Ng Ka Ling（吳嘉玲）v. Director of Immigration*（（1999）2 HKCFAR 4） 及 *Chan Kam Nga（陳錦雅）v Director of Immigration*（（1999）2 HKCFAR 82）兩案的判決。這兩案的判決與由人大常委會於 1999 年 6 月 26 日所作出的解釋（**“該解釋”**）有關。所涉及的《基本法》條款為第二十二條第四款及第二十四條第二款第（三）項。第二十二條第四款內容如下：

> “中國其他地區的人進入香港特別行政區須辦理批准手續，其中進入香港特別行政區定居的人數由中央人民政府主管部門徵求香港特別行政區政府的意見後確定。”

第二十四條（在第二款中）列出了六類人士為香港永久性居民，並（根據第三款）賦予他們享有在港的居留權。就本上訴案而言，只需引述首三類人士的資格，內容如下：

> “（一）在香港特別行政區成立以前或以後在香港出生的中國公民；
>
> （二）在香港特別行政區成立以前或以後在香港通常居住連續七年以上的中國公民；
>
> （三）第（一）、（二）兩項所列居民在香港以外所生的中國籍子女。”

308. 就與本上訴案有關的判決而言，本院於*吳嘉玲*案裁定憑藉第二十四條第二款第（三）項為香港永久性居民的人士，無須根據第二十二條第四款取得批准才可以由內地來港行使他們在港的居留權。然而，**該解釋**則闡明就算只是為了以上的情況，他們也必須取得批准才可出境。本院亦於*陳錦雅*案裁定當一名子女以第二十四條第二款第（三）項為依據，欲藉著其父母中至少一人的身份去爭取香港永久性居民身份時，其父或母是在其出生前或後取得永久性居民身份這點並無影響。然而，**該解釋**則闡明該名父親或母親必須在該名子女出生前取得永久性居民的身份。

309. **該解釋**並非是人大常委會因應本院提交釋法的請求而作出的，而是因應香港政府通過國務院向人大常委會請求釋法而作出的。不過，代表入境事務處處長的馬先生同意（本席認為他的做法恰當），第一百五十八條規定“在此以前作出的判決不受影響”的條文，同樣適用於人大常委會並非在本院提交釋法請求的情況下所作出的解釋，猶如人大常委會在本院提交釋法請求的情況下所作出的解釋一樣。

310. 正如本席較早時所指出的，就“在此以前的判決不受影響”的論據而言，所有上訴人都屬同一處境。理由如下：當本院頒下*吳嘉玲及陳錦雅*兩案的判決時，所有上訴人均為於內地出生的中國公民，他們的父母至少有一人為第二十四條第二款第（一）項或第（二）項類別的香港永久性居民。因此，根據本院在該兩案中的判決對《基本法》所作出的解釋，他們全部已擁有香港永久性居民的身份。簡言之，根據“在此以前的判決不受影響”這個論據，他們全部已可按照該兩項判決取得香港永久性居民的身份，而這個身份憑藉第一百五十八條第三款最後一句句子的效力，是不受**該解釋**影響的。

311. 倘若該“在此以前的判決不受影響”的論據是正確的話，那麼就會產生兩個後果。首先，所有的上訴人都有權要求法院宣告他們勝訴，即他們為香港永久性居民，在港享有居留權。其次，任何針對他們任何一人而作出的遣送離境令都必須撤銷。

312. 該等遣送離境令必須撤銷的理由如下。本院於*吳嘉玲*案中有以下的闡述（第 36 頁 F-H）：

> “然而，這並非表示“第 3 號條例”所引進的整個居權證計劃是違憲的。大家必須把享有居留權的永久性居民和*聲稱*是永久性居民的人士區別清楚。所以，立法當局引進一項計劃來核實某些人士聲稱擁有永久性居民的身份是合理的做法。我等認為在居權證計劃中，必須持有單程證的規定是違憲的，除此之外，計劃的其他部份都是符合憲法的，不能稱之為逾越核實範疇。因此，該計劃規定聲稱人須向入境事務處處長申請及領取居權證，並且只能在持有居權證後才能確立其永久性居民的身份都是符合憲法的。再者，居

權證計劃訂明這些人士必須留在內地申請居權證，以及在被入境事務處處長拒發居權證而提出上訴時，也必須留在內地，這方面也是符合憲法的。永久性居民因為擁有居留權而有權入境，但*聲稱*擁有這身份的人，其身份必須首先獲得核實。"

313. 但在本案中，當本院頒下*吳嘉玲*及*陳錦雅*兩案的判決時，所有的上訴人都是於內地出生的中國公民，他們的父母至少有一個為第二十四條第二款第（一）項或第（二）項類別的人士。因此，倘若該"在此以前的判決不受影響"的論據是正確的話，那麼，他們便全部都是擁有香港永久性居民身份的人士，而並非單純是聲稱擁有這個身份的人士。換言之，他們的身份便得以確立，無需核實。

314. 說明了有關的背景後，本席現就該"在此以前的判決不受影響"的論據是否正確表達我的看法。

315. 討論的起點為：倘若人大常委會沒有作出相反的解釋（或修訂《基本法》），*吳嘉玲*和*陳錦雅*兩案中的判決便成為先例，任何人士其情況符合該等判決中所闡述的有關法律的都可受惠，不論他們的情況是在甚麼時候符合有關的法律。（當本席提述在該等判決中所闡述的有關法律，所指的當然是判決就"出境批准"及"出生時間"這兩個問題所闡述的有關法律）。然而，當人大常委會作出**該解釋**後，該等判決便不再是關乎該等問題的先例。很明顯，這是必然的後果，因為根據第一百五十八條，香港法院有責任在引用人大常委會所解釋的《基本法》條文時，應以人大常委會的解釋為準。與此同時，毫無疑問，那些在該兩案中為具名當事人的居留權申請人，即使人大常委會作出了**該解釋**，他們仍然是有權獲按照在該等判決中所闡述的有關法律處理他們的個案。這個後果也是無法避免的。因為根據第一百五十八條的規定，"在此以前作出的判決不受"人大常委會在該等判決之後所作出的解釋"影響"。

316. 然而，很多時候，在兩個明顯的極端的中間，存在著一個沒有那麼明顯的情況，傾向於兩個極端的其中一方。在本案的情況中，那些位於這個中間處境的，包括那些在**該解釋**前符合*吳嘉玲*及*陳錦雅*兩案中的判決所闡述的有關法律所指的情況的人士。本案的上訴人正是該等人士，他們本來可以加入該等案件中為當事人。

317. 第一百五十八條第三款最後一句中的"判決"一詞的涵義為何？

318. 本席知悉在*R v. Ireland*（（1970）44 ALJR 263）一案中，澳洲首席大法官 Garfield Barwick 爵士於一項為所有其他澳洲高等法院大法官認同的判決中指出（第266頁A），"當正確使用有關字詞時，唯一稱得上是法院所頒下的判決是法院所作出的命令，〔並且〕判決的理由本身並不是判決；雖然這些理由可為法院提供作出決定的理由，並因而成為一個先例"。不過，他這番說話是在論及一條法定條文時所表達的看法，該法定條文規定，除非分別作出判決被視為合宜，否則法院只能頒下單一的判決。他說這番話，也是為了要解釋有關的見解（第266頁B），即"在〔該條文〕中所提述的'分別作出判決'，嚴格來說，並沒有準確地使用有關字詞，〔而〕只能是指以不同理由作出判決"。

319. 一如以往，必須切記首席大法官 Earl of Halsbury 於*Quinn v. Leathem*（〔1901〕AC 495第506頁）案中所闡述的著名忠告："〔在司法宣告中〕使用的語句所表達的一般性涵義，法院並無意視其為有關的全部法律的註解，有關的涵義須由出現這些語句的個案中的特定事實來加以管限和約制"。

320. 誠然，首席大法官 Garfield Barwick 爵士本人亦於*Moller v. Roy*（（1975）49 ALJR 311 第312頁D-F）案中指出有關語句上下文的相關性。在該案中，他所審理的是一條憲法條文，該條文賦予澳洲高等法院司法管轄權聆訊"針對任何一個州的最高法院的所有判決、判令、命令及判刑"而提出的上訴。他並且闡釋"判決等"這些字詞，指的是任何一個州的最高法院可作出的正式命令，亦即是"*與本案一樣的情況中*，該詞'判決'可被接受的涵義"。（文字斜體以示強調。）

321. 本席要提述一件稍為特別的案例，就是*Australian Consolidated Press Ltd v. Uren*（〔1969〕1AC 590），就本上訴案而言，此案具有啟發的作用。該案是由澳洲高等法院提交樞密院審理的上訴案。澳洲高等法院就該案頒下重審令，不過當事人並沒有針對這項命令提出上訴。在樞密院席前上訴人所質疑的只是澳洲高等法院的判決中的一部份，即裁定澳洲法院理應不依循英國上議院於*Rookes v. Barnard*（〔1964〕AC 1129）案中，就懲罰性損害賠償可在甚麼情況下追討所作出的決定。然而，根據《1833年司法委員會法令》（Judicial Committee Act 1833）第3條，樞密院裁定樞密院有司法管轄權聆訊該上訴案。該條條文規定，"任何針對或關乎任何法院、法官或司法人員所作出的裁定、判刑、規令或命令，向英皇陛下或英皇陛下會同樞密院"提出的上訴，須提交樞密院的司法委員會審理。在由大法官 Lord Morris of Borth-y-Gest 向英女皇所呈述的意見中，樞密院認為無需在該案的情況下界定該詞"裁定"的範圍，但儘管如此，樞密院認為（第633頁A）該詞"涵義廣泛"。"判決"一詞也應有同樣意思。其涵義亦取決於其上下文的語境。

322. 在文意方面，當然必須切記當人大常委會就《基本法》中任何一條條文作出解釋時，人大常委會所闡釋的是該條文從立法生效後一直以來的涵義。所以，該情況與法院將一條法定條文判定為不符合憲法時所帶來的情況有些相似之處。當法院這樣做時，法院是闡明該條文從開始便是無效的。就此情況而言，美國最高法院於*Chicot County Drainage District v. Baxter State Bank*（308 US 371（1939））案中的決定具有啟發的作用。首席大法官 Hughes 在頒下該院的判決時有以下的闡釋（第374頁）：

> "在考慮某一個隨後作出的判決指有關條文無效所帶來的影響時，得從不同層面作出考慮，就是關乎個人及法團的特定的關係，以及關乎私人及公務的特定的行為。法院必須審視與聲稱因以下情況而既得的權利有關的問題：因為某個身份而產生的權利；因為以往被視為終局並切實執行的裁定而產生的權利；因為有關的公共政策（鑑於有關法規及其以往被應用的性質）而產生的權利。這些問題是引致州政府法院及聯邦政府法院關注的問題中最難解決的；無數的司法決定顯示，採取一刀切的原則，視裁定某條文無效的判決具有絕對追溯力的說法，是沒有充分理由的。"

323. 不論法例也好（正如大法官 Deane 於*University of Wollongong v. Metwally*（（1984）158 CLR 447第478頁）案中所表達的看法），或是司法決定也好（正如大法官 Lord Browne-Wilkinson 於*Kleinwort Benson Ltd v. Lincoln City Council*（〔1999〕2 AC 349第359頁E）案中所表達的看法），都不能"抹殺過去或更改歷史事實"。

324. 為何《基本法》第一百五十八條規定"在此以前作出的判決不受"人大常委會以後所作出的解釋"影響"，當中必然有一個很好的理由，顯然是為了保障已具體確立的權利。這個情況屬於憲法性的，當中實在沒有任何根據要將該保障的範圍縮窄或視該保障的效力取決於法律條款的技術性細節。於*R v. Secretary of State for the Home Department, ex parte Shefki Gashi and*

Artan Gjoka（〔2000〕EWHC Admin 356）案中，法院要審理一項技術性的論據，該論據大意為法院不能因應答辯人提出要求而作出宣告。大法官 Collins 有以下的闡釋（第 6 段）："但這是個空洞的論據，因為當法院的判決已明確表達了主審法官對有關法律的見解時，法院便無需作出正式的宣告"。在該案的情況下，法院並沒有對"判決"一詞作出狹義或技術性的解釋。同樣，就本上訴案而言，亦不應有這類的情況出現。

325. *吳嘉玲及陳錦雅*兩案是憲法性的訴訟，關乎一項受捍衛的權利。本席認為，就關乎受捍衛權利的憲法訴訟的性質而言，任何人士倘若他們現時所處的境況可代入該訴訟的有關情況中，根據法院對該訴訟當事人所作出的勝訴判決，他們都有權取得已具體確立的權利。本席在任職大律師及法官多年來所處理的案件中，從未遇過本上訴案中關乎這部份的正反論據是如此的各有千秋，不相上下。本席尊重相反的見解。然而，就本人而言，本席無法認同第一百五十八條對已具體確立的權利所給予的保障，只局限於具名的當事人。

326. 有一點需要強調的是，倘若該"在此以前的判決不受影響"的論據，導致**該解釋**效力不大，或倘若該論據無論以甚麼方式去質疑一項明顯是無需質疑的事實，即人大常委會所具有不容置疑的權力，那麼，該論據就不可能被接納。但該論據是否有造成這些問題？本席信納該論據並沒有造成這些問題。該論據只適用於已具體確立的權利，並不涉及援引*吳嘉玲及陳錦雅*兩案的判決為先例。**該解釋**已將該等判決的先例效力除去，而該"在此以前的判決不受影響"的論據並無質疑此點。

327. 基於上述所有的理由，本席接納上訴人所提出的"在此以前的判決不受影響"的論據，並作出以下的裁定。任何人士於**該解釋**前的情況符合*吳嘉玲及陳錦雅*兩案中所闡述的有關法律所指的情況，都有權根據該兩案中的判決取得已具體確立的香港永久性居民身份。憑藉《基本法》第一百五十八條的"在此以前的判決不受影響"的條文的效力，這個身份不受**該解釋**影響。每名上訴人都為這類人士。

328. 據此，本席判決全部上訴人上訴得直，並（i）宣告所有上訴人均為香港永久性居民並有本地居留權；以及（ii）撤銷任何針對他們任何一人所作出的遣送離境令。

329. 倘若本席的判決為本院最少過半數的主審法官所接納的話，那麼本上訴案便就此審結。但既然事實並非如此，本席現處理上訴人就合理期望這點所提出的論據。

IV. 針對濫用權力 / 合理期望而給予的濟助：引言

330. 一般稱為"合理期望的法則"這個法則的主要功用，是針對行政機關濫用行政權力而給予司法濟助。倘若要名副其實地為這個法則的功用取名，大可以稱之為"針對濫用權力的法則"。然而，這個法則已按著某事項的名稱取名，因為忽視該事項可構成濫用權力，本席亦按該名稱提述此法則。

331. 簡言之，上訴人的"合理期望"論據為：

（i） 他們有合理期望，就是根據入境處處長所擁有的酌情決定權，他們至少在大體上可得到於*吳嘉玲及陳錦雅*兩案中申請居留權的具名當事人所得到的同一看待；

（ii） 當局沒有這樣的看待他們是濫用了行政權力；以及

（iii）法院應針對該濫用行政權力的情況給予他們濟助。

入境事務處處長就此論據所提出的反對理由涉及的廣度和深度，都必須就有關的法律作出相稱而全面的審視。為了解決本上訴案及為了之後處理所涉及的合理期望的聲稱所採用的做法，有幾點問題需在此先行澄清。

332. 合理期望的法則是普通法制中被確立的法則，源於法院在審理真實個案時，按著原則作出可切實執行的判決，並在此情況下發展。御用大律師 Lord Alexander of Weedon 在其著作《The Voice of the People》（1997，第 46 頁）按其一貫的風格，一針見血地指出"普通法其中一個強項是以真實的個案處境為基礎，確立權利和責任"。合理期望的法則中涉及一個責任，即管治者對受管治者有當負的責任。這個責任經由法院所確立，確保當局只會使用而不會濫用其行政權力，藉此進一步鞏固法治。細看之下，一般可見法院所付出的努力，標誌著 Thomas More 爵士所倡議的取向；他於其著作《Utopia》中（第一冊（1516））（本席摘錄 Paul Turner 的譯文（1965，第 63 頁）），提議"一個更文明的人生哲學，認識所謂人生如舞台的處境，不但設法與其接軌，並在現場演出時扮演一個合適的角色。"一般來說，法院已盡其當盡的本份，建立合理期望的法則，致使三權分立的原則得以保存，並避免與憲法的運作脫節，從而讓行政當局在憲法的安排上仍然專責處理行政政策。

333. Dawn Oliver 教授（在她的一本評論著作《A negative aspect to legitimate expectations》（〔1998〕PL Winter 558 第 562 頁））中有以下的詮釋：

> "英國普通法確立了合理期望的法則，為的是要加增公法的利益，這些利益是在該法則下才可以享有的；確立該法則的目的並非是要它作為享有現存民事權利的先決條件：因為在民事訴訟中，當事人無需證明他同時享有某項權利及合理期望才可以勝訴……"

因此，大法官 Simon Brown 於 *R v. Devon County Council, ex parte Baker*（〔1995〕1 All ER 73 第 89 頁 e）案中論及"在該等案件中，法院裁定就某特定程序而言（法例本來沒有要求在保障某項權益時必須依循該程序行事），倘若有一方作出了某些具體的承諾或做法，那麼就必須依循該程序行事"。但當然要切記一點，正如法律權威典籍《Wade & Forsyth on Administrative Law》，第 8 版（2000），第 496 頁中所闡述：基本上人們有權得到公平的看待，就算當中沒有人對他們作出過具體的承諾，並且沒有已被確立的做法；在此情況下，該"合理期望的法則……只是加重而並非取代要公平行事的責任"。

334. Yvonne Cripps 博士在她一篇名為"Some Effects of European Law on English Administrative Law"（（1994）2 Indiana Journal of Global Legal Studies 213 第 222 頁）的文章中指出"一些歐盟會員國家的本國法律，尤以德國的為然，都有承認'合理期望'"。至於"合理期望"這個法則的起源，本人不曾深入研究。要探討這個源頭肯定費煞思量。Norbert Rouland 在其著述"Legal Anthropology"（1988 年版）（英譯本完成於 1994 年）的第 1 頁這樣說：已知的不同法律制度為數有一萬個，〔雖然〕當中能夠找到較為確切資料的則只有幾百個。就英國普通法而論，"合理期望"這個法則第一次出現是在 1969 年。當時是在案例 *Schmidt v. Secretary of State for Home Affairs*（〔1969〕2 Ch. 149）中出現。英國上訴法院 Lord Denning MR（第 171 頁 A–B）說：外籍人士在獲得批准可以逗留英國一段指定的時期後，如果當局出乎爾反乎爾，考慮要在這段時期未屆滿之前取消有關的批准。那麼，該有關外籍人士應該"獲得給予機會表達意見，因為他會有合理期望，期望自己在該段批准逗留時間內，可以逗留在英國。"就是這樣，法院對合理期望在*程序上*予以執行。自此以後，這個法則一直演變到現時包括對合理期望在實體上予以執行。

335. 這兩種不同執行形式都會在以下的情況中產生，有關的行政部門都令致個別人士抱有合理期望，期望行政部門會允許他保有某些東西或會給與他某些東西。這兩種執行形式都是基於法治精神。正如大法官 Lord Steyn 在案例 *R v. Secretary of State for the Home Department, ex parte Pierson*（〔1998〕AC 539 第 591 頁 E）中所說，"法治是執行公平的最起碼準則，在實體上和程序上都是。"合理期望的程序執行，是法庭要有關的行政部門在作出可能影響某人的決定前，必須給與該有關人士表達意見的機會。可能因為某行政部門某些做法，令致他抱有合理期望，期望有關的行政部門在作出決定之前會給他表達意見的機會。又可能因為某行政部門某些做法，令致他抱有合理期望，期望有關行政部門會讓他保有或給與他本來想要取走或減少或撤回的某些實質東西。合理期望的實體執行，則是法庭要求有關的行政部門不得取走、減少或撤回某些實質東西以實現該合理期望。

336. 在案例 *R v. Secretary of State for Home Affaris, ex parte Hargreaves*（〔1997〕1 WLR 906）中，英國上訴法院（i）不同意任何決定的本質，可以因為決定本身不公平地令致合理期望落空，而受到質疑；（ii）設法把這等質疑局限於根據 Wednesbury 理由而提出的質疑。但法官 Sedley（大法官 Sedley 當時的官階）在案例 *R v. Ministry of Agriculture Fisheries and Food, ex parte Hamble（Offshore）Fisheries Ltd*（〔1995〕2 A11 ER 714）中則採用了相反的處理方法。對於這個相反的處理方法，上訴庭在案例 Hargreaveas 中予以批評時，一點也不客氣。但自此以後，Sedley 法官的處理方法一直都得到贊同。

337. 本席認為，合理期望的實體執行，不應以懷疑眼光來看待，或在執行時畏首畏尾，因為實體執行是從程序執行自然發展而來。說到底，合理期望本身都必會是實質的，除非陳述本身只不過是給機會該有關人士表達意見。而即使是表達意見，最終目的也是實質的。表達意見的機會是達致這個目的的唯一方法。正如上訴法院 Lord Denning MR 在案例 *Schmidt* 判詞中（第 171 頁 A–B）的一段（亦即本席所引述者）的見解所言：外籍人士所合理期望的，是可以在獲准逗留期間內逗留下來。表達意見的機會，只不過是防止當局撤消這個逗留批准的一個方法。新西蘭上訴庭庭長（英國上議院大法官 Lord Cooke of Thorndon 當時任此職）在案例 *Thames Valley Electric Power Board v. NZFP Pulp & Paper Ltd*（〔1994〕2 NZLR 641 第 653 頁 ）中有這樣的見解："實質不公平這個理據的優點是它提供了一個彈性的措施，對當局不適當運用行政權力時可以予以糾正，不然的話當局的行政權力便變成沒有制衡。"本席認為，合理期望的實體執行是一個補救方法，而這種補救方法，在整個公法法制裏（一如香港的法制裏），佔有一席很重要的地位。

338. 合理期望實體執行的一個主要例子（如果不是最主要的）可以在 1999 年英國上訴庭在 *R v. North and East Devon Health Authority, ex parte Coughlan*（〔2001〕1 QB 213） 案中頒下的裁決中看到。但英國上議院早於 1985 年在 *R v. Inland Revenue Commissioners, ex parte Preston*（〔1985〕AC 835）一案中已承認這樣的濟助是可以得到的。

339. 在 *Preston* 一案中，稅務局局長決定，根據《1970 年個人入息稅及公司利得稅法令》第 17 部份對有關納稅人提出訴訟，以便局長重新評估納稅人在 1974–75 年度和 1975–76 年度的稅務責任。有關納稅人申請司法覆核，聲稱稅務局人員曾向他陳述，謂納稅人如果撤回申索該兩個年度的利息濟助和資本損失，稅務局便不會重新評估他在該兩個年度的稅務責任。有關納稅人其後確實撤回申索，這一點雙方都沒有爭議。雙方的爭論點是該番陳述是否真的有作出。從大法官 Lord Templeman 的一番說話（其他上議院大法官亦表支持）看來，納稅人結果之所以敗訴，是因為諸位大法官認為這樣的陳述事實上未有作出過。大法官 Lord Scarman 的判詞（第 853 頁 A）則這樣說：如果納稅人能證明有這樣的陳述作出過，"那麼，基於稅務局對他不公平，濫用權力根據 1970 年法令第 17 部份提起訴訟，他便有權申請司法覆核要求濟助。"

340. 在法律權威典籍"Wade & Forsyth on Administrative Law"（第 7 版（1994））一書中，作者引述案例"*Preston's case*"時，強調（第 419 頁）合理期望這個法則，"證明是程序權利的源流，也是實質權利的源流"。而這本法律權威典籍的最新版（第 8 版（2000）），在書本中（第 494 至 495 頁）指出，合理期望這個法則"在合理理據的領域……以及在自然公義這個領域，都有長足的發展"。

341. 在 *Coughlan* 案中申請司法覆核的申請人是一個嚴重傷殘人士，獲得收留住在馬登健康院內—— 一間專門收容長期傷殘人士的國家醫療服務中心。醫務當局的前任局長曾向 Coughlan 小姐和馬登健康院內的其他病人承諾過，答應他們可以在該健康院內渡過餘生。這個承諾作出後，政府定下政策決議，對於可以獲得國家健康服務中心長期收容護理的資格標準，有所規定。受這個決策影響所及，國家醫療服務中心只是提供專科護理服務，至於普通科護理服務則應由地方的有關當局撥款資助。接著，醫務當局作出決定，指 Coughlan 小姐和馬登健康院內的其他病人並不符合這個資格。最後，經過公眾諮詢後，醫務當局決定關閉馬登健康院，並將 Coughlan 小姐和馬登健康院的其他病人所需要的長期普通科護理服務，轉交地方有關當局負責，但同時沒有說明會有其他的安置辦法。

342. Hidden 法官推翻醫務當局把馬登健康院關閉的決定。經上訴後，Hidden 法官的判決得到上訴庭的確認。上訴庭的判詞（第 260 頁 E–G）指出關閉馬登健康院的決定是非法的，而其中一個理由是：

> "……關閉健康院的決定不合理地破壞了醫務當局的前任局長曾經對 Coughlan 小姐清楚許下的承諾。前任局長答應她，可以在馬登健康院居住渡過餘生。醫務當局這樣不合理破壞承諾構成了不公平、等於濫用權力。"

343. 也許可以這樣說：*Coughlan* 案是由一個對公法有特別強烈感覺的審判團（當中有上訴法院 Lord Woolf MR（即現任首席大法官），大法官 Mummery 和大法官 Sedley）裁決。關於這個案例，大法官 Lord Hoffmann 在 *R v. Ministry of Defence, ex parte Walker*（〔2000〕1 WLR 806 第 816 頁 B）案中提述時，並沒有異議。特別要注意的是，在 *R v. Secretary of State for the Home Department, ex parte Hindley*（〔2001〕1 AC 410）案中各位法官對 *Coughlan* 案的看法。在判詞中大法官 Lord Steyn（其他大法官 Lord Browne-Wilkinson, Lord Nicholls of Birkenhead 和 Lord Hutton 亦表示贊同）這樣說（第 419 頁 A–B）：

> "代表 Hindley 的大律師以實質合理期望這個法則，即案例 *R v. North East Devon Health Authority, Ex p Coughlan*（〔2001〕QB 213）中所闡明者，作為依據。在案例 *In re Findlay*（〔1985〕AC 318）中法官的附帶意見，似乎跟代表大律師就實質合理期望所持的論據相違背。大律師請求本院裁定案例 *In re Findlay* 的判決可予區別，或裁定該判決錯誤。而代表內政部的大律師則試圖說服本席相信，根據本案中事實來看，並沒有法律爭論點需要判決。"

可以看到，甚至連要求推翻*Coughlan*一案的判決（跟要求區別案例*Findlay*或不依循*Findlay*案例判決的意思相反）這個問題也沒有提出。而在*Hindley*案中，第五位上議院大法官，Lord Hobhouse of Woodborough 把*Coughlan*案中的判詞描述為"有重大價值"的判詞。

344. 提供司法覆核以制衡行政權力的濫用，但另一方面又不會對這個權力的正常行使構成制（掣）肘，是法庭審理"合理期望"案件時所應關注的要點。但這個關注要點並不是新事物，亦非只局限於合理期望的案件。在案例*HTV Ltd v. Price Commission*（〔1976〕ICR 170）中（案件涉財政部徵收稅項），上訴法院Lord Denning MR 這樣說（第 185 頁 G）：

> "據我所知，大家一直都認為公共機構，既然是一個由國會委任，賦與（予）權力為大眾謀福祉的組織，不可能在行使這些權力時自我制（掣）肘，亦不可能阻止它履行公職。這樣就必須對公共機構有制約，以防止它濫用權力。如果公共機構對個別市民行事時不公平、不公正，但又不是因為顧全公眾利益這個理由而要這樣做，那麼它就是濫用權利了。"

上訴法院民事分院院長跟著引述（第 185 頁 H-186 頁 B）四宗案例，而當中每件案例都顯示，法庭不容許有關行政部門，在沒有合理理由的情況下，說話或行事出乎爾反乎爾。這四宗案例是：*Robertson v. Minister of Pensions*（〔1949〕1 KB 227）（案件涉及退休金）；*Wells v. Minister of Housing and Local Government*（〔1967〕1 WLR 1000）（案件涉及規劃圖則的批核）；*Lever Finance Ltd v. Westminster（City）London Borough Council*（〔1971〕1 QB 222）（案件也是涉及規劃圖則的批核）；以及*Congreve v. Home Office*（〔1976〕1 QB 629）（案件涉及電視牌照）。在退休金和規劃批核的案件中，當事人因倚賴當局的聲明或作為而蒙受損害（有關這個課題，本席在適當時候會再深入論述）。在有關電視牌照的案件中，所涉及的問題純粹是：電視牌照取消時，是否不用給予理由，又或是否理由不需要合理。

345. 上議院在*Findlay*案中的裁定，說明行政部門有需要能夠行使權力，就本身所認定的公眾利益，更改本身部門的政策。但這樣說並不表示因為有這個需要，所以就不能限制，甚至是有限度地限制，這個更改政策的權力；而之所以有需要這樣限制，目的是防止濫用權力。畢竟，只有在衡量過如何公平對待抱有合理期望的人，以及所依據的公眾利益能否凌駕乎個人的合理期望兩者後，如果認為前者重要，這個限制才會實施。而這方面的衡量則由獨立和公正無私的司法機關來負責。正如 M. J. Detmold 教授在其著述"The Nature of Judicial Power"（（2001）12 PLR 135 第 135 頁）中所言："法官審判案件所按照的只是法律原則，並無其他。"

346. 同樣必須緊記的是：不能純粹因為案件所牽涉的是行政政策事宜，就說有關的政策要受到徹底質疑。闡明這一點的好例子是案例*R v. Ministry of Defence, ex parte Smith*（〔1996〕QB 517）。在該案中，申請司法覆核的申請人被革除軍職，而革除他們的唯一理由是他們有同性戀的癖好。兩位申請人質疑把他們革除的決定，以及質疑該革除決定所根據的行政政策。他們所持的論據是：行政部門的決定和政策不合理，亦與《1995 年歐洲保護人權和基本自由公約》有抵觸，同時也違反了歐盟會議規定人人平等的指引。至於行政政策為顧全公眾利益，必須確保有運作效率高效益高的戰鬥部隊，這一點則沒有質疑。真正的問題是，大法官 Simon Brown 說：內政部長認為讓軍中存在同性戀有損公眾利益，這種說法是否合理呢？簡單地說，這個意見是不是有邏輯的意見呢？是正確的，還是錯誤的呢？（事情發展的結果是，申請人在本國法院的訴訟敗訴，但最後在歐洲人權法院卻勝訴，歐洲人權法院裁定，禁制軍隊中有同性戀，是違反該兩名軍人根據《1950 年歐盟保護人權和基本權利公約》所享有的權利。有關的案例是*Smith and Grady v. United Kingdom*（（2000）29 EHRR 493）和*Lustig-Prean and Beckett v. United Kingdom*（（2000）29 EHRR 548）。

347. 不論執行"合理期望"是以程序方式抑或是以實體方式，法院都是公正持平裁決案件。由於要公正持平裁決，因此要求在達至裁決的過程中必須認真考慮"合理期望"，也因此"合理期望"有時可能支配了這個裁決過程的結果。而最重大的分別就是這點。在實體（並非只是程序上）執行"合理期望"之時，法庭必須份外謹慎，避免侵犯行政部門政策領域。本席認為謹慎的程度，必須從法庭在司法覆核某一令致"合理期望"落空的有關行政決定時所引用的覆核準則反映出來。但本席不認為這番謹慎，是要求大家傾向裁定並無"合理期望"存在。本席亦不認為這番謹慎，是要求大家若發現合理期望沒有被納入考慮之列時，不要要求重新考慮。

V. 合理期望的十八個考慮點

348. 綜觀整個法律體系之時，本席竭力瞭解法律的過往發展，同時亦探索其未來發展趨勢。甚至在這樣努力鑽研之時，本席當然亦有確認法律本身的現況。正如大法官 Holmes 在其法律權威著述"The Common Law"（1881 年）的第一頁中所解釋者：要認識〔法律〕，我們必須認識它的過去，以及它的將來演變。弄清楚每個要素的來龍去脈後，可以看到"合理期望"這個法則包括有以下十八點，而當中有些是法律觀點，有些是原理的闡述，有些則是發展的範疇：—

349. <u>第一點</u>　三權分立意味著行政政策的制定、廢除、重訂或執行都是行政部門負責的。同時，法律原則規定法庭有責任確保個人由於行政部門令其抱有的合理期望，就可以得到有關的行政部門正式尊重，因為這樣地尊重合理期望，是法律規定的一部份，是政府和個人之間存在的憲法關係的一個重要特色。正如大法官 Lord Mustill 在*R v. Secretary of State for the Home Department, ex parte Fire Brigades Union*（〔1995〕2 AC 513 第 567 頁 E-G）一案中就三權分立表達見解時說：法庭並不管治人民，但保護人民不會受行政權力濫用的侵犯。而保護人民不受行政權力誤用或濫用的侵犯，就是貫徹執行"合理期望"這個法則的充分理由。但這個法則絕不能視為傾向於不利行政部門。另外，還有一個支持"合理期望"這個理念的原因。由於行政部門本身可能是第一個承認"合理期望"的存在，因此這個法則肯定有利政府的管治，因為人民覺得政府所說的和所做的都可以信賴。

350. <u>第二點</u>　假若行政部門令致任何人抱有合理期望，期望在任何影響他本人的決定作出之前，會獲得有關行政部門給與（予）機會表達意見，但結果期望卻落空了。如果是這樣的話，法庭一貫做法都會讓這個期望可以在程序上執行。如果有關行政部門仍未作出決定的話，法庭會考慮宣告，有關行政部門必須先給與（予）該人機會表達意見，然後才可作出決定。又如果有關部門已作出了不利該有關人士的決定，但之前卻未有給與他機會表達意見，那麼，法庭會推翻有關決定，並下令有關行政部門的決策人，必須先給與（予）該有關人士機會表達意見，然後重新作出決定。樞密院在*Attorney-General v. Ng Yuen Shiu*（〔1983〕2 AC 629）案例中就是採用這個處理方式，在宣告樞密院眾位大法官的集體意見時，大法官 Lord Fraser of Tullybelton（第 638 頁 F-G）提述一個原則，就是公眾機構就本身所依循的程序作出承諾時，得受所作出的承諾約束。但有關承諾不得與公眾機關本身的職責有抵觸。

351. 第三點　假若行政部門令致任何人抱有合理期望，期望有關的行政部門會給他一些實質的東西或讓他保有一些實質東西，那麼，有關的行政部門在未給與（予）這個實質期望正式考慮之前，不應撤回，拿走或減少該有關實質東西。這是合理期望實體執行的基礎。如果行政決策人對實質的合理期望不予考慮，而令致這個實質的合理期望落空，那麼，法庭一貫做法都會推翻他的決定，下令要他正式考慮有關的合理期望，然後再重新作出決定（正如英國上訴法院在 *R v. London Borough of Newham, ex parte Bibi*（〔2001〕EWCA Civ 607）案例中所判決的一樣）。倘若行政決策人在給與（予）實質合理期望考慮後，才作出令實質合理期望落空的決定（不論是初次考慮後或是重新考慮後），那麼，法庭就得依循適當的覆核準則，決定可否給予有關的合理期望實體執行。在Coughlan案中，法庭有給與（予）合理期望實體執行。

352. 第四點　"一貫做法"這個詞在第二點和第三點都有使用，因為第二點和第三點所說的事情都會有例外情況。這是難以避免的。而"難以避免"有兩方面。首先，如果可以看得出 —— 在極端的個案中 —— 即使有把合理期望列入正式考慮之列，亦難免出現不利抱有合理期望人士的最後結果，那麼，為免徒勞無功，法庭是不會只因為決策人漏掉合理期望沒有考慮，而推翻有關行政決定。除非法庭確實認為（i）有關的行政決策人把合理期望正式考慮後，所得的也是該項結果；以及認為（ii）針對決策而提出的行政上訴或質疑決策而進行的司法覆核都是註定失敗的，否則，不會設定對抱有合理期望人士會有不利的終局決定。這個有關"難以避免"的測試，是樞密院在 *Nguyen Tuan Cuong v. Director of Immigration*（〔1997〕1 WLR 68 第 77 頁 B）案中所定下的。

353. 第五點　另一個以不同和相反形式產生的難以避免情況如下：假若行政決策人沒有把合理期望加以考慮就對抱有實質合理期望人士作出不利的決定，又假若法庭確實認為合理期望一旦被正式列入考慮時，有關行政決策人就會對抱有合理期望人士作出有利的最後決定，又或如果沒有正式考慮合理期望，審理行政上訴的審裁處或法庭就會對抱有合理期望人士作出有利的終局決定，那麼，法院必然會推翻有關的行政決定。本席認為，法院在推翻有關的行政決定後，不一定要依循迂迴的做法，把問題交回有關行政決策人，讓他重新作出決定，因為法院知道，如果行政決策人或行政上訴審裁處重新作出的決定，並非有利於該抱有合理期望的人士時，毫無疑問法院會再次干預。這樣便會引起不必要的延誤。此外，這樣做亦會強調有關的行政決策人擔當著一個"橡皮圖章"的不光彩角色。本席認為，法院應該有權在假定的極端情況下，直接進行合理期望的實體執行：例如，以適當的宣告形式作出。

354. 第六點　正如大法官 Lord Diplock 在 *Hughes v. Department of Health and Social Security*（〔1985〕AC 776 at p.788 A-C）案中所指出者，事情的發生可以是，合理期望在有關的行政決定作出之前已經再不存在。如果是這樣的話，就沒有提供來質疑該有關決定的基礎。但是，不用說，合理期望所造成的結果，並不會單單因為行政決定，令合理期望落空這個事實而給抹掉。在法律權威典籍"de Smith, Woolf & Jowell on Judicial Review of Administrative Action"（第 5 版（1995）第 575 頁，第 13-035 段）一書中有這樣一段說話：雖然當局可以自由改變政策，但不可以漠視"合理期望的存在"。

355. 第七點　關於知情方面，這一點在法律權威著述"de Smith, Woolf & Jowell on Judicial Review of Administrative Action"5th ed（（1995）第 426 頁，第 8-058 段）一書中有所論述。文章指出：任何人如屬某些陳述對象中的類別，那麼，即使事實上他對於這一點並不知情，直至令致他的合理期望落空的決定作出後他才知道，也不能剝奪他憑藉有關陳述可得到的利益。本席贊同這番論述。在 *Minister for Immigration and Ethnic Affairs v. Teoh*（（1995）183 CLR 273）一案中，澳洲高等法院裁定：由於條約簽訂後得予追認，因此所產生的合理期望是行政部門行事會符合有關的條約。首席法官 Mason 和法官 Deane 說（第 291 頁）："毋需規定要尋求以"合理期望"為依據的人士必須〔對條約〕知情，或他本人應該抱有這個期望。只要能證明有關的期望是合理的，即是有足夠資料支持這個期望，便已足夠。"同樣，法官 Toohey 指出（第 301 頁）："合理期望在這種情況下並非取決於個人本身是否知情或他本人內心怎樣想。有關事情要從客觀角度評估……。"本席知道法律權威典籍"Wade & Forsyth on Administrative Law"，（第 8 版（2000）第 496 頁）一書有這樣的論述："如果個人沒有任何期望，那麼，'合理期望'這個法則就變成沒有甚麼可以保障了。因此，任何人若對公共機構所作的承諾不知情，就不能期望有關公共機構行事要符合該有關承諾。"但據我所理解，這番論述並不是一個向群體作出的陳述，就像 Teoh 案和本案中向群體作出的陳述一樣。任何人都不能純粹因為他本人，是在行政部門作出令合理期望落空的決定後，才知道有這個陳述，就被拒絕執行他所屬群體的合理期望。

356. 第八點　至於與這個問題對立的一面，這方面的意見在權威法律著述"de Smith, Woolf & Jowell on Judicial Review of Administrative Action"第 5 版（1995）一書中，在前文提述的第 426 頁第 8-058 段所提及的"向群體作出的陳述"的注釋中，有這樣的論述："相應地，合理期望可以透過通傳的方式正式傳達來撤回，表明陳述已經改變，而毋需申請人知情"。經考慮後，本席贊同應該是這樣。但仍然留下的問題是，怎樣才算是正式傳達呢？

357. 第九點　誘使合理期望產生可以經由：明示的陳述（正如在 *Attorney-General of Hong Kong v. Ng Yuen Shiu* 案中）；和隱含的陳述（正如在 *R v. Gaming Board, ex parte Kingsley*（〔1996〕COD 241 第 242 頁）案中的正確論述）；或經確立的常規（正如在 R v. Birmingham City Council, ex parte Dredger（〔1993〕COD 340）一案中）。

358. 第十點　任何人如果因為倚賴有關的合理期望而改變本身的先前狀況，結果因為合理期望落空而蒙受損害，那麼，支持執行合理期望的理據就份外強力了。但倚賴合理期望而蒙受損害這個理由，一般來說並非是絕對必要的，"特別是如果他曾經依賴該合理期望"。這是大法官 Bingham（Lord Binghamof Cornhill 當時的官銜）在 *R v. Inland Revenue Commissioners ex parte MFK Underwriting Agencies Ltd*（〔1990〕1 WLR 1545 at p.1569 H）案中所說的。法律權威著述"de Smith, Woodlf & Jowell's Principles of Judicial Review"（1999）一書中，在第 306 頁的注釋（41）提到，要留意案例 *R v. Secretary of State for the Home Department, ex parte Astif Mahmood Khan*（〔1984〕1 WLR 1337），案例 *Attorney-General v. Ng Yuen Shiu* 和案例 *R v. Secretary of State for the Home Department, ex parte Ruddock*（〔1987〕1 WLR 1482），並指出這些案例"很重要"，因為案中是以倚賴合理期望獲判勝訴，而沒有證明曾因為倚賴合理期望而蒙受損害。"

359. 第十一點　雖然倚賴合理期望而蒙受損害這個理由，一般來說不是絕對必要的理由，但也會有例外的情況，在某些案件中，以合理期望作為依據，如欲獲判勝訴就必須證明倚賴合理期望有蒙受損害。這種情況發生在案例 *R v. Secretary of State for*

Education and Employment, ex parte Begbie（〔2000〕1 WLR 1115）中。在該案中，政府的決策由於官員不稱職而被錯誤陳述，約五星期後才更正該錯誤。大法官 Laws 認為問題是“把錯誤更正是不是濫用權力的行為”。大法官的判決如下（第 1131 頁 F-G）：

> “如果有人依據這個錯誤陳述而結果蒙受損害，本席會裁定內政大臣濫用權力，沒有及早把錯誤陳述更正，但並沒有人倚賴這個錯誤陳述而蒙受損害。當然，合理期望落空會給人痛苦的感受，然而本席認為雖然事件令人寄與（予）莫大同情，但亦不至於可以把內政大臣更正錯誤的做法視為濫用權力。本院的職能並不是懲罰不稱職的公共機構，雖然不稱職有時確實會影響公法。”

因此在 *Begbie* 案中，行政部門在傳達部門本身的決策時犯錯誤，並繼而迅速更正有關錯誤。而法庭裁定：在該案的情況下，更正有關錯誤並不構成濫用權力。正如上訴法院副院長麥慕年在 *Chu Piu Wing v. Attorney General*（〔1984〕HKLR 411 第 417 頁 J-418 頁 A）案的判詞中所說：“必須促使政府官員履行他們*在完全明白交易會帶來甚麼後果的情況下*所作出的承諾，這樣做是明顯要顧全公眾利益”。（文字斜體以示強調）。這段判詞得到大法官 Lord Griffiths 在 *R v. Horseferry Road Magistrates' Court, ex parte Bennett* 案中（〔1994〕1 AC 42 第 61 頁 E-F）所贊同及援引。上訴法院副院長的說話（本席以斜體文字表示）正好說明了像 *Begbie* 案這類“行政部門犯錯後迅速更正”的案件的獨特性質。

360. <u>第十二點</u>　期望要稱得上合理就必須有道理。這是本席從樞密院在 *Attorney-General of Hong Kong v. Ng Yuen Shiu*（第 636 頁 E）案的判詞中所理解的意思。怎樣才稱得上有道理，這個問題得視乎有關案件的情況而定。大法官 Bingham 在 *MFK Underwriting Agents* 案（第 1570 頁 A-B）中這樣說：“本席認為，根據像本案一樣的案情事實，如果裁定稅務局要受一個並不完全清晰、模棱兩可、並無約制的陳述約束的話，這個裁定是不公平的。”英國民事上訴分院在 *R v. Jockey Club, ex parte RAM Racecourses Ltd*（〔1993〕2 All ER 225）案中亦說了意思大致相同的說話。本席認為，根本上大可以確立一個能夠普遍地應用的法律主張，規定陳述如果要產生合理期望，就必須非模棱兩可和無約制。但如果陳述的對象是一個廣大群眾，當中包括一些沒有多大學識的人，法庭便不應刻意尋找陳述中有沒有含糊或約制的成份。在以公平為標準的前提下，法庭應該視乎陳述本身所造成的真正衝擊。

361. <u>第十三點</u>　尋求以“合理期望”為倚賴的人士必須坦誠。在 *MFK Underwriting Agents* 案中，大法官 Bingham（第 1569 頁 D-E）說道：“開心見誠把事情全部交代”是其中一個納稅人通常必須遵照的條件，納稅人才可以成功爭辯說，稅務局在雙方接觸後已同意放棄徵收，或曾經陳述會放棄徵收，那些雙方根據條例的正式釋義爭持應否繳付的稅項。*在 R v. Inland Revenue Commissioners, ex parte Martrix-Securities Ltd*（〔1994〕1 WLR 334）案中，大法官 Lord Jauncey of Tullichettle（第 352 頁 F）說：他認為大法官 Bingham 的論述，無可置疑，是絕對正確的。同樣本席亦肯定該論述是正確的。即使是沒有多大學識的人，亦必須要坦誠。但在衡量他們是否坦誠之時，為公道起見，應該著重於他們是一群沒有多大學識的人這一點。

362. <u>第十四點</u>　通常來說，每當法庭被請求就合理期望給予實體執行時，都會產生覆核的適當標準和有關因素的問題。

363. <u>第十五點</u>　但這個問題，即使在法庭被請求就合理期望給予程序上執行時，也會產生。這方面的例子有上訴庭的 *Coughlan* 案。在該案中，上訴庭說（第 247 頁 A）：即使援用“合理期望”這個法則反映了程序上的合理期望，例如，關於諮詢方面，合理期望也會受公眾利益優先考慮所影響。在 *Council of Civil Service Unions v. Minister for the Civil Service*（〔1985〕AC 374）案中就是這樣的情況。在該案中，上議院裁定有關的公務員有合理期望，期望有關當局在決定是否要剝奪他們參加工會的權力之前會先向他們諮詢；但亦裁定基於國家安全的原因，有關當局並沒有責任要諮詢他們。

364. <u>第十六點</u>　合理期望會導致抱有這個期望的人士，要求有關行政部門履行責任，因此在這個範圍之內，合理期望就像權利一樣。而像權利一樣這點，跟合理期望在維護法治時所擔任的角色，完全相稱。合理期望和權利兩者之間的實際分別是，合理期望跟權利不同，有關行政部門可以以公眾利益優先考慮為理由，而把合理期望置於有關的公眾利益之後。這個實際分別與所涉及的概念上的分別相吻合。正如法律權威典籍“Lloyd's Introduction to Jurisprudence”（第 6 版）（（1994）第 392 頁）一書所指出者，雖然“每個權利嚴格來說都隱含著一個相互關聯的責任，但不是每個責任都隱含一個相互關聯的權利”。任何人士根據合理期望而取得的權利，跟有關的行政部門為符合合理期望而履行的責任，並沒有相互關聯。因為，正如三權分立所要求，不履行原本屬合理期望所要求的責任時，決策人可以指出當中所涉及的公眾利益要優先考慮，作為不履行合理期望的理由。這一點對於在覆核該令致合理期望落空的行政決策時，法庭所應援用的準則有莫大關係。正因為覆核的準則力求不使行政部門決策變成僵化而不利有效管治，所以覆核的準則不應放任有關政府行政部門作出陳述後違背前言，亦不應容許該有關部門濫用權力。

365. <u>第十七點</u>　不論所援用的是甚麼覆核準則，法庭都應該堅持公共機構在處理公眾人士的事情上，行事必須有明確的原則，以及公正持平一絲不苟。而公眾人士中個人與個人之間的交往，當然可以容忍這方面不用有十足的程度，但公共機構即使在上述這種情況中，對公眾行事仍須有明確的原則，以及公正持平一絲不苟。有關這個做法，英國上議院在 *R v. Tower Hamlets London Borough Council, ex parte Chetnik Developments Ltd*（〔1988〕1 AC 858）以及 *Woolwich Equitable Building Society v. Inland Revenue Commissioners*（〔1993〕AC 70）這兩宗有關復還的案件的裁決中，都有舉例說明，而上訴法院在 *R v. Inland Revenue Commissioners, ex parte Unilever Plc*（〔1996〕COD 421 第 423 頁）這件有關合理期望的案件中亦有說及。

366. <u>第十八點</u>　對於法庭在覆核令合理期望落空的行政決策時所援用的準則，（即使有關決策是初次考慮或一再考慮合理期望之後才作出者），有關這方面的法律仍未完全確立。已判決的案件和學者的著述中所主張的取向，各有不同；有些屬概括性的，有些則視乎案件的性質。這些取向（在 Craig 與 Schonberg 的法律權威論著“Substantive Legitimate Expectations after Coughlan”（〔2000〕PL Winter 684 第 698-700 頁）一書中，這方面的論述很有見地）有下列者：

（a）覆核行政部門有否濫用權力，以及覆核權力本身是否屬濫用；

（b）進行覆核看看有沒有慣例的 Wednesbury 案中那種不合理情況（根據上訴法院 Lord Greene MR 在 *Associated Provincial Picture Houses Ltd v. Wednesbury Corp.*（〔1948〕1 KB 223 第 230 及 234 頁））案中所定下的測試準則，只可因為行政決策“非常無理，是任何行事有道理的行政部門都不會推行的”，才可抨擊有關的行政決策）；

(c) 進行覆核看看案中有沒有經大法官 Lord Cooke of Thorndon 在 *R v. Chief Constabel of Sussex, ex parte International Trader's Ferry Ltd*（〔1999〕 2 AC 418 at p.452 E）案中重新制定的 *Wednesbury* 案那種不合理情況。（在該案中，"界定有關決策是不是一個合理的行政部門所會作出的"時，所採用的是限制沒有那麼嚴謹的測試準則）

(d) 進行覆核，看看是否有不成正比例的情況；和

(e) 進行覆核，看看公平對待抱有合理期望的人士，以及行政部門基於公眾利益優先考慮的理由而令致這個合理期望落空的做法，兩者之間是否失卻平衡。

另者，尤其應該注意的是，法律學者 Elliot 在其法律權威著述"Human Rights and Substantive Review"（〔2001〕CLJ 301 第 322 頁）一文中所提出的主張。他說：合理和成正比例這兩個原則是可以共存的，而兩者之間又互為補足，通過互相提供的法則來把實體覆核的準則修正，以便順應具體的現實狀況在憲法上和建制上的要求。

VI. 對令致合理期望落空的做法的覆核準則

367. 本訴訟案在現階段來說，仍未需要對覆核準則作出最後決定，因為入境事務處處長仍未就合理期望作出考慮。直至處長考慮過合理期望並作出決定，而有關決定又受到質疑之時，才要決定採用甚麼覆核準則。但是，即使在現階段，不單應該起碼考慮採用哪些準則是適當的，亦是有需要這樣做。採用哪些適當準則這一點，與入境事務處處長的另一個論據有關係；而處長的論據，是指即使有合理期望，但無可避免的結果是，在處長考慮過合理期望後，上訴人以合理期望作依據而提出的申請，最終亦要失敗。

368. 不管怎樣，在某程度上是完全可以把所主張過的各個覆核準則，調和同化，共冶一爐。本席認為有一點恆久不變的是，這個覆核的憲法基礎，永遠都是由法治、公平原則、以及法庭針對行政權力濫用而提供司法濟助時所履行的職責所構成。至於行政部門政策所涉及的政治層面，法庭永遠都不感興趣。但如果有投訴政策不合法，那麼法庭就會審理，而經審理後，如果事情證明屬實，法庭就會作出補救辦法。雖然法庭不是執掌行政權力，但法庭必會針對行政部門的作為或不作為所構成濫用權力因而被認定屬非法時給與（予）濟助，甚至在某程度上做到實體執行某些合理期望。所有這些事都必須在覆核準則的範圍內予以調和。

369. 如果 *Wednesbury* 案的"不合理"測試準則，用作進行覆核的準則，本席認為大法官 Lord Cooke of Thorndon 所重新制定的一個，較諸大法官 Lord Greene MR 原先制定的一個更為可取。從這個基礎出發，如果決策者行使權力因而令致合理期望落空，那麼，要決定他是否有濫用權力，就得視乎他所作的決定是不是一個合理決策者所會作出的。這點可能取決於法庭是否認為，受質疑的決定不成正比例。而這點反過來又得視乎法庭是否認為，抱有實質合理期望人士必須得到的公平對待，以及行政部門基於大多數市民的利益要優先考慮因而令致這個期望落空的做法，兩者之間所取得的平衡是否可以接受。

370. 再者，如果有涉及人權時，那麼（正如大法官 Simon Brown 在 *Reg v. Ministry of Defence, ex parte Smith*（第 540 頁 E）案中所說）"慣常採用的 *Wednesbury* 案準則，便得適應人權法的情況。" 本席並不完全信賴 *Wednesbury* 案測試準則，尤其是本席在留意到大法官 Lord Cooke of Thorndon 在 *R（Daly）v. Secretary of State for the Home Department*（〔2001〕2 AC 532 第 549 頁 C）中所給與（予）的告誡之後。大法官 Lord Cooke 說："大有可能是……在行政的領域裏，單靠裁斷所覆核的決定既非變幻莫測亦非荒謬這個做法，實難使法律達至令人滿意的程度。" 本席論述 *Wednesbury* 案的測試準則，目的是因應援用 *Wednesbury* 案測試準則的情況，作出準備或起碼繼續考慮，把 *Wednesbury* 案測試準則適當地重新制定或修正。

371. 對於這個法律領域可以怎樣發展，御用大律師 Jeffrey Jowell 教授在他那篇題為"Beyond the Rule of Law: Towards Constitutional Judicial Review"（〔2000〕P L Winter 671 第 682 頁）的文章中的談話，有很寶貴的貢獻。他說：

> "從新近的憲法訴訟案看來，法院問的問題主要有兩條，第一條問題是：有沒有違反基本的民主權利？如果答案"是"的話，第二條問題是，有關的決定是不是表面上似乎是打擊民主，事實上，是為了有一個合理抗衡的民主價值觀，在維護民主所需要的。在評估這些問題時，法庭得考慮界定有關決定是否合理時所進行的過程，以及考慮一個民主社會所固有的素質。這種覆核是從憲法上的協調來覆核決定，跟非具體、純粹基於決定是否可取而進行的覆核完全不同，兩者大相徑庭。"

372. 本席認為，一方面要完全避免有不確實的情況，但另一方面行事又要保存所必需的彈性以迎合不同個案中所可能遇到的各種情況，確實一點也不容易。但無論有甚麼困難，法官在真實的個案中仍得努力找出恰當的覆核準則 —— 而很大程度上，本席膽敢說，需要求助於那些一直密切注意法律這方面的重大發展，而又在這方面做學問功夫的律師的有關著述。也許 —— 本席聲明，本席提出這點只是試探性 —— 解決辦法是採用一些並非嶄新的方法來定下一些慣常準則，並容許在特別情況下，這些慣常準則可以不予依循。至於怎樣才算特別情況，這一點仍然是不能確實。但希望有多些不同個案判決後，這種不確實情況可以減少。

373. 鑑於"合理期望"這個法則在維護法治方面擔當了一個非常重要的角色，在有關"合理期望"的案件中所運用的覆核準則應該嚴謹。像本案這一類案件中，所涉及的合理期望是居留權，一個受捍衛的憲法權利，這個覆核準則應該更加嚴謹。關於這點，容許我這麼說，在 T.R.S. Allan 所著的"Constitutional Justice"（（2001）第 131 頁）一書中，作者論述實質合理期望時這樣說："如果問題涉及重大的憲法權利，那麼，合理性的範圍界定當然要更加嚴謹，而法庭對行政上的專門知識和合宜性所著意的程度亦得相應減少"。*Daly* 案在這方面有指引性的作用。該案涉及被囚禁人士的權利（根據《1950 年歐洲保護人權和基本自由公約》第 8（1）條，亦即《1998 年人權法令》第 1 附表中所列出者），有關他的通信權利，當局應予尊重。以下各點在大法官 Lord Steyn 的說話中出現（第 546-548 頁中敍述）。正如有關英國軍方禁制軍中同性戀一案（初時在倫敦，繼而在斯特拉斯堡）所顯示，以傳統基礎進行的司法覆核跟以正比例作基礎而進行的方式有所不同，兩者有時會產生不同的結果。因此，涉及傳統上的權利必須以正確途徑分析，這點非常重要。要做到這點而又不會令"覆核"轉為根據"案情的是非曲直"，亦不會侵蝕法官角色和行政官角色兩者之間的基本分別，是可以的。"

374. 本席意見認為，適用於傳統上權利的論述，同樣亦適用於《基本法》的權利。

VII. 例案和合理期望

375. 代表上訴人的 Robertson 先生陳詞謂上訴人等基於合理期望而提出的理據，如果需要加強的話，那麼，*吳嘉玲*案和*陳錦雅*案這兩個例案性質可以用來加強上訴人理據的說服力。

376. 終審法院首席法官在吳嘉玲案中頒下判詞時說（第 23 頁 J）："這些案件是例案"。而在*陳錦雅*案中，本席說出生時間所涉問題的答案不但會影響案中已具名的居留權申請人，亦影響現在和未來很多其他人。對"現在"（相對於未來）這個詞的提述，關乎那些情況與法院在裁判該兩宗例案時適合該案所闡釋的法律的人士。

377. 對於在公法的範疇內，有關例案中判詞的作用和效力，英國上訴法院在 *R v. Hertfordshire county Council, ex parte Cheung*（"The Times" 4 April 1986）案和最近的 *R v. Secretary of State for the Home Department, ex parte Zequiri*（〔2001〕EWCA Civ 342）案中，都有論述到。

378. 在第 10 頁（是原謄寫本，不是"時報"中的簡略報導）上訴法院 John Donaldson MR 爵士（其後冊封勳爵）在 *Cheung* 案中這樣說：

> "……如果例案在公法法院中正進行審理時，若有其他人士情況跟案中當事人相同的話，有關當局不應期望這等其他人士本身提出訴訟來保障自己的法律地位。本席這樣說有兩個理由。第一，其他人也提出訴訟，會造成公法法院資源緊張，達到爆破點。第二，也許是較重要的一點，根據良好公共行政的基本原則，所有情況相同的人，都應該得到相同的看待。因此，可以想當然地認為，例案的判決結果，同樣亦適用於這等其他人士；因此，他們不用提出訴訟，有關當局也會在他們的個案中援用判決結果，不然的話，法庭也會以這個判決作為完全合理的理據批准遲延提出的司法覆核申請。"

379. 在 *Zequiri* 案判詞中的第 43 段，上訴法院大法官 Lord Phillips of Worth Matravers MR 亦表示贊同 *Cheung* 案中的論述。在緊接表示贊同的話語之前的文句中，在同一個段落，現任上訴法院民事分院院長提述到"合理期望"這個用詞時，提供了他本人的表述。大法官這樣說：

> "一如其他案件，例案會按照"服從案例"這個法理來清楚確定法律原則。但是在公法的領域裏，例案產生的作用卻超逾上述這點。很多時，所爭論的問題都是涉及一些雙方無爭議的公法原則，是否可以適用於某些事實情況。在這樣的情況下，任何人暫時停止提起訴訟，等候例案有判決結果後才作打算，都會有合理期望，期望倘若例案中的申請人能夠證明有權向法庭取得某些濟助或得到某些看待時，他也能像申請人一樣得到同樣的看待。"

380. *Zequiri* 案一直上訴至上議院，案中大法官把判決押後宣告。直至此一刻判決仍未頒下。本席不想在上議院就 *Zequiri* 案和 *Cheung* 案宣告判決之前表達對該兩案的意見。本席只想就本案中這個問題表達以下意見。

381. 首先，*吳嘉玲*案和*陳錦雅*案的訴訟不僅是有關公法上的訴訟例案。正如本席在處理"在此以前作出的判決不受影響"這個理據時所說，*吳嘉玲*案和*陳錦雅*案的訴訟是針對受憲法捍衛的權利而進行的憲法訴訟。本案上訴人，有需要時，是可以用這些作為依據來加強他們的"合理期望"依據。

382. 其次是，在另一方面"合理期望"這個論據並非只局限於以*吳嘉玲*案和*陳錦雅*案訴訟的性質為依據。本案中的"合理期望"是基於明示的陳述，而*吳嘉玲*案和*陳錦雅*案訴訟的性質提供了這些明示陳述的有關背景。

VIII. 合理期望必須予以考慮

383. 本席現在論述代表答辯方的馬先生所依據的 *Lau Kong Yung v. Director of Immigration*（（1999）2 HKCFAR 300）案的法庭判決。馬先生以上述案例為依據，提出主張指入境事務處處長根據《入境條例》行使權力時，不須考慮"合理期望"。在該案中，法庭裁定（法庭以 4 比 1 大比數作出裁定，而本席是唯一一個持相反意見的法官）入境事務處處長根據《入境條例》中該條款行使權力時，雖然可以考慮人道理由，但無須一定要這樣做。如果本上訴案中大多數法官贊成這樣做，本席不擬再談*劉港榕*案這方面的問題。在現階段來說，本席只須說明，本席同意所有其他大法官意見認為，*劉港榕*案無論怎樣看，都不能成為案例，來支持入境事務處處長可以漠視合理期望這一個觀點。

IX. 本案中的有關陳述和合理期望

384. 在本案中所涉及的陳述有 4 個類別。入境事務處處長對於這等陳述完全沒有考慮。這等陳述是：

（i）政府作出陳述，向公眾一再保證，政府會服從法庭的決定；

（ii）入境事務處在給與居港權申請人的信件中作出陳述，說明由於訴訟在進行中，他們就居留權而提出的申請暫時未能決定；

（iii）保安局局長在一封日期為 1998 年 4 月 24 日寫給第 13 名代表申請人的信中作出的陳述。信中重複政府一再保證會服從法庭的決定；以及

（iv）法律援助署在寫給要求法律援助的申請人的信件中所作出的陳述。信中重複該項政府保證，並且說：申請人因此毋需參與現時進行的訴訟程序，亦毋需開展新的訴訟程序。

所有這等陳述，雖然形式上是通知個別人士，但實質上屬於以群體為對象而作出的通知。群體是指可以援用*吳嘉玲*案和*陳錦雅*案中判居留權申請人勝訴的判決書，並可因而受惠的人士所組成的群體。本案中所有上訴人都屬這個群體。

385. 正如本席所指出者，入境事務處處長對這幾個類別的陳述完全沒有考慮。因此，本席認為，要決定他在考慮過這等陳述後，會否設法把這等陳述詮釋為，並非"異常至可歸入不合理的類別"（並設法為這樣的詮釋辯護），實在言之過早。"異常至可歸入不合理的類別"這句話語乃引述自大法官 Lord Mustill 在 *R v. Monopolies and Mergers Commission, ex parte South Yorkshire Transport Ltd*（〔1993〕1 WLR 23 第 32 頁 H）案中的論述。這番話語同樣亦有被大法官 Lord Slynn of Hadley 在 *Walker* 案（第 813 頁 A）中援引。此外，要注意的是，不管怎樣，上述這兩件案例並不涉及對任何陳述的詮釋。

386. *Monopolies and Mergers Commission* 案所涉及的，是法例制定給委員會援用的準則的詮釋。大法官 Lord Mustill 的論述是，對於這個準則因為不明確而令致不同決策人，即使行事合理，在援用準則於實際個案時，會得出不同結論這種情況（第 32 頁 G）。大法官 Lord Mustill 接著引述案例 *Edwards v. Bairstow*（〔1956〕AC 14）。同樣，這件案例並不涉及"合理期望"。

387. *Walker* 案所涉及的，是英國國防部所實施的特惠金賠償計劃內，有關酌情決定權條款中一句短語的詮釋。這個賠償計劃是向在海外服役的英國軍人，因暴力罪行而受傷時，提供特惠金賠償。有關的一句短語，據大法官 Lord Slynn of Hadley 所言（第 813 頁 A），"意思並不明確因而可以有多個解釋"。值得注意的是，根據大法官 Lord Hoffmann 的見解（第 816 頁 B），*Walker* 案並不像 *Coughlan* 案那樣，當局在作出一個具體承諾後，有出乎爾反乎爾的情況。

388. 最後，在這方面而言，給政府說句公道話，本席必須指出政府也許不是要爭辯說，他們為安撫公眾人士而要作出的聲明事實上不明確，以致不能達到安撫目的。但行政部門把說話斷章取義，只是從當中抽取一些意思不甚明確的話，從而打擊公眾人士在聽到政府這些說話後，有理由因此亦合理地產生的期望。有關行政部門這種行為，可以說是濫用權力。這樣的事，如果法官給予支持和鼓勵，是會嚴重影響公眾對政府言論的信心！

389. 撇開"在此以前作出的判決不受影響"這個論據不談，本席現在只是論述"合理期望"這個論據，以下是本席的見解：根據本席看過的有關法律原則以及本案的實質情況，有關的四個不同陳述，均曾令致各上訴人產生合理期望。他們的合理期望是，像他們那樣情況的人應該獲得跟*吳嘉玲*案和*陳錦雅*案中的居留權申請人一樣的看待。即使在**該解釋**後，他們這個期望仍然是合理期望。而合理性亦已達到一定的程度，可以讓上訴人獲得這樣的看待。政府是可以給與他們這樣的看待，只需要 — 亦只要——入境事務處處長行使他的酌情決定權，不把他們遣送回內地，讓他們留在香港建立他們的家園，並在一般及連續居滿七年後，根據《基本法》第第二十四條第二款第(二)項，取得香港永久性居民身份；亦即是居留權。漠視他們仍然抱有的合理期望，就是濫用行政權力，這正是合理期望這個法則所要保障不受侵犯的。

390. 第（iii）和第（iv）類別的陳述，較諸第（i）和（ii）類別的更為直接。而第（iv）類別的陳述更超逾其他三個類別的陳述。根據本席對本案現時事情的觀察，本席毫不感困難地認為，入境事務處處長一旦正式考慮他們的合理期望，屬於第（iii）類別的受陳述者的申請，大有可能可以成功，而第（iv）類別的受陳述者的申請幾乎肯定地可以成功。至於屬第（i）和第（ii）類別的受陳述者的申請，他們的條件沒有第（iii）和第（iv）類別的那樣強，他們尋求入境事務處處長，就他們所提出來遲了的合理期望的聲請，給與開明的考慮。他們這個做法不能說是瑣屑和無意義的。正如本席曾努力證明和強調的，合理期望這個法則在維護法治方面扮演著一個非常重要角色。既然是這樣，本席認為，因此之故，如果法庭裁斷行政決定針對某人作出時，決策人並沒有正式考慮他的合理期望，那麼，法庭不應輕易拒絕給與他濟助。

391. 尤其在本案中，情況更是這樣。在一份表示異議但說服力強的判決書中（本席拜讀過後認為如果他現時仍未完全得到支持擁護，漸漸亦會完全得到支持擁護），大法官 Lord Nicholls of Birkenhead 在 *Briggs v. Baptiste*（〔2000〕2 AC 40 第 58 頁 B）案中這樣說："如果拒絕 Anthony Briggs 不讓他可以這樣做，就是拒絕他所享有的憲法權利。"美洲人權法院很有可能會頒下命令，把 Mr Briggs 死刑轉為終生監禁，讓 Mr Briggs 起碼可以用這個法庭命令，跟千里達、多巴哥島政府鬥爭。（至於 Mr Briggs 是否可以訴諸千里達、多巴哥法院來執行這個法庭命令，大法官 Lord Nicholls of Birkenhead 指出，這是一個必須另外決定的問題。）在本案中，有可能發生的事情是，（現時來說只局限於屬第（i）和第（ii）類別的受陳述者），入境事務處處長應就他們基於合理期望而提出的聲稱，作出讓他們受惠的決定。不然的話，就由法庭給與他們的聲請（稱）實體執行。

392. 現時來說，每一位上訴人要求他們的合理期望應該盡可能按照測試憲法權利就爭論問題的判決來看待，根據這判決他們的情況跟勝訴的人士相同。如果勝訴的話，他們日後便可以在住滿一段日子符合《基本法》的要求後，取得居留權。本席援用大法官 Lord Nicholls of Birkenhead 對分析這種情況所涉及問題時用的分析方法，本席的裁決如下：—— 舉例來說，如果有人尋求機會證明自己具有憲法權；或具有接近相等於憲法權的身份，而一般而言這身份最終會得到這個憲法權利，那麼，問題是有沒有可能 — 當然是真正的可能而不是純粹空想 — 如果他有這個機會的話，他就會勝訴；倘若有這個可能，不給與（予）他這個機會便等於拒絕給他憲法上的權力。

393. 根據手頭上的資料，本席認為入境事務處處長一旦考慮他們的合理期望，第（iii）類別的受陳述者大有可能獲得成功，而第（iv）類別的受陳述者則幾乎肯定可以成功。即使這樣，本席認為不能說他們的個案是極端的個案，因而說在現階段不用交予入境事務處處長處理，而可以直接進行合理期望的實體執行。

394. 本席認為不可以說——應該是更不可以說 —— 在現階段第（i）和第（ii）類別的受陳述者無法躲避的命運是，他們最終會失敗。他們每人都抱有合理的期望。如果堅持說入境事務處處長別無他途，只可以令他們的合理期望落空，那是基於甚麼道理呢？又如果堅持說法院亦別無他途，亦是只可以令他們的合理期望落空，那又是基於甚麼道理呢？本席看不到有甚麼道理。

395. 至於任何上訴人或入境事務處處長可能作出對其不利決定的上訴人，所提起的司法覆核程序會否勝訴，須於另一訴訟程序中作出決定。本席不知道入境事務處處長會否於重新考慮後，仍然作出對任何上訴人不利的決定；本席亦不知道，倘若入境事務處處長真的這樣做，在以優先考慮公眾利益為理由的情況下，並為了支持他對抱有合理期望人士作出不利的決定是合理的做法時，入境事務處處長會怎樣回應有關的質詢。本席並無意暗示任何其他上訴人的個案中的論據有任何弱點，不過本席認為，特別是對第（iv）類的受陳述者來說，公平的看法是，不論其他的情況怎樣也好，與任何其他類別的人士比較，從固有的可能性看來，這類人士更有可能在接收了有關的陳述後作出了反應，而這些反應致使他們可以援引因倚賴有關陳述而蒙受損失為論據，從而回應或進一步回應當局可能以任何所謂的公眾利益應被優先考慮為理由的解釋，但當局以這些公眾利益為理由，只不過是要設法證明對抱有合理期望人士作出令他們失望的決定是合理的做法。

396. 關乎"合理期望"這個理由，正如關乎"在此以前的判決不受影響"的理由一樣，所有遣送離境令都必須撤銷。然而，法院卻不能單就"合理期望"這個理由作出宣告（但卻可以就"在此以前的判決不受影響"這個理由作出宣告），即所有上訴人均為香港永久性居民並有居留權在港定居。倘若單就"合理期望"這個理由來作出宣告，法院所作出的宣告應為：入境事務處處長可行使酌情決定權，包括根據《入境條例》（第 115 章）第 13 條及第 19（1）（b）條所賦予他的權力。

397. 第 13 條規定：

> "處長可隨時授權在香港非法入境的人留在香港，不論該人是否已被裁定犯該罪，但有關授權須受處長認為適當的逗留條件規限，而第 11(5)、(5A)及(6)條須對該人適用，猶如對根據第11(1)條已獲准在香港入境的人適用一樣。"

第 19（1）（b）條規定處長"可"針對某人發出遣送離境令，規定該人必須離開香港，如處長覺得該人：

> "(i) 若非因為第 18(2)條所定的限期已過，該人本可根據第 18(1)條被遣離香港；或
>
> (ii) 已在香港非法入境(不論在《1981年人民入境(修訂)(第4號)條例》(1981年第75號)生效之前或之後)，或正違反或已違反向他施加的逗留條件；或
>
> (iia) 並不享有香港居留權亦未憑藉第 2AAA 條擁有香港入境權，但已違反第 42 條的規定；或
>
> 根據第 7(2)條的規定，倘無入境事務處主任或入境事務助理員的准許不得留在香港，而該人卻在未獲准許的情況

下留在香港。"

398. 就算不考慮上訴人"在此以前的判決不受影響"的論據，而只考慮他們"合理期望"的上訴理由，本席亦裁定他們有權獲得法院：（i）撤銷所有遣送離境令；以及（ii）宣告處長在行使酌情決定權，包括根據《入境條例》第 13 條及第 19 條所賦予他的權力時，必須考慮上訴人的合理期望，即他們大體上可得到在*吳嘉玲及陳錦雅*兩案中具名當事人的那些居留權申請人所得到的看待。

399. 可以說上述的情況涉及廣泛地行使一項通常只會在特殊情況下才行使的酌情決定權。但是該酌情決定權並不會因為上述理由而無法行使的。某項酌情決定權只可在特殊情況下行使，並不表示必須狹隘地行使該酌情決定權。倘若濫用權力的情況嚴重，以致要受保障的範圍廣泛時，那麼實在沒有任何理由，不可相應廣泛地行使一項可用來對付這些濫用權力情況的酌情決定權。首席大法官 Lord Mansfield 在頒下英皇皇座法院（Court of King's Bench）於 *Taylor v. Horde*（（1757）1 Burrow 60 第 119 頁；97 ER 190 第 223 頁）案中的判決時，闡述了一個著名的原則："並沒有任何損害或錯失是法律無法補救的。"本席並不認為濫用行政權力涉及的範圍廣泛這個事實，可構成一個理由，讓這些濫權的情況得過且過，並且不設法補救有關的損害或錯失。本席亦不認為有關條文的立法目的有任何一部份是要禁止引用該等條文，即使引用該等條文可以避免發生濫用行政權力的情況。

400. 倘若入境事務處處長在考慮過上訴人的合理期望後，所作出的決定仍然使上訴人失望時，會有甚麼事情發生，端視乎那些失望人士可能會提起的新訴訟程序是甚麼的程序。

X. 上訴人的其他論據

401. 本席除了裁定上訴人"在此以前作出的判決不受影響"和"合理期望"這兩個論據勝訴外，並在不偏離以上判決以免對任何一位上訴人不利的情況下，贊同本院其他法官就各上訴人，或他們任何一位就任何上訴人，在其他獲判勝訴的論據上所作出的每個決定，除此之外，本席不打算有任何補充。

XI. 結論

402. 本席感謝代表雙方的大律師及律師，他們擬備好呈交本院的材料和所呈述的論據；本席亦藉此機會向下級法院的法官致謝，本席從他們的判決中得到了所需的幫助。

403. 本席判決全部上訴人上訴得直。正如本席於上文所表達的，本席接納上訴人"在此以前的判決不受影響"的論據，並據此判決所有上訴人全面勝訴並上訴得直：（i）撤銷所有遣送離境令及（ii）宣告所有上訴人均為香港永久性居民並有本地居留權。

404. 即使本席只考慮"合理期望"這個理由，本席仍然判決所有上訴人上訴得直，亦即（i）撤銷所有遣送離境令及（ii）作出有利於*所有*類別的受陳述者，換言之，有利於*所有*上訴人的宣告。該宣告為入境事務處處長在行使酌情決定權時，包括行使《入境條例》第 13 條及第 19 條所賦予的權力時，必須考慮到所有上訴人均合理地期望，他們會得到如*吳嘉玲及陳錦雅*兩案中居留權申請人在大體上相同的看待。本席在該宣告命令中列明有關人士可得到下述的看待。入境事務處處長可行使其酌情決定權：（i）授權所有上訴人留在香港；以及（ii）不對他們任何一人作出遣送離境令。處長如此行使其酌情決定權，就能使他們全部留港，以香港為家，並藉此積累在香港通常居住連續七年的時間。根據《基本法》第二十四條第二款第（二）項，在香港通常居住連續七年可令他們全部得到香港永久性居民的身份，從而取得香港居留權。

405. 本席除了裁定上訴人"在此以前作出的判決不受影響"和"合理期望"這兩個論據勝訴外，並在不偏離以上判決以免對任何一位上訴人不利的情況下，贊同本院其他法官就各上訴人，或他們任何一位就任何上訴人在其他獲判勝訴的論據上所作出的每個決定。

406. 本上訴案為獲法律援助人士與政府之間的憲法訴訟，本席尊重並同意本院其他法官所作出的訟費令，即除了命令所有上訴人本身的訟費按有關法律評定外，不對訟費作出任何命令。

407. 從上文可見，本席所作出的判決，比較本院其他法官認為合適的判決，對所有上訴人來說是更為有利。並且無可否認，本席判決上訴人勝訴所涉及的情況頗為全面。然而，要說明一點，本席尊重不同的意見，並且是經過深思熟慮後，才會站在與同事法官不同的立場。

終審法院首席法官李國能：

408. 本院作出根據本席、常任法官陳兆愷、常任法官李義及非常任法官梅師賢爵士的判決中標題為"濟助"的結論（第 294-301 段）內所列出的命令及指示。本院判決有關上訴得直的決定是一致的，但判決有關上訴駁回則是多數的決定（常任法官包致金持不同意見）。

首席法官（李國能）

常任法官（包致金）

常任法官（陳兆愷）

常任法官（李義）

非常任法官（梅師賢爵士）

御用大律師 Geoffrey Robertson 先生及大律師郭瑞熙先生由貝嘉蓮律師行延聘，並由法律援助署委派代表終院民事上訴 2001 年第 1 號案中的上訴人

資深大律師李志喜女士及大律師郭瑞熙先生由賈偉林江令名律師行延聘，並由法律援助署委派代表終院民事上訴 2001 年第 2 號案中的上訴人

資深大律師李志喜女士及大律師郭瑞熙先生由彭思帝理律師行延聘，並由法律援助署委派代表終院民事上訴 2001 年第 3 號案中的上訴人

資深大律師馬道立先生、資深大律師霍兆剛先生及大律師溫考庭先生由律政司延聘代表終院民事上訴 2001 年第 1、2 及 3 號案中的答辯人

JT 3-02 FACV 1-3/2001

許詩蘆 對 入境事務處處長

HCAL 108/2001 *; CACV250/2001

楊銘陽 對 入境事務處處長

HCAL 116/2002 *; CACV250/2002

* 香港司法機構網站未有提供該判決書。

簡略案情

據資料顯示，上訴人許詩蘆於 1960 年 1 月 4 日在內地出生，出生時父母不是香港永久性居民。而上訴人楊銘陽於 1964 年 4 月 19 日在內地出生，出生時父母亦不是香港永久性居民。

裁決摘要

在此兩個案件中，上訴庭重申吳小彤案是終審法院的判決，是對上訴庭具約束力的案例。而人大常委會的解釋對特區法院也是有約束力，上訴庭亦需遵守。根據該案例及該解釋，永久性居民在香港以外所生的中國籍子女，只有符合下列三項其中一項條件的才可獲法庭給予協助：

申請人在 1997 年 7 月 1 日之前已抵達香港，而且申請人在出生時其父母之中最少一人已經是永久性居民。符合這條件者有權在香港申請或繼續申請獲取居留權，無須領取單程證；或

"有合法理期望者"：申請人曾收到（a）法律援助署在 1998 年 12 月 7 日至 1999 年 1 月 29 日間發出的有關公函，述明申請人不必參與當時的訴訟程序或展開新訴訟程序，或（b）保安局局長在 1998 年 4 月 24 日發出的有關信件，內容大意是入境事務處會依循法院的判決處理居留權的申請。對於符合這條件者，入境事務處處長應考慮行使《入境條例》第 11 條、第 13 條和第 19（1）條賦予他的酌情決定權，在決定前不把申請人遣送離開香港；或

"政府寬免政策受惠者"：（a）申請人在 1997 年 7 月 1 日至 1999 年 1 月 29 日期間在香港，和（b）在該段期間，他在香港曾向入境事務處提出居留權的聲稱，和（c）入境事務處存有該聲稱的記錄或聲稱由其他政府官員在執行職務時轉交予入境事務處。如果有文件可以明確（i）辨認出申請人是永久性居民的子女；（ii）提供有關申請人的資料，如出生日期和地點；和（iii）要求申請人來香港以便定居或要求給予申請人居留權，入境事務處處長應視之為居留權的聲稱。對於符合條件者，入境事務處處長應按照*吳嘉玲*和*陳錦雅*兩案的上述裁決考慮申請人的申請。

若申請人不能符合以上所述條件的任何一項，申請人就沒有居留權。即使在他出生時其父或其母已經是永久性居民，他也必須先向內地機關取得單程證，才可以在香港行使永久性居民的居留權。

在本案件中，兩位上訴人也不符合以上的任何一項條件，據此，他們的上訴被駁回。

CACV 250/2001

香港特別行政區
高等法院上訴法庭
民事司法管轄權
民事上訴

案件編號：民事上訴案件 2001 年第 250 號
（原高院憲法及行政訴訟案件 2001 年第 108 號）

申請人　許詩蘆
　　　　對
答辯人　入境事務處處長

主審法官：高等法院上訴法庭法官張澤祐
　　　　　高等法院原訟法庭法官鍾安德

聆訊日期：2002 年 8 月 1 日

判案書日期：2002 年 8 月 7 日

判案書

由高等法院原訟法庭法官鍾安德頒布上訴法庭判案書：

1. 就申請香港特別行政區居留權（"居留權"）的問題，1999 年 1 月 29 日終審法院判決了*吳嘉玲及其他人士對入境事務處處長* [1] 和*陳錦雅及其他人士對入境事務處處長* [2] 兩案。在*吳嘉玲*案，終審法院裁定《基本法》第 24 條第 2 款第（3）項並不受第 22 條第 4 款［須以國內機關簽發的單程證（"單程證"）來港］規限，香港永久性居民（"永久性居民"）在香港以外所生的中國籍子女申請居留權者不須先取得單程證才可獲取居留權。在*陳錦雅*案，終審法院裁定永久性居民在香港以外所生的中國籍子女，不論他們是在父母之中最少一人取得永久性居民身份之前或之後出生，均屬《基本法》第 24 條第 2 款第（3）項所述的人士，享有居留權。

2. 1999 年 6 月 26 日全國人民代表大會常務委員會對居留權問題作出解釋（"人大常委會解釋"），取代了終審法院上述的裁決，該等裁決不再適用。2002 年 1 月 10 日，終審法院在*吳小彤及其他人士對入境事務處處長* [3] 一案清楚闡述和解釋了*吳嘉玲*和*陳錦雅*兩案及人大常委會解釋的關係和效果，對居留權的問題作出了決定性的結論。

3. *吳小彤*案是終審法院的判決，是對本庭有約束力的案例，人大常委會的解釋對本庭也是有約束力的，本庭必須遵守。根據該案例及該解釋，永久性居民在香港以外所生的中國籍子女，只有符合下列三項其中一項條件的才可獲法庭頒發濟助：

（1）申請人在 1997 年 7 月 1 日之前已抵達香港，而且申請人在出生時其父母之中最少一人已經是永久性居民。符合這條件者有權在香港申請或繼續申請獲取居留權，無須領取單程證；或

（2）［有合法理期望者］申請人曾收到（a）法律援助署在 1998 年 12 月 7 日至 1999 年 1 月 29 日間發出的有關公函，述明申請人不必參與當時的訴訟程序或展開新訴訟程序，或（b）保安局局長在 1998 年 4 月 24 日發出的有關信件，內容大意是入境事務處會依循法院的判決處理居留權的申請。對於符合這條件者，入境事務處處長應考慮行使《入境條例》第 11 條、第 13 條和第 19（1）條賦予他的酌情決定權，在決定前不把申請人遣送離開香港；或

（3）［政府寬免政策受惠者］（a）申請人在 1997 年 7 月 1 日至 1999 年 1 月 29 日期間在香港，和（b）在該期間他在香港時向入境事務處提出居留權的聲稱，和（c）入境事務處存有該聲稱的記錄或聲稱由其他政府官員在執行職務時轉交予入境事務處。如果有文件可以明確（i）辨認出申請人是永久性居民的子女；（ii）提供有關申請人的資料，如出生日期和地點；和（iii）要求申請人來香港以便定居或要求給予申請人居留權，入境事務處處長應視之為居留權的聲稱。對於符合條件者，入境事務處處長應按照*吳嘉玲*和*陳錦雅*兩案的上述裁決考慮申請人的申請。

4. 若申請人不能符合以上第 3 段所述條件的任何一項，申請人就沒有居留權；即使在他出生時其父或其母已經是永久性居民，他必須先向國內機關取得單程證，才可以在香港行使永久性居民的居留權。

5. 本案資料顯示，申請人於 1960 年 1 月 4 日在國內出生。出生時父母不是香港永久性居民。申請人的情況不符合上述任何一項的條件。

6. 上訴無理據支持，本庭駁回上訴，不作出訟費命令。

高等法院上訴法庭法官（張澤祐）

高等法院原訟法庭法官（鍾安德）

申請人：自行應訊

答辯人：由律政司指派何展鵬政府律師代表

註：

1. (1999) 2 HKCFAR 4 (decision of CFA on 29 Jan 1999)

2. (1999) 2 HKCFAR 82 (decision of CFA on 29 Jan 1999)

3. Ng Siu Tung & others v. The Director of Immigration, FACV1-3/2001 (10 Jan 2002, unreported)

CACV 250/2002

香港特別行政區
高等法院上訴法庭
民事司法管轄權
民事上訴

案件編號：民事上訴案件 2002 年第 250 號
（原本案件編號：高院憲法及行政訴訟 2002 年第 116 號）

申請人　楊銘陽
　　　　對
答辯人　入境事務處處長

主審法官：高等法院上訴法庭法官胡國興
　　　　　高等法院上訴法庭法官張澤祐

聆訊日期：2002 年 7 月 3 日

判案書日期：2002 年 7 月 15 日

判案書

由上訴法庭法官胡國興頒發上訴法庭判案書：

1. 就申請香港特別行政區居留權（“居留權”）的問題，1999 年 1 月 29 日終審法院判決了***吳嘉玲及其他人士對入境事務處處長***[1] ***和陳錦雅及其他人士對入境事務處處長***[2] 兩案。在*吳嘉玲*案，終審法院裁定《基本法》第 24 條第 2 款第（3）項並不受第 22 條第 4 款 [須以國內機關簽發的單程證（“單程證”）來港] 規限，香港永久性居民（“永久性居民”）在香港以外所生的中國籍子女申請居留權者不須先取得單程證才可獲取居留權。在*陳錦雅*案，終審法院裁定永久性居民在香港以外所生的中國籍子女，不論他們是在父母之中最少一人取得永久性居民身份之前或之後出生，均屬《基本法》第 24 條第 2 款第（3）項所述的人士，享有居留權。

2. 1999 年 6 月 26 日全國人民代表大會常務委員會對居留權問題作出解釋（“人大常委會解釋”），取代了終審法院上述的裁決，該等裁決不再適用。2002 年 1 月 10 日，終審法院在***吳小彤及其他人士對入境事務處處長***[3] 一案清楚闡述和解釋了*吳嘉玲*和*陳錦雅*兩案及人大常委會解釋的關係和效果，對居留權的問題作出了決定性的結論。

3. *吳小彤*案是終審法院的判決，是對本庭有約束力的案例，人大常委會的解釋對本庭也是有約束力的，本庭必須遵守。根據該案例及該解釋，永久性居民在香港以外所生的中國籍子女，只有符合下列三項其中一項條件的才可獲法庭頒發濟助：

（1）申請人在 1997 年 7 月 1 日之前已抵達香港，而且申請人在出生時其父母之中最少一人已經是永久性居民。符合這條件者有權在香港申請或繼續申請獲取居留權，無須領取單程證；或

（2）[有合法理期望者] 申請人曾收到（a）法律援助署在 1998 年 12 月 7 日至 1999 年 1 月 29 日間發出的有關公函，述明申請人不必參與當時的訴訟程序或展開新訴訟程序，或（b）保安局局長在 1998 年 4 月 24 日發出的有關信件，內容大意是入境事務處會依循法院的判決處理居留權的申請。對於符合這條件者，入境事務處處長應考慮行使《入境條例》第 11 條、第 13 條和第 19（1）條賦予他的酌情決定權，在決定前不把申請人遣送離開香港；或

（3）[政府寬免政策受惠者]（a）申請人在 1997 年 7 月 1 日至 1999 年 1 月 29 日期間在香港，和（b）在該期間他在香港時向入境事務處提出居留權的聲稱，和（c）入境事務處存有該聲稱的記錄或聲稱由其他香港政府官員在執行職務時轉交予入境事務處。如果有文件可以明確（i）辨認出申請人是永久性居民的子女；（ii）提供有關申請人的資料，如出生日期和地點；和（iii）要求申請人來香港以便定居或要求給予申請人居留權，入境事務處處長應視之為居留權的聲稱。對於符合條件者，入境事務處處長應按照*吳嘉玲*和*陳錦雅*兩案的上述裁決考慮申請人的申請。

4. 若申請人不能符合以上第 3 段所述條件的任何一項，申請人就沒有居留權；即使在他出生時其父或其母已經是永久性居民，他必須先向國內機關取得單程證，才可以在香港行使永久性居民的居留權。

5. 本案資料顯示，本案申請人於 1964 年 4 月 19 日在國內出生。出生時父母都不是香港永久性居民。本案申請人的情況也不符合上述任何一項的條件。

6. 本案申請人的上訴無理據支持。本庭駁回上訴，不作出訟費命令。

高等法院上訴法庭法官（胡國興）

高等法院上訴法庭法官（張澤祐）

申請人：無律師代表。

答辯人：由律政司何展鵬政府律師代表。

註：

1. (1999) 2 HKCFAR 4 (decision of CFA on 29 Jan 1999)

2. (1999) 2 HKCFAR 82 (decision of CFA on 29 Jan 1999)

3. Ng Siu Tung & others v. The Director of Immigration, FACV1–3/2001 (10 Jan 2002, unreported)

Vallejos Evangeline Banao, also known as Vallejos Evangeline B v. Commissioner Of Registration & Registration Of Persons Tribunal

Vallejos Evangeline Banao 亦稱為 Vallejos Evangeline B 對 人事登記處處長及人事登記審裁處

HCAL 124/2010；CACV 204/2011

簡略案情

申請人是菲律賓人，自從 1986 年開始在香港從事家傭工作。在得到她服務超過 20 年的僱主的支持下，她嘗試根據《基本法》第 24（2）、（4）條向入境處申請永久性居民身份，及後亦向人事登記處申請永久性居民身份證。然而，《入境條例》第 2（4）（a）（vi）列明，受僱為外來家庭傭工（指來自香港以外地方者）而留在香港，不得被視為通常居於香港。此條例明確排除了申請人停留香港的期間符合通常居住的條件，因此，她的申請一概被拒絕。對於申請人的上訴，人事登記審裁處明確地指出如果不是因為《入境條例》第 2（4）（a）（vi）的關係，申請人是完全符合《基本法》第 24（2）、（4）的要求的。申請人遂向原訟庭申請司法覆核，要求裁定相關的《入境條例》違反《基本法》並判決其無效。

原訟庭法官在審理本案時強調，雖然公眾一直非常關心這起案件的發展，但是，他作為法官必須獨立、公正和無懼地履行他依法審理案件的責任，不受任何政治因素所影響。《基本法》第 24 條給予六類人士成為香港永久性居民的資格。而根據第 24（2）、（4）條規定，如果該人士並非中國籍，他必須持有有效旅行證件進入香港，同時在香港通常居住連續 7 年，並以香港為永久居住地。

原訟庭法官指出，除非有相關的人大常委的解釋，法庭有責任去釐清《基本法》的含義。他進而認為除非條款中有含糊的地方導致法庭不能以既自然又通常的字面含義去解釋該條文時，外部證據才會給予信納，但對於後期的外部證據必須額外小心，而僅僅因為《基本法》本身沒有對"通常居住"作出定義而判斷它是含糊不清是不對的。就算真的是有不清楚的地方，也不應該由《入境條例》作解釋。最後，法官接受申請人的陳詞認同海外僱傭在港停留的時間並非特殊而導致他們不應被納入在香港通常居住的類別中，因此，《入境條例》第 2（4）（a）（vi）被裁定違反《基本法》第 24（2）（4）而無效。

人事登記處處長對該判決提出上訴。

裁決摘要

對於《基本法》的解釋方法，上訴庭同意原訟庭在這方面的分析。可是，上訴庭認為在理解《基本法》的文理和目的的過程中，起草材料給予重大的幫助。上訴庭認為既然《基本法》並沒有對"通常居住"提供定義，必然期待法院根據不同的社會環境對該字義作出對應的解釋，不可能在通過後便一成不變。而作為對入境人士的良好管理，《基本法》第152條為《入境條例》第2（4）條提供了法律效力的基礎。而且，"通常居住"並非新的法律概念，在《基本法》通過前已經使用已久，起草文件中並看不出有不延續這法律概念的意圖。立法機構應該有充足的裁量權，因應社會的情況制定適當的管理措施。海外傭傭的出現有特殊的背景，對他們採取的政策也有特別的原因，所以，將他們從"通常居住"的類別中排除是可以理解的，並不違反《基本法》第24（2）（4）。

據此，上訴成功，申請人的司法覆核申請被駁回。

CACV 204/2011

IN THE HIGH COURT OF THE

HONG KONG SPECIAL ADMINISTRATIVE REGION

COURT OF APPEAL

CIVIL APPEAL NO 204 OF 2011
(ON APPEAL FROM HCAL 124/2010)

Between:

VALLEJOS EVANGELINE BANAO,
also known as VALLEJOS EVANGELINE B — **Applicant**

- and -

COMMISSIONER OF REGISTRATION — 1st Respondent
REGISTRATION OF PERSONS TRIBUNAL — 2nd Respondent

Before: Hon Cheung CJHC, Tang VP and Stock VP in Court

Dates of Hearing: 21 - 23 February 2012

Date of Judgment: 28 March 2012

JUDGMENT

Hon Cheung CJHC:

The issue

1. This is an appeal from Lam J's judgment dated 30 September 2011. In his judgment, the learned judge decided in the affirmative a single, important point of law, that is, whether section 2(4)(a)(vi) of the Immigration Ordinance (Cap 115) is inconsistent with article 24(2)(4) of the Basic Law and is therefore unconstitutional. The Commissioner of Registration, who is the only active respondent in the proceedings below and in this appeal, challenges that conclusion of law in this appeal. The applicant, a foreign domestic helper who has been working in Hong Kong as such since 1986, supports the judge's decision.

The facts

2. By the nature of the issue before the court, the underlying facts pertaining to the applicant's case assume secondary significance. The point of law decided by the judge affects not only the position of the applicant, but also that of other foreign domestic helpers working in Hong Kong, who are said to have been residing continuously in Hong Kong by reason of their employments for continuous periods of not less than 7 years. Indeed, there are pending cases before the Court of First Instance raising, amongst other issues, the same point of law. The court's decision in this appeal will bind these other proceedings.

3. In those circumstances, it is unnecessary to go into the facts pertaining to the applicant's case in any detail, save to mention that according to the Registration of Persons Tribunal:

(1) the applicant is not of Chinese nationality;

(2) the applicant has entered Hong Kong with a valid travel document;

(3) the applicant has ordinarily resided in Hong Kong for a continuous period of not less than 7 years – however, because of section 2(4)(a)(vi) of the Immigration Ordinance, she shall not, as a matter of law, be treated as ordinarily resident in Hong Kong;

(4) she has taken Hong Kong as her place of permanent residence.

4. Indeed, according to the Tribunal, but for the exclusionary provisions in section 2(4)(a)(vi) of the Ordinance relating to ordinarily residing in Hong Kong, the applicant would have satisfied the requirements for becoming a permanent resident of the Hong Kong Special Administrative Region ("HKSAR") set out in article 24(2)(4) of the Basic Law.

Article 24 of the Basic Law and permanent residents

5. Article 24, appearing at the beginning of Chapter III of the Basic Law which governs the fundamental rights and duties of the residents of the HKSAR, classifies residents into permanent residents and non-permanent residents: article 24(1). Permanent residents have the right of abode in the HKSAR and are qualified to obtain, in accordance with laws, permanent identity cards which state their right of abode: article 24(3). The right of abode means, in practical terms, that a permanent resident cannot be refused entry into Hong Kong, his stay in Hong Kong cannot be subjected to any conditions, and he cannot be deported or removed from Hong Kong.

6. On the other hand, non-permanent residents are persons who are qualified to obtain Hong Kong identity cards in accordance with laws, but have no right of abode: article 24(4). Unlike a permanent resident, a non–permanent resident does not have the right to vote or the right to stand for election in accordance with law: article 26.

7. Article 24(2) defines the permanent residents of the HKSAR:

> "The permanent residents of the Hong Kong Special Administrative Region shall be:
>
> (1) Chinese citizens born in Hong Kong before or after the establishment of the Hong Kong Special Administrative Region;
>
> (2) Chinese citizens who have ordinarily resided in Hong Kong for a continuous period of not less than seven years before or after the establishment of the Hong Kong Special Administrative Region;
>
> (3) Persons of Chinese nationality born outside Hong Kong of those residents listed in categories (1) and (2);
>
> (4) Persons not of Chinese nationality who have entered Hong Kong with valid travel documents, have ordinarily resided in Hong Kong for a continuous period of not less than seven years and have taken Hong Kong as their place of permanent residence before or after the establishment of the Hong Kong Special Administrative Region;
>
> (5) Persons under 21 years of age born in Hong Kong of those residents listed in category (4) before or after the establishment of the Hong Kong Special Administrative Region; and
>
> (6) Persons other than those residents listed in categories (1) to (5), who, before the establishment of the Hong Kong Special Administrative Region, had the right of abode in Hong Kong only."

8. Article 24(2)(4) is directly in issue in the present case. More specifically, the parties' arguments focus on one of the several

requirements for becoming a permanent resident pursuant to article 24(2)(4), that is, "have *ordinarily resided* in Hong Kong". This requirement is also found in article 24(2)(2) dealing with Chinese citizens.

"Ordinarily resident" and section 2(4) of the Immigration Ordinance

9. What constitutes "ordinarily residing" or "ordinarily resident" is not defined in article 24 or in any other parts of the Basic Law. Section 2(4) of the Immigration Ordinance gives (or purports to give) "ordinarily resident" a partial definition. Earlier, the Ordinance has, in section 2(1), defined "Hong Kong permanent resident" by reference to various classes or descriptions of persons specified in Schedule 1 to the Ordinance – paragraph 2 of which simply copies the six categories in article 24(2) of the Basic Law to define Hong Kong permanent residents. The partial definition of "ordinarily resident" given in section 2(4) of the Ordinance reads:

"(4) For the purposes of this Ordinance, a person shall not be treated as ordinarily resident in Hong Kong-

(a) during any period in which he remains in Hong Kong-

(i) with or without the authority of the Director, after landing unlawfully; or

(ii) in contravention of any condition of stay; or

(iii) as a refugee under section 13A; or

(iv) while detained in Hong Kong under section 13D; or

(v) while employed as a contract worker, who is from outside Hong Kong, under a Government importation of labour scheme; or

(vi) while employed as a domestic helper who is from outside Hong Kong; or

(vii) as a member of a consular post within the meaning of the Consular Relations Ordinance (Cap 557); or

(viii) as a member of the Hong Kong Garrison; or

(ix) as a holder of a prescribed Central People's Government travel document; or

(b) during any period, whether before or after the commencement of this Ordinance, of imprisonment or detention pursuant to the sentence or order of any court."

Lam J's decision

10. Specifically for our present purposes, it should be noted that a person shall not be treated as ordinarily resident in Hong Kong during any period in which he or she remains in Hong Kong "while employed as a domestic helper who is from outside Hong Kong": section 2(4)(a)(vi). As mentioned, Lam J held that this exclusionary provision is inconsistent with article 24(2)(4) of the Basic Law which does not contain any such exclusion vis–à–vis foreign domestic helpers. The exclusionary provision is therefore unconstitutional and has to be struck down. The judge recognised that his determination of law has potential read-across implications for other exclusionary provisions found in section 2(4).

11. Lam J held that "ordinarily resident" has a fixed common law meaning, that is, the meaning given to the expression by the House of Lords in *R v Barnet London Borough Council, Ex p Shah* [1983] 2 AC 309. The natural and ordinary meaning of "ordinarily resident", according to the House of Lords, refers to a man's abode in a particular place or country "which he has adopted *voluntarily* and for *settled purposes* as part of the regular order of his life for the time being, whether of short or long duration" (emphasis added): p 343G/H, per Lord Scarman.

12. Lam J pointed out that that definition given in *Shah* had been applied by the Hong Kong courts in immigration cases and, more specifically, by the Court of Final Appeal in *Fateh Muhammad v Commissioner of Registration* (2001) 4 HKCFAR 278 and in *Prem Singh v Director of Immigration* (2003) 6 HKCFAR 26 in relation to article 24(2)(4) of the Basic Law and section 2(4)(b) of the Immigration Ordinance. The judge concluded that it is therefore the correct test to apply in the present case. Needless to say, both the Court of First Instance as well as this court are bound by any relevant decisions of the Court of Final Appeal.

13. The judge took the view that whether a foreign domestic helper, including the applicant, can satisfy the voluntariness/settled purposes test propounded by the House of Lords in *Shah* is a question of fact to be determined in accordance with the facts and circumstances pertaining to each individual case. There is no "one-size-fits-all" answer. Therefore, reasoned the judge, the blanket exclusion of the periods of time spent by foreign domestic helpers in Hong Kong whilst working as such from the definition of "ordinarily resident" in section 2(4)(a)(vi) of the Immigration Ordinance is simply inconsistent with the proper meaning of "ordinarily resident" as used in article 24(2)(4) of the Basic Law. The former amounts to a more stringent or restrictive requirement for qualification as a permanent resident than that laid down in article 24(2)(4) of the Basic Law. It amounts to an additional requirement for qualification which is not found in the Basic Law itself. The legislature has no constitutional power to change the constitutional definition of permanent resident given in the Basic Law. Section 2(4)(a)(vi) is therefore unconstitutional and has to be struck down.

14. The judge did not think that the legislature has any power under article 154(2) of the Basic Law to impose the additional exclusionary provision. Article 154(2) permits the Government to apply immigration controls on entry into, stay in and departure from the HKSAR by persons from foreign states and regions.

15. The judge considered that no immigration controls can be used to trump the definition of permanent resident given in article 24(2) of the Basic Law. In this regard, he considered himself as bound by the Court of Final Appeal's decision in *Prem Singh*.

16. The judge also rejected a fallback argument of the Commissioner based on the *Shah* test. The Commissioner had argued that under the government scheme by which foreign domestic helpers are permitted to come to Hong Kong and work, a foreign domestic helper's abode in Hong Kong can never be classified, under the *Shah* test, as "ordinarily", as opposed to "extraordinarily", "out of the ordinary" or "far from regular".

17. The judge recognised that the government scheme imposes various restrictions on a helper's stay here in terms of her terms of contract of employment, term of employment, limit of stay, compulsory home leave, change of employment, departure from Hong Kong upon expiry of her term of employment or early termination thereof and prohibition on bringing in dependants to Hong Kong. However, the judge was of the view that in the

absence of a detailed examination of the facts pertaining to each individual case, these matters were not by themselves sufficient for the court, applying the *Shah* test, to conclude generally and without any exception, that no helpers could ever be regarded as "ordinarily resident" in Hong Kong.

18. Lam J did not find the extrinsic materials which were put in evidence before the court particularly helpful in shedding light on the true meaning of the expression "ordinarily resident" used in article 24(2)(4).

The parties' arguments

19. In this appeal, Ms Gladys Li SC (Mr PY Lo and Mr Benson Tsoi with her) supported the judge's decision on essentially the same grounds.

20. On the other hand, Lord Pannick QC (with him Mr Anderson Chow SC and Ms Eva Sit) contended that the judge was in error in relation to his reasoning and his conclusion.

21. In essence, Lord Pannick submitted that the judge failed to recognise that the Basic Law implicitly confers power on the legislature to exclude from the scope of "ordinarily resident" those persons who the legislature reasonably considers, having regard to relevant policy considerations, including considerations of immigration policy, are living in Hong Kong in circumstances which do not amount to ordinary residence, such as foreign domestic helpers admitted here under severely restricted conditions.

22. As a fallback position, Lord Pannick argued that even if article 24(2)(4) of the Basic Law does not confer a "discretionary area of judgment" for the legislature to define what is and what is not "ordinarily resident", the judge erred in law by failing to recognise that section 2(4)(a)(vi) correctly recognises that a foreign domestic helper is excluded from the scope of "ordinarily resident" under article 24(2)(4) because the circumstances of her residence in Hong Kong are "out of the ordinary" or exceptional, and far from regular.

23. Lord Pannick also invited the court, as he did before the judge below, to look at extrinsic materials which pre-date and post-date 1990, the year the Basic Law was promulgated, in case the court is of the view that the true meaning of article 24(2)(4) is ambiguous. Leading counsel submitted that the materials demonstrate the intention of the Chinese and British Governments, as a matter of interpretation or application of paragraph 159 in Part XIV of Annex I to the Joint Declaration signed on 19 December 1984 (which corresponds to article 24(2)(4) of the Basic Law), to authorize the local legislature to explain and implement the concept of "ordinarily resident". According to the materials, counsel submitted, by the time section 2(4)(a)(vi) was enacted, the two Governments had reached agreement in the Joint Liaison Group ("JLG") that foreign domestic helpers should be excluded by legislation from the scope of "ordinarily resident" in Hong Kong for the purposes of article 24(2)(4) of the Basic Law.

The principles of interpretation

24. The principles of interpretation of the Basic Law are not in doubt. They have been authoritatively laid down by the Court of Final Appeal in *Ng Ka Ling v Director of Immigration* (1999) 2 HKCFAR 4 and in *Director of Immigration v Chong Fung Yuen* (2001) 4 HKCFAR 211. They are well known and need not be repeated in detail. All I wish to emphasise here is that in the interpretation of a constitution such as the Basic Law a purposive approach is to be applied. This is because a constitution states general principles and expresses purposes without condescending to particularity and definition of terms. Gaps and ambiguity are bound to arise and, "in resolving them, the courts are bound to give effect to the principles and purposes declared in, and to be ascertained from, the constitution and relevant extrinsic materials": *Ng Ka Ling* at p 28E/F. The purpose of a particular provision may be ascertainable from its nature or other provisions of the Basic Law or relevant extrinsic materials including the Joint Declaration. The state of domestic legislation at the time of the Basic Law's enactment and the time of the Joint Declaration will often also serve as an aid to the interpretation of the Basic law. As to the language of its text, the courts must avoid a literal, technical, narrow or rigid approach. They must consider the context. Assistance can also be gained from any traditions and usages that may have given meaning to the language used. On the other hand, the courts will not on the basis of any extrinsic materials depart from the clear meaning and give the language of the text (when construed in the light of its context and purposes) a meaning which the language cannot bear.

25. In ascertaining the context and purpose of the Basic Law and of the provisions thereof in issue, it is right and proper to look at pre-enactment materials, that is materials brought into existence prior to or contemporaneous with the enactment of the Basic Law in 1990 although it only came into effect on 1 July 1997. However, as regards post-enactment materials, the use of them relating to context and purpose must be approached "cautiously".

26. As the Court of Final Appeal emphasised in *Chong Fung Yuen*, at p 224I-J, extrinsic materials, whatever their nature and whether pre or post-enactment, cannot affect interpretation where the courts conclude that the meaning of the language, when construed in the light of its context and purpose is clear. The meaning of the language is clear, the court explained, "if it is free from ambiguity, that is, it is not reasonably capable of sustaining competing alternative interpretations".

Article 24(2)(4) raises a prior question

27. Article 24(2)(4) of the Basic Law is a natural starting point to tackle the task of interpretation faced by the court. As mentioned, "ordinarily resident" is used both in article 24(2)(2) concerning Chinese citizens and in article 24(2)(4) in respect of non-Chinese nationals. The first important point to note is that the term, important as it is, is nowhere defined in article 24 itself or in any part of the Basic Law.

28. The natural question thus arises is: what is the meaning of "ordinarily resident"? But before one even attempts to supply a definition, a prior question arises: Does the term have one definite meaning, or put more specifically, is the term intended to have one and only one definite and unchanging meaning throughout the intended life of the Basic Law (50 years from 1997)? That this is a prior question is self-evident and affects how one would answer the definitional question about the term. Its significance lies not only in whether one should give one definition or more than one definition in answer to the ultimate question. Its significance lies also in its opening up of a distinct interpretative possibility that the legislature is intended by the Basic Law to have a (limited) say on what the term means at any given point of time. That, in my view, essentially captures the gist of Lord Pannick's primary argument.

29. This requires some elaboration. The fact that the expression "ordinarily resident" is undefined in the Basic Law does not mean as a matter of logic or of necessity, that on its proper interpretation, the Basic Law intends that the definition is to

be solely supplied by the court, or that its meaning is to remain unchanged and unchangeable for 50 years starting from 1997 (short of an amendment of the Basic Law).

30. Having one court-supplied meaning which is to hold good for 50 years is, of course, an interpretative possibility that must be seriously considered. However, that is not the only possible interpretative option. The other option, persuasively advocated by Lord Pannick, is that the framers of the Basic Law actually intended to leave it to the legislature to define, within bounds (if I may put it loosely for the time being), what "ordinarily resident" means according to its best judgment, which would no doubt be dependent on, amongst other things, policy considerations and the ever-changing political, economic and social conditions prevailing for the time being.

31. It is only after this prior question has been properly answered can one move on to define the expression "ordinarily resident" in the Basic Law or, as the case may be, to consider whether the legislature has acted outwith its power to define, refine, elaborate or adapt the meaning of "ordinarily resident" by enacting section 2(4)(a)(vi) of the Immigration Ordinance.

Genesis of article 24(2)

32.To better answer the prior question, several important matters should be borne in mind.

33.First, article 24(2) (including article 24(2)(4)) is not a new invention under the Basic Law. Its genesis can be traced to paragraphs 157 to 160 in Part XIV of Annex I to the Joint Declaration signed in late 1984. Article 24(2)(4) copies almost verbatim what has been set out in paragraph 159. Like the Basic Law, neither paragraph 159 nor the rest of Annex I, nor indeed any part of the Joint Declaration, defines the meaning of "ordinarily resident".

"Ordinarily resident" –pre–existing use and importance of context

34. Secondly, the term "ordinarily resident" was not a novel term whether back in 1990 or 1984, and whether in Hong Kong or in the UK in those days. Rather, it was an expression used in a variety of contexts in law, including immigration laws. As the judge pointed out in paragraph 42 of his judgment, in the 1970s, the expression "permanent resident" did not appear in our statute book. Instead, the Immigration Ordinance had a definition of "Hong Kong belonger". But there were already references to "ordinarily resident in Hong Kong", for instance, in the definitions of "Chinese resident" and "resident United Kingdom belonger". Further, section 2(4) of the Immigration Ordinance already existed although at that time only those who remained in Hong Kong unlawfully or in breach of a limit of stay, and those who were imprisoned or detained, were excluded from being "ordinarily resident in Hong Kong". See Ordinance No 55 of 1971.

35. Moreover, as the actual decision in *Shah* demonstrates, the term or concept is also commonly used in other areas of law. In *Shah*, the concept was crucial to whether overseas students in the United Kingdom were entitled to receive educational awards under the Education Act 1962 and Education Act 1980. As mentioned, Lord Scarman, who delivered the leading judgment, described the natural and ordinary meaning of the expression in terms of voluntariness and settled purposes. This, it should be noted, was not a new test; it was a test borrowed from two House of Lords cases which also dealt with the expression but in a different context, namely: *Levene v Inland Revenue Commissioners* [1928] AC 217 and *Inland Revenue Commissioners v Lysaght* [1928] AC 234. Both were tax cases. When his Lordship adopted the same test for the purposes of deciding the case before the House, Lord Scarman said at p 343G-H:

> "Unless, therefore, it can be shown that *the statutory framework or the legal context in which the words are used requires a different meaning*, I unhesitatingly subscribe to the view that 'ordinarily resident' refers to a man's abode in a particular place or country which he has adopted voluntarily and for settled purposes as part of the regular order of his life for the time being, whether of short or of long duration." (emphasis added)

36. Indeed, Lord Scarman went on to acknowledge that in different contexts, the same set of facts may give rise to different answers in terms of "ordinarily resident". He referred to the situation where the person's stay in a country was unlawful (eg in breach of the immigration laws). He pointed out that in that case, the person would not be regarded as ordinarily resident in the UK for the purposes of the Education Acts that he had to deal with (indeed there was an express exception to that effect in the Immigration Act 1971), but in the context of tax, his Lordship recognised, the same person, on the same facts, may well be regarded differently: pp 343H-344B. In *Fateh Muhammad*, a case which I will presently turn to, Bokhary PJ, in giving the leading judgment of the Court of Final Appeal, made a similar point at p 284B-C.

The meaning of "ordinarily resident" was not free from controversies

37. Thirdly, even in a given context, the meaning of "ordinarily resident" has not been necessarily clear. Again, taking *Shah* as an illustration, the decision of the House of Lords on this crucial point reversed both the decision of the Divisional Court (Ormrod LJ, Kilner Brown and McNeill JJ) and that of the Court of Appeal (Lord Denning MR, Eveleigh and Templeman LJJ). All the judges below took a narrower and more restrictive view on the meaning of "ordinarily resident" and placed great emphasis on the immigration status of the students and the limited purposes for which they were permitted to reside in the UK in determining whether they were "ordinarily resident" there – matters which, in the view of the House of Lords, were irrelevant to the proper meaning of the expression.

38. We now know, with the benefit of hindsight, that the test favoured by Lord Scarman, though regarded as too wide by equally eminent judges including Lord Denning and Templeman LJ (as Lord Templeman then was), has since been accepted and adopted by many courts including the courts in Hong Kong as representing good law in many different contexts where the term is found. However, the Joint Declaration was signed in 1984, and the *Shah* test was barely two years old then. That was the background that one should bear in mind in seeking to answer the prior question.

Common law meaning is always subject to statutory modification

39. Fourthly and more importantly, the undeniable fact is that common law (in the sense of case law) has never had an exclusive say on the meaning of "ordinarily resident". Lord Scarman recognised as much in *Shah*. In the passage quoted above, he said that the meaning he favoured was subject to "the statutory framework or the legal context in which the words are used". Very often, when the term is used in a statute, the statute itself provides either a complete or at least a partial definition of the term. For instance, when "ordinarily resident" was used in the original Immigration Ordinance when enacted in 1971, it already

contained the several exceptions mentioned above. Therefore, when a court is called upon to interpret the statutory term, it must bear those statutory exceptions in mind and read the relevant provisions in the statute as a whole, in deciding what meaning should be ascribed to the term. Where necessary, the common law meaning of the expression must be adjusted and adapted to suit the statutory text.

40. But not only that. The very history of the litigation in *Shah* demonstrates one further matter of great significance, that is, the common law meaning of "ordinarily resident" is always subject to subsequent statutory intervention. The actual decision in *Shah*, which was favourable to overseas students, was duly reversed by Parliament: see *R v Hereford and Worcester County Council, Ex parte Wimbourne*, The Times, 12 November 1983. And that was even before the Joint Declaration was signed in December 1984.

Pre-existing power to legislate on "ordinarily resident"

41. This leads me to my fifth point, which is of equal importance. Before 1997 and indeed before 1990 or 1984, the legislature has always enjoyed and indeed exercised the power to legislate on the meaning of "ordinarily resident", typically by adding exceptions to what might otherwise have been regarded as within the meaning of the expression.

42. As mentioned, when the Immigration Ordinance was first enacted in 1971, it already contained exceptions in section 2(4) as it then was. For instance, the exclusion of those imprisoned or detained from the expression was there from day one: section 2(4)(b). The exclusion relating to Vietnamese refugees permitted to remain in Hong Kong as refugees pending resettlement elsewhere pursuant to section 13A of the Ordinance was added in 1982: section 2(4)(a)(iii). A further exception relating to detained Vietnamese refugees pending decision as to permission to remain or pending removal under section 13D of the Ordinance was added in 1989, after the signing of the Joint Declaration in 1984 but before the promulgation of the Basic Law in 1990.

43. The impugned exception relating to foreign domestic helpers was added by the Provisional Legislative Council in 1997, together with other exceptions relating to contract workers under a government importation of labour scheme, members of a consular post and members of the Hong Kong garrison. The latest addition to the list of exclusions was made in 2002 in relation to a holder of a prescribed Central People's Government travel document.

44. Putting aside whether the provisions in the Basic Law are sufficiently wide to enable the legislature to add to the list of exclusions to the meaning of "ordinarily resident" in the Immigration Ordinance after the coming into effect of the Basic Law in 1997, the undeniable fact is that whether before or after 1984, 1990 and 1997, both the executive arm of government and the legislature have always proceeded on the assumption that the legislature is entitled to define, refine, elaborate or adapt, by means of ordinary legislation, the meaning of "ordinarily resident" to suit prevailing circumstances.

Immigration controls

45. This leads me to my sixth point. Article 154(2) of the Basic Law, which has its origin also in Part XIV of Annex I to the Joint Declaration, para 166, specifically provides:

> "The Government of the Hong Kong Special Administrative Region may apply immigration controls on entry into, stay in and departure from the Region by persons from foreign states and regions."

46. This is not at all surprising given the great importance of immigration controls in the context of Hong Kong, something which I sought to highlight in *MA v Director of Immigration*, HCAL 10/2010, 6 January 2011, para 97 (where other relevant cases were referred to).

47. Needless to say, political, economic and social conditions are not static. They do change. Almost by definition, they have a great bearing on the question of immigration and immigration controls. And the need to be able to respond, timeously and effectively, to changing circumstances in terms of immigration controls is self-evident, particularly in a geographically small yet highly sophisticated, populous city like Hong Kong. That need has never diminished or otherwise changed, whether before or after 1984, 1990 or 1997. Rightly or wrongly, the Government and the legislature have proceeded on the basis, post 1997, that they may, just as before 1997, legislate on the definition of "ordinarily resident" to effect immigration controls.

The theme of continuity

48. Are they wrong to proceed in this way? One important theme of the Basic Law is the theme of continuity. It is simply a manifestation of one of the guiding principles underlying the Joint Declaration and the Basic Law, that is, the previous capitalist system and way of life in Hong Kong shall remain unchanged for 50 years: article 5 of the Basic Law. Immigration controls and the question of who can and who cannot become permanent residents of the Special Administrative Region must be matters that have an impact, and conceivably a material impact, on the way of life in Hong Kong. In different contexts, the courts have referred to the theme of continuity in interpreting various provisions of the Basic Law: *HKSAR v Ma Wai Kwan David* [1997] HKLRD 761; *Secretary for Justice v Lau Kwok Fai* (2005) 8 HKCFAR 304, para 35; *Luk Ka Cheung v Market Misconduct Tribunal* [2009] 1 HKLRD 114, paras 32 and 36.

49. Certainly, the theme of continuity cannot be carried too far. Where a new regime is introduced by the Basic Law, the theme of continuity has no or little role to play. By definition, the old is replaced by the new. Our new Court of Final Appeal and the new office of the Chief Justice of the Court of Final Appeal are just two amongst many examples that can be given to illustrate the limitations of the theme of continuity under the new constitutional order. Ms Li, in the present context, argued that this is such a case in relation to article 24(2) of the Basic Law which provides a brand new definition of permanent resident of the Special Administrative Region. She also reminded the court of the non-adoption of the previous statutory definition of the term (permanent resident) in the Immigration Ordinance pursuant to article 160 of the Basic Law as from 1 July 1997.

50. I accept all this so far as it goes. However, whilst we have a new definition of permanent resident, this new definition uses, relevantly, familiar terms, that is, "ordinarily resident" in Hong Kong for a continuous period of not less than 7 years. Therefore, to this extent, one asks, did the framers of the Basic Law intend a clean break from the former practice, or did they intend some form of continuity with the past? The absence of a definition for "ordinarily resident" and the presence of article 154(2) in the Basic Law would tend to support the latter answer. The fact that article 154(2) is contained in Chapter VII of the Basic Law covering "External Affairs" should not mask its proximity to the provisions governing the definition of permanent resident in the Joint Declaration. To be exact, it is only seven paragraphs away from the crucial definition of permanent resident in question. The

intervening paragraphs in Part XIV of Annex I deal with passports, travelling documents and people coming to Hong Kong from other parts of the country.

51. A further point that can be made in relation to article 154(2) and immigration controls in general, under the present context (the theme of continuity), is that putting the case law aside (which I will return to), controlling and regulating who can and who cannot become a permanent resident must be one of the core businesses and purposes of immigration controls. Put another way, one of the main aims and purposes of having immigration controls in the first place is to enable society to control and regulate who can, and who cannot, immediately or in due course, become a national, citizen or, as the case may be, permanent resident with the right of abode, of that society.

A valuable status and right

52. This brings me to my last observation. For Hong Kong, the permanent resident status is a highly valuable status and right: *Fateh Muhammad*, p 284D/E. It makes the present context a very different context from one concerning educational award or taxation. Naturally one expects the Basic Law to intend a more cautious if not different approach to be adopted in determining what amounts to "ordinarily resident" as a condition for the concession by society of the valuable status and right.

53. This is all the more so, in the context of the impugned provisions, given the number of foreign domestic helpers already working in Hong Kong back in the 1980s–by 1986, there were 28,951 working in Hong Kong; that figure increased to 70,335 by 1990 when the Basic Law was promulgated. All this happened against the background that most if not all of them were not qualified to become Hong Kong permanent residents according to the then immigration laws, a fact which was made well known to the foreign domestic helpers even before their first arrival in Hong Kong. It is true that also excluded from potential permanent resident status were many other classes of people staying in Hong Kong under the then immigration laws. However, this does not detract from the fact that, for all practical purposes, at no time before 1997 were foreign domestic helpers entitled to the valuable status and right of a permanent resident. Nor does it detract from the fact that article 24(2)(4) of the Basic law is now said to have opened a real possibility for the acquisition of the valuable status and right by such a potentially large group of people (I use the word "potentially" advisedly as I am aware of the controversy on the implications, real or projected, of the present issue in terms of numbers and figures.)

One definite, immutable meaning?

54. I would now look at the position from a slightly different perspective. What are the implications of the Basic Law intending (for the sake of argument) that there should be a fixed meaning of "ordinarily resident" in article 24(2)(4), so that the court's only task is to discover that meaning by applying the normal canons of construction of the Basic Law? In that event, the legislature would have no or very limited role to play in shaping the meaning of the term. Indeed, that represents Ms Li's position. According to leading counsel, "ordinarily resident" has one definite and immutable meaning, good for all time, subject to any amendment of the Basic Law. That meaning has been fixed since 1990 (or 1984 when the Joint Declaration was signed?) Furthermore, she contended that that single, immutable meaning of the term is that given by the House of Lords in *Shah*. In other words, article 24(2)(4) has, on its proper interpretation, codified or constitutionally entrenched *Shah*.

55. Ms Li's position is best illustrated by her answer given to a hypothetical question posed to counsel during submission: what if the Supreme Court in the United Kingdom were to depart from *Shah* tomorrow and give the term a different meaning; what should the courts in Hong Kong do then? Counsel answered that the courts, in interpreting article 24(2)(4), should nonetheless follow the meaning given by *Shah* to the term. Although it was not posed to counsel during submission, I suppose counsel would have given the same answer if she had been asked what the position would have been if the Privy Council had, between 1990 and 1997, refused to follow *Shah* but instead adopted a different meaning for the term. For the sake of completeness, I also suppose the answer that counsel would have given would still be the same if she were asked whether the Court of Final Appeal would be at liberty to say that *Shah* was wrongly decided and "ordinary resident" in article 24(2)(4) should be given a different meaning in a post 1997 case.

56. I have difficulties with this approach. Not only does it represent a significant departure from the previous practice whereby the legislature is free to define, refine, elaborate or adapt the meaning of "ordinarily resident" to suit the needs of society for the time being, but this approach – whereby a single common law decision, albeit one by the House of Lords, is elevated to the status of an immutable, constitutional definition, which cannot be changed either by ordinary legislation or by normal development of case law–also represents a considerable departure from the traditions of common law. That is a very drastic position to take.

57. All this change is said to have taken place even though the Basic Law contains no definition of the term "ordinarily resident", and nowhere can we find in the Basic Law any references to the crucial elements of the *Shah* test, namely, voluntariness and settled purposes.

Pre-existing exceptions relating to imprisoned persons and Vietnamese refugees

58. Ms Li's contention has significant practical implications. Take the pre-existing exceptions to the definition of "ordinarily resident" in the Immigration Ordinance as examples. As mentioned, section 2(4)(b) excludes all periods of imprisonment or detention from the reckoning of ordinary residence. There can be no doubt that this exclusion is constitutional: *Fateh Muhammad* and *Prem Singh*.

59. Nor can it be doubted that the exclusion of Vietnamese refugees in section 2(4)(a)(iii) is constitutionally valid. Back in the 1980s, the presence of a very significant number of Vietnamese refugees stranded in Hong Kong awaiting resettlement was a real political, economic and social problem not only for Hong Kong, but also internationally. The exception was added to the Immigration Ordinance in 1982 under those circumstances. In the ensuing years, it became increasingly plain that the chances of many of these stranded refugees securing resettlement elsewhere were slim and short of repatriation to Vietnam, a great many of them would remain in Hong Kong indefinitely. Plainly this was an unacceptable situation given Hong Kong's small geographical size and huge population. Indeed the United Nations Refugees Convention 1951 was (and still is) never extended to Hong Kong and Hong Kong's "reached base" policy for Mainland illegal immigrants had been discontinued by 1980: *Attorney-General of Hong Kong v Ng Yuen Shiu* [1983] 2 AC 629, 633F to 634B. It therefore came as no surprise that many thousands of those stranded here were eventually repatriated to Vietnam. In those circumstances, it would be most startling a proposition

to suggest that the framers had, in the latter part of the 1980s when the Vietnamese refugee problem was at its height, actually intended to confer permanent resident status on those who had been stranded in Hong Kong for long enough. On a purposive interpretation of the Basic Law, therefore, bearing in mind the pre-enactment position, there can be little doubt that the exclusion relating to Vietnamese refugees is constitutionally valid. Ms Li has not sought to argue otherwise.

60. Yet, importantly, a strict and mechanical application of the *Shah* test, as enunciated by the House of Lords in 1982, would have yielded a very different result. Depending on the facts, and the right facts are not difficult to imagine, such a Vietnamese refugee, or for that purpose, an imprisoned or detained person, may well be able to satisfy the *Shah* test in terms of voluntariness and settled purposes even though one is a stranded refugee, and the other has been imprisoned or detained. It all depends on the facts.

61. It should not be forgotten that in *Fateh Muhammad*, the applicant who unsuccessfully applied for a permanent identity card in 1998 because he had been imprisoned for 3 years during the requisite 7 year period, had lived in Hong Kong since the 1960s. And in the subsequent case of *Prem Singh*, the applicant had been in Hong Kong since 1988, and the period of imprisonment in issue was only 2 weeks. One can easily think of more extreme facts to bring out the point here. And the point is: depending on the facts, such a person may well be able to satisfy the voluntariness/settled purposes test propounded by the House of Lords in *Shah*, if that test is indeed the proper test to apply for the purposes of article 24(2)(4). One only needs to compare the situation of such a person with that of a local person who has, for one reason for another, been imprisoned or detained for a period of time, and ask whether such a local person was still ordinarily resident in Hong Kong under the Shah test during his period of imprisonment or detention, in order to see that depending on the facts, the answer could well be "yes". In terms of analysis, again depending on the facts, there could be little difference between such a foreign national and a local person.

62. Likewise, a stranded Vietnamese refugee in Hong Kong with little or no realistic prospect of resettlement elsewhere in the near future may well regard his presence in Hong Kong as something he has adopted for settled purposes as part of the regular order of his life for the time being. And regardless of where he ultimately wants to go, his presence in Hong Kong may, in many cases, be regarded as voluntary under the *Shah* test. Yet, as analysed above, there can be no doubt about the constitutional validity of the exception relating to Vietnamese refugees.

63. These are real exclusions. They are sweeping exclusions which do not permit the individual from asking the authorities to examine the facts pertaining to his or her case individually. Yet they are constitutional.

64. The wholesale adoption of the *Shah* test as the correct, immutable definition of "ordinarily resident" in article 24(2)(4) cannot accommodate these two blanket exceptions. Certainly one cannot find any grandfather clause in the Basic Law to preserve them. In my view, the very presence of these admittedly valid statutory exceptions casts a serious doubt on the primary premise on which Ms Li's argument is founded, namely, that article 24(2)(4) has, in essence, constitutionally entrenched the *Shah* test, forever and ever.

Can new exceptions be created?

65. The practical implications of Ms Li's contention do not stop there. For it is counsel's primary contention, building on the *Shah* test, that no further exceptions can be created by the legislature after 1990 which are inconsistent with the immutable *Shah* test. That this is a startling proposition can best be brought out by illustrations. According to this argument, the legislature has since 1997 or even 1990 lost the power to add exceptions to "ordinarily resident" which are inconsistent with the *Shah* test regardless of changing political, economic and social circumstances. (I say 1990 because any such *new* exceptions added after the promulgation of the Basic Law in 1990 would not have survived the coming into effect of the Basic Law in 1997.) Not forgetting that the exclusion of refugees in section 2(2)(a)(iii) relates only to Vietnamese refugees, the legislature has no power to legislate against any refugees coming from elsewhere, or for that matter, economic migrants or torture claimants (whether screened in or otherwise), even if it wants to. As illustrated by the facts in *MA*, the possibility of mandated refugees and screened in torture claimants being stranded in Hong Kong for a prolonged period of time is not unreal at all. Yet, according to Ms Li's contention, the Government has no power to legislate on these matters in any way that is inconsistent with the *Shah* test; the only remedy lies with the amendment of the Basic Law.

66.Why should this be so, if one may ask rhetorically? Ms Li relied on the theme of continuity. But she relied on it to justify the continued adoption of the *Shah* test which had been adopted in some local cases prior to 1990.

67. For my part, I do not believe this is a correct way of understanding the theme of continuity or of applying it to the present case. It represents too narrow a view of what constituted the pre–Basic Law or pre–1997 position which is continued in the post-1997 era. As mentioned, the legislature, as recognised by common law, has always possessed and exercised the power to define, refine, elaborate or adapt the concept of "ordinarily resident" for the purposes of immigration controls, so as to meet ever–changing circumstances. The need to do so and to be able to do so has never changed whether before or after 1997. I do not believe it was the intention of the framers of the Basic Law to put an end to this power altogether. That would be counterproductive and it would amount to imposing a straitjacket on the Government of the Special Administrative Region.

68. What the framers intended, in my view, is that, on the one hand, article 24(2)(4) of the Basic Law defines relevantly the requirements for obtaining the status of permanent resident by reference to, amongst other things, "ordinarily resident", and on the other, it leaves it to the legislature to define, refine, elaborate or adapt the expression to meet the ever–changing needs of society. In that way, a balance is struck. By using the term "ordinarily resident", a certain degree of certainty is obtained and the legislature's freedom is curtailed. No further or other requirement can be added: *Prem Singh*. Furthermore, whatever refinement, elaboration or adaptation the legislature might wish to make to the term "ordinarily resident", it cannot go outside the core meaning of the term. As was remarked during submission, the legislature cannot call a swimming pool a lighthouse: *cf Australian Communist Party v The Commonwealth* (1951) 83 CLR 1, 249; *Singh v The Commonwealth* (2004) 222 CLR 322, para 153. However, within bounds, the legislature is given a free rein.

Inherent flexibility of the expression "ordinarily resident"

69. This approach accords well with the common law position, which, as explained, always assumes Parliament's power to

modify or even change a common law rule. Even Lord Scarman pointed out that his test of "ordinarily resident" is always subject to the relevant statutory framework or the legal context in which the words are used which may require or indicate a different meaning.

70. As Lord Pannick submitted, it would be a very strange thing to say that our Basic Law has, for some unknown reasons, chosen to adopt a particular meaning given to the expression "ordinarily resident" in an educational allowance case in the United Kingdom by way of statutory interpretation of some Education Acts there, as the immutable meaning for the same expression found in our article 24(2)(4). This is particularly so, when the common law definition so supposedly adopted is itself not free from controversies amongst eminent jurists, and when the expression is notorious for being capable of bearing different meanings in different contexts.

71. That the term "ordinarily resident" may reasonably bear different meanings is illustrated not only by the more restrictive meanings ascribed to the expression by the Divisional Court and by the Court of Appeal in Shah, but also by, for instance, the statutory definition given under the latest Australian Citizenship Act 2007 which reads:

> "... a person is taken to be ordinarily resident in a country if and only if:
>
> (a) he or she has his or her home in that country; or
>
> (b) that country is the country of his or her permanent abode even if he or she is temporarily absent from that country.
>
> However, the person is taken not to be so resident if he or she resides in that country for a special or temporary purpose only."

72. As Bokhary PJ recognised in *Fateh Muhammad*, at p 283G/H-284B:

> "The expression 'ordinarily resident' is to be given its natural and ordinary meaning. What that meaning is depends on the context in which the expression appears. The courts have often had to grapple with the expression's natural and ordinary meaning in legislation eg as in *Levene v IRC* [1928] AC 217 and *IRC v Lysaght* [1928] AC 234 (where liability to tax was concerned) and as in *R v Barnet LBC, ex p Shah* [1983] 2 AC 309 (where entitlement to educational allowance was concerned). Although residence and its nature can be highly relevant to the common law concept of domicil, it was pointed out by Lord Carson in *Gout v Cimitian* [1922] 1 AC 105 at p110 that the expression 'ordinarily resident' (found in that case in an order-in-council) could not be interpreted by the considerations which apply when determining domicil, and must be given its usual and ordinary meaning.
>
> No single judicial pronouncement or combination of such pronouncements in regard to the meaning of the expression 'ordinarily resident' can be conclusive for the purposes of every context in which that expression appears. But as a starting point at least, Viscount Sumner's observation in *IRC v Lysaght* [1928] AC 234 at p243 that 'the converse to 'ordinarily' is 'extraordinarily''is, I think, of wide utility. Serving a term of imprisonment, at least when it is not of trivial duration, is something out of the ordinary."

Singh – the Australian approach

73. In this regard, our situation is not wholly unlike the one faced by the Australian High Court in *Singh*. Section 51(xix) of the Australian Constitution confers upon the Parliament the power to make laws with respect to "naturalization and aliens". Section 10(2) of the Australian Citizenship Act 1948 (Cth), as amended by the Australian Citizenship Amendment Act 1986 (Cth), provided that a person born in Australia after 20 August 1986 shall be an Australian citizen by virtue of that birth only if a parent of the person was, at the time of the birth, an Australian citizen or a permanent resident, or if the person has been ordinarily resident in Australia throughout a period of 10 years commencing on the day the person was born. The plaintiff was born in Australia in February 1998. Her parents were citizens of India and were not Australian citizens or permanent residents. By virtue of her parents' citizenship of India, the plaintiff took Indian citizenship at birth. In 2003 she commenced proceedings to resist removal under the Migration Act 1958 (Cth) as an "unlawful non-citizen". At issue was whether the applicant was an "alien" within the meaning of section 51(xix) of the Constitution and therefore whether the Parliament had the constitutional power to make the relevant statutory provisions empowering her removal from Australia. The plaintiff contended that by virtue of her birthright in Australia, she was not an alien as the word was understood properly at the time the Constitution was made.

74. By a majority, her contention was rejected. Although different judges gave different reasons for their decisions, I find the judgment of Kirby J, one of the majority judges, most relevant for our present purposes, whilst bearing firmly in mind that the facts and contexts of the two cases are quite different.

75. Having pointed out in paragraph 250 of the judgment that even in 1901, there were two major legal theories concerning the legal status of aliens, in the sense of "belonging to" another place or person, Kirby J said in paragraph 251 that it was unconvincing to suggest that the federal Parliament in Australia was "forever to be limited to the approach of birthright", the approach favoured by the English courts (subject to statutory exceptions) at the time of confederation. Starting from paragraph 252, the learned judge asked a number of highly illuminating rhetorical questions:

> "252. Why could the Parliament not adopt, wholly or in part, elements of the alternative legal approach to the issue of alienage accepted by many legal systems of the world? After all, each approach was an endeavour to identify the feature of a relationship between the individual and a nation on the basis of which loyalty and membership could generally be imputed and demanded. Further, the common law rule of birthright had already admitted its own exceptions, namely for the children of a foreign monarch, diplomats and enemy aliens. Why, of its nature, could more exceptions never develop around the notion of 'aliens'? From medieval times, the English Parliament provided particular derogations from birthright in favour of the principle of descent. Why, as a matter of constitutional principle, should further exceptions be forbidden to the Australian Parliament? Why should it be forbidden in the absence of a clear indication that such was the purpose of those who made the Constitution and designed its basic notions?
>
> 253. In the nineteenth century, in the United Kingdom, inquiries had been launched relating to the need to modify the birthright rule. If this was in

the contemplation of the generation that adopted the Constitution, why did the use of the word 'aliens' forbid any further movement if later generations were convinced that movement was warranted? Within limits set by the unchanging, essential elements of the word 'aliens', it has been conventional in our constitutional law to acknowledge a large power on the part of the Parliament to give meaning to the language of the Constitution, subject always to consideration by the courts, which, in this respect, have the last say."

76. Drawing the threads together, Kirby J said:

"256. Because the Constitution, of its function and character, adapts to such changes, there is no reason why the word 'aliens' should not be capable of responding to such new circumstances. There is every reason why it should.

......

266. The recognition of this change in the notion of alienage is only consistent with an acceptance of the fact that the ambit of the word 'aliens' was not closed at the time of Federation. It was not a word devoid of meaning. But neither was its meaning fixed by what the word would have meant to lawyers, or the laity, in 1901 or even 1980. Addressing as it does a status, defined by reference to the relationship between the Australian people and each other as well as with the people of the rest of the world, it is inevitable that geo-political, technological and other developments will have an impact on the contemporary understanding of the meaning of 'aliens' and that appreciation of the meaning of that word will change over time.

.....

269. Should some future Parliament attempt to push the 'aliens' power into extreme instances, so as to deem a person born in Australia an 'alien' despite parental or grand-parental links of descent and residence, this Court can be trusted to draw the necessary constitutional line. Doing so is inherent in the task of constitutional interpretation. To avoid such dangers, it is not necessary to embrace a rigid, and now outmoded, meaning of a contested constitutional word."

77. As I have emphasised, the context and indeed the issues faced by the High Court in *Singh* are quite different from that in the present case. There are of course distinctions between the two cases. However, I do not think the fact that the Parliament in *Singh* is given an express power to make law with respect to "naturalization and aliens" provides a valid distinction. The simple reason is that no one contended in *Singh* that that express authorization by itself allows the Parliament to *define* who is or who is not an alien. On that point, the Australian Parliament is no different from the legislature in Hong Kong. It is permitted to legislate on the *definition* of alienage not because of the express power given to legislate with respect to "aliens", but only because of the fact that "the ambit of the word 'aliens' was not closed at the time of Federation" (para 266) and the Parliament is thus entitled to adapt the meaning of the word "aliens" to respond to changing circumstances over time.

Unchanging, essential elements or central characteristic of "ordinarily resident"

78. As Lord Pannick emphasised, the Commissioner is not advocating for a free-for-all position in respect of the power of the legislature to legislate on the meaning of "ordinarily resident". In *Singh*, the majority recognised that the word "aliens" is not devoid of meaning but has some unchanging, "essential elements" (para 253) or a "central characteristic" (para 200), that is, "owing obligations (allegiance)" (*ibid*). Likewise, the expression "ordinarily resident", when used in the Basic Law, is not devoid of meaning but has some unchanging, essential elements or a central characteristic. But subject to these unchanging, essential elements or the central characteristic, the legislature may, as before, define, refine, elaborate or adapt the expression to meet the changing needs of society.

79. The unchanging, essential elements or central characteristic means that once the essential elements or central characteristic is met, the person cannot be labelled by the Parliament in *Singh* as an alien, or in our present case, the foreigner cannot be regarded by the legislature as not "ordinarily resident" here. In other words, the unchanging, essential elements or central characteristic demarcates the outer limit of the word "aliens" in *Singh* or, of the expression "ordinarily resident" in our case. Beyond the outer limit, the legislature cannot go. Within the outer limit, however, the legislature has a free hand. In other words, if it so wishes, the legislature may choose to give the word/expression a more generous and liberal meaning than that required by its unchanging, essential elements or central characteristic. Thus, there is nothing to stop the Australian Parliament, if it so wishes, to adopt, even now, the place of birth as the sole criterion for determining alienage. Nor is there anything to stop the local legislature from giving the expression "ordinarily resident" a more liberal and generous meaning than that required by its unchanging, essential elements or central characteristic.

80. For reasons that I will continue to develop, the *Shah* test is indeed such a more liberal and generous test, which the legislature has *not*, however, chosen to adopt in the Immigration Ordinance. Rather it has chosen to add one exception after another to the expression "ordinarily resident" and make the door narrower and narrower. The present case raises the all–important question of whether the exception found in section 2(4)(a)(vi) has made the door narrower than is permitted by the unchanging, essential elements or central characteristic of the expression "ordinarily resident".

81. What then are those unchanging, essential elements or central characteristics of the expression "ordinarily resident" when used in article 24(2) of the Basic Law? In my view, they are not represented by the *Shah* test, which, as mentioned, is in fact a more liberal and generous test. In this regard, contrary to the view of the judge below, I do not understand the two Court of Final Appeal cases in *Fateh Muhammad* and *Prem Singh* as binding the court to come to a different conclusion. Rather, in my view, the two cases demonstrate precisely that the unchanging, essential elements or central characteristic of the term "ordinarily resident", when used in the Basic Law, is not limited to the two requirements of voluntariness and settled purposes or, put another way, the essential elements or central characteristic is only properly reflected by a more stringent or restrictive way of applying the two requirements than in other contexts.

Fateh Muhammad

82. In *Fateh Muhammad*, the applicant applied for a permanent identity card in 1998, claiming that he was a permanent resident under article 24(2)(4) of the Basic Law. He had lived in Hong

Kong since the 1960s, but between 1994 and 1997, he had been imprisoned for non-immigration offences. Seven years therefore had not elapsed since his release from prison at the time he applied for a permanent identity card. The issue therefore arose as to whether section 2(4)(b) of the Immigration Ordinance, which has the effect of excluding the period of imprisonment from counting toward the requisite 7 year continuous ordinary residence immediately before the application for a permanent identity card was made, was constitutional. The meaning of the term "ordinarily resident" in article 24(2)(4) was therefore at the forefront of the court's consideration.

83. The court unanimously held that section 2(4)(b) of the Immigration Ordinance is constitutional. Leaving aside those rare cases where the *de minimis* principle applies, the provisions are constitutionally effective in excluding any period of imprisonment or detention pursuant to a court sentence or order from the definition of "ordinarily resident". The constitutional challenge therefore failed.

84. It is important to note that in the judgment of Bokhary PJ, with whose judgment the other members of the court all agreed, the *Shah* test was not adopted as such. It was referred to only in the context of the judge's pointing out that the courts had had on many occasions to grapple with the natural and ordinary meaning of the expression "ordinarily resident" in legislation in different contexts, and *Shah* was given as an example of the context involving educational allowance: p 283H. The twin test of voluntariness/settled purposes was not referred to as such. Rather, the judge emphasised in the passage already extracted that there is no single judicial pronouncement or combination of such pronouncements in regard to the meaning of the expression "ordinarily resident" that can be conclusive for the purposes of every context in which that expression appears. Bokhary PJ then emphasised that as a "starting point" at least, the observation of Viscount Sumner in *IRC v Lysaght* (a tax case) that "the converse to 'ordinarily' is 'extraordinarily' " is of wide utility. In regard to the case in question, the judge then said that serving a term of imprisonment, at least when it is not of trivial duration, is "something out of the ordinary": p 283J-284B. Yet Bokhary PJ cautioned that he should not be taken to say that the fact of being imprisoned somewhere would of itself render a person not ordinarily resident there necessarily for all purposes and he gave the example of tax to illustrate his point. In other words, *for tax* purposes as opposed to the purposes of article 24(2)(4) of the Basic Law, the prisoner may well be treated, as a matter of law, to be ordinarily resident in the place where he was imprisoned. Yet, pausing here, it should not be forgotten that the *Shah* test, propounded by Lord Scarman, was borrowed from two *tax* cases.

85. It should also be remembered that the full quotation of Viscount Sumner's observation in *Lysaght* (at p 243) reads:

> "I think the converse to 'ordinarily' is 'extraordinarily' and that part of the regular order of a man's life, adopted voluntarily and for settled purposes, is not 'extraordinary'."

Ms Li submitted that, therefore, when he referred to the converse of "ordinarily" is "extraordinarily", Bokhary PJ was not suggesting any new test apart from the twin test of voluntariness/settled purposes, ie the *Shah* test.

86. I do not agree. In my view, the Court of Final Appeal was very careful in only singling out the first part of Viscount Sumner's observation as "a starting point" for discovering the true meaning of the expression "ordinarily resident" as used in our Basic Law. This is illustrated by the actual decision there. As already alluded to, depending on the facts, it is quite possible for a person who has been imprisoned for a substantial period of time in Hong Kong to be able to satisfy the twin test of voluntariness/settled purposes (if it is applied at face value). Thus, the very applicant in *Fateh Muhammad* has been in Hong Kong since the 1960s. There was no suggestion on the facts that between 1994 and 1997 when he was imprisoned, but for his imprisonment, he would have wanted to reside elsewhere.

87. In fact, his position, according to the facts, was no different from a local person (a permanent resident) who, for one reason or another, was sent to jail for a substantial period of time. To illustrate my point better, let us imagine that this local person is a hardened criminal, who has been imprisoned on many occasions. Can it be seriously suggested that he is not "ordinarily resident" in Hong Kong every time he is sent to jail, applying the *Shah* test at its face value? In my view, in every case, if one really were to apply the *Shah* test at its face value, the answer must depend on the facts. One simply cannot say, as a blanket statement, that no period of imprisonment can ever satisfy the *Shah* test or the "settled purposes" requirement.

88. By the same token, it is difficult to see how the applicant in *Fateh Muhammad* should be treated as not ordinarily resident in Hong Kong according to the *Shah* test (voluntariness/settled purposes), just because he was imprisoned during the relevant period of time, without any investigation of the underlying facts. In any event, one need not be bogged down by the facts in *Fateh Muhammad*. It is not difficult to imagine realistic examples of people still satisfying the twin test of voluntariness/settled purposes according to *Shah* even though he or she was imprisoned in Hong Kong for a substantial period of time.

89. Yet, the Court of Final Appeal had no difficulty in concluding that section 2(4)(b), which applies in a blanket way to exclude all periods of imprisonment or detention from the expression "ordinarily resident" regardless of the facts of individual cases, is constitutional.

90. This can only be explained by the fact that the Court of Final Appeal was applying a more stringent or restrictive test of "ordinarily resident" for article 24(2)(4) of the Basic Law than the twin test of voluntariness/settled purposes expounded in *Shah* (or, put another way, the court was applying the twin test in a more stringent or restrictive way than in an ordinary case involving a non-constitutional or different context).

91. Thus analysed, I do not think *Fateh Muhammad* stands in the way of the analysis put forward in this judgment. Rather, it supports the analysis.

Prem Singh

92. As for *Prem Singh*, one of the issues raised there was whether the applicant's 2 week imprisonment in May 1999 broke his continuous ordinary residence in Hong Kong. He came to Hong Kong in 1988 and the application for verification of his permanent resident status was (formally) made in May 2000. The question therefore arose as to whether the short period of imprisonment broke the period of ordinary residence by reason of section 2(4)(b) of the Immigration Ordinance.

93. Four of the judges took the view that the 2 week imprisonment was not trivial and the *de minimis* rule did not apply; whereas Bokhary PJ was more doubtful on this point. However, the actual decision did not turn on this as the court held that the applicant's

application for the permanent resident status had been made earlier than May 2000; rather, on the facts, it was made back in October 1998 when he applied for an extension of stay based on a new employment. The May 1999 imprisonment was therefore irrelevant.

94. For our present purposes, it is important to note what the court has, nonetheless, said, *obiter*, about the 2 week imprisonment. All the judges thought that section 2(4)(b) of the Immigration Ordinance was constitutionally effective to exclude the 2 week imprisonment from "ordinarily resident" (subject to Bokhary PJ's doubt regarding the application of the *de minimis* principle). Indeed, the majority (per Ribeiro PJ) explained why the *de minimis* rule did not apply in these terms:

> "75. In my judgment, the two week period of imprisonment in this case was not *de minimis*. Ms Eu sought to argue that the sentence brought about a trivial interruption because the period of two weeks represents a small fraction of the seven year qualifying period. However, the exclusion of periods of imprisonment from the ordinary and natural meaning of the words 'ordinary residence' in BL art 24(2)(4) does not depend on the duration of such periods being substantial or on their amounting to a substantial fraction of the seven year qualifying period. The exclusion is qualitative. The incarceration, reflecting sufficiently serious criminal conduct to warrant an immediate custodial sentence, falls outside what could qualify as 'the settled purposes' underlying a person's ordinary residence in the ordinary and natural sense of those words, referred to by Lord Scarman in *Akbarali v Brent London Borough Council, ex p Shah* [1983] 2 AC 309 at p 344. It is this qualitative aspect of time spent in prison that has led to such periods being excluded from the concept of 'ordinary residence' in successive statutory schemes and in the Basic Law."

95. It is true that in the above passage, the court referred to "settled purposes" in *Shah*. However, one must look carefully at how the court applied the "settled purposes" requirement. In the court's view, even though the applicant had been ordinarily residing in Hong Kong since 1988, yet during the 2 week imprisonment, he was not "ordinarily resident" in Hong Kong because the incarceration "falls outside what could qualify as 'the settled purposes' underlying a person's ordinary residence" for the purposes of the Basic Law. For by definition, the incarceration reflected "sufficiently serious criminal conduct to warrant an immediate custodial sentence".

96. Pausing here, it must be noted that this is a sweeping exclusion of any period of imprisonment, without any investigation into the underlying facts, from the ambit of "ordinarily resident". A person may be imprisoned for a variety of reasons. Contempt of court, non-payment of fines and unsuitability for non-custodial alternatives (such as community service order in the case of a young offender) and so forth, may all result in an offender being sent to jail rather than being given a non-custodial sentence. In a wholly different context, I have examined this aspect of imprisonment and the various factors at play: *Chan Kin Sum v Secretary for Justice* [2009] 2 HKLRD 166, paras 112-120.

97. In particular, in the case of a short sentence like the one faced by the applicant in *Prem Singh*, it is difficult to see how, without examining the relevant facts in the individual case concerned, one can safely conclude that the person's imprisonment must be outwith the "settled purposes" of his or her abode in Hong Kong during the period of imprisonment according to the *Shah* test. Certainly, all things would depend on the facts.

98. Yet I am *not*, for one moment, suggesting that the Court of Final Appeal has wrongly understood the "settled purposes" test in *Shah* or has incorrectly held that the 2 week imprisonment did not qualify for ordinary residence when the underlying facts have not been examined. Far from it – my point is precisely the opposite. My point is that the Court of Final Appeal has rejected the 2 week imprisonment regardless of the underlying facts precisely because the court was applying a more stringent or restrictive test than the ordinary Shah test, or put another way, it was applying the *Shah* test in a more stringent or restrictive way. That their Lordships have chosen to say that the incarceration falls outside what could qualify as "the settled purposes" underlying the applicant's ordinary residence in Hong Kong during the 2 week imprisonment is just another way of saying that *for the purposes and in the constitutional context of article 24(2)(4)* (as opposed to other purposes and contexts), the requirement of "settled purposes" assumes a different and indeed more stringent or restrictive meaning.

99. Therefore, as mentioned, my view is that the two Court of Final Appeal cases do not support Ms Li's contention that the *Shah* test as such has been adopted by the Court of Final Appeal in Hong Kong in interpreting article 24(2)(4). Rather, the two cases suggest that something more stringent or restrictive than the ordinary *Shah* test is applied, which results in the exclusion of all periods of imprisonment from counting towards ordinary residence regardless of the underlying facts.

Central characteristic of "ordinarily resident"

100. What then does "ordinarily resident" mean for the purposes of article 24(2)(4) of the Basic Law? Some clues can be gleaned from the approach of the Court of Final Appeal in the two cases, the imprisonment/detention exception upheld by the court as constitutional in those two cases, and also from the other pre-existing exceptions which formed part of the pre-existing background against which the Basic Law was enacted in the first place, in order to discover the relevant "central characteristic" (or "essential elements") of the expression "ordinarily resident".

101. This was indeed the approach of the majority in *Singh*. They discovered the central characteristic of the word "alien" by reference not to who was and who was not considered as an alien under British law in 1901, but rather by identifying the characteristics of the legal status to which the word referred back in 1901: paras 199-200.

102. In my view, underlying the pre-existing statutory exceptions, including the imprisonment/detention exception upheld by the Court of Final Appeal in the two cases, is the idea of being out of the ordinary, that is "extraordinarily", particularly in terms of the purpose for which the person resides or stays in Hong Kong *when viewed from the perspective of society* – this being a more important consideration than the person's own subjective purpose or intention.

103. This requires some elaboration. A refugee may well be staying in Hong Kong for a very settled purpose, that is, to seek refuge and await resettlement or even to await permission to remain in Hong Kong permanently. His residence in Hong Kong is, from his own point of view, something which he has adopted for a settled purpose as part of the regular order of his life *for the time*

being. Yet, the blanket statutory exception relating to Vietnamese refugees is regardless of their subjective settled purposes. This is because their stay in Hong Kong is, when viewed from Hong Kong's perspective, "out of the ordinary" in the sense that their stay in Hong Kong is for a special, limited purpose.

104. Take the case of a prisoner. Regardless of the subjective intent or purpose of the prisoner, and regardless of how settled his purpose is to stay in Hong Kong as part of his regular order of his life for the time being irrespective of his imprisonment, from an objective point of view, his stay in Hong Kong during the period of imprisonment is to serve a specific, limited purpose, that is, the need to punish him for his crime, regardless of whether, but for the imprisonment, he would have stayed or left Hong Kong or would have wanted to do so.

105. Having so described what is "out of the ordinary" or "extraordinarily", one arrives at, albeit from the other end, the central characteristic of "ordinarily resident" as used in article 24(2)(4) of the Basic Law. As Bokhary PJ said in *Fateh Muhammad* at p 284B, the converse to "ordinarily" is "extraordinarily".

106. So long as a statutory exclusion does not go against this central characteristic, it cannot be regarded as unconstitutional. This is, as mentioned, the approach in *Singh*. As Kirby J said in paragraph 253, within limits set by the unchanging, essential elements of the word "aliens" as used in the Constitution, it has been conventional in Australian constitutional law to acknowledge a large power on the part of the Parliament to give the meaning to the language of the Constitution, subject always to consideration by the courts, which, in this respect, have the last say. Should some future Parliament attempt to push the "aliens" power into extreme instances, the judge continued in paragraph 269, the court can be trusted to draw the necessary constitutional line. Doing so is inherent in the task of constitutional interpretation. To avoid such dangers, it is not necessary to embrace a rigid, and now outmoded, meaning of a contested constitutional word.

107. By way of contrast, the case of *Cheatle v The Queen* [1993] 177 CLR 541 illustrates how the Parliament cannot encroach upon the essential feature of a constitutional guarantee. At issue was the constitutional guarantee of trial by jury in criminal cases. The High Court of Australia identified, by reference to the law existing in 1900, as one of the essential features of the institution of trial by jury in criminal cases the requirement of unanimity. The court was able to distil from the law then many restrictions and qualifications, including the exclusion of women and unpropertied persons from serving as jurors, as non-essential features of the institution as at the turn of the century. It concluded that the relevant essential feature of the institution was the requirement of unanimity. The court also distinguished civil trials by jury which permitted the return of a majority verdict on the basis that the constitutional guarantee only extends to criminal trials. The offending statutory provision which allowed the return of a majority verdict in a criminal trial was read down by the High Court accordingly.

What the legislature is permitted to do

108. I believe the same approach applies with equal force in our present case, although as I have emphasised, the contexts are quite different. In the Hong Kong context, having so identified the central characteristic of the expression "ordinarily resident", so long as the legislature acts within the outer limit set by this central characteristic, the legislature has a free hand in defining, refining, elaborating and adapting the expression to meet changing political, economic and social needs. Existing statutory exceptions may be deleted, whereas new exceptions may be added. I believe this represents the correct interpretation of article 24(2)(4).

109. Adopting such an interpretation, it is not difficult to understand the various statutory exceptions now found in section 2(4) relating to the different types of people concerned. Putting aside those exceptions dealing with unlawful stays which are justified separately by the maxim *ex turpi causa non oritur actio* (an action does not arise from a base cause): *Shah*, at pp 343H to 344B), one common theme underlying all other statutory exceptions is that regardless of their own subjective purposes for staying here (whether settled or not), the stays of those covered, when viewed objectively from the perspective of society, are all for very specific, limited purposes; and they are far from "ordinary".

110. Admittedly, this interpretation would entitle the legislature to legislate against others who are otherwise not caught by the ordinary *Shah* test, such as a tourist who is visiting Hong Kong for a prolonged period of time. But that is precisely the point that I am trying to make, that is, when construing the expression "ordinarily resident" in the Basic Law, one does not apply the *Shah* test in an ordinary way. It is up to the legislative to decide, in accordance with prevailing political, economic and social conditions, whether to exclude others from the ambit of "ordinarily resident", so long as the central characteristic of the concept is not infringed.

111. In case of dispute, the courts will have the last say on whether the outer limit has been crossed: *Singh*, at para 253. They will draw the necessary constitutional line: *ibid*, at para 269.

112. Thus analysed, there is in fact no conflict between article 24(2)(4) and article 154(2). Nor does the decision of the Court of Final Appeal in *Prem Singh* stand in the way of this interpretation. It should be remembered that in *Prem Singh*, another issue in contention was whether an additional requirement that at the time of an application for verification of status, the applicant must have been permitted by the Director of Immigration to stay in Hong Kong unconditionally, was constitutional. The Court of Final Appeal held that the requirement of unconditional stay was an additional requirement alien to the requirements for acquiring permanent resident status laid down in article 24(2)(4). It could not be justified by article 154(2) as a means of immigration controls. It was therefore unconstitutional.

113. However, as analysed above, the present case concerns not the imposition of an additional requirement as a means of immigration controls. Rather, the expression "ordinarily resident" used by article 24(2)(4) itself invites and permits the legislature to legislate on the matter by way of definition, refinement, elaboration or adaptation in the implementation of the Basic Law, so long as the central characteristic of the term is not encroached upon.

Section 2(4)(a)(vi) is constitutional

114. Foreign domestic helpers as a class are excluded under section 2(4)(a)(vi). Ms Li argued that there is no reference to foreign domestic helpers imported under the Government's Foreign Domestic Helper Scheme detailed in the evidence. The scheme implements the Government's policy on foreign domestic helpers, described in detail in paragraphs 36-41 of the judgment below. According to the figures provided by the Commissioner, there were only 881 foreign domestic helpers in Hong Kong in 1974. As mentioned, by 1986 the number increased to 28,951.

By the end of 1990, there were 70,335 foreign domestic helpers. As at 31 December 2010, there were 285,681 foreign domestic helpers here. Amongst them, according to the Commissioner, 117,000 are estimated to have been continuously working in Hong Kong for more than 7 years – this estimate is not admitted by the applicant. All of them have been admitted to Hong Kong under the Foreign Domestic Helper Scheme, which includes the mandatory use of standard-form employment contracts.

115. In my view, there is no uncertainty as to the scope of application of section 2(4)(a)(vi). Given its known background and purpose, the exclusionary provision applies obviously to those who have been admitted to work in Hong Kong under the Government's Foreign Domestic Helper Scheme (for the time being). It is true that there have been changes in the details of the Scheme. However, for our present purposes, there is no suggestion that the answer to the constitutional issue raised turns on any of these minor changes.

116. In my view, the exclusion of foreign domestic helpers under section 2(4)(a)(vi) does not encroach upon the central characteristic of the term "ordinarily resident". It is a category of exclusion not different in kind, but only in degree, from the pre-existing categories of excluded persons, for instance, Vietnamese refugees and imprisoned or detained persons. Regardless of her own subjective intention or purposes, a foreign domestic helper's stay in Hong Kong is for a very special, limited purpose from society's point of view – to meet society's acute demand for domestic helpers which cannot be satisfactorily met by the local labour market. Hence, their stays in Hong Kong are highly regulated so as to ensure that they are here to fulfil the special, limited purpose for which they have been allowed to come here in the first place, *and no more*.

117. This is of course not to say that they enjoy no rights or freedom whilst working here. But that is not the point. From society's perspective, their stays here are all directed toward one objective and purpose – the purpose for which they have been allowed to come to Hong Kong in the first place. Whether compared with the abode of a local person or with the residence of a foreigner who has been given a work visa to come and take up employment here, a foreign domestic helper's stay is highly regulated, "out of the ordinary", exceptional or "far from regular", particularly from society's perspective. The central characteristic of the expression "ordinarily resident" as used in article 24(2)(4) of the Basic Law is therefore not infringed by the exclusion in section 2(4)(a)(vi).

118. For these reasons, I conclude that section 2(4)(a)(vi) of the Immigration Ordinance does not infringe article 24(2)(4) of the Basic Law. It is constitutionally valid.

Commissioner's fallback argument

119. It is therefore unnecessary to deal with Lord Pannick's fallback position, that is, even under the *Shah* test (applied in an ordinary way), as a class, foreign domestic helpers must be regarded as not being ordinarily resident in Hong Kong. For my part, I do not think one can draw such a sweeping conclusion without first having regard to the facts in individual cases. In this respect, I would simply indicate my agreement with the judge below on this fallback position. The judge's conclusion was essentially that despite the many restrictions on a foreign domestic helper's employment and activities in Hong Kong whilst staying here, on the ordinary *Shah* test, she should still be capable of being regarded as ordinarily residing in Hong Kong, depending on the facts. Therefore, a blanket exclusion of foreign domestic helpers from the expression would be too wide.

120. However, this does not affect the outcome of the case because I have concluded that the ordinary *Shah* test is not the test to apply, nor does it precisely represent the central characteristic of the term "ordinarily resident" as used in article 24(2)(4) of the Basic Law.

Extrinsic materials

121. This also renders academic Lord Pannick's further argument that in case of ambiguity, one may resort to pre-as well as post-enactment extrinsic materials.

122. I have already summarized the applicable principles of interpretation. It should be remembered that so far as pre-enactment materials are concerned, regardless of whether there are ambiguities, where relevant, they should be looked at for the purposes of ascertaining the purpose and context of the relevant provisions in the Basic Law under interpretation. However, the proviso is that where the meaning of the text as understood against the purpose and context so ascertained is clear, the extrinsic materials cannot give the text a meaning that it cannot bear. For post-enactment materials, their use even for the purposes of ascertaining the purpose and context of the provisions under interpretation is much more limited and the court must approach them with caution.

123. The relevant extrinsic materials include (chronologically):

(1) the comments of the convenor of the Special Sub-Group on Basic Rights and Duties of Hong Kong Residents under the Basic Law Drafting Committee in August 1986;

(2) the Secretary for Security's explanation to Legislative Council on 8 April 1987 on the amendments to the Immigration Ordinance and on further legislative proposals to be introduced before 1 July 1997 so as to comply with section XIV of Annex I to the Joint Declaration;

(3) an information note dated 3 January 1994 (paragraph 8) prepared by the Security Branch for the Legislative Council on the presentation by the British side of the JLG to the Chinese side proposals to set out precise definitions of foreign nationals who might acquire the right of abode in the HKSAR;

(4) the report of the Legal Sub-group of the Preparatory Committee dated 9 August 1996 which specifically stated that foreign domestic helpers would not be regarded as ordinarily resident in Hong Kong regardless of the length of their stay here;

(5) the Opinion of the Preparatory Committee dated 10 August 1996 (paragraph 2) to the effect that persons permitted to stay in Hong Kong under specific Government policies would not be regarded as ordinarily resident in Hong Kong;

(6) the approval by the National People's Congress on 14 March 1997 of the Working Report and the Opinions of the Preparatory Committee presented on 10 March 1997;

(7) the Immigration (Amendment) (No 3) Bill passed by the Provisional Legislative Council on 7 June 1997 which added to the Immigration Ordinance an exception relating to, amongst others, imported domestic helpers, from the definition of "ordinarily resident". The amendment, according to the Secretary for Justice elect, was to

implement the Basic Law by making detailed provisions in the local laws. The Secretary for Justice elect also referred to the decision of the Preparatory Committee, "the consensus arrived at by the JLG" and "the Right of Abode" booklet issued by the Immigration Department, which again excluded foreign domestic helpers from being regarded as "ordinarily resident" in Hong Kong, in explaining why the Bill was presented to the Provisional Legislative Council;

(8) the approval of the 1996 Opinion of the Preparatory Committee described above by the Standing Committee of the National People's Congress ("NPCSC") in paragraph 2 of its Interpretation on articles 22(4) and 24(2)(3) of the Basic Law given on 26 June 1999.

124. Given my above conclusion, it is not necessary to go into these materials, particularly those post-enactment materials relied on by Lord Pannick. Suffice it to say, these materials, when read as a whole, would tend to suggest that foreign domestic helpers were not intended to be given the status of permanent resident in the HKSAR regardless of how long they had been here. But in the light of my conclusion, it is not necessary to rely on the controversial post-enactment extrinsic materials, and I do not do so.

The 1999 NPCSC Interpretation

125. Equally academic is the question of whether the 1999 Interpretation given by the NPCSC, insofar as it refers to, with approval, the 1996 Opinion, which excludes foreign domestic helpers from those who are to be regarded as "ordinarily resident" in Hong Kong irrespective of their length of stay here, amounts to an interpretation of article 24(2)(4) of the Basic Law, binding on the local courts. On this important question which has significant implications for the proper interpretation of all other categories of people included in article 24(2) of the Basic Law as well, several observations need to be made.

126. First, the same issue arose but was conceded by the Director of Immigration in *Chong Fung Yuen* before the Court of Final Appeal. Having lost the same point twice in the courts below ([2000] 1 HKC 359 and [2000] 3 HKLRD 661), the Director conceded that the 1999 NPCSC Interpretation had only made a binding interpretation on articles 22(4) and 24(2)(3) of the Basic Law, despite its reference (with approval) to the 1996 Opinion. The Court of Final Appeal accepted the concession and proceeded to deal with the case, which concerned article 24(2)(1), on that footing: p 223C/D-E.

127. Secondly, this court has heard no argument on whether as a result, *Chong Fung Yuen* should be taken as a binding authority on the question of whether the 1999 Interpretation contains a binding interpretation of article 24(2)(4) in terms of the 1996 Opinion, given that the point was actually conceded before the Court of Final Appeal, which simply proceeded on that concession without commenting on whether the concession had been correctly made or whether the courts below had reached the correct conclusion on the point. (Absent a binding interpretation by the NPCSC, *Chong Fung Yuen* is of course a binding authority on the proper interpretation of article 24(2)(1).)

128. Thirdly, the Court of Appeal's decision on the point in *Chong Fung Yuen* is binding on this court but only to the extent explained by the Court of Final Appeal in *Solicitor (24/07) v Law Society of Hong Kong* (2008) 11 HKCFAR 117. The court has likewise heard no argument on whether it should follow or depart from its own previous decision that the 1999 NPCSC Interpretation had only made a binding interpretation on articles 22(4) and 24(2)(3) of the Basic Law, despite its reference (with approval) to the 1996 Opinion .

129. Fourthly, the lack of argument before this court was due to the fact that the Commissioner, for reasons of his own, did not wish to rely on the 1999 Interpretation insofar as it may have made such a binding interpretation. The Commissioner was simply content to reserve his position on the issue in case there should be a further appeal to the Court of Final Appeal, and to prosecute the present appeal on the grounds already described.

130. Fifthly, as the Commissioner is successful on his primary argument in this appeal, this court therefore does not deal with the question of whether it is bound to accept the Commissioner's position (or concession) – bearing in mind that unlike a private action, this is a public law litigation, the result of which binds not only the instant parties but affects, potentially, many others.

131. Finally, so far as this court is concerned, all these questions are left open.

Discrimination and article 25 of the Basic Law

132. As regards the applicant's argument based on discrimination and article 25 of the Basic Law (equality before the law), I agree with Lam J that this is not a case about discrimination and article 25 is simply not engaged. As was pointed out below, it must be up to the sovereign authority to decide the extent to which the status of permanent resident should be conceded to foreign nationals. It is a fundamental principle in international law that a sovereign state has the power to admit, exclude and expel aliens: *Januzi v Secretary of State for the Home Department* [2006] 2 AC 426, 439G. As Bokhary PJ said in *Fateh Muhammad* (at p 285I-J), different treatment of citizens and non-citizens in regard to the right of abode is a common if not invariable feature of the laws of countries throughout the world, including those with constitutions which prohibit discrimination. That difference of treatment flows inevitably from the fact of the political boundaries which are drawn across the globe. The question of who can and who cannot qualify for permanent resident status is governed by the same principles. There simply cannot be any complaint that article 24(2)(4) confers the permanent resident status on some people but not others.

Outcome

133. For these reasons, I would allow the appeal and set aside the order made below and, instead, dismiss the application for judicial review. On an order *nisi* basis, I would award the costs of this appeal, as well as the costs of the proceedings below, including all costs previously reserved, to the Commissioner, with a certificate for three counsel.

134. I would like to thank counsel and their supporting teams for their very helpful submissions.

Hon Tang VP:

135. I have had the advantage of reading the judgments of the Chief Judge and Stock VP in draft. I am in respectful and complete agreement with them. There is nothing which I can usefully add.

Hon Stock VP:

136. I respectfully agree with the judgment of the Chief Judge.

137. There is a single premise upon which the validity of the case postulated on behalf of the foreign domestic helpers rests. If the

premise is sound, the case succeeds; if it is flawed, the case fails.

138. The premise is that the phrase "ordinarily resident" in article 24(2)(4) of the Basic Law is hard-edged in that at the date of its promulgation it allowed for no meaning other than the common law meaning attributed by Lord Scarman in 1982 in *Shah*[1]. It must follow that for the helpers' case to succeed, they would have to show that at that point in time, the concept "ordinarily resident" was vested with a fixed legal meaning and, further, that it was intended for that meaning to remain fixed for the life of the constitution, for one can be confident that constitutions are not promulgated with a view to regular amendment whenever societal needs change.

139. In my opinion, the case falls at the first hurdle. It cannot seriously be denied that in the world of the common law, there then existed – and still exist – acceptable alternative interpretations of the phrase by distinguished jurists. Similarly it is not an issue that the concept's reach has in common law jurisdictions always been amenable to legislative definition and exception. This was expressly acknowledged by Lord Scarman himself in *Shah*[2]. Statutory definition or adjustment of the phrase has for long been recognised as a necessary and sensible tool by which to cater for issue–specific exigencies. And so it has been in this jurisdiction, especially though not exclusively in the sphere of immigration control.

140. It is said that all that is required is an application of the natural and ordinary meaning of the words. But that is to presuppose that the ascertainment of the natural and ordinary meaning allows of no reasonable debate; a supposition self–evidently laid to rest by the diverging views at the various curial levels at which the case of *Shah* itself rested from time to time and by the statement of Ormrod LJ in the Divisional Court that:

> "We have experienced considerable difficulty in ascertaining the "natural and ordinary" meaning of the words in question. To determine the "ordinary" meaning of "ordinarily" is something of a linguistic feat in itself. Nor is the word "resident" at all easy. It is not much used in ordinary speech, and then without precision." [3]

141. And in Hong Kong, we find the acknowledgment in *Fateh Mohammed v Commissioner of Registration and another*[4] that:

> "No single judicial pronouncement or combination of such pronouncements in regard to the meaning of the expression "ordinarily resident" can be conclusive for the purposes of every context in which the expression appears." [5]

142. This illustrates the first difficulty with the applicant's case; that it presupposes a single and exclusive definition or understanding of a phrase which, by its nature, does not lend itself to precision or to exclusive definition.

143. The second difficulty is that the argument for the applicant is based on a non–binding, albeit highly persuasive, judgment of another jurisdiction in the context of domestic legislation – not, be it noted, a constitutional instrument – of that jurisdiction, and which argument seeks to fix the definition encapsulated by that judgment as applicable for all time to a constitutional instrument governing this different jurisdiction. This, with respect, is an unrealistic and non–contextual approach.

144. Insofar as *Fateh Mohammed* reminds us of the importance of context, it echoes Lord Scarman's statement in *Shah* that his common law definition must necessarily give way to such alternatives and qualifications as are demanded by context. So it must be in any exercise of statutory and constitutional interpretation: context is all–important.

145. The context with which we are concerned is, first, a constitution; a law with its own function and character, different from that of ordinary statutes.[6] Essential to that character is its applicability to changing needs over time. That is not to say that black may be read as white whenever it appears convenient to do so, or that core fundamental freedoms may be undermined; but it is to say that where an interpretation is, in the context of the subject matter, inimical to reasonable responses to changing societal demands, the suggested interpretation is likely to be incorrect. And that is the problem with the interpretation which is advanced by the applicant: it is stultifying in its effect.

146. Further, the context is not merely article 24 (2)(4); nor is the context merely article 24. And the context is not a routine item of local legislation. Rather, the context is an article of a constitution and when interpreting a constitution, it is to the matrix of the entire constitution and its historical setting to which one looks to ascertain the purpose and then the meaning of a particular provision.

147. The context of this constitution, the Basic Law, includes its themes. As the Chief Judge emphasises, a central theme of the Basic Law is continuity: a smooth transition whereby the essence of societal structures and systems are intended to be preserved beyond resumption of the exercise of sovereignty subject only to such changes to the law as are necessarily incidental to that resumption. The Basic Law is replete with indicia of continuity, for example: the maintenance of the way of life (article 5); preservation of such laws previously in force as are consistent with the Basic Law (articles 8 and 18); maintenance of the judicial and other systems (articles 81; 124; 129; 136; 141; 142; 144; and 145); and the Preamble itself with its reference to the maintenance of the "prosperity and stability of Hong Kong."

148. Since it is common ground that an interpretation of a constitution and of its individual provisions must, if it is to be a valid interpretation, be purposive, any suggested interpretation of an article which clearly runs contrary to that central theme of continuity is a suspect interpretation and – unless the language used is unambiguous and allows of no clarification – it is an interpretation which is likely to be incorrect. In such a situation it is incumbent on the court to see whether there exists a viable alternative interpretation which does not offend the language of the provision, and which is consistent with the provisions and purposes of the constitution as a whole.

149. The interpretation of article 24(2)(4) of the Basic Law for which the applicant contends is not purposive for, rather than supporting a theme of continuity, it stands starkly against one:

(1) It abjures entirely the previous role of the legislature in adjusting the scope of ordinary residence in the immigration context, and it does so not just for a given point in time, but for all time;

(2) It brushes aside the previous provisions of the law by which certain categories of persons are deemed not to be ordinarily resident in the territory, leaving it open therefore to swathes of persons within those groups to become permanent residents or, at least, to challenge any post–resumption renewal of local legislation which excludes them;

(3) It imposes on the immigration authorities the burden of creating facts on the ground by which those who are allowed into the Region for specific purposes cannot become ordinarily resident within Lord Scarman's definition; in the case of domestic helpers, by ensuring that no series of contracts ever reaches the seven–year mark, the impact of which on individuals might well be viewed as unjust. In this regard, the proposed interpretation also assumes that the framers were content to leave to chance, or to the creation of facts on the ground, the question of ordinary residence of members of the Hong Kong Garrison and members of consular posts, an unlikely intention; and

(4) It attributes to the framers of the Constitution a blindness to the history of immigration pressures upon the confined space that is Hong Kong; for in denying the legislature the power to say that refugees, for example, are admitted for a special reason and that such a special reason falls outwith the concept of ordinary residence, it assumes bizarre confidence in a future absence of unusual immigration pressures or in the ability of the authorities to resolve such problems as do arise without the powers which previously they possessed.

150. These are the consequences which flow from the assertion, if correct, that Lord Scarman's definition was intended by the framers of the Basic Law as sacrosanct for the purpose of article 24 (2)(4), amenable to no qualification or narrowing. They are serious consequences and they are, viewed in the round, consequences that sit ill with any concept of continuity or historical reality and with the Constitution's objective of ensuring stability. That is not to diminish the valuable contribution to society made by groups permitted to enter the Region for special reasons: it is rather to recognize the ramifications of the wholly inflexible and wide interpretation which is that propounded by the applicant. In short, that interpretation is contrary to a purposive interpretation and for that reason it is an interpretation which in my opinion is incorrect.

151. It is not as if there are unacceptable alternative definitions. The Chief Judge has alluded to a provision of the Citizenship Act, Australia as an example: it excludes from the concept "ordinarily resident" those who reside in a country for a special or temporary purpose. It may well be – we have not researched it – that other jurisdictions have similar qualifications; but the point is that that narrowing of the scope does not offend the sense of the concept and the present provisions of s 2(4)(a) of the Immigration Ordinance fall within it and accord with the like approach of the Divisional Court and Court of Appeal in *Shah*.

152. As against the emphasis on continuity, Ms Li SC points to the fact that article 24(2) itself marks a major change for its intent was to create a new status, namely, that of permanent resident and to redefine the category of persons upon whom would be conferred the right of abode. That is true as far as broad categorisation goes, for the categories are fixed. But it does not flow logically from that fact that it was intended to impose a new and inflexible method by which to determine or delineate who was and who was not deemed to be ordinarily resident.

153. Ms Li further contends that it is misleading to say in opposition to her arguments that the framers of the Basic Law are unlikely to have intended adherence to the definition of a court of another jurisdiction, for that ignores the fact that prior to the promulgation of the Basic Law *Shah* had been followed in Hong Kong, for which proposition she cites *Director of Immigration v Ng Shun–loi*[7] which, as the name of the case suggests, was an immigration case. The gravamen of this argument is or must be that at or by the date of that decision (1987), Lord Scarman's test was adopted in Hong Kong and the drafters of the Basic Law must be taken to have recognised that fact.

154. There are several difficulties in the way of this argument. The first difficulty is that at that time, the phrase "ordinarily resident" was not confined to a common law definition; the Scarman test was subject to legislative refinement so that there is no logic in presuming that if the Basic Law drafters had the *Shah* definition in mind, they did not equally have in mind the availability of legislative adjustment.

155. The second difficulty is that this approach ignores the fact that article 24(2)(4) tracks the terms of and was no doubt intended to give effect to the Joint Declaration.[8] In this very particular, the Basic Law has been said to "[follow] the Joint Declaration faithfully."[9] Paragraphs 157 to 159 of the Joint Declaration, signed in December 1984 – before *Shah* was followed here in *Ng Shun–loi* – stated that amongst those who would have the right of abode in the Region were all Chinese nationals born or who had ordinarily resided in Hong Kong before or after the establishment of the Region for seven years or more as well as persons of Chinese nationality born outside Hong Kong of such Chinese nationals and:

> " – all other persons who have ordinarily resided in Hong Kong before or after the establishment of the [Region] for a continuous period of seven years or more and to have taken Hong Kong as their place of permanent residence before or after the establishment of the [Region]."

156. Not only were these provisions agreed before, as far as I am aware, the adoption of *Shah* by any Hong Kong court, but it is in my opinion singularly unlikely that the *Shah* definition had embedded itself in the mind of either signatory party and entirely unlikely that either party contemplated that test as the sole future standard to the complete exclusion of legislative adjustment, no matter how sensible, how consonant with previous practice, and how attuned to reasonable appreciation of the phrase, such adjustment might be.

157. Finally, an analogy has been drawn between the issues this case and that of *Chong Fung Yuen*[10]. The analogy is not apt. That was a case in which the courts were asked to say that 'born in Hong Kong' carried a qualification which was simply not there. Nothing in the wording of the provision there at issue or in its context permitted of a different meaning or adjustment. The analogy is not apt because it does not compare like with like.

158. Accordingly, I too would allow the appeal and make the orders proposed by the Chief Judge.

Hon Cheung CJHC:

159. The appeal is therefore allowed and the order made below is set aside. We further order that the application for judicial review be dismissed. There will be a costs order *nisi* in the terms proposed in paragraph 133 above.

Chief Judge of the High Court (Andrew Cheung)

Vice President (Robert Tang)

Vice President (Frank Stock)

Ms Gladys Li SC, Mr P Y Lo and Mr Benson Tsoi, instructed by Barnes & Daly, for the applicant

Lord Pannick QC, Mr Anderson Chow SC and Ms Eva Sit, instructed by the Department of Justice, for the 1st respondent

Attendance of the 2nd respondent was excused

Footnotes:

1. [1983] 2 AC 309, 343

2 *Ibid* at 343G

3 [1982] 1 QB 688 at 695E

4 (2001) 4 HKCFAR 278

5 At 283J – 284A

6 See *Grain Pool of Western Australia v Commonwealth* (2000) 202 CLR 479, 523, para [111]

7 [1987] HKLR 798

8 Joint Declaration para 159

9 Yash Ghai, *Hong Kong's New Constitutional Order* 2nd ed, p 161, fn 22

10 (2001) 4 HKCFAR 211

第二十五條

香港居民在法律面前一律平等。

案例

香港居民在法律面前一律平等。

對不同階層應用不同稅務政策是否違反"平等"原則？

Wong Tai Wai, David v. Commissioner Of Inland Revenue

Wong Tai Wai, David 對 稅務局局長

HCIA 2/2003；CACV 287/2003

簡略案情

申請人與其妻子的應課稅收入包括個人薪金和房屋租金。在 1998/1999、1999/2000 和 2000/2001 三個課稅年度裏，申請人選擇了以已婚人士身份的個人入息課稅評核計算應課稅款。該計算方法得出的應繳納稅款，低於以非個人入息課稅評核作為基礎的計算，但是卻比未婚應繳納的總共稅款為高。申請人認為稅務局應按照他們未婚的狀況作稅務評定，否則便違犯《基本法》第 25 條，法律面前一律平等的原則，即歧視已婚人士。稅務局局長否定了該主張。申請人遂向稅務上訴委員會提起申訴。在上訴委員會否定了申請人的請求後，他們再向原訟庭提起上訴。

裁決摘要

原訟庭法官認為在申請人夫婦共同選擇了個人入息課稅評核後，稅務局局長並沒有酌情權，不能不依據這選擇作稅務評定。法院亦認為稅務條例並未違反《基本法》第 25 條。事實上，稅務條例對所有已婚人士是一視同仁的，不能說因為某些人士在身份改變後，面對另一評核標準而認為是被歧視。不同收入人士可能面對不同的稅基，這是稅務政策，並不關乎平等與否。申請人的請求被拒絕，他們的上訴亦被上訴庭駁回。

CACV 287/2003

IN THE HIGH COURT OF THE

HONG KONG SPECIAL ADMINISTRATIVE REGION

COURT OF APPEAL

CIVIL APPEAL NO. 287 OF 2003
(ON APPEAL FROM HCIA 2 OF 2003)

Between:

Wong Tai Wai, David — Appellant

- and -

Commissioner of Inland Revenue — Respondent

Before: Hon Rogers VP, Hon Cheung JA and Hon Kwan J in Court

Date of Hearing: 10 June 2004

Date of Judgment: 23 June 2004

JUDGMENT

Hon Rogers VP:

1. I agree with judgment of Cheung JA and the order he proposes. The judge below had carefully set out his reasons and they were correct.

Hon Cheung JA:

2. The appellant, Mr. Wong Tai Wai, David ('Mr. Wong') and his wife ('Mrs. Wong') derived income from their employment and also rental income from a property which was jointly owned by them.

3. These two sources of income were subject to salaries tax and property tax for the years 1998/99, 1999/2000 and 2000/01. For each of the three years, Mr. Wong and his wife elected 'personal assessment'. As a result the total income of Mr. Wong and his wife was aggregated and the tax liability of Mr. Wong and his wife was accordingly assessed.

4. Mr. Wong and his wife raised objections against the personal assessment. The respondent by a letter dated 8 February 2002 made a determination and rejected the objection. Mr. Wong and his wife appealed to the Inland Revenue Board of Review ('the Board'). The appeal was dismissed on 25 September 2002. By way of Case Stated, Mr. Wong and his wife appealed against the board's decision to the Court of First Instance of the High Court. Deputy High Court Judge To dismissed the appeal. Mr. Wong now appeals against the decision.

The questions of law

5. The two questions of law stated for the judge's consideration are:

"(1) Whether the provisions in the *Inland Revenue Ordinance*, Cap. 112 ('the *Ordinance*') which enable a married couple to elect for personal assessment and which may produce the result that such married couple will end up having a greater tax liability on the same income than if they had not been married to each other are null, void and of no effect for the reason that they contravene the Basic Law, in particular, Articles 8, 11 and 25 thereof ("Question 1").

(2) Whether in making an assessment for tax against a married couple who have elected for personal assessment or in considering an objection against an assessment by such married couple, the Commissioner of Inland Revenue ('the Commissioner') is bound by the Basic Law, in particular, Articles 8, 11 and 25 thereof, to exercise her discretion to adjust the assessment in such a way so that the tax liability of such married couple is no different from their tax liability on the same income if they had not been such married couple ("Question 2").'

The judge answered both questions in the negative.

The complaint

6. The gist of Mr. Wong's complaint is that as a result of his and his wife's election for personal assessment they were required to pay a higher amount of tax than each of them is liable to pay if they had not been married. He claims that the result is unjust, absurd and contrary to the rules of construction of a tax statute. He further claims that this is contrary to certain provisions of the Basic Law.

The tax regime

7. Property tax is charged under section 5 of the *Ordinance*. Salaries tax is charged under section 8 of the *Ordinance*. Property tax is charged at the standard rate which since 1989/90 has been fixed at 15%. Salaries tax is charged at progressive rate set out in Schedule 2 of the *Ordinance*.

Personal assessment

8. A taxpayer may elect for 'personal assessment' of his total income from property, profits and employment. The main advantage of an election for personal assessment stems from the fact that the concessionary deductions, personal allowances and reduced marginal rates available for salaries tax are not available for property or profits taxes which are assessed at the standard rate without the benefit of progression. A person with a relatively low total income can, however, obtain the benefit of the same progression that is available for salaries tax by electing for personal assessment. Other benefits include the benefit of deduction of interest that has been paid on money borrowed for the purpose of acquiring land for the production of rental income and tax relief is not otherwise available: see Willoughby & Halkyard: *Encyclopaedia of Hong Kong Taxation* Vol. 3, Para. 628. The rate of tax charged on personal assessment is based on Schedule 2 of the *Ordinance*.

9. The following is a summary of the relevant principles in respect of personal assessment:

(1) An individual may elect for personal assessment on his total income (section 41(1));

(2) A married couple cannot elect for personal assessment separately if both have income and are not living apart. In other words there must be a joint election by such a married couple (section 41(1A));

(3) Where a married couple had made a joint election for personal assessment, the assessor is required to make a single assessment from the joint total income less the appropriate allowances (section 42A);

Interpretation of the *Ordinance*

10. There are numerous judicial expressions on the approach

to be adopted in construing a tax statute. There is no need to repeat them. The interpretation of a tax statute, like any statute, is for the court to ascertain the intention of the legislature. The fundamental point is that one is taxed no more and no less than is stated in the statute.

11. In this case the provisions dealing with personal assessment for married couple are very clear. A married couple must elect for personal assessment jointly and the assessor has to make a single assessment based on their joint income after deducting the prescribed allowances.

12. In this case, had Mr. Wong and his wife not elected for personal assessment, the total assessment of tax charged on them would be higher because they would not be able to deduct the interest expenditure of the property. This point can be shown in the following two tables showing the tax payable for the relevant years of assessment with and without personal assessment.

Tax payable with personal assessment

	1998/99	1999/00	2000/01
Mr. Wong	$62,914	$94,782	$12,460
Mrs. Wong	$55,627	$52,530	$44,704
Total tax payable by Mr. & Mrs. Wong	$118,541	$147,312	$57,164

Tax payable without personal assessment

		1998/99	1999/00	2000/01
Mr. Wong	Salaries tax	$62,135	$106,147	$973
	Property tax	$8,198	$7,072	$6,778
	Total tax	$70,333	$113,219	$7,751
Mrs. Wong	Salaries tax	$45,906	$30,665	$50,550
	Property tax	$8,198	$7,072	$6,778
	Total tax	$54,104	$37,737	$57,328
Total tax payable by Mr. & Mrs. Wong		$124,437	$150,956	$65,079

13. However, having elected for personal assessment Mr. Wong and his wife must take both the benefit and the burden resulting from such an assessment. Mr. Wong cannot turn around and say that had he not been married, he and his wife would be separately assessed for personal assessment and their total tax liability would have been less. This is not open to him because the legislation requires a married couple in the position of Mr. Wong and his wife to make a joint election and their tax liability will be based on their joint total income. A separate assessment is simply not open to them. This is the clear intention of the legislature and there is nothing inherently unjust or inequitable under the tax regime.

Discretion

14. The Assessor is required by section 42A to make a single assessment for personal assessment by a married couple. This being the case, neither he nor the Commissioner has a discretion to do otherwise.

Basic Law

15. Mr. Wong's reliance on the provisions of the Basic Law misses the point altogether.

16. Article 8 preserves the system of law that was in place before the unification in 1997. The system of law includes the 'rules of equity' which simply means the law historically developed by the Chancery Court in England in order to complement the law developed by the 'Common Law' Court. These two branches of law were applied in Hong Kong when it was under the former English rule. Equity is not synonymous with justice in the broad sense : see Hanbury & Martin: *Modern Equity*, 16th Ed. page 3.

17. Article 11 provides for the supremacy of the Basic Law over the other legislation in Hong Kong. I do not see how the provision on personal assessment of married couple can be in breach of the Basic Law.

18. Article 25 provides that all Hong Kong residents are equal before the law. Mr. Wong and his wife are indeed equal before the law. They are taxed no more and no less than is allowed by the law.

19. Another relevant provision is Article 37 which recognizes the freedom of marriage. In my view this does not provide the juridical basis for a challenge of the personal assessment provisions.

Conclusion

20. The judge was correct in his decision. I would dismiss the appeal with costs to the respondent.

Hon Kwan J :

21. I agree. Section 64(2) of the *Ordinance* relied on by Mr. Wong does not assist him. It cannot be construed as giving the Commissioner the power to determine an objection to an assessment in a manner contrary to the provisions for personal assessment in Part VII.

Vice-President (Anthony Rogers)

Justice of Appeal (Peter Cheung)

Judge of the Court of First Instance (Susan Kwan)

Appellant, in person, present

Mr. Eugene Fung, instructed by Department of Justice for the respondent

---

Secretary For Justice v. Yau Yuk Lung Zigo & Lee Kam Chuen

律政司司長 對 丘旭龍、李錦全

HCMA 107/2006；FACC 12/2006

簡略案情

兩位答辯人被指控違反《刑事罪行條例》第 200 章第 118F 條，即「任何男子與另一名男子非私下作出肛交，即屬犯罪，一經循公訴程序定罪，可處監禁 5 年。」答辯人在初審時申請中止訴訟，主張該條例第 118F 條違憲。裁判官最後撤銷了對兩人的指控。控方向高等法院上訴庭提出上訴。答辯人認為，相對於雙性戀和女同性戀者而言，第 118F 條是對男同性戀者的歧視與不平等的對待。上訴庭接受德沃金教授在其著作《認真對待權利》（R. Dworkin, *Taking Rights Seriously*）的觀點，認為很多人在沒有理由的前提下，單單基於偏見、不理性和個人的反感下排斥男同性戀者。在考慮了蘇偉倫一案後，上訴庭認為沒有正當理由，包括社會道德的考量，去容許第 118F 條偏離一般的平等原則，因此駁回控方的上訴。控方遂上訴至終審法院。

裁決摘要

終審法院重申蘇偉倫案的論據，平等原則的偏離，必須滿足以下的條件：

1. 該偏離是爲了達到一個有真確需要的合法目的；

2. 該偏離與該合法目的之間有理性的聯繫；

3. 該偏離的程度並不超越為達致該合法目的之需要。

終審法院認為在本案中並沒有任何真確需要作出偏離，原因是該立法的目的已經充分地包含在普通法的公眾不雅罪行中。據此，上訴人的上訴被駁回。

FACC No. 12 of 2006

IN THE COURT OF FINAL APPEAL OF THE HONG KONG SPECIAL ADMINISTRATIVE REGION

FINAL APPEAL NO. 12 OF 2006 (CRIMINAL)
(ON APPEAL FROM HCMA NO. 107 OF 2006)

Between:

SECRETARY FOR JUSTICE Applicant

- and -

YAU YUK LUNG ZIGO 1st Respondents
LEE KAM CHUEN 2nd Respondents

Court: Chief Justice Li, Mr Justice Bokhary PJ, Mr Justice Chan PJ, Mr Justice Ribeiro PJ and Sir Anthony Mason NPJ

Dates of Hearing: 25 and 26 June 2007

Date of Judgment: 17 July 2007

JUDGMENT

Chief Justice Li:

1. Equality before the law is a fundamental human right ("the right to equality"). Equality is the antithesis of discrimination. The constitutional right to equality is in essence the right not to be discriminated against. It guarantees protection from discrimination. The right to equality is enshrined in numerous international human rights instruments and is widely embodied in the constitutions of jurisdictions around the world. It is constitutionally protected in Hong Kong.

2. Discriminatory law is unfair and violates the human dignity of those discriminated against. It is demeaning for them and generates ill-will and a sense of grievance on their part. It breeds tension and discord in society.

3. The question in this appeal is whether s.118F(1) of the Crimes Ordinance, Cap. 200 ("s. 118F(1)"), which criminalises homosexual buggery committed otherwise than in private, is unconstitutional on the ground that it is discriminatory and infringes the constitutional right to equality.

The charges

4. The respondents were charged with having committed buggery with each other otherwise than in private, contrary to s. 118F(1). It is alleged that they had developed a liaison over the Internet and that they committed the act in a private car parked beside a public road. This case is the first prosecution under s. 118F(1) since its enactment in 1991.

The Magistrate

5. At the commencement of their trial before the Magistrate (Mr John Glass), the respondents challenged the constitutionality of s. 118F(1) and applied for a stay of the proceedings. The Magistrate upheld the constitutional challenge and dismissed the charges.

The Court of Appeal

6. The appellant appealed by way of case stated to challenge the Magistrate's conclusion of law. The Court of First Instance ordered that the appeal be heard by the Court of Appeal.

7. The Court of Appeal (Ma CJHC, Woo VP and Tang JA as he then was) upheld the conclusion that s. 118F(1) is unconstitutional and dismissed the appeal. *Secretary for Justice v Yau Yuk Lung and Another* [2006] 4 HKLRD 196.

Leave to appeal

8. The appellant appeals to the Court with the leave of the Appeal Committee which certified two questions of law:

> "1. Is [s. 118F(1)] discriminatory to the extent that it is inconsistent with the Basic Law and the Hong Kong Bill of Rights?
>
> 2. What is the proper order to be made when the charge against the defendant is found to be unconstitutional?"

In seeking leave, the appellant gave undertakings (i) not to seek remittal of the case; (ii) not to bring any charge in relation to the conduct alleged in this case; and (iii) not to seek an adverse costs order against the 1st respondent and to pay the reasonable costs of the 2nd respondent to be taxed if not agreed.

The constitutional provisions

9. The right to equality is guaranteed by art. 25 of the Basic Law which provides:

> "All Hong Kong residents shall be equal before the law."

10. Further, the right is protected by the Bill of Rights ("the BOR") contained in the Hong Kong Bill of Rights Ordinance, Cap. 383, which implements in accordance with art. 39 of the Basic Law the provisions of the International Covenant on Civil and Political Rights ("the ICCPR") as applied to Hong Kong. Article 22 of BOR (corresponding to art. 26 of the ICCPR) provides:

> "All persons are equal before the law and are entitled without any discrimination to the equal protection of the law. In this respect, the law shall prohibit any discrimination and guarantee to all persons equal and effective protection against discrimination on any ground such as race, colour, sex, language, religion, political or other opinion, national or social origin, property, birth or other status."

Article 1(1) of the BOR provides that the rights recognised therein:

> "shall be enjoyed without distinction of any kind, such as race, colour, sex, language, religion, political or other opinion, national or social origin, property, birth or other status."

As art. 22 itself guarantees the right to equality, it is unnecessary to rely on art. 1(1) in the present case.

11. Discrimination on the ground of sexual orientation would plainly be unconstitutional under both art. 25 of the Basic Law and art. 22 of BOR in which sexual orientation is within the phrase "other status".

Section 118F

12. Section 118M of the Crimes Ordinance abolished the offence of buggery at common law. However, s. 118F(1) criminalises homosexual buggery committed otherwise than in private. It provides:

> "A man who commits buggery with another man otherwise

> "than in private shall be guilty of an offence and shall be liable on conviction on indictment to imprisonment for 5 years."

Section 118F(2) is a supplementary provision. It prescribes two situations in which an act shall not be treated as done in private. The first situation provided for in subsection (2)(a) is when more than two persons take part or are present. However, this subsection was held to be unconstitutional by Hartmann J in *Leung v Secretary for Justice*[1] [2005] 3 HKLRD 657 at para. 99. The Government had so conceded before the judge. The second situation prescribed in subsection (2)(b) is where the act is done:

> "in a lavatory or bathhouse to which the public have or are permitted to have access, whether on payment or otherwise."

"Bathhouse" is defined by s. 118(F)(3) to mean:

> "any premises or part of any premises maintained for the use of persons requiring a sauna, shower-bath, Turkish bath or other type of bath."

Legislative history

13. In April 1983, the Law Reform Commission ("the Commission") published its Report on laws governing homosexual conduct. Its main recommendations included the decriminalisation of homosexual acts performed in private by consenting adult males and the enactment of measures to protect men and boys from sexual abuse and exploitation.

14. Some seven years later, in 1991, the Crimes (Amendment) Ordinance was enacted and came into force on 12 July 1991. It is significant to note that the Hong Kong Bill of Rights Ordinance came into force shortly before that date on 8 June 1991. As stated in the Explanatory Memorandum to the Bill, the Crimes (Amendment) Ordinance implemented the main recommendations of the Commission's Report.

15. Section 118F was enacted as part of the Crimes (Amendment) Ordinance in 1991 and criminalises only homosexual buggery otherwise than in private. Its provenance was not the Commission's Report. In fact, the Commission had recommended the creation of a new offence of indecent public behaviour which in contrast to s. 118F, would be neutral on sexual orientation. The Commission proposed the new offence in order to increase protection "for all members of the community from any public behaviour of a sexual nature, including homosexual behaviour, which offends the common standard of decency of the community." See paras 11.24 and 12.17 of the Commission's Report.

16. The circumstances in which s. 118F came to be proposed in the Bill and enacted are somewhat puzzling. It can be ascertained from the nature of the provision that its purpose is for the protection of public decency. By enacting this section, the Legislature was protecting the community from outrageous public behaviour. Yet, in introducing the Bill, which included this provision, the Government stated its position in the Legislative Council Brief to be that:

> "the existing law to safeguard standards of public decency adequate to ensure that public behaviour by homosexuals likely to cause offence to the public would continue to be an offence."

The existing law which the Brief then described was the common law offence of committing an act outraging public decency[2]. The Brief noted that it covers both homosexual and heterosexual behaviour in public. See para. 8 of the Legislative Council Brief on the Crimes (Amendment) Bill 1991 issued on 20 March 1991 by the then Security Branch of the Government.

The common law offence

17. It is an offence at common law to commit any act of a lewd, obscene or disgusting nature which outrages public decency. As Lord Simon observed in *Knuller (Publishing, Printing and Promotions) Ltd v Director of Public Prosecutions* [1973] AC 435 at 493 G–H and 495D, the offence is concerned with minimum standards of decency and its rationale is that:

> "... reasonable people should be able to venture into public without their sense of decency being outraged".

The maximum penalty for the offence is seven years imprisonment and a fine. Section 101I(1) of the Criminal Procedure Ordinance, Cap. 221.

18. On the authorities in England, the act must have been committed in public in the sense that at least two persons must have been able to see the act in question. *R v Mayling* [1963] 2 QB 717. There is a further requirement that the offence must have been committed in a place where there exists a real possibility that members of the general public might witness what happens. The place need not necessarily be one of public resort but must be one where the public are able to see what takes place there. *R v Walker* [1996] 1 Cr. App. R. 111 at 114 C–E. The question whether the common law offence in Hong Kong has the same requirements as those in England does not arise in this appeal. This is not the proper occasion to consider that question and no view is expressed on it.

Principles

19. In general, the law should usually accord identical treatment to comparable situations. As Lord Nicholls observed in Ghaidan v Godin-Mendoza [2004] 2 AC 557 at 566C:

> "Like cases should be treated alike, unlike cases should not to be treated alike."

20. However, the guarantee of equality before the law does not invariably require exact equality. Differences in legal treatment may be justified for good reason. In order for differential treatment to be justified, it must be shown that:

(1) The difference in treatment must pursue a legitimate aim. For any aim to be legitimate, a genuine need for such difference must be established.

(2) The difference in treatment must be rationally connected to the legitimate aim.

(3) The difference in treatment must be no more than is necessary to accomplish the legitimate aim.

The above test will be referred to as "the justification test". In the present case, the Court has had the benefit of submissions on its appropriate formulation. There is no material difference between the justification test and the test stated in *R v Man Wai Keung (No. 2)* [1992] 2 HKCLR 207 at 217 which was used by the Court in *So Wai Lun v HKSAR* (2006) 9 HKCFAR 530 at para. 20.

21. The burden is on the Government to satisfy the court that the justification test is satisfied. Where one is concerned with

differential treatment based on grounds such as race, sex or sexual orientation, the court will scrutinize with intensity whether the difference in treatment is justified. See *Ghaidan v Godin-Mendoza* at 568G (Lord Nicholls).

22. In requiring differential treatment to be justified, the view has been expressed that the difference in treatment in question is an infringement of the constitutional right to equality but that the infringement may be constitutionally justified. See the Court of Appeal's judgment in the present case at 208B–C (Ma CJHC) and in *Leung v Secretary for Justice* [2006] 4 HKLRD 211 at 234G–H. This approach is not appropriate. Where the difference in treatment satisfies the justification test, the correct approach is to regard the difference in treatment as not constituting discrimination and not infringing the constitutional right to equality. Unlike some other constitutional rights, such as the right of peaceful assembly, it is not a question of infringement of the right which may be constitutionally justified.

Difference in treatment

23. Section 118F(1) in criminalising only homosexual buggery otherwise than in private plainly gives rise to differential treatment on the ground of sexual orientation which requires to be justified. This is rightly accepted by McCoy SC for the appellant.

24. All persons, whatever their sexual orientation, are subject to the common law offence of committing an act outraging public decency. Irrespective of sexual orientation, a person may be exposed to criminal liability for this offence for committing in the required circumstances a sexual act of a lewd, obscene or disgusting nature which outrages public decency. But homosexuals alone are subject to the statutory offence in s. 118F(1) for committing buggery otherwise than in private. In contrast, heterosexuals are not subject to any criminal liability comparable to that prescribed in s. 118F(1) in relation to the same or comparable conduct, namely, vaginal intercourse or buggery otherwise than in private. Thus, as a result of s. 118F(1), a dividing line is drawn on the basis of sexual orientation between homosexuals on the one hand and heterosexuals on the other in relation to the same or comparable conduct. The point that the common law offence has a higher maximum penalty than the statutory offence in s. 118F(1) cannot affect the matter.

Justification

25. As s. 118F(1) gives rise to differential treatment on the ground of sexual orientation, justification for the difference in treatment is required. The justification test must now be applied. The first stage of that test is to consider whether the differential treatment pursues a legitimate aim. For this purpose, a genuine need for the difference in treatment must be made out.

26. Mr McCoy SC for the appellant submits that there is a genuine need for the differential treatment. The appellant's case is put in this way. The offence in s. 118F(1) is a specific form of the common law offence of committing an act outraging public decency. The specific offence punishes homosexual buggery otherwise than in private per se and obviates such difficulties as there may be in proving the common law offence. In enacting it, the Legislature must be taken to have considered that there was a genuine need for such a specific offence as part of the package to reform the law relating to homosexual conduct.

27. The appellant's submission does not address the critical question. What must be established is a genuine need for the differential treatment. That need cannot be established from the mere act of legislative enactment. It must be identified and made out. In the present case, no genuine need for the difference in treatment has been shown. That being so, it has not been established that the differential treatment in question pursues any legitimate aim. The matter fails at the first stage of the justification test.

28. In enacting a package of measures to reform the law governing homosexual conduct, the Legislature was entitled to decide whether it is necessary to enact a specific criminal offence to protect the community against sexual conduct in public which outrages public decency. But in legislating for such a specific offence, it cannot do so in a discriminatory way. Section 118F(1) is a discriminatory law. It only criminalises homosexual buggery otherwise than in private but does not criminalise heterosexuals for the same or comparable conduct when there is no genuine need for the differential treatment.

29. Homosexuals constitute a minority in the community. The provision has the effect of targeting them and is constitutionally invalid. The courts have the duty of enforcing the constitutional guarantee of equality before the law and of ensuring protection against discriminatory law.

30. Accordingly, s. 118F(1) is discriminatory and infringes the right to equality. It is unconstitutional. The answer to the first certified question is in the affirmative.

The proper order

31. Mr Justice Ribeiro PJ's judgment deals with the second certified question as to the proper order to be made when the charge against the defendant is found to be unconstitutional and I agree with his judgment.

Disposal

32. The appeal is dismissed. In accordance with the appellant's undertaking, an order is made that the 2nd respondent's costs be paid by the appellant.

Mr Justice Bokhary PJ:

Equality

33. Human rights are aptly named, being basic to and inherent in humankind. They consist of what were referred to in the *Barcelona Traction Case* (Second Phase), ICJ Rep. (1970) 3 at p.32 as "the principles and rules concerning the basic rights of the human person". And such rights, as Judge Tanaka explained in the *South West Africa Cases* (Second Phase), ICJ Rep. (1966) 5 at p.297, "have always existed with the human being... independently of, and before, the State". So they are not for the State to make. The State makes law. Of the many and varied purposes for which law is made, none is more important than that of declaring, protecting and realising the full potential of human rights. And there is no better way to secure these rights than ensuring that they are enjoyed by everyone in equal measure. History teaches us that, for so many violations of human rights have sprung from discrimination, and struggles for social justice have so often been based on claims to equal treatment.

34. I see that in his contribution to *The Rights of Peoples* (ed. James Crawford) (1988), Prof. Garth Nettheim observes (at p.123) that "non-discrimination... has recognition in international law as, perhaps, the primary human right". Dr W A McKean, at pp 185-186 of his article "The Meaning of Discrimination in International

and Municipal Law" (1970) 44 BYIL 177, puts forward the formula "arbitrary, invidious or unjustified distinctions, unwanted by those made subject to them" as the definition of discrimination accepted in the international sphere. That definition is, he says at p.186, "more advanced and sophisticated than that adopted in most municipal legal systems". In the field of human rights, municipal law has often walked in the footsteps of international law – and may in some jurisdictions have caught up with or even overtaken it.

35. Prejudice can be a very insidious thing. And discrimination is sometimes practised unwittingly. Coping with it requires a strong, straightforward and easily understood law. The entrenched protection of such a law is conferred by our constitution on everyone in Hong Kong. By art.25, the Basic Law guarantees in unlimited terms that "[a]ll Hong Kong residents shall be equal before the law". And by art.41, it extends this guarantee to all persons in Hong Kong even if they are not Hong Kong residents. These provisions set no limit on the matters in respect of which they guarantee equality before the law. And this Court has always recognised that fundamental rights and freedoms are to be interpreted generously.

36. Guaranteed in unlimited terms and interpreted generously, equality before the law inevitably amounts to an absolute right not to be discriminated against. So any departure from identical treatment is liable to scrutiny. And the ultimate test of whether any such departure offends against equality before the law is whether the departure amounts to discrimination against any person or category of persons: in short, whether it is discriminatory. If it is discriminatory, it will offend against equality before the law. It will so offend whether discrimination is its objective or merely its effect.

37. Within the ultimate test of whether the departure from identical treatment is discriminatory, it is possible and useful to identify various factors by reference to which any such departure can be examined with a view to determining whether it is non-discriminatory and therefore compatible with equality before the law. My earliest attempt to identify such factors was made in a case decided under the equality before the courts clause of art.10 of the Bill of Rights. It was the case of *R v. Man Wai–keung* (No.2) [1992] 2 HKCLR 207 where I said this (at p.217):

> "Clearly, there is no requirement of literal equality in the sense of unrelentingly identical treatment always. For such rigidity would subvert rather than promote true even–handedness. So that, in certain circumstances, a departure from literal equality would be a legitimate course and, indeed, the only legitimate course. But the starting point is identical treatment. And any departure therefrom must be justified. To justify such a departure it must be shown: one, that sensible and fair-minded people would recognise a genuine need for some difference of treatment; two, that the difference embodied in the particular departure selected to meet that need is itself rational; and, three, that such departure is proportionate to such need."

That was relied upon by both courts below in the present case and by Hartmann J in *Leung v. Secretary for Justice* [2005] 3 HKLRD 657 at p.689 A-E (where he rightly described equality before the law as "the constitutional protection against discrimination"). And it was cited in *So Wai Lun v. HKSAR* (2006) 9 HKCFAR 530 at p.539 D–G by Mr Justice Chan PJ and I in our joint judgment agreed to by the other members of the Court.

38. Of the *Man Wai–keung* factors, rationality and proportionality have long been well established legal concepts, informed by a large body of case law and academic opinion. They are of general application. But the "genuine need for some difference of treatment" factor is a concept specific to equality before the law. It is the first line of defence against discrimination. And it is the first step toward pluralism and respect for otherness. These are matters on which we must all guard against prejudice in ourselves. So I took the view in the early years of the Bill of Rights – and remain of the view – that it is preferable on such matters that the courts openly acknowledge that they are proceeding on the basis of that which is sensible and fair–minded in people. But the first *Man Wai–keung* factor could, I daresay, be expressed simply in terms of the sensible and fair–minded view being that there is a genuine need for some difference of treatment. What would be plainly unacceptable is for the courts to proceed on some unarticulated standard when deciding the question of genuine need.

39. In further explanation of why I prefer an express reference to that which is sensible and fair–minded in people, I would stress that these qualities are, after all, the life–force of human rights in action. So restrictions on fundamental rights and freedoms need to be, as Lord Nicholls of Birkenhead said in *R (Prolife Alliance) v. British Broadcasting Corp* [2004] 1 AC 185 at p.224 C, "examined rigorously by all concerned, not least the courts". In his contribution to *The Hong Kong Bill of Rights: A Comparative Approach* (eds Johannes Chan and Yash Ghai) (1993) Prof. Rajeev Dhavan, dealing with the post-emergency period in India, says (at p.465) that "the people have recast the chapter of human rights through judges". Tellingly Prof. Christopher Eisgruber concludes his book *Constitutional Self–Government* (2001) by referring (at p.211) to the United States Supreme Court's role of "speaking about justice on behalf of the American people".

40. When speaking about justice on people's behalf, a court should have regard to their sense of fairness. And I see no reason why the court should not openly acknowledge such regard. The United States Supreme Court famously made such an acknowledgment in *Hirabayashi v. United States* 320 US 81 (1943), saying (at p.100) that "[d]istinctions between citizens solely because of their ancestry are by their very nature odious to a free people whose institutions are founded upon the doctrine of equality." Their Honours immediately went on to identify that as the "reason" why legislative classification or discrimination based on race alone has often been held to be a denial of equal protection. There is much to be said for making the legal process as visibly participatory as practicable. In particular, the administration of constitutional justice is strengthened and enhanced when seen to be carried out according to the good in people.

41. Various expressions have been used by judges when invoking the good in people as a standard. In the constitutional case of *Snyder v. Massachusetts* 291 US 97 (1934), for example, Cardozo J spoke (at p.105) of "the traditions and conscience of our people" and (at p.122) of what is "acceptable to the thought of reasonable men". Another example is to be found in the common law case of *Davis Contractors v. Fareham Urban District Council* [1956] AC 696. There Lord Radcliffe said (at p.728) that " the spokesman of the fair and reasonable man, who represents after all no more than the anthropomorphic conception of justice, is and must be the court itself". Habits of speech change, and it is no reflection on those judges that nowadays we should speak instead of the reasonable "person". This we learn from the phraseology selected by Mason J (as he then was) in the equity case of *Commercial*

Bank of Australia v. Amadio (1983) 151 CLR 447 at p.467.

42. There are various ways in which to describe what would justify a departure from identical treatment. One would be to say that anything put forward for that purpose must be reasonable and objective. By "objective" I mean free from bias whether conscious or unconscious.

43. Turning to the circumstances of the present case, they are as follows. The prosecution's allegation against these respondents, both adult men, was that they had, as they subsequently admitted to the police, committed buggery with each other in a car parked in a dark and isolated spot at night. They were charged with homosexual buggery committed otherwise than in private, contrary to s.118F(1) of the Crimes Ordinance, Cap.200, which provides that "[a] man who commits buggery with another man otherwise other in private shall be quilty of an offence and shall be liable on conviction on indictment to imprisonment for 5 years." I have no hesitation in agreeing with the courts below that s.118F(1) discriminates against homosexual men and is unconstitutional by reason of such discrimination. That is my answer to the first certified question.

44. My reasons for that answer are these. Section 118F(1) has the effect of targeting a group defined by sexual orientation, namely homosexual men. Approached realistically, it has that effect even though it makes no mention of homosexuality. Indeed, it would have that effect even if it were to use the word "person" rather than the word "man". The relevant principle is to be found in the advisory opinion of the Permanent Court of International Justice in *German Settlers in Poland* PCIJ, Series B, No.6, 1923, p.5. This principle is succinctly put by Judge Schwebel in his book *Justice in International Law* (1994). Citing that advisory opinion, he says (at p.149) that "discrimination in fact is debarred even if discrimination in form is absent".

45. By its effect, s.118F(1) departs from identical treatment. And it does so in a particularly serious way since it is a penal law of some severity. But there is simply no demonstrable genuine need for this departure. Such non-discriminatory objective as can be attributed to this subsection is, at least is general, catered for by the common law offence of outraging public decency, which s.101I of the Criminal Procedure Ordinance, Cap.221, makes punishable by up to 7 years' imprisonment. This common law offence does not have the effect of targeting any group. The present appeal is not an occasion for identifying the full definition of this common law offence. Suffice it to say that, on the English cases, it would appear that this common law offence is committed when there is done, in a place where there is a real possibility of members of the public witnessing it, any act of a lewd, obscene or disgusting nature that outrages public decency. Given the existence of this common law offence and the maximum penalty for it, the alleged prevalence of homosexual buggery in public does not begin to give rise to a demonstrable genuine need for a provision like s.118F(1). So one cannot begin to justify this subsection.

46. Mr Gerard McCoy SC for the Secretary for Justice queries the adequacy of the common law offence of outraging public decency. There was, he says, no evidence of there having been any onlooker or potential onlooker to what the respondents did in the car. And he says that the absence of any onlooker or potential onlooker meant that the respondents probably could not have been prosecuted to conviction for outraging public decency. So, he argues, there is a need for a law like s.118F(1). But there is a fatal weakness in this argument of Mr McCoy's. It attaches importance to punishing persons who engage in sexual activities in public rather than to protecting persons who are outraged by the sight of such activities. Such an argument does not provide justification for a law that has the effect of targeting a particular group.

47. If law enforcement agencies and prosecuting authorities believe that the protection of the public calls for more than what the common law offence of outraging public decency provides, their proper course is to try to persuade the executive to introduce non-discriminatory legislation for the purpose. And if the executive saw fit to do that, the legislature could then consider the perceived problem in all its aspects – remembering always that law is a problem-solver while discrimination is a problem and never a solution.

48. On the first certified question, I agree with the Chief Justice that s.118F(1) of the Crimes Ordinance is unconstitutional, and regard my reasoning as in harmony with his.

49. Before parting with the question of equality, I would underline the fact that the present case concerns discrimination in the form of an unjustified departure from identical treatment. So the focus is on what it takes to justify a departure from identical treatment. But there can be cases in which the complaint is of discrimination in the form of a failure to accord different treatment in circumstances calling for it or in which affirmative action is involved. Such cases may raise other considerations as to what is called for by equality before the law. That is what I had in mind when I said in *Man Wai-keung's* case that in certain circumstances a departure from literal equality would be a legitimate course and, indeed, the only legitimate course. As the Permanent Court of International Justice said in its advisory opinion in *Minority Schools in Albania* PCIJ, Series A/B, No.64, 1935, p.4 at p.19, "[e]quality in law precludes discrimination of any kind; whereas equality in fact may involve the necessity of different treatment in order to attain a result which establishes an equilibrium between different situations". In her contribution to Human Rights Protection: Methods and Effectiveness (ed. Frances Butler) (2002), Dame Rosalyn Higgins underlines the recognition in that case of the linkage between special needs and equality in fact. And she says (at p.166) that it is "not fanciful ... to see in that linkage both the precursor of more contemporary notions of affirmative action and the response to suggestions that special protections themselves constitute a form of discrimination".

Order to be made on charge alleging offence declared unconstitutional at trial

50. That leaves the second certified question. What order should the trial court make where it is persuaded that the offence charged is unconstitutional and has so declared?

51. In the present case, the magistrate ordered that the information be dismissed, and the Court of Appeal held that he was right to make that form of order. Under the second certified question, the appellant originally contended that where a trial court holds that an offence charged is unconstitutional, it should quash that charge and discharge the accused in relation thereto. And the respondents had originally contended that the appropriate course is for the trial court, having declared an offence unconstitutional, to decline jurisdiction to proceed further on any charge alleging that offence, so declining jurisdiction on the basis that such charge alleges an offence unknown to the law. During the argument however, both sides came to accept that – subject to the possibility of an amendment to charge a constitutional offence – the appropriate course is to dismiss the information or so much of it as charges an unconstitutional offence. In my view,

the parties were right to accept that.

52. My reasons for taking that view are those expressed by Mr Justice Ribeiro PJ. All that I would add is a word about the reference to "nullity" made by Litton JA (as he then was) in *Commissioner for Labour v. Jetex HVAC Equipments Ltd* [1995] 2 HKLR 24 at p.32. I think that it was no more than the *obiter* precaution of declining to rule out the theoretical possibility of some extraordinary mishap generating a purported information that was not by any stretch of the imagination really an information at all.

Result

53. For the foregoing reasons, I concur in the result stated by the Chief Justice.

Mr Justice Chan PJ:

54. I agree with the judgment of the Chief Justice and that of Mr Justice Ribeiro PJ.

Mr Justice Ribeiro PJ:

55. I agree with the reasoning and judgment of the Chief Justice.

56. I address the second question arising on this appeal which was certified in the following terms:

> "What is the proper order to be made when the charge against the defendant is found to be unconstitutional?"

In context, it concerns the approach to be adopted where a finding of unconstitutionality is made by a magistrate.

The approach adopted below

57. Having heard submissions from counsel, the magistrate, Mr John T Glass, held that section 118F(1) of the Crimes Ordinance, Cap 200, under which the defendants were charged was unconstitutional and that he was consequently bound to dismiss the charges.[3] In the Court of Appeal,[4] both parties submitted that that was the wrong course to adopt. Mr Gerard McCoy SC submitted for the Government that section 19 of the Magistrates Ordinance, Cap 227 ("the Ordinance") required the magistrate to hear the entirety of the prosecution's case before he could properly dismiss it on a point of law. Mr Philip Dykes SC, appearing for the 1st respondent,[5] contended that the magistrate should simply have declined jurisdiction to avoid giving an unconstitutional provision any semblance of validity.

58. Their arguments were rejected by the Court of Appeal. Tang JA commented that summary trials are not designed with such niceties in mind and held that the magistrate had made the correct order, stating:

> "...the magistrate had to deal with the charge and the proper way to deal with it, when the charge has not been made out, whether on the facts or as a matter of law (including the constitutionality of the law), was to dismiss it." [6]

59. Ma CJHC also rejected the parties' procedural arguments but he drew attention to section 27 of the Ordinance ("section 27") as providing a possible basis for dealing with an information charging an unconstitutional offence. However, as the Court had not heard argument on that section, his Lordship left open the question of its applicability.

The parties' approach before the Court

60. Mr McCoy SC[7] and Mr Dykes SC[8] continue to represent their respective clients before this Court. Mr Stanley Ma appears for the 2nd respondent and again adopts the submissions made by Mr Dykes.

61. In the Government's printed case, it was submitted that where the offence charged is found to be unconstitutional, the magistrate should declare the relevant legislation unconstitutional, quash the charge as one unknown to law and discharge the defendant, it being contended that power to make such orders should be implied as necessary to the exercise of a magistrate's jurisdiction. Objection was taken to the magistrate's approach in that his dismissal of the charges was said to amount to an acquittal of the defendants, precluding their prosecution on any other charges on the ground of *autrefois acquit*. In their joint printed case, the respondents continued to submit that the only appropriate course was to decline jurisdiction.

62. Those arguments do not require to be examined in detail. The parties accepted in the course of argument that section 27 is capable of supplying the framework for dealing with findings of unconstitutionality. In my judgment, section 27 is indeed engaged. A number of incidental issues bearing on its application arise and it is desirable that they should be dealt with in this judgment.

Operating section 27

63. Section 27 is in the following terms:

> "(1) Where it appears to the adjudicating magistrate that there is–
>
> (a) a defect in the substance or form of any complaint, information or summons; or
>
> (b) a variance between the complaint, information or summons and the evidence adduced in support of it,
>
> he shall, subject to subsection (2)–
>
> (i) amend the complaint, information or summons if he is satisfied that no injustice would be caused by that amendment; or
>
> (ii) dismiss the complaint, information or summons.
>
> (2) The adjudicating magistrate shall amend the complaint, information or summons where–
>
> (a) the defect or variance mentioned in subsection (1) is not material; or
>
> (b) any injustice which might otherwise be caused by an amendment would be cured by an order as to costs, an adjournment or leave to recall and further examine witnesses or call other witnesses.
>
> (3) Following an amendment to a complaint, information or summons, the adjudicating magistrate shall–
>
> (a) read and explain the amended complaint, information or summons to the defendant;
>
> (b) give leave to the parties to call or recall and further examine such witnesses as may be reasonably required by a party having regard to the nature of the amendment;
>
> (c) grant such adjournment as may be reasonably

necessary to enable the parties to call or recall witnesses and to prepare their cases;

(d) if he thinks fit, make an order that the complainant or informant shall pay to the defendant such costs, not exceeding $5000, as may be occasioned by the amendment; and

(e) give judgment upon the substantial merits and facts of the case as proved before him, having regard to the offence charged in the complaint, information or summons as amended:

Provided that, if the amendment is made after the case for the complainant or informant is closed, no further evidence may be called by the complainant or informant other than evidence that would, apart from this section, be admissible in rebuttal.

(4) In this section, 'amend' includes the substitution of another offence in place of that alleged in the complaint, information or summons."

64. Where an information charges a defendant with an offence which is held to be unconstitutional, there is plainly a "defect in the substance ... of the information" so that section 27 is engaged. Leaving aside for the moment what should happen if the prosecution should wish at that point to challenge such determination, the scheme of section 27(1) requires the magistrate next to consider, subject to subsection (2), either amending the information or dismissing it. Subsection (2), which is given precedence, prescribes in mandatory terms that the magistrate should amend the information, removing the option of its dismissal, if an amendment can be made without causing injustice or where any potential injustice would be cured by the procedural measures referred to in section 27(2)(b).

65. In the context of a finding of unconstitutionality, it is important to note that "amendment" is given a very wide meaning by section 27(4) and includes "the substitution of another offence in place of that alleged in the ... information". It would therefore in principle be open to the magistrate to amend the information by substituting an offence which raises no constitutional difficulties in place of the unconstitutional offence, provided that this causes no injustice and that the section 27(3) procedures are then followed. If this can be done, the substitution relates back to the time when the information was laid and if it would not have been time-barred at that stage, the substituted charge would not be treated as time-barred even if the substitution occurred well after expiry of an otherwise applicable time-limit, so long as the substituted offence arises out of the same (or substantially the same) facts as the offence originally charged.[9]

66. Section 27 envisages a magistrate acting of his own motion, and this may be appropriate where an unproblematical alternative charge is plainly available. However, in practice, whether another offence can be substituted is likely to depend on whether the prosecution considers such a charge viable. If no suitable alternative offence can be found, or if the evidence is insufficient to support a suggested charge, amendment (assumed in the present context to take the form of substituting the offence charged) would not be a genuine option. In such cases, and in cases where a proposed amendment cannot be made without injustice, section 27(1) requires the magistrate to dismiss the information.

67. The magistrate did not apply section 27 in deciding to dismiss the charges. He evidently took the view (as did Tang JA) that since the charge could not be made out given the unconstitutionality of the offence, it ought simply to be dismissed. The question of amendment pursuant to section 27 was not addressed.

Appealing an unconstitutionality ruling

68. A decision that a statutory provision is unconstitutional is of the gravest import and generally calls for examination by the higher courts. It is therefore important to consider the correct procedural approach where a challenge to constitutionality is made in the magistrates' courts.

69. If the challenge fails, no particular problems arise. If the defendant is convicted of the offence as charged, the challenge to constitutionality can be renewed on appeal or, where appropriate, on a judicial review. However, if the challenge to constitutionality succeeds, the position is more complicated. As section 27 is engaged, the magistrate would be expected to follow the procedures prescribed by that section: considering whether an amendment can be made without injustice, and so forth. But if that course is followed without interruption and the trial proceeds on the basis of a substituted offence (especially to the point of an acquittal), difficulties may lie in the way of any challenge to the ruling that the offence originally charged is unconstitutional. Moreover, if that ruling is held on appeal to have been wrong, the opportunity of proceeding against the defendant on the original charge is likely to have been lost.

70. In my view, where the prosecution wishes to question a determination of unconstitutionality, the magistrate should generally, before proceeding to consider possible amendment as prescribed by section 27, accede to an application to state a case pursuant to section 105 of the Ordinance in respect of that determination, adjourning the proceedings pending the outcome of such appeal. Section 105 materially states as follows:

"Within 14 clear days after the hearing and determination by a magistrate of any complaint, information, charge or other proceeding which he has power to determine in a summary way, either party thereto or any person aggrieved thereby who desires to question by way of appeal any conviction, order, determination or other proceeding as aforesaid on the ground that it is erroneous in point of law, or that it is in excess of jurisdiction, may apply in writing to the magistrate to state and sign a case setting forth the facts and the grounds on which the conviction, order or determination was granted and the grounds on which the proceeding is questioned, for the opinion of a judge ..."

71. Adoption of this procedure enables the question of constitutionality to be examined at the highest levels of court while preserving the position in the magistrates' court. If the magistrate's decision is overturned, the appellate tribunal may remit the case for trial de novo on the original charge before another magistrate. And if the magistrate's ruling is affirmed, the appellate court may either remit the matter to the trial magistrate to consider possible amendment or it may itself[10] effect an amendment pursuant to section 27 and then remit the matter for trial de novo on the substituted charge. As is pointed out in *HKSAR v Tse So-so*,[11] a judgment of this Court handed down on the same day as the present judgment, this approach to amendment by an appellate court was followed (although not in relation to a constitutional challenge) in *Fai Ma Trading Co Ltd v L S Lai* (Industry Officer)[12] and (in the context of an incomplete review under section 104 of the Ordinance) in *Poon Chau Cheong*

v Secretary for Justice.[13]

72. In coming to the conclusion that an appeal by way of case stated may be brought upon the magistrate ruling that the offence is unconstitutional, I bear in mind the well-established principle, referred to by Mr McCoy, that such an appeal is not available to challenge interlocutory decisions, catering only for final determinations by the magistrate. After an extensive review of the authorities, Fuad VP, giving the judgment of the Court of Appeal in *R v Yeung Wai Hung,*[14] concluded that:

> "... upon the true construction of s 105 of the Ordinance (and there is no power elsewhere) a magistrate has no jurisdiction to state a case until there has been a final disposal of the case."

73. That decision was endorsed by this Court in *Yeung Siu Keung v HKSAR,*[15] where Chief Justice Li stated:

> "As with appeals using the case stated procedure under section 105, an appeal under section 113 must relate to a final decision on all matters in issue between the parties."

74. One can readily understand the concerns that underlie the requirement of finality. As Pickering J put it in Newton v Walker:

> "... it is not the intention of the subsection to permit appeals upon interlocutory matters arising in the magistrates' courts. Were it otherwise, appeals would proliferate like mushrooms at dawn to the impediment of the disposal of the work of the criminal courts." [16]

Nothing said in this judgment is intended to disturb that well-settled principle.

75. In my view, where a magistrate determines that the offence charged is unconstitutional, that determination is not merely interlocutory. It is the end of the case in respect of the offence charged so far as the magistrate is concerned. It is a final determination for the purposes of an appeal by way of case stated. The issue of constitutionality to be referred to the appellate court is qualitatively different from the sorts of interlocutory appeals that have attracted strictures against misuse of the case stated procedure. Examples mentioned in *Yeung Siu Keung v HKSAR* include appeals against rejection of a duplicity submission, against a ruling on admissibility of evidence and against the construction of a statute adopted in the course of a trial.[17]

76. It is accordingly my view that an appeal by way of case stated is available to challenge a magistrate's ruling of unconstitutionality before reconstitution of the information pursuant to section 27, and that this is consistent with the principles precluding appeals from interlocutory magisterial decisions.

Section 27 and "nullity"

77. A possible argument against the applicability of section 27 in the present context arises on the basis of the suggestion in certain cases that a defect in an information may be so fundamental as to render it a nullity which is incapable of being cured by amendment, leaving the court with no alternative but to dismiss the information. If that suggestion is correct, an information charging an unconstitutional offence might be regarded as so fundamentally defective as to amount to a nullity, precluding amendment under section 27.

78. *In AG v Wong Lau trading as Kin Keung Construction & Engineering Co,*[18] Stock J (as he then was) sought in the context of section 27 to distil from English authorities (referred to below) the propositions *inter alia* that:

> "1. A distinction is to be drawn between informations that are defective and those which are nullities.
>
> 2. An information will be a nullity if
>
> (i) the statutory provision creating the offence has been repealed and not re-enacted; or
>
> (ii) the statement and particulars of offence cannot be seen fairly to relate to, or be intended to charge, a known and subsisting criminal offence; or
>
> (iii) in some other way, it is so defective that it cannot be cured.
>
> ...
>
> 12. Informations which are a nullity cannot be amended."

79. That decision was followed in *R v Yeung Lee Transportation & Engineering Limited.*[19] And in *Jetex HVAC Equipments Ltd v Commissioner for Labour,*[20] Litton JA accepted the hypothetical proposition that "if the information were a nullity there is nothing to amend; section 27(1) of the Magistrates Ordinance cannot in those circumstances bite at all." It is however the case that none of the informations in these three cases were held to be nullities.

80. In formulating his categories of "nullity", Stock J cites a number of English cases,[21] which, it is true, do refer to certain indictments as containing defects which render them "nullities".[22] However, those authorities must be approached with great care. None of them was dealing with any enactment resembling our section 27, that is, a provision imposing a duty to amend as discussed above and conferring a power to amend which expressly includes substitution of the offence charged. And in none of them was the court concerned with the question whether the trial or appellate court was precluded from amending the relevant indictment or charge on the ground that it was so defective that it had to be treated as a nullity leaving nothing to amend.

81. Instead, in many if not all of them, any constraint on amendment was the constraint, recognized in the English case-law, against an appellate court amending the charge after the trial court had recorded a conviction, it being acknowledged that the defect *could* have been, but was not, cured by amendment prior to conviction below.[23] Plainly, in such cases, it was not the seriousness of the defect, but the unwillingness of appellate courts to re-cast a defective charge after conviction, that prevented amendment. As noted above, appellate courts are not so constrained in Hong Kong in the section 27 context, they having adopted the practice of ordering a trial *de novo* on the amended charge where the power to amend is exercised on appeal.[24] Given that, on English the authorities, the defective charge could not be cured by amendment on appeal, the point arising in some of the abovementioned cases was whether the defect was so serious as to render the indictment a nullity so as to exclude application of the proviso.[25] The issues addressed in those cases were, in other words, quite different from those before this Court and arose in a very different statutory environment.

82. Given the overall scheme of section 27 and the great width of the power of amendment it confers, it is hard to conceive of a

defect in an information which cannot in principle be amended, particularly by substitution of the offence charged.

(a) Stock J gives as his first example of nullity, a case where the statutory provision creating the offence charged has been repealed and not re-enacted.[26] However, if section 27(4) is kept in view, in such a case the question is whether there exists an alternative offence under a valid enactment or at common law which would be disclosed on the evidence to be called and which could be substituted without injustice for the defective charge. Of course in any particular case, this may not be possible. But defects of this nature are clearly in principle capable of being cured so that the proposition that they result in a nullity cannot be accepted.

(b) The same applies to Stock J's second example, involving a case where "the statement and particulars of offence cannot be seen fairly to relate to, or be intended to charge, a known and subsisting criminal offence." [27] If the offence charged is not known to law, the curability of the information must depend, in the section 27 context, on whether a valid offence can be substituted without injustice and pursued on the available evidence. There is again no reason in principle why a defect of this particular type should brand the information a nullity.

83. Indeed, it is hard to see what role there is at all for the notion of "nullity" in section 27. That provision creates a self-contained scheme which requires a defective information or one which is at variance with the evidence adduced to be dealt with either by amendment or by dismissal. It prescribes amendment in mandatory terms if this can be achieved without injustice. If not, section 27 itself stipulates that the information must be dismissed. It is hard to see what purpose would be served by injecting the notion of "nullity" into that scheme. To the extent that the three cases referred to support the view that informations may be so defective as to constitute nullities incapable of being amended pursuant to section 27 (and only to such extent) they are, in my respectful view, wrongly decided and should not be followed.

Autrefois acquit

84. As noted above, one of the prosecution's concerns with regard to the order made by the magistrate was that it might result in a plea of *autrefois acquit* in the event that an alternative offence was sought to be charged.

85.The application of section 27 to a determination of unconstitutionality largely meets that concern and certainly does not aggravate it.

(a) If (say, after confirmation of the unconstitutionality on appeal) the section 27 procedure is followed and the defendant is tried for a constitutionally valid offence substituted by amendment, he will have been tried on the substantial merits on the basis of an alternative offence without being allowed to raise a plea of autrefois acquit.

(b) If, on the other hand, no amendment is made (for instance, because no amendment can be made without injustice) and the information is dismissed pursuant to section 27, it does not follow merely from the fact of such dismissal that a plea of autrefois acquit would necessarily avail the defendant if, due to later developments or otherwise, the prosecution subsequently felt able to charge him with a different, constitutionally valid, offence. Whether at that stage, a plea of autrefois acquit or an objection on the ground of oppression and abuse of process might succeed would depend on the legal principles governing such objections.

Section 27 and the "adjudicating magistrate"

86. As noted in *Tse So-so*, section 27 deals specifically with the powers of the "adjudicating magistrate", meaning the magistrate seised of the substantive trial, to deal with defects in the information. The foregoing discussion has proceeded on the footing that a constitutional objection is taken before the magistrate at the trial. However, as held in *Tse So-so*, magistrates other than the trial magistrate have power to amend an information outside the confines of section 27. It follows that if the prosecution should wish to avoid a debate on the constitutionality of a particular offence charged, it could seek to amend the information in advance of the trial without relying on section 27, to charge a constitutionally uncontroversial offence. Whether such an amendment would be permitted would obviously depend on general principles and the usual discretionary considerations.

Disposal of the present case

87. As this Court has upheld the determination that the offence charged is unconstitutional, it could in principle exercise the magistrate's power under section 27 to consider amending the information by substituting, for instance, the charge of outraging public decency at common law.[28] If satisfied that such an amendment could be made without injustice, this Court could in principle make the amendment and remit the amended information for trial *de novo* before the same or a different magistrate. If not satisfied that such an amendment can be made without injustice, it could simply uphold the dismissal of the charge.

88. However, in the present case, these considerations do not arise since, in obtaining leave to appeal, the Government undertook that it would not seek remittal of the case and would not bring any charge in relation to the conduct alleged in this case. Accordingly, I would simply order that the appeal be dismissed with the order as to costs referred to in the Chief Justice's judgment.

Sir Anthony Mason NPJ:

89. I agree with the judgment of the Chief Justice and that of Mr Justice Ribeiro PJ.

Chief Justice Li:

90. The Court unanimously dismisses the appeal and makes an order that the 2nd respondent's costs be paid by the appellant.

Chief Justice (Andrew Li)

Permanent Judge (Kemal Bokhary)

Permanent Judge (Patrick Chan)

Permanent Judge (R.A.V. Ribeiro)

Non-Permanent Judge (Sir Anthony Mason)

Mr Gerard McCoy SC and Ms Annie Leung (instructed by the Department of Justice) and Ms Sally Yam (of that Department) for the appellant

Mr Philip Dykes SC and Ms Wing Kay Po (instructed by Messrs

Tang Tso & Lau and assigned by the Legal Aid Department) for the 1st respondent

Mr Stanley Ma (instructed by Messrs Tang Tso & Lau) for the 2nd respondent

---

Footnotes:

1. Hartmann J held the following provisions relating to homosexual conduct in Part XII of the Crimes Ordinance to be unconstitutional: (i) Section 118H to the extent that it applies to a man aged 16 or over and under 21; (ii) sections 118F(2)(a) and 118J(2)(a) and (iii) section 118C to the extent that it applies to a man aged 16 or over and under 21. The conclusions in (i) and (ii) were not appealed. The conclusion in (iii) was affirmed by the Court of Appeal in *Leung v Secretary for Justice* [2006] 4 HKLRD 211.

2. Although not referred to in the Brief, the existing law also included the statutory offence of indecency in public provided for in s. 148 of the Crimes Ordinance which was enacted in 1978.

3. Case Stated, §44.

4. [2006] 4 HKLRD 196. Pang J had directed that the prosecution's appeal by way of case stated should be argued before the Court of Appeal.

5. His submissions being adopted by Mr Stanley Ma, instructed for the 2nd respondent.

6. Judgment §36.

7. Appearing with Ms Annie Leung and Ms Sally Yam.

8. Appearing with Ms Wing Kay Po.

9. *Poon Chau Cheong v Secretary for Justice* (2000) 3 HKCFAR 121 at 131 and 132.

10. Exercising the powers of the magistrate as provided for by section 119(1)(d) of the Ordinance, powers which are in turn available to this Court by virtue of section 17(2) of the Hong Kong Court of Final Appeal Ordinance, Cap 484.

11. FACC 1/2007.

12. [1989] 1 HKLR 582.

13. (2000) 3 HKCFAR 121.

14. [1990] 2 HKC 86.

15. (2006) 9 HKCFAR 144 at 153.

16. [1975] HKLR 317 at 321-322.

17. These being examples mentioned in *Streames v Copping* [1985] 1 QB 920.

18. [1993] 1 HKCLR 257 at 268.

19. [1994] 2 HKC 556 (Keith J).

20. [1995] 2 HKLR 24.

21. *R v McVitie* [1960] 2 QB 483; *R v Nelson* (1977) 65 Cr App R 119 ; *R v Molyneux* (1981) 72 Cr App R 111 ; *R v McLaughlin* (1983) 76 Cr App R 42; *R v Ayres* [1984] 1 AC 447; and *R v Williams* (1991) 92 Cr App R 158.

22. *R v Ayres* [1984] 1 AC 447 at 461.

23. *R v Nelson* (1977) 65 Cr App R 119 at 122. See also *Meek v Powell* [1952] 1 KB 164.

24. *Fai Ma Trading Co Ltd v L S Lai (Industry Officer)* [1989] 1 HKLR 582; and *Poon Chau Cheong v Secretary for Justice* (2000) 3 HKCFAR 121.

25. *R v McVitie* [1960] 2 QB 483; *R v Molyneux* (1981) 72 Cr App R 111 ; *R v Ayres* [1984] 1 AC 447 at 461.

26. Evidently taken from *R v McVitie* [1960] 2 QB 483 at 495.

27. Evidently derived from *R v Ayres* [1984] 1 AC 447 at 461.

28. See footnote 10 above.

So Wai Lun v. HKSAR

蘇偉倫 對 香港特別行政區

HCMA 39/2004；FACC 5/2005

簡略案情

2002 年 7 月 28 日，25 歲的上訴人與一位 13 歲的女童發生了性關係。他因此被控觸犯《刑事罪行條例》第 200 章第 124(1) 條的罪名，即與 16 歲以下的女童發生性行為。審訊期間，裁判官認為如果被告能夠在相對可能性較高的基礎上（on a balance of probabilities）證明他不知道、也沒有理由懷疑與其性交的是 16 歲以下的女童，那麼這將對他的控告，構成為辯護理由。最後，裁判官認定被告人不知道、也沒有理由懷疑受害人是 16 歲以下兒童，因此對他做出了無罪的裁決。

控方不滿判決結果而向上訴法庭提請上訴。上訴庭認為《刑事罪行條例》第 200 章第 124（1）條是一條絕對法律責任的條文，因此，被告人知不知道、和有沒有理由懷疑受害人是 16 歲以下的女童，並不能對他的指控構成抗辯理由。最後，上訴庭將案件發回裁判處，指示對被告人作出判罪並施與適當判刑。上訴人決定上訴至終審法院，其理由有二：第一，《刑事罪行條例》第 124（1）條的規定與《基本法》第 25 條的“平等原則”相違背；第二，該絕對法律責任條文不單任意，而且嚴苛和不合理，沒有任何意義，因為刑法的目的不是去防止人們實施他們認為合法的行為。

裁決摘要

終審法院考慮了 *R v. Man Wai-keung No. 2* [1992] 2 HKCLR 207 一案，同意平等的起點是一視同仁，但不應局限於單純文字上的平等。有時候，偏離是恰當的。前提是如果依據一個合理的平常人的角度，偏離是有理性的需要；而且，偏離的程度合比例於該理性的需要。法院同時亦考慮了美國、加拿大和愛爾蘭跟上訴人情況類同的案例，在平等的原則上，它們皆以大比數裁定該相關刑事條文並不違憲，因此，終審法院亦認為第 124（1）條在平等原則上的偏離是具正當理由的。對於第二個理據，終審法院亦認為不能成立，因此《刑事罪行條例》第 124 條的規定是合乎憲法的。據此，上訴人的上訴被駁回。

FACC No. 5 of 2005

IN THE COURT OF FINAL APPEAL OF THE HONG KONG SPECIAL ADMINISTRATIVE REGION

FINAL APPEAL NO. 5 OF 2005 (CRIMINAL)
(ON APPEAL FROM HCMA NO. 39 OF 2004)

Between:

SO WAI LUN — **Applicant**

- and -

HONG KONG SPECIAL ADMINISTRATIVE REGION — **Respondents**

Court: Chief Justice Li, Mr Justice Bokhary PJ, Mr Justice Chan PJ, Mr Justice Ribeiro PJ and Sir Anthony Mason NPJ

Dates of Hearing: 10 – 11 July 2006

Date of Judgment: 18 July 2006

JUDGMENT

Chief Justice Li:

1. I agree with the joint judgment of Mr Justice Bokhary PJ and Mr Justice Chan PJ.

Mr Justice Bokhary PJ and Mr Justice Chan PJ:

2. Two lines of argument have been put forward by Mr Philip Dykes SC for the appellant. The appeal is against a conviction for unlawful sexual intercourse with the girl under the age of 16, contrary to s.124 of the Crimes Ordinance, Cap. 200. This section reads:

> "(1) Subject to subsection (2), a man who has unlawful sexual intercourse with a girl under the age of 16 shall be guilty of an offence and shall be liable on conviction on indictment to imprisonment for 5 years.
>
> (2) Where a marriage is invalid under section 27(2) of the Marriage Ordinance (Cap. 181) by reason of the wife being under the age of 16, the invalidity shall not make the husband guilty of an offence under this section because he has sexual intercourse with her, if he believes her to be his wife and has reasonable cause for the belief."

3. Initially the complaints raised by Mr Dykes on the appellant's behalf included a complaint of an infringement of his presumption of innocence as guaranteed by art. 87 of our constitution the Basic Law and art. 11(1) of the Bill of Rights as entrenched by art. 39 of the Basic Law. Eventually, however, the complaints advanced were of inequality and arbitrariness.

First line of argument: inequality

4. Shortly stated the first line of argument put forward on the appellant's behalf is that s.124 is unconstitutional because, for the act of both, it criminalises the conduct of the male to the exclusion of the female. This, it is argued, deprives the male of the equality before the law guaranteed by art. 25 of the Basic Law and art. 22 of the Bill of Rights as entrenched by art. 39 of the Basic Law.

5. Article 25 of the Basic Law provides that "[a]ll Hong Kong residents shall be equal before the law". And art. 22 of the Bill of Rights provides:

> "All persons are equal before the law and are entitled without any discrimination to the equal protection of the law. In this respect, the law shall prohibit any discrimination and guarantee to all persons equal and effective protection against discrimination on any ground such as race, colour, sex, language, religion, political or other opinion, national or social origin, property, birth or other status."

6. The essence of the complaint under the first line of argument is inequality.

Circumstances of the case

7. Before the second line of argument put forward on the appellant's behalf can be properly understood, it is necessary to say something about the circumstances of the case. These are, shortly stated, as follows. On 28 July 2002 the appellant, then aged 25, had sexual intercourse with a girl then aged 13. That led to his being charged under s.124 with unlawful sexual intercourse with a girl under the age of 16. He was tried in the Magistrate's Court.

8. Following legal submissions, the magistrate (William Ng, Esq) ruled that it would be a defence if the appellant were to prove on a balance of probabilities that he did not know and had no reason to suspect that the girl was under the age of 16.

9. The appellant then gave evidence in support of this defence. And the magistrate found that the appellant had proved on a balance of probabilities that he did not know and had no reason to suspect that the girl was under the age of 16. On that finding of fact and on the view of the law reflected in his ruling, the magistrate acquitted the appellant.

10. Dissatisfied with the magistrate's ruling on the law, the prosecution appealed against the acquittal by way of case stated. The questions posed in the case stated were:

> "(1) WHETHER I was correct in holding that for a charge of unlawful sexual intercourse with a girl under the age of 16 pursuant to section 124 of the Crimes Ordinance, it is a defence if the defendant proves on a balance of probabilities that he did not know and had no reason to suspect that the girl was under the age of 16.
>
> (2) WHETHER I was correct in holding that for all age-based sexual offences, it is a defence if the defendant proves on a balance of probabilities that he did not know and had no reason to suspect that the person was under the prescribed age.
>
> (3) WHETHER I was correct in acquitting [the defendant] in this case."

11. The Court of Appeal (Ma CJHC, Stuart-Moore VP and Lunn J), to whom the appeal had been referred by the High Court, allowed the appeal to: (i) answer questions (1) and (3) in the negative and (ii) remit the matter to the magistrate with a direction to convict and pass an appropriate sentence. Question (2) was not answered (because the parties accepted, and the Court of Appeal held, that it did not arise on the facts of the present case).

12. Pursuant to the remitter and direction, the magistrate

convicted the appellant. He sentenced the appellant to four months' imprisonment suspended for two years.

Second line of argument: arbitrariness

13. We turn now to the second line of argument put forward on the appellant's behalf, which would arise if the first line of argument put forward on his behalf were to fail.

14. Mr Dykes says that if the first subsection of s.124 could be construed in isolation, then, even without resort to any constitutional right or freedom, the offence under the section would fall [*sic*] to be regarded as one of strict, but not absolute, liability. So it would be a defence for the accused to prove on a balance of probabilities that he believed that the girl was aged 16 or older. Alternatively and at worst from the accused's point of view, it would be a defence for him to prove on a balance of probabilities that he reasonably believed that the girl was aged 16 or older.

15. But the first subsection of s.124 does not stand in isolation. And Mr Dykes concedes that, as a pure matter of statutory construction, s.124's legislative history and its second subsection leads inescapably to the conclusion that the offence under the section is one of absolute liability. However, moving beyond pure statutory construction, he argues that there are constitutional guarantees which force a defence upon s.124. This is, he argues, a defence to be made out by the accused on a balance of probabilities consisting of belief or, at worst from the accused's point of view, reasonable belief that the girl was aged 16 or older.

16. Absolute liability under s.124 is, Mr Dykes argues, not only harsh but harsh to no useful purpose since the criminal law does not deter people from doing what they believe to be lawful. That is the essence of the second line of argument put forward on the appellant's behalf. We will examine this argument in due course. But first we will look at the constitutional rights and freedoms invoked for its purposes.

17. These are rights and freedoms which the Basic Law enumerates and ones which, through art. 39, it incorporates by entrenching the Bill of Rights. They are: (i) freedom of the person and freedom from arbitrary or unlawful arrest, detention or imprisonment under art. 28 of the Basic Law; and (ii) the right to liberty and security of the person and freedom from arbitrary arrest or detention under art. 5(1) of the Bill of Rights.

18. Article 28 of the Basic Law provides:

> "The freedom of the person of Hong Kong residents shall be inviolable.
>
> No Hong Kong resident shall be subjected to arbitrary or unlawful arrest, detention or imprisonment. Arbitrary or unlawful search of the body of any resident or deprivation or restriction of the freedom of the person shall be prohibited. Torture of any resident or arbitrary or unlawful deprivation of the life of any resident shall be prohibited."

And art. 5(1) of the Bill of Rights provides:

> "Everyone has the right to liberty and security of person. No one shall be subjected to arbitrary arrest or detention. No one shall be deprived of his liberty except on such grounds and in accordance with such procedure as are established by law."

19. The essence of the complaint under the second line of argument is arbitrariness.

Complaint of inequality

20. The complaint of inequality leveled against s.124 is, as we have said, that for the act of both, the section criminalises the conduct of the male to the exclusion of the female. Dealing with equality, Bokhary J (as he then was) said this in *R v. Man Wai-keung* (No. 2) [1992] 2 HKCLR 207 at p.217:

> "Clearly, there is no requirement of literal equality in the sense of unrelentingly identical treatment always. For such rigidity would subvert rather than promote true even-handedness. So that, in certain circumstances, a departure from literal equality would be a legitimate course and, indeed, the only legitimate course. But the starting point is identical treatment. And any departure therefrom must be justified. To justify such a departure it must be shown: one, that sensible and fair-minded people would recognise a genuine need for some difference of treatment; two, that the difference embodied in the particular departure selected to meet that need is itself rational; and, three, that such departure is proportionate to such need."

That was said in the course of holding that a statutory provision was inconsistent with the Bill of Rights because it took away the power to award costs to the defence whenever a retrial is ordered.

21. We turn now to the decisions of the United States Supreme Court in *Michael M v. Superior Court of Sonoma County* 450 US 464 (1980), of the Supreme Court of Canada in *R v. Nguyen* (1990) 59 CCC (3d) 161 and of the Supreme Court of Ireland in *CC v. Ireland* [2006] IESC 33.

22. *Michael M's* case concerned California's statutory rape law. That law defined unlawful sexual intercourse as "an act of sexual intercourse with a female not the wife of the perpetrator, where the female is under the age of 18 years". Thus males but not females were made criminally liable. By a 5:4 majority it was held that the law did not violate the equal protection clause of the fourteenth amendment of the United States Constitution.

23. *Nguyen's* case concerned s.146(1) of the Canadian Criminal Code. That section provided that every male person who has sexual intercourse with a female person who is not his wife, and is under the age of 14 years, whether or not he believes that she is 14 years of age or more, is guilty of an indictable offence and is liable to imprisonment for life. It was however subject to a requirement, laid down elsewhere in the legislation, that the accused must be older than the complainant. Four sections of the Canadian Charter of Rights and Freedoms were considered, namely, sections 1, 7, 15 and 28 which provide:

> "1. The *Canadian Charter of Rights and Freedoms* guarantees the rights and freedoms set out in it subject only to such reasonable limits prescribed by law as can be demonstrably justified in a free and democratic society.
>
> ...
>
> 7. Everyone has the right to life, liberty and security of the person and the right not to be deprived thereof except in accordance with the principles of fundamental justice.
>
> ...

> 15(1) Every individual is equal before and under the law and has the right to the equal protection and equal benefit of the law without discrimination and, in particular, without discrimination based on race, national or ethnic origin, colour, religion, sex, age or mental or physical disability.
>
> (2) Subsection (1) does not preclude any law, program or activity that has as its object the amelioration of conditions of disadvantaged individuals or groups including those that are disadvantaged because of race, national or ethnic origin, colour, religion, sex, age or mental or physical disability.
>
> ...
>
> 28. Notwithstanding anything in this *Charter*, the rights and freedoms referred to in it are guaranteed equally to male and female persons."

24. As to liberty, all seven judges held that s.146(1) of the Code infringed s.7 of the Charter. Five of them held that s.146(1) of the Code was not, while two of them held that it was, saved as a reasonable limit under s.1 of the Charter.

25. Then, as to equality, four judges held that s.146(1) of the Code did not infringe s.15 of the Charter. Three judges held that s.146(1) of the Code did infringe s.15 of the Charter but was saved as a reasonable limit under s.1 of the Charter. None of the judges treated s.28 of the Charter as relevant.

26. *CC's* case concerned s.1(1) of Ireland's Criminal Law (Amendment) Act 1935. That section provided:

> "Any person who unlawfully and carnally knows any girl under the age of fifteen years shall be guilty of a felony, and shall be liable on conviction thereof to penal servitude for life or for any term not less than three years or to imprisonment for any term not exceeding two years."

Michael M's and *Nguyen's* cases were discussed, but the decision in *CC's* case did not turn on equality. It was held that the form of absolute liability provided in s.1(1) of the 1935 Act was, in all the circumstances, inconsistent with the Irish Constitution. And–in a strongly worded judgment which we bear in mind even more on the question of arbitrariness than on that of inequality–it was declared that that subsection was inconsistent with the provisions of that constitution.

27. We have examined the reasoning behind the majority and minority views in *Michael M's* case. And we have examined the reasoning in *Nguyen's* case, both for the view that equality was not infringed and for the view that it was infringed but justifiably so. Various considerations were canvassed. These included: the problem of teenage pregnancies; not criminalising the female's conduct because that might deter her from reporting the matter; the legislature's role in resolving issues engaging society's code of sexual morality; and the extent to which it was for the legislature to form a view on issues such as whether the initiative in these matters is generally taken by the male, often older than the female, sometimes very considerably so.

28. Considerations of that kind are ones which the legislature are entitled to take into account and weigh. In our view, the legislation under challenge, while it departs from identical treatment, is justified by reference to genuine need, rationality and proportionality. It does not violate the equality guarantees of the constitution. In so holding we are not deferring to the legislature. Rather are we acknowledging the legislature's proper role.

29. Accordingly the complaint of inequality fails.

Complaint of arbitrariness

30. We now turn to consider the complaint of arbitrariness. The essence of this complaint lies, as we have indicated, in Mr Dykes's argument that absolute liability under s.124 is not only harsh but harsh to no useful purpose since the criminal law does not deter people from doing what they believe to be lawful.

31. Arbitrariness was the basis of the constitutional challenges which this Court adjudicated upon in *Lau Cheong v. HKSAR* (2002) 5 HKCFAR 415. Two laws, one a rule of common law and the other a statutory provision, were attacked as unconstitutional for arbitrariness.

32. The common law rule was the one that intent to cause grievous bodily harm i.e. really serious injury sufficed for murder. And the statutory provision was s.2 of the Offences Against the Person Ordinance, Cap. 212, which lays down a mandatory sentence of life imprisonment for murder.

33. It was held that neither the "grievous bodily harm" rule nor mandatory life imprisonment for murder were arbitrary; and both were pronounced constitutional.

34. In arriving at those conclusions the Court in *Lau Cheong's* case examined what arbitrariness entails. This was done at pp 434C – 436B. The Court noted what the United Nations Human Rights Committee said in *Hugo van Alphen v. Netherlands* (Communication No. 305/1988, 23 July 1990), Official Records of the General Assembly, 45th Session, Supplement No. 40 (A/45/40) para. 5.8. Dealing with art. 9(1) of the International Covenant on Civil and Political Rights with which art. 5(1) of the Bill of Rights is identical, the Committee said "that 'arbitrariness'is not to be equated with 'against the law', but must be interpreted more broadly to include elements of inappropriateness, injustice and lack of predictability".

35. The Court also referred to this statement of Lord Cooke of Thorndon delivering the advice of the Privy Council in *Fok Lai Ying v. Governor in Council* [1997] HKLRD 810 at p.819G:

> "The expression 'arbitrary interference' can also extend to interference provided for under the law. The introduction of the concept of arbitrariness is intended to guarantee that even interference provided for by law should be in accordance with the provision, aims and objectives of the Covenant and should be, in any event, reasonable in the particular circumstances."

36. After a careful consideration and full appreciation of what arbitrariness entails, the Court held in *Lau Cheong's* case that neither the "grievous bodily harm" rule nor mandatory life imprisonment for murder were arbitrary and that both were constitutional.

37. Where the legislature has enacted an absolute offence, the judiciary will not strike down the offence merely on the basis of a view that it would be preferable for the offence to admit of a defence of belief or reasonable belief. The time may come when the legislature amends s.124 to provide some such defence. Additionally or alternatively, the legislature may enact that it be a condition of a prosecution being brought that the accused is older

than the girl, which appears to be the position in Canada.

38. Those and other legislative possibilities and permutations are matters fit for future public consultation and debate. But the question before the Court is whether, as things now stand, it is arbitrary for unlawful sexual intercourse with a girl under the age of 16 to be an absolute offence.

39. Imposing absolute liability is a strong course which the law is generally if not always reluctant to take. But it is not a course which the law is never willing to take whatever is to be achieved by it. We are unable to accept Mr Dykes's argument that absolute liability under s.124 would have no deterrent effect. The deterrent effect of the criminal law is not confined to deterring people from doing what they know is unlawful. It also encourages them to take care to avoid what may be unlawful. This idea is captured in the expression, used in the *Noise Control Authority v. Step In Ltd* (2005) 8 HKCFAR 113 at p.120H, "steer well away from the line between legality and illegality". In the context of s.124, care to avoid what may be unlawful and steering well away from the line between legality and illegality would add materially to the protection for young girls which the section provides.

40. Having regard to the vital importance of protecting young girls, and in all the circumstances, we feel unable to say that imposing absolute liability for unlawful sexual intercourse with a girl under the age of 16 is arbitrary. It is a choice constitutionally open to the legislature.

41. Accordingly the complaint of arbitrariness fails.

42. We will turn in a moment to the matter of penalty, Mr Paul Harris SC for the respondent having said that it would be unjust to pass a sentence of imprisonment, whether immediate or suspended, on a person who is morally blameless in that he believed the girl to be aged 16 or older. Before turning to penalty, we mention this. At one stage of the argument Mr Dykes said that on the basis of absolute liability the stigma of a conviction would of itself be degrading. But when asked if he submitted that such a conviction would amount to "degrading treatment" within the meaning of and as prohibited by art. 3 of the Bill of Rights, Mr Dykes said that he would be loath to so submit. He did not proceed to so submit, and we say no more on the point.

Penalty

43. In the light of what Mr Harris said about penalty, Mr Dykes indicated that, if this appeal against conviction were to fail, his client, on whom the magistrate passed a suspended sentence of imprisonment, would go to the High Court for leave to appeal against sentence out of time. Under s.118(1)(d) of the Magistrates Ordinance, Cap. 227, it would be open to the High Court to direct that such an appeal be argued before Court of Appeal. Of course, Mr Dykes observed, none of that would be necessary if, in the event of this appeal against conviction failing, the Secretary for Justice were to apply to the Court of Appeal under s.81A of the Criminal Procedure Ordinance, Cap. 221, for a review of the sentence on the ground that it is manifestly excessive.

44. It is obviously undesirable in the circumstances for us to say anything more about penalty, and we refrain from doing so.

Conclusion

45. In the result, we hold that s.124 of the Crimes Ordinance is constitutional even though the offence thereunder is one of absolute liability. The constitutional challenge on which it is based having failed, we would dismiss this appeal against conviction.

Mr Justice Ribeiro PJ:

46. I agree with the joint judgment of Mr Justice Bokhary PJ and Mr Justice Chan PJ.

Sir Anthony Mason NPJ:

47. I agree with the joint judgment of Mr Justice Bokhary PJ and Mr Justice Chan PJ.

Chief Justice Li:

48. The Court unanimously dismisses this appeal against conviction.

Chief Justice (Andrew Li)

Permanent Judge (Kemal Bokhary)

Permanent Judge (Patrick Chan)

Permanent Judge (R A V Ribeiro)

Non-Permanent Judge (Sir Anthony Mason)

Mr Philip Dykes SC and Mr Joseph Tse SC (instructed by Messrs Ho & Ip and assigned by the Legal Aid Department) for the appellant

Mr Paul Harris SC (instructed by the Department of Justice) and Mr David Leung and Ms Mickey Fung (both of that Department) for the respondent

---

第二十六條

香港特別行政區永久性居民依法享有選舉權和被選舉權。

案例

申請司法覆核的條件

莫泰基 對 香港特區政府政制事務局、選舉管理委員會及選舉署

HCAL 129/2004；CACV 343/2004

簡略案情

申請人認為立法會功能界別選舉的自動當選制度違反《基本法》第 26 條，遂向高等法院原訟法庭申請司法覆核許可。原訟法庭拒絕給予其申請許可。申請人於是向上訴庭提出上訴。根據該自動當選制度，若某功能界別只有一名候選人，選舉主任就會宣佈這名候選人當選，而該界別的選民不需要投票。申請人指自動當選制度是違反《基本法》第 26 條賦予香港永久居民的選舉權利及《公民權利和政治權利國際公約》第 25 條（即《香港人權法案》第 21 條）的同一性質權利。申請人指他曾經寫信給政府部門，包括香港特區政府政制事務局、選舉管理委員會及選舉署，要求不要公開宣佈確認自動當選的 11 位候選人，但有關部門沒有回應他的要求，這 11 位候選人已被宣佈當選及已成為立法會議員。

裁決摘要

上訴庭認為申請人既無足夠的權益，亦無充分的理據去支持他的申請。根據《高等法院規則》第 53 號命令第 3（7）條規則，對有關覆核事項，申請人必須有“足夠權益”，才能作司法覆核申請。然而，申請人並非以功能界別選民身份提出是次申請，他甚至不能肯定自己是否屬於某一功能界別，在這情況下，法院認定申請人並沒有足夠的權益對該制度作出爭議。至於申請人司法覆核的理據，法院認為亦不充分。法院指出在某功能界別只有一名候選人參選的情況下，選民是不可能有其他的選擇，候選人因此而自動當選也是理所當然的事，並沒有抵觸《基本法》第 26 條。最後，該上訴被駁回。

CACV 343/2004

香港特別行政區
高等法院上訴法庭
民事司法管轄權
民事上訴

案件編號：民事上訴案件 2004 年第 343 號
（原高等法院憲法及行政訴訟 2004 年第 129 號）

申請人　莫泰基
對
答辯人　香港特區政府政制事務局，
選舉管理委員會及選舉署

審理法官：高等法院上訴法庭法官張澤祐
高等法院上訴法庭法官袁家寧

聆訊日期：2005 年 1 月 21 日

判案書日期：2005 年 1 月 27 日

判決書

上訴法庭法官張澤祐頒發上訴法庭判案書：

1. 申請人向高等法院原訟法庭申請許可進行司法覆核，原訟法庭法官朱芬齡拒絕給予許可。申請人現就該裁決提出上訴。

自動當選制度

2. 申請人擬進行司法覆核的議題是有關立法會功能界別選舉候選人自動當選之事。在該制度下，若某功能界別只有一名候選人，選舉主任就會宣布這名候選人當選，而該界別的選民不需要投票選舉。申請人指自動當選制度是違反《基本法》第 26 條賦予香港永久居民的選舉權利及《公民權利和政治權利國際公約》第 25 條（即《香港人權法案》第 21 條）的同一性質的權利。申請人指他曾經寫信給政府部門，包括香港特區政府政制事務局、選舉管理委員會及選舉署，要求不要公開宣布確認自動當選的十一位候選人，但有關的部門沒有回應他的要求，這十一位候選人已被宣布當選及已成為立法會議員。

申請人無足夠權益

3. 司法覆核申請是一項特殊的程序，法律已經清楚說明，不是任何一位市民都可以根據這程序挑戰公眾事項。這類申請的其中一項先決條件是申請人必須證明他有“足夠權益”挑戰有關的事項，見：《高等法院規則》第 53 號命令第 3(7) 條規則。

4. 申請人指他是以香港永久居民身份及立法會選民的身份，而不是以功能界別選民身份提出是次申請，他指他不肯定自己是否屬於某一功能界別。本庭認為申請人單以香港永久居民及立法會選民的身份提出這次申請是不足夠的，因為這兩項身份都不能顯示他在功能界別選舉中具有足夠的權益，以致因權益受到損害而可以挑戰有關的事項。除非申請人可以提出他是屬於某個功能界別的證明，而該界別的唯一候選人是在自動當選的情況下獲選，否則申請人是不能提出司法覆核。

申請無充分的理由

5. 就算申請人具有足夠的權益，本庭不認為他就本申請提出了充分的理由以致法庭需要給予他進行司法覆核申請的許可。《基本法》第 26 條說明香港特別行政區永久性居民依法享有選舉權和被選舉權。另外，有關的國際公約亦賦予同樣的權利。本庭不認同申請人所說，自動當選是有違有關的權利。

6. 若某個功能界別有超過一名的候選人參選，這當然要經過正式的選舉過程來決定誰人當選。但若該功能界別只有一名候選人參選，這即是沒有其他候選人與他競爭。在這情況下，選民是沒有其他的選擇，而這名候選人獲自動當選也是理所當然的事。香港不是實行強制性的選舉制度，不能硬性規定每一位選民都要在選舉日進行投票。在這情況下，要求某一功能界別的選民在單一候選人的選舉中投票是沒有意義的，而這名單一候選人獲自動當選和選民的選舉權是沒有抵觸的。

7. 就算該界別的其他選民不投票或投廢票，但該候選人自己也有投票權，他亦可以憑自投的一票而獲選，故此自動當選制度沒有任何不公之處。

8. 申請人提出在澳門特別行政區行政首長的選舉中，就算在只得一名單一候選人參選的情況下，選舉團仍必須進行投票選舉。本庭認為每個選舉制度不同，不可以一概而論。申請人亦指當選的十一位人士在立法會的表現不佳，有違《基本法》及影響香港在國際的聲譽。本庭認為這兩項理由並不足以說服法庭批准他就有關的事項進行司法覆核申請。

總結

9. 本庭認為朱法官的裁決是正確的，故此本庭駁回申請人的上訴及不對訟費作出任何命令。

高等法院上訴法庭法官（張澤祐）

高等法院上訴法庭法官（袁家寧）

申請人，無律師代表，親自出席。

第二十七條

香港居民享有言論、新聞、出版的自由，結社、集會、游行、示威的自由，組織和參加工會、罷工的權利和自由。

案例

The Democratic Party v. The Secretary For Justice

民主黨 對 律政司司長

HCAL 84/2006

簡略案情

根據《公司條例》第 95 條，所有公司必須存有一本包括所有成員名字和地址的成員登記冊。而《公司條例》第 98 條再規定，所有公司必須允許他人查閱此登記冊。1994 年，一群有著共同政治理念的人以"民主黨"為名、並以有限公司形式成立了該黨，即本案的申請人。所有的黨員將會是公司的成員，換言之，成員登記冊亦即是黨員登記冊。因此，任何人想了解該黨成員身份，只需要行使《公司條例》第 98 條賦予的權利便可。然而，該黨黨員並不想向大眾公開自已身份，擔心因為他們的理念而受到他人不友善的對待。因此，申請人向法院申請，宣佈《公司條例》第 98 條的規管不能施加於政黨上，否則便違反了《基本法》第 27 條和第 30 條及違反了《香港人權法案》第 14 條和第 18 條，即結社自由和私隱的基本保護。

申請人提出，因為政治團體的敏感性，沒有限制的第 98 條，在程度上超出了其需要達到的合理目的。申請人作為政治團體，沒有營商性質，所以沒必要受到第 98 條的約束。然而，答辯人卻認為任何跟申請人交往的公眾也應有權知道它的成員身份，而且，申請人不是純粹以有限公司為名去追求政治理想，實質上還包涵一定的經濟利益，其中包括接受捐獻、籌款、借貸和商業買賣等。

裁決摘要

"有限公司"是一個獨立法律個體，獨自對債權人承擔責任，而不是其背後的成員。因此，第 98 條的合理目的，是讓公眾在跟這些公司交往前，可以了解它們的成員的身份，從而在有足夠認識與信心下作出決定。而第 98 條的限制，正正為了達到這個目的。法庭不同意申請人認為第 98 條只針對純粹是商業性質的公司，反之，法庭接受答辯人的分析，申請人有限公司的身份包含了一定的經濟利益。所以，第 98 條對它的約束，如同對其他公司一樣，是有合理的基礎的。

在考慮申請人提出的結社自由和私隱保護問題時，法官引述了歐洲人權法院於 *United Communist Party Of Turkey v. Turkey* [1998] 26 EHRR 121 案中的一段判詞：

> 在民主社會裏，政黨的目標是讓市民對國家面臨的困難表達意見，並提出解決的方案從而讓政府去採納。這一種精神不止適用於被肯定接受的、被認定為非冒犯性的或者是無足輕重的意見，還應包括那些冒犯性的、震撼性和困擾性的。這是多元化、包容與寬宏所需要的。沒有這些，

便沒有“民主社會”。

法庭確認，結社自由受《基本法》第 27 條和《香港人權法案》第 18 條的一致保護。但重申，這些保護並不是絕對的，是需要平衡各方利益的，而終審法院於*梁國雄*一案所釐定的均衡比例測試（Proportionality Test）正好作為考慮這平衡問題的標準。

在考慮平衡問題時，法官也注意到兩個方面：（1）並非任何情況下，申請人也要提供成員登記冊給予檢查。在濫用的情況下，法庭有酌情權拒絕依據第 98 條作出的要求；（2）在法律層面上，申請人並非被強迫以有限公司形式運作，它完全可以以另外一種方法存在，包括登記為社團，事實上歐洲人權法院在 *Le Compte, Van Leuven & De Meyere v. Belgium* [1981] 4 EHRR 1 裏也有相同的見解。現在申請人是一方面享受這選擇的好處，另方面又質疑它的壞處。

最後，法庭認為申請人現在的身份，是當時發起人的自由選擇，並非被強迫做出的選擇；而且，第 98 條亦有避免濫用的機制；因此，在平衡公眾利益的考慮下，認定《公司條例》第 98 條並不違憲。

HCAL 84/2006

IN THE HIGH COURT OF THE

HONG KONG SPECIAL ADMINISTRATIVE REGION

COURT OF FIRST INSTANCE

CONSTITUTIONAL AND ADMINISTRATIVE LAW LIST

NO. 84 OF 2006

Between:

THE DEMOCRATIC PARTY Applicant

- and -

THE SECRETARY FOR JUSTICE Respondent

Before: Hon Hartmann J in Court

Dates of Hearing: 26-28 March 2007

Date of Handing Down Judgment: 21 May 2007

JUDGMENT

Introduction

1. It is provided under the Companies Ordinance, Cap.32, that all companies must keep a register of members. S.95 of the Ordinance requires that, among other matters, a register must record the names and addresses of all m

embers.

2. It is further provided under the Ordinance that all companies must allow their registers to be inspected not only by persons who are members but also by the public; that is, by 'other persons' . Not only may members and other persons inspect the registers, they may require copies of them. S.98 of the Ordinance, the section which imposes these duties, provides for the imposition of civil and criminal sanctions if any inspection is refused or there is a failure to deliver up any requested copy of a register.

3. The purpose of these statutory requirements is fundamental. It arises, first, from the fact that a company is a separate legal person from its members, being liable for its own debts, and second, from the fact that the liability of the members is itself limited. That being the case, it has long been recognised that persons dealing with a company, if they are to trust that company, must be able to know who are its members; in short, who stands behind the company.

4. The linked concepts of separate juristic personality and limited liability may have their genesis in matters mercantile but today not all persons who come together in a body corporate do so purely for the purpose of trading in the market.

5. In 1994, a group of persons sharing common political ideas decided that they could best advance their interests by way of incorporation. In the result, under the name of the Democratic Party, they chose to be incorporated as a company limited by a guarantee, not having a share capital. That company is the applicant in this matter.

6. In choosing incorporation, the persons who at the time made up the Democratic Party also chose to order their affairs so that all persons becoming members of the political party would become members of the company. In short, the decision was made that membership of the political party and of the incorporated body would be one and the same.

7. In the result, upon incorporation, the register of members which the applicant is obliged to keep under s.95 of the Companies Ordinance, became at one and the same time both the register of members of the limited liability company and the register of members of the political party.

8. The consequence, of course, is that any person who wishes to learn the identity of the members of the political party need do no more than exercise his legal right under s.98 of the Companies Ordinance to inspect the applicant's register of members.

9. The applicant's members, however, do not accept that, in law, their political beliefs, and their affiliation with others to advance those beliefs, should be permitted to be laid open to the world in this way. On behalf of its members, the applicant has therefore brought the present application for judicial review. It has done so on the basis that s.98 of the Companies Ordinance, in so far as it gives to the public at large the legal right to inspect its register of members, undermines two constitutionally protected freedoms enjoyed by its members, the one being integral to the other; first, the freedom to associate with others and, second, the freedom to do so in circumstances in which there is no arbitrary interference with their privacy.

10. On behalf of the applicant it is said that very real inroads into these constitutionally protected freedoms are at stake. The Democratic Party advances political views that are not free from controversy. As a consequence, s.98 of the Companies Ordinance, in compelling revelation of the identity of all members, especially rank and file members, may leave those members open to various forms of hostility.

The factual background

11. The history of this application reveals that, in about mid–2006, the applicant received a number of requests from persons who were not members seeking to inspect and/or obtain copies of its register of members. It appears that the applicant was concerned as to the purpose behind these requests and did not accede, or did not immediately accede, to them.

12. At about the same time, the Companies Registry received enquiries from the press concerning the requirement of all companies to allow their register of members to be inspected, asking what enforcement action the Registry may take. On 24 May 2006, the Registrar wrote to the applicant and to two other political parties which had been incorporated. In the letter to the applicant, it was said that it had been brought to the Registrar's attention that the applicant's register may not have been made available for inspection. The letter continued with what may be described as a polite warning:

> "I would like to draw your attention to the provisions under sections 95 and 98 of the Companies Ordinance (the Ordinance) which require every company to keep a register of its members in its registered office and to make the same available for public inspection.
>
> Please be reminded that it is the obligation of the company and its officers to observe and comply with the statutory requirements in various provisions of the Ordinance, including sections 95 and 98, failing which the company and every officer in default will be liable to

prosecution..."

13. In light of these developments, the applicant canvassed the views of its current and past members. A significant number objected to the register being made available for general scrutiny. Indeed, in his affirmation of 31 July 2006, the applicant's chairman, Mr Lee Wing Tat, said that 'subsequently' 18 members withdrew their memberships.

14. In July 2006, fearing that the Registrar's warning letter would inevitably be followed by civil or criminal proceedings, the applicant sought leave to apply for judicial review.

15. Although it originally sought wider ranging remedies, in the end result the applicant sought only a declaration to the following effect:

> "...that s.98 of the Ordinance, to the extent that it applies to the political parties of Hong Kong which are registered as limited companies under the Ordinance, are inconsistent with arts. 27 and 30 of the Basic Law and arts. 14 and 18 of the Hong Kong Bill of Rights and are unconstitutional."

The central issue: has a fair balance been struck?

16. On behalf of the applicant, its leading counsel, Mr Erik Shum, accepted that the lawful regulation of corporate bodies may have to result in some diminishment of the fundamental interlocked freedoms of people to associate together in private. He contended, however, that, in respect of political parties, bearing in mind the special but sensitive role they play in our society, the unrestricted provisions of s.98 are not proportionate to any legitimate aim that the provisions seek to achieve.

17. Tensions of the kind exhibited in this case are not unusual in a modern, democratic society. What is to be sought, of course, is a fair balance between the demands of the legitimate interests of society and the requirements of the protection of an individual's fundamental rights. Whether in any particular case that fair balance is achieved is determined in Hong Kong, as it is in many other jurisdictions, by the use of what is called the proportionality test.

18. In my judgment, this application for judicial review falls squarely to be determined by the use of that test. I will come to its mechanics later in this judgment. But, as in the determination of all disputed matters of law, context–legal and factual–is everything. The context, therefore, must first be set.

Looking to the Companies Ordinance

19. As I have said earlier, a company is a separate legal person from its members. S.5A of the Companies Ordinance states that a company has the capacity and rights, the powers and privileges of a natural person. It may do anything which is permitted by its memorandum of association.

20. Once created, a company becomes a separate legal person from its members; it becomes a body endowed with perpetual succession. S.16(2) of the Ordinance states that:

> "From the date of incorporation mentioned in the certificate of incorporation, the subscribers of the memorandum, together with such other persons as may from time to time become members of the company, shall be a body corporate by the name contained in the memorandum, capable forthwith of exercising all the functions of an incorporated company, and having perpetual succession and a common seal, but with such liability on the part of the members to contribute to the assets of the company in the event of its being wound up as is mentioned in this Ordinance."

21. In terms of s.28 of the Ordinance, the members of a company are those persons who initially subscribe to its memorandum and those who subsequently agree to become members and have their names entered in the company's register of members. It is the act of entry into the register which constitutes both the taking on of membership and proof of that membership.

22. The sections of the Companies Ordinance of immediate relevance in the present matter are ss.95 and 98.

23. Under s.95, every company is required to keep a register of members. The register must contain specific information concerning the members. In this regard, s.95(1) directs that the register must contain:

> (a) the names and addresses of the members, and in the case of a company having a share capital a statement of the shares held by each member, distinguishing each share by its number so long as the share has a number, and of the amount paid or agreed to be considered as paid on the shares of each member;
>
> (b) the date at which each person was entered in the register as a member;
>
> (c) the date at which any person ceased to be a member:

24. It is important to recognise that information concerning those who have ceased to be members must be retained on the register and may only be destroyed after 30 years: see s.95(1) (c) (ii) .

25. The applicant does not challenge the constitutionality of the requirement to keep a register. The keeping is not its concern. Its concern is the obligation under s.98 to make the register available to all persons, whatever their purpose. In this regard, s.98(1) lays down the requirement to make the register available for inspection. In so far as relevant, it reads:

> "... the register, and the index of names, of the members of a company shall during business hours be open to the inspection of any member without charge and of any other person on payment of the appropriate fee..."[my emphasis]

26. S.98(2) lays down the requirement to deliver a copy of the register to any person who asks for it. It reads:

> "Any member of other person may require a copy of the register, or of any part thereof, on payment of the appropriate fee specified in the Fourteenth Schedule, or such less sum as the company may prescribe. The company shall cause any copy so required by any person to be sent to that person within a period of 10 days commencing on the day next after the day on which the requirement is received by the company." [my emphasis]

27. To refuse inspection or to refuse to deliver up a copy of the register may have criminal consequences. S.98(3) states:

> "If any inspection required under this section is refused or if any copy required under this section is not sent within the proper period, the company and every officer of the company who is in default shall be liable in respect of each offence to a fine and, for continued default, to a

daily default fine."

28. There may be civil consequences too. S.98(4) directs that:

> "In the case of any such refusal or default, the court may by order compel an immediate inspection of the register and index or direct that the copies required shall be sent to the persons requiring them." [my emphasis]

29. It is important, I think, to emphasise that the provisions of ss.95 and 98 apply to all companies irrespective of whether they are public or private and irrespective of their primary objects. The Companies Ordinance does not seek to regulate the nature of what companies may seek to do provided what they seek to do is lawful. The regulatory scheme contained in ss.95 and 98 applies therefore to companies in so far as they are companies.

The purpose of s.98

30. The register of members is a fundamentally important document because it is the document which proves the identity of the members of a company. As for the members, they are the persons who stand behind a company. They constitute the flesh and blood, the character of a company; they constitute its will. It is unlikely that a potential creditor, donor, partner or associate will place trust in a company if he can place no trust in its members.

31. It is for this reason that the Ordinance not only requires that every company must keep a register of members but that the register should be open to public scrutiny. In England, this requirement for public scrutiny was first contained in an Act of 1862. Shortly thereafter, Lord Cranworth, in his speech in *Oakes v. Turquand and Harding* (1867) LR 2 HL 325, at 366, explained the legislative intention behind the requirement in the following terms:

> "There is a similar obligation in the Act of 1862 as to keeping a register; but there is an important change; for, by the 32nd section of that Act, it is provided that the register shall be open to the inspection not only of shareholders, but, on payment of one shilling, of all other persons, which would therefore include creditors. This seems to me strongly to indicate the intention of the Legislature that the creditor were to look to this document as shewing them to what extent they might trust the company. Before the introduction of the principle of limited liability such a power of inspection was not necessary, or, certainly, not at all so necessary. A creditor could hardly fail to know who were some at least of the shareholders, and there was no limit to the extent to which he might obtain execution against shareholders of wealth. *But when the Legislature enabled shareholders to limit their liability, not merely to the amount of their shares, but to so much of that amount as should remain unpaid, it is obvious that no creditor could safely trust the company without having the means of ascertaining, first, who the shareholders might be, and, secondly, to what extent they would be liable. This is obviously the reason why the new statute opened the register to the inspection of all the world, indicating, as I think, very clearly that persons dealing with the company might trust to that register as containing a true exposition of the assets they had to rely on.*" [my emphasis]

32. During the course of submissions, it was suggested by Mr Erik Shum, leading counsel for the applicant, that the only valid reason why a register of members should be made open for inspection had to be commercial in nature. Essentially, he said, it was for the protection of persons who were, or stood to be, creditors. In my judgment, having regard to the fact that all manner of companies are incorporated today, that submission goes too far.

33. In his written submissions, Mr Benjamin Yu SC, leading counsel for the respondent, set out why it is that knowing who stands behind a company is important, not only for those who stand in the relationship of creditor to a company but for others too. I can do no better than adopt his words. It is natural, he said, that a third party who wishes to have dealings with a company–no matter of what nature–may wish to ascertain who lies behind, and is protected by, the corporate front. A third party may wish to know whether he agrees with the philosophy of the persons behind a company; whether the company is backed by many or few members; whether the members include particular persons, and so on. He may wish to have this information prior to dealing with the company, or even after having entered into relations with the company. He may wish to have this information when considering, for example, whether to make a donation to a company or take legal action against the company.

The applicant too has commercial objects

34. In any event, as Mr Yu emphasised, the members of the applicant do enjoy the benefit of limited liability in respect of commercial matters. That is because the applicant's memorandum of association, in addition to setting out objects of a political nature, sets out a substantial number of objects which enable it to act in the economic sphere. These objects are, in part, listed in para.3(q) of the memorandum of association as follows:

> "(i) to accept and receive donations, subscriptions and gifts from persons, corporations or organizations for any one or more of the objects set out in the foregoing and to give receipts therefor;
>
> (ii) to organize fund-raising projects and activities to promote, demonstrate, support and carry out any of the above objects and to pay and discharge payments and expenses incurred for such projects and activities;
>
> (iii) to organize campaigns and activities to promote, demonstrate, support and carry out any of the above objects and to pay and discharge payments and expenses incurred for such campaigns and activities;
>
> (iv) to purchase, sell, lease, mortgage, improve, manage or otherwise dispose of or deal in land, houses or other properties, whether leaseholds or otherwise and whether movable or immovable;
>
> (v) to borrow any money required for the purposes of the Party with or without security;
>
> (vi) to hire and employ all classes of persons necessary or expedient for the purposes of the Party and to pay them in return for the services rendered to the Party, salaries, wages, allowances and pensions in accordance with the laws governing employment for the time being in force in Hong Kong;
>
> (vii) to invest and deal with the money of the Party which is not immediately required in such manner as may from time to time be thought fit..."

35. It will be seen, therefore, that the memorandum of association anticipates the applicant receiving donations, borrowing money and entering into commercial agreements; in short, with the benefits of incorporation, participating in financial and commercial ventures of various kinds.

36. As to the issue of the members enjoying limited liability, para.6 of the memorandum of association reads:

> Every member of the Party undertakes to contribute to the assets of the Party, in the event of the same being wound up while he is a member or within one year after he ceases to be a member, for payment of the debts or liabilities of the Party contracted before he ceases to be a member, and of the costs, charges and expenses of winding up, and for the adjustment of the rights of the contributories amongst themselves, such amounts as may be required, not exceeding HK$10.00.

37. On the basis, therefore, that the applicant can, and no doubt does, use its corporate personality to advance not only its political objects but also its economic interests, Mr Yu submitted that there are good reasons why the provisions of s.98 of the Companies Ordinance should apply to it just as those provisions apply to all other corporate bodies.

Turning to the constitutionally protected freedoms

38. The applicant, as I have said, has based its application on the assertion that s.98 of the Ordinance–in so far as it applies to itself as a political party–is inconsistent with its members' freedom of association and freedom from arbitrary or unlawful interference with their privacy.

39. The two freedoms are to be read together, the one being essential to the other, because, of course, what is asserted by the applicant is that s.98 is inconsistent with the freedom of its members to associate together because it is inconsistent with their freedom to do so in private. In this regard, in *National Association for the Advancement of Coloured People v. Alabama* 357 U.S.449 (1958), the United States Supreme Court spoke of the vital relationship between freedom of association and privacy in one's associations. It went on to observe that 'inviolability of privacy in group association may in many circumstances be indispensable to preservation of freedom of association, particularly where a group espouses dissident beliefs' .

40. In considering these two freedoms in context, it must be recognised that political parties are a form of association essential to the proper functioning of an open, democratic society. In *United Communist Party of Turkey v. Turkey* (1998) 26 EHRR 121, the European Court of Human Rights observed:

> "In a democratic society, the aim of political parties is to enable citizens to express their views on all the problems facing the country, and to suggest concrete solutions which a government could adopt. This is applicable not only to opinions which are favourably received or regarded as inoffensive or as a matter of indifference, but also to those which offend, shock or disturb; such are the demands of that pluralism, tolerance and broad-mindedness without which there is no 'democratic society'."

Freedom of association

41. As to the fundamental right of freedom of association, art.27 of the Basic Law states that:

> "Hong Kong residents shall have freedom of speech, of the press and of publication; freedom of association, of assembly, of procession and of demonstration; and the right and freedom to form and join trade unions, and to strike."

42. Art.27 is complemented by art.18 of the Bill of Rights. The Bill of Rights is the incorporation into Hong Kong domestic law of the International Covenant on Civil and Political Rights ('the ICCPR'). That incorporation is constitutionally recognised by art.39 of the Basic Law. Art.18 itself, which is drawn in exact terms from art.22 of the ICCPR, provides that:

> "(1) Everyone shall have the right to freedom of association with others, including the right to form and join trade unions for the protection of his interests.
>
> (2) No restrictions may be placed on the exercise of this right other than those which are prescribed by law and which are necessary in a democratic society in the interests of national security or public safety, public *order* (ordre public), the protection of public health or morals or the protection of the rights and freedoms of others..."

43. The European Convention on Human Rights guarantees freedom of association. The jurisprudence of the European Commission (*Association X v. Sweden I* DR 1 (1978) E Com HR) defines the phrase as constituting a 'general capacity for citizens to join without interference by the state in association in order to attain various ends' . Those various ends, manifestly, include political ends.

44. In its judgment in *National Association for the Advancement of Coloured People v. Alabama*, the United States Supreme Court recognised that 'effective advocacy of both public and private points of view, particularly controversial ones, is undeniably enhanced by group association' . The Court went on to observe that:

> "It is beyond debate that freedom to engage in association for the advancement of beliefs and ideas is an inseparable aspect of the 'liberty' assured by the Due Process Clause of the Fourteenth Amendment, which embraces freedom of speech."

45. That being said, in respect of commercial activities, limitations on freedom of association which are necessary to protect the rights of others have been accepted as lawful. Some of the oldest recorded laws concern the regulation of the market place to ensure fairness. It is also one of the marks of a modern democratic society that its commercial markets, especially its financial markets, are transparent. In his commentary on the International Covenant on Civil and Political Rights, Dr Nowak has said (para.396):

> "With economic associations, all legal restrictions and ordinances under the commercial and trade law of the various socio–economic systems of the States Parties are permissible to protect the rights and freedoms of others (including property rights) to the extent that they may be deemed necessary in a democratic society."

46. While therefore the right to freedom of association is a fundamental constitutional right, it is not an absolute right.

47. In *Leung Kwok Hung and Others v. HKSAR* (2005) 8 HKCFAR 229,

the Court of Final Appeal, in considering the right to freedom of assembly, held that it was closely related to and overlaps with the freedoms of association, procession and demonstration. In the constitutional context, the Court held that there was no difference between the right of peaceful assembly guaranteed by the Basic Law and that provided for in the Bill of Rights.

48. By comparing the provisions of the Basic Law and Bill of Rights concerning freedom of association with the provisions in respect of freedom of assembly, I am satisfied that I can come to the same determination in respect of freedom of association; namely that there is no difference between the right guaranteed by the Basic Law and that provided for in the Bill of Rights.

49. Accordingly, as a right that is not an absolute right, freedom of association, whether under the Basic Law or the Bill of Rights, may be subject to restrictions provided two requirements are satisfied:

(i) The restriction must be prescribed by law.

(ii) The restriction (following the wording of art.18(2) of the Bill of Rights) must be necessary in a democratic society in the interests of national security or public safety, public order (*ordre public*), the protection of public health or morals or the protection of the rights and freedoms of others.

50. The first requirement; namely, that the restriction must be prescribed by law, presents no difficulties. The provisions of ss.95 and 98 of the Companies Ordinance have been accessible to the public over a long period of time. They are worded in precise, plain language.

51. The second requirement presents more difficulties. Its determination is the core issue in this matter. In respect of associations, such as political parties which choose to incorporate, do the provisions of s.98 achieve a fair balance between the legitimate interests of society and the requirement to protect fundamental freedoms accruing to every individual? That question, as I have said earlier, requires the application of the proportionality test.

The formulation of the proportionality test in the present case

52. In *Leung Kwok Hung and Others v. HKSAR*, the Court of Final Appeal, in respect of the right of assembly, said that the proportionality test should be formulated in the following terms:

(i) The restriction must be rationally connected with one or more of the legitimate purposes, and

(ii) The means used to impair the right of peaceful assembly must be no more than is necessary to accomplish the legitimate purpose in question.

53. Bearing in mind the similarities between the provisions concerning the right of assembly and freedom of association, I shall later in this judgment employ the same two-stage test.

The right to privacy

54. As to what may broadly be called the right to privacy, art.30 of the Basic Law states that:

"The freedom and privacy of communication of Hong Kong residents shall be protected by law. No department or individual may, on any grounds, infringe upon the freedom and privacy of communication of residents except that the relevant authorities may inspect communication in accordance with legal procedures to meet the needs of public security or of investigation into criminal offences."

55. It will be seen that art.30 does not seek to protect privacy simpliciter. It is more narrow in its scope. Art.30 protects only the right of Hong Kong residents freely and in private to communicate with others whether by the spoken word, in writing or by telecommunication. It includes therefore the right of persons who wish to associate together to attain a common goal to communicate with each other freely and in private. To that extent, it may be said that the right to freely associate must include the right to communicate, the one right being an essential part of the other.

56. Art.14 of the Bill of Rights, taken in exact terms from art.17 of the ICCPR, is drawn more widely. It reads:

"(1) No one shall be subjected to arbitrary or unlawful interference with his privacy, family, home or correspondence, nor to unlawful attacks on his honour and reputation.

(2) Everyone has the right to the protection of the law against such interference or attacks."

57. 'Privacy' is not the easiest concept to reduce to a legal definition. It speaks, of course, of that part of every person's life in which, without imposing on the rights and freedoms of others, personal autonomy may be expressed. It is that secluded part of every person's life in which, without outside interference, he or she may act independently. Privacy, in its intimacy, is normally to be enjoyed in the seclusion of family, home and friends. As a recognition of the independent nature of every individual, it is closely associated with the right to the protection of honour and reputation. In an article published in 'The International Bill of Rights' (Columbia University Press, edited by Louis Henkin), Femando Volio described it as a kind of 'spiritual zone' .

58. Art.8 of the European Convention, does not speak of 'privacy' but speaks instead of 'private life' . The two concepts, however, have been held to be indistinguishable. In *Niemietz v. Germany* (1992) 16 EHRR 97, para.29, the European Court did not consider it necessary to attempt an exhaustive definition of the notion of 'private life' . But the Court did say that:

"However, it would be too restrictive to limit the notion to an 'inner circle' in which the individual may live his own personal life as he chooses and to exclude therefrom entirely the outside world not encompassed within that circle. Respect for private life must also comprise to a certain degree the right to establish and develop relationships with other human beings.

There appears, furthermore, to be no reason of principle why this understanding of the notion of 'private life'should be taken to exclude activities of a professional or business nature since it is, after all, in the course of their working lives that the majority of people have a significant, if not the greatest, opportunity of developing relationships with the outside world."

59. Privacy in plain terms may be described as every individual's area of 'private space' . But, as such, of course, it has its limits. In respect of the present case, this has two consequences. First, it does not necessarily encompass every aspect of a person's life that he might wish to keep private: see *X. v. Iceland* (1993) 16

EHRR 97, at para.29. Second, respect for an individual's privacy will be narrower when it is brought into contact with public life or is in conflict with other protected interests. In this latter regard, in *Bruggerman and Scheuten v. Federal Republic of Germany* (1981) 3 EHRR 244, at paras.55 and 56, the European Commission said:

> "The right to respect for private life is of such a scope as to secure to the individual a sphere within which he can freely pursue the development and fulfilment of his personality. To this effect, he must also have the possibility of establishing relationships of various kinds, including sexual, with other persons. In principle, therefore, whenever the State sets up rules for the behaviour of the individual within this sphere, it interferes with the respect for private life and such interference must be justified in the light of Article 8(2) .
>
> However, there are limits to the personal sphere. While a large proportion of the law existing in a given State has some immediate or remote effect on the individual's possibility of developing his personality by doing what he wants to do, not all of these can be considered to constitute an interference with private life in the sense of Article 8 of the Convention. In fact, as the earlier jurisprudence of the Commission has already shown, *the claim to respect for private life is automatically reduced to the extent that the individual himself brings his private life into contact with public life or into close connection with other protected interests*." [my emphasis]

60. In my judgment, 'public life', as the term is contrasted with 'private life' in *Bruggerman and Scheuten v. Federal Republic of Germany*, must include life in the market place. As I have said earlier, it is one of the marks of a modern democratic society that its commercial markets, especially its financial markets, are transparent. In that sense transparency is the opposite to privacy. Put simply, it must be axiomatic, I think, that if a person seeks to deal in the market place, he must expect that the rules governing his conduct–rules intended to secure fairness for all–will impinge on his right to privacy. Doing business in the market place is not a private matter. Rights of privacy, however, should only be extended to those areas of life in respect of which a person has a reasonable expectation of privacy.

61. Art.14 of the Bill of Rights recognises, of course, that the right to privacy is not absolute. As with the right of freedom of association, it may be subject to limitations. In this regard, art.14 provides that no one shall be subjected to 'unlawful' or 'arbitrary' interference with his privacy.

62. The term 'unlawful', as it appears in the article, means that there can be no interference unless envisaged by law. In the present case, there is no dispute that the interference is envisaged by law. That is set out in plain terms in ss.95 and 98 of the Companies Ordinance.

63. The term 'arbitrary' may extend to an interference which is envisaged by law but is nevertheless capricious; an interference, for example, that is found to amount to an abuse of power.

64. The use of the terms 'unlawful' and 'arbitrary' implies, as with the right of freedom of association, that, in cases such as the present one, a fair balance must be sought between the demands of the general interests of society and the requirements of the protection of an individual's fundamental rights. The machinery to be employed in achieving that balance is the proportionality test.

65. Again, I believe, I can use the same two–stage proportionality test, formulating it in respect of the right to privacy, in the following terms:

> (i) The restriction must be rationally connected with one or more of the legitimate purposes, and
>
> (ii) the means used to impair the right of privacy must be no more than is necessary to accomplish the legitimate purpose in question.

Is the applicant powerless to prevent inspection of its register?

66. A factor of considerable relevance to the test of proportionality is the extent to which the fundamental rights in question are restricted.

67. If the law provides measures by which the seriousness of a restriction may, in appropriate circumstances, be limited, that, it seems to me, is a matter of considerable relevance; indeed, perhaps determinative.

68. As I have understood it, however, it is integral to the applicant's case that, in terms of s.98 of the Companies Ordinance, it has no power to prevent a member of the public inspecting its register of members even if the purpose of the inspection is so divorced from the purposes contemplated by the Ordinance as to amount to an abuse of the legal rights bestowed by that section.

69. In my judgment, however, the applicant is not left without any form of defence against demands to scrutinise its register which amount to an abuse. On a true construction of s.98, I am satisfied that persons who demand access to the register do not have an absolute right to do so, their reasons for demanding access being irrelevant to the exercise of that right. On a purposive construction of s.98, I am satisfied that it is not as supine as counsel for the applicant suggested.

70. S.98(1) of the Ordinance obliges a company to leave its register of members open for inspection both by members and third parties. S.98(2) directs that, if required by members or third parties, the company must supply a copy of the register to any member or third party who seeks it. A failure to comply with the obligations imposed under ss.98(1) and 98(2) attracts criminal liability. Clearly, therefore, s.98 creates a legal right on the part of members and third parties to be able to inspect the register and to obtain a copy of it. But s.98(4), in my judgment, on a true construction, reveals the legislative intention that the right should not be absolute. I say that because s.98(4) gives to the courts a discretion whether or not to make an order compelling inspection or delivery up. To cite it again, s.98(4) reads:

> "In the case of any such refusal or default, the court may by order compel an immediate inspection of the register and index or direct that the copies required shall be sent to the persons requiring them." [my emphasis]

71. Read in context, the discretion to refuse an order under s.98(4) may be a narrow one but, in my judgment, the courts must be able to exercise that discretion, either by refusing to make an order or by making one in qualified terms.

72. That a discretion under s.98(4) does exist has been pronounced by the Court of Appeal in *Pelling v. Families Need Fathers Ltd* [2002] 2 All ER 440, a judgment concerning provisions under the English statute; namely, s.356 of the Companies Act 1985, which is

to the same purpose and effect and almost identical in language to our s.98. S.356 of the English statute obliges companies to keep their register of members open for inspection and, upon request, to supply copies of the register to any member or other person. A failure to do so attracts criminal liability. S.356(6), however, gives to the courts the same discretion as that provided by s.98(4) of our Ordinance; that is, the discretion to refuse to make any order compelling inspection or delivery up. S.356(6) reads:

> "In the case of such refusal or default, the court may by order compel an immediate inspection of the register and index, or direct that the copies required be sent to the persons requiring them."

73. In giving the judgment of the Court of Appeal, Mummery LJ observed that the word 'may' appearing in the sub-section was normally to be read as conferring a discretionary power. He recognised that there are certain situations where a discretionary power is conferred for the purpose of enforcing a right and is coupled with an obligation to exercise that power only for the benefit of the person who possesses that right. But the word as it appeared in the sub-section, he said, was not to be construed in that manner. In this regard, he adopted the reasoning contained in an Australian judgment, *O' Brien v. Sporting Shooters Association of Australia (Victoria)* [1999] 2 VR 255, at 255, where Byrne J rejected the submission that the court had no discretion under a similarly-worded provision in s.1303 of the Australian Corporations Law. It was submitted to Byrne J that the word 'may' in that section was not permissive but merely signified that the jurisdiction of the court to make an order did not arise until there had been a contravention of the Law. Byrne J (at 255) held that –

> "the word 'may' means exactly that. It means that the court is empowered to make the order where a refusal in contravention of the Law has been established, as in the present case. Whether the power will be exercised must depend upon the proper discretionary considerations affecting the power in the light of the facts as are found by the court."

74. As to the discretion conferred by s.356(6) of the English statute, Mummery J held that the courts will generally make a mandatory order to give effect to the legal right conferred by the statute to seek inspection of the register of members or to obtain copies of it. But he went on to say that the legal right was not an unqualified one. As he expressed it:

> "There may be something special in the circumstances of the case which leads the court to refuse to make the usual order."

75. In whatever manner, s.98(4) of the Ordinance may have been construed in the past, I am satisfied that, since the coming into effect of the Basic Law, a purposive construction, indeed, in so far as it necessary, a remedial construction, is appropriate.

76. S.2A(1) of the General Clauses Ordinance, Cap.1, directs that:

> "All laws previously in force shall be construed with such modifications, adaptations, limitations and exceptions as may be necessary so as not to contravene the Basic Law..."

77. As to this court's power, in so far as is necessary, to employ a remedial interpretation, the matter has been placed beyond doubt by the Court of Final Appeal in its judgment in *HKSAR v. Lam Kwong Wai and Another* [2006] 3 HKLRD 808 in which, Mason NPJ said the following (para.73):

> "In the context of the Basic Law, which arms the HKSAR with a modern constitution including entrenched rights and freedoms, the concept of judicial power necessarily includes the making of remedial interpretations in the sense already discussed. It is recognized as an incident of the exercise of judicial power in other jurisdictions."

78. I am therefore satisfied that, if a demand is made for an inspection of the register of members of a company or for receipt of a copy of it, for purposes which amount to an abuse, in the sense that I have earlier used the term, a court has the power under s.98(4) to refuse to compel compliance with the demand.

79. I am further satisfied that, if a court concludes that a demand amounts to an abuse, that will not only go to any civil liability under s.98(4) but also to any criminal liability under s.98(3).

80. In summary, therefore, I am satisfied that, in certain important circumstances, s.98 does give to the applicant the means by which it may limit the seriousness of any restriction that the section places on the freedom of its members to associate in private.

The issue of choice

81. During the course of submissions, there was considerable argument on what I will call the issue of choice.

82. Mr Yu, for the respondent, raised the issue in the following way. In 1994, at the time when the decision was made to incorporate the Democratic Party, he said, the members of the political party had a number of choices open to them. It was for them at the time to inform themselves as to the most appropriate choice or, if the choice subsequently proved to be wrong, to correct it.

83. Mr Yu pointed to the fact that at no material time has there been a statutory requirement for political parties to be incorporated or registered in any way. Nor is there legislation regulating the operation of political parties.

84. In this regard, I am told that the matter has been debated in the Legislative Assembly with opinions divided. The Administration has concluded that, at this moment in Hong Kong's history, the introduction of statutory controls may do more to hinder rather than facilitate the development of political parties.

85. Mr Yu accepted that incorporation presented a number of administrative and economic advantages. But he emphasised that there were other routes. The members of the party could, for example, have registered the party as a society under the Societies Ordinance, Cap.151. The evidence showed that several associations of a political nature had chosen this route. No doubt registration under the Societies Ordinance has disadvantages, he said, but equally no doubt it has advantages too. There would, for example, be no need to leave a register of members open to public scrutiny.

86. Mr Yu went on to say that, even with incorporation, the members of the Democratic Party had open to them a number of alternatives as to how best to arrange matters so as to protect the anonymity of those, especially rank and file members, who did not wish the world to know of their affiliation. He set out a number of possibilities. It is, I think, sufficient to briefly map out two:

> (1) There was no need, he said, for all members of the political party to be members of the corporate body.

For example, founding members and office holders could constitute the membership. Rank and file members could be gathered under a separate scheme whereby they were members of the party, not the company.

(2) The Democratic Party, he said, could establish a company limited by share capital, and have each member own a share. When a member wants to remain 'off the register', the share may be held by a nominee. Indeed the Democratic Party could formally allocate a particular officer to hold shares on trust for those members who wish to remain 'off the register' . This would not affect members' voting rights.

87. These choices, said Mr Yu, would have ensured that the freedom of the applicant's members, certainly its rank and file members, to associate in private was not impinged. The applicant, however, had chosen the one way in which it was impinged. In such circumstances, having made its choice, the applicant had to accept the consequences of that choice.

88. Mr Shum did not contest that there had been, and remained, certain alternatives open to the applicant; effective and lawful alternatives, even if perhaps more cumbersome. Mr Shum, however, rejected the contention that, having made its choice, the applicant could not now be heard to complain. The right to freely associate in private, he said, was a right in a democratic society to do so in each and every way that the law provides. As it is, the law provides that the applicant may incorporate in the manner it has done. As such, having made that choice, the applicant was not obliged as a consequence to endure the diminishment of the fundamental freedoms of its members.

89. Mr Shum agreed that, if the choices open to the applicant all provided equal benefits, then there may be some validity in Mr Yu's submission. But, when each choice was problematic, each having advantages and drawbacks, then the 'you made your bed, you must lie on it' contention lost its validity. The applicant, said Mr Shum, was entitled to order its affairs as it saw best.

90. In my judgment, while there can be no hard and fast rule, if the state permits a choice, even if they do not all provide the exact same advantages, that must be a relevant factor in deciding whether there is a reasonable relationship of proportionality between the limitations that the state imposes; in this case, the obligations imposed by s.98, and the legitimate objectives that the limitations seek to attain.

91. In coming to this conclusion, I start from the fundamental approach that matters concerning human rights demand a sensible determination. If, as Lord Woolf said in *Attorney General of Hong Kong v. Lee Kwong Kut* [1993] AC 951 PC, at 975, issues concerning a Bill of Rights should be approached 'with realism and good sense, and kept in proportion', it seems to me that, whether or not the state leaves open other viable options, must be a matter that can assist the court in determining whether there has been a violation of a protected right.

92. Although it was not cited in the course of submissions, I note that the European Court of Human Rights, in *Le Compte, Van Leuven and De Meyere v. Belgium* (1981) 4 EHRR 1, in considering art.11 of the Convention which protects freedom of association, took the factor of viable alternatives into account. The Court held that an obligation to join the *Ordre de Medecins* in order to practice medicine did not violate art.11 because doctors were free to form their own associations even though they were also compelled to join the *Ordre*. The Court noted (para.65) that:

"However, there is a further requirement: if there is not to be a violation, the setting up of the Ordre by the Belgian State must not prevent practitioners from forming together or joining professional associations. Totalitarian régimes have resorted–and resort–to the compulsory regimentation of the professions by means of closed and exclusive organisations taking the place of the professional associations and the traditional trade unions. The authors of the Convention intended to prevent such abuses.

...in Belgium there are several associations formed to protect the professional interests of medical practitioners and which they are completely free to join or not. In these circumstances, the existence of the Ordre and its attendant consequence–that is to say, the obligation on practitioners to be entered on the register of the Ordre and to be subject to the authority of its organs–clearly have neither the object nor the effect of limiting, even less suppressing, the right guaranteed by Article 11..."

93. The factual circumstances are, of course, different to the present case. No doubt the decision of the European Court can be distinguished on a number of grounds. I have cited it for one reason only. In my view, it confirms that the availability of viable alternatives is a relevant factor to take into account.

Legislative provisions in other jurisdictions

94. During the course of submissions, Mr Shum, for the applicant, laid emphasis on the fact that, in a number of other common law jurisdictions, legislation reflecting the provisions of our ss.95 and 98 are more nuanced, making provision for the protection of members who are made the subject of improper applications. But the issue before this court is not whether there are more nuanced statutory regimes in other jurisdictions but whether the regime presently constituted under our Ordinance is inconsistent with the protected freedoms of members of political parties when those parties have incorporated and made the choice to make all members of the party members also of the corporate body.

95. The English Companies Act 2006, places the burden on a person seeking inspection to justify the request. However, as I have found earlier, s.98(4) of the Hong Kong Ordinance, while no doubt it places the burden on a company to justify a denial of inspection, nevertheless does provide a protection against claims that constitute an abuse.

96. I would add that the wide sweep of the statutory regime created by ss.95 and 98 of the Ordinance is not, by that reason alone, to be taken as being inconsistent with the fundamental freedoms advocated by the applicant on behalf of its members. Bright line rules which are easy to apply and ensure fairness in the great majority of cases may be permissible even if some hardship is demonstrated in individual cases. In *James v. United Kingdom* (1986) 8 EHRR 123, when considering expropriation legislation, the European Court observed that (para.68)–

"...legislation of wide sweep, in particular if it implements a programme of social and economic reform, is hardly capable of doing entire justice in the diverse circumstances of the very large number of different individuals concerned."

Looking to the authority of National Association for the

Advancement of Coloured People v. Alabama

97. During the course of submissions, Mr Shum placed considerable emphasis on the judgment of the Supreme Court of the United States in the case of *National Association for the Advancement of Coloured People v. Alabama*. While I have obtained much assistance from that judgment as to the integration and relative importance of the two freedoms of freedom of association and what, in broad terms, I have called the right to privacy, in my view, it has rendered limited assistance in respect of other matters essential to this judgment. I say that because the factual context in which the Supreme Court came to its judgment is very different from the factual context in the present case.

Employing the proportionality test

98. It is accepted that the restrictions imposed by s.98 on the applicant (and, through the applicant, its members) are prescribed by law.

99. It must equally be accepted, I believe, that the restrictions imposed by s.98 seek to achieve a legitimate purpose. I have explained that purpose at some length earlier in this judgment. That there is a rational connection between the restrictions imposed by s.98 and the legitimate purpose that the section seeks to achieve must also be accepted.

100. Members of a company, it seems to me, have a legitimate interest, in the great majority of cases, in knowing who are the other members. Members are entitled to know who they stand in association with. Inter-action between members is an essential part of the operation of a company. Equally, it seems to me that, in the great majority of cases, third parties have a legitimate interest in knowing who stands behind a company.

101. In respect of a political party (such as the applicant), it seems to me that the fundamental rationale must still apply. Persons dealing with an incorporated political party–whether, for example, to make a donation to it or enter into some commercial relationship with it–if they are to be able to place trust in the party, are entitled to learn who stands behind it.

102. The real issue, it seems to me, is whether it can be said that the restrictions imposed by s.98, in so far as they apply to incorporated political parties, are no more than is necessary.

103. In this regard, in setting out the various factors earlier in this judgment which I believe must go to determine the issue, and in explaining their dynamics in detail, I have been drawn to the conclusion that, to protect the rights and freedoms of others, the restrictions imposed by s.98, insofar as they may affect political parties that have chosen to incorporate, are no more than is necessary.

104. In my judgment, the difficulty faced by the applicant may be stated in the following terms:

(i) Those persons who chose to incorporate the Democratic Party, and who chose to make all members of the party members of the corporate body, and continue to abide by that decision, chose thereby to bring each and every member into substantial contact with matters public; in many ways, into potential conflict with the rights and freedoms of others. By making that choice, they chose to limit the seriousness of any restrictions placed on the freedom of members to associate in private.

(ii) I say this because it is to be remembered that the applicant has extensive powers under its memorandum of association to deal commercially; that is, to borrow money, to enter into contracts and the like. It has the power, as I have said, to accept donations. On top of that, it has the power to undertake associated activities such as to campaign to raise funds. In that regard, it can have no real complaint that, like all other companies which operate under the Ordinance, people dealing with it should be entitled to know who stands behind it.

(iii) What must be emphasised is that the persons who made the decisions to incorporate and to make every member of the political party a member of the corporate body were not under an obligation in law to do so. Put simply, they could have chosen a number of viable alternatives. Even if, having chosen incorporation, they wished to protect the identity of members, there were still options open to them to achieve this end.

(iv) The applicant's real complaint, as I have understood it, is that persons may seek, and have sought, access to the register of members for reasons which fall outside the parameters of matters contemplated by the Ordinance or which fall reasonably into its ambit. But, if that is the case, as I have said earlier, the applicant is not left entirely powerless. S.98(4) of the Ordinance does provide a shield against what I have described as abusive applications.

(v) In summary, the applicant and its members are able to enjoy the advantages that incorporation gives and, at the same time, are provided with a measure at least of protection by the statutory regime against demands which improperly, in terms of the Ordinance, invade their freedom to associate in private.

105. mpanies Ordinance do strike a fair balance between the demands of the legitimate interests of Hong Kong society, particularly in the commercial and financial sphere, and the requirement of the protection of the individual freedoms of the applicant's members.

106. It is accepted that s.98 may not provide the clear cut protections contained in the United Kingdom's Companies Act 2006. No doubt, there are strong arguments for saying that the statutory regime contained in our Ordinance can be improved. But that, as I have said, is not the issue. The issue is whether the regime, as presently constituted, is inconsistent with the fundamental freedoms of the applicant's members to associate in private. I do not find it to be so.

107. It is also to be remembered that bright line rules which are easy to apply and ensure fairness in the great majority of cases may, when fundamental freedoms are being considered, still be permissible if they ensure fairness in the great majority of cases and are to that extent justified in the general interests of society even if they impose a restriction on those freedoms.

Conclusions

108. For the reasons given in the body of this judgment, I am not prepared to make the declaration that has been sought.

109. I see no reason why costs should not follow the event and I make an order nisi to that effect. The order will be made final in 14 days from the date of this judgment unless an application is made within that time to set the matter down for argument.

Judge of the Court of First Instance, High Court (M.J. Hartmann

---

Mr Erik Shum and Ms Linda Wong, instructed by Messrs Ho, Tse, Wai & Partners, for the Applicant

Mr Benjamin Yu, SC and Ms Yvonne Cheng, instructed by Department of Justice, for the Respondent

---

Brian Alfred Hall v. Secretary for Justice

Brian Alfred Hall 對 律政司司長（代表懲教署署長）

HCAL 5/2006

簡略案情

申請人為尼日利亞籍人士，一名拉斯特法里教徒。於 1998 年 6 月在香港法院承認販賣毒品罪而被判 18 年監禁，現在赤柱監獄服刑。在服刑期間，申請人不滿懲教處對他作出的一連串處理方法，遂提出司法覆核的申請。他總共有 13 項投訴，其中包括歧視與違反他的基本人權。對於歧視的指控，申請人表示他曾申請在其囚室擁有播放器並播放宗教音樂，但此申請被拒絕，然而申請人指出，其他囚犯同樣的申請獲得准許，所以，應一視同仁地讓他也可以播放宗教音樂。其次，在服刑期間，申請人因違反紀律而被獨立監禁。申請人不滿他因此而不能閱報和聽廣播，他認為接觸和接受資訊是他的基本人權，懲教處不應該也不能剝奪此權利。

裁決摘要

原訟庭法官認為申請人的這起司法覆核申請有不能解釋的延誤，而且，他所有的指控，連最低的具爭議性的標準也不能達到，所以他的司法覆核申請不獲批准。對於申請人認為他被歧視的指控，法官接受懲教處的解釋，在一般情況下，沒有囚犯可以在囚室播放任何音樂，但是，在囚犯患病或極度情緒化的時候，如果音樂可以紓緩他的痛苦，是可以酌情考慮給予這種特殊待遇。申請人指出他有性格問題，他應該有相同的待遇，容許他在囚室內播放音樂。雖然，法官接受有報告顯示他有性格缺陷，卻沒有任何證據顯示音樂能紓緩他的問題，由此，歧視指控不能成立。

法官同意，除了那些因直接或者引申而被剝奪的權利，囚犯可繼續享有完整的公民權利。法庭援引了 *R. v. Home Secretary, Ex Parte Leech* [1994] QB 198 指出，良好的秩序和紀律是保證監獄能安全和有系統地運作的重要因素，因此，監獄守則賦予監獄處長很大的酌情權，從而以最好的方法執行這工作。在 *Chim Shing Chung v. Commissioner Of Correctional Services* [1996] 6 HKPLR 313 一案中，上訴庭清晰地指出，除非在很極端的情況下，法院才能安心地認定監獄處長的判斷與決定是濫用職權。法官清楚《基本法》第 27 條對言論自由的保障，但認為並非絕對而不受限制的。

法官亦注意到《香港人權法案條例》第 9 條也清晰註明，為了維護囚禁紀律，可以根據法律對服刑人士在該條例下被保障的權利加以限制。法官進而列舉了聯合國《對所有被任何形式拘押的人士的保護總則》第 28 條，“在公共資源條件容許下，及為了保證拘押或監禁地方的安全與良好秩序的合理條件外，被拘押或在囚人士應該有權獲得合理數量的教育、文化和資訊的材料。”說明監獄處長有權在對囚犯施予懲罰的情形下，限制其閱讀報章。據此，法官認為禁止獨立監禁的在囚人士獲取資訊的決定，是依法並且是維護良好秩序與紀律所必須的。因此，申請人的相關論據被否定。

HCAL 5/2006

IN THE HIGH COURT OF THE

HONG KONG SPECIAL ADMINISTRATIVE REGION

COURT OF FIRST INSTANCE

CONSTITUTIONAL AND ADMINISTRATIVE LAW LIST
NO. 5 OF 2006

Between:

BRIAN ALFRED HALL **Applicant**

- and -

SECRETARY FOR JUSTICE Respondent
(for Commissioner of Correctional Services Department)

Before: Hon Hartmann J in Court

Dates of Hearing: 16 and 30 June 2006

Date of Judgment: 30 June 2006

JUDGMENT

Introduction

1. This is an application for leave to apply for judicial review. The applicant is a serving prisoner held at Stanley Prison. In 1998 he was sentenced to 18 years for drug trafficking. He is a Nigerian national.

2. In his application, the applicant seeks to challenge various actions of Correctional Services officers, some of those actions dating back two years or more.

3. This is not the first application for judicial review brought against CSD officers by the applicant. Two previous applications have been dealt with by me: HCAL 140/2004 and HCAL 84/2004.

4. In addition to his applications for judicial review, the applicant has made numerous complaints about the conduct of CSD officers and others who have had the responsibility of dealing with him; for example, doctors who have had to attend to his medical complaints.

5. This new application, like the previous ones, has been handwritten by the applicant. It is prolix and often difficult to understand. That is why I have directed that there should be an oral hearing.

6. The Commissioner was informed of the hearing in support of the application for leave and told that, if he wished, he could be represented to assist the court where necessary. Mr Wesley Wong has appeared on his behalf.

7. The applicant has represented himself. I am informed that at one time he did apply for legal aid in respect of one or more of his various actions. However, he has now (apparently) been prohibited from seeking further assistance. This would suggest that the Director of Legal Aid has dealt with the applicant in terms of s.11 of the Legal Aid Regulations, Cap.91A, which provides that, if it appears to the Director that an applicant's conduct has amounted to an abuse of the facilities provided by the Ordinance, he may order that no consideration be given to any future application by that person, that prohibition to endure for a maximum of three years.

8. As the applicant knows, this is a hearing for leave only. It is for the applicant, in respect of each of his complaints, to demonstrate that, on the material he has placed before me, matters have been disclosed which on further consideration might demonstrate an arguable case for the grant of the relief sought.

The first complaint

9. It has taken some time to understand the basis of this complaint. It arises out of an incident which took place in Stanley Prison on 2 June 2004, some two years ago.

10. It seems that the applicant had a newspaper in his possession. An officer demanded that the applicant give it to him. The applicant refused to do so. There was a verbal exchange in which the applicant used bad language. A more senior officer, a Principal Officer, was summoned. He came to the applicant's cell and also demanded that the applicant hand over the newspaper. The applicant refused to do so and again, it seems, bad language was used. At this stage, CSD officers employed force to take the newspaper from the applicant. There was a struggle.

11. In the result, the applicant was charged with assaulting the CSD officers and was tried in the Magistrates Court by Mr T. Casewell. He was convicted and sentenced to six months' imprisonment, the sentence to run consecutively with the 18 year sentence he received for drug trafficking.

12. The applicant appealed both his conviction and sentence. His appeal was heard in February of this year. The appeal was dismissed. In his judgment, Deputy Judge Leong, a retired Chief Judge of this court, said the following:

> "The magistrate found the prosecution witnesses reliable, consistent and truthful and accepted their evidence. He found that the medical evidence was consistent with the struggle described by the prosecution witnesses and it did not support the appellant's case. He rejected the appellant's story that the prison officers had conspired to assault him as a revenge for his making complaints. He found the appellant concocted his story. He said in his findings: 'I find the prosecution witnesses to be truthful and reliable. The appellant did refuse to return the newspaper. He abused PW2 with foul language and threw the newspaper at him. Furthermore, he struck him at least three blows to the chest. These are clear and unequivocal assaults accompanied by an intention to do so.'"

13. One of the grounds upon which the applicant appealed was that the Principal Officer who was responsible for using force to obtain the newspaper had acted unlawfully. In this regard, in his judgment, Deputy Judge Leong said the following:

> "··· the magistrate had dealt with [this] in his findings. *He found it was not unlawful for PW2, who was a principal officer, to retrieve the newspaper from the appellant.* I agree with the finding of the magistrate. In any case, even if the officer had acted in breach of his duty in retrieving the newspaper, this was no excuse for the appellant to assault the officer. This ground must fail." [my emphasis]

14. How is it that, out of criminal proceedings in which the applicant himself was found guilty of assault, he now seeks to bring judicial review proceedings against the officers who

were responsible for physically subduing him and removing the newspaper from him?

15. As I understand it, the applicant's complaint is that the CSD officers were guilty of a breach of prison regulations in that, when initially the applicant refused to hand over the newspaper, there was a failure to immediately report that matter to a Superintendent so that he could investigate it. In this regard, the applicant has relied on a number of prison rules and regulations but I think that reference to Prison Rule 60, Cap.234A, illustrates the point. It reads:

> "Every offence against prison discipline shall be reported immediately and it shall be the duty of the superintendent to investigate such reports not later than the following day unless that day is a general holiday."

16. It appears to be the applicant's contention that, when the initial refusal to hand over the newspaper took place, accompanied by the use of bad language, the matter should – then and there – have been reported to a Superintendent so that the Superintendent could come to the scene and commence an investigation. In the meantime, of course, the applicant would have been left in his cell in possession of the newspaper.

17. There is nothing in this ground of complaint. A simple analogy makes it plain. What if, instead of a newspaper, the applicant had a knife in his possession or a syringe containing drugs? Was he to be left in possession of the items while a Superintendent was informed so that he could commence investigations or were the officers on the spot under a responsibility to take immediate action to enforce prison discipline (and if necessary to protect the safety of others) by removing the items?

18. Common sense dictates that in the ordinary course of events an incident which appears to contravene prison discipline must first be contained and only then reported to a Superintendent so that it may be investigated and, if required, criminal or disciplinary proceedings instituted. Whether the CSD officers would have been wiser to immediately report the matter – in this instance – to a Superintendent is not the issue, the issue is whether they acted unlawfully in failing to do so. And I do not see how it can be said they acted unlawfully.

19. There may not at any time have been any official report to a Superintendent which was restricted to the issue of the applicant refusing to hand over the newspaper. But in the present case, it is apparent that the initial refusal by the applicant to hand over the newspaper and his use of bad language escalated into a far more serious incident, one in which the applicant was accused of and prosecuted for criminal assault. The initial and lesser breach of discipline therefore became part of a more serious criminal offence; as lawyers would put it, it became part of the *res gestae*.

20. In addition to being satisfied that this first ground of complaint is misconceived, I am of the view that delay on the part of the applicant must result in leave being refused. In terms of Order 53 rule 4(1) of the Rules of the High Court, an application for leave to apply for judicial review shall be made promptly, and in any event within three months of the day when the grounds for the application first arose. This requirement to act promptly in public law matters applies unless the court considers that there is good reason for extending the period within which the application shall be made. Delay is a serious issue, one which puts an applicant in peril. In *R. v. Aston University Senate ex parte Roffey* [1969] 2 QB 538, 555, Donaldson J, as he then was, said :

> "The prerogative remedies are exceptional in their nature and should not be made available to those who sleep upon their rights."

21. The incident in question took place on 2 June 2004. The applicant filed this latest application for leave in January of this year, almost two years after the event.

22. The applicant complains that he has been unable to draft and file his complaint earlier. I do not accept that. He has filed two earlier judicial reviews, the first being filed on 30 June 2004, the second on 18 November 2004. His complaint could have been contained in one of those applications.

23. The applicant complains he was unable to take legal advice as he was unable to get legal aid. But, on the evidence before me, the applicant appears to have brought that upon himself. In any event, the applicant has been able to draft numerous grounds of complaint in his three applications to date. I do not see why he would have been handicapped with this one.

24. Finally, it seems to me, after a delay of nearly two years, even if I was to find the complaint was *prima facie* arguable, that nothing of substance turns on it. How at this late stage is the applicant to benefit, or is good administration to be enhanced, from the fact that disciplinary proceedings are taken against one or more CSD officers for what could be little more than a technical breach? The applicant will still remain convicted of criminal assault and must serve the sentence imposed on him.

25. As I have explained to the applicant, the exercise of this court's jurisdiction is discretionary. It does not follow that a remedy will be granted merely because some error of law has been identified. A remedy will only be granted when it is necessary or desirable to do so in the interests of justice. In the present case, even if I found that the applicant had a *prima facie* arguable case – which I do not – I do not see how the interests of justice could be advanced by granting leave.

26. Leave is refused.

The second complaint

27. This complaint also arises out of the incident which took place on 2 June 2004.

28. It appears that, after the incident, the officers who dealt with the applicant were photographed by a fellow CSD officer. The purpose of the photographs was to show their injuries. It appears, however, that the applicant was not photographed.

29. At some later time the applicant complained of this failure and photographs were taken. It has not been made clear to me the degree to which, if at all, these photographs showed any injuries.

30. When the criminal trial took place, the magistrate apparently came to a finding of fact that the applicant had originally refused to be photographed.

31. The applicant complains that this finding was perverse and should be quashed.

32. But the finding was a finding of fact, not law, and was simply one finding among many made in the course of criminal proceedings. The applicant had the opportunity to challenge that finding of fact on appeal and it appears that he did so. In his judgment, Deputy Judge Leong said:

> "On the third ground this is also a question of fact. There

is no evidence of collusion between the doctor and the prosecution witnesses on the injuries suffered by the appellant. Dr Chan found no head injuries when he examined the appellant on 2 June 2004. The medical report from the doctor indicated that the patch or mark as shown in the photographs after the appellant complained to Master de Sousa did not appear until the entry at 14 June 2004, which was almost two weeks after the incident of assault. The magistrate was entitled to find the mark or patch and any injury found later could not be attributed to the incident on 2 June 2004. There is no substance in this ground."

33. The matter of the photographs was therefore one for the criminal courts and it has been dealt with in those courts, both at first instance and on appeal. I can find no reason why this court should take the entirely exceptional step of now assuming jurisdiction.

34. Leave is refused.

The third complaint

35. This complaint also arises out of the incident which took place on 2 June 2004. The applicant complains that after the incident he wished to telephone a friend, a Mr Crawley, and a solicitor. He wished to inform them, he says, that he had been assaulted and framed. He was, however, denied permission to do so. Later, on 6 July 2004, the applicant complains that he wished to telephone his solicitor to tell him he had been formally arrested for assault. Again, permission was refused.

36. Documents were produced which, in a brief, bureaucratic way, spoke of these matters. They are prison forms.

37. In respect of the first refusal, there is a note to the effect that the applicant was interviewed in an isolation cell of the hospital wing of Stanley Prison. The interview took place on 3 June 2004, the day after the incident. On that occasion, the applicant submitted two written requests to make telephone calls. He sought to call Mr Crawley, apparently to try and get money to pay legal fees. He also sought to call a solicitor.

38. It appears that the prison authorities believed that the applicant only wanted to inform the solicitor of what he alleged had taken place. The applicant denies this, saying that he also wanted to obtain legal advice. The probabilities would, of course, suggest that the applicant did wish to obtain some form of advice.

39. The two requests, it seems, were considered but refused. One of the forms bears the endorsement that it would be more –

> "appropriate to advise the subject to write to Mr Crawley and Mr Midgley as telephone communication would only be utilised in case of urgency or in dearth of other means of communications."

40. The later request – the one dated 6 July 2004 – was also refused, the papers being endorsed :

> "He is not recommended to have his telephone call to his solicitor, as no sufficient grounds and his solicitor could visit him through the channel of legal visit."

When looking at the papers, I notice that the applicant had made three earlier requests to make telephone calls, two to the Nigerian Consulate and one described simply as an IDD call. All three had been granted.

42. The applicant complains that the refusal to let him make the telephone calls in order to arrange for and receive legal advice was a breach of his fundamental right to communicate with a lawyer and constituted an abuse of power.

43. Of course, the first problem that the applicant faces is again one of delay. I can find no good reason why the applicant could not have included this complaint in his second judicial review proceedings filed in November 2004. I shall return to the problems caused by delay shortly.

44. At this juncture, however, I do accept that the right to communicate with a lawyer is a fundamental right. Art.35 of the Basic Law enshrines the right to confidential legal advice. Any suggested denial or frustration of that right must therefore be considered with utmost care.

45. That being said, however, while no doubt there will be occasions when serving prisoners should have the right to telephone their counsel to receive legal advice, I have not been referred to any international convention or domestic law that says that serving prisoners, whether a matter is urgent or not, have the right always to seek legal advice *by telephone*.

46. If a matter is not urgent, legal advice is invariably given when counsel visits the serving prisoner. There may also, of course, be occasions when communication can be by letter.

47. The use generally of the telephone by serving prisoners must – for any number of good reasons – be controlled by the prison authorities. In this regard, for example, the Prison Rules provide that :

> "Heads of institution may under the following special circumstances and on being satisfied on the prisoner's genuine need for timely communication with his friends and relatives, allow a prisoner to make local or overseas phone calls on a case to case basis:
>
> (1) to inform them of the prisoner's detention or whereabouts;
>
> (2) to arrange for bail, fine payment or other legal matters..."

48. In short, each request must be considered in the context of its own particular circumstances. The basic criteria is the demonstration of a 'genuine need for timely communication'. That, in my view, must apply to communications with lawyers as well as 'friends and relatives'.

49. This, of course, is where the issue of delay becomes so important. The applicant appears to suggest that a timely meeting with his solicitor and his friend, Mr Crawley, would have enabled him to demonstrate that, despite the doctor's report, he did suffer bad injuries. As against that, however, if leave is granted, the CSD officers will have to look back over a two year period to try to recall how and why it was, in the circumstances as they existed at the time, that they believed it proper to come to the decisions they did.

50. I would also observe that nothing has been placed before me of any substance to demonstrate what sort of delay was occasioned by the refusal of the authorities to allow the applicant to telephone Mr Crawley and his solicitor.

51. Nor has anything been put before me to state what alternative steps were taken by the applicant. Was somebody else able to contact his solicitor for him, perhaps the prison welfare officer?

When did he eventually get to see his solicitor? Was the issue of delay – if indeed there was delay – raised with the criminal court before or at trial? If not, why not? If there had been prejudice to the applicant, surely that would have been raised. In this regard, I note that the applicant was represented at his trial by counsel. If it was raised, how was it dealt with by the magistrate and/or Deputy Judge Leong?

52. In respect of the refusal to allow the applicant to telephone his solicitor in July 2004, the applicant has accepted that he only wished to make the telephone call to inform his solicitor that he had been formally charged. He has not urged upon me any urgent or otherwise pressing circumstances which, at the time, demanded that a telephone call be made.

53. The applicant has referred to a notice given to persons under investigation – as he was at the time. But the notice does not promise that telephone communication is guaranteed. It speaks of private telephone calls or communication in person.

54. In summary, the applicant has put nothing before me to show on a *prima facie* basis that:

(a) he was unable to bring up his complaint in the criminal proceedings, the issue going directly, it would seem, to his ability properly to defend himself in those proceedings;

(b) he was unable to bring his challenge by way of judicial review within time.

55. Leave is refused.

The fourth complaint

56. This complaint arises out of an earlier application for judicial review made by the applicant: see my judgment dated 16 August 2005 (HCAL 140/2004 and HCAL 84/2004). In that judgment, I quashed certain disciplinary proceedings that had been taken against the applicant: see paragraphs 54 to 66 (inclusive). I concluded in paragraph 66 by saying the following:

> "The proceedings are vitiated as being unlawful. Any punishments imposed are quashed. I am not prepared to make an order that the matter be remitted for a new hearing. The circumstances do not warrant it."

57. Regrettably, when I delivered my judgment, I had not been able to dispose of all the applicant's various challenges and to deal with any consequential orders. That was why, in paragraph 93, I said:

> "There may, of course, be further submissions by the applicant as to consequential remedies that he thinks should flow from the matters already determined by me."

58. In the present application, the applicant now seeks the costs incurred by him in photostating documents which, he says, was a necessary procedure in order to prosecute his appeal before the Commissioner against his conviction of the disciplinary offences which, as I have said, I quashed in my earlier judgment. Three sets of costs, he says, were incurred by him in copying the transcripts of the disciplinary proceedings. They come to $58.50, $60 and $87.

59. The issue of these costs, of course, arose out of the earlier proceedings and should be part of those proceedings.

60. But leaving that aside, the difficulty the applicant faces, as I perceive it, is that he must be able to identify some provision in law which entitles him to payment. To put it another way, he must be able to identify some provision in law which enables the Commissioner, as a public officer, to make payment.

61. Mr Wong for the Commissioner has referred me to s.63(3) of the Prison Rules which deals with the hearing of appeals by the Commissioner. That provision reads:

> "Upon hearing the appeal, either by the prisoner in person or by him in writing, the Commissioner shall determine the appeal and may cancel, vary or confirm the order against which the appeal is made or may substitute therefor any other order which the superintendent was competent to make …"

62. Mr Wong has said that on his reading of the Prison Rules, he can find no provision which entitles the Commissioner, in law, to refund a prisoner any costs incurred by him in pursuing a successful appeal.

63. The applicant says that he can only approach the matter as a layman. He understands that, in any court, if a person is successful, costs follow. That may be a general rule in courts of the classic kind but it is not necessarily a rule in special tribunals such as the tribunals regulated under the Prison Rules. The applicant has not himself been able to identify any relevant provision in law. That being the case, I do not see how the applicant can mount a *prima facie* argument that his costs should be paid.

64. This may visit an injustice on the applicant. I appreciate that every dollar to a prisoner is important. But the fact remains that I would be unable to direct the Commissioner to make a payment when, in my judgment, the Commissioner has no power to make that payment.

65. Leave is refused.

The fifth complaint

66. As I can best understand this complaint, it relates to three alleged instances of assault. The applicant alleges that – on 2 June 2004 (the same date as the assault referred to in the earlier complaints), 23 March 2005 and 12 April 2005 – CSD officers assaulted him. It is suggested that the assaults were instigated by a Superintendent or some other senior officer; in short, that the assaults had a sinister origin.

67. However, as I have explained to the applicant, actions for wrongful assault should be instituted by way of writ not judicial review. Judicial review is not suited to the determination of complex factual issues of the kind described. Issues of that kind should be determined at a trial when witnesses can be called and cross-examined and, if necessary, when medical evidence can be called as to injuries suffered.

68. The applicant protests that other courts have found issues of trespass against the body to be suitable for judicial review. He has not given me any cases to support that assertion. But I do not dispute the fact that there may be cases where the lawfulness of physical assault is a proper matter for judicial review. One example might be the admitted forced feeding of a prisoner. In the present case, however, undoubtedly, the only issues will be contested issues of fact and it is those kind of cases which should be commenced by writ and should go to trial so that the evidence of the various witnesses can be tested and findings of fact made by the court.

69. By way of a footnote, even if judicial review was found to be the appropriate procedure, I refer again to the question of delay. The most recent alleged assault referred to by the applicant took place some eight months before the present leave application was filed.

70. Leave is refused.

The sixth complaint

71. This complaint refers to some 25 cases of disciplinary proceedings taken against the applicant by the prison authorities. The individual case numbers suggest that the earliest of these proceedings was in 1999, some seven years ago, while the latest was in 2005.

72. The applicant complains that the adjudicating officers were biased. They were biased because in every case they were judges in their own cause. The applicant seeks an order that all of the proceedings should be quashed.

73. Over the lunch adjournment, Mr Wong, for the Commissioner, has been able to examine some (but not all) of the proceedings. His examination appears to reveal the following :

a. Ta.Two of the cases were dismissed without the need for them to even go to trial. No question of a tribunal being a judge in his own cause arose.

b. In four of the cases, the applicant chose not to avail himself of the appeal procedure. In short, he chose not to take the issue of bias to a higher tribunal.

c. In one case, the applicant abandoned his appeal.

d. In six proceedings, the record shows that the tribunal asked the applicant if he had any objection to the adjudicating officer determining the matter and was told there was no objection.

74. I have also briefly considered the papers in one case: R/N 655 of 2004. On the face of the papers, the applicant, who was charged with assaulting a fellow Nigerian prisoner, pleaded guilty and gave evidence in mitigation. Some two years after he had been convicted on his own plea, he decided to appeal. His appeal was lodged on 6 October 2004 and determined on 2 November of that year. The applicant admits that he pleaded guilty. He says, however, that he was forced to do so.

75. I do not intend to become embroiled in the intricacies of each disciplinary case. The point that is revealed by Mr Wong's investigations is that the applicant's blanket accusation of bias is, even at this preliminary stage, shown at best to be wayward in respect at least of a number of the proceedings. It is not for this court to give general leave and then attempt at a substantive hearing to try and sort the wheat from the chaff. It is for the applicant to put his case in proper order when he applies for leave.

76. Delay, of course, is again a profound issue. This court is expected to forgive delays that are of several years.

77. In respect of each of the disciplinary proceedings the applicant, in terms of the rules and regulations, had an appeal process open to him. He was entitled to challenge any matter that he thought relevant in respect of his appeals. This would include the fact that he was pressured into pleading guilty, that there was a dishonest doctoring of the records, that he was otherwise dealt with unfairly and that the adjudicating officer was biased against him. If those allegations had been made, it was the responsibility of the appeal tribunal to consider those allegations and to come to a finding in respect of them. This court does not act as some sort of extra appeal court.

78. As for the appeals themselves, there is nothing to suggest that each of them was not properly considered in good faith. I notice that in two appeals the awards were varied.

79. Leave is refused.

The seventh complaint

80. The applicant professes to be a member of the Rastafarian religion. For an extended period of time he has sought permission to be able to play the music of his religion in his cell; that is, to have tapes and a tape recording machine in his cell. The prison authorities have refused him permission. The applicant complains that other prisoners have been allowed religious music in their cells and that he is being made the subject of discrimination.

81. In earlier judicial review proceedings brought by the applicant, I found that the Rastafarian religion should be considered a religion. I also found that certain reggae music was considered to be devotional music in the religion. In para.37 of my judgment of 16 August 2005, I said :

> "I have looked through certain of the material shown to me today by the applicant. In my judgment, certainly on the balance of probabilities, the evidence indicates that reggae music is integral as a means of expression to the Rastafarian faith. The lyrics of reggae, as written by certain reggae artists, are considered to be words of wisdom within the Rastafarian faith, just as the psalms of King David are meant to be part of the wisdom of the Hebrew faith. I mention this analogy because, as I understand it, Rastafarianism finds its ancient roots in the Hebrew faith."

82. In terms of Rule 23(1) of the Prison Rules, no prisoner is entitled to have in his possession any article without authority. It is not disputed that tapes and tape-recorders constitute "articles".

83. The prison authorities say that, as a general rule, no music may be played in cells. It does not matter – in principle at least – whether it is religious or secular. The purpose of the rule is to maintain good order and discipline.

84. The rule is, however, subject to exceptions which are decided on a case by case basis. For example, prisoners studying for examinations may be allowed educational material or prisoners suffering emotional difficulties may be allowed some solace in the form of tapes. As I said in my earlier judgment :

> "There may be a number of compassionate reasons; for example, if a prisoner is ill and is looking for solace in religious music or if he is having a difficult time in coming to terms with his predicament. But the fact remains that it does lie within the discretion of the prison authorities to allow individuals to possess tapes of religious music, that is not disputed. It is a discretion, however, which can only be set aside if shown to have been exercised in some unlawful way; for example, in a way that goes further than differentiating and actively discriminates."

85. It is, as I have said, the applicant's contention that the refusal to give him religious music was an act of discrimination as opposed to differentiation.

86. The applicant has shown me an authority card which apparently enabled him to play reggae music in his cell at some earlier time. But that sets no precedent. As I have said, a prisoner may be granted the privilege for a limited period only, for example, when he is studying or requires the solace of music during a time of emotional difficulty.

87. The applicant has shown me a newspaper article dated 24 January 2006. In part, it reads:

> "For many people, music is an avenue to release, soothe or indulge their emotions, be it through catchy guitar riffs, soulful jazz or the dramatic score of a classical composition. The Correctional Services Department believes that music plays an important role in the rehabilitation process of prisoners, and the Hong Kong Philharmonic Orchestra believes that the sounds of an orchestra can bring hope and meaning to life.
>
> With these beliefs in mind, the Pak Sha Wan Correctional Institution in Stanley in December opened its doors to 50 Hong Kong Philharmonic Orchestra players who performed two concerts for 400 inmates…"

88. The fact that the prison authorities from time to time put on musical concerts for an audience of prisoners does not advance the applicant's case that he should be granted leave. The applicant's complaint is that he is not permitted to have the music in his cell for his own enjoyment only. Quite clearly issues of good order in discipline are different when concerts are arranged from time to time for a large section of the prison population.

89. The applicant has gone on to say that, in any event, as a person with severe emotional difficulty, musical tapes will benefit him. In this regard, he has referred me to a report on his condition prepared by a psychologist. It reads :

> "The prisoner is a known case to the psychological unit. He has been given a diagnosis of dissocial personality disorder by a psychiatrist in 1999. People with such personality profiles are generally impulsive, irritable, aggressive, deceitful and irresponsible, having difficulties in conforming to rules and regulations. Institutional misbehaviour in the form of verbal violence and physical violence (against staff and fellow prisoners) were recorded. In view of the tension with the management and the chronicity of behavioural problems, BAU [whatever that may mean] may serve as a buffer at this juncture."

90. The applicant does not dispute the accuracy of this report. In fact, he appears to adopt it. If the report is correct it may explain why there has been so much friction between the applicant, the prison authorities and other prisoners.

91. The applicant says that, because he has been diagnosed as a person who is impulsive, aggressive, deceitful, irresponsible and liable to bouts of violence, it follows that he must be given music in his cell at night, if that music is of a religious nature, to soothe his troubled personality. However, there is nothing before me to suggest that, because of his diagnosed personality disorder, the ordinary rules of prison discipline should not apply equally to the applicant as it does to all other prisoners. Nor, importantly, is there anything before me to say that the ability to play music in his cell will materially assist his particular condition. There is, for example, no suggestion that a recommendation by a doctor has been refused.

92. In summary, no material has been put before me upon which to base any sort of argument that the applicant, by the denial to him of music in his cell, is suffering unlawful religious discrimination or discrimination of any other kind.

93. Leave is refused.

The eighth complaint

94 .In this complaint the applicant challenges a decision to refuse him permission to take $20 out of his compulsory savings account in order to file proceedings in the Small Claims Tribunal. He also challenges a decision to refuse him permission to transfer all the moneys in his compulsory savings account into his earnings account.

95. In respect of moneys earned in prison, I have an affirmation from a CSD officer, Mr Wan, who says that –

> "Prisoners are required to save up to $500 or more in their compulsory savings. If part of the compulsory savings is used resulting in the savings falling below the $500 ceiling, the prisoners will be required to save 10 per cent of their earnings until the ceiling is attained."

96. Mr Wan continues :

> "The applicant made an application on 24 November 2005 for a sum of $20 to be deducted from his compulsory savings in order to settle the filing fee for his amendment."

97. Mr Wan then explains:

> "The Department noted that the amount of the applicant's compulsory savings fell below the $500 ceiling while he had $200.60 in his property and the usable balance of his weekly earnings was $126.49 at the time. The prison authority was of the view that the alleged filing fee of $20 could be fully recovered by his money in his property or his weekly earnings and there was no urgency and no merit at all for converting the compulsory savings into his earnings."

98. Mr Wong, for the Commissioner, points out that – fundamentally – the more money prisoners have in their earnings account, the more they can spend in the canteen. Accordingly, it is often an advantage if they can somehow cash in their compulsory savings account and move the funds from that 'capital account' into their 'cash account'.

99. Mr Wong has also pointed out that the Correctional Services Department does its best to ensure that prisoners, upon their discharge, have at least $500 savings to help them when they have to face the world again.

100. A memorandum dated 6 December 2005 shows how the decision to refuse the applicant was reached:

> "On 1.12.2005, Prisoner HALL made a request to deduct HKD 20 from his compulsory saving for the charge of filing an amendment form to the court (Case: SCTC 32143/04). Besides, he requested to convert his compulsory saving into earning for purchasing additional basic necessities. His self-explanatory submission is attached.
>
> An assessment on Prisoner HALL's request had been conducted by the Management with the following

findings:–

(a) There was HKD 200.6 in his property;

(b) There was HK$126.49 in his usable balance in earnings before December's canteen purchase; and

(c) He earned HK$33.14 (CA) weekly.

In view that the charge in question is only HK$20.00 which can be fully covered by his money in property or earning, I see no merit in his case. For the request of converting the compulsory saving into his earning, his application had been assessed; there was no urgency and imminent need for his request as all the basic necessities were being provided. Therefore, his application for withdrawal of compulsory saving is not recommended."

101. On the face of it, the decisions reflected in this memorandum are rational and unexceptional. The applicant complains, however, that the decisions were irrational and discriminatory. He says that certain other prisoners were able to cash in their compulsory $500 savings in order, for example, to help victims of the Tsunami. The applicant, however, does not deny the fact that he had money in his earnings account which could have been used. Indeed, it would have still left him with $100 or so in his earnings account. He says that nevertheless he was treated unfairly.

102. There is nothing in this complaint. Being given permission to donate to disaster relief is not to be compared to a desire to use moneys in a compulsory savings account to help fund litigation when there is already sufficient in what I have described as the applicant's cash account. Indeed, on the face of it, it appears as if the applicant was trying to manipulate the system.

103. Leave is refused.

The ninth complaint

104. The applicant has on a number of occasions received a disciplinary punishment of 'separate confinement'. The person on the street would call it solitary confinement. When in solitary confinement, the applicant has been denied a daily newspaper or radio. It is his complaint that it is unlawful to deny a prisoner access to the media even if, for a limited period of time, that prisoner is serving a punishment for an infringement of discipline.

105. In my judgment, to suggest that, even when undergoing punishment for a disciplinary offence, all prisoners are at *all times* entitled as a basic right to a newspaper and/or other means of information is not *prima facie* arguable.

106. I accept, of course, that a convicted prisoner, in spite of his imprisonment, retains all civil rights which are not expressly or impliedly taken from him.

107. But that being said, it has to be recognised that the maintenance of discipline in prisons presents its own particular difficulties. As Lawton LJ said in *R. v. Camphill (Deputy Governor), ex parte King* [1984] 3 All ER 897, at 902 –

> "Management without discipline is a recipe for chaos. For a prison governor, however, the ultimate sanction used in industry, commerce and schools, namely dismissal, is not available. There is need for other sanctions."

108. Good order and discipline being so important in ensuring the safe and orderly running of prisons, the Prison Rules vest a large measure of discretion in the Commissioner to determine how best that can be secured. See, for example, *R. v. Home Secretary, ex parte Leech* [1994] QB 198 (*per* Steyn LJ at 202).

109. In *Chim Shing Chung v. Commissioner of Correctional Services* (1996) 6 HKPLR 313, at 322, Litton VP (as he then was) said that it would need "an extreme case" before a court could safely say that the Commissioner, in the purported exercise of his judgment and discretion, has abused his legislative or regulatory powers.

110. As I understand the applicant's case, it is premised on the basis that regular – that is, uninterrupted – access to the news via television, radio or newspapers is a fundamental right of all Hong Kong residents including serving prisoners. But I do not see how that proposition is *prima facie arguable*.

111. First, it is axiomatic that the freedom to receive information of all kinds may be subject to restriction. This is stated in art.16 of the Bill of Rights which reads:

> "(1) ...
>
> (2) Everyone shall have the right to freedom of expression: this right shall include freedom to ... receive ... information and ideas of all kinds, ... either orally, in writing or in print, ...
>
> (3) *The exercise of the rights provided for in paragraph (2) of this article carries with it special duties and responsibilities. It may therefore be subject to certain restrictions, but these shall only be such as are provided by law and are necessary;*
>
> (a) for respect of the rights or reputations of others; or
>
> (b) for the protection of ... public order (ordre public) ..." [my emphasis]

112 Indeed, s.9 of the Hong Kong Bill of Rights Ordinance, Cap.383 specifically recognises that serving prisoners may be subject to such restrictions on their rights protected by the Bill of Rights as are necessary "for the preservation of ... custodial discipline" :

> "... persons lawfully detained in penal establishments of whatever character are subject to such restrictions as may from time to time be authorized by law for the preservation of ... custodial discipline."

113. Put simply, the freedom to receive information through television, radio and newspapers is a qualified right. One of those qualifications quite clearly, in so far as it applies to serving prisoners, must be the need within penal establishments to maintain good order and discipline.

114. As for art.27 of the Basic Law – which guarantees freedom of speech, of the press and of publication – I do not see that article in any way taking away from the proposition that the freedom is a qualified one.

115. S.18(1) of the Prisons Ordinance makes it a criminal offence to bring unauthorised articles into a prison. These include 'papers' and 'books'. However, r.56 of the Prison Rules provides that :

> "Prisoners may receive such books, periodicals, newspapers or other publications from outside the prison as the Commissioner may determine."

116. The Commissioner may therefore impose conditions on the manner in which prisoners receive books, newspapers, periodicals and the like.

117. On a fair, large and liberal construction of r.56, looking to its purpose, the imposition of conditions will cover a wide range of matters. For example, in *Chim Shing Chung v. Commissioner of Correctional Services* (1996) 6 HKPLR 313, the Court of Appeal held that it was lawful for the Commissioner to permit the introduction into prison of newspapers under the condition that their horse racing supplements were first removed.

118. In my judgment, it is clear that the Commissioner may impose a condition which prohibits a prisoner from having access to newspapers when he is undergoing a form of punishment. By way of illustration, Principle 28 of the United Nations 'Body of principles for the protection of all persons under any form of detention' reads :

> "A detained or imprisoned person shall have the right to obtain within the limits of available resources, if from public sources, reasonable quantities of educational, cultural and informational material, *subject to reasonable conditions to ensure security and good order in the place of detention or imprisonment.*" [my emphasis]

119. R.63 of the Prison Rules provides that a Superintendent may punish a prisoner who has breached discipline with "separate confinement for any period not exceeding 28 days".

120. Separate confinement – solitary confinement – is therefore prescribed by law as a necessary provision for the enforcement of discipline.

121. As to the nature of the punishment, the Standing Orders (65–07(5)) provide –

> "Prisoners undergoing separate confinement will be permitted to retain only a grass mat, a night soil bucket (when there is no toilet in the cell), toilet paper and drinking water during the period between unlock and lock-up, a bible or any devotional books may be retained by the prisoner during the whole period of punishment."

122. Solitary confinement is therefore a Spartan regime under which literature – other than devotional literature – is specifically prohibited. That is a necessary part of the punishment. If it was not, it would lessen the reluctance of the average prisoner to undergo it.

123. In summary, despite what at first blush may seem to be a point that carries at least enough merit to be prima facie arguable, I am satisfied that it is beyond doubt that the prohibition against access to the media during solitary confinement is prescribed by law and is a necessary requirement to ensure good order and discipline.

124. Leave is refused.

The tenth complaint

125. The history of this complaint is to the following effect. When the applicant was in Shek Pik Prison, he was given a hair trimmer on loan, the trimmer to be for his use only. However, when the applicant was transferred to Stanley Prison and the trimmer was found to be in his possession, it was taken from him. When it was removed, it was either implied or a direct accusation was made that the applicant must have retained possession of the trimmer dishonestly. According to the applicant, he was accused of being a thief.

126. The issue of the hair trimmer was the subject of a complaint by the applicant. By letter dated 18 January 2006, the applicant was informed by the Government Secretariat that there had been an investigation and that he was cleared of any allegation of dishonesty on his part. The letter says:

> "According to the Correctional Services Department, it came to the attention of the management of the Stanley Prison that you were in possession of a hair trimmer, which was not of the type the prison management commonly permitted a prisoner to retain for personal use. In the absence of reasonable information showing that the hair trimmer was obtained with prior authority, the CSD staff handling the case, ... had reason to suspect that possession of it might be in breach of Prison Rule 61 and action had to be taken to retrieve the hair trimmer pending investigation."

It continues by saying the following:

> "Subsequently the management of the Stanley Prison conducted an investigation into the case and learnt that, although the hair trimmer was government property, it was lent to you by the management of the Shek Pik Prison while you were in prison there. As a result, the management of Stanley Prison decided that no disciplinary action should be instituted against you. The Complaints Investigation Unit of the CSD later received your complaint on the improper confiscation of the hair trimmer and conducted an independent inquiry. The CIU's findings were consistent with those of the management of Stanley Prison.

The letter concludes:

> "One of the duties of CSD staff is to uphold prison discipline and in doing so they might have to take action against any person who is suspected to have breached the prison rules. In your case, the concerned CSD staff had the obligation to explain to you clearly what he suspected before taking any action to retrieve the object in question and this should not be taken as a deliberate attempt to embarrass you."

127. Mr Wong, for the Commissioner, has informed me that, not only has the applicant's complaint been fully investigated, but he now has the use – if he applies for it – of a new hair trimmer.

128. The applicant's complaint appears to be, first, that he should never have been accused of stealing the original hair trimmer and, second, that, as he was previously allowed to retain full-time possession of the original hair trimmer, he should be allowed the same privilege in respect of the new trimmer.

129. In respect of the first aspect of the complaint, I do not see how this court can take matters further. There has already been a full official inquiry.

130. If the applicant believes he has been defamed then he should sue.

131. The fact that in Shek Pik Prison the applicant was allowed to permanently retain the original hair trimmer did not set up any form of legitimate expectation that he would be allowed to have permanent possession of a trimmer for his entire sentence no matter in which institution he was incarcerated.

132. As for the new trimmer, the old one apparently having been broken, the applicant appears to seek an order that he be entitled

to keep the trimmer in his possession for his sole use: I can find no *prima facie* arguable grounds for making any such order.

133. The applicant complains that, unless the trimmer is – without doubt – kept solely for his use, there is the risk that other prisoners with skin problems and the like may use it.

134. The applicant further complains that every time he wants to use the trimmer he has to make an application. That is a bureaucratic process and can result in delays. The CSD officers can make life difficult for him.

135. I observe at this juncture that the applicant is firmly of the view that there is some sort of conspiracy hatched by the prison authorities to make his life as difficult as possible. Indeed, he has concluded his general submissions by warning that his life is in danger, that his death is being plotted.

136. While it is more than apparent that the applicant has experienced a good deal of friction with the prison authorities, there is no objective evidence to suggest that the applicant's well being is under threat in the way he has suggested.

137. In a previous hearing, almost a year ago, the applicant spoke of a plot to cripple him.

138. As for the hair trimmer, it seems to me to be a matter for the management of Stanley Prison how such items are to be stored and utilised. No doubt one factor that is taken into account is that of hygene. I am told that the new trimmer is in fact kept for the applicant but the decision has been made that the trimmer should not be in the possession of the applicant at all times. Nothing has been put before me to even begin to suggest that such a decision is in any way unlawful.

139. I note, in passing, that the cells where the applicant is housed are not wired for electricity. In any event, therefore, with an electric instrument such as a trimmer, the applicant has to use a socket point outside his cell, no doubt having to receive permission to do so.

140. Leave is refused.

The eleventh complaint

141. When the applicant received punishment of solitary confinement, that punishment entailed a loss of privileges for the time he spent in confinement. In the result, so I am told, certain canteen purchases – biscuits, chocolate and the like – were removed from the applicant and only returned to him when he completed his punishment. This, the applicant complains, has constituted an abuse of power and was unlawful.

142. The applicant has asserted that by the time his period in solitary confinement was over the canteen purchases would often not be fit for consumption. It is therefore the applicant's case that a prisoner sentenced to solitary confinement for a breach of discipline has the right to take all his canteen purchases with him; in short, that, at least as far as fungibles are concerned, there should be no loss of privileges.

143. What must first be understood is that canteen purchases – with the exception of letter-writing materials and postage stamps – are classified as privileges. A serving prisoner has no absolute right to biscuits, chocolate, condensed milk or whatever purchased from a retail outlet.

144. Nothing has been put before me to suggest that ordering a temporary loss of privileges is in any way unlawful in Hong Kong or against international conventions. Indeed, the threat of a possible loss of privileges is recognised as one of the most effective ways of enforcing discipline.

145. If privileges may be lost then they may be lost immediately when the punishment commences. The loss of privileges is after all an inherent part of the punishment.

146. That order makes it plain that any items being enjoyed by way of privilege – for example, secular magazines or foodstuffs – are not available to a prisoner serving solitary confinement. Bearing in mind the need for discipline in a prison, I can identify no argument to suggest that such removal is in any way unlawful.

147. If it so happens that any fungibles purchased from the canteen become inedible that, it seems to me, is a consequence of the prisoner's breach of discipline. All forms of punishment, to a greater or lesser degree, carry with them subsidiary consequences.

148. Leave is refused.

The twelfth complaint

149. The applicant complains that the prison authorities have refused to supply him free of charge with a pair of spectacles. This refusal, he says, is unlawful.

150. The applicant, in fact, has a pair of spectacles. He obtained them through his friend, Mr Crawley. He says that Mr Crawley should be reimbursed the amount he paid for those spectacles, whatever that sum is.

151. Although his condition has not yet been finally diagnosed, at this time it appears that the applicant needs spectacles because he has myopia. This is a condition which causes short sightedness. It is a common enough condition.

152. In support of his contention that spectacles must be supplied to him free of charge, the applicant relies principally on Prison Rule 143. This rule directs that the Prison Medical Officer is responsible for the treatment, when sick, of all prison inmates. Rule 148 directs that the Medical Officer shall, when necessary, make recommendations to the prison management concerning the best treatment, or any change in treatment, for a prisoner, this to include recommending the supply of any additional articles to him.

153. Looking, first, to the background of this matter, it appears that the applicant did seek to obtain spectacles from the prison authorities. There is evidence to show that the prison authorities informed him that, if he had money of his own sufficient to purchase a pair of glasses, those funds would have to be used; in short, that the prison authorities did not supply spectacles free of charge. There is further evidence to show that the applicant was advised that, if he did not have sufficient funds, he could make application to the 'Prisoners Welfare Fund' for sufficient moneys to buy spectacles. This fund is established under section 21A of the Prisons Ordinance and is set up for the benefit of prisoners.

154. When the applicant asked for spectacles free of charge in December 2005, it was noted that he had $200 in his property. This was considered sufficient to purchase a pair of glasses. His application to obtain a pair of glasses free of charge was therefore refused. The applicant, so the evidence shows, was invited to apply to the Prisoners Welfare Fund and, on his part, it is said that he did so. The prison authorities, however, suggest that he may not have done so.

155. At this juncture such minor disputes of fact are not germane. The issue is whether the applicant has a *prima facie* arguable case to say that prisoners, even if they have their own moneys, are entitled in law to obtain those spectacles free of charge.

156. My first observation, obvious though it is, is that the applicant was not refused spectacles.

157. If a prisoner has money available to him, he can use that money to buy spectacles.

158. My second observation is that, if a prisoner does not have the money to buy spectacles, he is able to approach the Prisoners Welfare Fund. This is a statutory fund and therefore part of the legislative regime which is set in place to assist persons like the applicant.

159. In short, a prisoner who requires spectacles has avenues open to him.

160. As to the applicant's contention that, once in prison, all of a prisoner's medical needs of whatever kind must be supplied free of charge, I do not see how that is even *prima facie* arguable either in light of international conventions or Hong Kong domestic law.

161. I note, for example, that the Standard Minimum Rules for the Treatment of Prisoners adopted by the United Nations, while it provides that a medical officer shall have 'the care of the physical and mental health' of prisoners makes no mention of all such care having to be free of charge.

162. There must be many jurisdictions where it is simply not possible for the authorities to supply items such as spectacles to prisoners free of charge.

163. There is nothing that I can find in the Hong Kong legislation to suggest that items such as spectacles must be supplied to prisoners free of charge. Put another way, I can find nothing to prevent the prison authorities from directing, as a general rule, that if a prisoner has sufficient funds to pay for spectacles, then he should do so, or if he does not, then he may apply to a special fund for financing.

164. Leave is refused.

The thirteenth complaint

165. After the applicant had been convicted of drug trafficking, the trial court made a number of consequential orders. These included an order that certain of the applicant's personal effects should be returned to him.

166. On 23 June 1998, customs officials attempted to carry out this order. The applicant was then held at Shek Pik Prison. The applicant, it appears, disputed that all of his effects were being returned and refused to accept those that were offered.

167. It seems as if the customs officers took the applicant's refusal as a final refusal. In the result, in early 2002 an application was made to a magistrate for an order that the personal effects be destroyed. That order was granted on 1 March 2002.

168. That order, however, appears not to have been made in knowledge of the earlier Court of First Instance order that the items be returned to the applicant.

169. As it turns out, however, the applicant's personal effects have not yet been destroyed. In the circumstances, without getting involved in whether this is or is not a suitable matter for judicial review, it seems to me to be common sense that the problem can, in the main, best be dealt with as follows:

(a) The applicant's personal effects can be returned to him.

(b) If the applicant is of the view that certain items are missing, he will accept the items that are returned without prejudice to his right to seek return of the missing items or to claim compensation for their loss.

170. In the circumstances, by agreement, the applicant's personal effects should be delivered to him as soon as possible.

171. If there is to be a dispute as to missing items and that cannot be resolved then, it seems to me, that the applicant would be well advised to consider seeking return of the missing items or compensation for their loss via the Small Claims Tribunal. I say that because I have my doubts that it would be a suitable matter for determination by way of judicial review.

Costs

172. I have refused leave on each and every application for leave made by the applicant. Mr Wong for the Commissioner seeks payment of costs, those costs to be assessed summarily. I decline to make that order.

173. These proceedings, even though they have taken a day and a half, are essentially *ex parte* in nature. I informed the Commissioner of the application, not on the basis that he was obliged to be represented here, but on the basis that, if he wished, he could choose to be represented to assist the court in such manner as it thought appropriate. Mr Wong has appeared to discharge a public function of ensuring, as far as possible, that the ends of justice are met.

Judge of the Court of First Instance, High Court (M.J. Hartmann)

Applicant, in person

Mr Wesley W.C. Wong, of the Department of Justice, for the Respondent

---

香港特別行政區 對 吳恭劭、利建潤

HCMA 563/1998；FACC 4/1999

簡略案情

1998 年 1 月 1 日，兩名答辯人吳恭劭、利建潤參與遊行，期間他們手持並展示塗污了的國旗及區旗，在遊行結束時把塗污了的國旗及區旗縛在欄杆上。兩名答辯人其後被控兩項控罪。第一項控罪是侮辱國旗，指他們違反《國旗及國徽條例》第 7 條，公開及故意以玷污的方式侮辱國旗。第二項控罪是侮辱區旗，指他們違反《區旗及區徽條例》第 7 條，公開及故意以玷污的方式侮辱區旗。對於該指控，答辯人認為是限制他們發表言論自由的權利，質疑該條文是違反《基本法》第 27 條，保證"香港居民享有言論、新聞、出版的自由，結社、集會、遊行、示威的自由，組織和參加工會、罷工的權利和自由。"

答辯人認為根據《香港人權法案》條例第 16 條，即《公民權利和政治權利國際公約》第 19 條：

（一）人人有保持意見不受干預之權利。

（二）人人有發表自由之權利；此種權利包括以語言、文字或出版物、藝術或自己選擇之其他方式，不分國界，尋求、接受及傳播各種消息及思想之自由。

（三）本條第（二）項所載權利之行使，附有特別責任及義務，故得予以某種限制，但此種限制以經法律規定，且為下列各項所必要者為限：

（甲）尊重他人權利或名譽；或

（乙）保障國家安全或公共秩序，或公共衛生或風化。

裁決摘要

然而，此辯護理由並未為裁判官所接納，法院認為，雖然《國旗及國徽條例》第 7 條及《區旗及區徽條例》第 7 條均限制了該公約第 19 條所保障的權利，但根據該公約第 19（3）條，為了保障公共秩序，該限制是必要的，故具有充分理據支持，因此並非違憲，最後兩名答辯人均被裁定罪名成立。他們遂上訴至上訴法院。上訴庭考慮了其他普通法系國家並沒有將污損國旗刑事化，認為該法條並不能依靠該公約第 19（3）條加以合理化，因此接受答辯人的理據，並將其定罪撤銷。控方於是向終審法院提出上訴。

終審法院同意關乎如表達自由或言論自由的憲法性問題時，法院應該採納較寬鬆的解釋。因此，這種自由應包括發表令人反感或討厭的思想，及對政府機關和官員行為的批評。終審法院引述了“錫拉庫扎原則”（The Siracusa Principles）和美洲人權法院的意見以解釋“公共秩序（public order 或 ordre public）”一詞，同意這概念並不能非常清晰地界定，並認為它包含為保障大眾福祉或為符合集體利益所必須採取的措施，包括制定法規以維持社會安寧及良好秩序，安全、公共衛生、美學及道德層面的考慮，以及經濟秩序（消費者權益的保障等）；而此概念亦會隨著時間、地點及環境的改變而改變。終審法院亦認為《國旗及國徽條例》及《區旗及區徽條例》對發表自由的限制是有限度的而並非廣泛的。為保護作為國家獨有象徵的國旗，以及作為香港特別行政區獨有象徵的區旗，該限制是必要的，而且並沒有超乎相關的範圍或程度。事實上，有一些《公民權利和政治權利國際公約》的締約國，如意大利和德國，也把侮辱國旗列為刑事罪行。

據此，終審法院裁定上述兩項條文並不違憲，控方上訴得直。

[中譯本 - Chinese Translation]

FACC 4/1999

香港特別行政區
終審法院

終院刑事上訴 1999 年第 4 號
（原本案件編號：高院裁判法院上訴 1998 年第 563 號）

上訴人	香港特別行政區
	訴
第一答辯人	吳恭劭
第二答辯人	利建潤

審理法官：終審法院首席法官李國能
終審法院常任法官烈顯倫
終審法院常任法官沈澄
終審法院常任法官包致金
終審法院非常任法官梅師賢爵士

聆訊日期：1999 年 10 月 20、21 及 22 日

判案書日期：1999 年 12 月 15 日

判案書

終審法院首席法官李國能：

1.《基本法》載有憲法性條文，保障香港這個文明社會不可或缺的多項自由。我等要處理的是發表自由的權利。本上訴案的爭議點，是究竟把侮辱國旗和區旗的行為列為刑事罪行的法定條文，是否與發表自由的保障相抵觸。受質疑的法定條文為《國旗及國徽條例》（香港法例 1997 年第 116 號）（"國旗條例"）第 7 條及《區旗及區徽條例》（香港法例 1997 年第 117 號）（"區旗條例"）第 7 條。

旗幟所象徵的意義

2. 國旗是一個國家的象徵，是獨有的象徵。所有國家都有國旗，而國徽也很普遍。

3. 案中國旗是中華人民共和國的象徵，是國家和國家主權的象徵。它代表中華人民共和國，代表她的尊嚴、統一及領土完整。

4. 案中區旗是香港特別行政區，作為"一國兩制"方針下中華人民共和國不可分離部分的獨有的象徵。在本判案書中，本席在提及中華人民共和國時會採用全名或簡稱為"中國"，而在提及香港特別行政區時則會採用全名或簡稱為"香港特區"或"特區"。

5. 作為如此獨有的象徵，國旗及區旗對香港特區的固有重要性可見於 1997 年 7 月 1 日子夜來臨的歷史性時刻，在香港舉行，標誌著中華人民共和國恢復對香港行使主權的交接儀式上，以升起國旗及區旗揭開儀式序幕的這項事實。此外，中華人民共和國主席隨後的講話也以此作為開端：

> "中華人民共和國國旗和中華人民共和國香港特別行政區區旗，已在香港莊嚴升起。"

本案爭議點

6. 中華人民共和國這個社會，即包括香港特別行政區在內的整個國家，具有保護作為國家獨有象徵的國旗之合法利益。同樣地，香港特別行政區這個社區也具有保護區旗之合法利益；區旗是代表特區作為"一國兩制"方針下中華人民共和國不可分離部分的獨有象徵。在我等席前，並沒有人就這些合法利益的存在提出爭議。

7. 我等面對的爭議點，是究竟這些合法利益是否足以構成充分理據把侮辱國旗及區旗的行為刑事化來限制發表自由。如果缺乏上述充分理據的支持，有關的法定條文便與《基本法》相抵觸，違反憲法；而且，法庭有權力及責任作如是宣告。代表香港特區政府的資深大律師麥高義先生也同意這點。

國旗

中國國旗法

8.1949 年 9 月 27 日，即臨近 1949 年 10 月 1 日中華人民共和國建國之日，中國人民政治協商會議第一屆全體會議首次通過關於國旗的決議。決議第四段為：

> "全體一致通過：中華人民共和國的國旗為紅地五星旗，象徵中國革命人民大團結。"

9. 現時，有關國旗的條文於現行中國憲法第一百三十六條有所訂明。

10. 中國國旗法於 1990 年 6 月 28 日由全國人民代表大會常務委員會通過及由中華人民共和國主席公布，並自 1990 年 10 月 1 日起施行。第一條述明該法是"爲了維護國旗的尊嚴，增強公民的國家觀念，發揚愛國主義精神"而根據憲法制定的。第二條訂明國旗是五星旗，並須按指明的製法說明製作。第三條規定：

> "中華人民共和國國旗是中華人民共和國的象徵和標誌。
>
> 每個公民和組織，都應當尊重和愛護國旗。"

11. 國旗法對升掛國旗的事項，例如升掛地點、時間及方式，也有所規定。

12. 第十七條規定不得升掛破損、污損、褪色或者不合規格的國旗。第十八條禁止將國旗及其圖案用作廣告商標或用於私人喪事活動。第十九條規定：

> "在公衆場合故意以焚燒、毀損、塗劃、玷污、踐踏等方式侮辱中華人民共和國國旗的，依法追究刑事責任；情節較輕的，參照治安管理處罰條例的處罰規定，由公安機關處以十五日以下拘留。"

13. 1990 年 6 月 28 日，即通過及公布中國國旗法當天，《全國人民代表大會常務委員會關於懲治侮辱中華人民共和國國旗國徽罪的決定》也獲得通過及公布，作爲《刑法》的補充規定，其內容如下：

> "在公衆場合故意以焚燒、毀損、塗劃、玷污、踐踏等方式侮辱中華人民共和國國旗、國徽的，處三年以下有期徒刑、拘役、管制或者剝奪政治權利。"

有關方面認爲要就該刑事罪行訂定條文，最佳方法便是對《刑法》作出上述補充規定。參閱負責研究該法例草案的法制工作委員會所做的報告，報告日期為 1990 年 5 月 30 日，並於 1990 年 6 月 20 日舉行的第七屆全國人民代表大會常務委員會第十四次會議上提交。上述規定現已由《中華人民共和國刑法》第二百九十九條的類似規定所替代。

《基本法》

14. 全國性法律於香港特別行政區的適用範圍，受《基本法》第十八條第二款所管限：

> "全國性法律除列於本法附件三者外，不在香港特別行政區實施。凡列於本法附件三之法律，由香港特別行政區在當地公布或立法實施。"

15. 第十八條第三款規定，全國人民代表大會常務委員會在徵詢其所屬的香港特別行政區基本法委員會和香港特別行政區政府的意見後，可對列於《基本法》附件三的法律作出增減。條文進一步規定：

> "任何列入附件三的法律，限於有關國防、外交和其他按本法規定不屬於香港特別行政區自治範圍的法律。"

16. 1997 年 7 月 1 日，全國人民代表大會常務委員會依據第十八條第二款，將中國國旗法與其他法律一起增列於附件三的法律中。

國旗條例

17. 由於《基本法》附件三有了上述增補，根據《基本法》第十八條第二款的規定，香港特區必須通過公布或立法在本地實施中國國旗法。因此，立法機關（當時的臨時立法會）通過立法制定了國旗條例，在香港特區內實施。採用立法方式較公布為適當，因爲該全國性法律必須作適應化修改以便在香港特區實施。國旗條例對在特區内使用及保護國旗的事宜有所規定。國旗必須在各主要政府建築物展示。見第 3(1) 條。行政長官可規定必須展示或使用國旗的機構、場合及其他場所，以及展示或使用國旗所必須遵守的方式及條件。見第 3(2) 條。第 4 條規定不得展示或使用破損、污損、褪色或不合規格的國旗。供升掛的國旗在香港特別行政區内只可由中央人民政府所指定的企業製造，並必須按訂明的規格製造。見第 5(1) 及 5(2) 條。國旗或其圖案不得展示或使用於商標或廣告、私人喪事活動或行政長官規定的其他場合或場所，違反上述規定即屬刑事罪行。見第 6(1) 及 6(3) 條。本上訴案受爭議的條文，即第 7 條，規定：

> "任何人公開及故意以焚燒、毀損、塗劃、玷污、踐踏等方式侮辱國旗……，即屬違法，一經定罪，可處第 5 級罰款［即 50,000 元］及監禁 3 年。"

如有國旗的複製本並非與國旗完全相同，但其相似程度足以使人相信它就是國旗，則就本條例而言，該複製本被視為國旗。

18. 第 9 條規定：

> （1）香港特別行政區内觸犯有關國旗及國徽的規定的罪行，按香港特別行政區現行法律進行調查及予以檢控。
>
> （2）如本條例與根據《基本法》附件三公布的任何全國性法律有不相符之處，本條例須解釋為該全國性法律的特別實施或改編本，並如此實施。"

區旗

《基本法》

19.《基本法》第十條第一款及第十條第二款規定：

> "香港特別行政區除懸掛中華人民共和國國旗和國徽外，還可使用香港特別行政區區旗和區徽。
>
> 香港特別行政區的區旗是五星花蕊的紫荊花紅旗。"

20. 香港特別行政區籌備委員會於 1996 年 8 月 10 日第四次全體會議上通過有關區旗的規定。1990 年 4 月 4 日，《全國人民代表大會關於〈基本法〉的決定》通過《基本法》及香港特別行政區區旗及區徽的圖案。在該決定未通過之前，基本法起草委員會主任向全國人民代表大會致詞解釋時，曾述及區旗及區徽的選擇程序，並說明區旗及區徽的圖案。他在說到區旗時表示：

> "區旗是一面中間配有五顆星的動態紫荊花圖案的紅旗。紅旗代表祖國，紫荊花代表香港，寓意香港是中國不可分離的部分，在祖國的懷抱中興旺發達。花蕊上的五顆星象徵著香港同胞心中熱愛祖國，紅、白兩色體現了'一國兩制'的精神。"

區旗條例

21. 區旗條例旨在就使用及保護區旗事宜制定條文。該條例賦予行政長官類似國旗條例所賦予的權力。他有權規定區旗的展示及使用事宜。見第 3(1) 條。第 3(3) 條及附表 3 開列出區旗的使用及展示辦法。該等條文原先已獲籌備委員會通過為暫訂條文，制定目的在於"維護"區旗的"尊嚴"及確保人人正確使用區旗。條文述明區旗及區徽：

> "是香港特別行政區的象徵和標誌。每個香港居民和團體都應當尊重和愛護區旗、區徽。"

該條例規定了區旗與國旗同時懸掛時的使用及展示辦法，那就是，國旗必須置於較顯眼的位置。見第 3(2) 條及附表 3。任何人不得展示或使用破損、污損、褪色或不合規格的區旗。見第 4 條。區旗必須按照訂明規格製造。見第 5(1) 條。區旗或其圖案不得展示或使用於商標或廣告或行政長官規定的其他場合或場所，違反上述規定即屬刑事罪行。見第 6(1) 條及 6(2) 條。

22. 第 7 條，即本上訴案受爭議的條文，規定：

> "任何人公開及故意以焚燒、毀損、塗劃、玷污、踐踏等方式侮辱區旗或區徽，即屬犯罪 ——
>
> （a）一經循公訴程序定罪，可處第 5 級罰款［即 50,000 元］及監禁 3 年；及
>
> （b）一經循簡易程序定罪，可處第 3 級罰款［即 10,000 元］及監禁 1 年。"

區旗條例載有一條文與國旗條例條文相似，規定就該條例而言，區旗的複製本會被視為區旗。

控罪

23. 兩名答辯人被控兩項侮辱國旗及區旗罪，分別是違反國旗條例第 7 條及區旗條例第 7 條。每項罪行的詳情指兩名答辯人於 1998 年 1 月 1 日在香港公開及故意以玷污方式分別侮辱國旗及區旗。

定罪

24. 1998 年 5 月 18 日，兩名答辯人均被裁定該兩項罪行罪名成立。各人就每項罪行須自簽 2,000 元，守行爲 12 個月 [1999] 2 HKC 10 第 13–16 頁。

本案的事實

25. 在原審裁判官席前，控辯雙方對構成定罪基礎的事實並無爭議。就本上訴而言，只須把這些事實簡述。正如第二答辯人的案由述要所說的（第 2 及第 3 段）：

> "本案發生於 1998 年 1 月 1 日香港市民支援愛國民主運動聯合會組織的一次香港公開示威活動中。該次示威活動由一個公衆集會及一個從維多利亞公園至位於下亞厘畢道的

香港政府中區政府合署的公開遊行所組成。該公衆集會及公開遊行均屬合法及有秩序地進行。

公開遊行期間，有人看見兩名答辯人手上拿着兩件東西，看似一面塗污了的國旗及一面塗污了的區旗，並沿途揮舞。遊行終結時，他們把那兩件東西縛在中區政府合署的欄杆上。警方檢走了那兩件東西……"

26. 兩面旗幟均被嚴重塗污。國旗的中央被剪掉一個圓形部分；大顆的五角黃星被人塗上黑色墨水，星型圖案本身更被刺穿。旗幟的背面也有類似的損毀情況。還有，旗幟上的其餘四顆較小的星型圖案，均被人以黑色墨水寫上"恥"字，而在旗幟背面，四顆較小的星型圖案之中位置最低的那一顆被畫上一個黑色交叉。

27. 那面區旗則被撕去一截，失去部分紫荊圖案，該圖案更被畫上黑色交叉；餘下四顆紅星的其中三顆各被畫上黑色交叉；旗幟被人用黑色墨水寫上"恥"字；旗幟上面還有另一個中文字，但由於旗幟被撕毀，那個字已不能辨識。旗幟的背面也有類似的損毀情況。

28. 遊行期間，兩名答辯人高聲喊叫"建立民主中國"。據報導，第二答辯人對傳媒說，"撕毀及塗污國旗、區旗是表達對非民選執政者的不滿和抗爭行動"。

上訴法庭

29. 兩名答辯人就判罪向高等法院原訟法庭法官貝珊提出上訴。1998 年 12 月 8 日在雙方共同提出申請之下，她將有關上訴留待上訴法庭聆訊。上訴法庭（副庭長鮑偉華、上訴法庭法官梅賢玉及司徒冕）於 1999 年 3 月 23 日判決上訴得直並將兩名答辯人的定罪判決撤銷 [1999] 1 HKLRD 783，（同時編入 [1999] 2 HKC 10）。

30. 在裁判法院及上訴法庭的聆訊中，唯一的爭論點都是國旗條例第 7 條及區旗條例第 7 條究竟有沒有違反《基本法》。辯方在裁判法院及上訴法庭的聆訊中均爭辯說，這兩條條文與《公民權利和政治權利國際公約》（"該公約"）第十九條相抵觸，因而違反了《基本法》第三十九條。

上訴許可

31. 1999 年 5 月 20 日，上訴委員會（終審法院首席法官李國能、終審法院常任法官烈顯倫及沈澄）給予上訴人向終審法院提出上訴的許可。上訴委員會證明案件涉及兩個具有重大而廣泛重要性的法律論點：即 (1) 國旗條例第 7 條是否違反《基本法》？ (2) 區旗條例第 7 條是否違反《基本法》？這兩個爭論點與在裁判法院及上訴法庭的聆訊中所提出的爭論點相同。基本上，在申請上訴許可的聆訊中也只提出了這兩個爭論點。

新論點

32. 第二答辯人在其書面案由述要中首次提出一個新的論點，指稱根本沒有證據支持定罪的裁決。詳情如下：

"沒有證據顯示，任何一位答辯人公開以玷污方式侮辱該兩面旗幟。控辯雙方所同意的事實記載了兩名被告人攜帶着或揮舞着塗污了的國旗和區旗（第 8 段），從銅鑼灣遊行至中環期間他們繼續這樣做（第 10 段），及於遊行結束時兩名被告人將該兩面他們曾經揮動的旗幟縛在政府總部外的欄杆上。

公開及故意展示破損或污損的旗幟並非刑事罪行。雖然國旗條例第 4 條規定不得展示或使用破損或污損的國旗，但並沒有將之列為刑事罪行。區旗條例第 4 條在文字上與國旗條例第 4 條相近。第二答辯人在公開場合所做的事情正是第 4 條條文所指的情況。由於第 4 條沒有將這樣的行為列為刑事罪行，所以第二答辯人在公開場合所做的事情不能構成刑事罪行。"

33. 沒有在下屬法院提過的新論點，除非情況非常特殊，否則不會獲得終審法院處理。參閱 *Wong Tak Yue v. Kung Kwok Wai David* [1998] 1 HKC 1 一案。

34. 在裁判法院的聆訊中，兩名答辯人均有大律師代表。在上訴法庭的聆訊中，第一答辯人由法律援助署署長延聘的大律師代表，而第二答辯人則沒有出庭。在申請上訴許可的聆訊中，兩名答辯人均由法律援助署署長延聘的大律師代表，並反對該次申請。緊接該上訴許可申請之後，第一答辯人拒絕接受法律援助署的進一步協助。其後，他便沒有律師代表，在本院的聆訊中一直是親自出庭。

35. 代表兩名答辯人的大律師在此之前從來沒有提出這一新論點，而原審裁判官或上訴法庭也沒有提出這論點。

36. 大律師或法官在下屬法院中沒有提出這個新論點實不足爲奇。這論點完全缺乏理據。國旗條例及區旗條例第 7 條所指的罪行均為以玷污方式侮辱有關旗幟。"玷污"的一般涵義顯然包括玷辱在內。兩名答辯人在公開遊行中攜帶和揮舞那兩面塗污了的旗幟，然後在遊行結束時把旗幟縛在欄杆上，這樣做明顯是要玷辱那兩面旗幟。這些作爲明顯地構成了以玷污方式侮辱國旗及區旗。

言論自由和發表自由

37.《基本法》第二十七條保障了言論自由。該條規定：

"香港居民享有言論、新聞、出版的自由，結社、集會、遊行、示威的自由，組織和參加工會、罷工的權利和自由。"

38. 發表的自由載於《公民權利和政治權利國際公約》第十九條。該條條文如下：

（一）人人有保持意見不受干預之權利。

（二）人人有發表自由之權利；此種權利包括以語言、文字或出版物、藝術或自己選擇之其他方式，不分國界，尋求、接受及傳播各種消息及思想之自由。

（三）本條第（二）項所載權利之行使，附有特別責任及義務，故得予以某種限制，但此種限制以經法律規定，且為下列各項所必要者為限 —

（甲）尊重他人權利或名譽；或

（乙）保障國家安全或公共秩序、或公共衛生或風化。"

39. 正如代表政府的資深大律師麥高義先生所同意，"該公約"第十九條藉《基本法》第三十九條納入《基本法》之內。《基本法》第三十九條規定：

"《公民權利和政治權利國際公約》、《經濟、社會與文化權利的國際公約》和國際勞工公約適用於香港的有關規定繼續有效，通過香港特別行政區的法律予以實施。

香港居民享有的權利和自由，除依法規定外不得限制，此種限制不得與本條第一款規定抵觸。"

《香港人權法案條例》（香港法例第 383 章）事實上規定了將"該公約"的條文納入香港法例之內。《香港人權法案條例》第 II 部第十六條與"該公約"第十九條在文字上是完全相同。

40. 侮辱旗幟是一種非語言的言論或發表形式。代表政府的資深大律師麥高義先生同意本案涉及言論自由或發表自由。他認同該兩條法例的第 7 條把侮辱國旗和區旗的行爲列為刑事罪行，是對這兩種自由構成了限制。就本上訴而言，無論把該限制視為對言論自由的限制或發表自由的限制都沒有分別，因爲根據《基本法》第三十九條第二款的規定，對其中任何一種自由所施加的限制，均不可與“該公約”的條文抵觸。這點也獲麥高義先生接納。在措詞方面，原審裁判官及上訴法庭均取“發表自由”而捨“言論自由”。本席也會採納這一做法。但如將該限制視為對言論自由的限制，本席的判決也同樣適用。

41. 發表自由是民主社會的基本自由，也是文明社會及香港的制度和生活方式的核心。法院對其憲法性的保障必須採納寬鬆的解釋。這種自由包括發表大多數人認爲令人反感或討厭的思想，及批評政府機關和官員行爲的自由。

限制的範圍

42. 雙方均認爲把侮辱國旗和區旗的行爲列為刑事罪行的法定條文限制了發表的自由。在考慮該限制是否有充分理據支持之前，首先必須研究該限制的範圍，因爲在考慮是否有理可據這個問題時，必須了解須要充分理據支持的到底是甚麼，特別是須要充分理據支持的究竟是一個廣泛的限制，還是一個有限度的限制。限制的範圍越廣，便越難提出充分理據支持。上訴人陳詞說，由於只有一種發表的形式被禁止，發表的自由僅受到輕微影響。答辯人則爭辯說該限制是廣泛的。其論據是該限制不僅禁止了一種發表形式，而且通過將一種政治抗議形式列為非法行為，也禁止了可以發表的內容。

43. 如上所述，侮辱旗幟是一種象徵的發表或非語言的發表。以侮辱國旗作爲一種發表方法的人通常是要發表一個抗議的信息，但他想傳達的那個信息不一定清晰。那個信息可能是對一個國家的仇恨或反對，或是對當權政府的抗議；又或者該名有關人士欲對政府的一個現行政策表示抗議，或想表達某些其他信息。我等必須考慮圍繞該次侮辱旗幟事件的情況才能確定那人欲傳遞的信息到底是甚麼。就本案而言，兩名答辯人是對內地政府的體制表示抗議。這可以從兩面旗幟上均寫上“恥”字，加上遊行期間有人高聲喊叫“建立民主中國”和第二答辯人據稱向傳媒所講的那番話中顯示出來。

44. 有關法例禁止侮辱國旗及區旗，這並不是一個對發表自由的廣泛限制，而是一個有限度的限制。不論有關人士欲發表的是甚麼信息，該法例都只是禁止一種發表形式，即侮辱國旗及區旗這一形式，並沒有干預該名人士以其他形式去發表同樣信息的自由。況且，在國旗及區旗上塗劃讚美的字句（而不像通常的情況爲了傳達抗議的信息而寫的字句）也可能構成該兩條條例第 7 條所指的罪行，即以塗劃方式侮辱國旗及區旗的罪行。如果這理解正確，那麼，有關條文不但禁止以這一形式發表抗議的信息，而且也禁止以這種形式發表其他信息，包括讚美的信息。但是，一條旨在維護具象徵意義的旗幟的尊嚴而制定的法例，必須全面保護旗幟免遭侮辱，才能產生應有的效力。

該限制是否有充分理據支持？

45. 發表自由的權利並非絕對。《公民權利和政治權利國際公約》的前言承認個人對其他個體及對其所屬之群體須承擔義務。第十九條第三款本身也承認發表自由的權利之行使，附有特別責任及義務，故得予以某種限制，但此種限制必須是經法律規定，且為下列各項所必要者為限 ——

> “（甲）尊重他人權利或名譽；或
>
> （乙）保障國家安全或公共秩序、或公共衞生或風化。”

46. 要限制自由必須經過法律規定。本案所涉及的兩條條文是依法制定，故已符合這個要求。在考慮一個限制的範圍時，對發表自由的權利所施加的任何限制都必須取其狹義解釋，這是早已確立的法律原則。參閱*明報報業有限公司對香港律政司一案*〔*Ming Pao Newspapers Ltd v Attorney-General*〕[1996] AC 907（英國樞密院）第 917 頁 B-C。雙方均認爲無論施加任何限制，政府都有責任提出充分理據加以支持。

47. 在這方面，政府以該限制是保障公共秩序〔public order（ordre public(1)〕所必要為主要論據。由此引起兩個問題。第一，本席已經裁定保護國旗和區旗存在着社會及社區的合法利益，這些利益是否包含在公共秩序〔public order（ordre public）〕這個概念之內？第二，如果第一條問題的答案是肯定的話，該項對發表自由的權利的限制是否為保障上述利益所必要？

是否屬公共秩序〔public order（ordre public）〕範圍內？

48. 代表政府的資深大律師麥高義先生陳詞說，無論公共秩序〔public order（ordre public）〕所涵蓋的範圍多廣，其概念都包括保護國旗及區旗這合法利益。代表第二答辯人的資深大律師余若薇女士則持相反論點，指不論公共秩序涵蓋的範圍多廣，其概念都不可能包括上述利益。

49. 我們必須了解的是公共秩序〔public order（ordre public）〕的概念並不局限於治安範疇之內，這亦已廣為法律學者所確認，並為香港法院所認同。參閱*譚慶義對胡大偉一案*（*Tam Hing-yee v Wu Tai-wai*）[1992] 1 HKLR 185 第 190 頁及律政司司長訴東方報業集團有限公司一案 （*Secretary for Justice v Oriental Press Group Ltd*） [1998] 2 HKLRD 123 第 161 頁（初審時由高等法院首席法官陳兆愷及祁彥輝法官主審）（此案的判案書亦輯錄於 [1998] 2 HKC 627）以及此案在上訴法庭上訴時的*黃陽午對律政司司長一案*（*Wong Yeung Ng v Secretary for Justice*）[1999] 2 HKLR 293 第 307 頁 I（此案的判案書亦輯錄於 [1999] 2 HKC 24）。這裡涉及的用詞並非單單是“public order”，而是“public order（ordre public）”。把“ordre public”一詞也包括在內明顯表示有關概念較普通法概念中的治安廣泛。審理本案的裁判官及上訴法庭看來都把公共秩序〔public order（ordre public）〕的概念局限於治安的範疇，這種處理方法並不正確。

50. 大律師嘗試搜集本港或其他地區法院就公共秩序〔public order（ordre public）〕一詞所作的論述，但能找到的極之有限，當中包括*律政司司長訴東方報業集團有限公司一案* (*Secretary for Justice v Oriental Press Group Ltd*) 在原訟法庭初審的一段判詞，內容如下（參閱第 669 頁 C-H）：

> “⋯⋯據稱對施加限制提供充分理據的 [《香港人權法案條例》] 第十六條第三款（乙）段 [等同《公民權利和政治權利國際公約》第十九條] 的訂立目的是為了“保障⋯⋯公共秩序。條文把括號內的字眼（“ordre public”）也包括在內，顯示應給予“公共秩序”這詞一個比在普通法適用地區通常對該詞所理解的更為廣泛的涵義。“公共秩序”這詞的涵義應包含歐洲律師所熟悉的“*ordre public*”的概念。為“*ordre public*”下定義從來並非易事，尤其因為這詞在公法及私法所包含的意思都不同，並因其使用的文意而異。例如，在香港法例第 383 章《香港人權法案條例》第十條，公共秩序一詞的涵義較為近似防止騷亂；然而，在公法範疇內：

……ordre public 的意思包含國家組織的存在及運作，不僅容許國家組織在國內維持安寧及秩序，也透過滿足集體需要及保障人權從而確保公眾福祉。（參閱輯錄於 Henkin 所編的"The International Bill of Rights"(1981 年版，第 301 頁）一書內由 Kiss 所著的"Permissible Limitations on Rights"一文）

法院是"國家組織"中一個極其重要的機構。法院是法治的化身，在滿足社會"集體需要"及保障"人權"方面擔當關鍵角色。一旦為"public order"下如此定義後（即該詞並不限於防止騷亂），依我等之見，第十六條第三款（乙）段中"保障…公共秩序"一詞顯然包括維護法治這概念，至少在公眾對適當執行司法工作的信心被削弱以致法治遭破壞的情況下是如此……"

法院在該案裁定，屬普通法的"惡意中傷法院"，以及"干預法院使其不能繼續執行司法工作"的藐視法庭罪，對發表自由構成了可容許的限制。這項裁定獲上訴法庭確認。原訟法庭亦裁定適當執行司法工作屬公共秩序〔public order（ordre public）〕的範圍內，這點在上訴法庭亦獲得該案雙方接受（參閱第 39 頁 E）。

51. 上文判詞所引述的文章的作者說，公共秩序〔public order（ordre public）〕這概念"並非絕對，也不精確，且不能簡化為一成不變的公式，而是必須隨着時間、地點以及環境的改變而有所不同"。作者並以下文總結其論述：

"總括而言，若符合下述條件，則基於公共機構之妥善運作為集體所必要者的理由，"public order"可理解為一可限制某些指明的權利和自由的基準。上文列出了在社會人士眼中適宜納入 ordre public 範疇的例子包括：為維持社會安寧及良好秩序而制定法規、安全、公共衞生、美學及道德層面的考慮、及經濟秩序(消費者權益的保障等)。然而，必須緊記的是不論在大陸法系或普通法系地區，採用這概念均意味著這方面的事宜由法院處理，讓法院根據其對社會組織基本需要和文明社會價值觀的清楚認識，正確地發揮其職能，以監察和消除這方面的矛盾。"(Kiss 一文第 302 頁)

52. 就《公民權利及政治權利國際公約》中的限制及減免條文，一班專家在 1984 年議定了"錫拉庫扎原則"（The Siracusa Principles），當中包含下列關於"公共秩序〔public order（ordre public）〕"一詞的論述：

"22. 在"該公約"中，"公共秩序〔public order（ordre public）〕"一詞可界定為確保社會運作的規則的總體或建立社會的一套基本原則。尊重人權屬公共秩序〔public order（ordre public）〕之一環。

23. 詮釋公共秩序〔public order（ordre public）〕一詞的涵義時，必須針對以公共秩序為理由加以限制的那項人權的目的來考慮。

24. 負責維持公共秩序〔public order（ordre public）〕的國家機關或代理機構行使權力時，必須受國會、法院或其他有管轄權的獨立機構所約束。"

參閱（1985）7 *Human Rights Quarterly* 季刊第 3–14 頁。

53. 1986 年，美洲人權法院（Inter-American Court of Human Rights）在其發表的諮詢意見中（Advisory Opinion No. DC-6/86）就《美洲人權公約》（*American Convention on Human Rights*）第 30 條中"法規"一詞表達了以下意見：

"制定法規必須以公眾利益為依歸，這要求是指這些法規必然是為了'公眾福祉'才獲通過（第 32（2）條）。這概念在民主社會必須詮釋為屬於公共秩序〔public order（ordre public）〕的不可缺少的部分，而其主要目的是為了"保障人類必不可少的權利，並創造環境讓人類獲得精神及物質上的進步和幸福。（American Declaration of the Rights and Duties of Man，……First Introductory Clause）"（見諮詢意見第 29 段）

上述引文輯錄於（1986）7 *Human Rights Law Journal* 法律期刊第 231 頁。上述公約第 30 條訂明"除非有基於公眾利益而制定的法規為根據，並為此制定了限制措施"，否則便不可以對各種權利或自由予以限制。第 32(2) 條訂明，"在民主社會，個人的權利是受其他人的權利、整體的安全，以及牽涉大眾福祉的正當需求所規限。"

54. 從上述資料可歸納出下列數點。第一，公共秩序這概念既不精確，亦難以表述，其涵蓋範圍也不能準確地界定。第二，這概念包含為保障大眾福祉或為符合集體利益所必須採取的措施，例子包括為維持社會安寧及良好秩序而制定法規、安全、公共衞生、美學及道德層面的考慮、及經濟秩序（消費者權益的保障等）。第三，這概念必須隨着時間、地點及環境的改變而有所不同。

55. 就現在我們所處的時間、地點及環境而言，香港已經處於新的憲制秩序。1997 年 7 月 1 日中華人民共和國對香港這個與中華人民共和國不可分離的部分恢復行使主權，並根據"一國兩制"的方針設立香港特別行政區。《基本法》的序言描述恢復對香港行使主權是"實現了長期以來中國人民收回香港的共同願望"。在此情況下，保護國旗這合法的社會利益，以及保護區旗這合法的社區利益，兩者均屬公共秩序〔public order（ordre public）〕這概念所包含之範圍內。正如本席先前指出，國旗是一國 —— 中華人民共和國 —— 的獨有象徵，而區旗是"一國兩制"方針下香港特別行政區作為中華人民共和國不可分離部分的獨有象徵。上述這些合法利益是大眾福祉和整體利益的一部分。

是否必要

56. 即使上述合法利益是屬於公共秩序〔public order（ordre public）〕的範圍內，問題並未了結。我們必須探究，對受保障的發表自由的權利所施加的限制，是否為保障這些屬公共秩序〔public order（ordre public）〕範圍內的合法利益所必要者。

57. 英國樞密院及香港法院已裁定，"必要"一詞在這個驗證中，應以一般的涵義去理解，不必借助諸如"迫切社會需要"等用語來代替"必要"一詞。參閱*譚慶義對胡大偉一案*（*Tam Hing-yee v Wu Tai-wai*）第 191 頁，*明報報業有限公司對香港律政司一案*（*Ming Pao Newspapers Ltd v Attorney General of Hong Kong*）第 919 頁 G–H 及*黃陽午對律政司司長一案*(*Wong Yeung Ng v Secretary for Justice*) 第 40 頁 E–F，第 53 頁 C–D 以及第 59 頁 B。這種處理方法是正確的。

58. 1997 年 7 月 1 日，全國人大常委會把中國國旗法增補入《基本法》附件三內，香港特別行政區因此要透過公布或立法程序來在特區實施這法例。香港特區立法機關為履行這項責任而制定了國旗條例，同時認為制定區旗條例是恰當的做法。

59. 香港特區立法機關認為，鑑於人大常委會已通過將國旗法列入《基本法》附件三內，特區制定包括第 7 條在內的國旗條例的有關條文，以履行在香港實施這條全國性法律的責任，此舉是恰當的。本院在處理"是否必要"這問題時，應對這個看法予以充分考慮。同樣，本院對香港特區立法機關認為制定區旗條例是恰當的這看法，也應予以充分考慮。

60. 本院在驗證“是否必要”時必須考慮，對受保障的發表自由的權利所施加的限制，與施加限制所要達致的目的是否相稱。參閱*明報報業有限公司對香港律政司一案*（*Ming Pao Newspapers Ltd v Attorney – General of Hong Kong*）第 917 頁 D–E。正如前文結論所述，本案所涉及的法定條文將侮辱國旗及區旗列為刑事罪行是對發表自由的權利施加一種有限度的限制，所要達致的目的是保護作為國家獨有象徵的國旗，以及作為香港特別行政區獨有象徵的區旗，以符合保護這些旗幟為社會及社區帶來無可置疑的合法利益。既然這些施加於發表自由的權利的限制只是有限度，這也就通過“是否必要”驗證。這些有限度的限制與施加這些限制所欲達致之目的相稱，並沒有超越彼此相稱的範圍。

61. 中華人民共和國恢復對香港行使主權後，香港正處於一個新秩序的初期。貫徹“一國兩制”的方針極之重要，正如維護國家統一及領土完整亦是極之重要一樣。既然國旗及區旗具獨有的象徵意義，保護這兩面旗幟免受侮辱對達致上述目標也就起着重大作用。因此，有非常充足的理由斷定，將侮辱國旗及區旗的行為列為刑事罪行，對受保障之發表自由的權利施加限制，此舉是有充分理據支持的。

62. 此外，雖然本院所處理的是香港特別行政區作為中華人民共和國不可分離部分的事情，但本院亦留意到多個簽署確認《公民權利及政治權利國際公約》的民主國家亦有制定法例保護國旗，將侮辱國旗或類似的行為列為可處以監禁刑罰的刑事罪行。這些保護國旗的例子顯示，將侮辱國旗的行為列為刑事罪行在其他民主社會可視為保障公共秩序〔public order（ordre public）〕的必要措施。

63. 因此，制定國旗條例第 7 條及區旗條例第 7 條是為了保障公共秩序〔public order（ordre public）〕所必要，這兩條條文對發表自由的權利施加限制具有充分理據支持，亦符合憲法。

64. 既然已作出這結論，本席也無須在此處理其他曾經討論過的論點。

法院的命令

65. 因此，兩項經證明須交由本院審理的法律問題的答案如下：

（1）國旗條例第 7 條有沒有違反《基本法》？

答案是“沒有”。

（2）區旗條例第 7 條有沒有違反《基本法》？

答案是“沒有”。

66. 本席判上訴得直，回復裁判官的定罪判決及簽保守行為判令。

67. 最後，本院衷心感謝代表政府的資深大律師麥高義先生和代表第二答辯人的資深大律師余若薇女士分別領導的法律代表團。他們分別提交的書面及口頭論據和有關的資料為本院提供了非常寶貴的協助，本席特此鳴謝。我等亦多謝第一答辯人親自出庭陳詞。兩位資深大律師均沒有在上訴法庭辦理本案。據本席了解，在本院提出的論據及提交的資料，無論在範圍方面和深度方面，都遠遠超過上訴法庭在審理本案時所掌握的。可惜，上訴法庭因缺乏全面的論據和資料而未能受惠。

終審法院常任法官烈顯倫：

68. 本席同意終審法院首席法官李國能的判決。

終審法院常任法官沈澄：

69. 本席同意終審法院首席法官李國能的判決。

終審法院常任法官包致金：

70. 本席對本案的見解與終審法院首席法官的見解一致。

是否符合憲法的爭議

71. 本院要處理的爭議是保護國旗國徽及區旗區徽免受侮辱的本地法律是否符合憲法。這些法律包含在兩條法定條文內。第一條是《國旗及國徽條例》（香港法例 1997 年第 116 號）第 7 條，該條禁止公開及故意以焚燒、毀損、塗劃、玷污、踐踏等方式侮辱國旗或國徽。第二條是《區旗及區徽條例》（香港法例 1997 年第 117 號）第 7 條，該條同樣禁止對區旗及區徽作出以上行為。違反上述兩條條文的最高刑罰一樣，同是罰款 50,000 元及監禁 3 年。

控罪

72. 1998 年 1 月 1 日，兩名答辯人參與遊行，遊行期間他們手持塗污了的國旗及區旗，在遊行結束時把塗污了的國旗及區旗縛在欄杆上。

73. 兩名答辯人其後被控兩項控罪。每項控罪均同時指控兩人。第一項控罪是侮辱國旗，違反《國旗及國徽條例》第 7 條，詳情指他們公開及故意以玷污的方式侮辱國旗。第二項控罪是侮辱區旗，違反《區旗及區徽條例》第 7 條，詳情指他們公開及故意以玷污的方式侮辱區旗。

案件在下屬法院的審理過程

74. 答辯人以發表自由的權利為基礎，質疑用以檢控他們的兩項法定條文是否符合憲法，但在裁判法院審訊時未能成功。兩名答辯人均被定罪及各判簽保 2,000 元，守行為 12 個月。他們就定罪判決向高等法院提出上訴。高等法院將案件提交上訴法庭。上訴法庭就條文是否符合憲法這點判上訴得直，並將定罪撤銷。控方向本院提出上訴，故上述憲法爭議便交由本院處理。

是否僅僅違抗第 4 條的指令？

75. 代表第二答辯人的大律師除了就這項憲法方面的爭議提出論點外，亦從一個較低的層面提出如下的論點，就是答辯人的行為只是違抗上述兩項條例的第 4 條所包含的指令，即不得展示或使用破損、污損、褪色或不合規格的國旗、區旗、國徽或區徽的指令，而該條文並無規定違抗指令須受刑事制裁。

76. 本席無法接納這論點。第 4 條的指令旨在給予那些欲對國旗區旗及國徽區徽表示敬意的人士一些指導。但是與此相比，第 7 條卻截然不同，該禁制條文旨在保護國旗區旗及國徽區徽免遭蓄意侮辱。公開及故意在遊行時展示一面經刻意選擇的塗污了的旗幟或徽號，就是玷污這旗幟或徽號，亦因而侮辱了這旗幟或徽號。因此，本上訴案的關鍵所在是有關條文是否符合憲法。本席現在處理這項爭議。

發表自由：實質內容及形式

77.“言論”一詞在憲制方面所涵蓋的範圍廣泛，因此言論自由便等同發表自由。本席將採用“發表”這一詞語。香港的憲法《基本法》第二十七條及三十九條保障在香港的人士享有發表自由。《基本法》第二十七條規定：

> “香港居民享有言論、新聞、出版的自由，結社、集會、遊行、示威的自由，組織和參加工會、罷工的權利和自由。”

78.《基本法》第三十九條訂明《公民權利和政治權利國際公約》

（“該公約”）適用於香港的有關規定繼續有效，並通過香港的法律予以實施。《香港人權法案條例》（“人權法案”）正是“該公約”適用於香港的有關規定的化身，而與“該公約”第十九條完全相同的“人權法案”第十六條訂明：

> (一)人人有保持意見不受干預之權利。
>
> (二)人人有發表自由之權利；此種權利包括以語言、文字或出版物、藝術或自己選擇之其他方式，不分國界，尋求、接受及傳播各種消息及思想之自由。
>
> (三) 本條第(二)項所載權利之行使，附有特別責任及義務，故得予以某種限制，但此種限制以經法律規定，且為下列各項所必要者為限——
>
> (甲)尊重他人權利或名譽；或
>
> (乙)保障國家安全或公共秩序、或公共衛生或風化。

79. 必須注意的是，雖然“人權法案”第十六條有明文規定對其賦予的權利施加限制，但《基本法》第二十七條並沒有明文規定對其賦予的任何權利施加任何限制。因此，若《基本法》第二十七條對言論自由的保障與“人權法案”第十六條（此條獲《基本法》第三十九條支持）對發表自由的保障有所不同，則本席將第二十七條所賦予的保障視為比第十六條所賦予的保障更加有力。

80. 若以 ordre public（公共秩序）這概念作為驗證標準，則我們首先要面對以下問題。正如佳日思教授所指出（先在韋利文所編輯的“Human Rights in Hong Kong”（1992 年版）第 11 章《發表自由》一文第 391 頁；後在陳文敏及佳日思所編輯的“The Hong Kong Bill of Rights：A Comparative Approach”(1993 年版)第 8 章《香港人權法案中的減免及限制條文》一文第 162 頁），法文 ordre public 一詞涵蓋的範圍並不明確。本席同意，ordre public 作為一個包含公眾福祉的概念，其涵蓋的範圍較純粹是擾亂公共秩序的反面為廣。然而，較之廣泛多少？若某個概念不明確，則法院必須首先闡明這概念，才能以此概念作為驗證標準，來判斷對某項基本權利或自由可以施加何種限制而又符合憲法，如果該權利或自由是可以受到限制的話。為此，本席將 *ordre public* 視作一項為限制此種權利或自由提供充分理據的基準，而這基準不得比下文所述的基準寬鬆。

81. 本席認為，對第二十七條的權利或自由所施加的限制，必須以其能與該項權利或自由相容為基準，才算具充分理據；同時，除非限制的範圍狹窄而明確，否則根本不可能把此種限制視為與此種權利或自由相容。歸根結底，這顯然是規則與例外之間的問題；在此，規則保障了權利或自由，而例外則對該項權利或自由施加限制。本席將會在適當時候針對本案的特殊背景，就實質爭議對以上各點詳加闡述。

82. 發表的自由涵蓋發表的實質內容（即表達甚麼）及發表的形式（即如何表達）。據本席所理解，兩條保護國旗國徽及區旗區徽的法例均只影響後者。對發表的實質內容不施加任何限制，其重要性從澳洲一宗案件 *Levy v. Victoria (1997) 189 CLR 579* 可見一斑，儘管該案的情況與本案有別。該案涉及一些規例的有效性。這些規例為保障人身的安全而實施一個發牌制度管制人們進入獵鴨區。

83. Levy 先生企圖進入一個獵鴨區，通過電視轉播抗議法例容許射擊野生雀鳥，以及抗議非法射擊受保護的雀鳥。由於 Levy 先生沒有進入該區的牌照，因此當他企圖進入該區時便遭到阻止。其後，他提出訴訟質疑這些規例是否有效。代表他的律師爭辯說，這些規例阻止 Levy 先生進入該區進行抗議，便是阻止人們作出一些受通訊自由所保障的行為，該自由隱含於《澳大利亞聯邦憲法》(Constitution of the Commonwealth)。澳洲高等法院 (High Court of Australia) 拒絕接納這論據，並確認這些規例有效。首席法官 Brennan 說（見第 595 頁）：

> “一項禁制非語言行為的法例，若是旨在達到某個正當目的，*而非旨在壓制這行為所帶出的政治訊息*，又若是所施行的禁制是恰當和經調整以配合達致該目的之需要，則該條禁制非語言行為的法例便不受隱含的自由影響。”（文字斜體由本席加上）

84. 雙方亦向本院陳述了多個海外司法管轄區對有關問題所持的立場。

侮辱美國國旗案例

85. 基於《美國憲法第一修正案》(The First Amendment to the Constitution of the United States of America) 規定不得立法剝奪言論自由，美國聯邦最高法院 (The United States Supreme Court) 廢除了將侮辱美國國旗的行為刑事化的州法例及聯邦法例，根據這些法例，該等行為可處以罰款或監禁。不論在涉及州法例的案件 *Texas v. Johnson 491 US 397* (1988)，或涉及聯邦法例的案件 United States v. Eichman 496 US 310 (1989)，法院的判決均非一致，而僅僅是五對四的多數。此外，在涉及州法例一案中 Kennedy 法官贊同判決時特別說出以下這番話（見第 420 頁至 421 頁）：

> “有時我們必須作出一些我們不喜歡的判決，這是一個不得不面對的事實。我們這樣做是因為這樣的判決是正確的，正確的意思是根據我們所理解的法律和憲法，我們不得不作出這樣的判決。而且我們對這司法過程的承擔是如此重大，所以若非在不尋常的情況下，我們是不會表達對判決感到不快的。也許，這是因為我們恐妨這樣做會破壞了主宰着判決的寶貴原則。本案便是這種不尋常的案件之一。”

86. 雖然 Kennedy 法官透露了他對這項判決感到不快，但這不但沒有削弱反而加強了他贊同判決的說服力，因為這正顯示他必定確信若要維護言論自由則如此判決實無可避免。然而，從這位支持判決的多數派法官就判決透露的不快感受，以及從少數派法官的判決，可見這類案件正是法律界人士所指的“棘手案件”。

其他海外國家

87. 談到其他海外國家，應該注意到其中一些國家將侮辱旗幟列為刑事罪行，而另外一些國家則沒有這樣做。還應該注意到的是，在那些有法例將侮辱國旗列為刑事罪行，對違例者處以罰款或監禁的國家之中，包括一些《公民權利和政治權利國際公約》的締約國在內。“該公約”第十九條第二款規定人人有發表自由的權利。

88. 當然，只是有這樣的法例載於例書，並不等於該法例已經由法院透過處理有關憲法的爭議，而獲確定是符合憲法。故此，與上述兩個美國判例形成鮮明對比的是兩個歐洲判例。這兩個判例分別來自意大利和德國，法院均裁定保護國旗及對違例者處以罰款或監禁的法例符合憲法。意大利和德國都是“該公約”的締約國。意大利最高上訴法院（Corte Suprema di Cassazione）於 1988 年 7 月 14 日，在 *Re Paris Renato*, Judgment No. 1218, General Registry No. 3355/88 一案中，作出有關判決。德國則在 *The German Flag Desecration Case*, 81 Entscheidungen des Bundesverfassungsgerichts 278 (FRG) 一案中，由德國聯邦憲法法院（Germany's Federal Constitutional Court）於 1990 年 3 月 7 日作出判決。

89. 爲了進一步説明世界各國對這些事情的處理手法的多樣性，本席在此一提挪威的有關情況。這是另一個我等獲提供資料的國家。挪威沒有法例將侮辱其國旗列為刑事罪行，卻有法例（以罰款或不超過一年的監禁）懲罰在其境内公開侮辱其他國家的國旗或國徽的行爲。本席也順帶一提，日本像挪威一樣，也在其司法管轄範圍内保護外國的國旗及國徽，但沒有以同樣方式保護自己的國旗或國徽。

90. 最後，關於這方面，本席在此提出，即使在有立法保護國旗及國徽的國家之間，這些法例的實際條款看來也彼此存在着相當大的差異。本席現以一個對照來加以説明。上訴人曾給我等看過一封 1999 年 6 月 25 日由葡萄牙總檢察長寫給香港律政司的函件。信中引述了《葡萄牙刑法典》(Portuguese Penal Code) 第 332(1) 條，其中文譯文為："任何人以語言、姿勢、文字或任何其他公開傳播方式，侮辱共和國、國旗、國歌、代表葡萄牙主權的象徵或徽號、或以任何其他方式不給予它們應得的尊重，均須處以不超過 2 年的監禁或不超過 240 天的金錢上的懲罰。"

91. 當然，即使對其他國家的法律稍加評論也絕非本席分内之事。但純為作一比較，本席不揣冒昧，在此提出一點看法：表面看來《葡萄牙刑法典》中這條條文似乎將很多在我們的旗幟和徽號保護法例中均沒有列為刑事罪行的行為都列作刑事罪行。

兩種可以協調的取向

92. 依本席看來，在憲法上這一範疇似乎基本上有兩種可以協調的取向。其中一種取向就是，儘管總會有遠較侮辱國旗國徽或區旗區徽有效的表達意見方式，也不論這種侮辱行爲是何等粗魯和令人反感，都應當視作一種發表方式而加以容忍。另一種取向則是，鑑於國旗國徽及區旗區徽具有象徵意義，因而應予尊敬，況且保護國旗國徽及區旗區徽並不會妨礙任何人在林林總總的方法中以一種或多種方法將他 / 她的看法表達出來，故此國旗國徽及區旗區徽應該受到保護，免遭侮辱。

93. 這兩種取向雖然會帶來相反結果，但卻有共同之處。兩者均對國旗國徽及區旗區徽予以尊敬，也確認發表自由並不局限於發表的內容，也包括發表的方式。

驗證標準：可否相容

94. 當類似本案的事宜交由法院處理時，問題便不在於法官個人屬意哪種取向，而在於立法機關所選擇的取向是否為憲法所容。這並不牽涉到是否順從立法機關的問題，而只是維持三權分立的問題。

95. 既然立法機關選擇的取向是保護國旗國徽及區旗區徽免遭侮辱，並以制定法例來提供這種保護，因此，本案的問題是這些法例是否符合憲法；而以本席之見，這問題的答案在於這些法例能否與受憲法保障的發表自由相容，所以，要驗證的是相容性的問題。

結論

96. 本席衷心支持上訴法庭三位法官維護發表自由的決心。然而，本席判上訴得直，因為本席不能說這兩條被質疑的法例與該項自由互不相容。兩件事物可以在周邊部分相疊而在本質上於核心部分有基本差異。因此，旗幟、徽號或圖騰這類公平地代表整個群體的象徵，與一份傳達特定訊息的陳述之間，在內容和形式上，均存在固有及基本差異；不論該群體是一小撮人或偌大國家，也不論該特定訊息是平平無奇或具爭議性，情況亦然。社會希望保護其象徵物乃合乎常情，而考慮到本席在前文所述及關於象徵物與陳述之間的差異，依本席之見，社會是有可能在保護其旗幟及徽號的同時，也能夠維護言論自由，儘管要做到這點絕非易事。

97. 若保護旗幟及徽號的法例明確，且不影響所發表的實質內容，也在發表形式方面僅限於保持旗幟及徽號中立，免涉於政治及傾軋，便有可能達到上述情況。依本席之見，本港兩條保護國旗國徽及區旗區徽免遭公開及故意侮辱的法例合符這些準則。這兩條法例完全沒有對人們可以發表的內容施加限制。甚至關乎人們可以用何種發表形式這方面，法例所施加的唯一限制，只是禁止侮辱一些即使沒有法例禁止，人們連做夢也沒想過要侮辱的物件而已。這限制不會壓制任何思想的表達。不論是政治意見的坦率表達，還是任何其他意見的坦率表達，都不會因此而受到抑制。

98. 代表第二答辯人的大律師在其具說服力的陳詞中反詰，若容許限制，則止境何在？這問題完全合理，而問題的答案，依本席之見，就是這些限制只能到此為止，因為它們已到了憲法所能容許的極限了。在國旗國徽及區旗區徽之下，所有在香港的人士根據本港法律都享有平等機會就任何事情暢所欲言，不論話題是否涉及政治：喜歡說甚麼便說甚麼，喜歡怎樣說便怎樣說。而且，他們亦可以有信心這種情況會持續下去。

終審法院非常任法官梅師賢爵士：

99. 本席同意終審法院首席法官李國能的判決。

終審法院首席法官李國能：

100. 本庭一致裁定上訴得直。回復裁判官的定罪判決及簽保守行為判令。

首席法官（李國能）
常任法官（烈顯倫）
常任法官（沈澄）
常任法官（包致金）
非常任法官（梅師賢爵士）

資深大律師麥高義先生（由律政司委託）、律政司高級助理刑事檢控專員、資深大律師布思義先生以及大律師鄒燦基先生（由律政司委託）代表上訴人。

第一答辯人吳恭劭先生無律師代表，親自出庭答辯。

資深大律師余若薇女士以及大律師羅沛然先生、夏博義先生及劉偉聰先生（由何謝韋律師事務所延聘並由法律援助署委派）代表第二答辯人。

（1）譯者按，order public 一詞是法文

HKSAR v. Pearce, Matt James

香港特別行政區 對 Pearce, Matt James

HCMA 1029/2005；HCMA 313/2006

簡略案情

上訴人是一個名為“國際行動”的小規模政治團體的領袖。據稱，該組織的目的是“通過非暴力的方式喚醒公眾爭取社會公義、民主、人權和美好生活的意識。”於 2004 年 12 月 12 日，在沙田馬場的一個盛大年度賽馬比賽中，上訴人在公眾看台內身著馬形道具服裝，上寫著“現在就需要民主”的字樣，與在場人士接觸。當時在場的保安人員並沒有阻止。然而，在第 8 場比賽即將開始之前，上訴人突然衝入賽道奔跑，並與在場高叫和鼓掌的人士揮手。現場保安在很短時間內便把沒有作出反抗的上訴人制服，並交與在現場執勤的警員。

另一宗案件發生於“天安門事件”16 周年的前一天中午時分。上訴人裝扮成蜘蛛俠，並在沒有任何安全設施下攀爬到中環一棟商業大廈外牆的一個巨型電視螢幕上，同時展示了一幅 10 乘 16 尺的橫額，上面寫著“天安門 4-6-1989，公義必勝”的標語。事件擾攘兩個多小時，上訴人一直拒絕勸喻，堅持要在上面午餐後才離開；期間，警方需要封閉部份主要道路，所有途徑的車輛和行人也需要改道，消防人員奉召在該大廈外鋪設救生墊，防止意外發生，而且，吸引大批群眾圍觀，需要警員維持秩序。

在馬場這事件中，上訴人被控告破壞社會安寧和公眾滋擾罪；而在蜘蛛俠這件事中，上訴人被控告公眾滋擾罪。裁判法院經審訊後，三條控罪皆被判成立。上訴人遂向原訟庭提出上訴，他其中的一個論點，就是他的自由表達權應受《基本法》的保護。

裁決摘要

原訟庭法官在判詞內清楚提醒自己 Sedley L. J. 在 *Redmond-Bate v. Director Of Public Prosecutions* [1999] Crim LR 998 一案中的一段話，“不單非冒犯性的，言論自由還應包括刺激性的、具爭議性的、奇異的、不受歡迎的和挑釁性的，只要它不傾向引起暴力。”上訴人援引終審法院*楊美雲*一案中所說“僅僅因為集會、遊行和示威而引致通道的一些阻塞，不足以剝奪《基本法》第 27 條的保障。”並認為他的行為是合理地行使憲法權利，道路阻塞是由停下來的途人所引起的，原審裁判官錯誤地把合理性原則加於這些途人身上。對於這個論據，法官持不同的意見。法官認為上訴人應該預見他的行為會對公眾造成甚麼影響，這擁擠的情況完全由上訴人行為直接引起的。原訟庭法官也重申*楊美雲*的觀點，合理性是平衡個人與群眾間利益衝突的標準。最後，法官認為原審裁判官已經充分考慮了相關的法理和事實，尤其是衡量了上訴人行使其憲法權利的合理性，因此，否決了上訴人關於《基本法》的論點，並且駁回他最後一條公眾滋擾罪的上訴。

HCMA 1029/2005 &

HCMA 313/2006

IN THE HIGH COURT OF THE HONG KONG SPECIAL ADMINISTRATIVE REGION COURT OF FIRST INSTANCE

MAGISTRACY APPEAL NO. HCMA 1029 OF 2005
(ON APPEAL FROM STS 5073 & 5074 OF 2005) and
MAGISTRACY APPEAL NO. HCMA 313 OF 2006
(ON APPEAL FROM ESS 26710 OF 2005)

Between:

HKSAR **Respondent**

- and -

PEARCE, MATT JAMES **Respondents**

Before: Hon Beeson J in Court

Date of Hearing: 11 April 2006

Date of Judgment: 28 April 2006

JUDGMENT

1. The Appellant appeals against his conviction and sentence on each of 3 charges which were dealt with in two separate cases heard by different Magistrates. The first in time was HCMA 1029/2005 in which on 2 November 2005, the Appellant was convicted after trial on 2 summonses. The particulars were that:

(1) On 12 December 2004, in a public place at the Shatin Race Course, New Territories in Hong Kong, he behaved in a disorderly manner with intent to provoke a breach of the peace or whereby a breach of the peace was likely to be caused, contrary to S. 17B(2) of the Public Order Ordinance, Cap. 245.

(2) On the same date, at the same place, he caused a nuisance to the public by unlawfully running on the race-track dressed in a mock horse costume just before the start of the televised horse race No. 8 for the Cathay Pacific Hong Kong Cup, contrary to common law.

On each summons he was sentenced to one month's imprisonment, suspended for 18 months, to run concurrently.

2. The second case, HCMA 313/2006 concerned one count of Public Nuisance, contrary to common law. It was alleged that on 3 June 2005, the Appellant caused a nuisance to the public by unlawfully climbing up a big TV screen dressed as Spiderman at Luk Hoi Tung Building at No. 31 Queen's Road Central.

3. On conviction after trial, he was sentenced to 21 days imprisonment. The Magistrate did not suspend the sentence but granted bail pending appeal.

FACTS OF EACH INCIDENT

4. In neither case was there any dispute about what had occurred on the day of the alleged offences. I shall summarise the facts briefly for each case.

Background

5. The Appellant is aged 30 and is the leader of a small group (8) of self-appointed political activists "International Action" – an all-embracing, suitably vague title for an organization which the Appellant told the Probation Officer "aims at propagandising social justice, democracy, human rights and betterment of society through non-violent action arousing the attention and concern of the public". Such a description allows the group to protest about anything and everything that might fall, conceivably, within these well meaning libertarian parameters.

6. The non-violent action appears to consist of the Appellant drawing attention to the cause of the moment by dressing in costume and making a nuisance or a spectacle of himself, in some manner which satisfies his undoubted exhibitionistic streak. He was assisted in these activities by other members of the group, none of whom feature in starring roles.

Race-Track Incident

7. On 12 December 2004, the Appellant attended a big race meeting at the Shatin race-course dressed in a horse costume which incorporated a yellow shirt bearing the words 'demand democracy now'. He amused the crowds in the Public Enclosure by prancing about. His purpose was apparently to promote public awareness of democracy, although the efficacy of such equine gambolling in bringing democracy to the minds of the populace must be questionable.

8. At about 1709 hours, just before the scheduled start of Race 8 at 1710, the Appellant was assisted to scale the barrier fence on to the track. He ran along the track heading away from the starting gate towards the winning post. He was pursued, at a distance, by security guards, who had tolerated his earlier antics in the Public Enclosure. As he ran the Appellant waved to the crowd, who were applauding and calling out – the Appellant claims they were approving – the Magistrate surmised that some were annoyed or angry. When, as was inevitable, the Appellant was caught, he was pushed to the ground by the security guards without offering any resistance. He was handed to police officers carrying out crowd control at the race-course and arrested.

9. The incident took about 2 minutes in all and though the start was delayed by one minute to 1711, the race was run without incident. It was not disputed that the Appellant's behaviour was peaceful at all times; nor was it disputed that the force used to apprehend him was reasonable.

10. Although at trial an argument was advanced that the race-track was not a public place, (an argument properly rejected by the Magistrate), on appeal it was agreed that it was. The race meeting was agreed to be the biggest in the Racing Calendar that season; the maximum crowd at the race-course was 48,000 and the race was to be televised to more than 13 countries. No doubt that was why the Appellant chose that date for his performance.

11. Whether the spectators at the track, or television viewers who watched the incident, could read the T-shirt message was not clear. It was written in Chinese and English, red on yellow with key letters/characters about 5 inches and others about 2½ inches high. Those who saw the Appellant close-up in the Public Enclosure would have been able to read the message without difficulty.

Spiderman Incident (HCMA 313/2006)

12. On 3 June 2005 the Appellant, dressed in a Spiderman costume

and with assistance from an acolyte, used a ladder to mount to the 1st floor Podium of Luk Hoi Tung Building, a commercial building at 31 Queen's Road Central. A large Television screen erected on the podium was used to show commercial messages to passers-by.

13. At 1245, having climbed up the screen, the Appellant hung a banner 16 ft x 10 ft in front of it, effectively obscuring any messages that might be shown. The message on the banner, in Chinese and English stated:

> "Tiananmen Square 4-6-1989
>
> Justice Must Prevail
>
> Injustice anywhere is a threat to Justice everywhere www.thebiggerpicture.hk"

14. The incident occurred the day before the 16th anniversary of the Tiananmen Square murders, an anniversary well-known to Hong Kong residents and, in all likelihood, one for which they need no reminder.

15. The banner produced by the Appellant was a practical one – if the top line was painted out the accompanying text could apply to any cause the Appellant or his group chose to publicise. The Appellant stayed on top of the screen, walking, sitting, waving, clapping his hands and generally drawing attention to himself. He was not confined in any manner, nor was he secured by any harness or safety belt.

16. Queen's Road Central at that time of day is notoriously crowded with pedestrians and heavy, slow-moving vehicular traffic; no doubt that was Appellant's reason for choosing the screen as his platform. Unsurprisingly, large pedestrian crowds gathered to watch him and police were needed for crowd and traffic control.

17. At 1348, Fire Services came and placed a rescue cushion below the screen, in case the Appellant jumped or fell. It was necessary at that stage to cordon off that part of Queen's Road and Theatre Lane which ran off it and in consequence vehicular traffic had to be diverted into Pedder Street and away from D' Aguilar Street which met Queen's Road Central as a T-junction at that spot. Traffic lights were suspended and police officers directed traffic. Traffic congestion lasted for about 2 hours. Movement was slow, drivers unhappy.

18. Pedestrians had to be directed by a circuitous route from the building through to Theatre Lane – Exhibits P.5 and P.8 showed the route by sketch and photographs respectively. Theatre Lane offers MTR access. Access to and from shops in the building was impeded, some shops closed and staff of the management company were needed to shepherd pedestrians along the route of the detour. Shops in the vicinity experienced reduced lunchtime business or had no business at all.

19. A Senior Fire Service officer (PW5) was raised to Appellant's level via the hydraulic platform of a fire engine brought to the scene. He asked the Appellant to come down, but the Appellant refused to do so unless he was fed with dim sum. Dim sum were provided, arriving about 30 mins afterwards. During that time the Appellant continued his posturing and at intervals affected to read a newspaper. The serious congestion was pointed out to him – the Appellant apologised but continued eating. He finished the food and left the screen with the officer. The screen eventually had stopped working because the Appellant's banner, positioned as it was, caused it to overheat. No permission for access was sought by the Appellant, or granted by the management company of the building or the owner of the screen. The Appellant knew the building and screen were private property and expected that the police and fire services would arrive to bring him down. He knew and expected a crowd to gather .He considered his action justified.

GROUNDS OF APPEAL

20. The Appellant appealed against conviction and sentence in each case. Originally the appeals were listed to be heard separately, but shortly before the date fixed for the hearing of the appeal HCMA l029/2005, it was decided that the appeals should be heard together as the basis of the cases was similar and some of the authorities relied on were applicable to both cases

21. In HCMA 1029/2005, the Amended Grounds of Appeal dated 3 April 2006 can be summarized as follows:

First Summons

(1) The Magistrate erred in finding that the Appellant's behaviour whilst not disorderly while within the public enclosure, became disorderly behaviour within the meaning of s. 17B(2), Public Order Ordinance, when continued on the race-track.

(2) Alternatively, the Magistrate erred in finding that the disorderly conduct of the Appellant was conduct likely to cause a breach of the peace. It was fanciful for the Magistrate to infer from the evidence that violence would ensue or that there was a real risk of violence ensuing.

Second Summons

(3) The Magistrate erred in finding that the Appellant's going on to the race-track and behaving in a disorderly manner was an act "not warranted by law" as it was neither prohibited by common law or by statute.

(4) The Magistrate erred in finding the Appellant's conduct in jumping on to the race-track at the start of a race upset and inconvenienced a section of the public such that it constituted an obstruction of rights common to all. The finding was speculative as no evidence supported it.

(5) The Magistrate failed to make a finding that the Appellant knew, or should have known, that his conduct would or could delay the start of the race. It was imperative that the Magistrate state whether he accepted or rejected the Appellant's evidence that he deliberately timed his actions so as not to disrupt the race.

22. In HCMA 313/2006, the Grounds of Appeal can be summarized as follows:

(1) The Appellant accepted that the Magistrate could have found public nuisance established by finding foreseen or foreseeable highway obstruction without reasonable excuse and common injury alone, but contended he had erred in finding that Appellant's acts had obstructed the public in rights other than free passage i.e.

   (a) their right to enter commercial premises and purchase goods or services; and

(b) the right of the screen owner to broadcast screen images and the right of the public to view them.

(2) The Magistrate found correctly that congestion of the highway for pedestrian user occurred and occurred as a result of Appellant's activity, but erred in holding that the Appellant was criminally responsible for the same, or that the congestion was an unreasonable user.

(3) The Magistrate failed to address a core issue, which was not whether the Appellant's conduct was reasonable, but whether any obstruction caused as a consequence of his foreseen or foreseeable acts was unreasonable.

REMINDER

23. In considering these appeals, I bore in mind the comments of Sedley L.J. in *Redmond-Bate v Director of Public Prosecutions* [1999] Crim LR 998:

> "Free speech includes not only the inoffensive but the irritating, the contentious, the heretical, the unwelcome and the provocative provided it does not tend to provoke violence."

ANALYSIS–HCMA 1029/2005

First Summons

24. The Magistrate found the elements of 'public place' and 'disorderly conduct' established by the evidence. Despite the Appellant's contention to the contrary, the Magistrate was correct in finding that the appellant's conduct became disorderly when transferred to the race-track. The track was closed to anyone not specifically permitted to have access. That was particularly the case when races were being prepared for, or run. Such a measure was necessary for the good administration of the race meeting, particularly for ensuring the safety of jockeys, horse and spectators. Although the Appellant's behaviour on the track followed much the same pattern as his behaviour in the Public Enclosure, his repetition of such behaviour in proximity to horses and riders made it possible, or likely, that one or more horses would bolt and/or throw their riders. It was also possible that one or more horses would baulk at entering the starting gate(s). The Magistrate noted that for disorderly conduct in the context of the Public Order Act 1986:

> "There needs be no element of violence whether present or threatened; it covers conduct which is not necessarily, threatening abusive or insulting." [*Chambers and Edwards v DPP(unreptd)* 1995 Crim LR 896]

"disorderly conduct" is not defined in the Public Order Ordinance; it was a matter of fact for him to determine.

25. Having found that the Appellant's behaviour on the track was disorderly, the Magistrate considered whether the Appellant had the intention of provoking a breach of the peace and concluded he could not be sure he had such intention.

26. Thereafter he examined the question of whether a breach of the peace was likely to be caused by the Appellant's behaviour. Ultimately, he concluded that a breach was likely to be caused, because if the Appellant reacted violently to the efforts of the security guards to stop him, more guards would be called and a more violent response would occur. The Magistrate was also of the view that some spectators, angered by the delay to the start of Race 8, would be likely to jump down to the track in order to help subdue the Appellant.

27. Counsel for the Appellant contended on the basis of R v. Howell [1982] QB 416, that there must be violence or threatened violence apprehended, or likely to occur, for there to be a breach of the peace. The disorderly conduct must constitute a real provocation to third parties e.g. the security guards or disaffected spectators, to do harm to the Appellant or others through assault, affray, riot or some other kind of disturbance. Public alarm, excitement or disturbance is not of itself a breach of the peace unless it arises from actual or threatened violence. [Refd Smith & Hogan "Criminal Law" 11th ed. p. 573].

28. The Appellant at no time resisted capture and cooperated with the security guards, who themselves used only reasonable force to subdue him. The Respondent submitted that because the security guards were not police officers they could be equated with laymen, meaning that they were likely to be provoked to violence in the event the Appellant resisted them.

29. Clearly the security guards are not to be equated with laymen. They have specific duties to perform and are trained to deal with situations such as this incident. The head of RHKJC security was at the race-course supervising. It seems improbable that faced with a cooperative, non-resisting, unarmed, pantomime horse after a chase lasting less than 30 seconds, that security personnel would resort to violence. It is even less likely that they would resort to violence under the gaze of the head of security, 48,000 spectators and police officers dealing with crowd control.

30. As for angry spectators taking violent action against the Appellant, that appears even more unlikely. Given that Appellant's conduct was not directed at provoking, nor intended to provoke the public it would have been wholly unreasonable if any spectator had behaved as the Magistrate feared they might. The Magistrate had to be satisfied there was a real risk of a future breach of the peace, so any violence or the threat of violence must be a natural consequence of the conduct of the Appellant.

31. There was no specific finding made by the Magistrate about this matter. At best it is implicit in his comment:

> "Moreover, in case the defendant could not be subdued by security guards, certain angry spectators who longed to see the horse race start as soon as possible might jump on to the racetrack in order to help subdue the defendant."

The Magistrate does not set out cogent evidence from which he infers violence or likely violence–it appears that this comment is speculation.

32. As I cannot be satisfied with the basis for his finding that a breach of the peace was likely to be caused, I allow the appeal and quash the conviction on the First Summons.

HCMA 1029/2005 & HCMA 313/2006

Public Nuisance

33. "Public Nuisance" is defined as:

> "an act not warranted by law or an omission to discharge a legal duty, which act or omission obstructs or causes inconvenience or damage to the public in the exercise of rights common to all Her Majesty's subjects." (A Digest of Criminal Law (1877) Ch. XIX p. 108 Sir James Stephen)

34. That basic definition of the common law offence was more recently interpreted and applied by the House of Lords in R v Rimmington [2005] 2 WLR 982 which held it to be committed when

a person did an act not warranted by law, or omitted to discharge a legal duty, and the effect of the act or omission was to endanger the life, health, property or comfort of the public, or to obstruct the public in the exercise of rights common to everyone.

35. It was acknowledged that many offences once chargeable as common law offences, over the years had become the subject of express statutory provisions. Good practice and respect for the primacy of the statute required that unless there was a good reason, the statutory provision should be used. The court did not say that conduct falling within the confines of a statutory offence could never be prosecuted as a common law offence, although it expected future use of such offences to be rare.

36. An essential ingredient of the offence of causing a public nuisance was that it must cause common injury to the public – the community as a whole or a significant section of it. Individual acts causing injury to several different people could not constitute criminal public nuisance.

37. The mens rea which had to be proved against a defendant to convict him of causing a public nuisance was that he knew or ought to have known, because the means of knowledge were available to him, the consequence of what he did or omitted to do.

HCMA 1029/2005

Second Summons

Ground 3 – Act not warranted by law

38. The Magistrate found that a public nuisance had been established on the evidence. He was satisfied that the Appellant's act in running on the race-track constituted disorderly conduct not warranted by law. The Appellant's argument was that at most such behaviour may have amounted to a breach of the terms of the licence under which the Appellant gained entry to the course. Given the requirement that only persons specifically authorized could have access to the track, the Magistrate was correct in concluding that the Appellant's entering the track was "conduct unwarranted by law".

Ground 4–Common Injury

39. The magistrate fixed on the 1 minute delay in the start of Race 8 as the basis for finding "common injury". In Rimmington such injury was described as follows:

> "central to the content of the crime was the suffering of common injury by members of the public by interference with rights enjoyed by them as such."

40. The relevant consideration and ultimate finding by the Magistrate reads:

> "I am certain that a great number of the people seeing this mock horse running on the racetrack were bewildered and felt upset and/or angry, and that they were anxious and concerned about, during that one minute's interval, whether or not the real horse race would have to be delayed for a substantial period of time or even to be cancelled in the end, bearing in mind that they had betted on the horse race with expectations or great expectations."
>
> "I have no doubt that this one minute's interval had created material discomfort and concern to a great number of people who had an interest in the horse race on the material day and at the material time, and that the defendant had obstructed the people in the exercise of their enjoyment of the horse race on time and that he had caused much inconvenience to Hong Kong Jockey Club in the proper organization of the horse race." [S of F para 19]

41. With respect to the Magistrate that finding adopts an unduly sensitive view of what constitutes 'common injury'. Assuming, as he found, that the delay was caused by the Appellant, there was no evidence to show that the public were aware of the delay; that they experienced any problems with placing bets in consequence; that their enjoyment in watching the race had been interfered with; or that they had had any disappointed expectation that the race would begin precisely at the time fixed.

42. The evidence of PW1, Mr Neil Maconey, Manager of Integrity Services of HKJC, was that delays of one or two minutes at the start of a race were usual for a variety of reasons, although on this occasion he was aware only of Appellant's action as causing the delay. As delays were usual, it is highly improbable that the anxiety, concern, discomfort and disappointment which the Magistrate considered the likely result of one minute's delay, would have had time to manifest itself.

43. The position might have been different if in consequence of the Appellant's actions, the race had had a false start, or had had to be cancelled, or postponed for a significant period of time.

44. The finding that much administrative inconvenience had been caused to the Jockey Club personnel did not establish the significant number of persons required to be affected to substantiate common injury.

Ground 5–Mens Rea

45. Counsel for the Appellant, in this additional ground of appeal, contended that the Magistrate failed to make any finding that the Appellant had the requisite mens rea, i.e. that he knew, or ought to have known, that his action in running onto the track, would delay the start of the race. The Appellant had given evidence that he had not intended to delay or disrupt the race, but the Magistrate made no finding whether he accepted or rejected that evidence. Counsel submitted it was not clear therefore whether the Appellant had been convicted on the basis that he was responsible for the delayed start, or on the basis he had intended to, or should have known, he would delay the race.

46. The Magistrate in his Statement of Findings did not specifically state that he found mens rea established, but at para. 6(c) did repeat the evidence given by the Appellant relevant to that issue and at para. 18 made a finding that the Appellant's act caused the one minute's delay. He began his consideration of the evidence by reminding himself of the relevant case law and although he may not have spelled out therefrom the element of mens rea, implicit in his findings is that the Appellant knew, or ought to have known that his action in running on the track would delay the race.

47. In this context regard should be paid to the comments of Mortimer V-P:

> "… it is usually preferable when a judge is assessing the evidence, that he or she should start by setting out the elements of the offence which are specifically in issue. Those usually relate to intention or the mental element. Where the judge is a professional judge sitting alone, however, it can be assumed, unless there are indications to the contrary, that the judge is well aware

of the offence charged and that the reasons, pointing to where the evidence is accepted or rejected, are directed to those elements." (*HKSAR v. KWOK Chi-wah* [1999] 1 H.K.L.R.D. 481 @486)

48. For the reasons set out above I find that the Magistrate while correct in finding the Appellant's conduct was disorderly and not warranted by law, nevertheless erred in finding his delaying the start of the race amounted to public nuisance. On the evidence before him it was not possible to find the necessary common injury caused to the community as a whole, or to a significant portion of it. Although the Appellant was undoubtedly a tiresome nuisance, his behaviour cannot be characterised as constituting a public nuisance.

49. I allow the appeal in respect of the second summons. The convictions on each of the first and second summonses are quashed.

HCMA 313/2006

General

50. The prosecution contended that the Appellant's actions were not warranted by law, that they affected injuriously the exercise or enjoyment of rights of many people in the neighbourhood and that the Appellant knew, or ought to have known, the consequences of his actions.

51. It was inevitable that congestion would ensue as crowds gathered at the busiest time of the day either to watch the antics of the Appellant or to negotiate their way along Queens Road Central, and roads running off it in that area or both. The diverting of pedestrian and vehicular traffic, in an area with limited flexibility for alternative traffic on pedestrian flow was caused consequentially by the Appellant's actions.

52. The Appellant in giving evidence explained how his stunt was carefully planned. He had chosen the date, time and venue for maximum impact; had made no attempt to obtain permission either to use the screen or enter the building; was fully aware that police and fire services would try to dislodge him; that he had expected crowds and congestion and that he had intended to stay at the screen area for some time. Counsel for the Appellant at trial argued that the charge was misconceived given the circumstances, but that even if it were correct it was not clear that 'common injury' had arisen from the Appellant's acts.

ANALYSIS–HCMA 313/2006

Inappropriate Choice Of Charge

53. Counsel for the Appellant contended that the Appellant should not have been charged with the common law offence of public nuisance, when s. 4(28) Summary Offences Ordinance, Cap. 228 was 'tailor made' for the behaviour complained of. This submission appeared to rest on the disparity of the maximum penalties. If tried by a jury the offence of public nuisance has a maximum sentence of 7 years imprisonment plus a fine, whereas s. 4(28), Summary Offences Ordinance has a maximum of 3 months' imprisonment and a $5,000.00 fine. Counsel argued that the charge should not have been laid because even the limited penalty in the Magistracy was excessive when compared with the penalty under s.(2). As this case was tried in the Magistracy, the maximum sentence is 2 years imprisonment and a fine of $100,000.00, so it is difficult to see how the charge, or the venue can be considered inappropriate.

54. Counsel for the Appellant argued, on the basis of Rimmington, that if a statutory offence existed it should be used, rather than the common law equivalent, unless there was good reason not to do so. However as counsel for the Respondent pointed out the offence had not been abolished and could be charged in appropriate circumstances.

55. Article 63 of the Basic law provides:

"The Department of Justice of the Hong Kong Special Administrative Region shall control criminal prosecutions free from any interference."

56. The choice of charge and venue for trial is the responsibility of the Secretary for Justice and his designated officers. The prosecution has a wide discretion as to the charge or charges it may lay and in the absence of bad faith, abuse of process, or perverse decision a court is unable to question the decision. Charges are laid and venues chosen according to prosecution policy and guidelines taking into account the gravity of the offence, the elements that can be proved and other factors such as prevalence, deterrence community mores etc. The prosecutorial burden is a heavy one and it is for the Secretary for Justice to decide in what manner it is borne. Although the Appellant argued that the charge was inappropriate, it was not suggested that the common law offence was chosen, in the manner deprecated in *Rimmington*, to circumvent mandatory time limits, or limits on penalties.

57. The Respondent submitted that it was open to the Secretary for Justice to choose the charge, which, in the proper exercise of his discretion, he considered, properly reflected the gravity of the situation it was intended to deal with. Section 4(28) of the Summary Offences Ordinance, Cap. 228 was more commonly used to combat the mischief of hawkers or shop owners encroaching on and obstructing public space in some way, although it could be used, as it was in *Yeung May-wan and HKSAR* (2005) 8 HKCFAR 137, to deal with obstruction caused by demonstrators.

58. Nothing in the arguments put forward by counsel for the Appellant convinces me that the common law offence should not have been preferred. This ground of appeal fails.

USER OF THE HIGHWAY

59. Counsel for the Appellant submitted the Magistrate had erred by concentrating on whether Appellant's demonstration had caused congestion, rather than considering the reasonableness of the public stopping in the street to watch. He pointed out that the Appellant had not caused congestion by blocking the highway, or inciting others to do so, or by making a speech; rather the congestion was caused by people choosing to stop and look at the Appellant and his banner, which was a reasonable use of the highway.

60. Counsel was being disingenuous in submitting thus. As the Appellant knew or should have known, there was no need for him to do more than prance on top of the screen, safe in the knowledge that crowds would gather to see what was happening, read the banner, or, given that the Appellant was not restrained or secured in any way, simply watch in ghoulish hope or expectation that something more exciting such as a fall would occur. The crowds gathered as a direct consequence of and in response to the Appellant's activities.

61. No doubt there would be many pedestrians who stopped not because they had any interest in what was going on, but because the crowds watching the Appellant impeded their progress, or

blocked their access to shops, offices or MTR, or because the positioning of the Fire Services cushion obliged them to take a lengthy detour. The longer the Appellant remained aloft, the greater the crowds and congestion and the less reasonable their user of the highway.

62. Counsel for the Appellant in submitting that the Magistrate had focused in error, on the reasonableness of the Appellant's behaviour, rather than the reasonableness of the crowd's using the highway to observe him, referred to *Yeung May Wan & Others and HKSAR* (2005) 8 HKCFAR. There the Court of Final Appeal, examined a number of matters arising when Falun Gong demonstrators outside the Liaison Office of the Central Peoples Government had been charged and convicted under s. 4A of the Summary Offences Ordinance, Cap. 228 of obstruction of a public place and by doing an act whereby obstruction might accrue under s. 4(28) of the same Ordinance. The convictions were quashed.

63. The court's holding at (2) p. 138 was that:

> "for the purposes of s. 4(28) the defendants would only be guilty of such offence if they caused such obstruction without lawful excuse. The burden of proving that was on the prosecution. A person who created an obstruction was not acting without lawful excuse if his conduct involved a reasonable use of the public place. What was reasonable was a question of fact and degree depending on all the circumstances, including the obstruction's extent duration, time, place and purpose."

64. Further, he argued that the Appellant's acts were not unreasonable as he was simply exercising his right to demonstrate.

> "the mere fact that an assembly, a procession or a demonstration causes some interference with free passage along a highway does not take away its protection under Art. 27 of the Basic Law."

65. With those matters in mind the Magistrate examined the question of reasonableness in relation to the Appellant and the crowd. What the public can reasonably be expected to tolerate is a question of fact and degree and thus a matter for the Magistrate to weigh, balancing the rights of the Appellant to demonstrate peacefully, with the right of the public to freedom of the highway. The Magistrate spent some time considering the question of fact and degree. He concluded that the Appellant's demonstration lawful and peaceful as it was, was unduly lengthy, given the well-aired topic he wished to bring to public attention; the time and place chosen for the demonstration and the further lengthening of the time of disruption by his bizarre insistence on being fed as a condition of his leaving the podium.

66. He found that the Appellant's message, although important and legitimate, could have been conveyed within a much shorter time-frame than the 2 hours he was on top of the screen. The Appellant was aware before climbing to the top of the screen of the congestion his activities were likely to cause. Indeed it was an integral part of his demonstration that such congestion or disturbance would be caused. By refusing to come down when, after a lengthy period, congestion below was pointed out to him, he had extended the time by demanding dim sum. At a certain point the crowd's user becomes unreasonable – a direct result of Appellant's acts. That point is for the Magistrate to find.

67. *Rimmington* held that the mens rea which had to be established against a defendant on a public nuisance charge was that he knew or ought to have known, because the means of knowledge was available to him, the consequences of what he did or omitted to do. The Magistrate considered the question of Appellant's knowledge and drew what must have been an irresistible inference, that the Appellant had the requisite mens rea.

COMMON INJURY

68. To establish 'public nuisance'the effect of the act or omission must be shown 'to endanger the life, health, property or comfort of the public, or to obstruct the public in the exercise of rights common to everyone.'

69. Counsel for the Appellant submitted that the Magistrate erred in finding that the economic interest of the shopkeepers and the owner of the television screen were public rights and as such protected by the common law offence of public nuisance, when, at best, they gave rise to civil action in private nuisance. The Respondent did not attempt to argue otherwise on this appeal and the Magistrate's finding on these points is irrelevant for the purposes of this appeal.

70. The pertinent findings are at para. 59 and para. 64 of the Statement of Findings where the Magistrate excluded police, fire and ambulance personnel, management staff of the building and shop owners claiming economic loss from his consideration and found that:

> "the many road users and shopowners and customers in that vicinity plus the TV owner and customers as injuriously affected by Defendant's act to varying significant degrees were enough to constitute a substantial number of the public."

71. In fact the Magistrate could have found on the evidence before him that potentially all citizens, residents and visitors in Hong Kong could be regarded as suffering the public nuisance caused by the obstruction of the highway, which in normal circumstances was available for ordinary use by anyone as a pedestrian or driver. Such user was not limited to simple passing and re-passing.

72. In *D.P.P. v. Jones* [1999] 2 A.C. 240, Lord Irvine stated:

> "The public highway is a public place which the public may enjoy for any reasonable purpose, provided the activity in question does not amount to a public or private nuisance and does not obstruct the highway by unreasonably impeding the primary right of the public to pass and repass: within these qualifications there is a public right of peaceful assembly on the highway.
>
> Since the law confers this public right I deprecate any attempt artificially to limit its scope. It must be for the Magistrates in every case to decide whether the user of the highway under consideration is both reasonable in the sense defined and not inconsistent with the primary right of the public to pass and repass.
>
> ··· provided an assembly is reasonable and non-obstructive, taking into account its size, duration and the nature of the highway on which it takes place, it is irrelevant whether it is premeditated or spontaneous: what matters is its objective nature ... to stipulate in the abstract any maximum size or duration for a lawful assembly would be an unwarranted restriction on the right defined. These judgments are ever ones of fact and

degree for the court of trial."

73. In *Yeung May-wan* – Bokhary PJ gave instances of how various uses of the road or footpath may impede other persons using the highway to some extent but the law regards such cases by seeking

> "to strike a balance between possibly conflicting interests of different users of the highway based on a requirement of reasonableness. Whether any particular instance of obstruction goes beyond what is reasonable is a question of fact and degree depending on all the circumstances, including its extent and duration, the time and place where it occurs and the purpose for which it is done." (para. 43 p.157)

74. The court reiterated, in various ways that where an obstruction resulted from a peaceful demonstration, it was essential that the constitutionally protected right to demonstrate, which was enshrined in Article 27 of the Basic Law, was recognised and given substantial weight.

CONCLUSION

75. I am satisfied that the Magistrate in evaluating the evidence had borne in mind the important matter of the Appellant's right to demonstrate. He was aware of the elements of the offence and had found those elements established. He was apprised of the relevant case law and had directed himself accordingly. In particular he carried out the balancing exercise required of him, in which the Appellant's right to demonstrate had to be balanced against the public right to use the highway, not just to pass and repass, but to use if for what might be described as social and community purposes.

76. I have heard and considered the arguments advanced on behalf of the Appellant but am not persuaded by them that this conviction was wrong, or should be disturbed.

77. This appeal against conviction is dismissed.

Appeal Against Sentence–HCMA 1029/2005

78. It follows from the allowing of the appeal against conviction that the sentences on these summonses are quashed also. In passing, I would comment that if the convictions had been upheld, in principle, the 1 month's imprisonment on each charge seems unduly harsh for a first offender, although I note they were concurrent and suspended.

79. The magistrate sentenced on the based of *R v Nguyen Quang Tong and Others* [1992] 2 HKCLR 10 where Silke, V-P said @p. 13:

> "We accept that, if there be a rule of sentencing practice that a deterrent sentence should not be passed on a man with a clear record, there are exceptions and offences against public order is one of them."

80. However, given the particular circumstances of this incident, it is not the type of public order case which calls for a deterrent penalty. The court in *Nguyen* was considering sentences imposed for offences of S. 17 Wounding and affray committed in a Detention Camp. These offences, qualitatively, were much less serious. In my view, given the extent of his activities, this Appellant could have been sentenced adequately, by the imposition of a substantial fine, or a Community Service Order.

Appeal Against Sentence–HCMA 313/2006

81. The Magistrate treated the Appellant as a man of clear record and noted his monthly earnings were around $7,000. He considered that the Appellant had caused substantial inconvenience to a large number of people and took the view that a financial penalty was inappropriate, in that it would lead others to "think they can pay for executing their belief, even to an unreasonable and excessive extent". The Magistrate might have added that the Appellant was in no position to pay the sort of substantial fine the offence merited.

82. A Community Service Order was considered as an alternative for the short prison sentence the Magistrate found to be appropriate. However the Appellant claimed he had no time to carry out a CSO programme, nor as was required, did he consent to such an order being imposed.

83. The Magistrate noted the maximum penalty for the offence was 2 years imprisonment. He adopted 28 days as the starting point, gave credit for Appellant's clear record and sentenced him to 21 days imprisonment. He did not find any reason to justify suspending the sentence.

84. When sentencing the Magistrate was aware of the sentences imposed on the Appellant for the race course incident. This offence was a more serious one in terms of the disruption.

85. I have considered the Magistrate's Reasons for Sentence and agree that in principle a short term of imprisonment, in all the circumstances, is a proper sentence. However I am of the view that justice would be served as well by suspending that sentence for a period of 18 months. This would recognise what is in effect a first offence, but would have a lasting deterrent influence.

86. According I allow the appeal against sentence to the extent that the sentence of 21 days imprisonment imposed by the Magistrate be suspended for a period of 18 months.

Judge of the Court of First Instance (C-M Beeson)

Mr Cheung Wai-sun, PGC (Ag) and Ms Winnie Lam, GC, of the Department of Justice for the Respondent

Mr DYKES Philip John, instructed by Messrs Vidler & Co., assigned by D.L.A., for the Appellant

---

A Solicitor v. The Law Society of Hong Kong

事務律師 對 香港律師會

CACV 107/2005；FACV 24/2007

簡略案情

上訴人是一名在香港執業的律師。因為在小巴、報章廣告等媒體中自稱為離婚專家，讓雜誌訪問並拍攝全裸或半裸露照片及與同業比較收費等宣傳行為，香港律師會認為其違反了《香港律師會專業守則》（The Hong Kong Solicitors Guide to Prefessional Conduct）。他被控 1）不恰當的執業宣傳；2）行為損害法律界聲譽；3）行為顯示他不適宜當律師。

經過 17 天的紀律聆訊，律師紀律審裁組最後裁定上訴人面對的 8 項指控全部成立，需接受罰款和停業的處分。上訴人不服，遂向上訴庭提起上訴。根據其上訴理由，上訴人認為紀律審裁組不單採納了錯誤的舉證標準，還忽略了《基本法》和《香港人權法案》對公民自由表達的保護，當中包括宣傳的自由。

裁決摘要

關於公民擁有自由表達權利的論點，上訴庭引述了另一個類同案例 *The Law Society of Hong Kong v. A Solicitor*, CACV 280/2003，並重申律師在秉承公義的過程中扮演著一個很重要的角色，雖然執業宣傳或廣告推廣必然能向公眾提供更多的信息，但是，這些宣傳不能沒有限制，而律師的守則正好提供一個扼要、清晰的指引。法庭亦說明，指控針對的不是上訴人的言論，而是其發表言論的方法。上訴人所採用的方式，毫無疑問會給正直的同行和公眾有一種低俗的感覺。另方面，法庭在考慮某種限制是否合理的時候，必須綜觀整件事件的情況，不能斷章取義。專業守則的作用，不止是規管成員的操守，還能清楚讓大眾知悉該專業人士能給予的合理期待與信心。

在本案中，上訴人身為司法人員以及一個受公眾尊重的專業成員，卻大量發佈其裸露照片，從而廣泛宣傳其專業身份，這絕不能稱為一種純粹私人的舉動。法庭接受公眾的容忍度會隨著時間改變，但法庭不能相信公眾對律師行業的嚴肅態度會與日下降。法庭認為上訴人既然選擇成為一名律師，就應當明白他需要遵守其屬會的守則。其屬會規則對他的限制不單適當、而且合理，並沒有剝削他表達的自由。因此，該規則並沒有違反《基本法》或《香港人權法案》。據此，他關於《基本法》論據一概被上訴庭否決。

CACV No. 107 of 2005

IN THE HIGH COURT OF THE HONG KONG SPECIAL ADMINISTRATIVE REGION

COURT OF APPEAL

CIVIL APPEAL NO. 107 OF 2005
(ON APPEAL FROM THE ORDER OF THE SOLICITORS DISCIPLINARY TRIBUNAL DATED 15 MARCH 2005 AGAINST A SOLICITOR)

Between:

A SOLICITOR — Appellant

- and -

THE LAW SOCIETY OF HONG KONG — Respondent

Before: Hon Ma CJHC, Tang VP & Stock JA in Court

Dates of Hearing: 26 April 2007

Date of Handing Down Judgment: 18 May 2007

JUDGMENT ON COSTS

Hon Ma CJHC:

1.On 7 July 2006, judgment was handed down in an appeal brought by the Appellant under section 13 of the Legal Practitioners Ordinance, Cap.159 ("the LPO") against findings made by the Solicitors Disciplinary Tribunal ("the SDT") whereby eight Complaints of professional misconduct against the Appellant were established to the Tribunal's satisfaction. This court decided that the appeal should be allowed in relation to two of the eight Complaints. There are now before us for determination three matters : -

(1) The question of the correctness of the penalties that the SDT had imposed on the Appellant, this issue having been left open in the appeal pending our determination on whether the Tribunal's conclusion on the eight Complaints could stand.

(2) The costs of the appeal and of the proceedings before the SDT.

(3) The application made by the Appellant for leave to appeal to the Court of Final Appeal against our earlier decision on the Complaints (the Notice of Motion applying for leave was dated 24 July 2006).

2. As in the previous judgment, I will refer to the Appellant as "the Solicitor" and the Respondent as "the Law Society". This judgment should be read in conjunction with our previous one.

The penalties to be imposed on the Solicitor

3. The eight Complaints made against the Solicitor can be broadly classified into two groups:

(1) Those dealing with various aspects of the Solicitor's practice promotion over the period between October 1997 and July 1998 during which he was found to have embarked on an extensive advertising campaign and adopted such practices that were regarded as unacceptable. (Complaints 1 to 5).

(2) Those Complaints that focused on the Solicitor's activities over January and February 1999 in which he had posed nude or semi-nude for the press, and had given interviews and made television appearances following this, all to promote himself and his practice. (Complaints 6 to 8).

4. Having found each Complaint established in a Statement of Findings dated 30 September 2004, the Tribunal then heard the parties on the question of penalties. Having done so, it made the following order (contained in its Reasons and Order dated 15 March 2005): -

"**Order**

28. The Tribunal therefore makes the following order against the Respondent:

a. That the Respondent be censured,

b. That in relation to Complaint 1, the Respondent be suspended from practising as a solicitor for a period of 6 months;

c. That in relation to Complaint 2, the Respondent be fined HK$50,000;

d. That in relation to Complaint 3, the Respondent be suspended from practising as a solicitor for a period of 9 months;

e. That in relation to Complaint 4, the Respondent be suspended from practising as a solicitor for a period of 9 months;

f. That in relation to Complaint 5, the Respondent be suspended from practising as a solicitor for a period of 9 months;

g. That in relation to Complaint 6, the Respondent be suspended from practising as a solicitor for a period of 9 months;

h. That in relation to Complaint 7, the Respondent be suspended from practising as a solicitor for a period of 12 months;

i. That in relation to Complaint 8, the Respondent be suspended from practising as a solicitor for a period of 12 months;

j. That the periods of suspension in relation to Complaints 1, 3, 4 and 5 are to run concurrently;

k. That the periods of suspension in relation to Complaints 6, 7 and 8 are to run concurrently;

l. If the Respondent is to resume practice after the suspension, for the first two years of his resumed practice, the Respondent is prohibited from practicing as a sole proprietor and if he shall practise in partnership or be employed, his other partner(s) and employer shall at least be one other solicitor with at least 15 years' actual practice experience;

m. That the Respondent bears and pays two-third of the costs of the Applicant in these proceedings, such costs to be taxed, if not agreed, on a party-and-party basis; and

n. That the Respondent bears and pays for the costs of the Applicant in its investigation and the costs of the

Clerk."

5. We have allowed the appeal insofar as Complaints 1 and 2 are concerned; only Complaints 3 to 8 therefore remain. If the penalties imposed by the Tribunal were to remain for these Complaints, the effect, save as to costs (which is dealt with below), would be as follows: -

(1) The Solicitor would be censured.

(2) The Solicitor would be suspended for a total period of 21 months (it is clear that the Tribunal intended to impose two consecutive periods of suspension of 9 months (for Complaints 3 to 5) and 12 months (for Complaints 6 to 8) and although the Solicitor originally argued that the Tribunal did not order the periods of suspension to be made consecutive to one another, this point was not really pursued before us nor, I might add, was it a valid argument anyway).

(3) If the Solicitor were to resume practice after the suspension, he would be prohibited from practicing as a sole proprietor for the first two years and if he were to enter into partnership or be employed, his partner or partners, or employer (as the case may be) would have to possess at least 15 years' experience in practice.

6. The Solicitor appealed against the penalties that were imposed. As I have said earlier, this aspect was left to be resolved after our decision on the appeal against the Complaints. Following our judgment, the Solicitor has continued with the appeal on penalties.

7. In considering the question of the appropriate penalties or sanction to be imposed following the establishment of a complaint made against a solicitor, a Solicitors Disciplinary Tribunal should first consider the appropriate penalty for the individual complaint, any relevant mitigation regarding such complaint and, where a series of penalties are involved, the appropriateness of the resulting overall impact, making such adjustment to the end result as will be suitable.

8. A number of short points can first be made: -

(1) The penalties for Complaints 1 and 2 must in any event be set aside in view of our earlier decision.

(2) One of the penalties imposed by the Tribunal was that the Solicitor be censured. No arguments were raised regarding this penalty and that order will therefore remain.

9. I consider first the appropriateness of orders for suspension that were made in relation to Complaints 3 to 8. Here, as mentioned above, the Tribunal imposed periods of suspension of 9 months for each of Complaints 3 to 5, 9 months for Complaint 6 and 12 months apiece for Complaints 7 to 8. I will then deal with the order that was made regarding the restrictions that were imposed on the Solicitor following the periods of suspension (see sub-paragraph (l) of the Tribunal's order set out in paragraph above).

10. In relation to the periods of suspension, it is important to identify the factors that influenced the Tribunal. Here, it is clear from the Tribunal's Reasons that the following matters assumed considerable weight:-

(1) The Tribunal first made reference to (and found assistance in) the case of Allinson v General Council of Medical Education and Registration [1894] 1 QB 750. That was a case in which a doctor had published a number of advertisements in newspapers in which he criticized fellow doctors with a view to persuading readers to consult him instead. This conduct was found by the regulatory body (the General Council of Medical Education and Registration) as amounting to "infamous conduct" and he was ordered to be struck off. The Tribunal in the present case regarded that authority as being relevant on its facts and in context, this could only mean the aspect of the Solicitor having disparaged his fellow solicitors (the specific subject matter of Complaint 1). This point was emphasized in paragraph 22 of the Reasons and Order as well. I should add here that as far as the Tribunal was concerned, this aspect appears to have been relevant only to Complaints 1, 3, 4 and 5.

(2) Next, the SDT was of the view that the Solicitor had been dishonest. The Tribunal said this at paragraph 13 of the Reasons and Order: -

"13. Although the Respondent's conduct in question may not have been 'dishonest' in a narrow or literal sense, they were done for personal gain and tantamount to 'dishonesty' in the sense suggested by Briggs C.J. in *Re a Solicitor's Clerk* [1978] HKLR 160 and in any event dishonourable."

(3) The Tribunal's view of dishonesty was said to have been based on *Re A Solicitor's Clerk* [1978] HKLR 160, where at 162, Briggs CJ (in a dissenting judgment) said: -

"Various cases were brought to our attention. In the case of *In re A Solicitor* (1976) 120 Sol. J. 353 Lord Widgery said: -

'There are four basic penalties for professional misconduct by a solicitor; reprimand, fine, suspension and striking off. The great divide came between fine and suspension. Suspension and striking off could well mean professional disaster. As the solicitor had not been dishonest, he had not reached the stage where he ought to be suspended and, accordingly, a fine of £250 would be substituted for the tribunal's order.'.

This is not a very full report but in my view it shows that what His Lordship meant by 'dishonesty' was doing an act for personal gain. It is, strictly speaking, 'dishonest'to tell a lie. But I do not think that such conduct should result in a sentence of suspension. To impose a penalty of suspension in such a case would, in my view, be wrong in principle. Suspension should only be used when a client of the firm has been prejudiced, where there has been misapplication of funds or in such like cases."

(4) The Tribunal's conclusion that the Solicitor's conduct was dishonest appears to have permeated through all the Complaints.

(5) As a fallback (as the passage recorded in sub-paragraph (2) above demonstrates), the Tribunal also said that in any event, the Solicitor's conduct was "dishonourable" .

11 .In determining that suspension was the appropriate penalty for Complaints 1 and 3 to 8, the Tribunal referred to a number of previous cases of this court (namely *A Solicitor v The Law Society of Hong Kong*, unreported, CACV 2/1993, 7 May 1993 and *A Solicitor v The Law Society of Hong Kong*, unreported, CACV 11/2003, 25 September 2003) in which it was held that a

serious view had to be taken of any dishonest or dishonourable conduct and that where a solicitor's integrity, probity or trustworthiness fell below requisite standards, suspension would be an appropriate penalty.

12. Accordingly, the Tribunal imposed the suspension orders for the Complaints I have earlier set out. In arriving at its decision, the Tribunal took into account the submissions on mitigation made by the Solicitor. It also purported to apply the totality principle and this was put in the following terms in paragraph 19 of the Reasons and Order: -

> "19. In determining the length of the suspension periods, the Tribunal has taken into account the principles of totality. Had it not been for the Respondent's good record of voluntary community service and other mitigating factors advanced by his Counsel in his favour the Tribunal would have been minded to deal with the Respondent more severely."

13. Overall, the SDT took a very serious view of the Solicitor's conduct. In paragraph 18 of the Reasons and Order, it said this: -

> "18. The eight Complaints here constitute, in the opinion of the Tribunal, very serious professional misconduct. The Tribunal considers that the Respondent's various misconduct under the Complaints were disgraceful and not only ridiculed the Respondent himself but also seriously and adversely affected the reputation of the legal profession. Quite apart from sentences imposed in other cases, to show the Tribunal's disapproval of the Respondent's misconduct, and as a warning of the consequences and deterrent to others and to restore public confidence in the profession, the Tribunal has decided that the professional misconduct of the Respondent under all but one of the Complaints calls for the sanction of suspension rather than a fine."

14. In relation to the specific Complaints which remain relevant in this appeal, the SDT viewed them in the following way: -

(1) Complaints 3 to 5 were seen by the Tribunal as a "selfish and inconsiderate promotion" of the Solicitor and his firm. Mention was made not only of the frequency of the promotion but also of the interviews in which the Solicitor had allegedly disparaged other solicitors.

(2) As for Complaints 6 to 8, the Tribunal said that the Solicitor had ridiculed the profession as well as himself. It regarded the Solicitor as having brought the profession into disrepute and all this had demonstrated his "lack of integrity and probity".

15. With regard to the post-suspension order, the Tribunal said only this by way of justification : -

> "26.If the Respondent is to resume his practice after the suspension period, the Tribunal considers that he should practise under the supervision of at least an experienced member of the legal profession, his senior, so that he may be well-guided in professional conduct."

16. These, therefore, were the Tribunal's reasons on penalty. I have dealt with them at some length because in an appeal from a decision of the SDT on penalties, the approach of the Court of Appeal has always been one of caution. The starting point must be that the disciplinary tribunal of the professional body is in a far better position to decide on penalty than the court simply because it has the feel and sense of its members when it comes to weighing up the seriousness of any given conduct and the level of any penalty. That said, the court will, where the circumstances dictate, disturb the decision of a professional disciplinary tribunal even in relation to penalty. For example, if a tribunal has acted under an error of law or the penalty is obviously inappropriate or excessive, the court will then be obliged to disturb the decision. In practical terms, in order to disturb the penalties imposed by a disciplinary tribunal, it must be shown that the decision was obviously or plainly wrong. It is not enough simply for the court to take a different view, however forceful that view may be.

17. In the present case, however, I am of the view that this court should disturb the SDT's findings on penalty. My reasons are as follows: -

(1) As seen above, the Tribunal imposed a 6-month suspension in relation to Complaint 1 that was made concurrent with the 12-month suspension for Complaints 3 to 5. It is clear therefore that the Tribunal regarded there was an overlap between these Complaints. I have already referred to the fact that account was taken in sentencing of the aspect of the disparagement of fellow solicitors (see paragraph above). The reference to *Allinson and linking* this with the 12 October 1997 article (in Ming Pao Daily News) and the 17 July 1998 article (in Next Magazine) demonstrates in my view that the Tribunal regarded this feature as being relevant not only to Complaint 1, but also Complaints 3 to 5. Further, Complaints 4 and 5 referred specifically to Complaint 1 in their Particulars of Complaint.

(2) Accordingly, as there existed very much an element of Complaint 1 in Complaints 3 to 5 and that Complaint has now to be discounted (in view of our earlier decision), the penalties for Complaints 3 to 5 must accordingly be adjusted on this ground alone.

(3) The Tribunal was wrong to have regarded the Solicitor's conduct as being dishonest. As stated above, the Tribunal's view was coloured by its analysis of what Briggs CJ said in *Re A Solicitor's Clerk* (see paragraph above). The Tribunal thought that what the Chief Justice meant was to equate any conduct carried out with a view to personal gain as being conduct that was tantamount to dishonesty. I think this was an erroneous view. All that Briggs CJ meant was that in order to classify conduct as being truly dishonest, there had to be an element of personal gain as well (in other words there had to be not only dishonest conduct but also an element of personal gain). This is clear from the context of that case which involved a solicitor's clerk having dishonestly represented to the prison authorities that the firm (in which he was employed) was acting for a prisoner when this was not the case. His motive was to enable him and his wife to visit her brother who was in prison. The Chief Justice, who was in the minority in the Court of Appeal, did not regard such conduct as amounting to dishonesty for the purposes of imposing the penalty of suspension, since, presumably, no personal gain was involved (the clerk's firm had not been prejudiced and there was no misappropriation of client's funds). While Briggs CJ thought that only a fine and censure were appropriate, Huggins and Pickering JJA took a far more serious view: a period of suspension of 6 months was thought to be appropriate.

(4) I agree that dishonourable conduct, without an element

of dishonesty, may well justify suspension. Indeed some forms of dishonourable conduct may be worthy of greater censure than some forms of dishonesty. But the fact is that this was not a case of dishonesty and in so far as that error has been made, we must assume in the Solicitor's favour that that finding impacted to some degree on the Tribunal's approach to penalty. So some adjustment should be made for that reason alone. It is unnecessary to put a figure on it, because at the end of the day the question is one of the nature and total impact of the punishment imposed.

(5) The question has not been an easy one and views may respectfully differ, but in the event we have been able to reach a broad consensus. On the one hand, it is recognized that the Solicitor's conduct was markedly inappropriate for any solicitor and that there is displayed no contrition and one is bound to believe that to this day he does not think he has done anything professionally wrong. That being so, no-one could reasonably quarrel with suspension for a significant period. On the other hand, given that the Tribunal decided that the punishment should be suspension and no more, one has to take a realistic view of the effect of suspension for a lengthy period, for the longer the suspension the more difficult it is to re-establish practice; and in the case of suspension of, say, 12 months, it will be longer than that before this Solicitor is back on his feet as a practitioner. Taking that fact into account, as well in this case as the very significant costs implication of the Tribunal proceedings to the Solicitor (the Law Society's costs for the proceedings before the SDT are estimated at $4.1 million, the costs of the Clerk to the Tribunal are said to be about $1.1 million and the investigation costs of the Law Society are pitched at $140,000) and the various adjustments I have already identified, the view ultimately reached by us (see below) is that a period of suspension of 12 months is sufficiently condign in this case.

(6) I now move on to the post-suspension condition that was imposed to the effect that the Solicitor should not for a period of two years be permitted to practice as a sole proprietor and that if he were to enter into a partnership or be employed, his partner or partners or his employer would have to be a solicitor of at least 15 years' standing. The Tribunal's justification for this has already been set out above (see paragraph). Such orders have in the past been made. The jurisdiction to make such orders is found in section 10(2)(ba) of the LPO. Before the introduction of that provision in 1992, there was no power to impose such a condition: - see *A Solicitor v Law Society of Hong Kong* [1996] 3 HKC 98. In that case, Liu JA said that the conditions that may be made under section 10(2)(ba) could be "highly detrimental to [a solicitor's] practice". With respect, I agree. For the Solicitor in the present case, I would think that the condition that was imposed would be highly detrimental. The options open to him to resume practice would be significantly reduced. While obviously this is a consequence that a solicitor would have to put up with if such a condition were to be imposed, the question is really whether it is justified in the circumstances. It is perhaps appropriate where a solicitor is inexperienced and therefore in need of guidance. It may be appropriate also where a solicitor has been shown that he cannot be trusted to practice on his own when dealing with, say, clients' monies. An order such as the present may be justified therefore to protect clients and third parties. However, it is somewhat difficult to see why such an order is necessary in the present case. The Solicitor is experienced; he was called to the Hong Kong Bar in 1985 and became a solicitor in 1992. Though his conduct has in my view been appalling, no clients or third parties were involved : he has hurt his profession and himself, but no one else. One would assume that the Solicitor has learnt from these proceedings and their outcome. It is difficult to see what a monitoring solicitor would be able to point out that is now not obvious to the Solicitor. The nature of the condemned conduct is such that any repetition would at once be known to the Law Society and the consequences would be swift and obvious. I do not think that a post-suspension such as that imposed by the Tribunal is in these circumstances justified or necessary. Any guidance he may need can be given by the Law Society and if he were to continue not to heed or seek proper advice, he will just have to bear the consequences himself.

18. Given the conclusion that the SDT has erred in the present case, it then becomes open for this court to look at the question of penalties afresh. In the present case, in summary, I am of the view that the following penalties should be imposed: -

(1) The Solicitor be censured.

(2) On Complaints 3 to 5, the Solicitor should be suspended from practice for a period of 6 months but the suspension should run concurrently.

(3) On Complaints 6 to 8, the Solicitor should be suspended from practice for a period of 12 months for each Complaint, but the suspensions are to run concurrently as well.

(4) The total period of suspension should be 12 months.

19. My reasons are as follows (see also paragraph above): -

(1) As can be seen from the earlier judgment of this court, the Solicitor's conduct was excessive, disgraceful, dishonourable and simply unacceptable. It can be regarded as being in the very serious category. However, since one can reasonably envisage worse situations (such as dishonesty involving the appropriation of funds or dishonesty in dealings as an officer of the court), I feel that a suspension, rather than an order striking off the Solicitor, is appropriate.

(2) For Complaints 3 to 5, once the element of the disparagement of fellow solicitors is taken away, one is left simply with the massive and excessive advertising campaign that was embarked upon by the Solicitor. This, by itself, was very serious and certainly merits a suspension being imposed. In the circumstances, I am of the view that suspensions of 6 months are appropriate for each Complaint here. Given their similarity and the theme that runs through them, the suspension should run concurrently.

(3) For Complaints 6 to 8 which involved the aspect of the Solicitor having posed nude or semi-nude, a much more serious view must be taken, for here he was not only promoting himself and his practice, he was doing so in the most vulgar and provocative way possible. His conduct was, quite frankly, outrageous and went far beyond acceptable standards. The Tribunal, although it has erred in those respects set out above, was, however in my view, correct in imposing suspensions of 12 months for the Complaints. Like the Tribunal, I am also of the view that the three suspensions should be made concurrent.

(4) The Tribunal was of the view that the suspensions for the two sets of Complaints should be made consecutive to each other. Mr Duncan has urged us to adopt the same approach. He points to the difference when the subject matter of the Complaints were committed : the first set took place between October 1997 and July 1998 while the second set took place over the course of January and February 1999. Next, he highlights the very significant added feature in Complaints 6 to 8 of the nudity. Finally, he referred to the context of the second set of Complaints : they were committed at the time when the Solicitor could not have been under any mistake about how the Law Society regarded his advertising activities (they had afterall been in lengthy correspondence with each other). For the Solicitor, I suppose it could be argued that there was a common theme that ran through all the Complaints, namely, that it was all done for the purpose of publicity and advertising.

(5) I see the force of Mr Duncan's submissions that the two sets of Complaints ought to be treated separately and as a matter of principle, it can quite readily be understood just why the Tribunal made the suspensions consecutive. However, it is important to bear in mind the question of totality when deciding on the matter. A period of 12-month suspension overall meets, I feel, the justice of the situation (see paragraphs and (5)). This is a hefty penalty when one considers the obvious adverse impact on the Solicitor's practice. It is all the more so once one adds to that the costs that he will have to pay.

(6) It is, in my view for the reasons earlier stated, inappropriate to attach any conditions dealing with the Solicitor's practice subsequent to his suspension and I would not so order.

20. In arriving at the penalties just mentioned, I have taken into account the same mitigating factors that the Tribunal had taken into account.

21. I should also mention two other arguments that Mr Gerard McCoy SC (for the Solicitor) raised. First, he pointed to the length of time it had taken for the SDT to dispose of the matter. Secondly, he claimed that the Solicitor had been prejudiced by two matters, namely (a) the fact that from 15 to 30 March 2005, the Tribunal had failed to inform the Solicitor of its order for suspension (thus breaching rule 15 of the Solicitors Disciplinary Tribunal Proceedings Rules, Cap.159C), thus depriving him of the opportunity for two weeks to apply for a suspension of the filing of the Tribunal's ruling, pursuant to rule 16 of the Rules; (b) subsequent to our earlier judgment, the Registrar of the High Court mistakenly published in the Gazette on 14 July 2006, the fact that the Solicitor was to be suspended, although this was withdrawn the next day. The effect of those matters was that the Solicitor had already undergone two (albeit short) periods of suspension.

22. In my judgment, none of these arguments has force. The time it took the SDT to deal with the Complaints was accounted for at least in part by the Solicitor appealing (unsuccessfully) against certain decisions of the Tribunal. The delay factor is a factor neither in favour of the Solicitor nor against him. As for the prejudice alleged by the Solicitor, none was shown. He did not seek to adduce any evidence regarding this. The relevant periods in this context are so short that any prejudice cannot readily be assumed to have existed. Nevertheless, I should perhaps add that the two periods of suspension ought to count towards the total suspension to be served by the Solicitor.

23. For the above reasons, I would allow the appeal regarding penalties and substitute for the order made by the SDT, the penalties referred to in paragraph above.

The costs of the appeal and of the proceedings before the SDT

24. Two aspects have to be dealt with : first, the costs of the appeal and of the proceedings before the SDT as far as what may be called the liability issue (the issue as to whether the Complaints made against the Solicitor could be sustained) and secondly, the costs in relation to the penalty phase.

25. The Tribunal ordered that the Solicitor had to pay two-thirds of the Law Society's costs on a party and party basis (in relation of both liability and penalties). In addition, the Solicitor had to pay the costs of investigation of the Law Society and also the costs of the Clerk to the Tribunal.

26. In my view, the allowing of the appeal against liability in part (our earlier judgment) should be reflected in the order for costs both here and before the SDT. While the Law Society has largely succeeded, it has not succeeded on every aspect. I would accordingly order that the Solicitor pay to the Law Society in relation to the liability issues, three-quarters of the costs of the appeal, such costs to be taxed if not agreed. In relation to the costs of the proceedings before the SDT, I would order that the Solicitor do pay to the Law Society, three-fifths of the costs, such costs again to be taxed if not agreed. The orders made regarding the costs of investigation and of the Clerk to the Tribunal, will remain.

27. As for the costs of the appeal dealing with penalties, I am of the view that the Solicitor has on the whole succeeded and needed to come to this court in order to get a reduction. In these circumstances, I would make an order nisi that the Law Society should pay to the Solicitor the costs of this part of the appeal, such costs to be taxed if not agreed. As far as the penalty phase of the proceedings before the SDT are concerned, I would make an order nisi that the Solicitors should pay to the Law Society three-fifths of such costs. The penalty phase was really just a part of the overall proceedings before the Tribunal.

Application for leave to appeal to the Court of Final Appeal

28. The Notice of Motion dated 24 July 2006 taken out by the Solicitor deals with our earlier judgment on liability. Leave is sought under section 22(1)(b) of the Hong Kong Court of Final Appeal Ordinance, Cap.484 on the ground that the appeal would involve questions of great general or public importance.

29. These questions are identified in the Notice of Motion: -

"Standard of Proof

1. Whether as a matter of principle and/or law, the requisite standard of proof in solicitor's disciplinary hearings, is the criminal standard of proof?

2. If not the criminal standard of proof, whether the Solicitor's Disciplinary Tribunal nevertheless ought to have applied a standard within the flexible civil standard akin to proof beyond reasonable doubt?

Binding Nature of Previous Judgments: Stare Decisis

3. Is the Court of Appeal bound by its own decision(s) when that previous decision(s) was influenced or itself bound by a Privy Council decision(s), which has since been either overtaken and/or developed and/or departed from?"

30. I agree that the questions in the appeal are of great general or public importance. Mr Duncan did not suggest otherwise and in effect took a neutral stance.

31. I would therefore for my part grant leave to the Solicitor to appeal to the Court of Final Appeal from our earlier decision based on the said questions. I would also make an order nisi on the conditions for leave that the Solicitor is to, within 3 months of the date of the order giving conditional leave, provide security for the appeal in the sum of $400,000 and that the appeal be prosecuted with due expedition. There will also be an order nisi that there be a stay of execution of the order as to penalties (paragraph above) pending the determination of such appeal or until further order (I make an order nisi because although Mr McCoy had asked for a stay at the conclusion of the arguments before us, we did not hear Mr Duncan on this). I would also make a costs order nisi that the costs of this application be costs in the appeal.

32. The parties will be at liberty to apply to vary the various orders nisi as well as to apply for any further directions.

Hon Tang VP:

33. I agree.

Hon Stock JA:

34. I agree.

Hon Ma CJHC:

35. In view of the above, the following orders are made.

36. <u>The appeal on penalties</u>

(1) The appeal is allowed.

(2) The SDT's order on penalties is set aside and there be substituted the following order: -

(a) The Solicitor be censured.

(b) On Complaints 3 to 5, the Solicitor should be suspended from practice for a period of 6 months but the suspension should run concurrently.

(c) On Complaints 6 to 8, the Solicitor should be suspended from practice for a period of 12 months for each Complaint, but the suspensions are to run concurrently as well.

(d) The total period of suspension should be 12 months.

37. <u>Costs</u>

(1) On the costs of the liability issue : -

(a) The Solicitor is to pay to the Law Society three-quarters of the costs of the appeal relating to this issue, such costs to be taxed if not agreed.

(b) The Solicitor is to pay to the Law Society three-fifths of the costs relating to this issue in the proceedings before the SDT, such costs to be taxed if not agreed. The Solicitor is also to pay the investigation costs of the Law Society and the costs of the Clerk to the SDT relating to this issue.

(2) On the costs of the penalties issue, I would make an order nisi that: -

(a) The Law Society is to pay to the Solicitor the costs of the appeal relating to this issue, such costs to be taxed if not agreed.

(b) The Solicitor is to pay to the Law Society three-fifths of the costs relating to this issue in the proceedings before the SDT, such costs to be taxed if not agreed. For the avoidance of doubt, the Solicitor is also to pay the investigation costs of the Law Society and the costs of the Clerk to the SDT relating to this issue.

38. <u>Application for leave to appeal to the Court of Final Appeal</u>

(1) Leave to appeal to the Court of Final Appeal is granted to the Solicitor on the basis that the following questions of great general or public importance are involved: -

"Standard of Proof

1. Whether as a matter of principle and/or law, the requisite standard of proof in solicitor's disciplinary hearings, is the criminal standard of proof?

2. If not the criminal standard of proof, whether the Solicitor's Disciplinary Tribunal nevertheless ought to have applied a standard within the flexible civil standard akin to proof beyond reasonable doubt?

Binding Nature of Previous Judgments: Stare Decisis

3. Is the Court of Appeal bound by its own decision(s) when that previous decision(s) was influenced or itself bound by a Privy Council decision(s), which has since been either overtaken and/or developed and/or departed from?"

(2) The following orders nisi are also made: -

(a) Leave to appeal is granted on the condition that the Solicitor is to provide within 3 months of this order security for the appeal in the sum of $400,000 and that the appeal be prosecuted with due expedition;

(b) There be a stay of execution of the penalties imposed on the Solicitor pending the determination of such appeal or until further order;

(c) The costs of this application be costs in the appeal.

(3) The parties have liberty to apply.

Chief Judge, High Court (Geoffrey Ma)

Vice President (Robert Tang)

Justice of Appeal (Frank Stock)

Mr Gerard McCoy SC, Mr Richard Zimmern & Ms Kristeen Lau, instructed by Messrs Paul W Tse for the Appellant

Mr Peter Duncan SC & Mr Alfred K C Fung, instructed by Messrs Haldanes for the Respondent

---

Dr. Kwok-Hay Kwong v. The Medical Council of Hong Kong

鄺國熙醫生 對 香港醫務委員會

HCAL 46/2006；CACV 373/2006

簡略案情

香港醫務委員會（下稱“答辯人”）是依據《醫生註冊條例》所設立的機構，它其中的一個職能是監察香港註冊醫生的操守和行為。因此，它定時制定並發佈對醫生有規管效力的專業守則（下稱“守則”）。申請人為香港養和醫院副院長，其主要工作之一是負責向公眾介紹養和醫院的設施及服務，其中包括可提供的治療和技術。他認為香港市民對醫生及其執業沒有充足的資訊，所以難以對相關服務作出知情選擇，究其原因，是該守則（*Professional Code and Conduct* 2000 年 11 月修訂版本）第 5 章第 5 和 14 段關於執業推廣的事情，以紀律懲罰的手段，限制了醫生向公眾提供服務、技術與醫療科技的信息。申請人認為，這些限制違反了《基本法》第 27 條、《公民權利和政治權利國際公約》第 19 條和《香港人權法案》第 16 條關於意見和發表自由的權利。申請人遂對該守則的限制提起司法覆核，爭議包括四方面：

1）容許醫生在互聯網及其診所內及外發放資料，卻禁止醫生在報紙、雜誌等出版物上發佈，這規定是不合理的。

2）醫生最多只能展示其 5 項醫療服務，這限制並沒有任何依據。

3）雖然醫生有權通過講演、參加電視廣播節目或出版書籍等形式，向公眾介紹醫療衛生的發展狀況。但與此同時規定醫生在該過程中，不能涉及自身的工作經驗、技術水平、個人聲望和一切有可能提升自身形象的內容。這對於參與公開活動的醫生來說是不現實的。而且作為聽眾，也希望知悉該醫生在相關領域的經驗，這些資料必然導致公眾認為該醫生在其專業領域內具有聲譽。

4）對於跟醫生有財務或其他專業關係的醫療機構的宣傳和推廣，該醫生須對這些宣傳負絕對責任，不能以不知情及不在其控制範圍之內作為免責事由。因此，就算是小心在意的醫生，也有機會因其不能控制的事而違反該守則。

答辯人強調該守則已經過業內廣泛諮詢，是合理與盡責的結果。平衡了各方的利益，尤其是醫生，負有保障病人生命健康的使命，公眾對他們的信心與依賴和行業的尊嚴是非常重要的考慮。關於業務推廣這問題，法院應該秉承“裁量餘地”原則（margin of appreciation），把平衡的工作交給答辯人處理。

申請人與答辯人皆同意，由於醫生的社會地位，他推廣其服務和收費時應受到管制，尤其是公眾對醫生的信心可能被唯利是圖的商業態度所影響。而且，求醫的病人與家屬是特別容易受到誤導的。

裁決摘要

原審法官引述*吳恭劭*與*梁國雄*兩個終審法院案例，確認《基本法》和《香港人權法案》對基本人權的保護並非絕對的，有需要時，例如在“保障國家安全或公共秩序，或公共衛生或風化”領域裏，可以作出限制。但需要通過一個必須性的驗測標準：

1）該限制與為求達到的合法目的必須成比例；

2）該限制必須和這目的有合理的聯繫；

3）該限制的幅度不應超過為達到該目的所必須的要求。

法院指出《歐洲人權公約》第 10 條有關言論自由跟《香港人權法案》第 16 條是一致的，並援引歐洲人權法院案件 *Stambuck v. Germany*（2003）37 EHRR 845。該案的申請人是一名眼科醫生，在接受雜誌訪問關於他專長的眼睛鐳射矯形手術後，德國醫委會認為他違反了不能推廣的禁令而判處罰款。於是，他上訴到歐洲人權法院指該禁令違反了《歐洲人權公約》第 10 條。在考慮到醫生的地位與專業，人權法院認為對醫生的宣傳作出限制是合理的，但同時必須與公眾知情權之間作出平衡。雖然該篇報導，可能不經意間宣傳和提升了該醫生的工作，但這只屬於次要性質，並不應因此而剝奪公眾對準確和中肯的資訊的知情權，超乎為了維護醫生行業專業性的目的，因此罰款無效。

法官再引述加拿大最高法院於 *Rocket v. Royal College Of Dental Surgeons Of Ontario* [1990] 71 DLR (4th) 68 所述，“為提升專業性與防止對一些難以驗證的問題上的不負責任和誤導的宣傳，這目的並不需要以規則去排除這麼多的言論……”並且同意在宣傳問題上，法庭一般依賴專業團體去管理其會員的行為，但任何限制也必須在程度比例上合符情理，不能只單單反映團體裏大部份人的意見；再者，不能因為僅僅可能在不經意間提升了某醫生的業務而限制對公眾提供有關資訊。

對於答辯人提出的英國案例 *R v. General Medical Council, Ex Parte Colman* [1990] 1 All ER 489 和相關的歐洲人權公署報告（*Report Of The European Commission Of Human Rights*）in *Colman v. United Kingdom*（1994）18 EHRR 119，法官認為這不僅過時，而且他認為舉證責任在申請人一方，是明顯違反*吳恭劭*一案的，所以不予採納。最後裁定申請人得直，答辯人遂提起上訴。

上訴庭重申任何對基本人權的限制都必須有足夠的正當理由。在衡量是否有足夠的正當理由時，法庭往往需要依賴和尊重決策者的專業知識。對表達自由的範圍和限制行使該自由的措施，法庭必須監督其正當理由和程度。因此，對任何限制，都應該通過均衡比例測試（Proportionality Test）。最後，上訴庭認為原審法院已經充分考慮了相關的法律和案例，裁決並沒有不妥的地方，因此駁回了答辯人的上訴。

CACV 373/2006

IN THE HIGH COURT OF THE

HONG KONG SPECIAL ADMINISTRATIVE REGION

COURT OF APPEAL

CIVIL APPEAL NO. 373 OF 2006
(ON APPEAL FROM HCAL NO. 46 OF 2006)

Between:

Dr. KWOK-HAY KWONG **Applicant**

- and -

THE MEDICAL COUNCIL OF HONG KONG Respondents

Before: Hon Ma CJHC, Tang VP & Stock JA in Court

Dates of Hearing: 24 and 25 October 2007

Date of Handing Down Judgment: 24 January 2008

JUDGMENT

Hon Ma CJHC:

1. The present appeal raises important issues for the medical profession in relation to practice promotion (that is, advertising). The Applicant, a medical practitioner (formerly the Assistant Medical Superintendent of the Hong Kong Sanatorium and Hospital and whose position mirrors that of the Hospital and many other doctors in Hong Kong), has sought in these judicial review proceedings to challenge certain restrictions contained in the Professional Code and Conduct for the Guidance of Registered Medical Practitioners, as updated from time to time, ("the Code") as being contrary to the freedom of expression guaranteed under the Basic Law, the International Covenant on Civil and Political Rights ("the ICCPR") and the Bill of Rights contained in the Hong Kong Bill of Rights Ordinance, Cap. 383. The freedom of expression includes as one of its facets the right to advertise.

2. For its part, the Respondent (the Medical Council) has maintained in the relevant decisions in these proceedings that the restrictions are consistent with the said constitutional right and are considered by a Medical Council (as the governing body for doctors) to be appropriate. This considered view, says the Respondent, ought to be given due respect by the courts. However, as will presently be seen, the Respondent has in this appeal somewhat retreated in its stance in at least one respect.

3. Both parties rely on the public interest to justify their positions. Essentially, while the Respondent recognizes that the public is entitled to be provided with relevant information about doctors to enable informed choices to be made by patients, it is anxious that practice promotion should not be permitted to reach a stage where commercialism takes over at the expense of public confidence and trust in the medical profession or, worse still, gives rise to the exploitation or manipulation of the sick and the vulnerable. For its part, the Applicant is not advocating a free for all in terms of practice promotion for doctors. Far from it, the intention is merely to provide the public in more media forms with the same information to which the public now has access and which is expressly permitted under the Code, and also to remove unreasonable restrictions on the freedom of speech. The basic legal issue for the court to resolve in these proceedings becomes whether the dividing line between what is acceptable and what is not (these being the restrictions maintained by the Respondent) is constitutionally justified.

4. Before going into the issues that still divide the parties, it is right to point out that the evidence before this court has changed substantially from the position that prevailed before Reyes J in the court below. The evidence on appeal, substantial in both content and volume, provides for the first time the thinking and reasoning behind the Respondent's decision to maintain the restrictions. In an earlier judgment on 5 September 2007 (the Reasons for Judgment were handed down on 27 September 2007), this court had given leave to the Respondent to adduce this evidence for the purposes of the appeal.

The Restrictions

5. There are four restrictions under challenge in the present proceedings. All are found in the Code. These restrictions mark the four issues which divide the parties in this appeal.

The first restriction: the medium of information

6. In the course of counsel's arguments, it became clear that this was the main issue on appeal. At present, certain basic information about doctors (name, address, qualifications, specialities, consultation hours, languages spoken and telephone and fax numbers) may be notified to the public on signboards or service information notices outside medical surgeries, stationery, telephone directories, doctor's directories and medical practice websites. In the case of doctor's directories, websites and service information notices, fee schedules are also permitted. This is the effect of paragraph 5 and Appendices E and F of the Code.

7. The Applicant's complaint is that doctors are, however, forbidden from providing the same information to the public if such appears in newspapers, magazines or other print media. The only occasion permitted under the Code when doctors are able to advertise in newspapers (but not any other form of print media) is to announce the commencement of practice or changes in the conditions of practice (meaning changes in address, telephone number, partnership details etc.) Mr David Pannick QC (for the Applicant) has emphasized that the information which his client wishes to be able to advertise is information that is accurate and basic. There is no question or danger of any misleading or potentially misleading information being provided to the public; the Applicant seeks only to be able to provide to the public in newspapers, magazines and other printed media the same information as is currently available (and sanctioned by the Respondent to be made available) to the public.

8. It is important to bear in mind that this was the limit of the Applicant's challenge on this ground. He does not in these proceedings seek to advance any argument to the effect that doctors should be allowed to promote themselves by providing material that is not accurate, basic or objectively verifiable.

The second restriction: the number of services

9. At present, doctors are permitted to inform the public (limited of course by the methods of doing so referred to above) of the medical services they provide in and out of their surgeries (or 'offices' as they are known in the Code) and the medical procedures and operations they perform. However, in relation to each of these aspects, a doctor is limited to a maximum of five items: - see paragraphs 5.2.3.5 (practice websites), 5.2.3.6 (service information notices), 5.2.3.7 (doctors directories) and Appendices E and F of the Code. In other words, a maximum of five

items can be identified for each of the medical services provided in surgeries, medical services provided outside surgeries, and medical procedures and operations – a maximum, as the Respondent has reminded the court, of 15 items. The Applicant's complaint is simply to question the restriction to five items for each of the three aspects: his case is that there is no logic or justification to restrict the numbers in this way.

The third restriction: educational vehicles

10. 1.This issue involves the aspect of public health education, which it is accepted by both parties should be encouraged. Paragraphs 5.1 and 5.2 of the Code state:

5. Books, lectures, mass media appearances, electronic publications

5.1 Doctors in their capacity as registered medical practitioners may give public lectures, participate in radio or television programmes, or publish in print or electronically for the fulfilment of public health education. Doctors' full names, identifiable photographs, together with the specialist title, qualifications, and appointments approved by the Council, may be used. However, doctors should ensure that reference is not made to the doctor's experience, skills and reputation, or practice, in a manner which can be construed as promotional.

5.2 Doctors should ensure the material in whatever form does not imply that he is especially recommended for patients to consult." (emphasis added)

11. The complaint was that the highlighted words of paragraph 5.1 rendered it virtually impossible for a doctor to reveal details of (in particular) his experience, skills, qualifications and reputation without falling foul of the prohibition on practice promotion in that paragraph. This is particularly so given the broad definition of "practice promotion" contained in section 5.2.2 of the Code (as updated in March 2006):

5.2.2 Practice promotion

5.2.2.1 Practice promotion means publicity for promoting the professional services of a doctor, his practice or his group, excluding communication with registered medical and dental practitioners, Chinese medicine practitioners, chiropractors, nurses, midwives, pharmacists, medical laboratory technologists, radiographers, physiotherapists, occupational therapists and optometrists. Practice promotion in this context will be interpreted by the Medical Council in its broadest sense, and includes any means by which a doctor or his practice is publicized, in Hong Kong or elsewhere, by himself or anybody acting on his behalf or with his forbearance (including the failure to take adequate steps to prevent such publicity in circumstances which would call for caution), which objectively speaking constitutes promotion of his professional services, irrespective of whether he actually benefits from such publicity."

12. This issue can in a sense be said to be academic in that it is clear from the Respondent's evidence now before the court that the highlighted words will in due course be deleted. There appears to be an amendment that the Respondent has in mind. In the first affidavit of Dr David Fang (the Chairman of the Ethics Committee of the Respondent), it is said that as part of the Respondent's continuing review process of the Code, it was proposed on 5 October 2005, (before the present judicial review proceedings were instituted), that the following amendments should replace the provisions set out above:

"29. The Council and the Ethics Committee are continually reviewing the Code to ensure that it maintains the standards and morals of the medical profession in a modern context. As part of this review process, on 5th October 2005 the Council approved the deletion of the last sentence of paragraph 5.1 of the Code and replaced it with the following which will become section 6.2 in an updated Code. The amendment has not come into effect because of the judicial review but the Council intends that it should come into effect as soon as the Judicial Review is finally deposed of:

'Doctors should take proper steps to ensure that the published or broadcasted materials, either by their contents or the manner they are referred to, do not give the impression that they are recommended to the audience for medical consultation. They should also ensure that the materials are not used directly or indirectly for the promotion of products or services of other persons or organizations.'"

The fourth restriction: individual responsibility for organization advertisting

13. This restriction is concerned with the relationship between doctors and organizations such as private hospitals. Paragraphs 14.1 and 14.1.1 of the Code read: -

"14. Relationship between doctors and organizations

14.1 Medical services are offered to the public not only by individual doctors but by a wide variety of organizations such as hospitals, screening centres, nursing homes, medical scheme administrators, insurance companies, healthy administration companies, managed care companies and counselling centres. Such organizations may be providing the medical service itself directly or through middlemen; or may be acting as an agent or a middleman itself. Some of them advertise their services to the public and the principles and rules set out in paragraph 4.2 above, concerning the advertising of medical practitioner services, apply also to such advertising.

14.1.1 Doctors who have any kind of financial or professional relationship with such an organization, or who use its facilities, bear responsibility to ensure the organization's advertising conforms to the principles and rules set out in paragraph 4.2 above. This also applies to doctors who accept for examination or treatment patients referred by any such organization. All such doctors must therefore make it their responsibility to acquaint themselves with the nature and content of the organization's advertising, and must exercise due diligence in an effort to ensure that it conforms with this guidance. Should any question be raised about a doctor's conduct in this respect, it will not be sufficient for any explanation to be based on the doctor's lack of awareness of the nature or content of the organization's advertising, or lack of ability to exert any influence over it." (emphasis added)

14. The complaint is over the highlighted words of the final sentence of paragraph 14.1.1. Mr Pannick contends that as currently drafted, strict liability can arise: for example, where an organization (such as a private hospital) with whom a doctor has a financial or professional relationship, advertises in a way that does not conform with the Code, that doctor will be himself subject to charges of misconduct notwithstanding that he may have exercised due diligence and is unaware of the content of the relevant advertisement or is unable to exert any information over the organization. It is said that liability being strict, this is in the circumstances, completely unwarranted and unfair.

15. As will be seen later when I come to resolve each issue, this argument was all but conceded by Mr Michael Beloff QC (for the Respondent) and can, again, in a sense be deemed academic.

The relevant decision of the Respondent

16. The relevant decision of the Respondent was contained in a letter dated 27 January 2006 from the Respondent to the Applicant's solicitors, in which the Respondent maintained that the restrictions were justified. This letter was the culmination of correspondence over the course of some four months between the Applicant (through his solicitors) and the Respondent over the question of restrictions on advertising. The Applicant had attempted to persuade the Respondent by enclosing extracts of an opinion from Queen's Counsel as well as a Joint Submission of some 78 doctors. As stated earlier, the Applicant's interests mirror those of the Hong Kong Sanatorium and Hospital; indeed, the correspondence from the solicitors representing the Applicant stated also that they were acting on behalf of the Hospital.

17. The Respondent is a statutory body established under the Medical Registration Ordinance, Cap. 161. In terms of its duties to supervise medical ethics and conduct, it is advised by an Ethics Committee. The provisions of Part IIID of the Medical Registration Ordinance deal with the functions of the Ethics Committee.

Relevant legal principles

18. At the risk of repetition, it is important to bear in mind the role of the court in judicial review proceedings when decisions are under challenge. The court does not function as an appellate body looking into the merits of a decision as such. There is therefore in general no question of the court agreeing or disagreeing with policy considerations or the principles under which a decision maker has acted. This general statement is, however, qualified by the limited role of the court in judicial review, for, within those parameters, it may sometimes be necessary to examine aspects of policy considerations or principles. The court's role is limited to reviewing a decision by reference to only three aspects: - first, the legality of the decision, in other words whether the decision complies with the law; secondly, whether in arriving at the relevant decision, the decision maker has followed all due procedural requirements and has been fair; thirdly, whether the decision itself on the merits is rational or, as lawyers usually refer to it, whether the decision is *Wednesbury* unreasonable.

19. We are in this appeal only concerned with the first aspect, namely, whether the decision of the Respondent complies with the law. Here, the relevant law is, as stated earlier, the Basic Law, the ICCPR and the Bill of Rights. The challenge is of course a constitutional one based on the freedom of expression.

20. A constitutional challenge is no less a challenge based on illegality than, say, a challenge based on the misapplication by the decision maker of a statute. However, the approach of the court may be quite different. A challenge based on the decision maker having misapplied a statute may simply require the court to construe the relevant statute and then see whether the decision maker has got the law right. This will usually provide the answer to whether or not the decision maker has acted properly. A constitutional challenge is often more complicated for the court. Constitutionally guaranteed rights such as the freedom of expression are usually couched (deliberately) in wide terms. Even given the approach that such rights must be generously construed (and the freedom of expression is no exception: see *HKSAR v Ng Kung Siu* (1999) 2 HKCFAR 442, at 455H-I), the court still has nevertheless to construe the relevant right to see whether it is relevant to the decision or matter under review. However, where the right is construed to be applicable, this does not necessarily dispose of the question whether or not the decision maker has acted properly or in accordance with constitutionally accepted norms. In many instances where a constitutionally protected right is involved, a two-stage inquiry is therefore required, namely:

> "(1) First, has a right protected by the Basic Law or the Bill of Rights (the ICCPR) been infringed?
>
> (2) Second, if so, can such infringement be justified?"

See: *Secretary for Justice v Yau Yuk Lung & Another* [2006] 4 HKLRD 196, at 208 B-C (paragraph 45); *Leung v Secretary for Justice* [2006] 4 HKLRD 211, at 234 G-H (paragraph 43).

In other words, although there may be an infringement of a constitutionally protected right, sufficient justification may be provided by the decision maker for the infringement. In the case of the right to equal treatment, the correct analysis may be that once justification is shown, there may not have been an infringement at all: - cf *Secretary for Justice v Yau Yuk Lung* [2007] 3 HKLRD 903, at 913J-914B (paragraph 22).

21. The question whether sufficient justification has been shown can be a complicated one. In the determination of the issue of justification, the court will of course have to look at the evidence adduced by the decision maker. Where a constitutionally guaranteed right has been shown to be relevant, the burden is on the decision maker to justify any restriction on that right. Here, the courts apply the proportionality test which was formulated in the following terms in the judgment of the Court of Final Appeal in *Leung Kwok Hung & Others v HKSAR* (2005) 8 HKCFAR 229, at 253I (paragraph 36) (a case dealing with the right of peaceful assembly):

> "36. As the legitimate purposes that may be pursued by any restriction on the right of peaceful assembly have been constitutionally specified in Hong Kong, the proportionality test should be formulated in these terms: (1) the restriction must be rationally connected with one or more of the legitimate purposes; and (2) the means used to impair the right of peaceful assembly must be no more than is necessary to accomplish the legitimate purpose in question."

22. In the determination of the issue of justification, the court

will, in practical terms, also have to accept the fact that proper respect must be accorded to the expertise of the decision maker. This is a manifestation of the limited role of the court in judicial review proceedings and acknowledges the pertinent fact that courts do not possess the necessary expertise or knowledge that the decision maker has. This approach is sometimes referred to as the margin of appreciation or deference that a court must allow to a decision maker when judicially reviewing decisions. It is an aspect that Mr Beloff very much relies on in the present case. He points out, rightly, that the courts have consistently recognized that medical regulatory bodies (such as the Respondent) are the best placed to determine the boundaries of medical professional conduct.

23. Many authorities in Hong Kong, from the United Kingdom and from the European Court of Human Rights, unnecessary to enumerate full, make out this principle. The following points, however, emerging from the judgment of Reyes J in the court below, have to be borne firmly in mind when considering arguments based on margin of appreciation: -

(1) While the starting point is that the court will of course give due deference to the views of the decision maker, it is the court that has the ultimate responsibility to determine whether constitutionally guaranteed rights have been infringed, grappling as it does with questions of proportionality. This is a matter of law and it is not for the decision maker to make this determination.

(2) Accordingly, the decision maker must provide cogent reasons to justify any interference with a constitutionally guaranteed right for the court to scrutinize.

(3) The burden is on the decision maker to justify; it is not for the applicant to prove that the restriction is not justifiable or proportionate.

24. It follows from these points that given the burden on the decision maker, it becomes incumbent on it to provide the court and the Applicant with all relevant materials. I dealt with this aspect in the judgment of this court allowing the Respondent to adduce further evidence on appeal, see the Reasons for Judgment dated 27 September 2007 at paragraph 6 (the need to place "all the cards face upwards on the table"). Stock JA in his judgment in the same appeal put the matter, with respect, entirely correctly:

> "18. Where there is an infringement on the freedom of expression (or, for that matter, on any other fundamental freedom) but it is argued that the infringement is lawful, it is for the body imposing the restriction – in this case, the Council – to show a justifiable societal objective for the restriction, and that the restriction goes no further than is necessary to achieve that objective. It is difficult, if not impossible, to envisage an infringement that could be justified without a clearly explained rationale, even though the depth of the explanation required will vary according to the nature of the restriction and its context. But to state merely that the decision accords with the majority view of a professional body as revealed in a consultation exercise comes nowhere close to an acceptable rationale. And to say that the court should allow the Council a margin of appreciation is fine so far as it goes, but means nothing in a vacuum. One can only accord a degree of appreciation if one is told what it is one is being asked to appreciate."

25. Lastly, on the aspect of margin of appreciation, Mr Pannick drew our particular attention to *RJR-MacDonald Inc v AG of Canada* (1995) 27 DLR (4)1, a decision of the Supreme Court of Canada. There, the Supreme Court was concerned with the constitutionality of legislation which prohibited tobacco advertising (the Tobacco Products Control Act 1988). The point of emphasis was that even in an area where the courts could be expected to allow the legislature maximum leeway in terms of margin of appreciation, the court recongnized its constitutional duty. This appears in the judgment of McLachlin J (now Chief Justice) in two passages highlighted in the judgment of Reyes J, but which bear repetition:

> "[129] The bottom line is this. While remaining sensitive to the social and political context of the impugned law and allowing for difficulties of proof inherent in that context, the courts must nevertheless insist that before the state can override constitutional rights, there be a reasoned demonstration of the good which the law may achieve in relation to the seriousness of the infringement. It is the task of the courts to maintain this bottom line if the rights conferred by our constitution are to have force and meaning. The task is not easily discharged, and may require the courts to confront the tide of popular public opinion. But that has always been the price of maintaining constitutional rights. No matter how important Parliament's goal may seem, if the state has not demonstrated that the means by which it seeks to achieve its goal are reasonable and proportionate to the infringement of rights, then the law must perforce fail.
>
> ......
>
> [136] As with context, however, care must be taken not to extend the notion of deference too far. Deference must not be carried to the point of relieving the government of the burden which the Charter places upon it of demonstrating that the limits it has imposed on guaranteed rights are reasonable and justifiable. Parliament has its role: to choose the appropriate response to social problems within the limiting framework of the constitution. But the courts also have a role: to determine, objectively and impartially, whether Parliament's choice falls within the limiting framework of the constitution. The courts are no more permitted to abdicate their responsibility than is Parliament. To carry judicial deference to the point of accepting Parliament's view simply on the basis that the problem is serious and the solution difficult, would be to diminish the role of the courts in the constitutional process and to weaken the structure of rights upon which our constitution and our nation is founded."

26. In the present case, the court's approach will require an examination of the ambit of the freedom of expression and also whether there has been a justifiable and proportionate infringement of that right. In the consideration of whether there has been an infringement, it will be necessary to evaluate the justification said to exist for the four restrictions referred to above.

27. The freedom of expression is constitutionally guaranteed by the Basic Law and is contained in the Bill of Rights:

<u>*Basic Law*</u>

> *"Article 27*

Hong Kong residents shall have freedom of speech, of the press and of publication; freedom of association, of assembly, of procession and of demonstration; and the right and freedom to from and join trade unions, and to strike."

Bill of Rights

"Article 16

Freedom of opinion and expression

(1) Everyone shall have the right to hold opinions without interference.

(2) Everyone shall have the right to freedom of expression; this right shall include freedom to seek, receive and impart information and ideas of all kinds, regardless of frontiers, either orally, in writing or in print, in the form of art, or through any other media of his choice.

(3) The exercise of the rights provided for in paragraph (2) of this article carries with it special duties and responsibilities. It may therefore be subject to certain restrictions, but these shall only be such as are provided by law and are necessary -

(a) for respect of the rights or reputations of others; or

(b) for the protection of national security or of public order (ordre public), or of public health or morals."

This article is in the same terms as Article 19 of the ICCPR, as embraced by Article 39 of the Basic Law.

This article is in the same terms as Article 19 of the ICCPR, as embraced by Article 39 of the Basic Law.

28. Unlike some other constitutionally guaranteed rights, Article 16 of the Bill of Rights actually sets out the scope of permissible restrictions on the right: see Article 16(3). We are in this appeal concerned with the aspect of public health.

29. The freedom of expression includes the right to advertise and this is so even where the intention is for personal financial gain: see the decision of the European Court of Human Rights in *Casado Coca v Spain* (1994) 18 EHRR 1, at 20 (paragraph 35), a decision concerning the rights of lawyers to advertise.

30. Developing this theme of personal financial gain, Mr Beloff emphasized at the outset of his submissions that where commercial gain was involved (and practice promotion was in reality for this purpose), less justification was required for restrictions than would otherwise be the case where more serious aspects of the freedom of expression were at stake. The right of free expression would in such cases be at the lower or even lowest end of the spectrum of this protected right. He relied on a passage in the speech of Lord Steyn in *R v Secretary of State for the Home Department ex p Simms* [2000] 2 AC 115, at 126F-127A:

"Freedom of expression is, of course, intrinsically important: it is valued for its own sake. But it is well recognised that it is also instrumentally important. It serves a number of broad objectives. First, it promotes the self-fulfilment of individuals in society. Secondly, in the famous words of Holmes J. (echoing John Stuart Mill), 'the best test of truth is the power of the thought to get itself accepted in the competition of the market: '*Abrams v. United States* (1919) 250 U.S. 616, 630, *per* Holmes J. (dissenting). Thirdly, freedom of speech is the lifeblood of democracy. The free flow of information and ideas informs political debate. It is a safety valve: people are more ready to accept decisions that go against them if they can in principle seek to influence them. It acts as a brake on the abuse of power by public officials. It facilitates the exposure of errors in the governance and administration of justice of the country: see *Stone, Seidman, Sunstein and Tushnet, Constitutional Law*, 3rd ed. (1996), pp. 1078-1086. It is this last interest which is engaged in the present case. The applicants argue that in their cases the criminal justice system has failed, and that they have been wrongly convicted. They seek with the assistance of journalists, who have the resources to do the necessary investigations, to make public the wrongs which they allegedly suffered.

The value of free speech in a particular case must be measured in specifics. Not all types of speech have an equal value. For example, no prisoner would ever be permitted to have interviews with a journalist to publish pornographic material or to give vent to so-called hate speech."

31. For my part, I can accept this passage as a general proposition. There are, however, other factors to be considered in the present case other than just commercial gain for doctors. To start with, I would repeat the point that (certainly as far as the first restriction is concerned) all the Applicant seeks is to be able to provide the same objective, accurate and basic information in various printed media as is now permissible to be provided to the public under the existing rules.

32. Next, it is important also to recognize the following facets of advertising which I believe to be relevant considerations in the present case:

(1) The public interest as far as advertising is concerned lies in the provision of relevant material to enable informed choices to be made. This was described in the decision of the US Supreme Court in *Virginia State Board of Pharmacy v Virginia Citizens Consumer Council Incoporated* (1976) 425 US 748, at 770 (footnote 24) as "the flow of truthful and legitimate commercial information". In his judgment, Reyes J referred to a number of authorities that made out this basic proposition, among them, the decisions of the Supreme Court of Canada in *Rocket v Royal College of Dental Surgeons of Ontario* [1990] 71 DLR (4th) 68, at 79c and 81g and in *RJR MacDonald* at 80g; and of the European Court of Human Right in *Stambuck v Germany* (2003) 37 EHRR 845, at 954 (paragraph 39).

(2) The provision of relevant material to enable informed choices to be made includes information about latest medical developments, services or treatments. *Stambuck* provides a good example of this. There, an ophthalmologist gave an interview to a journalist about an eye laser operation technique. He was fined in professional disciplinary proceedings as being in breach of the provisions against advertising. The European Court of Human Rights, however, held that this fine constituted a violation of the freedom of expression guaranteed under Article 10 of the European Convention on Human Rights (the equivalent to Article 16 of the Bill of Rights). The court referred to the provision of information to the public on a matter of general medical interest as being desirable: at 855 (paragraph 46).

33. In contrast to these what may be called the advantages of advertising just highlighted, it is, however, also important to bear in mind the need to protect the public from the disadvantages of advertising. Misleading medical advertising must of course be guarded against. In *Rocket*, McLachlin J referred (at 81g) to the danger of "misleading the public or undercutting professionalism". In *Stambuck*, the European Court of Human Rights said, "nevertheless, it [advertising] may sometimes be restricted, especially to prevent unfair competition and untruthful or misleading advertising". There were references made in both cases to the need to limit commercialism to enable high standards of professionalism to be maintained.

34. The body that imposes restrictions (in our case the Respondent) must therefore carefully balance the interests of the person who seeks the right to exercise the freedom of expression (such as the Applicant) against other aspects of the public interest. Where the public interest is in favour of allowing advertising, the fact that the person who places the advertisement will incidentally benefit is no reason to justify restrictions. I should also add this. In the context of medical advertising, there is in addition the important consideration that the "public" which is exposed to advertising will include particularly vulnerable members of society, namely, the sick and infirm. The interests of these persons must be particularly borne in mind. The balancing exercise may not always be easy to perform, and in any given case, the scales may be tipped one way or the other by the importance of any factor in the circumstances.

35. Before applying the legal principles just stated to the particular four restrictions that have to be considered in the present case, I ought first to refer to relevant principles contained in the Code.

Relevant principles contained in the Code

36. The paramount theme in the Code is the public interest. The Introduction to the Code refers to the need to protect the public and to maintain public confidence in the medical profession. It can therefore be assumed (and there is no dispute about this) that the Code (and the application and enforcement of it by the Respondent) seeks to reflect what is seen to be in the public interest.

37. The provision of information to patients is recognized in the Code. In Part III of the updated Code, it is said that communication with patients is a basic responsibility of doctors. Section 5.1.1 states that good communication between doctors and patients, and also as between doctors, is fundamental to good patient care. This is developed in section 5.1.2 where emphasis is laid on the desirability of patients being able to make an informed choice:

> "**5. Professional communication and information dissemination**
>
> 5.1 The need for good communication and accessible information
>
> 5.1.1 ...
>
> 5.1.2 A key aspect of good communication in professional practice is to provide appropriate information to users of a doctor's service and to enable those who need such information to have ready access to it. Patients need such information in order to make an informed choice of doctors and to make the best use of the services the doctor offers. Doctors, for their part, need information about the services of their professional colleagues. Doctors in particular need information about specialist services so that they may advise patients and refer them, where appropriate, for further investigations and/or treatment."

38. Of course, the Code also expressly warns against the dangers of misleading information. This is a point already made above, that in the context of health care, there are likely to be a large number of people who will be vulnerable to misleading information. Paragraphs 5.1.3 and 5.2.1 state:

> "5.1.3 Persons seeking medical service for themselves or their families can nevertheless be particularly vulnerable to persuasive influence, and patients are entitled to protection from misleading advertisements. Practice promotion of doctors' medical services as if the provision of medical care were no more than a commercial activity is likely both to undermine public trust in the medical profession and, over time, to diminish the standard of medical care.
>
> 5.2 Principles and rules of good communication and information dissemination
>
> 5.2.1 Information refers to information of any form, computer-related information, internet modalities, telemedicine related items and any other form of electronic transmission. Any information provided by a doctor to the public or his patient:
>
> (a) shall be legal, decent, honest, truthful, factual, accurate, and not exaggerated; and
>
> (b) shall not claim superiority over or disparage other doctors or their work."

39. The reference in paragraph 5.1.3 to "commercial activity" is an important qualification to the right to provide information (and this will of course cover advertising): the intention here is clearly that while good communication and the provision of information are to be encouraged, the more subjective features of advertising (or, as was described by Ralph Gibson LJ in *R v General Medical Council ex p Colman* [1990] 1 All ER 489, at 493f "laudatory material") must be guarded against.

40. It can therefore be seen from those parts of paragraph 5 of the Code referred to above that within the confines of the provision of good communication and the provision of objectively verifiable information, practice promotion is, as a matter of principle, permitted for doctors. This is an important point to bear in mind in case it should be thought that the Respondent's position proceeds on the premise that as a matter of principle, advertising ought not be permitted. As reflected in the Code, the medical profession, like certain other professions, have moved on from this stance, although I daresay it is one that is perhaps still held by some doctors.

41. The evidence filed by the Respondent confirms the above analysis. In his first affidavit, Dr Fang says this:

> "**<u>Overall justifications</u>**
>
> 7. The medical profession is distinguished from other professions because of the special moral duty with

which it is invested by society. This special moral duty is the duty of care to save life and to relieve suffering. Because of this special duty of care, the medical profession has developed a code of ethics which emphasizes the priority of this moral ideal over and above considerations of personal freedom, interest and private gain of individual medical practitioners. The Code is developed with the objective to uphold this moral ideal in order to ensure public trust in the profession and to achieve the common good of public health in society.

8. Placing constraints on advertising, medical marketing and practice promotion to limit commercialism and to prevent exploitation or manipulation of the sick and the vulnerable, is considered essential to upholding this moral principle. It is firmly believed that a robust professional culture, based on reasonable self-regulation to safeguard the public interest and the public trust, is far more effective for governing the practice of medicine than by the norms and rules of a trade or a commodity in open market competition."

42. For his part, the Applicant and those doctors of whom he is representative, agree with these statements. The difference between the Applicant and the Respondent in relation to the four restrictions is accordingly in reality fairly narrow. As I say, both sides rely on the public interest to justify their respective positions. In the application of the legal principles which are set out above, are the restrictions constitutionally justifiable?

The first restriction

43. As earlier stated, the Applicant seeks only to be able to provide to the public in newspapers, magazines and other print media the same accurate, basic and objectively verifiable information as doctors are now permitted under the Code to provide to the public on signboards and service information notices outside surgeries, stationery, telephone directories, doctors directories and websites.

44. The Applicant's position is therefore ultimately a straightforward one. Given that the same information can (and I should say, is encouraged to) be conveyed to the public by other means, there is no reason or logic why the same information cannot be made available to the public by a wider means of circulation. If it is accepted that such information benefits the public by enabling informed choices to be made, then surely making the same information <u>more</u> accessible to <u>more</u> members of the public must be acceptable? Afterall, many people read newspapers or magazines, while fewer numbers may have access to telephone directories, doctors directories or computers. For example, it was at one stage suggested that doctors directories may be readily available to members of the public either in libraries or hospitals. Even if this were the case (and there is considerable doubt as to this: the evidence before us if anything showed the contrary), it simply cannot be said that the provision of information in newspapers, magazines and other printed media would not reach more members of the public.

45. For my part, I agree with these submissions, as did Reyes J in the court below.

46. Before us, the Respondent adduced further evidence to explain fully the reasons for maintaining this restriction. With respect, these reasons are simply insufficient to displace the force of the arguments going the other way:

(1) By far the major concern of the Respondent is the danger of misleading advertisements being placed by doctors in newspapers, magazines and other printed media. As Dr Fang rightly points out, misleading advertisements, particularly in the context of the vulnerable and the infirm, may lead to danger to health and life. However, in my view, in the language of the proportionality test (see paragraph above) the restriction is admittedly rationally connected to a legitimate purpose (in this case, the danger of misleading advertisements) but the means used (a total and absolute ban on all advertising, irrespective of whether the information provided is misleading or not) is much more than is necessary to achieve the legitimate purpose. A more prosaic way of putting it (though less precise) is that a sledgehammer has been used to crack a nut.

(2) One can think of a number of restrictions that can be imposed that can go some way in preventing misleading advertisements. The extent and justification for such restrictions must of course depend on the particular or potential problems of misleading advertisements by doctors (as to which there was no evidence before us).

(3) Then it is said that the Respondent simply does not have the resources to police or supervise every newspaper or magazine that may carry advertisements from doctors. Dr Fang points to the fact there are some 48 newspapers and 691 magazines in Hong Kong. By contrast, it is relatively easy for the Respondent and its staff to check the veracity and accuracy of entries in doctors directories. I do not regard this as a valid ground of objection at all. No evidence was adduced before us of the extent of the problem or potential problem nor of the financial resources of the Respondent. The court simply does not know whether the propensity of doctors is such that particularly careful vigilance is required. One is also left in the dark as to how the Respondent at present monitors the accuracy of signboards, websites, notices or telephone directories in which doctors' advertisements may be found. Mr Beloff submits that the modes of dissemination of information at present permitted can be "properly and confidently policed". One is tempted to remark that if this be the case, then the policing of newspapers and magazines would surely not add a significant burden to the Respondent's responsibilities in this regard.

(4) In this context, Mr Beloff also submitted that whereas at present, the source of any misleading advertisements could quite easily be traced (say, in the case of doctors directories, enquiries could be directed at the relevant medical organization publishing such directory, where co-operation could be expected), the same could not be said as far as the publishers of newspapers or magazines were concerned. The difficulties of proving allegations of misconduct do not appear to me to be a valid reason to restrict the constitutional right. In any event, one would have to question the problem alleged here. Surely, one perhaps should be able to assume in most cases that the doctor whose services are advertised, was the person responsible for placing such advertisement in the first place, unless proven otherwise.

(5) Another facet of misleading advertising relied on by the Respondent was the possibility that medical information provided to the public, even though accurate, may sometimes not be readily understood by laymen, and

therefore become in a sense misleading. Dr Fang stated in his affidavit that while assistance could be sought from medical organizations that published directories, this would not be possible in the case of newspapers or magazines. This is not a valid point. Quite apart from the complete lack of particularity as to the extent of this perceived problem and as to how assistance is in fact at present obtained in the case of medical directories (or for that matter, signboards, notices and telephone directories), I see no reason why members of the public cannot telephone the doctor who placed the advertisement (for his or her telephone number will be advertised) for any further clarification that may be required.

(6) It was also submitted that allowing doctors' advertisements in newspapers and magazines may enable such advertisements to be juxtaposed with other advertisements for medical or other products that may mislead the public into thinking that the products were endorsed by the doctor in question. An example given was the placing of an oncologist's advertisement next to one advertising a cure for cancer. I can understand the point being made, but an outright and total ban appears to me to be out of all proportion. No explanation was given as to why it was unacceptable, for example, for a requirement to be imposed on doctors wishing to advertise, to insist with publishers that their advertisements should not be placed in such a way that would be seen as unacceptable. Much the same argument applies to the concern that doctors' advertisements may be found in publications that are totally inappropriate for such advertisements to appear in.

(7) Finally, Dr Fang observed that the purpose of dissemination of information was to enable patients to make an informed choice "when they required a doctor's services, not to attract patients to a doctor when they do not need such a service". There is admittedly a superficial attraction to this argument but on reflection, it bears scarce analysis. First, nothing in the Code makes this distinction. Secondly, persons who at present do not require immediate medical attention, may at some stage need such assistance or they may know of relatives or friends who do. Thirdly, there is no evidence to suggest that only persons in need of medical services read the information contained in the currently permitted modes of advertising.

47. In the circumstances, the first restriction is in my judgment not constitutionally justifiable. There must be less intrusive means of dealing with the concerns of the Respondent other than a total ban. What those means might be, is a matter for the Respondent and not the courts.

48. Before leaving this issue, I would like to make the following final observations: -

(1) Like Reyes J, I have derived very little assistance from *R v General Medical Council ex p Colman* (see paragraph above), a case referred to us by Mr Beloff. Ultimately, this case was relied on more for the decision on the facts (the Court of Appeal in England upheld the General Medical Council's ban on advertising in newspapers by a doctor) than any proposition of law. Although there was some discussion on proportionality, the case was resolved largely on the basis of whether the General Medical Council's decision was *Wednesbury* unreasonable. The only point of note, however, is the fact that the dispute was eventually compromised just before the European Court of Human Rights had to determine the question whether the restrictions in that case contravened Article 10 of the European Convention on Human Rights. It is also interesting to note that in the United Kingdom now, advertising by doctors in the printed press is permitted.

(2) Even though much emphasis was laid by Mr Beloff on the margin of appreciation that the court ought to allow the Respondent in relation to this restriction, it is clear on the materials now before the court that at one stage, the Respondent was itself seriously contemplating relaxing the restriction to enable advertisements to be made in newspapers, magazines and other print media. In October 2005, the Respondent issued a letter to all doctors in Hong Kong stating that the Ethics Committee was prepared to relax the restriction but sought the views of the profession. The rationale behind this was to encourage doctors to benefit from the Mainland and Hong [*sic*] Closer Economic Partnership Agreement (CEPA). This was rejected by the majority of doctors. However, the position of the Ethics Committee is not entrenched. Far from it. Dr Fang says this in his third Affidavit, "the Ethics Committee would continue to find more acceptable ways to relax the relevant restrictions in the Code, but deliberations have since been put on hold pending the outcome of the judicial review".

The second restriction

49. This restriction cannot, in my view, be justified. There is no sense or logic in a doctor being restricted to just five items when he or she can, legitimately and accurately, point to more. Mr Pannick must be right when he observes that such a restriction goes very much against one of the cornerstones of the Code: the desirability of good communication and the passage of information to patients to enable informed choices to be made. Dr Fang indicated that the information about the services or medical procedure operations a doctor could perform was not intended to be comprehensive, merely to give a "fair indication". With respect, this is not a valid argument. It is difficult to see why the provision of comprehensive (and therefore fuller and more accurate) information should be regarded as less desirable than merely a "fair indication".

50. In articulating the Respondent's concerns, Mr Beloff referred again to the dangers of misleading information being provided to the public, as well as the difficulties that could arise when laymen may not understand medical terms or are confronted with what was called "information overload". Connected to this point was the fear that the public may associate the quality or ability of any doctor with the number of services or operations or procedures advertised. These were similar concerns to those expressed in relation to the first restriction and can really be answered in much the same way. Inasmuch as the concerns are real concerns, the Respondent can impose conditions (particularly against the provision of misleading or inaccurate information) without having an arbitrary cut off point of five items. Furthermore, with regard to the use of medical terms that may be confusing, it should be noted that in the description of medical procedures and operations in medical directories, it is stated in the Code that the nomenclature for procedures and operations should follow as far as possible those adopted by the Colleges of the Hong Kong Academy of Medicine. The risk of confusion should therefore be minimized at least in this respect.

51. Finally, one might also add that even within the present limit of five items, this is not to say that the Respondent's concerns will not materialize. The perceived problems, accordingly, do not really relate to the number of items that can be stated at all.

52. In the court below and before us, emphasis was given to the argument that somehow a line had to be drawn and it was the considered view that five items (or in total 15 items) was a reasonable limit to set, as was the limit of two A3 sheets of paper for medical information in service information notices. I respectfully adopt the reasoning of Reyes J contained in paragraphs 158 and 159 of his judgment:

> "158. ...The question is why there should be any limit on the number of available services which a doctor can mention in a Service Information Notice at all.
>
> 159. As far as I can see on the material before me, there is simply no good reason for interfering with the freedom of expression by imposing a limit of 5 items. ..."

The third restriction

53. The main objection here from the Applicant was that while on the one hand the Code recognized the benefits of promoting public health education for members of the public (as well as for fellow doctors), the restrictions contained in paragraphs 5.1 and 5.2 of the Code were such that a doctor would fall foul of the prohibition against advertising almost every time he referred (even indirectly) to his personal experience, skills, qualifications or reputation. The definition of practice promotion in the Code and the wide meaning that the Respondent would give to it (see paragraph 5.2.2.1 of the Code – paragraph above) strongly supported this fear. The risk of disciplinary proceedings in these circumstances had the effect that, according to the Applicant, many doctors were discouraged from activities that furthered public health education. This, in the end, would not be in the public interest. It constituted an unjustifiable restriction on the freedom of expression in that it would significantly, if not effectively, deprive the public or fellow doctors of the benefit of health education. Analyzed in this way, the complaint made here by the Applicant is not directed so much at the right to advertise but at the right to impart relevant information on matters of public interest.

54. There is much force in these arguments. I agree with the judge below that in order for the public (or fellow doctors) to attach any weight to what is being said about, say new medical developments or techniques, a reference to a doctor's experience, skills, qualifications and reputation may well be essential. The fear of the Applicant is justified and arises from the true construction of those provisions of the Code I have highlighted.

55. In my judgment, this restriction is not justifiable. The effect of paragraphs 5.1 and 5.2 of the Code does put any doctor at risk of disciplinary proceedings on charges of unacceptable practice promotion whenever reference is made to his experience, skills, qualifications or reputation. I accept nevertheless the legitimacy of the Respondent's concerns, namely, that the giving of lectures, participating in radio or TV programmes or publication of articles may sometimes merely be a transparent or shambolic cloak to disguise an ulterior motive (blatant advertising). However, the wording of paragraphs 5.1 and 5.2 goes too far and constitutes a disproportionate response.

56. I have found of assistance the case of *Stambuck* (see paragraph above) where the European Court of Human Rights accepted that the interview given by the ophthalmologist which led to a newspaper article on a laser operation technique, did deal with a matter of public health education. The fact that the article also had the effect of giving publicity to the doctor was not sufficient to displace the legitimacy of the article. At paragraph 49, the court said:

> "In the Court's opinion, it is not possible to isolate the passage of the article concerning the applicant's past success rate in applying this operation technique and the appearance of the accompanying photograph from the article as a whole in order to argue the necessity to take disciplinary action for a breach of professional duties. The article may well have had the effect of giving publicity to the applicant and his practice, but, having regard to the principal content of the article, this effect proved to be of a secondary nature."

57. Ultimately, the Respondent, I believe, also recognizes the difficulties identified by the Applicant. In Dr Fang's first affidavit (which was not before Reyes J), he states that the Respondent now intends to amend paragraph 5.1 of the Code. Details of this proposed change have already been set out in paragraph above.

58. This amendment has not yet come into effect and, although Mr Beloff invited us now to determine whether it would be acceptable from a constitutional point of view, I would decline to do so. It was not before the court below, it is not referred to in the Form 86A Application for Leave to Apply for Judicial Review and there is little evidence before us in relation to it. It is not even clear whether in the light of the judgment of this court the Respondent may wish to consider its position further.

The fourth restriction

59. I have already set out the gist of the Applicant's complaints (see paragraph above). Reyes J was of the view that the last sentence of paragraph 14.1.1 of the Code imposed a strict liability. The judge said this:

> "173. Mr. Pannick accepts that, if paragraph 14.1.1 ended with the sentence which Mr. Blanchflower has highlighted, Dr. Kwong would have no quarrel with paragraph 14.1.1. The difficulty (Mr. Pannick says) lies in the last sentence of paragraph 14.1.1. That imposes strict liability for the defaults of an organisation even where a doctor has taken all due diligence to ensure that the Code's rules on advertising are followed by an organisation.
>
> 174. Given the last sentence of paragraph 14.1.1, a doctor cannot say that, despite all reasonable care to keep himself informed of his organisation's activities, the organisation suddenly put out an advertisement without reference to the doctor. That (according to paragraph 14.1.1) will be no defence.
>
> 175. Nor can a doctor say that there is nothing more that he could have done to prevent the issue of by an organisation of non-conformist advertising. Paragraph 14.1.1 indicates that will not amount to a defence either.
>
> 176. There is (Mr. Pannick submits) no justification for imposing such strict liability. If a doctor has done everything that can reasonably be done to prevent a contravention of the Code, what purpose could be served by making him strictly liable for what an organisation

has nonetheless done?

177. It seems to me that Mr. Blanchflower has no answer to Mr. Pannick's point."

60. With respect, I agree with the judge's analysis. The imposition of strict liability in these circumstances is another disproportionate response to dealing with unacceptable practice promotion.

61. Mr Beloff submitted that it was never the intention of the Respondent to impose strict liability. He suggested that the mandatory words "it will not be sufficient" in paragraph 14.1.1 really meant "it may not be sufficient...". In a letter to the Applicant's solicitors dated 21 March 2006, the Respondent stated, "Furthermore, it failed to recognize that paragraph 14.1.1 of the Code imposes on a doctor a responsibility to exercise due diligence to prevent, not a strict liability for, advertising by organizations with which he has a financial or professional relationship".

62. With respect to these submissions, this stated position does not reflect the position hitherto adopted by the Respondent. That was certainly not the position advanced in the court below. The affidavit evidence now before the court is also unclear. In Dr Fang's first affidavit, he states that, "The last sentence in paragraph 14.1.1 is necessary to prevent a doctor from simply relying on ignorance or lack of influence". The perceived abuse consists of doctors shielding behind limited companies to benefit from uncontrolled advertising or from uncontrolled medical centres. One would have thought that suitable conditions could be drafted to deal with these problems without the imposition of strict liability even where due diligence has been exercised.

63. In view of the Respondent's position as clarified by Mr Beloff, this issue is in a sense academic as it seems tolerably clear that the Respondent will have to re-examine the wording of paragraph 14.1.1.

Conclusion

64. For the above reasons, I would dismiss the appeal and make an order nisi that the Respondent (the appellant in this appeal) pay the costs of the Applicant in the appeal, such costs to be taxed if not agreed. I should perhaps just say that the genuineness of the concerns expressed by the Respondent have not been in dispute in these proceedings. Rather, it is the means by which these concerns are addressed in the Code that have been the focus of the opposition.

65. Finally, by way of postscript, we have, since the handing down of our Reasons of Judgment on 27 September 2007 been apprised of a number of matters in relation to the conduct of the case below by counsel formerly instructed by the Respondent. In case it be thought that any criticism of counsel appears in that judgment (whether express or implied), I should record that there is some disagreement as to exactly what transpired. Neither side has attached any significance to this aspect insofar as the outcome of the present appeal is concerned and I am therefore content to leave the matter there.

Hon Tang VP:

66. Freedom of expression protects the communicator as well as the recipient. We are not concerned with the dissemination of information which is in itself harmful. That being the case I would assume that:

"... people will perceive their own best interests if only they are well enough informed, and that the best means to that end is to open the channels of communication rather than to close them." Blackmun J delivering the opinion of the U.S. Supreme Court in *Virginia State Board of Pharmacy et al. v Virginia Citizens'Consumer Council et al.* [1976] 425 U.S. 748 at 770.

67. For this reason as well as the reasons given by the Chief Judge, I would dismiss the appeal.

Hon Stock JA:

68. The restrictions imposed by the Council upon the extent to which doctors may publish information about their medical practices constitute an infringement upon freedom of expression; a freedom that connotes the right to impart as well as to receive information. The fact of infringement is common ground. That being so, the questions are these:

(1) Do the restrictions pursue a legitimate societal objective?

(2) If so, are the restrictions rationally connected to that objective?

(3) If so, has the Council discharged the burden of showing that the restrictions go no further than is necessary to achieve that objective?

69. The answer to the first question is clear. The aim of the restrictions is the protection of public health and the reputation of the profession. That is self-evidently a legitimate aim. It is clear also that the restrictions imposed are rationally connected to the legitimate aim thus identified. The sole question in the case is therefore the third.

70. What is or is not a proportionate restriction upon any fundamental right is always a matter of context. That is because the competing values and interests at stake in any one case will be different from those in another. The interests at stake in this case are profound, and require, in my opinion, a particularly sensitive approach, such that the courts should be slow before disturbing a mature judgment of those entrusted and equipped by experience to strike the balance. The interests of patients and potential patients are the overwhelming consideration. What we are concerned with, as indeed are the doctors, is the protection of the public in a realm in which that public is vulnerable. That is a fact that does not, in my judgment, change with the passage of time. It is the standing of the profession and the assumed expertise of each member that renders the patient or potential patient highly susceptible to persuasion; and in this regard, professionally correct in their approach that most medical practitioners no doubt are, it must be accepted that there may be some, a small minority no doubt, who may be tempted to push information about their services beyond accurate bounds. Doctors do not dispense standardized products but, rather, they 'render professional services of almost infinite variety and nature, with the consequent enhanced possibility for confusion and deception if they were to undertake certain kinds of advertising': *Virginia State Board of Pharmacy v Virginia Citizens Consumer Council* 425 U.S. 748 (1976) at 773, n.25 and there is a duty upon, let alone a right in, the medical profession to guard against commercialisation and exploitation. If the profession did not itself do so, the State no doubt would. There is in other words a powerful interest 'in restricting the advertising of health-care services to those which are truthful, informative and helpful to the potential consumer in making an intelligent decision': *Talsky* 68 Ill. 2d

at 585, referred to in *Desnick v The Department of Professional Regulation* 665 N.E. 2d 1346 in which, at 1356, was emphasized the fact that "the State has substantial interest in maintaining professional standards and preventing undue influence, overreaching and the invasion of its citizens' privacy," with the added reminder, citing In re *American Medical Association* 94 F.T.C. 701, 1034–35, that "Physicians... have an ethical duty to subordinate financial reward to social responsibility. A physician should not engage in practices for pecuniary gain that interfere with his medical judgment."

71. With such considerations at play, restrictions on advertising by doctors will not be difficult to justify. But there is a countervailing consideration, with the same interests in view, namely, the right of members of the public to receive information with which to make an informed choice on a matter of such individual importance. The question then becomes one of balance: how to provide an informed choice whilst at the same time protecting the most vulnerable from influence that may be detrimental; detrimental where it is misleading, or lures the individual from a secure and competent existing relationship, or provides false hope, or confuses in its language or by competing claims, or because 'the doctor most successful at achieving publicity may not be the most appropriate to consult' (*R v General Medical Council ex parte Colman* [1990] 1 All E R 489 at 484) or because the advent of advertising itself may force others into what has been called (*Semler v Oregon State Board of Dental Examiners* 294 U.S. 608 (1935)) 'unseemly rivalry which would enlarge the opportunities of the unscrupulous.' Put thus, it is easy to understand why the courts tread carefully where regulatory judgments have been made by experts in a field outwith the court's own expertise. Nonetheless the court's function is to determine legality and whilst the profession's evaluation as to where the proper balance lies will be accorded significant weight, the professional body is required to show that it has gone no further than is necessary to achieve the legitimate objective. That does not mean that it has to show that it has taken the least intrusive route but rather that it has chosen from a range of solutions which, whilst commensurate with the legitimate objective, infringes upon the right as little as is reasonably possible: *Attorney General of Hong Kong v Lee Kwong-kut* [1993] A.C. 951 at 972.

72. It is in this respect that the appellant Council has, in my judgment, failed in this case: it has failed to demonstrate that the restrictions as they presently stand go no further than are reasonably necessary. The Council accepts that doctors may place notices in newspapers when they open or move their practices and that they may have websites and that the latter may contain information about the services they provide; but not that the same information may be provided in newspapers. I am not dismissive of the logic of the distinction drawn, namely, that there is a difference between a patient seeking information on the one hand and on the other a prospective patient having information thrust upon him. That said, the Council accepts – and it must be the case – that the individual is better served by having readily available the tools with which to make informed choices about his or her health care, and it is to that end that Doctors' Directories are published and it is to that end that websites are available. But as matters presently stand, it is difficult to see that the Directories begin to serve that purpose. The sample Directory we have seen is not user-friendly. There is no index to it, divided, say, by category of health care; there is no indication which independent body might be approached for further information; and the question of where these directories are available in hard copy (as opposed to the internet, to which many will not have ready access) is entirely unclear on the evidence; nor is there any suggestion that publicity is given to their availability. On the evidence we have, the Directories, as presently distributed, available and composed seem to me to be an inadequate vehicle for providing the public with the tool for making an informed choice.

73. Moreover, I am far from convinced that the Council is itself convinced that the present restrictions go no further than are necessary. The history of the professional body's consideration of the issue reveals that its Ethics Committee was at one stage in favour of allowing media advertising, suitably controlled. An opinion survey was conducted, the method for which was criticised by some within the Council but, nonetheless, as a result of the survey the Council determined in November 2005 not to pursue the proposal 'for the time being and directed the Ethics Committee to further consider the matter.' (Affirmation of Au Hing Yuen, 19 July 2006 para. 38). In his affidavit of 13 April 2007, Dr Fang refers to that decision and explains the position thus: "The Ethics Committee would continue to find more acceptable ways to relax the relevant restrictions in the Code, but deliberations have since been put on hold pending the outcome of the judicial review." That is, as one would expect, a frank statement of the position, but that statement and the history of the matter suggests to me that the Council is at a half-way house in its consideration of where the proper balance can be struck.

74. It is perfectly clear that untruthful speech is not protected (*Virginia State Board of Pharmacy*, above, at 771–772) and the Council's objective of safeguarding the public against misleading or confusing information is an objective that, in my estimation, is bound to receive judicial support. But what we have at this stage of the Council's history of deliberations is insufficient to show that the restrictions are no broader than reasonably necessary to prevent the dangers that quite understandably agitate the Council's mind. This is not to say that the Council has an all or nothing choice. It is to say rather that the Council should go back to the drawing board. Its concerns about policing, indirect promotion of other services or products, comprehensibility, accuracy, and frequency are suspectible to practical and reasonable solution; whether by way of a much more sophisticated and readily accessible form of directory system, or by permitting advertisements whilst limiting to particular publications where they may be placed, and regulating the size of them, their frequency, the language used, the method by which a reader may secure further and reliable information, a requirement to provide copies of advertisements to the Council: such are some of the tools available for striking a reasonable balance. That is not a balance that has presently been struck or, in my judgment, adequately addressed.

75. For these reasons, I agree that in relation to the first restriction (the medium of information), the appeal should be dismissed. I agree also for the reasons given by the Chief Judge that the other restrictions challenged cannot in their present form stand.

Hon Ma CJHC:

76. For the above reasons, the appeal is dismissed. There will also be an order nisi that the Respondent (the appellant in this appeal) pay the costs of the Applicant in the appeal, such costs to be taxed if not agreed.

Chief Judge, High Court (Geoffrey Ma)

Vice President (Robert Tang)

Justice of Appeal (Frank Stock)

Mr David Pannick QC and Mr Alfred Fung, instructed by Messrs Johnson Stokes & Master for the Applicant

Mr Michael J Beloff QC and Mr Nicholas Cooney, instructed by Messrs Wilkinson & Grist for the Respondent

---

The Law Society Of Hong Kong v. A Solicitor

香港律師會 對 一名事務律師

CACV 280/2003

簡略案情

上訴人為香港一名執業事務律師。他須於 2001 年 3 月 1 日出席香港律師會對他提出的紀律聆訊。上訴人在此前曾要求該聆訊以公開形式進行，但律師紀律審裁組認為，根據法定程序，聆訊須在錄影下進行，因此該要求被拒絕。上訴人於是發函件通知其法律界同行，他將於聆訊當天在會場外抗議自己所受到的不公正及不公平待遇，該函件還批評律師會的打壓和官僚行為。他並邀請同行出席當日下午三時律師紀律審裁組對其進行的不公開聆訊。

在聆訊當天，上訴人在會場外大街舉行抗議。他當時只穿了泳褲，並以寫著“我也有天賦的權利”的橫幅遮擋其下體。上訴人這行為吸引了大批圍觀人士，最後原定的紀律聆訊並不能按照計劃進行。香港律師會認為被告的抗議與邀請業界出席閉門聆訊行為損害了法律界的聲譽，違反了《香港律師會專業守則》第 1.02 條，遂對上訴人作出罰款懲款。

然而，上訴人認為其行為是體現《基本法》和《香港人權法案》所賦予的發表與言論的自由；上訴人亦認為《香港律師會專業守則》第 1.02 條模糊不清，並不能以此作為對他行為約束的法律依據。

裁決摘要

各方皆不質疑《基本法》第 27 條和《香港人權法案》第 16 條同時保障公民有不同方法去表達個人意見的自由。上訴庭重申終審法院在 *吳嘉玲*一案中的主張，即以寬鬆和帶目的的方法去解釋這些憲法性條文；反之，在解釋限制這些權利的條文時，卻應嚴格審視並須有足夠的正當理由支持。然而，這些權利並非絕對的和沒有限制的，誠如《香港人權法案》第 16 條（三）所述，行使該權利時必須恪守的是“（甲）尊重他人權利或名譽；（乙）保障國家安全或公共秩序，或公共衛生或風化。”簡而言之，必須在個人與大眾之間的利益取得一個平衡。法律在保障公眾利益的同時，亦需考慮律師作為社會與法律的橋樑，在公眾擁有崇高的地位，有必要規範其行為而確保其他同業的尊嚴不受影響。因此，給予律師會權限通過專業守則去限制律師的行為是具有正當理由的。法院認定上訴人作為律師和一名司法人員，當天的行為既不恰當也不體面，所以律師紀律審裁組對他的裁決是不能質疑的。上訴庭認為，作為律師和司法人員，上訴人理應服從律師紀律審裁組依法作出的決定，如果他對該決定有任何不滿，他更加應該選擇以法律手段去挑戰，而不是以此等藐視行為對抗。對比一般市民，他應該對個人的行為更小心在意。

在憲法條文的法律確定性問題上，法庭考慮了終審法院在 *Shum Kwok Sher v. HKSAR* [2002] 2 HKLRD 一案的裁決後，重複強調任何限制基本自由的條文都必須有足夠的準確度，否則公眾難以預計其行為的後果；可是，不能因為需要確定性而出現過度僵化，應該視乎其影響的範疇、社會階層與人數作出平衡。作為律師，在專業與個人之間，這問題尤為突顯。據此，上訴庭認定《香港律師會專業守則》第 1.02 條足夠清晰，並沒有抵觸《基本法》第 39 條。上訴人的上訴因此被駁回。

CACV280/2003

IN THE HIGH COURT OF THE

HONG KONG SPECIAL ADMINISTRATIVE REGION

COURT OF APPEAL

CIVIL APPEAL NO. 280 OF 2003
(ON APPEAL FROM THE ORDER OF THE SOLICITORS DISCIPLINARY TRIBUNAL DATED 10 SEPTEMBER 2003 AGAINST A SOLICITOR)

IN THE MATTER OF a Solicitor of the High Court of the Hong Kong Special Administrative Region

- and -

IN THE MATTER OF THE LEGAL PRACTITIONERS ORDINANCE (CAP.159)

Between:

THE LAW SOCIETY OF HONG KONG — Applicant

- and -

A SOLICITOR — Respondents

Before: Hon Ma CJHC, Woo VP & Cheung JA in Court

Date of Hearing: 23 March 2004

Date of Handling Down Judgment: 25 November 2004

JUDGMENT

Hon Ma CJHC:

1. On 10 September 2003, the Respondent was found guilty by a Solicitors Disciplinary Tribunal ("the SDT") of having breached Principle 1.02 of the Hong Kong Solicitors' Guide to Professional Conduct issued by the Law Society ("Principle 1.02") in relation to two complaints. These decisions were contained in a document headed "FINDINGS AND ORDER" ("the Findings") of that date. Both complaints related to incidents that had taken place on 1 March 2001.

2. The complaints were as follows:

> "1. That you, [the Respondent], on the 1st March, 2001, conducted yourself in a manner likely to bring the profession into disrepute in breach of Principle 1.02 of the Hong Kong Solicitors' Guide to Professional Conduct and Rule 2(d) of the Solicitors' Practice Rules.
>
> Particulars
>
> a) At approximately 2.30 p.m. outside Wheelock House, Pedder Street, you stood demonstrating in the street wearing no clothes other than your swimming trunks.
>
> b) You held a banner covering your lower parts with a template that stated in both English and Chinese 'Legal rights are inborn mine too'.
>
> 2. That you, [the Respondent], on the 1st March, 2001, conducted yourself in a manner likely to bring the profession into disrepute in breach of Principle 1.02 of the Hong Kong Solicitors' Guide to Professional Conduct and Rule 2(d) of the Solicitors' Practice Rules.
>
> Particulars
>
> a) On or about the 1st March, 2001, you published or caused to be published a circular in your name which was distributed to members of the profession.
>
> b) The circular stated that a protest would be staged outside Wheelock House at 2.30 p.m. against what you alleged to be the unjust and unfair conduct of the Law Society.
>
> c) You invited members of the profession to attend the disciplinary hearing notwithstanding that there were previous rulings by the Tribunal that the hearings were to be held in camera.
>
> d) The circular contained disparaging and improper remarks against the Law Society."

3. Insofar as the complaints were based on Rule 2(d) of the Solicitors' Practice Rules, Cap.159, this was rejected by the SDT as a basis for substantiating the complaints. The reason was that Rule 2(d) only applied where the solicitor was acting "in the course of practising as a solicitor". The subject matter of the two complaints with which we are concerned did not involve the Respondent having acted in that capacity. At all material times on 1 March 2001, the Respondent was facing another set of disciplinary proceedings that had been brought against him by the Law Society. The SDT did not regard this as involving the Respondent practising as such.

4. The basis on which the Respondent was found guilty of the two complaints in the proceedings relevant to this appeal was Principle 1.02, which states as follows:

> **"1.02 Conduct subject to discipline**
>
> A solicitor is an officer of the Court (see s 3(2) of the *Legal Practitioners Ordinance* (Cap.159), and should conduct himself appropriately in professional and private matters.
>
> **Commentary**
>
> A solicitor, whether practising or not, is an officer of the Court. Certain standards of behaviour are required of a solicitor, as an officer of the Court and as a member of the profession, in his business activities outside legal practice and in his private life."

5. The Respondent was fined $90,000 in relation to the first charge and $40,000 in relation to the second. He was also ordered to pay two-thirds of the costs of and incidental to the disciplinary proceedings, such costs to be taxed on a party and party basis.

6. In this appeal, the Respondent was represented by Mr Johnny Mok and Miss Joyce Leung, the Applicant (The Law Society of Hong Kong) was represented by Mr Paul Carolan.

The facts surrounding the complaints

7. The hearing before the SDT took place over the course of two days. No evidence was adduced and the matter proceeded on the basis of the following agreed facts:

> "1. On or about the 1st March, 2001, the Respondent published or caused to be published in his name a circular which was distributed to members of the profession.

2. The circular states that a protest would be staged outside Wheelock House at 2:30 p.m. against what the Respondent alleged to be unjust and unfair conduct of the Law Society.

3. The Respondent invited members of the profession to attend the disciplinary hearing notwithstanding that there were previous rulings by the Tribunal that the hearings were to be held in camera.

4. A true copy of the circular is annexed herewith marked 'Annexure A'.

5. On the 1st March, 2001 at approximately 2:30 p.m. outside Wheelock House, Pedder Street, the Respondent stood demonstrating in the street wearing no clothes other than his swimming trunks.

6. At the time, the Respondent held a banner covering his lower part with a template that stated in both English and Chinese 'Legal rights are inborn mine too'.

7. On the afternoon of the 1st March, 2001, the Solicitors Disciplinary Tribunal did not proceed with the hearing as scheduled."

8. The circular dated 1 March 2001 referred to above ("the Circular") was annexed to the document containing the agreed facts. Insofar as relevant to the present appeal, the Circular stated the following:

"To All Fellow Colleagues:

You are hereby invited to attend the Solicitors' Disciplinary Tribunal Hearing against me, the details which are as follows:-

Date: 1st March, 2001

Time: 3:00p.m. – 7:00p.m.

Venue: 4/F., Central Conference Centre, Wheelock House,

20 Pedder Street, Central.

A PROTEST will be staged at outside the Wheelock House Building at 2:30p.m. against the unjust and unfair conduct of the Law Society, including:

1. Insisting on a secret hearing when the Law Society had right at the outset publicized its intention to institute and the fact of Disciplinary Proceedings against me;

2. Maintaining its opposition to an open hearing when I have clearly indicated my wish to waive the protection of a hearing in camera which afterall is for my own benefit;

3. ...

4. ...

5. ...

All of you who feel you have been oppressed by the Law Society's disciplinary regime or are disillusioned by its bureaucratic attitude are specially invited."

9. The following points arise from the agreed facts and should be noted:

(1) On 1 March 2001, the Respondent was engaged in disciplinary proceedings that had been brought against him by the Applicant before another Solicitors Disciplinary Tribunal. It is clear that the Tribunal in those proceedings had ruled on a number of occasions that any hearings were to be conducted in camera. This, I interpose, is entirely consistent with the requirements of section 9B(4) of the Legal Practitioners Ordinance, Cap.159 ("the LPO"), which states: -

"(4) The Tribunal shall sit in camera in the places and at the times it directs."

(2) Despite the said rulings that any hearings were to be held in camera, the Respondent issued the Circular to all solicitors inviting them:

(a) to attend the hearing of the disciplinary proceedings against him that day between 3:00 pm and 7:00 pm on 1 March 2001; and

(b) to attend a protest he was staging outside Wheelock House (on Pedder Street) at 2:30 pm that day to protest against the "unjust and unfair conduct" of the Applicant. One of the bases for the protest was the fact that the Tribunal had ruled that hearings should take place in *camera*.

(3) Accordingly, the protest that was held by the Respondent on the day in question was in the context of the disciplinary proceedings against him and specifically, of the rulings made by the Tribunal that any hearings were to take place in camera.

10. As a matter of inference from the agreed facts, it can readily be seen that by his actions on 1 March 2001, the Respondent intended to protest in some of the strongest and most graphic ways possible his dissatisfaction with the rulings of the SDT. It is also clear that by the Circular and the invitation contained in it to fellow solicitors to attend the disciplinary hearing, he intended to flout the rulings. He was not just inviting other solicitors to protest; he was actually asking them to attend the hearing itself, details of which (time, duration and place) he provided.

11. Based on the agreed facts, were the complaints justified? The Respondent says not.

Issues

12. In this appeal, at the forefront of Mr Mok's arguments on the Respondent's behalf in relation to both complaints have been the submissions based on freedom of expression. Essentially, two arguments were raised in this context:

(1) The Respondent's actions on 1 March 2001 were no more than the exercise of his right of freedom of expression guaranteed under the Basic Law and the Hong Kong Bill of Rights. Principle 1.02 (or indeed any other provision) should not be permitted to stifle this fundamental right (**Issue 1: The freedom of expression and its limits in relation to professional discipline**).

(2) In any event, Principle 1.02, inasmuch as it referred to appropriateness as the test for solicitors' conduct both professionally and privately, was much too vague a provision with which to limit fundamental rights such as the freedom of expression. The principle was not "prescribed by law" within the meaning of Article 39 of the Basic Law. (**Issue 2: Is Principle 1.02"prescribed by law"or is it too vague?**)

13. In addition, a number of points were raised specifically in relation to each of the two complaints. As to these, I have had the advantage of reading in draft the judgments of Woo VP and that of Cheung JA. I agree with them and accordingly intend to deal just briefly with those issues under the following headings: **Issue 3: The First Complaint, Issue 4: The Second Complaint.**

14. On the day of the appeal, we granted leave to the Respondent to raise an additional ground of appeal which was in the following terms:

> "3. Having regard to the terms of the two Complaints made against the Respondent, namely, that he conducted himself in a manner likely to bring the profession into disrepute, the Tribunal was not entitled (as it did) to find those Complaints 'proved in respect of only Principle 1.02 of the Hong Kong Solicitors' Guide to Professional Conduct' after it had found that Rule 2(d) of the Solicitors' Practice Rules is not applicable."

15. For the reasons contained in the judgment of Woo VP, I agree that this ground has no merit and in any event adds little to the other grounds of appeal raised by the Respondent.

Issue 1: The freedom of expression and its limits in relation to professional discipline

16. Both parties have assumed the Basic Law, the International Covenant on Civil and Political Rights (the "ICCPR") and the Bill of Rights to be relevant in the present case in considering the Hong Kong Solicitors' Guide to Professional Conduct. Neither party has questioned the limits of the application of these laws or the human rights concepts within them to professional bodies such as the Law Society. As far as the Hong Kong Bar Association is concerned, it has been held by the Barristers Disciplinary Tribunal in *Hong Kong Bar Association v Anthony Chua* (1994) 4 HKPLR 637 that the Association is not a public authority for the purposes of section 7(1)(b) of the Hong Kong Bill of Rights Ordinance, Cap.383. I express no view one way or the other on these matters nor on the question of the limits of the applicability of the Basic Law, the ICCPR and the Bill of Rights to disciplinary tribunals such as the SDT. In the latter respect, the decisions of this Court in *Dr Ip Kay Lo v Medical Council of Hong Kong* [2003] 3 HKLRD 851 and *A Solicitor v The Law Society of Hong Kong*, unreported, CACV 302/2002, 18 February 2004, Court of Appeal, are relevant. I am however content, given the parties' approach just stated, likewise to assume the relevance and applicability of the Basic Law, the ICCPR and the Bill of Rights.

17. Article 27 of the Basic Law guarantees as a fundamental right the freedom of speech. Article 39 of the Basic Law stipulates that the ICCPR remains in force in Hong Kong and requires that convention (among others) to be implemented through the laws of Hong Kong. The relevant provision in the ICCPR engaged in the present case is Article 19 which states:

> "Article 19
>
> 1. Everyone shall have the right to hold opinions without interference.
>
> 2. Everyone shall have the right to freedom of expression; this right shall include freedom to seek, receive and impart information and ideas of all kinds, regardless of frontiers, either orally, in writing or in print, in the form of art, or through any other media of his choice.
>
> 3. The exercise of the rights provided for in paragraph 2 of this article carries with it special duties and responsibilities. It may therefore be subject to certain restrictions, but these shall only be such as are provided by law and are necessary:
>
> (a) For respect of the rights or reputations of others;
>
> (b) For the protection of national security or of public order (ordre public), or of public health or morals."

This provision is reproduced in Hong Kong legislation in Article 16 of the Bill of Rights.

18. The freedom of expression, like all fundamental rights contained in the Basic Law, must be given a generous and purposive meaning, for such rights lie at the heart of Hong Kong's existence: - see *Ng Ka Ling & Others v Director of Immigration* (1999) 2 HKCFAR 1, at 28D-29B. Any restrictions on such rights must be closely scrutinized and fully justified.

19. The above said, the freedom of expression is not, however, an absolute one. The limitations to it are contained in Article 19 of the ICCPR itself. In addition, in paragraph 6 of the Preamble to the ICCPR, it is expressly stated that individuals have duties to "other individuals and the community to which he belongs".

20. The specified limitations contained in Article 19 of the ICCPR are that any restrictions on the freedom of expression must be: -

(1) "provided by law" (or, as Article 39 of the Basic Law states, "prescribed by law" – the two terms have the same meaning); and

(2) necessary for respect of the rights or reputations of others, or for the protection of national security or of public order *(ordre public)* or of public health or morals.

These limitations are reproduced in Article 16 of the Bill of Rights and are permitted under Article 39 of the Basic Law.

21. These limitations have recently been extensively analyzed in two decisions of the Court of Appeal: *HKSAR v Yeung May Wan & Others*, unreported, HCMA 949/2002, 10 November 2004 and *HKSAR v Leung Kwok Hung & Others, unreported*, HCMA 16/2003, 10 November 2004. I do not intend to repeat what has been dealt at length in the judgments in those cases, but for the time being, emphasize one point. The said limitations to the freedom of expression reflect the need to balance the rights of the individual against the general interests of the community. Here, I would repeat what Lord Bingham of Cornhill said in *Brown v Stott (Procurator Fiscal, Dunfermline) and another* [2003] 1 AC 681, at 704F-G:

> "The court has also recognised the need for a fair balance between the general interest of the community and the personal rights of the individual, the search for which balance has been described as inherent in the whole of the [European Convention for the Protection of Human Rights and Fundamental Freedoms]".

22. Issue 2 deals with whether Principle 1.02 satisfies the "prescribed by law" test. I would therefore for the time being confine myself to the other limitations on the right of freedom of expression.

23. The two limitations most relevant here are the requirement to "respect the rights or reputations of others" and the protection of "public order (*ordre public*)". The first limitation is particularly pertinent when considering Principle 1.02 because the rationale

behind this provision is clearly to ensure that the standing and dignity of solicitors within the community are preserved. It will be noted that the two complaints made against the Respondent alleged that his conduct on the day in question was "likely to bring the profession into disrepute". I accept that the term "rights or reputations of others" in the ICCPR is principally intended to offer protection against defamatory remarks being made but I think the term to be sufficiently wide to apply to the general reputation of a professional body. This is particularly so when the profession is seen in the context of the general community to which it belongs, an aspect I now address.

24. The term "*ordre public*" was extensively discussed in the Court of Final Appeal's decision in *HKSAR v Ng Kung Siu & Another* (1999) 2 HKCFAR 442, at 457E-460E. In particular, at 459I-460A, the Chief Justice said this:

"The following points can be drawn from the materials referred to above. First, the concept is an imprecise and elusive one. Its boundaries cannot be precisely defined. Secondly, the concept includes what is necessary for the protection of the general welfare or for the interests of the collectivity as a whole. Examples include: prescription for peace and good order; safety; public health; aesthetic and moral considerations and economic order (consumer protection, etc). Thirdly, the concept must remain a function of time, place and circumstances."

25. I emphasize the reference to the need to protect the general welfare and interests of the community. Lawyers, whether barristers or solicitors, occupy a central role in the administration of justice in Hong Kong. Solicitors enjoy the respect of the community and, for most people, provide the only link with the law. And, where citizens encounter the courts, it is often the solicitors who provide the only comfort with what is often regarded as a daunting experience. In *Nikula v Finland*, Application No. 31611/1996, 21 March 2002, the European Court of Human Rights said this at paragraph 45 of its judgment:

"45. The Court reiterates that the special status of lawyers gives them a central position in the administration of justice as intermediaries between the public and the courts. Such a position explains the usual restrictions on the conduct of members of the Bar. Moreover, the courts – the guarantors of justice, whose role is fundamental in a State based on the rule of law – must enjoy public confidence. Regard being had to the key role of lawyers in this field, it is legitimate to expect them to contribute to the proper administration of justice, and thus to maintain public confidence therein (see the Schopfer v Switzerland judgment of 20 May 1998, Reports of Judgments and Decisions 1998-III, pp.1052-1053, paras 29–30, with further references)."

26. In *Casado Coca v Spain* [1994] 18 EHRR 1, the European Court of Human Rights was faced with a challenge made by a lawyer based on Article 10 of the European Convention for the Protection of Human Rights and Fundamental Freedoms (the equivalent to Article 19 of the ICCPR) against a warning that had been issued to him by the Barcelona Bar Council for advertising. The warning was challenged without success in the Spanish Courts. The Court upheld the decision of the Spanish Courts. In doing so, the Court made a number of general observations:

(1) Rules of discipline and conduct (in that case the rules of the Barcelona Bar) were "designed to protect the interests of the public, while ensuring respect from members of the Bar": at paragraph 46.

(2) Lawyers (in that case, the reference was to members of the Spanish Bar) have a special status giving them "a central position in the administration of justice as intermediaries between the public and the courts". It was this special position that justified the restrictions on them and the monitoring and supervising powers vested in their professional bodies. See here: paragraph 54.

27. I find the reasoning of the European Court of Human Rights in the two decisions compelling to justify the necessity and legitimacy for rules or principles of conduct such as Principle 1.02 to exist. In my view, the public interest requires such rules of conduct to be in existence and indeed, I would even go so far as to say that the Law Society would be failing in its public duty and responsibilities were such rules not in place.

28. I would perhaps also add here that decisions of the European Court of Human Rights on provisions in the European Convention that bear similarity to the Basic Law and the ICCPR are of considerable persuasive authority. As Sir Anthony Mason said in *Shum Kwok Sher v HKSAR* (2002) 5 HKCFAR 381, at 401E-F (paragraph 59):

"59. In interpreting the provisions of chap.III of the Basic Law and the provisions of the Bill [of Rights], the Court may consider it appropriate to take account of the established principles of international jurisprudence as well as the decisions of international and national courts and tribunals on like or substantially similar provisions in the ICCPR, other international instruments and national constitutions".

29. For the above reasons, I am of the view that Principle 1.02 cannot be said to constitute an unjustifiable limitation on the freedom of expression enjoyed by solicitors such as the Respondent. It does not of course prohibit solicitors from exercising this freedom at all (if it had purported to do so, very different considerations would arise), but seeks to restrict this freedom where inappropriate conduct is involved.

30. But is the standard of inappropriateness too vague? It is this issue to which I now turn.

Issue 2: Is Principle 1.02"prescribed by law"or is it too vague?

31. Mr Mok submits that the requirement in Principle 1.02 that solicitors should conduct themselves "appropriately in professional and private matters" is so vague and uncertain so as not to be "prescribed by law" within the meaning of Article 39 of the Basic Law. It is argued that this term is very much a subjective one and therefore uncertain. Such subjective criteria were criticized in the Consultation Paper on Legal Services published by the Attorney General's Chambers in 1995: see paragraph 6.7, 6.17 and 6.19(b).

32. The constitutional principle of legal certainty was dealt with in the judgment of Sir Anthony Mason in *Shum Kwok Sher* at 401J-403J (paragraphs 60-65) and by this Court in *HKSAR v Leung Kwok Hung & Others*. Again, it is not necessary to go through what has been dealt with at some length in the two decisions but I would emphasize the following:

(1) Any restriction on a fundamental freedom must be formulated with sufficient precision so that a person may be able to regulate his conduct and foresee to a reasonable

degree the consequences that any given action on his part may entail. However, consequences need not be foreseeable with absolute certainty for this is unattainable.

(2) The need for certainty, albeit desirable, must however be balanced against the danger of excessive rigidity (where provisions are so inflexible as to be unable to keep pace with changing circumstances). In the case of the conduct of professionals such as solicitors in both their professional and private capacities, this balance is particularly acute.

(3) As the European Court of Human Rights said in Hashman and Harrup v United Kingdom (2000) 30 EHRR 241, at 256 (paragraph 31):

"The level of precision required of domestic legislation – which cannot in any case provide for every eventuality – depends to a considerable degree on the content of the instrument in question, the field it is designed to cover and the number and status of those to whom it is addressed."

33. In my judgment, Principle 1.02 is not too vaguely worded so as to offend against the principle of certainty:

(1) It is important to construe the terms "should conduct himself appropriately in professional and private matters" in context. Principle 1.02 is to be found in that part of the Solicitors' Guide to Professional Conduct under the heading "PRINCIPLES OF PROFESSIONAL CONDUCT". It can therefore readily be seen that it is in the context of the conduct of solicitors (and correspondingly, misconduct) that the principle operates and against which the appropriateness of a solicitor's conduct in professional and private matters is to be gauged.

(2) The appropriateness of a solicitor's conduct is also to be seen in the context of his being an officer of the Court. Principle 1.02 itself (which contains an important commentary) makes it clear that certain standards of behaviour are expected of a person who is an officer of the Court and also the member of a profession (I add here an honourable profession at that).

(3) Seen in the context I have just referred to, Principle 1.02 is in my view readily understandable and of sufficient clarity to enable solicitors to regulate their conduct. Though the terms used are wide, this is necessary given the flexibility that is required to regulate the conduct of solicitors. Solicitors, like everyone else, are part of the community in which the people in Hong Kong live and work. The myriad of situations a solicitor will encounter in the course of his professional and private life cannot easily nor comprehensively be identified. A large degree of flexibility is therefore required in any rules to ensure the proper standards of behaviour are adhered to. The point I have just made as to the desirability of having flexibility in relation to professional conduct situations was precisely the point made by the Privy Council in *John Roylance v General Medical Council* [2000] 1 AC 311 at 330 F-H per Lord Clyde.

(4) Inappropriate conduct is conduct that is unbefitting to an honourable profession, a profession in which trust is reposed by the public and in which dignity is to be maintained. It is a form of professional misconduct (see paragraph (1) above) which itself is conduct "which would reasonably be regarded as disgraceful or dishonourable by solicitors of good repute and competency": - see *Myers v Elman* [1940] AC 282, at 288-9 per Viscount Maugham (cp. here section 2(2) of the LPO). The complaints made against the Respondent in the present case charge that his conduct was such as to be likely to bring the profession into disrepute. This is yet another way of connecting the appropriateness of behaviour or conduct to the standards expected of officers of the Court, to the fact that the solicitors profession is an honourable one and this profession's role in the community.

(5) Finally in this context, I would perhaps just add that for many years, the Courts and professional disciplinary bodies have dealt with concepts such as "conduct disgraceful to him in a professional respect"(see for example *Marten v Royal College of Veterinary Surgeons'Disciplinary Committee* [1966] 1 QB 1) and "serious professional misconduct" (see for example *Roylance*) without any difficulties caused by vagueness. The words "should conduct himself appropriately in professional and private matters" should likewise cause few difficulties. They are neither "unintelligible" (see here *R v Nova Scotia Pharmaceutical Society*, (1992) 74 CCC (3d) 289, at 310B-C) nor "incomprehensible" (*see Committee for the Commonwealth of Canada v Canada* (1991) 77 DLR (4th) 385, at 438).

34. These general objections disposed of (they being Mr Mok's main arguments in this appeal), I now deal with the other aspects of the individual complaints.

Issue 3: The First Complaint

35. In dealing with this complaint, the SDT bore firmly in mind the submission that the Respondent was exercising his freedom of expression but saw the need also to recognize the fact that he was a professional solicitor. As the Chairman said in the Findings, "The Respondent cannot be right in trying to arbitrarily distinguish his conduct as complained of him as a solicitor and of him as a man in the street/an individual citizen of the community".

36. The Respondent's behaviour in wearing only swimming trunks in public holding a banner was regarded by the SDT as inappropriate behaviour. Tribunals such as the SDT are in the best position to adjudicate on the appropriateness of a fellow professional's behaviour. This has long been recognized in Hong Kong: see *The Law Society of Hong Kong v A Solicitor*, unreported, Civil Appeal 130/1995, 9 November 1995, Court of Appeal. As Chan J (now Chan PJ) said in that case, "There is very good sense in the practice that the propriety of the conduct of a professional man is to be judged by his peers". The SDT referred to this case in the Findings. It is clear that the SDT assumed the responsibility of deciding whether or not the Respondent's behaviour was appropriate. Further, although Mr Mok seized upon references in the Findings to newspaper reports to suggest that the SDT may have taken into account facts which were extraneous to the agreed facts, I think that when the reasons of the SDT are read as a whole, it is reasonably clear that it based its findings on the agreed facts. Specific reference was made to paragraphs 5 and 6 of the agreed facts (see paragraph 7 above) which refer to the Respondent having worn only swimming trunks and carrying a banner. I would add here that the demonstration that was held on 1 March 2001 was in the context of the Respondent seeking to flout (certainly not accepting) rulings that had been made that the hearing in the disciplinary proceedings he faced that day was to be held *in camera*.

37. We are only entitled to disturb the SDT's findings if they are plainly wrong: see *Re a Solicitor* [1988] 2 HKLR 137, at 144.

For my part, I am far from satisfied this is the case. On the contrary, I agree with the SDT's findings on the first complaint. The Respondent's behaviour was unbecoming, undignified and completely inappropriate given his position as an officer of the Court and the member of an honourable profession. Much was made by Mr Mok of the lack of evidence from members of the public as to whether what the Respondent did was likely to bring the profession into disrepute. I doubt whether it was suggested this was some sort of evidential requirement every time a complaint is made to this effect. If it was so suggested, I would reject it. The determination of whether or not any act is likely to bring the profession into disrepute is a matter entirely for the Tribunal to determine on the basis of the facts before it. It is not crucially dependent on evidence being adduced of what members of the public may think any more than where the issue of liability in a negligence case has to be determined by reference to the reasonable man on the Star Ferry.

38. For the above reasons, I am of the view that the SDT's findings on the first complaint cannot be impugned.

Issue 4: The Second Complaint

39. The gravamen of this complaint was seen by the SDT to be the invitation to other solicitors to attend a hearing that had been ruled (on at least two occasions) should be held *in camera*. The SDT said this in the Findings:

> "Although we take lightly The Respondent's disparaging and improper remarks against the Law Society, we are of the opinion that for a solicitor, being an officer of the Court, very high standards of behaviour, ethical too apart from professional and private, are expected of him from the court, from his fellow solicitors and from the public including abiding by and respecting rulings made by a Tribunal. The Respondent's failure of abiding by the ruling was part and parcel of the conduct inappropriate of a solicitor".

40. Again, I cannot fault the reasoning of the Tribunal here and find myself in total agreement with the sentiments expressed by it. A solicitor is an officer of the Court. He is expected to abide by rulings made by a court of law or, in the present case, by a statutory tribunal. The public expects lawyers at least to abide by rulings. If there is dissatisfaction with a ruling, any appellate or review measures can be taken. If the law is somehow deficient, again appropriate measures may be taken or representations can be made to the authorities concerned. What legal practitioners cannot do is to flout rulings that are made. Unfortunately, this was what the Respondent was inviting fellow practitioners to do. Mr Mok sought to argue that no solicitor receiving the Circular would actually have turned up (at least this had not been proved by the Applicant). This misses the point because the focus of the complaint was not what would have happened had any solicitor turned up but the Respondent's conduct in sending out the Circular in the first place. In another sense, Mr Mok's arguments here reinforce the complaint against the Respondent in that it impliedly recognizes the fact that most solicitors would not have turned up at the disciplinary hearing on 1 March 2001 for the very reason of this being in contravention of the express rulings made by the Tribunal (and of section 9B(4) of the Ordinance).

41. Mr Mok also submitted that as the Circular was not directed at members of the public but only issued to other solicitors, somehow the complaint that this act was likely to bring the profession into disrepute could not be made out. I confess not easily being able to understand this point. In determining whether or not conduct is likely to bring the profession into disrepute, a disciplinary tribunal is not confined to conduct that is directed at the public in general. It looks to conduct that, were it known by the public, would or might bring the profession into disrepute.

42. As with the first complaint, again I am of the view that the SDT's findings cannot be impugned.

Conclusion

43. For the above reasons, I would dismiss the appeal and make a costs order nisi that the Respondent is to pay the Applicant's costs of this appeal, such costs to be taxed if not agreed.

44. Lastly, it was faintly suggested by Mr Mok that perhaps the penalties that were imposed on the Respondent were too harsh. In my view, given the nature of the complaints and in particular the gravity of the second complaint, the Respondent can consider himself quite fortunate that the penalties imposed were not heavier.

Hon Woo VP:

Introduction

45. The respondent, who was at all material times and is a member of the Law Society, the applicant, and a solicitor in active private practice in Hong Kong, faced two complaints before the Solicitors Disciplinary Tribunal ("Tribunal").

46. Both complaints were in respect of the respondent's conduct that took place on 1 March 2001. Both complaints were that he conducted himself in a manner likely to bring the profession into disrepute in breach of Principle 1.02 of the Hong Kong Solicitors' Guide to Professional Conduct ("Principle 1.02") and Rule 2(d) of the Solicitors' Practice Rules ("Rule 2(d)").

47. The particulars of his conduct under the first complaint were that:

(a) at approximately 2.30 pm outside Wheelock House, Pedder Street, he stood demonstrating in the street wearing no clothes other than his swimming trunks; and

(b) he held a banner covering his lower parts with a template that stated both in English and Chinese "legal right are inborn mine too".

48. The particulars of his conduct under the second complaint were as follows:

(a) on or about 1 March 2001, he published or caused to be published a circular in his name which was distributed to members of the profession;

(b) the circular stated that a protest would be staged outside Wheelock House at 2.30 pm against what he had alleged to be an unjust and unfair conduct of the Law Society;

(c) he invited members of the profession to attend the disciplinary hearing notwithstanding that there were previous rulings by the Tribunal that the hearing was to be held in camera; and

(d) the circular contained disparaging and improper remarks against the Law Society.

49. The hearing in camera referred to the hearing on 1 March 2001, starting at 3 pm.

50. The hearing of the complaints, the subject matter of the

present proceedings, took place before the Tribunal on 4 April, 6 June and 10 September 2003. On 10 September 2003, the Tribunal found the first and second complaints against the respondent proved for contravening Principle 1.02, and proceeded to order the respondent to pay a fine of $90,000 in respect of the first complaint and $40,000 in respect of the second complaint. The Tribunal further ordered that the costs of and incidental to the proceedings, including all prior enquiries and investigations in relation to the matter and including but not limited to costs of the Tribunal, the Tribunal Clerk and the applicant, be taxed on a party and party basis with a two–thirds contribution from the respondent.

51. The respondent now appeals.

Grounds of Appeal

52. By the re–amended notice of appeal, the respondent has raised three grounds of appeal, as follows:

(1) The Tribunal erred in law in holding that respondent had brought the profession into disrepute by reason of conduct, which not being "conduct in the course of practising as a solicitor", constituted breaches of Principle 1.02, on various bases in respect of each of the complaints.

(2) The Tribunal should have held that:

(a) The respondent, albeit a solicitor, does enjoy the fundamental right and freedom of speech and expression under Article 16 of the Hong Kong Bill of Rights and Article 27 of the Basic Law.

(b) Objective evidence from the community ought to have been adduced to establish that the respondent's conduct complained of had brought the profession into disrepute.

(c) The Tribunal was obliged, as a matter of law, to take into account and/or give effect to the views and standard of the community as a whole on the conduct of the respondent.

(d) The Tribunal ought to have considered the matter from the point of view of persons outside the legal profession and not or not merely that of persons within the legal profession.

(e) The circulation of a letter only to members of the profession would not, as a matter of law and fact, have the effect of bringing the profession into disrepute.

(3) Having regard to the terms of the two complaints, namely that the respondent conducted himself in a manner likely to bring the profession into disrepute, the Tribunal was not entitled (as it did) to find those complaints proved in respect of only Principle 1.02 [after it had found that Rule 2(d) is not applicable] (the part in parenthesis was deleted when counsel addressed us).

53. The bases that are relied on as the Tribunal's errors of law alleged in ground (1) are varied. Some are repetitive of the matters raised in ground (2). The others contend that the Tribunal erred in law by placing a wider restriction on the respondent's right and freedom of expression than that applicable to a man in the street because the respondent was a solicitor and an officer of the court, and by the Tribunal's examination of the respondent's conduct in the light of the fact that he was a solicitor.

Ground (3)

54. Ground (3) can be disposed of first. It was added by way of a re–amendment to the notice of appeal. Leave was granted to the respondent when the hearing commenced. As originally drawn, this ground was abstruse and gave me the impression that what was challenged was that there was the inconsistency between the finding by the Tribunal that the respondent was not in breach of Rule 2(d) and its finding that he was in breach of Principle 1.02, or that Principle 1.02 could not stand alone because of the way the complaints were framed, as stated in paragraph 2 above.

55. Rule 2 of the Solicitors Practice Rules provides:

> "A solicitor shall not, in the course of practicing as a solicitor, do or permit to be done on his behalf anything which compromises or impairs or is likely to compromise or impair –
>
> (a) his independence or integrity;
>
> (b) the freedom of any person to instruct a solicitor of his choice;
>
> (c) his duty to act in the best interests of his client;
>
> (d) his own reputation or the reputation of the profession;
>
> (e) a proper standard of work; or
>
> (f) his duty to the court."

56. This Rule 2 appears in terms identical to Principle 1.01 under the heading of Principles of Professional Conduct in the Hong Kong Solicitors' Guide to Professional Conduct. Principle 1.02 that follows provides:

> "1.02 **Conduct subject to discipline**
>
> A solicitor is an officer of the court (see section 3(2) of the Legal Practitioners Ordinance (Cap. 159), and should conduct himself appropriately in professional and private matters."

57. It can be seen that Rule 2(d) (Principle 1.01) deals with a solicitor's conduct "in the course of practising as a solicitor", whereas Principle 1.02 deals with his conduct in both "professional and private" matters.

58. Both complaints related to the respondent's conducts that were "likely to bring the profession into disrepute" which were alleged to be in breach of Principal 1.02 and Rule 2(d). It is therefore clear that the complaints related only to the respondent's conducts that were alleged to be likely to bring the profession into dispute, which were within the ambit of Rule 2(d) and also had the effect of circumscribing the ambit of the word "appropriately" in Principle 1.02. The way that the complaints were framed had the effect of limiting the scope of the inappropriate conduct being alleged to be in breach of Principle 1.02. In my judgment, the complaints directing at the breach of Principle 1.02 were properly framed in making it clear to the respondent that his conducts that were subject to the complaints were inappropriate and likely to bring the profession into disrepute. This fairly and adequately informed the respondent of the true nature of the complaints against him as regards his alleged breach of Principle 1.02.

59. The Tribunal found that there was no breach of Rule 2(d), simply because Rule 2(d) only directs at conducts of a solicitor, in the course of practising as a solicitor, and the Tribunal found

that the conducts of the respondent complained of and as proved against him did not amount to conducts in the course of his practising as a solicitor. The basis of the Tribunal's finding that there was no breach of Rule 2(d) was not that the respondent's conducts complained of were unlikely to bring the profession into disrepute. The Tribunal found him to be in breach of Principle 1.02 because the conducts of the respondent as found were in the course of the respondent's private matters, as opposed to in the course of his practice as a solicitor. The finding that the respondent was not in breach of Rule 2(d) on the one hand and that he was in breach of Principle 1.02 was not at all inconsistent. There is no logic to support the contention that as the Tribunal had found that Rule 2(d) did not apply, they had to find similarly that there was no breach of Principal 1.02.

60. The lack of logic might have been the reason why Mr Mok, on behalf of the respondent, deleted the part of the ground in parenthesis when he sought leave before us. He clarified what he meant by this ground. His point is that while the words in both complaints "likely to bring the profession into disrepute" are not contained in Principle 1.02 though such words form part of Rule 2(d), those words appeared as particulars of the "inappropriateness" of the conducts complaint of. He contended that the Tribunal, however, did not make any specific finding regarding the second complaint that the conducts of the respondent in issuing the circular was likely to bring the profession into disrepute, and therefore the second complaint, as thus particularized, could not have been found proven.

61. This contention is similarly without substance, because the Tribunal was obviously considering all along the inappropriateness of the respondent's conduct in the second complaint in the context of whether it was likely to bring the profession into disrepute. It was not necessary for the Tribunal to expressly state at every stage of its consideration that the conduct had that effect, especially at the time when it concluded that it was inappropriate.

62. Ground (3) fails.

Grounds (1) and (2)

(a) The freedom of expression

63. The main thrust of grounds (1) and (2) is the respondent's reliance on his freedoms of speech and expression enshrined in Article 16 of the Hong Kong Bill of Rights and Article 27 of the Basic Law.

64. Article 27 of the Basic Law provides:

> "Hong Kong residents shall have freedom of speech, of the press and of publication; freedom of association, of a assembly, of procession and of demonstration; and the right and freedom to form and join trade unions, and to strike."

65. Article 16 of the Bill of Rights provides:

> "(2) Everyone shall have the right to freedom of expression; this right shall include freedom to seek, receive and impart information and ideas of all kinds, regardless of frontiers, either orally, in writing or in print, in the form of art, or through any other media of his choice.
>
> (3) The exercise of the rights provided for in paragraph (2) of this Article carries with it special duties and responsibilities. It may therefore be subject to certain restrictions, but these shall only be such as are provided by law and are necessary –
>
> (a) for respect of the rights or reputation of others; or
>
> (b) for the protection of national security, or of public order (ordre public), or of public health or morals."

66. There is no doubt, and the applicant does not seek to gainsay, that a solicitor, as a member of the community of Hong Kong, is entitled to protection of his freedom of expression and freedom of speech. For ease of reference, and since for the purpose of these proceedings, freedom of expression covers freedom of speech, I shall use the term freedom of expression to cover both freedoms in this judgment. The applicability of the Bill of Rights and Article 35 of the Basic Law to the Tribunal in its exercise of powers was recently affirmed by this Court in *A Solicitor v The Law Society of Hong Kong, CACV 302/2002* (18 February 2004), see paras 76, 109 and 214.

67. There are two aspects of the freedom of expression that has to be examined in this case, namely, whether Principle 1.02 is a necessary and legitimate restriction of this freedom, and secondly, if it is, whether its applicability by the Tribunal in the present case was proper.

68. Mr Mok contends that Principle 1.02 is too vague and uncertain, with little guidance as to its applicability to members of the profession, including the respondent, wherefore it is an improper restriction of the freedom.

69. Mr Mok submits that the word "appropriately" in Principle 1.02 is so vague and constitutes a subjective criterion on the part of members of the Tribunal that it falls foul of the requirement that any restriction of a solicitor's freedom of expression must be prescribed by law.

70. He refers us to *Shum Kwok-sher v HKSAR* [2002] 2 HKLRD 793 at 810–821 in support. That case related to the appellant's challenge of the propriety of the offence of "misconduct in public office" for being too vague and uncertain. In Mason NPJ's judgment, with which all judges of the Court of Final Appeal agreed, a number of passages are relevant to the consideration of the appeal before us, as follows:

> "60. International human rights jurisprudence has developed to the point that it is now widely recognised that the expression 'prescribed by law', when used in the context such as art.39 of the Basic Law, mandates the principle of legal certainty. This principle is likewise incorporated in the expression 'according to law' in art.11(1) of the Bill."
>
> "64. In *Hashman and Harrup v. United Kingdom* (1999) 30 EHRR 241, where conduct contra bonos mores was held to be too vague and imprecise to justify a restriction on the applicants' liberty of action in the form of an order binding them to keep the peace and be of good behaviour, the European Court of Human Rights pointed to the tension between requiring a law to be formulated with sufficient precision and the desirability of avoiding rigidity in the law. The Court said (at para.31):
>
> > The Court recalls that one of the requirements flowing from the expression 'prescribed by law' is foreseeability. A norm cannot be regarded as a 'law' unless it is formulated with sufficient precision to

enable the citizen to regulate his conduct. At the same time, whilst certainty in the law is highly desirable, it may bring in its train excessive rigidity and the law must be able to keep pace with changing circumstances. The level of precision required of domestic legislation – which cannot in any case provide for every eventuality – depends to a considerable degree on the content of the instrument in question, the field it is designed to cover and the number and status of those to whom it is addressed."

"89. ... a law must be adequately accessible in the sense that it gives a person an adequate indication of the law relevant to his situation so that (if need be with advice) he can regulate his conduct. On the other hand, it is well settled that the degree of precision required will vary according to the context of the law. In *Sabapathee v Mauritius*, Lord Hope of Craighead, speaking for the Privy Council, said (at p.1843):

"But the precision which is needed to avoid [striking down as unconstitutional] will necessarily vary according to the subject matter. The fact that a law is expressed in broad terms does not mean that it must be held to have failed to reach the required standard. In an ideal world it ought to be possible to define a crime in terms which identified the precise dividing line between conduct which was, and that which was not, criminal. But some conduct which the law may quite properly wish to prescribe as criminal may best be described by reference to the nature of the activity rather than to particular methods of committing it. It may be impossible to predict all these methods with absolute certainty, or there may be good grounds for thinking that attempts to do so would lead to undesirable rigidity. In such situations a description of the nature of the activity which is to be penalised will provide sufficient notice to the individual that any conduct falling within that description is to be regarded as criminal. The application of that description to the various situations as they arise will then be a matter for the courts to decide in the light of experience."

71. Mr Mok also refers us to *Elloy de Freitas v Permanent Secretary of Ministry of Agriculture, Fisheries, Lands and Housing* [1999] 1 AC 69, 77C–79A, for the proposition that the freedom of expression is delicate and vulnerable, as well as supremely precious in our society, that in fairness it should not be left to the hazard of individual decision by the members of the Tribunal, that the guidance given to solicitors must be sufficiently precise and clear, and that any restriction of the freedom can only be made with narrow specificity.

72. On the other hand, Mr Carolan, on behalf of the applicant, refers us to Casoda Coca v Spain [1994] 18 EHRR 1, where the European Court of Human Rights considered the Spanish Bar's rules in restriction of advertising by Spanish lawyers. Mr Carolan relies on the observations of the court that the restriction of advertising was "designed to protect the interests of the public while ensuring respect from members of the profession ... taking into account their special rights and position as officers of the court", and the Spanish "Bar Authorities and Courts were in a better position than an international court to determine how the balance should be struck between protection of the requirements of the public administration of justice, the dignity of the legal profession, the right of everyone to receive information about legal existence and affording lawyers the possibility of advertising their practices" on the one hand, and an individual lawyer's unrestricted freedom to advertise on the other.

73. In my judgment, as is expressly provided for in Article 16 of the Bills of Rights, the freedom of expression may be subject to certain restrictions. Although Principle 1.02 was not designed specifically to restrict the freedom of expression, it does, as in the present case, impose such a restriction insofar as the conduct subject to complain is an exercise of that freedom. While generally speaking, an "appropriate" conduct may appear to be vague, the meaning of appropriateness was in the present case circumscribed by "conduct likely to bring the profession into disrepute" as specified in the complaints. In other respects, the word "appropriateness" can also be viewed together with Principle 1.01 which is an identical repetition of Rule 2(d). I am not saying that the word "appropriately" can only be read in conjunction with the various items of conducts set out under Rule 2(d); however, the items will afford ready guidance to members of the solicitors' profession. As such, I am not persuaded that Principle 1.02 is so vague or uncertain that no clear guidance was afforded to solicitors to know what may amount to professional misconduct or unprofessional conduct. Moreover, any member of the profession should be able to discern what is and what is not appropriate in accordance with the prevailing circumstances. Circumstances may change, social norms and even practising norms may change with time, and "appropriateness" of conduct has the flexibility that can cater for these changing circumstances and, indeed, the changing views of members of the profession on conducts of its members. It is impossible to define all kinds of conduct that will be considered inappropriate, just as it is impossible to define all kinds of unprofessional conduct and professional misconduct.

74. After all, a solicitor's conduct is normally judged by his peers of good standing and competence, those whose reputation will be affected by the conducts of others in the same profession. What better hands would he expect to be in when questions of his conduct arise for consideration, also with the remedy of an appeal to the Court of Appeal when he doubts whether his peers that sat in judgment on him had reached a correct or proper decision.

75. In its written decision of 10 September 2003, the Tribunal cited the following two decisions of this Court on appeal from the Solicitors Disciplinary Tribunal in support of the proposition that "Members of the profession are indeed the best people to judge their own peers" that it adopted.

76. In the case of the *Law Society of Hong Kong v A Solicitor*, Civil Appeal No. 130 of 1995 (9 Nov 1995, unreported), Nazareth VP said:

"... it is also pertinent to note the limited role of this Court on appeal. It is for the Solicitors Disciplinary Tribunal to deal with such disciplinary matters and to decide whether the conduct was unbefitting a solicitor judged by the standards which responsible legal opinion demanded of its own profession. A decision to such effect will only be interfered with on appeal if plainly wrong. Re a Solicitor [1988] 2 HKLR 137 at 144A–E and *In re A Solicitor* (1924) 93 LJKB 761. Furthermore, as Channell J said *In re A Solicitor, ex parte the Law Society* (1913) 29 TLR 354 at 355, with reference to persons in a position similar to the Tribunal have:

'... These gentlemen were the most competent to decide upon professional matters of this kind, ...'

That is an important consideration that has been repeatedly recognised by the courts."

77. Also in *A Solicitor v The Law Society of Hong Kong*, Civil Appeal No. 2 of 1993 (7 May 1993, unreported), Bokhary JA (as he then was) observed:

> "Each professional body entrusted with responsibility for professional discipline is in a uniquely advantageous position to discharge its duty: first, to set and maintain professional standards; secondly, to view each offence against discipline in its proper context from time to time as times change; thirdly, to gauge the effect of each offence on the profession and the public; and, fourthly, to assess the penalty required to mark professional disapproval, restore public confidence and provide effective deterrence. That is why they are entrusted with such responsibility in the first place."

78. With respect, I agree with these observations. They have been applied in Hong Kong and they are consonant with the views of the European Court of Human Rights in *Casoda Coca v Spain* cited above. In particular, in the present context, the word "appropriately" in Principle 1.02 prevents excessive rigidity so that the provision can cater for and keep pace with changing circumstances and the changing attitude of members of the profession in the light of changing social circumstances and attitude of the community. It enables the profession itself to gauge the conduct of its professional colleagues in accordance with such ever-changing circumstances.

(b) Was the freedom of expression applied?

79. Now I turn to Mr Mok's contention that the Tribunal erred in law in the following passage in that the Tribunal excluded the freedom of expression that should be enjoyed by the respondent from its consideration:

> "... as a solicitor is an officer of the court, he should conduct himself appropriately in <u>professional and private matters</u> as stated in Principle 1.02 of the Hong Kong Solicitors' Guide to Professional Conduct. We are here dealing with the conduct of a professional man, a solicitor, not a case where the high-sounding principle of freedom of an individual citizen is at issue. The cases submitted by the Respondent deal mainly with freedom of expression (<u>Ng Kung Siu</u>), free speech (the US case of <u>Fred H. Edenfield</u>), human rights and fundamental freedoms and permissible restrictions prescribed by law (<u>Shum Kwok Sher as well as Gurung</u>): a generous approach should be adopted to the interpretation of those rights while restrictions to them should be narrowly interpreted. All these cases [involving freedom of expression] would be relevant if the Respondent is a man in the street but not a professional man and being a solicitor makes him more than an ordinary professional. He is also an officer of the court."

80. However, the passage above must be read in its context. The Tribunal went on:

> "From the cases produced by the prosecution, notably <u>New South Wales Bar Association v Cummins</u> [2001] NSWCA 284 (Professional misconduct may include acts which do not occur in the ordinary course of practice but which are sufficiently closely connected to practice or <u>which manifest the presence or absence of qualities which are incompatible with, or essential for, the conduct of practice.</u>) and <u>Barristers' Board v Darveniza</u> [2000] QCA 253 (On the Respondent's behalf, it was submitted that the relevant acts happened in private, and that such acts did not scandalise the public unless and until there was a conviction. That submission is far from convincing .... What is relevant are the acts committed by the respondent and <u>the extent to which they reflect upon his character as a barrister who is expected to play an important role in the administration of justice</u>.), the cardinal principle that a professional man should behave properly is clear and we are of the opinion that he should behave more cautiously than a man in the street because of the particular constraint over him for rules meant to be observed whether in public or private as the profession requires of him. The Respondent cannot be right in trying to arbitrarily distinguish his conduct as complained of him as a solicitor and of him as a man in the street/an individual citizen of the community. The Respondent seems to have been trying to get the best of both worlds to suit his purposes and hopes to be benefited from two incompatible sets of ideas and circumstances, i.e. those of a solicitor who is additionally constrained and those of an individual citizen of the community who, being not a professional, is not required to be similarly constrained. The Respondent is not entitled to do so as a solicitor. ... We find that the conduct was in breach of the said Principal 1.02."

81. What I understand the Tribunal to be saying is that although a man in the street, not being a member of the profession, was not subject to Principle 1.02, the respondent, as a solicitor, was subject thereto. Members of the profession expected the respondent, a fellow solicitor, to abide by the rules imposed by their professional organisation, which rules might impose a restriction on his freedom of expression to which, but for the fact that he was a solicitor, he would not be so subject as a man in the street. The restriction imposed on the respondent was more stringent than that to which an ordinary citizen would be subjected. As a solicitor, and an officer of the court, the respondent should behave more cautiously than a man in the street and heed such restrictions.

82. The Tribunal is a statutory body set up by the Legal Practitioners Ordinance, and its members were appointed by the Chief Justice in accordance with that Ordinance. They are entrusted with the power to deal with professional discipline. As observed by Nazareth VP and Bokhary JA, the Tribunal is in a uniquely advantageous position to discharge its duty regarding professional discipline and to set and maintain professional standards. Unless the Tribunal's decision is totally unreasonable or is plainly wrong or is clearly against any principle of law, it would be ill advised for this Court to interfere. The Tribunal, when sitting in discharge of its functions and duties on professional disciplinary matters, represents the view of the profession over the conduct of one of its professional colleagues. Moreover, the Tribunal is in the most advantageous position to gauge the effect of such conduct on the profession and the public from the perspective of the profession itself.

(c) The first complaint

83. Under the first complaint, the conduct involved was that the respondent was demonstrating outside Wheelock House in Central at about 2.30 pm on a working Thursday, almost naked, save that he covered his lower parts in swimming trunks with a template

bearing a statement in both English and Chinese "legal right are inborn mine too". The place was as public a place and one can expect: it was a busy area with a large number pedestrians and heavy vehicular traffic. While such a conduct was not in contravention of the criminal law relating to indecency in a public place, I would venture to say, as was apparently the view of the Tribunal, that conduct would adversely affect the public's view of the solicitors' profession and even render members of the profession to becoming a laughing stock in the community. I have no hesitation to say that the Tribunal was correct in finding that the respondent's conduct in that manner was likely to bring the profession into disrepute.

84. I do not agree with Mr Mok's contention that the Tribunal was obliged, in the absence of objective evidence from the community regarding the respondent's conduct, not to find the respondent's said conduct to be in breach of Principle 1.02.

85. Mr Mok complains that the Tribunal took into account inadmissible evidence of newspaper clippings on the respondent's almost naked demonstration as evidence of the public's view on the subject. He points to a passage in the Tribunal's findings where the Tribunal referred to the newspaper clippings exhibited to the affidavit for laying the complaints on behalf of the Law Society, and submits that the evidence before the Tribunal was and should be limited to the Agreed Facts made between the parties. In fact, these clippings were referred to by Mr Mok when he addressed the Tribunal on behalf of the respondent. He carefully made known to the Tribunal that he referred to the clippings not as evidence but to demonstrate that there was a need to adduce evidence to show whether or not the image of the profession was brought into disrepute generally.

86. I consider that the Tribunal's comments on those clippings were to counter the arguments in Mr Mok's submissions. It is sufficiently clear from the passage below that the Tribunal was merely looking at the agreed facts and applying its own knowledge of the profession's standards to the facts as agreed:

> "Paragraphs 5 and 6 of the Agreed Facts referred. Such conduct was likely to compromise or impair Respondent's own reputation or the reputation of the profession."

(d) The second complaint

87. Another contention that needs to be dealt with is that the sending of the circular, the subject of the second complaint, only to members of the profession would not, as a matter of law and fact, have the effect of bringing the profession into disrepute. What I understand the contention to mean is that even if its contents were inappropriate, since the circular was sent only to members of the profession and there was no evidence that it had come to the notice of any member of the public, it would not have the effect of bringing the profession into disrepute in the eyes of the public. Mr Mok also places great reliance on the finding of the Tribunal that solicitors who received the circular were unlikely to attend the hearing despite the invitation.

88. I am afraid I do not agree. Although the addressees of the circular were limited to members of the profession, it did contain disparaging and improper remarks against the Law Society. It alleged that the Law Society was unjust and unfair and contained an invitation to fellow solicitors to attend the hearing fixed at 3 pm on the very day. The invitation was, in my view, in patent disregard of the ruling of the Tribunal that the hearing of the then complaints against the respondent was to be held in camera. While right-thinking members of the profession might well have disregarded the remarks against the Law Society and the invitation in the circular, even these members could have harboured the feeling that the dignity of the Tribunal and of the profession as represented by the Law Society and the respect for them would be undermined or lowered. Some might think that they could openly defy the rulings of the Tribunal, as the respondent did. Some might form the view that the Law Society was unfair and unjust and was oppressive to its members and bureaucratic, as the circular stated. I have little doubt that the Law Society and the solicitors' profession can thus be brought into disrepute, although the circular was only sent to its own members. The conduct was to be judged against the discipline of the profession for ensuring respect for it and protecting its dignity. Where the conduct undermines that respect and dignity, it adversely affects the reputation of the profession and its members.

89. Mr Mok has also strenuously argued that the Tribunal's ruling that the hearing was to be in camera did not impose any injunction on the respondent against sending an invitation to his fellow members to attend the hearing. He argues that the ruling of conducting the hearing in camera was only made to announce the Tribunal's own procedure, as opposed to an order prohibiting the respondent from inviting other persons to attend the hearing. He refers us to a passage in para 52/1/16 of the 2004 Hong Kong Civil Procedure regarding contempt of court for breaching a court order that states:

> "Any ambiguity in the order or undertaking will be resolved in favour of the alleged contemnor ..."

90. That, of course, is an indisputable rule, but it only applies to contempt of court. Here, we are dealing with a conduct of the respondent who is a member of the solicitors' profession and an officer of the court. He well knew that the Tribunal had made a ruling of hearing in camera after hearing his objections to that course being taken. By his circular to fellow solicitors, he intended or at least hoped that they would attend in the face of the Tribunal's ruling. Mr Mok argues that the invitation could not be flouting the ruling because other solicitors could just attend and apply or make a request to the Tribunal for allowing them to stay in at the hearing if they wished, and it was then entirely a matter for the Tribunal to decide whether their requests would be acceded to. The Tribunal knew full well that it was not dealing with a situation of contempt of court, it was dealing with the conduct of the respondent in order to decide whether it constituted inappropriate conduct that was likely to bring the profession into disrepute. The respondent is a solicitor and an officer of the court. He could find the ruling wrong in law and against principle and disagree with it, just as he can disagree with any judgment of the courts and consider it wrong in law, principle or fact. However, his invitation was to his fellow solicitors to attend the hearing, without intimating anything of the necessity of applying or requesting the Tribunal to allow them to stay in, contrary in fact to what Mr Mok has argued. It is clear that the respondent intended other members of the profession to attend the hearing so as at least to disturb the Tribunal. Even if the attending members requested the Tribunal to allow them to stay at the hearing in the most civil manner, the proceedings would have to be disrupted for the Tribunal to deal with such requests. As a solicitor and an officer of the court, the respondent should have well known that his invitation to other members of his profession in the face of the ruling was a wanton and disrespectful disregard of the ruling and a manifest attempt to cause disruption to the proceedings. Moreover, the letter stated that the Law Society was unjust and

unfair in "insisting on a secret hearing when the Law Society had right at the outset publicised its intention to institute and the fact of Disciplinary Proceedings against me". The use of the term "secret hearing" helps demonstrate the attitude of the respondent and his intention as aforesaid.

91. The gravamen of the complaint relating to the circular was not whether there was a risk of other solicitors accepting the respondent's invitation to attend the hearing, it was his intention and conduct of sending the circular that was inappropriate, as found by the Tribunal. In all the circumstances, I am not persuaded that the Tribunal was wrong to so find.

92. Grounds (1) and (2) fail.

The last ground

93. In the afternoon of the hearing before us, Mr Mok raised a new ground, which is that where this Court finds that the Tribunal had erred in any respect, then even if this Court finds that the Tribunal's findings could otherwise be supported, the disciplinary offences that the respondent had committed were so minor that no sanction should have been imposed by the Tribunal. Having stated my views above, this ground necessarily fails.

Conclusion

94. For the above reasons, I would dismiss the appeal. I agree with the order for costs as proposed in paragraph 43 of the CJHC's judgment.

Hon Cheung JA:

The real issue

95. The solicitor clearly had a right to demonstrate in public and send a circular to his fellow lawyers. These are his right of expression which is guaranteed by the *Basic Law and the Hong Kong Bill of Rights Ordinance*.

96. What is at issue is that this right of expression is subject to legitimate limitation. The limitation is provided by Rule 2 of the *Solicitors' Practice Rules and Principle 1.02 of the Hong Kong Solicitors' Guide to Professional Conduct* both of which are to ensure that this exercise of the right of expression does not constitute a misconduct in his professional duty or in private matters.

Rule 2

97. Rule 2 provides that:

> "A solicitor shall not, in the course of practising as a solicitor, do or permit to be done on his behalf anything which compromises or impairs or is likely to compromise or impair–
>
> (a) his independence or integrity;
>
> (b) the freedom of any person to instruct a solicitor of his choice;
>
> (c) his duty to act in the best interests of his client;
>
> (d) his own reputation or the reputation of the profession;
>
> (e) a proper standard of work; or
>
> (f) his duty to the court.'

Principle 1.02

98. Principle 1.02 provides that

> 'Conduct subject to discipline
>
> A solicitor is an officer of the Court (see s 3(2) of the Legal Practitioners Ordinance (Cap. 159)), and should conduct himself appropriately in professional and private matters.'

The challenge on Principle 1.02

99. It is not argued that Rule 2 does not constitute a legitimate limitation on the solicitor exercising his right of expression. The challenge is directed towards Principle 1.02. It is submitted by Mr. Mok, counsel for the solicitor, that the words 'appropriate conduct' are too vague and if a solicitor is to be charged for a misconduct, he should know the precise misconduct that he is alleged to have committed.

100. In my view, since Principle 1.02 is concerned with conduct subject to discipline, the inappropriate behaviour cannot be any trivial misbehaviour but serious misconduct of a solicitor committed by him in professional or private matters. Rule 2 deals with those serious misconducts committed by solicitor in the course of his practice, while serious misconduct under Principle 1.02 may be committed by him, apart from those committed by him in the course of his practice, in connection with his practice and in private matters. Such misconduct may bring his reputation or that of the profession into disrepute.

101. View in this manner, Principle 1.02 clearly constitutes a legitimate limitation.

Professional matters

102. Under Principle 1.02, serious misconduct in professional matters may arise in respect of

a) the actual legal work performed by the solicitors, for example, the performance was below the required standard;

b) or connected to his practice, such as failure to notify the client of the development of the case; breach of confidentiality and putting himself in conflict of interest situations.

Private matters

103. Private matters are covered as well because a solicitor is an officer of the court and obviously misconduct in private matters has an effect on this important role. The misconduct may involve

(a) either moral turpitude, such as sexual misconduct committed by a solicitor in his private capacity;

(b) or conduct short of moral turpitude but nonetheless outrageous or disgraceful to him in a professional respect.

104. The case of *Raylance v. General Medical Council* [2000]1 A.C. 311 contained examples of misconduct of a professional man in his professional and private capacity. Whether a conduct constitutes a serious misconduct has to be judged by the facts of the case. One can only give examples of misconduct and they are not exhaustive.

Reputation

105. In case of professional misconduct, one can readily see that apart from the solicitor's own reputation, the reputation of the legal profession is also affected. Public confidence in both the

solicitor and the profession is prejudiced by the misconduct.

106. The same will equally be true in situations involving serious misconduct of a solicitor in his private matters. Both his own reputation and that of the profession are equally affected.

107. It is difficult to envisage situations where the tarnish of the solicitor's own reputation will not also affect that of the profession. The connection exists because he is a member of the profession which is used as a yardstick in judging his conducts.

The 1st complaint

108. Anyone who appears in business Central wearing only his swimming trunks is bound to raise eyebrows, let alone a member of an honourable professional.

109. The skills of a lawyer are based on his knowledge of the law and his ability to communicate both verbally and in writing. The conduct of the solicitor demonstrating in this manner was more appropriate in a show business setting. It appealed to sensation rather than a genuine expression of his grievances against the Law Society or the Tribunal. The action was directed towards a decision of the Tribunal. Considering the context in which the demonstration was made, what had happened went beyond what was merely a matter of bad taste. The conduct was disgraceful and was a serious misconduct subject to discipline. It was a mockery of the high standard one expects from the solicitor profession. The episode brought the solicitor's own reputation and that of the profession into disrepute. In my view this first complaint was clearly substantiated.

The 2nd complaint

110.A lawyer plays a vital role in the administration of justice. The rule of law depends on the efforts of everyone involved with the justice system. It is important that a high standard is maintained by members of the legal profession.

111. Whether the decision to hold a private hearing is correct or not is not the issue here. A lawyer should know how a decision can be lawfully challenged. He should further know how a third party who wishes to intervene in a case should proceed. In a usual case, the third party has to lodge a written application to the court or tribunal first. These are basic principles.

112. The solicitor invited members of his profession to attend the hearing when the Tribunal had already held that the hearing was to be in private. Clearly what the solicitor intended to do by the circular was to challenge the ruling of the Tribunal by way of confrontation at the hearing itself. He intended non-parties to be present despite the ruling by the Tribunal. This is tantamount to saying to the Tribunal: 'I don't care about your ruling. Here are the non-parties and what are you going to do about it.' It was not intended to be an impassionate discussion of legal principles on the right of intervention by non-parties.

113. In my view it is serious misconduct on the part of the solicitor to try to engineer a situation of confrontation with the Tribunal in respect of a decision that it had made. It lowers the public confidence in the legal system. It brings his reputation and that of the profession into disrepute.

114. As we learnt from another disciplinary case involving another lawyer from the solicitor's firm, 40 members of the solicitor's firm had attended the hearing that day resulting in it being aborted.

Penalties

115. The penalties imposed in this case are totally appropriate to the complaints.

Conclusion

116. I too would dismiss the appeal with costs.

Hon Ma CJHC:

117. It follows from the above judgments that this appeal is dismissed with a costs order nisi that the Respondent is to pay the Applicant's costs of this appeal, such costs to be taxed if not agreed.

Chief Judge, High Court (Geoffrey Ma)

Vice President (K H Woo)

Justice of Appeal (Peter Cheung)

Mr Paul Carolan instructed by Messrs Boase, Cohen & Collins for the Applicant/ Respondent

Mr Johnny S L Mok & Miss Joyce Leung instructed by Messrs Paul W Tse for the Respondent/ Appellant

---

Yeung May Wan & Others v. HKSAR

楊美雲等 8 人 對 香港特別行政區

HCMA 949/2002；FAMC 62/2004；FACC 19/2004

簡略案情

上訴人均為“法輪功”學員，法院明白法輪功學員和支持者經常在香港示威的行為一直是被容許的。2002 年 3 月 14 日，上訴人在西環干諾道西 160 號中央人民政府駐香港特別行政區聯絡辦公室（下稱“大樓”）正門外的行人道上示威。開始不久，大樓的保安人員便報警求助，警員到達後，在上訴人身後以鐵馬阻擋通入大樓的道路。及後，不單參加示威的人數不斷增加，亦出現圍觀的人群，其中包括途人、記者和新聞媒體。從早上 10 時到下午 1 時，警員曾多次警告示威者離開現場，但得不到理會。最後，警員決定拘捕並企圖帶走上訴人，過程遇到強烈反抗。最終，警員成功用兩輛警車把他們送到西區警署，然而，部份女上訴人拒絕離開警車，導致警員需使用武力帶她們離開。可是，暴力情況在警署內再度出現，引致部份警員受傷。

針對示威者的行為，警方決定起訴他們全部阻礙公眾地方罪、部份妨礙警員執行職務罪和第 6 上訴人襲擊警員罪。案件原審時，裁判官裁定所有上訴人全部罪名成立並處以罰款。上訴人遂提出上訴，案件後來轉介到上訴庭審理。上訴庭重申及肯定《基本法》第 27 條、《公民權利和政治權利國際公約》第 21 條和《香港人權法案條例》第 17 條對集會遊行和示威自由的保障，任何與這些條例有衝突的法例皆無效。上訴庭亦援引終審法院在*吳恭劭*一案的分析，集會遊行和示威自由的權利並非絕對，亦受限制，同樣地，除非必要與合情理，否則也不能隨意限制這些權利。總體來說，是一種平衡個人與公眾間利益的問題。

經分析，上訴庭認為沒有充分證據顯示當時警員有合理理由去壓制該示威，而且，原審裁判官並沒有充分考慮上訴人所提供的能描述當時環境的證據，從而對上訴人的行為是否達到合理標準作出適當的衡量。據此，上訴庭推翻各上訴人阻礙公眾地方的定罪。對於後兩項罪名，上訴法庭認為，有足夠證據證明執行拘捕的警員，是合理地相信上訴人觸犯了阻礙公共地方罪行。然而，就算警員的拘捕不合法，上訴人也沒有權利逗留在警車內或襲擊其他在警署內執行職務的警員，所以上訴庭維持各項妨礙及襲警罪的定罪。受影響的上訴人獲得終審法院的特准，對他們的定罪提出上訴。

裁決摘要

終審法院肯定上訴庭對於阻礙公共地方罪的分析和決定，但否定了上訴庭認為對上訴人的拘捕合法與否不影響其他控罪的論點。終審法院強調人身自由是《基本法》第 28 條所保障的重要公民權利，非法拘捕引起的扣留本身就是非法的禁錮，因此，不論接下來的行動是由原來不知情的警員執行或由其他同袍接手，都不能改變該行動的“非法”性質，因此不能認為進行該非法行動是在執行警員職責。而且，任何被非法羈押的公民，也有權力以合理而適當的武力去自我解救。

終審法院再指出，《基本法》第 28 條保障公民不會受到非法逮捕，所以，警員在執行拘捕任務時，必須有合理理由懷疑被捕人士有觸犯可判處監禁的行為，他不能麻木執行上司的指示。在通盤考慮案件中的證據後，終審法院認為在客觀基礎上不能證明在拘捕時相關警員思維上有此合理懷疑。因此，上訴人是被非法拘捕。據此，警員往後一連串的行動不能被視為執行職務的行為，所以，妨礙警員執行職務和襲擊警員罪均不能成立。由此，上訴得直。

No.19 of 2004

IN THE COURT OF FINAL APPEAL OF THE HONG KONG SPECIAL ADMINISTRATIVE REGION

FINAL APPEAL NO. 19 OF 2004 (criminal)
(ON APPEAL FROM HCMA No. 949 of 2002)

Between:

YEUNG MAY-WAN	1st Appellant
LU JIE	2nd Appellant
TSE LAI-SIM	3rd Appellant
TSO CHI-SIN	4th Appellant
TSANG HAU-SIM	5th Appellant
LAU YUK-LING	6th Appellant
CHAU SING	7th Appellant
LEE JENNY	8th Appellant
- and -	
Hong Kong Special Administrative Region	Respondent

Court: Chief Justice Li, Mr Justice Bokhary PJ, Mr Justice Chan PJ, Mr Justice Ribeiro PJ and Sir Anthony Mason NPJ

Dates of Hearing: 4, 6 - 8 April 2005

Date of Judgment: 5 May 2005

JUDGMENT

Chief Justice Li, Mr Justice Chan PJ, Mr Justice Ribeiro PJ and Sir Anthony Mason NPJ:

1. The freedom to demonstrate is a constitutional right. It is closely associated with the freedom of speech. These freedoms of course involve the freedom to express views which may be found to be disagreeable or even offensive to others or which may be critical of persons in authority. These freedoms are at the heart of Hong Kong's system and it is well established that the courts should give a generous interpretation to the constitutional guarantees for these freedoms in order to give to Hong Kong residents their full measure.

2. In this case, the appellants were engaged in a peaceful demonstration in exercise of their constitutional right. This appeal concerns the extent of their right to do so on a public highway and the scope of police powers to curtail a demonstration on the ground that such persons were causing an obstruction.

3. The demonstration in question took place on 14 March 2002 on the public pavement outside the main entrance to the Liaison Office of the Central People's Government at No 160 Connaught Road West ("No 160"). The demonstrators were members of an association known as the Falun Gong and the number of persons taking part varied from four to 16. Following upon the events described more fully below, all 16 demonstrators were arrested by the police.

The charges

4. All of them were charged with obstruction of a public place contrary to s 4A of the Summary Offences Ordinance, Cap 228 ("the first charge") which materially provides as follows:

> "Any person who without lawful authority or excuse sets out ...... any matter or thing which obstructs, inconveniences or endangers, or may obstruct, inconvenience or endanger, any person ...... in a public place shall be liable to a fine of $5000 or to imprisonment for 3 months."

The particulars charged were that, at the relevant location, the defendants:

> "...... without lawful authority or excuse, set out a banner of about 5 feet x 10 feet which might obstruct, inconvenience or endanger persons in the said public place."

5. All 16 defendants were also charged with a public place obstruction offence under s 4(28) of the same Ordinance ("the second charge") which is relevantly in the following terms:

> "Any person who without lawful authority or excuse ...... does any act whereby ...... obstruction, whether directly or consequentially, may accrue to a public place ...... shall be liable to a fine of $500 or to imprisonment for 3 months."

The particulars alleged that, at the relevant location, the defendants:

> "...... did an act, namely assembling together and displaying a banner of about 5 feet x 10 feet outside the said entrance, whereby obstruction, whether directly or consequentially, might accrue to a public place."

6. After being arrested and taken in police vehicles to the nearby Western Police Station ("WPS"), some of the defendants refused to alight and resisted being removed from those vehicles. Some of them also resisted being subjected to routine processing procedures inside the station. This led to nine of the defendants, including all eight of the present appellants, being charged with wilfully obstructing a police officer contrary to s 36(b) of the Offences Against the Person Ordinance, Cap 212 ("the third charge"). That section materially provides:

> "Any person who ...... wilfully obstructs any police officer in the due execution of his duty ...... shall be guilty of an offence ...... and shall be liable to imprisonment for 2 years."

The particulars were that the relevant defendants had:

> "...... on board the vehicle AM8258 at Western Police Station, ... wilfully obstructed Inspector Ho Ming-yan, a police officer ......, in the due execution of his duty."

7. The fourth charge was brought against Madam Lu Jie, the 2nd appellant. It was alleged that, while on board the police vehicle, she committed an assault against Woman Police Constable Wong Mei-po (WPC1453), a police officer acting in the execution of her duty, contrary to s 63 of the Police Force Ordinance, Cap 232. The 2nd appellant was accused of biting the constable on her forearm.

8. The fifth and sixth charges were also brought under s 63. They were preferred against Madam Lau Yuk-ling (the 6th appellant), it being alleged that while on board the police vehicle, and also in the station car park, she committed two separate assaults against police officers, namely WPC Wong Mei-po (mentioned above) and Chan Wai-man (WPC56952) respectively, each acting in the due execution of her duty. Those assaults were alleged to have involved the actions of grabbing the officers.

9. Section 63 relevantly provides:

> "Any person who assaults ...... any police officer acting in the execution of his duty ...... shall be liable on summary conviction to a fine of $5000 and to imprisonment for 6 months."

The proceedings below

10. On 15 August 2002, Mr Symon Wong, a permanent magistrate sitting at Western Magistracy, convicted the defendants on all charges after a 27-day trial. All the defendants (each of whom was of good character) were fined $1,300 for the public place obstruction offences. Those convicted of wilful obstruction of a police officer were each additionally fined $500 and the convictions for assaulting a police officer drew fines of $1,000 for each assault. The largest total fine was in the sum of $3,800, ordered against the 6th appellant.

11. On 19 August 2002, the defendants lodged an appeal and, on 4 April 2003, they filed their preliminary grounds of appeal. Pang J, before whom the appeal had been listed, decided on 16 June 2003 that it should be transferred for hearing to the Court of Appeal. The appeal (HCMA 949/2002, Ma CJHC, Woo V–P and Stock JA) was heard in early September 2003 and, on 10 November 2004, the Court of Appeal handed down its reserved judgment, unanimously quashing the obstruction convictions on the first and second charges, but upholding (again unanimously but on varying grounds) the relevant defendants' convictions on the third to sixth charges.

12. The Court of Appeal therefore decided that although the public place obstruction convictions could not be sustained, the police officers had nevertheless been wilfully obstructed and assaulted while acting in the due execution of their duty.

13. On 22 December 2004, the Appeal Committee granted the present appellants leave to appeal to this Court against the wilful obstruction and assault convictions.

The demonstration

14. Members of the Falun Gong had, since about August 2001, been demonstrating in the vicinity of the Liaison Office. In accordance with arrangements made by the police, they had been occupying a position on the pavement outside the building next door, at No 162 Connaught Road West ("No 162").

15.The demonstration was political in nature. The magistrate described its purpose (made evident by banners, leaflets and other materials) in the following terms:

> "They protested at the treatment of their [Falun Gong] co–practitioners and asserted that the Central People's Government, the Chairman Jiang Ze Min, in particular, had persecuted the [Falun Gong] by ordering brutal killings of its members in China."

16. In the morning of 14 March 2002, four Falun Gong practitioners from Switzerland decided to conduct their demonstration (in the form of a proposed three–day hunger strike) seated on the pavement outside No 160, some 2 or 3 metres in front of a flag podium on which the national flag was hoisted. This was obviously a more prominent location than that occupied by the demonstrators in front of No 162. The Swiss demonstrators were joined by other Falun Gong members who stood in a compact group behind them, displaying a banner bearing the words: "Jiang Zemin: Stop Killing!" The demonstrators varied in number, but the group did not exceed 16 persons in total. The demonstration was peaceful and largely static, with the participants assuming postures apparently associated with Falun Gong rituals.

17. The flag podium (which covers an oblong–shaped area of about 4 square metres) was situated some 8 or 9 metres in front of the main entrance to the Liaison Office building. It was flanked by lamp installations each covering a similar–sized area on either side, leaving gaps of about 3 metres between each lamp installation and the flag podium. The width of the pavement in front of the flag podium and lamp installations was about 9.5 metres, making it a wide pavement in Hong Kong terms.

18. There was vehicular as well as pedestrian access to No 160 from Connaught Road West. Vehicles could enter and leave a basement car–park using driveways situated to the left and right of the main entrance, passing to the outside of the lamp installations. Some pedestrians might gain access to the main entrance from the pavement by walking through the gaps between the flag and lamp installations described above. Others might gain access from the pavement by crossing the vehicular driveways diagonally, skirting the lamp and flag installations.

19. Plainly, pedestrian access was to some extent physically obstructed by the 14 March demonstration although pedestrians continued to be able to use the building's main entrance by making a slight detour around the group of demonstrators. This does not, of course, amount to saying that the demonstrators were necessarily committing the offence of obstructing a public place, as discussed more fully below.

Events leading to the charges

20. At about 08:50 hrs on 14 March 2002, private security guards employed by the Liaison Office saw the four Swiss demonstrators take up their positions in front of No 160. They immediately made a series of telephone complaints to the police at the nearby WPS, alleging that office workers seeking access to the building and others were being obstructed.

21. WPS was under the command of Superintendent Chiu Kai–ting, Divisional Commander, Western District ("Supt Chiu"). As he acknowledged in evidence, Supt Chiu acted as the overall commander at the scene and was responsible for all the actions taken in relation to the demonstrators. Having been told of the complaints, he, together with Senior Inspector Wong Tak–hung ("SIP Wong"), inspected the scene at about 09:00 hrs. After some 15 minutes' observation, Supt Chiu concluded that the demonstrators were causing an obstruction. This was because he saw people wishing to enter the Liaison Office having to use the vehicular driveway to do so. He also testified that he saw local residents using the pavement being compelled to make detours to avoid the demonstrators at the scene.

22. One of the first measures ordered by Supt Chiu involved erecting pedestrian barriers between the demonstrators and the main entrance to the Liaison Office. This took place at about 09:20 hrs and was done to avoid repetition of an incident which had taken place a fortnight earlier, on 26 February 2002, when a female Falun Gong member dashed several times into the Liaison Office building, chanting slogans and carrying a banner. However, such barriers also had the effect of denying all access to the main entrance through the gaps between the flag and lamp installations. Thereafter, access to that entrance could only be gained by crossing the vehicular driveways.

23. The demonstration attracted media attention and, by 10:00

hrs, some 30 or so reporters had come to the scene, adding to the numbers outside No 160.

24. An attempt was made, by a series of verbal warnings given by various police officers, to persuade the demonstrators to return to their previous location outside No 162. They were told that the demonstration in the present location constituted an offence of obstruction and that, unless they moved immediately, steps would be taken to remove and arrest them for that offence. All such warnings were ignored.

25. The services of the Police Tactical Unit ("PTU") were enlisted. At about 10:54 hrs, members of the PTU's Z Company were ordered to attend at the WPS. There, at about 11:25 hrs, Supt Chiu briefed Superintendent Patrick Hodson, and Inspector Ho Ming-yan ("Insp Ho") on the situation. They were commander of the PTU's Z Company and platoon commander of Unit 3 of Z Company, respectively. Supt Chiu told them that complaints had been received from security officers at the Liaison Office and that a group of more than ten protestors consisting of Falun Gong members had gathered outside No 160 and were causing an obstruction. He said that warnings had been given but were ineffective so that removal and arrest action would have to be taken.

26. After inspecting the scene with Supt Chiu, a briefing was held at about 12:25 hrs at which Supt Hodson briefed the other ranks in PTU, Z Company and officers attached to WPS who were to take part in the operation. Officers were told that there was a Falun Gong demonstration outside the Liaison Office which had caused obstruction and that the demonstrators would be warned to leave, failing which they would be arrested and removed using minimum force. Similar briefings of the police officers involved were held by Insp Ho. PTU officers were assigned to several removal teams, each comprising a sergeant and three constables, and WPS officers were given the task of cordoning off the area and taking charge of any arrested persons. The officers then took up a position outside Kwan Yick Building at 271-285 Des Voeux Road West, to await further instructions.

27. After further verbal warnings had no effect, Supt Chiu gave the order to arrest and remove the demonstrators. This was conveyed to Insp Ho who instructed members of his platoon to proceed. The relevant team of arresting officers was led by Woman Police Sergeant Ma Pui-man ("Sergeant Ma") and included three Woman Police Constables, namely, Wong Mei-po ("WPC Wong"), Chan Wai-man ("WPC Chan") and Chan Hoi-lei (referred to in evidence as "WPC57215"). They had the task of removing female demonstrators.

28. When arrest action began, the demonstrators linked arms with each other, sat on the ground and struggled physically to prevent members of their group from being taken to waiting police vehicles. As part of their efforts to extract individual demonstrators from the group, the police applied what is known as the hypoglossal nerve pressure technique which is intended to overcome resistance by causing pain to the person being arrested. Eventually, after a struggle lasting about half an hour, all the demonstrators were loaded on board police vehicles and taken back to WPS.

29. When they got back to the station, the female demonstrators, including all the present appellants, refused to leave the vehicle in question. After police warnings did not persuade them to alight, officers took action to carry them bodily off the vehicle. The appellants resisted by hanging on to the seats and other fixtures in the vehicle. This was the conduct which resulted in the wilful obstruction charge. It was also in the course of their removal from the vehicle that the relevant appellants were alleged to have assaulted the police officers in question.

The continuing importance of the obstruction charges

30. As previously noted, the Court of Appeal quashed the convictions for public place obstruction. However, for reasons developed more fully below, it remains analytically important for the disposal of the present appeal to examine the basis upon which those convictions were quashed and to consider the impact of such quashing on the lawfulness of the arrests, these being matters which bear directly on the prosecution's contention that when obstructed or assaulted, the police officers in question were acting "in the due execution of their duty".

The constitutional guarantees

31. Central to the case is the fact that the arrests were made and the charges of public place obstruction laid against the defendants because of their conduct in the course of a peaceful public demonstration. This was not a simple case of obstruction, for instance, by inconsiderate parking of a vehicle or by dumping waste building materials on a road or by a hawker impeding pedestrians on a pavement. Here, the fact that the defendants were at the time of arrest engaged in a peaceful demonstration meant that the constitutionally protected right to demonstrate was engaged. Indeed, a peaceful demonstration, may also engage the closely related guaranteed freedoms of opinion, expression and assembly. Such fundamental rights, when engaged, have an important bearing on the scope of the offence of obstruction and consequentially on the scope of police powers of arrest on suspicion of that offence.

32. Article 27 of the Basic Law is directly in point and relevantly states:

> *Article 27*
>
> "Hong Kong residents shall have freedom of speech, ...
> of assembly, ... and of demonstration......"

33. By Article 39 of the Basic Law, constitutional protection is also given to freedom of opinion, of expression and of peaceful assembly as provided for in Articles 16 and 17 of the Hong Kong Bill of Rights, those articles being the equivalents of Articles 19 and 21 of the International Covenant on Civil and Political Rights and representing part of the ICCPR as applied to Hong Kong.

34. For present purposes, it will be sufficient to focus on the interaction between the obstruction convictions on the one hand and the constitutional right to demonstrate enshrined in Article 27 of the Basic Law on the other. As the foregoing description of the relevant events indicates, the facts are straightforward, involving an essentially static demonstration alleged to constitute a public place obstruction. The restrictions on the right to demonstrate sought to be upheld by the prosecution are those contained in the Summary Offences Ordinance and it has correctly not been suggested that those provisions in themselves go beyond what is constitutionally permissible. The present focus is therefore on how those statutory provisions were applied in the context of an exercise of fundamental rights.

The quashing of the obstruction convictions in the Court of Appeal

35. The Court of Appeal unanimously quashed the public place obstruction convictions principally on the basis of Stock JA's

analysis. However, Ma CJHC (with Woo V-P agreeing) sought additionally to support the conclusion reached by reference to the Public Order Ordinance, Cap 245, in the context of the permitted restrictions in the Hong Kong Bill of Rights. We are respectfully unable to support that approach. The Public Order Ordinance was not applicable on the facts and not relied on by either party. And, as indicated in the preceding paragraph, it was correctly accepted that the statutory restrictions do not themselves exceed the scope of the constitutionally permitted restrictions. Accordingly, reference to the Public Order Ordinance regime was not relevant in the context of the present case.

36. Nonetheless, the quashing of the obstruction convictions on the basis of Stock JA's accurate analysis of the offence in the context of the fundamental right to demonstrate, coupled with his exhaustive analysis of the facts (at paras 61 to 118 of the Judgment), is unassailable.

37. The conviction on the first charge was quashed on the ground that it was factually unsustainable. As Stock JA put it, the suggestion that the banner itself could constitute an unreasonable obstruction was "nonsensical". No further discussion of the first charge is called for.

38. The real issues arose from the second charge which alleges that, by assembling together for the demonstration outside the Liaison Office, the defendants (including the present appellants) caused an obstruction to a public place. It should be noted that while the particulars of the second charge were couched in terms of the assembly constituting an act "whereby obstruction, whether directly or consequentially, might accrue to a public place", the prosecution's case proceeded entirely on the basis that there had been an actual, and not merely a potential, obstruction.

The law relating to obstruction of a public place

39. Leaving aside for the moment the constitutional right to demonstrate, the offence created by s 4(28) has two main limbs: (i) there must be an act which directly or consequentially causes an obstruction to a public place; and (ii) that act must have been done without lawful authority or excuse. Although s 4(28) refers to conduct whereby an obstruction "may accrue", this does not mean that the mere possibility of obstruction may be sufficient. As was pointed out by Stock JA (para 60), this simply means that where it is clear that obstruction will be caused, there is no need to wait until obstruction is actually caused before an offence is committed. For the purposes of considering the applicable authorities, obstructing the highway may be taken as the paradigm example of obstructing a public place, and no distinction needs to be drawn between the two.

40. So far as the first limb is concerned, the authorities indicate that any physical occupation of a road which interferes (to an extent which is more than de *minimis*) with the use of that road by others constitutes an obstruction: *Nagy v Weston* [1965] 1 All ER 78 at 80; *Hirst and Agu v Chief Constable of West Yorkshire* (1987) 85 Cr App R 143 at 151.

41. It is, however, the second limb which is of importance for present purposes. The fact that someone physically obstructs the highway or some public place *does not* in itself constitute an offence. It is only where this takes place without lawful authority or excuse that a breach of s 4(28) occurs. Accordingly, while the impeding of pedestrian access to the Liaison Office amounted to a physical obstruction for the purposes of s 4(28), the demonstrators would only be guilty of an offence under that section if they caused the obstruction without lawful excuse. The burden of proving that it was without lawful excuse lies on the prosecution: *Hirst and Agu*, at 150 and 151. One might add in parentheses that questions concerning lawful authority (relevant to cases involving statutory permits or licences for market and street traders, and the like: see *Hirst and Agu*, at 151) do not arise on this appeal.

42. It is clear that a person who creates an obstruction cannot be said to be acting without lawful excuse if his conduct involves a reasonable use of the highway or public place: *Nagy v Weston*, at 80; *Hirst and Agu*, at 150. The suggestion in some of the earlier reported cases that the public's right to use the highway is limited to the right of passage and re-passage and acts incidental or ancillary thereto, is too narrow. It is now established that "......the public have the right to use the public highway for such reasonable and usual activities as are consistent with the general public's primary right to use the highway for purposes of passage and repassage" (*DPP v Jones* [1999] 2 AC 240 at 255E–G per Lord Irvine of Lairg LC; see also Lord Clyde at 279F, and Lord Hutton at 290H).

43. Many examples of obstructions which may nevertheless constitute reasonable use of the highway can be found in the cases: two friends stopping for a chat when they happen to meet on the street, people handing out leaflets for commercial purposes, collecting money on a charity's flag-day, stopping on the street to look into shop windows, to take a photograph or to make a sketch, and so forth. While other users of the road or footpath may be to some extent impeded by such conduct, the law looks upon such cases applying what Stock JA (citing *Harper v G N Haden and Sons Limited* [1933] 1 Ch. 298, 320) called "the law of give and take". It seeks to strike a balance between possibly conflicting interests of different users of the highway based on a requirement of reasonableness. Whether any particular instance of obstruction goes beyond what is reasonable is a question of fact and degree depending on all the circumstances, including its extent and duration, the time and place where it occurs and the purpose for which it is done: *Nagy v Weston*, at 80, *DPP v Jones*, at 257E–G, 281E–F and 293B–C.

44. Where the obstruction in question results from a peaceful demonstration, a constitutionally protected right is introduced into the equation. In such cases, it is essential that the protection given by the Basic Law to that right is recognized and given substantial weight when assessing the reasonableness of the obstruction. While the interests of those exercising their right of passage along the highway obviously remain important, and while exercise of the right to demonstrate must not cause an obstruction exceeding the bounds of what is reasonable in the circumstances, such bounds must not be so narrowly defined as to devalue, or unduly impair the ability to exercise, the constitutional right.

The flawed approach to obstruction

45. Stock JA identified as the applicable legal principles, propositions corresponding to those summarised above. He held, with the concurrence of the other members of the Court of Appeal, that there was reason to doubt:

> "...... whether the fact and the centrality of the requirement of showing an unreasonable impediment to the primary right of passage, was appreciated by the police officers who on 14 March 2002 asserted that an offence had been committed, or by the prosecutor in the presentation of the case; and whether the true issues were addressed by the magistrate." (para 93)

46. He concluded that the proper issues had not been sufficiently appreciated:

> "......the transcript in this case reveals an assumption on the part of the prosecution witnesses who alleged obstruction, and also on the part of prosecuting counsel, that all that had to be shown was that pedestrians were diverted from the path which but for the presence of the demonstrators they would have taken; and that since there was a space available down the road for the Falun Gong to demonstrate, an obstruction contrary to section 28(4) of the Summary offences Ordinance was proved." (para 94)
>
> "......With respect to the magistrate, whose task was not made easier by some unhappy exchanges between counsel, I find scant assurance from the Statement of Findings that give and take as between two rights was accorded adequate consideration: indeed, there is a strong assertion in that Statement that the demonstrators were disrespectful of the rights of those seeking access to the offices – a conclusion against which the testimony tended – with no concomitant recognition of the tolerance and respect demanded by the right to assemble and protest guaranteed in terms by the Basic Law." (*ibid*)

47. The principal factual conclusions reached by Stock JA were summarised as follows:

(1) that the objective indicia and the facts which are common ground show clearly enough that there was ample room for pedestrians as well as office workers safely to pass and to gain access to the building;

(2) that that situation was not likely materially to change;

(3) that the court below failed to take into account relevant evidence;

(4) that the court below accorded too little regard to the right of assembly and protest;

(5) that the court below applied too restrictive a test to the issue of reasonableness as it arises when two fundamental rights compete for space on a highway;......"

48. Accordingly, the Court of Appeal quashed the convictions on the second charge, holding that the magistrate had failed to conduct the necessary evaluation of the reasonableness of the obstruction in deciding that the demonstrators had acted without lawful excuse; or, if he did make such an evaluation, that no reasonable tribunal properly directing itself could have arrived at the conclusion reached by him. As indicated above, we endorse the Court of Appeal's findings and conclusions in this regard.

Consequence of quashing the obstruction convictions

49. It is clear that the demonstrators, including the appellants, were arrested on the footing that they had committed public place obstruction offences. Given that the convictions for those offences have been quashed, the question arises as to whether the arrests which had been based on suspicion of those offences were lawful. And if they were not lawful, one must ask whether the act of removing the appellants from the police vehicle at WPS was action taken by the police officers concerned in the due execution of their duty. If not, an essential element of the offences for which the appellants were convicted on the third to sixth charges would be missing.

50. The Court of Appeal, on grounds which were not unanimous, held that the wilful obstruction and assault convictions could be upheld notwithstanding the setting aside of the public place obstruction convictions.

The"no nexus"argument

51. The first contention, accepted by Ma CJHC and Woo V-P, but not Stock JA, was that it did not matter whether the original arrests for public place obstruction were lawful. Woo V-P put this as follows:

> "Factually and logically, there can be no nexus between the arrests of the appellants by the police on the pavement outside 160 Connaught Road West and the conduct of the appellants after the vehicle carrying them had arrived at the Western Police Station.
>
> Even though three officers (PW13, PW15 and PW17), the complainants of the obstruction and assault charges 3, 4, 5 and 6, took part in the arrest of the appellants, their asking the appellants to alight from the vehicle at the police station had nothing to do with the arrest. The obstruction under charge 3 did not occur on the pavement outside 160 Connaught Road West when the appellants were arrested; it occurred after the appellants had arrived at the Western Police Station when the three complainants and their colleagues requested the appellants to leave the vehicle. Whether the appellants had been lawfully arrested, the requesting police officers must be executing their lawful duties when requesting the appellants to alight (see section 51 of the Police Force Ordinance). Even if the appellants had been unlawfully arrested, they had no right to remain on the vehicle. PW15 and PW17, who were assaulted as charged in charges 4, 5 and 6, were lawfully executing their duties in using reasonable force to carry the appellants concerned out of the vehicle, but they were bitten, scratched and grabbed on the neck by these appellants." (paras 48 and 49)

Ma CJHC made a similar point at para 40.

52. With respect, this argument is unsound. The starting point is that every resident is entitled to freedom of the person. Anyone who seeks to interfere with that freedom can only do so with proper legal justification. This was well-established at common law and is now laid down in Article 28 of the Basic Law:

> *Article 28*
>
> The freedom of the person of Hong Kong residents shall be inviolable.
>
> No Hong Kong resident shall be subjected to arbitrary or unlawful arrest, detention or imprisonment. ......

53. If a person is subjected to an unlawful arrest by a police officer, the continued detention of that person pursuant to the arrest perpetuates the unlawfulness and constitutes a false imprisonment. It matters not that the continued detention is placed in the hands of officers other than the original arresting officers and it is irrelevant that the latter officers may know nothing of the circumstances of the arrest. The act of maintaining custody which is unlawful forms no part of the duty of any police officer and if he is obstructed or assaulted while doing so, he is

not obstructed or assaulted while acting in the due execution of his duty. On the contrary, persons unlawfully in custody are entitled to use reasonable force to free themselves.

54. In *Christie v Leachinsky* [1947] AC 573, Lord Simonds stated:

> "Putting first things first, I would say that it is the right of every citizen to be free from arrest unless there is in some other citizen, whether a constable or not, the right to arrest him. And I would say next that it is the corollary of the right of every citizen to be thus free from arrest that he should be entitled to resist arrest unless that arrest is lawful." (at 591)

Lord Du Parcq put it as follows:

> "The principles established by the authorities are agreeable to common sense, and follow from the governing rule of the common law that a man is entitled to his liberty, and may, if necessary, defend his own freedom by force. If another person has a lawful reason for seeking to deprive him of that liberty, that person must as a general rule tell him what the reason is, for, unless he is told, he cannot be expected to submit to arrest, or blamed for resistance. The right to arrest and the duty to submit are correlative." (at 598)

55. That it makes no difference that custody is handed over to a different officer has long been recognized. Thus, in *Griffin v Coleman* (1859) 4 H&N 265, a prisoner who had been arrested by a constable in circumstances which did not give rise to a power of arrest, was taken to the police station where some hours later, the prisoner was handcuffed and taken by the superintendent before the magistrates who eventually dismissed the case. The superintendent had not made any inquiries as to the circumstances of the arrest and was held liable for trespass to the person. Pollock CB held that "the imprisonment was utterly illegal" and that "the defendant was a party to it". Martin B cautioned: "Every person who takes part in an unlawful imprisonment acts at his peril."

56. In the present case, when the demonstrators were taken to WPS, they were being detained pursuant to their arrest outside No 160. This remained the case when action was taken to remove them from the relevant vehicle at WPS. It follows that if the original arrests were unlawful, such action (taken with a view to subjecting the demonstrators to processing procedures while keeping them in custody) were also unlawful and could not have been carried out by the relevant officers in the due execution of their duty. It is quite untenable to suggest that the action taken in the car-park of WPS had "nothing to do with" the original arrest.

The arguments for holding that the original arrests were lawful

57. The other arguments set out in the Court of Appeal judgments proceed on the basis that the original arrests were lawful so that the subsequent actions were taken in the due execution of the officers' duty. These arguments all relate to the power of arrest conferred on police officers by s 50 of the Police Force Ordinance, Cap 232 ("PFO s 50"), which materially states:

> *Section 50*
>
> (1) It shall be lawful for any police officer to apprehend any person who he reasonably believes will be charged with or whom he reasonably suspects of being guilty of –
>
> (a) any offence for which the sentence is fixed by law or for which a person may (on a first conviction for that offence) be sentenced to imprisonment; or
>
> (b) ...
>
> (1A) A police officer may exercise the power to apprehend a person under subsection (1) without any warrant for that purpose and whether or not he has seen any offence committed."

58. Three arguments require consideration, namely:

(a) That the arrests were justified on the basis that the arresting officers reasonably believed that the demonstrators would be charged with obstruction (per Ma CJHC, at para 39);

(b) That, as appears from the evidence of Supt Chiu and SIP Wong, all the police officers concerned had a reasonable suspicion that the offence of obstruction had been committed by the demonstrators (per Ma CJHC, at para 38); and,

(c) That although Supt Chiu, who gave the order to arrest, did not himself have reasonable grounds for suspecting that an obstruction offence had occurred (para 119), the arresting officers had the necessary reasonable suspicion, making the arrest lawful (per Stock JA, para 145).

These will be referred to as "the first, the second and the third arguments" respectively.

The first argument: the"would be charged"limb of PFO s. 50

59. Ma CJHC touched lightly on this argument, stating merely that:

> "Sight should not be lost either of the other limb of section 50(1), namely, a reasonable belief that the relevant Appellants would be charged (the Appellants were of course eventually charged)."

60. It would appear that his Lordship was suggesting that even if reasonable suspicion of guilt could not be shown, the arrests would be within the statutory power on the basis that the arrests were carried out in the belief (which was in fact vindicated) that the demonstrators would be charged with public place obstruction. With respect, such an argument cannot be accepted.

61. It is true that, on its face, PFO s 50 appears to provide two alternative bases for the exercise of the power of arrest: (i) where the officer reasonably believes that the arrested person will be charged with a relevant offence; and (ii) where the officer reasonably suspects that person of being guilty of a relevant offence.

62. However, Article 28 of the Basic Law prohibits arbitrary arrest (as does Article 5 of the Hong Kong Bill of Rights). If PFO s 50 were to be construed as permitting a resident to be arrested where there is no reasonable suspicion that such person has committed any relevant offence, but merely where the arresting officer believes that (notwithstanding the absence of reasonable suspicion) the person in question will be charged with an offence, PFO s 50 would open the door to arbitrary arrest.

63. The need for there to be some acceptable objective

justification for an arrest, as reflected in a requirement of reasonable suspicion of guilt, is essential if residents are to be safeguarded from arbitrary arrest. As the European Court of Human Rights ("ECHR") stated (in connection with Article 5(1) of the European Convention on Human Rights) in *Fox, Campbell and Hartley v UK* (1990) 13 EHRR 157, at para 32:

> "The 'reasonableness' of the suspicion on which an arrest must be based forms an essential part of the safeguard against arbitrary arrest and detention which is laid down in Article 5(1)(c). The Court agrees with the Commission and the Government that having a 'reasonable suspicion' presupposes the existence of facts or information which would satisfy an objective observer that the person concerned may have committed the offence. What may be regarded as 'reasonable' will however depend upon all the circumstances."

64. This was echoed in *O' Hara v UK* (2002) 34 EHRR 32, at para 34. In both of these cases, the ECHR emphasised the requirement for reasonable suspicion in order to avoid arbitrary arrest even in the context of anti–terrorist legislation. In *O' Hara* (at para 35), the court acknowledged that terrorist crime poses special problems since there will often be constraints on disclosing information as to the basis of the suspicion for fear of jeopardising the safety of informants. The court nonetheless stated:

> "Even in those circumstances, the respondent Government has to furnish at least some facts or information capable of satisfying the Court that the arrested person was reasonably suspected of having committed the alleged offence."

65. The ECHR stated in Fox, *Campbell and Hartley* (above) at para 32, that domestic courts may be justified in applying less stringent "reasonable suspicion" standards in such terrorist cases, but that some objective basis for asserting a reasonable suspicion remained essential.

66. If PFO s 50 is to be construed consistently with our constitutional guarantees against arbitrary arrest, the provision authorising a police officer to apprehend a person "who he reasonably believes will be charged" must be read to mean "who he reasonably believes will be charged *on the basis of* a *reasonable suspicion that the arrested person is guilty of the offence to be charged*". So understood, the first limb of PFO s 50 encompasses the second limb and does not eliminate or dilute the requirement for there to be a reasonable suspicion of guilt.

The second and third arguments: Arrests in fact based on reasonable suspicion

67. The second and third arguments are closely related and can be dealt with at the same time. As to the second argument, Ma CJHC (at para 38) stated:

> "Insofar as the focus should be on the validity of the arrests, while doubt exists as to whether the police had reasonable grounds to stop the demonstration when they did, there was never any doubt that the police had reason to believe that an offence had been committed. Both Senior Inspector Wong and Superintendent Chiu gave evidence not only as to the obstruction, but also to the potential dangers caused by the demonstration. These dangers may have been given a prominence that, on a careful balancing exercise, might not have been merited, but to say that the police did not have any reasonable grounds to believe that an offence had been committed, is simply not supported by the facts."

His Lordship therefore evidently held that all police officers concerned had met the reasonable suspicion requirement at the time of arresting the demonstrators. However, he did not proceed to any analysis of the facts relied on in support of that conclusion.

68. Turning to the third argument, the essential reason why Stock JA decided (with the concurrence of the other members of the court) that the public place obstruction convictions had to be quashed was that there had been a failure on the part of the police – and particularly on the part of Supt Chiu who had ordered the arrests – properly to appreciate "the centrality of the requirement of showing an unreasonable impediment to the primary right of passage" (para 93). Stock JA held that this entailed the conclusion that Supt Chiu could not have had a reasonable suspicion that the demonstrators had committed public place obstruction offences. However, his Lordship went on to state that it did not necessarily follow that those who effected the arrests themselves had also fallen foul of the objective test of reasonable suspicion (para 129(1)).

69. The issue identified by Stock JA concerned the nature of:

> "......the circumstances in which junior officers can be said to be acting in the execution of their duty in relation to a suspect when it is not adequately shown that the test is satisfied in relation to the officer supervising the same operation." (para 129(2))

He expressed regret that such issue had received sparse attention in argument before the Court of Appeal.

70. After careful consideration of *O' Hara v Chief Constable of the Royal Ulster Constabulary* [1997] AC 286 (*"O' Hara"*), his Lordship held that the arresting officers *did* have a sufficient basis for reasonably suspecting that the demonstrators had committed a public place obstruction offence at the time of the arrests. In particular, it was held that information imparted at the briefing attended by those officers, plus the evidence of what they saw for themselves at the scene, permitted them reasonably to suspect that at an earlier point in time, the demonstrators had committed an obstruction offence. His Lordship put it thus:

> "On the evidence placed before us, I am satisfied that, despite such flaw as [there] may have been in the Superintendent's approach to the issue of public place obstruction, there is enough upon which the magistrate could properly conclude that the arresting officers themselves had reasonable cause to suspect the commission of an offence under section 4(28) of the Summary Offences Ordinance. They had been briefed and they went to the very scene where the demonstration was still afoot. Mr Haynes points to the fact that at the time the arresting officers went to the scene, the situation had changed, in that barriers had been erected, and that therefore the facts upon which the original view had allegedly been formed that an obstruction had been caused were no longer the same facts. This he says is highly material. The answer is that for the purpose of section 50 of the Police Force Ordinance it might not be material at all. The question for the arresting officers was not necessarily whether they reasonably suspected that an offence was in the course of commission at the very time of arrest, but rather whether they reasonably suspected that one had been committed. I think that

it can reasonably be said that an officer who is given a briefing that an obstruction has taken place, and is told that those who were obstructing are still in situ, and then himself or herself sees persons fitting the description of the described group actually occupying the described place has reasonable, even if mistaken, grounds for suspecting the earlier commission of the offence ......" (para 145)

The relevant principles

(i)Need for genuine suspicion on reasonable grounds

71. An examination of the legal principles relevant to the two foregoing arguments may begin with the proposition, well-established in relation to powers of arrest which are exercisable on reasonable suspicion of guilt, that the arresting officer must have both a genuine suspicion that the offence in question has been committed and reasonable grounds for that suspicion.

72. Leaving aside for the moment a question concerning the relevance of judicial review (mentioned later in this judgment), Woolf LJ in *Castorina v The Chief Constable of Surrey* (CA), The Times 15 June 1988, identified the relevant questions as follows:

" (1) Did the arresting officer suspect that the person who was arrested was guilty of the offence? The answer to this question depends entirely on the findings of fact as to the officer's state of mind.

(2) Assuming the officer had the necessary suspicion, was there reasonable cause for that suspicion? This is a purely objective requirement to be determined by the judge if necessary on facts found by a jury."

(ii) Suspicion in the mind of the arresting officer

73. The House of Lords in *O'Hara* made it clear that when considering whether these subjective and objective requirements have been met, one is concerned solely with what was in the mind of the arresting officer. The House of Lords was dealing in that case with a provision requiring the arresting constable to have "reasonable grounds for suspecting [the person arrested] to be a person who is or has been concerned in ...... acts of terrorism" and Lord Steyn stated (at 292) that provisions employing such language "categorise as reasonable grounds for suspicion only matters present in the mind of the constable."

74. Lord Hope of Craighead (at 298) elaborated upon this as follows:

"My Lords, the test which section 12(1) of the Act of 1984 has laid down is a simple but practical one. It relates entirely to what is in the mind of the arresting officer when the power is exercised. In part it is a subjective test, because he must have formed a genuine suspicion in his own mind that the person has been concerned in acts of terrorism. In part also it is an objective one, because there must also be reasonable grounds for the suspicion which he has formed. But the application of the objective test does not require the court to look beyond what was in the mind of the arresting officer. It is the grounds which were in his mind at the time which must be found to be reasonable grounds for the suspicion which he has formed. All that the objective test requires is that these grounds be examined objectively and that they be judged at the time when the power was exercised.

This means that the point does not depend on whether the arresting officer himself thought at that time that they were reasonable. The question is whether a reasonable man would be of that opinion, having regard to the information which was in the mind of the arresting officer. It is the arresting officer's own account of the information which he had which matters, not what was observed by or known to anyone else."

75. As Lord Steyn pointed out, it is by virtue of "the longstanding constitutional theory of the independence and accountability of the individual constable" that the law has come to fasten on the mind of the arresting officer himself:

"The information which causes the constable to be suspicious of the individual must be in existence to the knowledge of the police officer at the time he makes the arrest. ...... The executive 'discretion' to arrest or not, as Lord Diplock described it in *Mohammed-Holgate v Duke* [1984] A.C. 437, 446, vests in the constable, who is engaged on the decision to arrest or not, and not in his superior officers." (*O'Hara* at 293D–E)

(iii) Who is the arresting officer?

76. The arresting officer is the constable who actually effected the arrest. Where several constables take part, they each qualify as an arresting officer. In *Hussien v Chong Fook Kam* [1970] AC 942 at 947, Lord Devlin explained what in law amounts to an arrest:

"An arrest occurs when a police officer states in terms that he is arresting or when he uses force to restrain the individual concerned. It occurs also when by words or conduct he makes it clear that he will, if necessary, use force to prevent the individual from going where he may want to go. It does not occur when he stops an individual to make inquiries."

(iv) Reasonable suspicion must relate to the material elements of the relevant offence

77. For the arresting officer to meet the statutory requirements of PFO s 50, the facts reasonably suspected by him to exist must be such that, if true, they would constitute the necessary elements of the offence for which the power of arrest is sought to be exercised. As Sedley LJ in *Clarke v Chief Constable of North Wales Police* [1997] EWCA Civ 2432 (7 October 1997) put it:

"......the power of arrest without warrant depends on the existence in the mind of the arresting officer of reasonable suspicion of the material elements of an arrestable offence ......"(para 23)

78. This is illustrated by Chapman v DPP (1988) 153 JP 27 where the power of arrest depended on the constable having a reasonable suspicion that the person to be arrested had committed an arrestable offence, meaning an offence punishable with 5 years' imprisonment. Bingham LJ pointed out that it was:

"...... therefore necessary to consider ...... what arrestable offence, or what facts amounting to an arrestable offence, [the constable] reasonably suspected to have occurred." (at 33)

79. The magistrates found that, on the basis of information received from fellow officers, the constable suspected and had reasonable grounds for suspecting either a common assault or an assault on a police officer in the execution of his duty. However,

neither of those offences were arrestable offences. An assault with the additional element of occasioning actual bodily harm was an arrestable offence. But there was no evidence and no finding by the magistrates that the constable had acted on suspicion or had reasonable grounds for suspecting that bodily injury was a material element of the offence for which he was making the arrest. Bingham LJ added:

> "It is not of course to be expected that a police constable in the heat of an emergency, or while in hot pursuit of a suspected criminal, should always have in mind specific statutory provisions, or that he should mentally identify specific offences with technicality or precision. He must, in my judgment, reasonably suspect the existence of facts amounting to an arrestable offence of a kind which he has in mind." (at 34)

80. The requirement is therefore one of substance and not of technicality. It complements the related rule that upon making an arrest, the arresting officer must in ordinary circumstances inform the person arrested in substance (without the necessity of using technical or precise language) of the reason for the arrest: see *Christie v Leachinsky* [1947] AC 573 at 587.

81. In relation to a public place obstruction offence, a material element is that the obstruction was unreasonable and the fact that the constitutional right to demonstrate was being exercised has to be given substantial weight when assessing reasonableness.

(v) The standard of reasonable suspicion

82. As noted above, the standard set by PFO s 50 is one requiring the arresting officer to have formed, at the time of arrest, a genuine suspicion of guilt held on grounds which are objectively reasonable. What is needed to meet that standard in any particular case is a question of fact and degree.

83.In *Hussien v Chong Fook Kam* [1970] AC 942 at 948 (PC), Lord Devlin emphasised that proving a reasonable suspicion is not the same as showing a prima facie case, describing the latter as importing "a much stiffer test". His Lordship continued:

> "Suspicion in its ordinary meaning is a state of conjecture or surmise where proof is lacking: 'I suspect but I cannot prove.' suspicion arises at or near the starting-point of an investigation of which the obtaining of prima facie proof is the end. When such proof has been obtained, the police case is complete; it is ready for trial and passes on to its next stage." (at 948)

84. Lord Devlin (at 949) also pointed out that prima facie proof consists of admissible evidence whereas suspicion can take into account matters that could not be put in evidence at all.

85. The requirement that the suspicion be "reasonable" stiffens the test. As Sir Fredrick Lawton pointed out in *Castorina v The Chief Constable of Surrey* (above):

> "Suspicion by itself, however, will not justify an arrest. There must be a factual basis for it of a kind which a court would adjudge to be reasonable."

(vi) The source and grounds for reasonable suspicion

86. Where the factual basis for the suspicion is within the arresting officer's own knowledge, for instance, where he witnesses a crime in progress, the application of the reasonable suspicion test is straightforward. However, in a modern police force, officers necessarily operate as a team subject to a chain of command. The information upon which arrests are made may come from a variety of sources, for instance, calls for assistance from fellow officers picked up on a beat radio, surveillance and detection reports by other police units, information from Interpol and reports from informants and members of the public. Often, as in the present case, a team of officers will be briefed about suspected offences by superior officers just prior to an operation.

87. These are matters which have received recognition in the case-law. The focus remains on the mind of the arresting officer who must be shown to have a genuine and reasonable suspicion that the person arrested has committed a relevant offence, having in mind the material elements of that offence. But that officer's reasonable suspicion may properly be based upon any of those sources of hearsay information provided that such information leads him to form a genuine suspicion on grounds which an objective observer would regard as reasonable.

88. Lord Steyn in *O'Hara* (at 293) stated:

> "In order to have a reasonable suspicion the constable need not have evidence amounting to a prima facie case. Ex hypothesi one is considering a preliminary stage of the investigation and information from an informer or a tip-off from a member of the public may be enough: *Hussien v Chong Fook Kam* [1970] AC 942, 949. ...... Hearsay information may therefore afford a constable reasonable grounds to arrest. Such information may come from other officers: *Hussien's case, ibid.*"

89. Lord Hope put it thus:

> "The information acted on by the arresting officer need not be based on his own observations, as he is entitled to form a suspicion based on what he has been told. His reasonable suspicion may be based on information which has been given to him anonymously or it may be based on information, perhaps in the course of an emergency, which turns out later to be wrong. As it is the information which is in his mind alone which is relevant however, it is not necessary to go on to prove what was known to his informant or that any facts on which he based his suspicion were in fact true. The question whether it provided reasonable grounds for the suspicion depends on the source of his information and its context, seen in the light of the whole surrounding circumstances." (*O'Hara* at 298)

90. Dealing with police teamwork, Lord Hope added:

> "Many other examples may be cited of cases where the action of the constable who exercises a statutory power of arrest or of search is a member of a team of police officers, or where his action is the culmination of various steps taken by other police officers, perhaps over a long period and perhaps also involving officers from other police forces. For obvious practical reasons police officers must be able to rely upon each other in taking decisions as to whom to arrest or where to search and in what circumstances. The statutory power does not require that the constable who exercises the power must be in possession of all the information which has led to a decision, perhaps taken by others, that the time has come for it to be exercised. What it does require is that the constable who exercises the power must first have equipped himself with sufficient information so that

he has reasonable cause to suspect before the power is exercised."(at 301–302)

91. In an operation such as that conducted in the present case, the arresting officers may be subject to the supervision of superior officers throughout and it may be on the order of a superior officer that they initiate the arrest action. It is recognized that, realistically, the arresting officer will generally not be in a position to question that order. Indeed every police officer is under a statutory duty to obey all lawful orders of his superior officers and is liable to dismissal for failure to do so: see ss 30 and 31 of the Police Force Ordinance, Cap 232. As Lord Roskill noted in *McKee v Chief Constable for Northern Ireland* [1984] 1 WLR 1358 at 1361:

> "The arresting officer is not bound and indeed may well not be entitled to question those instructions or to ask upon what information they are founded."

92. However, this does not mean that the arresting officer is entitled simply to rely on the fact that a superior officer has ordered the arrest. It remains essential that the arresting officer must be equipped with a sufficient factual basis to found, in his own mind, the requisite reasonable suspicion. It follows that where, for instance, a briefing precedes the arrest action, the officer giving the briefing must be careful to impart sufficient information to provide a proper factual basis for a reasonable suspicion. And where the lawfulness of the arrest is subsequently challenged, evidence of the contents of the briefing may be important.

93. Lord Steyn dealt with orders from superior officers as follows:

> "Given the independent responsibility and accountability of a constable under a provision such as section 12(1) of the Act of 1984 it seems to follow that the mere fact that an arresting officer has been instructed by a superior officer to effect the arrest is not capable of amounting to reasonable grounds for the necessary suspicion within the meaning of section 12(1). It is accepted, and rightly accepted, that a mere request to arrest without any further information by an equal ranking officer, or a junior officer, is incapable of amounting to reasonable grounds for the necessary suspicion. How can the badge of the superior officer, and the fact that he gave an order, make a difference? In respect of a statute vesting an independent discretion in the particular constable, and requiring him personally to have reasonable grounds for suspicion, it would be surprising if seniority made a difference. ...... Such an order to arrest cannot without some further information being given to the constable be sufficient to afford the constable reasonable grounds for the necessary suspicion."(at 293–294)

(vii) Applicability of judicial review principles

94. The provisions of PFO s 50 give the police officer the power to arrest upon the reasonable suspicion condition being met. But he obviously has a discretion and is not obliged to make an arrest in every case where such condition is satisfied. Indeed, the authorities show that there may be cases where, notwithstanding the existence of a reasonable suspicion of guilt, an arrest may be made in bad faith or otherwise be made in circumstances justifying a judicial review on the basis laid down in *Associated Provincial Picture Houses Ltd v Wednesbury Corporation* [1948] 1 KB 223. In *Mohammed–Holgate v Duke* [1984] AC 437 at 443, Lord Diplock, having noted that the conditions precedent for an arrest had been fulfilled in the case at hand, continued as follows:

> "...... since the wording of the subsection under which he acted is 'may arrest without warrant,' this left him with an executive discretion whether to arrest her or not. Since this is an executive discretion expressly conferred by statute upon a public officer, the constable making the arrest, the lawfulness of the way in which he has exercised it in a particular case cannot be questioned in any court of law except upon those principles laid down by Lord Greene M.R. in [the *Wednesbury* case]..... The *Wednesbury* principles, as they are usually referred to, are applicable to determining the lawfulness of the exercise of the statutory discretion of a constable under section 2(4) of the Criminal Law Act 1967, not only in proceedings for judicial review but also for the purpose of founding a cause of action at common law for damages for that species of trespass to the person known as false imprisonment, for which the action in the instant case is brought."

95. Given the way the arguments were presented in the present case, the Court is not concerned with any consideration of such judicial review powers. The issue is as to whether, on the evidence and in the light of the applicable legal principles, the Court of Appeal was correct to hold (on the second and third arguments) that the condition precedent of a reasonable suspicion that the demonstrators had committed an offence of obstruction under s 4(28) was fulfilled.

Application of the principles

96. Initially, Mr Paul Harris (who appeared with Mr Cheung Yiu Leung for the 1st, 2nd, 3rd and 7th appellants) submitted in argument that Supt Chiu should be regarded as the arresting officer since he had given the order to make the arrests. He also sought to suggest that Supt Chiu did not genuinely suspect the demonstrators of any obstruction offence but had ordered the arrests merely with a view to sparing the sensitivities of the Liaison Office and therefore had issued the order for an improper reason.

97. In his reply submissions, Mr Harris correctly withdrew the argument that Supt Chiu should be regarded as the arresting officer in the light of the authorities canvassed. We are in any event not prepared to entertain the suggestion that Supt Chiu ordered the arrests in bad faith. This case has throughout proceeded on the footing that the relevant officers did (as they testified) genuinely suspect obstruction, the issue focussing on whether that suspicion was held on reasonable grounds. A suggestion of bad faith is a serious allegation. It was not advanced either before the magistrate or in the Court of Appeal. Neither was it fairly put to Supt Chiu in the witness–box.

98. The arresting officers in the present case were the four–officer team comprising Sergeant Ma, WPC Wong, WPC Chan and Chan Hoi–lei (WPC57215). They were the officers who actually effected the arrest of the appellants and it is to their states of mind that one looks in deciding whether the arrests were carried out on reasonable suspicion of guilt. All except Chan Hoi–lei gave evidence so that an examination of the basis upon which they took arrest action may be made.

99. In relation to the second argument, Ma CJHC appears to have focussed instead on the evidence of Supt Chiu and SIP Wong for his conclusion that "there was never any doubt that the police had reason to believe that an offence had been committed." He did not mention the arresting officers themselves and offered no factual

analysis in support. As the authorities reviewed above show, that was an erroneous approach.

100. Stock JA recognized that "the person who has to house the reasonable suspicion is the arresting officer himself" (para 138) but he was hampered by the fact that the Court of Appeal did not have before it transcripts of the evidence of either Insp Ho or WPC Wong. It is no doubt for this reason that he treated Insp Ho as one of the arresting officers. That was not consistent with the evidence. In the transcript (which was made available to this Court), this exchange is to be found in Insp Ho's cross-examination:

Q. Officer, it appears from your evidence that you were the arresting officer of a number of these defendants; is that correct?

A. No, I gave instruction to my subordinate to do the arrest operation.

101. As previously indicated, Stock JA felt able to uphold the wilful obstruction and assault convictions on the footing that the arrests had lawfully been made on reasonable suspicion supplied by the contents of the briefing and by what the arresting officers were able to see with their own eyes at the scene. His Lordship considered that the available information gave the arresting officers "reasonable, even if mistaken, grounds for suspecting the earlier commission of the offence." We are respectfully unable to accept that conclusion.

102. The authorities certainly support the view that an officer may properly form a reasonable suspicion based on what he has been told at a briefing, supplemented, if necessary, by what he then sees at the scene. However, it must be borne in mind that the suspicion stimulated must relate to the material elements of the offence, in this case, an offence which involved obstructing a public place *without lawful excuse in the context of an exercise of the constitutional right of public demonstration*. As noted above, the Court of Appeal unanimously held that the evidence did not sustain the finding that the obstruction was without lawful excuse. Stock JA, moreover, correctly held that Supt Chiu did not sufficiently have in mind the elements indicated in italics and could not, if he had himself effected the arrests, have demonstrated a reasonable suspicion of the offence in question.

103. The evidence as to what was said at the briefing was sparse. Nothing in that evidence indicates that the briefing addressed facts which might enable the arresting officers reasonably to suspect that the obstruction caused by the demonstrators was of such character, dimensions or duration as to amount to an unreasonable use of the highway and therefore to have been without lawful excuse, bearing in mind their constitutional right to demonstrate.

104. Insp Ho gave evidence of two briefings he had attended. The first was at 11:25 hrs when he was briefed by Supt Chiu. That briefing is not directly relevant since the arresting officers were not present. However, that evidence indicates the boundaries of the information made available to the officers concerned:

Q. At about 1125 hours on that day, were you given a briefing in relation to a complaint of obstruction outside 160 Connaught Road West?

A. Yes. Yes, I was briefed by the commander of Western Police Station. He briefed me that earlier on complaints have been received from LOCPG [ie, the Liaison Office] concerning obstruction.

Q. And did he give you any further particulars about the nature of the obstruction?

A. A part of it at that time. Superintendent Chiu Kai-ting briefed me that there was a group of more than 10 protesters gathered at the pavement outside No. 160 Connaught Road West. And that group of people consisted of Falun Gong members and the complainant is one of the security officers of LOCPG.

Q. Were you given any particular instructions at this stage?

A. Superintendent Chiu told me that earlier on warning or warnings had been given to this group of people concerned but the warning or warnings was not effective. And he briefed me that I had to make some arrangement relating to the removal operation and arrest action.

105. Then in relation to the 12:25 hrs briefing which was attended by the arresting officers, Insp Ho's evidence was as follows:

Q. Did you later attend a briefing in relation to this demonstration that was taking place at 160?

A. Yes.

Q. Remember what time that briefing took place?

A. The time was 12.25 pm to 12.35 pm.

Q. Who gave the briefing?

A. My commander, that is Superintendent Ho Tak-shing, Patrick Hodson.

Q. And who did he brief and what did he brief them about?

A. He mainly told me that my team, that is sub-unit 3, would be responsible for the removal action and the escort of the prisoners-I'm sorry, it should be the escort of (Witness continues in English) prisoner escort...

106. Insp Ho was obviously not given any factual details bearing on the material element of lawful excuse in relation to the suspected offence. There was no mention of the demonstrators' constitutional right of peaceful demonstration nor of any facts which might render its exercise unreasonable.

107. Sergeant Ma, who led the team of arresting officers, gave evidence about two briefings which she attended. The first, held at about 12:25 hrs was attended by officers of the rank of sergeant and up:

Q. At about 12.25 pm that day, were you given a briefing?

A. Yes.

Q. Who gave you the briefing?

A. The commander of my sub-unit, Inspector Ho Man-yan.

Q. Did he give a briefing to you and to your platoon members?

A. Yes.

......

Q. Now, during this briefing that was given, what was said to you, as best as you can recall, the general gist of what was said?

A. At that time I was briefed by Inspector Ho Man-yan that a group of people had caused obstruction at the Liaison Office of the Central Peoples Government of the Special Administrative Region at No 160 Connaught Road, West.

108. In relation to the briefing held for other ranks, Sergeant Ma's evidence was to like effect:

Who gave this briefing and what was said at that briefing?

A. Also by Inspector Ho. Likewise, the content of it was that there was a group of people causing obstruction at the aforesaid location, that is No. 160 Connaught Road, West.

109. Sergeant Ma was also asked about what she saw at the scene:

Q. What did you see at the scene?

A. At that time I saw there was a group of people sitting outside No. 160 Connaught Road West. At that time they were holding a banner with a white background.

Q. Can you tell us whether you observed what some of them were doing and what positions they were in, whether they were sitting or standing?

A. Amongst them most of them were sitting and some of them were standing and holding the banner. For the location where they were standing, it was at the middle of the pedestrian passageway outside the office.

Q. Did you make any assessment of the conduct of the demonstrators, how that might affect users of the road or of the pavement?

A. Yes.

Q. What was that?

A. At that time I had made the assessment since that location was the main passageway for going in and out. And for the location which was occupied by them, they occupation two-thirds of the passageway horizontally. And I had reason to believe that obstruction would be caused to the people who went in and out of the office.

Q. ...... On viewing this, did you form any view as to whether any offence had been committed?

A. Yes, obstruction.

Q. On the assessment of the situation that you saw, was that a suspicion that you had formed, that the offence of obstruction had been committed?

A. Yes.

110. Sergeant Ma's evidence was therefore to the effect that at the briefing, information about the offence of obstruction went little beyond the assertion that it had been committed without any reference to the material element of lawful excuse. The evidence of WPC Wong and WPC Chan did not take the matter any further.

111. Stock JA's suggestion that there was sufficient to found a reasonable suspicion that the demonstrators had, at an *earlier stage*, committed the offence of obstruction without lawful excuse, is not supportable. None of the arresting officers testified to harbouring any such suspicion. On the contrary, they all stated that when arriving at the scene, they considered that the offence was in the course of being committed. The warnings given by the police, some within the hearing of the arresting officers, involved stating in the present tense that the demonstrators were then causing an obstruction. From the beginning, reference had been made to a group of "more than ten" demonstrators, an apt description given the maximum of 16 participants. There was nowhere any suggestion that the demonstration had earlier been larger and so possibly more obstructive.

Conclusion

112. The inescapable conclusion is accordingly that the objective requirement of reasonable suspicion of a public place obstruction without lawful excuse cannot be made out either on the basis of what had been said at the briefings or of what was self-evident at the scene. It follows that the arrests for obstruction contrary to s 4(28) were unlawful. This in turn means that the actions taken by the officers to remove the appellants from the vehicle while keeping them in police detention were not performed in the due execution of their duty. The appeal must therefore be allowed and the convictions on the 3rd to 6th charges inclusive must be quashed.

Common assault

113. Consideration was given to the possibility of substituting convictions for common assault in respect of the 4th to 6th charges. In appropriate cases this is possible since a person who assaults a police officer who is not acting in the execution of his duty may nevertheless commit the offence of common assault on that officer.

114. A substituted conviction would not be appropriate in the present case. As noted above, the law permits individuals to use reasonable force to resist being subjected to unlawful detention. The assaults in the present case occurred in circumstances where the relevant appellants were resisting detention and attendant procedures. Their acts would amount to common assaults if more than reasonable force was used. It is possible that their acts may have amounted to common assaults. However, whether this was the case involves a factual assessment that this Court is in no position to make, the issue never having been examined below. Such evidence as has been placed before us falls far short of establishing unequivocally that excessive force was used.

Conduct of the police

115. This judgment should serve to clarify the law on the public obstruction offence and the law of arrest. We wish to make clear that no criticism of the conduct of any of the police officers is intended by this judgment. They had to cope with a difficult situation in relation to an area of the law which has been developing. It should be acknowledged that as is shown by the evidence including the video recordings, they acted with restraint and with disciplined professionalism throughout.

The Court of Appeal's delay in handing down judgment

116. The trial before the Magistrate had taken 27 days and the appeal involved complex issues of fact and law. On 5 September 2003, the Court of Appeal reserved judgment after a three day hearing. About six months later, in early March 2004, the

appellants' solicitors wrote to the clerk of the court to inquire when judgment would be handed down. In the absence of a reply, they wrote again in the middle of August 2004. The reply indicated this was likely to be in September 2004. This was later revised to October. Judgment was eventually handed down on 10 November 2004. There was thus an interval of over 14 months between the conclusion of the hearing and the delivery of judgment.

117. The appellants rely on the delay involved as an independent ground for challenging the convictions on the obstruction and assault charges. It is submitted that as a result of such delay, their right to be tried without delay had been breached and that the appropriate remedy is the quashing of the convictions in question.

Article 11(2)(c) of the Bill of Rights

118. Article 11(2)(c) of the Bill of Rights Cap 383 provides:

> "In the determination of any criminal charge against him, everyone shall be entitled to the following minimum guarantees, in full equality–
>
> (c) to be tried without undue delay."

119. Article 11(4) provides that everyone convicted of a crime shall have the right to his conviction and sentence being reviewed by a higher tribunal according to law. These articles are equivalent to Art 14.3(c) and 14.5 of the International Covenant on Civil and Political and Rights (ICCPR).

120. In the present context, the appeal provides the review envisaged in Art 11(4). A criminal charge is not determined within the meaning of Art 11(2)(c) until there has been a determination on appeal. Accordingly, the guarantee of trial without delay in the determination of a criminal charge includes the appellate process. This is consistent with General Comment 13 on Art 14 of the ICCPR (21st session 1984). Paragraph 10 of that Comment stated that to make the right to be tried without delay effective, "a procedure must be available in order to ensure that the trial will proceed without undue delay, both in first instance and on appeal". This view was applied by the Human Rights Committee in *Rogerson v Australia UN Human Rights Committee Reference 802/98* (15 April 2002). In that case, it was held that an unexplained delay of almost two years by the Northern Territory Court of Appeal in giving judgment on a contempt of court matter violated the party's right to be tried without delay in Art 14.3(c) of the ICCPR. It also held that such finding of violation constituted a sufficient remedy (paras 9.3 and 11).

The reason for delay

121. In his judgment, the Chief Judge expressed regret for the delay. He stated that the reason for delay was that he wanted to wait until after the Court of Appeal (Ma CJHC, Stock and Yeung JJA) had heard the appeal in *HKSAR v Leung Kwok Hung* [2004] 3HKLRD 729 which concerned freedom of expression and peaceful assembly and limits to their exercise so that the principles from that case could be borne in mind in dealing with the present case. (The Chief Judge and Stock JA sat in both appeals.) That appeal was heard on 24 to 27 February and 24 and 25 June 2004 and judgment was handed down on 10 November 2004, the same day as the judgment in the present case.

122. Whilst we, of course, accept that the Chief Judge believed that the reason he gave justified the delay, the matter must be objectively judged. Having regard to our conclusion that the permitted restrictions in the Public Order Ordinance are irrelevant to the public place obstruction offence, the reason given is not objectively a sufficient justification for the delay.

123. We have concluded that the convictions in question should be quashed on the ground that the police officers were not acting in the execution of their duty. Having regard to this conclusion, the challenge on the ground of undue delay does not arise for decision and it is unnecessary to determine whether there was undue delay in the present case and, if so, the proper remedy. The question of undue delay involves a consideration of many factors. In this respect, we note that there are extensive comparative materials on the matter. The Court would wish to hear comprehensive argument and examine carefully these materials before deciding these issues should they arise for decision in a future case.

Duty to give judgments within a reasonable time

124. However, it must be clearly and firmly reiterated that judges at all levels of court have a duty to give judgments within a reasonable time after the conclusion of the hearing. This is important not only for ensuring that justice is done to the parties but also for the maintenance of public confidence in the Judiciary and the judicial system.

125. An interval of over 14 months between the conclusion of the hearing and the delivery of judgment in a criminal appeal is most exceptional. Irrespective of whether Art 11(2)(c) was breached in this case, a question on which it is unnecessary to express any view, even taking into account the complexity of the issues involved and the fact that the appellants were not in custody, we think that delay of this order is unacceptable and should not occur again.

Costs

126. As the parties are agreed that costs should follow the event in this Court, the costs of this appeal are awarded in favour of the appellants with an order for legal aid taxation of the costs of those appellants who are on legal aid. As for the costs in the courts below, the parties are at liberty to make any necessary application in writing to this Court.

Mr Justice Bokhary PJ:

127. On 14 March 2002 a number of demonstrators including these appellants were staging a demonstration on the pavement along a public road. As it happens, the demonstrators were followers of the Falun Gong movement. The demonstration was being staged right outside the main entrance to the Liaison Office of the Central People's Government at No. 160 Connaught Road West. And it took the form of a protest against what the demonstrators said was happening to Falun Gong followers in the Mainland. But subject to one question, the politics (if any) behind a demonstration are irrelevant to the legal issues to which it may give rise. It can happen that the demonstrators' cause is itself intolerant. If so, there would arise the question mentioned by Gendall J at p.630 in *Police v Beggs* [1999] 3 NZLR 615, a decision of a two–judge division of the High Court in New Zealand hearing an appeal from the District Court. Should the law "in the name of tolerance tolerate the intolerant" ? Subject to this question the freedoms of assembly, procession and demonstration are enjoyed irrespective of the participants' politics. That question does not arise in the present case. Nor in fact did it arise in *Beggs*' case which involved a student protest about education funding.

128. Article 27 of our constitution the Basic Law guarantees

freedom of assembly, procession and demonstration for Hong Kong residents. These appellants are Hong Kong residents but some of the other demonstrators were from abroad. So it should be mentioned that art. 41 extends the guarantee of these and other freedoms to persons in Hong Kong other than residents, thus matching the common law approach. This approach can be seen in *R v Chiswick Police Station Superintendent, ex parte Sacksteder* [1918] 1 KB 578, a deportation case heard by the Court of Appeal in England during the First World War. Scrutton LJ's judgment in particular lays stress (at pp 589–590) on the anxious care that the courts will always give to any interference with liberty whether the person affected is a citizen or a foreigner temporarily within the sovereign's protection.

129. 1.While staging their demonstration the appellants and the other demonstrators were arrested for public place obstruction. The Summary Offences Ordinance, Cap. 228, lays down two offences of public place obstruction, one under s.4(28) and the other under s.4A. Charges were brought under both in the present case.

130. Section 4(28) provides that any person who without lawful authority or excuse does any act whereby any injury or obstruction, whether directly or consequentially, may accrue to a public place or to the shore of the sea, or to navigation, mooring or anchorage, transit or traffic shall be liable to a fine of $500 or to imprisonment for 3 months. The allegedly obstructive act consisted of gathering together in a group of 16 demonstrators: four on a hunger strike and 12 supporting them.

131. Turning to s.4A, it provides that any person who without lawful authority or excuse sets out or leaves, or causes to be set out or left, any matter or thing which obstructs, inconveniences or endangers, or may obstruct, inconvenience or endanger, any person or vehicle in a public place shall be liable to a fine of $5,000 or to imprisonment for 3 months. The allegedly obstructive thing consisted of a banner displayed by the hunger strikers. It is common ground that the banner would not have been obstructive if the gathering of persons was not obstructive.

132. The Court of Appeal (Ma CJHC, Woo VP and Stock JA) held, rightly in my view, that the demonstration did not amount to offences under those sections. And they quashed the demonstrators' convictions in the Magistrate's Court (Symon Wong, Esq.) for public place obstruction. The respondent has not cross-appealed against the quashing of those convictions. But the arguments presented on behalf of the respondent in resisting the appeal makes it necessary to examine the inter-relationship between free assembly and public place obstruction. And I will do so in due course.

133. After the demonstrators were arrested they were all taken in police vehicles to a police station. Upon arrival there the police ordered them to alight from the vehicles and enter the station for processing as persons under arrest. Some of the demonstrators complied with that order. But the appellants declined to do so. Instead they remained in a vehicle linking arms, holding on to their seats and chanting slogans. They physically resisted when the police prised them from the vehicle and carried them into the station. So in addition to public place obstruction outside the Liaison Office, all the appellants were charged with obstructing a police officer in the due execution of his duty, contrary to s.36(b) of the Offences Against the Person Ordinance, Cap. 212. And some of them were also charged with assaulting a police officer in the due execution of his duty, contrary to s.63 of the Police Force Ordinance, Cap. 232. The Court of Appeal has quashed the convictions for public place obstructions. So this appeal is against their judgment affirming the convictions for obstructing a police officer in the due execution of his duty and for assaulting a police officer in the due execution of his duty.

Reasonable obstruction

134. The presence of these demonstrators did not prevent persons from passing and re-passing along the pavement in front of the Liaison Office. Nor did it prevent persons from entering or leaving the Liaison Office by its main entrance. But persons passing or re-passing along the pavement might have had to make a detour around the demonstrators. And so might persons entering or leaving the Liaison Office. So the presence of the demonstrators did cause an obstruction. But public place obstruction does not consist of mere obstruction. It consists of unreasonable obstruction in the sense of obstruction that the public cannot reasonably be expected to tolerate. I say so for the following reasons.

135. It is by no means easy to imagine a meaningful assembly, procession or demonstration that would not cause some measure of obstruction in the ordinary sense of the term. What then would happen if it were to be held that people inevitably commit public place obstruction whenever they cause anything that would in common parlance be called an obstruction? The consequence, I think, would be that the freedoms of assembly, procession and demonstration would be unacceptably curtailed.

136. The Irish case of *Lowdens v Keaveney* [1903] 2 IR 82 is instructive. It was decided by the Divisional Court of the Queen's Bench Division of the High Court of Justice in Ireland. Lowdens was the leader of a band which had played political party tunes through the streets of Belfast. He was charged under a statutory provision (14 & 15 Vict. c. 92, s.13) which made it an offence for any person wilfully to prevent or interrupt the free passage of persons or carriages in a public street. The trial magistrates convicted him.

137. But the Divisional Court quashed his conviction. They quashed it because the trial magistrates had omitted to consider whether his user of the street was, under the circumstances, reasonable. Lord O' Brien CJ referred (at p.87) to instances in which "the whole street... may be swept and the greatest physical obstruction caused – traffic brought absolutely to a standstill". The examples which he gave were "the funeral of some distinguished man", "a regiment of soldiers marching along a street, playing a martial air", "some great civic pagent" and "a trades procession [by which] cabs and carriages are brought to a standstill whilst the procession was passing". And he then said:

> "These instances show that taking part in a procession which has caused obstruction in the street and the natural and probable consequence of taking part in which was that obstruction would ensue is not enough to create liability under the statute. There must be something more. What more must there be. What other condition is necessary? This, namely, that the user of the street was an unreasonable one. The necessity for the existence of this condition is obvious, and the law on the subject is clear."

For that last proposition Lord O' Brien CJ cited Sir George Jessel MR's judgment in *Original Hartlepool Collieries Co. v Gibb* (1877) 5 Ch D 713 (a first instance decision concerning a navigable river as a public highway).

138. *Lowdens' s* case was applied by the Court of Criminal Appeal in *R v Clark* (No. 2) [1964] 2 QB 315 (in which Lord Parker CJ said at p.321 that "*Lowdens v Keaveney* is valuable as setting out the true position"). Clark was the field secretary of the Campaign for Nuclear Disarmament. He had been convicted of inciting persons to commit a public nuisance by obstructing the highway in and around Whitehall in the course of a demonstration. His conviction was quashed on the ground that the trial judge had failed to leave to the jury the question of whether or not, granted obstruction, the highway user involved was unreasonable.

139. In *Hirst v Chief Constable of West Yorkshire* (1987) 85 Cr App R 143 two animal rights supporters obstructed free passage along a street while demonstrating outside a furrier's shop. They were convicted of wilfully obstructing free passage along a highway without lawful authority or excuse. Their appeal to the Divisional Court of the Queen's Bench Division succeeded on the ground that the trial magistrates had omitted to consider the question of reasonableness.

140. None of that is to deny that the primary purpose of a highway is 3/4 as the Divisional Court of the Queen's Bench Division held in *Ex parte Lewis* (1888) 21 QBD 191, as the English Court of Appeal held in *Hickman v Maisey* [1900] 1 QB 752 and as the House of Lords held in *Director of Public Prosecutions v Jones* [1999] 2 AC 240— free passage. The police have the important and sometimes difficult duty of preserving such free passage. But highway user does not end with passing or repassing or even with matters incidental thereto. There is more. In *Hague v Committee for Industrial* Organization 307 US 496 (1938) at p.515 Roberts J, in a judgment which enjoyed the concurrence of Black J, said in the United States Supreme Court that:

> "Wherever the title of streets and parks may rest, they have immemorially been held in trust for the use of the public and, time out of mind, have been used for purposes of assembly, communicating thoughts between citizens, and discussing public questions."

This statement including highways among traditional public fora was endorsed (at pp 480–481) in the majority judgment of the United States Supreme Court delivered by O' Connor J in *Frisby v Schultz* 487 US 474 (1987). To these statements made in the United States Supreme Court may be added one made in the High Court of Australia. As Brennan CJ observed in *Levy v Victoria* (1997) 189 CLR 579 at p.594, "actions as well as words can communicate ideas".

141. I am aware that in the Scottish case of *M' Ara v Magistrates of Edinburgh* 1913 SC 1059 decided by the Inner House of the Court of Session some 90 years ago the Lord President (Lord Dunedin) said (at p.1073) that "the right of free speech is a perfectly separate thing from the question of the place where the right is to be exercised". But coming to more recent times, I agree with Lamer CJC's statement in the Supreme Court of Canada in *Committee for the Commonwealth of Canada v Canada* (1991), 77 DLR (4th) 385 at p.394 a–b. He said that "the freedom of expression··· necessarily implies the use of physical space to meet its underlying objectives". And then there is the approach of the European Commission of Human Rights to the inter-relationship between freedom of expression and freedom of assembly. That is dealt with in Lester and Pannick: *Human Rights Law and Practice,* 2nd ed.(2004) at p. 380, para. 4.11.2. There it is said that "[w]here applicants have complained of violations of their right to freedom of expression under art 10 in cases concerning meetings or assemblies, the Commission analysed the complaint in terms of art 11 [on freedom of peaceful assembly and association] being the operative provision, subsuming the right to freedom of expression within it."

142. To that may be added what Hughes CJ said when delivering the opinion of the United States Supreme Court in *De Jonge v Oregon* 299 US 353 (1937). He said (at p.364) that "[t]he right to peaceable assembly is a right cognate to those of free speech and free press and is equally fundamental." Much the same sort of point is made by Prof. Manfred Nowak in his book *UN Covenant on Civil and Political Rights: CCPR Commentary* (1993) at p.370. There he says that "the focus of freedom of assembly is clearly on its democratic function in the process of forming, expressing and implementing political opinions". (Emphasis in the original).

143. From what I have seen of its jurisprudence on freedom of assembly, the United States Supreme Court has tended to give almost extreme illustrations when indicating the degree of interference with free passage along a highway that is to be regarded as unacceptable. Thus in *Schneider v State* 308 US 147 (1939) at pp 160–161 it was put like this in the opinion of the court delivered by Roberts J:

> "Municipal authorities, as trustees for the public, have the duty to keep their communities' streets open and available for movement of people and property, the primary purpose to which the streets are dedicated. So long as legislation to this end does not abridge the constitutional liberty of one rightfully upon the street to impart information through speech or the distribution of literature, it may lawfully regulate the conduct of those using the streets. *For example, a person could not exercise this liberty by taking his stand in the middle of a crowded street, contrary to traffic regulations, and maintain his position to the stoppage of all traffic; a group of distributors could not insist upon a constitutional right to form a cordon across the street and to allow no pedestrian to pass who did not accept a tendered leaflet*; nor does the guarantee of freedom of speech or of the press deprive a municipality of power to enact regulations against throwing literature broadcast in the streets." (Emphasis supplied).

144. The mere fact that an assembly, a procession or a demonstration causes some interference with free passage along a highway does not take away its protection under art. 27 of the Basic Law. In my view, it would not lose such protection unless the interference caused is unreasonable in the sense of exceeding what the public can reasonably be expected to tolerate. As to that, I think that the participants in a large or even massive assembly, procession or demonstration will often be able to say with justification that their point could not be nearly as effectively made by anything on a smaller scale. Subject to this, the most obviously relevant considerations are, I think, how substantial the interference is and how long it lasts. But other considerations can be relevant, too. These include, I think, whether the interference concerned had been recently preceded by another act or other acts of interference on another occasion or other occasions. What the public can reasonably be expected to tolerate is a question of fact and degree. But when answering this question, a court must always remember that preservation of the freedom in full measure defines reasonableness and is not merely a factor in deciding what is reasonable.

145. This approach is, I think, consistent with the one adopted by the Privy Council in *Francis v Chief of Police* [1973] AC 761, a

constitutional appeal from St Christopher, Nevis and Anguilla. The Privy Council's decision in that case was informed by decisions of the courts of Canada (*Roncarelli v Duplessis* (1959) 16 DLR (2d) 689), India (principally *Gopalan v State of Madras* [1950] SCR 88 and *Indulal v The State AIR* (50) (1963) Gujarat 259), Pakistan (*Safdar v Province of West Pakistan* (1964) 16 All Pak LD (Lahore) 718) and the United States (including the cases of *Saia v New York* 334 US 588 (1948) and *Kovacs v Cooper* 336 US 77 (1949) which appear to be in conflict).

146. Francis had used a loudspeaker at a public meeting without having obtained permission from the Chief of Police to do so. A local statute made it an offence to use any "noisy instrument" at a public meeting or procession without such permission. Did that requirement of permission contravene the guarantee of freedom of communication conferred by s.10 of the St Christopher, Nevis and Anguilla Constitution? The Privy Council declined to strike down the requirement but limited its operation. Delivering their Lordships' advice, Lord Pearson said this (at pp 772H–773A):

> "Whatever may be the exact construction of section 10, it must be clear that (1) a wrongful refusal of permission to use a loudspeaker at a public meeting (for instance if the refusal is inspired by political partiality) would be an unjustified and therefore unconstitutional interference with freedom of communication, because it would restrict the range of communication, and (2) some regulation of the use of loudspeakers is required in order that citizens who do not wish to hear what is said may be protected against 'aural aggression' if that might reach unbearable intensity."(Emphasis supplied).

147. The law calls upon ordinary highway users to accommodate demonstrators' freedom to demonstrate by tolerating some interference with their own right to pass and repass along the highway. They are expected to show such tolerance even if they do not sympathise with the demonstrators' cause. Hopefully they will do so with patience born of the sentiment expressed in the English Court of Appeal in *R v Home Secretary, ex parte O' Brien* [1923] 2 KB 361. There Scrutton LJ famously said (at p.382) that "[i]t is indeed one test of belief in principles if you apply them to cases with which you have no sympathy at all".

148. Then there is the other side of the coin. The law also calls upon demonstrators to accommodate other people's rights, especially ordinary highway users' right of free passage. For that purpose demonstrators have to tolerate some interference with their own freedom to demonstrate. Such tolerance is expected of demonstrators however strongly they may feel about their cause. Hopefully they will understand the point made by John Stuart Mill in his timeless essay *On Liberty* (1859). He wrote — I take it from p.72 of ISBN 1–85715–081–3 — that "[a]s soon as any part of a person's conduct affects prejudicially the interests of others, society has jurisdiction over it, and the question whether the general welfare will or will not be promoted by interfering with it, becomes open to discussion."

149. Having looked at both sides of that coin, one is reminded of what the Privy Council said in *Attorney General v Lee Kwong-kut* [1993] AC 951 at p.975 C–D and we repeated in the mandatory life sentence case of *Lau Cheong v HKSAR* (2002) 5 HKCFAR 415 at p.449 D–E. This is that the courts often are required "to maintain the balance between the individual and the society as a whole".

Powers of arrest

150. Section 50(1) of the Police Force Ordinance, Cap. 232, says:

> "It shall be lawful for any police officer to apprehend any person who he reasonably believes will be charged with or whom he reasonably suspects of being guilty of –
>
> (a) any offence for which the sentence is fixed by law or for which a person may (on a first conviction for that offence) be sentenced to imprisonment; or
>
> (b) any offence; if it appears to the police officer that service of a summons is impracticable because –
>
> (i) the name of the person is unknown to, and cannot readily be ascertained by, the police officer;
>
> (ii) the police officer has reasonable grounds for doubting whether a name given by the person as his name is his real name;
>
> (iii) the person has failed to give a satisfactory address for service; or
>
> (iv) the police officer has reasonable grounds for doubting whether an address given by the person is a satisfactory address for service."

151. To be constitutional those powers of arrest have to be read in a sense consistent with freedom of the person and freedom from arbitrary arrest, both guaranteed by art. 28 of the Basic Law. Read literally s.50 appears to consist of two discrete bases for arrest: one being reasonable belief that a person will be charged with an offence and the other being reasonable suspicion that he is guilty of an offence. But it would be sinister if a police officer reasonably believed that a person would be charged with an offence even though he did not reasonably suspect him of being guilty of it. I cannot imagine that any right-thinking police officer would wish to effect an arrest in that state of mind. Section 50(1) must therefore be read as requiring reasonable suspicion of guilt. Of course the fact that a person is eventually acquitted of an offence does not necessarily mean that the police officer who arrested him for that offence could not have reasonably suspected him of being guilty of it.

Reasonable suspicion of an unreasonable obstruction

152. As I have noted, pedestrians might have had to make a detour past these demonstrators. Was the presence of these demonstrators open to a reasonable suspicion of amounting to an unreasonable obstruction? "Yes" argued the respondent's first leader Mr Gerard McCoy SC. Ably as always, he urged everything that can possibly be put forward in support of that argument. But he properly volunteered a concession. He conceded that not every gathering of demonstrators at the spot in question would have been open to a reasonable suspicion of amounting to an unreasonable obstruction. For example, he said, a gathering of two elderly ladies could not possibly be open to such a suspicion.

153. Whereupon Mr Paul Harris for the appellants pertinently pointed to a counter-proposal made to the police's proposal that the demonstrators move to a nearby spot. This counter-proposal was that the four hunger strikers be permitted to remain for three days where they were. The respondent's second leader Mr Kevin Zervos SC properly conceded that a hunger strike is a legitimate form of demonstration. Demonstrators naturally want their demonstration to make an impact. And the hunger strikes that make an impact tend to be ones lasting at least a few days. Each of them sitting peaceably on the ground in the lotus position, these four hunger strikers were positioned side-by-side

and close together. I see no material difference between such a gathering and the one in Mr McCoy's example of two elderly ladies. And I do not think that it would be right to ignore the counter-proposal when deciding whether this demonstration was open to a reasonable suspicion of amounting to an unreasonable obstruction. But even if the counter-proposal were ignored, I would still be of the view that this demonstration was not open to such a suspicion.

154. Albeit wrongly, the magistrate found the demonstrators guilty of public place obstruction. Not surprisingly therefore, he did not consider the question of whether, although they were not guilty, the arresting officers nevertheless reasonably suspected that they were. Having quashed the public place obstruction convictions, the Court of Appeal had to answer that question. They had to do so in order to deal with the other convictions. For it was an essential ingredient of the other offences that the police officers concerned were acting in the due execution of their duty. They would be if, but only if, the arrests for public place obstruction were lawful. And those arrests would be lawful if, but only if, the arresting officers reasonably suspected that the demonstrators were guilty of public place obstruction.

155. Taking a view which I feel unable to share, Woo VP said that "there can be no nexus between the arrests of the appellants by the police on the pavement outside 160 Connaught Road West and the conduct of the appellants after the vehicle carrying them arrived at the Western Police Station". So he omitted to consider whether the arresting officers reasonably suspected that the demonstrators were guilty of public place obstruction. Regrettably therefore, we do not have the benefit of his views on the question of reasonable suspicion.

156. Chief Judge Ma thought that there was a basis for reasonable suspicion. It is clear that he thought that Superintendent Chiu and Senior Inspector Wong had such suspicion. The superintendent gave the order to arrest, and the chief inspector communicated it to the arresting officers i.e. those who physically executed the arrests. Although he did not say so in terms, I think that the Chief Judge should be understood to have thought that the arresting officers, too, reasonably suspected that the demonstrators were guilty of public place obstruction.

157. Mr Justice Stock JA said: "I do not accept that such suspicion as the Superintendent may have nursed that a public place obstruction offence had been committed was reasonably based". Later on in his judgment Stock JA said:

> "We have not been taken to the evidence of the officers named in charges 3 to 6 (charge 7 did not involve an arresting officer) as part of any attempt to demonstrate that they could not have harboured the requisite state of mind. Indeed, we do not have the transcript of the testimony of Inspector. Ho (charge 3) or of WPC Wong (charges 4 and 5), but only of WPC Chan (charge 6) and Inspector Chan (charge 7). In so far as it seems clear that the magistrate did address the question of the states of mind of the arresting officers, it seems to me to be difficult for the appellants to demonstrate, without reference to the effect of their testimony that his conclusion was erroneous."

Now the immediate problem with that is this. The magistrate did not consider the question of whether, although the demonstrators were not guilty of public place obstruction, the arresting officers nevertheless reasonably suspected that they were. And even if the magistrate had considered that question, the Court of Appeal were in as good a position as he was to decide the objective element of the question i.e. the reasonableness of the suspicion. So the Court of Appeal should have considered that element afresh. They should have done so by examining all the material evidence. That task is now for us to perform.

158. Still later on in his judgment Stock JA dealt with the briefings which the arresting officers had received and with the conduct of the two witnesses the transcript of whose testimony the Court of Appeal did not have, saying:

> "I think that it can reasonably be said that an officer who is given a briefing that an obstruction has taken place, and is told that those who were obstructing and still in situ, and then himself or herself sees persons fitting the description of the described group actually occupying the described place has reasonable, even if mistaken, grounds for suspecting the earlier commission of the offence. It must follow from this that the conduct of Inspector Ho who was party to the arrests and of WPC Wong in effecting arrests was lawful; and it is. therefore difficult to conclude other than that their conduct in taking the appellants to the police station, and in removing them from the van, was other than conduct in the lawful execution of their duty."

We have the transcript of those two witnesses' testimony. And their testimony does not advance the respondent's case beyond the point to which the other evidence takes it.

159. Section 50(1) of the Police Force Ordinance is to be described in the way in which Lord Steyn described s.12(1) of the Prevention of Terrorism (Temporary Provisions) Act 1984 in *O' Hara v Chief Constable of the Royal Ulster Constabulary* [1997] AC 286. In a speech with which Lords Goff of Chieveley, Mustill and Hoffmann agreed while also agreeing with Lord Hope of Craighead's speech, Lord Steyn said (at p.292F) that "... section 12(1), and similar provisions ··· categorise as reasonable grounds for suspicion only matters present in the mind of the [arresting officer]".

160. I would not attempt an exhaustive definition of arresting officer. But I think that this much can be said. Essentially an arresting officer is the one who takes an accused into custody by conduct such as, typically, laying hands on him. But it can be by conduct such as pointing a weapon at him. Indeed it can be by conduct such as directing a verbal command at him backed by an obvious preparedness to use physical force if necessary.

161. Constitutionally and obviously, s.50(1A) of the Police Force Ordinance states that a police officer may exercise his power to apprehend a person under subsection (1) "whether or not he has seen any offence committed". I call that obvious because it is inherent in the concept of reasonable suspicion. Reasonable suspicion can be — and I expect usually is — generated by information. Both in the House of Lords and in the European Court of Human Rights (where it is constituted as *O' Hara v United Kingdom* [2002] 34 EHRR 32), *O' Hara' s* case was treated as one of reasonable suspicion generated by information.

162. What information or assessment given to him at a briefing would suffice to generate reasonable suspicion in an arresting officer's mind must depend on the circumstances of each case. Suppose a briefing fails to generate a reasonable suspicion in an arresting officer's mind. Even so, it can happen that the situation that he finds at the scene of arrest will, on its own or together with the briefing, generate such a suspicion. Conversely it can happen that a reasonable suspicion generated in an arresting

officer's mind by a briefing will be dispelled by the situation that he finds at the scene.

163. There is no evidence that the briefings in the present case dealt adequately if at all with the element of reasonableness. Those briefings suffice for a conclusion that the arresting officers formed a reasonable suspicion that the demonstration amounted to an obstruction. But they do not suffice for a conclusion that the arresting officers formed a reasonable suspicion of an unreasonable obstruction. And the evidence as to the situation which these arresting officers found at the scene of arrest does not reveal a situation capable of causing or contributing to a reasonable suspicion of an unreasonable obstruction. Indeed the situation was more apt to dispel any suspicion of an unreasonable obstruction. The being so, the arrests of the demonstrators were unlawful.

164. I have every sympathy for all the police officers in this case. But I do not feel able to say that they were acting in the due execution of their duty. That being so, the convictions for obstructing a police officer in the due execution of his duty and for assaulting a police officer in the due execution of his duty cannot stand. It is unnecessary to consider whether, on the charge of obstructing a police officer in the due execution of his duty, the appellants would in any event have a defence on the basis that they were innocent demonstrators merely resuming the exercise of their freedom of demonstration.

Substitution

165. In regard to the convictions for assaulting a police officer in the due execution of his duty, there remains the question of substituting convictions for common assault. But the problem with such a course is this. There was never any focus at the trial on the question of common assault. Defence counsel's efforts were concentrated on the issue of whether the police officers were acting in the due execution of their duty. The material evidence was not as clear as it might have been. Substitution is more naturally within the province of an intermediate appellate court than a final appellate court. And we do not have the benefit of the Court of Appeal's opinion on substitution in the present case. All things considered, I do not think that it would be appropriate for us to order substitution now.

Delay

166. The appellants succeed without having to rely on their complaint of delay developed in a balanced argument which Mr Philip Dykes SC presented and Mr Harris adopted. So all that I would say about delay is this. A heavy workload can make delay difficult to avoid. So can other factors. Even so, it always remains important to give judgment expeditiously. I agree with what the other members of the Court say in this connection.

Conclusion

167. For the foregoing reasons, I would allow the appeal to quash all the convictions without substituting any other conviction. As to costs, I agree with the other members of the Court.

168. While justice to the appellants requires the quashing of their convictions without any substitution, justice to the police officers involved in this case requires this acknowledgement. They were, as police officers so often are, confronted with an extremely difficult situation. Far from deserving any criticism, they deserve praise for the patience and restraint with which they conducted themselves.

Chief Justice Li:

169. The Court unanimously allows the appeal. The costs of this appeal are to be paid by the respondent to the appellants with an order for legal aid taxation of the costs of those appellants who are on legal aid. In relation to the costs in the courts below, the parties are at liberty to make any necessary application in writing to this Court.

Chief Justice (Andrew Li)

Permanent Judge (Kemal Bokhary)

Permanent Judge (Patrick Chan)

Permanent Judge (R A V Ribeiro)

Non-Permanent Judge (Sir Anthony Mason)

Mr Philip Dykes SC and Mr Paul Harris (instructed by Messrs Ho, Tse, Wai & Partners, assigned by the Legal Aid Department) for the 4th, 5th, 6th and 8th appellants

Mr Paul Harris and Mr Cheung Yiu Leung (instructed by Messrs Ho, Tse, Wai & Partners) for the 1st, 2nd, 3rd and 7th appellants

Mr Gerard McCoy SC (instructed by the Department of Justice), Mr Kevin P Zervos SC and Mr Robert KY Lee (of that Department) for the respondent

---

Wong Yeung Ng v. The Secretary For Justice

律政司司長 對 東方報業集團有限公司等

HCMP 407/1998；CACV 161/1998；FAMC 8/1999

簡略案情

被告人等對於一宗關於淫褻物品審裁處的裁定和一宗與《蘋果日報》的訴訟的裁決感到不滿，遂針對相關審理的高等法院上訴法庭法官進行"狗仔隊"式廿四小時跟蹤採訪、並發表大量批評文章，甚至侮辱司法機關和法官。律政司司長遂以藐視法庭罪中醜化司法機關罪行，起訴相關報社、編輯及其主要負責人。

在審訊過程中，被告提出普通法的"醜化法庭罪"，違反《基本法》第 27 條有關言論自由的規定，以及抵觸了《香港人權法案》。然而，法庭認為該條規定的言論自由並非絕對，《基本法》第 27 條中"居民的基本權利和義務"，應被視為《基本法》所要保障的一系列基本權利和自由，但並不表示不能制定法律對這些權利和自由進行限制。《基本法》第 39 條的作用，正是確保這些限制權利和自由的法律，並不違反各個國際公約的規定。最後，法庭裁定報社的行為構成普通法定義下的醜化法庭罪，判處報社罰款港幣五百萬和該社編輯、即第六被告人 Wong Yeung Ng，即時入獄 4 個月。第六被告人對判罪與判刑皆提出上訴。

裁決摘要

上訴人認為除非其行為對法院秉承公義的責任引起實質、嚴重和即時的影響，上訴人的言論和出版自由並不應該受到限制，而上訴人在本案中的行為並不構成這種危險。

可是，上訴庭卻同意原審法官的看法，同意上訴人的行為會降低公眾對司法機關執行公義的信心，認定此等明顯的行為極其嚴重，目的只是希望將來在法庭的審理中得到優待，以所謂的公眾輿論要脅法庭。

上訴庭進一步指出，如果為了達到一個合法的目的，比如彰顯公義，《基本法》第 27 條及《香港人權法案》第 16 條所賦予的言論和出版自由是可以受到限制的。據此，該上訴被駁回。

CACV 161A/1998

IN THE HIGH COURT OF THE HONG KONG SPECIAL ADMINISTRATIVE REGION COURT OF APPEAL

1998, No. 161 (Civil)

Between:

Wong Yeung Ng	Applicant
- and -	
The Secretary For Justice	Defendant

Coram: Mortimer V-P, Mayo and Leong JJA in Court

Dates of Hearing: 1-3 December 1998

Date of handing down Judgment: 9 February 1999

JUDGMENT

Mortimer V-P: On 23 June 1998 the appellant, Wong Yeung Ng, was convicted of two contempts of court and sentenced to a total of 4 months imprisonment by a Divisional Court (Chan CJHC and Keith J). At the time of the contempts, the appellant was editor of the *Oriental Daily News*. The Oriental Press Group Ltd, a public listed company, is the de facto owner publisher and controller of the *Oriental Daily News*. The Oriental Press Group was also convicted and fined $5m but does not appeal.

The Amended Notice of Motion were that the appellant, the Oriental Press Group and others (who were acquitted) committed contempts of court:

> "(a) by seeking to threaten, harass and/or intimidate Godfrey JA during 13, 14 and 15 January 1998 (by having him pursued by their employees and/or agents and/or others) in order to influence his future judicial decisions, all by reason of a judgment which he had previously delivered, thereby wrongfully interfering with the administration of justice, and
>
> (b) in printing, publishing or instigation such printing or publishing the articles, considered in isolation and considered cumulatively, as set forth in the copy <u>Amended</u> statement ('the <u>Amended</u> Statement') served herewith used on the application for leave to issue this Notice of Motion, in the issues of the Oriental Daily News on 11 December 1997, 12 December 1997, 13 December 1997, 15 December 1997, 12 January 1998 and 13 January 1998 upon the grounds set forth in the <u>Amended</u> Statement."

The contempt alleged in (a) became known below on "the pursuit of Godfrey JA' and (b) as "scandalising the court".

In each case it was said that the conduct of the defendants had interfered with the due administration of justice as a continuing process. It was not suggested that any attempt was made to influence the outcome of particular proceedings either pending or in progress.

Further, to avoid repetition, interference with the administration of justice as a continuing process may take many forms which include diminishing the authority of the court, bringing the count into disrepute and reducing public confidence in the system.

The appellant and the Oriental Daily News

The *Oriental Daily News* is the most popular daily newspaper in Hong Kong with 2.3 million readers and 53% of the vibrant newspaper market. It is obviously influential.

The appellant was the editor of the *Oriental Daily News* at the time of the events complained of and he was fully responsible for them.

The background

The second contempt was the first in time. Re–acting to adverse decisions of the court and the Obscene Articles Tribunal, prolonged attacks were made upon the judiciary and the court. The Divisional Court described the articles as follows:

> "Apart from being abusive, offensive and scurrilous, the remarks contained racial slurs. There can hardly be any justification or basis for such remarks in what members of the OAT and the judges did and there was nothing in the article purporting to explain why they should be given such descriptions. These remarks were neither rational nor reasonable. Secondly, the article impugned the integrity of the judges and members of the OAT. Thirdly, what was said in the last two paragraphs of the article amounted to a threat to members of the OAT and the judges. The phrase 'to wipe you all out', coupled with the warning in the last sentence at the end of the article, particularly when they were repeated in English, strongly smack of a threat to do something harmful or unpleasant to members of the OAT and the judges."

Mr Sydney Kentridge QC, who appears for the appellant, has no quarrel with that description. In his submissions he did not seek to minimise the offensiveness of the articles which he described as "shocking, reprehensible and greatly to be deprecated".

By the first alleged contempt, the Oriental Press Group and the appellant sought to punish Godfrey JA for a judgment he had delivered by having him beset and pursued round–the–clock by numbers of their reporters and photographers.

The Faye Wong case

These contempts followed two cases before the Hong Kong courts. In the first, known as the *Faye Wong* case, a photograph of the singer was taken by an Oriental Daily News reporter at Beijing Airport without her consent. She was pregnant. The photograph was published on the front cover of the *Sunday Weekly* published by Oriental Sunday Publisher Ltd, a subsidiary of the Oriental Press Group. *Apple Daily*, a competitor, published the front page including the photograph. The Oriental Press Group and the publisher brought an action for breach of copyright. Rogers J (as he then was) awarded them $8,001 damages but on the basis of a previous offer he ordered them to pay *Apple Daily's* costs.

The Oriental Press Group and the publisher appealed. On 19 September 1997 the Court of Appeal dismissed the appeal on damages and later varied the order for costs by making no order for costs below, but ordering the Oriental Press Group and the publisher to pay two–thirds of the costs of the appeal.

Godfrey JA delivered the judgment of the court, towards the end of which are some obiter remarks upon the privacy of public figures:

"Public sentiment has turned, or seems to be turning, against those who are guilty of invasion of the privacy of public figures by taking their photographs for large sums which reflect the cupidity of the publishers and the prurience of their readers. The time may come when, if the legislature does not step in first, the court may have to intervene in this field (as Lord Bingham of Cornhill, LCJ, has recently suggested in England); for example, by holding that the protection of copyright will not be extended to photographs of public figures taken on private occasions without their consent."

On 8 January 1998 the same court refused an application by the Oriental Press Group and the publisher for leave to appeal to the Court of Final Appeal. The case had progressed no further at the time of the contempts.

The obscene articles case

The second case involved the Obscene Articles Tribunal (OAT). In June 1996 the *Oriental Daily News* published several photographs of women in the nude. These photographs were classified as indecent by the OAT. The same photographs were published in another local Chinese newspaper and were similarly classified. The other newspaper successfully appealed but the case was remitted to the OAT who again classified the photographs as indecent.

The publisher of the *Oriental Daily News* also appealed to the High Court. This was dismissed. On 28 October 1997 a further appeal to a court differently constituted to that in the *Faye Wong* case dismissed the appeal. The court accepted the publisher's submission that the OAT was obliged to give reasons but held that those given were sufficient. On 10 December 1997 the Court of Appeal refused the publisher's leave to appeal to the Court of Final Appeal. That is as far as the second case had progressed before the contempts.

The earlier articles

There were earlier articles before those complained of on the same subject matter. The Divisional Court thought "they set the tone for what was to come". The first of these on 22 September 1997, a few days after the Court of Appeal had dismissed the Oriental Press Group's appeal in the copyright case. Apart from arguing that Godfrey JA's judgment was in error, it wrongly suggested that the judge equated the photographer of Faye Wong with *paparazzi* who pursued Princess Diana. There were extravagant personal attacks on the judge who was described variously as "ignorant, unreasonable, ridiculous, arbitrary, prejudicial and arrogant". It was said that the Judiciary were unfair to the Oriental Press Group and that since 1995 the British-Hong Kong Government had intensified its persecution of the Oriental Press Group through the police and the Obscene Articles Tribunal.

On 30 October 1997, two days after the newspaper's appeal had been dismissed in the obscene articles case, the Oriental Daily News published a special feature – "Special Page on the Denouncement of the Tribunal". Earlier cases were described and hostility, persecution and discrimination by the Tribunal against the Oriental Press Group was alleged.

The next day, 31 October 1997, several pages of photographs were published with short articles. Included were photographs previously classified as indecent in respect of which appeals to the court had failed. As the Divisional Court said,

"The re-publication of these photographs was nothing less than a defiance of the court's decision and a challenge to the rule of law".

The articles from 1–7 November focused on the Obscene Articles Tribunal. The names of the 157 members were published and they were generally reviled. For example, they were described as "scumbags".

On 10 November 1997, with increasing enthusiasm an article described the members of the Tribunal variously "dogs and bitches", "tortoises having retreated into their shells", "having to run for cover like a rat in the gutter", "scumbags", "public enemy of freedom of the press and a public calamity to the six million citizens" (of Hong Kong).

On 9 December 1997 the Court of Appeal set aside the costs order of Rogers J. On 10 December, another division refused leave to appeal to the Court of Final Appeal in the obscene articles case. These events "rekindled the fire ..." and led to a series of articles between 11 December 1997 and 15 December 1997, the subject of complaint.

The articles complained of

I gratefully accept the Divisional Court's unchallenged account of these articles, the impact of which can only be appreciated if set out in detail:

"(1) <u>11th December 1997</u>. On that day, two articles were published in the *Oriental Daily News*. The first article was published in the Kung Fu Tea column with the heading: 'The Swinish White-skinned Judges and the Canine Yellow-skinned Tribunal'. The article criticised the OAT and the two judges, namely, Rogers J and Godfrey JA for attacking the Oriental Press Group. The OAT and its members were described as 'mangy yellow-skinned dogs' which wrongly accused the Group of publishing indecent and obscene articles. The two judges were described as 'British white ghosts' and 'white-skinned judges' or 'pigs' who deliberately ruled against the Oriental Press Group resulting in it having to incur huge legal costs to pursue its actions. Towards the end of the article, there were the following passages:

'Oriental does not care if you are yellow-skinned or white or a pig or a dog. In our self-defence, we are determined to wipe you all out!

Here, Kung Fu Tea warns the pigs and dogs: don't you bother me again. Otherwise, when I counterattack in self-defence, you will regret it exceedingly – *you will regret it! I repeat: you will regret it very much!*'

The article was written in Chinese but the latter part of the last sentence quoted above was expressed in English which is commonly used as or understood to mean a spiteful warning.

Apart from being abusive, offensive and scurrilous, the remarks contained racial slurs. There can hardly be any justification or basis for such remarks in what members of the OAT and the judges did and there was nothing in the article purporting to explain why they should be given such descriptions. These remarks were neither rational nor reasonable. Secondly, the article impugned the integrity of the judges and members of the OAT. Thirdly, what was said in the last two paragraphs of the article amounted to a threat to members of the OAT and the judges. The phrase 'to wipe you all out', coupled with the warning in the last sentence at the end of the article, particularly when they were repeated in English, strongly smack of a threat to do something harmful or unpleasant to members of the OAT and the judges. It must be borne in mind that the newspaper had in an earlier article published all the names of the OAT members. While judges are professional and experienced persons, members of the OAT are laymen. Even if judges may not treat such warnings seriously, the effect on lay members of the OAT who are performing a public function as part of the administration of justice could be quite intimidating.

Another article which was published on the same day was entitled 'Rogers' Despicableness and Godfrey's Derangement'. It was written by the newspaper's commentators. The article criticised the decisions of Rogers J and Godfrey JA in the copyright case. It alleged that Rogers J had deliberately ruled against the Oriental Press Group and was guilty of 'such a despicable act of abstract confirmation and concrete negation by way of double dealings (which) has always been characteristic of British politicians.'It also contained the following passages:

> 'The crux of the problem is that there exists in the Hong Kong judicial sector a bloc of colonial remnants. They harbour animosity towards Oriental.
>
> The Obscene Articles Tribunal is attached to the judiciary system. It is merely a tail-wagging dog outside the judiciary. All of the adjudicators kept by the Tribunal are stupid men and women who suffer from congenital mental retardation and have no common knowledge worth mentioning.
>
> The Obscene Articles Tribunal is the main culprit in wronging Oriental. We have the name list of those ignorant adjudicators, and we will punish them on just grounds. The masters of those yellow-skinned canine adjudicators are none other than the likes of Rogers and Godfrey, the sheltering and condoning judicial scumbags and evil remnants of the British Hong Kong Government.
>
> After 1st July, they have continued to occupy their stolen prominent places in the judicial sector. They, together with the vicious yellow-skinned adjudicators, have methodically attacked, harassed, and persecuted the publications under the Oriental News Group.
>
> Here, we solemnly issue a warning: irrespective of race and status, effective action to restore full righteousness will be taken against those scumbags and demons who oppress freedom of the press.'

There was hardly any rational discussion in these articles. It can be seen that the abusive and scurrilous attacks were intensified and the racial slurs were repeated. The status of the OAT was depreciated and its members were insulted. The repute of the judges was smeared and their integrity cast into doubt. They were accused of having deliberately abused their position for illicit motives. Members of the OAT were also threatened that their names were in the hands of the newspaper and that they would be 'punished'.

(2) 12th December 1997. There was an article written in the Kung Fu Tea column on that day. It was entitled 'Readers voiced their support in slapping canine adjudicators'. This article claimed to have received many phone calls and letters of support from their readers. It referred to 'the Kung Fu Tea (having) stripped off (the judges') wigs and trampled them underfoot, and has also separated their flesh from their bones and boiled them in a soup'. The article also quoted a letter from a reader called Mr Leung. It quoted from the letter as follows:

> 'Capitalising on the pre-eminent status, the justices treat the law as a game. They can wreak whatever havoc they like, and they complacently dare anyone who has the courage to challenge them. *Oriental Daily News* has given them a sound tongue-lashing. ... Someone has had the courage to pull off the tiger's whiskers and remove the dragon's scales. ... Someone has torn off their designer briefs that conceal their deficiencies and expose the ringworm, scabies and syphilis that they have hidden under their solemn black gowns.'

The article also referred to the judges and members of the OAT as having 'become street rats who are being spat on and cursed everyday.'

It is quite clear that the article adopted the contents of the reader's letter by quoting them verbatim. If there were indeed such letters from readers, as the newspaper claimed, the campaign had apparently taken effect on the public confidence in the administration of justice. The language used was increasingly vulgar and the threat on the judges and members of the OAT was most vivid and alarming.

(3) 13th December 1997. The next article was published on 13th December 1997 which was shortly after the Court of Appeal refused leave to appeal to the Court of Final Appeal in relation to the OAT case. The article criticised the decision of the Court of Appeal in refusing leave. It also alleged that the judges of the Court of Appeal were prejudiced against the Oriental Daily Group and sided with the OAT to harm them.

(4) 15th December 1997. On that day, the newspaper published another article in the Kung Fu Tea column in response to a report in the *South China Morning Post* written 2 days previously saying that the Judiciary and the Department of Justice were considering prosecuting the *Oriental Daily News* for spreading racism in its articles. The article purported to justify the allegations which the newspaper had previously made. It accused Rogers J of having shown animosity to and deliberately attacked the Oriental Press Group and Godfrey JA of showing prejudice against them. However it went further and said:

> 'All of the charges were unwarranted and aimed at letting out anger at Oriental's refusal to obey British Hong Kong Government and its insisting independence in the operation of its newspaper.
>
> The Tribunal became an implement used by the British Hong Kong Government to attack political

dissidents. It persecuted Oriental unceasingly. Following his assumption of office, Chris Patten attempted to rope Oriental in and turn it into his political tool, but Oriental rejected him. He nursed hatred in his heart and directed various Government departments to harass and provoke Oriental non-stop!

After 1st July, Hong Kong is PRC territory, but centipedes remained supple after death. Having left the corpse of the colonial government, the ferocious demons in the form of the Tribunal and the justices have resettled in the body of the SAR Government. As before, they treat Oriental viciously. The verdicts of the *Faye Wong* case and that concerning the three photographs were passed after the transfer of sovereignty on 1st July, which, in turn, indicates that even though Hong Kong has become PRC territory, the demons are still careering frantically and are very active. Under the SAR Government and Chief Executive Tung Chee-hwa, the demons carry on the British Hong Kong authorities' unfinished business and continued to let out the anger on Oriental.

Last week, the likes of Rogers and Godfrey were soundly and righteously denounced by Kung Fu Tea. Oriental treats all evil influences equal. We will absolutely not administer lighter blows on white-skinned pigs while hating Chinese yellow-skinned dogs more. In our counterattack of self-defence, we strike heavy blows and do not care if they are officials or not!

After the handover of sovereignty on 1st July and under the SAR Government and Tung Chee-hwa administration, those white skinned pigs and yellow-skinned dogs who are evil remnants of the former government have not ceased their attack of Oriental.'

The allegation of animosity and bias was again repeated. The abusive, offensive and scurrilous attacks with their racial slurs persisted. The OAT and the judges were accused of having continued the persecution of the Oriental Press Group which was begun by the former Governor. They were alleged to have been the instruments of political persecution of the British Hong Kong Government and perpetrated such persecution by their decisions and judgments. They had a political motive to serve while they were discharging their judicial duty."

After the Court of Appeal refused leave to appeal to the Court of Final Appeal in the *Faye Wong* case, on 8 January 1998 an article appeared in the Oriental Daily News under a heading containing the words "...the Judiciary Contravenes Society's Laws and Principles; Oriental Is Prepared to Sacrifice Everything in the Final Battle". The article contained the following passages:

"For years, the Oriental Press Group was subjected to the methodical political persecution inflicted by the Hong Kong judiciary system that was manipulated by the former colonial Government. Such persecution had a long history. The so-called Obscene Articles Tribunal, which was under the Judiciary, harassed Oriental repeatedly.

Oriental has spared no efforts in destroying the public authority of the so-called Obscene Articles Tribunal. Its image has been torn to shreds, and it is on the verge of disintegration and extinction. Each of the so-called adjudicators has become a public enemy like a street rat.

Although the Tribunal, which is under the Judiciary, has collapsed entirely, High Court and Court of Appeal judges like Rogers and Godfrey and certain yellow-skinned judges of Chinese descent have continued to exercise their political role of persecuting Oriental. Personalities at increasingly senior levels are involved, and the extent has broadened. What is especially adverse is that such a form of political persecution has not terminated with Hong Kong's reversion to Chinese rule upon 1st July 1997. Very much the opposite, the Hong Kong SAR Government under the People's Republic of China has adopted a condoning attitude and given the Judiciary system that has sheltered a large number of evil remnants of the former Government a free hand in persecuting Oriental endlessly. More blatantly than ever, they have passed sentence after sentence that is tinged with prejudice and indifferent to public righteousness.

The Tribunal and the Justices followed in the footsteps of the political influences that were persecuting Oriental. The Judiciary of the Hong Kong SAR is a member of the political bloc that persecutes Oriental. The judicial measures it has employed after 1st July 1997 to continue to attack Oriental are part of the entire operation.

It was at that time that the so-called Obscene Articles Tribunal started to harass Oriental nonstop. After the transfer of Hong Kong's sovereignty to China on 1st July last year, the despicable role of persecuting Oriental has been formally assumed by judges of the High Court and the Court of Appeal. They have inherited the mantle of that role and taken up the unfinished anti-Oriental historical mission of Ford the racist and Patten the colonial governor.

Under the SAR administration, the biased attitude of the Hong Kong judicial system has remained unchanged and even intensified. They do not restrain themselves from treating Oriental unfairly, and they are getting increasingly extreme.

We are utterly disgusted with the incessant persecution dealt out by the HKSAR Judiciary, and our toleration is quite limited.

To staunchly defend the truth, we are determined to fight to the last bullet to wipe out the enemy and defend ourselves."

The effect of the articles

The meaning is clear. For the reasons set out, it was said the Oriental Press Group was the target of a biased Judiciary which was pursuing a conspiracy of political persecution started under the former colonial government. The Oriental Press Group had destroyed the authority of the Obscene Articles Tribunal and would now attack the Judiciary in every possible way in order to destroy its authority.

As the Divisional Court pointed out, the last article was a preclude to the harassment of Godfrey JA. On 13 January 1998, the next day, a number of articles on the subject repeated the earlier (erroneous) allegation that Godfrey JA had accused the taker of the Faye Wong photographer of being a *paparazzo* and announced that it would begin a pursuit of the judge. It described what later happened.

A team of reporters started to pursue the judge around the clock in his daily life. He was advised in the newspaper not "to take any false steps". Photographs and articles appeared the next day detailing the judge's movements to and from court, the cases in which he was involved and the times when he left the court building and returned at lunch time. Brief extracts of dialogue with the judge were reported together with descriptions of his composure.

Other media organisations were invited to send their reporters to join in. They came to report the event. The operation continued on 14 and 15 January 1998, accompanied by articles. But on 15 January 1998 an editorial repeated the conspiracy allegations but said that the operation had achieved its purpose of educating Godfrey JA upon the meaning of *paparazzi* and therefore the operation would cease at midnight. It did.

The motive

The avowed purpose of the harassment was to educate Godfrey JA but the nature of the articles written before, during and after the pursuit and the times of some compared with the progress of the cases demonstrated otherwise. Consequently the Divisional Court found that the real purpose of the "pursuit" was to take revenge for the court's decision against the Oriental Press Group and punish the judge for his decision. Put more bluntly it was "to teach the judge a lesson" for finding against the Oriental Press Group in the *Faye Wong* case.

I note in passing that the judicial process in neither the *Faye Wong* case nor the Obscene Articles Tribunal was then complete. Later, leave to appeal was granted by the Court of Final Appeal in each, and in due course, both appeals were allowed.

The Divisional Court's decision

The Divisional Court found the appellant guilty of both contempts. The second (but first in time) was for scandalising the court and thereby undermining public confidence in the administration of justice by publishing the articles between 11 December 1997 and 12 January 1998. It found that there was "a real risk" that the articles complained of would undermine confidence in the administration of justice in the minds of "at least some of the persons who were likely to have become aware of the particulars of the acts complained of".

The second was for interfering with the administration of justice as a continuing process. This concerns the pursuit of Godfrey JA and the light thrown upon it by the accompanying articles. Again, the court held that the pursuit of Godfrey JA constituted a real risk that the administration of justice as a continuing process would be interfered with in the sense that public confidence in its due administration would be undermined. Indeed, the court decided that there was "a very real likelihood" of this. It added that there was no risk that the administration of justice would be actually affected but some of the readership would think it a possibility and that if tolerated, the conduct would give rise to the misconception that such conduct by a losing party to litigation is permissible.

Arguments that these offences were incompatible with both the Bill of Rights Ordinance (Cap. 383) and the Basic Law were rejected.

Scandalising the court – the appellant's case

In *Secretary of State for Defence v Guardian Newspaper Ltd* [1985] AC 339, 347A Lord Diplock was of the opinion that contempt for publishing material which scandalises the court was "virtually obsolescent". But Mr Kentridge does not seek to argue for the appellant that such contempt no longer exists. He submits that the court below was wrong to hold on the facts of this case that this contempt had been committed under Hong Kong law. In short, he submits that the Divisional Court's finding that in order to establish this contempt it was necessary to show that the conduct involved a "real risk" of inference with the administration of justice was wrong. Further, that if the correct test had been applied the offence is not made out.

Given that the attacks were *mala fide*, scurrilous, abusive, shocking and reprehensible, he submits that the fundamental rights of freedom of expression and freedom of the press given under Article 16 of the Bill of Rights, Article 27 of the Basic Law and the International Covenant of Civil and Political Rights as incorporated in the Basic Law, protect the appellant unless it can be shown that the statements and conducts were "necessary" exceptions to the rule. This cannot be demonstrated unless on the evidence the risk to the administration of justice was real, substantial and immediate.

The substance of the submission is that the "real risk" test is insufficient to establish a "necessary" exemption to the fundamental rights provided by Article 19 of the ICCPR and Article 16 of the Bill of Rights Ordinance:

"(2) Everyone shall have the right to freedom of expression; this right shall include freedom to seek, receive and impart information and ideas of all kinds, regardless of frontiers, either orally, in writing or in print, in the form of art, or through any other media of his choice.

(3) The exercise of the rights provided for in paragraph (2) of this article carries with it special duties and responsibilities. It may therefore be subject to certain restrictions, but these shall only be such as are provided by law and are *necessary* –

(a) ...

(b) for the protection ... of public order (order public), ..."

Mr Kentridge rightly concedes that "public order" includes the due administration of justice.

For these submissions he relies heavily upon the majority decision in *R v Kopyto* (1988) 47 DLR 213 in the Ontario Court of Appeal. This decided that scandalising the court as charged was unconstitutional and contrary to the Canadian Charter. The offence could survive as an exemption to the right of free expression only if there was a "clear, serious and immediate" danger to the administration of justice. As the Canadian Charter, the Hong Kong Bill of Rights and the Basic Law (incorporating the ICCPR) are in this respect in *pari materia* the correct test in Hong Kong law is that suggested in *Kopyto*. It follows, says Mr Kentridge, that in adopting the lower test of "real risk" the Divisional Court fell into serious error.

He supported his eloquent argument with persuasive, but not binding, authority. Many of his preliminary submissions on the fundamental rights are uncontroversial. The freedom of expression and of the press are given specific protection in the Bill of rights and the Basic Law. In our society their importance cannot be over-estimated. This, in my view, must be the starting point. I cannot better the way it is put by Hoffmann LJ (as he then was) in *R v Central Television Plc* (CA) [1994] Fam 192 at 202H to 203C:

> "The motives which impel judges to assume a power to balance freedom of speech against other interests are almost always understandable and humane on the facts of the particular case before them. Newspapers are sometimes irresponsible and their motives in a market economy cannot be expected to be unalloyed by considerations of commercial advantage. Publication may cause needless pain, distress and damage to individuals or harm to other aspects of the public interest. But a freedom which is restricted to what judges think to be responsible or in the public interest is no freedom. Freedom means the right to publish things which government and judges, however well motivated, think should not be published. It means the right to say things which "right-thinking people" regard as dangerous or irresponsible. This freedom is subject only to clearly defined exceptions laid down by common law or statute.
>
> Furthermore, in order to enable us to meet our international obligations under the Convention for the Protection of Human Rights and Fundamental Freedoms (1953) (Cmd. 8969), it is necessary that any exceptions should satisfy the tests laid down in article 10(2). They must be 'necessary in a democratic society' and fall within certain permissible categories, namely: ..."

He recognised that it was necessary for any exemptions under the international covenants to fall within defines categories including "the maintenance of the authority and impartiality of the judiciary" and added at 203D-E:

> "It cannot be too strongly emphasised that outside the established exceptions, or any new ones which Parliament may enact in accordance with its obligations under the Convention, there is no question of balancing freedom of speech against other interests. It is a trump card which always wins."

The argument before us has concentrated upon whether having regard to the Basic Law, the ICCPR and the Bill of Rights it was open to the Divisional Court to hold that the contempts came within "necessary" exemptions. Mr Kentridge urged the application of the ordinary meaning of "necessary" rather than other formulations under international covenants. I agree. See *Ming Pao Newspapers Ltd v AG* [1996] AC 906.

In determining what are necessary exemptions in Hong Kong a number of points have been urged upon us. The first is that the test will differ accordingly to the needs of the jurisdiction concerned. This was recognised by Lord Morris in *McLeod v St Aubyn* [1899] AC 549, 561.

Then, it is rightly said that the courts and judges are not immune from criticism. They must rely upon merited good reputation for protection against *bona fide* censure even if it is fierce and misguided. Such criticism is not contempt. In *Ambard v AG for Trinidad and Tobago* [1936] AC 322 at 335 Lord Atkin put it thus:

> "But whether the authority and position of an individual judge, or the due administration of justice, is concerned, no wrong is committed by any member of the public who exercises the ordinary right of criticising, in good faith, in private or public, the public act done in the seat of justice The path of criticism is a public way: the wrong headed are permitted to err therein: provided that members of the public abstain from imputing improper motives to those taking part in the administration of justice, and are genuinely exercising a right of criticism, and not acting in malice or attempting to impair the administration of justice, they are immune. Justice is not a cloistered virtue: she must be allowed to suffer the scrutiny and respectful, even though outspoken, comments of ordinary men."

Salmon LJ (as he then was) expressed similar sentiments in *R v Commissioner of Police ex parte Blachburn (No. 2)* [1968]2 QB 150 at 155F:

> "It follows that no criticism of a judgment, however vigorous, can amount to contempt of court, providing it keeps within the limits of reasonable courtesy and good faith. The criticism here complained of, however rumbustious, however wide of the mark, whether expressed in good taste or in bad taste, seems to me to be well within those limits."

Or, as Cory JA put it in *Kopyto* (above) "but the courts are not fragile flowers that will wither in the heat of controversy".

In this context Mr Kentridge invites us to consider the effect of justified, strong, bona fide criticism of the court and judges. What could be more effective, he says, in interfering with the administration of justice as a continuing process and diminishing the authority of the court? Therefore, he argues, the fact that the conduct may diminish the authority of the court is not enough by itself. Sound and warranted criticism is necessary for the improvement of any public institution including the courts.

Drawing together these reasons, Mr Kentridge urges the conclusion that the approach of the majority in *Kopyto* is correct under Hong Kong law. At most, the only protection consistent with the fundamental rights afforded by the law against scandalising the court, is if the conduct complained of is such as to involve a real, substantial and immediate danger to the administration of justice. This, Mr Kentridge equates with "clear and present danger"— the test applied in the United States courts which is only referable and relevant to cases pending or already in process.

R v Kopyto considered

Mr Kentridge's heavy reliance upon this case is founded upon the similarity of the Canadian Charter with the relevant provisions in Hong Kong, and the exhaustive consideration by that court of authorities in other commonwealth jurisdictions and in the United States. The five member Ontario Court of Appeal was unanimous that the momentary but excessive reaction of a disappointed lawyer was not made out as a contempt. In its consideration of the necessary ingredients of contempt by way of scandalising the court it is impressive. Mr Kentridge submits that it is also highly persuasive and ought to be followed.

It is necessary to examine the judgments in a little detail for the reason that on issues other than the result the court was split three ways. Cory and Goodman JJA were of the view that in order to accord with the fundamental freedoms in the Charter the contempt must be shown to involve a "real, substantial and immediate" (Cory) or "real, significant and present or immediate" (Goodman) danger to the administration of justice.

Houlden JA stood alone in deciding that no offence of scandalising the court, however framed, could be consistent with the Charter and therefore there could be no such contempt.

Brooke and Dubin JJA on the other hand considered the offence to be a necessary exemption provided that the statement complained of is calculated to bring the administration of justice in disrepute and it is shown that there is a "serious risk that the administration of justice would be interfered with – that risk could be expressed as serious, real or substantial".

The majority view that such a contempt could not be committed unless it interferes with the fair trial of present or pending proceedings was influenced in varying degrees by American jurisprudence and its test of "clear and present danger". Dubin JA (with whom Brooke JA agreed) was dismissive of this approach. He preferred the commonwealth authorities for the reasons he gives at 285:

> "The result of the majority ruling is that in this jurisdiction there is, at present, no limit on what is permissible with respect to comments made which are intended to interfere seriously with the administration of justice and the rule of law unless the comment is made in the face of the court, or would interfere with the fair trial of pending proceedings. With respect, I see no basis for such a distinction."

He then points out that the distinction had been rejected in *Solicitor–General v Radio Avon Ltd* [1978]1 NZLR 225 at 232–3 where Lord Diplock's analysis in *Attorney General v Times Newspaper Ltd* [1974] AC 273 is cited with approval.

In *Kopyto* at 287 Dubin JA refers to the erroneous assumption in American jurisprudence (*Bridges v State of California*, 62 S Ct 190, 314 US 252 (1941) at 217) that scandalising contempt is to "preserve the dignity of the bench":

> "But, with respect, the criminal offences of contempt of court, with which we are dealing, is not for the purpose of 'preserving the dignity of the bench' as the many cases to which I have referred demonstrate, and, with respect, I think has been misinterpreted in the American jurisprudence. It is apparent in reading American jurisprudence that the constitutional tradition and the philosophy underlying the manner in which justice is administered in the United States is different in many ways from that in Canada and throughout the Commonwealth. I need not dwell on those many differences."

He adopts the summary of the different approaches in *Radio Avon* at 234:

> "*The American courts appear to have directed their attention to the existence of a clear and present danger of a court being influenced, intimidated, impeded, embarrassed or obstructed in the administration of justice. English law, on the other hand, has also attached great importance to the need to preserve public confidence in the administration of justice generally. This court should not depart from that attitude subject, of course, in the type of contempt now under consideration, to the public right of fair comment and criticism, and to the possible defence of justification earlier referred to in this judgment.*" (emphasis supplied)

I refuse to enter the lists on the question whether the American approach involves a misapprehension of the nature of scandalising but the majority in *Kopyto* were much influenced by it.

Is scandalising contempt as found by the Divisional Court a "necessary" exemption in Hong Kong?

The Bill of Rights and the Basic Law distinguish the law in Hong Kong from that of the United Kingdom, Australia and so far as *Radio Avon* is concerned New Zealand because that case was decided before its Bill of Rights came into force. The question is whether the commonwealth approach to scandalising contempt as applied by the Divisional Court survives the Bill of Rights and the Basic Law as a necessary exemption to freedom of expression. As became clear in *Kopyto*, what is a "necessary" exemption depends upon the nature of the contempt – what must be proved to establish it and the local circumstances in which the due administration of justice has to be maintained.

It seems that American law provides no protection for the administration of justice as a continuing process. Yet, the American system is well respected and appears not to be under any obvious disability consequent upon the absence of this protection. If this protection is unconstitutional in Canada, Mr Kentridge asks how can it be necessary in Hong Kong?

The answer, I believe, lies partly in the commonwealth tradition and partly in what is necessary in the particular circumstances in Hong Kong. It is abundantly clear from the authorities relied upon by the Divisional Court, that the commonwealth traditional attaches great importance to the preservation of all the factors which contribute to the due administration of justice as a continuing process – as well as the integrity of proceedings in progress or in contemplation. Also, the "real risk" test can be regarded as well established by those authorities.

I can discern no practical difference between the "real risk" test in *Radio Avon* at 239 line 11 (the commonwealth tradition) and that held to be constitutional by Dubin and Brooke JJA in *Kopyto* in their impressive minority judgment at 289 to 209:

> "It was essential for the Crown to prove that the statement made by the appellant was calculated to bring the administration of justice into disrepute. That is the *actus reus* of this offence. The mere fact the words are capable of bringing the administration of justice into disrepute does not suffice. What must be shown is that, by reason of the statement made by the appellant, there was a serious risk that the administration of justice would be interfered with. The risk or prejudice must be serious, real or substantial."

I have already referred to the passage in which Dubin JA points out what he considers to be the flaw in the American approach. In summary, the Divisional Court held that in order to establish the contempts alleged, proof was necessary that the statement (or conduct) was calculated to interfere with the administration of justice in its widest sense; that it involved a "real risk" that the due administration of justice would be interfered with and (the mental element) that there was an intention to interfere with the administration of justice, or recklessness by appreciating this possible consequence and ignoring it. This requisite mental element will almost always be implicit in the statement or conduct itself.

I readily accept Mr Kentridge's point that the administration of justice in Hong Kong is held in high repute both at home and abroad. There is every reason to think that it enjoys general confidence and respect. Therefore, it has little to fear from *bona fide*, temperate, and rational criticism. Indeed, the appellate process itself involves this and yet tends to increase confidence in the system. Further, like many other public institutions, it stands to benefit from, rather than be damaged by, such criticism — especially if constructive. Nor do I think that isolated excesses of disappointed litigants or their lawyers which are neither in the face of the court nor related to proceedings either pending or in progress, ought necessarily to be condemned as scandalising contempts. But, the spirit in which the attack is made is relevant.

Mr Kentridge's point that a rational attack is more likely to result in risk than a scurrilous and preposterous attack which may be recognised for what it is I do not accept as generally correct. *Bona fide*, balanced and justified criticism is susceptible to reasoned answer or even acceptance. Sustained scurrilous, abusive attacks made in bad faith, or conduct which challenges the authority of the court, are not susceptible to reasoned answer. If they continue unchecked they will almost certainly lead to interference with the administration of justice as a continuing process.

Further, the relatively small size of the Hong Kong's legal system is important. As is demonstrated in this case communication with a very substantial proportion of the population is easily achieved. Proceedings in court are widely publicised. Many judges are known by name because of this reporting. Confidence in our legal system, the maintenance of the rule of law and the authority of the court are matters of special importance in our society. There are frequent, if misconceived, expressions of anxiety in this respect. There is reason to believe that the ordinary citizen in Hong Kong regards the court as his ultimate and sure refuge from injustice and oppression.

One need go no further than to consider the likely effect upon the confidence of the ordinary citizen or an ordinary litigant in the administration of justice in its widest sense if an unsuccessful litigant, who is also a powerful subject, indulges in sustained attacks upon the court or judges which go unchecked.

Also, on the "necessity" point, Mr Kentridge was asked in his submissions whether a judge trying a case ought to be in the position of knowing that the losing party may indulge in a scurrilous attack upon him, or seek to punish him by harassment. His bold answer is that the fundamental right to freedom of expression means that a judge must endure such treatment and that it must be regarded as "coming with the job". This I unhesitatingly reject not only for the reasons already given. There is a further aspect of the administration of justice not touched upon in argument but nevertheless of importance. It is to be found in *Arlidge, Eady & Smith on Contempt*, 2nd Edn at 16 — 8. The authors put it in this way and I adopt their formulation:

> "While it is true that the law of contempt is not concerned with the dignity of individuals taking part in the judicial process, or even with upholding respect for the law in any purely deferential sense, *the administration of justice needs to proceed in circumstances of calm and dignity in order to be effective.*" (emphasis added)

The respondent's answer

Mr Ronny Tong SC, for the Secretary for Justice, has made cogent and detailed submissions upon the "necessity" point and supporting the judgment below. In brief, he submits that the scurrilous and abusive attacks made in this case cannot amount to a genuine exercise of the freedom of speech and that a modern, civilised society such as Hong Kong, relies upon the authority of and respect for the rule of law. The moment this respect is challenged, or the standing of the court is demeaned, this supremacy of the law is in doubt. This, he submits, is calculated to seriously interfere with the due administration of justice and in the circumstances of this case amounts to a necessary exemption from the right of free speech and freedom of expression. He supports both the reasoning and the conclusions of the court below.

For my part, I am indebted for some of my reasoning in this judgment to Mr Tong's submissions which I accept in substance.

Conclusion on scandalising contempt

I reject Mr Kentridge's main submissions without difficulty. For the above reasons, I would hold that the contempt defined by the Divisional Court is a necessary exemption to the fundamental rights of freedom of expression and freedom of the press under the Basic Law and the Bill of Rights. The Divisional Court considered the applicable law and authority with great care and rightly concluded that "real risk" of interference with the due administration of justice was the correct test. I do not repeat the reasoning and the conclusions with which I entirely agree, and I would uphold the decision.

I would only add that in this case that I doubt whether a detailed consideration of the type of readership of the newspaper was necessary. To my mind, a consideration of the nature of the articles with a readership of 2.3 million people inevitably involves a real risk. As to the necessary mental element, this is expressly established by the articles themselves. See for example the article of 8 January 1998 when the newspaper expressed the intention to destroy the authority of the Judiciary.

The pursuit of Godfrey JA

As to the pursuit of Godfrey JA, Mr Kentridge first submits that the court wrongly found the appellant guilty of conduct which was calculated to undermine public confidence in the due administration of justice whereas the contempt charged was wrongfully interfering with the administration of justice. With respect, this is a bad point. As I have already indicated, the ways in which the administration of justice as a continuing process are many. They certainly include undermining public confidence.

Essentially, however, Mr Kentridge's point is that there is no risk that the judge would be adversely influenced by this conduct either generally or in respective of a particular case. He criticises the Divisional Court's reliance upon those cases of contempt in which witnesses or jurors have been threatened or victimised on the basis that such people may well have been influenced whereas a judge certainly would not.

He cites a number of cases in support in which eminent judges have indicated that judges are not influenced by statements or comments in the media. By way of example, he relies upon Lord Salmon in *Attorney General v British Broadcasting Corporation* [1981] AC 303, 342:

> "I am and have always been satisfied that no judge would be influenced in his judgment by what may be said by the media."

Although the harassing conduct directed at Godfrey JA was much more serious than the statements in the media, for my part I accept, as did the Divisional Court, that no judge in Hong Kong would be influenced in his judgment by it or anything like it.

On this Mr Kentridge suggests that the Divisional Court was therefore wrong in holding that there was a real risk that public confidence would be undermined because

> "... it was inevitable that at least some sectors of the newspaper's readership would think that there was a possibility that Godfrey JA might be affected by the treatment of him, and that that might have affected his future handling of cases involving the *Oriental Daily News* in particular, and the press in general. If such conduct as in the present case is tolerated, it would also give rise to a misconception that it is permissible to resort to similar tactics after a person has lost his cause in court."

But the Divisional Court was not considering the narrow question whether this particular judge would have been influenced in his judgment but the much wider and equally important question whether this conduct would lead to the undermining of public confidence.

Conclusion on the pursuit of Godfrey JA

Much of the reasoning under scandalising contempt is relevant to this contempt. It is not necessary to repeat it.

For my part, therefore, I am satisfied that the Divisional Court applied the correct principles of law and that it was correct in finding that the necessary acts had been done with the requisite intention. I would dismiss the appeal on this contempt.

Finally, in spite of all the arguments raised, these contempts were plain, obvious and extremely serious.

The appeal on sentence

These examples of this type of contempt by the media are unprecedented. The attacks were made by those who normally are vociferous in seeking to uphold the rule of law and fundamental freedoms, not in seeking to damage them. They represent gross abuses of freedom of expression and freedom of the press.

They were rightly described by the Divisional Court as follows:

> "The campaign which the Oriental Daily News waged against the Judiciary was without parallel in modern times. The features of this prolonged and sustained campaign which made it so unique include the venom of the language which was used, the outrageousness of the motives which it ascribed to its targets, and ... the impact which the campaign had on public confidence in the ability of Hong Kong's judges to dispense justice conscientiously and impartially.
>
> ... what was at stake in the *Oriental Daily News*' campaign was not the outcome of an individual case but nothing less than the rule of law itself. ... It was this ultimate challenge to the rule of law which makes these contempts probably the most serious examples of 'media' contempts which the courts in the common law world have ever encountered."
>
> "The contempt of court consisting of the pursuit of Godfrey JA was equally unprecedented. We know of no case in which a judge has been harassed in the way in which Godfrey JA was. What made the pursuit of him particularly serious was that it was done, not as was suggested to educate him in the ways of *paparazzi*, but to pay him back for not going along with all of the Oriental Press Group's arguments in the case which he had heard."

Having outlined the seriousness of these matters, the Divisional Court reviewed and took into account the mitigating features advanced on the appellant's behalf, which included his acceptance of prime responsibility together with his unreserved public apology, his genuine remorse, his high reputation and unimpeachable character. Additionally, the court generously took into account certain matters in his favour which were not advanced on his behalf in that it had reservation over the extent of Mr Wong's responsibility for the contempts. It had a suspicion that the impetus for the campaign may not have come from him and that in this respect he did not enjoy full editorial independence.

Taking all these matters into account, including the unprecedented gravity of the contempt the court treated the publication of the various articles as one contempt and the harassment as another. It took a total of eight months imprisonment as the starting point. Having regard to the substantial mitigation, this was reduced to four months imprisonment which was achieved by passing 3 months imprisonment for each contempt, one month of which was to be served consecutively, making four months in all.

In this sentence, the court also took into account of its order that Mr Wong should pay four–fifths of the costs incurred by the Secretary for Justice for the prosecution, but it is to be noted that an order was also made against the Oriental Press Group Ltd which had to be enforced first. The order against Mr Wong cannot be enforced without a further order from the Divisional Court.

Mr Kentridge submits that eight months imprisonment was manifestly too high as a starting point, and that in the circumstances of the case a suspended sentence and a fine was the appropriate order. He recognised that the Divisional Court had been generous in finding mitigating factors but submitted that they were given insufficient weight. He emphasised Mr Wong's unreserved apology, his genuine and repeated remorse and his acceptance of full responsibility although he was not the writer. Emphasis was placed upon the fact that these proceedings will ensure that such contempts are never repeated in the future and that a fine is an éffective deterrent together with costs on an indemnity basis.

It was further pointed out that these offences were not motivated by financial gain but by a genuine resentment over unfair decisions. Finally, it was submitted that Mr Wong had not only made a public apology but had suffered public humiliation as a major item of news and he had suffered the indignity of three days in custody which had been serious punishment to him.

It was suggested that the standing of the court would be enhanced by showing mercy. Cases were cited supporting the proposition that in cases in other jurisdictions more lenient sentences had been passed.

Conclusion on sentence

With respect to the submissions made, it is impossible for this Court to say that eight months imprisonment as a starting point was manifestly excessive for offences of this persistence and seriousness. I would conclude that eight months was in all respects moderate. Thereafter, the Divisional Court gave generous weight to the substantial mitigating factors. Nothing that Mr Kentridge has advanced persuades me that these unprecedented contempts did not merit immediately custodial sentences. Not without regret for Mr Wong's personal position, I would hold these sentences to be temperate, proper and in all the circumstances necessary. For these reasons, I would dismiss this appeal against sentence.

Mayo JA: It is useful to bear in mind the two charges which were laid against the Appellant. They were that the Appellant was guilty of contempt of court in that:

"(1) They sought to threaten, harass and/or intimidate Godfrey JA during 13, 14 and 15 January 1998 (by having him pursued by their employees and/or agents and/or others) by reason of a judgment which he had previously delivered, thereby wrongfully interfering with the administration of justice.

(2) They published articles which contained passages of crude and vicious abuse of the judiciary as set out in paragraphs 9(2) to (8), with little if any reasoned argument, and which alleged systematic bias and wilful abuse of power (those allegations being without any justification whatsoever). The articles also contained threats to the judiciary. The articles, considered separately and cumulatively, were calculated to undermine public confidence in the administration of justice in Hong Kong."

This appeal was greatly simplified by the fact that Mr. Kentridge, Q.C. for the Appellant accepted at the outset that the newspaper articles were abusive, intemperate and shocking and that the campaign against the Judiciary had been conducted over a period of some time. Also it was accepted that the articles had not been written in good faith. They had been actuated by resentment at what the paper perceived to be its persecution by the Judiciary. Likewise it was accepted that the treatment of Godfrey, J.A. referred to in charge 1 had not been to "educate" him in the ways of the so called Paparazzi. It had been an attempt to reek revenge upon him for not accepting the submissions which had been made to him on their behalf. A further important factor which was accepted was that the circulation of the *Oriental Daily News* was and is very extensive. It enjoys a daily readership in excess of 2 million people. It is possible to state that none of the court below's findings of fact were in any way subject to challenge.

The approach adopted by Mr. Kentridge to this was that the articles complained of were of such an excessive nature that the allegations were preposterous and that it was unlikely that they would constitute a real danger to the administration of justice.

The main issue which was ventilated on this appeal was the law which is applicable to contempts of court of this nature. It related to Article 16 of the Bill of Rights and the extent (if any) to which Article 16 had modified the existing common law on the subject of scandalising the court.

Article 16 reads as follows:

"**Article 16**

Freedom of opinion and expression

(1) Everyone shall have the right to hold opinions without interference.

(2) Everyone shall have the right to freedom of expression; this right shall include freedom to seek, receive and impart information and ideas of all kinds, regardless of frontiers, either orally, in writing or in print, in the form of art, or through any other media of his choice.

(3) The exercise of the rights provided for in paragraph (2) of this article carries with it special duties and responsibilities. It may therefore be subject to certain restrictions, but these shall only be such as are provided by law and are necessary

(a) for respect of the rights or reputations of others; or

(b) for the protection of national security or of public order (ordre public), or of public health or morals.

[cf. ICCPR Art. 19]"

Mr. Tong, S.C. for the Respondent argued that the exceptions referred to in Article 16 (3)(b) were such that the existing common law had not been modified as a consequence of the enactment of the Bill of Rights. This being so all the various cases based upon *R v. Gray* [1900] 2 QB 36 were still applicable to this situation.

According to Mr. Tong a contempt of court is committed where the publication was calculated to impair the confidence of the people in the Judiciary or the administration of justice or there is a risk that the publication tended to lower the authority of the court as a whole or that of its judges and excites misgivings as to the integrity, propriety and impartiality of the judicial office. In all these matters the test was not what the writer intended but the likely result of the publication. I have taken this from the very helpful skeleton argument prepared by Mr. Tong and he cites these cases in support of the propositions he advances.

"1. *R v. Odhams* [1957] 1 QB 73, Div Ct.

2. *AG v. Mundey* [1972] 2 NSWLR 887

3. *SG v. Radio Avon Ltd* [1978] 1 NZLR 225, NZCA

4. *Chokolingo v. Law Society of Trinidad and Tobago* [1978] 30 WIR 372, C.A. of Trinidad and Tobago

5. *Badry v. DPP* [1983] 2 AC 297, P.C.

6. *SG v. Radio New Zealand* [1994] 1 NZLR 48, Full Court

7. *AG v. Lingle* [1995] 1 SLR 696"

Mr. Kentridge accepted that the crime of contempt of court still existed which included scandalising the court. It was his contention however that for the offence to have been committed it had to be established that there was a substantial risk to the administration of justice.

Mr. Kentridge also accepted that freedom of speech under the Basic Law and the Bill of Rights was not absolute. A balancing exercise had to be undertaken to determine whether there were legitimate constraints. Any deviation had to be based upon necessity rather than convenience or desirability. What was meant by necessity was that the court had to be satisfied that the publication constituted an imminent and substantial danger to the administration of justice.

All of this was separate to the question of interference with the administration of justice. He readily accepted the necessity to restrict publications relating to impending jury trials and prevent threats to witnesses to proceedings or parties thereto or jurors or any attempts to influence judges.

In relating these propositions to the facts of the instant case Mr. Kentridge contended that the question which had to be asked was – Did the articles pose such a danger that they constituted a necessary constraint on freedom of speech? He accepted that you had to look at the meaning and context of the articles to determine whether they constituted a clear and imminent danger to the administration of justice. In doing so one had to bear in mind the effect the articles would have on a reasonable person of average intelligence and disposition and then ask oneself the question whether it was necessary to criminalise conduct of this nature.

In formulating his propositions on the law Mr. Kentridge placed heavy reliance upon the Canadian case of *R v. Kopyto* [1988] 47 DLR (4th) 213. This case involved a consideration of the Canadian Charter of Rights and Freedoms and it is clear that some of the Judges were influenced by the jurisprudence of the United States of America. It has to be said however that the Canadian Charter is in many respects similar to our Bill of Rights.

It will be appreciated from all of this that the main difference in the approach adopted by respective counsel is whether guidance is to be sought from the Canadian model or from other sources.

Mr. Tong submitted that the New Zealand Bill of Rights had more in common with the Hong Kong Bill of Rights than the Canadian Charter. Perhaps the most important consideration was that both pieces of legislation have been modelled upon the International Covenant on Civil and Political Rights (ICCPR). Other considerations also have to be borne in mind. Our Article 16 (2) is identical to Article 19 of the ICCPR and is very similar to Article 10 of the European Convention on Human Rights. Having given the matter careful consideration I have come to the conclusion that the New Zealand Bill of Rights and the cases based upon that legislation provide better guidance than the Canadian Charter.

Having said this I do not accept the validity of the contention advanced by Mr. Tong that Article 16 does not supplant or modify the law of contempt. In my view the focus of attention has to be Article 16 and a balancing exercise is required to determine whether it is necessary to curtail the freedoms provided by Article 16 (2). In this connection it is apparent from the decision of the European Court of Human Rights in *The Sunday Times v. The United Kingdom* [1979] 2 EHRR 245 that it was accepted the papers freedom of expression could in certain circumstances be interfered with. This was in the context of contempt of court. This was perhaps hardly surprising as Article 10 of the Bill of Rights guarantees a fair and public hearing by a competent independent and impartial tribunal and it may well be the case that the rights conferred by Article 16 may be incompatible with those conferred by Article 10.

What is however clear is that any restriction must be in accordance with the provisions of Article 16 (3) and must be necessary to achieve the legitimate objects to be pursued.

These questions were considered by Rogers, J. (as he then was) in the *AG v. CHEUNG Kim–hung* [1997] 7 HKPLR 295. He said at p.303:

> "As Mr Kwok has submitted, if the law of contempt is to prohibit the publication of an article such as is in issue in the present case, the restriction on the publication must satisfy each of the following tests:
>
> (a) it must be provided by law
>
> (b) the law of contempt must intend to achieve one of the permissible objectives set out in article 16(3) and
>
> (c) it must be necessary for the achievement of the relevant objective or objectives and be proportionate to the legitimate aim pursued.

In my view the law of contempt *in so far* [*sic*] as it is sought to be applied in these proceedings does fulfil all these three tests.

So far as the requirement that it is provided by law is concerned, it seems to me that the law of contempt is provided by law. The law satisfies the criteria because the law can be reasonably ascertained and the consequences of any given action can be foreseen to a reasonable degree. In this respect I have regard to what was said by the majority [of the European Court of Human Rights] in interpreting art 10 [of the European Convention on Human Rights] in the case of *Sunday Times v. United Kingdom* (1979) 2 EHRR 245 at 271 para 49 where they said:

> 'In the Court's opinion, the following are two of the requirements that flow from the expression "prescribed by law". First, the law must be adequately accessible: the citizen must be able to have an indication that is adequate in the circumstances of the legal rules applicable to a given case. Secondly, a norm cannot be regarded as a "law" unless it is formulated with sufficient precision to enable the citizen to regulate his conduct; he must be able – if need be with appropriate advice – to foresee, to a degree that is reasonable in the circumstances, the consequences which a given action may entail. Those consequences need not be foreseeable with absolute certainty; experience shows this to be unattainable. Again, whilst certainty is highly desirable, it may bring in its train excessive rigidity and the law must be able to keep pace with changing circumstances. Accordingly, many laws are inevitably couched in terms which, to a greater or lesser extent, are vague and whose interpretation and application are questions of practice.'

One of the exceptions in art 16(3) is for the respects of rights of others.

Article 10 of the Bill of Rights articulates in my view one of those rights. It provides as follows:

'All persons shall be equal before the courts and tribunals. In the determination of any criminal charge against him, or of his rights and obligations in a suit at law, everyone shall be entitled to a fair and public hearing by a competent, independent and impartial tribunal established by law. The press and the public may be excluded from all or part of a trial for reasons of morals, public order (*ordre public*) or national security in a democratic society, or when the interest of the private lives of the parties so requires, or to the extent strictly necessary in the opinion of the court in special circumstances where publicity would prejudice the interests of justice; but any judgment rendered in a criminal case or in a suit at law shall be made public except where the interest of juvenile persons otherwise requires or the proceedings concern matrimonial disputes or the guardianship of children.'

Finally, the Privy Council in the case of *Ming Pao Newspapers Ltd v Attorney General* (1996) 6 HKPLR 103 approved the Court of Appeal's approach in giving the word 'necessary' its normal meaning. As regards the question of proportionality; of course the fundamental right of freedom of speech must be given as generous an application as possible and any restriction must be narrowly interpreted and be proportionate to the aims sought to be achieved, but in my view that test is also satisfied."

With respect I would agree with this statement of the law.

Turning to the publications referred to in the 2nd charge it is helpful to consider the New Zealand case of *The Solicitor–General v. Radio New Zealand Ltd.* [1994] 1 NZLR 48 which is a post Bill of Rights case. When considering what they referred to as 'Proof of Corrosive "tendency" 'the Court had this to say.

"Proof of corrosive 'tendency'

In argument there was some discussion regarding the meaning of 'tendency' in this context, and how it was to be proved. We take the meaning adopted in *Solicitor–General v Radio Avon Ltd* at p 234 which of course is binding on us, a real risk as distinct from a remote possibility that the broadcast items would undermine public confidence in the administration of justice. A similar approach has been followed in Australia where the expressions used include a real risk of interference with the administration of justice, a substantial risk of serious injustice or a real and definite possibility that the conduct may prejudice the administration of justice; see *Hinch v Attorney–General (Vic)* at pp 23, 34, and 47. Direct proof will rarely be possible. The Court must consider all the circumstances of the publication: *Attorney–General v New Statesman and Nation Publishing Co Ltd* at p 10, following *Attorney–General v Leveller Magazine Ltd* per Lord Edmund–Davies at p 465. Relevant factors include the statements published, the timing of their publication, the size of the audience they reached, the likely nature, impact and duration of their influence; see *Hinch v Attorney–General* [1987] VR 721, 740, 742."

As can be seen they did in that passage also consider the case of *Solicitor–General v. Radio Avon Ltd.* [1978] 1 NZLR 225 which involved a question of scandalising the court. In that case Richmond P. said at p.233 of the report.

"Contempt by 'scandalising'the court is, of course, conduct which, in Lord Diplock's words, is calculated to undermine the public confidence in the proper functioning of the courts. It is to be noted that Lord Diplock, like Lord Russell, makes no distinction between one form of contempt and another from the point of view of the intent of the defendant. In the light of the approval given in *Ambard v Attorney–General* to Lord Russell's definition we doubt whether it would in any event be open to this court to introduce a special requirement of mens rea into this one branch of the law of contempt. We would not in any event be prepared to do so as we think that the public interest in the administration of justice is so important that it justifies the attitude which has been taken by the English courts.

We shall now refer to another passage in Lord Diplock's speech in *Attorney–General v Times Newspapers Ltd.* After describing some of the features of the summary remedy for contempt of court, Lord Diplock said:

'The courts have therefore been vigilant to see that the procedure for committal is not lightly invoked in cases where, although a contempt has been committed, there in no serious likelihood that it has caused any harm to the interests of any of the parties to the litigation or to the public interest. Since the court's discretion in dealing with a motion for committal is wide enough to entitle it to dismiss the motion with costs, despite the fact that a contempt has been committed, if it thinks that the contempt was too venial to justify its being brought to the attention of the court at all, the distinction between conduct which is within the general concept of "contempt of court" and conduct included within that general concept, which a court regards as deserving of punishment in the particular circumstances of the case, is often blurred in the judgments in the reported cases. The expression 'technical contempt' is a convenient expression which has sometimes been used to describe conduct which falls into the former but outside the latter category; and I agree with my noble and learned friend, Lord Reid, that, given conduct which presents a real risk as opposed to a mere possibility of interference with the due administration of justice, this is at very least a technical contempt. The seriousness of that risk is relevant only to the question whether the contempt is one for which the court, in its discretion, ought to inflict any punishment and, if so, what punishment it should inflict' ([1974] AC 273, 312; [1973] 3 All ER 54, 74–75).

The views which had been expressed by Lord Reid and with which Lord Diplock concurred in the foregoing passage were as follows:

'I think the true view is that expressed by Lord Parker CJ in *Reg v Duffy, Ex parte Nash* [1960] 2 QB 188, 200, that there must be "a real risk, as opposed to a remote possibility". That is an application of the ordinary *de minimis* principle. There is no contempt if the possibility of influence is remote. If there is some but only a small likelihood, that may influence the court to refrain from inflicting any punishment. If there is a serious risk some action may be necessary. And I think that the particular comment cannot be considered in isolation when considering its probable effect. If others are to be free and are likely to make similar comments that must be taken into account' ([1974] AC 273, 298–299).

In *Attorney–General v Times Newspapers Ltd* their Lordships were not directly concerned with the type of contempt which is in issue in the present appeal. Indeed, Lord Morris of Borth–y–Gest noted that on behalf of the respondents it had been accepted that there must be no 'scandalising' of the court ([1974] AC 273, 303; [1973] 3 All ER 54, 67). Even so, we accept Mr Palmer's submission that in the present case the appellants ought not to have been convicted of contempt unless the facts established beyond reasonable doubt that there was a real risk, as opposed to a remote possibility, that the broadcast item would undermine public confidence in the administration of justice. But we think that a real risk of that kind was established. It is true, as Mr Palmer said, that this broadcast was ephemeral and lasted only for about 40 seconds. Nevertheless, one of the affidavits shows that the listening audience of Radio

Avon represents some 50,000 people of the ages of 10 years and upwards. In our opinion the broadcasting of an imputation of judicial partiality to an audience of that size and nature certainly carried with it a real risk, as opposed to a remote possibility, that public confidence in the administration of justice would be undermined. For that reason we think that Radio Avon was properly found guilty of a contempt of court in the present case."

I am satisfied that this is a correct statement of the law and that it is applicable following the enactment of the New Zealand Bill of Rights. I am also satisfied that having regard to the scurrilous and abusive nature of the articles complained of and the duration of the attack on the Judiciary there can be no doubt that the court below was right to hold that the contempt of court complained of in the 2nd charge had been established. This is particularly the case having regard to the duration of the campaign against the Judiciary and the wide reach of the publication.

It is also perhaps worth adding that having regard to these factors it may well be the case that even if I am wrong in finding that the New Zealand Bill of Rights approach is the correct one the result may well have been the same under the Canadian Charter. I say this because the articles complained of in this case were very much more serious than the subject matter of the proceedings in *Kopyto*. In that case it was accepted that the outburst of the lawyer who made the offending remarks had been made in good faith. That is in sharp contrast to the publications in the present case. It is also evident from the majority judgments of the court that the offence of scandalising the courts was consistent with the Canadian Charter. In an extreme case such as the present one it is likely that the Appellant would have been found guilty of contempt of court even under the Canadian Charter.

That then leaves outstanding the 1st count of harassing and/or intimidating Godfrey, J.A. in what has been described as the Paparazzi Campaign. Mr. Tong placed heavy reliance upon the case of the *Attorney General v. Butterworth & Others* [1963] 1QB 696. He placed particular reliance upon a passage at p.725. from the judgment of Donovan, L.J.:

"The administration of justice is, after all, a continuing thing. It is not bounded by the day's cases. It has a future as well as a present. And if somebody pollutes the stream today so that tomorrow's litigant will find it poisoned, does he appeal to the court in vain?

There are indeed decisions which say that he does not. *Reg. v. Martin* is one, and I can see no essential difference between an attempt to punish a juror for having done his duty in court and an attempt to punish a witness for having done the same thing.

Kay J. said, in *Rowden v. Universities Co-operative Association Ltd.*, that he could not imagine a grosser offence against a court of justice than to exercise a power, legal or illegal, in order to punish a witness for giving evidence, and he made no distinction in this regard between pending proceedings and proceedings that are concluded, though it is true that more were to come in that case."

He also placed reliance upon a passage from Lord Denning's judgment at p. 723:

"It seems to me that the intimidation of a witness is only a contempt of court if it is done with the purpose of deterring him from giving evidence or influencing him to give it in a sense different from that in which he would otherwise have given it, and the victimisation of a witness is only a contempt of court if it is done with the purpose of punishing him for having given evidence in the sense he did.

But when the act is done with mixed motives, as indeed the acts here were done, what is the position? If it is done with the predominant motive of punishing a witness, there can be no doubt that it is a contempt of court. But even though it is not the predominant motive, yet nevertheless if it is an actuating motive influencing the step taken, it is, in my judgment, a contempt of court. I do not think the court is able to, or should, enter into a nice assessment of the weight of the various motives which, mixed together, result in the victimisation of a witness. If one of the purposes actuating the step is the purpose of punishment, then it is a contempt of court in everyone so actuated."

While it is true that this case involved "punishing" a witness I can see no reason why the observations which were made by Donovan, L.J. and Lord Denning should not be equally applicable to an attempt to "punish" a Judge.

It was undoubtedly conduct which manifested an intent to interfere with the administration of justice. It was imperative that action should be taken to demonstrate that this type of behaviour would not be tolerated. Again I am satisfied that the court below was right to find the Appellant guilty of contempt of court on this count.

So far as sentence is concerned I have no doubt that a severe penalty was called for. I can see no reason to believe that the sentences which were imposed on these counts were either wrong in principle or manifestly excessive. In my view the appeal against sentence should also be dismissed.

Leong JA: The appellant was found guilty of two charges of contempt of court. The first charge of contempt relates to the pursuit of Godfrey J.A. and this is said to be wrongful interference of the administration of justice. The second charge is contempt by scandalizing the court and this relates to the publication within a period of one month, of seven articles in the *Oriental Daily News* (ODN). These articles are said to be calculated to undermine public confidence in the administration of justice in Hong Kong. The present appeal is against those convictions.

The judges below found the articles in the second charge "were not spontaneous, unconsidered reaction of a disappointed litigant, but amounted to a deliberate and persistent campaign of vilification of Hong Kong's Judiciary" and " ... on any view this was not criticism, albeit outspoken and trenchantly expressed, of the Judiciary. The articles were a series of personal attacks on the Judiciary in abusive, intemperate and shocking language. They contained no reasoned argument to speak of, and the allegations which they made were without foundation."

The appellant accepts these findings on the nature of the articles and he accepts full responsibility for their publication.

It is accepted that at common law, as laid down by Lord Russell in *R v. Gray* [1900] 2 QB 36, "any act done or writing published calculated to bring a Court or Judge into contempt or to lower his authority is a contempt of court" and "any act done or writing published calculated to obstruct or interfere with the due course of justice or the lawful process of the court is a contempt of court." Thus scurrilous abuses of judges and courts constitute contempt by scandalizing the court. But this is subject to the qualification that criticism of judges and courts for the public good would not amount to contempt if they lie within the bounds of "reasonable argument or expostulation" (*R v. Gray*) and "within the limits of reasonable courtesy and good faith" (*Metropolitan Police Comr. Ex p. Blackburn (No. 2)* [1968] 2 QB 150). In AG for *NSW v Mundey* [1972] NSWLR 887, Hope LA, quoting Rich J in *R v Dunbabin Ex parte Williams* [1935] 53 CLR 434, made it clear that the "law permits in respect of courts, as of other institutions, the fullest discussions of their doings so long as that discussion is fairly conducted and is honestly directed to some definite public purpose ... ." But he added (at p.910) that there are two qualifications to the right of criticism, the first is "criticism will constitute contempt if it is merely scurrilous abuse" but it must be "a very strong one". In the second place, the criticism may amount to contempt if it "excites misgivings as to the integrity propriety and impartiality brought to the exercise of the judicial office."

On the findings of the judges on the nature of the articles in the second charge, publication of the articles undoubtedly constituted contempt by scandalising the court at common law and the appellant can find no shelter behind the qualifications of the right to criticise on matters of public concern.

However, the appellant contends that the common law offence of scandalizing the court has become "virtually obsolescence in England" (per Lord Diplock p.347 *Secretary for State for Defence v. Guardian Newspapers Ltd.* [1985] 1 AC 339 at 347) and merely scurrilous abuses no long constitute contempt by scandalising the court.

The appellant's submission is that Article 16(2) of the Bill of Rights and Article 27 of the Hong Kong Basic Law now guarantee the right to freedom of speech in Hong Kong and these afford him protection from liability in contempt for the publication of those article.

Mr. Kentridge for the appellant is not contending that contempt by scandalizing the courts no long exists under the Bill of Rights. He accepts that even though the right to freedom of expression is guaranteed under the Bill of Rights, it may be restricted if it is necessary for the protection of the administration of justice. But he contends that restriction on publication by way of an offence of contempt of court is only necessary where the articles are such as to constitute a real, substantial and imminent danger to the administration of justice. That being the test, it is submitted, publication of the articles in the second charge, crude and scurrilous abuses of the judiciary as they are, constituted no contempt of court because the evidence does not justify any finding that the articles posed a danger to the administration of justice that was real, substantial and immediate. The case against the appellant did not pass that threshold. The appellant's test is based on the majority decision of the Canadian case of *R v. Kopyto* [1987] 47 DLR (4th) 213.

The judges below did not accept this test. They preferred the New Zealand test in *Solicitor General v. Radio Avon Ltd and Anr* [1978] 1 NZLR 255 that to restrict the right to freedom of expression, there must be "a real risk, as opposed to a remote possibility, that the ... item would undermine public confidence in the administration of justice." This followed the approach in *AG v. Times Newspapers Ltd.* [1974] AC 273 where the Court of Appeal held that to amount to contempt of court, "there must be a real risk as opposed to a mere possibility of interference with the due administration of justice." With these cases in mind, the judges below adopted a test along the New Zealand approach. It is this: "Was there a real risk that the acts complained of would undermine confidence in the due administration of justice in the minds of at least some of the persons who were likely to become aware of the publication or acts complained of?" Their answer to the question they posed to themselves was in the affirmative and they found contempt by scandalizing the court had been proved.

The appellant contends the judges were wrong to follow *Solicitor General v. Radio Avon Ltd and Anr.* which was decided before the New Zealand Bill of Rights came into being. The judges, it is submitted, should have followed the Canadian view in *Kopyto* where the provisions in the Canadian Charter of Rights and Freedoms are similar to the Bill of Rights in Hong Kong.

The question is that were the judges wrong to prefer the New Zealand approach and if not, whether the publication of the articles constitute contempt of court under their test.

Article 19 of the International Covenant on Civil and Political Rights 1966 (ICCPR) recognises freedom of expression but it is expressed to be subject to any "necessary" legal restrictions for the respect of the rights and reputations of others. The Hong Kong Bill of Right affirms the ICCPR and in Article 16(2) the right to freedom of expression is guaranteed but subject to restrictions provided by law and which are "necessary" for the protection of other rights, national security or public order. "Necessary" in the context of Article 16, it has been held, should be given its normal meaning *(Ming Pao Newspaper Ltd v. A.G.* [1996] AC 906). The New Zealand Bill of Rights Act 1990 which also affirms the ICCPR provides that the right to freedom of expression is subject to "such reasonable limits as can be demonstrably justified in a free and democratic society". In *Solicitors General v. Radio New Zealand* [1994] 1 NZLR 48, a case decided after the enactment of the New Zealand Bill of Rights, the Full Court held that the test of that limit is proof beyond reasonable doubt that there was "a real risk as distinct from a remote possibility that the conduct would undermine public confidence in the administration of justice". The European Convention on Human Rights in Articles 10 provides for the right to freedom of expression but the exercise of this right carries with it duties and responsibilities and may be subject to restrictions as are prescribed by law and are "necessary in a democratic society for the prevention of disorder ... or for maintaining the authority and impartiality of the judiciary." In *Sunday Times v. The United Kingdom* [1979] 2 EHRR 245, the European Court of Human Rights decided that "maintaining the authority and impartiality of the judiciary is one purpose of the law on contempt of court". The test is whether there is pressing social need for such restrictions.

In Singapore, its Constitution guarantees in section 14 the right to freedom of speech and expression but subject to Parliament may by law impose restrictions as it considers it necessary and expedient in the interest of the security of Singapore or ... public order. But "any one [*sic*] exercising that right must observe a corresponding duty of responsibility. No one is entitled under the guise of freedom of speech and expression to make irresponsible accusations against *inter alia* the judiciary" (*AG v. Lingle* [1995] 1 SLR 696 at 761). The Canadian Charter of Rights and Freedoms guarantees the right to freedom of expression subject only to "such reasonable limits prescribed by law as can be demonstrably justified in a free and democratic society" and this is expressed as the aspiration of the Canadian people.

In the United States, freedom of speech is an absolute guarantee under the American Bill of Rights and contempt by scandalizing the court is not recognised and other types of contempt of court require proof that the words or statement constitute a real and imminent danger to the administration of justice. The United Kingdom has no expressed constitutional guarantee of freedom of expression. But Lord Reid in *AG v. Times Newspapers Ltd.* said that "freedom of speech should not be limited to any greater extent than is necessary but it cannot be allowed where there would be real prejudice to the administration of justice." Contempt of court in the United Kingdom is now provided in the Contempt of Court Act 1981 under which publications which create a substantial risk that the course of justice in the proceedings in question will be seriously impeded or prejudiced is contempt of court with strict liability. In Australia there is no constitutional guarantee of freedom of speech, but in *Gallpher v. Durack* [1983] 45 ALR 53, Murphy J. said this, "The absence of a constitutional guarantee does not mean that Australia should accept judicial inroads upon freedom of speech which are not found necessary or desirable in other countries. At stake is not merely the freedom of one person; it is the freedom of every one to comment rightly or wrongly on the decisions of the courts in a way that do not constitute a clear and present danger to the administration of justice." The test suggested was there must be a "clear and present danger to the administration of justice".

Thus different countries guarantee the right to freedom of expression in different ways but each country does permit restrictions to be imposed by way of the offence of contempt of court if it is necessary to protect its administration of justice and each country adopts its own test according to the people's aspiration and the country's social circumstances. But it would seem that the "real risk" test is preferred among common law countries.

As may be seen from above, the Hong Kong position on the legal restrictions on freedom of expression is not similar to that in Canada where the restrictions must be such as are "reasonable and demonstrably justified in a free and democratic society. The Canadian case of *Kopyto* was decided in the light of the Canadian Charter according to the Canadian social circumstances and therefore decided against a background totally different from that of Hong Kong. Goodman J.A. found the words complained of in *Kopyto* "no more than an expression by the appellant of an unfavourable opinion with respect to a court decision" and "if such opinion were expressed by such person in a respectful, albeit firm manner ... it would not have constituted contempt of court even before the Charter came into effect." This is in stark contrast to the articles in the second charge which are wholly abuses directed at the judges and the courts. In any case, the Canadian approach should be treated as providing guidance and it cannot be said that the judges were not justified in refusing to follow *Kopyto*. Also, I see no reason why the judges below should not have applied the test they had decided upon. The appellant would be protected if the publication of the articles survives that test.

Was there a real risk that the published articles would undermine public confidence in the administration of justice? In *Solicitors General v. Radio New Zealand*, the court was of the opinion that direct proof of such a risk will rarely be possible and the court must consider all the circumstances of the publication. However, the court identified a number of relevant factors which included, "the statements published, the timing of their publication, the size of the audience they reached, the likely nature, impart and duration of their influence." It should be noted that the judges below were aware of these relevant factors when they decided on the evil consequences of the publication of the articles. Suffice to say, having regard to the fact that the *Oriental Daily News* has a large circulation with a readership of over 2.3 million, and the newspaper is intended for the reasonable and average person in Hong Kong and that the publication was in the nature of a sustained campaign for over a month against the Judiciary, the judges were entitled to conclude that "the newspaper clearly wanted its readers and the public to believe, that the Judiciary was an instrument of political persecution and that the judges had no integrity at all" and if that were believed, "there would be very little left in the confidence of the public in the administration of justice in Hong Kong." Their finding was clearly supported by the evidence and their conclusion that the second charge has been proved cannot be challenged.

The 1st charge is direct interference with the due administration of justice. The pursuit and harassment of Godfrey J.A. lasted over a period of four days. This received widespread media coverage including television coverage. The motive and real purpose behind such an operation was found by the judges as "to take revenge for the court's decisions against the Oriental Press Group and to meet out a punishment to the judge for his judgments against the Group. The so called educational purpose of the operation was clearly an excuse which cannot hold up to scrutiny". This finding is not challenged by the appellant. In *AG v. Butterworth* [1963] 1 QB 696 Pearson L.J. had this to say as regards intimidation of witnesses, "In my judgment, however, such victimisation, because it tends to deter persons from giving evidence as witnesses in future proceedings, and giving that evidence frankly and fully and without fear of consequences, is an interference with the due administration of justice as a continuing process and does constitute contempt of court." Thus in direct interference, it is the effect of the conduct complained of on others that is material and not whether the person to whom the conduct has been directed had in fact been affected by it. Whether or not Godfrey J.A. took the harassments unperturbed is immaterial. On this finding, there must be a real risk that the public may have been led to think that judges may not act independently or fairly for fear of punishment for their decision by those against them the decision has been made, and thereby confidence in the due administration of justice would be undermined. The judges cannot be faulted in their conclusion that this charge of contempt of court is also proved.

On the sentences imposed, having regard to the nature of the offences and the scale in which the acts of contempt have been carried out, they are neither wrong in principle nor manifestly excessive and there is no justification for suspending the sentences. I would dismiss both the appeal against conviction and the appeal against sentence.

Mortimer V-P: The appeal on both liability and sentence is dismissed.

We make an *order nisi* for costs against the appellant.

The appellant is on bail pending appeal and until 10 days after this judgment. This was granted by Liu JA on 3 July 1998 on the terms that he must surrender to the High Court within 10 days after this judgment. Because of the intervening holidays and for the sake of clarity, we order that the appellant shall surrender to the High Court before P. Chan CJHC on Friday, 19 February 1999 at 10 a.m. The order of Liu JA of 3 July 1998 is varied accordingly.

Vice President (Barry Mortimer)

Justice of Appeal (Simon Mayo)

Justice of Appeal (Arthur Leong)

Mr Sydney Kentridge QC, Mr Cheng Huan SC and Mr Jason Pow (M/s Iu, Lai & Li) for Respondent/Appellant

Mr Ronny Tong SC and Mr Johannes Chan (Dept of Justice) for Applicant/Respondent

---

第二十八條

香港居民的人身自由不受侵犯。

香港居民不受任意或非法逮捕、拘留、監禁。禁止任意或非法搜查居民的身體、剝奪或限制居民的人身自由。禁止對居民施行酷刑、任意或非法剝奪居民的生命。

案例

香港特別行政區 對 關健森

HCMA 263/2005

簡略案情

上訴人被控違反《侵害人身罪條例》第 36（b）條，即“襲擊在正當執行職務的警務人員”罪。據控方指，第二證人與另一警員在案發日著便裝在街上巡邏時，看見上訴人急步從衍慶街轉入富源街向崇齡街方向走去，認為上訴人形跡可疑，懷疑其攜帶毒品，遂上前截查。但上訴人拒絕讓警員搜身，並強調不要阻礙他去馬會投注。在上訴人企圖離開時，第一證人（一名警長）途經現場，勸告上訴人合作，但上訴人認為他是良好市民，沒有理由被搜身。在其企圖強行離開時，跟第一證人發生肢體踫撞。第二證人便連同另一名警員將上訴人制服並拘捕，期間上訴人不斷掙扎。

但據上訴人辯稱，其在案發時正前往馬會投注站投注六合彩，遇到控方第二證人要求他出示身份證和讓其搜身。可是搜查完畢後，他們還拖延時間，不讓上訴人離開，由於上訴人尚在上班期間，便要求控方第二證人盡快完成調查。雙方因此發生衝突，後來第一證人還誣衊他襲擊。經裁判處審訊後，上訴人被判有罪。他不服裁決，遂向原訟庭提起上訴。上訴理據是：1）裁判官沒有充分考慮第一證人在被襲擊時是否屬於正當地執行職務；2）沒有足夠證據證明控方第一證人有合理理由懷疑上訴人犯有危險藥物罪。

裁決摘要

對於上訴人的第一個上訴理由，法官雖然同意答辯人引述終審法院案例 *Chung Wai Leung v. HKSAR* FAMC 64/2004 指出裁判官不需提及所有案情，才能顯示他已考慮相關的事實，但法官認為對於罪行的主要元素之一，裁判官理應作出明確的分析、裁斷。若裁判官當時曾經作出分析考慮，應會提及當時第二證人是否有權截查上訴人及其是否在正當地執行職務，進而可引申至究竟控方第一證人是否也在正當地執行職務。而上訴人的第二個上訴理由，關於《基本法》第 28 條對上訴人人身自由的保護，法官同意根據終審法院在*香港特別行政區對楊美雲及其他人士* [2005] 2 HKLRD 212 一案中的裁定，指警員在行使《警隊條例》第 54（2）條所賦予的權力時，都必須具備相應的“合理地懷疑”。而“合理地懷疑”是指真正的懷疑和有合理理由的懷疑。

然而，在本案中，根據第二證人的證供，上訴人只是“急步”行走，並沒有其他客觀的證據，比如一名人士在看見穿著軍裝的警察時便立刻低頭轉身急步離開、或被有經驗的警員看見他與區內“知名”的販毒者有接觸等等，均可構成合理懷疑。因此，法官認為警員當時並不能說是“在正當執行職務”，所以警方當時是無權截查上訴人的。進而考慮到上訴人當時所作的所謂“襲擊”，其實僅僅是“推”了第一證人一下，在此情況下，上訴人是在作出合理反抗，不構成“襲擊”罪。據此，法庭判上訴得直，定罪撤銷，刑罰擱置。

然而，法官在判詞末段亦指出，“上訴人當然有權維護他的人身自由，但他在行使此權利時，應作出合理堅持，而非大吵大鬧、以粗言穢語辱罵警員。須知在香港的環境情況，若某人在公眾地方大吵大鬧，尤其是辱罵警員，勢必引來群眾（駐）足圍觀。除了有可能造成阻礙，更可能引致秩序大亂、防礙公眾安寧。本席絕不鼓勵上訴人當時的表現及行徑，且對上訴人的言行作出（譴）責。”

HCMA 263/2005

香港特別行政區
高等法院原訟法庭
刑事上訴司法管轄權
判罪上訴

案件編號：裁判法院上訴案件 2005 年第 263 號
（原九龍城裁判法院案件 2004 年第 13753 號）

香港特別行政區
訴
被告人　關健森

主審法官：高等法院原訟法庭暫委法官張慧玲

聆訊日期：2005 年 7 月 7 日

宣判日期：2005 年 7 月 25 日

判案書

背境

1. 上訴人被控一項「襲擊在正當執行職務的警務人員」罪，違反香港法例第 212 章《侵害人身罪條例》第 36(b) 條。他否認控罪，經審訊後被裁定罪名成立。上訴人就定罪不服，提出上訴。

控方案情

2. 在案發當天下午約 5 時 20 分，控方第二證人（警員 33167）和同僚穿着便裝，在新蒲崗富源街執行反罪惡巡邏任務時，見到上訴人急步由衍慶街轉入富源街向崇齡街方向行去。控方第二證人認為上訴人形跡可疑，懷疑上訴人身上可能藏有毒品，便示意同僚一起上前截查。

3. 控方第二證人稍後在富源街某號的樓梯口把上訴人截停，向他出示警察委任證；並對他說因懷疑他身上藏有毒品，要向他搜身。上訴人聽罷，不但拒絕搜身，更高聲以粗言喝斥控方第二證人不能隨便搜查良好市民，也不要阻礙他去投注賽馬。控方第二證人於是向上訴人解釋搜查的原因，但上訴人依然不肯合作，再次高聲粗言喝令控方第二證人不要妨礙他前往投注，更作勢起步離開。控方第二證人於是張開雙手阻止，並和同僚把上訴人帶往更靠近樓梯口內，但上訴人繼續以粗言穢語破口大罵。

4. 此時控方第一證人（警長 9167）剛巧在執行穿着便裝巡邏中，他由崇齡街右轉入富源街時，看見他的兩名下屬（即控方第二證人及警員 53820）正和上訴人站在該樓梯口講話，而上訴人不時以手指向控方第二證人他們，並似嘗試在他們之間的空隙離開，但為警員 53820 張手阻止。

5. 控方第一證人遂上前查問究竟。當他到達他們身旁時，見到上訴人神情兇惡，高聲粗言穢語指斥警察不能隨便搜查良好市民，並不要阻礙他往投注賽馬。控方第一證人於是出示警察委任證，勸說上訴人不要高聲呼叫，冷靜下來。

6. 控方第一證人向控方第二證人查詢發生何事。控方第二證人向控方第一證人作出報告後，控方第一證人向上訴人解釋說控方第二證人他們只是依法執行職務，希望上訴人合作。但上訴人不單不聽勸說，反而變本加厲，高聲用粗言穢語喝令控方第一證人不可阻礙他去投注賽馬，並企圖離開。控方第一證人遂張開雙臂阻止，說上訴人不能就此離開。此時上訴人突然以右手向前伸展，打向控方第一證人面部；力度雖不大，但也足以令控方第二證人畧（略）失重心，只是沒有跌倒而矣。

7. 控方第二證人和警員 53820 立即用手控制上訴人，在上訴人左右兩邊，緊握上訴人的手臂；但上訴人依然不肯就範，不斷擺動身軀。最後在控方第一證人的協助下，他們終於成功制服了上訴人。事件中無人受傷。

辯方案情

8. 上訴人選擇作供，但沒有傳召其他證人。上訴人為髮型師，以往無刑事紀錄。他指在案發時他正前往馬會投注站投注六合彩。在途經富源街時遇上控方第二證人及其同僚。控方第二證人要求他出示身分證和讓控方第二證人搜身。上訴人遂出示身分證和讓他們搜身。

9. 當搜查完畢後，控方第二證人還拿着上訴人的身分證在檢視。由於上訴人還在上班期間，便要求控方第二證人快些完成調查，好讓他盡快返回工作崗位。但控方第二證人他們故意拖延，要上訴人站在一旁；且態度欠佳，把上訴人當成壞人看待。上訴人便出言拒絕，說「要查就在這裡查」。此時控方第一證人已經來到，而控方第二證人及其同僚以不想阻礙途人為由硬把他拉往樓梯底。

10. 上訴人恐怕他們可能會誣衊他，所以高叫：「差佬屈人呀！」但對方有人回應說：「屈你咪屈你囉！」然後控方第一證人就捉着上訴人的手去輕觸他本人（控方第一證人）的臉，並立即裝成疼痛的樣子。在旁的其中一位警員立即指上訴人襲警，並將他雙手扣上手銬。上訴人開始情緒激動，對控方第一證人他們說：「你哋咁樣屈良好市民，我實告你！」事發後兩天左右，上訴人前往警察投訴課投訴控方第一證人他們行為不當。

上訴理由

11. 上訴人代表魏龍傑大律師提出兩項上訴理由指定罪不安穩

上訴理由（一）

12. 裁判官沒有或沒有充份考慮控方第一證人在被襲擊時是否正在正當執行職務。

13. 魏大律師指從裁斷陳述書第 11 至 16 段可見，裁判官在考慮證據時，只將注意力集中於考慮兩位控方證人和上訴人誰是誠實可靠的人。由此可見，裁判官在作出事實的裁斷時，沒有或沒有充份考慮控方第一證人在被襲擊時是否在正當執行職務。

上訴理由（二）

14. 裁判官錯誤裁定控方第一證人在被襲擊時是在正當執行職務：

（a）沒有或沒有足夠證據證明控方第一證人有合理理由懷疑上訴人干犯了管有危險藥物罪；或

（b）根據香港法例第 134 章《危險藥物條例》第 52(9) 條，上訴人可反對在公眾場所被搜查。

15. 魏大律師指裁判官可能認為兩位控方證人的證供已清楚顯示控方第一證人在被襲擊時是在正當執行職務，因而沒有在裁斷陳述書內為此詳細解釋。若是如此，裁判官就控方第一證人在被襲擊時是在正當執行職務的裁定是錯誤的。

16. 就上述上訴理由 (2)(a)，魏大律師指控方沒有或沒有足夠證據證明控方第一證人有合理理由懷疑上訴人干犯了管有危險藥物罪或身上藏有毒品。

17. 魏大律師指根據控方證人的證供，控方第一證人在被襲擊時所執行的職務是扣留上訴人以作身體搜查，因為上訴人被懷疑身上藏有毒品。

18. 魏大律師陳詞指上訴人的人身自由受《基本法》保障（參看《基本法》第 28 條），而控方第一證人搜查上訴人的權力來自香港法例第 232 章《警隊條例》第 54(2) 條；及第 134 章《危險藥物條例》第 52(1)(f) 條。

19. 魏大律師引用權威著作 *Hong Kong Archbold*，（第 15–16 段）陳詞指由於普通法並不賦予警方搜查的權力，因此警方行使搜查權力時必須嚴格遵守法例的要求。

20. 如控方第一證人當時是行使《警隊條例》第 54(2) 條所賦予的權力，則他必須「合理地懷疑」上訴人干犯了管有危險藥物罪。

21. 魏大律師引用案例 *HKSAR v. Yeung May Wan and Others*, FACC19/2004, 5 May 2005，第 71 至第 75 段支持他指《警隊條例》第 54(2) 條要求的「合理地懷疑」是指真正的懷疑和有合理理由的懷疑此論點。

22. 魏大律師指控方第一證人的證供沒有提及他有否真正懷疑和基於什麼合理理由懷疑上訴人干犯了管有危險藥物罪。控方第一證人只是說他是基於控方第二證人的報告而要阻止上訴人離開並搜查上訴人，他的證供沒有提及他從控方第二證人得到什麼資料、也沒有提及所得的資料是否令他合理地懷疑上訴人干犯了管有危險藥物罪。

23. 魏大律師指假設控方第一證人已從控方第二證人獲得全部有關資料，從裁斷陳述書第 8 段及控方第二證人的證供可見，控方第一證人只知上訴人被控方第二證人形容為「形跡可疑」，以及被控方第二證人懷疑身上藏有毒品。由於這些資料都是控方第二證人的主觀描述或懷疑，沒有客觀的事實基礎支持，所以控方第一證人對上訴人身上藏有毒品的懷疑並不合理。

24. 魏大律師亦指如控方第一證人當時是行使《危險藥物條例》第 52(1)(f) 條賦予的權力，他必須「有理由懷疑」上訴人實際保管有危險藥物。《危險藥物條例》第 52(1)(f) 條內的「有理由懷疑」是客觀的準則，魏大律師指應與《警隊條例》第 54(2) 條內的「合理地懷疑」作同一詮釋。故此，控方第一證人對上訴人身上藏有毒品的懷疑並不合理。

25. 就上訴理由 (2)(b)，魏大律師指根據《危險藥物條例》第 52(9)(c) 條，上訴人可反對在公眾場所被受搜查，因此控方第一證人是沒有合法權力為了在案發地點搜查上訴人而阻止上訴人離開。

答辯人回應

26. 答辯人代表高級政府律師林少明就上訴理由作出回應：

上訴理由（一）

27. 林律師指上訴人不能單憑裁判官在其裁斷陳述書中並無提及控方第一證人在被襲擊時是否在正當執行職務，便批評他沒有或沒有充分考慮這點。因為這點正正就是控罪及控罪條文所指控的「襲擊在正當執行職務的警務人員」，也是最關鍵的控罪元素之一。這點實在太明顯不過。裁判官怎會連這點也忽略呢？

28. 林律師指終審庭在 *Chung Wai Leung v. HKSAR*, FAMC64/2004 案中引述 *HKSAR v. Singh Balraj* [2003] 3 HKC 621 並明確指出，法官在判詞中沒有提及某些事情並不等於他沒有想及有關事情。

上訴理由（二）（a）

29. 林律師指從控方第二證人口中去瞭解事件的經過（即控方第二證人所指見到上訴人急步向崇齡街行及形跡可疑並懷疑他身上藏有毒品等），控方第一證人已有足夠證據合理地懷疑上訴人干犯了管有危險藥物罪。所以控方第一證人（及其同事）有權根據《危險藥物條例》第 52(1)(f) 條或《警隊條例》第 54(2) 條搜查上訴人。

30. 林律師根據 *A.G. v. Kong Chung Shing* [1980] HKSR 533 的案例，《警隊條例》第 54 條可以是純屬主觀性的，而《危險藥物條例》則須執法人員說出其懷疑理由。本案的情況均符合兩者要求。

31. 本席特此一提，在魏大律師指出有關的《警隊條例》54 條在 *Kong Chung Shing* 一案後曾作出修改，林律師不再堅持他的「主觀論」，但他陳詞指控方證人有合理懷疑理由。

32. 林律師指雖然控方第一證人的證供中除了得知上訴人被懷疑身上藏有毒品外，並沒有詳細提及他從控方第二證人得到什麼資料，但在現實的執法情況下他不可能詳細詢問控方第二證人的所見所聞然後才判斷其懷疑上訴人是否合理，他理應可以倚賴其同事的判斷去對上訴人執行正當職務（即搜查行動）。林律師指控方第二證人及第一證人兩人「合而為一」，一同正當執行職務。

33. 林律師亦指另一方面，若要求執法人員凡事要親自耳聞目睹才可執行正當職務是不合情理及不符現實的。

上訴理由（二）（b）

34. 林律師指雖然根據《危險藥物條例》第 52(9) 條，上訴人可反對在公眾場所被搜查，但這點並不適用於本案，因為由始至終上訴人只是想強行離去，根本上是完全拒絕接受搜查，並非只是反對在公眾場所進行搜查（例如要求前往警署接受搜查）。

裁決

35. 本席已詳細考慮魏大律師及林律師的詳盡陳詞。首先，就上訴理由（二）（a），本席認同並接納魏大律師的陳詞見解。

有關法例

36. 根據香港法例第 232 章《警隊條例》第 54 條：

「(1) 警務人員如在任何街道或其他公眾地方、或於任何船隻或交通工具上，不論日夜任何時間，發現任何人行動可疑，該警務人員採取以下行動，乃屬合法——

(a) 截停該人以要求他出示身分證明文件供該警務人員查閱；

(b) 扣留該人一段合理期間，在該期間內由該警務人員查究該人是否涉嫌在任何時候犯了任何罪行；及

(c) 如該警務人員認為以下行動乃屬必需——

(i) 向該人搜查任何可能對該警務人員構成危險的東西；及

(ii) 扣留該人一段為作出該項搜查而合理需要的時間。

(2) 警務人員如在任何街道或其他公眾地方、或於任何船隻或交通工具上，不論日夜任何時間，發現任何人是他合理地懷疑已經或即將或意圖犯任何罪行者，該警務人員採取以下行動，乃屬合法——

(a) 截停該人以要求他出示身分證明文件供該警務人員查閱；

(b) 扣留該人一段合理期間，在該期間內由該警務人員查究該人是否涉嫌在任何時候犯了任何罪行；

(c) 向該人搜查任何相當可能對調查該人所犯或有理由懷疑該人已經或即將或意圖犯的罪行有價值的東西 (不論就其本身或連同任何其他東西)；及

(d) 扣留該人一段為作出該項搜查而合理需要的期間。」(本席以橫線加以強調)

37. 根據 54(1) 條，若警員發現任何人行動可疑時，警員可依據 54(1) 條文內容所賦予的權力截查該人。而搜查是限於如該警務人員認為「向該人搜查任何可能對警務人員構成危險的東西及扣留該人一段為作出該項搜查而合理需要的期間」是必需的行動。

38. 就 54(1) 條，法例只是就搜查時段列出了「合理需要」此要求，就警員發現任何人行動可疑，法例並無列明該發現需為合理。看來警員可「主觀」地認為某人「行動可疑」。

39. 反之，根據 54(2) 條，若警員發現任何人是他合理地懷疑已經或將或意圖犯任何罪行，警員可依據 54(2) 條文內容賦予的權力截查該人「向該人搜查任何相當可能對調查該人所犯或有理由懷疑該人已經或即將或意圖犯的罪行有價值的東西」，而搜查是包括該人「本身或連同任何其他東西」。明顯可見，警員的「懷疑」須是「合理」的。

40. 由於本案的警員 (控方第二證人) 指他當時懷疑上訴人身藏毒品而要向上訴人作出搜身，相關的條文應是 54(2) 條而非 54(1) 條。控方必需證明警員合理地懷疑上訴人身藏毒品。

41. 而根據香港法例第 134 章《危險藥物條例》第 52(1)(f)(i) 條：

「(1) 為施行本條例，任何警務人員及海關人員可——

(f) 截停及搜查任何人，以及搜查該人的財物，如——

(i) 他有理由懷疑該人實際保管有可予扣押的物件；……」

42. 根據上述《危險藥物條例》第 52(1)(f)(i) 條，警員是需要有理由懷疑某人實際保管有危險藥物的。

43. 控方第二證人的證供是上訴人「急步」行走，他認為上訴人「形跡可疑」，但他從無提及上訴人如何形跡可疑。誠言，某人是否形跡可疑，某程度上是一主觀看法，但這並不表示不會有客觀事實支持。譬方說，一名人士在看見穿着軍裝的警察時便立刻低頭轉身急步離開、或被有經驗的警員看見他與區內「知名」的販毒者有接觸等等，均可構成合理懷疑。

44. 在本案，控方第二證人當時是穿着便裝在富源街巡邏。當時是下午約 5 時 20 分。無證據指上訴人在「急步」由衍慶街轉入富源街向崇齡街方向行去時，他知悉控方第二證人的警員身分。控方第二證人從無指出他為何認為上訴人「形跡可疑」，更無指出為何他懷疑上訴人身上可能藏有毒品。

45. 本席裁定控方不能提出足夠證據顯示當時控方第二證人是「合理地懷疑」上訴人身藏毒品，或「有理由懷疑」上訴人「實際保管有危險藥物」，他不是依據法律賦予他的權力而為，他當時截查上訴人並不是「在正當執行職務」。

46. 控方第一證人從無顯示他本人「合理地懷疑」上訴人身藏毒品或「有理由懷疑」上訴人「實際保管有危險藥物」，他只是從控方第二證人處得悉控方第二證人有懷疑上訴人身藏毒品而已。再者，證據顯示控方第二證人並無將上訴人曾「急步」行走、他（控方第二證人）認為上訴人「形跡可疑」等資料告知控方第一證人。明顯控方第一證人當時亦非「在正當執行職務」。本席不接納林律師指控方第二及第一證人「合而為一」此論點。

47. 上訴人當時所作的「襲擊」其實是「推」了控方第一證人一下。以警方當時是無權截查上訴人，而上訴人是「推」開攔阻他的控方第一證人一下而言，在該情況下上訴人亦只是作出合理反抗，不構成「襲擊」罪。

48. 就上訴理由（一），裁判官在本案確只是說控方第一、第二證人證供可信可靠，繼而裁定上訴人罪名成立。雖然裁判官不需提及所有案情，但上訴人面對的罪行是襲擊「在正當執行職務的警務人員」，當時控方第一證人是否在正當執行職務是罪行的主要元素之一，裁判官是理應就此作出分析裁斷的。

49. 若裁判官當時曾經作出分析考慮，他應會顧及到究竟當時控方第二證人是否有權截查上訴人及他是否在正當執行職務，而引申至究竟控方第一證人是否在正當執行職務？

50. 就上訴理由（二）(b)，本席並不認同魏大律師的陳詞見解，而接納認同林律師的論點。由於上訴人由始至終只是想強行離去，完全拒絕接受搜查，上訴人並非反對在公眾地方進行搜查，警員是無須向上訴人表示上訴人可要求前往警署接受搜查的。

51. 本席特此強調，雖然在本案，警方人員未能顯示他們合理地懷疑上訴人身藏毒品或有理由懷疑上訴人實際保管有危險藥物，他們無權將上訴人截查，上訴人當時的反應亦極其不恰當。上訴人當然有權維護他的人身自由，但他在行使他此權利時，應作出合理堅持，而非大吵大鬧、以粗言穢語辱罵警員。須知在香港的環境情況，若某人在公眾地方大吵大鬧，尤其是辱罵警員，勢必引來群眾注（駐）足圍觀。除了有可能造成阻礙，更可能引致秩序大亂、防礙公眾安寧。本席絕不鼓勵上訴人當時的表現及行徑，且對上訴人的言行作出衍（譴）責。

52. 基於上述理由，本席裁定上訴得直，定罪撤銷，刑罰擱置。

高等法院原訟法庭暫委法官 (張慧玲)

控方：由律政司林少明高級政府律師代表香港特別行政區。
辯方：由聶柏仁律師行委派魏龍傑大律師代表被告人。

Lau Cheong, Lau Wong v. HKSAR

Lau Cheong、Lau Wong 對 香港特別行政區

CACC 646/1998；FACC 6/2001

簡略案情

第一上訴人和第二上訴人持刀共同搶劫被害人，在掙扎中，被害人和第二上訴人均受刀傷。隨後被害人被發現死亡，頸部、腕部和腿部均縛有繩索，其死因不是刀傷，而是頸部被繩索捆綁至窒息而死。第一上訴人承認搶劫罪，同時也承認為防止被害人逃走以及復仇，遂以繩索捆綁被害人，但不承認其具有殺死被害人或對其造成嚴重傷害是故意的。第一上訴人同時作證稱第二上訴人在當時已暈厥，並沒有參與捆綁被害人。雖然第二上訴人否認搶劫和殺人罪，但證據顯示，他身上藏有被害人財物，及經法醫鑒定，從第二上訴人身上發現被害人的血跡及被害人衣服的纖維，這些證據均證明第二上訴人參與了上述搶劫行為。在審訊中，第二上訴人選擇不出庭作供，只依賴第一上訴人對其有利的供詞。最終陪審團裁定兩名上訴人均謀殺罪成立。按照香港法律，謀殺罪只有強制性終身監禁一種判罰，因此，法官判處兩名上訴人終身監禁，同時因搶劫罪分別判處 6 年和 9 年監禁。

在向上訴庭的上訴中，兩名上訴人提出了兩個和憲法性權利相關的上訴理由：1）在普通法下，在認定謀殺罪時，並不需要加害人有殺死被害人的主觀故意，而只需要有對被害人施加嚴重肉體傷害的主觀意圖，且客觀上造成了被害人的死亡，則可構成謀殺罪（下稱“嚴重傷害規則”）。兩名上訴人認為“嚴重傷害規則”違反了《基本法》第 28 條和第 87 條，以及《香港人權法案條例》第 5 條、第 10 條和第 11 條。《基本法》第 28 條規定：“香港居民不受任意或非法逮捕、拘留、監禁。禁止任意或非法搜查居民的身體、剝奪或限制居民的人身自由”。《香港人權法案條例》第 5（1）條亦有類似規定。《香港人權法案條例》第 10 條和第 11 條則是分別關於法律面前人人平等的權利、公開審判和無罪推定的原則。

兩名上訴人的第二個上訴理由是關於“強制性終身監禁”的判刑。香港法律規定對謀殺罪的判罰是“強制性終身監禁”，亦即對謀殺罪只有終身監禁一種判罰。上訴人認為該法例亦違反《基本法》第 28 條給予香港居民的不受“任意或非法”拘禁的保障。同時，根據《刑事訴訟程序條例》第 83G 條規定，除法定判刑控罪外，其他任何被判有罪的人可對其判刑向上訴法庭上訴。申請人認為《刑事訴訟程序條例》第 83G 條違反了《香港人權法案條例》第 11（4）條規定，任何經判定犯罪者有權就判刑向上級法院申請覆核判刑。

裁決摘要

上訴庭

主觀故意部份

上訴法庭援引 *HKSAR v. Coady*, [2002] 2 HKLRD 195 一案，認為上訴法庭在該案中已經裁決“嚴重傷害規則”並未違反《香港人權法案》第 5（1）條、第 10 條和第 11 條，而上訴人亦承認上訴法庭受該判決約束。雖然第二上訴人主張其在本案中屬於從犯（Secondary Party），沒有直接實施犯罪行為，和 *Coady* 一案的情況有所不同，不應受該判決約束。但上訴法庭認為從陪審團確認的事實來看，第二上訴人其實參與了犯罪行為。而且在另一個上訴庭案件中 *HKSAR v. Pun Ganga Chandra & Anr* [2001] 2 HKLRD 151，法庭已經詳盡考慮了從犯的問題，仍然認定“嚴重傷害規則”不違反《香港人權法案》第 5（1）條。《香港人權法案》的規定是“任何人”不受任意或非法拘禁，因此是否是從犯在本案中並無差別。

判刑部份

上訴法庭援引 *Pun Ganga Chandra & Anr* 一案，認為該案已經就“強制性終身監禁”判罰做出裁決，認為其不違反《香港人權法案》第 5（1）條以及《基本法》第 25 條“香港居民在法律面前一律平等”和第 28 條的規定，上訴法庭受該判決約束。針對申請人主張第 83G 條違憲的部份，上訴法庭認為香港已經設立委員會，覆核在押犯的情況，以確定他們能否被提早釋放。對於被判“強制性終身監禁”的罪犯，在其服刑後 5 年就可得到覆核，以後至少每兩年一次。在覆核中當事人會被告知所有委員會會考慮的因素，並有機會為自己做出陳述。因此即使被判強制性終身監禁，當事人仍然享有《香港人權法案》第 11（4）條下的向更高層仲裁組織覆核的權利。因此，《刑事訴訟程序條例》第 83G 條並不違憲。兩名上訴人的上訴被駁回。但容許上訴至終審法院。

終審法院

終審法庭首先回顧了謀殺罪的主觀要素，指出在普通法的歷史發展中“嚴重傷害規則”確實存在爭議，但是在多年來的判決和立法中，經反覆辯論和考慮後，仍舊得以保留。至於認為“嚴重傷害規則”違反《香港人權法案》第 11 條的無罪推定原則，終審法院認為該“嚴重傷害規則”並未假設當事人有意殺人或者假定其犯有謀殺罪，所以並不違反無罪推定原則，它僅為一項主觀要件的判斷標準，其本身以及構成犯罪的其他要素均需要證據證明。

對於《基本法》第 28 條和《香港人權法案》第 5（1）條的部份，終審法院指出，第 5（1）條的行文只包含逮捕（arrest）和拘禁（detention），而第 28 條的規定則擴展到包括監禁（imprisonment）。而監禁從字面上則包含了經法庭定罪而被合法剝奪自由的情況，當然，第 28 條的目的不是用於保護經合法判決有罪的罪犯。然而，第 28 條的規定是香港居民不受“任意或非法”的拘禁，因此，除非法外，如果是合法但任意的監禁，亦屬法律所排斥的情形。因此，如果實體法律內包涵了任意的成份，亦可能抵觸第 28 條而無效。終審法院援引新西蘭上訴法庭在 *Neilsen v. Attorney-General* [2001] 3 NZLR 433 一案中的意見，認為判定是否“任意”拘禁的標準在於，拘禁是否“反覆無常的、無原因的，缺乏合理理由的（capricious, unreasoned, without reasonable cause）”。終審法院認為，對於“嚴重傷害規則”而言，行為的人具有造成他人身體上嚴重傷害的主觀故意且最終造成他人死亡，從法律角度看這種行為屬於謀殺，決不是“反覆無常的”或“無理由的”。所以“嚴重傷害規則”

並未違反《基本法》第 28 條。對於“嚴重傷害規則”違反《基本法》第 25 條的“法律面前人人平等”的主張，終審法院認為這樣的主張不可能獨立於“不得任意拘禁”的規定。因此，上訴人針對“嚴重傷害規則”違反《基本法》的上訴全部被駁回。

關於“強制性終身監禁”違反《基本法》的上訴理由，終審法院首先回顧了普通法及香港法律對謀殺罪判刑的發展，指出在 1993 年之前，對謀殺罪的唯一判罰是死刑，後經過激烈的討論後，從死刑轉為“強制性終身監禁”。因此，“強制性終身監禁”的法律規定，是經過反覆討論並平衡了各種社會利益後的結果。對本案而言，在考慮“強制性終身監禁”是否違憲的問題上，焦點在於其是否“顯而易見地不合比例（manifestly disproportionate）”。對於按照法律規定作出的判罰，必須是明顯的不合比例，才能推斷它依據的法律是“反覆無常的、無原因的，缺乏合理理由的”。上訴人主張，謀殺罪具有各種各樣的情形，從以對兒童性侵犯為目的的殘暴殺害、造成多人死亡的恐怖主義行為，到為解除無法治癒的愛人的痛苦而實施的安樂死，這些行為具有不同的罪責度（culpability），對其適用相同的“終身監禁”判罰，這意味著“任意”實施拘禁。然而，終審法院認為，在考慮是否“顯而易見地不合比例”時，罪責度並不是唯一考慮的因素，除了犯罪行為本身的實質和嚴重程度以外，也需考量對公眾的保護、防治其他犯罪及社會譴責等問題。因此，不能因為不同的謀殺個案存在不同的罪責度而認定“強制性終身監禁”的判罰不合比例。是故上訴人該申請理由亦被駁回。

FACC 6 / 2001

IN THE COURT OF FINAL APPEAL OF THE HONG KONG SPECIAL ADMINISTRATIVE REGION

FINAL APPEAL NO. 6 OF 2001 (criminal)
(ON APPEAL FROM CACC No. 646 of 1998)

Between:

LAU CHEONG	1st Appellant
LAU WONG	2nd Appellant
- and -	
HKSAR	Respondent

Court: Chief Justice Li, Mr Justice Chan PJ, Mr Justice Ribeiro PJ, Mr Justice Fuad NPJ and Sir Anthony Mason NPJ

Dates of Hearing: 15-19 April 2002

Date of Judgment: 16 July 2002

JUDGMENT

Chief Justice Li and Mr Justice Ribeiro PJ:

1. In this appeal, a challenge is made to the legal and constitutional validity of two aspects of the offence of murder, namely, an intention to cause grievous bodily harm as a sufficient form of *mens rea*; and life imprisonment as the mandatory penalty under section 2 of the Offences Against the Person Ordinance, Cap 212.

The facts and the decisions below

2. The prosecution's case at the trial was that the appellants, both armed with knives, had acted in concert in robbing the victim Kei Wai-heung. A violent struggle had ensued, during which both the victim and the 2nd appellant had suffered knife injuries. The victim was later found dead, tied up with rope which bound his neck, wrists and legs. His death was found to have resulted, not from the knife wounds, but from ligature strangulation caused by the rope around his neck.

3. The 1st appellant pleaded guilty to robbery and admitted in evidence that he had tied up the victim to prevent him from getting away and taking revenge. However, he denied that he had any intention to kill or cause grievous bodily harm. He was prepared to plead guilty to manslaughter but this was not accepted by the prosecution. He also said that the 2nd appellant had fainted at the material time and did not take part in tying up the victim.

4. The 2nd appellant denied robbery and any participation in causing the victim's death. However, there was evidence, including his possession of the victim's property, blood stains and evidence of contact, which indicated that he had been involved in both the robbery and the events leading to the victim's death. He did not testify but relied on those parts of the 1st appellant's evidence which were favourable to him.

5. At the trial, Mrs Justice Bokhary, delivered a summing-up which the Court of Appeal described as impeccable, in our view rightly so, subject to the legal issues raised in this appeal. In accordance with the usual practice in murder cases, it included the direction that a killing accompanied by an intention to cause grievous bodily harm constitutes murder. In respect of the 2nd appellant, the jury was directed as to participation in a joint enterprise. Although the summing-up inclined markedly towards manslaughter verdicts, the jury convicted both appellants of robbery and murder.

6. The appellants received mandatory sentences of life imprisonment for murder. They were also given concurrent sentences for robbery: 6 years' imprisonment in the case of the 1st appellant (reflecting his guilty plea) and 9 years' imprisonment in the 2nd appellant's case.

7. The Court of Appeal dealt with their appeal in two parts. A number of grounds involving various aspects of the summing-up were dealt with first and rejected in a judgment delivered in June 2000. The second part raised the constitutional issues with which we are now concerned and was adjourned pending the Court of Appeal's decisions in *HKSAR v Coady* [2000] 2 HKLRD 195; and *HKSAR v Pun Ganga Chandra* [2001] 2 HKLRD 151, where similar issues had been raised.

8. After publication of those judgments, the Court of Appeal re-convened and, after hearing further submissions, dismissed the appeal (*HKSAR v Lau Cheong and Lau Wong* [2002] 2 HKLRD 869).

Leave to appeal

9. Leave to appeal to this Court was granted by the Appeal Committee on the basis of four certified questions of law.

10. The first two questions address the mens rea for murder. The appellants seek first to challenge the sufficiency, as a matter of common law, of an intention to cause grievous bodily harm as such *mens rea*. Secondly, they seek to argue that the grievous bodily harm rule contravenes provisions of the Basic Law and the Bill of Rights which prohibit, among other things, arbitrary detention or imprisonment.

11. The second pair of questions arise in relation to the sentence for murder. The appellants seek here to contend that mandatory life imprisonment falls foul of our constitutional safeguards against arbitrary imprisonment, cruel, inhuman or degrading punishment and inequality before the law. They also seek to contend that such a mandatory sentence violates their constitutional right to a review by a higher tribunal. Furthermore, they allege that the system unconstitutionally denies them access to a court to challenge the lawfulness of their detention.

12. At the hearing of the appeal, the challenges to the grievous bodily harm rule and the mandatory life sentence were made on behalf of the 1st appellant by Ms Audrey Eu SC and her team, instructed by the Director of Legal Aid. The 2nd appellant appeared in person, having declined legal aid representation. He addressed us on points relating to the evidence. Those were points not open to him as the Appeal Committee had only granted leave on points of law. In any event, the points made by the 2nd appellant were of no merit. However, all of Ms Eu's legal arguments are equally relevant to his case.

Grievous bodily harm and the mens rea of murder

13. Criminal liability at common law usually requires proof of relevant prohibited conduct causing certain prohibited consequences (the *actus reus*), accompanied by a defined state of mind on the part of the accused in relation to that conduct and its consequences (*the mens rea*).

14. In the case of murder, the *actus reus* crucially involves causing the death of another person. Of course, if the accused intentionally causes that death, the *mens rea* requirement is satisfied. However, as the law stands, he may be convicted of murder without ever intending or foreseeing death as the consequence of his acts or omissions. It is sufficient if he intends to cause grievous bodily harm and death in fact results. It is this apparent lack of symmetry between what constitutes the *mens rea* of the offence and the consequence of death as part of the actus reus that is the subject of criticism.

The mens rea of murder historically

15. Such absence of symmetry has been a feature of the law of murder for centuries. The *mens rea* of murder (previously referred to as "malice aforethought" in line with Sir Edward Coke's definition of murder: 3 Inst 47) has not been confined to an intention to kill or to states of mind requiring foresight of death as a consequence. The acceptance, in modern law, of an intention to cause grievous bodily harm as sufficient actually represents the culmination of a long process whereby the range of mental states capable of sustaining a murder conviction has been progressively and drastically narrowed down.

16. Accounts of this narrowing process often begin with Coke's view in the 17th century that a person who caused death in the course of performing *any unlawful act* was guilty of murder. The width and constructive nature of such liability is demonstrated by the following passage in the *Institutes*:–

> "Homicide by misadventure is when a man doth an act that is not unlawful, which without any evil intent tendeth to a man's death .... If the act be unlawful it is murder. As if A. meaning to steal a deer in the park of B., shooteth [*sic*] at the deer and by the glance of the arrow killeth [*sic*] a boy that is hidden in a bush, this is murder, for that the act was unlawful, although A. had no intent to hurt the boy, nor knew not of him. But if B., the owner of the park had shot at his own deer, and without any ill intent had killed the boy by the glance of his arrow, this had been homicide by misadventure, and no felony." (3 Inst 56)

17. In the 18th century, Sir Michael Foster limited the doctrine to cases where the unlawful act amounted to a felony (many of which were in any event punishable by death) and, although subject to criticism, the "felony–murder rule" remained an important basis for liability during the 19th century (see Stephen, *A History of the Criminal Law of England*, Vol 3, p 57; and *Stephen's Digest of the Criminal Law*, 9th Ed, Art 264(c), p 212). The intention required was therefore not necessarily an intention to kill, but an intention to commit the relevant felony which resulted in a person's death. Alongside felony–murders generally, the common law recognized as a specific class of "malice aforethought" the intention to inflict grievous bodily harm: for an historical discussion see *Stephen' s Digest*, Art 264(a), *R v Vickers* (at 670) and *R v Cunningham* [1982] AC 566 at 575–577.

18. In the 20th century, legal writers argued for the felony–murder rule to be further restricted to felonies *of violence*: (eg, Kenny, *Outlines of Criminal Law*, 13th Ed (1929), p 140). It became recognized that this represented the law in *DPP v Beard* [1920] AC 479, where Lord Birkenhead LC stated:–

> "...... the evidence established that the prisoner killed the child by an act of violence done in the course or in the furtherance of the crime of rape, a felony involving violence. The Court held that by the law of England such an act was murder. No attempt has been made in your Lordships' House to displace this view of the law and there can be no doubt as to its soundness." (at 493)

19. A separate but related head of constructive liability for murder involved causing death in the course of resisting an officer of justice (see Russell on Crime, 12th Ed, Vol 1, p 477).

20. The most significant narrowing of the categories of murder occurred by statute. By section 11 of the Homicide Act 1957 in the United Kingdom, reproduced in 1963 in Hong Kong by s 2 of the Homicide Ordinance, Cap 339, constructive liability for murder on the basis of the felony–murder rule and of the rule on causing death in the course of resisting an officer of justice was abolished. The provision states:–

> "(1) Where a person kills another in the course or furtherance of some other offence, the killing shall not amount to murder unless done with the same malice aforethought (express or implied) as is required for a killing to amount to murder when not done in the course or furtherance of another offence.
>
> (2) For the purposes of subsection (1), a killing done in the course or for the purpose of resisting an officer of justice, or of resisting or avoiding or preventing a lawful arrest, or of effecting or assisting an escape or rescue from legal custody, shall be treated as a killing in the course or furtherance of an offence."

Grievous bodily harm after the Homicide Ordinance

21. This legislative change radically re–structured the offence of murder. Liability could no longer be founded simply on proof that death was caused in the course of committing some other offence. An accused had to be shown to have acted with a state of mind described as "malice aforethought (express or implied)". But this was an unhappy phrase. What did "implied malice" mean? Did it preserve an intention to cause grievous bodily harm as a head of *mens rea* or had that category been swept away along with liability based generally on killing in the course or furtherance of some other offence?

22. This question was addressed by a five–member Court of Appeal in *R v Vickers* [1957] 2 QB 664. It was held that an intention to cause grievous bodily harm survived as a category of mens rea for murder. That judgment was upheld in *DPP v Smith* [1961] AC 290, a decision of the House of Lords which proved controversial on other grounds. However, that controversy did not affect their Lordships' ruling that "grievous bodily harm" means "really serious harm" or their rejection of the argument that an intent to do an act "obviously dangerous to life" or "likely to kill" was required (at 334–5).

23. The issue was re–opened in *Hyam v DPP* [1975] AC 55, another decision that was to prove troublesome regarding other aspects of the mental element in criminal liability. As to the question now under discussion, the minority, comprising Lord Diplock and Lord Kilbrandon, held that *DPP v Smith* had been wrongly decided and that the Homicide Act 1957 had abolished the grievous bodily harm rule. Lord Diplock concluded (at 93) that for the accused to be convicted of murder, it was necessary to show that he had either intended to kill or intended or foresaw that human life would be endangered as a likely consequence of his acts. Lord Kilbrandon's view (at 98) was that an intention to cause grievous bodily harm was sufficient only if "grievous bodily harm means

some injury which is likely to cause death." However, the majority, led by Lord Hailsham LC, held that the grievous bodily harm rule had survived. They considered that the changes proposed by the minority could only be effected by Parliament. This, Lord Hailsham explained, was partly because:–

> "...... before passing legislation, it would be desirable for Parliament to investigate policy considerations more widely than is desirable or possible in the course of a judicial investigation based on a single case" (at 69).

24. The views of the majority were confirmed in *R v Cunningham*. Lord Hailsham LC expressed doubts as to whether changing the rule from one requiring an intention to cause grievous bodily harm to one requiring an intention to endanger life would be beneficial. Such a change might give rise to:–

> "...... endless opportunity for fruitless and interminable discussion of the question whether the accused intended to endanger life and thus expose the victim to a probable danger of death, or whether he simply intended to inflict really serious injury." (at 579)

These doubts were shared by Lord Wilberforce who commented:–

> "...... whatever defects the present law may possess, that particular change would in my opinion be for the worse, not for the better, in providing a test both uncertain and practically unworkable." (at 581)

25. *The R v Cunningham* position represents settled law in Hong Kong, having been adopted by the Privy Council in *Chan Wing–Siu v The Queen* [1985] 1 AC 168. As Sir Robin Cooke put it:–

> "In the common law of England, which for all purposes material to this case applies in Hong Kong, it is now settled by the decision of the House of Lords in *R v Cunningham* [1982] AC 566 that killing with the intention of inflicting on the victim grievous bodily harm–that is to say, really serious bodily harm–is murder." (at 174)

26. As a result of these and other related developments (which do not require elaboration), the mens rea of murder, both in Hong Kong and in England and Wales, is now confined to two alternatives: an intention to kill or an intention to cause grievous bodily harm. This was made clear in R v Hancock [1986] AC 455, where Lord Scarman, referring to the earlier decision in *R v Moloney* [1985] AC 905, stated:–

> "...... the House cleared away the confusions which had obscured the law during the last 25 years laying down authoritatively that the mental element in murder is a specific intent, the intent to kill or to inflict serious bodily harm. Nothing less suffices: and the jury must be sure that the intent existed when the act was done which resulted in death before they can return a verdict of murder." (at 471)

The appellants'challenge at common law

27. Given the state of the authorities, the appellants face insurmountable obstacles in seeking to persuade this Court that it should, as a matter of common law, develop the mens rea of murder so as to require nothing less than an intention to kill or an intention to endanger life.

28. It is true that Ms Eu is able to point to recent dicta from eminent judges expressing dissatisfaction with the grievous bodily harm rule, largely on the ground that it results in a lack of symmetry between the *mens rea* of murder and the actus reus element of causing death, particularly when contrasted with the *mens rea* requirements of attempted murder and murder as a secondary participant: see Lord Edmund–Davies in *R v Cunningham* (at 582); Lord Mustill in *Attorney–General's Reference (No 3 of 1994)* [1998] AC 245 at 250, 258–9; and Lord Steyn in *R v Powell* [1999] 1 AC 1 at 14–15; and in *R v Woollin* [1999] 1 AC 82 at 90.

29. These dicta do not, however, make good the argument. Notwithstanding their criticisms, the very same judges recognize that in the light of the authorities, the grievous bodily harm rule is settled law and that no further judicial narrowing of the mens rea requirement is permissible. As Lord Edmund–Davies put it in *R v Cunningham* (at 583), any such change must be left to the legislature "as the constitutional organ best fitted to weigh the relevant and opposing factors". Accordingly, the common law challenge to the grievous bodily harm rule must fail.

30. One may note in passing that in recent times, the legislature has intervened in relation to the common law definition of murder on three occasions but has left the grievous bodily harm rule untouched. The radical redefinition of murder in the Homicide Ordinance has already been discussed. Then in 1971, following Westminster's initiative of undoing by statute the unsatisfactory aspects of the House of Lords decision in *DPP v Smith*, the Legislative Council enacted s 65A of the Criminal Procedure Ordinance, Cap 221, to re–iterate the subjective quality of the mental elements in murder and other offences. Then in the year 2000, following a recommendation of the Law Reform Commission, the legislature enacted s 33C of the Offences Against the Person Ordinance, abolishing the "year and a day" rule which had formed part of the common law definition of murder.

The constitutional challenge to the grievous bodily harm rule

31. The constitutional safeguards said by the appellants to have been infringed by the grievous bodily harm rule derive from the Basic Law ("BL") and the Bill of Rights ("BOR") contained in the Hong Kong Bill of Rights Ordinance, Cap 383. The rights relied on fall into three groups, namely the rights to:–

(a) protection against arbitrary detention or imprisonment under BL art 28 and BOR art 5(1);

(b) equality before the law under BL art 25 and BOR art 10; and,

(c) the presumption of innocence under BOR art 11.

32. BL art 39(1) provides, among other things, that the provisions of the International Covenant on Civil and Political Rights ("ICCPR") as applied to Hong Kong shall remain in force and be implemented through the laws of the HKSAR. Article 39(2) furthermore provides that the rights and freedoms of Hong Kong residents shall not be restricted unless as prescribed by law and that such restrictions shall not contravene the provisions of BL art 39(1). The Hong Kong Bill of Rights Ordinance effects the necessary incorporation into our domestic laws of the ICCPR as applied to Hong Kong: see *HKSAR v Ng Kung Siu* (1999) 2 HKCFAR 442 at 455. Accordingly, as Mr Blanchflower SC, leading for the respondent, accepts, a statutory provision is liable to be constitutionally invalidated on the ground of inconsistency with the BOR.

Presumption of innocence

33. The right to be presumed innocent can briefly be dealt with

first. BOR art 11 provides:–

> "Everyone charged with a criminal offence shall have the right to be presumed innocent until proved guilty according to law."

34. As indicated above, the grievous bodily harm rule constitutes one of two independent heads of mens rea for the offence of murder. It does not give rise to any presumption, whether, for example, a presumption that the accused intended to kill or a presumption that he is guilty of murder. No presumption as to an intention to kill is necessary since proof of an intention to cause grievous bodily harm itself suffices. No presumption of guilt arises either, since such intention has to be proved and its proof does not of itself establish murder. All the elements of the offence require to be established. The constitutionality of the grievous bodily harm rule therefore has nothing to do with the presumption of innocence and BOR art 11 is not engaged.

Arbitrary imprisonment

35. The main constitutional attack on the grievous bodily harm rule focuses on whether imprisonment of an offender following his conviction for murder on the basis of that rule (without any necessary reference to an intention to kill or to endanger life) amounts to arbitrary imprisonment.

36. This question is most appropriately dealt with under BL art 28. No material difference exists in the central concept of arbitrariness which occurs in both BL art 28 and BOR art 5(1), but, as the discussion below indicates, complications which occur in relation to the latter article do not arise in relation to BL art 28. As appears below, we are also of the view that the analysis is not assisted by referring to the right to equality protected by BL art 25 and BOR art 10.

37. Article 28 of the Basic Law provides as follows:–

> "The freedom of the person of Hong Kong residents shall be inviolable. No Hong Kong resident shall be subjected to arbitrary or unlawful arrest, detention or imprisonment. ......"

It is found in Chapter III of the Basic Law which sets out the fundamental rights and freedoms which are constitutionally guaranteed and which lie at the heart of Hong Kong's separate system. As this Court held in *Ng Ka Ling v Director of Immigration* (1999) 2 HKCFAR 4 at 28J–29A, these provisions should be generously interpreted to ensure that Hong Kong residents enjoy the full measure of those rights and freedoms.

Preliminary points on the scope of BL art. 28

38. Two related preliminary points of interpretation should be addressed. They concern the scope of the protection afforded by BL art 28 as compared with BOR art 5(1) and the doubts voiced in *R v Coady* (at 203B–207B) and echoed in *R v Chandra* (at 158) as to whether BOR art 5(1) extends to invalidate substantive legal provisions like the grievous bodily harm rule.

39. Article 5(1) of the Bill of Rights provides:–

> "Everyone has the right to liberty and security of person. No one shall be subjected to arbitrary arrest or detention. No one shall be deprived of his liberty except on such grounds and in accordance with such procedure as are established by law."

40. The argument in the two Court of Appeal cases proceeded on the basis of BOR art 5(1) and involved asking (i) whether that article extends its protection to offenders lawfully imprisoned after conviction by a court; and (ii) whether it is capable of invalidating, on the grounds of arbitrariness, substantive criminal laws founding a conviction and consequent imprisonment, such as the grievous bodily harm rule in the present case. Both questions are better answered under BL art 28.

41. The terms of BL art 28 differ from those of BOR art 5(1). Article 28 expressly provides a constitutional guarantee against arbitrary "imprisonment" and not just against arbitrary "arrest or detention" as in the case of BOR art 5(1). Plainly, "imprisonment" covers incarceration pursuant to a sentence lawfully imposed by a court after a criminal conviction. The first question is therefore plainly answered in the affirmative in relation to BL art 28, whatever may be the position under BOR art 5(1).

42. The second question must also be answered affirmatively. Article 28 prohibits not merely "unlawful" imprisonment but "arbitrary or unlawful" imprisonment. It envisages that a term of imprisonment lawfully ordered may nonetheless be "arbitrary". It follows that such arbitrariness may reside in the substantive rules of criminal liability whose breach led to the imprisonment ordered.

43. This conclusion is consistent with interpretations of article 9(1) of the ICCPR (which is identical to BOR art 5(1), prohibiting "arbitrary arrest or detention"). Thus, in *Hugo van Alphen v The Netherlands* (Communication No 305/1988, 15 August 1990), the United Nations Human Rights Committee (dealing with a case of detention without prior conviction) stressed that arbitrariness is not excluded merely because detention is pursuant to lawful procedures:–

> "The drafting history of article 9, paragraph 1, confirms that 'arbitrariness' is not to be equated with 'against the law', but must be interpreted more broadly to include elements of inappropriateness, injustice and lack of predictability." (para 5.8)

This approach was also adopted in *A v Australia* (Communication 560/1993) (UN HRC) 4 BHRC 210, at para 9.2.

44. In *Fok Lai Ying v Governor in Council* (1997) 7 HKPLR 327, the Privy Council was concerned with a challenge to a land resumption in Hong Kong pursuant to the Crown Lands Resumption Ordinance. The challenge was mounted on the basis of BOR art 14 which prohibits "arbitrary or unlawful interference" with (among other things) one's home. For the purposes of the argument, the Privy Council was prepared to assume that article 14 applied to the land resumption. Lord Cooke, giving the advice of the Board, referred to the Human Rights Committee's opinion as to the meaning of "arbitrary", noting:–

> "The expression arbitrary interference can also extend to interference provided for under the law. The introduction of the concept of arbitrariness is intended to guarantee that even interference provided for by law should be in accordance with the provisions, aims and objectives of the Covenant and should be, in any event, reasonable in the particular circumstances." (at 339–340)

Lord Cooke also referred to the interpretation of "arbitrary" in the *Hugo van Alphen* case, and stated that the Privy Council was prepared, without so deciding, to accept its correctness, the appeal then being disposed of on the footing that the challenge failed on the facts. His Lordship explained the Board's reluctance to lay down firm principles in the following terms:–

"The reason for proceeding by way of assumption rather than decision is that the present case touches on far-reaching issues. Within a few days the structure of the Hong Kong judicial system is to change. It is inappropriate for their Lordships to offer opinions on issues which may well in future cases fall to the Hong Kong courts to resolve, unless such opinions are necessary for the disposal of the case before the Board." (at 340)

45. In the light of the foregoing, the precise scope and effect of BOR art 5(1) do not require further discussion in the present case. While some authorities on the meaning of "arbitrariness" in relation to BOR art 5(1) and its ICCPR art 9 equivalent are helpful and will be referred to below, the doubts expressed by the Court of Appeal do not arise in relation to BL art 28 which caters sufficiently for the allegations of arbitrariness.

The grievous bodily harm rule and the meaning of "arbitrary" in BL art. 28

46. As noted above, the approach of the Human Rights Committee is to interpret the concept of arbitrariness broadly "to include elements of inappropriateness, injustice and lack of predictability". The scope of the arbitrariness concept is a matter to which we will return when we deal with the mandatory life sentence, where it arises in a different context. A strand of the developing jurisprudence in this area introduces the concept of manifest or gross disproportion as part of "arbitrariness", a matter of importance to the mandatory life sentence but not relevant to the debate on the grievous bodily harm rule.

47. A helpful way in which the concept of arbitrariness may be approached for present purposes can be found in dicta in *Neilsen v Attorney–General* [2001] 3 NZLR 433, a decision of the New Zealand Court of Appeal. This was a case where the decision of the police to arrest a suspect was challenged. One ground of challenge was that it was arbitrary and in contravention of s 22 of the New Zealand Bill of Rights Act 1990 which provides "Everyone has the right not to be arbitrarily arrested or detained." The Court in fact disposed of the case on the narrower basis of Wednesbury unreasonableness. However, on the meaning of "arbitrary" Richardson P, giving the judgment of the Court, stated as follows:–

"Whether an arrest or detention is arbitrary turns on the nature and extent of any departure from the substantive and procedural standards involved. An arrest or detention is arbitrary if it is capricious, unreasoned, without reasonable cause: if it is made without reference to an adequate determining principle or without following proper procedures." (para 34)

48. In our view, in the context of the grievous bodily harm debate, this is a useful formulation which is consistent with and adds flesh to the approach adopted in the *Hugo van Alphen* opinion. Applying it to the present case, one asks: Can it be said, given the asymmetry resulting from the grievous bodily harm rule, that such rule is arbitrary in that it is capricious or unreasoned or without reasonable cause? Can the imprisonment which followed be said to have been imposed without reference to an adequate determining principle?

49. In our view, the answer is clearly "No". A person convicted of murder under the rule is one who acts with the intention of causing someone really serious bodily harm and whose actions in the event cause another's death. A person who takes another's life in such circumstances brings to realisation the risk which is necessarily inherent in his conduct. In our view, there is nothing capricious or unreasonable in classing such conduct as murder as a matter of legal policy. A person may not subjectively intend or even foresee that he will cause death. He may desire to limit the consequences of his actions to the infliction of grievous bodily injury. However, as a matter of commonsense it is impossible to predict that the consequences of an intentional infliction of really serious bodily harm will necessarily be successfully limited and will not prove to be life–threatening.

50. Judges who have expressed a preference for abolishing the grievous bodily harm rule have nevertheless recognized that a contrary view is tenable. For example, in *R v Cunningham*, after commenting that he found the rule "passing strange", Lord Edmund Davies stated:

"But I recognise the force of the contrary view that the outcome of intentionally inflicting serious harm can be so unpredictable that anyone prepared to act so wickedly has little ground for complaint if, where death results, he is convicted and punished as severely as one who intended to kill. So there are forceful arguments both ways. ......" (at 583)

51. A contrary argument was also recognized in *R v Powell* [1999] 1 AC 1, by Lord Steyn, one of the rule's sternest critics. His Lordship stated:–

" There is an argument that, given the unpredictability whether a serious injury will result in death, an offender who intended to cause serious bodily injury cannot complain of a conviction of murder in the event of a death." (at 15)

Lord Steyn however thought it preferable to deal with such an offender under the manslaughter and discretionary life sentence regime.

Two Canadian cases on the mens rea of murder

52. The appellants rely on two decisions of the Canadian Supreme Court in support of striking down the grievous bodily harm rule as unconstitutional. They are *R v Vaillancourt* (1987) 47 DLR (4th) 399, and *R v Martineau* (1990) 58 CCC (3d) 353 respectively. Both were concerned with challenges to the constitutionality of provisions of the Canadian Criminal Code, RSC 1970, c C–34, then defining the offence of murder. Such challenges were mounted under various provisions of the Canadian Charter of Rights and Freedoms with particular reliance being placed on the principles of fundamental justice given force by s 7 of the Charter as follows:–

"Everyone has the right to life, liberty and security of the person and the right not to be deprived thereof except in accordance with the principles of fundamental justice."

53. In *R v Vaillancourt* the accused was convicted of second degree murder under s 213(d) of the then Criminal Code, on the footing that he and an accomplice had committed an armed robbery during which the accused had been armed with a knife and the deceased had been shot by his accomplice. The liability of the accused was doubly constructive and virtually absolute. He had personally not done the act of killing but was liable as the killer's accomplice (pursuant to s 21(2) of the Code). He had not formed any subjective mental state in relation to killing or harming the victim (which had taken place in a different part

of the premises), but was constructively held liable for murder because he had had a weapon on his person while committing the robbery. He argued that a conviction on such a basis under s 213(d) was inconsistent with the principles of fundamental justice.

54. The material provisions of the then-existing Criminal Code, taken from the principal majority judgment delivered by Lamer J in *R v Vaillancourt* (at 409–410), were as follows:–

> "212. Culpable homicide is murder
>
> (a) where the person who causes the death of a human being
>
> (i) means to cause his death,
>
> (ii) means to cause him bodily harm that he knows is likely to cause his death, and is reckless whether death ensues or not;
>
> (b) ......
>
> (c) where a person, for an unlawful object, does anything that he knows or ought to know is likely to cause death, and thereby causes death to a human being, notwithstanding that he desires to effect his object without causing death or bodily harm to any human being. ......
>
> 213. Culpable homicide is murder where a person causes the death of a human being while committing or attempting to commit high treason or treason or an offence mentioned in [various sections of the code including] section 302 (robbery), ... whether or not the person means to cause death to any human being and whether or not he knows that death is likely to be caused to any human being, if
>
> (a) – (c) ......
>
> (d) he uses a weapon or has it upon his person
>
> (i) during or at the time he commits or attempts to commit the offence, ...
>
> and the death ensues as a consequence."

55. As Lamer J notes (at 408–410) sections 212 and 213 contain "a very interesting progression" with respect to the mental state required to be proved. They start with someone who "means to cause death". They then progress to a lesser requirement, catching someone who "means to cause [the victim] bodily harm that he knows is likely to cause his death, and is reckless whether death ensues or not". The requirement is then further relaxed so as to catch someone who "for an unlawful object, does anything that he knows or ought to know is likely to cause death, and thereby causes death to a human being, notwithstanding that he desires to effect his object without causing death or bodily harm to any human being". Finally, by section 213, the net is cast so widely as to catch anyone who causes death while committing or attempting one of the enumerated offences in combination with satisfying one of the specified conditions. The mental elements of murder so defined therefore range from an intention to kill to the constructive liability of the defendant in *R v Vaillancourt*.

56. Having pointed to the severity of the punishment for murder and the peculiar stigma attached to that offence, Lamer J stated:–

> "I am presently of the view that it is a principle of fundamental justice that a conviction for murder cannot rest on anything less than proof beyond a reasonable doubt of subjective foresight." (at 415)

However, the Court did not at that stage consider it necessary to lay down such a principle. Section 213(d) did not even meet the lower threshold test of objective foreseeability and so was held on that basis to have infringed s 7 of the Charter without any saving justification.

57. *R v Vaillancourt* taken on its own does not advance the appellants' case. As Lamer CJC later explained in *R v Martineau* (at 359), it decided that "...... it is a principle of fundamental justice that before a person could be convicted of murder there must be proof beyond a reasonable doubt of at least objective foreseeability of death." The requirement in Hong Kong law of an intention to cause grievous bodily harm is a subjective form of mens *rea* far-removed from the constructive liability created by s 213(d). *R v Vaillancourt* was however the decision which set the stage for *R v Martineau* which is more directly on point.

58. The facts in *R v Martineau*, were similar to those in *R v Vaillancourt*. They also involved two participants in an armed robbery with the killing actually carried out by Martineau's accomplice. Although it was not strictly necessary, the Court decided to take the step it had foreshadowed in *R v Vaillancourt* and to identify positively which of the *mens rea* provisions for murder in the Code were consistent with the principles of fundamental justice. Lamer CJC stated:–

> "[In *R v Vaillancourt*] I concluded that objective foreseeability of death was the minimum threshold test before a conviction for murder could be sustained. I went on to state, however, that it was my view that the principles of fundamental justice require more; they demand that a conviction for murder requires proof beyond a reasonable doubt of subjective foresight of death. ...... I am still of that view today, and indeed, while I agree with the Alberta Court of Appeal and could dispose of this appeal on the basis of objective foreseeability, it is on the basis of the principle of subjective foresight of death that I choose to dispose of this appeal."(at 359)

59. The appellants rely on Lamer CJC's reference to principle in the following terms:–

> "The rationale underlying the principle that subjective foresight of death is required before a person is labelled and punished as a murderer is linked to the more general principle that criminal liability for a particular result is not justified except where the actor possesses a culpable mental state in respect of that result: see *R v Bernard* [1988] 2 SCR 833, per McIntyre J, and *R v Buzzanga* and *Durocher* (1979), 49 CCC (2d) 369 (Ont CA), per Martin JA. In my view, in a free and democratic society that values the autonomy and free will of the individual, the stigma and punishment attaching to the most serious of crimes, murder, should be reserved for those who choose to intentionally cause death or who choose to inflict bodily harm that they know is likely to cause death." (at 360)

60. The appellants submit that these decisions support the proposition that an asymmetrical *mens rea* for murder, meaning a mental state which does not involve contemplation of death as a consequence of the accused's conduct offends principles of fundamental justice which would include a principle against

arbitrary imprisonment, making the grievous bodily harm rule unconstitutional in Hong Kong.

61. We do not accept that view of these Canadian cases. Properly understood, they do not bear on the validity of the grievous bodily harm rule as a head of *mens rea* for murder.

62. The Canadian Supreme Court was examining the constitutional validity of the specific provisions of sections 212 and 213 of the Criminal Code. As Lamer J had indicated in *R v Vaillancourt*, these sections set out "an interesting progression" of required mental states ranging from an intention to kill down to liability that was constructive and virtually absolute. When Lamer CJC in *R v Martineau* concluded that the principles of fundamental justice required the offence of murder to be "reserved for those who choose to intentionally cause death or who choose to inflict bodily harm that they know is likely to cause death", he was echoing the language of the Code and drawing a line which affirmed the constitutionality of ss 212(a)(i) and (ii) as well as that part of s 212(c) which imposed liability on a subjective basis (see Lamer CJC at 362–363). Drawing the line at that point invalidated or at least cast doubt on the constitutionality of the other, less stringent mental requirements provided for by s 212(c) and 213.

63. An intention to cause grievous bodily harm does not feature as a category of *mens rea* in sections 212 or 213 and the Canadian cases provide no basis for postulating that if, hypothetically, the grievous bodily harm rule had represented a point on the progression, it would have been considered unconstitutional. It is therefore incorrect to conclude that on the reasoning of these cases, the grievous bodily harm rule offends any principles of fundamental justice.

Equality before the law

64. The right of equality before the law is provided for by BL art 25 which states: "All Hong Kong residents shall be equal before the law". Similarly BOR art 10 materially provides: "All persons shall be equal before the courts and tribunals...."

65. It is unnecessary to explore the scope of these articles or to consider whether they are engaged. The appellants' argument based on these provisions in relation both to the grievous bodily harm rule and the mandatory life sentence mirrors and does not add to their argument based on arbitrariness. Unless the imprisonment is held to be arbitrary, it is not suggested that any infringement of the equality protection arises. These grounds therefore require no further discussion in this judgment.

Conclusion on challenge to grievous bodily harm rule

66. For the reasons given above, the challenges to the grievous bodily harm rule mounted at common law and on constitutional grounds both fail.

Mandatory life sentence

67. Upon their conviction for murder, the appellants were sentenced to life imprisonment. The judge had no choice as the sentence is fixed by law: Offences Against The Person Ordinance, s 2. If a judge is of the opinion that matters relating to the appellants or the offence exist which should be recorded for the purpose of reviewing the sentence in the future, he must make a report in writing to the Chief Executive specifying those matters: Criminal Procedure Ordinance, s 67B(2). No such report was made in this case.

68. Being a sentence fixed by law in respect of an indictable offence, a mandatory life sentence cannot be appealed independently of an appeal against conviction: Criminal Procedure Ordinance, s 83G.

Constitutional challenge to the mandatory life sentence

69. The appellants seek to subject this mandatory regime to a constitutional challenge. The argument is put in various ways, but in essence, the appellants argue that the culpability of those convicted of murder varies greatly, ranging from the mercy killing to the contract or sadistic killing. Therefore, relying primarily on BL art 28, they contend that in depriving the judge of all sentencing discretion and compulsorily requiring the imposition of life imprisonment in all murder cases, whatever the degree of culpability of the individual involved, such imprisonment is arbitrary and unconstitutional.

70. Putting the same complaint in another way, they contend that such laws and the sentence of life imprisonment constitute cruel, inhuman or degrading punishments contrary to BOR art 3.

71. It is also argued that the right given by BOR art 5(4) to persons under detention to contest the lawfulness of his detention is infringed by the mandatory life sentence regime.

72. Furthermore, the statutory exclusion of a right of appeal has attracted a challenge under BOR art 11(4) which gives persons convicted of a crime the right to have their conviction and sentence reviewed by a higher tribunal according to law.

73. Finally, the mandatory regime is said to infringe the requirement of BOR art 6(3) that the treatment of prisoners in our penitentiary system should have as its essential aim, their reformation and social rehabilitation.

74. As indicated above, it is unnecessary to consider further the complaints put in terms of BOR art 5(1) (involving arbitrary detention) or BL art 25 and BOR art 10 (regarding equality before the courts) since, in the context of this particular appeal, those articles add nothing to the discussion under BL art 28. The same applies to BOR art 22 (relating to equal protection of the law and non-discrimination) which was mentioned in the course of submissions.

History of the sentence for murder in Hong Kong

75. Murder is and has throughout the years been regarded by our community as the most serious of crimes. The offence is unique in that, for adult offenders, it has always carried a mandatory sentence. An understanding of the history and framework within which the sentence for murder operates is important to an assessment of its constitutionality.

76. Prior to 1993, in respect of adults, the mandatory sentence for murder was the death penalty. This had been the position since 1842 when the common law became applied to Hong Kong, the mandatory death sentence being part of the common law: see Hawkins, *Pleas of the Crown*, Book 2, Ch 48. As from 1865, the sentence became statutory: Offences Against the Person Ordinance, s 2 (Originally Ord No 4 of 1865). The mandatory death penalty was also the punishment for treason and piracy with violence: Crimes Ordinance, Cap 200, ss 2 and 19 (prior to amendment in 1993).

77. There was an exception for pregnant women. Where a woman convicted of an offence punishable by death was found to be pregnant, the sentence was still mandatory but she was sentenced to imprisonment for life instead: Criminal Procedure Ordinance, s

77 (repealed in 1993).

78. Persons who were under 18 when the offences were committed were also differently treated. Instead of the mandatory death penalty for murder, they were ordered to be detained during Her Majesty's pleasure: Criminal Procedure Ordinance, s 70 (repealed in 1993). The judge again had no choice in the matter.

79. By the Homicide Act 1957, the United Kingdom restricted the application of the mandatory death penalty. It retained the sentence for capital murders which were defined to include murders done in the course of theft, done by shooting or causing an explosion or done in the course of resisting lawful arrest or effecting escape from legal custody, as well as murder of a police or prison officer on duty. It also remained the sentence for persons convicted of murder for a second time. For other murders, the penalty became the mandatory life sentence.

80. In 1965, the United Kingdom abolished capital punishment altogether and replaced it with mandatory life imprisonment: Murder (Abolition of Death Penalty) Act 1965. However, capital punishment remained on the statute book for treason and piracy with violence until 1998 when it was substituted by a discretionary life sentence: Crime and Disorder Act 1998 s. 36.

81. Hong Kong, although then a British colony, did not follow those changes. The death penalty remained on our statute book until 1993. Indeed, in 1966, a year after its total abolition in the United Kingdom, the death penalty for murder was carried into effect. This was to be the last execution in Hong Kong.

82. In 1973, there occurred the celebrated case of Tsoi Kwok–cheung. Tsoi was convicted of murder and the Governor refused to exercise the prerogative of mercy. Tsoi petitioned the Queen who, acting on the advice of the Secretary of State, granted a pardon. This was a controversial and unprecedented intervention. The Secretary of State believed that if advice were given that the death penalty should be carried out in Hong Kong, this would not be supported in the British Parliament to which he was answerable. Thereafter, although there were calls from time to time in Hong Kong for the death penalty to be carried out, the Governor invariably commuted death sentences to imprisonment for life or a fixed term of imprisonment. The Hong Kong Administration had taken the view that given the state of opinion in the British Parliament, the right to petition the Queen would secure a reprieve: see Athena Liu, *The Right to Life, in Human Rights in Hong Kong* (ed Wacks 1992) pp 264 at 270 ff.

83. In 1990 the Basic Law was adopted to come into effect on 1 July 1997. In June 1991, the Legislative Council enacted the Hong Kong Bill of Rights Ordinance incorporating the ICCPR as applied to Hong Kong. At that time, the mandatory death penalty was still part of our law. The Bill of Rights in effect tolerated preservation of the death penalty. In dealing with the right to life, BOR art 2(2) provides that the sentence of death may be imposed only for the most serious crimes. However, BOR art 2(6) makes it clear that nothing in the article should be invoked to delay or to prevent the abolition of capital punishment in Hong Kong.

84. In June 1991, a few weeks after the Hong Kong Bill of Rights Ordinance came into effect, a member of the Legislative Council moved a motion urging the Administration to resume immediately the carrying out of the death penalty. There was extensive debate. At the end of the day, the motion was not supported by the majority. What carried the day (by a majority of 24 to 12 with 5 abstentions) was an amendment to the motion moved by the Honourable Mr Martin Lee. The amended motion called for legislative measures to abolish the death penalty and to replace it with life imprisonment. The mandatory quality of the penalty would remain but the sentence of death would be replaced by a life sentence.

85. During the debate, differing views were expressed. Many legislators expressed the community's serious and widespread concern about the problem of violent crime and what was perceived to be a deteriorating situation. In particular, there was concern that criminals were coming to commit serious violent crime in Hong Kong from the Mainland where the regime on crime and punishment was harsher than in Hong Kong. A number of legislators were advocating the carrying out of the death penalty in murder cases, stressing that the circumstances of Hong Kong were different from those in the United Kingdom. As is reflected in the terms of the amended motion, those in favour of abolition of the death penalty recognised both the need to deter and prevent crime and the importance of maintaining the highest standards of a modern and humane society. They favoured abolition but only on the basis that it would be replaced by mandatory life imprisonment. They believed that having regard to its severity, a mandatory life sentence would be the appropriate penalty by way of replacement.

Enactment of legislation

86. In November 1992, responding to the majority view in the 1991 motion debate, the Administration introduced the Crimes (Amendment) (No 3) Bill 1992. It proposed abolition of the mandatory death penalty and its replacement by mandatory life imprisonment, not only for murder but also for treason and piracy with violence.

87. A Bills Committee was set up to study the bill and its Chairman reported to the Legislative Council at the debate on the bill in April 1993: see Official Record of Legislative Council Proceedings (commonly called "Hong Kong Hansard"), 21 April 1993, p 2935 ff. The Committee had received different views from the Bar Association, the Law Society and a group called the Hong Kong Citizen Alliance. The Alliance was totally against the abolition of capital punishment. The Bar Association considered that the only offence for which there should be a mandatory life sentence was murder. The Law Society believed that life imprisonment should only be the maximum sentence for murder.

88. The Bills Committee took the view that murder stands in a different category from treason and piracy with violence. It concluded that mandatory capital punishment should be replaced by a mandatory life sentence for murder but by a discretionary life sentence for treason and for piracy with violence.

89. Further, the Bills Committee "felt strongly" that legislation should be enacted to put on a statutory basis the Board of Review of Long Term Prison Sentences which provided individual scrutiny of cases on reviews of sentence. Under the then s 69A of the Prison Rules, various categories of sentences were required to be reviewed at regular intervals, including life sentences. The Board had been established in 1959 as an advisory body to review each sentence in those categories and to make recommendations to the Governor on the exercise of the prerogative to commute or remit sentences. It was considered that a statutory scheme for review was needed.

90. During the debate on this Bill, views were again expressed both for and against the abolition of mandatory capital punishment and its replacement by the mandatory life sentence. One member, the Honourable Mr Simon Ip, spoke in favour of a discretionary

life sentence on the ground that a mandatory sentence was unsatisfactory as it would cover convicted persons of different degrees of culpability and would also blur the separation of powers.

91. At the end of the debate, the Administration accepted the views of the Bills Committee and gave an assurance that the legislation it required would be introduced.

92. In April 1993, the Crimes (Amendment) Ordinance was passed (with 40 votes in favour, 9 votes against and 2 abstentions). It prescribes mandatory life imprisonment only for murder. A discretionary life sentence is prescribed for treason and for piracy with violence. It should be noted that persons under 18 years of age were at that stage, like adults, subject to the mandatory life sentence for murder, unlike previously when they were subject to mandatory detention during Her Majesty's pleasure instead of the mandatory death penalty for adults.

The Long-term Prison Sentences Review Ordinance

93. Pursuant to the assurance given, the Long-term Prison Sentences Review Ordinance, Cap. 524 ("the Review Ordinance") was enacted in June 1997, with the intention of enhancing the transparency, efficiency and fairness of the prison sentence review and remission systems: Hong Kong Hansard, 23 June 1997, p 238.

94. The Review Ordinance established the Long-term Prison Sentences Review Board ("the Board"), specifying that it is not part of the Government: s 5. The Board's essential function is to give individual consideration to offenders and their cases in relation to certain sentences, including life sentences, both mandatory and discretionary: s 7. The Board, consisting of eight to ten members appointed by the Chief Executive, is required to have a range of expertise. It must include two judges or former judges of the Court of First Instance (as its President and Deputy President), a psychiatrist, a psychologist, a social worker, a barrister or solicitor, an educator and a person engaged in industry or commerce. Among the members appointed, at least one must have expertise and experience in the rehabilitation of offenders: s 6.

95. The Board has a statutory duty to consider each individual case at the regular intervals prescribed. In the case of a mandatory life sentence, this begins 5 years after the start of the sentence and takes place at least every 2 years thereafter: s 11(2). To facilitate its review, it can call for reports from the Commissioner of Correctional Services, the Commissioner of Police, the Registrar of the High Court and the Director of Social Welfare: s 14.

96. In conducting its review of each sentence, the Board is required to have primary regard to the following principles: (a) where the prisoner's rehabilitation is not complete, the rehabilitative effect of release; (b) the benefits to the prisoner arising from supervision after release with a view to securing rehabilitation and reintegration into the community; (c) whether the part of the sentence served is sufficient to warrant consideration of early release; (d) the need to protect the community from reasonably foreseeable harm by the prisoner as a result of early release: s 8. The Board is also permitted to take into account various matters set out in regulations which reflect these principles and any other matters which the Board considers relevant: Long-Term Prison Sentences Review Regulations, s 2.

97. There are procedural safeguards for the prisoner. He must be told the date of the review and is entitled to make written and, subject to the Board's consent, oral representations: ss 12(4) and 12(5). In the case of prisoners serving a mandatory life sentence, no regulations have yet been made to apply to them the procedural safeguard presently enjoyed by prisoners serving other sentences, whereby, subject to exceptions, they are provided the materials to be considered by the Board prior to the review. The statute contemplates that this safeguard is to be extended to life prisoners. Appropriate regulations should therefore be made as soon as practicable. Even in the absence of such regulations, this safeguard can and should be applied administratively.

98. Upon a review of a life sentence, the Board may recommend to the Chief Executive substitution of a determinate sentence and thereafter, it may further recommend remission of all or part of the determinate sentence: s 15(1)(a). When acting on the Board's recommendation, the Chief Executive exercises his powers under BL art 48(12) to pardon persons convicted of criminal offences or to commute their penalties. Where the Board wishes to defer recommending conversion of a life sentence into a determinate one, it may make a conditional release order: s 15(1)(b). Such conditional release orders take effect directly and without need for a recommendation to the Chief Executive. The order may be for up to two years and may be subject to conditions, for example, as to prescribed places of residence and employment, etc: s 18. Where the life sentence has been converted into a determinate sentence and the prisoner has served not less than two thirds of it, the Board may make an order directing the prisoner's early release under supervision: ss 15(1)(c) and 18. As with a conditional release order, such an order takes effect directly and is not a matter of recommendation to the Chief Executive.

Exceptions for persons under 18

99. As mentioned above, under the Crimes (Amendment) Ordinance, persons under 18 convicted of murder were made subject to the mandatory life sentence. In 1997, when the Review Ordinance was enacted, the legislature decided that this should be changed. For those who were under 18 at the time of the offence, the court is now given a discretion whether to sentence them to life imprisonment or imprisonment for a shorter term: s 44, Schd 2, para 2.

The role of the legislature

100. Before turning to the specific constitutional provisions relied on, the question of the weight which the court should give to the view of the legislature in the context of the present constitutional debate is an important facet of that debate.

101. The Basic Law enshrines the principle that there must be a separation of powers as between the executive, the legislature and the judiciary. The legislature is constitutionally entitled to prescribe by legislation what conduct should constitute criminal offences and what punishment those found guilty by the courts should suffer: *R v Hinds* [1977] AC 195 at 225G–226D. But in the exercise of their independent judicial power, the courts have the duty to decide whether legislation enacted is consistent with the Basic Law and the Bill of Rights. If found to be inconsistent, the duty of the courts is to hold that legislation invalid: *Ng Ka Ling v Direction of Immigration* (1999) 2 HKCFAR 4 at 25G–I.

102. It is also established that when deciding constitutional issues, the context in which such issues arise may make it appropriate for the courts to give particular weight to the views and policies adopted by the legislature. In *R v DPP, Ex p Kebilene* [2000] 2 AC 326, speaking of the Human Rights Act 1998 which

took effect on 2 October 2000, incorporating the European Convention on Human Rights ("ECHR"), Lord Hope stated:–

> "In this area difficult choices may have to be made by the executive or the legislature between the rights of the individual and the needs of society. In some circumstances it will be appropriate for the courts to recognise that there is an area of judgment within which the judiciary will defer, on democratic grounds, to the considered opinion of the elected body or person whose act or decision is said to be incompatible with the Convention." (at 381B–C)

103. This approach has been compared to the doctrine of according a "margin of appreciation" to national institutions, adopted by the supra-national European Court of Human Rights in exercising its supervisory function. As Lester and Pannick put it:–

> "Just as there are circumstances in which an international court will recognise that national institutions are better placed to assess the needs of society, and to make difficult choices between competing considerations, so national courts will accept that there are some circumstances in which the legislature and the executive are better placed to perform those functions." (Lester and Pannick, *Human Rights Law and Practice* (1999), p 74)

104. This was acknowledged by Lord Bingham in Brown v Stott [2001] 2 WLR 817, in the following terms:–

> "Judicial recognition and assertion of the human rights defined in the Convention is not a substitute for the processes of a democratic government but a complement to them. While a national court does not accord the margin of appreciation recognised by the European Court as a supra-national court, it will give weight to the decisions of a representative legislature and a democratic government within the discretionary area of judgment accorded to those bodies ..." (at 834–835)

Lord Steyn shared this view:–

> "... national courts may accord to the decisions of national legislatures some deference where the context justifies it." (at 842F)

105. The context and circumstances of the present case render this approach relevant and justify the courts giving proper weight to the decision of the legislature. As is clear from the legislative history of the mandatory life sentence provisions, the question of the appropriate punishment for what society regards as the most serious crime is a controversial matter of policy involving differing views on the moral and social issues involved. The legislature has to make a difficult collective judgment taking into account the rights of individuals as well as the interests of society. It has to strike a balance bearing in mind the conditions and needs of the society it serves, including its culture and traditions and the need to maintain public confidence in the criminal justice system. As Lord Woolf pointed out in *Attorney-General v Lee Kwong Kut* [1993] AC 951:–

> "In order to maintain the balance between the individual and the society as a whole, rigid and inflexible standards should not be imposed on the legislature's attempts to resolve the difficult and intransigent problems with which society is faced when seeking to deal with serious crime. It must be remembered that questions of policy remain primarily the responsibility of the legislature." (at 975 C–D)

106. In prescribing punishments for criminal offences, the legislature usually prescribes the maximum penalties that may be imposed by the courts. However, the punishment for murder stands in a special position. Continuing the position at common law, the legislature in Hong Kong has always provided for a mandatory sentence in respect of adult murderers. When it passed the Crimes (Amendment) (No 3) Bill in 1993, it decided that mandatory life imprisonment should be the penalty for murder. It arrived at that decision when the Bill of Rights had been part of our law for nearly two years. And in 1997, when it enacted the exception for those under 18 years of age, the legislature implicitly confirmed its decision to impose a mandatory life sentence in the case of adults.

107. In the extensive debate that had taken place, different views had been expressed, including the view (which had support which was not insignificant) that the mandatory death penalty should not only be retained, but should be carried into effect. Ultimately, the opposing school which favoured abolition of the death penalty carried the day but this was achieved only on the basis that it would be replaced by the mandatory life sentence.

108. The legislative history also makes it clear that the legislature's intention was to mark out murder as a uniquely serious offence by attaching only to that offence the mandatory life sentence. Manslaughter and offences falling short of the full offence of murder such as conspiring or soliciting to commit murder attract only a discretionary life sentence: ss 5 and 7 of the Offences Against the Person Ordinance. And when the original bill proposed that treason and piracy with violence should equally be made subject to a mandatory life sentence, the legislature rejected that proposal and made the sentence for those offences discretionary life imprisonment.

109. These are matters to which due weight should be given. The Court ought also to give proper weight to the fact that it was part and parcel of the legislature's decision that a statutory regime for the individualised review of each sentence after its mandatory imposition should be put in place. It was on the basis of the Administration's assurances that the legislation necessary for such a scheme would be introduced that the mandatory life imprisonment provisions were passed into law. That scheme is now embodied in the Review Ordinance.

Mandatory life sentences, "arbitrariness" and BL art. 28

110. The test of arbitrariness adopted in relation to the grievous bodily harm rule focuses on whether the legal provision challenged can be said to be "capricious, unreasoned or without reasonable cause", in line with the approach of the New Zealand Court of Appeal in *Neilsen v Attorney-General*. In the present context, of particular relevance is a strand of authority that introduces the concept of "disproportion" and equates with arbitrary imprisonment, sentences of imprisonment which are manifestly disproportionate.

111. Thus, in *R v Governor of Brockhill Prison, ex p Evans (No 2)* [2001] 2 AC 19, Lord Hope, discussing the jurisprudence of the European Court of Human Rights on the meaning of "arbitrary detention" in ECHR art 5(1), notes that it encompasses cases where the detention "was resorted to in bad faith or was not proportionate" (at 38). This was re-iterated by his Lordship in the Privy Council in *Anderson et al v The Scottish Ministers and the*

Advocate General for Scotland, DRA Nos 9, 10 and 11/2000 (15 October 2001), para 22.

112. Deprivation of liberty can be attacked on the separate ground that it is unlawful. But where imprisonment is lawful, that is, where it is ordered pursuant to duly constituted laws, a high threshold must be crossed before those laws can be struck down on the basis that the imprisonment pursuant thereto is disproportionate. It must be sufficiently disproportionate to justify describing the law as "arbitrary" – a disproportion so great as to reduce the law virtually to something capricious, unreasoned or without reasonable cause. As Dr Manfred Nowak puts it, the disproportion must be "manifest". Discussing arbitrariness in the context of art 9(1) of the ICCPR, he states:–

> "… arbitrariness is to be interpreted broadly. Cases of deprivation of liberty provided for by law must not be manifestly unproportional, unjust or unpredictable. …" Nowak, UN Covenant on Civil and Political Rights: CCPR Commentary (N P Engel 1993, at p 173)

Why the appellants say mandatory life sentences are arbitrary

113. Citing the comments made by Lord Bingham in relation to the mandatory death penalty in *Patrick Reyes v The Queen* [2002] 2 WLR 1034, Ms Eu points out that the range of moral culpability in murder cases is very extensive:–

> "It covers at one extreme the sadistic murder of a child for purposes of sexual gratification, a terrorist atrocity causing multiple deaths or a contract killing, at the other the mercy–killing of a loved one suffering unbearable pain in a terminal illness or a killing which results from an excessive response to a perceived threat." (at para 11)

The same point is made in other cases (eg, per Simon Brown LJ in *R (on the application of Anderson) v Home Secretary* [2002] 2 WLR 1143, 1160: "...... the spectrum is a wide one with multiple sadistic murders at one end and mercy killings at the other.")

114. The appellants contend that for s 2 of the Offences Against the Person Ordinance to require the court to impose the same sentence on the mercy killer as the contract or sadistic killer is to make compulsory a punishment that is grossly disproportionate and therefore arbitrary (as well as cruel, inhuman or degrading, as discussed below) in the case of an offender at the lower end of the culpability scale, such as the mercy killer. Accordingly, they argue, since cases with such an outcome are inevitable, the section is unconstitutional and must be struck down or at least "read down" to convert the mandatory sentence to one that is discretionary.

Key aspects of the appellants' argument

115. Two important features of the appellants' argument must be addressed. In the first place, it is an argument that implicitly challenges not merely the sentence prescribed for murder, but the permissible scope of the offence as a matter of substantive criminal law. The argument regards it as objectionable that one should define murder so as to include persons considered to be at the lower end of the culpability scale, such as mercy killers and those who kill from using excessive force in self–defence.

116. Whether such killings should be treated as murder of course raises highly controversial issues of moral, social and legislative policy which are debated in many countries. Various groups can be found championing the retention of murder and the mandatory life imprisonment (or even the death penalty) for such cases, or advocating that such cases be treated as manslaughter or arguing for the de-criminalization of some such cases (for instance, cases of consensual euthanasia).

117. In Hong Kong, the law classifies as a murderer, someone who causes the death of another either intending to cause death or intending to inflict really serious bodily harm. We have already rejected the argument that mens rea so defined is unconstitutionally wide. Statutory exceptions exist which reduce the liability to manslaughter where the killing is done while suffering from diminished responsibility, or as a result of provocation or as the survivor of a suicide pact, significantly narrowing the classes of homicide which constitute murder: Homicide Ordinance, ss 3, 4 and 5.

118. Murder, with such a focused definition, is regarded by the legislature as a crime apart, involving the infliction of death the most serious harm than one human being can cause to another with a mental element carrying a very high degree of moral blameworthiness. The legislature has accordingly prescribed the uniquely serious punishment of a mandatory life sentence which is reserved for the crime of murder and which is a response to the crime itself, irrespective of the circumstances of the offence or the offender, notwithstanding an undoubted recognition that there will inevitably be a range of culpability among different offenders. As the European Court of Human Rights, referring to the mandatory life sentence in the United Kingdom noted in *Wynne v UK* (1994) 19 EHRR 333, such a sentence is imposed "because of the inherent gravity of the offence." While evolving United Kingdom practice (discussed below) has made this description of the mandatory life sentence no longer applicable in England and Wales (see *Stafford v UK*, ECtHR Application No 46295/99, 28 May 2002, para 79), it remains relevant in the Hong Kong context.

119. To stay with the example of mercy killings as homicides at the lower end of the culpability scale, it remains the policy of the law, a policy that is quite constitutional, that in the absence of one of the statutory exceptions, a mercy killer should be held liable for murder. The law is presently not prepared to exempt from murder, someone who takes it upon himself to kill another on what he perceives to be mercy killing grounds, even where the victim consents. Such a killing is caught by the definition of murder, since the perpetrator undoubtedly intends to cause death. Some may disagree with that policy. But whether persons such as mercy killers at the lower end of the culpability scale should or should not be classified as murderers is a question which falls pre-eminently within the area where, as discussed above, weight should be given to the legislature's view when assessing the constitutionality of legislation enacted. Different sectors of the community may legitimately wish to have their voices heard. In the legislature, the full range of policy considerations can be considered with much greater efficacy than a court can achieve in the course of deciding a single case.

120. Secondly, the appellants' argument proceeds on the basis that the existence of a wide range of moral culpability separating defendants in different murder cases is in itself a complete and sufficient basis for a finding of arbitrariness. We do not agree in respect of the offence of murder. The fact that a mercy killer can point to there being more heinous killings does not of itself mean that his own sentence was arbitrary and unconstitutional.

121. An assessment of alleged arbitrariness by reason of manifest disproportion involves weighing the severity of the punishment (life imprisonment) against not only the nature and seriousness of

the offence, but also other legitimate sentencing objectives (such as protection of the public, preventing repetition of the offence, deterring others from committing like offences and societal denunciation of the offence). It is, in other words, not merely a question of looking at the offender's culpability in comparison with the culpability of others convicted of the same offence. We would emphasise that this is particularly so in relation to murder which, as indicated above, is a crime apart.

122. The mandatory life sentence performs deterrent and denunciatory functions in support of the existing policy of the law. To return to the example of the mercy killing, while it is in the nature of such an offence that a mandatory life sentence is unlikely to serve the object of protecting the public from the offender since he is unlikely to repeat the crime, such a sentence will undoubtedly have a considerable deterrent effect on others who may be contemplating what they perceive to be mercy killings. It is also a sentence conveying emphatic denunciation of what continues to be regarded in our society as the most serious of crimes.

Conclusion as to BL art. 28

123. Taking into account the inherent and unique gravity of the offence and the sentencing objectives of a mandatory life sentence as a whole, we are unable to accept that mandatory life imprisonment represents a manifestly disproportionate sentence so as to contravene BL art 28 on the grounds of arbitrariness. The legislative judgment that the offence of murder, having regard to its gravity, calls for a sentence of mandatory life imprisonment, even allowing for the different circumstances in which it may be committed, is tenable and rational. As such it is a legislative judgment which this Court should respect.

124. As Borins DCJ put it in *R v Guiller* (1985) 48 CR (3d) 226 (cited with approval by Lamer CJC in *R v Smith (Edward Dewey)* (1987) 34 CCC (3d) 97 at 137, and in *R v Luxton* (1990) 58 CCC (3d) 449 and 460):–

> "It is not for the court to pass on the wisdom of Parliament with respect to the gravity of various offences and the range of penalties which may be imposed upon those found guilty of committing the offences. Parliament has broad discretion in proscribing conduct as criminal and in determining proper punishment. While the final judgment as to whether a punishment exceeds constitutional limits set by the Charter is properly a judicial function the court should be reluctant to interfere with the considered views of Parliament and then only in the clearest of cases where the punishment prescribed is so excessive when compared with the punishment prescribed for other offences as to outrage standards of decency."

125. In accepting the legislative judgment, we give particular weight to the legislature's insistence on a statute-based regime for review by an independent board of all life sentences, with power to recommend conversion of such sentences to fixed terms and to direct conditional releases in appropriate cases.

Cruel, inhuman or degrading punishment

126. Article 3 of the Bill of Rights provides:–

> "No one shall be subjected to torture or to cruel, inhuman or degrading treatment or punishment...."

127. The appellants argue in the alternative that the mandatory life sentence for murder represents a cruel, inhuman or degrading punishment because it will inevitably be wholly disproportionate in some cases.

128. Prohibitions of "cruel and unusual" or "cruel, inhuman or degrading" punishments were originally regarded as being directed against punishments which were cruel or degrading in their nature or in the manner or conditions in which they were imposed. As Wilson J explained in *R v Smith (Edward Dewey)* (1987) 34 CCC (3d) 97:–

> "The rack and the thumbscrew, the stocks, torture of any kind, unsanitary prison conditions, and prolonged periods of solitary confinement were progressively recognized as inhuman and degrading ......" (at 147)

129. However, it is now clear that punishments which are not cruel in the abovementioned sense, but are "grossly disproportionate" fall also to be treated as within the prohibited class. It has been so held by, among others, the Canadian Supreme Court in *R v Smith (Edward Dewey)*, the European Court of Human Rights *(Soering v UK* (1989) 11 EHRR 439, paras 103–104), the Constitutional Court of South Africa (*State v Makwanyane* 1995 (3) SA 391, para 94) and the Privy Council (*Patrick Reyes v The Queen*).

130. In our view, the threshold for establishing such disproportionality as would suffice to make a punishment which is prescribed by law cruel, inhuman or degrading (ie, "grossly disproportionate"), is either the same or higher than the threshold for arbitrariness ("manifestly disproportionate"). Thus, in *R v Smith* (*Edward Dewey*) a mandatory minimum sentence of 7 years' imprisonment for importing narcotics was challenged as disproportionate and in violation of s 12 of the Canadian Charter which prohibits "cruel and unusual treatment or punishment". Lamer J, giving the main majority judgment, explained that the test for such cruelty is:–

> "...... to use the words of Laskin CJC [in Miller and Cockriell (1976) 31 CCC (2d) 177 at 183] 'whether the punishment prescribed is so excessive as to outrage standards of decency'. In other words, though the state may impose punishment, the effect of that punishment must not be grossly disproportionate to what would have been appropriate." (at 138–139)

131. Moreover, Lamer J also pointed out that in assessing whether a sentence is grossly disproportionate one looks first at the circumstances of the offence and of the particular offender but that this:–

> "...... does not mean that the judge or the legislator can no longer consider general deterrence or other penological purposes that go beyond the particular offender in determining a sentence, but only that the resulting sentence must not be grossly disproportionate to what the offender deserves." (at 139)

132. Accordingly, the appellants' case based on BOR art 3 also fails. Having fallen at the hurdle of arbitrariness, they face an equal or higher obstacle in seeking to establish that the mandatory life sentence is cruel, inhuman or degrading punishment. The approach to assessing disproportionality is the same in each case, with the court not being confined to considering individual culpability but factoring in also other legitimate penological aims and giving due weight to the legislative choice of sentence.

Cases on the mandatory death penalty

133. We note in passing that considerable reliance was placed at the hearing on assessments of disproportionality in relation to mandatory death penalty cases: eg, *Mithu v State of Punjab* AIR 1983 SC 473; *Patrick Reyes v The Queen; United States v Burns and Rafay* (2001) 151 CCC (3d) 97; and *R v Hughes* [2002] 2 WLR 1058, see also *Fox v The Queen* [2002] 2 WLR 1077.

134. In our view, because they are concerned with the death penalty, such assessments proceed on a qualitatively different footing and provide no authority for the assessment of proportionality regarding mandatory life sentences. For example, Chinnappa Reddy J in *Mithu v State of Punjab*, decided that the mandatory character of the death penalty in that case was objectionable because: –

> "So final, so irrevocable and so irresistible is the sentence of death that no law which provides for it without involvement of the judicial mind can be said to be fair, just and reasonable." (para 25)

135. Similarly, Lord Bingham in *Patrick Reyes v The Queen* cited numerous authorities that highlighted the peculiar gravity and irreversibility of the death penalty and stressed that the Privy Council was not considering the constitutionality "of any mandatory penalty other than death" (at para 43). Indeed, while the Privy Council struck down the mandatory death sentence in that case, the effect of its order was to remit the case to the trial judge for re-sentencing where the judge's options were either to impose a death sentence afresh as a matter of discretion or in default of doing so, imposing a mandatory life sentence under s 102 of the Belize criminal code (see paras 4 and 43). The *Patrick Reyes* case is therefore certainly no authority for the proposition that a mandatory life sentence is to be regarded as inhuman or degrading punishment.

Decisions of the Supreme Court of Canada

136. The conclusions we have reached above are consistent with decisions of the Supreme Court of Canada in *R v Luxton* (1990) 58 CCC (3d) 449 and *R v Latimer* (2001) 150 CCC (3d) 129, where it held that the mandatory life sentence for murder does not infringe relevant provisions of the Canadian Charter of Rights and Freedoms.

137. Under the Canadian Criminal Code as enacted at the times material to those judgments (RSC 1970, c C-34 and RSC 1985, c C-46 as amended) the sentence for murder was (and remains) mandatory life imprisonment: Criminal Code, s 235. The Code goes on to sub-divide murder into first and second degree murder. Murder is in the first degree when it is planned and deliberate. Furthermore, irrespective of whether it is planned and deliberate, murder is in the first degree where the victim is a police officer or a prison officer on duty; or where death is caused by the accused while committing or attempting to commit certain specified offences including, for example, sexual assault or kidnapping and forcible confinement. Murder that is not first degree murder is second degree murder: Criminal Code, s 231.

138. The convicted person is ineligible for parole, in the case of first degree murder, until he has served 25 years of his sentence; and in the case of second degree murder, until he has served 10 years, although the judge at the time of sentencing can specify a longer period of up to 25 years: Criminal Code, ss 745 and 754.4. However, after serving at least 15 years of the sentence, the offender may apply to the court for a reduction in the period of ineligibility for parole: s 754.6(1).

139. It follows that the Canadian system is one where, in respect of all murders, the mandatory life sentence, coupled with statutory minimum periods of ineligibility for parole, must be imposed by the court irrespective of the circumstances of the offence or the offender and notwithstanding differences in culpability in different cases. Thus, in the case of a mercy killing, the judge would have no choice but to impose a life sentence to which the statutory period of parole ineligibility will apply.

140. In *R v Luxton*, the appellant was convicted of first degree murder on the basis that he had killed the deceased in the course of forcible confinement, one of the specified first degree murder offences. His consequent liability to be sentenced mandatorily to life imprisonment without eligibility for parole for 25 years was challenged as an infringement of the principles of fundamental justice mandated by s 7 of the Charter as well as a violation of sections 9 (right not to be arbitrarily imprisoned) and 12 (right not to be subjected to cruel and unusual punishment). These arguments can be dealt with compendiously.

141. In submissions that found an echo in the present case, counsel for Luxton submitted that the principles of fundamental justice "require that differing degrees of moral blameworthiness in different offences be reflected in differential sentences, and that sentencing be individualized" (at 456). He argued that it was such a principle that "...... a just sentencing system contains a gradation of punishments differentiated according to the malignity of offences and that sentencing be individualized" (*Ibid*).

142. Lamer CJC (giving the principal majority judgment) accepted a need for proportionality but stressed that such proportionality did not rest on culpability alone but also on the pursuit of applicable principles of sentencing:–

> "There is no doubt that a sentencing scheme must exhibit a proportionality to the seriousness of the offence, or to put it another way, there must be a gradation of punishments according to the malignity of the offences. However, a sentencing scheme also must take into account other factors that are of significance for the societal interest in punishing wrongdoers." (at 457)

Lamer CJC found support in a passage from La Forest J in *R v Lyons* [1987] 2 SCR 309, 328–9 as follows:–

> "...... it cannot be considered a violation of fundamental justice for Parliament to identify those offenders who, in the interests of protecting the public, ought to be sentenced according to considerations which are not entirely reactive or based on a 'just deserts' rationale. The imposition of a sentence which 'is partly punitive but is mainly imposed for the protection of the public'...... seems to me to accord with the fundamental purpose of the criminal law generally, and of sentencing in particular, namely, the protection of society. In a rational system of sentencing, the respective importance of prevention, deterrence, retribution and rehabilitation will vary according to the nature of the crime and the circumstances of the offender." (cited at 457)

143. Lamer CJC concluded that the mandatory life sentence with the mandatory minimum periods of ineligibility for parole were not unconstitutional, stating: –

> "In my view the combination of [the relevant sections] clearly demonstrates a proportionality between the

moral turpitude of the offender and the malignity of the offence, and moreover it is in accord with the other objectives of a system of sentencing identified by La Forest J in Lyons." (at 457–8)

The Court reached this conclusion pointing out that such murder cases all concern persons killing with a mens rea which involves subjective foresight of death, that the first degree murder category of killing in the course of committing offences like forcible confinement was a relatively narrow class and that Parliament had provided for a post–sentencing procedure whereby the offender could apply after 15 years to the court for his period of ineligibility for parole to be reduced. In relation to this latter consideration, the Court gave weight to the fact that Parliament had thereby "provided for some sensitivity to the individual circumstances of each case" (at 457).

144. *R v Latimer* was a case of mercy killing. The appellant was convicted of the second degree murder of his 12 year old daughter who was suffering from acute cerebral palsy and, although having the mental capacity of a four month old baby and most severely disabled, was not terminally ill. She was completely dependent on others for her care and suffered a great deal as a result of her condition, having had to undergo repeated surgeries. After learning that the doctors wished to perform an additional surgery, the appellant took his daughter's life by seating her in the cab of his pick–up truck and inserting a hose from the truck's exhaust pipe into the cab.

145. On conviction for second degree murder, he was liable to mandatory life imprisonment without eligibility for parole for a minimum of 10 years. However, the appellant contended that in the circumstances of the case, such a sentence amounted to cruel and unusual punishment contrary to s 12 of the Charter. The trial judge agreed and sentenced the appellant to one year's imprisonment and one year on probation, confined to his farm. The Court of Appeal reversed the judge and imposed the mandatory life sentence, carrying the mandatory minimum of 10 years without parole.

146. The appeal to the Supreme Court was dismissed. In a judgment of all its members, the Court noted that "...... the questions that arise in Mr. Latimer's case are the sort that have divided Canadians and sparked a national discourse" (para 4). The Court discussed the "grossly disproportionate" test for "cruel and unusual punishment", citing *R v Smith (Edward Dewey)* and later cases, as follows (para 76):–

> "While the test is one that attributes a great deal of weight to individual circumstances, it should also be stressed that in weighing the s 12 considerations the court must also consider and defer to the valid legislative objectives underlying the criminal law responsibilities of Parliament (*R v Goltz* [1991] 3 SCR 485, at p 503). In this regard, Cory J, for the Court in *Steele v Mountain Institution*, [1990] 2 SCR 1385 at p 1417, stated:
>
> 'It will only be on rare and unique occasions that a court will find a sentence so grossly disproportionate that it violates the provisions of s 12 of the Charter. The test for determining whether a sentence is disproportionately long is very properly stringent and demanding. A lesser test would tend to trivialize the Charter.'"

147. While it took all relevant factors into account, including "Mr Latimer's good character and standing in the community, his tortured anxiety about [his daughter's] well–being, and his laudable perseverance as a caring and involved parent" (para 85), the Court nonetheless stressed the culpability of the appellant notwithstanding the mercy killing features of the case:–

> "...... even if the gravity of second degree murder is reduced in comparison to first degree murder, it cannot be denied that second degree murder is an offence accompanied by an extremely high degree of criminal culpability. In this case, therefore, the gravest possible consequences resulted from an act of the most serious and morally blameworthy intentionality. It is against this reality that we must weigh the other contextual factors, including and especially the particular circumstances of the offender and the offence." (para 84)

The Court held that the sentence was not grossly disproportionate.

The position in England and Wales

148. The legal regime for the treatment of mandatory life sentences for murder in England and Wales is in a state of flux. The regimes in Scotland and Northern Ireland have diverged from the English position as a result of statutory changes and need no further discussion here (see *Stafford v UK* paras 48–49). However, an understanding of the English position, which differs materially from the position in Hong Kong, requires a brief survey of its evolution.

149. A sentence of life imprisonment is on its face an indeterminate sentence. Traditionally, that is how it has in fact taken effect. The court sentences the offender to prison for an indefinite period, exercising its judicial power in a system which embraces the principle of the separation of powers. Thereafter, in the execution of the sentence, the constitutionality of non–judicial intervention in appropriate cases in pursuit of legitimate policy aims has been accepted. Thus, executive clemency, a system of sentence remission and a parole system to encourage the rehabilitation and re-integration into society of offenders who have been sufficiently punished, have been accepted as part of the institutional framework in which an indeterminate sentence is served. By the operation of such non–judicial measures, the life prisoner may, in appropriate cases, be released either unconditionally or on licence.

150. Mandatory life imprisonment has been the sentence for murder in the United Kingdom since 1965, when the mandatory death penalty was ultimately abolished. Like other life sentences, it was treated as an indeterminate sentence along traditional lines. However, in 1983, the Home Secretary announced that he would adopt the practice of fixing a "tariff" for each case of life imprisonment, both mandatory and discretionary, after consulting the trial judge and the Lord Chief Justice. The tariff would represent the punitive element of the sentence, reflecting what was required by way of retribution and deterrence. It would be the minimum period which the offender was to spend in prison. At its expiry, he would be released unless it was considered that there were grounds to continue his imprisonment. The decision as to whether to release the prisoner at the post–tariff stage was also to be made by the Home Secretary.

151. This practice, which has not been adopted in Hong Kong, inevitably raised important legal questions: see *R v Home Secretary, ex parte Doody* [1994] 1 AC 531. Did it alter the status of the judge's sentence and did the fixing of the tariff by the Home Secretary form part of the sentencing process? If so, was this a violation of the separation of powers principle? If it was to be treated as a sentence, what were the prisoner's rights at the

expiry of the tariff period? On what grounds could he be kept in detention at that stage? Who ought to make that decision and subject to what procedures?

152. A number of challenges, both in the domestic courts and in the European Court of Human Rights in Strasbourg, followed. The first targets were discretionary life sentences. In Ex parte Doody, the rationale of the tariff system in relation to such discretionary sentences was described by Lord Mustill. A judge would impose such a sentence:–

> "...... to reflect his appraisal that even a long fixed term of years may not adequately protect the public against the risk that when the term has been served the prisoner will continue to be a danger to the public. Such a sentence ensures that the prisoner will be kept in custody until it is thought safe to release him.
>
> The discretionary life sentence may thus be regarded as the sum of two sentences, to be served consecutively. First, a determinate number of years appropriate to the nature and gravity of the offence. This is often called the 'tariff' element of the sentence. ...... The second component is an indeterminate period, which the offender begins to serve when the penal element is exhausted. I will call this the 'risk element.'." (at 550)

153. In *Weeks v UK* (1987) 10 EHRR 293; and *Thynne, Wilson and Gunnell v UK* (1990) 13 EHRR 666, the Strasbourg Court held that this regime attracted the protection of ECHR art 5(4) which provides:–

> "Everyone who is deprived of his liberty by arrest or detention shall be entitled to take proceedings by which the lawfulness of his detention shall be decided speedily by a court and his release ordered if the detention is not lawful."

The tariff approach raised the possibility that post-tariff detention might be unjustified by any legitimate purpose, where, for instance, the prisoner poses no risk to the public. Such detention might raise new issues as to its lawfulness. It would follow in such cases that ECHR art 5(4) requires there to be access to a body with judicial characteristics to determine whether continued detention is lawful. The United Kingdom practice was held to violate the article since the decision to continue the imprisonment was taken by the Home Secretary, a member of the executive, and not by a court or a sufficiently judicial body.

154. These decisions led to the United Kingdom's enactment of the Criminal Justice Act 1991 (later replaced by the Crimes Sentences Act 1997) which provides that discretionary life sentence prisoners are to have their tariffs fixed by the trial judge in open court and, that, at the expiry of the tariff period, it is the Parole Board which decides whether they should be released (the Parole Board being constituted with a sufficiently independent and judicial character for this purpose). Subsequently, after similar challenges in the Strasbourg Court (see, eg, *Hussain v UK* (1996) 22 EHRR 1 and *V v UK* (1999) 30 EHRR 121) juvenile murderers who had been sentenced to detention at Her Majesty's pleasure were assimilated by statute to the discretionary life sentence regime.

155. However, mandatory life prisoners continued to receive different treatment. The United Kingdom Government's justification in 1991 for excluding mandatory life sentences from the statutory scheme for discretionary life sentences was that mandatory sentences are different in principle. The Minister of State offered to the House of Commons the following explanation:–

> "...... In a discretionary case, the decision on release is based purely on whether the offender continues to be a risk to the public. The presumption is that once the period that is appropriate to punishment has passed, the prisoner should be released if it is safe to do so. The nature of the mandatory sentence is different. The element of risk is not the decisive factor in handing down a life sentence. According to the judicial process, the offender has committed a crime of such gravity that he forfeits his liberty to the state for the rest of his days. If necessary, he can be detained for life without the necessity for subsequent judicial intervention. The presumption is, therefore, that the offender should remain in custody until and unless the Home Secretary concludes that the public interest would be better served by the prisoner's release than by his continued detention. In exercising his continued discretion in that respect, the Home Secretary must take account not just of the question of risk, but of how society as a whole would view the prisoner's release at that juncture. The Home Secretary takes account of the judicial recommendation, but the final decision is his." (quoted in *ex parte Doody* at 555)

156. As Lord Mustill pointed out, the government's stated position made it difficult to see why the 1983 decision to fix tariffs should be applied to such ostensibly indeterminate sentences: *Ex parte Doody*, at 551. Nonetheless, it remained the practice in England and Wales for a tariff to be fixed by the Home Secretary after conviction and imposition of the mandatory life sentence by the court, and for the post-tariff release decision to continue to be taken by him. In 1994, notwithstanding such controversy (of which it was aware), the Strasbourg Court in *Wynne v UK* accepted the United Kingdom's rationale for the difference in treatment and ruled that there was no violation of ECHR art 5(4) in cases where, by decision of the Home Secretary, a prisoner serving a mandatory life sentence continued to be detained in prison after expiry of the tariff period.

157. After the Human Rights Act 1998 entered into force, the executive's treatment of mandatory life cases came under attack in the domestic courts. They were asked to recognize that in reality, mandatory life sentences were not indeterminate sentences but, like discretionary life cases, were sentences determined on a tariff-fixing approach. In *R (on the application of Anderson) v Home Secretary* [2002] 2 WLR 1143, the court was invited to hold that the existing system violated ECHR art 6(1) in that tariff-fixing amounted to a sentencing function that could not properly be carried out by a member of the executive. In *R (Lichniak) v Home Secretary* [2001] 3 WLR 933 (CA), the court was asked to rule that where an offender had served the tariff period and was considered not to represent a danger, continued detention was arbitrary and an inhuman and degrading punishment which violated articles 3 and 5 of the ECHR. The appellants failed in each case because the Court of Appeal felt constrained by the acceptance of the Home Secretary's role in *Wynne v UK* and were awaiting clarification from Strasbourg in *Stafford v UK*, then pending. However, in the course of arguing the *Anderson* case, the Government's position as to the nature of a mandatory life sentence shifted to one of accepting that it was in reality a sentence determined on the tariff approach.

158. In *Stafford v UK*, a decision published after conclusion of

the argument in the present case, the European Court of Human Rights has held, after a detailed review, that the United Kingdom's treatment of mandatory life sentences contravened ECHR arts 5(1) and 5(4). The Court held (a) that *Wynne v UK* was not definitive and should be re-examined; (b) that the domestic jurisprudence in England and Wales showed that there was in reality no difference in principle between mandatory and discretionary life sentences; (c) that the tariff-fixing exercise was part of the sentencing process; (d) that, accordingly, post-tariff period detention raised issues of potential unlawfulness and required compliance with ECHR 5(4), the UK being in contravention in that the decision whether to release after the tariff period was not taken by a body qualifying as judicial, but by the Home Secretary; and (e) that continued imprisonment pursuant to the Home Secretary's decision after expiry of the tariff period where there was no risk of violent offending infringed ECHR 5(1) which limits the deprivation of liberty, inter alia, to lawful detention after conviction by a competent court.

159. It is not at present possible to say what legal changes in England and Wales will result from the *Stafford v UK* decision. It may, for instance, be that mandatory life sentences will also be assimilated to the statutory regime currently in force for discretionary life sentences, in which case, the sentence for murder will remain a mandatory life sentence but the trial judge will fix a tariff period in open court and post-tariff release will be decided by the Parole Board. It is also quite possible that the sentence for murder may be changed to make it discretionary life imprisonment. For our purposes, it suffices to note that the system in Hong Kong is materially different. No tariff is fixed and mandatory life imprisonment continues to take effect as an indeterminate sentence along the traditional lines described above.

Mandatory life imprisonment and BOR art 5(4)

160. The appellants' next complaint is that the mandatory life sentence in Hong Kong contravenes BOR art 5(4) which provides:-

> "Anyone who is deprived of his liberty by arrest or detention shall be entitled to take proceedings before a court, in order that that court may decide without delay on the lawfulness of his detention and order his release if the detention is not lawful."

161. This article obviously bears a close resemblance to ECHR art 5(4) and is designed to take effect where an issue of unlawfulness may arise in relation to someone's detention. The survey of the position in England and Wales has shown how that article can be engaged even in relation to detention pursuant to an order for imprisonment lawfully made by a court, but only in the special circumstances thrown up by the tariff approach adopted in the United Kingdom. The article was engaged only in relation to the post-tariff period where fresh issues of possible unlawfulness could arise.

162. In Hong Kong, the tariff approach has never been applied and BOR art 5(4) is therefore not engaged in relation to prisoners serving mandatory life sentences. Detention of such prisoners is pursuant to the lawful order of the court made at the trial and on any subsequent appeal. Such proceedings satisfy the requirements of BOR art 5(4).

Mandatory life sentences and the right of review by a higher tribunal

163. Article 11(4) of the Bill of Rights provides:-

> "Everyone convicted of a crime shall have the right to his conviction and sentence being reviewed by a higher tribunal according to law."

164. As the mandatory life sentence is a sentence fixed by law, there is no right of appeal solely against sentence: Criminal Procedure Ordinance, s 83G. But this produces no inconsistency with BOR art 11(4). What that article confers on persons who have been convicted of a crime is the safeguard of a second tier of judicial scrutiny. A convicted person is entitled to a review of his conviction and sentence by a higher tribunal with powers to overturn them. Such a safeguard exists in the present case. A person convicted of murder and sentenced to mandatory life imprisonment is entitled to appeal to the Court of Appeal which may, on allowing the appeal, overturn the conviction and sentence. BOR art 11(4) does not confer a separate right to launch an appeal limited to an appeal against sentence so as to prohibit sentences fixed by law. The requirements of the article are therefore satisfied by the existing procedure for appeal to the Court of Appeal.

Article 6(3) of the Bill of Rights

165. Article 6(3) of the Bill of Rights provides:-

> "The penitentiary system shall comprise treatment of prisoners the essential aim of which shall be their reformation and social rehabilitation. Juvenile offenders shall be segregated from adults and be accorded treatment appropriate to their age and legal status."

166. Leaving aside the question whether and to what extent BOR art 6(3) is intended to confer rights on individuals, there are no materials before the Court to suggest that the system does not meet its requirements. The Prison Rules, Cap 234, indicate that the system is directed at the prisoners' reformation and rehabilitation. The extent of a prisoner's reformation and rehabilitation is also of central importance in the statutory scheme for review of sentences under the Review Ordinance.

Conclusion as to the mandatory life sentence for murder

167. For the reasons given above, the challenges to the constitutionality of the mandatory life sentence for murder fail.

168. We wish to emphasise that this conclusion is confined to the mandatory sentence for murder, arrived at taking into account the unique seriousness of the offence, the legal policies embodied in the sentence for such offence, the peculiar legislative history of such sentences and the statutory framework in which they are implemented. This reasoning would not be applicable to any other crime or any other sentence fixed by law.

169. We also wish to make two observations on current practice. First, as previously stated, regulations providing procedural safeguards for prisoners in relation to sentence reviews to be conducted should be promulgated as soon as practicable and in the meantime, the safeguards operated in respect of other prisoners should be applied administratively to prisoners serving mandatory life sentences.

170. The second observation concerns the judge's report. Where a mandatory life sentence is imposed, if the judge is of the opinion that there are matters relating to the person or the offence which should be recorded for the purpose of reviewing the sentence in the future, the judge must make a report in writing specifying those matters: Criminal Procedure Ordinance, s 67B(2). Any report made by a judge would be of assistance in reviewing the

sentence. It is important for a judge to give consideration to the question of whether a report should be made. If he is minded to make one, the convicted person should, so far as practicable, be given an opportunity to be heard, represented by counsel if possible, before the report is made. Unless there are exceptional circumstances, he should also be provided with a copy of any report which is made.

Disposal of the appeal

171. Accordingly, the appellants' appeal is dismissed. There shall be an order for taxation of the 1st appellant's costs in accordance with the Legal Aid Regulations.

Mr Justice Chan PJ:

172. I agree with the judgment of the Chief Justice and Mr Justice Ribeiro.

Mr Justice Fuad NPJ:

173. I agree with the judgment of the Chief Justice and Mr Justice Ribeiro.

Sir Anthony Mason NPJ:

174. I also agree with the judgment of the Chief Justice and Mr Justice Ribeiro.

Chief Justice:

175. The Court unanimously dismisses the appellants' appeal. There shall be an order for taxation of the 1st appellant's costs in accordance with the Legal Aid Regulations.

Chief Justice (Andrew Li)

Permanent Judge (Patrick Chan)

Permanent Judge (R A V Ribeiro)

Non-Permanent Judge (K T Fuad)

Non-Permanent Judge (Sir Anthony Mason)

Ms Audrey Eu SC, Mr John Mullick and Mr PY Lo (instructed by the Legal Aid Department) for the 1st appellant

2nd appellant, Lau Wong, in person

Mr MC Blanchflower SC, SADPP, Mr Gavin Shiu, SGC and Miss Diana Lam, SGC (of the Department of Justice) for the respondent

---

李元虹 對 香港特別行政區政府

HCA 677/2005；CACV 196/2005

簡略案情

原告聲稱受到周邊的人的迫害與監視，令她感到精神困擾並活在惶恐中。她認為這些事情都是被告人香港特別行政區政府所指使的，是政府密謀針對她和家人。因此，原告人向被告人發出傳訊令狀要求法庭針對被告人的非法行為：1）頒發人身安全禁制令，強令被告人即時停止一切任意非法剝奪她和她家人的人身安全、人身自由的侵權行為；2）聲明她與她家人享有天賦的生命權、人權和自由；不容許任何政府予以任意非法剝奪；和 3）損害賠償。在其申索陳述書及多份誓章和書面陳詞中，原告人對該等違反《基本法》第 28 條的行為作出詳細的描述。她指出政府以潑毒粉、異形物體、跟蹤、偷聽、攝錄監察與飛虎隊行動等手段，動用大批人力、物力謀害她和她家人。後來，應被告人的申請，經內庭聆訊後，高等法院司法常務官下令剔除原告人本案的申索陳述書及傳訊令狀。原告人不服，提出上訴，亦是經內庭聆訊，原訟法庭法官駁回其上訴，維持原判。原告人遂向上訴法庭提出上訴，指稱在高等法院前兩次沒有律師的“內庭”聆訊，是違反《基本法》的“秘密審訊”，對她不公平、不公正，法官判決錯誤。

裁決摘要

上訴庭推斷，原告人所說的“秘密審訊”，是投訴高等法院前兩次的“內庭”聆訊違反《基本法》第 35 條，即“香港居民有權得到秘密法律諮詢、向法院提起訴訟、選擇律師及時保護自己的合法權益……”但上訴庭指出，該條所說的秘密法律諮詢是指，按當事人的意願，他尋求法律意見時是有權只與法律代表進行，他們談話和通訊的內容，除得當事人同意外，是絕對保密、不能公開的，亦不能用以對當事人不利，這與內庭聆訊並沒有關連。根據《高等法院規則》，一般非正審程序或訴訟，皆以內庭聆訊處理，並沒有不公平、不公正之處。至於她沒有律師代表的問題，法庭認為香港有法律援助的機制，這裏並沒有不公平的地方。

在考慮原告人的申索陳述書時，法庭指出必須竭力捍衛《基本法》第 28 條對香港居民的保障。但原告人的指控充其量只是她一些很初步的懷疑，缺乏具體性，如具體的人物身份、時間、地點等，在這情況下，被告人是難以抗辯的，這屬於《高等法院規則》第 18 號命令第 19 條規則內載的“瑣屑無聊或無理纏擾”及“可能會對有關訴訟的公平審訊造成損害、妨礙或延遲”的情況。而且，原告人指控的人及其行為即使存在，也沒有明顯具體的事實或證據足以支持政府是同謀者或指使者，所以原告人對政府的申索是注定失敗的，就算法庭容許她繼續進行本案也是徒然，只會令她和被告人無謂地浪費時間、金錢及精力而已。這也是《高等法院規則》第 18 號命令第 19 條規則內含的情況，構成“濫用法庭的法律程序”，所以剔除本案的申索陳述書及傳訊令狀是理所當然的。據此，上訴被駁回。最後，法庭順帶提出“聲稱者具舉證之責”的原則，認為在沒有科學鑑證的情況下，法庭有權拒絕接納呈堂的東西載有毒粉或毒物的說法，但反之，內庭審理的法官認為那些呈堂的皆是垃圾廢物，也有“越俎代庖”之嫌。

CACV 196/2005

香港特別行政區
高等法院上訴訟法庭
民事司法管轄權
民事上訴

案件編號：民事上訴案件 2005 年第 196 號
（原高等法院原訟法庭民事訴訟 2005 年第 677 號）

原告人　李元虹
　　　　及
被告人　香港特別行政區政府

主審法官：高等法院上訴法庭副庭長胡國興
　　　　　高等法院上訴法庭法官張澤祐

聆訊日期：2005 年 10 月 7 日

判案書日期：2005 年 10 月 12 日

判案書

高等法院上訴法庭副庭長胡國興頒發上訴法庭判案書：

序言

1. 2005 年 5 月 9 日，應被告人的申請，經內庭聆訊後，高等法院司法常務官陳爵下令，剔除原告人本案的申索陳述書及傳訊令狀。原告人不服，提出上訴。2005 年 6 月 1 日，經內庭聆訊後，原訟法庭暫委法官杜淮峰駁回上訴，維持原判。現原告人向本庭提出上訴。

背景

2. 2005 年 4 月 15 日，原告人向被告人發出傳訊令狀要求法庭針對被告人（1）頒發人身安全禁制令，強令被告人即時停止一切任意非法剝奪她和她家人的人身安全、人身自由的侵權行為；（2）聲明她與她家人享有天賦的生命權、人權和自由；不容許任何政府予以任意非法剝奪；（3）損害賠償。

3. 在申索陳述書及多份誓章和書面陳詞中，原告人詳細道出她的案情。杜法官在他的判案書有以下的描述：

> "3. 聆訊本上訴時，原告人重覆她在傳訊令狀及她所存檔的六份誓章的陳述。她的陳述荒謬絕倫；令人難以置信。她指居於她隔鄰與上層的鄰居向她散播白色毒粉，使她全屋鋪滿毒粉，毒粉發出的香味使她感到不適、頭痛及幾乎窒息。雖然她把門窗關上，毒粉仍可從天而降。她打開門時便遭他人撥毒粉。她在家中聽到滴水聲，但找不到滴水的源頭。當她觸摸門鎖時，她的手感到劇痛，她指門鎖遭人下毒，而門後亦發現大量毒粉。她又指居於上層的鄰居曾利用攝錄機與偷聽器監察她的行動。當她擬割斷攝錄機與偷聽器時，上層的鄰居便把該等儀器收回。她在公園時，一名女子向她打開一個袋，她便嗅到毒粉的香味使她感到頭暈。她在街上遭一群青年干擾。她在百佳超級市場遭穿保安員制服的人跟蹤。她在火車上亦遭多人跟蹤，她發現其中一名男子背部有很多毒粉。她問該名男子他是不是警員時，該名男子向她回答他是警員並向她查問「到底她知到什麼國家機密」。她在麥當奴餐廳進食時發現碟上載滿毒粉，她又發現一些黑色異形物體，那些異形物體可由小變大並會走到她身上咬她。她在大家樂餐廳遭警察下毒，警察並召來救護車強行把她送到北區醫院；幸好她的丈夫把她從醫院拯救出來。她前往高等法院途中遭一名女子撥毒粉，她把該名女子抓緊，但卻遭警員指控她向該名女子施襲。她在高等法院的廁所內又嗅到毒粉的香味。她在高等法院的餐廳吃牛腩時，她的舌頭感到麻痺，她指遭人在食物中下毒。她回想到一至兩年前曾有三名飛虎隊警員在她對面單位從天而降。她認為所有發生在她身上的事；如撥毒粉、異形物體、跟蹤、偷聽與攝錄監察與飛虎隊的行動等均屬特別行政區政府的所為。她感到極度驚荒，她憂慮會遭受殺害，她為她與家人的人身安全感到擔憂。所以她向法庭申請禁制令與聲明。"

4. 本庭細閱原告人向法庭所呈交的所有文件，認為她聲稱的案情可歸納為以下幾點：

> （1）她的鄰居、所住大廈的保安人員、修理工人和處理垃圾的人、在天空飛過大廈的飛機、街上一些人和商店及食肆等都向她撤（撒）毒粉和放毒藥，使她感到不適、便秘、頭痛、頭暈、麻痺、幾乎窒息、胃部劇痛、不能移動、不能說話和有口吃及失憶的後遺症等等。
>
> （2）有關的人在她暈厥時召救護車送她入醫院，並有時假稱她暈厥召救護車送她入醫院的精神病科，企圖誣陷她有精神病、有忘想症，企圖把她關進精神病院而整治她，而醫生又誤斷或誣陷她有精神病，該些人欲謀殺她，等等。
>
> （3）在她的家中有人佈下了監視監聽儀器，監控她及家人的一舉一動、一言一行。
>
> （4）所有上述發生的事情都是政府（即被告人）所指使，是政府針對她和家人的圖謀，政府動用大批人力物力謀害和暗殺她和家人。

5. 在本庭前，原告人強調，她在街上買菜、買水果，發覺那些東西上都放有毒藥，飛機向她撒毒粉有廿多次。她告訴本庭，她受到這些災難八年了，受了很多苦。有人用先進的技術，噴毒粉、毒藥害她，也不只害她一人。

6. 本庭只需引述原告人的上訴陳述書數段，從中她的投訴便可見一斑：

> "陳生［鄰居］兩次叫搬垃圾的兩個男人、兩個电器青年工、一次兩個整鎖人來找我了！想弄死我由倒垃圾的人把我弄到堆填區，讓我'人間蒸發'！
>
> "政府不惜財力、人力動用飛機、警方、……多個政府部門，甚至高等法院……來謀害我們一家人！規模之大，比美國對付拉登的規模都小不到哪裏去吧！"
>
> "差人叫白車來，指揮人要同我打針，我不肯打，被抬上担架捆起雙手雙脚搬上救護車，送我到了北區急診室精神病人治療處，意圖關我在小房毒死我，我反抗掙下床坐地下，之後又讓三个女保安一面帶白膠手套、一面圍向我，我想她們可能要弄死我，大叫'她們要謀殺我呀！'"
>
> "補充：新發現！

飛機固定停在我家窗前的天空上：

> 八月十五日晚上，……我自己下楼去看月亮。……天上很多厚厚的白雲行過，我好像見到有閃著燈光的飞机（機）飞

過……，一刹那就不見了！

……不久，厚厚的白雲飄走了，天空露出一大块青天，我向右轉頭看月亮，却同時見到……有一顆火紅色'星星'，格外显眼，我被它吸引著，不去看月亮了！它正在我家窗户的上方天空，我看到它像有尾一樣，是長條的！我很奇怪：……到球場，兩个青年在打兰（籃）球，我問其中一个：請他看那个火紅色的是不是星星？青年說那是飞机（機）！……他說可能是用衛星……他說：成日都是這樣子的啦！

……问（問）過青年之後，我才發現、明白到：原來有飞机（機）停在天空看著我家！……

……

第二天上午…剛寫了幾天'陳詞'，寫完後很累了，這天白天下樓散步，晒晒太陽，輕鬆下！一下樓，就見到……地上一塊約十多平方米大的地方，白華華，給用鐵馬給圍住了！我經過看時，像是飛機撒的大白片藥物，它們大多給黏貼在地上了！……我拾了小塊看，與我在樓梯間撿拾的一樣物品！風（一號風球）把這些藥物給吹偏了，離目的地五十米開外了！我又走，走遍了……邨所有樓，見到也有幾處這樣子！（按：原文為簡體字）

但這些給鐵馬圍住的地方，絕對不是現在正在進行用白漆油大鐵管的工程，地方流下的白漆！我想：可惜沒有人會來作調查！"（按：原文為簡體字）

上訴理由

7. 在上訴通知書中，原告人提出她的上訴理由，如下：

"高等法院對我個案的兩次"內庭"聆訊，正是"23"條中所說的：（我在）沒有律師的情形下的"秘密審訊"！有絲毫的公平、公正嗎？

我覺得：陳官的判決，為政府繼續謀害我和家人開了綠燈！杜官的判決，幫政府把我置於死地（在他判詞結論前的所言中，可見到他的用心）！"

秘密審訊

8. 首先，第1段的上訴理由好像是包含兩個投訴：（1）"秘密審訊"，即原告人所指在高等法院前兩次的"內庭"聆訊；（2）原告人在該兩次聆訊均沒有律師代表；因此對她不公平、不公正。

9. 就"秘密審訊"一詞，這並非中華人民共和國香特別行政區《基本法》第23條內載的。原告人向本庭澄清，她說該段中所說的第23條是指她是被落實第23條的人，這看來是暗示政府謀害她。

10. "秘密"兩字可見於原告人申索陳述書所依賴的《基本法》第35條。第35條規定：

"香港居民有權得到<u>秘密</u>法律諮詢、向法院提起訴訟、選擇律師及時保護自己的合法權益或在法庭上為其代理和獲得司法補救。"（劃線後加）

11. 條款所說的秘密法律諮詢是指，按當事人的意願，他尋求法律意見時是有權只與法律代表進行，他們談話和通訊的內容，除得當事人同意外，是絕對保密、不能公開的，亦不能用以對當事人不利。法庭的內庭聆訊並不類同，不可混為一談。

12. 一般而言，對民事案件的處理，法庭的聆訊分為開庭聆訊和內庭聆訊兩大類。在正審時，除非案情涉及機密或有關孩童身份、身世或利益問題之外，所有審訊均在公開法庭中進行。另一方面，處理就有關正審前與訟各方程序上的問題或紛爭，統稱非正審程序，法庭是在內庭進行聆訊的，這是遵從香港法律第4章《高等法院規則》的規定辦事，也是法庭的一貫做法。概括地說，這些內庭聆訊所涉事情多關於各與訟者在該案程序上的爭辯，與其他案件的與訟人無關，與公眾的關係更是微乎其微，因而不須公開審理，但如有需要，法庭可公開聆訊或公開判決：參閱《實務指示》25.1。因本案被告人申請剔除原告人的令狀及申索陳述書是非正審程序，故也如其他非正審程序一樣，在內庭聆訊，並非如原告人所指的"秘密審訊"。

13. 在本庭，原告人問本上訴是否公開審訊，本席答覆她那是肯定的，但她指出，庭上沒有記者，是法庭有人攔在法庭門口，不給人進入。本席數次請她出外察看，她都拒絕，最後說她不欲再談這點了。

無律師代表

14. 有關原告人所指的沒有律師代表她進行聆訊，這是個人的資源問題。若她有足夠資源，她可自僱律師，若她資源不足，她可申請法律援助。法律援助署會按照香港法律第91章《法律援助條例》的規定審查申請者資產資料和案件的成功質素用以決定是否提供法援，這是合法而保障公帑的程序及做法。原告人在她的文件中提及，她生活拮据，而法律援助署又三次拒絕她的法援申請，所以無法律代表。這是事實，但並不等如她沒有律師代表就受到或會受到不公平不公正的對待。

15. 本庭認為，以本案的情況觀之，第1段上訴理由不成立。

兩位法官判決的對錯

16. 第2段上訴理由雖以怨言表達，實質是指陳、杜兩位法官的判決犯錯，這是本庭先要處理的。

17. 原告人的申索陳述書依賴《基本法》第28條支持她的申索。第28條規定：

香港居民的人身自由不受侵犯。

香港居民不受任意或非法逮捕、拘留、監禁。禁止任意或非法搜查居民的身體、剝奪或限制居民的人身自由。禁止對居民施行酷刑、任意或非法剝奪居民的生命。

18. 誠然，這是《基本法》對香港居民的保障，也是法庭必須竭力捍衛的。

19. 原告人指她的鄰里、大厦的保安人員、修理工人和處理垃圾的人、在天空飛過大厦的飛機、街道上一些人和商店及食肆等都向她撤（撒）毒粉和放毒藥、謀害她及家人，甚至想令她"人間蒸發"，但她未能提出任何證據，以玆證明這些人的行為是政府指使的，或這干人等是政府派遣來對付她的。即使原告人指控其所針對的行為是政府人員所作的，這極其量只是她一些很初步的懷疑，她的指控缺乏具體性，如具體的人物身份、時間、地點等，在這情況下，被告人是難以抗辯的，這屬於《高等法院規則》第18號命令第19條規則內載的"瑣屑無聊或無理纏擾"及"可能會對有關訴訟的公平審訊造成損害、妨礙或延遲"的情況。

20. 原告人的指控即使屬實，這些對她不利甚至誣陷或意欲或意圖把她置諸死地的人及其行為即使存在，但並無明顯具體的事實或證據足以支持政府是同謀者或指使者，所以原告人對政府的申索是註定失敗的，就算法庭容許她繼續進行本案也是徒然，只會令她和被告人無謂地浪費時間、金錢及精力而已。這也是《高等法院規則》第18號命令第19條規則內含的情況，構成"濫用法庭的法律程序”，所以剔除本案的申索陳述書及傳訊令狀是理所當然的。

21. 因此，陳、杜两（兩）位法官判決的結論，都沒有犯錯，都是合法合理的。

忘想、幻覺

22. 在第 2 段上訴理由中，原告人用詞激動，有埋怨或不滿杜法官之言：

> “杜官的判決，幫政府把我置於死地（在他判詞結論前的所言中，可見到他的用心）！”

23. 很明顯，原告人所不滿杜法官判詞的部份是以下一段：

> “此外，當觀察到原告人在庭上的舉止神態、她所呈堂指稱載有毒粉的文件及信封與所謂黑色異形物體，本席相信原告人心存妄想，她在傳訊令狀及誓章的陳述全屬幻覺。被告人不須因原告人的狂妄思想而浪費公帑就這無理訴訟答辯。”

24. 原告人在上訴陳述書指，杜法官不是藥物專家，但是卻說原告人所呈堂指稱載有毒粉的文件及信封與所謂黑色異形物體是垃圾、廢物，是她的忘想及幻覺，把她形容成一個狂人，這是不公平不公正的，希望法庭把她呈堂的藥物拿去化驗。在本上訴聆訊時，她也向本庭作出同樣要求。

25. 法官與市民無異，看見垃圾廢物時定知道該些是垃圾廢物，但是如訴訟一方堅持己見，認為有關物體是毒粉、毒藥，在無科學鑑證的情況下，法官雖然有權不接納該方意見，但也不應斷言該物體是垃圾廢物，令人以為他僭越了法官而非藥物專家的位置。而且，雖然法官所說的“心存妄想”只指原告人想把物體說成毒粉，但原告人卻認為法官以“妄想”、“幻覺”等詞把她形容成一個狂人、瘋子，因而感到怨憤、不滿。在這情況下，本庭認為杜法官該段言詞確有商榷之處。

26. 然而，聲稱者具舉證之責，若原告人堅持有關物體乃毒粉毒藥，而她自己也不是藥物專家，她便須提供藥物專家的化驗報告，以支持她的說法。法庭無權也不會把她具呈的物體拿去化驗。

27. 無論如何，以上的情況對杜法官剔除原告人的申索陳述書及傳訊令狀的判決本身並無影響，不能挽救本上訴的命運。

結論

28. 基於上述理據，本庭駁回原告人的上訴，維持原判。但因上文第 24 及 25 段所述情況，原告人提出本上訴也不無道理，所以本庭作出暫准訟費命令，本上訴的訟費由雙方各自負責。

高等法院上訴法庭副庭長（胡國興）

高等法院上訴法庭法官（張澤祐）

原告人（上訴人）：無律師代表，親自出席。

被告人（答辯人）：由律政司署政府律師王華宜代表。

香港特別行政區 對 蕭逸良

HCMP 549/2002

簡略案情

申請人因搶劫和無牌藏有槍械或彈藥罪，等候高等法院原訟庭的審訊。在拘留期間，申請人曾向裁判官申請保釋候審，但遭拒絕。他繼而向原訟庭申請覆核被拒絕保釋的裁決，亦遭拒絕。在往後的程序中，他沒有再向主審裁判官申請保釋。當案件的交付程序完成後，在等候正審期間，申請人再次根據《刑事訴訟程序條例》第 9J 條，再次向原訟庭申請保釋候審。

裁決摘要

原訟庭法官指出，依據前上訴庭案例 *Chung Tse Ching v. Commissioner Of Correctional Services* [1988] HKC 251，他沒有權力去覆核前一位原訟庭法官拒絕他保釋申請的決定。而且，由於案件已交付原訟庭進行審訊，裁判官對此案的權責已終結（functus officio），申請人已無權再重新向裁判官提出保釋申請。但法官鑑於《基本法》第 28 條對人身自由的保護和《香港人權法案》第 5（3）條“因刑事罪名而被逮捕或拘禁之人，應迅即解送法官或依法執行司法權力之其他官員，並應於合理期間內審訊或釋放。候訊人通常不得加以羈押，但釋放得令具報，於審訊時、於司法程序之任何其他階段、並於一旦執行判決時，候傳到場。”即對一般等候審訊人士不作羈押的要求，認定作為一個擁有無限管轄權的法庭，不需要成文法的授權，也能給候訊人保釋，這應該建立在法院的固有管轄權上。可是，在考慮行使該管轄權前，申請人必須向法庭證明有“相關情況的實質改變”因素。在全面考慮所有相關事實後，法官拒絕了申請人的申請。

FOR REFERENCE

HCMP 549/2002

IN THE HIGH COURT OF THE

HONG KONG SPECIAL ADMINISTRATIVE REGION

COURT OF FIRST INSTANCE

MISCELLANEOUS PROCEEDINGS NO. 549 OF 2002

IN THE MATTER OF Kowloon City Magistracy Court Case No. KCCC3721/2001

- and -

IN THE MATTER OF application for bail under Section 9J of the Criminal Procedure Ordinance Cap. 221 of the Laws of Hong Kong

---

BETWEEN

HKSAR Respondent

- and -

SIU YAT LEUNG Applicant

Before: Deputy High Court Judge McCoy SC in Chambers

Date of Hearing: 15 April 2002

Date of Judgment: 15 April 2002

Date of Reasons for Judgment: 19 April 2002

REASONS FOR JUDGMENT

1. This application for bail, which I dismissed with short form reasons at the hearing, has raised significant and previously unresolved questions of jurisdiction under Part 1A Criminal Procedure Ordinance, Cap. 221. I now hand down my formal reasons, in accordance with s11 High Court Ordinance Cap 4.

2. On 11 April 2002, the applicant, who was and is still presently detained in Lai Chi Kok Reception Centre awaiting trial, took out a summons, supported by a short affirmation returnable on 15 April 2002, applying for bail. His application was expressly brought in terms of s.9J Criminal Procedure Ordinance.

3. That section provides:

"Review of refusal of bail or conditions of bail

S9J

(1) Where a District Judge or magistrate has refused to admit a person to bail or has so admitted a person subject to any condition, that person may in the case of a refusal, apply to a judge to be admitted to bail or in the case of an admission to bail subject to any condition, apply to a judge to be admitted to bail without bail being subject to that condition.

(2) On the hearing of an application under subsection (1), a judge may by order confirm, revoke or vary the decision of the District Judge or magistrate, and may make such other order in the matter including an order as to costs as he thinks just."

4. This section gives the Court of First Instance statutory jurisdiction to review, at the behest of a defendant, the decision made by either a District Judge or a magistrate, under s.9D(1) Criminal Procedure Ordinance. The jurisdiction under s.9J is not appellate. The judge of the Court of First Instance must review the matter afresh: s.9J(2).

5. It is apparent that s.9J(1) precludes the judge of the Court of First Instance from reviewing under that section an earlier decision of another Court of First Instance judge made under and in accordance with s.9J. This is consistent with the general common law principle that no court of co-ordinate jurisdiction may sit in review of itself: *Re Kray* [1965] Ch 736, 745A, per Lord Gardiner LC, *Chung Tse Ching v. Commissioner of Correctional Services* [1988] HKC 251, 255D (CA) per Cons VP. Of course, this does not (outside the s9J jurisdiction) preclude a judge of the Court of First Instance varying, granting or revoking bail which had been earlier granted by the Court of First Instance, if the circumstances warrant that course; that is "for sufficient reason": *Chung Tse Ching* at 254D–E.

History

6. The applicant is now facing an indictment, dated 4 April 2002, which alleges the serious offences of incitement to rob, contrary to common law and punishable under s.101I Criminal Procedure Ordinance and possession of arms without a licence, contrary to s.13(1) and (2) Firearms and Ammunition Ordinance, Cap. 238. The case, HCCC 109/2002, is pending a trial fixture in this Court.

7. The applicant was arrested on 18 December 2001. An application for bail on 1 February 2002 to a Magistrate was unsuccessful. The applicant by a summons dated 7 February 2002, returnable on 15 February 2002, asked the Court of First Instance, pursuant to s.9J Criminal Procedure Ordinance, to review the decision of the Magistrate. On 15 February 2002 Jackson J refused to grant him bail, because of the strength of the prosecution evidence and the nature and seriousness of the alleged offences.

8. Subsequent to the decision of Jackson J the applicant appeared before a Magistrate on 15 March 2002. He made no application for bail and was remanded to 28 March 2002 for committal proceedings. On that day he was committed to face trial in the Court of First Instance. He made no application for bail.

9. The present application before me is purportedly brought pursuant to s.9J However, this Court cannot review the decision of Jackson J, which was itself a review of the decision of the Magistrate on 1 February 2002. The primary decision of the Magistrate has been reviewed and affirmed. That jurisdiction to review has been exhausted. That primary decision of the Magistrate was made pursuant to s.9D(1). Since the decision of Jackson J, understandably, there has been no application for bail to any Magistrate. I therefore conclude that the present application fails for want of statutory jurisdiction under s.9J(1) Criminal Procedure Ordinance.

Other jurisdiction to apply for bail

10. However, so jealously does the Court inquire into any decision restricting liberty of a person entitled to the presumption of innocence, that the Court on its own motion, *nunc pro tunc*, amended the summons so that it now sought bail under s.9D Criminal Procedure Ordinance and/or the inherent jurisdiction of the High Court. Since the completion on 28 March of his committal proceedings under Part III Magistrates Ordinance Cap 227, the magistracy has become *functus officio* and indisputably so by the

time of the filing of the indictment, a week later, in this Court.

Inherent Jurisdiction to Grant Bail

11. There can be no doubt that Part 1A Criminal Procedure Ordinance is not a code. Indeed as Dr Robert Sharpe stated (now Sharpe JA in the Ontario Court of Appeal) in *The Law of Habeas Corpus*, 2nd ed at p. 134.:

> "... the summary procedure, designed particularly for the purpose of bail and which is now used in most jurisdictions, is undoubtedly an offspring of habeas corpus. It is really nothing more than a simplified habeas corpus application, and in a sense, all bail applications are rooted in the law of habeas corpus."

Further, it has been said, even in the Victorian era, that it would take unmistakably clear and precise language to abrogate the inherent jurisdiction of the Court of First Instance to grant bail: *R v. Spilsbury* [1898] 2 QB 615, 622 per Lord Russell of Killowen CJ.

12. However, I venture to suggest, that as a matter of constitutional law, because of the overriding imperatives in

(a) Article 28 Basic Law

> "The freedom of the Person of Hong Kong residents shall be inviolable.
>
> No Hong Kong resident shall be subjected to arbitrary or unlawful arrest, detention or imprisonment."

and (b) Article 5(3) Bill of Rights, Cap 383

> "It shall not be the general rule that persons awaiting trial shall be detained in custody, but release may be subject to guarantees to appear for trial, at any other stage of the judicial proceedings, and, should occasion arise, for execution of the judgement."
>
> and (c) as a bail application is but a vestigial form of habeas corpus under common law, (see s22A(14) High Court Ordinance and 054 RHC)

this Court could never be lawfully denied, by the Legislature, its quintessential power of adjudication in relation to liberty. That power is self-referentrial of its existence, and the Rule of Law depends on its undiminished virility and muliebrity. The very right to grant bail is innate in a superior court of unlimited jurisdiction: s.3(2) and s.12(3)(a) and (b), High Court Ordinance, Cap. 4. There is, and remains, a general right to bail at common law, independent of statute: *Re Wong Tai* (1911) 6 HKLR 67, 69 per Sir Francis Piggott CJ. It is a residual jurisdiction and is not therefore parallel to Part 1A Criminal Procedure Ordinance. See also *R v. Reading Crown Court ex parte Malik* [1981] QB 451 per Donaldson LJ, *R v. Croydon Crown Court ex parte Cox* [1997] 1 Cr App R 20 per Pill LJ, *Re Di Stefano* (1976) 30 CCC (2d) 310, 313 (NWT:SC), *Tobin v. Minister for Correctional Services* (1980) 24 SASR 389, 391-393 (SA: FC).

13. Therefore, in my judgment, in the window of opportunity between the decision of Jackson J under s9J and the completion of the applicant's committal s85A Magistrates Ordinance, although no application had been made to any magistrate, the applicant would have been entitled to apply to this Court for bail under its inherent jurisdiction. However, this Court would have, as a matter of jurisdiction (not discretion) during that period, required the applicant to establish "a material change in relevant circumstances" –the enduring common law test.

Principles at Common Law:Successive Bail Application

14. Until 1994, s.12B Criminal Procedure Ordinance provided:

> "12B
>
> If an accused person is refused or denied bail by the court or a judge, he shall not thereafter be entitled to make a fresh application for bail –
>
> (a) before the commencement of his trial, except to the court or a judge and only if he satisfies the court or judge that since the refusal or denial, there has been a material change in relevant circumstances;
>
> (b) during the trial, except to the court conducting his trial."

That section was simultaneously repealed by the enactment of the new Part 1A Criminal Procedure Ordinance.

15. By the former s.12B a further application for bail could not be made without "a material change in relevant circumstances". In my judgment that repealed statutory test was and is declaratory of the true common law position for the determination of a repeated bail application before the Court of First Instance. It would continue to apply to an application for bail to the Court of First Instance brought under the inherent jurisdiction, where there had been a previous decision refusing bail by this Court, under the inherent jurisdiction.

16. Section 9G(11) is essentially an epexegesis of the common law test. This test ensures that access to the Court is not a revolving door. A serious issue of judicial resources arises. Deserving cases may be needlessly postponed by repeated and legally frivolous applications by others for bail. The test is "a sensible and necessary adjunct to a coherent legal system, which would otherwise be prey to a proliferation of speculative bail applications on issues already decided": *R v. Ng Yiu Fai* [1992] 2 HKCLR 122, 125.

Part 1A Criminal Procedure Ordinance Cap 221

17. Part 1A of the Criminal Procedure Ordinance introduced new statutory bail provisions into Hong Kong law.

18. In s.9C "court" is defined as including a magistrate and District Court. Plainly, therefore the Court of First Instance is included in s.9C. But the structure and thrust of the s.9D jurisdiction shows that "court" when meaning the Court of First Instance, only means the Court when not sitting on review under s.9J.

19. Further therefore the statutory restrictions against multiple bail applications in s9G(11), by a person alleging himself entitled to bail, do not apply to a s.9J review, as the s.9G(11) limitations are directed at the primary decision-making court under s9D only and not the Court of First Instance when exercising the review jurisdiction given by s.9J, despite the literal wording in s9G(11) "at any hearing".

> s9G(11)
>
> "If at any hearing the court refuses to admit an accused person to bail the court shall, at each subsequent hearing while the accused remains in custody, consider the question of whether or not he ought to be admitted to bail and –
>
> (a) on the first occasion after that upon which the court first refused to so admit, the court shall hear any argument as to fact or law put to it in support of his

admission to bail, whether or not it has previously heard that argument;

(b) on the second or any subsequent occasion after that upon which the court first refused to so admit, the court need not hear any argument as to fact or law put to it in support of his admission to bail, if it has previously heard that argument."

s9D(1)(b) Criminal Procedure Ordinance

20. But the present application could be brought properly under s.9D(1)(b) Criminal Procedure Ordinance, as once the indictment has been filed in this Court, it has the trial jurisdiction over the accused and he is therefore now in "the Court before which he is accused". It follows the applicant would now have to qualify under s9G(11) in any further application.

21. How does the present applicant suggest he now qualifies for bail? Under a s9D(1)(b) application the decision-maker is plainly entitled and required to consider all the circumstances, including the previous bail application history. The only different circumstance is that he has now been in custody longer since the hearing before Jackson J and he is much closer to his trial in this Court than he was before. This is a wholly inadequate basis and cannot possibly qualify. Being committed by a Magistrate for trial in the Court of First Instance is not a development in favour of the applicant's position; indeed as it now presupposes the existence of a *prima facie* case against him of an indictable offence, it may very well be an adverse change of material circumstances. True, a "radical" change in the trial fixture date may qualify: per Bokhary J (as he then was), in *R v. Chu Kwok Wah*, 22 December 1989, HCMP 2006/89, but the allocation of a trial date "after a bail refusal will materially change the circumstances only if the delay to trial is excessive in itself or, if not excessive, then beyond the likely contemplation of the judge refusing bail": *R v. Ng Yiu Fai* at p. 124–125.

Disposition

22. Bail refused: applicant remanded in jail custody pending trial in the Court of First Instance.

23. I am grateful to Ms Catherine Ko, Senior Government Counsel, for both the considerable skill and care with which she assisted the Court in this matter.

Deputy High Court Judge (Gerard McCoy SC)

Ms. Catherine Ko, Senior Government Counsel of Department of Justice, for the Respondent

Mr. Siu Yat Leung, Applicant in person

第二十九條

香港居民的住宅和其他房屋不受侵犯。禁止任意或非法搜查、侵入居民的住宅和其他房屋。

案例

政府能否為了履行監督樓宇結構的責任而進入私人地方

P.415 | 香港特別行政區 對 林東

香港特別行政區 對 林東

HCMA 851/2005

簡略案情

上訴人是一個連天台物業的業主。屋宇署曾分別於 2000 年及 2001 年期間三次派員到訪該處視察，發現天台上加建了三個違章建築物。在第三次巡查後，發現違章搭建物仍然存在的情況下，屋宇署職員遂根據《建築物條例》第 24（1）條規定，在單位的鐵閘外張貼了要求上訴人於 60 天內拆除上述違章建築物的命令，及要求上訴人須修復有關樓宇受上述建築工程影響的部份；而該命令亦以掛號郵遞方式寄給上訴人。至 2003 年，屋宇署職員再次巡查該處時，發現上訴人並沒有遵從該命令。於是根據《建築物條例》第 40（1B）（b）條，對上訴人作出檢控。最終在裁判處被判罰款 4,000 元。上訴人不服定罪，向高等法院原訟庭提出上訴。

上訴人其中一個理據是屋宇署職員到該物業巡視前沒有得到上訴人的批准，亦無法庭的搜查令，因此，這些擅自進入其住所巡視、拍照及張貼告示的行為是違反《基本法》第 29 條，即“香港居民的住宅和其他房屋不受侵犯，禁止任意及非法搜查，侵入居民的住宅和其他房屋”的規定。

裁決摘要

法庭認為，申請人對於屋宇署職員擅闖民居是違反《基本法》的指控不能成立。

屋宇署職員均獲書面授權進行監督樓宇情況的工作，這授權已經由《建築物條例》第 22 條所規定、並詳細紀錄於他們的委任證上。據此授權，他們可以代表建築事務監督，隨時進入、並於必要時在警務人員陪同下，強行進入任何樓宇或任何地方執行公務。因此，他們進入上訴人住所的天台是有法可依、合情合理的行為，不屬於任意或非法的搜查。因此，上訴被駁回。

HCMA851/2005

香港特別行政區
高等法院原訟法庭

刑事上訴司法管轄權
判罪上訴
案件編號：裁判法院上訴案件 2005 年第 851 號
（原荃灣裁判法院案件 2004 年第 8724 號）

香港特別行政區
訴
被告人 林東

主審法官：高等法院原訟法庭暫委法官潘敏琦

聆訊日期：2005 年 10 月 27 日

判案日期：2005 年 10 月 27 日

判案書

1. 上訴人在聆訊後被裁定一項「身為樓宇擁有人，無合理辯解，而沒有遵從建築事務監督根據《建築物條例》第 123 章第 24（1）條的條文所送達的命令，即拆除有關的違例的建築工程，並按照建築事務監督核准的圖則，修復該樓宇受影響的部份」罪，罪名成立，違反香港法例第 123 章《建築物條例》第 40（1B）（b）條，被判罰款 4,000 元。上訴人不服定罪，提出上訴。

控方案情

2. 上訴人是傳票所指的單位連天台其中一位的樓宇擁有人。

3. 屋宇署測量主任分別於 2000 年 12 月 15 日、2001 年 9 月 19 日及 2001 年 12 月 5 日到該處所視察，發現天台上加建了 3 個搭建物。證人在首兩次拍下照片，及在圖則上作紀錄。第二次更量度了搭建物的高度。在第三次的巡查中，證人發現搭建物仍然存在。她再拍下照片存檔，並在單位的鐵閘外張貼了一份由建築事務監督根據香港法例第 123 章《建築物條例》第 24（1）條規定頒佈的命令，著令業主在 60 天內拆除上述建築工程，及須根據建築事務監督批准的圖則，修復有關樓宇受上述建築工程影響的部份，此限期於 2002 年 2 月 2 日屆滿。該命令亦以掛號郵遞方式寄給上訴人。

4. 2003 年 6 月 26 日及 2003 年 12 月 13 日，屋宇署測量主任及測量師及其他同事視察該天台處所，發現清拆工程仍未展開，違例搭建物仍未拆除，上訴人沒有遵從命令。他們拍下照片及在圖則上作紀錄。

辯方案情

5. 上訴人選擇不作供及不傳召證人。

上訴理據

6. 上訴人所提出的書面及口述上訴理由，可歸納如下：

（1）裁判官錯誤地在他未決定是否作供前，已宣佈表面證供成立；

（2）證人擅自進入其處所巡視、拍照及張貼告示，有違《基本法》第 29 條；

（3）控方呈遞的照片並不能顯示搭建物的真實呎吋，證人的量度存在疑點；及

（4）證人承認他們曾討論此案，所以他們的證供吻合實不足為奇。裁判官不應倚仗此點而作出證人為誠實可靠的結論。

答辯人回應

7. 答辯人指出上訴人並無提出實際理據指出定罪不穩妥。至於上訴人重複所指屋宇署人員在執法時違反基本法的指控，裁判官在口述判詞及裁斷陳述書中已作出適當的裁斷。

裁決

8. 根據香港法例第 123 章《建築物條例》第 2 條，建築工程是「包括任何種類的建築物建造工程、地盤平整工程、附表所列地區內的土地勘察、基礎工程、修葺、拆卸、改動、加建以及各類建築作業，此外，亦包括排水工程」。

9. 憑此闡釋，則加建於該處所天台上的 3 個搭建物，均屬建築工程。但在某些情況下，包括高度少於 1.5 米和不影響結構的情況下，申請是會獲考慮接納的。

10. 根據上述條例第 14 條的規定，任何人未事先獲得建築事務監督的書面批准及同意，不得展開或進行任何建築工程，除非是屬於第 41（3）條內所載的豁免工程外。在本案中，上訴人並無爭議該處天台上存在 3 個搭建物。

11. 上訴人在上訴理由中，質疑有關人員對搭建物量度的準確性，與本案的關鍵點無關。而有關照片亦確切地顯示了實況。上訴人並無預先取得屋宇署的許可，進行任何建築工程，亦是不爭的事實。

12. 證人可信性的問題乃是事實的裁斷。裁判官亦已考慮證人承認同事間有討論過本案，但她認為證人商討案件實屬無可厚非，而本案並無證據顯示他們曾就此案互相串通，甚至捏造證據。再者，上訴人在聆訊時，既不爭議該處所天台上存在 3 個搭建物，亦無爭議他沒有遵從屋宇署發出的命令著令他把搭建物拆除及修復。裁判官絕對有權作出證人是誠實可靠的證人的裁斷。

13. 上訴人在上訴理由中，指有關人員在作出視察前，沒有得到上訴人的批准，亦無法庭的搜查令，有違《基本法》第 29 條這點，裁判官判詞中已作出處理。有關之《基本法》第 29 條，節錄如下：

> 「香港居民的住宅和其他房屋不受侵犯，禁止任意及非法搜查，侵入居民的住宅和其他房屋。」

14. 然而，根據香港法例第 123 章《建築物條例》第 22 條的規定，因屋宇署職員均已獲書面授權代表建築事務監督，有權隨時進入，並於必要時在警務人員陪同下，強行進入任何樓宇或任何地方，這授權已詳細紀錄於他們委任證的背面，故此，他們進入上訴人處所的天台是有法可依，合情合理的，並非任意或非法搜查。本席認同裁判官的觀點。上訴人對於屋宇署職員擅闖民居，違反《基本法》的指控，純因其對法例一知半解所致。

15. 至於上訴人所指裁判官錯誤地在他未決定是否作供前，已宣佈表面證供成立的上訴理由，亦不成立。裁判官在控方案情完結後，給予上訴人中途陳詞的機會。上訴人有作出陳詞，裁判官裁定表面證據成立。然後裁判官再詳細解釋上訴人的權利，他清楚表明選擇不自辯、不傳召證人，謄本紀錄一目了然。此乃一貫既定的審訊程序。被告人並沒有權利在裁判官宣佈表面證據成立<u>之前</u>選擇作供與否。

16. 裁判官正確地提醒自己不應因上訴人選擇不作供及不傳召證人而對他作出不利的揣測，又提醒自己舉證的責任和準則，最後認定上訴人在天台搭建 3 個搭建物是違法，和信納由於在有關時段，上訴人並無遵從有關命令拆除及按照建築事務監督核准的圖則，和把之修復。亦沒有合理辯解，沒有遵從建築事務監督向他送達的命令拆除 3 個違例建築物，所以裁定上訴人罪名成立。裁判官並無犯錯。

17. 上訴理據不足，駁回，維持原判。

高等法院暫委法官（潘敏琦）

控方：由律政司政府律師鄭凱聰代表香港特別行政區

辯方：無律師代表，親自出庭

第三十條

香港居民的通訊自由和通訊秘密受法律的保護。除因公共安全和追查刑事犯罪的需要，由有關機關依照法律程序對通訊進行檢查外，任何部門或個人不得以任何理由侵犯居民的通訊自由和通訊秘密。

案例

民主黨 對 律政司司長

HCAL 84/2006（判決書參考 P.269.）

簡略案情

根據《公司條例》第 95 條，所有公司必須存有一本包括所有成員名字和地址的成員登記冊。而《公司法》第 98 條再規定，所有公司必須允許他人對此登記冊進行檢查。1994 年，一群有著共同政治理念的人以民主黨名字並以有限公司形式成為申請人。他們的構思是所有的黨員也將會是公司的成員，換言之，成員登記冊亦即是黨員登記冊。結果，任何人想了解該黨成員身份，只需要行使第 98 條賦予的權利便可。然而，該黨黨員並不想讓其身份向廣大的公眾公開，恐怕因為他們的理念而受到不友善的對待。因此，申請人向法院申請，宣佈第 98 條的規管不能施加於政黨上，否則便違反了《基本法》第 27 條和第 30 條及違反了《香港人權法案》第 14 條和第 18 條，即結社自由和私隱保護的基本保護。

申請人提出，因為政治團體的敏感性，沒有限制的第 98 條，在程度上超出了其需要達到的合理目的。作為政治團體，申請人沒有營商的性質，所以沒必要受到第 98 條的約束。然而，答辯人卻認為任何跟申請人交往的公眾也應有權知道它的成員的身份，而且，申請人不是純粹依賴它的有限公司身份去追求政治理想，它還包涵一定的經濟利益，其中包括接受捐獻、籌款、借貸和商業買賣等等。

裁決摘要

“有限公司”是獨立的法律個體，獨自對債權人承擔責任，而其背後的成員的責任是有限的。因此，第 98 條的合理目的，是讓公眾在跟這些公司交往前，能對其成員有更多的認識。而第 98 條的限制，正正為了達到這個目的。法庭不同意申請人認為第 98 條只針對純粹是商業性質的公司，反之，法庭接受答辯人的分析，申請人有限公司的身份包含了一定的經濟利益。所以，第 98 條對它的約束，如同對其他的公司一樣，是有合理的基礎的。但這種約束，不能超過必須的程度。關於私隱保護問題，法官注意到《基本法》第 30 條相對《香港人權法案》第 14 條，對私隱的保護比較狹義。第 30 條保護的是通訊溝通內容的保密，但第 14 條保護的重點是私人的生活，其中包括了家庭、朋友等元素。法官再引用案例 *Bruggerman And Scheuten v. Federal Republic Of Germany* [1981] 3 EHRR 244 說明當把私人的生活注入了公眾生活後，它的保護便相對減少。而且，法官又認為，在第 14 條中，“非法”、“無理”的用詞，顯示大眾利益和個人權利間需要取得一個平衡，而法庭認為終審法院於*梁國雄*一案所釐定的均衡比例測試（Proportionality Test）正好作為考慮這平衡問題的標準。

在審訊時，法官也注意到兩個方面：1）並非任何情況下，申請人也要提供成員登記冊給予檢查。在濫用的情況下，法庭有酌情權拒絕依據第 98 條作出的要求；2）在法律層面上，申請人並非被強迫以有限公司形式運作，它完全可以以另外一種方法存在，包括登記為社團，事實上歐洲人權法院在 *Le Compte, Van Leuven And De Meyere v. Belgium* [1981] 4 EHRR 1 裏也有相同的見解。現在申請人是一方面享受這選擇的好處，另方面又質疑它的壞處。

最後，法庭認為申請人現在的身份，是當時發起人的自由選擇，並非被強迫做出的選擇；而且，第 98 條亦有避免濫用的基制；因此，在平衡公眾利益的考慮下，認定《公司條例》第 98 條並不違憲。

香港特別行政區 對 李萬德及陳財成

DCCC689/2004；CACC 303/2005

簡略案情

上訴人李萬德及其他三名被告在區域法院被指控串謀行賄。四人向 ING 的一名基金經理提供報酬從而促使 ING 購買並繼續持有上訴人擔任執行董事的上市公司的股份，並向 UBS AG 的一名分析員提供報酬從而促使其發佈推薦該上市公司股份的報告。

在區域法院的審理過程中，辯方就證據的可接納性提出了質疑。在案件調查過程中，廉政公署針對上訴人及其他被告在飯館的兩次會面進行了秘密監視與監聽，獲取了有關被告賄賂他人的證據。辯方認為該等秘密監視所得的證據不能在案件審理過程中使用，原因是違反了《基本法》第 30 條。

辯方認為《基本法》第 30 條中的“法律程序”指的應當是法例，包括具體指引和守則等，目的是規範需要監聽私人談話的有關政府部門的行為，但目前香港沒有相關的法例。然而，控方卻認為只要獲取了犯罪信息，獲取信息過程中的程序缺陷即可被補救。

裁決摘要

原審法官認定獲取該監視證據的手法違反了《基本法》第 30 條的規定。法官援引了歐洲法院的案例 *Malone v. United Kingdom* [1984] 7 EHRR，其中對《歐洲人權公約》第 8 條裏規定的“依照法律”做出了明確的解釋。法官認為《基本法》第 30 條即來源於《歐洲人權公約》的第 8 條，且其中的“依照法律”與《基本法》第 30 條中的“依照法律程序”是同一個意思。該案例指出“依照法律”即暗示必須有明確的法律保證，公共機構不得隨意干涉第 8 條賦予的公民權利，並使得公民可知悉在何種情況和條件下，公共機構才可採取秘密的、且具有潛在危險性的手段來干預公民的生活和通信私隱。法官認為英國普通法已考慮歐洲法院的判決，同時隨著英國人權法的頒佈，英國議會通過了《調查權力法案》以及法定指引，其中詳細地列明有關秘密監視的授權、書面記錄，以及資料保管的規定。而香港並沒有類似的監管秘密監視行為的法例，因此法官認為廉政公署的兩次監視行為未能“依照法律程序”進行，從而違反了《基本法》第 30 條。

然而，根據嚴格的證據排除規則，法官認為採納兩次監視的記錄作為證據並不會導致審判的不公平。同時，辯方也承認廉政公署並不是在明知的情況下故意侵犯被告的權利，根據英國的案例，一般認為如果獲取證據的過程中只是存在善意的錯誤手法，就不應排除該等非法獲取的證據。因此，法官決定採納該監視證據。但是，法官進一步補充，鑒於法院已經做出了在沒有遵從法律程序的情況下，秘密安裝監視設備違反了《基本法》的判決，除非該判決被推翻，否則，日後廉政公署在沒有法例依據的情況下，繼續進行這種監視行為，則很有可能被認定為具有惡意。上訴人不滿法庭的裁決遂向上訴庭提起上訴，認為原審法官雖然正確地裁定秘密監視的行為違反了《基本法》第 30 條，卻未能正確地在審訊中排除使用此等證據。

上訴庭援引 *Leung Kwok Hung & Another v. Chief Executive Of HKSAR* CACV 73/2006，CACV 87/2006，確認了廉政公署秘密監視的行為違反了《基本法》規定的隱私權。但是，上訴庭同樣認為獲取證據的程序違反《基本法》並不必然導致證據不可被採納。上訴庭認為法院必須在保護憲法性權利及發現和懲治犯罪這兩方面取得平衡。上訴庭同意原審法官的看法，即隱私權的保護有時可能需要讓位於調查嚴重犯罪行為的公共利益。而在行使其酌情權時，法院亦必須保證審判的公平性。上訴庭認為該案件是非常嚴重的犯罪行為，涉及上市公司的董事和國際財務機構。同時，上訴庭同意原審法官的意見，認為採納秘密監視記錄作為證據，不會導致對上訴人的不公平審判，因此駁回了上訴人的上訴。

CACC 303/2005

IN THE HIGH COURT OF THE
HONG KONG SPECIAL ADMINISTRATIVE REGION
COURT OF APPEAL

CRIMINAL APPEAL NO 303 OF 2005
(ON APPEAL FROM DCCC 689 of 2004)

Between:

HKSAR	Respondent
- and -	
Li man tak (李萬德)	1st Applicant
tan chue seng, nicholas (陳財成)	2nd Applicant

Before: Hon Stuart-Moore VP, Yeung JA and Suffiad J in Court

Date of Hearing: 25-27 July 2006

Date of Judgment: 13 September 2006

JUDGMENT

Hon Yeung JA (giving judgment of the Court):

Background

1. SBI E2-Capital China Holdings Ltd. ("SBI-E2") specialised in the placements of shares of public listed companies to major investors, including asset management companies. Kwong Hing International Holdings (Bermuda) Ltd ("Kwong Hing"), a public listed company and ING Investment Management Asia Pacific (Hong Kong) Ltd ("ING"), a global asset management company, were SBI-E2's clients.

2. UBS AG and one of its subsidiaries-UBS Securities Asia Ltd. ("UBS Securities"), provided wealth and asset management, and investment banking and securities services to corporate and individual clients, (including the supply of research reports on public listed companies) to assist them in their investment decisions.

3. SBI-E2, ING and UBS AG did not allow their employees to accept any secret commission/payment from clients.

4. The 1st applicant-Lee Man-tak Michael, the executive director of Kwong Hing, together with his family, controlled 45% of Kwong Hing's issued shares. The 2nd applicant-Nicholas Tan Chye Seng was a research analyst of UBS AG, heading its small capitalization department.

5. Louis Lin Chak Pui ("Louis Lin") and Vincent Yum were employees of SBI-E2 and were in charge respectively of its Corporate Finance Department and its Equity Capital Market Department. Adrian Foo Tiang Hock ("Adrian Foo") was a fund manager working for ING.

6. In June 2003, SBI-E2 made two placements of Kwong Hing shares to corporate investors, including ING, one on 13 June 2003 of 33.6 million shares at $0.84 per share and one on 11 July 2003 of 19.7 million shares at $1.01 per shares. Under the placement agreements, ING had to hold onto the shares for not less than six months.

7. Between 1 July 2003 and 26 February 2004, ING, through various funds under its management, purchased another 18 million Kwong Hing shares.

8. On 12 February 2004, UBS Securities Asia, as an affiliate of UBS AG, published a bullish report on Kwong Hing, forecasting substantial increase in its year to year turnover with a target price of its shares at $2.31 in one year against the then market price of $1.57 per share. The report also carried a rating of "Buy 2" for the Kwong Hing shares when there was no previous rating.

The Prosecution Allegations

9. It was the prosecution case that the 1st applicant conspired with Louis Lin, Adrian Foo and Vincent Yum to offer advantages to Adrian Foo as a reward for causing ING to purchase the 18 million Kwong Hing shares, and conspired with Louis Lin and Vincent Yum to offer advantages to Adrian Foo as a reward for causing ING to continue to hold the placed Kwong Hing shares after the expiration of the six-month period.

10. The prosecution also alleged that the 1st and 2nd applicants, together with Louis Lin, Adrian Foo and Vincent Yum conspired to offer advantages to the 2nd applicant for causing UBS AG and UBS Securities to publish a bullish report on Kwong Hing shares and/or to recommend such shares to their clients.

11. There were other allegations against Vincent Yum and/or Adrian Foo.

The Charges

12. Arising out of the aforesaid allegations, the 1st and 2nd applicants (D1 and D4 at trial), together with Louis Lin and Adrian Foo (D2 and D3 at trial) appeared before Judge Sweeney in the District Court on an indictment consisting of seven charges.

13. Charge 1 against the 1st applicant, Louis Lin and Adrian Foo alleged that they conspired with Vincent Yum to offer a bribe to Adrian Foo as a reward for causing ING to purchase the 18 million Kwong Hing shares.

14. Charge 2, with the alternative charges 2A and 2B, against the 1st and 2nd applicant, Louis Lin and Adrian Foo, alleged that they conspired with Vincent Yum to offer a bribe to the 2nd applicant for procuring the publication of a bullish report on Kwong Hing shares and/or for promoting the Kwong Hing shares.

15. Charge 3 against the 1st applicant and Louis Lin alleged that they conspired with Vincent Yum to offer a bribe to Adrian Foo for causing ING to continue to hold the placed Kwong Hing shares.

16. Charges 4 and 5 were directed at Adrian Foo only.

17. Louis Lin pleaded guilty to charges 1 and 2A. Adrian Foo pleaded guilty to charges 1 and 4. They denied the other charges and those charges were left on file and not proceeded with.

18. The 1st applicant was convicted of charges 1 and 2B but acquitted of charge 3. The 2nd applicant was convicted of charge 2B.

19. The 1st and 2nd applicant sought leave to appeal against conviction.

20. Vincent Yum was not charged as the prosecution accepted his offer as a witness under immunity, and he gave evidence against the applicants at trial.

The Prosecution Evidence

21. Not surprisingly, the direct evidence against the applicants

came from Vincent Yum, one of the alleged co-conspirators. He described his dealings with the applicants and the other co-conspirators whom he knew quite well as business acquaintances.

22. Vincent Yum described how the 1st applicant agreed to pay commissions, as a reward, to fund managers who would buy Kwong Hing shares. The reward took the form of share options of 3.8 million Kwong Hing shares at the exercise price lower than the market price.

23. Louis Lin, Adrian Foo and Vincent Yum then shared the substantial profits generated from the exercise of the share options.

24. Vincent Yum testified that he kept his share of the money and part of Adrian Foo's share (at Adrian Foo's request) in safety deposit boxes separate from his regular income as the money "came from monkey business".

25. Vincent Yum also said that shortly before his arrest on 25 February 2004, the 1st applicant handed Louis Lin P1, a piece of paper recording the calculation of the profits from the exercise of the share options. The 1st applicant also gave him a paper bag containing $594,500 in cash, which was recovered by the ICAC.

26. Vincent Yum mentioned the 1st applicant's request to Adrian Foo for his funds to continue to hold the Kwong Hing shares after the expiration of the six-month period stipulated in the placement agreements.

27. However, up to the time of their arrests on 25 February 2004, no conclusion was reached as Adrian Foo had yet to make a final decision.

28. According to Vincent Yum, in order to promote the Kwong Hing shares, the 2nd applicant would be asked to procure the publishing of a bullish report on Kwong Hing by UBS AG. The agreement was that the 1st applicant, as a reward for such a favourable report, would grant a 10 million share options at the below market price of $1.08 per share. The profits derived from the exercise of such options were to be shared, one-sixth to Louis Lin and five-sixths to the 2nd applicant, Vincent Yum and Adrian Foo.

29. The 1st applicant also agreed to make an advance payment of $1 million, which sum would be deducted from the profits when the share options were exercised.

30. In late 2003, the 1st applicant did hand over $1 million in cash to Vincent Yum who then gave $800,000 to the 2nd applicant through Adrian Foo, leaving $200,000 to be shared by Vincent Yum and Adrian Foo. According to Vincent Yum, the 2nd applicant had acknowledged his request for the return of the $200,000 allegedly as payment to the co-author of the report. However, by the time of their arrest, the $200,000 had not been returned.

31. Ms Ada Poon, responsible for research in UBS AG, described how the 2nd applicant was instrumental to the publication of a bullish report on Kwong Hing, forecasting a 50% increase of price in one year. The tenor of her evidence was that the 2nd applicant was eager to publish the bullish report on Kwong Hing and was in frequent contact with the Kwong Hing management at the material time.

32. Ms Poon described how the 2nd applicant amended her draft financial model on Kwong Hing with far more optimistic estimates for future turnover and profits. According to Ms Poon, the 2nd applicant said he obtained the figures after talking to the Kwong Hing management.

33. Another officer of UBS AB, Julian Pickstone, who headed the UBS committee that approved the publication of research reports ("IRC") said Kwong Hing was the company with the smallest capital that they had ever approved for research reports, as they did not usually do reports for companies with less than US$100 million market capitalisation.

34. The 1st applicant, Louis Lin, Adrian Foo and Vincent Yum were under ICAC covert surveillance before they were arrested. Their telephone conversations were secretly taped although the records relating to the taping had been destroyed before trial.

35. With the information obtained from the telephone taping, the ICAC was able to make an audio-visual record of a dinner meeting of the 1st applicant, Louis Lin, Adrian Foo and Vincent Yum on 4 November 2003 at the Tang Court restaurant in Langham Hotel (the Tang Court meeting) and of another meeting of the 1st applicant, Louis Lin and Vincent Yum on 20 February 2004 at the Hunan Garden Restaurant at Exchange Square (the Hunan Garden meeting).

36. The records of the meetings supported Vincent Yum's allegations against the applicants.

37. The ICAC also video recorded and took pictures of a meeting of the 1st applicant with Louis Lin and Vincent Yum at the Star Ferry Pier on 25 February 2004 at about 1750 hours (the Star Ferry meeting).

38. At the Star Ferry meeting, the 1st applicant, with a piece of paper in his hand, was explaining its contents to Louis Lin and Vincent Yum. They then got into the 1st applicant's car and the 1st applicant handed over a brown paper bag containing $594,500 in cash to Vincent Yum, who put it in his yellow knapsack. They were then arrested.

39. The 1st applicant was found to have, on his person, cash of $208,500, including a hundred of $1,000 notes with serial numbers BZ 624301 to BZ 624400. His co-director in another company, Mr Chiu Ka-chun was found to be in possession of a further three hundred $1,000 notes from the same series.

40. Louis Lin had P1 and Vincent Yum had $594,500, including five hundred $1,000 notes from the same series as those from the 1st applicant and Mr Chiu. Subsequently, the ICAC recovered a further $2.3 million in cash from a wardrobe and in safe deposit boxes under Vincent Yum's control. Adrian Foo also had $700,000 in a safe deposit box.

41. The 2nd applicant was arrested on 26 February 2004 shortly after midnight. In one of the subsequent interviews, the 2nd applicant described his role in procuring the research report on Kwong Hing. He denied having received any advantages to assist the 1st applicant.

42. The 2nd applicant emphasized that the report on Kwong Hing was based on their interim results and that he was not responsible for the "pricing issues", which was Ada Poon's responsibility. Indeed, he said he had to push down the forecasted price of the Kwong Hing shares, as he did not believe they worth that much. The 2nd applicant also tried to distance himself from the Kwong Hing management.

Defence Case

43. Only the 1st applicant gave evidence at trial. He admitted explaining the contents of P1 to Louis Lin and Vincent Yum at the Star Ferry meeting and then handing it over to Louis Lin. He also

admitted to have paid Vincent Yum on four occasions the large sums of money mentioned by him. The 1st applicant, however, denied there was any element of corruption.

44. The 1st applicant said there was an agreement between Louis Lin and a good friend of his, Mr Chiu, who held 20 million Kwong Hing shares and that Louis Lin would purchase 3.8 million Kwong Hing shares from Mr. Chiu at $0.92 per share, with the completion of the agreement in one year's time. If the price of the Kwong Hing share fell below 92 cents, Louis Lin had to pay the difference to Mr Chiu and, if the price went up, Mr Chiu had to pay him the difference. The 1st applicant said at the time of the agreement, the Kwong Hing shares were trading at between 80 cents to $1 a share.

45. The 1st applicant said he approved the agreement even though that would breach the company rules and the SFC regulations, as their agreement demonstrated confidence of the security people in Kwong Hing and would in turn lead to more fund managers investing in Kwong Hing.

46. The 1st applicant said he helped Mr Chiu to pass on the money, sometimes to Vincent Yum after the Kwong Hing shares acquired by Louis Lin were realized at a profit.

47. The 1st applicant was asked why Mr Chiu did not pay Louis Lin himself or why Louis Lin did not collect the money from Mr Chiu directly, and his reply was that it was part of the arrangement. He said he did not know if the agreement relating to the 3.8 million shares had been registered. He also said it was Mr Chiu who asked him to hand over P1 to Vincent Yum on 25 February 2004.

48. The 1st applicant denied having paid the 2nd applicant money for a bullish UBS AG report on Kwong Hing. He said in the summer of 2003, Louis Lin mentioned that UBS had shareholding in Kwong Hing and might be interested to introduce Kwong Hing to their clients. There was a suggestion that UBS AB might take up 10% of the Kwong Hing shares and then request a seat on the company board. Louis Lin also mentioned that UBS would charge $1 million, which payment was approved by the Kwong Hing directors. However, there was in fact no payment. The 1st applicant said he never talked to Vincent Yum about the $1 million.

49. The 1st applicant admitted that he wished ING would hold onto the Kwong Hing shares for a further 3 to 6 months. However, he denied paying or agreeing to pay any reward to anyone to achieve his wish.

50. The 1st applicant was asked to explain the reference to "advances", "payments", and "additional dessert" mentioned in the taped conversations of the Tang Court meeting. He said he was referring to possible additional placement of Kwong Hing shares to fund managers at below market price, which shares would then be sold at a profit.

51. The 1st applicant said Vincent Yum and Louis Lin were interested in promoting Kwong Hing as it was SBI E2's client and that they might benefit from a rise of the Kwong Hing share price.

52. The 1st applicant was unable to give a satisfactory explanation to the contents of the conversations at the Tang Court meeting.

53. It was part of the admitted facts that when the ICAC surveillance records showed that the 1st applicant handed over money to Vincent Yum on 5 December 2003 and 25 February 2004 in paper bags, he had earlier collected the paper bags from the home of Mr Chiu.

54. Apart from putting forward the aforesaid evidence, it was also the defence's case that the audio and video records of the Tang Court meeting and the Hunan Garden meeting should not be admitted as evidence as they infringed the 1st applicant's right to freedom and privacy of communication protected under the Basic Law and the Hong Kong Bill or Right Ordinance ("the Bill of Rights"), Cap. 383.

55. The 1st applicant also applied for a permanent stay of the proceedings as a result of the non-disclosure and destruction of the records of telephone interceptions leading to the covert surveillance of the Tang Court meeting and the Hunan Garden meeting.

56. There were also applications by both applicants to exclude certain records of interviews.

The Judge's Findings

57. The judge concluded that the ICAC had not conducted the covert surveillance in accordance with legal procedures, thus infringing the 1st applicant' right to freedom and privacy of communication. However, the judge refused to exclude the audio and video records of the Tang Court meeting and the Hunan Garden meeting as evidence.

58. The judge said he could not find any unfairness in admitting such evidence in all the circumstances of the case.

59. The judge noted the concession by the 1st applicant's senior counsel at trial that "the ICAC officers did not knowingly and wilfully breach the defendant's right". The judge further pointed out that the right to privacy might be outweighed by the public interest in the detection of serious crime.

60. The judge rejected the 1st applicant's application for a permanent stay. The judge ruled some of the applicants' records of interviews admissible, and some inadmissible.

61. The judge was mindful of the "despicable" character of Vincent Yum who he described (adopting the defence submission) in the following terms:

> "He was a trusted professional with a bright future, but on his own evidence he has proved himself to be greedy, self-interested, deceitful and manipulative.He has cheated those around him and has breached every trust reposed in him. On his own version he invented a 'UBS syndicate' and lied as to how many people were involved in order to increase his slice of the pie."

62. The judge agreed with the defence suggestion that Vincent Yum's dishonest dealings in the Stock Market went well beyond Kwong Hing and he had not been too forthcoming with the ICAC on those dealings, and that his criminality was far wider and more serious than those of the applicants.

63. The judge accepted that Vincent Yum was vague on some detail and there were inconsistencies in some of his evidence.

64. However, the judge accepted Vincent Yum's evidence against the applicants. The judge pointed out that his evidence was supported by the tape conversations of the Tang Court meeting and the Hunan Garden meeting.

65. In summarising Vincent Yum's evidence against the 1st applicant, the judge said in his reasons for verdict the following:

> "49. Shortly after Vincent Yum became acquainted with D1 (the 1st applicant), he dined with him and D2 (Louis

Lin). In the course of the meal D1 and D2 asked if Vincent Yum knew any fund manager interested in buying the shares of Kwong Hing. D2 also mentioned at the time that some commission would be payable to the relevant fund manager. Vincent Yum said he knew some fund managers and he would introduce them. He knew that his friend Adrian Foo had already bought in Kwong Hing shares via the funds that he controlled, 'partially because he liked the shares and partially because D1 had promised him share options as a "kick back" that the market would not notice' . Also, he knew that D3 (Adrian Foo) had previously inquired of opportunities to co-operate. D1 made it clear that he was keen to have institutional fund managers buy and hold his shares as such purchases by blue chip institutions would give his company kudos in the market and encourage other fund managers to join in.

50. Two weeks later, Vincent and D2 arranged a dinner in Tsim Sha Tsui in which they talked with D1 and D3. D1 did not have a good command of English and D3 did not know Cantonese, so Vincent and D2 had to act as interpreters. In the course of discussions an agreement was reached. Michael offered advantages calculated by reference to 'options' over 1 per cent of Kwong Hing's market issue of shares, that is, about 3.8 million shares. There would be an exercise price of 92 cents in return for D3's arranging the purchase by his employers ING of 5 per cent of Kwong Hing's shares, that is, about 19 million shares. However, D3 had to hold onto the shares and not put them back on the market for 6 months. It was agreed at the time that the options would be exercised in stages and the profit (that is the difference between the market price and option price of 92 cents) would then each time be divided between D2, D3 and Vincent Yum."

66. The judge pointed out that if Vincent Yum only accepted the payments arising out of proper share option arrangement as suggested by the 1st applicant, there was no reason for Vincent Yum to admit to serious criminal offence when what he did only amounted to unethical conduct of a minor nature.

67. The judge adopted the "co-conspirators rule" and took into account the record of the Tang Court meeting as evidence against the 2nd applicant. In so doing, the judge referred to the following extrinsic evidence:

"(1) The evidence of Vincent Yum of his sporadic contacts and discussions on this conspiracy with D4 (the 2nd applicant), whether by telephone or, once, meeting him at Adrian's house, to discuss the report and the reward for the same.

(2) By contrasting the (uncontradicted) evidence of PW 18, Ada Poon, to the effect that it was her boss, Nicholas Tan (the 2nd applicant), who was radically amending upwards all of her estimates for future turnover and profits of Kwong Hing with what D4 told the ICAC in his cautioned statement (P66). There he lays all the blame on her for coming up with figures that were too high and which he had to 'push downwards'.

68. In so far as the contents of the 2nd applicant's cautioned interview contradicted the evidence of Ada Poon on the pricing issues and on his relationship with the Kwong Hing management, the judge found that they were deliberate lies. The judge took the view that such lies related to a central issue in the case and therefore not only provided a foundation for the receipt of the records of the Tang Court meeting as evidence against him under the co-conspirator's rule, but also strengthened the inference of guilt against him.

69. The judge rejected the 1st applicant's evidence. He pointed out that it made no financial sense for Mr Chiu to agree to the option agreements mentioned by the 1st applicant and that there was no reason for the 1st applicant to be involved in the manner when he had no personal interest. The judge also emphasized that the suggested share option agreement was never put to Vincent Yum.

70. The judge was satisfied that charges 1 and 2B against the 1st applicant and charge 2B against the 2nd applicant had been proved and he accordingly convicted them on those charges.

71. The judge acquitted the 1st applicant of charge 3, not because he had any doubt about the evidence of Vincent Yum, but because his evidence did not show that the parties had made a final decision.

Grounds of Appeal

72. Mr Andrew Macrae SC, together with Mr Joseph Tse SC and Ms Maggie Wong, for the 1st applicant, relies principally on two grounds, namely (1) that the judge was wrong to admit the records of the Tang Court meeting and the Hunan Garden meeting as evidence; and (2) that the judge, by adopting a substantial part of the Prosecution Opening in his reasons for verdict, had demonstrated a lack of impartial and independent assessment of the evidence.

73. Mr Macrae submits that without the record of the meetings, the judge would not have convicted the 1st applicant, in the light of his misgivings about Vincent Yum's evidence.

74. Mr Macrae argues that the judge, having rightly ruled that the ICAC covert surveillance contravened the right of privacy guaranteed under Article 30 of the Basic Law and of the Bill of Rights, adopted a wrong test on the issue of admissibility. The suggestion is that by adopting the approach as enunciated in *R v. Sang* [1980] AC 402 and *R v. Kuruma* [1955] AC 197, the judge had failed to take into account the significant shift in approach arising out of human rights legislation.

75. Mr Macrae submits that the judge had failed to carry out a proper evaluation of the relevant factors, and had wrongly placed the burden on the applicants to show unfairness.

76. Mr Macrae further suggests that the judge had misunderstood the evidence of Vincent Yum and had made findings unsupported by evidence. To support his argument, Mr Macrae makes reference to paragraphs 49 to 50 of the judge's reasons for verdict (See: paragraph 65 above) as an example to demonstrate the judge's lack of independent and impartial judgment.

77. Mr Gary Plowman SC, together with Ms Wing Kay Po, for the 2nd applicant, associated themselves with Mr Macrae's main grounds and argument, and put forward further grounds.

78. Mr Plowman SC suggests that the incriminating evidence from Vincent Yum against the 2nd applicant was confused, imprecise, contradictory and unreliable, and therefore should not be relied upon.

79. Mr Plowman argues that the judge was wrong to conclude that

the 2nd applicant had lied on the two matters mentioned by the judge and alternatively, even if those lies had been established, the judge was wrong to rely on them as an indication of guilt, or as evidence capable of strengthening an inference of guilt, or as the foundation for the reception of the record of the Tang Court meeting as evidence against the 2nd applicant. Mr Plowman further says that the judge had failed to consider the possible innocent explanation for the "lies", even if they were indeed "lies".

80. Mr Plowman also relies on what he claims to be numerous misstatements and omissions of evidence to show the judge's lack of independent and impartial judgment.

Discussion

Admission of Evidence Obtained in Breach of Freedom and Privacy of Communication

81. There is no dispute, as confirmed by the Court of Final Appeal in *Leung Kwok Hung & Another v. Chief Executive of HKSAR* CACV 73 and 87 of 2006, that the ICAC's covert surveillance infringed the freedom and privacy of communication, as protected by the Basic Law and the Bill of Rights.

82. However it is important to bear in mind that evidence obtained in breach of the right of privacy is not inadmissible *per se*. The court has to carry out a balancing exercise "in which the fact that there has been a breach of the accused's guaranteed right is a very important but not necessarily determinative factor". (Per Blandchard J in *R v. Shaheed* [2002] 2 NZLR 377 at p. 419)

83. Mr Macrae suggests, relying on *R v. Sang* [1980] AC 402 and *R v. Cheung Ka Fai* [1995] 3 HKC 214, that the common law approach obliges the court to admit relevant and cogent evidence even if such evidence is obtained unfairly. He further suggests that the common law approach has been modified by human rights legislation that confers upon the court a residual discretion. However, the judge failed to consider such residual discretion.

84. With respect, the common law approach is not as rigid as Mr Macrae suggests.

85. Whilst under common law it is no part of a judge's function to exercise disciplinary powers over the police or prosecution regarding the ways in which evidence to be used at the trial is obtained, the judge has a discretion to exclude evidence to ensure that the accused has a fair trial. Lord Goddard CJ said in *Kuruma v. The Queen* [1955] AC 197 at p. 204:

> "No doubt in a criminal case the judge always has a discretion to disallow evidence if the strict rules of admissibility would operate unfairly against an accused."

86. In *Sang* (supra), Lord Salmon and Lord Scarman said at p.444 and 456 respectively the following:

> "I consider that it is a clear principle of the law that a trial judge has the power and duty to ensure that the accused has a fair trial. Accordingly, amongst other things, he has a discretion to exclude legally admissible evidence if justice so require."

> "The question remains whether evidence obtained from an accused by deception, or a trick, may be excluded at the discretion of the trial judge. Lord Goddard CJ thought it could be: *Kuruma v. The Queen*..Lord Parker CJ and Lord Widgery CJ thought so too: see *Callis v. Gunn* [1964] ! QB 495, 502 and *Jeffrey v. Black* [1978] QB 490. The dicta of three successive Lord Chief Justices are not to be lightly rejected."

87. In *R v. Lee Yi Choi* [1985] 1 HKC 578 the Court of Appeal was concerned with the admissibility of a confession allegedly obtained by an undercover police officer introduced into the accused's cell under the guise of a fellow prisoner. In concluding that the trial judge had a discretion to exclude the confession, McMullin VP said at p. 588

> "We believe that more often than not, unfair evidence will be excluded as involuntary.Further,we would emphasize that while subterfuge is a recognised and often indispensable weapon in the police armoury for the detection of crime, stricter standards must apply when a suspect is in custody.Public confidence in the integrity of the judicial process must not be prejudiced.
>
> Applying the approach outlined by the House of Lords in *R v. Sang* [1980] AC 402 and of this court in *R v. Leung* (Crim App 194/83..), it is apparent to us that the admission in evidence of the applicant's confession did endanger the principles which exist in law to secure fair trials and that the administration of justice was thereby brought into disrepute. The end, being the conviction of the applicant, did not justify the means employed. The learned judge was wrong both in directing himself that he could not, as the law presently stood, exclude it, as he apparently wished, and, sequentially, in failing to do so."

88. The Court of Final Appeal in *Secretary for Justice v. Lam Tat Ming & another* (2003) 3 HKCFAR 168 also confirmed the common law approach, emphasizing the importance of the circumstances of each case and the 'overriding duty' of the court to ensure a fair trial (see the judgment of Li CJ at 178–182).

89. The Court of Appeal in *HKSAR v. Chan Kau-tai* [2006] 1 HKLRD 400 considered the impact of the rights guaranteed under the Basic Law and the Bill of Rights on the common law approach. The court observed that the breach of the constitutional rights can be an important factor, but at the same time emphasized the two important features identified in *Sang* (supra), namely, (1) the existence of a discretion to exclude as well as to admit; and (2) the importance to ensure a fair trial for the accused. The Court of Appeal doubted that the human right provisions "marks a dramatic reversal of what has hitherto been the common law approach in Hong Kong. Rather, we perceived it as a natural development of the common law."

90. Ma CJHC, in considering the effect of the provisions of the Basic Law and ICCPR on the exercise of discretion to exclude evidence in criminal matter and in emphasizing that the human right provision is not conclusive, but just one of the relevant factors in the balancing exercise, made the following observation at p. 443:

> "In our view, the questions posed in the previous paragraph fall to be answered in the following way. First, account must of course be taken by the court of any breaches of rights contained in the Basic Law or the ICCPR. Second, any breach as aforesaid will not, however, automatically result in the exclusion of the evidence obtained in consequence of the breach: the court still retains discretion to admit or exclude the evidence. Third, the discretion in the court to admit or exclude evidence involves a balancing exercise in which the breach of constitutional rights is an important factor whose weight will depend on mainly two matters: the

nature of the right involved and the extent of the breach".

91. On how the balancing exercise should be conducted, the Chief Judge further observed at p. 444:

"(4) One of the fundamental themes of a constitutional document such as the Basic Law (and the ICCPR) is the recognition that society has many different interests to be taken into account and very often, a balance must be struck. Derogations from constitutional rights are sometimes permitted where they can be justified as being necessary, rational and proportionate. This is in no way to undermine the importance of constitutional rights but a court must at times perform what can be a delicate balancing exercise.

(5) In the present context, there are two main competing interests, both facets of what can broadly be called the public interest: on the one hand the interest in protecting and enforcing constitutionally guaranteed rights; on the other, the interest in the detection of crime and bringing criminals to justice. This latter aspect has been highlighted in many cases, among them *HKSAR v. Lee Ming Tee & Securities and Future Commission (Intervener)* (2003) 6 HKCFAR 336 at p. 396 A–C (para. 187); *R v. Khan (Sultan)* [1997] AC 558; *Mohammed (Allie) v. State of Trinidad and Tobago* [1999] 2 AC 111 at p. 123 F–G. It is hardly surprising that this latter facet of the public interest receives prominence. It is not only commensurate with commonsense, the wording of the Basic Law also supports this. In art. 30 of the Basic Law, the concept of the 'investigation into criminal offences' is expressly mentioned, albeit in the context of legal procedures allowing an invasion into the right of privacy.

(6) The balancing exercise that faces the court in the exercise of its discretion in each case where there has been a breach of or derogation from constitutional rights, involves a consideration of the two facets mentioned in the last paragraph. The objective of the exercise of judicial discretion is to ensure that a fair trial of the accused takes place. We have already referred to the relevant passages in the decision of the House of Lords in *R v. Sang & Another and that of the Court of Final Appeal in Secretary for Justice v. Lam Tat Ming & Another* (2000) 3 HKCFAR 168 (see paras. 112 and 114 above). In R v. Khan (Sultan), a case involving covert surveillance, Lord Nicholls of Birkenhead referred to the discretion to admit or exclude evidence and the right to a fair trial contained in art. 6.1 of the European Convention as being concerned to ensure that those facing criminal charges would receive a fair trial: at p. 583 B–C. he added at p. 583 C–D:

In the present case the decision of the European Court of Human Rights in *Schenk v. Switzerland*, 13 EHRR 242 confirms that the use at a criminal trial of material obtained in breach of the rights of privacy enshrined in article 8 does not itself mean that the trial is unfair.

...

(8) In considering the fairness of a trial, the court must take a broad view of the overall circumstances. The court must look at the fairness of the actual trial itself: for example, whether the evidence obtained in breach of constitutional rights is reliable in the first place. Thus, for example, evidence which has been 'tricked' out of a person (say, by inducements improperly made) may be so inherently unreliable that it ought to be excluded.

(9) However, the court does not just look at procedural fairness in the actual trial. It is also entitled to look at the overall behaviour of the investigating authority or the treatment of the accused. Thus, circumstances may be such that it would simply be unfair to an accused person to allow certain evidence to be used at trial, for example, where an innocent person has been enticed to commit a crime. There can be situations in which it would be such an affront to the public conscience or the integrity of the criminal justice system is so compromised that the court must step in to put a stop to it...

(10) On the other hand, the breach of or derogation from constitutional guaranteed rights may be outweighed by the public interest in ensuring that crimes are detected and punished. Here, one needs to look closely at two inter-related aspects: the right that has been breached and the extent of the breach. Though all rights guaranteed by a constitution are to be accorded great respect and any breach or derogation must always be considered a cogent factor in excluding evidence, one must bear in mind that some rights are more fundamental and important than others and that where a right is breached, this can occur in a multitude of different situations...

(11) Where the gravity of a breach or derogation is small but the crime involved is a serious one, the public interest will lean more favourably towards the latter factor with the consequence that any evidence obtained as a result of the breach or derogation will be admitted..."

92. Ma CJHC's approach in *Chan Kau Tai* (supra) is similar to the approach of English courts with regard to the right to a fair trial guaranteed under s. 78(1) of the Police and Criminal Evidence Act, 1984 and Article 6 of the European Convention. Blackstone's *Criminal Practice 2006* summaries the position at p. 2202 as follows:

"In *Khan* [1997] AC 558 the police made a recording of an incriminating conversation relating to the importation of heroin, by means of a secret electronic surveillance device. The House of Lords held that the fact the evidence has been obtained in apparent or probable breach of the right to privacy set out in ECHR, Article 8, or for that matter the law of a foreign country, is relevant to the exercise of the s. 78 power, but the significance of such conduct is its effect, if any, upon the fairness of the proceedings. It therefore upheld the decision of the trial judge that the circumstances, in which the evidence had been obtained, even if they constituted a breach of Article 8, did not require exclusion. In *Khan v. United Kingdom* (2001) 31 EHRR 1016, the European Court of

Human Rights held that, although the recording was obtained in breach of Article 8, its use at the trial did not violate the right to a fair hearing under Article 6. The court, repeating what it had said in previous judgments such as *Schenk v. Switzerland*, held that the central question was whether the proceedings as a whole were fair. Noting that the accused had had the opportunity to challenge the admissibility of the evidence under s. 78, as well as its authenticity, the court found that the use of the evidence did not conflict with the requirements of fairness guaranteed by Article 6(1) . Similar conclusion have also been reached by the European Court of Human Rights in respect of evidence obtained in breach of Article 8 by the unlawful installation of a listening device in the applicant's home (*Chalkley v. United Kingdom* [2003] Crim LR 51) and by the unlawful use of covert listening devices at a police station (*PG and JH v. United Kingdom* [2002] Crim LR 308). See also *Mason* [2002] 2 Cr App R 628. In *Button* [2005] Crim LR 571, the proposition that the court is bound to exclude any evidence obtained in breach of art. 8 because otherwise it would be acting unlawfully, was rejected on the basis that any breach of art. 8 is subsumed by the art. 6 duty to ensure a fair trial. As to covert filming, see also *Perry v. United Kingdom* [2003] Crim LR 281, in which the police, infringing official guidelines, filmed the applicant covertly in order that he might be identified by witness; *Loveridge* [2001] 2 Cr App R 591 in which the accused was covertly and unlawfully filmed at court; and *Marriner* [2002] EWCA Crim 2855, in which undercover journalists had made secret videos (as well as tape–recordings) of the accused.

In *P* [2002] 1 AC 46, the House of Lords rejected an argument that the admissibility of telephone intercepts made overseas, in accordance with both the laws of the country in question and the ECHR, would infringe Article 6. It was held that (1) the criterion of fairness under Article 6 is the same as that to be applied by a judge under s. 78; (2) the fair use of intercept evidence at a trial is not a breach of Article 6 even if the evidence was unlawfully obtained; (3) it is a cogent factor in favour of the admission of such evidence that one of the parties to the conversation is to be a witness and gave evidence of what was said during it; and (4) there is no principle of exclusion of intercept evidence in English Law independent of the Interception of Communications Act 1985 (see now the Regulation of Investigatory Powers Act 2000). In *Sargent* [2003] 1 AC 347, a decision under the 1985 Act, it was held that there is no rule prohibiting the use of inadmissible intercepts at police interviews and that, subject to s. 78, such use will not render the interview evidence inadmissible."

93. Mr McWalters, SC for the respondent, initially seeks to persuade us that, in so far as the Court of Appeal's decision failed to distinguish the relevant factors pertaining to an application to permanently stay the proceedings and an application to exclude evidence, *Chan Kau Tai* was wrongly decided. He, however, compromises his position and suggests that the balancing exercise mentioned by the Chief Judge is just the exercise of discretion after considering all the relevant factors.

94. With respect, the compromised position of Mr McWalters is a correct one.

95. The court must balance the two main competing interests; the interest in protecting and enforcing constitutionally guaranteed rights and the interest in the detection of crime and bringing criminals to justice. In the exercise of the judicial discretion, the court must ensure that the accused has a fair trial.

96. The judge could not have made any direct reference to all the factors mentioned in *Chan Kau Tai* as the judgment was only pronounced over six months after the judge gave his ruling.

97. However, the judge had been referred extensively to the relevant authorities by the prosecution and the defence. The judge was aware of the "double breach" of the right of privacy emphasized by Mr Macrae, namely the telephone interception and the covert surveillance resulting therefrom.

98. The judge referred to the evidence of Mr Tony Lui, an ICAC principal investigator, that "covertly recording the meeting was the only means by which the ICAC could obtain important evidence of this very serious corruption offence", and then quite rightly pointed out that the right to privacy might be outweighed by the public interest in the detection of serious crime.

99. The judge made reference to defence counsel's concession that "the ICAC officers did not knowingly and wilfully breach the defendant's right. What they did was at best a deliberate act done in ignorance of those rights", indicating the judge had the overall behaviour of the investigating authority or the treatment of the applicant in mind.

100. The judge noted that the applicants did not contend that the records of the meetings were unreliable or inauthentic and that they had the opportunity to challenge them if they so wished.

101. What is perhaps most important is that the judge, in referring to *Sang* (supra) and other common law cases, was clearly placing importance on the fairness of the trial. Having considered all those factors and then having conducted a balancing exercise, the judge concluded that he could not find any unfairness in admitting the records of meetings as evidence.

102. We do not agree with Mr Macrae's submission that the judge had adopted a wrong approach and/or failed to properly evaluate the relevant factors. On the contrary, the approach adopted by the judge is a correct one, certainly broadly in line with the decision in *Chan Kau Tai* (supra).

103. We also reject Mr Macrae's complaint that the judge had wrongly placed the burden on the 1st applicant to show unfairness. The judge simply was stating, as a matter of fact, that the 1st applicant was unable to show how unfairness would follow if the challenged evidence was admitted.

104. If the judge were simply operating on the burden of proof, he would not have referred to the factors hereinbefore identified.

105. When the court considers the exercise of discretion, the court is acting on its own motion and the concept of the burden of proof has no application. That was how the English court approached the issue in the exercise of the discretion under s. 78 of the Police and Evidence Act, 1984 as demonstrated in Archbold, Criminal Pleading, Evidence and Practice 2006, 15–462:

> "section 78 places no burden on the prosecution to disprove unfairness: see *Vel v. Owen* [1987] Crim. L. R. 496, DC. But does the burden fall on the defence? In *R v. Keenan*..., the judgment of the Court of Appeal suggests, perhaps not intentionally, that the burden shifts depending on the circumstances. In *R (Saifi) v.*

Governor of Brixton Prison [2001] 1 WLR 1134 DC, it was said that the concept of burden of proof has no part to play in the exercise of the discretion under section 78.There seems no reason why the trial court cannot exercise its discretion of its own motion, although there is no equivalent in section 78 to 76(3). In most cases the defence will raise the issue with the trial judge. Therefore the evidential burden of satisfying the court that there is an issue to be decided, as in self–defence will rest on the defence, if no more."

106. If it was the 1st applicant's contention that the admission of the evidence constituted unfairness, the shifting of the evidential burden was logical and accorded with common sense.

107. The judge's exercise of his discretion to admit the records of the Tang Court meeting and the Hunan Garden meeting cannot be faulted.

108. At trial, counsel for the 1st applicant was unable to show how unfairness would follow by the admission of the evidence and Mr Macrae is in the same position in this appeal.

109. Indeed other than pointing out the undisputed infringement of the right to privacy, neither Mr Macrae nor Mr Plowman is able to point to any factor supportive of the exclusion of the surveillance records of the Tang Court meeting and the Hunan Garden meeting.

110. The case is a very serious case of corruption, involving the managing director of a public listed company and senior employees of leading international financial houses in Hong Kong.

111. It is a fraud against not just the company and its shareholders or the respective financial houses, but the public at large and thus has huge impact on Hong Kong's image as a world–class financial centre.

112. At the time of the covert surveillance, there were ongoing criminal activities and we wish to echo what the Chief Justice said in *Lam Tat Ming* (supra) at p. 180:

> "The law recognises that the use of undercover operations is an essential weapon in the armoury of the law enforcement agencies; particularly their use when the criminal activities are ongoing but also their use after crimes are completed to obtain evidence to bring the criminal to book. The use of undercover operations plays an important part in society's struggle to combat crime especially serious crime, whether it be corruption, trafficking in dangerous drugs or terrorism. But the success and indeed viability of such undercover operations depend upon the concealment of the true identity of the law enforcement officer in order to establish the appropriate relationship with the alleged wrongdoers. They therefore unavoidably involve elements of subterfuge, deceit and trickery. The law accepts that law enforcement agencies may find it necessary to resort to tactics of that kind.

113. On the prosecution's case, the full and correct records of the Tang Court meeting and the Hunan Garden meeting were produced. Vincent Yum, one of the participants in the meetings gave evidence of what was said during the meetings, a cogent factor in favour of admission according to *P* [2002] 1 AC 46. Vincent Yum's evidence could of course be tested with reference of the records of the meetings and to that extent the production of the records of the meetings would certainly lead to a fairer trial.

114. There is no suggestion of any oppressive conduct or inducement on the part of the ICAC nor is there any suggestion that the 1st applicant was acting involuntarily in saying what he said during the meetings.

115. Any reasonable tribunal, adopting the proper approach, would have admitted the records of the meetings as evidence albeit such evidence was obtained in breach of the right to privacy.

116. This ground of appeal fails.

Plagiarism

117. Undoubtedly the judge, in his reasons for conviction, had reproduced a substantial portion of the Prosecution Opening and Mr Macrae's estimate of 45% of the relevant parts is not challenged. Further, such extensive reproduction contains prosecution allegations not supported by evidence and thus, in so far as they purported to be findings by the judge, they were mistakes.

118. However, in the context of this application, plagiarism is only relevant if it shows that the judge had abdicated his responsibility to adjudicate, leading to the applicants not having a fair trial by an independent and impartial tribunal, a right guaranteed under Articles 85 and 87 of the Basic Law and Article 10 of the of the Bill of Rights.

119. Mr Macrae refers to the decision of the Court of Final Appeal in *Nina Kung v. Wong Din Shin* (2005) 8 HKCFAR 387. It was, with respect, an unusual case with most peculiar facts. It is perhaps necessary only to refer to a small part of the judgment of Ribeiro PJ, who, having referred to the copying of over 95% of counsel's submissions by (the judge), said at p. 517:

> "453. Legitimate concerns as to whether (the judge) did bring an independent mind to his judicial function do arise in the present case. Two instances which have been examined above in some detail illustrate the grounds for such doubt.
>
> (a) It will be recalled that (the judge) inexplicably reversed himself when reproducing verbatim a submission to such effect, he called the appellant's concerns causing her to resist opening of the sealed envelope 'daft and illogical' whereas he had previously fully accepted those concerns as legitimate in a ruling made prior to the start of the trial.
>
> (b) It will also be recalled that, again copying verbatim from Mr Chan's submissions, he once more reversed himself, going so far as to accuse Professor Jia of dishonesty when he had in the course of the hearing secured acknowledgment from Mr Chan that Professor Jia's rejection of a suggestion would be 'an end of the matter' .
>
> 454. The point about these examples is that they suggest that the judge reproduced the copied material without giving any genuine thought to the issue at hand. If in each of these cases (the judge) had thought independently about the issue rather than merely copying the respondent's submissions, he would surely not have made findings wholly incompatible with considered positions he had

previously taken unless he was able to articulate grounds for changing his stance."

120. In our view, the observation of the Court of Final Appeal in *Nina Wang v. Wong Din Shin* (supra) can have no application in the present case.

121.The trial took a long time and there were significant numbers of pre-trial applications with consequential rulings by the judge. There were also extensive admitted facts. The 1st applicant did not challenge much of the prosecution evidence.

122. The adoption of part of the Prosecution Opening, particularly those uncontroversial parts and/or admitted facts, is not objectionable. It certainly does not support any suggestion that the judge had abdicated his judicial duties.

123. The judge was careful to make necessary adjustments and had referred to the evidence presented by the parties at trial.

124. The judge made a summary of the records of the Tang court meeting and the Hunan Garden meeting and their impact on the charges. The judge referred to the evidence of the 1st applicant and the contents of the 2nd applicant's records of interview. He made separate findings in respect of the different charges.

125. It must not be ignored that the main issue that the judge had to decide was a narrow one, namely whether Vincent Yum was telling the truth in his allegations against the applicants.

126. In assessing the truthfulness and/or reliability of Vincent Yum's evidence, the judge was assisted by the unchallenged and/or indisputable evidence relating to the payments by the 1st applicant and the records of the Tang Court meeting and the Hunan Garden meeting.

127. It is also important to bear in mind that there was no suggestion that Vincent Yum lied against the 1st applicant. Counsel's suggestion that it was a common practice to pay fees or other benefits to fund managers so that they would promote the share of a company indicated that Vincent Yum's evidence was not being challenged.

128. There was then the direct suggestion that Vincent Yum was possibly present when the 1st applicant was asked for $1 million for the promotion of the Kwong Hing shares.

129. The defence case that the payments in question were made in pursuance to a private share option agreement between Louis Lin and Mr Chiu was never even suggested to Vincent Yum.

130. The 2nd applicant did not give or call any evidence.

131. Nevertheless, the judge had analysed in detail the evidence presented by both sides. The judge explained why he accepted the evidence of Vincent Yum and why he rejected the evidence of the 1st applicant. In particular, the judge posed a most pertinent question, "why on earth would a sensible, educated man invent an elaborate criminal conspiracy in order to cover up a mild ethical infringement?"

132. We reject entirely the submissions that the judge had abdicated his judicial function or that the applicants had been denied a fair trial.

Vincent Yum's Evidence Against the 1st Applicant

133. Vincent Yum was a person of dubious character, as recognised by the judge. That did not, of course, mean that his evidence against the applicants must be rejected. The judge had carefully evaluated Vincent Yum's evidence, in particular with reference to the records of the Tang Court meeting and the Hunan Garden meeting.

134. Mr Macrae complains that the judge had misstated Vincent Yum's evidence in paragraphs 49 to 50 of his reasons for verdict, in particular as to what happened in the Tang Court meeting, (1) the suggestion that the 1st applicant asked Vincent Yum if he knew any fund manager interested in buying Kwong Hing shares; (2) that the 1st applicant mentioned the payment of commission to fund manager; and (3) that the 1st applicant had promised share options as a "kick back" that the market would not notice; and as to what happened in the Hunan Garden meeting, that there was an agreement to offer advantages calculated by reference to options.

135. It must be remembered that in four full-days' evidence with transcripts occupying not less than 230 pages in the appeal bundle, Vincent Yum talked about many meetings that he had with Louis Lin and/or Adrian Foo and/or the 2nd applicant before the Tang Court meeting took place.

136. Vincent Yum frankly admitted that he was unable to be precise as to when the meetings took place or what was actually decided. He was, however, adamant that one of the reasons for ING to acquire the 18 million Kwong Hing shares was the 1st applicant's promise of fees in the form of share options. Vincent Yum was also adamant that the agreement that he had with Louis Lin and/or Adrian Foo on the payments of fees was put to the 1st applicant and he agreed to it.

137. Vincent Yum confirmed that as a result of the Tang Court meeting in which the 1st applicant took part, he came away with idea that the 1st applicant was aware of all the detail leading to the payment by him of $2.3 million.

138. Vincent Yum also described in detail why he thought the 1st applicant was prepared to pay large sums of money for the Kwong Hing shares to be held by institutional buyers.

139. Vincent Yum's evidence was supported by the contents of the record of the Tang Court meeting. There was no dispute about the various payments made by the 1st applicant and the contents of P1, which were consistent with Vincent Yum's evidence.

140. There was ample evidence upon which the judge could conclude as he did that there was an agreement for the 1st applicant to pay substantial fees as an inducement for causing ING to purchase the 18 million Kwong Hing shares.

The Judge's Misstatement of Part of the Evidence of Vincent Yum

141. It is perhaps unfortunate that in his attempt to recite the evidence of Vincent Yum, the judge had reproduced the relevant part of the prosecution opening, instead of referring to his evidence at trial and in so doing, appeared to have misstated part of his evidence. It is clear that Vincent Yum was unable to be precise as to who said what at the various meetings.

142. However, as Mr McWalters quite rightly points out, the judge's misstatements are limited only to the exact circumstances in which the 1st applicant agreed to pay the fees for ING to purchase the further 18 million Kwong Hing shares.

143. In the light of Vincent Yum's evidence about the 1st applicant's payments to induce Adrian Foo to purchase the 18 million Kwong Hing shares, the indisputable and/or unchallenged evidence that the 1st applicant did pay out large sums of money, what transpired at the Star Ferry meeting and the contents of the

Tang Court meeting, the conclusion that the 1st applicant was a party to the conspiracies was inescapable.

144. The judge was entitled to accept the evidence of Vincent Yum and to reject the evidence of the 1st applicant.

145. Indeed as the judge quite rightly observed, there could be no conceivable reason for Vincent Yum to lie and in so doing not only unjustifiably wrong the 1st applicant, but at the same time link himself to serious criminal offences when what he did was no more than the breach of certain company or regulatory rules.

146. In any event, the record of the Tang Court meeting almost demonstrated conclusively that the 1st applicant was indeed involved in the conspiracies, the subject matters of charges 1 and 2B and Mr Macrae does not seek to argue otherwise.

147. We are of the view the 1st applicant was fairly and properly convicted of charges 1 and 2B and there is nothing unsafe or unsatisfactory about those convictions.

Vincent Yum's Evidence Against the 2nd Applicant

148. Mr Plowman may well be right in suggesting that Vincent Yum's evidence against the 2nd applicant is not too satisfactory.

149. In his evidence-in-chief, Vincent Yum talked about the direct contact he had with the 2nd applicant when the 2nd applicant confirmed that he had received $800,000 and then subsequently asked for the return of $200,000 so that he could give it to Ada. He also talked about a meeting prior to his arrest with the 2nd applicant and Adrian Foo at the latter's house to convince the 2nd applicant to publish a research report.

150. Vincent Yum was unable to remember the exact time and circumstances in which the 2nd applicant confirmed the receipt of $800,000 or acknowledged the demand for the return of $200,000. He was also unable to recall the exact time of the meeting at Adrian Foo's house.

151. However, we do not agree with Mr Plowman's suggestion that Vincent Yum had retracted his evidence and we set out the following questions and answers in Vincent Yum's testimony to illustrate the point.

In-chief:

"Q. Who is the person 'Nick' who is referred to–188?

A. That's Nicholas Tan (the 2nd applicant).

Q. And what's the advance that's referred to, as far as you' re aware?

A. It's the payment for the research report.

Q. Who paid for the research report?

A. Michael. Michael did.

Q. How much did he pay?

A. He gives $1 million.

Q. And who did Michael give the money to?

A. To me.

Q. And who did you give it to?

A. I gave it to Adrian.

Q. And when was the payment made, approximately? Very approximately?

A. I cannot remember. Maybe sometimes in...towards the end of the year 2003.

Q. And how did you know or become aware that the 4th defendant had received–well, how much money was to be paid on to the 4th defendant by you and Adrian?

A. We have agreed to give him HK$800,000.

Q. And how did you become aware that the 4th defendant had received that money?

A. I didn't until weeks after that, when we get to speak, and also the day of 25 February, when I spoke to him...

Q. Yes, how did you learn from the 4th defendant he' d received the money?I' m not talking about the day of your arrest, I' m talking about before your arrest. When you speak, speak to whom?

A. Okay. I can't remember exactly. I don't think I have spoken to him about–or maybe in casual conversation I have spoken to him previously to February confirming that he has received the 800,000

...

Q. Did D4 ever mention Ada in respect of the report or payment?

A. Yes.

Q. What did he say to you?

A. He said that he needs to pay Ada some...some money for her work in constructing the report.

Q. And when did he say that to you, approximately, very approximately?

A. A telephone conference sometime in December or something, or may be even January. I' m not...

...

Q. How much did D4 ask to be paid in respect of Ada?

A. He just said that the 200,000 which were kept by myself and Adrian needs to give it back to him so that he can give it to Ada.

...

Q. Can you tell us about them–about the conversation you had, please.

A. I remember that as I said in my testimony last week, there was a conversation, telephone conversation between myself and Nicholas. And I also recalled that there is a short meeting at Adrian's house with myself, Adrian and Nicholas there, and that's probably it. May be one more telephone conversation and that's probably it.

Q. All right. Tell us what happened at the meeting at Adrian's house. If can't remember exactly what was said please just give us the gist.

A. The–I can't remember exactly what it's–why we

need to call up a meeting but it would definitely be related to the research report. And, basically, it's we wanted Nicholas to publish a research report from UBS and Adrian felt that having me there is probably better than just all by himself doing the convincing Nicholas. So he dragged–sort of dragged me in and holds the meeting in his house.

Q. Was this before or after D1 had paid you the million dollars to give to D4?

A. The–I have to think about the sequence of event but it's likely that it's after.

Q. What did Adrian say–what did D4 say in this meeting. Everything you can recall, even if it's only the gist, of what D4 said at this stage.

A. Again he thinks that–he thinks that the company–well, the company being UBS, his company, are looking closely at what listed companies they can cover. So again we are discussing on when we can come out with the report, if we could, and what are the conditions–requirements. Is it better to–we were asking him whether it is better to wait a little bit longer until the interim comes out or when we see a larger market cap of the company, etc., before he can come out with the report. Again he would be just telling us why he can't do it at the moment. And he also gave us–I remember he also told us about his travelling plan, that he might be going away so unlikely that he will have time to do a report, like, in the next week or two. Something like that. That's all I can remember."

In cross–examination:

Q. What was the purpose of this meeting?

A. I can't remember exactly now.

Q. That's exactly what you said when Mr Fitzpatrick asked you that same question in your evidence in chief, wasn't it? 'I can't remember exactly.' You cannot tell us the purpose of the meeting.

A. I...

Q. Is that right?

A. Yes, to be very accurate, yes, I can't remember exactly. I don't want to.

Q. You can't tell us the date of the meeting?

A. No, I can't remember the date of the meeting but I remember that we have talked about, you know, a couple of issues and I already said that in–when Mr Fitzpatrick asked me.

Q. What do you mean by a couple of issues?

A. The–he mentioned about···

Q. He is who?

A. That's the 4th defendant. That the 4th defendant mentioned about his plans in leaving Hong Kong and whether–it's, you know, in relation to the research report.

Q. You can't tell us whether the meeting took place before or after the alleged $1 million payment. Is that right?

A. I can't remember exactly, unless you can show me the date.

...

Q. ..The first answer–the question was asked of you twice and your first answer was, 'I didn't until weeks later when we got to speak and on the day of 25 February.' Remember that answer?

A. Correct.

Q. The question was repeated. You said, 'I can't remember. I don't think I spoke to him. May be some casual conversation before 25 February.' Remember that evidence?

A. Yes, I remember that but that's also the truth.

Q. The truth is what? That you can't remember?

A. No.

...

Q. Would you answer it in the way I've suggested?

A. I would answer in a similar way, yes. It is true...

Q. Thank you. That will do for the moment. You would answer it in a similar way. 'I can't remember. I don't think I spoke to him.'

A. I reality is I really can't remember. I have confirmed him that he has received the 800,000. It is true, but maybe through causal conversation we have talked about that.

Q. Maybe.

A. May be.

Q. You are not sure about that.

A. I'm not sure. I did confirm with Adrian and Adrian said that he has given the money to...

Q. Of course, but as you concede, you wouldn't know whether Adrian was telling you the truth or not. So you're saying that you're unsure as to whether you had any such conversation. Is that right?

A. Yes, I guess you can say that.

...

Q. I suggest that you did not have any telephone conference in either December 03 or January 04 with the 4th defendant in which he told you that he needed money to pay Ada for her work in constructing the report.

A. No, there was no–he did not ask me that I need to pay Ada.

...

A. In the telephone conversation I had with him, he did not ask me to pay him back the 200,000 for Ada because the defendant already told me before the–before the call.

Q. My suggestion is that there was no such telephone conference, no such call.

A. There is a call but there is no such line say–said in the call.

Court. Well what was said then?

A. The–before the–the call was made sometimes in year 2000–year 2003 when Adrian Foo after–soon after Adrian Foo told me that the 4th defendant wanted us to pay him back that $200,000 for Ada Poon, and I took it as in that's want the 4th defendant wants. So soon after that, there was a telephone call between myself and the 4th defendant. But answering Mr Plowman's question, the 4th defendant did not ask me to pay him back that 200,000 for Ada.

Court. Was there any mention of the 200,000?

A. I think I have mentioned it to the 4th defendant by saying–because I have automatically thought that he knew, according to what Adrian told me. So I did–during the call, may be towards the end of the call, I did mention something like, 'Oh, about that"–something like 'about that 200,000, well, Adrian told me already', something like that. Yes, that's what I have said.

...

Q. So it came from you, not from him

A. That's correct. It came from me."

152. Vincent Yum had a recollection of the 2nd applicant admitting the receipt of $800,000 and acknowledging the demand for the return of $200,000. He was sure of the meeting at Adrian Foo's house. What he was unsure about was the time, the circumstances and the exact manner in which such matters took place. He was clearly not able to remember the full contents of the conversations.

153. Vincent Yum gave evidence on topics covering a long period of time and involving a number of people on varying occasions. His contacts with the 2nd applicant were very often not direct, but via Adrian Foo. Because of the nature of the dealings, Vincent Yum and the others might not want to be too "explicit".

154. However, Vincent Yum was adamant that he had contacts with the 2nd applicant when he confirmed the receipt of the $800,000 and when the payment of the $200,000 to Ada was mentioned.

155. Vincent Yum was also adamant about the meeting with the 2nd applicant at Adrian Foo's house where there was discussion on several issues, including the publishing of a bullish research report on Kwong Hing, although he could not remember the date or the exact purpose of the meeting.

156. One could easily conclude that Vincent Yum was a truthful witness, trying to account to the court the detail of his dealing with the 2nd applicant, albeit with an imperfect recollection. If he were to lie about the 2nd applicant, it could have been so easy for him to be more forthcoming and more direct.

157. However, in analysing charge 2B against the 2nd applicant, the judge only very briefly mentioned Vincent Yum's evidence as follows:

"Some time in late 2003, D1 handed $1 million in cash to Vincent Yum, again at the Star Ferry Pier. Vincent Yum then, through Adrian, gave D4 $800,000, leaving $200,000 to be divided between himself and Adrian. Later, D4 let it be known to Vincent and Adrian that he wanted the $200,000 back, allegedly to pay a person at UBS called 'Ada' who, he said, had been the co-author of the report. Vincent testified that he did not know who Ada was. However, neither he nor Adrian had returned that $200,000 by the time of their arrest. Vincent was asked in-chief if he knew whether or not D4 had received this $800,000. Answer, 'I didn't, until weeks after that, when we got to speak', and,

'I can't recall exactly. May be in casual conversations I spoke to him previously to February to confirm that he had received the $800,000. Also, we–that is Nick, Adrian and I–had a short meeting at Adrian's house shortly after the $1 million had been paid over. That meeting definitely concerned the research report from UBS. We want Nick to publish it. Adrian felt that it would help him to convince Nick if I went along to the meeting as well."

158. In assessing the prosecution evidence against the 2nd applicant, the judge only mentioned, in connection with ruling a case to answer, "the evidence of Vincent Yum of his sporadic contacts and discussions on this conspiracy with D4, whether by telephone or, once, meeting him Adrian's house, to discuss the report and the reward for same".

159. The judge did not conduct a critical analysis of Vincent Yum's evidence against the 2nd applicant at all and he did not state if or to what extent he accepted Vincent Yum's evidence against the 2nd applicant. Instead, the judge concentrated on what he found to be "lies" of the 2nd applicant in his cautioned statement.

160. We find the judge's approach to Vincent Yum's evidence on charge 2B against the 2nd applicant unsatisfactory.

<u>The 2nd Applicant's Lies and Such Lies as a Foundation for the Receipt of the Record of the Tang Court Meeting as Evidence Against The 2nd Applicant Under the Co-conspirators' Rule</u>

161. Despite Mr Plowman's effort, we are satisfied that the judge was entitled to find that the 2nd applicant had lied in his cautioned interview on his role in the publication of the bullish report on Kwong Hing and his contact with its management at the material time.

162. The 2nd applicant was the direct superior of Ada Poon and was the head of the "small cap" department in UBS.

163. On Ada Poon's evidence, there could no doubt that the 2nd applicant was concerned with and instrumental to the publishing of a bullish report on Kwong Hing and that it was the 2nd applicant who introduced the Kwong Hing management to her.

164. Ada Poon was adamant that the 2nd applicant, upon introducing Kwong Hing to her, said it was all along growing. He also made arrangement for her to meet the Kwong Hing management, including the 1st applicant.

165. When Ada Poon indicated reluctance to write a report on Kwong Hing, the 2nd applicant said the company would develop in a very aggressive way and would be getting bigger and bigger

with an increased market value.

166. The 2nd applicant wanted the report to carry the title "A Cinderella Stock" and adjusted upward the targeted figures of Kwong Hing's turnover and net income. The 2nd applicant chose not to appear to persuade the IRC in UBS to agree to the publishing of the report despite the fact that he was obviously concerned about it and was visibly happy when it was approved.

167. Yet in the cautioned interview, the 2nd applicant suggested that Kwong Hing was just a number to him and he had no access to its management. He emphasized that as he did not speak Cantonese, he could hardly communicate with the 1st applicant. When the 2nd applicant was asked about the "pricing issues", he gave the following answer:

> "... she, she-we-she come out with herself and-in fact, she came out with much higher price-target. I actually push it down because I didn't think the company was worth as much. So it went through downward revision..."

168. The 2nd applicant further tried to suggest that the 1st applicant was close to Ada Poon and would share with her trade secret. He even suggested that Ada Poon had conviction in Kwong Hing whereas he didn't.

169. In so far as the 2nd applicant tried to distance himself from the Kwong Hing management and tried to blame Ada Poon for the bullish view on Kwong Hing, his evidence clearly contradicted that of Ada Poon.

170. The judge was entitled to conclude that the 2nd applicant was lying on those issues upon finding Ada Poon a truthful witness.

171. Mr Plowman's attempt to distinguish the judge's reference to revising downward "the estimates for future turnover and profits" when 2nd applicant was talking about "push down...the much higher price target" is, in our view, unrealistic when the price target of a company's share must be directly related to the estimates for its future turnover and profits.

172. In any event, as Mr McWalters rightly points out, the 2nd applicant was responsible for the forecast of Kwong Hing's performance and the price target, there could therefore be no question of Ada Poon coming out with a much higher price target that had to be pushed down by the 2nd applicant.

173. In the light of Ada Poon's evidence, the judge's mistake on the date of a meeting could hardly have any bearing on his conclusion that when the 2nd applicant tried to distance himself from the Kwong Hing management, he was lying.

174. One can of course argue that being confronted with the ICAC allegation of accepting a bribe as a reward for publishing a bullish report on Kwong Hing, it would be natural for the 2nd applicant to try to distance himself from the Kwong Hing management and to avoid any suggestion that he was instrumental in the bullish view taken about Kwong Hing even though he might have in fact done nothing wrong.

175. However, the judge had clearly considered the possibility of the 2nd applicant having an innocent explanation for his "lies". The judge rejected such possibility in all the circumstances of the case and he was entitled to do so.

176. Having said that, we are concerned with the way in which the judge relied on the 2nd applicant's "lies" as a foundation for the receipt of the record of the Tang Court meeting as evidence against him.

177. In his assessment of the prosecution evidence against the 2nd applicant, the judge said:

> "As already indicated, there has been ample evidence of the statements of co-conspirators to urge upon D4 the publication of a favourable research report and to have paid for that service (see annex to this verdict). Such evidence is normally hearsay and is inadmissible as against any person who was not present at the time unless there is a solid foundation of independent evidence, outside and beyond the restaurant conversations, of D4's participation in the conspiracy (the co-conspirators rule')."

178. The judge concluded that the 2nd applicant's "lies" not only (a) strengthened the inference of guilt against him, but (b) provide a foundation for the receipt of hearsay evidence. Was the judge right?

179. Mr McWalters submits that (i) the evidence of Vincent Yum, (ii) the favourable report, and (iii) the 2nd applicant's concern about the publishing a bullish report on Kwong Hing constituted prima facie evidence under the co-conspirator's rule to justify the admission of the record of the Tang Court meeting as evidence against the 2nd applicant.

180. Mr McWalters fairly points out that "lies" of an accused only has a supporting role to play. Negatively, it affects the credibility of the accused and positively, it can assist the prosecution case or strengthen an inference of guilt against the accused.

181. Mr McWalters relies on *HKSAR v. Yuen Kwai Choi* (2003) 6 HKCFAR 113 and argues that the judge was entitled to rely the 2nd applicant's "lies" as supporting evidence linking him to the conspiracy.

182. The publication of a bullish report on Kwong Hing and the 2nd applicant's concern about such publication are, in our view, innocuous and do not constitute independent evidence linking the 2nd applicant to the conspiracy charged. After all the report was prepared jointly by the 2nd applicant and Ada Poon and had gone the usual procedure, including the approval by the IRC department of UBS.

183. In any event, the judge did not rely on such matter in his deliberation of the co-conspirator's rule.

184. The judge only referred to the evidence of Vincent Yum in ruling a case to answer against D4. The judge did not refer to Vincent Yum's evidence in identifying the "foundation for the receipt of hearsay evidence" at all.

185. We agree that he judge could have relied on the 2nd applicant's "lies" to strengthen Vincent Yum's evidence against him but we do not agree that the "lies" itself could provide a foundation for the receipt of hearsay evidence.

186. "Lies", as Mr McWalters concedes, can never, on its own, be sufficient to found a conviction. "Lies" *per se*, in our view, cannot constitute a sufficient foundation for the reception of hearsay evidence under the co-conspirator's rule as "lies" cannot be independent evidence linking an accused to the conspiracy charged.

187. A fair reading of the judge's reasons for verdict, particularly paragraph 109 suggests that the judge did rely on the 2nd applicant's "lies" as the sole foundation for the receipt of the record of the Tang Court meeting under the co-conspirator's rule.

In our view, the judge was in error.

188. We do not wish to speculate about the extent to which the judge would rely on Vincent Yum's evidence in determining if a "prima facie" case to prove the 2nd application's participation in the conspiracy or how such evidence could be strengthened by the 2nd applicant's "lies". That was essentially a matter for the judge and he did not deal with it.

189. However, without the record of the Tang Court meeting as evidence, the prosecution case on charge 2B against the 2nd applicant would have been seriously dented.

190. In the light of the judge's error in relying on the 2nd applicant's "lies" as the foundation for the admission of the recording of the Tang Court meeting as evidence, we find the conviction on charge 2B against the 2nd applicant unsafe and unsatisfactory.

Conclusion

191. We dismiss the 1st applicant's application for leave to appeal against conviction but grant that of the 2nd applicant. We treat the 2nd applicant's application as the appeal proper and allow his appeal. The conviction against the 2nd applicant is quashed, and the sentence and order relating thereto are set aside.

Vice-President (M. Stuart-Moore)

Justice of Appeal (W Yeung)

Judge of the Court of First Instance (A.R. Suffiad)

Mr IC McWalters SC(DDPP) of the Department of Justice for the Respondent.

Mr Andrew Macrae SC, Mr Joseph W.Y. Tse SC and Ms Maggie Wong Pui Kei instructed by Messrs Tai Mak & Partner for the 1st Applicant.

Mr Gary Plowman SC and Ms Po Wing Kay instructed by Messrs Haldanes for the 2nd Applicant.

Mo Yuk Ping v. Secretary For Justice

毛玉萍 對 律政司司長

HCAL 111/2005；CACV 270/2005

簡略案情

上訴人因串謀詐騙、串謀妨礙司法公正和行為上顯示與企圖妨礙司法公正三項指控在區域法院接受審訊。在審訊開始時，上訴人便向法官提出永久終止該審訊的申請，理由是，上訴人認為在訴訟過程中存在濫用權力的情況，嚴重違反公義和人權，為了維護健全的法律制度，該檢控必須終止。

上訴人所指的濫權行為就是廉政公署在調查上訴人的過程中，竊聽她的電話。據法院的理解，所有政府部門監聽的目的只是為了收集情報，而不會使用那些電話錄音作為訴訟證據。在監聽完成後，除了少量筆記大綱會交予相關部門跟進外，所有錄音和資料皆會被銷毀，以保障當事人的私隱。

但上訴人認為廉政公署竊聽其電話的行為違反了《基本法》第 30 條。上訴人指出，根據《基本法》第 30 條，電話監聽行為必須依照"法律程序"進行，然而，廉政公署只是依據行政長官按 1963 年實施的《電訊條例》第 33 條所授權的程序進行。該條例賦予行政長官簽發命令各執法機構，進行監聽疑犯電話對話。上訴人認為該監聽行為只是"行政程序"而非遵從《基本法》的要求，由法律條例所訂定的程序。

裁決摘要

區域法院認為廉政公署按照既定的程序進行電話監聽並不存在惡意，同時認為無需就《電訊條例》第 33 條是否違反《基本法》第 30 條做出裁決，因為即使其違反了《基本法》第 30 條，也並不說明廉政公署濫用權利損害健全的司法制度；同時，即使違反了《基本法》第 30 條也不會導致上訴人無法受到公正的審判。因此，區域法院拒絕了上訴人的申請。

上訴人遂向原訟庭提出司法覆核的請求，要求推翻區域法院的決定。但原訟庭法官認同區域法院的見解，為保護刑事審訊的健全性，否決了該請求。

上訴人繼而向上訴庭提起上訴。法官認為如何界定《基本法》第 30 條中所述的"法律程序"並不是一個簡單的問題，尤其是因為《電訊條例》授予了行政長官頒佈截取電話錄音命令的權力，以及設立了公平合理地行使該權力的制度。但上訴庭引用終審法院案例 *HKSAR v. Lee Ming Tee & Another* [2001] 4 HKCFAR 133 認為，除非有十分充足的理據，單純有違反《基本法》的情況出現並不足以終止一個公平的刑事審訊。上訴庭認為《電訊條例》第 33 條是否違反《基本法》第 30 條，需要留待將來在具體的案件中才能作判斷。最後，上訴庭認為本案並非特殊或適當的案件去行使他們的酌情權去干預原訟庭的決定，因此駁回了上訴人的上訴。

CACV 270/2005

IN THE HIGH COURT OF THE

HONG KONG SPECIAL ADMINISTRATIVE REGION

COURT OF APPEAL

CIVIL APPEAL NO. 270 OF 2005
(ON APPEAL FROM HCAL 111 OF 2005)

BETWEEN:

MO YUK PING — Applicant

- and -

SECRETARY FOR JUSTICE — Respondent

Before: Hon Stuart-Moore Ag CJHC, Stock and Tang JJA in Court

Date of Hearing: 2 September 2005

Date of Judgment: 2 September 2005

Date of Reasons for Judgment: 6 September 2005

REASONS FOR JUDGMENT

Hon Tang JA (giving the reasons for judgment of the Court):

1. The Applicant is on trial in the District Court together with several other Defendants. She faces three charges, one of conspiracy to defraud, one of conspiracy to pervert the course of public justice and one of "doing an act tending and intended to pervert the course of justice". On 2 August 2005 and before the commencement of the trial before Judge Wright, she applied for a permanent stay of proceedings. Judge Wright refused a stay.

2. On 24 August 2005, the Applicant applied *ex parte* on notice for leave to apply for Judicial Review against the decision of Judge Wright. Hartmann J refused leave on the same day. The trial began on 25 August 2005, however, just before the lunch break, the Applicant became sick and the case was adjourned. The trial would have re–commenced on 1 September 2005 but for the fact that the Applicant decided to change her lawyers and Judge Wright granted an adjournment to Wednesday, 7 September 2005 in order to enable her new lawyers to prepare her defence. Hartmann J's extemporary judgment was typed and provided to the applicant on 31 August 2005. On 2 September 2005, the Appellant filed her Notice of Appeal and sought an early hearing. We heard and dismissed the appeal in the afternoon of the same day. The reason given for the urgency was that the trial would resume on Wednesday, 7 September 2005.

Judge Wright's Ruling

3. The application arose in this way. From the disclosure of unused materials to the Applicant, she became aware that she had been the subject of telephone intercepts, that the tapes of those intercepts had been destroyed, and all that remains is a synopsis. Judge Wright held that although the disclosure:

> "may have been belated, I am satisfied that that was not due to any attempt at concealment by the prosecution." (para. 39)

She applied for a permanent stay relying on the 2 well known grounds which have been considered and explained in *HKSAR v. Lee Ming Tee and another* (2001) 4 HKCFAR 133 (*Lee Ming Tee No. 1*), namely, notwithstanding the range of remedial measures available at the trial, a fair trial was impossible (first basis). Secondly, this was one of those rare cases where the circumstances of the prosecution involved an abuse of power which so offended justice and propriety that, to protect the integrity of the justice system, the prosecution should be stopped (second basis).

4. Judge Wright has ruled that a fair trial was not impossible and that this was not one of those rare cases which required the prosecution to be stopped.

5. The hearing before Judge Wright took several days. There were 2 days of evidence, some of which was heard in camera, followed by 5 days of submissions. Judge Wright found that intercepted telephone calls were made on one or more of the Applicant's telephones, and that those intercepts were authorized by the Chief Executive under section 33, Telecommunications Ordinance, Cap. 106. He also found that the ICAC followed, as they were obliged to, an established Government policy laid down by the Security Bureau, which applied to all law enforcement agencies. It is part of this policy that the intercepts are not used for the purposes of gathering evidence for use in criminal proceedings but solely for the purposes of gathering intelligence in regard to criminal activities. Furthermore, the material gathered (principally, tapes of the intercepts) are subsequently destroyed. Judge Wright said in para. 20 of the Ruling:

> "This destruction is designed in order to protect the privacy of those whose privacy has been invaded by the interception."

6. Essentially the applicant relies on the destruction of the tapes in support of her claim that a fair trial was impossible. Judge Wright concluded that a fair trial was not impossible. It is said that he was arguably wrong because he said that it was for the applicant to establish:

> "Firstly, she has been prejudiced or potentially prejudiced and, secondly, that that prejudice or potential prejudice will result in it being impossible for her to have a fair trial" (para. 46)"

7. Mr Dykes SC has referred us to *R v. Carosella* [1997] 1 SCR 80 where it is said a majority of the Canadian Supreme Court (5 to 4) has held otherwise. But Mr Dykes accepted that the dictum of Lord Lane CJ in *Attorney General's Reference (No. 1 of 1990)* [1992] QB630 at 644, represents the position in England, namely that:

> "...no stay should be imposed unless the defendant shows on the balance of probabilities that owing to the delay he will suffer serious prejudice to the extent that no fair trial can be held: in other words, that the continuance of the prosecution amounts to a misuse of the process of the court"

8. But that is also the position in Hong Kong. The same dictum was cited with apparent approval in *Tan v. Cameron*, by the Privy Council on appeal from Hong Kong, [1992] 2 AC 205 at 224B, and also by the Court of Final Appeal in *Lee Ming Tee (No. 1)* at 149E. Nor is there any reason in principle why this dictum is applicable only to delay. In *R (Ebrahim) v. Feltham Magistrates Court* [2001] 2 Cr. App. R 427, which concerned the power to stay proceedings for abuse of process on the basis of destruction of video tape evidence, reliance was placed on the same dictum by Brooke LJ in the Judgment of the Court at 435, L.28.

9. Hartmann J has noted the powerful dissenting judgments in *Carosella* at para. 54 of his judgment, which lends further support for Judge Wright's view. We do not believe that Judge Wright was

even arguably wrong.

10. Judge Wright has held that the Applicant has failed to show any prejudice. That is a decision based on the evidence before him. He concluded in para. 54 with those words:

> "In the circumstances, on the basis of demonstrating the impossibility of a fair trial, the Accused fail. Of course, if cross-examination of one or more or any of the witnesses were to bear fruit during the course of the trial in the sense that an apprehension of the existence of materials in the monitored telephone conversations which may or might have furthered cross-examination or otherwise assisted an Accused is raised, that is an aspect which may be dealt with at that stage even, and this is an observation rather than an invitation, by way of renewing an application for permanent stay."

Judge Wright had left open the possibility of a further application before him if circumstances warrant it. This underlines the fact sensitive nature of the decision. Judicial review is rarely appropriate for such decisions.

11. Regarding the second issue, the issues which are said to arise on Judicial Review are:

> "(1) Whether there was bad faith on the part of the Administration and/or the ICAC (so that the criminal proceedings against the Applicant should be stayed solely on this ground);
>
> (2) Whether the telephone interceptions violate Article 30 Basic Law and has infringed the Applicant's right to privacy; and
>
> (3) If yes, whether to allow the continuation of the trial is consistent with the Court's duty to preserve the integrity of the criminal justice system and to foster public confidence in the administration of justice."

12. Section 33 of the Telecommunications Ordinance was enacted in 1963. The Hong Kong Bill of Rights Ordinance, Cap383 was enacted in June 1991. Article 14 of that Ordinance provides:

> "(1) No one shall be subjected to arbitrary or unlawful interference with his privacy, family, home or correspondence, nor to unlawful attacks on his honour and reputation.
>
> (2) Everyone has the right to the protection of the law against such interference or attacks"

The Basic Law, of course, came into force on 1 July 1997.

13. Whether authorization by the Chief Executive under section 33 and the policy laid down by the Security Bureau or the procedures prescribed by the ICAC constitute "legal procedures" as contemplated by Article 30 may require consideration in an appropriate case. Judge Wright found it unnecessary to decide whether section 33 was inconsistent with Article 30 of the Basic Law (Article 30) or whether the interception had infringed the Applicant's right to privacy. However, Judge Wright has made it perfectly clear that he would have decided the question had he found it necessary to do so. We do not believe Judge Wright could be faulted.

14. Judge Wright held that there was no bad faith. More importantly, he also held that even if Article 30 had been contravened this is not a case where he would stay the prosecution. These were decisions made by him on the basis of all the material available to him. We do not believe there is any ground for judicial review. As Lord Steyn said in *R v. Latif* [1996] 1 WLR104 at 112H:

> "The law is settled. Weighing countervailing considerations of policy and justice, it is for the judge in the exercise of his discretion to decide whether there has been an abuse of process, which amounts to an affront to the public conscience and requires the criminal proceedings to be stayed."

See also *HKSAR v. Lee Ming Tee and Securities and Futures Commission*, where this dictum was cited by Sir Anthony Mason NPJ at Para. 182.

15. *Lee Ming Tee (No. 1)* is clear authority that even if there had been a breach, a stay on the second basis would only be granted in very rare cases. There, the Court of Final Appeal was concerned with the right to a trial without undue delay which is protected by Article 39 of the Basic Law and the Hong Kong Bill of Rights Ordinance. Ribeiro PJ said at 151G:

> "The public interest lies in the guilt or innocence of the accused being fairly and openly determined at trial. For this to be displaced, powerful reasons must exist for concluding that such a trial, although fair, would nonetheless constitute an intolerable abuse of the court's process. The instances where such an argument has any prospect of success must necessarily be very rare."

16. If it be suggested that a stay of prosecution must be granted if a contravention of Article 30 is shown, we do not believe that to be reasonably arguable.

Appeal from Hartmann J

17. It is said that Hartmann J erred because although he held that the Applicant has clearly established a prima facie or arguable case, he held that the present case was not an exceptional one which would justify the grant of leave with the inevitable postponement of the proceedings. Hartmann J was of the view that the criminal proceedings in the District Court should continue and that the Applicant could argue the issues in the Court of Appeal if she was eventually convicted.

18. Mr Dykes argued that an exceptional case was not required. Nor was the possibility of appeal a good reason to refuse leave. He submitted that in an appropriate case the existence of an arguable or prima facie case is sufficient. Lastly, he submitted this is an exceptional case so leave should be granted.

19. Hartmann J was of the view that the integrity of the criminal process must prevail. He said

> "When a criminal trial has commenced, it is accepted that only in exceptional cases will the trial be interrupted–perhaps for many months–to enable a matter of law to be resolved."

20. That also was the view of Keith J in *Secretary for Justice v. Lee Wai Man and others* [1999] 1 HKLRD 572, where he refused application for leave to apply for Judicial Review brought by the Secretary for Justice who was dissatisfied with a Magistrate's decision to exclude certain evidence. He said at 575 at B:

> "However, to interrupt a criminal trial to enable a party disappointed by a ruling on the admissibility of evidence to challenge that ruling in the course of the case is extremely rare. That is because it is thought to be highly undesirable to interrupt the ebb and flow of the trial. If there exists an alternative route by which the injustice

done to the party adversely affected by the ruling can be remedied, that route should be taken."

21. In *Commissioner for Labour and Arron v. Jetex HVAC Equipment Limited* [1994] 3 HKC, Litton JA (as he then was) was of the view that Hartmann J could properly have refused leave. He was of the view that although what was called a jurisdictional point was invoked, the Magistrate should have gone on with the trial and the defendant, if convicted, should appeal.

22. It is helpful to note what this Court has said about section 81 of the Criminal Procedure Ordinance, Cap. 221, under which a question of law which may arise on the trial of any indictment could be reserved by the Court of First Instance or the District Court for determination by the Court of Appeal. In *R v. Sin Yau Ming* [1992] 1 HKCLR127 at 136 L. 34, Silke V-P observed:

> "It is by far the better practice, while this unfortunate section remains on our statute books, that, where such a question of law does arise, it is reserved at the conclusion of the trial when all the evidence is in, and is therefore available to this court, and the judge has come to a decision upon the matter. It can then, and it should be, part of the appellate procedure."

He added:

> "While it is not for this court to fetter a discretion conferred upon a judge, nevertheless recourse to and reservation under section 81 should be the subject of the most careful scrutiny and orders made only in the rarest of cases.
>
> It is not helpful to reserve a question of law...and to require this court to consider its decision on the question raised before any evidential background is available."

23. These authorities support the view that criminal trials should not be interrupted and that points of law should be decided when all the evidence is in. These authorities also support Hartmann J's view that only in exceptional cases should criminal proceedings be permitted to be interrupted by proceedings for judicial review. Mr Dykes argued that an exceptional case was not required. He said leave should be granted in an appropriate case. We doubt if there is any difference between them. In any event we are of the view that this is neither an exceptional nor an appropriate case for leave.

24. Mr Dykes submitted that *R v. Hereford Magistrates Court, ex parte Rowlands* [1998] QB 110, shows that the availability of alternative remedies is not a good reason to refuse leave. There, the complaints were that the applicants did not have a fair trial before a Magistrate who had convicted them. The question was whether they should be refused Judicial Review because they had the alternative remedy of an appeal.

25. In *R v. Peterborough Magistrates' Court ex parte Dowler* [1997] QB 911, relief by way of Judicial Review was refused because there was an equally effective and convenient remedy, namely, an appeal. But in *ex parte Rowlands*, Lord Bingham of Cornhill CJ in delivering the judgment of the divisional court said at 123:

> "While we do not doubt that ex *parte Dowler* [1997] QB 911 was correctly decided, it should not in our view be treated as authority that *a party complaining of procedural unfairness or bias* in the magistrates' court should be denied leave to move for judicial review and left to whatever rights he may have in the Crown Court. So to hold would be to emasculate the long-established supervisory jurisdiction of this court over magistrates' courts, which has over the years proved an invaluable guarantee of the integrity of proceedings in those courts. The crucial role of the magistrates' courts, mentioned above, makes it the more important that that jurisdiction should be retained with a view to ensuring that high standards of procedural fairness and impartiality are maintained.
>
> Two notes of caution should however be sounded. First, leave to move should not be granted unless the applicant advances an apparently plausible complaint which, if made good, *might arguably be held to vitiate the proceedings in the magistrates' court*. Immaterial and minor deviations from best practice would not have that effect, and the court should be respectful of discretionary decisions of magistrates' courts as of all other courts. This court should be generally slow to intervene, and should do so only where good (or arguably good) grounds for doing so are shown. Secondly, the decision whether or not to grant relief by way of judicial review is always, in the end, a discretionary one." (emphasis added)

26. *Ex parte Rowlands* was concerned with situations where the complaint was that the trial was unfair. In effect, the applicants had been denied a trial. Thus, the unfair trials were quashed so that they should have a fair trial before the Magistrates. Here, the complaint is not that the trial before Judge Wright was unfair but that it was unfair to try the Applicant. See: *R v. Horseferry Road Magistrates' Court, ex parte Bennett* [1994] AC 42 at 74L, where Lord Lowry underlined the distinction.

27. *R v. Bradford Justices, ex parte Wilkinson* [1990] 1 WLR692, was also a case where the Applicant had not had a fair trial.

28. Here, as we have said the complaint is not that the applicant has not had a fair hearing before Judge Wright. We are also of the view that the availability of an alternative remedy is relevant to the exercise of discretion whether to grant leave.

29. Mr Dykes also relied on *Tan v. Cameron* (above) as a case where leave to apply for Judicial Review to stay criminal proceedings was granted. There is no doubt that in a suitable case, which will be very rare, the Court will permit its supervisory jurisdiction to be invoked. But for the reasons given by Hartmann J, we are of the view that this is not a suitable case.

30. We do not believe Hartmann J has erred in refusing leave. He did so after making the generous assumption that there are relevant arguable grounds, we see no reason to interfere. Indeed, if we were to exercise our discretion, we would also refuse leave. First, because we do not believe there are any relevant arguable grounds. Secondly, even on the basis that there are arguable grounds, we would also refuse leave for the reasons given by Hartmann J and expanded on by us.

31. For the above reasons we dismissed the appeal.

Ag Chief Judge, High Court (M. Stuart-Moore)

Justice of Appeal (Frank Stock)

Justice of Appeal (Robert Tang)

Mr Philip Dykes, SC and Mr Hectar Pun, instructed by Messrs Rowland Chow, Chan and Co., for the Applicant/Appellant.

Mr Alex Lee, SADPP, of Department of Justice, for the Respondent/ Respondent.

HCAL 111/2005

IN THE HIGH COURT OF THE

HONG KONG SPECIAL ADMINISTRATIVE REGION

COURT OF FIRST INSTANCE

CONSTITUTIONAL AND ADMINISTRATIVE LAW LIST
NO. 111 OF 2005

BETWEEN:

MO YUK PING	Applicant
– and -	
SECRETARY FOR JUSTICE	Respondent

Before: Hon Hartmann J in Court

Date of Hearing: 24 August 2005

Date of Judgment: 24 August 2005

JUDGMENT

1. This is an urgent application to seek leave to apply for judicial review. The decision that is sought to be challenged is the decision of His Honour Judge Wright given yesterday, refusing an application made by the applicant for a permanent stay of criminal proceedings against her.

2. The relief sought is described in the papers as follows:

> 1. An order of *certiorari* to bring up and quash the decision of His Honour Judge Wright, a Judge of the District Court, made on 23rd August 2005 refusing the application of the Applicant for a permanent stay of the criminal proceedings against her before His Honour in the District Court;
>
> 2. An order of Prohibition prohibiting His Honour Judge Wright from continuing the criminal proceedings against the Applicant;
>
> 3. An order under O.53 r.3(10)(a) of the Rules of the High Court that the criminal proceedings against the Applicant in DCCC 367/2004 and DCCC 636/2005 be stayed pending determination of this Application;
>
> 4. An expedited hearing of this Application be granted.

3. As the trial before Judge Wright is intended to be continued tomorrow, I have agreed to hear this application and to determine upon it today.

4. In the trial before Judge Wright, the applicant is one of several defendants. Not all have sought a permanent stay, only the applicant and one other.

5. The applicant faces two charges, one of conspiracy to defraud and one of conspiracy to pervert the course of public justice. The first charge, I am told, arises out of allegations of stock market manipulation.

6. When the trial commenced before Judge Wright, the application for a permanent stay was made. It was made on two grounds. First, notwithstanding the range of remedial measures available at the trial, a fair trial for the applicant was impossible. Second, that this was one of those rare cases where the circumstances of the prosecution involved an abuse of power which so offended justice and propriety that, to protect the integrity of the justice system, the prosecution should be stopped.

7. In a judgment of 38 pages, Judge Wright held that a fair trial remained possible and that, in his view, this was not a rare case that demanded a stay in order to protect the integrity of the criminal justice system.

8. Leave is sought to challenge Judge Wright's decision on the basis that the matter should finally be determined in law before the trial is allowed to proceed further.

9. When a criminal trial has commenced, it is accepted that only in exceptional cases will the trial be interrupted–perhaps for many months–to enable a matter of law to be resolved. Matters of law constantly arise in criminal trials. Trials after all are legal proceedings. But if rulings of law made by a trial judge are disputed they can be challenged on appeal. The criminal justice system is designed to this end.

10. It is also a founding principle of the judicial review jurisdiction that applications for judicial review should in most cases be applications of last resort. Other remedies should first be exhausted.

11. In the present case, however, it is submitted that exceptional circumstances exist warranting this court exercising its discretion in favour of the application for leave.

12. In order to consider this application in context, something briefly needs to be said of how it has arisen.

13. I am told that in or about April 2003, officers of the ICAC–acting under telephone interception warrants, as I think they are called–intercepted telephone calls made on one or more of the applicant's telephones.

14. There can be no suggestion that the officers were acting in bad faith. The warrants had been issued by the Chief Executive in accordance with set procedures. Those warrants were issued pursuant to s.33 of the Telecommunications Ordinance, Cap.106. It reads as follows:

> "Whenever he considers that the public interest so requires, the Chief Executive, or any public officer authorised in that behalf by the Chief Executive either generally or for any particular occasion, may order that any message or any class of messages brought for transmission by telecommunication should not be transmitted or that any message or any class of messages brought for transmission, or transmitted or received or being transmitted, by telecommunication shall be intercepted or detained or disclosed to the Government or to the public officer specified in the order."

15. I am told that s.33 has been in existence since 1963 and, to date, its lawfulness in the context of the Bill of Right and/or the Basic Law has not been challenged.

16. In an open and free society, covert surveillance is a matter of sensitivity. Indeed, I have granted leave recently in respect of two applications which go to the constitutional validity of covert surveillance. The applicant's challenge is therefore one of public interest, a point emphasised by Mr Cheng Huan SC, leading counsel for the applicant.

17. But public interest, of course, on its own, can rarely be good reason to take the exceptional step of interrupting an on-going criminal trial.

18. In respect of authorised telephone interceptions, I am told that the ICAC, and all other law enforcement bodies, use the information gathered for intelligence purposes only and not for evidential purposes in criminal prosecutions. The distinction is important.

19. In respect of the applicant, therefore, any information obtained was never–at any time–intended to be used to support a prosecution.

20. The system employed was, I think, roughly as follows. The tapes of the intercepted calls were studied by officers in the special unit authorised to do this work. A paraphrase of what was heard was produced and from that paraphrase a synopsis was produced. In short, a process of distillation took place. The purpose was to isolate relevant intelligence, inculpatory or exculpatory.

21. Once this was done, in accordance with set procedures, the tapes were destroyed together with all the resulting written material other than those notes which were, it seems, the final distillation.

22. The destruction was not an act of bad faith. The purpose was to protect the privacy of third parties. It was done in accordance with set procedure.

23. In respect of this applicant, it appears that the intercepts were conducted on the basis that she may be involved in matters of corruption. No intelligence of this kind was obtained. However, as I am told, intelligence was obtained to the effect that the applicant may–and I stress 'may'–be involved in illegal stock market manipulation.

24. In the result, the intelligence unit gave to the investigative branch of the ICAC a very distilled piece of intelligence to enable a criminal investigation to commence. Evidentially, of course, the investigation was starting from square one.

25. Once the intelligence was passed, all that was left, I understand, were a few notes.

26. I state again that the destruction of the great bulk of the intelligence material was not arbitrary. The destruction of the material was in terms of an administrative or executive policy created by the Security Bureau to ensure that the rights of privacy of third parties were protected and, in addition, to ensure, as the Security Bureau saw it, a consistency of approach by all investigating agencies and, through that, a fairness of approach.

27. In the run-up to the criminal trial, the applicant was informed of the notes held by ICAC that concerned the earlier intelligence gathering. The notes were disclosed as unused material. For the prosecution, they had no evidential value.

28. It is a fundamental common law principle that the defence is entitled to access to unused material. As Mr Cheng Huan puts it, it is the prosecution's duty to disclose to the defence relevant material which includes information which may undermine its case or advance the defence case. This duty is not limited solely to the disclosure of admissible evidence. Information may not be admissible but may lead–by a train of inquiry–to evidence which is admissible. Material which is not admissible may be relevant, nevertheless, and may be useful for cross-examination of a prosecution witness on credit.

29. In the present case, says counsel, the prosecuting authority was obliged by fundamental principles of disclosure under the common law to disclose all unused material, including all material created by the telephone interceptions, the tapes and notes and the like. This was material which the applicant wished to see because it could be directly relevant to her defence.

30. The material, of course, is no longer in existence. It has been destroyed.

31. Mr Cheng Huan submits that the applicant would have wanted access to the material not simply because it was her common law right but because in her case it could have been of direct and material assistance to her. What was said in the conversations had given rise to the criminal investigation. More than that, one or more of the prosecution witnesses–accomplices–may have been recorded in those conversations.

32. What is argued is that the destruction of the material not only thereby denies the applicant a fair trial but is such a fundamental breach of the applicant's constitutional rights that the prosecution cannot be allowed to proceed.

33. How does this asserted breach of constitutional rights come about? It is said that s.33 of the Telecommunications Ordinance is inconsistent with art.30 of the Basic Law. Art.30 reads:

> "The freedom and privacy of communication of Hong Kong residents shall be protected by law. No department or individual may, on any grounds, infringe upon the freedom and privacy of communication of residents, *except that the relevant authorities may inspect communication in accordance with legal procedures to meet the needs of public security or of investigation into criminal offences.*" [Emphasis added]

34. If, therefore, there are to be interceptions of private telephone calls they must be in accordance with 'legal procedures' . It is argued, I presume, that the phrase is narrower than the phrase 'in accordance with law' and implies procedures dictated by legislation.

35. But there were no 'legal procedures' in place, says Mr Cheng Huan, only administrative procedures and we do not have rule by executive decision, we have rule by law.

36. What amounts to 'legal procedures' in terms of art.30 is, I anticipate, not an easy issue, especially as the Telecommunications Ordinance gives power to the Chief Executive to order intercepts and thereby to set up a system for the rational and fair exercise of that power.

37. But, says Mr Cheng Huan, easy or not, in order to decide the application for a stay, Judge Wright was obliged to decide the issue of whether the procedures in place in respect of covert surveillance did or did not breach the Basic Law. However, he refused to do so. For that alone, his decision to refuse a stay is fundamentally flawed.

38. This brings me to a brief consideration of the judgment itself. In my view, it is in many respects an impressive document, logical and articulate. It has been of much assistance to me.

39. In respect of the possibility of a fair trial, the judge said:

> "The only evidence before me in respect of these applications is that adduced by the prosecution. Neither

accused gave or led any evidence in support of her application, particularly in support of the contention that it is impossible to obtain a fair trial or to show how non-disclosure may, in some practical way, have prejudiced the defence. In the case of the 1st accused [the applicant] whose telephone conversations were undoubtedly monitored, there was no evidence dealing with the existence of exculpatory content in the monitored telephone conversations which allegedly had been omitted from the intelligence information."

The judge continued:

"In simple terms, these applications are entirely speculative. The accused are simply unable to point to anything whatsoever which enables either to say, other than on a purely assumptive or speculative basis, what material there was, which, by virtue of being deprived of it, results in the inevitability of the impossibility of a fair trial. That, of course, is a matter of simple logic. If the material no longer exists, for whatever reason, an accused may be unable to identify any material which is capable of use in the discharge of the onus."

He then went on to say:

"It is important to retain at the forefront of one's mind the fact that it is the accused who bear the onus to establish for the purposes of this first basis that, firstly, she has been prejudiced or potentially prejudiced and, secondly, that the prejudice or potential prejudice will result in it being impossible for her to have a fair trial."

He concluded by saying:

"To discharge the onus, it is, in my judgment, simply inadequate to come to court to say that it is not known whether there is or is not material contained in that which has been destroyed, that the court must therefore assume that there was something that may have been of assistance to the accused and that the court must therefore assume that the accused is prejudiced by the deprivation of whatever that might have been."

40. On behalf of the applicant, it is argued that the judge may have been wrong in law in putting the onus on the applicant to establish potential prejudice. That, of course, is another issue of law arising in the course of the trial, again perhaps not an easy one.

41. In respect of the second limb of the application; namely, that there had been an abuse of power by the prosecuting authorities which must result in the prosecution being halted, the judge, as I understand it, said that the ICAC in this instance had been doing no more than following a policy which was incumbent upon it to do, that there was no suggestion it had acted in bad faith, and that the policy, whether consistent with the Basic Law or not, was inherently rational.

42. He therefore held as follows:

"The destruction of materials about which complaint is made was effected by the ICAC in pursuance of a policy with which it was required to comply if it wished to engage in telecommunications intercepts. Even assuming, but without deciding, that sec. 33 were to be inconsistent with the Basic Law and consequently no longer of any force or effect that fact taken on its own would neither assist the Accused in establishing that it is impossible for them to have a fair trial nor alter the nature of the conduct of the ICAC, in carrying out the telecommunications intercepts or destroying the subsequent product, so as to characterise that conduct as unconscionable, being possessed of 'serious fault' or *mala fide*.

It follows that, as interesting as the debate about sec. 33 may be, the position of the Accused will not be affected by any decision."

43. In summary, having heard certain evidence and having heard submissions, the judge decided the matter on the two issues before him: first, is a fair trial possible? He believed it was. Second, had there been an abuse of process which went to undermine the integrity of the justice system? He said no, there had not.

44. As to the constitutional validity of s.33, the judge, it seems to me, was saying in plain terms: even if there is an inconsistency, having regard to all the circumstances, it is not so profound in the case now before me that it denies the applicant a fair trial or so shocks the conscience of the court as to demand a stay.

45. It is difficult to criticize the judge for his conclusion. Not all breaches of the Basic Law or the Bill of Rights demand remedial action, not all such breaches should bring criminal trials to a halt. It is a question of weighing all relevant matters. If it was otherwise it would become a game of 'spot the constitutional slip and avoid the trial' . The Basic Law is not such a draconian document.

46. I come now to look to whether, in all the circumstances and against this background, leave should be granted.

47. The standard test for leave is whether the material before me discloses matters which, on further consideration, might disclose an arguable case. It is not a high test. It is intended only to eliminate vexatious or hopeless cases.

48. As to the merits of the decision made by Judge Wright, there is clearly a prima facie arguable case. It is not a hopeless case. The issues before the judge were complex, both factually and legally, also in constitutional terms.

49. But, as I have said earlier, issues of law arise in criminal trials all the time and in many cases it may properly be argued that the decision in law should have been other than the one made by the trial judge. But that is why the appeal process exists.

50. Mr McWalters SC, who has appeared for the respondent to assist me in so far as I ay require it, has shown me a judgment of the Court of Appeal–*Dairy Farm Company Limited v. Director of Food and Environmental Hygiene*, unreported, CACV283/2004–in which in paragraph 28, per Rogers VP, the following is said:

"It is undesirable that there should be appeals and applications at an interlocutory stage of prosecution with a view to stifling the prosecution. This court is mindful that it is undesirable to encourage judicial review proceedings in such circumstances as it would have a tendency to prolong proceedings and make what should be comparatively simple prosecutions into long, drawn–out litigation with consequential satellite litigation."

51. In earlier judgments, I have said that the criminal process must be allowed to continue and only in very exceptional cases–

invariably when matters go to fundamental jurisdiction–will the collateral process of judicial review be permitted. In the present case, the fundamental jurisdiction of the court to conduct the trial cannot be questioned. The stay of application was a matter for the judge to determine in his discretion. He had the power to do so and his decision does not undermine his jurisdiction. Whether he was right or wrong does not go to fundamental jurisdiction. It is a matter which–if necessary–can be dealt with on appeal.

52. It is also important, in my view, to consider not only whether there is an alternative procedure, that is, by appeal, but whether the real issue can be conveniently determined by that means. If it can then clearly the alternative procedure–appeal–should prevail and should be the route adopted by the aggrieved person. If, on the other hand, the alternative procedure is not apt to deal with the real issue then there is nothing to prevent an application for judicial review. In the present case, I am satisfied that the alternative procedure is the entirely correct procedure to deal with the real issues arising out of the stay application and the judge's decision in that regard. As I have said, the criminal division of the Court of Appeal deals regularly with profound constitutional issues and, I believe, in the criminal jurisdiction is the appropriate court. Considerable caution must be exercised by this court before it allows the integrity of the criminal process to be interrupted by reason of the exercise of its supervisory jurisdiction. It has been said that judicial review is a remedy of last resort. That must be emphasized. It is not a remedy of first resort although all too often attempts are made to make it so.

53. During the course of submissions, Mr Cheng Huan has placed considerable reliance on the decision of the Supreme Court of Canada in *R. v. Carosella* [1997] 1 SCR 80. It is said that this judgment goes directly against Judge Wright, both in respect of his finding that the onus of establishing a fair trial was on the applicant and his finding that the application for a stay on the grounds of a fair trial being impossible was 'speculative'.

54. However, in my judgment, it is important to bear in mind that *Carosella* was a majority judgment of the Supreme Court of Canada–indeed, it was a majority judgment, I think, by a majority of one–and there were powerful dissenting judgments by judges, including La Forest J, which suggest that the approach of Judge Wright is the approach to be preferred. In this regard, I cite the minority judgment:

> "While the production of every relevant piece of evidence might be an ideal goal from the accused's point of view, it is inaccurate to elevate this objective to a right, the non-performance of which leads instantaneously to an unfair trial. Where evidence is unavailable, the accused must demonstrate that a fair trial, and not a perfect one, cannot be had as a result of the loss. *He must establish a real likelihood of prejudice to his defence. It is not enough to speculate that there is the potential for harm.* Materials can be easily lost and setting too low a threshold for finding a breach of the right to full answer and defence would bring the justice system to a halt. While it is true that, with regard to certain rights, a court can infer the necessary degree of prejudice, this is not uniformly so." [Emphasis added]

The judgment goes on to say:

> "To demonstrate that a breach has actually occurred often demands a finding and measuring of the prejudice suffered. Given the nature of the action which is being challenged in the present case–the actual pursuing of the prosecution–it seems quite appropriate to require a demonstration of a real likelihood of prejudice. There are ample legal and policy reasons for placing this onus upon the accused. The burden is not an unmanageable one and is consistent with established jurisprudence. For missing evidence to cause a violation of the Charter, therefore, the accused must demonstrate upon a balance of probabilities that the absence of the evidence denies him a fair trial...It is not proper to state that a Charter right has been violated and that a fair trial cannot be had based on pure speculation."

55. I have been told that the s.33 issue has not yet been resolved. If the issue falls to be determined in the context of criminal proceedings, which way will our courts go? Will they follow the majority or the dissenting minority? If the views of the minority are chosen then it seems to me that a decision can best be made within a full factual context and that context must be created by allowing the trial to be completed and evidence led. Perhaps then the applicant will be able to demonstrate–on the evidence–that she has been prejudiced or has suffered the real likelihood of prejudice.

56. To my understanding, applications for a stay are not confined to the beginning of a trial. Judge Wright is master of his own court and can act at any time to protect the integrity of process in his court.

57. I am satisfied, therefore, even though a *prima facie* arguable case has been demonstrated, that this is not an exceptional case which requires this court to exercise its supervisory jurisdiction at this time.

58. In my judgment, the imperatives point to the fact that justice in the longer term will be assured by having this trial completed and then, if necessary, having the issues resolved on appeal against a fully realised evidential background.

59. I understand the argument that a reasonably long trial lies ahead. I understand that if the issue of a stay can be determined finally it may–only 'may'–make the trial redundant. But these are not matters, in my view, which should persuade this court to exercise its jurisdiction. Whether there will be a saving in time, cost and concern is in this case problematic.

60. In my judgment, in this case, the integrity of the criminal process must prevail. Leave is refused.

61. If it is necessary, I will hear from the parties on a separate occasion concerning costs.

Judge of the Court of First Instance, High Court (M.J. Hartmann)

Mr Cheng Huan, SC leading Mr Bernald Chung and Mr Hectar Pun, instructed by Messrs S Y Wong & Co., for the Applicant

Mr I C McWalters, SC of the Department of Justice, for the Respondent

---

第三十一條

香港居民有在香港特別行政區境內遷徙的自由，有移居其他國家和地區的自由。香港居民有旅行和出入境的自由。有效旅行證件的持有人，除非受到法律制止，可自由離開香港特別行政區，無需特別批准。

案例

Gurung Kesh Bahadur v. Director Of Immigration

Gurung Kesh Bahadur 對 入境事務處處長

HCAL 11/2000；CACV 216/2000；FACV 17/2001

簡略案情

《基本法》第 24 條規定，香港特別行政區的居民包括永久性居民和非永久性居民。永久性居民享有居留權，非永久性居民為"有資格依照香港特別行政區法律取得香港居民身份證，但沒有居留權的人"。除第 24 條提及的居留權和第 26 條牽涉的選舉權和被選舉權之外，《基本法》第三章（該章名為"居民的基本權利和義務"）沒有區分永久性居民和非永久性居民的權利，因此，無論是永久性居民還是非永久性居民，同等享有該章所保障的權利和自由。

上訴人為尼泊爾公民，1994 年曾在港服役於英國啹喀兵團（Gurkha）。他於 1995 年再度到訪香港，因為其妻子為香港永久性居民，所以他獲准以家屬簽證繼續在香港延長逗留至 1999 年 1 月 9 日。雖然他沒有香港特區居留權，但有資格按照香港法律取得香港居民身份證，因此，根據《基本法》他是非永久性居民。事實上，自 1995 年起，他已經持有了香港居民身份證。

1997 年 10 月他離開香港前往尼泊爾。同年 11 月 5 日，他回港但被拒絕入境，儘管當時他的逗留期限到 1999 年才屆滿。其後，他在港被羈押並被控提供假資料，違反《入境條例》，但經審訊後被裁定無罪。入境事務處處長（下稱"處長"）於 1998 年 12 月根據《入境條例》第 11（10）條向他發出遞解令，即他的逗留批准在他離開香港時便失效，企圖驅逐他出境。上訴人針對處長 1997 年 11 月 5 日拒絕給予入境許可的決定和 1998 年 12 月發出的遞解令提出司法覆核申請。2000 年 5 月，原訟庭駁回上訴人的申請。他遂提起上訴，並獲上訴法庭於 2001 年 6 月判其勝訴，上訴庭裁定處長拒絕給予上訴人入境及企圖發出遞解令的決定侵犯了其根據《基本法》第 31 條享有的權利。處長決定向終審法院提出上訴。

裁決摘要

處長的主要論據是，《基本法》第 31 條所規定的居民權利受第 39 條限制。根據第 39（2）條，居民所享有的權利和自由並非絕對的，而是可以受到限制的，但必須符合所載的兩項要求，即 1）該限制必須依法規定；2）該限制不得違反適用於香港的國際公約。處長認為其中第二項與本案無關，原因是旅行和入境自由並未在《公民權利和政治權力國際公約》中作出規定。因此，處長認為入境處依法根據《入境條例》第 11（10）對上訴人發出遞解令，是符合第一項要求。

在考慮處長的這一論據時，終審法院認為需先確定《基本法》第三章（包含第 31 條和第 39 條）的解釋。根據前終審法院 *Ng Ka Ling v. Director Of Immigration* [1999] 2 HKCFAR 4 和 *HKSAR v. Ng Kung Siu* [1999] 2 HKCFAR 442 在此兩案中確立的原則，對於權利和自由的解釋應採取寬泛的方法，反之，對其施加的限制應採取狹義的解釋方法。通過《香港人權法案條例》而在香港適用的《公民權利和政治權力國際公約》僅僅規定了國際公認的權利的最低標準，而《基本法》可以在此最低標準的基礎上增加規定權利。因此，終審法院認為香港居民的權利和自由可能有以下三種規定方式：1）在《基本法》和《香港人權法案條例》中均有規定；或 2）僅在《基本法》中規定；或 3）僅在《香港人權法案條例》中規定。旅行和入境自由即屬於第二種。《基本法》第 39（2）條並未暗示只要依法規定就能隨意限制僅由《基本法》保障的權利。終審法院認為，如果處長這論據正確，就意味著僅由《基本法》規定的權利可以被本地法律排除，那麼《基本法》所保障的權利將遠遠不及《香港人權法案條例》所規定的權利穩固可靠。終審法院認定這絕對不可能是《基本法》的用意。因此，駁回了處長此論據。

處長的補充論據是，“均衡比例原則”（The principle of proportionality）應當適用於對旅行和入境權利施加的限制。這意味著在每個個案中，入境事務主任必須考慮是否存在相對重要的公眾利益足以使他拒絕給予有關人士入境許可，即使該有關人士是非永久性居民，如果沒有《入境條例》第 11（10）條的規定，該人士可在逗留批准仍然有效的期間回港。同時，入境事務主任還應考慮該人士回港的全部原因。對於這一補充論據，終審法院認為，即使假定《基本法》第 31 條所規定的旅行和入境權利是可以限制的，而“均衡比例原則”又是恰當的驗證標準，本案中爭議的限制仍非如《基本法》第 39（2）條所要求的“依法規定”。根據終審法院 *Shum Kwok She v. HKSAR*, FACC 1/2002 一案，要滿足“依法規定”的要求，該限制必須有足夠的可預見性，而入境事務人員拒絕有關人士進入香港時，所依據的是《入境條例》中為出入境管理而設的一般酌情權，在此情況下，“足夠的可預見性”這一要求顯然是不足的，必須有一個特定的法定明文計劃才足夠。故此，處長的補充論據也被駁回。

終審法院進一步認為，如果第 11（10）條適用於逗留批准期限尚未屆滿的非永久性居民，則難免導致該居民因行使《基本法》賦予他的旅行權利而喪失其非永久性居民的身份。原因是，隨著先前給予的逗留批准在該名居民離開香港後自動失效，他就再無資格取得香港居民身份證。因該名非永久性居民離開香港外訪而剝奪其再次進入香港的權利，即侵犯其根據《基本法》第 31 條享有的旅行和入境權利，因此是違憲和無效的做法。

最後，終審法院補充指出第 11（10）條本身並非違憲，但將該條文應用於逗留批准期限尚未屆滿的非永久性居民，則抵觸《基本法》第 31 條賦予他們的權利。但第 11（10）條仍然有效及適用於逗留期限尚未屆滿的非永久性居民以外的人士。

據此，處長的上訴被駁回。

FACV No. 17 of 2001

IN THE COURT OF FINAL APPEAL OF THE HONG KONG SPECIAL ADMINISTRATIVE REGION

FINAL APPEAL NO. 17 OF 2001 (CIVIL)
(ON APPEAL FROM CACV NO. 216 OF 2000)

Between:

GURUNG KESH BAHADUR — Applicant (Respondent)

- and -

DIRECTOR OF IMMIGRATION — Respondent (Appellant)

Court: Chief Justice Li, Mr Justice Bokhary PJ, Mr Justice Chan PJ, Mr Justice Ribeiro PJ and Sir Anthony Mason NPJ

Dates of Hearing: 10 and 11 July 2002

Date of Judgment: 30 July 2002

JUDGMENT

Chief Justice Li:

Introduction

1. The Basic Law provides that residents of the Hong Kong Special Administrative Region shall include permanent residents and non-permanent residents. Permanent residents have the right of abode in Hong Kong. Non-permanent residents are persons who are qualified to obtain Hong Kong identity cards in accordance with the laws of the Region but have no right of abode. Art.24.

2. There are approximately one million non-permanent residents. They include Mainland Chinese who, not enjoying the right of abode in Hong Kong, have been permitted to come to Hong Kong on one-way permits for settlement and in many cases to reunite with their families. They do not become permanent residents until they have ordinarily resided for a continuous period of not less than seven years and they are, in the meanwhile, non-permanent residents. Non-permanent residents also include persons from many jurisdictions who have come to work in Hong Kong which is an international centre of business, finance and trade.

3. Chapter III of the Basic Law provides for the rights and freedoms of residents. Apart from the right of abode (art.24) and the rights to vote and to stand for election (art.26) which are enjoyed only by permanent residents, Chapter III does not distinguish between permanent and non-permanent residents. The rights and freedoms provided for are enjoyed by all residents, both permanent and non-permanent. As the Court has emphasised in previous judgments, these rights and freedoms lie at the heart of Hong Kong's separate system.

4. This appeal concerns the freedom to travel and to enter Hong Kong guaranteed by art.31 of the Basic Law in respect of a non-permanent resident who had been granted permission to stay with a limit of stay which had not expired. The essential question is whether the immigration authorities could lawfully refuse such a non-permanent resident permission to land, when he returns during the unexpired period of the limit of stay previously granted after travelling outside Hong Kong.

5. The applicant in the judicial review proceedings is the respondent in this appeal and will be referred to as "the respondent". The Director of Immigration, the respondent in the judicial review proceedings, is the appellant in this appeal and will be referred to as "the Director". The Immigration Ordinance, Cap.115, will be referred to as "the Ordinance".

The facts

6. The detailed facts are set out in the judgment of Rogers V-P in the Court of Appeal. It is unnecessary to set them out here. For the purposes of this appeal, the essential facts can be shortly stated.

7. The respondent is a citizen of Nepal. He had served in Hong Kong for some years as a member of the Gurkha Regiment in the British Army before retiring in early 1994.

8. During 1994, he visited Hong Kong on two occasions when he tried unsuccessfully to change his status from visitor to resident. In 1995, he visited again and was allowed to change his status from visitor to dependant of his wife who was a permanent resident of the HKSAR. He was given a limit of stay of twelve months. Subsequent extensions were granted. The last extension was given on 2 July 1996 to expire on 9 January 1999. Since June 1995, he has resided in Hong Kong operating two businesses, an employment agency and a construction business.

9. On 28 October 1997, the respondent left Hong Kong for Nepal. On 4 November 1997, he returned and after questioning, was refused permission to land on 5 November 1997. The respondent was however kept in Hong Kong and was prosecuted for offences under the Ordinance. The charges related to alleged false declarations of his date of birth when he arrived in 1992 and 1994. He was acquitted. The magistrate accepted his evidence that he knew the declared dates of birth to be wrong but he had followed the dates on his passport at the time which had resulted from a mistake made by the Nepalese authorities and which he had unsuccessfully tried to persuade them to correct.

10. On 10 December 1998, the Director made a removal order against the respondent under s.19(1) (b) of the Ordinance. The respondent appealed to the Immigration Tribunal which can only entertain and allow appeals on limited grounds. When he appealed, the Director gave reasons relevant to such limited grounds for the removal order pursuant to the Immigration Regulations. The Tribunal allowed his appeal. But on the Director's application for judicial review, the Tribunal's decision was quashed. In January 2000, the Tribunal, reconsidering the matter, dismissed the respondent's appeal.

11. The respondent then brought the present judicial review proceedings challenging the Director's decision to refuse him permission to land on 5 November 1997 and his decision to make the removal order on 10 December 1998. In affidavits filed on behalf of the Director, immigration officials deposed to the reasons for refusing him permission to land and for the removal order. These reasons, which had not been given earlier, included the ground that the respondent was a person of dubious character having engaged in dubious activities as an immigration consultant.

The judge and the Court of Appeal

12. In May 2000, Hartmann J. dismissed the respondent's challenge. In June 2001, the Court of Appeal (Rogers V-P, Le Pichon JA and Yuen J) allowed his appeal, holding that his rights under art.31 of the Basic Law had been infringed.

Non-permanent resident

13. The respondent was a non-permanent resident. This was accepted by the Director. He had no right of abode but was qualified to obtain a Hong Kong identity card in accordance with the laws of Hong Kong. He has in fact held an identity card since 1995. Every person who is in Hong Kong is required to be registered and to apply for an identity card unless exempted or excluded by the Regulations. Section 3 of the Registration of Persons Ordinance, Cap.177 and s.3 of the Registration of Persons Regulations. The respondent was not within any exemption or exclusion. It should be noted that persons granted permission to remain in Hong Kong by the Director for a period of not more than 180 days are exempted. But the respondent was not within this exemption since he had been granted permission to remain for more than 180 days. It should be emphasised that when he was refused permission to land on 5 November 1997 and when the removal order was made against him on 10 December 1998, the permitted limit on his stay had not expired. It would only expire on 9 January 1999.

The Immigration Ordinance

14. The Ordinance provides for a scheme of immigration control. It is only necessary to refer to the provisions relevant to this appeal. An immigration officer or assistant has the power to examine any person on his arrival or landing in or prior to his departure from Hong Kong. Section 4(1) (a) . He may not land without the permission of an immigration officer or assistant. Section 7(1) . The definition of "land" includes "enter by land". Section 2. Whilst either official has the power to give permission, only the more senior official, the immigration officer (as opposed to the immigration assistant) has the power to refuse permission. Section 11(1) .

15. Where a person is refused permission to land, an immigration officer or a chief immigration assistant has the power to remove him from Hong Kong. But the power vested in them is only exercisable within two months of the date on which the person landed. Sections 18(1) and (2). After two months, a removal order can be made against him but it must be made at a high level in the Immigration Department, namely, by the Director, defined for this purpose to include any Deputy Director or any assistant director of immigration, who has to be satisfied that the person might have been removed under s.18 if the two months time limit provided for therein had not expired. Sections 19(1) (b) (i) and 19(6). As has been mentioned, where the Director makes a removal order, there is a right of appeal to the Immigration Tribunal but only on limited grounds.

16. Where permission to land is given to the person concerned, an immigration officer or assistant may impose a limit of stay and such other conditions of stay as he thinks fit. Section 11(2). Once permission has been given with a limit of stay, as in the case of the respondent, the position during the unexpired period of the limit of stay is as follows. First, only the Chief Executive has the power to curtail the permitted period of stay. Section 11(6). Secondly, the Chief Executive has the power to make a removal order if it appears to him that the person concerned is an undesirable immigrant who has not been ordinarily resident for three years or more. Section 19(1) (a). "Immigrant" is defined to mean a person who is not a Hong Kong permanent resident and would therefore include a non-permanent resident. Section 2. Thirdly, the Chief Executive has the power to make a deportation order against the person concerned if (a) he has been found guilty in Hong Kong of an offence punishable with imprisonment for not less than two years; or (b) the Chief Executive deems it to be conducive to the public good. Section 20(1) . In summary, during the unexpired period of the limit of stay imposed on the person concerned, only the Chief Executive can curtail the period or make a removal or deportation order against him.

17. Section 11(10) is a crucial provision. It provides:

> "Any permission given to a person to land or remain in Hong Kong shall, if in force on the day that person departs from Hong Kong, expire immediately after his departure."

A central question in this appeal is whether its application to the respondent is inconsistent with his freedom to travel and to enter guaranteed by art.31 of the Basic Law.

Articles 31 and 39 of the Basic Law

18. Article 31 of the Basic Law provides:

> "Hong Kong residents shall have freedom of movement within the Hong Kong Special Administrative Region and freedom of emigration to other countries and regions. They shall have freedom to travel and to enter or leave the Region. Unless restrained by law, holders of valid travel documents shall be free to leave the Region without special authorization."

19. Article 31 confers on residents, permanent and non-permanent, a number of rights and freedoms. The second sentence guarantees "the freedom to travel and to enter or leave the Region". "The freedom to travel" on its own in relation to a jurisdiction would involve the freedom to depart from and return to that jurisdiction. In any event, this is expressly provided for by the words "and to enter or leave the Region" in the second sentence after "the freedom to travel". This appeal concerns the "freedom to travel and to enter the Region".

20. Article 39 of the Basic Law provides:

> "The provisions of the International Covenant on Civil and Political Rights...as applied to Hong Kong shall remain in force and shall be implemented through the laws of the Hong Kong Special Administrative Region.
>
> The rights and freedoms enjoyed by Hong Kong residents shall not be restricted unless as prescribed by law. Such restrictions shall not contravene the provisions of the preceding paragraph of this Article."

21. The provisions of the International Covenant on Civil and Political Rights ("the ICCPR") as applied to Hong Kong were implemented through the Hong Kong Bill of Rights Ordinance, Cap.383, which contains the Hong Kong Bill of Rights ("the Bill"). That Ordinance effects the incorporation of the ICCPR as applied to Hong Kong into our laws. See *Shum Kwok Sher v. HKSAR* FACC No.1 of 2002 (10 July 2002) para.53, *HKSAR v. Ng Kung Siu* (1999) 2 HKCFAR 442 at 455.

22. The ICCPR as applied to Hong Kong was subject to the reservation, originally made by the United Kingdom, that immigration legislation as regards persons not having the right to enter and remain could continue to apply. It is unnecessary to set out the terms of the reservation in full since it is reflected in s.11 of the Hong Kong Bill of Rights Ordinance. This provides:

> "As regards persons not having the right to enter and remain in Hong Kong, this Ordinance does not affect any

immigration legislation governing entry into, stay in and departure from Hong Kong, or the application of any such legislation."

A person with the right of abode and hence the right to enter and remain is provided for in art.8(4) of the Bill in these terms:

"No one who has the right of abode in Hong Kong shall be arbitrarily deprived of the right to enter Hong Kong."

Non-permanent residents of course do not enjoy the right of abode and art.8(4) is inapplicable to them. Article 8(4) of the Bill is based on art.12(4) of the ICCPR which provides: "No one shall be arbitrarily deprived of the right to enter his own country".

The Director's primary submission

23. The primary submission of Mr David Pannick QC for the Director is that the rights in art.31 are subject to art.39. He argues that on its plain language, art.39(2) permits the restriction of all rights and freedoms enjoyed by residents (whether contained in the Basic Law itself or in the Bill incorporating the ICCPR as applied to Hong Kong), provided the two requirements prescribed therein are satisfied, namely, (i) the restrictions must be prescribed by law and (ii) the restrictions must not contravene the ICCPR as applied to Hong Kong. In other words, the rights (or at any rate most rights excepting those which are by their nature absolute, such as the right not to be subjected to torture) are only prima facie rights, as he calls them, and can be restricted provided the two requirements are met. The second requirement is not relevant to the right to travel and the right to enter conferred on non-permanent residents by art.31. This is because those rights are not provided for in the ICCPR as applied to Hong Kong and their restriction would not therefore contravene the Covenant. It follows, so the argument runs, that only the first requirement is relevant to the rights in question which may therefore be restricted without any limitation so long as the restrictions are prescribed by law. Here, the restrictions are prescribed by law as contained in the Immigration Ordinance, including s.11(10). If this makes these rights of non-permanent residents precarious, Mr Pannick points out that the status of non-permanent residents is itself precarious as it is defined in the Basic Law by reference to domestic legislation which may be changed from time to time. Mr Pannick submits that there is nothing surprising in this arrangement, bearing in mind that the standards in the ICCPR as applied to Hong Kong already provide for a strong body of rights.

24. In considering the Director's primary submission, the starting point must be the proper approach to the interpretation of Chapter III of the Basic Law in which arts.31 and 39 are contained. A generous approach should be adopted to the interpretation of the rights and freedoms whilst restrictions to them should be narrowly interpreted *Ng Ka Ling v. Director of Immigration* (1999) 2 HKCFAR 4 at 28I–29A and *HKSAR v. Ng Kung Siu* (1999) 2 HKCFAR 442 at 457B. (In this context, right and freedom are used interchangeably). So, art.31 providing for the right to travel and the right to enter should be generously interpreted. On the other hand, art.39(2), which deals with the question of restrictions to rights and freedoms, should be narrowly interpreted.

25. Article 39(1) provides for the incorporation into the laws of Hong Kong of the ICCPR as applied to Hong Kong. As has been pointed out, the Hong Kong Bill of Rights Ordinance containing the Bill has effected such incorporation. The ICCPR as applied to Hong Kong as incorporated by the Bill only provides for minimum standards for rights which are internationally recognised. The Basic Law can provide for rights additional to such minimum standards.

26. When art.39(2) proceeds to deal with the question of restrictions on rights and freedoms, it refers to "the rights and freedoms enjoyed by Hong Kong residents". A right may be provided for (i) in both the Basic Law and the Bill; or (ii) only in the Basic Law and not in the Bill; or (iii) only in the Bill but not in the Basic Law. An example of (i) is the freedom of speech or the freedom of expression. It is to be found both in the Basic Law (art.27) and in the Bill (art.16). Here, one is concerned with the right to travel and the right to enter conferred on non-permanent residents. These rights are an example of (ii) above. They are not provided for and are additional to those in the Bill. They are created by the Basic Law and are only provided for therein.

27. Article 39(2) is protective of the rights and freedoms of Hong Kong residents. Its provisions make it clear first, that such rights and freedoms may not be restricted unless as prescribed by law. Secondly, even if the restrictive measures are prescribed by law, art.39(2) provides that the restrictions shall not contravene provisions of the ICCPR as applied to Hong Kong, that is, as incorporated by the Bill. Thus, in the context of rights recognized by the ICCPR as applied to Hong Kong, (whether or not such rights are also enshrined in the Basic Law), art.39(2) spells out the two requirements which any purported restriction must satisfy.

28. But where as in the present case, one is concerned with rights conferred by the Basic Law, which are not found in and are additional to those provided for by the ICCPR as applied to Hong Kong, art.39(2) does not imply that such rights may be freely qualified or limited simply by restrictions which are prescribed by law. In the context of rights contained only in the Basic Law, the second requirement in art.39(2), which any purported restriction must satisfy, has no application because the rights in question are conferred by the Basic Law and not by the ICCPR as applied to Hong Kong. But it does not follow that rights found only in the Basic Law can be restricted without limitation provided the restrictions are prescribed by law. The question of whether rights found only in the Basic Law can be restricted and if so the test for judging permissible restrictions would depend on the nature and subject matter of the rights in issue. This would turn on the proper interpretation of the Basic Law and is ultimately a matter for the courts.

29. If it were otherwise and the Director's primary submission were correct, it would mean that where the Basic Law has chosen to confer rights additional to the minimum guarantees provided for in the ICCPR as applied to Hong Kong incorporated by the Bill, these additional rights could be swept away by domestic legislation and would therefore be much less secure than the rights in the Bill, whether or not they are also provided for in the Basic Law. This could not have been the intention of the Basic Law. The intention of the Basic Law was to entrench constitutionally the rights and freedoms in Chapter III, rights and freedoms which are essential to Hong Kong's separate system, and the courts have the duty of safeguarding and protecting them by adopting a generous approach to their interpretation.

30. Two further points should be mentioned. First, it is of no assistance to the Director's case that the class of non-permanent residents is defined in the Basic Law by reference to domestic legislation governing those who are qualified to obtain Hong Kong identity cards and that such domestic legislation may expand or reduce the class from time to time. The fact is that the status of non-permanent residents is one that is recognised by the Basic Law and they enjoy rights and freedoms guaranteed by the Basic

Law.

31. Secondly, in support of the Director's primary submission, Mr Pannick relies on the following passage in the judgment of Chan, CJHC (as he then was) and Keith J in *Secretary for Justice v. The Oriental Press Group Ltd* [1998] 2 HKLRD 123 at 164J–165A.

> "...art.27 merely identifies a particular group of fundamental rights and freedoms which the Basic Law guarantees. It does not purport to prevent the enactment of restrictions on those rights. The effect of art.39 is to permit restrictions on the rights protected in Chap. III, provided that those restrictions are provided by law (for example, art.16(3) of the Bill of Rights) and are compatible with various international instruments, including the [ICCPR]."

That case concerned the offence of contempt by scandalising the court and the freedom of expression. That freedom is guaranteed both by the Basic Law and the Bill incorporating the ICCPR as applied to Hong Kong and it was in the context of such a freedom that the passage referred to restrictions being permissible provided both requirements are satisfied. The passage was not discussing rights such as the right to travel and the right to enter which are guaranteed only in the Basic Law and not in the ICCPR as applied to Hong Kong.

32. Accordingly, the Director's primary submission must be rejected.

The Director's supplementary submission

33. If his primary submission fails, Mr Pannick, in seeking to uphold the decisions to refuse the respondent permission to land and to remove him, advances in the alternative a supplementary submission which runs as follows: The principle of proportionality should apply to restrictions on the right to travel and the right to enter. This means that on the facts of a particular case the following questions must be asked (i) whether the legislative objective is sufficiently important to justify limiting a fundamental right; (ii) whether the measures designed to meet the legislative objective are rationally connected to it; and (iii) whether the means used to impair the right or freedom are no more than is necessary to accomplish the objective. In the present context, such a test would mean that the immigration officer must ask himself whether there is a sufficiently strong State interest requiring the refusal of permission to enter even though the person concerned is a non-permanent resident who would be returning within the currency of an existing leave but for s.11(10) of the Ordinance, and having regard also to all the reasons why the individual is returning to Hong Kong (home, family, business etc). In dealing with the matter, a fair procedure would have to be adopted.

34. The Director's supplementary submission can be disposed of shortly. Assuming (without deciding) that having regard to their nature and subject matter, the right to travel and the right to enter in art.31 of the Basic Law could be subject to restrictions and that the test of proportionality is the appropriate test for judging the extent of permissible restrictions, the restrictions must be "prescribed by law". In the present context, this would have to involve the introduction of a statutory scheme specifically designed for the purpose of prescribing restrictions on the constitutional rights of non-permanent residents to travel and to enter together with such safeguards as may be thought appropriate. The expression "prescribed by law" was recently considered by this Court in *Shum Kwok Sher v. HKSAR* para.60–65. The expression signifies that a law must be formulated with a sufficient degree of precision–just how much depends upon the nature and content of the subject matter in question–so that the individual is given some indication as to how he may regulate his conduct. The requirement that restrictions must be "prescribed by law" could not be satisfied by the existence of general discretionary powers for immigration control vested in immigration officials under the Ordinance and by their undertaking administratively the exercise of considering the imposition of restrictions on such constitutional rights of non-permanent residents on a case by case basis at immigration counters at entry points. Accordingly, the Director's supplementary submission must also be rejected.

35. The question of whether such a scheme needs to be introduced is of course not a matter for the courts, which ultimately have the task of determining the constitutional validity of any scheme. In this connection, it must be borne in mind that there already exists powers in the Ordinance for curtailing the stay of any non-permanent resident whose limit of stay has not expired.

Article 31 and s.11(10)

36. Having rejected both the Director's primary and supplementary submissions, the scope of the constitutional rights in question must now be examined. One is concerned with the right to travel and the right to enter guaranteed by art.31 of a non-permanent resident who has been granted permission to stay where the limit of stay has not expired. If s.11(10) of the Ordinance were to apply to such a non-permanent resident, the permission already granted to him would expire immediately after his departure. Upon his return, he would have to seek permission to land afresh. This would be the statutory consequence, notwithstanding that the original permitted limit of stay had not expired at the time of his re-entering, and irrespective of the purpose or duration of his travel outside Hong Kong. This would be the inevitable consequence if, for example, he departed just for a few hours to play golf on the Mainland. Indeed, as submitted by Mr Philip Dykes SC for the respondent, by departing for however short a time, he would lose his status as a non-permanent resident altogether. This is because on the automatic expiry of the permission previously granted immediately after departure, he would cease to be qualified to obtain an identity card under the relevant legislation.

37. The rights to travel and to enter are constitutionally guaranteed by art.31 of the Basic Law and the courts must give them a generous interpretation. In the case of a non-permanent resident whose permitted limit of stay had not expired, his right to re-enter Hong Kong after travelling is an essential element of these rights. To deprive such a non-permanent resident of his right to re-enter Hong Kong by reason of his travelling outside Hong Kong is to contravene his rights to travel and to enter under art.31. Any application of s.11(10) to such a non-permanent resident would contravene these rights. This is because that provision fastens on the exercise of his right to travel, that is his departure, as the reason which triggers automatically the termination of the permission previously granted to him with a limit of stay which had not expired. Indeed, by effecting such termination, the application of s.11(10) to him would destroy his status as a non-permanent resident which is the foundation of the rights conferred by art.31.

38. It is unnecessary to consider in this case whether the rights to travel and to enter under art.31 could be subject to restrictions and if so, the test for judging permissible restrictions. Even

assuming the rights in question can be restricted, the application of s.11(10) to him as discussed above would not merely amount to restrictions on his rights to travel and to enter. Such application would be totally inconsistent with his rights and indeed would have the effect of abrogating the rights in question. Accordingly, the application of s.11(10) to him would infringe his constitutional rights to travel and to enter under art.31 and such application would be unconstitutional and invalid.

39. After travelling outside Hong Kong, such a non-permanent resident has the right to re-enter Hong Kong on the basis of the permission previously granted with a limit of stay which had not expired. Since s.11(10) does not apply to him, the previous permission would not have expired by virtue of departure. The previous permission with the unexpired limit of stay would, notwithstanding his departure for travelling, continue to be effective. Section 7(1) of the Ordinance must be construed consistently with art.31. Accordingly, the word "permission" in s.7(1) must be construed to include permission previously given where a limit of stay is still current at the time of re-entry. Since s.11(10) does not apply to him, a non-permanent resident with such previous permission is therefore entitled to land and does not need a further grant of permission to land under s.7(1) .

40. Section 11(10) itself is not unconstitutional. It is its application to a non-permanent resident, whose permitted limit of stay has not expired, which is inconsistent with his rights under art.31 of the Basic Law. Section 11(10) continues validly to apply to persons who are not non-permanent residents with an unexpired limit of stay, for example, to visitors.

41. As with any person, including a permanent resident who enjoys the right of abode, a non-permanent resident with an unexpired permitted limit of stay may be examined by immigration officials under s.4 of the Ordinance. But he does not require permission to land under s.7 because the previous permission with the unexpired limit of stay remains effective. As pointed out by Mr Pannick, such a non-permanent resident in effect would enjoy an important element of the right of abode. See ss.2A(1) (a) and 7(1) . But this is only one of the elements of the right of abode and is enjoyed by such a non-permanent resident during and only during the unexpired permitted limit of stay. There is nothing surprising in this result. It follows from his rights to travel and to enter guaranteed by art.31. These rights in the new order were created by the Basic Law.

42. It must be emphasised that this judgment only concerns a non-permanent resident in a position like the respondent, whose permitted limit of stay has not expired. A person whose limit of stay has expired would cease to be a non-permanent resident and would be in a very different position. Further, as has been pointed out, as regards a non-permanent resident in the position of the respondent, the Ordinance contains powers for curtailing the period of his permitted limit of stay as well as for his removal and deportation.

43. Having regard to the conclusion reached, it is unnecessary to deal with other arguments advanced by Mr Dykes in support of his contentions on art.31 or to deal with the separate issue concerning the reasons that should be given when an appeal is made to the Immigration Tribunal against a removal order.

Result

44. The Director's appeal must be dismissed.

Costs

45. There shall be an order nisi for costs in favour of the respondent. Any party challenging it should lodge written submissions within 21 days. If no written submissions are received, the order nisi shall become absolute.

Mr Justice Bokhary PJ:

46. Despite the arguments so ably presented by Mr David Pannick QC for the Director of Immigration, I respectfully agree with the Chief Justice's judgment dismissing this appeal with costs nisi. All that I would add is the following.

47. This case concerns Hong Kong's non-permanent residents. In particular, it concerns their position when, after travelling outside Hong Kong, they return here within the period for which they have been given permission to be here. They do not have the right of abode. So they rely on their permission to remain. Permission to enter must be understood as an inherent antecedent of permission to remain. And permission to remain so understood is obviously an essential element of non-permanent residents'status as residents. Axiomatically, therefore, their very status as residents is coterminous with their permission to remain. What if, as the Director contends, such permission expires merely because they travel out of Hong Kong? It would mean that exercising their constitutional freedom to travel (under art.31 of the Basic Law) would destroy their constitutional status as residents (under art.24 of the Basic Law).

48. Such a consequence would be plainly unconstitutional. For it would so inhibit or penalise travel on the part of non-permanent residents as virtually to abrogate their freedom to travel. Section 11(10) of the Immigration Ordinance, Cap.115, provides that permission to remain expires immediately after departure. So s.11(10) would have to be struck down if it had to be read as applicable even to non-permanent residents within the period for which they have been given permission to be here. But s.11(10) can intelligibly-and therefore should properly-be given the limited reading referred to in the Chief Justice's judgment.

49. Having said that the consequence of accepting the Director's contention in the present case would be the virtual abrogation of the freedom concerned, I should guard strongly against giving the impression that nothing is liable to be adjudged unconstitutional unless it goes so far as virtually to abrogate the right or freedom concerned. Let us assume that the right or freedom concerned is susceptible of some restriction. And let us assume also that the way in which the legislation in question touches upon such right or freedom stops well short of virtually abrogating the same. Even so, it does not mean that such legislation is immune from constitutional review by the courts. For there would still be the question of whether such legislation is unconstitutional on some other basis. It might, for example, be unconstitutional because it unreasonably burdens or restricts the right or freedom concerned. Having offered that example, I should present its credentials.

50. In the course of the argument, I drew counsel's attention to certain decisions of the United States Supreme Court on the constitutional freedom of citizens of the United States to travel from one State to another. *Shapiro v. Thompson* 394 US 618 (1969) struck down Connecticut, District of Columbia and Pennsylvania requirements of one year's residence in those respective jurisdictions before receiving any welfare benefit there. *Dunn v. Blumstein* 405 US 330 (1972) struck down a Tennessee requirement of one year's residence in that State before being entitled to vote in State elections. *Memorial Hospital v. Maricopa County* 415 US 250 (1974) struck down an Arizona requirement of one year's residence in a county before being entitled to non-

emergency hospitalisation or medical care at that county's expense. *Saenz v. Roe* 526 US 489 (1999) struck down a California limitation by which the welfare benefits payable to a family which had less than a year's residence in that State were limited to the amount payable by the State of the family's prior residence.

51. As I understand the essentials of those decisions, their common starting point is this. Although the word "travel" does not appear in the text of the United States Constitution, it is nevertheless firmly embedded in American jurisprudence that citizens of the United States have a constitutional freedom to travel from one State to another. Beyond this common starting point, there appears to be room for debate as to which provision of the United States Constitution is most obviously engaged when a statute impinges upon this freedom. Two clauses of section one of the Fourteenth Amendment appear to be principal among the provisions which have been invoked in the relevant cases. One is the privileges or immunities clause which provides that "No State shall make or enforce any law which shall abridge the privileges or immunities of citizens of the United States". The other is the equal protection clause which provides that "No State shall… deny to any person within its jurisdiction the equal protection of the laws".

52. In his book *The Rehnquist Court and the Constitution* (2000), Prof. Tinsley E. Yarbrough observes (at p.244) that in *Saenz v. Roe* Stevens J (who delivered the judgment of the majority) "rested the interstate travel guarantee the statute was found to inhibit on what the Court apparently considered the more concrete foundation of the Fourteenth Amendment's long-neglected privileges or immunities clause rather than on the equal protection standard more traditionally invoked in travel cases". In their book *Constitutional Law*, 6th ed. (2000) Prof. John E. Nowak and Prof. Ronald D. Rotunda predict (at pp 989–990) that "the analysis used in the equal protection right to travel cases will still be used by the Supreme Court, even if that analysis will be given the label of privileges or immunities clause analysis".

53. However that may be, our constitutional arrangements are such that the American "freedom to travel" cases repay study. It is true that we do not have a provision like the privileges or immunities clause. But we find ourselves at the appropriate position without any such provision. This is because Hong Kong is a single jurisdiction rather than a union of jurisdictions. And all Hong Kong residents enjoy all Basic Law rights and freedoms apart from the three Basic Law rights reserved exclusively to permanent residents, namely the right of abode, the right to vote and the right to stand for election. As for equality, art.25 of the Basic Law provides that "All Hong Kong residents shall be equal before the law". And art.31 of the Basic Law confers freedom to travel upon "Hong Kong residents", not upon Hong Kong *permanent* residents only.

54. The United States Supreme Court said in *Shapiro v. Thompson* (at p.629) and repeated in *Saenz v. Roe* (at p.499) that their Honours

> "...long ago recognized that the nature of our Federal Union and our constitutional concepts of personal liberty unite to require that all citizens be free to travel throughout the length and breadth of our land uninhibited by statutes, rules, or regulations which *unreasonably burden or restrict* this movement." (Emphasis supplied)

55. Whatever standard of constitutional review is applied, whether a right or freedom is unconstitutionally affected by any given piece of legislation will always depend in part on the scope of that right or freedom. And as to that, the principle by which Basic Law guarantees of rights and freedoms are interpreted is as so cogently and memorably stated by the Chief Justice in delivering the Court's judgment in *Ng Ka Ling v. Director of Immigration* (1999) 2 HKCFAR 4 at pp 28J–29A and repeated and applied in subsequent cases including by him in the present case. My Lord described them as "the constitutional guarantees for the freedoms that lie at the heart of Hong Kong's separate system", and said that the courts should give them "a generous interpretation… in order to give to Hong Kong residents the full measure of fundamental rights and freedoms so constitutionally guaranteed".

Mr Justice Chan PJ:

56. I agree with the judgment of the Chief Justice.

Mr Justice Ribeiro PJ:

57. I also agree with the judgment of the Chief Justice.

Sir Anthony Mason NPJ:

58. I too agree with the judgment of the Chief Justice.

Chief Justice Li:

59. The Court unanimously dismisses the Director's appeal and makes the order nisi set out in the concluding paragraph of my judgment.

Chief Justice (Andrew Li)

Permanent Judge (Kemal Bokhary)

Permanent Judge (Patrick Chan)

Permanent Judge (R.A.V. Ribeiro)

Non-Permanent Judge (Sir Anthony Mason)

Mr David Pannick, QC, Mr William Marshall, SC, (instructed by Department of Justice, and Mr Tin Yan Lee, GC of that Department), for the appellant

Mr Philip J. Dykes, SC and Mr Paul Harris (instructed by Messrs Jal N Karbhari & Co) for the respondent

---

陳國雄 對 香港警務處處長曾蔭培

HCAL 86/2003

簡略案情

申請人是一位警務人員。在 2000 年 9 月至 2001 年 7 月期間，申請人先後 20 次前往澳門。除其中兩次外，其餘均未有在事前或事後向警隊作出申報。2001 年 7 月，申請人透過律師向法庭申請破產，並於同年 10 月份被法庭頒佈破產令。2002 年 10 月 21 日，申請人接受警隊的紀律研訊，共被指控 26 項違反紀律行為，其中包括在沒有給予通知的情況下前往澳門，違反警隊《2000 年總部通令》第一部第 105 號。雖然申請人承認所有控罪，但申請人卻就兩項懲罰向警務處處長提出減免懲罰申請，然而該申請最後被拒絕。

申請人遂於 2003 年 8 月 26 日向高等法院原訟法庭申請逾期提出司法覆核的許可，並要求法庭宣佈所有違反紀律的指控及相關的懲罰一概無效。申請人要求宣佈警隊《2000 年總部通令》第一部第 105 號、《警員（紀律）規例》第 9（11）條、《警員通令 6-01（8）》因違反《基本法》、《香港人權法案》而無效。

案件其中一個爭議焦點，在於警隊《2000 年總部通令》第一部第 105 號，要求警務人員如以私人身份前往澳門，須在出發前提交通知書予單位指揮官，如在緊急及無可避免的情況下，警務人員也須在回港後不遲於 48 小時內給予單位指揮官事後通知，這個規定有否違反《基本法》第 31 條和《香港人權法案》第 8 條關於香港居民的遷徙往來、旅行和出入境自由。

裁決摘要

法庭認為，警隊《2000 年總部通令》第一部第 105 號僅要求警務人員以私人身份前赴澳門時給予通知，而且通知可以在事後補發。該《通令》並不要求警務人員在獲得批准後才能夠前往澳門。這項通令不構成限制警務人員旅行和出入境的自由。事實上，申請人並不是因為前往澳門而面對違反紀律的控罪，他是因為沒有給予通知而被裁定違反紀律。

基於這個理由，原訴法庭認為申請人提出的警隊《2000 年總部通令》第一部第 105 號違反《基本法》、《香港人權法案》的申請理由不能成立。

此外，法庭同時認為申請人就延誤提請司法覆核申請的解釋並不充分，不具備法律上的良好理由，因此拒絕給予他進行司法覆核申請的許可。

HCAL 86/2003

香港特別行政區
高等法院原訟法庭

憲法及行政訴訟 2003 年第 86 號

申請人　陳國雄

訴

答辯人　香港警務處處長曾蔭培

主審法官：高等法院原訟法庭法官朱芬齡

聆訊日期：2004 年 3 月 8 日

判決日期：2004 年 5 月 17 日

判決書

1. 申請人申請給予許可，以進行司法覆核的申請。

案件背景

2. 申請人在 1986 年 8 月 4 日加入警隊成為警員。

3. 在 2000 年 9 月 5 日至 2001 年 7 月 2 日期間，申請人先後廿次前赴澳門，除其中兩次外，申請人均未有在事前或事後向警隊作出申報。在 2000 年 9 月 9 日，申請人向警察儲蓄互助社申請貸款 50,000 元，在填報貸款申請書時，申請人沒有填報其他貸款。2001 年 7 月 10 日，申請人透過律師向法院申請破產。

4. 其後在 7 月 13 日，申請人向所屬小隊指揮官報告已申請破產和他的欠債情況。據申請人所報，他在當時共欠銀行、財務公司和信用咭共 808,333 元，即共月薪 (22,210 元) 的 36 倍，而他每月最少須還款 42,000 元。2001 年 7 月 18 日開始，分區副指揮官免除申請人執行需要配槍、處理金錢和貴重財物的職務。申請人被調派到報案室內工作。2001 年 10 月 4 日，申請人被法院頒令破產。

5. 2002 年 10 月 21 日，申請人接受警隊的紀律研訊。申請人共被控 26 項違反紀律罪如下：

（1）（a）－（x）項：在沒有給予通知的情況下前往澳門，違反警隊《2000 年總部通令》第一部第 105 號；

（2）（y）項：不審慎理財引致嚴重財務困難而令工作效率受損，違反《警察通令 6-01(8)》；

（3）（z）項：向警察儲蓄互助社申請貸款時沒有披露其他借貸，致使公共服務聲譽受損。

6. 申請人在紀律聆訊中由一名高級督察作辯護代表。申請人承認所有控罪，並同意有關的「案情簡要」和接納主控人員呈交的文件證據。主審官裁定 26 項控罪成立。2002 年 10 月 22 日，申請人的辯護代表向主審官提交減免懲罰的求情書，以及 7 封求情信。主審官決定把案件交高級警務人員決定懲罰。

7. 2002 年 10 月 30 日，油尖區指揮官確認罪名成立的裁定，並作出懲罰如下：

（1）（a）－（x）項：　每項為嚴厲譴責

（2）（y）項：　迫令退利（福利延期發放）

（3）（z）項：　迫令退利（福利延期發放）

8. 2002 年 11 月 19 日，警隊紀律主任有鑑於出入境記錄顯示申請人有兩次是前往內地而非澳門，取消 (c) 及 (d) 項的控罪和懲罰。至於其他各項定罪的裁決和懲罰，紀律主任則予以確認。

9. 2003 年 1 月 1 日，申請人就 (y) 和 (z) 項的懲罰向警務處長提出上訴，要求減免懲罰。2003 年 1 月 28 日，上訴申請被拒絕。這項決定在 2003 年 1 月 30 日通知申請人。

司法覆核許可的申請

10. 申請人在 2003 年 8 月 26 日提出申請，要求法院批予許可，以便進行司法覆核。申請人在表格 86A 中，要求法庭宣佈違反紀律罪成立及懲罰的所有決定悉數無效。申請人尋求的濟助如下：

（1）批准申請人逾期提出司法覆核的申請。

（2）宣佈警隊《2000 年總部通令》第一部第 105 號（"HQO Pt I 105/2000"）因違反《香港特別行政區基本法》（"基本法"）和《香港人權法案條例》（"人權法"）無效；因此申請人對 (a) 至 (x) 項控罪的認罪亦無意義。

（3）宣佈《警察（紀律）規例》第 9(11) 條因違反基本法及 / 或人權法而無效，因此申請人對所有控罪的認罪無意義。

（4）宣佈《警察通令 6-01(8)》（"PGO 6-01(8)"）因違反基本法、人權法、《警隊條例》及 / 或法則法規而無效，因此申請人對 (y) 項控罪的認罪無意義。

（5）宣佈基於 (z) 項控罪沒有足夠案情予以支持，申請人對該項控罪的認罪無意義。

（6）因申請人的懲罰較同類案件明顯為重（尤以 (z) 項控罪為甚），而應獲減罰。

（7）如單憑文件和表格 86A 所述理據不能說服法庭批矛（予）許可進行司法覆核，申請人要求就許可申請展開聆訊。

11. 2003 年 8 月 27 日，法庭指令許可申請以訴訟各方之間的程序進行聆訊。其後申請人申請法律援助，申請在 11 月 6 日拒絕。基於法庭檔期的情況，許可申請要待 2004 年 3 月 8 日才進行聆訊。

申請人的論據

12. 申請人提出申請所持的論據可歸納如下：

（1）申請人是在休假期間前往澳門。按基本法第 31 條和人權法第 8 條，他享有旅行和自由出入境的權利。HQO Pt I 105/2000 是限制了他這方面的權利。

（2）申請人在加入警隊時，曾按《警察條例》第 26 條的規定作出宣誓詞，惟誓詞內容沒有要求他理財得宜。再者，《警察條例》第 10 條所列的警察職責也不包括要懂得理財。因此，PGO 6-01(8) 的規定不合情理和違反條例第 26 條的精神。警務處長以不懂得理財等同不能履行警員職務是不合理的。

（3）申請人與政府之間的僱傭契約沒有要求申請人懂得理財。《警察條例》第 19(3) 條就警員破產時薪金和津貼的處理作出規定，從而可推斷立法者認為破產的警員仍有能力執行警務工作，而且即使申請人破產，他仍可留職。申請人指 PGO 6-01(8) 是近年新加入的，是單方面修改了他與政府之間的契約的重要條款，於法不合。

（4）基於上述理由，PGO 6-01(8) 也違反了《警察條例》第 19(3) 條的規定，故屬無效。

（5）在現今社會，破產並非出奇之事，PGO 6-01(8) 以不審慎理財推論破產者工作受損是不合邏輯和乖乎常理。

（6）PGO 6-01(8) 敵視破產的警員，違反人權法第 1 條而無效。

（7）《警察（紀律）規例》第 9(11) 條規定警員只可在警司級以下的警務人員中挑選辯護代表。然而，警司級的警務人員卻可從其他政府部門、不論職級地挑選代表。申請人稱這些規定不合理地限制了他挑選辯護代表的選擇權，使他失去了公平審訊的機會。

（8）申請人作為警察儲蓄互助社的社員，向互助社借款是社員之間的私事，與公共服務聲譽無關。而且借款社員的其他債項不是互助社決定借貸時考慮的因素，所以 (z) 項控罪並沒有足夠事實基礎予以支持。

（9）申請人的懲罰與其他類型案件的懲罰相比，明顯較重，其中尤以 (z) 項控罪的懲罰為甚。

判決理由

（1）時限問題

13. 申請人要求法庭批准逾時作出司法覆核的申請。他表示在 2003 年 2 月 7 日離開警隊時，因為面對失業和財務困境，感到十分徬徨，精神受到壓力。幸好其後成功覓得工作，並經朋友介紹下認識了本地督察協會的廖督察和另一位劉先生，在與他們商談後決定採取法律行動，時為 2003 年 5 月、6 月間。申請人同時表示他因為沒有法律知識，也沒有獲得法律意見，所以在認識廖督察等之前不知悉有司法覆核申請的渠道，而且他也不知道有關時限的規定。申請人在表格 86A 和誓章中並沒有提及上述有關延遲申請的解釋。

14.《高等法院規則》第 53 命令第 4 條規則如此規定：

「（1）申請司法覆核許可，須從速提出，並無論如何均須在申請理由首次出現的日期起計三個月內提出，但如法庭認為有好的理由延展提出該申請的期限，則屬例外。

（2）凡所尋求的濟助是就任何判決、命令、定罪判決或其他法律程序作出移審令，則申請理由首次出現的日期，須視為該判決、命令、定罪判決或法律程序的日期。」

15.《高等法院規則》第 21K(6) 條同時規定：

「凡原訟法庭認為在提出一項申請司法覆核時有不當的延遲，如法院認為批予所尋求的濟助相當可能會對任何人造成實質困難或在實質上對任何人的權利造成損害，或會有損良好的行政運作，可拒絕批予 —

（a）提出該項申請的許可；或

（b）該項申請所尋求的任何濟助。」

16. 申請人是在 2002 年 10 月 21 日被裁定各項控罪罪名成立。有關的懲罰是在 2002 年 10 月 31 日作出。警隊紀律主任的裁決則是在 2002 年 11 月 19 日作出。2003 年 1 月 30 日申請人獲悉警務處處長拒絕他的上訴。申請人在 2003 年 8 月 26 日才提出本申請時，是明顯超逾了法例規定的時限。即使以拒絕上訴日期起計，申請人的申請也逾時 6 個多月，屬嚴重的延遲。答辯人反對法庭延展申請人提出申請的時限，並指出為了警隊的良好行政運作，針對其決定的司法覆核申請必須從速提出。袁律師也指出針對紀律研訊的司法覆核申請，在警隊中並不罕見，申請人稱不知悉有此渠道令人存疑。

17. 本席認為，即使申請人確如其所述，在最初不知道可以提出司法覆核的申請，他就延遲所作的解釋也並不充份。申請人並沒有說明何以在 2003 年 5、6 月間知道有關法律情況後，仍要待 8 月下旬才作出申請，這與從速提出申請的法例規定不符。申請人是否知悉有關時限的法律規定並不重要，因他在任何情況下仍得迅速地作出申請。申請人在離開警隊後面對的困境，雖可以理解，但不構成良好的解說，以延長提出司法覆核申請的時限。總括而言，申請人不具法律上可接受的良好理由，在規定時限外作出本申請。單就本申請涉不當延遲而申請人又未具良好解釋理由一點，本申請便得予以駁回。

（2）警隊《2000 年總部通令》第一部第 105 號

18. HQO Pt I 105/2000 第 4 段要求警務人員如以私人身份前往澳門，須在出發前提交通知書予單位指揮官。第 5 段列明如在緊急及無可避免情況下，警務人員也須在回港後不遲於 48 小時內給予單位指揮官事後通知。第 2 段說明此項通令是為維持警隊的良好管理效能及紀律水平。

19. 基本法第 31 條規定：

「第三十一條　香港居民有在香港特別行政區境內有遷徙的自由，有移居其他國家和地區的自由。香港居民有旅行和出入境的自由。有效旅行證件的持有人，除非受到法律制止，可自由離開香港特別行政區，無需特別批准。」

20. 人權法第 8 條如此規定：

「（1）合法處在香港境內的人，在香港境內有遷徙往來之自由及擇居之自由。

（2）人人應有自由離去香港。

（3）上列權利不得限制，但法律所規定、保護國家安全、公共秩序、公共衛生或風化、或他人權利與自由所必要，且與人權法案所確認之其他權利不抵觸之限制，不在此限。

（4）具有香港居留權的人進入香港之權，不得無理褫奪。」

21. 上述基本法和人權法的條文所保障的是香港居民的遷徙往來、旅行和出入境的自由。HQO Pt I 105/2000 第 4 和第 5 段僅要求警務人員以私人身份前赴澳門時要給予通知，而且通知可以在事後補發。通令並不要求警務人員在獲得准許下才前往澳門。這項通令不構成限制警務人員旅行和出入境的自由。事實上，申請人並不是因為前往澳門而面對違反紀律的控罪，他是因為沒有給予通知而被裁定犯上違紀的行為。有關 HQO Pt I 105/2000 的申請理由沒有可供爭辯之處。

（3）警察通令 6-01(8)

22. 現時的 PGO6-01(8) 雖是在 1999 年修訂，但它的前身（即警察通例 6-02(4D)）卻早於 1984 年已發出，在申請人加入警隊前已存在。GPO6-01(8) 說明警務人員如因不審慎理財招致嚴重財務困難，致使工作效率受損，將會面對紀律處分。

23.《警隊條例》第 30 條及第 46 條如此規定：

「30. 所有警務人員須服從其上級人員以口頭或書面發出的一切合法命令，亦須服從及遵守根據本條例訂立的警察規例及命令。

…

46（1）…，處長可不時發出他認為適宜於管理警隊、使警隊有效率地履行職責及達致本條例的目的和規定等的命令，…

（2）根據本條訂立的任何命令須稱為"警察通例"（police general orders），…。」

24. GPO6-01(8) 是警務處處長按《警察條例》第 46 條所授予的權力而訂立。按《警察條例》第 30 條，包括申請人在內的警務人員均有責任和必須予以遵守。而且它亦是警務人員聘用條件的一部份，並在申請人加入警隊前已訂立，因此是申請人僱傭契約的一部份，故不存在警隊藉引入 GPO6-01(8) 單方面更改契約條款的情況。

25. 每名警務人員按《警察條例》第 26 條所作的就職誓言，當中包括承諾「毫不懷疑地服從上級長官的一切合法命令」。GPO6-01(8) 既屬一項由處長依法訂立的命令，警務人員按就職誓言須予以服從。申請人稱通令與第 26 條的精神有違背一點，不能成立。再者，雖然 GPO6-01(8) 的條文不在《警察條例》第 10 條所列的職責內，但它是一項警務人員在條例下須遵守的紀律要求。

26. 至於 GPO6-01(8) 的合理性，上訴法庭在 *Leung Fuk Wah Oil v. Commissioner of Police* [2002] 3 HKLRD 653 第 78 和 79 段指出，此項通令所針對的是因不審慎理財招致的嚴重財務困難；而警隊重視警務人員的嚴重財務困難的原因，是因為它被視為構成警務人員效率受損的一個情況。判案書的第 80 至 83 段引用警隊的一些內部指示，說明嚴重財務困難對警隊人員在工作和誠信方面的潛在影響。上訴法庭的判決肯定了 GPO6-01(8) 的需要性和合理性。

27. 至於《警察條例》第 19(3) 條，它是規管警員在遭頒令破產時，其薪津的安排事宜。GPO6-01(8) 的主旨是警務人員須審慎理財以避免嚴重財務困難。雖然理財不當可能導致破產，但通令非為針對破產的警務人員。兩項條文之間沒有矛盾，可以並行不悖，GPO6-01(8) 沒有違反第 19(3) 條。

28. 就人權法第 1 條而言，它指明「人人得享受人權法案所確認之權利，無分……財產……等」。GPO6-01(8) 規定警務人員因不審慎理財而陷於嚴重財政困難，以致有損工作的效率，可構成違紀的行為。通令的內容和目的在於避免警務人員因債務問題而影響工作和誠信，不存在歧視或敵視破產人士，與人權法第 1 條沒有抵觸。

29. 有關 GPO6-01(8) 不合法和不合理的申請理由，並沒有可供爭辯之處。

（4）《警隊（紀律）規例》第 9(11) 條

30.《警察（紀律）規例》第 9(11) 條對辯護代表的安排有如下的規定：

「違紀者可由以下人士代表他進行辯護—

（a）他所選定的督察或其他初級警務人員；或

（b）他所選定的任何具有大律師或律師資格的其他警務人員。」

31. 第 9 條適用於包括申請人在內的初級警務人員。就高級警務人員而言，他們的紀律研訊則按《公務人員（紀律）規例》進行。他們可選擇不具有法律專業資格的公務人員作為辯護人。

32. 答辯人方面指出，這兩項不同的安排是基於實際的需要和考慮。首先，涉及警務人員的紀律聆訊在本質上是適宜由警隊人員處理，惟在高級警務人員方面，由於人數有限和須考慮主審官、主控人員和辯護代表的職級，故需在警隊外處理。然而，兩類警務人員的辯護代表都是由公務人員出任，而且都是不具法律專業資格。

33. 申請人在表格 86A 中稱如他能向其他政府部門的人員求助，他很有可能是不會認罪的。他又稱他錯誤地認罪，主要是因為選擇辯護代表的權利受到限制，因此得不到最合適的意見。

34. 如袁律師指出，《警察（紀律）規例》第 9(11) 條只是就出席紀律聆訊的辯護代表作出規定，它沒有限制警務人員向外界尋求意見和協助的自由和權利。申請人是否尋求警隊以外的人士的協助和他是否獲得恰當的意見和幫助，與第 9(11) 條就聆訊時辯護代表的規定，沒有必然的關係。申請人的申請文件和陳詞都沒有說明第 9(11) 條如何引致他錯誤地承認控罪，甚或使他得不到公平的聆訊。

35. 申請人在聆訊時援引歐洲人權法庭在 *Grieves v. The United Kingdom* (Application No.57067/2000) 一案中的判決。申請人和答辯人其後分別就此案提交補充陳述書。申請人指從這案可見，香港警隊紀律研訊的機制有違人權法第 10 條，而且存在很多不完善和不公平之處。答辯人則認為 *Grieves* 一案與本案有根本分別，判決內容不適用於本案。答辯人亦認為人權法不適用於警隊的紀律聆訊。

36. *Grieves* 案所涉的審裁體是英國海軍軍事法庭。該案的申請人因惡意傷害他人身體違反英國的刑事法，在海軍軍事法庭接受審訊，被判監禁三年。他向歐洲人權法庭投訴海軍軍事法庭在組成上不是獨立無私，所以聆訊程序是不公平，有違歐洲人權公約第 6(1) 條。第 6(1) 條與人權法第 10 條內容相若。歐洲人權法庭裁定申請人的投訴成立，主要原因是海軍軍事法庭中的主審官代訴人 (Judge Advocate) 的委任機制不足以確保軍事法庭的獨立性。這些主審官代訴人 (Judge Advocate) 的主要職責是向軍事法庭的主審官提供法律意見和協助，傳統上是從現役海軍人員中委任，他們在軍事法庭審訊中的表現是受到上級軍官的評核。歐洲人權法庭認為這些主審官代訴人 (Judge Advocate) 在軍事法庭的聆訊中扮演重要角色，因此由現役海軍人員出任是不足以確保軍事法庭的獨立性和公正性。

37. 香港警隊的紀律聆訊並沒有如英國海軍軍事法庭主審官代訴人 (Judge Advocate) 的制度。主審官代訴人 (Judge Advocate) 的角色和功能，與警隊紀律聆訊中違紀者的辯護代表全然不同。歐洲人權法庭在 *Grieves* 案的判決書中，只是就英國海軍軍事法庭的組成作出針對性的分析。它並沒有就人權公約第 6(1) 條作出原則性的分析，也沒有就一般紀律部隊的紀律研訊作出任何原則性的說明。*Grieves* 一案的裁決和歐洲人權法庭在判決書中的考慮不適用於申請人的情況，也無助他對《警察（紀律）規例》第 9(11) 條的立論。

38. 至於申請人在補充陳述書中所臚列有關警隊紀律研訊制度的批評，申請人並沒有指出這些不足處如何影響他的紀律聆訊過程和結果。這些一般性的論點無助他的司法覆核申請。

（5）'Z' 項控罪的基礎

39. 'Z' 項控罪指申請人在向警察儲蓄互助社申請貸款時，沒有披露他的其他債項。按《警察（紀律）規例》第 3(2)(m) 條的規定，違紀行為指致使公共服務聲譽受損的行為。條文中所指的「公共服務聲譽」乃是指整個警隊的聲譽。

40. 如 *Chu Ping Tak Tim v. Commissioner of Police* [2002] 3 HKC 663 一案指出，一名警務人員的行為是否構成第 3(2)(m) 條的違紀行為，關鍵的考慮是有關的行為是否低於公眾合理期望的標準，以致整個警隊的聲譽可能受損：見 678 頁 C-G 段及 679 頁 I 段。申請人指他向警察儲蓄互助社貸款是他們之間的私事，與公共服務沾不上關係，是曲解了第 3(2)(m) 條的意思。

41. 申請人也指警察儲蓄互助社並不關注借款社員的債項情況。就這點，申請人沒有提交任何資料或證據支持。在紀律聆訊時提交的案情第 13 段中指出，公眾有權期望一名警務人員在向互助社申請借貸時，會如實地提供資料。但申請人卻蓄意不申報他的債項，他的行為遂令警隊聲譽受損。紀律主任復指出申請人蓄意瞞報債項，使人對他的誠信有所懷疑。

42. 法庭過往在許多司法覆核申請中重複強調，司法覆核程序是有別於上訴程序；法庭只具有監察的角色（supervisory role）。因此，只有在審裁體的決定從行政法的角度看來是全然不合理的情況下，法庭才會給予濟助。

43. 本席認為就申請人 'z' 項控罪的定罪決定，紀律聆訊的主審官和紀律主任所持的理由，從行政法的規定看來，不能說是全然不合理的。申請人稱定罪沒有基礎的說法不能成立。

（6）申請人的懲罰

44. 申請人指他所受的懲罰，較諸同類型案件中所作的為重，但他沒有就此點作出具體說明。在包括違反 GPO6-01(8) 的違紀案件中，懲罰的方式會因應所涉事實的性質和情況輕重而有所區別。抽空的比較無助於衡量懲罰是否得宜。而且，在涉及專業人士或紀律部隊人員的紀律研訊的司法覆核案件中，法庭在處理懲罰是否得宜的問題時，一般會尊重專業團體或紀律部隊的成員的判斷：見 *Wong Wai Tak v. The Secretary for the Civil Service*，(unreported)，CACV611/2001，第 23 段。再者，一項懲罰即使是嚴厲，也不構成對懲罰進行司法覆核的理由。

45. 申請人懲罰過重的申請理由，並沒有可爭議性。

總結

46. 有鑑於申請人的申請涉不當延遲，和申請人就此沒有良好的解釋理由，以及申請人的申請理由不具有可爭議性，本席認為不應批予申請司法覆核的許可。本席拒絕申請人的許可申請。就訟費問題，本席不擬作出指令，此為暫准令。

高等法院原訟法庭法官（朱芬齡）

申請人：無律師代表，親自出席。
答辯人：由律政司袁國良政府律師代表。

Ng King Tat Philip v. Post-Release Supervision Board Secretary For Security

Ng King Tat Philip 對 監管釋囚委員會

HCAL 47/2010

簡略案情

申請人為香港永久性居民。1998 年因為企圖偷運毒品進入美國關島而被判監 14 年。然而，基於美國政府跟香港政府在 1999 年簽訂的在囚人士轉介協議，申請人於 2005 年要求遣送回港服刑。在申請人被送回香港繼續服刑前，保安局已經向其發出書面通知，根據《監管釋囚條例》（"該條例"），為了他將來重新融入社會的需要，監管釋囚委員會可能會在他刑滿出獄後對他施予一定時間的監管。事實上，在申請人出獄前，委員會最後亦決定對他頒佈 12 個月的監管令，其中的限制包括申請人如想離開香港，必須通知監管主任；居住與工作亦必須得到他的批准；而且除非有合理的理由，否則必須聽從他的指示從事有酬勞的工作。

在釋放後，申請人通過律師，要求委員會取消該頒令但遭拒絕。因此，申請人對委員會的決定申請司法覆核。

申請人認為該條例對他的個案並不適用，而且，頒令中對他的個人限制違反了《基本法》第 31 和第 33 條，非法干預他的行動和就業自由。

裁決摘要

在仔細考慮了相關法律的歷史發展，尤其是相關的在囚人士轉介安排，在 1997 年回歸前已經存在，原訟庭法官認為該條例的立法目的是要幫助釋囚更新和再投入社會，並保障公眾的安全，這些因素完全適用於申請人的情況，認為轉介的囚犯跟本地的囚犯並無分別，因此該條例同樣適用於申請人。

至於違反《基本法》第 31 條和第 33 條的論點，法院認為該頒令對申請人的限制是有理據的。而且，法院指出除非沒有合法合理的原因，違反頒令中的限制也並非必然引起重召入獄的後果。為求達到一個合法目的去幫助釋囚重入社會和避免他們再次犯罪，該條例對他們的自由所作出的限制是必要的和適度的。因此，該條例並沒有違反《基本法》第 31 條和第 33 條。

據此，該司法覆核申請被拒絕。

HCAL 47/2010

IN THE HIGH COURT OF THE HONG KONG SPECIAL ADMINISTRATIVE REGION COURT OF FIRST INSTANCE

CONSTITUTIONAL AND ADMINISTRATIVE LAW LIST
NO 47 OF 2010

BETWEEN:

NG KING TAT PHILIP **Applicant**

- and -

POST-RELEASE SUPERVISION BOARD **Respondents**
SECRETARY FOR SECURITY **Interested Party**

Before: Hon Lam J and Andrew Cheung J in Court

Dates of Hearing: 12 July 2010

Date of Judgment: 23 August 2010

JUDGMENT

Hon Lam J:

1. For the reasons given by Andrew Cheung J, I agree that the application should be dismissed.

Hon Andrew Cheung J:

1 Introduction

2. This application for judicial review raises questions about the power of the Post-Release Supervision Board ("the Board") to make a supervision order against a transferred prisoner, that is to say, a person who is sentenced in a place outside Hong Kong and has been transferred to Hong Kong in order to serve the sentence imposed on him or any part thereof; and the conditions that may be imposed by way of supervision.

3. The applicant is a permanent resident of Hong Kong. In 1998, he was convicted on his own plea on a charge of "attempted importation of methamphetamine in the United States Territory of Guam". He was sentenced by the United States District Court for the District of Guam to 168 months' (14 years') imprisonment.

4. On 17 April 1999, the Agreement for the Transfer of Sentenced Persons between the Government of Hong Kong and the Government of the United States of America came into force. It provides for the transfer of sentenced persons between Hong Kong and the United States. Article 8 of the Agreement provides, amongst other things, that the receiving party shall enforce the sentence as if the sentence had been imposed in the receiving party; and that the continued enforcement of the sentence after transfer shall be governed by the laws and procedures of the receiving party, including those providing for the reduction of the term of imprisonment by parole, conditional release, remission or otherwise.

5. In about 2005, the applicant applied for transfer to Hong Kong pursuant to the Agreement with the view to serving the remainder of his sentence in Hong Kong. The Security Bureau received the relevant letter of application from the US Department of Justice on 31 July 2006, and after processing, the Secretary for Security issued an Inward Warrant with respect to the transfer of the applicant on 31 July 2007. The Inward Warrant, issued under section 3 of the Transfer of Sentenced Persons Ordinance (Cap 513), provided for the bringing in of the applicant into Hong Kong, the taking of the applicant into the penal institution stipulated therein, and the detention of the applicant until the stipulated day of release. In the course of processing the application, the applicant was supplied with a "Statement indicating the basis that the transfer may take place" ("the Annex B Statement"), which he was asked to read and sign. The Annex B Statement provided:

> "[3]C. **Post-Release Supervision in the HKSAR**
>
> In accordance with the Post-Release Supervision of Prisoners Ordinance (Chapter 475, Laws of the HKSAR), a prisoner serving a sentence of 6 years or more or sentenced to 2 years or more for specific types of offences, such as triad related offences, sexual offences or crimes of violence will be considered by the Post-Release Supervision Board for post-release supervision. The period of supervision will not be longer than the remitted part of his sentence permitted under the Prison Rules. The scheme aims at assisting prisoners concerned to reintegrate into society.
>
> 4. **Sentence Remaining to be Served in the HKSAR**
>
> ...
>
> ... As your sentence falls into the sentences specified in the Post-release Supervision of Prisoners Ordinance, the Post-release Supervision Board will consider your case and you may be subject to a period of supervision following your release. This period will not be longer than the remitted part of your sentence."

6. Originally, it was thought that the earliest and latest dates of discharge of the applicant were respectively 27 November 2009 and 10 November 2010. However, after clarification with the US authorities regarding the applicant's "jail time credit" and "good conduct time", the earliest and latest dates of discharge were revised to 7 October 2009 and 12 October 2010. In short, the earliest date of discharge took into account the benefit of remission which the applicant would earn pursuant to rule 69 of the Prison Rules (Cap 234A) for industry and good conduct.

7. The applicant was indeed released from prison on 7 October 2009. However, on 10 September 2009, prior to his release from prison, the Board made a supervision order in respect of the applicant pursuant to the Post-Release Supervision of Prisoners Ordinance (Cap 475) ("the Ordinance"). By paragraph (c) of the supervision order, the applicant was ordered to comply with the following conditions for 12 months from his release:

> "(1) You shall place yourself under the supervision of a supervising officer nominated for this purpose and any other officer replacing him from time to time.
>
> (2) You shall meet with your supervising officer in accordance with that officer's instructions.
>
> (3) You shall inform your supervising officer at once of any changes in your home and office address or any employment particulars including dismissals.
>
> (4) You shall be of good behaviour and keep the peace.
>
> (5) You shall inform your supervising officer of the

intention to leave Hong Kong for a specified period or of the intention to take up residence abroad.

(6) You shall reside at an address approved by your supervising officer.

(7) You shall undertake only such employment as approved by your supervising officer.

(8) You must meet with your supervising officer at least once a month.

(9) You shall not, without reasonable excuse, fail to engage yourself in gainful employment in accordance with the instructions of your supervising officer.

(10) You shall not commit any offence against the Laws of Hong Kong."

8. The supervision order was made by the Board after considering the representation of the applicant who opposed the making of the order. After his release, the applicant continued to object to the supervision order. By a letter dated 22 December 2009, the applicant through solicitors asked the Board to review the supervision order and to discharge the same, pursuant to the Board's powers under sections 7(4) and 11(1) of the Ordinance, on the ground that the Ordinance does not apply to transferred prisoners and therefore the Board had no power to make the supervision order in respect of him.

9. By a letter dated 15 January 2010, the Board replied that it considered it was empowered to make the supervision order and the applicant's requests were refused.

10. The applicant's application for legal aid took time and, eventually, on 30 April 2010, he took out an application for leave to apply for judicial review to challenge the Board's supervision order and refusal to discharge the order. The Court extended the time for the making of the application and granted leave to mount the judicial review. The Court did not accede to an application for interim relief but ordered an expedited hearing of the substantive application instead.

2 Applicant's arguments

11. The applicant essentially takes three points.

12. First, the applicant argues that the Board has no power under the Ordinance to make a supervision order in respect of a transferred prisoner. He contends that the Ordinance does not apply to a transferred prisoner. Unlike the Prisons Ordinance (Cap 234) (see the definition of the word "prisoner" in section 2), the Prisoners (Release under Supervision) Ordinance (Cap 325) (see the express provisions regarding a transferred prisoner in section 7) and the Long-term Prison Sentences Review Ordinance (Cap 524) (see sections 2(d) and 3 thereof), the Ordinance contains no express provisions to cover the position of a transferred prisoner.

13. The applicant argues that as a matter of statutory construction, since the Ordinance is penal in nature, any ambiguity about the scope of application of the Ordinance should be resolved in favour of a transferred prisoner like himself.

14. Secondly, the applicant argues that he was misled by the documents provided to him for his information into consenting to the transfer. He contends that he understood from paragraph 3C of the Annex B Statement that the provisions under Hong Kong law for post-release supervision would not apply to him because on return to Hong Kong the balance of his sentence to be served would be less than 6 years.

15. The applicant argues that the Board must have failed to take this into account in deciding whether to make a supervision order; alternatively, the Board has made a supervision order which is unreasonable in the *Wednesbury* sense; and in either event, the supervision order should be quashed.

16. Thirdly, the applicant argues that conditions (3), (5), (6), (7) and (9) in paragraph (c) of the supervision order infringe his right to emigrate and to leave Hong Kong guaranteed by article 31 of the Basic Law and article 8(2) of the Hong Kong Bill of Rights, his freedom to choose his place of residence guaranteed by article 12(1) of the International Covenant on Civil and Political Rights (ICCPR) and article 8(1) of the Hong Kong Bill of Rights, his freedom of choice of occupation guaranteed by article 33 of the Basic Law, and his right to privacy guaranteed by article 14(1) of the Hong Kong Bill of Rights.

3 The Ordinance

17. It is helpful to first look at the Ordinance.

18. The Ordinance was enacted in 1995 (as Ordinance No 36 of 1995), and came into force on 30 November 1996. According to its preamble, it is an Ordinance to provide for the release under supervision of certain categories of prisoners, on the order of a board established for the purpose.

19. Section 2 of the Ordinance defines the word "prisoner" to include a person who has been released from imprisonment subject to supervision under the Ordinance. There is no other definition for the word.

20. Section 3(1) provides that the Ordinance applies to every prisoner who was 21 or over at the time of being sentenced to imprisonment, or has since attained the age of 25 and is serving a sentence of a kind specified in the Post-Release Supervision of Prisoners Regulation (Cap 475A). The specified sentences comprise a sentence of imprisonment of 6 years or more; and a sentence of imprisonment of 2 years or more but less than 6 years in respect of various specified common law and statutory offences, as well as accessory offences in relation to them: regulation 2 of Cap 475A. The application of the Ordinance is subject to several exceptions set out in section 3(1)(c) to (e) and (2). Amongst other things, it does not apply if the prisoner is already subject to supervision by virtue of an order made under section 7(1) of Cap 325, or to a prisoner who was sentenced or detained under an indeterminate sentence within the meaning of Cap 524 and whose sentence is subsequently converted by the Chief Executive to a determinate sentence.

21. Section 5 of the Ordinance sets out the functions of the Board:

"(1) The functions of the Board shall be –

(a) to consider whether any prisoner to whom this Ordinance applies should be granted early release under supervision, and if so, to order his release in accordance with this Ordinance; and

(b) to consider applications for the variation, suspension or discharge of supervision orders in accordance with this Ordinance.

(2) In the discharge of its functions under this Ordinance the Board shall have regard to –

(a) the desirability of securing prisoners' rehabilitation and their re-integration into society; and

(b) the need to protect the public from serious harm from offenders."

22. Under section 6 of the Ordinance, the Board may order early release of a prisoner on the ground of his industry and good conduct, subject to supervision under the Ordinance. A supervision order may provide for the release under supervision of a prisoner at any time after he has served not less than two-thirds of the total of the actual term of his sentence.

23. In this regard, the grant of remission of sentence under rule 69 of the Prison Rules (Cap 234A) need be borne in mind. Rule 69 provides that a prisoner serving a sentence of imprisonment for an actual term of more than one month may, on the ground of his industry and good conduct, be granted remission. The remission granted under rule 69 shall not exceed one-third of the total of the actual term of imprisonment. However, no remission shall be granted in respect of a prisoner to whom the Ordinance applies: rule 69(4B). In other words, if a supervision order is made in respect of a prisoner under the Ordinance, no remission would be granted under rule 69, but the prisoner would be given an early release subject to supervision under the Ordinance. However, if no supervision order is made under the Ordinance, remission may be granted under rule 69.

24. Section 7(1) of the Ordinance provides, amongst other things, that a supervision order shall specify the conditions as to supervision "which the Board considers to be necessary or desirable in the case of the prisoner having regard to the considerations specified in section 5(2)(a) and (b)", that is to say, the desirability of securing a prisoner's rehabilitation and his re-integration into society; and the need to protect the public from serious harm from offenders.

25. Section 9 the Ordinance provides that a prisoner who is released from imprisonment subject to a supervision order shall, until the expiration of the order, be subject to supervision by a supervising officer and comply with the supervision order. Section 10 goes on to stipulate that upon the expiration or discharge of a prisoner's supervision order, any unserved balance of his sentence shall be deemed to be remitted.

26. Section 13(1)(a) provides that where the Board is satisfied as regards a person who is subject to a supervision order that the person has "without lawful authority or reasonable excuse failed to comply with any term or condition of the order", it may order that the supervision order be suspended for a specified period not exceeding the unexpired term of the Order. In that event, the Commissioner of Correctional Services shall recall the person to prison and re-imprison him for the period of the suspension: section 13(2).

27. There are elaborate provisions governing the procedure for suspending a supervision order and recalling the person involved to prison and re-imprisoning him, as well as the making of temporary recall orders and summary recalls.

4 Rule 69 of the Prison Rules – remission without supervision

28. The Ordinance is not the only piece of legislation in Hong Kong to deal with early release of prisoners (subject to supervision). As mentioned, rule 69 of the Prison Rules provides for the early release of prisoners by way of remission. However, it does not involve any post-release supervision. On the other hand, as described, if a supervision order is made under the Ordinance, no remission would be granted under rule 69.

5 Cap 325 – voluntary supervision

29. The Prisoners (Release under Supervision) Ordinance (Cap 325) is indeed an earlier piece of legislation to the Ordinance dealing with the release of prisoners under supervision. It was enacted in 1987 (as Ordinance No 59 of 1987) and came into effect on 1 July 1988. The word "prisoner" is again defined as including a person who has been released from imprisonment under Cap 325.

30. Cap 325 provides for the release under supervision of certain categories of prisoners. A main difference between a supervision order made under Cap 325 and one made under the Ordinance is that under the former, supervision is voluntary. A supervision order under Cap 325 is only made upon an application by the prisoner to the Chief Executive through the Supervision Board established under Cap 325 for an order for his release under Cap 325 under supervision.

31. Importantly for our purposes, section 7(2A), (2B) and (5), which were added by an amendment to Cap 325 in 1995, contain provisions on counting the length of the sentence of imprisonment being served by the prisoner concerned, "where the prisoner is a transferred prisoner", for the purposes of determining whether he is eligible to apply for release under supervision under Cap 325.

6 Cap 524 – indeterminate and long-term prisoners

32. The Long-term Prison Sentences Review Ordinance (Cap 524) is an Ordinance enacted in 1997 (as Ordinance No 86 of 1997). It came into force on 30 June 1997. It establishes a board to review indeterminate and long-term prison sentences and the detention of persons detained at Executive discretion and certain other kinds of prison sentences. It defines the word "prisoner" to include a person who is released under a conditional release order or a supervision order (section 4(1)).

33. One of the specific purposes of the Ordinance is (section 2(d)):

> "to provide for the review of sentences of prisoners who, having been convicted of offences outside Hong Kong and sentenced to indeterminate or long-term sentences for those offences, are serving all or part of those sentences at prisons in Hong Kong."

34. Section 3 of Cap 524 specifically provides that the Ordinance applies to and in relation to all long-term prisoners, prisoners serving indeterminate sentences, juvenile prisoners and "transferred prisoners".

35. Parts IV and V of Cap 524 go on to provide for the conditional release of a prisoner and the circumstances in which a supervision order may be made.

7 Cap 513 – transfer of sentenced persons to and from Hong Kong

36. As regards the transfer between Hong Kong and places outside Hong Kong of persons detained in institutions by virtue of orders made by courts in the exercise of their criminal jurisdiction, domestically the matter is governed by the Transfer of Sentenced Persons Ordinance (Cap 513), which was enacted in 1997 (as Ordinance No 51 of 1997) and came into effect on 6 June 1997. By itself, it should be remembered, an international treaty governing the transfer of prisoners has no domestic force.

37. Section 3 of that Ordinance provides that the Chief Executive may, pursuant to any arrangements for the transfer of sentenced

persons, issue an Inward Warrant providing for the transfer of a sentenced person into Hong Kong from the place outside Hong Kong to which those arrangements are applicable.

38. Section 4(1) sets out the restrictions on the issue of an Inward Warrant. Amongst other things, the acts or omissions constituting the conduct in respect of which the sentence was imposed must amount to conduct which, if the conduct had occurred in Hong Kong, would constitute a criminal offence under the law of Hong Kong. Furthermore, the sentenced person must be a holder of a Hong Kong permanent identity card or is a person who, in the opinion of the Chief Executive, otherwise has close ties with Hong Kong. Moreover, the sentence imposed must be for life; an indeterminate period; or a fixed period.

39. Section 5(1) of Cap 513 provides that an Inward Warrant shall be sufficient authority for the bringing of the sentenced person into Hong Kong from the place outside Hong Kong; the taking of the sentenced person to the institution in Hong Kong which is specified in the Warrant; and the detention of the sentenced person in accordance with the terms of the Warrant. It is of significance to note that Cap 513, which was enacted subsequent to the making of rule 69 of the Prison Rules, and the enactment of Cap 325 and the Ordinance, only made consequential amendments (via section 11 of and Schedule 2 to Cap 513) to the Prisons Ordinance (Cap 234) and to Cap 325, but not to the Ordinance, relating to the position of transferred prisoners.

40. Thus in relation to the Prisons Ordinance, a definition of the word "prisoner" has been added to section 2 and it defines the word as including a person who is sentenced in a place outside Hong Kong and is brought into Hong Kong in order to serve the sentence imposed upon him (or any part thereof) in that place. Given that definition and the absence of any other relevant definitions or provisions in the Prison Rules, there can be no doubt that the provisions relating to remission set out in rule 69 of the Prison Rules apply equally to a transferred prisoner.

41. As described, Cap 325 was amended in 1995 in that section 7 of that Ordinance, concerning the categories of prisoners who may apply for release under a supervision order, depending on their length of sentence, to include express provisions to deal with how the length of sentence of a transferred prisoner should be counted for the relevant purposes. It was further amended by Cap 513 by way of consequential amendments to bring the relevant provisions in line with Cap 513.

42. However, no relevant consequential amendments were made by Cap 513 to the Ordinance on that occasion.

43. As mentioned, Cap 524, dealing with long-term prison sentences review, also has express provisions dealing with the position of transferred prisoners. However, it should be noted that Cap 524 was actually enacted after Cap 513, and therefore one cannot find any consequential amendments made by Cap 513 to Cap 524. Nonetheless, like the amended Cap 325 and Prisons Ordinance, the position of transferred prisoners is specifically catered for in Cap 524.

8 History of transferred prisoners detained in Hong Kong

44. Although the Ordinance , which was enacted prior to Cap 513, does not, in the circumstances described, contain any express or specific provisions to deal with the position of transferred prisoners, it does not mean that prior to or at the time the Ordinance was enacted, Hong Kong did not have transferred prisoners. Indeed, the legal basis for transferred prisoners in Hong Kong may be traced to the Repatriation of Prisoners Act 1984. As has been explained by the Court of Final Appeal in *Re Yung Kwan Lee* (1999) 2 HKCFAR 245, 248, there were two relevant United Kingdom Orders-in-Council made under the 1984 Act. They were the Repatriation of Prisoners (Overseas Territory) Order 1986 and the Repatriation of Prisoners (Overseas Territory) Amendment Order 1987. The 1986 Order extended the 1984 Act, with certain adaptations, to a list of British overseas territories, whereas the 1987 Order added Hong Kong to that list. The Governor was empowered to issue warrants under the 1986 Order (as amended) for the transfer of prisoners to and from Hong Kong and for the detention here of prisoners transferred to Hong Kong.

45. As the case also demonstrated, prior to the enactment of the Ordinance, there were already bilateral international treaties covering the transfer of prisoners to and from Hong Kong and for their detention here, such as the Anglo-Thai Treaty signed on 22 January 1990, which was dealt with by the Court of Final Appeal in that case.

46. In other words, at the time the Ordinance was enacted, the transfer of overseas prisoners back to Hong Kong to serve their sentences here had already been happening. The Ordinance, when first enacted, did not have any provisions to deal specifically with transferred prisoners. The consequential amendments made by Cap 513 when it was enacted in 1997 did not cover the Ordinance. This, therefore, sets the scene for the first issue raised by the applicant in this application of judicial review, namely, whether the Ordinance applies to transferred prisoners or not.

9 1st issue: Does the Ordinance apply to transferred prisoners?

9.1 Applicant's arguments

47. This is essentially a question of construction of the Ordinance. In essence, Mr S H Kwok, appearing for the applicant, argues that there are no express provisions in the Ordinance to say that it covers a transferred prisoner, that is to say, that a supervision order may be made under the Ordinance in relation to a transferred prisoner. Absent such a supervision order, a transferred prisoner's position falls to be governed by the provisions in rule 69 of the Prison Rules. He may be granted remission on the ground of his industry and good conduct, and such remission (under rule 69) is not subject to any post-release supervision.

48. Mr Kwok argues that unlike the Prisons Ordinance (as amended by Cap 513), there is no expanded definition of the word "prisoner" to specifically cover a transferred prisoner. Likewise, unlike Cap 325, there are no specific provisions to govern the position of a transferred prisoner when it comes to determine whether they qualify for the making of a supervision order under that Ordinance.

49. Mr Kwok likewise argues that unlike Cap 524 (concerning long-term prison sentences and the making of relevant conditional release and supervision orders), which was enacted subsequent to the Ordinance, there are no specific provisions in the Ordinance to deal with transferred prisoners.

50. Mr Kwok argues that a supervision order made under the Ordinance is penal in nature, and any ambiguity in relation to its scope of application should be resolved in favour of a transferred prisoner. Counsel relies on *Bennion on Statutory Interpretation* (5th ed), sections 271 and 273.

51. Mr Kwok also contends, by reference to the conditions typically imposed under a supervision order, that the order seeks to restrict

the released person's fundamental rights and freedoms under the Basic Law and the Hong Kong Bill of Rights. Such rights, counsel argues, cannot be overridden by general or ambiguous words. In the absence of express language or necessary implication to the contrary, counsel contends, the court would rather presume that even the most general words were intended to be subject to the basic rights of the individual. *R v Secretary of State for the Home Department, ex parte Simms* [2000] 2 AC 115, 131.

9.2 Matter of statutory construction

52. The question raised is essentially one of statutory construction. As has been pointed out by the Court of Final Appeal on repeated occasions, the modern approach in interpreting a statute is to adopt a purposive interpretation. The Court's task is to ascertain the intention of the Legislature as expressed in the language of the statute. The statutory language is construed, having regard to its context and purpose. Words are given their natural and ordinary meaning unless the context or purpose points to a different meaning. Importantly, context and purpose are considered when interpreting the words used and not when an ambiguity may be thought to arise. Context and purpose must be considered in the first instance, especially in the case of general words, and not merely at some subsequent stage when ambiguity may be thought to arise. Indeed, the mischief rule is an example of the purposive approach, which is reflected in Hong Kong in section 19 of the Interpretation and General Clauses Ordinance (Cap 1). The context of a statutory provision should be taken in its widest sense and certainly includes the other provisions of the statute and the existing state of the law. The purpose of a statutory provision may be evidenced from the provision itself. Where relevant, materials such as a law reform commission report, the explanatory memorandum to the bill, and a statement made by the responsible official of the Government in relation to the bill in the Legislative Council may be referred to and used in order to identify the purpose of the legislation. *HKSAR v Cheung Kwun Yin* [2009] 6 HKC 22, paras 11 to 14; *HKSAR v Lam Kwong Wai* (2006) 9 HKCFAR 574, para 63; *HKSAR v Ho Yau Yin* [2010] 4 HKC 160, para 14.

9.3 General context

53. It is therefore necessary to adopt a purposive interpretation of the Ordinance to determine whether it applies to transferred prisoners. In this regard, one must examine the relevant context and purpose. I have, in the above discussion, explained in some detail the various legislative schemes governing early release of prisoners and release under supervision. I have also dealt with the statutory regime for the transfer of prisoners to and from Hong Kong and the detention here of prisoners transferred to Hong Kong. They form the relevant context of the Ordinance in general.

9.4 Purpose of the Ordinance

54. It is necessary to look at the purpose of the Ordinance and the provisions contained therein in slightly greater detail.

55. As mentioned, section 5 of the Ordinance sets out the functions of the Board. It is plain from section 5(2), already extracted above, that two matters are of particular significance in deciding whether a supervision order should be granted. First, the desirability of securing the prisoner's rehabilitation and his re-integration into society. Secondly, the need to protect the public from serious harm from offenders.

56. Indeed, according to the Legislative Brief of the Bill, those two matters are the objectives of the post-release supervision scheme designed under the Ordinance. Paragraph 6 of the Brief specifically states:

> "6. Under the proposed scheme, certain categories of adult prisoners may be placed under supervision after their release. The objectives are to protect the public from discharged prisoners considered still to represent a potential threat to public safety, and to help prisoners reintegrate into society and thereby to prevent recidivism."

57. According to another Legislative Council Brief in relation to the Post-Release Supervision of Prisoners Regulation made under the Ordinance,

> "3. The Post-Release Supervision of Prisoners Ordinance (Chapter 475) was enacted on 31 May 1995 to establish a Post-Release Supervision scheme to place certain categories of prisoners under supervision after their early release. The objective is to provide discharged prisoners with guidance and assistance to help them return to society and lead a normal, useful life, thus minimizing recidivism. There is a need for this scheme because many prisoners, after serving long periods in prisons and with limited preparation for what to expect after their release, often do not know how best to reintegrate into society in a law abiding manner.
>
> ...
>
> 6. Under the current penal system, prisoners may have up to one-third of their sentences remitted, subject to good conduct and industry. The Board will consider the cases of prisoners within the target group before their earliest date of discharge. If early release under supervision is granted under the scheme, the prisoner will be released on the date when his sentence would otherwise have been remitted. The supervision order will cover a period no longer than the remitted portion of the sentence. Hence, the period of supervision is not an extension of the prisoner's sentence because the original sentence imposed by the court will not be increased. The granting of early release under supervision may be viewed as an alternative method of completing the punishment set by the court."

58. In *Lui Tat Hang Louis v The Post-Release Supervision Board* [2010] 1 HKC 297, 315, Stock J (as he then was) described the post-release supervision scheme under the Ordinance in these terms:

> "35. The scheme to which the Ordinance gives effect is essentially rehabilitative. I believe that to be so even though there are controls and limitations on the lifestyle and habits of the released prisoner, and even though there is a right to recall. In my judgment, those limitations and controls, and the power of recall for breach of a supervision order, are adjuncts to rehabilitation. They are there as tools by which to render the scheme, rehabilitative in intent, effective. It is to be remembered that those who fall under the scheme's umbrella are those who have been imprisoned for more than six years, or who have committed specified offences and have been sentenced to terms of imprisonment for between two to six years. The nature of the specified offences are in many instances of a kind which, for a variety of reasons, carry a particular recidivist risk – triad offences or offences which tend to be triad related

where, in the absence of fruitful support, the danger of falling back into bad company upon release may be real; or sexual offences where a particular offender might have a disposition to an offence of that kind. The scheme is and, as the various papers make clear, is intended to be, rehabilitation oriented, to assist discharged prisoners to re-integrate into society and to discourage them from re-offending. What is intended is that assistance be given to the prisoners to secure employment or to enroll in training courses and to find accommodation. Upon discharge, apart from periodic acts of supervision, welfare requests are received and, where appropriate, referrals are made; for example, referral to psychological services."

59. Putting aside the question of whether the Ordinance applies to transferred prisoners for the time being, given the categories of prisoners covered by the Ordinance in terms of their lengths of imprisonment or the types of offence committed, it is not difficult to understand the purpose of the Ordinance and the objective of the post-release supervision of prisoners scheme. Many of the prisoners covered by the Ordinance would be long-term prisoners who have been, by definition, separated from society for a long period of time. They are likely to encounter adjustment difficulties upon discharge. According to the evidence, the scheme would provide counselling, advice and available services as well as support which are necessary to help them re-integrate into society, to discourage them from re-offending and to help them lead a law abiding life after discharge.

60. Furthermore, understandably, some of the targeted prisoners are hard-core criminals and recidivists, and they still represent a potential threat to public safety after discharge. There must be reasonable protection for the public, which may be achieved through supervision under the Ordinance.

61. Indeed, they are the two matters specifically singled out for consideration under section 5(2) of the Ordinance.

9.5 Purpose of the arrangement for the transfer of sentenced persons

62. This being the purpose and objective of the Ordinance, the next logical question to ask is whether the intention of the Legislature as expressed in the language of the Ordinance is to cover transferred prisoners who otherwise fall within the targeted categories.

63. In this regard, one must inquire into the purpose or objective of the regime for the transfer of prisoners and for the detention here of prisoners transferred to Hong Kong.

64. In this regard, the purpose or objective behind the transfer arrangements have been succinctly put by the Court of Final Appeal in *Re Yung Kwan Lee*, at p 252D:

> "For humanitarian reasons Hong Kong had an interest in enabling Hong Kong permanent residents imprisoned abroad to return here to serve their sentences in our own prisons rather than in foreign prisons."

65. This has been elaborated in the standard information about the transfer arrangements provided by the Security Bureau of the Government to those who are interested in applying for a transfer. Paragraph 1 of the information puts the purpose of the transfer arrangements in these terms:

> "The above transfers are based on the humanitarian belief that the elimination of difficulties which may arise through language barriers, alienation from local culture and customs and non-contact with relatives, would facilitate the sentenced persons re-integration into society."

66. Indeed the Hong Kong-US Agreement in question, for instance, also refers to facilitating prisoners' successful re-integration into society of which they are citizens, nationals or permanent residents, as the rationale for the transfer of sentenced persons.

9.6 Harmony of purpose

67. Given the respective purposes or objectives of the post-release supervision of prisoners scheme under the Ordinance and the arrangements for the transfer of sentenced persons under Cap 513, not only is there no conflict or inconsistency between the scheme and the arrangements, but also the purpose or objectives of the arrangements for the transfer of sentenced persons is in full harmony with and is indeed enhanced by the post-release supervision scheme under the Ordinance, which aims at, amongst other things, helping the released prisoner to re-integrate into society.

68. In terms of purpose or objective, one can immediately see that a transferred prisoner, who is, by definition, a Hong Kong permanent resident or somebody otherwise having close ties with Hong Kong, stands in no different position from a local prisoner. In terms of rehabilitation and re-integration, their needs are essentially the same.

69. In terms of the need to protect the public from harm from offenders, again there is no distinction between the two types of prisoner.

70. Mr Kwok argues that unlike a local prisoner, a transferred prisoner has not committed any crime in Hong Kong, and he is only detained here on the authority of an Inward Warrant issued under Cap 513.

71. With respect, this is an immaterial distinction in the present context. In the present context, that is to say, in terms of rehabilitation, re-integration and reasonable protection against re-offending, there is no material distinction between a transferred prisoner and a local prisoner. As mentioned, the purpose or objective of the arrangements for the transfer of prisoners is in perfect harmony with that of the post-release supervision scheme under the Ordinance.

9.7 Context and relevance of other legislation

72. As regards the relevant context, I have already described the existing state of the law when the Ordinance was enacted, and the subsequent amendments made to the Prisons Ordinance and Cap 325, following the enactment of Cap 513 in 1997, as well as the subsequent enactment of Cap 524 on 30 June 1997.

73. However, it is important to bear in mind that when the Ordinance was enacted in 1995, the arrangements for the transfer of prisoners and the detention here of prisoners transferred to Hong Kong had already been in place for almost a decade on the basis of the relevant Orders-in-Council. It is true that the Legislative Briefs relating to the Ordinance did not specifically mention the position of transferred prisoners. However, given that, as analysed above, there is simply no material distinction between the position of a transferred prisoner and a local prisoner in terms of rehabilitation, re-integration and protection against

re-offending, the absence of any special mentioning is not surprising at all. Indeed, one would think otherwise and assume that if the Administration had intended to exclude transferred prisoners from the intended scope of operation of the post-release supervision scheme, it would have said so in the relevant Legislative Bills, bearing in mind that both the Administration and the Legislature were well aware that detained in our penal institutions were not only local prisoners, but also transferred prisoners.

74. One may legitimately debate whether the true interpretation of the Ordinance in relation to its scope of application, which was enacted in 1995, could be dependent upon whether and what consequential amendments were made to other legislation in 1997 following the enactment of Cap 513, or whether the proper interpretation could be affected by the enactment of Cap 524 on the last day before the resumption of the exercise of sovereignty. The point made by Mr Kwok is all the more debatable when one bears in mind that Cap 513 did not *introduce* into Hong Kong for the first time the arrangements for the transfer of prisoners and the detention here of prisoners transferred to Hong Kong. It simply *replaced* the pre-existing legal basis for the transfer and detention arrangements, which had been in place before the Ordinance was enacted: para 10 of the Legislative Council Bill on the Cap 513 Bill.

75. *Bennion*, at pp 708 to 710, deals with the use of later Acts *in pari materia* to aid the interpretation of an earlier Act. The principle underlying the treatment of Acts which are *in pari materia* is based on the idea that there is continuity of legislative approach in such Acts, and common terminology. On the facts of the present case, what is plain from the subsequent enactment history is that the Legislative Council did intend the various post-release supervision schemes as well as the regime of remission to apply to transferred prisoners. The question therefore becomes whether the Legislative Council, in the light of the subsequent legislative history, did intend to create an exception in the case of the Ordinance, and if that really was the case, what the Legislature's purpose or justification for such an exception was. Approaching the matter from that perspective, it is quite plain that there is no discernible reason, purpose or justification for the Legislature not intending to apply the Ordinance to transferred prisoners, when the Prison Rules, Cap 325 and Cap 524 are all applicable to transferred prisoners. In other words, to the extent that the subsequent enactment history is relevant and is of assistance, it actually points against the contention of the applicant; rather it suggests that the absence of any similar consequential amendments to the Ordinance was due to an accidental omission on the part of the Legislature/Administration in its rush to pass the relevant legislation before the resumption of the exercise of sovereignty on 1 July 1997.

76. As for section 7(2A), (2B) and (5) of Cap 325, they were added by section 57 of the Administration of Justice (Miscellaneous Provisions) (No 2) Ordinance (Ordinance No 68 of 1995), which was enacted on 24 July 1995. The relevant Bill was first read in the Legislative Council on 10 May 1995. By then, the Bill for the Ordinance ("the Cap 475 Bill") had already been drafted and tabled at the Legislative Council (its first reading took place on 19 January 1993). The Ordinance was enacted on 31 May 1995. In other words, it would appear that the Cap 475 Bill, which eventually was enacted as the Ordinance, was modelled on the unamended Cap 325, and when Cap 325 was amended in 1995, the Cap 475 Bill had already become law, and no amendment had been made to that Bill to bring it in line with the proposed amendments to Cap 325.

9.8 Plain meaning of the text

77. Whilst purpose and context are of great significance in the proper interpretation of a statute, it does not mean that one can distort or even ignore the plain meaning of the text and construe the statute in whatever manner that achieves a result which is considered desirable. As Lord Millett NPJ has reminded the courts in *China Field Ltd v Appeal Tribunal (Buildings) (No 2)* [2009] 5 HKLRD 662, para 36, purposive construction means only that statutory provisions are to be interpreted to give effect to the intention of the Legislature, and that intention must be ascertained by proper application of the interpretative process. This does not permit a court to attribute to a statutory provision a meaning which the language of the statute, understood in the light of its context and the statutory purpose, is incapable of bearing.

78. In other words, even though I have come to the view that in terms of the purpose or objective of the Ordinance (as well as that of the arrangements for the transfer of prisoners and their detention in Hong Kong), there is no material distinction between transferred prisoners and local prisoners in similar situations, and although I have also reached the conclusion that in terms of the context of the Ordinance and the relevant provisions, there is really nothing to indicate that the Ordinance is not to apply to transferred prisoners, one must still look at the provisions and the words used to arrive at their proper construction.

79. Here, an important word used is the word "prisoner", which is only given a partial definition in section 2 of the Ordinance. The crucial question is whether one would be distorting or even ignoring the meaning of the word if one were to construe the Ordinance as applying also to transferred prisoners. In this regard, one must look at the ordinary and natural meaning of the word. The literal or dictionary meaning of "prisoner" is a person who is being kept in prison as the result of some legal process: *Shorter Oxford English Dictionary* (6th ed), p 2351. Certainly, a transferred prisoner is detained in a penal institution as the result of some legal process, namely, the issue of an Inward Warrant pursuant to the provisions in Cap 513.

80. In my view, construing the word "prisoner" to include a transferred prisoner would not do any unjustified violence to the ordinary and natural meaning of the word.

81. As mentioned, the Ordinance only applies to a prisoner who is serving a sentence of a kind specified in the Post-Release Supervision of Prisoners Regulation. This means a sentence of imprisonment of 6 years or more, or that of 2 years or more but less than 6 years in respect of a conviction for any of the offences specified in Schedule 1. The specified offences are statutory offences under 7 different Ordinances in Hong Kong, together with the common law offences of murder and manslaughter. It should also be remembered that under Cap 513, one of the restrictions on the issue of an Inward Warrant is that the act or omission constituting the conduct in respect of which the foreign sentence was imposed must amount to conduct which, if the conduct had occurred in Hong Kong, would constitute a criminal offence under the law of Hong Kong.

82. In my view, the wordings of section 3(1)(b) of the Ordinance and the provisions in the Regulation made thereunder are more than apt to cover the case of a transferred prisoner. Indeed neither section 3 nor any other provisions in the Ordinance or the Regulation place any geographical restrictions in respect of

the sentencing court or the place where the relevant offence was committed (except, of course, where a specified *statutory* offence is involved).

83. In conclusion, I take the view that construing the Ordinance as applicable not only to local prisoners but also to transferred prisoners would not do any unacceptable violence to the ordinary and natural meaning of the language used by the Ordinance.

84. That being the case, and given the context and purpose of the Ordinance, in my view, on a proper interpretation of the Ordinance, it applies to a transferred prisoner just as it applies to a local prisoner.

9.9 Interpretative presumptions

85. In other words, on a purposive interpretation of the Ordinance and its relevant provisions, there is no doubt that the Ordinance applies to a transferred prisoner. That being the case, the aids to statutory interpretation relied on by Mr Kwok simply are not engaged.

86. In particular, I do not accept Mr Kwok's argument that the supervision order to be made under the Ordinance is penal in nature. Both local and overseas authorities are to the effect that it is not penal or criminal in nature: see *Lui Tat Hang Louis, supra; R (West) v Parole Board* [2005] 1 WLR 350.

87. In relation to the presumption that even the most general words in a statute were intended to be subject to the basic rights of the individual, I would make two observations. First, whether the suggested encroachment on fundamental rights can be justified will be dealt with as the third issue below. In other words, if the suggested interference can be justified, it is difficult to see why as a matter of interpretation, the Ordinance has to be construed as to exclude transferred prisoners from its scope of operation despite clear wording to that effect.

88. Secondly, insofar as Mr Kwok is actually saying that because of some ambiguity in the wording of the Ordinance, it should be construed as not applying to transferred prisoners given that fundamental rights are potentially involved, the short answer is that on a purposive interpretation of the Ordinance, there is no such ambiguity.

9.10 Conclusion on the 1st issue

89. In conclusion, on the first issue, I hold that as a matter of proper interpretation of the Ordinance and its relevant provisions, it applies to transferred prisoners just as it applies to local prisoners.

10 2nd issue: Applicant misled?

90. This issue may be disposed of shortly. The applicant claims that he has been misled by the documents provided to him for his information prior to his consenting to the transfer. He alleges that he understood from paragraph 3C of the Annex B Statement that the provisions under Hong Kong law for post-release supervision would not apply to him because on return to Hong Kong, the balance of his sentence to be served would be less than 6 years. He says he has been misled. He argues that the Board must have failed to take all this into account in deciding whether to make a supervision order; alternatively, the Board has made a supervision order which is *Wednesbury* unreasonable; and in either case, the supervision order should be quashed.

91. The applicant can only blame himself for any misunderstanding of what the Annex B Statement says. The Statement, which is in both English and Chinese, clearly says in paragraph 3C that a prisoner serving a sentence of 6 years or more or sentenced to 2 years or more for specific types of offences, such as triad related offences, sexual offences or crimes of violence, will be considered by the Board for post-release supervision. The fact that after returning to Hong Kong, the remainder of the applicant's sentence would be less than 6 years does not alter the fact that he had been serving a sentence of more than 6 years, and was thus within the scope of the Ordinance. Indeed paragraph 4 of the Statement clearly states that the applicant's sentence falls within the Ordinance and the Board will consider his case and he may be subject to a period of supervision following his release.

92. In those circumstances, it is difficult to see how the Board can be criticised for not giving any weight to this complaint by the applicant. In fact, the Board has clearly in its letter dated 14 July 2009 replied to the applicant about the alleged misrepresentation.

93. There is no merit in the second ground of challenge.

11 3rd issue: Compatibility of supervision conditions with fundamental rights

94. The last ground of challenge relied on by the applicant is directed against conditions (3), (5), (6), (7) and (9) of the supervision order. Although the right to privacy has also been mentioned in the Form 86, Mr Kwok has essentially relied on the right to freedom of movement and of choosing one's residence, the right to travel, and the right to freedom of choice of occupation, in support of his challenge.

95. Mr Kwok argues that the conditions in question restrict the rights of the applicant and are unconstitutional.

11.1 Movement, travel and choice of residence

96. Conditions (3), (5) and (6) may be taken together. Condition (3) requires the applicant to inform his supervising officer at once of any changes in his home and office address or any employment particulars including dismissals. Condition (5) requires the applicant to inform his supervising officer of the intention to leave Hong Kong for a specified period or of the intention to take up residence abroad. Condition (6) stipulates that the applicant shall reside at an address approved by his supervising officer.

97. Mr Kwok argues that those conditions (leaving the employment aspect thereof aside for the time being) interfere with the applicant's right to freedom of movement and right to travel, as well as his freedom of choice of residence guaranteed under article 31 of the Basic Law and article 8(1) and (2) of the Hong Kong Bill of Rights.

98. Mr Kwok accepts that under the Ordinance, a breach of a condition in the supervision order does not automatically lead to a recall of the released prisoner. As described, it is only where the Board is satisfied that the released prisoner has "without lawful authority or reasonable excuse" failed to comply with any term or condition of the relevant supervision order that it "may" order that the supervision order be suspended, in which event the Commissioner of Correctional Services shall recall the released prisoner to prison and re-imprison him for the period of the suspension.

99. To this extent, the present case may be distinguished from *Official Receiver & Trustee in Bankruptcy of Chan Wing Hing v Chan Wing Hing* (2006) 9 HKCFAR 545 and *Yao Man Fai George v The Director of Social Welfare*, HCAL 69/2009, 21 June 2010,

Andrew Cheung J, where the relevant sanction in each case followed automatically from any departure from the stipulated mode of exercising the right to travel.

100. However, Mr Kwok also relies on the earlier case of *The Association of Expatriate Civil Servants of Hong Kong v The Chief Executive of HKSAR* [1998] 1 HKLRD 615, 624 to 625, where Keith J (as he then was) took the view that the right protected by article 8(2) of the Hong Kong Bill of Rights is a right to leave Hong Kong "without suffering any disadvantage as a result of exercising that right". In that case, the relevant colonial regulation required an officer under interdiction not to leave Hong Kong during the interval before he was reinstated or dismissed, "without the permission of the Governor". If he left Hong Kong without first obtaining permission to leave, the disadvantage he suffered was the *possibility* of having to face disciplinary action, which could result in his dismissal and forfeiture of all claims to any pension or gratuity. The learned Judge held that the relevant colonial regulation amounted to a restriction on the officer's right to leave Hong Kong.

101. Mr Kwok therefore argues that the conditions restrict the applicant's relevant rights, even though a breach of the conditions does not lead automatically to a suspension of the order or a recall. A mere possibility that this could happen is sufficient to constitute a restriction on the applicant's right.

102. For my part, I accept that in order to constitute a restriction, the sanction following non-compliance with the direct or indirect requirement placed on the exercise of the right to movement or to travel need not be automatic. On the other hand, a mere possibility of sanction following non-compliance may or may not be sufficient to found a case of restriction. In my view, it really turns on the facts of each case.

103. In the present case, I am prepared to proceed on the assumption that the conditions in question do amount to a restriction on the relevant rights. The important question is whether the restrictions can be justified.

104. In this regard, one notes that unlike the position with article 31, the justification permitted under article 8 of the Hong Kong Bill of Rights is limited by article 8(3). In other words, the permitted justification is limited to the protection of national security, public order, public health or morals or the rights and freedoms of others. This difference does not assume any significance in the present case because one is concerned with re-integration and prevention of re-offending, and therefore the protection of public order and of the rights and freedoms of others is engaged.

105. Justification is determined in terms of a legitimate aim; a rational connection between the legitimate aim and the restriction in question; and whether the restriction is no more than is necessary to achieve the legitimate aim.

106. Here, the legitimate aims are quite obviously the re-integration of the prisoner and the prevention of re-offending.

107. Conditions (3), (5) and (6) obviously have a rational connection with re-integration and the prevention of re-offending.

108. As has been explained in the evidence, one of the main aims of the post-release supervision scheme is to provide counselling and advice to discharged prisoners to assist them in adjusting to the life after discharge and in re-integrating into society. To that end, the supervisee is required to meet his supervising officer regularly so that the supervising officer can monitor his progress and offer him assistance or advice on the relevant services available as and when they are required, including, for instance, comprehensive social security assistance, public housing assistance, or counselling services where there are adjustment problems in the supervisee's family or employment settings. Those meetings will also enable the supervising officer to detect, in as early a stage as possible, any deterioration in the performance of the supervisee, so that the officer can offer the necessary counselling to discourage him from re-offending, and in an appropriate case to bring the matter to the attention of the Board to consider whether the conditions in the supervision order have been satisfied and whether it would be a proper case to recall the supervisee, so that the public could be protected.

109. In those circumstances, conditions concerning information on the whereabouts and movement of the supervisee to be supplied to the supervising officer are really ancillary to and essential for the effective implementation of the supervision order, for the supervising officer need to be able to locate the supervisee timeously for the purpose of carrying out the various means of supervision, including home and workplace visits.

110. The right to approve the supervisee's residence (condition 6) is, according to the evidence, necessary as it enables the supervising officer to monitor the environment and the individuals that the supervisee associates with after discharge. According to the evidence, normally the supervising officer will only disapprove a supervisee from residing in a suspected vice establishment or gambling establishment, or any other premises where unlawful activities are suspected to be taking place. According to the evidence, the place where a supervisee resides is of significance to the successful supervision of a supervisee, in order to achieve the ultimate goal of re-integration and the prevention of re-offending. Therefore, for instance, a request to live apart from the family, in the case of a young supervisee, may not be entertained, unless it is with the consent of the family. In any event, a supervising officer would be interested to find out whether there are friends living together with the supervisee and their identities, for better supervision to the supervisee. Home visits and "surprise checks" are carried out regularly.

111. In this regard, one must bear in mind that the rights and powers given to a supervising officer under the conditions are subject to the control of public law. In other words, approval of residence cannot be withheld unreasonably (in the public law sense) or for any other reasons that may be challenged under public law.

112. According to the evidence, the supervising officer will also have to be informed of the details of the supervisee's plans to travel outside Hong Kong because he has to ascertain whether the supervisee's intended travel outside Hong Kong or emigration plan is genuine or is merely a way to evade supervision. It should be noted that there is no power to stop a supervisee from leaving Hong Kong or from emigrating to other places if the supervising officer is properly informed of such plans. In the absence of other matters satisfying the requirements in section 13(1) of the Ordinance, there is no power to recall the supervisee solely on the ground of his departure from Hong Kong.

113. For all these general and practical reasons, I take the view that not only are the conditions rationally connected to the legitimate aims of re-integration and prevention of re-offending, but they are also no more than is necessary for the achieving of those aims, when the matter is considered in the round and

realistically.

11.2 Employment

114. As for conditions (3) (insofar as it requires the reporting of any employment particulars including dismissals), (7) and (9), they relate to article 33 of the Basic Law which stipulates that "Hong Kong residents shall have freedom of choice of occupation".

115. Condition (7) requires the applicant to undertake only such employment as approved by his supervising officer. Condition (9) provides that the applicant shall not, without reasonable excuse, fail to engage himself in gainful employment in accordance with the instructions of his supervising officer.

116. In *Cheng Chun-ngai Daniel v Hospital Authority*, HCAL 202/2002, 12 November 2004, Hartmann J (as he then was) said of article 33 in the following terms:

> "However, as I read the article, even when it is interpreted generously and purposively, it is not to be interpreted in an active sense, by which I mean that it does not guarantee the right of employment in any particular field of occupation. Whether employment can in fact be obtained will depend on the laws of supply and demand as they apply in the market place. The article, in my view, is to be interpreted rather in the light of what it seeks to prevent; namely, outside of issues of national service, should they ever arise, any form of conscription to particular fields of occupation."

See also Yash Ghai, *Hong Kong's New Constitutional Order, The Resumption of Chinese Sovereignty and the Basic Law* (2nd ed), 435 to 436.

117. I therefore doubt very much whether the right prescribed by article 33 is engaged in the present case at all. However, even if it is, I take the view that the relevant restrictions can be justified. Again the legitimate aims of the restrictions are not in doubt, namely, rehabilitation, re-integration and the prevention of re-offending.

118. As for rational connection and "no-more-than-is-necessary", according to the evidence, it is important that the supervisee should take up gainful employment where his personal circumstances, such as health, permit, so that he would be able to re-integrate into society as soon as is practicable. Moreover, the requirement that the supervisee should undertake only such employment as approved by the supervising officers is to ensure that the supervisee will not be working in a vice establishment or any other illegal trade. The requirement to provide employment particulars including dismissals is ancillary to these matters.

119. From the perspective of a supervising officer working in the field, frequent change of employment is not advisable. According to the evidence, in approving a proposed change of employment, a satisfactory reason has to be given, such as better working condition or prospect, higher income, greater travelling convenience, close down of the existing employer's business and so forth. The power to withhold approval of change of employment is therefore of practical significance.

120. As employment situations may vary, a general approval requirement is imposed in order to maintain the necessary flexibility in terms of proper supervision.

121. The withholding of approval is controlled by public law.

122. Moreover, one must not look only at the conditions in isolation in determining whether they bear a rational connection to the legitimate aims or whether they are no more than is necessary for achieving the aims. One must also bear in mind the statutory provisions in the Ordinance itself governing the suspension of a supervision order and the recall of the released prisoner to prison following suspension. In particular, the Board may only order the suspension of a supervision order if the supervisee has "without lawful authority or reasonable excuse" failed to comply with the supervision conditions.

123. Having considered the matter globally and robustly, I have come to the conclusion that the conditions in question are both rationally connected to the legitimate aims and are no more than is necessary to achieve those aims.

11.3 Privacy

124. I have already mentioned that Mr Kwok accepts that his reliance on the right to privacy does not add anything to his arguments based on the other rights. I need not deal with the right to privacy separately.

11.4 Conclusion on the 3rd issue

125. For the above reasons, I take the view that the ground of challenge based on the fundamental rights also fails.

12 Outcome

126. For these reasons, I would dismiss the application for judicial review, and make a costs order nisi that the applicant pay to the respondent and the interested party their costs of the application, including all costs previously reserved, to be taxed if not agreed (the respondent and the interested party are represented by the same team and one set of legal costs only is involved). I would also order legal aid taxation of the applicant's own costs.

127. I thank counsel for their assistance.

Judge of the Court of First Instance, High Court (M H Lam)

Judge of the Court of First Instance, High Court (Andrew Cheung)

Mr Kwok Sui Hay, instructed by Brian Kong & Co, for the applicant

Ms Eva Sit, instructed by the Department of Justice, for the respondent and interested party

---

第三十二條

香港居民有信仰的自由。

香港居民有宗教信仰的自由，有公開傳教和舉行、參加宗教活動的自由。

案例

對教會僱用境外人員進行審批會否構成干預信仰自由

P.473 | Karlo Joanani Dauz 對 入境事務處處長

Karlo Joanani Dauz v. Director Of Immigration

Karlo Joanani Dauz 對 入境事務處處長

HCAL 86/2008

簡略案情

申請人為菲律賓籍人士，他以訪客身份進入香港後向入境處申請受聘於某教會作為常駐傳教士。根據當時的入境政策，在此等申請中，僱主必須證明有實質需要從境外聘用於本港無法找到的擁有特殊技能的僱員。該申請最後被拒絕，入境事務處處長認為在提交的資料中，顯示該教會規模甚小，其發展並不足以支持它僱用境外人員，而且它也沒有健全的經濟能力。雖然申請人及其教會其後曾多次提供補充資料予入境事務處處長，但其申請仍然被拒絕。申請人遂向原訟庭申請司法覆核，企圖推翻入境事務處處長的決定。

根據申請人的論據，入境事務處處長以其教會的規模和財政來考慮他的申請是一種歧視，而且，教會的信徒也有權利得到神職人員的服務。申請人進一步認為該決定違反了《基本法》第 32 條對宗教自由的保障。

裁決摘要

在有限的和不能核實的資料下，原訟庭法官認為入境事務處處長的決定是有理據的，並無不妥。雖然申請人不能來港服務該教會的信徒，但是他們並沒有因此被剝奪繼續其信仰的自由，事實上，入境事務處也沒有向申請人施加壓力，迫使他離開香港。據此，該司法覆核申請被拒絕。

HCAL 86/2008

IN THE HIGH COURT OF THE

HONG KONG SPECIAL ADMINISTRATIVE REGION

COURT OF FIRST INSTANCE

CONSTITUTIONAL AND ADMINISTRATIVE LAW LIST
NO. 86 OF 2008

BETWEEN:

KARLO JOANANI DAUZ — Applicant

- and -

DIRECTOR OF IMMIGRATION — Respondents

Before: Hon Saunders J in Court

Dates of Hearing: 25 May 2009

Date of Judgment: 25 May 2009

JUDGMENT

The application

1. This application for judicial review is brought by Mr Dauz, a Philippine national. Mr Dauz sought permission from the Director of Immigration, (the Director), to change his immigration status to enable him to take up employment work as a missionary for the Love of Jesus Mission Church, Hong Kong Limited (the Church).

The background

2. Mr Dauz first came to Hong Kong in September 2006, and again in October 2006. On a third visit to Hong Kong on 20 October 2006, he was permitted to remain as a visitor until 23 October 2006. On that day he lodged the application with the Director to change his status.

3. Initially insufficient information was submitted with the application and, despite reminders by the Director, no further information was supplied. In late December 2006, the application was treated as cancelled.

4. On 10 January 2007, the Church resubmitted the application. The Director considered the application and by letter on 15 February 2007, the Church was informed that the application was refused.

The Policy

5. The evidence establishes that under the existing immigration policy the factors relevant in considering the application of a person seeking to enter Hong Kong include the following:

(a) whether the person possesses special skills, knowledge or experience of value to Hong Kong and which is not readily available in Hong Kong;

(b) whether the job can be filled locally; and

(c) whether it is justified for the employer to bring in expatriate staff.

The grounds for refusal

6. The Director was not satisfied that the application met these elements of the criteria. The key points upon which the Director relied were:

(a) the Church was not sufficiently established to justify importing expatriate staff because:

(i) the Church was a small-scale church with a membership of only 100;

(ii) the Church did not occupy its own premises, and the tenant recorded in the tenancy agreement produced was not the Church;

(iii) the Church had no staff;

(iv) the Church had no bank account;

(b) the church was not sufficiently financially sound to justify importing expatriate staff because:

(i) unaudited financial statements for the period July–December 2006 reflected a monthly income ranging between $25,300 and $53,700;

(ii) the salary offered to Mr Dauz of $15,600, on average cost 50% of the Church's monthly income.

(c) there was no evidence that any attempt had been made to recruit for the post locally, and no indication that the post could not be filled locally;

(d) although the Church claimed to be a charitable organisation entitled to a tax exemption under s 88 of the Inland Revenue Ordinance, there was no evidence to substantiate the assertion;

(e) Mr Dauz's qualifications and working experience did not indicate that he possessed special skills, knowledge or experience of value to Hong Kong, and not readily available in Hong Kong.

The first reconsideration

7. On 23 February 2007 the Church requested the Director to reconsider the application and submitted further information. That information was considered and on 16 August 2007, the Church was informed that the refusal decision still stood.

8. In particular, the Director took into account the following:

(a) no new information concerning the financial status of the Church was submitted;

(b) there was no new information concerning the qualifications of Mr Dauz, and a course stated to have been undertaken by Mr Dauz had already been taken into account.

The second reconsideration

9. On 10 April 2008, the Church requested the Director to reconsider the application again, and submitted further information. On 7 May 2008, the Director informed Church that refusal was maintained. The following matters were taken into account:

(a) although now contending it had 148 members, the Director had been unable to verify that membership, and remained of the view the Church was small-scale;

(b) the financial status of the Church was unstable with a negative balance recorded;

(c) there was no new information concerning Mr Dauz.

The grounds for review of the decisions

10. Ms Chow says first that no grounds of relief are stated in the Notice of Application for Judicial Review, (Form 86A), and says that Mr Dauz cannot rely on any grounds not set out in the notice: O 53 r 6(1) and see Hong Kong Civil Procedure § 53/14/51. That is strictly correct, but by O 53 r 6(2) I may at the hearing permit an applicant to amend his grounds. I bear in mind that Mr Dauz is not legally represented. There is no suggestion that there is any prejudice to the Director.

11. Ms Chow says, and Mr Dauz accepts, that the grounds upon which he challenges the refusal of the Director are:

(a) Mr Dauz was appropriately qualified;

(b) of the church is sufficiently established and qualified;

(c) there is no security objection, neither is there any record that Mr Dauz has committed any serious crimes;

(d) on the evidence Mr Dauz will not become a burden to Hong Kong;

(e) the discrepancies in the papers relied upon by the Director arose as a result of confusion on the part of the Director in relation to the documents submitted.

I treat these grounds as being an allegation that the Director has failed to properly consider the information submitted to him, and that the decision is Wednesbury unreasonable.

12. Mr Dauz also considers that the Director has discriminated against both him and the Church in the following ways:

(a) he has treated evangelical pastors/missionaries in the same way as Anglican or Catholic priests, when they are quite different;

(b) by comparing the Church financially with Anglican or Catholic churches he has treated the Church less favourably;

(c) as the members of the Church are residents of Hong Kong they are entitled to have a Christian worker in Hong Kong.

In support of these contentions Mr Dauz refers to Article 32 of the Basic Law and the right of freedom of religion.

Is the application out of time

13. Pursuant to O 53 r 4, an application for leave to apply for judicial review must be made within three months of the decision to be challenged. But that three-month period is not a time limit, because the application must also be made promptly. There may be circumstances in which even if an application is made within the three-month period, the court will hold that it has not been made promptly. This is not such a case.

14. Ms Chow complains that the application is out of time, arguing that it has not been filed until 16 months after the first decision was made refusing the application.

15. The original application to the Director was made on 23 October 2006, but lapsed for want of information. It was treated as resurrected on 10 January 2007, when information was supplied and was refused on 15 February 2007. Further information was submitted by the Church and the first reconsideration was requested on 23 February 2007. The decision to refuse the application was confirmed by the Director on 6 August 2007. On 10 April 2008, further information was submitted and reconsideration requested for the second time. On 7 May 2008, the application was refused for a second time.

16. The application for judicial review was not filed until 18 August 2008, a little over three months after the final decision, but 16 months after the original decision.

17. The court will not permit an applicant to "resurrect" an old decision, simply by asking the Director to reconsider the application, and thereby artificially bring himself within time, by relying upon the reconsideration decision. This is not a case of "resurrection", but a case in which additional information has actually been submitted, and each application treated as a new application by the Director.

18. Consequently, I am satisfied that time should not start to run from the time of the first decision. Time did start to run however, on 7 May 2008, and the application for leave was not made until 18 August 2008, 11 days after the expiry of the three-month period. Although technically out of time, the delay is not such as to cause any prejudice, and I do not reject the application for judicial review on a time basis.

The power of the court on judicial review

19. It is quite clear that on an application for judicial review the court cannot substitute its decision for the decision of the Director. In relation to immigration applications the position is appropriately set out by Stock J in *Santosh Thewe v Director of Immigration* [2000] HKLRD 717 at 723 A–D:

> "The applicant has no right in law to remain in Hong Kong as a resident and the decision is one within the discretion of the Director ... .The legislature has entrusted to the Director a discretionary power to grant permission to reside to individuals who, in the first instance, have no right to reside here and that discretion is a very wide one. It must not be exercised in bad faith, or arbitrarily, or perversely and the policy which the Director has adopted is one which must not be exercised without considering the circumstances of each individual case. To that extent the courts will review the exercise of the discretion, but the courts are concerned with legality not with merits. Where determination of facts are left to the Director and the facts sweep across a range, from the obvious to the debatable to the just conceivable, it is the duty of the court to leave the decision of that fact to the public body save in a case where it is obvious that the public body are acting perversely."

20. The judge went on to say, at p 723E–F:

> "Where a person seeks to obtain permission to reside in Hong Kong, the burden is on him to show such facts as might persuade an immigration officer that his circumstances are such as to fall within a policy adopted by the (Director). It is not for the (Director) to have to show that an applicant or an application falls outwith such a policy."

Discussion

21. The financial information presented to the Director was sparse, unaudited, and unsupported by bank statements, because the Church did not have a bank account. While assertions were made as to a regular but very modest income, it was certainly open to the Director to conclude that the financial information

submitted was insufficient to satisfy him that the Church was not sufficiently financially sound to employ expatriate staff. That is particularly so when the financial information submitted showed the Church to be in deficit.

22. It may well be that if the Church had operated its accounts through a bank account, with proper accounting information in which the expenditure and income were verifiable, the Director might come to a different conclusion. But on the evidence, the decision of the Director in saying that he could not be satisfied on this matter, is justifiable.

23. An assertion was made to the Director that nobody could be found locally to fill the job. But there was no evidence given to the Director as to the steps taken in that respect. Again, on the evidence, the decision of the Director is justifiable.

24. When the application was originally made the Church asserted to 102 members. A list of names were supplied, but the list contained merely names and no other details which might enable the Director to undertake any verification. On the second reconsideration application a further list of 46 names was supplied, bringing the claim of the Church to a membership of 148. The list of 46 additional names were supplied with Hong Kong identity card numbers in relation to those names. A record check undertaken by the Director demonstrated that only 70% of those 46 were Hong Kong residents.

25. And unverifiable list, and a deficient list, are matters upon which the Director was entitled to rely for his conclusion that the Church was of a small-scale, and was not well established in Hong Kong.

26. Consequently, it may well have been, on the facts presented to the Director by the Church, open to the Director to come to the conclusion that the Church was sufficiently established, that it had sufficient funds and that was in the interests of Hong Kong that an expatriate missionary should be brought in to serve the Church. But it was plainly open to the Director to conclude that none of those criteria were established.

27. On the evidence that was presented both to the Director and to the court, I cannot say that the Director has acted perversely or unreasonably in reaching his decision. He has plainly considered all of the relevant matters, and weighed them appropriately in the balance, and reached a conclusion. He has not acted unlawfully in so doing. The decision was once the Director to reach, and having concluded that he has considered all of the relevant matters, it is not open to me to substitute my own view in place of that of the Director.

28. I am satisfied that there has been no confusion on the part of the Director in assessing the papers submitted by the Church. If there was any confusion, it was on the part of the Church in failing to properly understand the Director's policy and requirements, and in failing to submit to the Director information to meet that policy. That is not a basis upon which the Director's decision may be challenged.

The discrimination argument

29. While I understand the argument made by Mr Dauz on discrimination, it cannot be said that the decision to refuse his permanent residency in Hong Kong impacts or infringes upon the rights of any Hong Kong residents to enjoy freedom of religious belief.

30. Article 32 of the Basic Law provides:

> "Hong Kong residents shall have freedom of conscience.
>
> Hong Kong residents shall have freedom of religious belief and freedom to preach and to conduct and participate in religious activities in public."

The Hong Kong Bill of Rights provides in Article 15(1):

> "Everyone shall have the right to freedom of thought, conscience and religion. This right shall include freedom to have or to adopt a religion or belief of his choice, and freedom, either individually or in community with others and in public or private, to manifest his religion or belief and in worship, observance, practice and teaching."

31. Two matters may be noted.

32 .First, the rights given by the Basic Law are rights given to Hong Kong residents. Consequently, Mr Dauz may not rely upon the Basic Law in support of his application, simply because he is not a Hong Kong resident.

33. Second, the provisions of s 11 of the Hong Kong Bill of Rights Ordinance make it quite clear that the rights given thereunder may not be called in aid by Mr Dauz, as he presently has no right to enter and remain in Hong Kong. Section 11 provides:

> "As regards persons not having the right to enter and remain in Hong Kong, this Ordinance does not affect any immigration legislation governing entry into, stay in and departure from Hong Kong, or the application of any such legislation."

34. The Church is already in existence, and its members, Hong Kong residents, are not in any way restricted from continuing to practice their religious beliefs as they have done in the past. It may be that they may consider that they will be better served with a resident missionary, but that is not the issue. They are free to continue to enjoy freedom of religious belief, even if Mr Dauz does not come to Hong Kong permanently.

35. Far from being "forced to leave Hong Kong" as Mr Dauz asserted, it is plain that the Director has not insisted upon Mr Dauz leaving. He would have been perfectly entitled to do so but has been reasonable and generous in the circumstances.

36. I have considered carefully Mr Dauz's submission that the Church has been compared unfavourably with the Anglican and Catholic churches. First, there is nothing whatsoever in the papers to justify a submission that such a comparison was even made. The determination of the Director that the Church was small in scale was made simply upon the basis of its membership size and was entirely justified. The issue of a comparison between the established churches and the Church was raised only by Mr Dauz in his affidavit in support of the application. I am satisfied that such a comparison did not form part of the Director's consideration.

37. For these reasons the application for judicial review must be dismissed.

Costs:

38. Having dismissed the application for judicial review, I invited the Director to consider whether, in the circumstances, he wished to pursue the order for costs that would usually follow upon dismissal of the application. I asked the Director to consider the fact that the Church was small-scale, that it did appear to be a genuine religious organisation, and with very limited funds,

not entitled to legal aid, in which Mr Dauz had undertaken the proceedings himself.

39. Ms Chow informed me, having taken instructions, that the Director pressed for a costs order upon the basis that he if did not do so he would be in a difficult situation, and unable to protect the public purse, in any application with a religious connotation.

40. I have to confess that I found the Director's reluctance to exercise his discretion in the circumstances difficult to follow. This was not merely a case with "a religious connotation", but an application by a genuine religious organisation that was plainly impecunious. I would have thought the Director would have been capable of separating such a case from one in which there was an unjustified religious connotation.

41. But that said, the discretion in the court in respect of costs is a discretion which must be exercised judicially. None of the factors referred to by at Atkin LJ, (as he then was) in *Ritter v Godfrey* [1920] 2 KB 47, which might otherwise entitled me to deprive the Director of his costs, were present.

42. In those circumstances there must be an order that Mr Dauz must pay the Director's costs of the application, to be taxed on a party and party basis.

Judge of the Court of First Instance, High Court (John Saunders)

Mr Karlo Joanani Dauz, the Applicant, in person

Ms Grace Chow, instructed by the Department of Justice, for the Director of Immigration

---

第三十四條

香港居民有進行學術研究、文學藝術創作和其他文化活動的自由。

案例

如何確保進行文化活動的自由得到體現？

P.479 | 大紀元集團有限公司 對 入境事務處處長

Epoch Group Limited v. Director Of Immigration

大紀元集團有限公司 對 入境事務處處長

HCMP 52/2011；HCMP 2475/2010；HCAL 43/2010

簡略案情

申請人為大紀元時報的出版者，亦是積極參與法輪功組織活動的本地註冊公司。在申請人的邀請和贊助下，以紐約為總部的神韻藝術團（“神韻”）打算在香港演藝學院提供 7 場表演。根據資料顯示，神韻曾在全球上百個國家表演，以劃時代的數碼背景演示傳統的中國舞蹈。

為了這次演出，申請人遂替神韻的 93 名工作人員向入境處根據一般就業政策（“General Employment Policy”）申請工作簽證。然而，除一名舞台製作經理和 87 位原舞蹈和音樂表演者獲得簽證外，餘下的 6 名後台工作人員的申請卻被拒絕。該 6 名被拒絕的後台工作人員中有 3 位分別是燈光、音響和投射工程師，而剩下的 3 位既是舞蹈員也是他們的助理。入境處認為申請人未能提供足夠資料證明他們擁有的專長在香港的勞工市場找不到相關的替代。

針對這個決定，申請人向原訟庭申請司法覆核。申請人認為入境事務處處長忽視了這 6 位申請人擁有的特殊技術和經驗，尤其是默契和一貫的排練要求並非臨時的本地僱員可以填補的；而且錯誤地考慮本地相關勞工團體可能的不滿，從而導致了這極不合理的決定。申請人也認為該決定違反了《基本法》第 34 條，是對文藝藝術創作自由的干預。

裁決摘要

原訟庭法官重新強調，因為香港的特殊地理、經濟和社會環境，法院不會輕易干預入境事務處處長的政策和酌情權。而且，《基本法》第 154 條也授權香港政府作出適當的入境管制措施。可是，這些權力並非不受約束，入境事務處處長的決定亦不能是乖張的、不合情理的、隨意的或者是麻木跟從指引。

法官認為在現有的工作簽證申請類別中，沒有一種切合本案申請人情況的，入境事務處處長應該個別地、彈性地考慮和處理。對於一個在本港作短暫表演的團體的申請，入境事務處處長應釐清個別職位的申請是該團體的整體不能分割的部份，還是表面不構成實體的部份。因此，入境事務處處長單純考慮本地勞工市場能否提供相關人才是不足的，尤其是他忽略了前期排練的重要性。最後，申請人的司法覆核申請被批准，入境事務處處長相關決定被推翻。至於違反《基本法》第 34 條的論點，法官認為在現階段不需要，也不應該作出考慮。應該留待將來一併和第 140，144 和 149 條作全面的分析和解讀。

HCAL 43/2010

IN THE HIGH COURT OF THE
HONG KONG SPECIAL ADMINISTRATIVE REGION
COURT OF FIRST INSTANCE

CONSTITUTIONAL AND ADMINISTRATIVE LAW LIST
NO 43 OF 2010

BETWEEN:

EPOCH GROUP LIMITED	Applicant
- and -	
DIRECTOR OF IMMIGRATION	Respondents

Before: Hon Andrew Cheung J in Court

Dates of Hearing: 24 and 25 January 2011

Date of Judgment: 9 March 2011

JUDGMENT

Facts

1. The applicant, a company registered locally, is involved in the activities of Falun Gong in Hong Kong and, in particular, with the activities of the Hong Kong Association of Falun Dafa. The Hong Kong Association of Falun Dafa is the organisation which represents local Falun Gong followers of whom, it is said, there are about 500. Mr Kan Hung Cheung is the chairman of the board and the president of the applicant. He is also the chairman of the Hong Kong Association of Falun Dafa.

2. The applicant publishes a newspaper, the Epoch Times, and is involved in the organisation of many public activities in Hong Kong usually involving Falun Gong adherents. These activities include performing arts events.

3. In 2009, the applicant invited Shen Yun Performing Arts to give 7 shows in Hong Kong. The shows were scheduled for 27 to 31 January 2010, and the Lyric Theatre of the Hong Kong Academy of Performing Arts was booked as the venue for the shows.

4. Shen Yun is based in New York. It was founded in 2006, and according to the materials placed before the Court, its annual audiences increased from 200,000 in that year to 800,000 in 2009. Shen Yun now considers itself to be the world's premier Chinese dance and music company. According to Shen Yun, it seeks to revive Chinese classical and traditional dance and music traditions while producing entirely new programmes of dances, songs and musical scores. Its choreography and routines range from "grand processions to ethnic dances with dancers moving in synchronized patterns". A feature of the performances, according to the evidence, is the "state-of-the-art digital backdrops, often animated, and designed to match the story line, lighting and choreography of particular dancers" (Form 86, para 10).

5. According to materials supplied by Shen Yun and the applicant, Shen Yun conducts annual world tours and has been invited to perform in some 100 cities around the world. Venues in which it has performed include the Royal Festival Hall in London, the John F Kennedy Center in Washington and the Palais des Congrès in Paris.

6. The planned shows were publicly announced at a press conference on 4 October 2009. They were jointly presented by the applicant, the Hong Kong Association of Falun Dafa, New Tang Dynasty Television and Ms Vina Lee of Shen Yun. Public ticket sales opened on 2 December 2009 and apparently all 7 shows were sold out within several days.

7. From 13 October to 1 December 2009, the applicant submitted to the Immigration Department a total of 95 employment visa applications on behalf of members of Shen Yun to take part in the shows. 69 applications were submitted on 13 October 2009 at a meeting between 3 representatives of the applicant and 2 immigration officers. Another batch of 16 applications was submitted on 4 November 2009. A third batch of 8 applications was submitted on 11 November 2009. The last batch of 2 applications was submitted on 1 December 2009.

8.On 7 and 19 January 2010, 2 applications were withdrawn respectively. As a result, the total number of employment visa applications made was 93. All of them were applications for entry for employment as professionals in Hong Kong.

9. Pausing here, it is necessary to point out that whilst there are many policies and guidelines published by the Director of Immigration governing various categories of foreigners (aliens) seeking permission to enter Hong Kong, none of them provide for a specific category to cater for travelling performing groups, such as dance troupes, orchestras, choruses, opera companies, musical companies and pop music groups. Nor, for that matter, is there any specific category to deal with sports teams. The Director's practice and policy is to require members of a travelling performing group to apply "for entry for employment as professionals in Hong Kong". They may do so under one of the three available schemes, namely, the Immigration Arrangements for Non-local Graduates (IANG); General Employment Policy (GEP); and Admission Scheme for Mainland Talents and Professionals (ASMTP). All three schemes are quota-free and non-sector specific. They are applicable to talents and professionals in, amongst other sectors, the arts, culture and sport sectors as well as those in the culinary profession. Furthermore, the GEP and ASMTP schemes are both applicable irrespective of the duration of employment.

10. Under the existing policy, applicants (other than Chinese residents of the Mainland) who are not "non-local graduates" but "possess special skills, knowledge or experience of value to and not readily available in Hong Kong" may apply to come to work under the GEP scheme. The application would be favourably considered if:

> "(a) there is no security objection and no known record of serious crime in respect of the applicant; and
>
> (b) the applicant has a good education background, normally a first degree in the relevant field, but in special circumstances, good technical qualifications, proven professional abilities and/or relevant experience and achievements supported by documentary evidence may also be accepted; and
>
> (c) there is a genuine job vacancy; and
>
> (d) the applicant has a confirmed offer of employment and is employed in a job relevant to his/her academic qualifications or working experience that cannot be readily taken up by the local work force; and
>
> (e) the remuneration package including income,

accommodation, medical and other fringe benefits is broadly commensurate with the prevailing market level for professionals in the HKSAR."

(Affirmation of Wong Yin Sang dated 8 July 2010, para 9)

11. According to the evidence filed on behalf of the Director, in processing applications to admit individual members of an overseas performing arts troupe to perform in Hong Kong, the Department of Immigration would need, amongst other things, information on the background of the performance group, the nature and characteristics of the shows intended to be given in Hong Kong, the venue arrangements and the financial arrangements of the sponsor, so as to establish whether the invitation of an overseas performing arts troupe with expatriate members to give shows in Hong Kong is justified. Furthermore, each individual application also needs to be considered on a case-by-case basis in accordance with the prevailing immigration policy and established procedures including, amongst other things, consideration of the individual applicant's educational background, relevant working experience, details of the position and role(s) of the individual in the show.

12. As mentioned, the applications, which were all made under the GEP scheme, were submitted from 13 October to 1 December 2009. Following further meetings and contacts by telephone and correspondence, supplementary information and supporting materials were requested for and supplied in relation to the applications. To cut a long story short, by a letter dated 30 December 2009, the Director informed the applicant that 5 applications had been approved. By another letter dated 31 December 2009, the Director informed the applicant that another 5 applications had been approved. By further letters dated 18, 19 and 20 January 2010, the Director informed the applicant that another 40, 28 and 8 applications respectively had been approved. However, on 21 January 2010, the Director by letters rejected the applications of 7 individuals. One of them (Mr Xu's) was approved on the following day upon reconsideration by the Director. But not so with the remaining 6. Upon 2 reconsiderations, the Director maintained his refusals of the 6 applications. The 6 individuals involved were Mr Deng Yu ("audio engineer"); Mr Tsai Chia Hwa ("production staff – lighting" / "lighting engineer"); Ms Li Ai Ni ("projection engineer"); Mr Brian Nieh ("dancer/audio assistant"); Mr Liu Mingye ("dancer/audio assistant") and Mr Mark Simon Abbott ("dancer/projector assistant").

13. It should be noted that with the exception of Mr Xu, a stage/production manager, the 87 individuals whose applications had been approved by the Director were all dancers/musicians or other stage personnel of Shen Yun. Only the 6 individuals whose applications were refused were related to backstage work. According to the applicant and Shen Yun, without these key individuals, the shows could not be performed and as a result, it was impossible, it is said, for the show tour in Hong Kong to go ahead. The shows were cancelled and steps were initiated to refund the ticket sales, which apparently exceeded $5 million.

Application for judicial review

14. The applicant, as the promoter or joint organiser of the shows, and the "sponsoring employer" of the 6 individuals whose applications were refused, now challenges the Director's refusals of the 6 applications on a number of grounds, namely, irrationality; failure to have regard to relevant considerations; failure to give adequate reasons; unfair procedure and illegality (delay); legitimate expectation (since abandoned); and breach of article 34 of the Basic Law ("freedom to engage in ⋯ cultural activities"). The grounds relied on, apart from the last ground based on the Basic Law, are essentially conventional public law grounds. In particular, the first two grounds are based squarely on *Wednesbury* unreasonableness. The case as presented by the applicant at the substantive hearing has little if anything to do with the Falun Gong background of this case.

Reasons for the refusals

15. In order to understand the grounds of challenge and the issues involved, it is necessary to go into the reasons for the Director's decisions under challenge. The initial refusals were made on 21 January 2010. By a letter dated 6 January 2010, Shen Yun had explained to the Director the various roles to be played by the 6 individuals concerned:

"(a) We do not have reserve dancers. All of our 38 dancers will perform on stage.

(b) Similarly we do not have reserve musicians and all of our musicians will perform on stage.

...

(d) The job of audio assistant is to help audio engineer to move and test audio equipment, cables, and microphones. This job is only performed during the setup and disassembling time, not during the show. During the show time they will only perform as dancers. Audio assistant is a minor position which we only require basic training. Both Mr Nieh, Brian and Mr Liu, Mingye are full time students at Fei Tian Academy of the Arts since 2006 and has been sufficiently trained to assume this position.

(e) The job of projector assistant is to help projection engineer to move and test projection equipment, cables. This job is only performed during the setup and disassembling time, not during the show. During the show time Mr Abbott will only perform as dancer. Projector assistant is a minor position which we only require basic training. Mr Abbott, Mark is a full time student at Fei Tian Academy of the Arts since 2006 and has been sufficiently trained to assume this position.

(f) The job of projection engineer is to prepare and examine projection equipment before the show and operate projection equipment during the show. Our show includes large projected image/animation on the backdrop as an integrated part of our programs. Since 2007 Ms Li, Ai Ni has been a full time student of Fei Tian Academy of the Arts and has been subject to extensive training in the area. For the past 3 years she has participated in over 100 Shen Yun Shows around the world.

...

(h) The job of audio engineer is to prepare and examine audio equipment before the show and operate audio equipment during the show. Mr Deng, Yu's credential is attached.

(i) Mr Tsai, Chia-Hwa's job is to prepare and examine lighting equipment before the show and operate lighting equipment during the show ..."

16. The letters of refusal were very brief. They were almost

identical in content. The letter of refusal relating to Mr Deng's application, for instance, read:

> "Under existing policy, a person seeking to enter the Hong Kong Special Administrative Region (HKSAR) for employment should among other things, possess a special skill, knowledge or experience of value to and not readily available in the HKSAR. Besides, other criteria to be considered include whether the job can be filled locally and whether it is justified for the employer to bring in an expatriate staff.
>
> Having considered the information made available and all circumstances of the case, we are not satisfied that his case meets the aforesaid criteria. His application is therefore refused. I should be grateful if you would inform him accordingly."

17. The internal minutes of the Immigration Department relating to the refusal were more informative:

> "This concerns entry employment visa application from an applicant who is one of the members of Shen Yun Performing Arts of USA. He is <u>audio engineer</u> of performance ...
>
> <u>Performance Group</u>
>
> 6. Applicant is member of Shen Yun Performing Arts (former[ly] known as Divine Performing Arts). It is based in New York with mission to rediscover the essence of true, traditional Chinese culture. The group travels the world, performing across Europe, the Americas, Oceania and Asia.
>
> <u>Position</u>
>
> 7. The job duties of the applicant as audio engineer is to prepare and examine audio equipment before the show and operate audio equipment during the show.
>
> ...
>
> <u>Considerations and Recommendations</u>
>
> 10. On the basis of documents and the information made available, I am not satisfied that the applicant meets the criteria for entry to Hong Kong under General Employment Policy in view of the following considerations:–
>
> - The duties of applicant as an audio engineer are of general nature and the knowledge, experience and skills required for the post do not meet the requirement that they are not readily available in Hong Kong.
> - There are a number of venues in Hong Kong for performances and concerts, and many of the performances and concerts are supported by local technical staff. There is no information showing that there is a lack of local supply of this category of work force.
>
> Therefore, I recommend this employment application be refused."

18. The internal minutes relating to Mr Tsai (production – lighting) and Ms Li (projection engineer) were similar in content, save that in relation to Ms Li, an additional consideration for rejecting her application was mentioned in the minutes:

> "Applicant is a 17–year–old full time student and there is no proof, academic or otherwise on the alleged expertise and skills."

19. In relation to the remaining 3 individuals who performed dual role, the content of the relevant internal minutes was similar. Thus, for instance, in relation to Mr Brian Nieh (dancer/audio assistant), the relevant internal minutes read:

> "This concerns entry employment visa application from an applicant who is one of the members of Shen Yun Performing Arts of USA. He is <u>dancer/audio engineer</u> of performance ...
>
> <u>Position</u>
>
> 7. The position of the applicant is Dancer/Audio Assistant. The job duties of audio assistant is to help audio engineer to move and test audio equipment, cables and microphones during the setup and disassembling time. During the show time, he will only perform as dancer.

...

> <u>Considerations and Recommendations</u>
>
> 10. On the basis of documents and the information made available, I am not satisfied that the applicant meets the criteria for entry to Hong Kong under General Employment Policy in view of the following considerations:–
>
> - The duties of applicant as an audio assistant are of general nature and the knowledge, experience and skills required for the post do not meet the requirement that they are not readily available in Hong Kong.
> - There are a number of venues in Hong Kong for performances and concerts, and many of the performances and concerts are supported by local technical staff. There is no information showing that there is a lack of local supply of this category of work force.
> - Taking into consideration that a dancer usually has to be engaged in various preparation works before the show, such as rehearsal, practice, make up etc., it is not satisfied that the applicant would be capable of performing the dual role of audio assistant and dancer as claimed.
>
> Therefore, I recommend this employment application be refused."

20. After notification of the initial refusals, the applicant, on behalf of the individuals concerned, sought a reconsideration by the Director of his refusals. This was supported by, amongst other things, a letter dated 21 January 2010 from the applicant to the Director. It said:

> "1 Shen Yun Performing Arts Company is based in New York and its members, including all production personnels such as Associate Company Manager, Projection Engineer and their assistants, Audio engineer and their assistants, and Lighting personnels, and of course, the Artists all undergo months of

rigorous training TOGETHER in their production. Programs for the show are new and original every year. All members have to closely train, work and rehearse with each other as a team in preparing the shows. They also have to do so in a well co-ordinated, co-operative, and synchronized manner, both in the production and during the performance of the shows. None of them is hence replaceable in the production and their performance in Hong Kong. They are unique, not replaceable and special by virtue of their extended training and co-operation TOGETHER in the preparation. It is therefore impossible, in this context and circumstances, for us to hire such personnels locally on a temporary basis, even assuming these skills are available. The reason for refusal may perhaps be relevant to a local arts group but is definitely irrelevant in our case.

(Appended to this letter, we have listed some detail information to substantiate why and how their skills are so special for Shen Yun shows. No one else can replace them to run the shows without these special skills.)

2 The three applicants who are both dancers and production assistants should be treated consistently with other applicants who are only dancers and we note all applications for dancers are approved.

3 The Projection Engineer and her assistant have to operate a state-of-the-art 3-dimensional backdrop and they have to possess special skill, knowledge or experience not available in HKSAR.

4 Finally we would like to mention the refusals have not taken into account all relevant factors as explained above. The refusal has also taken into account irrelevant factors such as that explained to us by you in the meeting, namely, the approvals would draw complaints from local workforce in the "relevant" field. As explained above the perceived concern has no ground under the context and circumstances of our applications. We want to put on record this stance of ours above is not refuted by you in the meeting. It is also worth mentioning the timing of refusal and notification of reason for refusal (summary of events as outlined in the letter handed to you in the meeting) has denied us the opportunity of a fair hearing, in terms of time and substance, and this is a serious procedural impropriety."

21. The letter contained further information regarding the individuals' roles in the shows:

"Lighting (Chia Hwa Tsai):

1. Based on the special design & content of show programs, and the venue's lighting conditions, to design the special lighting plot, and supervise the installation & adjustment on site according to the design;

2. During the show, following the dance and music changes in the programs, control all the changes in lighting to make every action on stage in agreement with their meaning and design.

All these need to have:

1) Special technical skills in lighting, show production knowledge;

2) Special deep understanding of every program of Shen Yun shows, from dance to music in detail, from the meaning to the artistic formality.

Audio Engineer (Yu Deng):

1. Based on the special design & content of show programs, and the venue's sound conditions, to design the special sound control setup, and supervise the installation & adjustment on site according to the design;

2. During the show, following the dance and music changes in the programs, control all the changes in sound to make every action on stage in agreement with their meaning and design.

All these need to have:

1) Special technical skills in lighting, show production knowledge;

2) Special deep understanding of every program in the show, from dance to music in detail, from the meaning to the artistic formality.

Projection Engineer: (Ai Ni Li)

1. Based on the special design & content of show programs, to design the detail projection contents;

2. On site, to install projection equipment and adjust the quality of projection;

3. During the show, following the dance and music changes in the programs, control all the changes on projection to make every action on stage in agreement with their meaning and design.

All these need to have:

1) Special technical skills in projection, show production knowledge;

2) Special deep understanding of every program in the show, from dance to music in detail, from the meaning to the artistic formality.

Mr. Mark Simon Abbott/Brian Nieh/Minye Liu: their major roles are dancers for Shen Yun shows. They help production staff as assistant only during the setup period before the show. As dancers for Shen Yun show, they need to perform on stage."

22. On the following day (22 January 2010), the applicant supplied to the Director further reasons in support of the request for reconsideration:

"Dancer cum technical assistants (3 numbers) –

1 Immigration Department asked us for clarification on 4th January 2010 on the break down of work for these applicants for the two posts. We clarified they are full time dancers. They help production staff as assistant only during the setup period before the show. They are therefore no different from other full time dancers and these dancers are all approved. The fact that they perform additional post should not jeopardize their position in terms of meeting approval criteria.

Company Manager and Projection, Audio, Lighting Engineers and personnels (4 #) –

2 These are key personnels who are on long term commitment with Shen Yun Performing Arts and deeply involved in the production, training, rehearsal, co-ordinating, co-operating and synchronizing during the preparation and during the performance of the shows with other members of the group, including all the Artists. They are all of high skill and are specialist and their skills and experience are not available in Hong Kong. Even if they were available, it is impossible to replace them in Hong Kong because it is impossible for them, during the brief stay of the Arts Group in Hong Kong of only ten days, to go through the long term process described above for the purpose of putting up the show in Hong Kong. Therefore your rationale for refusal should not apply to these personnels."

23. On the same day, the Director maintained his refusals upon reconsideration. In each of the letters informing the applicant of the results, the Director wrote:

"After careful reconsideration of all information made available and circumstances of the case, we cannot find a reason or justification for reversing our decision. The decision previously conveyed to you on 21 January 2010 still stands."

24. In other words, no additional reasons were given for maintaining the refusals.

25. The internal minutes of the Immigration Department simply noted the grounds for the initial refusals and the additional information/documents submitted in support of the request for reconsideration, and stated that "on the basis of the available information and documents, there is no justification for us to grant entry/employment visa to the applicant". According to the minutes, "there is no change in substance of the application which warrants a reversal of our previous decision."

26. As mentioned, there was a request for a second reconsideration. It was made on 22 January 2010. No fresh material was supplied in support of the second request. It was refused on the following day. The letters of refusal, all identical in content, stated that the Director could not find any reason or justification for reversing his earlier decisions. The internal minutes relating to each application also stated that there was no change in substance of the application which would warrant a reversal of the previous decision.

27. In the evidence filed in these proceedings, what was said at the meeting held on 21 January 2010, when the initial refusals were conveyed to the applicant's representatives, was recounted:

"(a) Mr. Au Yeung explained to the four representatives of the Applicant that the reasons for refusal of the applications of the said 7 applicants were because of their failure to meet the eligibility criteria for entry to Hong Kong for employment under the GEP, which required, *inter alia*, that the applicant should possess a special skill, knowledge or experience of value to and not readily available in the HKSAR.

(b) Mr. Au Yeung also explained that other criteria to be considered include whether the job can be filled locally. Mr. Au Yeung said that in processing entry applications for taking up employment in Hong Kong under the GEP, ImmD had to strike a proper balance between bringing in talent and professional to Hong Kong and protecting the local labour market. ...

(c) At the said meeting, Mr. Au Yeung lastly told the four representatives of the Applicant that it was after careful consideration of:– (i) all the relevant information made available to the Director at the material time, and (ii) all the relevant circumstances of the case that the decisions to refuse the applications of the said 7 applicants were made on ground that the 7 applicants could not prove to the satisfaction of ImmD that they possessed a special skill, knowledge or experience of value to and not readily available in Hong Kong."

(Affirmation of Fung Kit Wa dated 8 July 2010, para 27)

28. In relation to the first reconsideration, the evidence filed on behalf of the Director stated:

"33. The decisions to refuse all the 6 applications were maintained upon reconsideration because Mr. Au Yeung was not satisfied that they met the eligibility criteria for entry to Hong Kong for employment under the GEP. ···

34. According to the said 6 sets of file minutes M3 and M4 dated 22 January 2010, Mr. Au Yeung was of the view, common to all 6 cases, that, notwithstanding the supplementary information submitted as referred to in paragraphs 28–30 above, there was no change in substance of the application which warrant a reversal of the previous decisions. Indeed, in three cases, the latest submission that the persons were "full time dancers" had also cast doubts on the earlier claims made by the Applicants (please also see paragraph 41 below). Therefore, the refusal decisions were maintained."

(Affirmation of Chan Shiu Keung Ellis dated 8 July 2010)

29. As regards the second reconsideration, the evidence filed on behalf of the Director read:

"38. The decisions to refuse all the 6 applications were upheld upon the 2nd reconsideration because the Director was not satisfied that they met the eligibility criteria for entry to Hong Kong for employment under the GEP. ···

39. According to the said 6 sets of file minutes M.2 and M.3 dated 23 January 2010 and M.4 dated 24 January 2010, I held the view, common to all 6 cases, that, notwithstanding the documents submitted as referred to in paragraphs 35 and 36 above, there was no change in substance of the application which warrant a reversal of the previous decision. Therefore, I decided to maintain the refusal of the applications."

(Affirmation of Chan Shiu Keung Ellis dated 8 July 2010)

Counsel's arguments

30. Mr Paul Harris SC, appearing for the applicant, submits, in relation to the first two grounds of challenge, that the nature of a touring performing dance troupe is that its members rehearse together before they arrive at their tour destination.

The jobs of those who rehearse together cannot realistically be filled by recruiting replacements locally when they arrive for their tours, nor by sending Hong Kong recruits to rehearse with them overseas. The knowledge of the performance which the performing troupe has is the collective knowledge required to produce a properly choreographed performance. Senior counsel emphasises that these points are so obvious that they do not really need spelling out, but they were in fact set out in relation to Shen Yun and the present case in the letters referred to above. Mr Harris also stresses that the Director was aware that the troupe had very few production staff and that, by refusing those individuals whom he refused, he was depriving the troupe of its entire production staff except the production manager.

31. Mr Harris argues that the decision to refuse all production staff except the production manager on the ground that they can be replaced by local recruits, ignores the simple but obvious fact that being able to operate the lighting, sound effect or backdrop for a stage event is not just a matter of knowing how to operate them, but is also a matter of knowing when to operate them. Knowing when to operate them, it is said, can only be achieved by rehearsing together with the dancers and knowing extremely well the sequences of the performances they are to perform. Mr Harris also submits that the Director has drawn no distinction whatsoever between a person seeking entry for residence in Hong Kong for employment purposes and a person seeking to visit for a few days as a member of a visiting arts troupe. No account has been taken of the special characteristics of visiting performing arts troupes, including in particular the short duration of their stay in Hong Kong and their need to rehearse together as a group before arrival in Hong Kong.

32. Mr Harris therefore argues that the refusals were irrational and the Director has failed to have regard to all relevant considerations.

33. As regards the third ground of challenge (inadequate reasons), Mr Harris argues that the stated reasons (not the reasons set out in the internal minutes) were not really reasons but just mere statements of the applicable policy. They were unhelpful and deprived the applicant of a meaningful reconsideration by the Director of the initial refusals.

34. Mr Johnny Mok SC, for the Director, argues that the Director has a wide discretion to exercise, and the courts, in accordance with the relevant case law, do not lightly interfere with either his policy or his exercise of discretion in accordance with his policy. Mr Mok submits that unless the Director's decisions can be described as perverse, they should not be disturbed. He accepts that in relation to members of a performing group, the eligibility criteria set out in the relevant guidebook have to be applied flexibly, particularly in relation to those performing on stage. However, in relation to the production staff, counsel argues that the Director's decisions cannot be challenged as being perverse. In his written submissions, Mr Mok has also drawn attention to various unsatisfactory aspects in relation to the materials submitted by the individuals in support of their applications.

35. As regards reasons, Mr Mok's fundamental point is that in immigration matters, the Director is, as a matter of law, not obliged to give any reasons at all for his decisions. If he is minded to give reasons, he is not obliged to reveal all the reasons. He can give some reasons and withhold others. Mr Mok relies on *Chu Woan Chyi v Director of Immigration* HCAL 32/2003, 23 March 2007, Hartmann J, paras 60 to 71 (and the cases cited therein) in support of his propositions.

General principles

36. It is of course true, as this Court has recently reiterated in *MA v Director of Immigration* HCAL 10/2010, 6 January 2011, a case relied on by Mr Mok, that generally speaking, the courts will not lightly interfere with the Director's policies or exercise of discretion. The courts recognise that in the light of Hong Kong's small geographical size, huge population, substantial daily intake of immigrants from the Mainland, and relatively high per capita income and living standards, and given Hong Kong's local living and job market conditions, almost inevitably Hong Kong (through the Director) has to adopt very restrictive and tough immigration policies and practices. This approach reflects not only the general limitation on the courts' supervisory jurisdiction under conventional public law, but also represents an acknowledgment on the part of the courts that the legislature has entrusted the Director with very wide discretions in performing the unenviable task of manning Hong Kong's immigration controls. Further still, the courts recognise that under the Basic Law, it is the executive which has been given the right and the responsibility to administer the affairs in Hong Kong generally. Article 154(2) of the Basic Law specifically authorises the Government to apply immigration controls on entry into, stay in and departure from Hong Kong by persons from foreign states and regions. The role to be played by the courts is essentially supervisory in nature. See paragraph 97 of the judgment.

37. All this, however, does not mean that the decisions of the Director are beyond the control of the courts. Within bounds, the Director is free to exercise his various powers and discretions as he and his officers see fit. Nonetheless, general principles of public law still govern the Director's decisions and decision-making process, just as they govern those of other decision-makers.

38. In particular, in making a decision, the Director has to take into account all relevant considerations and disregard all those that are not relevant. His decision must not be unreasonable (in the public law sense), perverse, irrational, arbitrary or unlawful, nor can it be motivated by bad faith.

39. Moreover, the decision-making process must be fair. In its classic formulation, unreasonableness in the public law sense, or *Wednesbury* unreasonableness, refers to a decision that is so unreasonable that no reasonable authority could ever come to it: *Associated Provincial Picture Houses Limited v Wednesbury Corporation* [1948] 1 KB 223, 229 to 230. There have been recent attempts to reformulate the *Wednesbury* unreasonableness test which it is not necessary in this judgment to go into: see *de Smith's Judicial Review* (6th ed) paras 11-018 to 11-024 and in particular, para 11-024.

40. There is no objection to a decision-maker, who is entrusted with wide discretions, to formulate and apply guidelines in relation to how he would exercise his discretions: *Wise Union Industries Ltd v Hong Kong Science and Technology Parks Corp* [2009] 5 HKLRD 620, paras 31 to 33 and the authorities cited therein. However, the decision-maker must not fetter his discretion. Describing the last point from a different perspective, when a decision-maker allows his guidelines to blind him from matters and circumstances which he ought to have regard to before deciding how to exercise his discretion, he fails to take into account all relevant considerations. Guidelines are what they are. They constitute "guidance and not tramlines": *R v Wakefield Metropolitan District Council, ex parte Pearl Assurance Plc* [1997] EWHC (Admin) 228, para 9, per Jowitt J. They must not be allowed

to preclude the decision-maker from departing from them or from taking into account relevant circumstances and merits of the case in question.

Applying the principles to the facts

41. Bearing these general principles in mind, I would approach the issues raised in these proceedings as follows.

42. It is plain that the Director's guidelines governing entry for employment as professionals in Hong Kong (the GEP scheme) are ill-suited to deal with applications for entry by members of a travelling performing group to perform in Hong Kong for a short duration only. Unquestionably, the guidelines are directed at those who wish to seek the Director's permission to enter and stay in Hong Kong for the purposes of taking up employment or otherwise working here as professionals. After all, GEP, it should be recalled, stands for "General Employment Policy". Thus the guidelines refer to the applicant's possessing "special skill, knowledge or experience of value to and not readily available in the HKSAR". They require the applicant to have a "good education background" or, in special circumstances, "good technical qualifications, proven professional abilities and/or relevant experience and achievements supported by documentary evidence". More importantly, one needs to demonstrate that "there is a genuine job vacancy" in Hong Kong and the applicant has to have a confirmed offer of employment and is employed in a job "that cannot be readily taken up by the local work force". Moreover, the applicant's remuneration package has to be "broadly commensurate with the prevailing market level for professionals in the HKSAR".

43. All this makes perfect sense when one has in mind an applicant seeking permission to come to Hong Kong to reside and work for a local employer. But the requirements become inapposite when one is concerned with, for instance, a pop music band, a singing group, a ballet company or a professional football team from overseas seeking permission to come to Hong Kong to give one or several performances during a short period of stay, or, as the case may be, to take part in a football tournament. It is, in those cases, not quite meaningful to speak in terms of whether the visa applicant really possesses special skills, knowledge or experience of value to and not readily available in Hong Kong; neither is it quite sensible to ask whether what he or she seeks to do in Hong Kong "cannot be readily taken up by the local work force". Nor does it make sense to compare his remuneration for his performances in Hong Kong with that offered to local artists, or, football players.

44. Carried to extreme, the guidelines would mean that unless, for instance, a violinist in an overseas orchestra is of such skill and experience that is not readily available in Hong Kong, he could not be allowed in as a member of an orchestra invited to perform in Hong Kong for one or two nights. Likewise, unless an overseas footballer can demonstrate that his skills are superior to that of all footballers in Hong Kong, he cannot be allowed in as a team member of his club invited to come to Hong Kong to participate in an international tournament or a friendly match. These (hypothetical) examples can be easily multiplied.

45. Fortunately, none of these happen in real life. In practice, and this has been confirmed by Mr Mok, this is not how the Director or his officers would apply his guidelines. Apparently, the Director recognises the self-evident value of cultural and artistic exchanges and international sports activities, and, according to Mr Mok, the Director applies commonsense in applying and adopting his guidelines when dealing with the sort of application just described. Take the present case as an example. The fact that all the dancers and musicians belonging to Shen Yun have been given entry visas does not mean that in the Director's view, they or anyone of them necessarily possesses "special skills, knowledge or experience of value to and not readily available in the HKSAR". The Director was not saying, when granting the visas, that he had been satisfied that no other local dancers or musicians in Hong Kong could dance or play their instruments as good as these overseas dancers and musicians after rehearsal. The Director recognised, counsel submits, that he was dealing with applications by members of a dance troupe from overseas, which had been invited to come to Hong Kong to give 7 shows only. He understood that after the shows, the entire group would depart Hong Kong, none of its members would stay behind to work here, and during their short stay in Hong Kong (planned for 10 days only), none of them would work in Hong Kong other than to give the shows.

46. In my view, this is the correct approach to take. As I see it, first, there is no obligation on the part of the Director to devise a separate scheme or category of visitors to specially cater for visiting performing groups and their members, or for that matter, visiting sports teams. Whilst it is desirable to have guidelines in the case of wide discretion, it remains a matter for the decision-maker to decide whether he should have guidelines.

47. Secondly, a court cannot force the Director to have guidelines, still less can it tell the Director what the content of the guidelines should be.

48. Thirdly, it is perfectly legitimate for the Director, in the absence of specific guidelines to deal with a particular category of visa applicants, to process each application on its individual merits. He need not force the application into any existing categories and apply guidelines designed for those categories to the application.

49. Fourthly, if the Director chooses to decide the visa application on its own merits without forcing it into any exiting categories, he must of course take into account all relevant considerations and disregard all those that are not relevant. Amongst the relevant considerations that should be taken into account are two that merit specific mention on the facts of the present case. First, the distinct value of cultural and artistic exchanges and activities (and international sports activities) to society generally, a matter not disputed by counsel. Second, the unique fact that the individual visa applicant is, unlike any other individual employment visa applicant, actually applying to come in as member of a visiting cultural or arts performing group (or sports team) invited to Hong Kong to perform or otherwise take part in a cultural or artistic (or sports) activity or exchange for a very short duration of time. Each visa applicant is and forms part of the whole, and the whole is more than the sum of its parts.

50. Fifthly, if, on the other hand, the Director chooses to apply guidelines or criteria designed for some broad category of application to the visa application, he must take care in applying those guidelines or criteria, lest he may apply them too rigidly, resulting in his failing to take into account considerations that are relevant and peculiar to the type of application in question, or in his taking into account considerations that are not relevant. In particular, he must not allow those guidelines or criteria to blind him from or otherwise obscure the two considerations specifically mentioned in the preceding paragraph.

51. In my view, the whole case essentially turns on this last point.

Discussion on the facts

52. As described, the Director has applied his relevant GEP guidelines to the 87 dancers, musicians and other miscellaneous stage personnel whose applications he has approved sensibly and flexibly in accordance with the last point made. As Mr Mok puts it, the Director did not require these 87 members to seriously prove that their artistic or musical skills were such that they were not readily available in Hong Kong. The Director recognised that they were coming in as a dance troupe, and they were to dance in Hong Kong onstage as a group or to play the relevant music accompanying the dances as musicians forming part of the group. The fact that there may be (or may well be) local dancers or musicians who after rehearsal can dance or play their instruments as well as, or even better than, those dancers and musicians from Shen Yun, would be quite beside the point. I have no difficulty with the Director's approach in relation to these dancers and musicians whatsoever.

53. However, when it comes to the backstage or production personnel of Shen Yun, the Director has apparently lost sight of this important point.

54. In this regard, it is important to remember that a group is a group. Whilst there are, by definition, different roles to be played by different members and naturally there would be a division of labour amongst members of the same group, they together make up and form the group. Moreover, as mentioned, the whole is more than merely the sum of its parts. It is as incongruous as it is impertinent for a local organiser to just invite part of the group to come to Hong Kong to perform on the ground that the rest of the group can be replaced by locals, and in any event, one wonders how many travelling performing groups of any reputation would be prepared to accept such an invitation. Given the essential character of a group, what is important is not so much whether an individual member's role can be readily taken over by an outsider, but rather whether the role in question forms an integral part of the group or its performance.

55. In my view, therefore, the considerations that apply to stage performers and musicians comprising the performing group apply similarly to backstage or production personnel of the group who play an integral role in the group or its performance. I have used the word "integral" here because certainly, there may be jobs within the performing group that can be easily done by anyone without affecting materially the integrity of the group as such. If a group employs a tea lady to serve refreshments to its members, then in all but the most exceptional of cases, one would not consider the tea lady as somebody other than of peripheral significance to the group, and the Director would be quite entitled to consider her application for entry accordingly. A more marginal case would be a cook employed by the group. Depending on the facts, the Director would have to make up his mind as to how he should exercise his discretion and what considerations are relevant and what are not.

56. Illustrating my point further, assume one has an overseas football club invited to come to Hong Kong to participate in a tournament, and the club wishes to bring in not only the footballers, the manager and the coach, but also its medical doctor, physiotherapist, masseur, cook and accountant (to handle the gate receipts), it would be up to the Director to decide, amongst other things, whether any of these individuals perform an integral role in the football club even though they do not play on the field, or whether he or she just plays a peripheral role in the club, and decide the applications for entry accordingly.

57. There can be no hard and fast rule. But one thing is clear. The Director has to bear in mind all considerations that are relevant, including the two that have been specifically mentioned in the preceding section of this judgment, and should ignore all those that are not. Moreover, if he applies guidelines that are meant for a broad or even different category to the applications in question, he must be careful in doing so, lest he may ignore some relevant considerations or take into account others that are irrelevant. What he should not do, reverting to the examples given above, is to reject the applications simply on the ground that there is an abundant supply of qualified medical doctors, physiotherapists, masseurs, chefs and accountants in Hong Kong, just as he should not refuse the entry of the goalkeeper or reserve goalkeeper of the foreign club to Hong Kong on the ground that there are many excellent local goalkeepers available to play for the team in the relevant games. To do so would be to miss entirely the point of having an international sports event in the first place. In my view, the same considerations apply to an international cultural event.

58. Whether a member plays an integral or peripheral production role in the group is a matter for the Director to decide. In accordance with general principles, the Court would not lightly interfere with any such decision. However, in deciding that question, one does not focus on whether the individual's job can be filled by local people. That is not the focus. The focal point here is whether, to the group, the individual performs an integral role and carries out production duties important to the performance in question, in whom the group reposes trust and confidence. To ignore such a question or to focus on whether the role or duties could be readily filled locally is to fail to take the relevant consideration into account.

59. In this regard, the group's own assessment and belief must be given due weight.

60. Furthermore, where, as here, the performing group informs the Director that the individual has been involved in rigorous rehearsals with the rest of the group, that must be a highly relevant matter to bear in mind in assessing whether the individual plays an integral production role important to the performance, regardless of whether his duties, skill or knowledge can be readily filled or matched by some local people.

61. I am, of course, restricting the Court's reasoning and observations here to the situation where a performing group is invited by some local promoter to come to Hong Kong to perform over a short duration only.

The production personnel

62. The problem with the Director's decisions in relation to the applications of the 3 production personnel involved in the present case (namely, Mr Deng, Mr Tsai and Ms Li) is that he has apparently focused on the wrong questions. I will not repeat the reasons given by the Director's officers in the letters of refusal, or the more detailed reasons set out in the internal minutes, or the relevant part of the evidence that has been given on his behalf in these proceedings. They have been set out in the earlier part of this judgment. It is plain from those materials that the Director has throughout concentrated on whether the 3 production personnel "possess a special skill, knowledge or experience of value to and not readily available in the HKSAR"; and "whether the job can be filled locally and whether it is justified for the employer to bring in an expatriate staff". These were the reasons given in the letters of refusal of 21 January 2010. For reasons given above, these were questions that did not quite address the specific characteristics of a visiting performing group and its

members, in the context of their seeking permission to come to Hong Kong to give a few shows. These questions overlooked and indeed obscured the much more pertinent question of whether the individual visa applicant played an integral production role in the performances of Shen Yun and his or her application should, therefore, like that of the dancers, be favourably considered, or whether the individual merely played a peripheral role in the shows. In this regard, the subjective assessment of Shen Yun itself must carry significant weight. Just as in the case of an overseas orchestra, where one does not ask whether there are no violinists or cymbals players in Hong Kong who are skilful and experienced enough and are readily available to replace any of the violinists or the cymbals player employed in the orchestra, one should not, in the present context, be bogged down by whether a production member's duties cannot be competently performed by a local person.

63. The more detailed reasons revealed in the internal minutes suffered from the same focusing problem. They spoke of whether "the knowledge, experience and skills" required for the job were not "readily available in Hong Kong", and whether there was a "lack of local supply" of technical staff to replace the individuals in question. In the evidence filed, it is clear that the oral explanations given to the applicant on 21 January 2010 again centred on whether the individuals' jobs could be "filled locally" and whether they possessed "a special skill, knowledge or experience of value to and not readily available in Hong Kong". The evidence also explained that "the Director was not satisfied that [the individuals] met the eligibility criteria for entry to Hong Kong for employment under the GEP", and he therefore decided to maintain the refusals in the two reconsiderations.

64. In short, the Director ought to have considered, in each application, whether the individual concerned played an integral production role in the performances of Shen Yun, and in this regard, he ought to have given Shen Yun's own assessment its proper and due weight; and if the answer was in the affirmative, the Director ought to have taken that consideration seriously into account, together with the fact that he was dealing with a performance group seeking to come to Hong Kong to perform in a few shows only, when deciding whether he should allow the individual concerned to come to Hong Kong for that particular purpose only. He should, of course, also bear in mind, amongst other considerations, the general value of cultural and artistic activities and exchanges.

65. In the present case, at least according to Shen Yun and the applicant, the lighting and sound personnel were of essential significance to the shows that Shen Yun was invited to perform in Hong Kong. Amongst other things, they were required, during the show, to follow the dance and music changes in the programmes and control all the changes in lighting and sound to make every action on stage in agreement with their meaning and design. In other words, as Mr Harris has put it, it was not simply a matter of being able to operate the lighting, sound effects or backdrop, but also a matter of knowing when to operate them, and that knowing when to operate them could only be achieved by rehearsing together with the dancers and knowing extremely well the sequences of the performances they were to perform.

66. The internal minutes show that the Director's officers paid very little attention and gave almost no weight to the information and clarification supplied by the applicant after the initial refusals regarding the various roles that the individuals in question were to play in the shows. Rather, the officers treated them as "bare assertions" from the applicant. In my view, clarification coming straight from Shen Yun (through the applicant), the very performing group in question, could not be regarded simply as bare assertions. In the absence of any suggestion that Shen Yun is anything other than a genuine and reputable dance group with an impressive record (or that the applicant has misrepresented any matter relating to Shen Yun), the officers should have given the clarification and explanations from Shen Yun their due weight. They could not be ignored as such.

67. It is to be remembered that of the 93 applications made, apart from one production manager, the 6 individuals involved were the only people involved in the production side of the shows. In particular, Mr Deng, Mr Tsai and Ms Li were the only full time production personnel of Shen Yun who were applying for entry. This fact alone would tend to suggest that their roles in the performances were of some significance.

68. In my view, the Director and his officers have, unfortunately, allowed themselves to be bogged down in the eligibility criteria under the GEP guidelines, which, as mentioned, are not primarily designed to deal with visiting performing groups, when deciding the applications of the 3 production personnel.

69. It is true that in the internal minutes, the Director's officers doubted Ms Li's claimed qualifications and experience. In itself, that was a valid consideration that the Director was fully entitled to take into account. However, this fact alone does not detract from the fact that in determining Ms Li's application for entry, the Director had focused on the wrong questions. It is not the Director's case in these proceedings that irrespective of the focusing problem, the application of Ms Li was doomed to fail because of the doubt over her qualifications and experience. After all, Shen Yun has itself written in to confirm that Ms Li has taken part in over 100 shows as its projection engineer. Perhaps more telling is the fact that this doubt over Ms Li's qualifications and experience did not even feature in the letter of refusal as a reason, let alone a primary one, for rejecting her application for entry.

70. For similar reasons, although Mr Mok has in his written submissions referred to various doubts over the respective qualifications and experiences of the 3 production individuals involved, with the exception of Ms Li's case, none of the doubts featured in the initial refusals, the internal minutes or the evidence filed in these proceedings, as reasons for rejecting the individuals' applications. Whilst I fully accept that the Director was entitled to take them into account, and one should proceed on the assumption that the Director did take those doubts into account, this does not, at the end of the day, make any difference to the result, given the serious focusing problem that the decision-making process suffered from.

The dancers with dual role

71. As regards the 3 dancers with dual role, in essence, the Director refused their applications on the ground that their production duties could be readily taken up by local technical staff. In the minutes, a further reason was mentioned, which was not stated in the refusal letters, namely, that the Director was not satisfied that the 3 individuals would be capable of performing their dual role.

72. As to this last point, I believe it has been sufficiently addressed in the information supplied after the initial refusals. As mentioned above, it was clarified that the individuals were full time dancers, they would only help production staff as assistants during the set up period before the shows. During the shows, they would be no different from other full time dancers.

The clarification by Shen Yun (through the applicant) should, for reasons explained, have been given due consideration.

73. In my view, putting aside their separate roles as dancers, the Director was perfectly entitled not to be satisfied that the 3 individuals played anything other than a peripheral production role in the shows. Indeed, this is quite plain from the applicant's own clarification supplied after the initial refusals.

74. However, this is not the end of the matter. This is because the 3 individuals also applied to come in as full time dancers during the shows. This part of their duties in the group could not be brushed aside without considering whether they really were full time dancers in the shows, and therefore played integral roles in the shows as stage performers, just like the other dancers and musicians who were all allowed in. The fact that they, if allowed to, would also perform some peripheral production duties that could be filled by others, does not detract from the fact that they were applying to come in also as full time dancers playing integral stage roles. I see nothing in the doubt as to whether one of them (Mr Brian Nieh) was a "lead dancer" – a claim made in the materials supplied after the initial refusal. Irrespective of whether he was a lead dancer or not, there is no suggestion that he was not a dancer to perform in the shows. It has to be remembered that all the dancers, whether they be lead dancers or supporting dancers, were allowed in. The same rationale must apply to these 3 individuals.

75. It would have been perfectly open to the Director to impose a condition to allowing these 3 individuals' entry to the effect that they could not perform any production role whether before, during or after the shows. Or, put the other way, they could only come in as dancers. However, it is plain from the refusal letters, the internal minutes and the evidence filed in these proceedings that this option was never considered by the Director or his officers.

76. For these reasons, unfortunately, I take the view that the Director and his officers have failed to take into account relevant considerations.

Conclusion

77. It would not lie in the mouth of the Director, and I hasten to add that it is not the case of the Director, that the individuals concerned had applied under the wrong scheme and therefore had themselves to blame when the Director applied the eligibility criteria under the GEP scheme to their cases.

78. As mentioned, there was no other applicable scheme under which the applicants could have made their applications. The GEP scheme is the normal scheme under which performing groups apply for entry visas. Moreover, there have been many contacts between the applicant and the Director's officers, in none of which it was ever suggested that the individuals were applying under the wrong scheme or there was a more suitable scheme or category under which they could make their applications. Nor is that suggested in the evidence filed in these proceedings.

79. For the reasons given above, the Director's decisions are challengeable and prima facie, they should be quashed. I recognise that the decisions related to a one-off event, but that alone, on the facts of the present case, is an insufficient reason not to quash the decisions. Mr Mok has not contended otherwise.

Adequacy of reasons

80. Given my conclusion, I do not need to go into the question of adequacy of reasons. As mentioned, Mr Mok has argued, by reference to authorities, that the Director is under no duty to give any reasons for his refusals. And if he decides to give some reasons, he is not obliged to provide all reasons. Mr Mok accepts that this does not mean that the Director need not have any or any proper reasons for his decisions: *Chu Woan Chyi v Director of Immigration* [2009] 6 HKC 77, para 16.

81. To put the argument in context, it has been Mr Harris' argument that the initial refusals only gave fairly general reasons that were nothing more than a recitation of the eligibility criteria in the guidelines. No substantive reasons were supplied. The more substantive reasons, counsel argued, were only found in the internal minutes and in the evidence filed in these proceedings.

82. I recognise the force of the authorities relied on by Mr Mok Although I can readily see some potential distinctions between the situations faced by the courts in these authorities and the instant type of situation, I have not heard detailed arguments on them and the possible distinctions that one may make. Given my conclusion above, it is quite unnecessary to rely on the present ground of challenge to decide this case. In those circumstances, I do not propose to address further the relevant law here, or to rely on the present ground in support of the conclusion that I have already reached.

Delay

83. That leaves two further grounds of challenge, namely delay and article 34 of the Basic Law.

84. In relation to delay, all I would say is that it is unnecessary for the Court to rely on this ground in support of its conclusion. It is a highly fact–sensitive point. I note from the evidence that the Director's officers had been most helpful in relation to the applicant's applications, and many documents and information had indeed come late. The Director was faced with a sizable number of applications, and had a practical deadline to meet.

85. I do not think this question of delay or alleged delay would by itself be sufficient to found a case against the Director.

Article 34

86. Finally, as regards article 34, I am, for the following reasons, reluctant to base my decision on this ground or to express any definite view on the article.

87. Article 34 has not been judicially interpreted. As Mr Harris submitted, one is on virgin territory. With due respect to counsel, the Court has only heard very general submissions on the true interpretation of the article. For his part, Mr Mok has argued that the article is not engaged at all because it does not give Hong Kong residents a constitutional right to any particular performance as such. The article would only be engaged if the Government were to, for instance, ban performing groups playing a particular type of music from visiting Hong Kong. On the other hand, Mr Harris has submitted that not only do Hong Kong residents have a right to cultural activities and performances in Hong Kong so that any interference with such a right would engage article 34 (subject to the proportionality test), but the Government also has a positive duty to facilitate residents to enjoy that right.

88. These are submissions of general significance. I am reluctant to go into these matters without the fullest assistance. It should also be noted that article 34 is not the only article in the Basic Law which touches on cultural activities. Articles 140, 144 and

149 may also have a bearing on the issues raised. The Court has heard no submissions on these other articles or their possible relationships with article 34.

89. Given my conclusion on the first two grounds of challenge, it is not necessary at all to go into article 34.

90. For these reasons, I do not base my decision on article 34, and I do not wish to express any view on it. Issues pertaining to the proper interpretation of article 34 and how the freedom guaranteed thereunder may possibly be restricted must await another day.

Oral application for cross–examination

91. During the hearing, Mr Harris made an oral application to cross–examine Ms Chan Shiu Keung Ellis, who had made several affidavits filed in these proceedings. Mr Harris wished to cross–examine Ms Chan on the reason why the relevant applications for entry were referred by the handling immigration officers to other Government departments for comment. Mr Harris wondered whether that was only done because of the Falun Gong background of the applicant or it was in accordance with general practice. The Court refused the application.

92. Very briefly, first, it was an extremely late application. It related to a matter which did not even form one of the grounds of challenge. It was a typical fishing expedition. The Court appreciated that the internal minutes of the Director had not been made available to the applicant when the present challenge was first mounted. But after its disclosure, the applicant could have taken out an interlocutory application for further discovery or even for leave to cross–examine Ms Chan. That was not done. It was simply too late for Mr Harris to attempt to do the same at the substantive hearing. (The Court is not, however, implying that if it had been made earlier, the application would have been granted.)

93. Secondly, as mentioned, the matter sought to be clarified by cross–examination had nothing to do with the pleaded grounds of challenge. At the substantive hearing, none of the grounds relied on had anything to do with the applicant's Falun Gong background, and the Court was not concerned with it, apart from regarding it as forming part of the general factual matrix of the case. As this judgment demonstrates, despite the Falun Gong background of the case, the issues raised and the Court's decision thereon have nothing to do with that background.

94. Thirdly, and in any event, it is clear from the eligibility criteria of the GEP scheme that one of the considerations that the Director, under his guidelines, takes into account is whether there is any security objection and known record of serious crime in respect of the person seeking entry. Therefore, on the face of it, the Director's referral of the applications to other departments for comment accorded perfectly well with this consideration.

95. For those reasons, the oral application was refused.

Outcome

96. For these reasons, the present application for judicial review is allowed to the extent that the Director's decisions refusing the 6 individuals' applications for permission to entry should be brought up and quashed. I so order.

97. This does not mean that if the Director had taken into account all relevant considerations and ignored all those that were not, the applications of the 6 individuals would necessarily have been successful. Nor does it mean that the Court would have lightly interfered with the Director's decisions if he had taken into account all relevant considerations and ignored all those that were not relevant.

98. As regards the applicant's claim for damages, as has been previously directed, it is to be dealt with separately, regarding which the parties are at liberty to seek further directions from the Court, if the matter is to be pursued. Amongst other things, the applicant would have to plead a good cause of action, establish causation and prove the quantum of its claim.

99. As regards costs, I make a costs order nisi that the respondent do pay to the applicant the costs of these proceedings, including all costs previously reserved, to be taxed if not agreed.

100. I thank counsel for their assistance.

Judge of the Court of First Instance of the High Court (Andrew Cheung)

Mr Paul Harris SC, instructed by Ho, Tse, Wai & Partners, for the applicant

Mr Johnny Mok SC, instructed by the Department of Justice, for the respondent

---

第三十五條

香港居民有權得到秘密法律諮詢、向法院提起訴訟、選擇律師及時保護自己的合法權益或在法庭上為其代理和獲得司法補救。

香港居民有權對行政部門和行政人員的行為向法院提起訴訟。

案例

"法院"的含義

證券監察委員會是否"法院"？

秘密法律諮詢的限制

濫用訴訟權利時的限制

選擇法律代表的權利是否絕對

Lam Siu Po v. Commissioner of Police

Lam Siu Po 對 警務處長

HCAL 7/2003；CACV 340/2005；FACV 9/2008

簡略案情

上訴人於 1988 年加入香港警隊。於 2000 年，因為股票市場投資失敗而欠下巨債，上訴人遂申請破產。2000 年 12 月，香港警務處以其違反《警察通例》第 6 章第 6-01（8）條（1999 年版），即“警務人員務必謹慎處理其個人財務。如不謹慎理財而導致嚴重財政困難，以致影響人員的工作效率，有關人員將因而遭受紀律處分。”向上訴人啟動了紀律聆訊。2001 年 3 月，該指控被裁定成立，並即時解除上訴人的職務。同年 8 月 9 日（約 5 個月後），警務處撤銷了原裁定，並下令就該指控重新聆訊。重新聆訊於 2001 年 12 月 14 日舉行，申請人在沒有律師代表的情況下於 2002 年 3 月 27 日被判有罪。原本的處罰為強制退休並押後發放退休金，緩期 12 個月執行。後來警務處卻將處罰加重為立即執行，因此，上訴人於 2002 年 10 月 23 日被強制退休。

上訴人於 2004 年 10 月申請司法覆核。他其中的一個申請理由是《警察（紀律）規例》第 232 章附屬法例 A 第 9（11）和（12）條規定違紀者只可選擇警務人員或具律師或大律師資格的警務人員代其進行辯護，限制了他選擇法律代表的自由，所以違反《基本法》第 35 條。上訴人認為在此條例裏，“法庭”的意思應被解釋為具有司法功能的審裁處。根據案件 *Dr. Ip Kay Lo Vincent v. Medical Council Of Hong Kong (No. 2)* [2003] 3 HKC 579 和 *A Solicitor v. The Law Society Of Hong Kong* CACV 302/2002，上訴庭皆認為《基本法》第 35 條中的“法庭”包括醫務委員會和律師紀律審裁組。答辯人反對此論點，認為警察紀律審裁小組身份特殊，組成人員基本非專業人士，不應視為第 35 條所述的“法院”。而且，根據《基本法》第 103 條，即“…… 香港原有關於公務人員的招聘、僱用、考核、紀律、培訓和管理的制度，包括負責公務人員的任用、薪金、服務條件的專門機構，除有關給予外籍人員特權待遇的規定外，予以保留。”該《警察（紀律）規例》在《基本法》實施前已經被執行，理應繼續有效。最後，原審法官駁回上訴人的申請。上訴人向上訴庭提出上訴。

上訴庭援引終審法院案例 *The Stock Exchange Of Hong Kong Ltd. v. New World Development Co. Ltd. & Others* [2006] 9 HKCFAR 234，認為並非任何面對嚴重紀律後果的人也有絕對的權利得到全面的法律代表。對於上訴人依賴《香港人權法案條例》第 10 條（被《基本法》第 39 條確認）支持其受到不平等限制的新論據，法院認為在本案中上訴人於聆訊中有否法律代表，結果也將是一樣，因此，否定了他因不平等限制而導致聆訊出現不利後果的主張，拒絕了他的上訴。但上訴庭最後亦批准上訴人就他們的裁決上訴至終審法院。

裁決摘要

根據之前同是終審法院案件 *New World Development Co. Ltd.* 的判詞，終審法院重申確認《基本法》第 35 條內"法庭"一詞的意思僅包括那些具"司法能力"的個體，並非如上訴人所堅持的包括紀律審裁組織，所以，《基本法》第 35 條在本案中並不適用。可是，終審法院也認為 *Chan Keng Chau v. Commissioner Of Police* HCMP 2824/2004 裁定《香港人權法案條例》第 10 條不適用於紀律聆訊亦是誤判，尤其是當指控成立時，上訴人很可能會被解僱，從而影響了他的公民權利和義務，所以，該案例應予推翻。上訴人的工作效率有否受影響也是控罪的重要部份，如果上訴人不是被不公平地剝奪了法律代表的權利，對他的指控很有可能不成立。而且，法院亦考慮到如果給予上訴人法律代表的權利，並不會影響警隊的運作，因此，本案案情跟 *New World Development Co. Ltd.* 一案有明顯分別，沒有客觀的原因要排除他行使這個憲法上的權利。據此，法院一致裁定上訴得直，強制退休決定被取消。

FACV No. 9 of 2008

IN THE COURT OF FINAL APPEAL OF THE HONG KONG SPECIAL ADMINISTRATIVE REGION

FINAL APPEAL NO. 9 OF 2008 (Civil)
(ON APPEAL FROM CACV No. 340 of 2005)

Between:

LAM SIU PO — Appellant

- and -

COMMISSIONER OF POLICE — Respondent

Court: Chief Justice Li, Mr Justice Bokhary PJ, Mr Justice Chan PJ, Mr Justice Ribeiro PJ and Lord Woolf NPJ

Dates of Hearing: 10-11 March 2009

Date of Judgment: 26 March 2009

JUDGMENT

Chief Justice Li:

1. I agree with the judgment of Mr Justice Ribeiro PJ.

Mr Justice Bokhary PJ:

2. There can be circumstances in which a hearing would be unfair if legal representation (by which I mean representation by a legal practitioner) is not permitted. The natural expectation is that if and when such unfairness occurs, the courts would provide a remedy to redress the consequences of that unfairness. But what if there appears to be a statutory provision by which legal representation is barred at hearings of the type concerned?

Provision barring legal representation

3. The validity of a statutory bar to legal representation is under challenge in the present case. It is contained in subsidiary legislation, being the one to be found in regulation 9(11) and (12) of the Police (Discipline) Regulations made by the Chief Executive in Council under the regulation-making power conferred by s.45 of the Police Force Ordinance, Cap.232. I will refer to it as "the reg.9(11) and (12) bar". Regulation 9 lays down the procedure to be followed when a defaulter (ie a police officer charged with a disciplinary offence) has pleaded not guilty. Paragraphs (11) and (12) of reg.9 read:

"(11) A defaulter may be represented by –

(a) an inspector or other junior police officer of his choice; or

(b) any other police officer of his choice who is qualified as a barrister or solicitor, who may conduct the defence on his behalf.

(12) Subject to paragraph (11), no barrister or solicitor may appear on behalf of the defaulter."

Material facts

4. Shortly stated, the material facts of the present case are as follows. The appellant, a police constable, engaged in stock market dealings. He lost heavily, found himself deeply in debt, petitioned for his own bankruptcy and was adjudicated bankrupt in September 2000. Consequently he was charged in December that year with a disciplinary offence. It was the offence of contravening Police General Order 6–01(8) ("PGO 6–01(8)") which at that time read:

"A police officer shall be prudent in his financial affairs. Serious pecuniary embarrassment stemming from financial imprudence which leads to the impairment of an officer's operational efficiency will result in disciplinary action."

PGO 6–01(8) is one of the provisions of the Police General Orders made by the Commissioner of Police under the general order-making power conferred on him by s.46 of the Police Force Ordinance.

Conviction at disciplinary hearing

5. There were two disciplinary hearings. The first hearing ended in the appellant being convicted on 2 March 2001. But that conviction was set aside by the Force Discipline Officer for procedural irregularity. The police officer who had represented the appellant at the first hearing was not available at the second hearing, which commenced on 14 December 2001. That police officer was replaced by another defaulter's representative. But the appellant lost confidence in that replacement. And after being told that he could not engage a legal practitioner to defend him, the appellant appeared in person at the second hearing.

6. On 27 March 2002 the appellant was again convicted. The penalty imposed on him was compulsory retirement with deferred benefits. Originally the penalty was suspended for 12 months. But it was subsequently varied so as to come into earlier effect. Consequently the appellant was compulsorily retired from the Police Force on 23 October 2002 with deferred benefits.

Judicial review fails in the courts below

7. On 21 January 2003 the appellant took out an application for leave to bring judicial review proceedings for the quashing of the decisions by which he was convicted and compulsorily retired. He obtained leave to do so on certain grounds. Then he sought leave to do so on additional grounds as well. The proceedings for which leave had been granted and the application to apply on additional grounds as well were heard together. Both were dismissed with costs *nisi* by Chung J on 23 August 2005. Judgment was not given until that date even though the hearing had ended on 11 November 2004. That lack of expedition is to be contrasted with the expedition displayed when Tang VP delivered the judgment of the Court of Appeal (consisting of himself, Yeung JA and Yam J) on 8 November 2007 after hearing the appellant's appeal to them on the 2nd of that month. They dismissed that appeal with costs *nisi*. By the leave which they granted him, the appellant now appeals to us.

Appellant's argument

8. The argument presented by Prof. Johannes Chan SC for the appellant involves questions as to (i) the validity of the statutory bar against legal representation with which the appellant was confronted and (ii) the elements of the offence of which he was convicted. Shortly stated, the argument runs thus. First, the reg.9(11) and (12) bar is invalid. Secondly, the impairment of operational efficiency is an element of the offence under PGO 6-01(8). Thirdly, legal representation should have been permitted. Fourthly and finally, if the appellant had been legally represented, he might have been acquitted by reason

of the evidence as a whole being insufficient to prove that his operational efficiency had been impaired within the meaning of PGO 6-01(8). So there are four parts, so to speak, to the argument.

Vires

9. As I have pointed out, the first part of the argument consists of a challenge to the validity of the reg.9(11) and (12) bar. At first instance and in the appeal to the Court of Appeal, that challenge was made on two bases. These were that the reg.9(11) and (12) bar is (i) *ultra vires* as being beyond the regulation-making power conferred by s.45 of the Police Force Ordinance and (ii) inconsistent with art.10 of the Bill of Rights Not having pursued the *ultra vires* argument when applying for and obtaining the Court of Appeal's leave to appeal to us, the appellant did not include that argument in his printed case. As set out in his printed case, the challenge to the validity of the reg.9(11) and (12) bar rests solely on his submission that it is inconsistent with art.10 of the Bill of Rights. Nevertheless we have heard oral argument on the question of *vires*.

10. The regulation-making power concerned, namely the one conferred by s.45 of the Police Force Ordinance, is in extremely wide terms. It includes "power to make regulations providing for appropriate tribunals to inquire into disciplinary offences by [police officers below the rank of superintendent] and generally for the procedure in cases where [such an officer] is alleged to have committed any of the disciplinary offences specified in the regulations". Regulation 9 has always barred legal representation in defaulter proceedings. That bar was introduced in 1977 when it was provided by reg.9(11) that no barrister or solicitor may appear on behalf of a defaulter. In 1982 it was provided (or perhaps spelt out for the avoidance of doubt) that a defaulter may be represented by a police officer even if that police officer happens to be qualified as a barrister or solicitor. That is not equivalent to being represented by a legal practitioner. So it is not legal representation.

11. On the question of *vires*, Mr Anderson Chow SC for the respondent submits as follows. The *vires* of subsidiary legislation is to be determined by reference to the law as it stood at the time when the subsidiary legislation in question was made. And as the law stood in 1977 when it was first provided by reg.9 that no barrister or solicitor may appear on behalf of a defaulter, so providing by subsidiary legislation was permitted. That appears by the decisions of the English Court of Appeal in *Fraser v. Mudge* [1975] 1 WLR 1132 and *Maynard v. Osmond* [1977] 1 QB 240.

12. As to the common law's exposure to legislative modification in the absence of any entrenched guarantee against such modification, I do not think that the correctness of those decisions was doubted in Hong Kong in 1977, in 1982 or indeed at any time thereafter. Until the advent of the Bill of Rights in 1991 these things were seen in much the same way as they were seen in 1977. It is therefore necessary to turn to the Bill of Rights.

Article 10 of the Bill of Rights

13. Article 10 of Bill of Rights reads:

> "All persons shall be equal before the courts and tribunals. In the determination of any criminal charge against him, or of his rights and obligations in a suit at law, everyone shall be entitled to a fair and public hearing by a competent, independent and impartial tribunal established by law. The press and the public may be excluded from all or part of a trial for reasons of morals, public order (ordre public) or national security in a democratic society, or when the interest of the private lives of the parties so requires, or to the extent strictly necessary in the opinion of the court in special circumstances where publicity would prejudice the interests of justice; but any judgment rendered in a criminal case or in a suit at law shall be made public except where the interest of juvenile persons otherwise requires or the proceedings concern matrimonial disputes or the guardianship of children."

14. At first instance, the appellant had also relied on art.35 of our constitution the Basic Law, which article reads:

> "Hong Kong residents shall have the right to confidential legal advice, access to the courts, choice of lawyers for timely protection of their lawful rights and interests or for representation in the courts, and to judicial remedies.
>
> Hong Kong residents shall have the right to institute legal proceedings in the courts against the acts of the executive authorities and their personnel."

But when this case reached the Court of Appeal, the appellant abandoned his reliance on art.35 because we had by then held in *Stock Exchange of Hong Kong v. New World Development Co. Ltd.* (2006) 9 HKCFAR 234 that the reference to "the courts" in art.35 is a reference to the judiciary and nothing else.

Bill of Rights and the ICCPR

15. As is well established, the Bill of Rights is the embodiment of the application to Hong Kong of the International Covenant on Civil and Political Rights ("the ICCPR") from which it is taken almost verbatim. Consequently the Bill of Rights is – and has always been – entrenched. Today it is entrenched by art.39 of the Basic Law which provides, relevantly to present purposes, that the ICCPR as applied to Hong Kong shall remain in force and that the rights and freedoms thereunder may not be restricted. The Bill of Rights was introduced by the Hong Kong Bill of Rights Ordinance, Cap.383, which came into effect on 8 June 1991. By s.3 of that Ordinance, all pre-existing legislation inconsistent with the Bill of Rights was expressly repealed. The legislation thus repealed was of course not revived upon s.3 ceasing to exist as from 1 July 1997. What about subsequent legislation? In pre-handover times (when Hong Kong's constitutional instruments were the Letters Patent and the Royal Instructions) the entrenchment of the Bill of Rights was by art.VII(3) of the Letters Patent. That article was added to the Letters Patent simultaneously with the coming into effect of the Bill of Rights. It prohibited the Legislative Council from making any law that restricts the rights and freedoms enjoyed in Hong Kong in a manner inconsistent with the ICCPR as applied to Hong Kong. That arrangement lasted until 1 July 1997 when the Basic Law came into effect, and art.39 thereof took over the entrenchment of the Bill of Rights.

16. It was said in the course of the argument before us and has often been said before – no doubt truly – that the text of the ICCPR involves a considerable measure of compromise between different systems. The article of the ICCPR from which we got art.10 of the Bill of Rights is no exception to that and is, indeed, a good example of it. But then there is the question of why, despite the differences between their systems, so many nations have set out to achieve, succeeded in achieving and subscribed to the ICCPR. There must have been a powerful idea at work. Perhaps it was the idea that rights and freedoms are shared things, so that unless everyone has them in due measure, nobody's position

would be what it should. True it is that some people would, through the possession of raw power, still have privileges. But such privileges would be selfish and ultimately insecure. The ICCPR employs a largeness of language by which fundamental values are appropriately moulded into and presented as enforceable rights and freedoms. Neither its content nor its context suggests anything narrow. Certainly I would not attribute a narrow meaning to any of the rights and freedoms contained in the ICCPR as applied to Hong Kong through the Bill of Rights entrenched by the Basic Law. They are to be approached generously.

17. If there was ever any doubt as to that approach, it was laid to rest by the famous statement of the Chief Justice for the Court in *Ng Ka Ling v. Director of Immigration* (1999) 2 HKCFAR 4 at p.29A that "the courts should give a generous interpretation" to the rights and freedoms contained in the fundamental rights and freedoms chapter of the Basic Law in order to give persons in Hong Kong "the full measure of fundamental rights and freedoms so guaranteed". The rights under art.10 of the Bill of Rights are among those rights, being guaranteed by art.39 of the Basic Law, which article is in that chapter.

Article 10 applies to disciplinary proceedings

18. Article 10 of the Bill of Rights is taken word for word from art.14(1) of the ICCPR and closely resembles art.6(1) of the European Convention on Human Rights. We have been shown what the European Court of Human Rights has said about art.6(1) of that Convention and the Human Rights Committee has said about art.14(1) of the ICCPR. Looking in particular at *Eskalinen v. Finland* (2007) 45 EHRR 43 and *General Comment No.32* (90th Session) (2008) Vol.15 No.1 IHRR 1, it would appear that the European Court of Human Rights has arrived at the view that art.6(1) has application to proceedings such as disciplinary proceedings while the Human Rights Committee has not – or at least has not yet – arrived at such a view in regard to art.14(1).

19. Mr Chow contends that if it were held that art.10 applies to disciplinary proceedings, the consequences would be (i) that such proceedings must be heard in public and (ii) that the result of such proceedings must be made public subject only to the exceptions spelt out in art.10. Quite simply, I do not think that either of those consequences would ensue. No provision, especially not one that guarantees a fundamental right or freedom, should be interpreted so that its components trip each other up and defeat its purpose. Every provision, especially one of that nature, should be interpreted so that its components operate in harmony to achieve its purpose. Article 10 of the Bill of Rights is entrenched for the purpose of guaranteeing the protection of the individual in an important context. And it is to be interpreted and applied to further that purpose. Fairness at disciplinary hearings is an aspect of that purpose. So is sparing the individual from harmful publicity unless, exceptionally, publicity is in the interest of the individual or is so much in the public interest as to override any individual interest in privacy. There are various types of art.10 suits at law. Disciplinary proceedings are of a sort in which, while fairness is always needed, privacy is usually appropriate. If art.10 applies to disciplinary proceedings, it would mandate fairness at disciplinary hearings but would not mandate publicity at such hearings or for their results.

20. As to the competence, independence and impartiality required by art.10, there can be no objection in principle to disciplinary proceedings against police officers being heard by tribunals consisting of police officers without any non-police element. Whether any objection can be taken to any given adjudicating police officer in any given case depends on the circumstances.

21. It should be mentioned that an appeal to the courts where such an appeal is available, or judicial review by the courts where no such appeal is available, can supply any essential element such as independence or publicity that might otherwise be missing from a tribunal's arrangements.

22. True it is that legal representation is not permitted at hearings before the Labour Tribunal or the Small Claims Tribunal. But there are in this connection crucial differences between those two tribunals on the one hand and disciplinary tribunals on the other. Neither the Labour Tribunal nor the Small Claims Tribunal award punishment. An element of mediation features prominently in the process of the Labour Tribunal and, in practice, to some extent in the process of the Small Claims Tribunal too. Hearings before each of those two tribunals have an inquisitorial element. Each of them is empowered to transfer claims to a court, whereupon legal representation becomes permissible. And appeals from each of them lie to the courts.

23. The fair hearing clause of art.10 of the Bill of Rights guarantees the fairness of the hearings to which it applies. Whether it applies to disciplinary proceedings depends on whether such proceedings are determinations of rights and obligations in suits at law within its meaning. If they are, then the fairness of such proceedings is secure. Let it be remembered that fairness does not always carry a right to be legally represented. It only carries a right to be legally represented when denying that right would be unfair. The rights typically involved in disciplinary proceedings are important ones extending to the right to remain in a profession, service or occupation.

24. Having regard to their context, the words "determination of ... rights and obligations in a suit at law" call for a generous interpretation. The fundamental question is whether our constitution permits legislation that brings about unfairness at disciplinary proceedings. My answer is that our constitution does not permit that. In my view, disciplinary proceedings – whether in respect of professions, disciplined services or occupations – are determinations of rights and obligations in suits at law within the meaning of art.10. So art.10 applies to disciplinary proceedings. In fairness to the Court of Appeal in the present case, it should be mentioned that they felt bound by their own decision in *Chan King-chau v. Commissioner of Police*, HCMP 2824 of 2004, 29 December 2004 (unreported) that art.10 does not apply to the hearing of defaulter proceedings. Their judgment in the present case was given before we held in *Solicitor (24/07) v. Law Society of Hong Kong* [2008] 2 HKLRD 576 that the Court of Appeal may depart from a previous decision of their own if they are satisfied that it is plainly wrong.

Bar to legal representation has gone. Now a matter of discretion

25. Procedural fairness works because it is flexible. Whether it calls for legal representation in any given instance depends on the circumstances. As a bar to legal representation at defaulter hearings no matter what the circumstance, the reg.9(11) and (12) bar was inconsistent with the fair hearing clause of art.10 of the Bill of Rights. Accordingly the reg.9(11) and (12) bar was repealed by s.3 of the Hong Kong Bill of Rights Ordinance for such inconsistency or, if one does not regard it as having been repealed, is to be treated as void for unconstitutionality by reason of such inconsistency. Subsidiary legislation that was *intra vires* when made may be impliedly revoked by subsequent legislation inconsistent with it. That was the situation in *Attorney General v.*

Chan Kei-lung [1977] HKLR 312 decided by the Court of Appeal. The present situation goes beyond implied revocation, although ever that would be enough. Legal representation at defaulter hearings is now a matter of discretion. Whether a defaulter should be permitted to be legally represented depends on whether fairness so requires in all the circumstances. That is primarily for the disciplinary tribunal to assess. And no court would disturb such an assessment except for plainly compelling reasons.

26. As I see it, the legal position in the present situation bears comparison with the one under the decision of the Court of Appeal in *R v. Man Wai-keung (No.2)* [1992] 2 HKCLR 207. In that case a constitutional challenge was brought against a provision in the Criminal Procedure Ordinance, Cap.221, which barred the awarding of costs to a certain category of appellants whose convictions have been quashed, namely those who have been ordered to be retried. That bar was struck down for inconsistency with the equality clause of art.10 of the Bill of Rights. So the absence of finality due to a retrial having been ordered ceased to be a bar to an award of costs. And it became instead a discretionary factor to be taken into account when deciding whether to withhold costs from an appellant even though his conviction had been quashed. Similarly the repeal of the reg.9(11) and (12) bar does not mean that persons facing disciplinary charges can simply insist on being permitted to be legally represented. What it means is that the disciplinary tribunal has a discretion to permit such a person to be legally represented, and should do so if refusing such permission would be unfair.

27. There are some disciplinary tribunals before which legal representation is quite common. Legal practitioners understand, as they should, that their duty is not only to their clients but also to those tribunals. Such are the traditions and responsibilities of professional advocates. Their role is a constitutional one, always to be approached as such and never to be abused. Most of them certainly need no reminder of that. But just in case some of them might sometimes need such a reminder, I have seen fit respectfully to issue one, meaning of course no offence thereby.

Assessment primarily for the tribunal to make

28. It is always to be remembered that whether fairness requires that legal representation be permitted at a disciplinary hearing is primarily for the disciplinary tribunal to assess, and that no court would disturb such an assessment except for plainly compelling reasons. It may transpire that defaulter proceedings in which fairness requires that the defaulter be permitted to be legally represented will not be numerous. Anyway it depends on the circumstances of each case.

Impairment of operational efficiency is an element of the offence

29. Being of the view that the appellant's attack against the reg.9(11) and (12) bar – and therefore the first part of his argument – succeeds, I turn to the second part of his argument. It is that the impairment of operational efficiency is an element of the offence under PGO 6–01(8). Since PGO 6–01(8) is a penal provision, any ambiguity in it would have to be resolved in favour of a person charged under it. As it happens however, the appellant does not even need to rely on that canon of construction. PGO 6–01(8) says in plain terms that what will result in disciplinary action is "[s]erious pecuniary embarrassment stemming from financial imprudence which leads to the impairment of an officer's operational efficiency". If the embarrassment does not lead to such impairment, then it is plainly not what PGO 6–01(8) says will result in disciplinary action. In my view, the impairment of operational efficiency is an element of the disciplinary offence under PGO 6–01(8). It should, in fairness to the Court of Appeal in the present case, be mentioned that they were confronted by previous decisions of theirs, including *Leung Fuk Wah v. Commissioner of Police* [2002] 3 HKLRD 653, to the effect that, as Tang VP put it in the present case, "serious pecuniary embarrassment would *necessarily* lead to impairment of operational efficiency". (Emphasis supplied.)

30. Since the impairment of operational efficiency is an element of the offence, the burden of proving it is on those who bring a charge. As to the standard of proof, nothing need be added to what we said in the *Solicitor (24/07)* case. In so far as Stone J held in *Ng Kam Chuen v. Secretary for Justice* [1999] 2 HKC 291 that the impairment of operational efficiency is an element of the disciplinary offence under PGO 6–01(8), he was right. But I am unable to accept his view (expressed at p.297A–D) that "upon the demonstration of serious pecuniary embarrassment... the evidential burden then shifts to the accused officer to establish that his efficiency as an officer has *not* been impaired" or, alternatively, that there is a "rebuttable presumption" of such impairment. (Emphasis in the original) In my view, that is not so. The position is straightforward. Drawing inferences is legitimate. But the position is not complicated by any presumption or the shifting of any onus, evidential or otherwise.

Legal representation should have been permitted

31. Having held in favour of the second part of the appellant's argument, I turn to the third part of his argument. It is that he should have been permitted to be legally represented at the disciplinary hearing. Since they regarded the reg.9(11) and (12) bar as valid, neither the disciplinary tribunal nor either of the courts below made an assessment of whether, in the circumstances of the present case, fairness required that the appellant be permitted to be legally represented at the disciplinary tribunal. Such an assessment has to be made here and now.

32. In granting the appellant leave to appeal to us, the Court of Appeal expressly and rightly declined to treat the appellant's points of law as academic. I am of the view that in all the circumstances fairness required that the appellant be permitted to be legally represented at the disciplinary hearing. Accordingly, I am of the view that the third part of the appellant's argument succeeds.

Might have been acquitted if legally represented

33. What remains is the fourth and final part of the appellant's argument. It is that if he had been legally represented, he might have been acquitted by reason of the evidence as a whole being insufficient to prove that his operational efficiency had been impaired within the meaning of PGO 6-01(8).

34. In this connection, too, it is pertinent to note that in granting the appellant leave to appeal to us, the Court of Appeal expressly and rightly declined to treat the appellant's points of law as academic. Suppose the appellant had been legally represented at the disciplinary hearing. Might he then have been acquitted by reason of the evidence as a whole being insufficient to prove that his operational efficiency had been impaired within the meaning of PGO 6–01(8)? The question of impairment of operational efficiency is of course pre-eminently to be resolved by an assessment to be made by the disciplinary tribunal. A court would normally be very slow to disturb such an assessment since the subject-matter is by definition an operational matter. But in the present case there is a real possibility that the state of the

evidence would have been crucially different if the appellant's defence at the disciplinary hearing had been in the hands of a legal practitioner. In other words, the difference might well have been the difference between an acquittal and a conviction. Accordingly I am of the view that the fourth and final part of the appellant's argument – and therefore the whole of his argument – succeeds.

Equality

35. As Prof. Chan has observed, there is nothing in reg.9 or elsewhere to prevent the case against a defaulter being presented by a Government lawyer or indeed a lawyer in private practice. So the bar to legal representation operates only against defaulters. And that, Prof. Chan said, means that the reg.9(11) and (12) bar is also inconsistent with the equality clause of art.10 of the Bill of Rights even though the invariable practice appears to be for the case against a defaulter to be presented by a police officer. This point as to an inequality of arms does not appear to have been canvassed below. And there is no need to pronounce on it since the challenge to the validity of the reg.9(11) and (12) bar succeeds without it.

Result

36. For the foregoing reasons, I would allow the appeal and quash the decisions by which the appellant was convicted and compulsorily retired. It is accepted on the appellant's behalf that the quashing of those decisions does not preclude a fresh – and fair – hearing before the disciplinary tribunal. Whether that or some other course offers the best way forward hereafter is not a question before the Court. I would make no order as to costs as between the parties but order that the appellant's costs be taxed under the Legal Aid Regulations. Finally, I wish to express my thanks to both legal teams for the very helpful arguments which they have prepared and presented.

Mr Justice Chan PJ:

37. I agree with the judgment of Mr Justice Ribeiro PJ.

Mr Justice Ribeiro PJ:

38. In this appeal, the applicability and operation of Article 10 of the Bill of Rights ("Article 10") fall to be considered in connection with police disciplinary proceedings. The appellant, a police constable, complains that the exclusion of professional legal representation by the relevant regulations deprived him of a fair hearing. He therefore challenges the constitutional validity of that exclusion and the lawfulness of the disciplinary proceedings.

A. The disciplinary proceedings

A.1 The conduct of the appellant

39. The appellant joined the Force in 1988 and had a commendable record of service, consistently rated as "very good". However, in the six-month period between November 1999 and May 2000, he engaged in speculation on the stock market and incurred significant losses. He had a monthly salary of $22,210 but was placing buy and sell orders in five-figure (and occasionally in low six-figure) amounts. Such trading was initially financed from his own savings, but he went on to incur debts by drawing on seven credit cards and taking personal loans from five finance companies. He bought shares for the total sum of $1,827,508.49 and sold them for $1,340,375.69 and so lost $487,127.80 on his trades. When he realised that his indebtedness had become unmanageable, he made a full report of his situation to his superior officers, disclosing an indebtedness of $621,404. On 26 September 2000, he was declared bankrupt upon his own petition.

A.2 The policy of the Police Force

40. The appellant is, unfortunately, not the only police officer to find himself in such a predicament. Policies and procedures have been established for dealing with "officers with unmanageable debts", abbreviated in police terminology to "OUDs". It is recognized that an OUD may be compromised or susceptible to corrupt overtures. And in a number of cases, the stresses of such debts have tragically driven officers to suicide. These considerations have resulted in detailed administrative instructions being issued from time to time[1] aimed at preventing officers from incurring unmanageable debts, at identifying and managing those who have done so and at dealing with the disciplinary aspects of such conduct. They provide guidance as to the appropriate deployment of OUDs so as to avoid, for instance, postings where public money may be handled or where greater opportunities may exist for corruption. Consideration also has to be given as to whether an OUD should be allowed to carry firearms.

41. The administrative instructions state that officers have the responsibility not to incur expenses they are unable to afford, including expenses in relation to "speculation in the stock, financial and property market". While a sympathetic view is taken of officers who become indebted due to unforeseen or compassionate circumstances, there is "no sympathy for officers who ... have had unmanageable debts due to financial imprudence, resulting in the impairment of the officers' operational efficiency".

A.3 The disciplinary provisions

42. The Police Force is of course a disciplined force. By section 30 of the Police Force Ordinance,[2] every police officer is required to obey all lawful orders of his superior officers and to obey and conform to police regulations and orders made under the Ordinance.

43. By section 45, powers are given to the Chief Executive in Council to make regulations including those providing for discipline and punishments, for appropriate tribunals to inquire into disciplinary offences and for the procedure to be followed.

44. Section 46 empowers the Commissioner of Police to make such orders (known as "police general orders" or "PGOs") as he thinks expedient to enable him to administer the police force and render it more efficient.

45. The Police (Discipline) Regulations made under section 45 create disciplinary offences including the offence under regulation 3(2)(e) of "contravention of police regulations, or any police orders, whether written or verbal". The Regulations lay down detailed rules as to the procedure to be followed at disciplinary hearings and, most importantly for present purposes, by regulations 9(11) and 9(12), they provide that:

> "(11) A defaulter[3] may be represented by–
>
> (a) an inspector or other junior police officer of his choice; or
>
> (b) any other police officer of his choice who is qualified as a barrister or solicitor,
>
> who may conduct the defence on his behalf.

(12) Subject to paragraph (11), no barrister or solicitor may appear on behalf of the defaulter.

Mr Anderson Chow SC, appearing with Mr Louie Wong SGC for the Commissioner, realistically accepts that these regulations represent a total ban on professional legal representation. An officer who has acquired legal qualifications may have many fine qualities but the services which he can provide cannot in general be equated with professional legal representation. Moreover, legally qualified officers are in any event in very short supply. At present, only one such officer has publicly indicated a readiness to act in the role of representative.

46. The police general order issued in respect of unmanageable debts is PGO 6–01(8) which, in the version applicable at the material time, provided:

"A police officer shall be prudent in his financial affairs. Serious pecuniary embarrassment stemming from financial imprudence which leads to the impairment of an officer's operational efficiency will result in disciplinary action."

A.4 The disciplinary proceedings

47. The charge against the appellant was that, contrary to regulation 3(2)(e):

"... on 26 September 2000, in Hong Kong, you did fail to be prudent with your financial affairs by incurring unmanageable debts of about HK$620,000 that resulted in serious pecuniary embarrassment as evidenced by the making of a bankruptcy order against you whereby your operational efficiency as a police officer was impaired contrary to PGO 6–01(8)."

48. In fact, two sets of disciplinary proceedings were held. The first took place in January 2001 before Superintendent Cheng Po-yan sitting as the Adjudicating Officer. The prosecutor was Inspector Yeung Chun-po who called witnesses including three of the appellant's superior officers, namely, Sergeant Yeung Kai-kwong, Inspector Li Hon-man and Chief Inspector Wong Koon-ho. Pursuant to regulation 9(11), the appellant was represented by Senior Inspector Wong Wai-hung. The appellant was found guilty and on 13 March 2001, he was sentenced to be dismissed. That was the most severe punishment available[4] and would have involved not only termination of the appellant's employment but also the loss of his pension rights.

49. However, on 19 August 2001, the appellant was told that it had been decided to set aside his conviction and to have a re–hearing. He was later told that this was because the Force Discipline Officer considered there to have been procedural irregularities or potential unfairness at the hearing, but that prima facie evidence to support the charge nevertheless existed.

50. The second set of proceedings started in December 2001 and, with various adjournments, ran into March 2002. The Adjudicating Officer this time was Superintendent Lo Tat–fai. The prosecutor and police witnesses called were the same. However, the Senior Inspector who had represented the appellant was not available and the appellant had difficulty finding someone to represent him. He eventually secured the assistance of Senior Inspector Wong Kwok–ming but, lacking confidence in him, asked him to withdraw at an early stage. On 22 January 2002, he asked the tribunal whether he could employ a solicitor (or an auxiliary officer or a civil servant from another department) to represent him and was told that he could only have a solicitor who was a serving regular officer and that otherwise, the answer was "no". He therefore represented himself at the hearings.

51. On 27 March 2002, the tribunal found the appellant guilty and referred the case to a senior police officer[5] for sentence. He was initially given a sentence of compulsory retirement with deferred benefits, suspended for 12 months.[6] However, this was considered inadequate by the Force Discipline Officer who, on 26 July 2002, increased it to an immediate sentence of compulsory retirement with deferred benefits. This meant that the appellant's employment as a police officer was terminated and, while his accrued pension rights were not lost, his pension could not be drawn until he reaches what would have been the normal age of retirement. The sentence was ratified by the Commissioner on 21 October 2002.

B. The appellant's complaint and the decisions below

52. On 21 January 2003, the appellant lodged what was described at first instance as a "homemade" notice of application for judicial review. After legal aid was obtained and various extensions of time granted, a formal application prepared by counsel was lodged on 5 October 2004. This sought orders of certiorari quashing the convictions and sentences and a declaration that regulations 9(11) and 9(12), to the extent that they restricted the appellant's choice of representative at the hearing, are unconstitutional and void.

53. The matter came before Chung J who dismissed the application for judicial review.[7] His decision deals with grounds that are no longer relied on and does not address any of the issues that have become material in the present appeal.

54. In the Court of Appeal,[8] Ms Margaret Ng, then appearing as counsel for the appellant (now assisting Mr Johannes Chan SC on the present appeal), advanced the argument which is at the core of this appeal, namely, that in depriving the tribunal of any discretion to permit legal representation, regulations 9(11) and 9(12) prevented the appellant from having a fair hearing in contravention of Article 10. This was rejected by Tang VP (giving the Court's judgment) on the ground that the Court was bound by the unreported Court of Appeal decision in *陳庚秋 訴 香港警務處處長* (*Chan Keng-chau v. Commissioner of Police*).[9] In that case, Yeung JA considered the protection afforded to an officer on disciplinary charges sufficient on the basis that judicial review was available and that officers in a disciplined force are better equipped and more suitable than judges for determining whether one of their number has breached discipline. He therefore held that Article 10 "does not apply to a police officer facing [a] disciplinary hearing..." [10]

55. Tang VP also rejected the argument that regulations 9(11) and 9(12) are *ultra vires* section 45 of the Ordinance, noting that at the time when the regulations were made, the exclusion of legal representation in disciplinary hearings, especially within a disciplined force, was considered justifiable and would have fallen within relevant rule-making powers, as indicated in *Maynard v. Osmond*.[11]

56. The Court of Appeal went on to hold that, in any event, judicial review should be refused since on the construction of PGO 6–01(8) adopted in earlier Court of Appeal decisions[12] and on the admitted facts, the appellant's conviction in the present case was inevitable.

57. However, the Court of Appeal granted leave to appeal to this Court.[13] Three questions of great general or public importance

were identified, namely:

(1) whether Article 10 is engaged in police disciplinary proceedings;

(2) whether regulations 9(11) and 9(12) are consistent with Article 10; and,

(3) whether it is necessary or permissible to adduce evidence to prove or disprove an 'impairment of operational efficiency' as a police officer (in addition to 'serious pecuniary financial embarrassment stemming from financial imprudence') in establishing a disciplinary offence under PGO 6-01(8).

C. Article 10 and related treaty provisions

58. Article 10 provides:

"All persons shall be equal before the courts and tribunals. In the determination of any criminal charge against him, or of his rights and obligations in a suit at law, everyone shall be entitled to a fair and public hearing by a competent, independent and impartial tribunal established by law. The press and the public may be excluded from all or part of a trial for reasons of morals, public order (*ordre public*) or national security in a democratic society, or when the interest of the private lives of the parties so requires, or to the extent strictly necessary in the opinion of the court in special circumstances where publicity would prejudice the interests of justice; but any judgment rendered in a criminal case or in a suit at law shall be made public except where the interest of juvenile persons otherwise requires or the proceedings concern matrimonial disputes or the guardianship of children."

59. Article 10 is in terms identical to Article 14.1 of the International Covenant on Civil and Political Rights ("ICCPR"),[14] which I will refer to simply as "Article 14.1". It follows that the General Comments and published Communications of the Human Rights Committee ("HRC") concerning Article 14.1 give guidance to an understanding of Article 10.

60. Article 39 of the Basic Law gives constitutional force to Article 10, stipulating that the ICCPR's provisions "as applied to Hong Kong" shall remain in force and "shall be implemented through the laws of the HKSAR", and that:

"The rights and freedoms enjoyed by Hong Kong residents shall not be restricted unless as prescribed by law. Such restrictions shall not contravene the provisions of the preceding paragraph of this Article."

61. Article 6(1) of the European Convention for the Protection of Human Rights and Fundamental Freedoms ("ECHR"),[15] which I shall refer to as "Article 6(1)", is in very similar terms:

"In the determination of his civil rights and obligations or of any criminal charge against him, everyone is entitled to a fair and public hearing within a reasonable time by an independent and impartial tribunal established by law. Judgement shall be pronounced publicly but the press and public may be excluded from all or part of the trial in the interest of morals, public order or national security in a democratic society, where the interests of juveniles or the protection of the private life of the parties so require, or the extent strictly necessary in the opinion of the court in special circumstances where publicity would prejudice the interests of justice."

62. In my view, the jurisprudence of the European Court of Human Rights at Strasbourg ("the European court" or "the Strasbourg court") in relation to Article 6(1) is of immediate relevance to an understanding of Article 14.1 and Article 10, notwithstanding certain differences in wording.

63. Differences appear in the English texts of the two treaties particularly in relation to the conditions which trigger engagement of the respective articles.

(a) In Article 6(1), the right to "a fair and public hearing within a reasonable time by an independent and impartial tribunal established by law" is activated if the person claiming its protection faces "a determination of his *civil rights and obligations*".

(b) And in Article 14.1 (and, it goes without saying, in the identical wording of Article 10), the entitlement "to a fair and public hearing by a competent, independent and impartial tribunal established by law" is triggered where the individual concerned faces a "determination of ... his *rights and obligations in a suit at law*".

64. However, the rendering of the words I have italicised is precisely the same in the French texts of both treaties. They both refer to "*droits et obligations de caractère civil*".[16] As the Joint Dissenting Opinion of the European court in *Feldbrugge v. The Netherlands*[17] explains, the English text of Article 6(1) had originally also followed the wording of Article 14.1, referring to "rights and obligations in a suit at law". It was changed at the last moment to refer instead to "civil rights and obligations" merely to align the English text more closely with the language of the French text and not to effect any substantive change.

65. Moreover, in my view, even without having regard to the drafting history of the two articles, the ordinary meaning of the two phrases in the English text, understood in the context of each article, is the same. They both refer to determinations of civil rights and obligations distinguishing them from determinations of criminal charges which are also dealt with in juxtaposition by the two articles. In other words, the words "suit at law" referred to in the ICCPR are intended to convey the meaning of "a *civil* suit at law", as opposed to the determination of a criminal charge.

D. The legal principles

D.1 When is Article 10 engaged?

66. As noted above, the Article 10 protections come into play (leaving aside criminal charges) when a person is subject to "a determination of his rights and obligations in a suit at law". This formula has spawned considerable uncertainty.

D.1.a Article 10 and the rule of law

67. Article 10 gives effect to the rule of law. When it is engaged, it enables the individual faced with a determination by a governmental or public authority[18] which may affect his civil rights and obligations to say: "I am entitled to the protections of Article 10, including the right to a fair and public hearing by a competent, independent and impartial tribunal established by law". As Lord Hoffmann, referring to Article 6(1), puts it in *Runa Begum v. Tower Hamlets LBC*:[19]

"One of the purposes of article 6, in requiring that

disputes over civil rights should be decided by or subject to the control of a judicial body, is to uphold the rule of law and the separation of powers..."

And as the Strasbourg court stated in one of its earlier decisions:

"... in civil matters one can scarcely conceive of the rule of law without there being a possibility of having access to the courts."[20]

D.1.b A historical gap

68. It is against this backdrop, recognizing the basic importance of Article 10 and its equivalents to the rule of law, that the difficulties encountered in establishing when the protections are engaged should be viewed.

69. Those difficulties stem from a gap in the protections contained in the text of the ICCPR (which, as we have seen, was duplicated in the ECHR). That gap, which has been traced in the international jurisprudence,[21] concerns the scope of the words "rights and obligations in a suit at law" and "civil rights and obligations". To a common lawyer, the existence of such a gap may not be obvious since one might assume that the phrase "civil rights and obligations" encompasses all rights and obligations outside the sphere of the criminal law. However, in many countries subscribing to the ICCPR and the ECHR, "civil rights and obligations" would not be understood to be so all-embracing. Distinctions may be drawn, for instance, between public and private law rights and between the law administered in civil and administrative courts. As Lord Hoffmann explains:

"... the term 'civil rights and obligations' was originally intended to mean those rights and obligations which, in continental European systems of law, were adjudicated upon by the civil courts. These were, essentially, rights and obligations in private law. The term was not intended to cover administrative decisions which were conventionally subject to review (if at all) by administrative courts. It was not that the draftsmen of the Convention did not think it desirable that administrative decisions should be subject to the rule of law. But administrative decision-making raised special problems which meant that it could not be lumped in with the adjudication of private law rights and made subject to the same judicial requirements of independence, publicity and so forth. So the judicial control of administrative action was left for future consideration."[22]

70. The need for certain administrative processes which affect the rights and obligations of individuals to be dealt with on a separate and different footing was spelt out, for instance, in the Joint Dissenting Opinion in *Feldbrugge v. The Netherlands* as follows:[23]

"The judicialisation of dispute procedures, as guaranteed by Article 6(1), is eminently appropriate in the realm of relations between individuals but not necessarily so in the administrative sphere, where organisational, social and economic considerations may legitimately warrant dispute procedures of a less judicial and formal kind. The present case is concerned with the operation of a collective statutory scheme for the allocation of public welfare. As examples of the special characteristics of such schemes, material to the issue of procedural safeguards, one might cite the large numbers of decisions to be taken, the medical aspects, the lack of resources or expertise of the persons affected, the need to balance the public interest for efficient administration against the private interest. Judicialisation of procedures for allocation of public welfare benefits would in many cases necessitate recourse by claimants to lawyers and medical experts and hence lead to an increase in expense and the length of the proceedings."

71. While common law systems may not distinguish between administrative and "judicialised" processes affecting civil rights and obligations in terms of the structure of their courts or the legal classifications used, the distinction between the processes is nevertheless real and the need to avoid the "over-lawyering" or "over-judicialisation" of procedures in certain administrative and disciplinary tribunals is recognised.[24]

72. As the *travaux préparatoires* of the ICCPR[25] show, it was acknowledged by the delegations concerned that the proper approach to determinations of rights and obligations by administrative bodies "had not been fully thrashed out and should be examined more thoroughly". Such "thrashing out" has, however, not occurred–hence, the gap.

D.1.c Filling the gap

73. The existence of such a gap presented a risk that the protections intended to be conferred by Article 10 and its equivalents might be wholly undermined. As the European court stated (in a slightly different context) in *Golder v. United Kingdom*:[26]

"Were Article 6 para 1 (art 6-1) to be understood as concerning exclusively the conduct of an action which had already been initiated before a court, a Contracting State could, without acting in breach of that text, do away with its courts, or take away their jurisdiction to determine certain classes of civil actions and entrust it to organs dependent on the Government. Such assumptions, indissociable from a danger of arbitrary power, would have serious consequences which are repugnant to the aforementioned principles and which the Court cannot overlook ..."

74. It is accordingly not surprising that the unmistakeable trend of the international jurisprudence has been to close the gap and to extend the protection of the equivalents of Article 10 in a variety of ways. Whereas the drafting history of Article 14.1 and Article 6(1) indicates that the "right to a court" provided by those articles was originally not intended to apply to decisions by administrative tribunals or to the legal relations between, for instance, civil servants and the State which employs them, that restrictive approach, as Lord Walker of Gestingthorpe pointed out,[27] "is now of no more than historical interest".

75. A significant early step taken by the European court and the HRC towards enlarging the scope of Article 10 protections involved establishing that the concepts which trigger the protections had an "autonomous" meaning under the conventions and could not be evaded by use of domestic law definitions.[28] As Lord Millett points out:

"According to the consistent case law of the Strasbourg court the concept of 'civil rights and obligations' is autonomous. Its scope cannot be determined solely by reference to the domestic law of the respondent state... Any other conclusion could lead to results incompatible with the object and purpose of the Convention, since it would be open to contracting states, by reclassifying the rights granted by their own domestic legal systems, to exclude particular categories of civil actions from the operation of article 6(1)." [29]

76. In *Yvon Landry v. Canada,*[30] the HRC extended Article 14.1's scope in two additional ways. First, it rejected the governmental or public status of one of the parties as a basis in itself for excluding the protections and secondly, (as was pointed out by Mr Anderson Chow SC) it held that the protections are applicable where a case which might otherwise have fallen outside the article is in fact adjudicated upon by a tribunal having judicial characteristics. The well-known passage in the Communication runs as follows:

> "... the concept of a 'suit at law' or its equivalent in the other language texts is based on the nature of the right in question rather than on the status of one of the parties (governmental, parastatal or autonomous statutory entities), or else on the particular forum in which individual legal systems may provide that the right in question is to be adjudicated upon, especially in common law systems when there is no inherent difference between public law and private law, and where the Courts normally exercise control over the proceedings, either at first instance or on appeal specifically provided by statute or else by way of judicial review. In this regard, each communication must be examined in the light of its particular features."[31]

77. Another step taken towards plugging the gap has involved the Strasbourg court deciding that Article 6(1) is engaged where the determination involves elements of both public and private law, but where the latter are found to be predominant. Thus, in *H v. Belgium,*[32] a case concerning the application of a disbarred *avocat* to be readmitted to the roll of *avocats*, the Court found that aspects of the profession of *avocat* and thus of the determination undoubtedly had public law features, but that they were outweighed by other features of a private law character.

78. A major extension was made in *Ringeisen v. Austria (No 1)*[33] which was concerned with the regulation of land transfers by a District Land Transactions Commission with an appeal to a Regional Commission. It therefore involved, as Lord Hoffmann notes in *R (Alconbury Developments Ltd) v. Secretary of State for the Environment,*[34] "a classic regulatory power exercisable by an administrative body". The European court nevertheless held that Article 6(1) was engaged and that it could intervene on the ground that the administrative decision was "decisive" for the enforceability of the private law contract for the sale of land. "Thus," as Lord Hoffmann points out, "a decision on a question of public law by an administrative body could attract article 6(1) by virtue of its effect on private law rights." [35] This has had a major impact since many decisions by administrative bodies and disciplinary tribunals[36] have a direct impact on the civil rights and obligations of the individual concerned, attracting the protection of Article 10.

79. This extended approach has been held to apply to planning cases.[37] It has also been adopted in relation to claims for non-contributory welfare benefits, as in *Salesi v. Italy* [38] and *Mennitto v. Italy.*[39] As Lord Millett explains in relation to those two cases:

> "The decisions had the effect of extending article 6(1) to disputes in connection with non–contributory welfare schemes. In each case the critical feature which brought it within article 6(1) was that the claimant 'suffered an interference with her means of subsistence and was claiming an individual, economic right flowing from specific rules laid down in a statute giving effect to the Constitution' (26 EHRR 187, 199, § 19)." [40]

D.1.d The Eskelinen decision

80. In its recent decision in *Vilho Eskelinen v. Finland,*[41] the Grand Chamber of the Strasbourg court took a major step towards extending the protection of Article 6(1) to civil servants generally, adopting an approach which may indicate the course which later developments in the jurisprudence might take.

81. As previously noted, the relationship between civil servants and the State as employer had originally not been intended to come within the relevant articles. However, the process of gradual extension of the protections has also occurred in this context. *Lombardo v. Italy,*[42] was a case involving the claim for an enhanced pension by a *Carabinieri* officer who had been invalided out of service. The Italian government contended that Article 6(1) was not engaged, arguing that as a civil servant, the claimant's relationship with the State had been of a public law nature, his appointment having been a unilateral act by the State pursuant to special legislation. The Court nonetheless held that Article 6(1) applied, treating the pension claim as a pecuniary or economic claim falling outside the civil service relationship.[43]

82. In *Pellegrin v. France,*[44] the European court proceeded to reduce substantially the number of civil servants excluded from protection by propounding a new "functional criterion". It noted that certain civil servants "wield a portion of the State's sovereign power" and reasoned that in relation to that category of persons, the State may have a legitimate interest "in requiring of these servants a special bond of trust and loyalty" thereby justifying the State in removing their relationship with such employees from the scrutiny of an Article 6(1) tribunal. It stated:

> "The Court therefore rules that the only disputes excluded from the scope of Article 6(1) of the Convention are those which are raised by public servants whose duties typify the specific activities of the public service in so far as the latter is acting as the depositary of public authority responsible for protecting the general interests of the State or other public authorities. A manifest example of such activities is provided by the armed forces and the police.[45]
>
> The Court made an exception, even within the excluded category, in respect of pension claims since "on retirement employees break the special bond between themselves and the authorities ..." [46]

83. While the motivation behind this new "functional criterion" was to expand the coverage of Article 6(1), it was plainly not a satisfactory or easily workable means for delineating when the article's protections are engaged. It is inherently discriminatory as between civil servants and based upon the somewhat mystical concept of "a special bond of trust and loyalty" with the State.

84. The unsatisfactory features of *Pellegrin* were prominently exposed in the *Eskelinen* case [47] which involved claims by five police officers and a civilian office assistant working as a public servant for wage supplements as compensation for being posted in a remote part of the country. As the Grand Chamber noted:

> "On a strict application of the *Pellegrin* approach it would appear that the office assistant applicant in the present case would enjoy the guarantees of Art 6(1), whereas

> there is no doubt that the police officer applicants would not. This would be so irrespective of the fact that the dispute was identical for all the applicants."[48]

85. It observed that:

> "Arts 1 and 14 of the Convention stipulate that 'everyone within [the] jurisdiction' of the contracting states must enjoy the rights and freedoms in Section I 'without discrimination on any ground'."

And it expressed the opinion that:

> "As a general rule, the guarantees in the Convention extend to civil servants";[49] and that "... there should therefore be convincing reasons for excluding any category of applicant from the protection of Art 6(1)." [50]

86. Accordingly, the *Pellegrin* functional criterion was replaced by a two-fold test:

> "...in order for the respondent State to be able to rely before the Court on the applicant's status as a civil servant in excluding the protection embodied in Art 6, two conditions must be fulfilled. First, the State in its national law must have expressly excluded access to a court for the post or category of staff in question. Secondly, the exclusion must be justified on objective grounds in the State's interest." [51]

Putting it another way:

> "There will, in effect, be a presumption that Art 6 applies. It will be for the respondent Government to demonstrate, first, that a civil servant applicant does not have a right of access to a court under national law and, secondly, that the exclusion of the rights under Art 6 for the civil servant is justified."[52]

87. In giving an indication of when objective grounds justifying exclusion might exist, the Court did mention that it would be "for the State to show that the subject matter of the dispute in issue is related to the exercise of state power or that it has called into question the special bond",[53] a statement relied on by the respondent in the present case. However, as stated above, I find it difficult to give practical meaning to this abstract notion of a "special bond".

88. Of more concrete value is the Court's statement[54] which followed upon its observation that "there should therefore be convincing reasons for excluding any category of applicant from the protection of Art 6(1)". The Court said:

> "In the present case, where the applicants, police officers and administrative assistant alike, had, according to the national legislation, the right to have their claims for allowances examined by a tribunal, *no ground related to the effective functioning of the State or any other public necessity* has been advanced *which might require the removal of Convention protection* against unfair or lengthy proceedings."[55] (italics supplied)

89. The *Eskelinen* case therefore, in my view, lays down the principled approach of (i) placing the onus on the State to specify, in legislation, the particular class of civil servants who are to be excluded from the Convention's protection; and (ii) subjecting such legislation to scrutiny by the Court which asks whether objective grounds related to the effective functioning of the State or some other public necessity which justify removal of Convention protection have been established. As the Grand Chamber stated:

> "If a domestic system bars access to a court, the Court will verify that the dispute is indeed such as to justify the application of the exception to the guarantees of Art 6. If it does not, then there is no issue and Art 6(1)will apply."[56]

90. This is clearly an area of developing jurisprudence and the *Eskelinen* decision, although followed in subsequent cases[57] and highly significant, is obviously not the last word on the subject. I pause to note that the HRC has evidently fallen behind the European court in developments in this area. In its General Comment No 32 dated 23 August 2007,[58] it continues to adopt a piecemeal and necessarily disjointed approach to the phrase "in a suit at law", listing various instances when the protections are engaged, including in that list cases involving "the termination of employment of civil servants for other than disciplinary reasons". [59] I would respectfully adopt in preference the *Eskelinen* approach as the more principled. It is obviously more satisfactory not to discriminate against some classes of civil servants in connection with their access to a judicial tribunal unless there is strong justification for doing so. To recognize, as General Comment No 32 does, an entitlement to protection where the employment is terminated for *other than* disciplinary reasons appears to me to acknowledge that entitlement where it is least needed and to refuse protection where (in disciplinary proceedings) it is most likely to be important.

D.1.e Purely disciplinary matters vs civil rights and obligations

91. Since Article 10's engagement depends on whether an individual's civil rights and obligations are to be determined (or whether he is facing a criminal charge) in a specific instance, Article 10 may be engaged only in relation to some, but not all, the matters dealt with by a particular administrative authority or administrative tribunal.

92. In other words, a specific charge brought before a particular disciplinary tribunal may or may not attract Article 10 protections depending on whether it involves determination of a criminal charge or of the individual's civil rights and obligations. This is well-recognized in cases concerned with drawing the line between criminal charges and the enforcement of internal discipline[60] and similar considerations arise in relation to disciplinary measures affecting the individual's civil rights and obligations. However, it has been emphasised that it is for the court to decide on which side of the line any particular case falls, whatever the domestic classification of the offence may be. As the Strasbourg court stated in *Campbell and Fell v. United Kingdom*:[61]

> "... If the contracting states were able at their discretion, by classifying an offence as disciplinary instead of criminal, to exclude the operation of the fundamental clauses of Arts 6 and 7, the application of these provisions would be subordinated to their sovereign will. A latitude extending thus far might lead to results incompatible with the object and purpose of the Convention."

E. Is Article 10 engaged in the present case?

93. In my view, Article 10 is clearly engaged in relation to the disciplinary proceedings in present case. The Administrative Instructions referred to above[62] make it clear that punishment

for the disciplinary offence under PGO 6–01(8) with which the appellant was charged is "normally terminatory". Such was in fact the nature of the punishment meted out in this case. Although the relevant jurisprudence is still in the course of development, it has developed sufficiently to enable us to say that the appellant undoubtedly faced a determination of his rights and obligations in a suit at law, meaning his civil rights and obligations.

94. This conclusion can be reached by adopting the approach developed in *Ringeisen v. Austria (No 1)*[63] since the disciplinary proceedings have a direct and highly adverse impact on the appellant's civil rights and obligations. As Baroness Hale of Richmond, held in *R (Wright) v. Secretary of State for Health*,[64] by analogy with cases in which civil rights and obligations have been held by the Strasbourg court [65] to include the right to practise one's profession: "The right to remain in the employment one currently holds must be a civil right ..." Moreover, where pension rights of civil servants have been affected, the relevant protections have readily been held applicable, as in *Lombardo v. Italy* [66] and *Pellegrin v. France*.[67]

95. The same conclusion is reached adopting the approach in *Vilho Eskelinen v. Finland*,[68] whereby one asks whether the protection of Article 10 has expressly been excluded in respect of police officers such as the appellant facing disciplinary proceedings; and if so, whether the exclusion is justified on objective grounds related to the effective functioning of the State or some other public necessity which justifies removal of the article's protection.

96. In the present case, there has been an express prohibition by subordinate legislation of any legal representation which undoubtedly bears on the right to a fair hearing protected by Article 10 (as further discussed below). To that extent, I am prepared to accept that the first *Eskelinen* condition is complied with. However, the second condition has not been met: the Commissioner has not provided sufficient justification for excluding Article 10 protections in the disciplinary proceedings.

97. The justification offered, as expressed in the Respondent's printed case, is that Article 10's requirements:

> "... would not be compatible with the character of police disciplinary proceedings, which are essentially domestic or internal hearings of a disciplined service where all participants have knowledge and experience of the procedures and demands of the police force, and where proceedings ought to be dealt with expeditiously and with a minimum of formality."

98. That submission echoes views which were current in the English Court of Appeal in the 1970's. Thus, in *Fraser v. Mudge*,[69] a case dealing with prison discipline, Lord Denning MR stated:

> "We all know that, when a man is brought up before his commanding officer for a breach of discipline, whether in the armed forces or in ships at sea, it never has been the practice to allow legal representation. It is of the first importance that the cases should be decided quickly. If legal representation were allowed, it would mean considerable delay. So also with breaches of prison discipline. They must be heard and decided speedily. Those who hear the cases must, of course, act fairly. They must let the man know the charge and give him a proper opportunity of presenting his case. But that can be done and is done without the matter being held up for legal representation. I do not think we ought to alter the existing practice."

99. About a year later, in *Maynard v. Osmond*,[70] a police discipline case, Lord Denning MR expressed the view that a person on disciplinary charges ought in general to be entitled to legal representation or at least be permitted such representation at the discretion of the tribunal. But his Lordship nevertheless accepted that it was legitimate for Parliament or a minister to decree otherwise, particularly where a disciplined force was concerned.[71] Rejecting the argument that regulations forbidding legal representation were ultra vires, his Lordship stated:

> "In a disciplined force it is important that those responsible for maintaining discipline should have the conduct of disciplinary proceedings. So long as they are conducted fairly and in accordance with natural justice, the trial of disciplinary offences can safely be left to them.[72]"

Orr LJ agreed and Waller LJ considered it appropriate to have "a commanding officer dealing with the discipline of his force, facing his men without the intervention of lawyers" as "an extension of everyday discipline."

100. The law has moved on since then. While (as noted above) the need to avoid the "over–lawyering" or "over–judicialisation" of procedures in certain disciplinary tribunals, including those of disciplined services, is fully acknowledged, it has to be recognized that the special needs of such tribunals must be pursued with proper regard for the constitutional safeguards conferred by Article 10.

101. Thus, speaking of prison discipline, the Strasbourg court in *Campbell and Fell v. United Kingdom* [73] stated:

> "[The Court] is well aware that in the prison context there are practical reasons and reasons of policy for establishing a special disciplinary regime, for example security considerations and the interests of public order, the need to deal with misconduct by inmates as expeditiously as possible, the availability of tailor–made sanctions which may not be at the disposal of the ordinary courts and the desire of the prison authorities to retain ultimate responsibility for discipline within their establishments.
>
> However, the guarantee of a fair hearing, which is the aim of Art 6, is one of the fundamental principles of any democratic society, within the meaning of the Convention ... As the *Golder* judgment shows, justice cannot stop at the prison gate and there is, in appropriate cases, no warrant for depriving inmates of the safeguards of Art 6."

102. And this Court, noting the special requirements of a disciplinary committee of the Hong Kong Stock Exchange, stated:

> "SEHK's policy, reflected in the Listing Rules and the Disciplinary Procedures, of limiting (at least in the first instance) the role of lawyers at the hearing is based upon the belief that limited representation suffices in most cases; that an informal, expert, lay tribunal, steeped in the ways of the stock exchange, is best placed to deal effectively and swiftly with disciplinary issues; that the public interest in maintaining confidence in the market requires swift investigation and treatment of suspected infringements; and that "over–lawyering" the procedures would undermine many of these objectives, substantially lengthening and complicating proceedings,

> "…and making it difficult to persuade qualified individuals to accept unremunerated appointment to a Disciplinary Committee. These are plainly legitimate concerns. But they can only be pursued with proper regard for the needs of procedural fairness and for proportionality in any procedural restrictions imposed." [74]

103. I do not accept that the requirements of the police disciplinary tribunals in Hong Kong justify a total ban on legal representation regardless of the requirements of fairness. There seems to me to be little doubt that the effective functioning of the Police Force as a disciplined service will not be impaired by allowing its disciplinary tribunals a discretion to permit an officer to be legally represented where fairness so dictates. No ground of public necessity has been suggested as a basis for excluding the constitutional protection.

104. It is noteworthy that other police forces permit such legal representation with no apparent difficulty. Thus, in the United Kingdom, under the Police (Conduct) Regulations 1999, where an officer possibly faced the sanctions of dismissal, a requirement to resign or reduction in rank at the hands of the disciplinary tribunal, he had to be given notice of this and allowed to elect to be legally represented at the hearing.[75] And if he did so elect he could be represented by counsel or a solicitor at the hearing.[76] Those arrangements came into force some 10 years ago and were renewed (with some elaboration) in the current Police (Conduct) Regulations 2004.[77] Such renewal suggests that the 1999 Regulations have not had any harmful effect on policing in the United Kingdom.

105. In British Columbia, the courts went further. A provision in the relevant disciplinary regulations excluded legal representation in cases where a police officer was accused of a disciplinary offence carrying a maximum penalty other than dismissal, resignation or reduction in rank. It was held that even this restriction, limited to cases carrying lesser punishments, was incompatible with the requirements of fairness and therefore ultra vires.[78] There is no indication that this has impeded the effective functioning of the British Columbia police force.

106. I therefore conclude that that no objective grounds have been established to justify excluding the disciplinary proceedings in the present case from the protection of Article 10. To the extent that the Court of Appeal held in *陳庚秋 訴 香港警務處處長 (Chan Keng-chau v. Commissioner of Police)*[79] that Article 10 is inapplicable to police disciplinary proceedings, I would overrule that decision.

F. Compliance with Article 10 in general

107. Before turning to consider whether Article 10 is contravened in the present case, it is worthwhile considering what that article requires by way of compliance.

108. Where Article 10 is engaged, the person concerned becomes entitled to "a fair and public hearing by a competent, independent and impartial tribunal established by law". This has sometimes been so interpreted as to give rise to an anxiety that giving effect to Article 10 would be to "over-judicialise" and therefore destroy or radically alter the entire administrative system by requiring decisions to be taken publicly by independent and impartial tribunals imported into the administrative structure for that purpose. Such a fear was voiced in the Respondent's printed case:

> "If police disciplinary tribunals are to be chaired or presided by 'independent' persons and conducted in accordance with the requirements of Article 14(1) of the ICCPR (or the equivalent Article 10 of HKBOR), they will lose their essential character of being domestic or internal hearings of a disciplined service and become much more formal and legalistic."

F.1 Compliance viewing the entire determination process

109. It is, however, clear that Article 10 does not operate with such an undesirable effect. It does not require every element of the protections conferred to be present at every stage of the determination of a person's rights and obligations, but only that such protections should be effective when the determination is viewed as an entire process, including as part of that process such appeals or judicial review as may be available.

110. Thus, in *Le Compte, Van Leuven and de Meyere v. Belgium*,[80] the point was made as follows:

> "Whilst Article 6(1) embodies the 'right to a court' … it nevertheless does not oblige the Contracting States to submit *'contestations'* (disputes) over 'civil rights and obligations' to a procedure conducted at each of its stages before 'tribunals' meeting the Article's various requirements. Demands of flexibility and efficiency, which are fully compatible with the protection of human rights, may justify the prior intervention of administrative or professional bodies and, *a fortiori*, of judicial bodies which do not satisfy the said requirements in every respect; the legal tradition of many member States of the Council of Europe may be invoked in support of such a system."

111. In *Albert and Le Compte v. Belgium*,[81] the Strasbourg court held that Article 6(1) was engaged where a professional association exercised the power of determining the right of a member to practise medicine. It held that this was compatible with the ECHR provided that suitable judicial supervision was in place:

> "… the Convention calls at least for one of the two following systems: either the jurisdictional organs themselves comply with the requirements of Article 6(1), or they do not so comply but are subject to subsequent control by a judicial body that has full jurisdiction and does provide the guarantees of Article 6(1)."[82]

112. The HRC has adopted a similar approach to Article 14.1. In *Yvon Landry v. Canada*,[83] proceedings before a pension review board were challenged as inconsistent in various ways with Article 14.1. But since the Canadian legal system subjected such proceedings to judicial review and since the complainant had not sought to suggest that the remedies the court could provide "would not have availed in correcting whatever deficiencies may have marked the hearing of his case before the lower jurisdictions", the committee concluded:

> "… the Canadian legal system does contain provisions in the Federal Court Act to ensure to the author the right to a fair hearing in the situation. Consequently, his basic allegations do not reveal the possibility of any breach of the Covenant."

113. As Lord Clyde pointed out in *R (Alconbury Developments Ltd) v. Environment Secretary*:[84]

> "…the opening phrase in article 6(1), 'in the determination', refers not only to the particular process

of the making of the decision but extends more widely to the whole process which leads up to the final resolution."

His Lordship cited *Zumtobel v. Austria,*[85] where the Commission recalled that:

"... article 6(1) of the Convention does not require that the procedure which determines civil rights and obligations is conducted at each of its stages before tribunals meeting the requirements of this provision. An administrative procedure may thus precede the determination of civil rights by the tribunal envisaged in article 6(1) of the Convention."

114. And as Lord Millett noted in *Runa Begum v. Tower Hamlets LBC*.[86]

"Where an administrative decision is determinative of the claimant's civil rights, including his or her right to social security benefits or welfare assistance, the Strasbourg court has accepted that it may properly be made by a tribunal which is not itself possessed of the necessary independence, provided that measures to safeguard the impartiality of the tribunal and the fairness of its procedures are in place and its decisions are subject to ultimate judicial control by a court with 'full jurisdiction'."

115. I pause to note that in Hong Kong, this approach has been adopted by the Appeal Committee in *Chow Shun Yung v. Wei Pih*,[87] and by the Court of Appeal in *Tse Wai Chun Paul v. Solicitors Disciplinary Tribunal.*[88]

F.2 A "court of full jurisdiction"

116. The position is therefore that Article 10 can be given effect without demanding radical changes to the administrative system provided that the process of determining a person's rights and obligations beginning with the administrative process is subject to control by "a court of full jurisdiction".

117. When then, can a court be said to have "full jurisdiction" ? The answer, provided by Lord Hoffmann in *R (Alconbury Developments Ltd) v. Environment Secretary*[89] is: When it has "full jurisdiction to deal with the case as the nature of the decision requires":

"The reference to 'full jurisdiction' has been frequently cited in subsequent cases and sometimes relied upon in argument as if it were authority for saying that a policy decision affecting civil rights by an administrator who does not comply with article 6(1) has to be re-viewable on its merits by an independent and impartial tribunal. ... But subsequent European authority shows that 'full jurisdiction' does not mean full decision-making power. It means full jurisdiction to deal with the case as the nature of the decision requires."

118. A court of full jurisdiction may deal with the case in the manner required in at least two different ways. It may do so by supplying one or more of the protections mandated by Article 10 which were missing below, for instance, by assuming the role of the necessary independent tribunal or by giving the individual concerned the needed public hearing. Or it may do so by exercising its supervisory jurisdiction so as to correct or quash some non-compliant aspect of the determination by the authority or tribunal concerned, for instance, where there has been a want of impartiality or some unfairness in the original process. If in assuming such a role, the court is armed with full jurisdiction to deal with the case as the nature of the challenged decision requires, there is compliance with Article 10's requirements.

119. Thus, in *Le Compte, Van Leuven and de Meyere v. Belgium,*[90] the Strasbourg court having reiterated that the ECHR does not require the protections to be present at every stage, went on to consider whether the appeals tribunal and subsequently the Court of Cassation supplied the missing elements. It found that both these bodies did provide the necessary independence but that the needed publicity was still wanting.[91]

120. The House of Lords has pointed out that in many situations it is inevitable and in no way improper that the initial administrative determination of a person's civil rights and obligations should be taken by someone who is part of the administrative body concerned and so is plainly not independent. For instance, in the *Runa Begum* case,[92] a decision had to be taken, in the context of a local council's duty to house the homeless, as to whether the accommodation offered to the applicant was suitable and whether it was reasonable for her to accept it. If it was, the authority would be discharged from its duty if the offer was nevertheless refused. That decision was taken by a housing manager who was obviously not independent since, as Lord Millett noted, "She was an officer of the very council which was alleged to owe the duty." [93] However, the Article 6(1) requirement of independence was in the circumstances met by the availability of judicial review.

121. The principle may also be illustrated by reference to the requirement of publicity. As the Strasbourg court recently re-iterated in *Gulmez v. Turkey,*[94] publicity is a highly important aspect of a fair trial:

"The Court reiterates that the holding of court hearings in public constitutes a fundamental principle enshrined in Article 6 § 1. This public character protects litigants against the administration of justice in secret with no public scrutiny; it is also one of the means whereby confidence in the courts can be maintained. By rendering the administration of justice transparent, publicity contributes to the achievement of the aim of Article 6 § 1, namely a fair trial, the guarantee of which is one of the fundamental principles of any democratic society, within the meaning of the Convention..."

But this does not mean that there must be publicity at the original hearing or at every stage. Where the matter proceeds to a public hearing before a court of full jurisdiction, the protection against secret trials is achieved.[95] This was the approach correctly adopted by the Court of Appeal in *Tse Wai Chun Paul v. Solicitors Disciplinary Tribunal,*[96] holding that whereas the Tribunal's hearing had been held *in camera*, the requirement of publicity was fulfilled on the statutory appeal to the Court of Appeal.

122. It should however be stressed that the court giving the complainant the eventual public hearing must be a "court of full jurisdiction" with sufficient powers to "deal with the case as the nature of the decision requires". Where the public hearing comes before a court with limited jurisdiction so that important aspects of the decision cannot be publicly reviewed, the article's requirements may not be met. This is what the Strasbourg court held to have occurred in *Albert and Le Compte v. Belgium,*[97] notwithstanding the public hearing before the Court of Cassation:

"The public character of the cassation proceedings does not suffice to remedy the defect found to exist at the stage of the disciplinary proceedings. The Court of Cassation does not take cognisance of the merits of the case, which means that many aspects of *'contestations'* (disputes) concerning 'civil rights and obligations', including review of the facts and assessment of the proportionality between the fault and the sanction, fall outside its jurisdiction."

123. Where the original determination is marred by a lack of impartiality or by unfairness, the court of full jurisdiction may have to quash that determination to ensure compliance. The fact that the reviewing court is itself impartial or will itself act fairly may not be sufficient since the original defects may have resulted, for instance, in skewed factual findings or materials wrongly excluded, preventing the court from fully addressing the decision in the manner demanded.

124. The requirements for proper compliance emerging from the Strasbourg court's jurisprudence are summarised by Lord Hoffmann (in the context of the requirement of independence) as follows:[98]

> "The Strasbourg court ... has said, first, that an administrative decision within the extended scope of article 6 is a determination of civil rights and obligations and therefore prima facie has to be made by an independent tribunal. But, secondly, if the administrator is not independent (as will virtually by definition be the case) it is permissible to consider whether the composite procedure of administrative decision together with a right of appeal to a court is sufficient. Thirdly, it will be sufficient if the appellate (or reviewing) court has 'full jurisdiction' over the administrative decision. And fourthly, as established in the landmark case of *Bryan v. United Kingdom* (1995) 21 EHRR 342, 'full jurisdiction' does not necessarily mean jurisdiction to re-examine the merits of the case but, as I said in the *Alconbury* case [2003] 2 AC 295, 330, para 87, 'jurisdiction to deal with the case as the nature of the decision requires'."

F.3 Compliance through judicial review

125. In Hong Kong, as in the United Kingdom, virtually every administrative determination is potentially subject to judicial review. Given that the court does not, on a judicial review, conduct afresh any fact-finding exercise underlying the impugned decision, is the court which exercises its judicial review function to be regarded as a "court of full jurisdiction"?

126. As we have just seen, Lord Hoffmann emphasises that it is erroneous to believe that a decision has to be reviewable on its merits before the reviewing court can be considered a court of full jurisdiction. Furthermore, as we have noted, in *Yvon Landry v. Canada*,[99] the HRC considered the availability of judicial review under the applicable Canadian statute sufficient to make the decision-making process compliant with Article 14.1. It is in my view clear, subject to what is stated below, that where a Hong Kong court is able to exercise its full powers on judicial review it is likely to qualify as a court of full jurisdiction for Article 10 purposes. This proposition assumes that there is no statutory restriction on the judicial review powers available to the court, a matter of obvious relevance to the present appeal to which I will return.

127. As Lord Millett points out, judicial review powers are substantial and include powers to intervene based on the decision-maker's unsatisfactory treatment of the facts:

> "A decision may be quashed if it is based on a finding of fact or inference from the facts which is perverse or irrational; or there was no evidence to support it; or it was made by reference to irrelevant factors or without regard to relevant factors. It is not necessary to identify a specific error of law; if the decision cannot be supported the court will infer that the decision-making authority misunderstood or overlooked relevant evidence or misdirected itself in law. The court cannot substitute its own findings of fact for those of the decision-making authority if there was evidence to support them; and questions as to the weight to be given to a particular piece of evidence and the credibility of witnesses are for the decision-making authority and not the court. But these are the only significant limitations on the court's jurisdiction, and they are not very different from the limitations which practical considerations impose on an appellate court with full jurisdiction to entertain appeals on fact or law but which deals with them on the papers only and without hearing oral evidence." [100]

128. Such powers have been held sufficient in the international jurisprudence. Thus, in *Bryan v. United Kingdom*,[101] the Strasbourg court noted that an appeal to the English High Court on points of law "was not capable of embracing all aspects of the inspector's decision" and that:

> "... there was no rehearing as such of the original complaints submitted to the inspector; the High Court could not substitute its own decision on the merits for that of the inspector; and its jurisdiction over the facts was limited." [102]

However, the breadth of the reviewing court's powers were noted:

> "... apart from the classic grounds of unlawfulness under English law (going to such issues as fairness, procedural propriety, independence and impartiality), the inspector's decision could have been quashed by the High Court if it had been made by reference to irrelevant factors or without regard to relevant factors; or if the evidence relied on by the inspector was not capable of supporting a finding of fact; or if the decision was based on an inference from facts which was perverse or irrational in the sense that no inspector properly directing himself would have drawn such an inference."[103]

Given that there were administrative safeguards at the level of the inspector's decision-making process and that there were no disputes as to primary fact, the argument being largely concerned with questions of policy, the Court held that the powers exercisable on judicial review were sufficient to qualify the process of determination as Article 6(1) compliant.

129. In the *Runa Begum* case, Lord Bingham of Cornhill concluded on the basis of his review of relevant European decisions, that:

> "... taken together they provide compelling support for the conclusion that, in a context such as this, the absence of a full fact-finding jurisdiction in the tribunal to which appeal lies from an administrative decision-making body does not disqualify that tribunal for purposes of article 6(1)." [104]

130. Lord Hoffmann, in the same case, commented that:

> An English lawyer can view with equanimity the extension of the scope of article 6 because the English

conception of the rule of law requires the legality of virtually all governmental decisions affecting the individual to be subject to the scrutiny of the ordinary courts.[105]

His Lordship's view was that on principle, judicial review, even with its limitations, is generally sufficient:

"The concern of the court, as it has emphasised since *Golder's* case 1 EHRR 524 is to uphold the rule of law and to insist that decisions which on generally accepted principles are appropriate only for judicial decision should be so decided. In the case of decisions appropriate for administrative decision, its concern, again founded on the rule of law, is that there should be the possibility of adequate judicial review. For this purpose, cases like *Bryan* and *Kingsley* make it clear that limitations on practical grounds on the right to a review of the findings of fact will be acceptable." [106]

131. Lord Hoffmann did, however, make it plain (echoing the Strasbourg court in *Bryan*) that the sufficiency of judicial review is dependent on the subject matter of the challenged decision, the manner in which it was arrived at, its content and the proposed grounds of challenge.[107] Different considerations may apply depending, for instance, on whether the impugned decision relates to administrative policy or to the way the facts were found:

"If, therefore, the question is one of policy or expediency, the 'safeguards' [in the decision-making process] are irrelevant. No one expects the inspector to be independent or impartial in applying the Secretary of State's policy and this was the reason why the court said that he was not for all purposes an independent or impartial tribunal. In this respect his position is no different from that of the Secretary of State himself. The reason why judicial review is sufficient in both cases to satisfy article 6 has nothing to do with the 'safeguards' but depends upon the *Zumtobel* principle of respect for the decision of an administrative authority on questions of expediency. It is only when one comes to findings of fact, or the evaluation of facts, such as arise on the question of whether there has been a breach of planning control, that the safeguards are essential for the acceptance of a limited review of fact by the appellate tribunal." [108]

132. In *R (Wright) v. Secretary of State for Health*, Baroness Hale of Richmond summarises the position as follows:

"What amounts to 'full jurisdiction' varies according to the nature of the decision being made. It does not always require access to a court or tribunal even for the determination of disputed issues of fact. Much depends upon the subject matter of the decision and the quality of the initial decision-making process. If there is a 'classic exercise of administrative discretion', even though determinative of civil rights and obligations, and there are a number of safeguards to ensure that the procedure is in fact both fair and impartial, then judicial review may be adequate to supply the necessary access to a court, even if there is no jurisdiction to examine the factual merits of the case." [109]

133. The powers enjoyed by a Hong Kong court on a judicial review are very similar to those exercised by the courts of England and Wales which have been held to constitute courts of full jurisdiction. Accordingly, it is my opinion that in Hong Kong, a court exercising its judicial review jurisdiction without statutory interference is likely to qualify for most purposes as a court of full jurisdiction.

G. Has Article 10 been contravened in the present case?

134. Given that the disciplinary proceedings faced by the appellant bring Article 10 into play, was his entitlement to "a fair and public hearing by a competent, independent and impartial tribunal established by law" met, looking at the process as a whole?

G.1 Matters which are not contraventions

135. The police disciplinary tribunal is obviously "established by law". It has furthermore never been suggested that either of the disciplinary tribunals convened was lacking in competence or impartiality. The only complaint is that the hearing was not fair because of the exclusion of legal representation in circumstances where, the appellant submits, fairness demanded that he be permitted such representation.

136. But before addressing that question, it is worth noting that there might have been a complaint concerning publicity and independence. The proceedings before the tribunal were held in private and the police superintendents who sat as the adjudicating officers cannot be regarded as independent, being officers subordinate to the Commissioner in whose name the disciplinary charges were brought. However, it was in my view right not to contend that those features of the disciplinary proceedings constituted a contravention of Article 10. Viewing the process as a whole, the protections of independence and publicity are achieved without any deficit through recourse to judicial review. Judges in the Court of First Instance and in the appellate courts are plainly independent of the Police Force and of the executive and legislative arms of government in general. The courts are open to the public and every relevant aspect of the charges, the evidence and the rulings made by the disciplinary tribunal can be (and have been) publicly discussed.

G.2 Legal representation and a fair hearing

137. Returning to the central complaint, one must ask: what are the requirements of a fair hearing under Article 10? In particular, what is required in terms of legal representation at disciplinary proceedings such as those under discussion? It is my view that the well-developed common law principles of procedural fairness supply the answer. An arrangement which satisfies the requirements of the common law will almost certainly conform with the fairness requirements of Article 10.

138. At common law and in the absence of inconsistent legislative intervention, administrative and domestic tribunals are generally regarded as masters of their own procedure possessing a flexible discretion to take whatever procedural course may be dictated by the requirements of fairness.[110]

139. The common law requirements regarding legal representation at disciplinary proceedings were recently examined in *The Stock Exchange of Hong Kong Ltd v. New World Development Co Ltd*,[111] and it is unnecessary to repeat the discussion of the authorities to be found in that judgment. The Court decided that there is no absolute right to legal representation, this being a matter to be dealt with in the tribunal's discretion in accordance with principles of fairness. The factors to be taken into account in deciding whether fairness requires such representation to be permitted include the seriousness of the charge and potential

penalty; whether any points of law are likely to arise; the capacity of the individual to present his own case; procedural difficulties; the need for reasonable speed in making the adjudication; and the need for fairness among the individuals concerned. It was recognized that no list of factors could be exhaustive and that the common law principles operate flexibly, requiring the tribunal to respond reasonably to the requirements of fairness arising in each case, balancing any competing interests and considering what, if any, limits may proportionately be imposed on legal representation in consequence.[112]

G.3 Regulations 9(11) and 9(12) inconsistent with Article 10

140. As I noted in section A.3 above, Mr Chow SC realistically accepts that regulations 9(11) and 9(12) impose a blanket restriction on professional legal representation in police disciplinary proceedings. The vice which results is that in a case where the common law principles and compliance with Article 10 compel the conclusion that the tribunal's discretion ought to be exercised in favour of allowing legal representation, regulations 9(11) and 9(12) prevent that course from being followed. In other words, they make it part of the disciplinary scheme that the tribunal is prevented from complying with its duty of fairness where such duty calls for legal representation to be permitted.

141. Furthermore, the regulations prevent the court on a judicial review from remedying non–compliance by quashing the decision on the ground of unfairness. Being sanctioned by subordinate legislation, the refusal of legal representation could not be said to be unlawful as a matter of common law. Therefore, so long as they remain in force, the regulations divest the reviewing court of the status of a "court of full jurisdiction", depriving it of the power necessary to deal with the case as the nature of the decision (involving an unfair refusal of legal representation) requires. Non–compliance would therefore be unremedied unless the regulations are struck down so as to remove the obstacle to conformity with Article 10.

142. Regulations 9(11) and 9(12) are therefore systemically incompatible with Article 10. Pursuant to section 6(1) of the Bill of Rights Ordinance, the Court is empowered to make such order in respect of this violation of the Bill of Rights as it considers appropriate and just in the circumstances. In my view, it is appropriate and just that regulations 9(11) and 9(12) be declared unconstitutional and invalid with the result that the tribunal, as master of its own procedure at common law, is able to exercise a discretion unfettered by those regulations to permit legal or other forms of representation where fairness requires this. I have been focussing on objections to the exclusion of professional legal representation by regulation 9(12). However, there is no reason why the tribunal should be restricted to permitting non–professional representation only by fellow officers as envisaged by regulation 9(11). The tribunal ought to be able, in its discretion, to permit other appropriate forms of representation if asked for, whether by a fellow officer or by a person from outside the Force who would in a courtroom setting be called a McKenzie friend.[113]

G.4 The appellant did not have a fair hearing

143. If the invalidity of the constraints imposed by the offending regulations had been established before the hearing the tribunal would have been obliged, pursuant to its duty to ensure that the appellant had a fair hearing in accordance with Article 10, to consider, by reference to factors such as those mentioned in the *Stock Exchange* case, whether his was a case calling for legal representation to be permitted.

144. Believing, no doubt on the footing of regulations 9(11) and 9(12), that it had no such discretion, the tribunal never considered the possibility of its exercise and obviously never examined the factors relevant to such exercise. In my view, this omission made the proceedings inherently unfair. On this basis alone, the conclusion must be reached that the appellant was indeed deprived of a fair hearing so that his conviction and sentence must be quashed.

145. I do not consider it necessary for this Court (or any reviewing court) to undertake the exercise of applying relevant discretionary factors to the evidence in order to decide whether it would itself, in the tribunal's position, have exercised the discretion in favour of permitting legal representation. Much less do I consider it necessary to demonstrate that a refusal by the tribunal to exercise its discretion would have been irrational. In taking this view, I am respectfully in agreement with the approach adopted by Hartmann J in *Rowse v. Secretary for the Civil Service.*[114] As his Lordship pointed out, when deciding whether the requirement of a fair hearing is met, the court is simply concerned with deciding whether the constitutional standard has been complied with. The standard, as his Lordship stated, is one of fairness and not irrationality.

146. Nor do I consider it necessary or profitable to enter into the inevitably speculative realm of trying to determine how the evidence or the case might have progressed differently if a lawyer had been acting for the appellant.

147. I might add that if I had arrived at a different view and decided that this Court ought to examine the factors bearing on the exercise of the discretion, my conclusion would have been that the factors substantially favour allowing legal representation.

(a) The charge and the potential penalty were obviously very serious, punishment for an offence under PGO 6–01(8) being "normally terminatory". The actual sentence was undoubtedly severe, involving the loss of his pensionable employment as a policeman after 12 years of commendable service and deferral for many years of his enjoyment of the pension rights which had so far accrued.

(b) As the Court of Appeal's decision as to the meaning of PGO 6–01(8) (discussed below) shows, a point of law does arise. A sound grasp of the true construction of the PGO was a necessary starting–point for deciding how the evidence should be developed and the case handled.

(c) The fact that a re-hearing was involved with potential inconsistencies in the testimony of witnesses appearing on both occasions, especially viewed against the background of a fresh set of Administrative Instructions, ought to have raised questions as to the appellant's capacity to present his own case.

H. The suggested inevitability of conviction

H.1 The Court of Appeal's approach

148. In the Court of Appeal, Tang VP accepted the argument that there was "a simple answer" to the appeal, namely, that relief by way of judicial review had to be refused since the appellant's conviction was inevitable.[115] As I understand it, his Lordship's approach was that even if regulations 9(11) and 9(12) were to be struck down as unconstitutional, the result would still be no different because, on what he considered to be the true construction of PGO 6–01(8), a conviction was inevitable. The

tribunal itself did not adopt the construction advocated by Tang VP, so the present discussion addresses the position adopted by the Court of Appeal in support of its "inevitability" proposition and not the tribunal's position.

149. As noted above, the version of PGO 6-01(8) promulgated on 22 September 1999 ("the 1999 version") defined the disciplinary offence with which the appellant was charged as follows :

> "A police officer shall be prudent in his financial affairs. Serious pecuniary embarrassment stemming from financial imprudence which leads to the impairment of an officer's operational efficiency will result in disciplinary action."

150. On its face, the disciplinary offence has three elements: (i) the officer must be guilty of conduct amounting to "financial imprudence"; (ii) such conduct must result in "serious pecuniary embarrassment"; and (iii) the serious pecuniary embarrassment must lead to impairment of that officer's operational efficiency.

151. Tang VP pointed out that there was no dispute as to elements (i) and (ii) and held that this was sufficient, with no need for any evidence of element (iii):

> "This court has consistently held that serious pecuniary embarrassment would necessarily lead to impairment of operational efficiency of a police officer within the meaning of PGO 6-01(8). See, for example, *陳庚秋 [Chan Keng-chau] and Leung Fuk Wah v. Commissioner of Police* [2002] 3 HKLRD 653." [116]

His Lordship added:

> "We do not believe legal representation could have resulted in a different outcome. His conviction under PGO 6-01(8) was inevitable. So we would in any event have refused relief." [117]

152. The Court of Appeal's decision regarding the "inevitability" of the appellant's conviction is therefore apparently based (a) on its construction of PGO 6-01(8); (b) on the authority of the *陳庚秋 (Chan Keng-chau)* and *Leung Fuk Wah* decisions; and (c) on a factual observation that an officer who finds himself in serious pecuniary embarrassment necessarily has his operational efficiency impaired.

H.2 Construction of PGO 6-01(8)

153. The construction adopted by the Court of Appeal seems contrary to the ordinary meaning of the words of the applicable version of PGO 6-01(8). As noted above, it has, on its face three elements. Its language suggests that those three elements are causally linked and occur in a sequence: financial imprudence causing serious pecuniary embarrassment causing the impairment of operational efficiency. Thus, the serious pecuniary embarrassment "stems from" financial imprudence and in turn "leads to" the impairment of operational efficiency. The Court of Appeal's approach does not reflect this.

H.3 The two authorities cited

154. The first authority relied on, *Leung Fuk Wah v. Commission of Police,*[118] was not in fact concerned with 1999 version of PGO 6-01(8). It was dealing with the preceding version issued on 30 January 1993 ("the 1993 version") which read as follows:

> "A police officer shall be prudent in his financial affairs. Serious pecuniary embarrassment from whatever cause is regarded as a circumstance which impairs the efficiency of an officer."

155. The 1993 version obviously differs significantly from the 1999 version. It centres on serious pecuniary embarrassment as the basis of the disciplinary offence "from whatever cause". The 1999 version, on the other hand, only treats serious pecuniary embarrassment as a disciplinary matter if it stems from financial imprudence. Moreover, while the 1999 version refers to impairment of operational efficiency as something which serious pecuniary embarrassment "leads to", the 1993 uses quite different language. It states that serious pecuniary embarrassment "is regarded as a circumstance which impairs the efficiency of an officer".

156. PGO 6-01(8) in its 1993 version was described by the Court of Appeal in *Ng Kam Chuen v. The Commissioner of Police,*[119] as suffering from a "lack of clarity" as "not an easy provision to apply" and as "obscure".[120] The Court of Appeal thought its construction was highly arguable and so reversed the earlier judgment of Keith J and granted the applicant leave to apply for judicial review. At the substantive judicial review hearing,[121] Stone J construed the 1993 version as placing an ultimate legal burden on the Commissioner "of establishing both serious pecuniary embarrassment stemming from financial imprudence and consequent impairment of efficiency of the officer" and, upon proof of serious pecuniary embarrassment, as placing an evidential burden on the officer "to establish that his efficiency as an officer has not been impaired".[122]

157. This was the fray which the Court of Appeal in *Leung Fuk Wah* entered. Cheung JA (apparently for the Court) overruled Stone J and held:

> "... as serious pecuniary embarrassment is regarded as a circumstance impairing efficiency, it is not necessary to adduce further evidence on the impairment of efficiency."

Like the earlier cases cited above, this was addressing the meaning and effect of the 1993 version.

158. Since we are only concerned with the 1999 version, I would prefer to say nothing as to the true construction of the 1993 version (as to which we have heard no argument). It is relevant to state this because PGO 6-01(8) was in fact further amended on 2 July 2003 (as a result of *Leung Fuk Wah*) to assume a form which has features in common with 1993 version and may require discussion in some future case.

159. The point for present purposes is that since *Leung Fuk Wah* was concerned only with the 1993 version, it is not an authority on the meaning and effect of the 1999 version and provides no support for the Court of Appeal's view as to the inevitability of the appellant's conviction in the present case.

160. In the second authority relied on, *陳庚秋 訴 香港警務處處長 (Chan Keng-chau v. Commissioner of Police)*[123] which was concerned with the 1999 version, the Court of Appeal was alive to the differences in the wording of the 1993 and 1999 versions. However, there was little analysis of the language of the latter. Yeung JA (for the Court) merely pointed to the need for special arrangements to be made for OUDs such as avoiding the handling of money or property or restrictions on carrying firearms and concluded (in translation):

> "It is reasonable for the Commissioner to take the abovementioned measures. As such, it is inevitable that serious pecuniary embarrassment would impair the work

efficiency of a police officer."[124]

161. The Court of Appeal in *Chan Keng-chau* did not rule on whether evidence of an impairment of operational efficiency was necessary or whether impairment would be presumed simply from the fact of serious pecuniary embarrassment. Instead, the Court declared itself satisfied that the Commissioner had in fact presented sufficient evidence of such impairment, pointing to various items of evidence adduced.[125]

162. I am therefore not persuaded that these two authorities provide any basis for the Court of Appeal's "inevitability" conclusion.

H.4 Inevitable Impairment as a matter of fact

163. The evidence does not support the conclusion that from the point of view of the Police Force, impairment of operational efficiency inevitably follows whenever an officer finds himself in a state of serious pecuniary embarrassment. On the contrary, the policy statements and other materials current at the time of the appellant's disciplinary proceedings suggest that it was regarded as a question of fact and evidence as to whether there was such impairment. Two examples will serve to illustrate this. I would emphasise that I do not refer to them for any view which they might express as to the proper construction of the relevant PGO but as demonstrating that it was evidently accepted by the Force that impairment of operational efficiency did not necessarily follow but could and should be separately established as a matter of fact.

164. Thus, shortly after Stone J's judgment, a memo from the Commissioner dated 15 April 1999 stated:

> "... automatic restrictions placed on an officer, which flow from establishment of the latter's indebtedness but fail to take into consideration his specific circumstances, may not be capable of supporting a finding of impaired efficiency.
>
> The essence of PGO 6–01(8) is that the officer's inefficiency results from his/her financial imprudence ... not from matters outwith his/her control. ... Where ... a Formation Commander has not considered the officer's ability to perform his duties and has restricted the officer as a 'matter of course', based solely on the officer's indebtedness, it can be said that the officer's efficiency has been impaired by circumstances outwith his control. This latter situation would not support establishment of the impairment to efficiency 'pillar'." (underlining in the original)

The 1999 version of PGO 6–01(8) was issued a few months later, reflecting this policy.

165. In the Administrative Instructions issued on 17 April 2000, during the period when the appellant was engaging in his share trading, there is discussion of how bankrupt officers (who must be by definition in serious pecuniary embarrassment) are to be treated. Paragraph 81 states that if bankruptcy is due to financial imprudence "which leads to impairment of an officer's operational efficiency, disciplinary action in accordance with PGO 6–01(8) should be contemplated." Significantly, paragraph 82 goes on to state:

> "If there is no evidence to show that the operational efficiency of the bankrupt officer has been impaired but there is evidence that the bankruptcy is due to some reprehensible causes (eg gambling, overspending, high risk speculative investments, etc) ... disciplinary action for an offence of 'Conduct Calculated' [to lower the reputation of the Force], contravening respondent 3(2)(m) of the [Regulations] should be considered."

166. Accordingly, I am with respect unable to accept the Court of Appeal's views as to the "inevitability of conviction". A conviction could not be secured simply by pointing to the absence of dispute as to the elements of financial imprudence and serious pecuniary embarrassment and holding that impairment of operational efficiency followed automatically. Giving effect to the ordinary meaning of the words used in the 1999 version, proof of impairment of the officer's operational efficiency as a separate element of the offence, flowing from his serious pecuniary embarrassment was required. I do not consider that there was any evidential burden on the officer charged. The impairment alleged by the Commissioner had to be proved by him. He would not have lacked the means of doing this as evidence could be adduced from colleagues and superiors of the officer charged to show the ways in which his operational efficiency was said to have been impaired.

I. Ultra vires

167. In the light of my conclusions, it is unnecessary to deal with the alternative argument that regulations 9(11) and 9(12) are ultra vires the rule–making power in section 45 of the Ordinance.

J. Conclusion

168. For the foregoing reasons, I conclude that:

(a) Article 10 is engaged in respect of the appellant's disciplinary proceedings.

(b) The requirement of a fair hearing means that the disciplinary tribunal ought to have considered permitting the appellant to be legally represented.

(c) In excluding the possibility of the tribunal exercising such a discretion, regulations 9(11) and 9(12) are inconsistent with Article 10 and must be declared unconstitutional, null and void.

(d) Since the tribunal failed to consider and, if appropriate, to permit legal representation for the appellant, he was deprived of a fair hearing in accordance with Article 10 so that the disciplinary proceedings were unlawful and the resulting convictions and sentences must be quashed.

169. I would accordingly allow the appeal and make the following Orders:

(a) That the following orders or decisions be quashed, namely:

(i) The finding dated 2 March 2001 by the Adjudicating Officer that the appellant was guilty of the disciplinary offence charged and the award of dismissal dated 13 March 2001 made pursuant thereto.

(ii) The finding dated 27 March 2002 by the Adjudicating Officer that the appellant was guilty of the disciplinary offence charged, the consequent award of compulsory retirement with deferred benefits suspended for 12 months made on 4 April 2002 and the subsequent increased award of immediate compulsory retirement with deferred benefits made on 26 July 2002 and ratified by the Commissioner on 21 October 2002 to take effect from 23 October 2002.

(b) That a Declaration be granted declaring that regulations 9(11) and 9(12) of the Police (Discipline) Regulations (Cap 232) are inconsistent with Article 10 of the Bill of Rights and Article 39 of the Basic Law and are unconstitutional, null, void and of no effect.

(c) That there be no order as to costs as between the parties, but that the appellant's costs be taxed in accordance with the Legal Aid Regulations.

Lord Woolf NPJ:

170. I agree with the judgment of Mr Justice Ribeiro PJ. Although there are differences in the treatment of some issues in the judgments of Mr Justice Bokhary and Mr Justice Ribeiro PJJ, the differences do not appear to me to be of significance to the outcome of this appeal and I also agree with the judgment of Mr Justice Bokhary PJ, without expressing any preference as to the views in the judgments as to which there are differences.

Chief Justice Li:

171. The appeal is unanimously allowed. We make the orders set out in the final paragraph of the judgment of Mr Justice Ribeiro PJ.

Chief Justice (Andrew Li)

Permanent Judge (Kemal Bokhary)

Permanent Judge (Patrick Chan)

Permanent Judge (R A V Ribeiro)

Non-Permanent Judge (Lord Woolf)

Mr Johannes Chan SC and Ms Margaret Ng (instructed by Messrs Lau Pau & Co and assigned by the Legal Aid Department) for the appellant

Mr Anderson Chow SC (instructed by the Department of Justice) and Mr Louie Wong (of that department) for the respondent

---

FACV 9/2008

LAM SIU PO and COMMISSIONER OF POLICE

[1] The Administrative Instructions on the Management of Indebtedness distributed under cover of the Commissioner's Memo dated 17 April 2000 were those in force at the relevant time.

[2] Cap 232.

[3] Defined by regulation 2 as "a police officer charged with a disciplinary offence".

[4] Under regulation 13.

[5] Defined by regulation 2 to mean "a chief superintendent, assistant commissioner or senior assistant commissioner".

[6] Suspended sentences are dealt with by regulation 28.

[7] HCAL 7/2003 (23 August 2005).

[8] [2008] 2 HKLRD 27 (Tang VP, Yeung JA and Yam J).

[9] HCMP 2824/2004, Yeung JA and Tang J (29 December 2004).

[10] §§48-51.

[11] [1977] 1 QB 240.

[12] *陳庚秋 訴 香港警務處處長 (Chan Keng-chau v Commissioner of Police)* HCMP 2824/2004, Yeung JA and Tang J (29 December 2004); and *Leung Fuk Wah v Commissioner of Police* [2002] 3 HKLRD 653.

[13] CACV 340/2005 Tang VP, Yeung JA and Yam J (13 May 2008).

[14] Adopted and opened for signature, ratification and accession by United Nations General Assembly Resolution 2200 A (XXI) of 16 December 1966.

[15] Opened for signature by member states of the council of Europe at Rome on 4 November 1950.

[16] The French text of Article 14.1 relevantly provides: "Tous sont égaux devant les tribunaux et les cours de justice. Toute personne a droit à ce que sa cause soit entendue équitablement et publiquement par un tribunal compétent, indépendant et impartial, établi par la loi, qui décidera soit du bien–fondé de toute accusation en matière pénale dirigée contre elle, soit des contestations surses *droits et obligations de caractère civil*." And the French text of Article 6(1) relevantly states: "Toute personne a droit à ce que sa cause soit entendue équitablement, publiquement et dans un délai raisonnable, par un tribunal indépendant et impartial, établi par la loi, qui décidera, soit des contestations sur ses *droits et obligations de caractère civil*, soit du bien–fondé de toute accusation en matière pénale dirigée contre elle."

[17] (1986) 8 EHRR 425 at 444-445, §§20-22.

[18] This limitation deriving from section 7 of the Bill of Rights Ordinance (Cap 383).

[19] [2003] 2 AC 430 at 445,§27.

[20] *Golder v United Kingdom* (1975) 1 EHRR 524, §34.

[21] See the Joint Dissenting Opinion in *Feldbrugge v The Netherlands* (1986) 8 EHRR 425 at 444-445, §§19-22; and the

Dissenting Opinion of Ms Ruth Wedgwood in *Wolfgang Lederbauer v Austria*, Communication No 1454/2006 (2008) Vol 15, No 1, IHRR, §§4.1-4.10.

[22] *Runa Begum v Tower Hamlets LBC* [2003] 2 AC 430 at 445, §28.

[23] (1986) 8 EHRR 425 at 443, §15.

[24] Eg, *The Stock Exchange of Hong Kong Ltd and New World Development Co Ltd* (2006) 9 HKCFAR 234 at 271, §109.

[25] Relating to the fifth session of the United Nations Commission on Human Rights held on 1 June 1949.

[26] (1975) 1 EHRR 524 at §35.

[27] *Runa Begum v Tower Hamlets LBC* [2003] 2 AC 430 at 464, §109, citing Lord Hoffmann in *R (Alconbury Developments Ltd) v Secretary of State for the Environment* [2003] 2 AC 295 at 327-330, §§78-88.

[28] *Konig v Federal Republic of Germany* (1978) 2 EHRR 170, §88; *Feldbrugge v The Netherlands* (1986) 8 EHRR 425, §26.

[29] *Runa Begum v Tower Hamlets LBC* [2003] 2 AC 430 at 459, §82, citing *König v Federal Republic of Germany* (1978) 2 EHRR 170 at 192-193, §88; and *Benthem v The Netherlands* (1985) 8 EHRR 1 at 9, §34.

[30] (Communication No 112/81) (8 April 1986).

[31] At §9.2. See also the Dissenting Opinion of Ms Ruth Wedgwood in *Wolfgang Lederbauer v Austria*, Communication No 1454/2006 (2008) Vol 15, No 1, IHRR, §§5.5 and 5.6; and *Perterer v Austria*, Communication No 1015/2001 (2005) Vol 12, No IHRR 80, §9.2.

[32] (1987) 10 EHRR 339 at 347-349, §§45-48.

[33] (1971) 1 EHRR 455.

[34] [2003] 2 AC 295 at 328, §80.

[35] At §80.

[36] As in *Konig v Federal Republic of Germany* (1978) 2 EHRR 170.

[37] Eg, *Bryan v United Kingdom* (1995) 21 EHRR 342.

[38] (1993) 26 EHRR 187.

[39] (2000) 34 EHRR 1122.

[40] *Runa Begum v Tower Hamlets LBC* [2003] 2 AC 430 at 460-461, §90.

[41] (2007) 45 EHRR 43.

[42] (1992) 21 EHRR 188.

[43] At §17.

[44] (2001) 31 EHRR 26.

[45] At §66.

[46] At §67.

[47] (2007) 45 EHRR 43.

[48] At §51.

[49] At §58.

[50] At §59.

[51] At §62.

[52] Ibid.

[53] At §62.

[54] At §59.

[55] Ibid.

[56] At §61.

[57] See, eg, *Mitin v Ukraine* [2008] ECHR 38724.02; and *Cvetkovic v Serbia* [2008] ECHR 17271.04.

[58] HRC, 90th Session, Geneva, 9 to 27 July 2007.

[59] At §16.

[60] *Engel v The Netherlands(No 1)* (1976) 1 EHRR 647; *Campbell and Fell v United Kingdom* (1985) 7 EHRR 165; *Ezeh and Connors v United Kingdom* (2004) 39 EHRR 1.

[61] (1985) 7 EHRR 165 at §§68-69.

[62] At section A.2 of this judgment.

[63] (1971) 1 EHRR 455.

[64] [2009] 2 WLR 267 at §19.

[65] *Le Compte, Van Leuven and de Meyere v Belgium* (1981) 4 EHRR 1; *Bakker v Austria* (2004) 39 EHRR 548.

[66] (1992) 21 EHRR 188.

[67] (2001) 31 EHRR 26.

[68] (2007) 45 EHRR 43.

[69] [1975] 1 WLR 1132 at 1133.

[70] [1977] 1 QB 240.

[71] At 253-254.

[72] At 254.

[73] (1985) 7 EHRR 165 at §69.

[74] *The Stock Exchange of Hong Kong Ltd v New World Development Co Ltd* (2006) 9 HKCFAR 234 at 271, §109.

[75] Regulation 17.

[76] Regulation 21.

[77] Regulations 18(1)(b), 23(3) and 24(3).

[78] *Joplin v Chief Constable of the City of Vancouver* (1985) 20 DLR (4th) 314.

[79] HCMP 2824/2004, Yeung JA and Tang J (29 December 2004).

[80] (1981) 4 EHRR 1 at §51(a).

[81] (1983) 5 EHRR 533.

[82] At §29.

[83] Communication No 112/81 (8 April 1986).

[84] [2003] 2 AC 295 at 349, §152.

[85] (1993) 17 EHRR 116, § 64.

[86] [2003] 2 AC 430 at 463, §100.

[87] (2003) 6 HKCFAR 299, §37.

[88] [2002] 4 HKC 1, §10. The Court of Appeal assumed without deciding that the Solicitors Disciplinary Tribunal was a "public authority" for the purposes of section 7 of the Bill of Rights Ordinance (Cap 383). This issue does not arise on the present appeal and references to the Court of Appeal's decision in the present judgment are not intended to imply acceptance that the Tribunal should be so categorized.

[89] [2003] 2 AC 295 at 330, §87.

[90] (1981) 4 EHRR 1.

[91] At §§57 and 60-61.

[92] [2003] 2 AC 430.

[93] At §96.

[94] [2008] ECHR 16330/02, §34.

[95] See eg, *H v Belgium* (1987) 10 EHRR 339 at §54.

[96] [2002] 4 HKC 1 at §26. See footnote 88 above as to the assumed basis of this decision.

[97] (1983) 5 EHRR 533 at §36.

[98] *Runa Begum v Tower Hamlets LBC* [2003] 2 AC 430 at §33.

[99] Communication No 112/81 (8 April 1986).

[100] *Runa Begum v Tower Hamlets LBC* [2003] 2 AC 430, §99.

[101] (1995) 21 EHRR 342.

[102 At §44.

[103] Ibid.

[104] [2003] 2 AC 430, §11.

[105] Ibid, §35.

[106] Ibid, §57.

[107] *R (Alconbury Developments Ltd) v Secretary of State for the Environment* [2003] 2 AC 295, §116.

[108] Ibid, §117.

[109] [2009] 2 WLR 267 at §23.

[110] *Enderby Town Football Club Ltd v Football Association Ltd* [1971] Ch 591; *Maynard v Osmond* [1977] 1 QB 240; *R v Home Secretary, ex parte Tarrant* [1985] QB 251.

[111] (2006) 9 HKCFAR 234.

[112] At §95 to §101.

[113] *McKenzie v McKenzie* [1971] P 33; *R v Home Secretary, ex parte Tarrant* [1985] QB 251 at 298.

[114] [2008] 5 HKC 405 at 433, §134.

[115] [2008] 2 HKLRD 27, §22.

[116] At §27.

[117] At §28.

[118] [2002] 3 HKLRD 653.

[119] CACV 241/1997 (17 February 1998), Nazareth VP, Liu and Leong JJA.

[120] At pp 5, 6 and 7 respectively.

[121] *Ng Kam Chuen v Secretary for Justice* [1999] 2 HKC 291.

[122] At 296-297.

[123] HCMP 2824/2004, Yeung JA and Tang J (29 December 2004).

[124] At §§34-35.

[125] At §37.

The Stock Exchange Of Hong Kong Limited v. New World Development Company Limited and others

香港聯合交易所有限公司 對 新世界發展有限公司及其他人

HCAL 79/2003；CACV 170/2004；FACV 22 /2005

簡略案情

上訴人香港聯合交易所有限公司（下稱“聯交所”）經《證券及期貨條例》第 19 條授權設立香港證券交易所並制定了《上市規則》，任何在聯交所上市交易的公司均須同意遵守該《上市規則》。答辯人是一家在聯交所掛牌交易的上市公司及其董事。聯交所上市科負責執行《上市規則》並調查違反該規則的行為，而上市委員會（由獨立的證券期貨從業員和專家組成）負責審理違反《上市規則》的行為。

2002 年 10 月，聯交所上市科向上市委員會提交了一份報告，要求審理答辯人涉嫌違反《上市規則》洩露價格敏感資訊的行為。上市委員會收到報告後組成了紀律委員會審理此案。答辯人要求在紀律委員會審理過程中獲得無限制的全面法律代表。紀律委員會主席根據《紀律程序》（此乃依據《上市規則》制定）的規定，僅批准答辯人在紀律委員會的審理中，可以聘請律師並隨時向律師諮詢，但是其律師不得向紀律委員會陳詞或替代答辯人回答紀律委員會的提問。答辯人遂向高等法院原訟庭申請司法覆核，認為紀律委員會限制答辯人獲得法律代表的決定違反了《基本法》第 35 條，亦違反了《香港人權法案》第 10 條（被《基本法》第 39 條確認）以及普通法下的公平審訊原則，因此請求法院認定該等限制無效，並指令紀律委員會允許答辯人獲得全面的法律代表的權利。

針對《基本法》第 35 條，答辯人指出，聯交所設立紀律審查程式和制裁乃是基於《證券及期貨條例》的要求，並受法定機構證券及期貨事務監察委員會（下稱“證監會”）的監督，為的是保護公共利益，而並非私人間的基於合同的利益，因此，紀律委員會應屬於《基本法》第 35 條規定的“法院”，因此，該條例適用於本案中。再者，針對《香港人權法案》第 10 條以及普通法下的公平和程序正義原則，答辯人指出，上市科的成員均為律師、會計師等專業人士，而答辯人作為外行人士需要自行進行陳詞和回答問題，違背了雙方“平等手段”原則（Equality of Arms），無法保證公平審理。

裁決摘要

原訟庭援引 *Dr Ip Kay Lo Vincent v. Medical Council Of Hong Kong (No. 2)* [2003] 3 HKC 579 和 *Attorney General v. British Broadcasting Corporation* [1981] A.C. 303，認為“法院”應指根據法例設立的司法機構，別無其他解釋。原訟庭認同聯交所提出的理由，包括：i）紀律委員會乃根據《上市規則》而非依據法例所設立；ii）其權力來源於上市公司與聯交所的協議而非法例；iii）雖然法例要求聯交所設立規則管理交易所，並不意味該等規則本身是法例；iv）有關紀律審查程序完全由聯交所自行制定；v）上市委員會並非政府許可機構及 vi）所有紀律覆核和上訴程序均是內部程序，因此從任何一個角度來講紀律委員會的性質都屬於民間審裁處，而不屬於《基本法》第35條規定的"法院"。針對《香港人權法案》第 10 條以及普通法下的公平和程序正義原則，原訟庭認為聯交所的紀律審查程序僅僅針對答辯人應當非常熟悉的《上市規則》，而不受證據規則和其他法律程序的約束，同時以書面陳詞為主，亦可由律師陪同並在口頭陳詞前向律師諮詢，因此並未違背答辯人主張的"平等手段"原則。原訟庭亦認同聯交所的看法，即紀律審查程序乃基於雙方的合意，這也是判斷程序公平與否時需要考慮的一個重要因素。因此，原訟庭不認為紀律委員會的決定違反了公平和程序正義原則。答辯人的司法覆核請求被原訟庭駁回。

答辯人隨後向上訴庭提出上訴，上訴庭一致撤銷了原訟庭的裁決，支持答辯人的請求。上訴庭重申了其在 *Dr Ip Kay Lo Vincent* 以及 *A Solicitor* v. *The Law Society Of Hong Kong*（Civil Appeal No.302 of 2002）中的觀點，認為對於《基本法》這樣的憲法性規定"作解釋時，應考慮當初立法的目的（目的性解釋）"，尤其是考慮到審裁處在香港的普遍性，《基本法》第 35 條規定的"法院"應不限於司法機構，同時包括行使司法職能的審裁處。法庭進一步認為此案中聯交所制定制度的權力不僅來自於上市公司的同意，也是基於《證券及期貨條例》的要求，紀律委員會是香港金融立法框架下的組成部份，有義務行使司法職能。因此，認定紀律委員會並非民間審裁處，而屬於《基本法》第 35 條所指的"法院"。針對《人權法》第 10 條以及普通法下的公平和程序正義原則，法庭引述 *R* v. *Hong Kong Polytechnic, Ex Parte Jenny Chua Yee Yan* (1992) 2 HKPLR 34，認為公平審理的要求包括了答辯人在紀律審查程序中應獲得法律代表的權利。法官再補充指出，紀律委員會行使的是司法職能，其決定可能對答辯人的名譽和職業有重大影響，且其管轄權來自於《證券及期貨條例》的規定而非當事人合意，因此，紀律委員會應屬於《基本法》第 35 條所指的"法院"。而且，法庭同意案件審理過程中的口頭陳詞很重要，如果一個面臨嚴重指控的外行人希望通過律師來進行口頭陳詞和詢問，該權利不應該被限制，因此認定限制答辯人獲得全面法律代表的規定違反了《基本法》第 35 條，也違反了公平審判的原則。

聯交所於 2006 年 3 月向終審法院提出上訴，終審法院一致撤銷了上訴庭的裁決。法庭認為《基本法》第 35 條應在整個《基本法》的背景和目的下進行解釋。《基本法》的目的包括在香港建立不同於中國大陸的法律制度，保證原有與現有法院和司法系統的連貫性以及增強司法獨立性。在此目的下，《基本法》眾多其他條款中提及到的"法院"均無例外地是指司法系統下行使司法職權的法院。而第 35 條目的是保證公民被《基本法》賦予的基本權利及以前生效的法律權利和義務，可在法院審理和強制執行，從而使有關設立法院行使獨立司法權的條款可被實際操作和實施。因此，該條中的"法院"僅指行使獨立司法權的法院，而不包括紀律委員會。

終審法院同時推翻 *Dr Ip Kay Lo Vincent* 以及 *A Solicitor* 兩案中的判決，認為醫務委員會和律師紀律審裁組並非《基本法》第 35 條所指的"法院"。最後，終審法院認為現階段針對案件審理的公平性申請司法覆核時機尚未成熟，因此駁回答辯人的司法覆核申請。然而，法庭亦順帶提及堅持公平審判的原則，並不代表在任何情況下也必須保證有全面的法律代表。以本案為例，為了有效地挽回公眾對證券市場的信心，迅速調查是符合公眾利益的，因此有需要簡化程序，一個非正式的並以專家為主導的聆訊可能更為合適。

FACV No. 22 of 2005

IN THE COURT OF FINAL APPEAL OF THE HONG KONG SPECIAL ADMINISTRATIVE REGION

FINAL APPEAL NO. 22 OF 2005 (Civil)
(ON APPEAL FROM CACV No. 170 of 2004)

Between:

THE STOCK EXCHANGE OF HONG KONG LIMITED	**Appellant**
- and -	
NEW WORLD DEVELOPMENT COMPANY LIMITED	1st **Respondent**
DATO' DR CHENG YU TUNG	2nd **Respondent**
DR CHENG KAR-SHUN, HENRY	3rd **Respondent**
DR SIN WAI-KIN, DAVID	4th **Respondent**
LIANG CHONG-HOU, DAVID	5th **Respondent**

Court: Mr Justice Bokhary PJ, Mr Justice Chan PJ, Mr Justice Ribeiro PJ, Sir Noel Power NPJ and Lord Woolf NPJ

Dates of Hearing: 21 and 22 March 2006

Date of Judgment: 6 April 2006

JUDGMENT

Mr Justice Bokhary PJ:

1. I agree with the judgment of Mr Justice Ribeiro PJ allowing the appeal with costs here and below. In adding something in words of my own, I do so out of respect for the Court of Appeal, having regard to how vigorously they stated the views which we feel unable to support. Article 35 of the Basic Law is to be found in the chapter containing the constitutional rights and freedoms enjoyed in Hong Kong. These rights and freedoms are safeguarded by a judiciary whose independence is maintained by the structural provisions of the Basic Law. So when art. 35 refers to "the courts" it obviously means the judiciary and nothing else. This does not run in any way counter to the importance which the Court of Appeal rightly attached to procedural fairness. The rules of procedural fairness extend to the disciplinary committee before which the respondents find themselves. But the committee has not yet had an opportunity to consider, in a position of knowledge rather than speculation, how the rules of procedural fairness are properly to be applied in the respondents' situation. So, even leaving aside any question of having first to exhaust the avenues of review and appeal available under the regulatory regime concerned, the respondents' resort to judicial review is plainly premature.

Mr Justice Chan PJ:

2. I agree with the judgments of Mr Justice Bokhary PJ and Mr Justice Ribeiro PJ.

Mr Justice Ribeiro PJ:

3. This appeal arises out of the respondents' challenge mounted by way of judicial review against certain procedural directions issued by the chairman of a Disciplinary Committee of the Stock Exchange. The directions were given before the start of the disciplinary hearing which, as a result, has been held in abeyance. The respondents claim to be entitled to full legal representation by lawyers at the hearing for the purposes of examining and cross-examining witnesses and making oral submissions. Whether Article 35 of the Basic Law ("Art 35") confers such an entitlement upon them falls to be determined. The Court must also decide whether (as the respondents contend) the directions in question infringe the respondents' right to a fair hearing under Article 10 of the Hong Kong Bill of Rights ("Art 10") and/or the common law principles of procedural fairness; or whether (as the appellant submits) no such infringement is, or can presently be, made out, the challenge having been brought prematurely and without first exhausting alternative remedies.

A. The parties

4. The 1st respondent ("New World") is a company listed on the stock exchange operated by the appellant ("SEHK"). The other four respondents are executive directors of New World (collectively "the directors").

5. SEHK, which is a company incorporated under the Companies Ordinance, Cap 32, operates the exchange pursuant to authority conferred by s 19 of the Securities and Futures Ordinance, Cap 571 (the "SFO"). It is supervised, monitored and regulated by the Securities and Futures Commission ("SFC"): SFO s 5(1)(b). By SFO s 21, SEHK is under a duty "to ensure ... so far as reasonably practicable, an orderly, informed and fair market" acting "in the interest of the public, having particular regard to the interest of the investing public." It is required to prefer the interest of the public over its own interests.

6. SEHK is empowered (subject to SFC approval) to make rules including rules for the regulation and efficient operation of the market and for the regulation of exchange participants and holders of trading rights. Express power is given to make rules for (among other things) laying down standards of conduct, imposing sanctions for breach of the rules and establishing procedures (SFO s 23). Pursuant to these provisions, rules known as the "Listing Rules" (here cited as "LR") have been made.

7. SEHK's Board has arranged for its functions and powers, including operation and enforcement of the Listing Rules, to be discharged by a committee known as the "Listing Committee" (LR2A.01 and LR2A.27). The Listing Committee is composed of 25 members, comprising individual participants in the exchange, directors of listed companies, market practitioners and experts, as well as the chief executive of SEHK's holding company (Hong Kong Exchanges and Clearing Limited, "HKEC") who is a member ex officio. Only the latter is an employee of the Stock Exchange. The others participate on a voluntary basis, appointed by virtue of their experience, their standing in their profession or occupation and their availability to carry out the duties of a member (LR2A.17 and 18).

8. The Listing Committee has in turn arranged for certain functions to be discharged by the Listing Division which consists of employees of SEHK (LR2A.02). Thus, the Listing Division administers and enforces the Listing Rules, its duties including the investigation and pursuit of disciplinary matters. Where the Listing Division believes that an infringement has occurred, it reports to the Listing Committee which, when sitting in a disciplinary capacity, comprises a sub–committee with a quorum of five members, all drawn from the Listing Committee. It is convenient to refer to it here as a "Disciplinary Committee" although in various rules, it is referred to simply as "the Listing Committee".

9. As a condition of being allowed to trade their shares on the Stock Exchange, issuing companies must enter into an agreement

with SEHK, known as a Listing Agreement which sets out certain covenants, including an undertaking to comply with the Listing Rules (para 2(3)). New World duly entered into such an agreement.

10. Another condition for being listed is that the issuing company's directors must give an undertaking to SEHK which is materially in the following terms:

> "... in the exercise of my powers and duties as a director of the issuer, I shall (i) comply to the best of my ability with the Rules Governing the Listing of Securities on The Stock Exchange of Hong Kong Limited from time to time in force (the 'Listing Rules'); (ii) use my best endeavours to procure that the issuer shall so comply; ..."

Such an undertaking was given by each of the directors.

B. The factual background

11. New World's interim results for the 6 month period ended 31 December 2000 were expected to be published in mid-March 2001. As is usual, financial analysts in investment houses provided their own forecasts of the expected figures. On 9 March 2001, one such investment house, Goldman Sachs, forecast [*sic*] interim profits of $730 million. Another, Vickers Ballas, put the figure at $628 million on 12 March. However, on 14 March 2001, it appears that those analysts and certain others circulated sharply reduced forecasts, placing the expected interim profits at around $300 million. According to the Listing Division, 33.5 million New World shares (representing 1.6% of its issued capital) were traded on that day, more than 4.4 times the average trading volume over the 10 preceding days. New World's share price fell to $10.10 on 14 March, having traded at $13.40, $12.60 and $11.60 on the 9, 12 and 13 March respectively. New World announced that it was unaware of the reasons for the fall in price and increase in trading volume.

12. Interim profits of $311.4 million were officially announced on 15 March. That morning, and again on 16 March, articles appeared in the press suggesting that those results had selectively been leaked to certain analysts.

C. The Listing Division's case against the respondents

13. On 17 May 2002, drawing on statements and materials obtained in the course of an investigation by the SFC into possible insider dealing, the Listing Division wrote to New World's board of directors expressing the view that New World and the directors had breached certain obligations to the Stock Exchange and stating that it was minded to commence disciplinary proceedings against them. The respondents sought unsuccessfully to refute those suggestions by letter dated 24 June 2002, and, on 4 October 2002, the Listing Division delivered a detailed report to the Listing Committee ("the Report"), confirming its view that the respondents had infringed certain rules and recommending sanctions against them by way of public censure. Subsequently, the Listing Division invited the Disciplinary Committee additionally to impose remedial measures on New World with a view to preventing future leakage of price sensitive information.

14. In the Report, the Listing Division asserts that, on 13 March 2001, in advance of New World's publication of the results, Mr Terence Kwok, an employee in its Corporate Communications Department, telephoned a number of analysts and disclosed to them the interim profit figures leading to publication of their revised forecasts. Mr Kwok denies having made such disclosures.

15. By paragraph 2 of the Listing Agreement, New World was obliged to provide to its members and to the general investing public any price sensitive information relating to the group as soon as reasonably practical. It provided in particular that:

> "Information should not be divulged outside the Issuer [i.e. New World] and its advisers in such a way as to place in a privileged dealing position any person or class or category of persons. Information should not be released in such a way that Exchange transactions may be entered into at prices which do not reflect the latest available information" ... (§2.1)

16. Since (so the Listing Division contends) Mr Kwok made the alleged disclosures in the course of his employment, New World must be held responsible for the leakage and accordingly, held to be in breach of paragraph 2. This is denied by New World.

17. The Listing Division asserts that the directors were in breach of their abovementioned undertaking by failing to cause New World to put appropriate controls in place to prevent improper disclosure of price sensitive information. The directors deny that allegation.

D. The contested procedural directions

18. In May 2003, the chairman of the Disciplinary Committee sent to the parties draft procedural directions for the hearing, inviting comments. The draft proposed limiting the role of legal advisers at the hearing "in accordance with the usual practice provided for in the disciplinary procedures", such advisers not being permitted "to address the Committee (whether in respect of oral submission, the examination of witnesses of fact or otherwise)."

19. In their earlier written submissions (of 3 December 2002), the Listing Division had indicated that if witnesses were to be called, it would be appropriate for them all to be examined and cross-examined by counsel, adding "although ... this is a matter for the Listing Committee". The respondents wrote seeking to persuade the chairman to make various changes to the draft directions, including permitting unrestricted use of lawyers at the hearing, but without success.

20. On 25 June 2003, the chairman gave the procedural directions which triggered the respondents' application for judicial review ("the Directions"). After requiring the parties to define the factual issues dividing them and to disclose the substance of the evidence of witnesses to be called with such disclosures to stand as evidence-in-chief, the Directions continue in the following terms:

> "3. Cross-examination of any witnesses of fact by the Listing Division, [New World] and the [directors] will be allowed at the substantive hearing only on those factual issues identified by the parties as being in issue ... and [identified in the disclosures relating to the evidence mentioned above].
>
> 4. Attendance of all witnesses at the substantive hearing is the sole responsibility of those parties proposing to call them.
>
> 5. Submissions by the Listing Division, [New World] and the [directors] will otherwise be presented in accordance with the usual practice provided for in the Disciplinary Procedures (a brief opportunity to consult with legal advisers, upon the conclusion of any oral evidence and prior to presentation of closing submissions will be allowed).

6. Legal advisers will not be permitted to address the [Disciplinary] Committee (whether in respect of oral submissions, the examination of witnesses of fact or otherwise).

7. Leave is granted to the Listing Division, [New World] and the [directors] to be accompanied by legal advisers (with no limitation as to number at the substantive hearing)."

21. Hartmann J read the Directions as not prohibiting examination (which I will generally use to include "cross-examination" in this judgment) of witnesses by legal representatives but leaving that question open. By letter dated 4 May 2005 written on his behalf in response to a query by Cheung JA, confirmation was received from the chairman that it had been "deliberately left open for any application for examination or cross-examination, whether by Counsel or otherwise, to be made to the Committee at the substantive hearing." However, Mr John Griffiths SC (appearing with Mr Richard Zimmern and Ms Amanda W M Li for the respondents) submitted that the Court should approach this appeal solely on the basis of the Directions, ignoring the letter dated 4 May 2005. The Court, he argued, should judge the lawfulness of the procedural arrangements on the basis that the Directions have definitively excluded all examination and oral submissions by the respondents' legal advisers. Whether this is the correct approach is considered later in this judgment.

22. The respondents contend in any event that the limitations on legal representation are unlawful and ask the court to hold that in principle the Disciplinary Committee must permit legal advisers to examine witnesses and to address it orally at the hearing without restriction.

E. The disciplinary powers of the Listing Committee

23. The contested procedural directions must be understood in the context of the Listing Rules and the Disciplinary Procedures referred to below.

24. The Listing Rules provide for a range of sanctions to be imposed for a breach (LR2A.09). They range from a private reprimand, escalating through a public censure (which is sought by the Listing Division in this case) to orders aimed at removing individuals from further participation in stock exchange activities. The ultimate sanctions involve suspension or cancellation of a company's listing.

25. The Listing Rules provide for such sanctions to be imposed not only on listed companies and their directors (who have a contractual nexus with SEHK) but also on others, including substantial shareholders and professional advisers (LR2A.10).

26. Where such a sanction has been imposed, the person concerned is given "the right to have the decision against him referred to the Listing Committee again for review" and, in relation to most of the sanctions, there is additionally a right to "a further and final review of the decision against the appellant by the Listing Appeals Committee" (LR2A.11). The intermediate review is conducted by a committee (referred to here as a "Review Committee") consisting of members of the Listing Committee who had not sat on the Disciplinary Committee at first instance. The Listing Appeals Committee comprises the chairman and two other members of the board of HKEC (LR2A.29).

F. The Disciplinary Procedures

27. The Listing Rules touch only briefly on the conduct of disciplinary proceedings. But they do so indicating that only a limited role is to be played by lawyers at the hearing. LR2A.16 provides:

"In any disciplinary proceedings of the Listing Committee and on any further review of the decision resulting from those proceedings by the Listing Committee or the Listing Appeals Committee, the party the subject of such proceedings shall have the right to attend the meeting, to make submissions and to be accompanied by its professional advisers. In all disciplinary proceedings the Listing Division will provide the parties with copies of any papers to be presented by it at the meeting, in advance of the meeting."

28. Detailed procedures are prescribed by the "Disciplinary Procedures" (here cited as "DP") which are rules made by the Listing Committee pursuant to LR2A.15 (DP2.3) and are referred to in paragraph 5 of the Directions.

29. The function of the Disciplinary Committee (defined by DP2.7) is "to decide whether there is a breach of the Listing Rules in light of the facts before it and to determine the appropriate sanction to be imposed in case of a finding that breaches of the Listing Rules have occurred." It must "have regard to all relevant circumstances, including the facts as contained in the written submissions, the documentary evidence appended to the submissions, and any oral evidence and submissions made" at the hearing.

30. DP2.5 stipulates that the hearing "is primarily by way of written submissions". It elaborates as follows:

"Whilst the procedures allow for limited oral submissions to be made at the hearing, all submissions should, so far as possible, be contained in the written submissions which are delivered to the [Disciplinary Committee] in advance of the hearing ... This gives the other parties to the hearing fair notice of the case and ensures that the hearing is kept as brief as possible. Given the nature of the tribunal, the [Disciplinary Committee] discourages lengthy oral submissions and in so far as they are deemed necessary at all, oral submissions should be limited to matters not contained in the written submissions."

31. The chairman's approach to legal representation in the Directions reflects DP5.1 and DP6.3 which are materially in the following terms:

"A Party may be accompanied by his/her legal adviser. The Representatives [i.e. of the Listing Division] will not normally be accompanied by an independent legal adviser, but may be, in which case the Party(ies) will be notified in accordance with paragraph 4.5 above. Whilst a Party may confer with his/her legal adviser at any stage during the first instance hearing, all submissions should be made by the Party(ies) and all questions addressed to a Party by the Chairman and/or any members of the [Disciplinary Committee] present at the first instance hearing must be answered directly by that Party and not through his/her legal adviser." (DP5.1)

"The procedural steps of a first instance hearing are as follows: ...

- members of the [Disciplinary Committee] present may ask the Representatives, the Party(ies) and any persons attending the first instance hearing any question relevant to the disciplinary enquiry. Any person to whom a question is directed shall answer such question directly, and not through his/her legal adviser, although any party accompanied by a legal adviser may confer with his/her legal adviser prior to answering such questions. However, any member of the [Disciplinary Committee] present may request any legal adviser present to clarify or elaborate upon any answers given by their clients;

- the Representatives, to be followed by the Party(ies) may make a final oral submission relating to matters arising at the first instance hearing if they so wish. Any Parties accompanied by a legal adviser may confer with his/her legal adviser prior to making that final submission." (DP6.3)

32. The Disciplinary Procedures emphasise the informality of the disciplinary proceedings as follows:

"The Listing Committee is a lay and informal tribunal, and it is the intention of the Listing Committee to keep the first instance hearing informal." (DP6.1)

"Rules of Evidence do not apply. The Listing Committee may receive any material, written or otherwise, and attach such weight as it thinks appropriate to these materials, notwithstanding that such material may not be admissible in civil or criminal proceedings." (DP6.2)

G. The characteristics of the Disciplinary Committee summarised

33. The characteristics of the Disciplinary Committee which emerge from the foregoing survey may be summarised as follows.

(a) While the Disciplinary Committee is not itself a statutory creation, its purpose and existence derive from the duty imposed by the SFO on SEHK to regulate the securities market, acting in the interests of the investing public. It is part of the machinery for protecting those interests.

(b) To the same end, SEHK has made the Listing Rules which, while not themselves statutory, were expressly authorised by the SFO. The Listing Division brings alleged infringers before the Disciplinary Committee which has the task of deciding whether the rules have been breached and if so, what sanctions are appropriate.

(c) In carrying out that task, the Disciplinary Committee must (as everyone accepts) act fairly and in a judicial manner, taking proper account of all relevant circumstances. It has developed Disciplinary Procedures which establish general procedural rules applicable to its proceedings.

(d) The Disciplinary Committee has powers to impose sanctions which range from minor reprimands to orders having serious repercussions for the reputation and professional status of the person in question. The Listing Rules assert power to impose such sanctions not merely against those who (like the respondents) have a contractual nexus with SEHK, but others involved in the market.

(e) Where a sanction is imposed, there is a right to a fresh hearing before the Review Committee and, if necessary, before the Listing Appeals Committee.

(f) Members of the Disciplinary, Review and Listing Appeals Committees are not judges or lawyers but market practitioners and experts. They are chosen for their knowledge, experience and standing in relation to market activities.

H. The relief sought

34. Referring to the making of the Directions as "the Decision" challenged, the respondents sought the following relief in the judicial review proceedings:

"1. A declaration that insofar as the Decision purports to deny legal representation, or proper and effective legal representation, to the [respondents] at the hearing of the Disciplinary Proceedings against the [respondents], the Decision in null, void or otherwise of no legal effect on the ground that it is calculated to deprive (or in the circumstances is bound to deprive) the [respondents] of a fair hearing and the right to fair legal representation, in breach of the Basic Law and the Hong Kong Bill of Rights Ordinance, Cap 383, as well as the fundamental rules of natural justice.

2. An order of certiorari to quash the Decision.

3. An order of mandamus to compel the Disciplinary Committee to allow the [respondents] full and unencumbered legal representation, by legal representatives of the [respondents'] own choice, at the Disciplinary Proceedings against the [respondents], including in particular the recognition of the entitlement of the [respondents'] legal advisers, as of right, to address the Disciplinary Committee (including the making of both oral and written submissions) and to examine witnesses of fact at all hearings conducted by the Disciplinary Committee against the [respondents] in the Disciplinary Proceedings."

I. The decisions in the courts below

35. Hartmann J (whose decision is reported at [2004] 2 HKLRD 1027) held that the Disciplinary Committee was not "a court" for the purposes of Art 35. He also held that the procedural arrangements catered for by the Directions and the Disciplinary Procedures do not deny the respondents a fair hearing and involve no breach of either Art 10 or the common law principles of fairness. Accordingly, although his Lordship held that the circumstances justified the bringing of an application for judicial review even at this early stage, he refused the relief sought and dismissed the application.

36. The Court of Appeal (reported at [2005] 2 HKLRD 612), while agreeing that the case merited judicial review at the present stage, unanimously reversed Hartmann J. The Disciplinary Committee was held to be a "court" within Art 35, giving the respondents a right to legal representation which had unlawfully been abridged by the Directions. The Directions were also held to have infringed the right to a fair hearing conferred by Art 10 and the common law principles. By its Order dated 27 May 2005, the Court of Appeal substantially granted all the relief sought by the respondents.

J. Is the Disciplinary Committee a "court" within the meaning of Art 35?

(i) A question of constitutional interpretation

37. As is apparent from the foregoing, whether Art 35 avails the

respondents depends on whether the Disciplinary Committee is "a court" within the meaning of its provisions. Art 35 states as follows:

> "Hong Kong residents shall have the right to confidential legal advice, access to the courts, choice of lawyers for timely protection of their lawful rights and interests or for representation in the courts, and to judicial remedies.
>
> Hong Kong residents shall have the right to institute legal proceedings in the courts against the acts of the executive authorities and their personnel."

38. The question whether the Disciplinary Committee is "a court" within Art 35's reference to "the right to ... choice of lawyers ... for representation in the courts" is first and foremost a question of constitutional interpretation.

39. The Court's approach to that task is explained in *Director of Immigration v. Chong Fung Yuen* (2001) 4 HKCFAR 211. As Li CJ stated:

> "The courts' role under the common law in interpreting the Basic Law is to construe the language used in the text of the instrument in order to ascertain the legislative intent as expressed in the language." (at 223)

In doing so, the courts "do not look at the language of the article in question in isolation" but consider the language "in the light of its context and purpose"; and:

> "To assist in the task of interpretation of the provision in question, the courts consider what is within the Basic Law, including provisions in the Basic Law other than the provision in question and the Preamble. These are internal aids to interpretation." (at 224)

40. This is particularly apposite in the present case. The Basic Law contains numerous other provisions making reference to "the courts" which form the context in which Art 35 is found and which may provide important guidance as to what the provisions of Art 35 intend. One asks: What are the institutions referred to as "courts" in those other provisions? Construing the language of Art 35 in the light of those provisions, is it referring to the same or to some different institutions when it speaks of "representation in the courts"?

(ii) The bodies referred to as "the courts" in the other provisions of the Basic Law

41. There can be no doubt as to the identity of the bodies referred to as "the courts" in the other provisions of the Basic Law. Moreover, the principal purposes of the Basic Law underpinning those Articles are clear.

42. The first evident objective of the Basic Law is the establishment of the HKSAR as a Region having a legal system which is separate from the legal system of the Mainland in accordance with the principle of "one country two systems". Thus:

(a) By Art 2, the National People's Congress authorizes the Region "to exercise a high degree of autonomy and to enjoy executive, legislative and independent judicial power, including that of final adjudication, in accordance with the provisions of this Law".

(b) Art 19 elaborates, making it plain that such independent judicial power is to be exercised by our courts:

> "[The HKSAR] shall be vested with independent judicial power, including that of final adjudication. The courts of the [HKSAR] shall have jurisdiction over all cases in the Region, except that the restrictions on their jurisdiction imposed by the legal system and principles previously in force in Hong Kong shall be maintained. [Subject to certain exceptions not presently material]"

(c) Art 80 then makes it clear that the courts in question are the courts of judicature, constituting the judicial system of the Region:

> "The courts of the [HKSAR] at all levels shall be the judiciary of the Region, exercising the judicial power of the Region."

(d) Art 81 specifically identifies the courts in question:

> "The Court of Final Appeal, the High Court, district courts, magistrates' courts and other special courts shall be established in the [HKSAR]. The High Court shall comprise the Court of Appeal and the Court of First Instance..."

43. Secondly, the Basic Law aims to provide for continuity between the pre-existing and the present courts and judicial systems. Thus, for example:

(a) Art 81 states that "... The judicial system previously practised in Hong Kong shall be maintained except for those changes consequent upon the establishment of the Court of Final Appeal of the [HKSAR]."

(b) Art 87 provides that "In criminal or civil proceedings in the [HKSAR], the principles previously applied in Hong Kong and the rights previously enjoyed by parties to proceedings shall be maintained" with the courts adjudicating cases in accordance with the laws previously in force in Hong Kong (Art 8 and Art 18), referring to precedents of "other common law jurisdictions" (Art 84) and with judges and other members of the judiciary remaining in employment and retaining their seniority, pay and so forth (Art 93).

44. A third evident purpose of the Basic Law in relation to the courts is to entrench the independence of the judiciary who operate those courts.

(a) This is made express by Art 85 which provides:

> "The courts of the [HKSAR] shall exercise judicial power independently, free from any interference. Members of the judiciary shall be immune from legal action in the performance of their judicial functions."

(b) It is also reflected in provisions such as Art 88 which lays down the machinery for appointing judges; Art 92 which stresses that judges must be chosen on the basis of their judicial and professional qualities; and Art 89 which establishes that judges can only be removed on limited grounds.

45. It is therefore entirely clear that when, in such Articles, the Basic Law refers to "the courts" it is referring to the courts of judicature: the institutions which constitute the judicial system, entrusted with the exercise of the judicial power in the HKSAR. I will refer to them simply as "courts of law". The purpose of the Basic Law provisions referred to is to establish the constitutional architecture of that system revolving around the courts of law, catering for the system's separation from that of the Mainland, its continuity with what went before and safeguarding the

independence of the judiciary.

46. The characteristics of the Disciplinary Committee have been summarised in Section G above. It plainly does not exercise the independent judicial power conferred on the Region by the Basic Law. It is therefore perfectly plain that the provisions discussed above do not apply to that tribunal notwithstanding any judicial functions it may perform.

(iii) Interpretation of Art 35

47. How does Art 35 fit in with those provisions? Should its reference to "the courts" be given a different and wider meaning so that, unlike the other Basic Law provisions discussed, Art 35 encompasses a tribunal like the Disciplinary Committee? Mr Griffiths suggests that the answer to the latter question is "Yes", pointing to the fact that it is found in Chapter III which is concerned with Fundamental Rights and Duties of Residents, separated from the other provisions.

48. There are two dimensions to Art 35 that should be noted for present purposes. In the first place, it lays down constitutional rights which need have nothing to do with court proceedings. Thus, for instance, the right to confidential legal advice is a right which is protected even where such advice does not bear on any existing or contemplated court proceedings. This was recognized in the decision recently handed down in *A Solicitor v. The Law Society of Hong Kong* (FACV 23 of 2005; 22 March 2006), which concerned the constitutionality of provisions empowering an inspector, appointed by the Law Society to investigate disciplinary complaints against a solicitor, to inspect documents which may contain privileged information derived from a client who is not involved in the disciplinary complaint. That client's privilege qualifies for independent protection notwithstanding the absence of his involvement in any related proceedings whether in a court of law or in any tribunal. These aspects of Art 35 do not bear on the issues in this appeal and nothing said in this judgment is intended in any way to affect the free-standing vigour of those rights.

49. What is of prime relevance to this appeal is the second dimension of Art 35. As appears from its language, Art 35 is also concerned with entrenching the individual's rights in relation to "the courts": individuals are to have the right of "access to the courts", the right of "choice of lawyers ... for representation in the courts", the right "to judicial remedies" and "the right to institute legal proceedings in the courts against the acts of the executive authorities and their personnel".

50. This is a crucial additional feature of the constitutional architecture of the Basic Law in relation to the judicial system of the Region. Art 35 ensures that the fundamental rights conferred by the Basic Law as well as the legal rights and obligations previously in force and carried through to apply in the HKSAR are enforceable by individuals and justiciable in the courts. It gives life and practical effect to the provisions which establish the courts as the institutions charged with exercising the independent judicial power in the Region. This dimension of Art 35 is therefore concerned with ensuring access to the courts for such purposes, buttressed by provisions aimed at making such access effective. The "courts" in this context are plainly the courts of law. They are the same bodies as those referred to in the other provisions of the Basic Law discussed above. I therefore reject Mr Griffiths' argument to the contrary.

51. Reliance was placed on the principle that "the courts should give a generous interpretation to the provisions in Chapter III that contain constitutional guarantees of freedoms that lie at the heart of Hong Kong's separate system" (*Director of Immigration v. Chong Fung Yuen* (2001) 4 HKCFAR 211 at 224). That principle is of course well-established and beyond question. However, one must establish what the essential right or freedom in question consists of. As a matter of constitutional interpretation, the Basic Law is plainly not concerned in Art 35 with entrenching rights to legal representation in respect of tribunals which are not courts of law. No measure of generosity in the interpretation process can extend its width to the point required by the respondents.

52. It follows that the Disciplinary Committee, not being a court of law, is *not* a "court" within the meaning of Art 35. This is decisive of the issue under discussion. However, in deference to the Court of Appeal which reached a different conclusion below relying on two previous Court of Appeal decisions, it is appropriate to examine those decisions and the some of the case-law on which they are founded.

K. The earlier Court of Appeal decisions

(i) Dr Ip's case

53. In *Dr Ip Kay Lo Vincent v. Medical Council of Hong Kong (No 2)* [2003] 3 HKC 579, the appellant was found guilty of professional misconduct by the Medical Council and was disqualified from practice for three years. At the disciplinary hearing, he had been refused an adjournment which he had sought on the ground that he wanted to arrange for legal representation. The question of whether the Medical Council was "a court" for the purposes of Art 35 was raised by the Court of Appeal one day before hearing the appeal and leading counsel appearing for the Medical Council was unable to provide any assistance on that important issue. The appellant was appearing in person.

54. Cheung JA nevertheless felt able to decide that the Medical Council *is* a "court" within Art 35 and that refusal of the adjournment had infringed Dr Ip's constitutional rights. Yuen JA did not consider it necessary to base her decision on Art 35. Burrell J stated that he agreed with both of the other judgments. I should make it plain that the comments in this judgment relate solely to the Court of Appeal's ruling that the Medical Council is "a court" within Art 35. Nothing said here is intended to suggest that the result arrived at by the Court of Appeal on principles of fairness was incorrect.

55. In reaching his decision, Cheung JA makes two observations as to the general approach to be adopted.

(a) First, he appears to adopt as a starting point a presumption in favour of treating tribunals as "courts" within Art 35, stating:

> "The use of tribunals are so prevalent in Hong Kong that it will need a strong case to justify the exclusion of tribunals from coming under the general word "courts". (§6)
>
> I would say at once that I cannot see any basis for such an approach. The fact that numerous tribunals exist suggests instead a need for distinguishing among their various functions and characteristics rather than lumping them together as presumptive "courts".

(b) Secondly, he states that since Art 35 is concerned "with the legal rights of a Hong Kong resident ... the word 'courts' should not be confined solely to [the courts of law]" (§7). However, with respect, this begs the question what are the rights–representation in respect of what tribunals – conferred by the Article.

56. Cheung JA concludes that the Medical Council is "a court" for Art 35 purposes because it is "performing judicial functions", that is, making decisions "according to rules and not policies" (citing Wade & Forsyth on *Administrative Law* 8th Ed. page 40) (§8); it is a "statutory tribunal" with procedures governed by statutory provisions (§9); and its decisions affect the doctor's rights and may involve severe penalties. (§10)

57. I return to discuss the significance of such factors later. However, it may be noted for present purposes that the decision on Art 35 was reached without seeking to interpret that Article in the context of the Basic Law and without citation of any relevant authority.

(ii) The Law Society case

58. Section 10(2)(e) of the Legal Practitioners Ordinance, Cap 159, gives the Solicitors Disciplinary Tribunal ("SDT") power to order a party to pay the costs of a disciplinary hearing on a full indemnity basis. In *A Solicitor v. The Law Society of Hong Kong* (CACV 302/2002 Woo VP, Cheung JA and Burrell J; 18 February 2004) it was contended that exercise of that power in the case at hand was unconstitutional. It was argued that exposure to a risk of having to pay costs of a large magnitude inhibited a solicitor's defence against misconduct charges and so impaired his rights of access to, and of a fair hearing in, the SDT, infringing Art 35 (among other constitutional provisions): §60–§63. I should likewise state that the comments in this judgment address solely the question of whether the SDT is "a court" for the purposes of Art 35. It is not intended to say anything as to the correctness or otherwise of the other aspects of the decision.

59. Although Woo V-P was inclined to the view that the SDT is not "a court" within the meaning of Art 35, he considered himself bound by *Dr Ip's case* and therefore concluded that Art 35 applies to that tribunal: §74–76. Woo V-P did not advance any independent grounds for that conclusion.

60. Cheung JA stated that he maintained the views he had expressed in *Dr Ip's case* (§172). It appears that the amicus accepted that "the word 'courts' in Art 35 includes tribunals" (§173). Cheung JA continued in the following terms (in §§174–175):

> "It is not necessary to elaborate further on this issue. It is sufficient to recognize that Article 35 is one of the provisions of the Basic Law under the heading of 'Fundamental Rights and Duties of the Residents'. In construing these rights it is in my view permissible and relevant to take into account the provisions dealing with fundamental rights in international covenants which are binding on Hong Kong such as the ICCPR. The principles on human values are universal in nature and the protection of human rights is based on the rule of law. This Court (Nazareth VP, Liu and Mayo JJA) in *Cheung Ng Sheong Steven v. Eastweek Publisher Ltd and Another* (1995) 5 HKPLR 428 recognized that our law should be developed by taking into consideration the international treaty obligations imposed on Hong Kong.
>
> Article 14 of ICCPR guarantees a right of fair hearing before courts and tribunals. It is not confined to 'courts' only. This right obviously includes the right of access to courts and tribunals. Hence it would be artificial to the extreme to confine the 'courts' in Article 35 to those in the traditional sense."

61. Cheung JA therefore accepted in this case that the question whether the SDT was a "court" within the meaning of Art 35 required interpretation of a provision of the Basic Law. However, his Lordship did not refer to other provisions of the Basic Law dealing with "courts", but embarked on an interpretation which relies solely on Art 14 of the ICCPR (which is enacted in Hong Kong as Art 10). His reasoning was as follows: Because Art 14 of the ICCPR applies to both courts and tribunals, Art 35 should also be interpreted to extend to courts and tribunals, since its interpretation should be consistent with the Region's international obligations.

62. I cannot accept such reasoning. Article 14 of the ICCPR, enacted as Art 10, is expressly incorporated by Art 39 of the Basic Law. It is therefore through Art 39 that the Basic Law addresses the relevant international obligations and gives constitutional status to Art 14 of the ICCPR implemented in Hong Kong as Art 10. Art 35 is plainly concerned with other issues. As previously stated, it is concerned with the constitutional architecture of the courts entrusted by the Basic Law with the exercise of the judicial power in the HKSAR. Tribunals like the Medical Council and the SDT are not part of that architecture and Article 14 of the ICCPR is not relevant in this context.

63. Other than stating the abovementioned approach to interpretation, Cheung JA returned to his approach of identifying factors tending to justify the conclusion that a given tribunal is "a court":

> "In my view a tribunal will fall within Article 35 if it exercises a judicial function and its jurisdiction is not private or consensual. The exercise of judicial function clearly means that it will make determinations affecting the rights of the parties before it and such determination will be made on the basis of the rules of law and following proceedings conducted in a prescribed manner. This definition will exclude those organizations such as private members clubs whose decisions may also affect the 'rights' of its members in matters such as the removal of membership." (§177)

I return to consider this approach later in this judgment.

64. Burrell J agreed with the conclusion on Art 35 although he differed on other matters not presently material.

L. The decision of the Court of Appeal below

65. In the Court of Appeal below, Cheung JA summarizes his approach to what constitutes a "court" for Art 35 purposes as follows:

> "Article 35 recognizes the importance of legal assistance and specifically the right of legal representation in legal proceedings. While this provision clearly applies to court proceedings, in deciding whether it also applies to proceedings other than those held in courts such as in tribunals, the matter has to be approached on a case by case basis. The framework of a particular tribunal has to be examined. However, within the confines of this approach, the following principles are relevant:
>
> 1. The Basic Law being a constitutional document must be given a purposive approach in its interpretation. Where the provisions are concerned with the fundamental rights of the residents, a generous approach in interpretation

should be adopted.

2. The use of tribunals alongside courts is so prevalent in Hong Kong that it will need a strong case to justify the exclusion of tribunals from coming under the general word of 'courts' in Article 35.

3. A tribunal may be known by different names, the name given to a tribunal is irrelevant in this context.

4. Many of the tribunals are set up expressly by statute but a statute-created tribunal is not the only criterion for coming within Article 35. What is equally important is that such a tribunal is an integral part of a legislative framework which is concerned with and takes into account matters of public interest.

5. The tribunal to be subject to Article 35 does not need to be a part of the judicial organ of the government. A tribunal will fall within its ambit if it exercises a judicial function and its jurisdiction is not private and consensual.

6. A judicial decision is made according to rules and not administrative policies. The exercise of judicial function means the tribunal will make determinations affecting the rights of parties before it and on the basis of rules of law and following proceedings conducted in a prescribed manner." ([2005] 2 HKLRD 612, §39)

66. Reyes J provided a reasoned judgment in which he concurred with Cheung JA's conclusion on Art 35's applicability. His Lordship approaches that question on the basis of three "insights" for deciding whether a tribunal is a "court" for Art 35 purposes derived from *Dr Ip's case* and the *Law Society case* (§§103–115). The first is that the function of a forum rather than its label is what matters. The second is that helpful tests for characterising the tribunal include asking (i) whether it is exercising a judicial as opposed to an administrative function in making decisions (applying rules rather than merely administrative policies); (ii) whether its basis of power is consensual or statutory; and (iii) whether the consequences of its decision may have a serious impact on a person's reputation or career. The third insight is that even if a tribunal is an Art 35 "court", the right to legal representation is not absolute but subject to legitimate proportional limitations.

67. It is clear from Point 1 in his summary that Cheung JA again recognizes that a question of constitutional interpretation arises. He stresses the need for a purposive interpretation and for a generous approach to construing fundamental rights. However, it appears that he may have in mind the same approach as that adopted by him in the *Law Society case*, namely, construing "courts" in Art 35 to extend to "tribunals" to achieve congruence with Art 14 of the ICCPR (equivalent to Art 10). That is an approach which I have rejected on the grounds set out above.

68. I have also rejected the approach of treating tribunals presumptively as courts (Point 2). Crucially, in my view, when purposively interpreted in the context of other relevant Basic Law provisions, Art 35 leads to a conclusion diametrically opposed to the proposition in Point 5: For a tribunal to be subject to Article 35 it *does* need to be an organ forming part of the judicial system, exercising the judicial power of the Region.

69. In my opinion, the same fundamental flaw regarding Art 35 affects the judgments in the Court of Appeal below as well as the relevant judgments in *Dr Ip's case* and the *Law Society case*. They do not adopt the correct approach to interpreting Art 35 and consequently fail to interpret it in the context of the Basic Law's evident purposes which involve laying the constitutional foundations for the exercise of the judicial power in the HKSAR.

M. Case-law on the concept of a "court"

70. The focus of the Court of Appeal's judgments has instead been on identifying factors (drawn from the English case-law) capable of serving as indicators that a given tribunal is "a court". The factors favoured by Cheung JA and Reyes J are summarised in Section L above.

71. For the purposes of the present case, that approach was inapposite. When considering reported cases dealing with whether a particular tribunal may be regarded as "a court", the context in which that issue arises is all-important. Different questions, requiring quite different approaches to their solution may be involved. Different answers may be given to what may superficially appear to be the same question. For example, one issue that often arises is whether certain recognized attributes of a court of law are applicable to a tribunal whose status as "a court" is in question. This is of course very different from the question of constitutional interpretation required to be addressed in this case. As it happens, in certain other contexts, the concept of a body exercising the judicial power of the state is the criterion adopted by the common law or by statute for deciding whether a tribunal is a "court" for the purposes there relevant. But in other cases, a different, and perhaps wider, notion of what qualifies as "a court" may be employed. The importance of context and the different approaches generated may be illustrated in the examples which follow.

(i) A "court" for the purposes of the law of contempt

72. In *Attorney-General v. BBC* [1981] AC 303, the question was whether a body, created by the Local Government Act 1948 as a "local valuation court", could claim the protection of the law of contempt so that the BBC might be restrained from making a broadcast which might prejudice a pending valuation appeal.

73. The House of Lords held that in the interests of freedom of expression, the law of contempt should not be extended beyond the protection of courts of law, meaning only those courts which form part of the judicial system and exercise the judicial power of the state. Applying that test, local valuation courts did not qualify:

> "... in my opinion, the class of inferior courts protected by the law against contempt should be limited to those which are truly courts of law, exercising the judicial power of the state." (per Lord Fraser of Tullybelton at 353)

> "I would identify a court in (or 'of') law, i.e. a court of judicature, as a body established by law to exercise, either generally or subject to defined limits, the judicial power of the state. In this context judicial power is to be contrasted with legislative and executive (i.e. administrative) power. If the body under review is established for a purely legislative or administrative purpose, it is part of the legislative or administrative system of the state, even though it has to perform duties which are judicial in character. Though the ubiquitous presence of the state makes itself felt in all sorts of situations never envisaged when our law was in its formative stage, the judicial power of the state exercised through judges appointed by the state remains

an independent, and recognisably separate, function of government. Unless a body exercising judicial functions can be demonstrated to be part of this judicial system, it is not, in my judgment, a court in law." (per Lord Scarman at 359–360)

74. The same criterion was adopted by s 19 of the Contempt of Court Act 1981 which states:

> "In this Act – 'court' includes any tribunal or body exercising the judicial power of the state and 'legal proceedings' shall be construed accordingly..."

75. As Robert Walker LJ pointed out in *General Medical Council v. BBC* [1998] 1 WLR 1573:

> "Although that definition applies, at first sight, only for statutory purposes, it was recognised by Lord Donaldson of Lymington MR in *P v. Liverpool Daily Post and Echo Newspapers Plc* [1991] 2 AC 370, 380 as having a wider significance and being 'intended to reflect the common law concept of what is a "court" for the purposes of the common law jurisdiction of the courts in relation to contempt of court.' The expression 'the judicial power of the state' is in fact a clear reflection of language used in the House of Lords in *Attorney-General v. British Broadcasting Corporation* [1981] AC 303, in which their Lordships held that a local valuation court established for rating purposes was not a court in law (or a court of law) and so was not an inferior court for the purposes of RSC, Ord 52, r 1." (at 1578)

76. Accordingly, the common law has adopted the concept of a "court" as a body "exercising the judicial power of the state" in the context of contempt, which, as it happens, is the same concept adopted by the Basic Law.

(ii) Where only "a court" can exercise the judicial power

77. Another context in which the concept of "a court" may be in issue concerns cases where a challenge is made to a tribunal's jurisdiction on the ground that it is performing a function which involves exercise of the judicial power whereas it is not a properly constituted "court" and therefore cannot lawfully exercise such power.

78. Thus, in *Shell Company of Australia Ltd v. Federal Commissioner of Taxation* [1931] AC 275, the question was whether the Board of Review set up under Australian tax legislation to review decisions of the Commissioner of Taxation was exercising the judicial power of the Commonwealth within the meaning of s 71 of the Constitution. If so, the taxpayer contended that it was not a properly constituted "court" since the terms of appointment of its members lacked the entrenched security of tenure enjoyed by judges. The challenge was unsuccessful since the Board of Review was held not to be exercising the judicial power but merely acting administratively.

79. In our own jurisdiction, a challenge based on similar grounds succeeded in *Lai Hung Wai v. Secretary for Security* (Unreported, HCAL 1596/2001, Hartmann J; 9 September 2002; see also *Yau Kwong Man & Lai Hung Wai v. Secretary for Security* CACV 377/2002, 2 July 2003). Young persons who had been convicted of murder had been made subject to an indefinite sentence of imprisonment. Legislation (s 67C of the Criminal Procedure Ordinance, Cap 221) was passed to modify that sentence so that there would be a fixed minimum term. It was provided that this task would be performed by the Chief Executive on the recommendation of the Chief Justice. The constitutionality of that legislation was successfully challenged on the basis that the fixing of the term imprisonment involved an exercise of the judicial power which had to be exercised by a court of law as provided for by Art 80 of the Basic Law and not by the Chief Executive. Section 67C was consequently further amended to vest the function in the court instead.

80. Issues arising in this context are again obviously different from those arising in relation to whether a Disciplinary Committee is a "court" within the meaning of Art 35. In this category of cases, there is no doubt that if the function in question involves exercising the judicial power, only a court of law is qualified to exercise it. The argument is about the nature of the function and whether the body performing it is in fact a court of law.

81. These cases also highlight a difficulty with holding that tribunals like the Disciplinary Committee constitute "courts" for the purposes of the Basic Law. If that were so, it might be thought logically to follow that their composition might be subject to challenge on the ground that they are not manned by judges or other members of the judiciary, which would of course be absurd.

(iii) "A court" for the purposes of absolute privilege

82. *Royal Aquarium and Summer and Winter Garden Society Ltd v. Parkinson* [1892] 1 QB 431, may be taken as a final example. In that case, a wider basis for qualifying as a "court" was adopted. The question was whether a meeting of the London County Council for granting music and dancing licences under a certain statute was "a court" for the purposes of conferring absolute privilege on members in respect of defamatory statements made in the course of its proceedings. Lord Esher MR held that the immunity extended not only to courts of justice, but to tribunals with "similar attributes":

> "It is true that, in respect of statements made in the course of proceedings before a Court of justice, whether by judge, or counsel, or witnesses, there is an absolute immunity from liability to an action. The ground of that rule is public policy. It is applicable to all kinds of Courts of justice; but the doctrine has been carried further; and it seems that this immunity applies wherever there is an authorized inquiry which, though not before a Court of justice, is before a tribunal which has similar attributes." (at 442)

83. It is unclear what the criteria for qualifying in this wider category are. However, even on this wider test, the LCC, which was obviously not "a court", did not qualify for the immunity. This suggests that bodies which count as "courts" for the purposes of the absolute privilege against suit for defamation may not count as "courts" for other purposes, such as for the purposes of the law of contempt.

N. The indicators identified by the Court of Appeal

84. Both Cheung JA and Reyes J lay considerable emphasis on "acting judicially" as an indicator of "a court". But, as previously discussed, the real question is one of constitutional interpretation. However, even in contexts where a search for qualifying attributes is relevant, it would appear that the guidance which the concept of "acting judicially" provides is very limited.

(a) Thus, in *Royal Aquarium and Summer and Winter Garden Society Ltd v. Parkinson* (cited above), the argument that absolute privilege applied to licensing proceedings in the LCC because it had to act judicially and therefore was "a court" was rejected. As Lopes LJ explained, the fact that a body acts judicially does not make it "a court":

"The word 'judicial' has two meanings. It may refer to the discharge of duties exercisable by a judge or by justices in court, or to administrative duties which need not be performed in court, but in respect of which it is necessary to bring to bear a judicial mind–that is, a mind to determine what is fair and just in respect of the matters under consideration." ([1892] 1 QB 431 at 452)

(b) Fry LJ pointed out that using an "acting judicially" criterion for defining a "court" for the purposes of the immunity would catch far too many tribunals, referring in passing to the General Medical Council:

"It would apply to assessment committees, boards of guardians, to the Inns of Court when considering the conduct of one of their members, to the General Medical Council when considering questions affecting the position of a medical man, and to all arbitrators. Is it necessary, on grounds of public policy, that the doctrine of immunity should be carried as far as this? I say not." (at 447)

(c) This was reiterated by their Lordships in *Attorney-General v. BBC* (cited above). As Viscount Dilhorne (referring to a local valuation court) put it:

"It has to act judicially but that does not make it a court of law. The fact that it has to act judicially means as Fry LJ said in *Royal Aquarium and Summer and Winter Garden Society Ltd v. Parkinson* [1892] 1 QB 431 that its proceedings must be 'conducted with the fairness and impartiality which characterise proceedings in courts of justice, and are proper to the functions of a judge' and not, though established by law, that it is a court of law and part of the judicial system of the country." ([1981] AC 303 at 340) (See also Lord Edmund-Davies at 351; Lord Scarman at 360)

85. The Court of Appeal also stressed the seriousness of the sanctions available to the Medical Council, the SDT and the Disciplinary Committee as an indicator in the three cases. It is unfortunate, particularly in *Dr Ip's case*, that the Court of Appeal did not have the benefit of having *General Medical Council v. BBC* (above) cited to it. That case concerns the question whether contempt applies to the Professional Conduct Committee of the UK's General Medical Council which closely resembles the Medical Council in Hong Kong in relation, among other things, to the severity of potential sanctions administered. That feature did not, however, bring the PCC into the category of a court of law protected by contempt. Robert Walker LJ, giving the judgment of the court, stated:

"[Counsel] submitted correctly, that the PCC of the GMC has to adjudicate in a formal and judicial manner on very serious issues which are of public importance and may also have the gravest effect on the reputation and career of an accused medical practitioner. Mr Henderson was correct in submitting that the PCC is exercising a sort of judicial power but in our judgment it is not the judicial power of the state which is being exercised. ... the PCC is a statutory committee of a professional body specially incorporated by statute. It exercises a function which is recognisably a judicial function, and does so in the public interest. It acts in accordance with detailed procedural rules which have close similarities to those followed in courts of law. Nevertheless it is not part of the judicial system of the state. Instead it is exercising (albeit with statutory sanction) the self-regulatory power and duty of the medical profession to monitor and maintain standards of professional conduct." ([1998] 1 WLR 1573 at 1580)

86. Some reliance was also placed by the Court of Appeal on the statutory basis of a tribunal as a qualifying criterion. However, while it is true that a purely domestic tribunal derived wholly from private contractual relations is most unlikely to be considered "a court", the fact that a tribunal has been created by statute or is integral to a statutory scheme is plainly not sufficient to qualify it as "a court" for any requisite purpose.

87. Mr Griffiths submitted on the respondents' behalf that the Court should essentially adopt the approach of the Court of Appeal decisions mentioned above. Indeed, he sought to cast a wider net, suggesting that any tribunals which carry out judicial functions as opposed to administrative functions should be held to fall within Art 35. For the foregoing reasons, I reject that submission.

O. Conclusion on Art 35 and the Disciplinary Committee

88. Interpreted in the light of the Basic Law as a whole, Art 35 only applies to courts of law, that is, the courts exercising the independent judicial power conferred on the Region by the Basic Law. The Disciplinary Committee is not a court of law. Art 35 therefore does not apply to it.

89. Neither are the SDT and the Medical Council courts of law. Therefore, to the extent that the judgments in *Dr Ip Kay Lo Vincent v. Medical Council of Hong Kong (No 2)* [2003] 3 HKC 579, and *A Solicitor v. The Law Society of Hong Kong* (CACV 302/2002 Woo VP, Cheung JA and Burrell J; 18 February 2004), hold otherwise, they are wrong and should not be followed.

P. The applicability of the common law principles of procedural fairness

90. I have dealt at some length with the Art 35 argument because of the need to address the case-law developed by the Court of Appeal on this important constitutional subject.

91. However, as all the parties correctly accept, the common law principles of procedural fairness provide an appropriate framework for dealing with the issues dividing them. As Reyes J points out: "An inquiry into whether art.35 rights have been transgressed by a court's procedure does not end with mere identification of a tribunal as a 'court'. As Cheung JA stresses, there remain questions of proportionality." (§113) It follows that even assuming the respondents succeeded in maintaining that the Disciplinary Committee is a court for Art 35 purposes, they would still have to address the question whether it may be proportionate to restrict legal representation in given circumstances–an inquiry which mirrors the inquiry that is undertaken at common law. Legal representation is not invariably an attribute of a court of law. Thus in tribunals dealing with small claims or employment matters, lawyers are often dispensed with for wholly legitimate policy reasons (usually while providing for the possible transfer of proceedings and appeal to more formal courts where justice requires).

92. Moreover, this is not a case where the respondents face a prohibition against legal representation. On the contrary, as the provisions of the Disciplinary Procedures set out in Section

F above indicate, persons appearing can avail themselves of legal assistance and advice before and during the hearing. The proceedings being primarily by way of written submissions (DP 2.5), their lawyers can and may be expected to draft the same. Their lawyers can accompany them and can confer with them at any stage of the hearing (DP 5.1). The lawyers may also, at the Disciplinary Committee's request, clarify or elaborate upon any answer given by their client (DP 6.3). And, prior to final submissions, the client can confer with the lawyer who will no doubt prepare submissions to be advanced (DP 6.3). One should bear in mind in this context that in many states which are signatories to relevant human rights conventions, the rule is that parties have no right to examine witnesses.

93. The issue in the present case therefore concerns the precise mode and extent of legal representation which should be permitted at the hearing. The answer must depend on what is fair and proportionate, applying the common law approach. This case is therefore distinguishable from *Dr Ip's case* where upon refusal of an adjournment, Dr Ip was left without any legal representation at the hearing. It is also quite different from the *Law Society case*, where the court was concerned with the purported impact of indemnity costs on the right of access to a tribunal and where the solicitor in question actually had counsel appearing on his behalf (§3).

94. It is also convenient at this stage to deal with Art 10. In my view, the applicability of the common law principles of fairness makes it unnecessary to embark on a parallel inquiry into the applicability of Art 10. Certain questions arise as to Art 10's scope and applicability to disciplinary proceedings (which, for instance, may or may not be "a suit at law"). But even assuming that it does apply, the parties are agreed that it does not add anything to the common law rules on procedural fairness. I therefore propose to say nothing more about Art 10.

Q. Legal representation and the common law principles of fairness

95. Mr Griffiths based his submissions on a dictum of Lord Denning MR in *Pett v. Greyhound Racing Association Ltd* [1969] 1 QB 125. After emphasising the value and importance of legal representation to a layman, his Lordship stated:

> "... when a man's reputation or livelihood is at stake, he not only has a right to speak by his own mouth. He also has a right to speak by counsel or solicitor." (at 132)

96. On that basis, Mr Griffiths suggested that in the circumstances of the present case, the respondents were entitled to legal representation as of right.

97. I am unable to accept that submission. The authorities have not developed along the lines suggested by Lord Denning MR. Indeed, as was pointed out by Webster J in *R v. Sec of State for the Home Department ex p Tarrant* [1985] QB 251 at 273–274, in *Pett's case* the Court of Appeal was dealing with an interlocutory appeal against an interim injunction and was dealing "only with the question whether it was arguable that the trainer was entitled, as of right, to legal representation ..." Webster J points out that at the substantive hearing, Lyell J found (see *Pett v. Greyhound Racing Association Ltd (No 2)* [1970] 1 QB 46 at 63–66) that the defendant association had not acted contrary to the rules of natural justice in refusing the plaintiff legal representation at the inquiry, preferring the decision of the Privy Council in *University of Ceylon v. Fernando* [1960] 1 WLR 223, to the dicta in *Pett (No 1)*.

98. More recent authority clearly establishes that there is no absolute right to have counsel address the tribunal or to question witnesses, any such entitlement depending on whether such procedures are required as a matter of fairness.

99. Thus, in *R v. Board of Visitors of HM Prison, the Maze, ex p Hone* [1988] AC 379, the House of Lords was concerned with a case involving prisoners charged with offences against prison discipline (which would also constitute criminal offences). The cases were referred to the prison's board of visitors and the prisoners were refused legal representation before them. Their argument that they were entitled as of right to legal representation at the hearing was rejected. Lord Goff of Chieveley (with whom the other Law Lords agreed) stated:

> "... though the rules of natural justice may require legal representation before a board of visitors, I can see no basis for Mr Hill's submission that they should do so in every case as of right. Everything must depend on the circumstances of the particular case, as is amply demonstrated by the circumstances so carefully listed by Webster J in *Reg v. Secretary of State for the Home Department, Ex parte Tarrant* [1985] QB 251 as matters which boards of visitors should take into account. But it is easy to envisage circumstances in which the rules of natural justice do not call for representation, even though the disciplinary charge relates to a matter which constitutes in law a crime, as may well happen in the case of a simple assault where no question of law arises, and where the prisoner charged is capable of presenting his own case. To hold otherwise would result in wholly unnecessary delays in many cases, to the detriment of all concerned including the prisoner charged, and to wholly unnecessary waste of time and money, contrary to the public interest." (at 392)

100. As his Lordship stated, the common law position is that such tribunals have a discretion whether to permit legal representation, depending on the needs of fairness:

> "In English law, we are fortunate in having available to us a discretionary power, so often employed when it is necessary to weigh the effect of different factors; and it is established that disciplinary tribunals have, in the exercise of their discretion, and having regard to a broad range of factors including those mentioned by the European Court, to decide whether natural justice requires that a person appearing before the tribunal should be legally represented." (at 394)

101. The matters listed in *Ex p Tarrant* (above at 285–286) referred to by Lord Goff include (with modifications to make the point more general): the seriousness of the charge and potential penalty; whether any points of law are likely to arise; the capacity of the individual to present his own case; procedural difficulties; the need for reasonable speed in making the adjudication; and the need for fairness among the individuals concerned. This approach was adopted in Hong Kong by Mayo J in *R v. Hong Kong Polytechnic, ex p Jenny Chua Yee-yen* (1992) 2 HKPLR 34. Plainly, as these judgments emphasise, no list of such factors can be comprehensive. The common law principles of fairness operate flexibly, requiring the tribunal to respond reasonably to the requirements of fairness arising in each case, balancing any competing interests and considering what, if any, limits may proportionately be imposed on legal representation in consequence.

102. Mr David Pannick QC (appearing with Mr John Scott SC for SEHK), made it plain that he fully accepts the Disciplinary Committee's obligation to act fairly and that considerations of fairness may well require it to permit the witnesses, or some of them, to be cross-examined by counsel or to permit submissions to be made by counsel. His fundamental objection is that these judicial review proceedings are premature in two essential respects. I return later to deal with that argument which is central to this appeal. I deal first with the approach of the Court of Appeal and the respondents.

R. The approach of the Court of Appeal and the respondents to the common law principles of fairness

103. The respondents invite the Court to find that they have, here and now, made good the case that unless their lawyers are given the unrestricted right to address the Disciplinary Committee and to examine and cross-examine witnesses, the common law principles of fairness will necessarily be infringed. The Court of Appeal adopted this approach and found that such case had been made out.

104. Cheung JA's view was that the Disciplinary Committee's procedure of allowing lawyers to advise but not to act as advocates for the respondents at the hearing would result in cumbersome and unsatisfactory to-ing and fro-ing between lawyer and client and that this "simply does not work" (§43). He listed the factors identified by Mayo J in the *Hong Kong Polytechnic case* (above) and appears to have held that they militated in favour of a finding of unfairness. He did not, however, engage in any specific analysis of such unfairness.

105. Reyes J considered the restrictions contained in the Disciplinary Procedures to be unjustified, founding himself in the first place on the dictum of Lord Denning MR in *Pett (No 1)*. He points out that that dictum was applied in *Joplin v. Chief Constable of the City of Vancouver* (1982) 2 CCC (3d) 396 (and upheld in the British Columbia Court of Appeal at (1985) 20 DLR (4th) 314) where a provision in police disciplinary regulations which excluded legal representation was held to be ultra vires [*sic*]. As I have stated above, the development of English and Hong Kong authority has not proceeded along the lines of giving an absolute entitlement to full legal representation whenever someone may be faced with serious disciplinary consequences. It may in any event be noted that in *Joplin*, one is concerned with regulations seeking to impose a blanket exclusion of legal representation. It may well be that such an exclusion is likely in most cases to offend against the principles of fairness. But that is not this case where, as stated above, the debate is as to the specific mode of legal representation to be permitted at a hearing.

106. Reyes J evidently gave weight to the potentially serious consequences of a public censure in the present case and to the likelihood that the directors, being laymen, would feel at a disadvantage presenting their cases.

107. In his submissions, Mr Griffiths pointed to a list of features in the present case which, he argued, meant that there would inevitably be unfairness at the hearing in the absence of full legal representation. I shall return to consider those features more fully later.

S. The SEHK's approach to the common law principles of fairness

108. As I have previously indicated, Mr Pannick accepts that the Disciplinary Committee is obliged to observe the common law principles of fairness. He accepts that, depending on circumstances which may arise, unfairness may result if counsel is not permitted to examine witnesses or to make submissions at the hearing. Equally, limiting representation by counsel may, depending on the circumstances, involve no breach of the principles.

109. It is therefore common ground, and obviously correctly so, that what fairness requires depends on the circumstances. SEHK's policy, reflected in the Listing Rules and the Disciplinary Procedures, of limiting (at least in the first instance) the role of lawyers at the hearing is based upon the belief that limited representation suffices in most cases; that an informal, expert, lay tribunal, steeped in the ways of the stock exchange, is best placed to deal effectively and swiftly with disciplinary issues; that the public interest in maintaining confidence in the market requires swift investigation and treatment of suspected infringements; and that "over-lawyering" the procedures would undermine many of these objectives, substantially lengthening and complicating proceedings, and making it difficult to persuade qualified individuals to accept unremunerated appointment to a Disciplinary Committee. These are plainly legitimate concerns. But they can only be pursued with proper regard for the needs of procedural fairness and for proportionality in any procedural restrictions imposed.

110. Mr Pannick's objection to the respondents' position is two-fold. First, he argues that the state of the evidence and other materials placed before the Disciplinary Committee is such that it is presently not possible to form a view as to whether fairness does or does not require the examination of witnesses by counsel. He submits that the chairman is fully justified in deciding to leave open that question. Secondly, he contends that the respondents ought to be required, in accordance with the general rule in judicial review proceedings, to exhaust the domestic remedies provided by the Listing Rules before seeking the court's intervention by judicial review. It is contrary to the policy of the law to permit these proceedings to be brought at such an early stage.

111. These objections are related but distinct. The first involves what is essentially a practical question. Since, in relation to the operation of the principles of fairness, everything must depend on the circumstances of the particular case, it must follow that an assessment of what procedures are dictated by fairness can only be made where those circumstances are known.

112. This approach was adopted by the House of Lords in *R (Roberts) v. Parole Board* [2005] 3 WLR 152, a case where a life sentence prisoner was to come before the Parole Board with a view to being released on licence. Information was to be placed before the Board suggesting that he was involved in drug dealing and infractions of prison discipline. The Board decided that revealing the sensitive information to the prisoner would put the informant at risk and decided that it would instead be shown to a special advocate appointed to look after his interests. Judicial review proceedings were brought on the ground that this decision infringed the prisoner's rights under Art 5(4) of the European Convention of Human Rights. The House of Lords held that the challenge was premature and that it was not possible to say in advance that the proposed procedure would necessarily be incompatible with Art 5(4).

(a) Lord Bingham put it thus, identifying various possible outcomes which would not lead to any incompatibility:

"... I would decline the appellant's invitation to rule, at this stage, that the adoption of the proposed procedure is necessarily incompatible with article 5(4). The practice of the European Court is to consider the proceedings in question as a whole, including the decisions of appellate courts: *Edwards v. United Kingdom* 15 EHRR 417 para 34. Thus its judgment is almost necessarily made in retrospect, when there is evidence of what actually happened. This reflects the acute sensitivity of the Court to the facts of a given case. Save where an issue of compatibility turns on a pure question of statutory construction, the House should in my opinion be similarly reluctant to rule without knowing what has actually happened. This seems to me important because there are some outcomes which would not in my opinion offend article 5(4) despite the employment of a specially appointed advocate. It might, for instance, be that the Board, having heard the sensitive material tested by the specially appointed advocate, wholly rejected it. Or having heard the material tested in that way the Board might decline to continue the review unless the sensitive material, or at least the substance of it, were disclosed at least to the appellant's legal representatives .... Or the board might, with the assistance of the specially appointed advocate, devise a way of anonymising, redacting or summarising the sensitive material so as to enable it to be disclosed to the appellant or his legal representatives. Or the board might, in a manner that was procedurally fair, reach a decision without relying at all on the sensitive material. If any of these possibilities were to eventuate, I do not think there would be a violation of article 5(4)." (§19)

(b) Lord Woolf CJ made the point as follows:

"So far as article 5(4) is concerned the need to examine the facts as a whole, including any appellate process, before coming to a decision is critical as Lord Bingham points out in his speech (at para 19). The same is true in domestic law. To make rulings in advance of the actual hearing would be to introduce a rigidity that would make the task of the Board extraordinarily difficult. The position has to be looked at in the round examining the proceedings as a whole with hindsight and taking into account the task of the Board." (§77)

"If a case arises where it is impossible for the Board both to make use of information that has not been disclosed to the prisoner and, at the same time, protect the prisoner from a denial of his fundamental right to a fair hearing then the rights of the prisoner have to take precedence, but we have not in my view reached the stage in this case where we can say this has happened. Certainly we cannot say it has happened without considering at least the closed as well as the open judgment of Maurice Kay J. The appellant has chosen to make the issue that which I identified at the outset. He is saying in no circumstances can a SAA be engaged at a hearing and this is putting the case too high."(§78)

(c) And Lord Rodger stated:

"So far as the argument based on the European Convention is concerned, substantially for the reasons given by Lord Bingham, I consider that the House cannot decide in advance whether the full hearing, involving the specially appointed advocate, meets the requirements of article 5(4). The same competing interests fall to be considered for the purposes of article 5(4), but the weight to be attached to the various factors may well depend, in part at least, on what happens at the hearing." (§112)

113. The first argument is therefore well-supported in law. Whether it applies on the present facts is examined later.

114. The doctrine referred to in Mr Pannick's second argument is also well known and is not disputed in principle by the respondents. In the Court of Appeal and before the Court, the parties were content to argue the point on the basis of the principles set out in *Stock Exchange of Hong Kong Ltd v. Onshine Securities Ltd* [1994] 1 HKC 319. In that case, a firm of stock brokers had been found guilty by the Disciplinary Committee of certain breaches of the rules. Instead of bringing an appeal to the Disciplinary Appeals Committee ("DAC") as provided for in the rules, it brought judicial review proceedings complaining that those findings were unfair. The Court of Appeal proceeded on the assumption that the complaints could be made good so as to warrant quashing the Disciplinary Committee's decision. Nevertheless, since there was a domestic right of appeal to the DAC, it refused to intervene "unless and until Onshine has exhausted that remedy and it can be seen that it has still not received fair treatment." (ibid)

115. Power VP (as Sir Noel Power NPJ then was), giving the judgment of the court, noted that the appellant could only say, "not that is *impossible* for the DAC to redress its grievances; only that there is a danger that it *might* not." He concluded: "In our judgment, this will not do." (at 329) In a valuable summary accepted by both sides in this Appeal, his Lordship pointed out that it is only in extraordinary or highly exceptional circumstances that the court allows departure from this rule, providing some illustrative instances:

"It is neither advisable nor possible to define 'extraordinary circumstances', but if the appeal available is adequate to deal with all the alleged flaws in the original proceedings, this will weigh heavily against the granting of leave. However, this cannot be decisive. For example, the applicant may show that immediate intervention is required because the appeal procedure is flawed by delay or some other extraneous matter. Similarly, if the court's immediate intervention will result in abating the litigation, this will also be an important–perhaps decisive–consideration. We have in mind cases where the tribunal had no jurisdiction to entertain the proceedings or where the proceedings were based on an obvious and fundamental error of law. In such circumstances it would not be possible to start the same proceedings again and justice and convenience may require that the decision is struck down immediately." (at 329)

116. Basing himself on *Calvin v. Carr* [1980] AC 574 and *R v. Chief Constable of the Merseyside Police, ex p Calveley* [1986] QB 424, Power VP stated the principle in the following terms:

"Where in the case of a domestic body like the Stock Exchange the appellate procedure may, or may not, ensure justice for the party aggrieved by the lower tribunal's decision, then, generally speaking, the court should not be asked to second–guess the appellate tribunal's decision. In the absence of exceptional circumstances requiring immediate intervention by the court, the aggrieved party should be told to wait and see what happens before the appellate tribunal. If that tribunal can, and does, quash the decision of the lower tribunal, that will be an end of the matter. If the appellate tribunal affirms the decision of the lower tribunal, the aggrieved party can then apply for a judicial review; but he will succeed only if, taking the procedure (original and appellate) as a whole, it can be seen that the aggrieved party has still not been fairly treated." (at 330)

117. It is to be noted that while the rule requiring exhaustion of domestic remedies is generally to be applied, a degree of flexibility exists to cater for cases (likely to be highly unusual) where it can starkly be shown that an exception must be made if substantial injustice is to be avoided. Mr Griffiths contends (as has been accepted by Hartmann J as well as the Court of Appeal) that the respondents have shown exceptional circumstances justifying their early launching of this judicial review. He also contends, as noted above, that the proceedings are not premature and that the court is now in a perfectly good position to rule on the inevitability of unfairness. Mr Pannick contends to the contrary. The facts must therefore be examined to decide who is correct.

T. Procedural fairness and the exhaustion of alternative remedies on the facts

(i) What did the chairman in fact direct?

118. It is first necessary to resolve the point of controversy raised by Mr Griffiths at the hearing mentioned in Section D above. The contested procedural directions have been described in that Section. The chairman issued the Directions which provided, among other things, that:

> 6. Legal advisers will not be permitted to address the [Disciplinary] Committee (whether in respect of oral submissions, the examination of witnesses of fact or otherwise).

119. It will be recalled that Hartmann J took this to mean that the chairman had left open the question whether lawyers would be allowed to cross-examine witnesses and that, after clarification sought by the Court of Appeal, this was confirmed to be the chairman's position in a letter written on his behalf. The Court of Appeal (at §34 and §176) accepted this and dealt with the appeal on the basis that the question had been kept open. Notwithstanding this background, Mr Griffiths submitted that the Court should proceed on the footing that the only relevant direction being contested is §6 of the Directions set out above which should be read as definitively excluding any examination of witnesses and any submissions by lawyers on the respondents' behalf.

120. With respect, that proposition is untenable and Mr Griffiths did not advance any legal basis for it. While it is true that on their face a few of the Disciplinary Procedures (such as DP5.1 and DP6.3) lay down general procedures which envisage lawyers playing a restricted and purely advisory role at the hearing, it is clear that the Listing Committee (whether sitting as a Disciplinary Committee or otherwise) can modify those rules. Thus, LR2.04 relevantly states:

> "It is emphasised that the Exchange Listing Rules are not exhaustive and that the Exchange may impose additional requirements or make listing subject to special conditions whenever it considers it appropriate. Conversely, the Exchange may waive, modify or not require compliance with the Exchange Listing Rules in individual cases (to suit the circumstances of a particular case), as a variety of circumstances may exist which require it to make ad hoc decisions..."

Such flexibility is obviously intended not only for the Listing Rules but also for the Disciplinary Procedures made thereunder.

121. Moreover, the Disciplinary Procedures themselves (in DP6.1 and DP6.2) emphasise the informality of the tribunal's proceedings which are conducted without the constraints of the rules of evidence. The Disciplinary Committee whether acting through the chairman or as a committee in session, must be master of its own informal procedures, subject always to the underlying obligation to act fairly. Its very informality and the need for it to meet the requirements of fairness give it an implicit discretion to modify directions previously made and to issue fresh directions as required by the circumstances.

122. In *R (D) v. Secretary of State for the Home Department* [2006] EWCA Civ 143, a similar approach was adopted. Although the matter arose in quite a different context (involving the procedures for conducting an inquiry set up by the Home Secretary into events in a prison), the comments of Sir Anthony Clarke MR on the role of the chairman are helpful. Giving the judgment of the court, his Lordship noted that the applicable Act did not give a right to parties represented at the inquiry to cross-examine witnesses so that this was a matter to be decided by the chairman in accordance with the principles of fairness. In consequence, he held:

> "It is a matter for the chairman of the particular inquiry to decide whether and to what extent to permit interested parties or their representatives to ask questions of witnesses.
>
> We see no reason why an inquiry conducted in such a way should not be compatible with Art 2 of the Convention. The underlying obligation of the chairman is to act fairly. In discharging that obligation, the chairman may or may not allow others to question witnesses, depending upon the circumstances of the particular case. In some cases it may be appropriate to do so and in others it may not." (§§40–41)

In my view, a similar procedural latitude is open to the Disciplinary Committee acting through its chairman or as a whole.

123. Mr Griffiths' submission is surprising since the respondents plainly accepted Hartmann J's reading of the Directions in the letter dated 27 May 2005 from their solicitors to the chairman. It referred to the relevant paragraphs in Hartmann J's judgment and "by reason of the said paragraphs" sought further directions permitting examination of witnesses by legal representatives which obviously assumed power to modify earlier directions. As it happens, they did not follow up that letter since they took the decision shortly afterwards to launch the judicial review application and obtained a stay of the disciplinary proceedings.

(ii) Is an assessment of the fairness of the hearing possible at this stage?

124. The steps taken by the Listing Division in bringing its case against the respondents have been described in Section C above. This was followed by the making of the Directions as described in Section D above. The respondents' initial written submissions indicated a legal challenge to the admissibility of the statements

obtained from the SFC and a general challenge to the reliability of the deponents particularly in the light of alleged deficiencies in the way those statements were taken. The Listing Division intimated that it was (in December 2002) intending to call four named witnesses, being two analysts from Goldman Sachs and one each from J P Morgan and DBS Vickers (Hong Kong) Ltd. It was in that submission that the Listing Division indicated its view that if these witnesses should be called, it would be appropriate for them to be examined and cross-examined by counsel, although that was a matter for the Disciplinary Committee.

125. On 2 July 2003 the Listing Division delivered its List of Factual Issues. This proved to be the first and last procedural step taken in the disciplinary proceedings after issue of the Directions. The proceedings were thereafter stayed, giving way to the judicial review proceedings culminating in this Appeal.

126. The Listing Division stated in its List that it was only able to identify a single factual dispute at that stage, namely, "whether [New World] disclosed its interim profit figure to Goldman Sachs and/or JP Morgan and/or Vickers Ballas in advance of its formal publication on 15th March 2001." It added in a Note:

> "To date submissions by the Parties concerned have not challenged any of the factual assertions made in paragraph 7 of the Listing Division's Report ... in respect of the complaint against the [directors] regarding their failure to put in place adequate control procedures to prevent selective disclosure of price sensitive information..."

127. It is obviously true that the judicial review application was launched at a very early stage in the disciplinary proceedings. There was no List of Factual Issues from the respondents. Neither the Listing Division nor the respondents had served witness statements or summaries disclosing the substance of the evidence to be given by each witness intended to be called. There was only a voluminous collection of statements and other documents in the Listing Division's Report and argumentative replies from the respondents. It is in this context that the letter of 4 May 2005 written on the chairman's behalf stated: "Upon compliance with Mr Cheng's other directions, the Committee would have been in a better position to consider the exercise of their discretion..."

128. In my view, it was perfectly within the chairman's discretion to take this wait-and-see position without any necessary infringement of the principles of fairness resulting. In leaving open the question of counsel examining witnesses, he did not exclude that course. He was merely deferring his decision until the issues and scope of the proceedings were better defined. If and when notice is given of the witnesses to be called, with disclosure of the substance of their evidence, the respondents could apply (possibly with support from the Listing Division, in the light of what they have previously said) for them to be dealt with by counsel, stating the grounds relied on. Of course if in future, the chairman or the Disciplinary Committee should give directions that are incompatible with the principles of fairness there would be grounds for judicial review to be initiated at an appropriate stage. That stage may or may not (depending on the nature of the infringement and the then prevailing circumstances) be after the review and appeal procedures provided for by the Listing Rules have been exhausted, the position being governed by the *Onshine* principles discussed above.

129. I am unable to accept that the features of this case identified by Mr Griffiths compel the Court to conclude that unfairness inexorably follows if directions authorizing full legal representation are not given at this point. To take these features in series:

(a) Seriousness of the sanctions: I agree that in considering what fairness requires, the seriousness of the sanctions must be taken into account. That remains a factor that should guide the chairman and the Disciplinary Committee not only regarding the handling of witnesses, but on its procedure generally when the issues are better defined.

(b) Difficult points of law exist: Assuming this to be so, written arguments have already been exchanged, obviously prepared by lawyers on both sides. Such submissions may or may not be enough to enable the Disciplinary Committee to decide the point. If not and if fairness so requires, it has a discretion to allow oral argument by legal representatives when the legal issues are better defined and the written submissions have been examined.

(c) The respondents are laymen who will not be able properly to present their own cases: Until the issues are well-defined and the substance of the evidence of any live witnesses is known, the court is in no position to assess whether this is the case. If such difficulties in fact arise, then it may well be proper to permit legal representation to the extent necessary.

(d) There is no equality of arms since the Listing Division would be represented by individuals who, while not court lawyers, are trained as lawyers and have experience of disciplinary cases while the respondents are laymen: if this is so at the hearing and if a risk of unfairness arises, it may well be proper to permit legal representation to the extent necessary.

(e) There is a material dispute of facts so that cross-examination is required: Mr Griffiths pointed to the fact that the Report runs to some 750 pages, involving 11 deponents and 16 records of interview, with the defence possibly calling additional witnesses. If anything, this supports the chairman's wait-and-see approach. The Listing Division has indicated that it is only going to call four witnesses, and not the 11 whose 16 statements have been made available. When it becomes clear what evidence the witnesses actually to be called are expected to give, fairness may or may not require some or all of them to be cross-examined by counsel for the respondents. The chairman and the Disciplinary Committee will have to give careful consideration to that question, which has been left open.

130. I also respectfully disagree with the view taken in the courts below that this is a case where exceptional circumstances justify judicial review proceedings at this early stage. No reason has been provided for saying that immediate intervention by the court is required. Correctly interpreted, Art 35 places no constitutional impediment in the way of the disciplinary proceedings. It cannot be said that proceeding on the basis that examination of witnesses by counsel has been left open involves any obvious and fundamental error of law. In short, there is nothing exceptional to justify judicial review now. On the contrary, given the lack of definition in the issues and lack of disclosure regarding the likely evidence, a judicial review requiring the court to assess the likely procedural fairness of the disciplinary proceedings cannot sensibly be undertaken at present.

Conclusion

131. It is accordingly my view that the attack on the Directions is premature in both of the senses contended for by Mr Pannick. I would therefore allow the appeal, set aside the Orders of the Court of Appeal dated 27 May 2005 and dismiss the application for judicial review. As the parties are agreed that the costs should follow the event of this Appeal, I would order the respondents to pay the appellant's costs here and in the courts below.

Sir Noel Power NPJ:

132. I agree with the judgments of Mr Justice Bokhary PJ and Mr Justice Ribeiro PJ.

Lord Woolf NPJ:

133. I agree with the judgments of Mr Justice Bokhary PJ and Mr Justice Ribeiro PJ.

Mr Justice Bokhary PJ:

134. The Court is unanimous. We allow the appeal, set aside the Court of Appeal's orders, dismiss the respondents' application for judicial review and award the appellant costs here and in the courts below. In the course of holding that the Listing Committee is not a court within the meaning of art. 35 of the Basic law, we have held that neither are the Medical Council or the Solicitors Disciplinary Tribunal. To the extent that the Court of Appeal held otherwise in *Dr Ip Kay Lo, Vincent v. Medical Council (No. 2)* [2003] 3 HKC 579 and *A Solicitor v. Law Society*, CACV NO. 302 of 2002, 18 February 2004, those two Court of Appeal cases are overruled.

Permanent Judge (Kemal Bokhary)

Permanent Judge (Patrick Chan)

Permanent Judge (R A V Ribeiro)

Non-Permanent Judge (Sir Noel Power)

Non-Permanent Judge (Lord Woolf)

Mr David Pannick QC and Mr John Scott SC (instructed by Messrs Richards Butler) for the appellant

Mr John Griffiths SC, Mr Richard Zimmern and Ms Amanda W. M. Li (instructed by Messrs Woo, Kwan, Lee & Lo) for the respondents

---

A Solicitor v. The Law Society Of Hong Kong

事務律師 對 香港律師會

CACV 246/2004；FACV 23/2005；FAMV 54/2007

簡略案情

上訴人是一名執業事務律師，因未能按照《法律執業者條例》第 8AA 條的規定，向香港律師會指派的調查員提交所要求的文件，面臨一項違紀指控。在聆訊過程中，有證據顯示上訴人不但沒有知會該文件的相關當事人，以確定當事人會否願意提供相關文件，更故意拖延。律師紀律審裁組認定指控成立，並譴責上訴人及處以罰款 10 萬元，責令他停業 4 個月或直至完成準備相關文件為止。上訴人遂提出上訴，辯稱香港律師會指派的調查員所要求提交的文檔侵犯了法律專業保密權，因對其當事人負有保密義務而不能提交。依照第 8AA 條的規定，香港律師會有權指派調查員去確認某律師是否遵從香港律師會發出的執業指引，而該等調查員在具有合理懷疑時，可命令律師提交其持有的文件。根據《法律執業者條例》第 8B（2）條，律師不得以享有律師與當事人間特權（下稱"律師特權"）為由拒絕提交，但是所涉及律師特權的文件只能被用於香港律師會調查之目的。上訴人認為律師特權不能被立法所侵犯，同時該等規定違背了《基本法》第 35 條，"香港居民有權得到秘密法律諮詢、向法院提起訴訟、選擇律師及時保護自己的合法權益或在法庭上為其代理和獲得司法補救"。

上訴庭援引英國上議院 *R (Morgan Grenfell & Co. Ltd.) v. Special Commissioner Of Income Tax & Another* [2000] 2 WLR 1299 一案，以及新西蘭最高法院 *Commissioner Of Inland Revenue v. West-Walker* [1954] NZLR 191 一案，確認律師特權包含一種公共利益，由於其存在才能鼓勵公眾尋求獨立的法律幫助而無需擔心秘密遭到披露。但上訴庭認為第 8B（2）條已經規定律師披露的資訊僅能被用於調查的目的，披露資訊的保密性得到了保證。因此，並不違反律師特權，再者，如果真有違反，也只是一種出於合法目的、合乎比例的技術性違反。上訴庭指出，律師特權應受到公共政策的限制，例如客戶向律師披露的資訊涉及進一步的犯罪或欺詐，則不在律師特權的涵蓋範圍內。同樣的，律師會對會員律師的調查權亦含有公共利益。第 8B（2）條已經限制了披露資訊的使用範圍，在上訴法庭看來，這種保護已經足夠。因而第 8B（2）條並不違背《基本法》第 35 條，上訴駁回。上訴人進而上訴至終審法院。

裁決摘要

終審法院認為律師特權在普通法裏早已被確立，同時亦為《基本法》第 35 條規定的憲法性權利。其實質上並非律師的特權，而是客戶的基本權利，必須受法庭保護。但是香港律師會亦應享有足夠權力來保證律師按照規定行事和執業。本案爭議在於，即便第 8B 條限制了調查員所獲得資訊的用途，其是否仍然違反《基本法》第 35 條下的"秘密法律諮詢保障"。終審法院援引歐洲人權法庭 *Roemen And Schmit v. Luxembourg*, Application No. 51772 of 1999 一案，關於涉及對律師辦公室的搜查，認為即便這種搜查是有法律規定的、是出於合法目的且必要的，亦須考慮其是否合乎比例，且是否附帶了足夠的保護措施。雖然本案涉及律師特權的文件不能被用於對當事人不利的目的，法庭相信在大多數情況下，當事人仍舊不會願意披露這些資訊，這在某些情況和某種程度上會抑制當事人與律師的坦誠溝通，但法庭認為這樣的情況並不會很多，程度也不會很嚴重。終審法院認為，第 8B（2）條的規定具有一項基本且重要的目的，即維持律師執業的高水準，加上獲得的相關資訊，需要在律師會的監督下處理，並且嚴格限制了其保密性，所以，從該等規定所想達到的合理目的來看，是合乎比例的。因此終審法院認為《法律執業者條例》的相關規定不違背《基本法》第 35 條，且是合憲的。上訴因此被駁回。

FACV No. 23 of 2005

IN THE COURT OF FINAL APPEAL OF THE HONG KONG SPECIAL ADMINISTRATIVE REGION

FINAL APPEAL NO. 9 OF 2008 (Civil)
(ON APPEAL FROM CACV NO. 246 OF 2004)

Between:

A SOLICITOR — Appellant

- and -

THE LAW SOCIETY OF HONG KONG — Respondent

Court: Mr Justice Bokhary PJ, Mr Justice Chan PJ, Mr Justice Ribeiro PJ, Sir Noel Power NPJ and Lord Woolf NPJ

Dates of Hearing: 15 March 2006

Date of Judgment: 22 March 2006

JUDGMENT

Mr Justice Bokhary PJ:

Introduction

1. There are two aspects to this appeal. One is a constitutional challenge to legislation attacked principally as incompatible with the right to confidential legal advice. The other, on which the appeal will turn if the constitutional challenge fails, concerns how certain statutory powers are to be exercised. They arise in the following circumstances.

2. The appellant ("the Solicitor") is a practising solicitor. He faced a disciplinary charge. The charge was of conduct unbefitting of a solicitor. He had, the charge ran, breached s.8AA of the Legal Practitioners Ordinance, Cap. 159, by failing to produce certain documents required by inspectors whom the Council of the Law Society of Hong Kong ("the Council") had appointed under that section. The Solicitor sought to defend his failure to produce the documents concerned primarily, although not solely, on the basis that they are subject to legal professional privilege which he said that his client was unwilling to waive.

3. Following a disciplinary hearing, the Solicitors Disciplinary Tribunal convicted the Solicitor. By way of penalty it censured him, fined him $100,000, ordered that he be suspended for four months or until he produced the documents concerned (whichever period proved shorter) and awarded costs against him.

4. Contending that he should not have been convicted, the Solicitor appealed to the Court of Appeal (Rogers VP, Le Pichon JA and Sakhrani J). They dismissed his appeal with costs. He now appeals to this Court.

5. Two grounds are put forward on the Solicitor's behalf with a view to justifying non-production. Shortly stated, the first ground, which is advanced by way of a constitutional challenge, runs thus. The documents concerned are covered by legal professional privilege. And s.8B(2) of the Legal Practitioners Ordinance, which provides for production or delivery of documents for inspection notwithstanding such privilege, is unconstitutional as being incompatible with the right to confidential legal advice guaranteed by art. 35 of our constitution the Basic Law. Is the statutory encroachment justifiable as a proportionate limitation of the right, particularly taking into account the safeguard provided by s.8B(2) which limits the use of privileged documents produced thereunder to use for the purposes of an inquiry or investigation under the Legal Practitioners Ordinance? The Solicitor contends that the right is insufficiently safeguarded and the encroachment cannot be justified while the respondent the Law Society of Hong Kong ("the Law Society") contends to the contrary.

6. As for the second ground, it concerns how the power to require the production or delivery of documents for inspection is to be exercised. Section 8AA(1) empowers the Council to appoint inspectors. And s.8AA(2)(b)(i) empowers the inspectors to require the production or delivery of documents if they reasonably suspect that the documents are relevant and the Council directs them to require such production or delivery. Shortly stated the second ground is that the Council acted beyond its powers because what it did amounted to appointing inspectors and at the same time requiring production. The Council says that production was required by the inspectors after they had reasonably formed a suspicion that the documents were relevant and had been duly directed to require production. So, the Council says, it had acted within its powers.

Sections 8AA and 8B

7. Although not every part of them is material, I should set out sections 8AA and 8B in their entirety so as to make the full context apparent.

8. Headed "Appointment and powers of inspector", s.8AA deals with the powers of the Council and with the powers of inspectors appointed by the Council.

9. Dealing with the Council's powers, subsection (1) of s.8AA reads:

> "The Council may appoint a person as an inspector to assist the Council –
>
> (a) in verifying compliance by a solicitor, a foreign lawyer, a trainee solicitor or an employee of a solicitor or foreign lawyer with the provisions of this Ordinance or any practice direction issued by the Society;
>
> (b) in determining for the purpose of section 9A whether the conduct of any solicitor, foreign lawyer, trainee solicitor or employee of a solicitor or foreign lawyer should be inquired into or investigated; or
>
> (c) in relation to an inquiry or investigation under section 9B."

10. Subsections (2) and (3) of s.8AA, dealing with the inspectors' powers, including the power exercisable only under the Council's direction to exercise it, read:

> "(2) For the purposes of subsection (1), an inspector may
>
> (a) in relation to any person who acts or purports to act as an employee of a solicitor in the premises of any court or place of lawful detention –
>
> (i) question there and then the person as to his name, identity card number, the identity of any client for whom he acts or purports to act on that occasion and the name of the firm of which he acts or purports to act as the employee; and
>
> (ii) require the person to produce for inspection there

and then all documents in his possession that the inspector reasonably suspects to be relevant to any matter referred to in subsection (1)(a), (b) or (c) and copy or seize any of the documents; and

(b) (i) subject to subsection (3), require a solicitor, a foreign lawyer or an employee of a solicitor or foreign lawyer to produce or deliver to him for inspection, at a time and place specified by him, all documents in the possession of the solicitor, foreign lawyer or employee of a solicitor or foreign lawyer that the inspector reasonably suspects to be relevant to any matter referred to in subsection (1) (a), (b) or (c) and specifies particularly or generally; and

(ii) copy or seize any of the documents produced or delivered under subparagraph (i).

(3) An inspector shall not exercise his power under subsection (2)(b)(i) except under a direction of the Council to do so."

11. Finally, subsections (4) and (5) of s.8AA read:

"(4) No liability shall be incurred by any person in respect of anything done or omitted to be done by him in good faith in the exercise of any power under this section.

(5) In this section, 'identity card' (身 份 證) means an identity card issued under the Registration of Persons Ordinance (Cap. 177)."

12. Headed "Document production and privilege", s.8B reads:

"(1) For the purpose of enforcing the production of documents required by the Council under section 8A, section 11 applies and references in section l 1 to the Solicitors Disciplinary Tribunal and to the Chairman of the Solicitors Disciplinary Tribunal shall be deemed to be references respectively to the Council and to the President of the Society.

(2) Documents required by the Council under section 8A or by an inspector under section 8AA shall be produced or delivered notwithstanding any claim of solicitor–client privilege but documents that are subject to a solicitor–client privilege may only be used for the purposes of an inquiry or investigation under this Ordinance."

Since subsection (2) of this section refers to s.8A, I should mention that s.8A pertains to the position where the Council considers that a solicitor or a foreign lawyer may be unfit to practise. And it deals with the Council's power to require a solicitor, a foreign lawyer or his firm to produce or deliver documents necessary for the purpose of investigating the matter.

13. Section 8B(2) makes the situation before us unlike the one before the Privy Council in *B v. Auckland District Law Society* [2003] 2 AC 736. That case concerned an attempt, which proved unsuccessful, to override legal professional privilege otherwise than by statute. The questions in the present case go to the constitutionality of the statutory provisions engaged and, if they are constitutional, how they work.

Compatibility with the right to confidential legal advice

14. It is obviously conducive to the due administration of justice that clients candidly reveal the unvarnished truth to their lawyers. And of course the law is not so naïve as to imagine that such candour can confidently be expected in practice if disclosure of the contents of client–lawyer communications may be compelled, to a client's prejudice and contrary to his wishes. I borrow the formula "to a client's prejudice and contrary to his wishes" from the speech of Lord Nicholls of Birkenhead in *R v. Derby Magistrates' Court, ex parte B* [1996] AC 487 at p.510E. What is prohibited is not simply disclosure contrary to a client's wishes but disclosure to his prejudice as well as contrary to his wishes.

15. Legal professional privilege is the name given to the common law rule which protects client–lawyer communications from disclosure to a client's prejudice and contrary to his wishes. Although too well established to be abandoned lightly, this name is perhaps not a happy one, for it might conjure up the image of a questionable advantage enjoyed by lawyers. But in truth legal professional privilege, as Lord Denning MR emphasised in *Attorney General v. Mulholland* [1963] 2 QB 477 at p.489, "is not the privilege of the lawyer but of his client". And the rule constituted by this privilege is a rational and practical one which exists in the public interest and involves an important right belonging to the client. In Hong Kong this right is a constitutional one. It is contained in the confidential legal advice clause of art. 35 of the Basic Law. By this clause it is provided that "Hong Kong residents shall have the right to confidential legal advice"– a right which our courts will always be vigilant to accord proper protection.

16. The Solicitor seeks to buttress his constitutional challenge by relying also on the right to a fair hearing and freedom from unlawful interference with privacy provided for by arts 10 and 14 respectively of the Hong Kong Bill of Rights. That right and that freedom are entrenched (in the manner explained in many cases including *Shum Kwok Sher v. HKSAR* (2002) 5 HKCFAR 381 at p.400 D-H) by art. 39 of the Basic Law. But in circumstances like these neither that right nor that freedom, whether taken separately or together, can result in, or contribute to, success for the Solicitor if the right to confidential legal advice cannot bring him success on its own. The client is not a party to the disciplinary hearing for which disclosure of the documents is sought. And, in circumstances like these, whether any interference with privacy resulting from such disclosure is lawful or unlawful depends on whether or not the disclosure is compatible with the right to confidential legal advice.

17. Not unnaturally the raising of legal professional privilege involved us in renewing our acquaintance with decisions like those of the House of Lords in R *(Morgan Grenfell & Co. Ltd) v. Special Commissioner of Income Tax* [2003] 1 AC 563 and *Three Rivers District Council v. Bank of England (No. 6)* [2005] 1 AC 610. Properly understood this privilege is indeed, as Lord Taylor of Gosforth CJ so memorably characterised it in the *Derby Magistrates' Court* case at p.507D, "a fundamental condition on which the administration of justice as a whole rests". It is of course not the *only* such condition. There are a number of others. Among them is the existence of a legal profession of efficiency and integrity. The Law Society has a very important role to play in maintaining standards within the solicitors' branch of the legal profession. Acting through its Council, the Law Society has frontline responsibility to ensure compliance by solicitors with the rules governing their conduct and activities. And it is necessary for the Council to have adequate powers to do that.

18. One such power is the Council's power under s.8AA to appoint inspectors to assist it in verifying such compliance and in determining whether conduct should be inquired into or investigated. Allied to that power of the Council's are the inspectors' powers under the same section. These include their power to require production or delivery to them of documents for

inspection.

19. It can happen that the documents which the inspectors reasonably suspect are relevant to the performance of their task will include documents subject to solicitor–client privilege. In that sort of situation s.8B does two things. First, in aid of the inspectors'task, the section provides that documents "shall be produced or delivered notwithstanding any claim of solicitor–client privilege". Secondly, in protection of the client's interests, the section provides that "documents that are subject to a solicitor–client privilege may only be used for the purposes of an inquiry or investigation under [the Legal Practitioners] Ordinance".

20. Is that requirement of production or delivery incompatible with the confidential legal advice clause even though use is limited in that way? The cases cited on the Solicitor's behalf on this question include *Roemen and Schmit v. Luxembourg*, Application No. 51772 of 1999, 25 February 2003, concerning, among other things, a search of a lawyer's office. The European Court of Human Rights held that even where such a search was prescribed by law, in pursuance of a legitimate aim and necessary, it still had to be proportionate and attended by special procedural safeguards.

21. It is true that the privileged documents produced or delivered cannot be used against the client. But human nature being what it is, I am prepared to believe that a significant percentage of clients would nevertheless instinctively prefer that nobody sees the documents. So I feel unable to rule it out that the susceptibility of the documents to production or delivery, albeit not for use against the client, would in some instances and to some extent inhibit the candour of communications by the client to his solicitor. But I do not think that such instances would be many or such extent large.

22. It is submitted on the Solicitor's behalf that the client might suffer prejudice even though the documents cannot be used as evidence against him. Such prejudice, this submission runs, could flow from the information contained in the documents becoming known to, for example, a private complainant who might use such information to his own advantage and the client's disadvantage. In my view, that is adequately met by the strict confidentiality which the inspectors and all concerned should–and doubtless would–accord to the documents. The private complainant has no right to see privileged documents and, in the absence of a direction by the Solicitors Disciplinary Tribunal giving him access to the documents where such access is essential to the fairness of proceedings, they should not be shown to him. It is true that in *Delhaise v. Solicitors*, CACV No. 147 of 2004, 8 June 2005, the Solicitors Disciplinary Tribunal allowed a private complainant to act as the prosecutor in disciplinary proceedings against solicitors. But the error of that course was emphatically pointed out by the Court of Appeal in that case. And there is no danger of any repetition.

23. I would add a word on the Solicitors Disciplinary Tribunal Proceedings Rules. In any instance where it is feared that a party's right (under rule 10) to inspect and be furnished with documents included in any other party's rule 9 list of documents might result in inappropriate access to privileged information, such access can be avoided. It can be avoided by the Solicitors Disciplinary Tribunal directing (under rules 9 or 32) that no such list need be furnished.

24. Nor is it to be forgotten that the Council, without whose direction inspectors cannot require production or delivery, would never lightly so direct. Composed as it is, the Council will be fully aware of–and always act with due respect for–the great importance of legal professional privilege.

25. Section 8B(2) production or delivery serves a fundamentally important purpose, namely the maintenance of high standards within the solicitors' branch of the legal profession. With the safeguard built into s.8B(2), the need for the Council's direction and the strict confidentiality to be accorded to documents produced or delivered, I do not consider s.8B(2) disproportionate to what is needed in the service of that purpose. I am therefore of the view that s.8B(2) production or delivery is compatible with the confidential legal advice clause and that s.8B(2) is constitutional.

26. So, despite the skill with which the Solicitor's constitutional challenge has been prepared and presented on his behalf, it fails. With it fails the first of the two grounds put forward on his behalf with a view to justifying non–production, and I turn now to the second one.

How the power to require production or delivery is to be exercised

27. Under the second ground, the question is how the power under s.8AA to require production or delivery of documents for inspection is to be exercised. This is by no means an ordinary question of procedure. It goes importantly to how the powers under that section are distributed between, on the one hand, the Council and, on the other hand, inspectors appointed by the Council. I refer to inspectors in the plural because three inspectors were appointed in this case. If only one inspector had been appointed, then what I say about inspectors in the plural would apply to an inspector in the singular.

28. It is submitted on behalf of the Solicitor that the regime laid down by s.8AA for requiring the production or delivery of documents for inspection is as follows. The Council appoints inspectors. Then the inspectors form a view as to whether they reasonably suspect that the documents in question are relevant. If they do not so suspect, then that is the end of the matter. But if they do so suspect, the Council comes into the picture again. And if the Council then directs the inspectors to require production or delivery of the documents for inspection, the inspectors will proceed to require such production or delivery.

29. Plainly no production or delivery can be required unless the inspectors reasonably suspect that the documents are relevant and the Council directs production or delivery. This is not disputed by the Law Society. What the Law Society disputes is the submission made on the Solicitor's behalf that the reasonable suspicion must precede the direction. In my view, the Law Society is right. Provided that both the reasonable suspicion and the direction are in place before production or delivery is required, it does not matter whether the reasonable suspicion precedes or comes after the direction. One course would be for the Council to direct the inspectors to require production or delivery if they reasonably suspect that the documents are relevant. Another course would be for the Council, having learned that the inspectors reasonably suspect that the documents are relevant, to direct them to require production or delivery. The Council may adopt either course. Both are permissible under s.8AA.

30. The course adopted in the present case is to be gathered by reading, fairly and in context, the Investigation Committee's report of 4 October 2002, the minutes of the Council's meeting of 18 October 2002 and the notice for inspection of 4 November 2002 signed by one of the inspectors. I say at once that despite the submission to the contrary made on the Solicitor's behalf, it is plain that the inspector who signed that notice did so on behalf of

all three inspectors.

31. In *Hakansson and Sturesson v. Sweden* (1991) 13 EHRR 1 the European Court of Human Rights said (in para. 66) that a waiver of legal privilege could not be effective if it is equivocal. The same is true, it is submitted on the Solicitor's behalf and I accept, of any direction by the Council to require production or delivery of documents, especially privileged ones. But I see nothing equivocal in the direction in the present case.

32. Giving the 4 October report, the 18 October minutes and the 4 November notice the reading they deserve, it is plain that the course adopted in the present case—and lawfully so—was as follows. The Council directed the inspectors, in regard to documents identified with due specificity, to require production of those documents if they reasonably suspected that the same were relevant. So suspecting, the inspectors lawfully required production of the documents concerned.

33. So the second ground, too, fails.

Conclusion

34. Accordingly I would dismiss the appeal with costs, the parties having accepted at the hearing that costs should follow the event.

Mr Justice Chan PJ:

35. I agree with the judgment of Mr Justice Bokhary PJ.

Mr Justice Ribeiro PJ:

36. I agree with the judgment of Mr Justice Bokhary PJ.

Sir Noel Power NPJ:

37. I agree with the judgment of Mr Justice Bokhary PJ.

Lord Woolf NPJ:

38. I agree with the judgment of Mr Justice Bokhary PJ.

Mr Justice Bokhary PJ:

39. The Court unanimously dismisses the appeal with costs.

Permanent Judge (Kemal Bokhary)

Permanent Judge (Patrick Chan)

Permanent Judge (R A V Ribeiro)

Non-Permanent Judge (Noel Power)

Non-Permanent Judge (Lord Woolf)

Mr Philip Dykes SC, Mr Johannes Chan SC and Mr Stanley Ma (instructed by Messrs Solomon C Chong & Co.) for the appellant

Mr John Scott SC and Mr Paul Carolan (instructed by Messrs Boase Cohen & Collins) for the respondent

---

Ng Yat Chi v. Max Share Ltd. & China Resources (Holdings) Co. Ltd.

Ng Yat Chi 對 Max Share Ltd. 及華潤（集團）有限公司

HCA 2039/2002；CACV 414/2002；CACV 306/2002；FACV 5/2004

簡略案情

上訴人於 1999 年 9 月起訴答辯人，請求法庭根據《公司條例》第 177 條判決第一答辯人清盤，並於原訟庭獲得勝訴。然而，上訴法庭卻推翻了原審法官的判決。上訴人為恢復原審判決，遂向終審法院請求上訴准許，但遭到拒絕。上訴人遂於 2002 年 10 月再次向原審法院重新起訴兩名答辯人，理由是上訴法庭及終審法院上訴委員會“欺詐性地搶奪在原審中的成果”，以編造事實的手段致使其敗訴。答辯人指出上訴人的再起訴理由和申請清盤時所提出的理由一樣，所以向法庭申請“*Grepe* v. *Loam*”禁令，即除非得到法庭的許可，上訴人將被禁止在往後以同一事由或主張再提起新的訴訟。

法庭認為，上訴人以上訴庭和終審法院“欺詐”為由再次就同一問題提起訴訟是濫用司法程序的行為，因此決定向上訴人發出“*Grepe* v. *Loam*”禁令處理該無理的上訴纏擾。上訴人再向上訴庭提起上訴但被駁回，他遂將案件重新上訴至終審法院。

裁決摘要

上訴人以《基本法》第 35 條，即“香港居民有權得到秘密法律咨詢、向法院提起訴訟、選擇律師及時保護自己的合法權益或在法庭上為其代理和獲得司法補救。香港居民有權對行政部門和行政人員的行為向法院提起訴訟”及第 39 條，即“《公民權利和政治權利國際公約》、《經濟、社會與文化權利的國際公約》和國際勞工公約適用於香港的有關規定繼續有效，通過香港特別行政區的法律予以實施。香港居民享有的權利和自由，除依法規定外不得限制，此種限制不得與本條第一款規定抵觸。”質疑“*Grepe* v. *Loam*”禁令的效力。終審法院同意，因濫用訴訟權利而提起的訴訟會導致時間與精力的無謂消耗，同時也消耗了有限的司法資源，造成對其他訴訟當事人的不公。《基本法》第 35 條雖然賦予了提起訴訟的憲法性權利，但並不意味著此訴權可以被濫用，事實上不當行使訴訟權正會妨礙他人正當行使訴訟權。

終審法院認為此處存在兩點爭議：1）《基本法》第 35 條規定的當事人提起訴訟的權利是否可以受到限制；2）即便當事人訴訟權可以受到一定限制，"*Grepe v. Loam*"禁令不能確切地建立在法律基礎上，與《基本法》第 39 條"除依法規定外不得限制"相衝突。終審法院援引歐洲人權委員會 *H v. UK* [1985] 45 DR 281 以及英國上訴法庭 *AG* v. *Covey*；*AG* v. *Mathews* [2001] EWCA Civ 254 等案例的判決認為，當事人提起訴訟的權利不是一項絕對權利，應受到一定限制，但這種限制必須具有合法目的，與該合法目的成比例，且沒有侵害該權利的關鍵部份，那麼該類限制就是合法有效的。

就濫用訴訟權的司法監察，不應被視為對訴訟權的否定，而是一種必要的管轄權，這類權力可以被認為是出於合法的目的。對於《基本法》第 39 條的爭議，法庭認為只要在本案中確定了禁令適用的相關原則，則不存在該等禁令的規定不明確而出現違反《基本法》第 39 條的情況。最後，終審法院一致裁定上訴被駁回。

FACV No. 5 of 2004

IN THE COURT OF FINAL APPEAL OF THE HONG KONG SPECIAL ADMINISTRATIVE REGION

FINAL APPEAL NO. 5 OF 2004 (Civil)
(ON APPEAL FROM CACV Nos. 306 & 414 of 2002)

Between:

NG YAT CHI — Appellant

- and -

MAX SHARE LIMITED — 1st Respondent

China Resources (holdings) Company Limited — 2nd Respondent

Court: Chief Justice Li , Mr Justice Bokhary PJ, Mr Justice Chan PJ, Mr Justice Ribeiro PJ and Lord Scott of Foscote NPJ

Date of Hearing: 29 November 2004

Date of Judgment: 20 January 2005

JUDGMENT

Chief Justice Li:

1. The judgment of Mr Justice Ribeiro PJ deals comprehensively with the inherent jurisdiction of the court to make an extended order and how that jurisdiction should be properly and effectively exercised. I am in complete agreement with his judgment. Having regard to the importance of the subject in the proper administration of justice in our courts, I wish to make some observations on certain aspects of this jurisdiction. These observations are intended to be and should be read as entirely consistent with what is contained in Mr Justice Ribeiro PJ's judgment.

Abusive proceedings

2. It is not difficult to recognise the activities of the vexatious litigant. The person concerned will almost invariably be unrepresented and will pursue abusive proceedings which usually exhibit some of the following features. Hopeless claims are instituted. Totally misconceived appeals are launched. Judgments of the court, both interlocutory and at trial and both first instance and appellate, may not be accepted. There are likely to be attempts, often repeated, to re-litigate the same matters as have already been determined. The materials filed will often be irrelevant, incoherent or scandalous. When present at a hearing, some vexatious litigants are unable to conduct themselves with decorum and may hurl abuse at the opposite parties and/or the judge.

3. Abusive proceedings are oppressive to the other parties and result in unfairness to them. To protect themselves against such proceedings, time, effort and stress are involved and costs have to be incurred. They may be in a weak position to cope. Often, there may be little prospect of recovering the costs incurred.

4. Quite apart from causing unfairness to the other parties, abusive proceedings lead to unfairness to other litigants before the courts. Judicial resources are inevitably finite. The time which judges and their supporting staff have is of course limited. Where much needed resources are diverted to dealing with abusive proceedings, litigants with cases of real merit suffer as a result. It will take a longer time for their cases to be dealt with. Courts should concentrate their resources in dealing with meritorious cases. Their attention should not be unnecessarily diverted to dealing with abusive proceedings.

The right of access

5. The constitutional right of access to the courts is well established under the common law and is guaranteed by the Basic Law (Article 35). But it would be absurd to suggest that the right of access involves a right to abuse the court's process. The pursuit of abusive proceedings would be an improper exercise of the right of access and may be regarded as adversely affecting the right of access of others with meritorious cases.

The prevention of abuse of process

6. The categories of abuse of process are never closed. In the context of the civil justice system as it evolves from time to time, there is an infinite variety of abuse that may arise. The courts are equipped with various powers by legislation, including rules of court, to deal with abuse of process. In addition to and in parallel with the statutory powers, there is no doubt that the courts have an inherent jurisdiction to prevent abuse of process. The proper and effective exercise of the courts' jurisdiction to prevent abuse, both statutory and inherent, is essential to the prevention of injustice to the other parties to the litigation in question as well as the operation of a fair and efficient judicial system. In exercising such jurisdiction, the courts should be flexible in developing remedies which are proportionate to the abuse that has to be dealt with.

Grepe v. Loam orders

7. The courts of course have the inherent jurisdiction to deal with abusive proceedings that have already commenced. The power to make a *Grepe v. Loam* order is well established and is widely accepted in many jurisdictions. Such an order relates to existing proceedings. The party subject to the order is not allowed to make any further application in the proceedings already instituted without the leave of the court. The order is preventive in nature and constrains future applications in existing proceedings, requiring the party concerned to obtain the court's leave. The justification for controlling future applications in this way is that, having regard to the party's past conduct in making abusive applications, it is apprehended that future abusive applications may be made.

Extended orders

8. There is no reason in principle why the inherent jurisdiction should be confined to dealing with anticipated abusive applications in existing proceedings. In my view, there is every reason in principle why it should also extend to preventing abusive proceedings which have not been commenced but are anticipated. See *Ebert v. Venvil* [2000] Ch 484 at 496F–497D (Lord Woolf). I agree with Mr Justice Ribeiro PJ that for the reasons explained in his judgment, the courts have the inherent jurisdiction to make an extended order. Just as the court can protect itself against anticipated abuse by making a preventive order directed at future applications in existing proceedings, so it can similarly protect itself by making a preventive order directed at abusive proceedings that may be instituted in the future. The justification is that in view of the past conduct of the party concerned, it is apprehended that that party may commence fresh proceedings which may be abusive. The extended order does not bar the institution of any new proceedings. Its scope is limited

to constraining new proceedings which may be abusive.

9. In his able submissions as an *amicus*, Mr Bernard Man advanced the arguments referred to by Mr Justice Ribeiro PJ as the statutory displacement argument and the constitutional right argument in support of the contention that there is no inherent jurisdiction to make an extended order and that the making of such an order requires statutory authority. As to the latter argument, once it is understood that the constitutional right of access to the courts plainly cannot involve a right to abuse the court's process, that argument must be rejected.

10. The question arising in relation to the statutory displacement argument is whether the suggested inherent jurisdiction to make an extended order has been abrogated by implication by s.27 of the High Court Ordinance, Cap 4. Under this provision, on an application by the Secretary for Justice and upon being satisfied of the prescribed criteria, the court may make an order prohibiting any new proceedings without leave. Such an order is a blanket order prohibiting all new proceedings in the absence of leave. The smaller the difference between the statutory jurisdiction and the inherent jurisdiction contended for, the stronger is the argument of implied abrogation. Here, having regard to the material differences between the statutory jurisdiction to make a blanket order and the inherent jurisdiction to make an extended order, including the differences between the two kinds of order, the statutory provision has not ousted the court's inherent jurisdiction in this regard.

Prohibited class of proceedings

11. The focus of an extended order is on a defined class of proceedings which is prohibited without leave. The class should be defined with clarity. Its permissible scope is laid down in Mr Justice Ribeiro PJ's judgment. That being its focus, an extended order is capable of protecting persons who were not parties to the original proceedings in which the extended order was made. If after the order was made, fresh proceedings are instituted against such persons, they would be protected by the extended order if the proceedings fall within the defined class.

Prevention of further abuse

12. A *Grepe v. Loam* order and an extended order are intended to prevent further abuse of process. It would be unfortunate if the orders, particularly the requirement for leave thereunder, give rise to yet further abuse. It is important that arrangements are put in place as part of the court system to prevent this from occurring, such as the issue of an appropriate practice direction and effective use of the courts' information technology system. At the same time, it is essential that in individual cases, orders are formulated with appropriate supporting directions to ensure that the orders can be effectively implemented and that the opportunity for further abuse is minimised.

Requirement for leave

13. The requirement for leave is of course a central feature of an extended order, as it is for a *Grepe v. Loam* order. It is a mechanism to prevent further abuse as well as a safeguard to ensure that meritorious claims are not shut out. In relation to an extended order, the leave requirement would be dealt with as follows:

(1) Where leave is sought, the first question for the court to determine is whether the new proceeding is within the prohibited class of proceedings specified in the order. In considering this question, the court should look at the substance of the matter.

(2) Where the court concludes that the new proceeding is not within the specified class, it directs that leave is not required, allowing the proceeding to be issued. An extended order does not envisage the court scrutinizing a new proceeding outside the class to decide whether it is arguably meritorious. The defendant could of course take such steps as is considered appropriate after the institution of the new proceeding, such as applying to strike it out.

(3) Where the court concludes that the new proceeding is within the specified class, the court should proceed to consider whether it is arguably meritorious, that is, whether there is a reasonably arguable case.

The above comments relate to an extended order. In relation to a *Grepe v. Loam* order, all new applications in the existing proceedings are prohibited without leave. Where leave is applied for, the court should consider whether the application is a reasonably arguable one.

Levels of court and the making of orders

Grepe v Loam orders

14. A court in which proceedings were instituted may obviously make a *Grepe v. Loam* order in relation to new applications in that court in those proceedings. Thus, the Court of Appeal, the Court of First Instance and the District Court may make a *Grepe v. Loam* order to prohibit new applications without leave at their respective levels. Further, the Court of Appeal may make a *Grepe v. Loam* order to prohibit not only new applications before the Court of Appeal but also new applications in the first instance court in which the proceedings were originally commenced, that is, the Court of First Instance or the District Court, as the case may be.

Extended orders

15. As to the making of an extended order, the Court of Appeal may make such an order to prohibit the institution of new proceedings of the specified class both in the Court of First Instance and the District Court. The Court of First Instance may make such an extended order to prohibit not only the institution of new proceedings in that court but also in the District Court. And the District Court may of course make an extended order in relation to new proceedings in that court.

Procedural fairness

16. In exercising the inherent jurisdiction to make a *Grepe v Loam* order or an extended order, it goes without saying that procedural fairness must be observed. The party concerned should be put on notice and be given the opportunity to be heard before an order is made.

Exercise of the jurisdiction

17. *Grepe v. Loam* orders and extended orders would usually be made on the application of a party. But there may be circumstances where it may be appropriate for the court to act on its own motion. In acting on its own motion, the court would initiate the process by informing the parties that it is considering whether a *Grepe v. Loam* order or an extended order should be made, indicating the possible basis of such order and giving the parties a sufficient opportunity to make submissions. Usually an oral hearing would be held, although written submissions could be called for beforehand. As has been noted, procedural fairness must be observed and the court should proceed with particular

caution where it is acting of its own motion.

18. The right of access to the courts must of course be strongly safeguarded. But where the circumstances are appropriate, the courts should not be reticent in making *Grepe v. Loam* orders and extended orders and should act firmly. It must be emphasized that it is essential for courts to exercise their jurisdiction to prevent abuse of process properly and effectively.

Judicial review proceedings

19. The use of *Grepe v. Loam* orders and extended orders has been developed by the courts under the inherent jurisdiction to prevent abuse of process in the context of private law proceedings. The case law developed so far in this area, including the present judgment, should be regarded as confined to that context.

20. The question whether it is appropriate for *Grepe v. Loam* orders and extended orders to be used to prevent abuse of process in judicial review proceedings does not arise in this appeal. That question would require careful consideration. The important differences between private law proceedings and public law proceedings would have to be borne in mind. The differences include the requirement that leave of the court has to be obtained for a judicial review application. This requirement, which enables unarguable claims to be filtered out, is already a mechanism in public law proceedings for preventing abuse of process.

Section 27

21. Section 27 of the High Court Ordinance, Cap 4, was based on s.51 of the Supreme Court of Judicature (Consolidation) Act 1925 in England. (The position in England is now governed by s.42 of the Supreme Court Act 1981.) Section 27 has stood in our statute book since 1975 and has not been reviewed. There is an urgent need to reform it by widening its scope. In particular, any person affected by vexatious conduct should have the right to apply for a statutory order without involving the Secretary for Justice. It is for consideration that the right of the Secretary for Justice to apply should be retained as an alternative so that where the person affected is in a weak position to take action or where the public interest so requires, the Secretary could apply to seek protection for the person affected against further abuse of process.

Contempt and Injunctions

22. Mr Justice Ribeiro PJ refers to the well established proposition that the court may in appropriate circumstances grant an injunction to restrain an anticipated interference with the administration of justice amounting to a contempt. See *Attorney-General v. Times Newspapers* [1974] AC 273, *Attorney-General v. Ebert* [2002] 2 All ER 789 at para. 35. This could be relevant to abusive conduct by vexatious litigants. Interference with court officials who are conducting their duties in the administration of justice, such as writ issuers, listing officers and process servers, may be a contempt of court. Whether it amounts to a contempt and the seriousness of such a contempt would obviously depend on the circumstances. See *Re de Court* [1997] Times Law Reports 601. (The transcript of the judgment is available on Lexis.) As Lord Scott, then Vice Chancellor, pointed out in that case, the administration of justice depends not only on judges and counsel in court, but also on court officials discharging essential functions for the purpose of enabling cases to come to court. Where a contempt of the nature being discussed is threatened, the court may grant appropriate injunctive relief to restrain future conduct. Of course, where it has already occurred, the court may also consider the imposition of punishment for the past conduct.

23. In *Re de Court,* the litigant had made over a hundred attempts at instituting ridiculous and incomprehensible legal proceedings based on documents described by the judge as gibberish. When court officials declined to entertain them or to treat them as serious legal documents, he became angry. He spat at a court official and this physical assault was held to be a contempt. He had a medical condition and was regarded as a person under a disability under the rules of court. The court did not impose any punishment but granted two orders. As set out in the transcript of the judgment (which contains a fuller version of the orders than the Times Law Reports), the first order restrained him from bringing any action or making any claim in an action he has already brought except by a next friend who can act for him. He was not allowed to do so in person. The second order restrained him from entering any civil court premises save as may be necessary to answer court subpoenas. The orders covered both the High Court and the County Court. The court held that it had a duty to protect court officials by such orders.

24. In Hong Kong, instances of interference by litigants with court officials who are conducting their duties in the administration of justice are unfortunately not unknown. In future, when faced with conduct of a sufficiently serious nature, the courts should be alert to the existence of the jurisdiction to grant injunctions to restrain threatened conduct amounting to a contempt of court. Apart from the question whether punishment should be imposed for past conduct amounting to contempt, appropriate injunctions may be most effective for preventing similar conduct in the future.

Mr Justice Bokhary PJ:

25. I agree with the Chief Justice's judgment and Mr Justice Ribeiro PJ's judgment. Access to the courts must always be carefully safeguarded. Especially for persons to seek judicial relief against executive misuse of state power, such access being, as Lord Nicholls of Birkenhead said in *Wilson v. First County Trust Ltd (No. 2)* [2004] 1 AC 816 at p.835E, "one of the checks on the danger of arbitrary power". This appeal is not about that kind of case. In private litigation it is the plaintiff who invokes state power, doing so by resorting to the coercive provisions of the court's process. A court is, as Sir Edward Coke said (in *Co. Litt.58a*), "a place where justice is judicially ministered". It is not a place for inflicting vexation or wasting the resources available to the judiciary for serving those who seek justice at its hands. To protect others from vexation and its resources from wastage the judiciary can constitutionally curb the private litigation court access of persons who have a history of initiating such litigation vexatiously. There is inherent jurisdiction unsuperseded by statute to do that by way of extended *Grepe v. Loam* orders operating as explained by the Chief Justice and Mr Justice Ribeiro PJ.

Mr Justice Chan PJ:

26. I agree with the judgment of the Chief Justice and the judgment of Mr Justice Ribeiro PJ.

Mr Justice Ribeiro PJ:

27. The appellant was the plaintiff in High Court Action No 2039 of 2002 ("the Action") which he brought against Max Share Limited ("Max Share") and China Resources (Holdings) Company Limited ("China Resources"). Max Share and China Resources are respectively the 1st and 2nd respondents to this Appeal.

28. On 28 October 2002, Deputy High Court Judge Carlson struck out the Statement of Claim in the Action and made an order ("the subject order") in the following terms:

"It is ordered that the Plaintiff be prohibited from commencing any further new legal proceedings in respect of the same claim or subject-matter in High Court Action No HCCW 321 of 1996 or the action herein without the leave of the Court and if notice of any such proceedings shall be given to the Defendants without such leave being obtained, the Defendants shall not be required to appear in such proceedings, which shall be dismissed without being heard."

29. The Judge invoked the court's inherent jurisdiction as the basis for the subject order and adopted the wording of similar orders made in *Tse Jeekeen v. HK Alliance in Support of Patriotic Democratic Movement of China* [2000] 2 HKC 339 (Chung J); CACV No 246 of 2000, 27 October 2000, (Wong and Woo JJA); and in *Lily Ann Chan v. Henry Chan*, HCMP 2921 of 2001, 31 July 2001 (Kwan J). In turn, those courts had drawn on orders deriving originally from the decision in *Grepe v. Loam* [1887] Ch 168.

30. The appeal from Deputy Judge Carlson to the Court of Appeal was dismissed: CACV No 306/2002, 10 September 2003 (Yeung JA, Stone and Lugar-Mawson JJ).

31. The issue on this Appeal is as to whether the court had power to make the subject order on the basis of its inherent jurisdiction.

The events which led to the making of the subject order

32. The relevant events commence in June 1996 with the appellant's presentation of a petition in High Court Companies Winding-up No 321 of 1996 ("the Petition") whereby the appellant, a minority shareholder in Max Share, made a series of complaints against China Resources (which held the majority through a nominee company). He sought an order that Max Share be wound up on the just and equitable ground or alternatively, an order under s 168A of the Companies Ordinance, Cap 32, requiring China Resources to purchase his shares in Max Share on the ground that the affairs of that company had been conducted in a manner unfairly prejudicial to his interests as a member.

33. The facts and arguments canvassed at the trial of the Petition are set out in the judgment of Yuen J (HCCW 321/1996, 24 May 2000) and, on appeal, that of Rogers VP (with whom the other members of the Court of Appeal agreed): see [2001] 1 HKLRD 561. The appellant succeeded before Yuen J on a single ground. Her Ladyship held that a large increase in the company's share capital in May 1992 had been effected for the purpose of diluting the appellant's shareholding in Max Share at a time when he was unable to subscribe for more shares, with a view to rendering his shares unattractive and worthless to a Mr Choy Bing Wing, who had become beneficially entitled to the appellant's shares. This was held to be unfairly prejudicial to the interests of the appellant as a shareholder and that the appropriate relief was for Max Share to be wound up on the just and equitable basis.

34. In their Notice of Appeal, the respondents asserted that Yuen J had had no evidential basis for her conclusion. They contended that the evidence established that the increase in share capital was essential for Max Share's survival and had occurred pursuant to recommendations made by independent professional accountants in a share valuation report obtained by the parties prior to the new issue. The Notice of Appeal continued:

"... even if (which is denied) the purpose of the share capital increase was to dilute the Petitioner's interest in the 1st Respondent and render his shares unattractive and worthless to Mr Choy, the learned Judge ought nevertheless to have held that ... there could have been no or no unfair prejudice to the Petitioner, since immediately before the share capital increase the 1st Respondent's shares were of negative value with no real prospect of recovery ..."

35. The respondents succeeded in the Court of Appeal. Rogers VP held that the Judge's conclusion had been arrived at without examining the effect of the increase in capital on the underlying value of the appellant's shares when, on the evidence (which he reviewed in detail), those shares had been valueless or of negative value so that the injection of capital could only have increased their worth. As the share valuation report had made plain, the increase in capital was essential if Max Share was to avoid a compulsory winding-up. Accordingly, the Judge's conclusion regarding unfair prejudice to the appellant was factually unsustainable.

36. The appellant sought leave from the Court of Appeal to appeal to this Court. When that application failed, he unsuccessfully renewed his application to the Appeal Committee. By its Determination dated 17 September 2001 (FAMV 19/2001), the Appeal Committee endorsed the approach of the Court of Appeal, holding that they were clearly entitled to substitute their finding that there had been no unfair prejudice. No question of great general or public importance was found to arise on the proposed appeal.

37. By section 18 of the Hong Kong Court of Final Appeal Ordinance, Cap 484, the Appeal Committee exercises the power of the Court to determine any application for leave to appeal. Its decision is final and not subject to appeal. Accordingly, the Petition proceedings ought to have come to a definitive end with the Appeal Committee's refusal of leave to appeal.

38. However, the appellant was not prepared to accept that result. Between October 1991 and May 1992, he, together with Mr Choy Bing Wing and a Mr Brumen Li, sent a barrage of letters to, among others, the Chief Executive, the Chief Justice, all 60 members of the Legislative Council, the Bar Association, the Law Society, the President and Prime Minister of China, and the Prime Minister and Lord Chancellor of the United Kingdom. In those letters, he accused the Court of Appeal and the Appeal Committee of "inventing facts", "cheating", "dishonesty" and "fraudulent conduct" in reversing Yuen J's decision and refusing leave to appeal to the Court of Final Appeal.

39. On 29 May 2002, he issued the Writ in the Action. The Statement of Claim repeated the allegations of fraud against the two tribunals concerned and sought, by way of relief, declarations aimed at undoing the increase in share capital of Max Share, nullifying the orders of the Court of Appeal and the Appeal Committee and restoring Yuen J's order in the Petition proceedings.

40. On 14 June 2002, the respondents served on the appellant a statutory demand in the sum of $1,432,994.23 in respect of part of their taxed costs in the Petition proceedings. Simultaneously, they took out a summons to strike out the Action as frivolous, vexatious or an abuse of the court's process on the basis that it was an unsustainable attempt at re-litigating those proceedings.

41. The appellant applied to set aside the statutory demand contending again that the relevant tribunals had acted fraudulently so that the judgments were incapable of founding the statutory demand. Refusal of that application by Deputy High Court Judge Woolley on 15 July 2002 led to an appeal against that

decision, lodged on 23 July 2002.

42. In the meantime, the respondents' striking out summons came on for hearing and, as indicated above, on 28 October 2002, Deputy High Court Judge Carlson made the striking-out and subject orders. He held that the allegations of fraud against the two appellate tribunals were without foundation and continued:

> "Stripped of its invective by the plaintiff, this is a straightforward case of *res judicata*. The plaintiff had applied for a winding-up of the 1st respondent. He succeeded at first instance, lost on appeal and the Court of Final Appeal has refused to take it further. This must be the end of the matter. These identical proceedings, for this is what they are, must be struck out as an abuse of the process of the court."

43. The Judge, in making the subject order, commented as follows:

> "I was concerned that where this is the first of such actions by him, it might be going too far to suggest that there might be more to come. I had wondered whether it might be premature to make the strong order asked for by the defendants. But given the nature of the correspondence and the allegations to the effect that the highest courts of Hong Kong and their judges have conducted themselves fraudulently and have played fast and loose with the legal system since 1 July 1997, which it seems to me are allegations made without any pause for reasoned reflection by the plaintiff, that there is every prospect that he will seek to revisit again the issues raised in this action and in the action tried by Yuen J. Some restraint should be applied now so that at least he has to show merit before the defendants are required to expend time and costs to defend and the wider public interest should also be addressed in the sense that the court's time and lists should not be burdened with thoroughly unmeritorious claims."

44. The appellant appealed (CACV 414/2002) against Deputy Judge Carlson's orders. This was heard on 10 September 2003 by the Court of Appeal (Yeung JA, Stone and Lugar-Mawson JJ) simultaneously with his appeal against Deputy Judge Woolley's refusal to set aside the statutory demand (CACV 306/2002). The Court of Appeal unanimously dismissed both appeals, holding that the allegation of fraud was manifestly unfounded, as was an allegation that the Appeal Committee had acted ultra vires. It held that:

> "In view of the background of the case as outlined in this judgment, a *Grepe v. Loam* order is a proper order to make in order to avoid further abuses of the process of the court."

45. Not satisfied with that result, the appellant applied to the Court of Appeal for leave to appeal to the Court of Final Appeal. That application was dismissed on 28 November 2003 and, on 17 December 2003, the appellant renewed that application before the Appeal Committee.

46. The Registrar of the Court of Final Appeal invoked rule 7 of the Hong Kong Court of Final Appeal Rules on the basis that the application disclosed no reasonable grounds for the grant of leave to appeal and required the appellant to show cause why it should not be summarily dismissed. Operation of that rule is discussed in *Chow Shun Yung v. Wei Pih* (2003) 6 HKCFAR 299. When the application was referred to it in the usual course, the Appeal Committee dismissed the application for leave to appeal except in respect of the subject order. Leave to appeal to this Court was granted on the sole question of whether there was jurisdiction to make the subject order.

Litigants who vexatiously abuse the process of the courts

47. It is unfortunately the experience of the courts in many jurisdictions that problems caused by litigants who repeatedly abuse the court's process are on the increase. I shall refer to such litigants as "vexatious litigants", including within such class, not merely those who have formally acquired the statutory status of vexatious litigant by order of the court (in Hong Kong, pursuant to s 27 of the High Court Ordinance, Cap 4 – "HCO, s 27"), but more generally, those who persistently engage in the abuse of the court's process.

48. There are many variants of such abuse and of what motivates it. It may represent a calculated attempt by a defendant to delay an inevitable judgment or its execution. Or it may be a malicious campaign of harassment directed against a particular adversary. Actions which are unintelligible or wholly frivolous may be commenced by litigants who are unfortunately mentally unbalanced. Sometimes the vexatious conduct springs from some deeply-felt sense of grievance left unassuaged after unsuccessful litigation. The vexatious litigant typically acts in person and characteristically refuses to accept the unfavourable result of the litigation, obstinately trying to re-open the matter without any viable legal basis. Such conduct can become obsessive with the litigant not shrinking from making wild allegations against the court, or against the other side's legal representatives or targeting well-known public personalities thought to be in some way blameworthy. Numerous actions may be commenced and numerous applications issued within each action.

49. In *Attorney-General v. Barker* [2000] 1 FLR 759 Lord Bingham of Cornhill CJ, identified some of the features of vexatious proceedings brought in England and Wales:

> "The hallmark of a vexatious proceeding is in my judgment that it has little or no basis in law (or at least no discernible basis); that whatever the intention of the proceeding may be, its effect is to subject the defendant to inconvenience, harassment and expense out of all proportion to any gain likely to accrue to the claimant; and that it involves an abuse of the process of the court, meaning by that a use of the court process for a purpose or in a way which is significantly different from the ordinary and proper use of the court process." (at §19)

50. Brooke LJ's description of one such litigant in *Bhamjee v. Forsdick (No 1)* [2003] EWCA Civ 799, strikes a chord which is all too familiar:

> "He appeared to me to ignore the basis on which the planning inspectors and the High Court judges had held against him. He returned again and again to points which he had argued unsuccessfully on previous occasions. He was an example of a litigant who will not take no for an answer, will not consider the reasons which have been given in clear language as to why his claims have not been successful, and is willing, not only to seek to re-litigate them again and again and again, but also, to bring what, in my judgment, are completely misconceived claims for damages for negligence and other relief against the lawyers who have been instructed on the other side to resist his various appeals and

applications. (at §17)"

51. Given the history of the present proceedings, the courts below were entitled to regard the appellant as a vexatious litigant in the sense described above. He obstinately refused to take "No" for an answer. When faced with a statutory demand for the respondents'taxed costs, he sought to re-open the very issues that had led to the relevant costs orders. He started the Action in a further attempt to re–litigate those issues. He did not hesitate to make wholly unfounded allegations of fraud and dishonesty against the judges who had decided against him. The scope, scale and content of his letter–writing campaign indicated the obsessive nature of his conduct and the likelihood that his efforts to re–litigate the matter would continue. At each stage, as each of his attempts at re–opening the Petition was dismissed, he lodged an appeal, seeking each time to take the matter all the way to this Court.

52. Such abusive activities are obviously very oppressive to the parties on the receiving end in terms of time, effort, costs and stress. They also make grossly disproportionate demands on the judicial system for spurious purposes. Such an unproductive diversion of limited judicial resources results in what may be damaging delays to *bona fide* litigants with serious actions to try. In *Bhamjee v. Forsdick (No 2)* [2004] 1 WLR 88 ("*Bhamjee (No 2)*"), Lord Phillips of Worth Matravers MR voiced the English courts' concerns in this context:

> "... the courts are facing very serious contemporary problems created by the activities of litigants like Mr Bhamjee who are bombarding them with applications which have no merit at all. ... The problem created by these hopeless applications is not only a serious financial one, for the reasons set out in para [25] of the judgment in *Bhamjee (No 1)*. It is also that the court is having to divert the skilled attention that ought to be paid to cases of real merit which warrant early hearings to cases which have no merit at all. A further problem is created by the fact that these litigants are often without the means to pay any costs orders made against them, and the parties in whose favour such costs orders are made are disinclined to throw good money after bad by making them bankrupt, particularly as the vexatious conduct may spill over into the bankruptcy proceedings themselves." (§3)

53. The financial problem caused to the court system by such litigants is illustrated by Brooke LJ's estimate, in §25 of *Bhamjee (No 1)* cited above, that:

> "... the true economic cost of handling each of these hopeless applications, when one takes into consideration the accommodation and staffing costs, salaries of the judges, the government lawyers, judicial assistants and the court's administrative staff, must be well over £ 1,000."

If a similar calculation were to be undertaken in Hong Kong, the results would no doubt be at least comparable.

The need to stop such abuse

54. The public interest plainly requires such abuse to be stopped. The increasing problem indicates that the measures presently available are insufficient.

55. Two such measures involve:

(a) the court's power to strike out interlocutory applications as well as fresh proceedings, on the basis that such applications or proceedings are an abuse of process ("the power to strike out"); and,

(b) its power, under HCO, s 27 to make an order ("the statutory order") prohibiting a person who is held to be a vexatious litigant from bringing any legal proceedings against any other person in any court without the leave of the Court of First Instance, with such leave to be refused unless the court is satisfied that the proceedings are not an abuse of the process and that there is prima facie ground for them.

56. The power to strike out is an aspect of the court's inherent jurisdiction to prevent abuse of its process. In *Connelly v. DPP* [1964] AC 1254, Lord Morris of Borth-y-Gest provided a much-cited explanation of such inherent powers:

> "There can be no doubt that a court which is endowed with a particular jurisdiction has powers which are necessary to enable it to act effectively within such jurisdiction. I would regard them as powers which are inherent in its jurisdiction. A court must enjoy such powers in order to enforce its rules of practice and to suppress any abuses of its process and to defeat any attempted thwarting of its process." (at p 1301)

57. But while an essential feature of any civil justice system, the power to strike out is not a sufficient answer to the problem of vexatious litigants. It is a reactive power aimed at curtailing abuse. It requires the party vexed to incur the expense and trouble of bringing a striking-out application and requires the court to entertain an *inter partes* hearing before such abuse can be brought to an end. The striking-out order which results does not prevent future abuse. The costs and inconvenience to the applicant and the absorption of judicial resources attendant on this process defines, rather than solves, the vexatious litigant problem.

58. A statutory order is preventive and imposes a blanket requirement for the court's leave before any proceedings can be brought by the vexatious litigant. However, it has in practice also proved to be an inadequate response to the vexatious litigant problem. HCO, s 27 provides:

(1) If, on an application made by the Secretary for Justice under this section, the Court of First Instance is satisfied that any person has habitually and persistently and without any reasonable ground instituted vexatious legal proceedings, whether in the Court of First Instance or in any inferior court, and whether against the same person or against different persons, the Court of First Instance may, after hearing that person or giving him an opportunity of being heard, order that no legal proceedings shall without the leave of the Court of First Instance be instituted by him in any court and that any proceedings instituted by him in any court before the making of the order shall not be continued by him without such leave and such leave shall not be given unless the Court of First Instance is satisfied that the proceedings are not an abuse of the process of the Court and that there is prima facie ground for the proceedings.

(2) A copy of any order made under subsection (1) shall be published in the Gazette.

59. Statutory orders are not readily obtainable. A party vexed

by abusive conduct cannot apply for one. Only the Secretary for Justice can apply. This requires representations to be made by the vexed party to the Department of Justice and requires someone from that Department who is wholly unfamiliar with the background, to read into the case in order to decide whether the Secretary should make the application. This is likely to take a comparatively long time since, like the courts, the resources of the Department are limited and heavily committed in many fields. This gives the vexatious litigant ample opportunity to pile on the abuse. Significantly, the Final Report on Civil Justice Reform issued by the Chief Justice's Working Party in March 2004 ("the Final Report") reported that between 1994 and April 2003, only two such applications were made by the Secretary (§434).

60. Another problem with taking the statutory route involves the high threshold set for the making of a statutory order. It must be shown that the person in question has habitually and persistently and without any reasonable ground instituted vexatious legal proceedings. This is so since the current legislation is evidently aimed at extreme cases of vexatious conduct, providing matching relief in the draconian form of a blanket restraining order. An application may therefore not satisfy the statutory conditions where the vexatious conduct complained of, though damaging and calling for protective measures, is not yet of such an extreme character. Indeed, of the two applications referred to in the Final Report, one failed to satisfy the threshold conditions. Examples of similar failures under comparable legislation can be found in *Foy v. Foy (No 2)* (1979) 102 DLR (3d) 342; and *AG v. Wentworth* (1988) 14 NSWLR 481. It is additionally to be noted that the statutory order relates only to the institution of fresh proceedings and gives no relief where the vexation relates to the unjustified issuing of numerous applications in the same action. What this indicates is that the coverage of HCO, s 27 is too limited. Measured intermediate responses, tailored to different variants and degrees of abuse by vexatious litigants, are needed.

Grepe v. Loam orders

61. In *Grepe v. Loam* [1887] Ch 168, the English Court of Appeal took steps to increase the courts' armoury against vexatious abuse. Having dismissed as frivolous the application of Hector Grepe and his brothers and sisters (who were acting in person) to set aside the judgments in two actions which had gone against them, and having heard that they had repeatedly made such applications without the respondents having any possibility of recovering their costs, the Court of Appeal ordered:

> "That the said Applicants or any of them be not allowed to make any further applications in these actions or either of them to this Court or to the Court below without the leave of this Court being first obtained. And if notice of any such application shall be given without such leave being obtained, the Respondents shall not be required to appear upon such application, and it shall be dismissed without being heard."

62. Unlike the striking-out orders discussed above, this type of order aims to prevent future abuse by requiring the vexatious litigant to obtain leave to issue any fresh application before that application needs to be noticed either by the proposed respondent or by the court. This is a useful protective measure. Where leave is applied for and refused, the intended respondent is spared further vexation. Where an application is issued without leave having first been obtained, the *Grepe v. Loam* order deems that application dismissed without being heard, avoiding further wastage of the court's resources and vexation of the respondent.

63. The legal foundations of the *Grepe v. Loam* order are not in doubt. It is plainly a legitimate exercise of the court's inherent jurisdiction to prevent its process being abused. Thus, in *Lord Kinnaird v. Field* [1905] 2 Ch 306, a case in which the defendant had made some 29 interlocutory applications and had sought to strike out the Statement of Claim on entirely frivolous grounds, the English Court of Appeal upheld a *Grepe v. Loam* order, Vaughan Williams LJ stating (at p 309) that "no question can possibly be raised as to the jurisdiction" to make such orders.

64. More recently, the availability of *Grepe v. Loam* orders was re-iterated by Lord Woolf MR in *Ebert v. Venvil* [2000] Ch 484 at 493; and by Lord Phillips MR in *Bhamjee (No 2)*. In the latter case (at p 99), such orders were given the new name of "civil restraint orders". Other common law jurisdictions have generally accepted the validity of *Grepe v. Loam* orders. These include Australia: *Commonwealth Trading Bank v. Inglis* (1974) 131 CLR 311; New Zealand: *Stewart v. Auckland Transport Board* [1951] NZLR 576; and Singapore: *Chua Choon Lim Robert v. MN Swami* [2000] 4 SLR 494. The courts in some Canadian provinces appear to be the exception: see *Shaward v. Shaward* (1988) 8 ACWS (3d) 412 (Manitoba); *Midwest Property Management v. Moore* (2003) Alta DJ 16023 (Alberta).

Extended Grepe v. Loam orders

65. An important limitation of *Grepe v. Loam* orders is that they are only directed against abuse which takes the form of repeated applications made within existing proceedings (whether before or after judgment). They do not address abuse which involves vexatiously issuing a series of fresh actions (or other proceedings) against the same defendants or in relation to the subject–matter of the proceedings already disposed of. One response to such abuse might be that the defendant has to resort to HCO, s 27 and try to persuade the Secretary for Justice to apply for a statutory order restraining such conduct. However, for the reasons already noted, this will often not be an effective option.

66. A different response has been to apply for what has come to be known as an "extended *Grepe v. Loam* order", referred to in this judgment as an "extended order". When faced with a litigant who vexatiously issues a series of fresh actions with a view to re–litigating a case which he has already lost, the courts have imposed a restraint against commencing such proceedings without the leave of the court, once more invoking the inherent jurisdiction to prevent abuse of process. This approach was pioneered by Lord Woolf MR in *Ebert v. Venvil* (above), and elaborated upon by Lord Phillips MR in *Bhamjee (No 2)* (where the order was named the "extended civil restraint order" at §41). Although in the present case, the courts below have referred to the subject order as a "*Grepe v. Loam* order", it is actually an extended order. It seeks to constrain the issue of fresh proceedings and not merely applications within an existing action.

67. Whether there is power to make extended orders by virtue of the court's inherent jurisdiction and without any statutory basis is the subject of this appeal. While stating that such a power is "highly desirable", the Final Report noted that some uncertainty (discussed below) existed as to whether the inherent jurisdiction could be relied on for restricting the right of access to the courts (see §§438 to 462). It recommended that the uncertainty be removed by improving the accessibility of HCO, s 27 statutory orders and widening their scope.

The Basic Law and extended orders

68. The appellant, who was not legally represented, submitted a

medical certificate indicating that he was unwell and asked that his associate, Mr Brumen Li (who is not a lawyer), be allowed to address the Court on his behalf. The Court exceptionally agreed to hear Mr Li. It should be noted that the Court was in any event much assisted by the helpful research and submissions of Mr Bernard Man who acted as *amicus curiae* and who set out to place before the Court all arguments reasonably available to the appellant. The Court is also grateful for the assistance of Mr Alan Leong SC, appearing with Ms Alexandra Norton for the respondents.

69. The appellant sought to challenge extended orders on the basis that they offend against Articles 35 and/or 39 of the Basic Law. That argument was, however, not one advanced by the *amicus*.

70. Those Articles relevantly provide as follows:

> *BL 35*
>
> Hong Kong residents shall have the right to ... access to the courts, ... and to judicial remedies.
>
> Hong Kong residents shall have the right to institute legal proceedings in the courts against the acts of the executive authorities and their personnel.
>
> *BL 39*
>
> The provisions of the International Covenant on Civil and Political Rights, ... as applied to Hong Kong shall remain in force and shall be implemented through the laws of the Hong Kong Special Administrative Region.
>
> The rights and freedoms enjoyed by Hong Kong residents shall not be restricted unless as prescribed by law. Such restrictions shall not contravene the provisions of the preceding paragraph of this Article.

71. The reference in BL 39 to the ICCPR as applied to Hong Kong makes relevant Article 10 of the Hong Kong Bill of Rights (reflecting ICCPR Art 14.1) which is materially in the following terms:

> BOR 10
>
> All persons shall be equal before the courts and tribunals. In the determination of any criminal charge against him, or of his rights and obligations in a suit at law, everyone shall be entitled to a fair and public hearing by a competent, independent and impartial tribunal established by law. ...

72. As I understand the appellant's position, reflecting some of the concerns raised in the Final Report, two arguments are advanced. In the first place, it is asserted that extended orders are inconsistent with the right of access to the courts guaranteed by BL 35 and BOR 10. Secondly, it is argued that even if such orders might otherwise be valid as limitations on the right of access, they are not established at law with sufficient certainty to qualify, in BL 39 terms, as a restriction "prescribed by law".

73. In my view, neither argument succeeds. In relation to BL 35 and BOR 10, it has firmly been established in the jurisprudence of the European Court of Human Rights in relation to the closely analogous right of access under Art 6(1) of the European Human Rights Convention, that such right is by its nature not absolute, but may be subject to limitations. Such limitations are valid if they pursue a legitimate aim, are proportionate to that aim and are not such as to impair the very essence of the right: *Ashingdane v. UK* [1985] 7 EHRR 528 at §57; *Tolstoy-Miloslavsky v. United Kingdom* (1995) 20 EHRR 442 at §59.

74. In *H v. UK* [1985] 45 DR 281, this principle was applied by the European Commission of Human Rights to declare inadmissible an Article 6(1) challenge to the validity of an order made under the Vexatious Actions (Scotland) Act 1898. The Commission pointed out that:

> "... the vexatious litigant order ... did not limit the applicant's access to court completely, but provided for a review by a senior judge of the Scottish judiciary of any case the applicant wished to bring. The Commission considers that such a review is not such as to deny the essence of the right of access to court; indeed, some form of regulation of access to court is necessary in the interests of the proper administration of justice and must therefore be regarded as a legitimate aim.
>
> Further, the Commission finds that in the present case the means employed in regulating access to court by the applicant were not disproportionate to the aim of ensuring the proper administration of justice ..."

75. The abovementioned principles were adopted by the English Court of Appeal in *AG v. Covey; AG v. Mathews* [2001] EWCA Civ 254, 19 February 2001 at §§60–61, in upholding the validity of vexatious litigant orders made under s 42 of the Supreme Court Act 1981.

76. In my view, those principles are plainly appropriate for application in Hong Kong both with regard to statutory orders made under HCO, s 27 and extended orders. Such orders pursue the legitimate aim of preventing harm to the proper administration of justice and preventing the vexatious oppression of other litigants. They are proportionate measures and do not impair the very essence of the right in that they provide a judicial mechanism for allowing proper cases to be brought forward.

77. Turning to the BL 39 argument, any relevant uncertainty that there may previously have been in relation to the validity of extended orders falls to be dealt with in the present appeal. If and in so far as the Court upholds such orders and formulates the relevant principles in the present case, no room would remain for arguing that such orders are unconstitutional by reason of uncertainty and hence inconsistency with BL 39. The Final Report was of course written from a different perspective. The Working Party was identifying possible uncertainties with a view to suggesting reforms and, unlike this Court, was not in a position to resolve any relevant doubts.

78. It is accordingly my view that the use of extended orders is consistent with the Basic Law and the Hong Kong Bill of Rights.

Extended orders and the inherent jurisdiction

79. One may accordingly return to the central question in this appeal: Does the inherent jurisdiction provide a sufficient foundation for the making of extended orders or must they be authorized by statute?

(a) The statutory displacement argument

80. Two arguments supporting the need for a statute have been raised. I shall refer to the first of these as the "statutory displacement argument" which proceeds as follows:

(a) While the court undoubtedly has an inherent jurisdiction to prevent abuse of its process, there may be cases where the legislature has intervened to regulate some matter which might otherwise have been dealt with under the inherent jurisdiction.

(b) HCO, s 27 is one such example. The legislature has laid down the conditions for obtaining orders to restrain a vexatious litigant from issuing fresh proceedings. Such conditions include the requirement that applications be made by the Secretary for Justice and the high threshold requirements.

(c) In this area, the court's inherent jurisdiction must be regarded as having been displaced by the statute. The court cannot purport, in reliance on its inherent jurisdiction, to grant relief which is the same as that provided for by s 27 on the basis of different and less stringent conditions.

(d) Any party who wants to restrain fresh proceedings must therefore take the statutory route.

81. As Lord Woolf MR accepted in *Ebert v. Venvil* at p 493 (after recording that the parties did not dispute the court's inherent jurisdiction to make an ordinary *Grepe v. Loam* order):

> "This does not mean that intervention of Parliament may not have cut down the inherent jurisdiction of the court. If there was an application for an order of the same width as the statutory jurisdiction, the court could only appropriately deal with such an application under the statutory jurisdiction."

(b) The constitutional right argument

82. The second argument in support of a requirement for statutory intervention may be called the "constitutional right argument". It centres on the contention that because extended orders restrict the right of access to the courts they can only validly be made if expressly authorized by statute.

83. There is certainly ample authority that the right of unimpeded access to the courts is regarded at common law as a constitutional right and that abrogation of that right requires express statutory provision. Thus, in *Pyx Granite Co Ltd v. Ministry of Housing and Local Government* [1960] AC 260 at 286, Viscount Simonds stated:

> "It is a principle not by any means to be whittled down that the subject's recourse to Her Majesty's courts for the determination of his rights is not to be excluded except by clear words."

Similarly, in *Raymond v. Honey* [1983] 1 AC 1 at 14, Lord Bridge noted that:

> "... a citizen's right to unimpeded access to the courts can only be taken away by express enactment."

As Laws J explained in *R v. Lord Chancellor ex p Witham* [1998] QB 575 at 585:

> "... the common law has clearly given special weight to the citizen's right of access to the courts. It has been described as a constitutional right, though the cases do not explain what that means. In this whole argument, nothing to my mind has been shown to displace the proposition that the executive cannot in law abrogate the right of access to justice, unless it is specifically so permitted by Parliament; and this is the meaning of the constitutional right."

84. These principles were applied in *Commonwealth Trading Bank v. Inglis* (1974) 131 CLR 311, where the bank had sought an order:

> "... 'pursuant to the inherent jurisdiction' of the Court that no legal proceedings should be instituted or applications in existing proceedings made or appeals lodged by the plaintiffs in the action or either of them without leave of a justice of the Court 'by reason of their having habitually and persistently and without any reasonable ground instituted vexatious legal proceedings, made repeated vexatious applications in pending actions and conducted legal proceedings in a vexatious and time-wasting manner'." (pp 311–2)

The High Court of Australia held that the inherent jurisdiction did not confer power on the court to make such an order:

> "In our opinion, it is not surprising that the Courts do not appear (so far as we have been able to discover) to have taken the further step of intervening in a summary way to prevent the commencement, except by leave, of actions and other proceedings by a particular person or persons but have limited themselves to exercising their powers in relation to proceedings which have been taken in a Court and have thus been placed under its control. It may be that the exercise of supervision, by means of a requirement that leave should be obtained for the bringing of proceedings, could have been justified logically as a proper safeguard against abuse of the Court's process in cases where it was shown to be probable that a person would continue bringing groundless proceedings. But, in our opinion, it is apparent that the Courts, both in England and in this country, have declined to regard themselves as having power to do so, except where such power has been conferred upon them by an Act of Parliament or by Rules promulgated under statutory authority. This is demonstrated, not merely by the absence of reported cases in which such orders have been made under the inherent power of the Court, but by the fact that it has been thought necessary to deal with specific cases of the bringing of numerous unfounded proceedings by legislation rather than by invoking the inherent power of the Court. There have been cases in which the vexatious character of the proceedings was so clear that it cannot be supposed that the Court would have hesitated to exercise such a power if it had been regarded as existing." (pp 314–5)

85. An earlier attempt in New Zealand to obtain an order "to prevent the plaintiff's commencing of any further action against the [defendant] Board without the precedent leave of the Court" had also failed for similar reasons: see *Stewart v. Auckland Transport Board* [1951] NZLR 576.

(c) Extended orders properly made in the inherent jurisdiction

86. The principles discussed above, underlying both the statutory displacement argument and the constitutional right argument, are plainly well-established. However, that is not to say that those arguments themselves are to be accepted. The crucial question is whether the application of those principles does result in excluding extended orders from the courts' inherent jurisdiction. This requires first an examination of the essential features of such orders.

87. The terms of the extended order made by Neuberger J and upheld by the Court of Appeal in *Ebert v. Venvil* [2000] Ch 484 are set out at pp 491-2 of the report. In *Bhamjee (No 2)*, Lord Phillips

MR described the essential features of that order as follows:

> "(i) It extended not only to applications in the current proceedings but also to taking any steps (including the issuing of new proceedings) in any division of the High Court or in any county court against the defendant bank or its legal representatives in or arising out of or concerning a wide range of matters defined in the order without the leave of a judge being first obtained.
>
> (ii) Any application for leave had to be made without notice in writing to one of two named judges of the Chancery Division and would be dealt with on paper.
>
> (iii) Six clear working days' written notice of any such application had to be given to the bank's solicitors, and if they replied in writing their response had to accompany the application." (at p 96)

Later in that judgment, when summarising the guidance given as to the making of extended civil restraint orders, Lord Phillips MR described them as orders which:

> "... will restrain the litigant from instituting proceedings or making applications in the courts identified in the order in or out of or concerning any matters involving or relating to or touching upon or leading to the proceedings in which it is made without the permission of a judge identified in the order." (at p 102)

88. While the subject order was not drawn up in such terms and suffers from certain deficiencies considered below, it is appropriate in the present case to proceed on the footing that the extended orders under discussion exhibit the features described by Lord Phillips MR above. I would add that the court's permission to proceed should be understood to cover two situations: (i) where the court directs that no leave is needed (the new matter falling outside the defined class of proceedings requiring leave); and (ii) where the court considers the new proceedings to fall within the relevant class but, in its discretion, allows them to go forward notwithstanding. The decision to grant leave is necessarily without prejudice to any *inter partes* application that the defendant may wish to mount to strike out the proceedings or to set aside the leave, as appropriate.

89. The blanket effect of statutory orders prohibiting any kind of legal proceedings without leave against any person has already been mentioned. They also make it a condition of such leave that the court must be satisfied that the proceedings are not an abuse and that there is prima facie ground for them. An extended order is therefore significantly narrower.

(a) First, it is not directed against any type of action whatsoever. It requires leave to be obtained only in respect of fresh proceedings which are an attempt at re–litigating specified proceedings which have already been determined (including fresh proceedings where there may be added elements which do not detract from the reality that they are in truth an attempt at such re-litigation). Extended orders are therefore limited by reference to the subject–matter of the new proceedings.

(b) Secondly, even where the proposed claim falls within the prohibited class of proceedings, it may nevertheless be allowed to go forward if it is arguably meritorious.

(c) Although (as discussed below) the abovementioned process will in practice require that all fresh proceedings issued by a litigant subject to an extended order be judicially examined, those proceedings would only be looked at for the limited purpose of giving effect to the extended order and not with a view to screening out every proposed action which is not shown to be viable.

90. In my view, these are important differences which lead to the conclusion that the statutory displacement argument is inapplicable. Extended orders are not of the same width or effect as orders made under HCO, s 27. This was the view taken by Lord Woolf MR in *Ebert v. Venvil*, at p 490. The statutory jurisdiction caters for the significantly wider blanket orders referred to above, and therefore does not by implication cut down on the court's inherent jurisdiction to make the more limited extended orders.

91. I note in passing that the headnote to the report of *Tse Jeekeen v. HK Alliance in Support of Patriotic Democratic Movement of China* [2000] 2 HKC 339, suggests that the application for an extended order in that case was "in effect" an application for a statutory order under HCO, s 27 to be made by virtue of the court's inherent jurisdiction "prohibiting a vexatious litigant from commencing new proceedings without the leave of the court". That statement is incorrect. Neither the order made by Chung J (at 346G) nor extended orders in general seek to impose a blanket prohibition against commencing new proceedings without leave. The headnote also fails to reflect Chung J's citation (at 344G–H) of Lord Woolf MR's observation that extended orders are more restricted than statutory orders and that orders of the same width as statutory orders can only appropriately be made under the statutory jurisdiction.

(d) The juridical basis of extended orders

92. As with simple *Grepe v. Loam* orders, extended orders are founded on the court's inherent jurisdiction to prevent abuse of its process. This was the starting–point of Lord Woolf MR when addressing the juridical basis of such orders in *Ebert v. Venvil* (at 496):

> "We prefer to approach the issues from a standpoint of principle. Doing so, the starting point must be the extensive nature of the inherent jurisdiction of any court to prevent its procedure being abused. We see no reason why, absent the intervention of a statute cutting down the jurisdiction, that jurisdiction should apply only in relation to existing proceedings and not to vexatious proceedings which are manifestly threatened but not yet initiated."

93. Pointing to the fact that the court has undoubted injunctive powers to restrain anticipated proceedings, both within the jurisdiction and abroad, in order to protect an applicant from serious and imminent anticipated damage, his Lordship continued:

> "We can see no reason in principle why it should not also, in accord with the general approach to the granting of *quia timet* injunctions, exercise that power to prevent the serious loss that anticipated but unidentified proceedings could cause the defendants to those proceedings." (at p 497)

94. While this means imposing abnormal constraints on the vexatious litigant, Lord Woolf MR pointed out that the constraints are not absolute and that such orders, with their limiting features, reflect and are a response to the type and degree of abuse which

they seek to restrain:

> "The making of an extended *Grepe v. Loam* order or a *Grepe v. Loam* order in its usual form does involve a serious inhibition on a prospective litigant exercising his normal rights of access to the courts. However, the extent of this interference should not be exaggerated. First it is only an inhibition on bringing proceedings without the leave of the court. If the proceedings are arguably meritorious leave will be forthcoming. Secondly, the court will not make an order unless there are serious grounds for doing so and if there are no serious grounds, the order will be capable of being set aside on appeal." (at 497)

95. I respectfully agree with these comments. In my view, once the nature of the extended order is appreciated, it is evident that cases like the *Pyx Granite* case, *Raymond v. Honey and ex p Witham* (discussed above in the context of the constitutional right argument) are distinguishable. The constitutional right which they address is the right of access to the court for the vindication of legal rights and interests. The vexatious litigant is only subjected to restraint under an extended order where he is engaged in an abuse of the court's process. Often, that litigant will already have fully exercised the right of access before vexatiously seeking to re-litigate the exhausted proceedings. Such restraint does not involve interference with any constitutional right and the cases cited do not require such orders to be placed on a statutory footing.

96. In *Attorney-General v. Vernazza* [1960] AC 965 at 977, Lord Denning drew a clear distinction between a legitimate exercise of the right of access and conduct abusive of the court's process:

> "The courts of this country have an inherent power to 'prevent the abuse of legal machinery which would occur, if for no possible benefit the defendants are to be dragged through litigation which must be long and expensive', see *Willis v. Earl Beauchamp* (1886) 11 PD 59, 63; by Bowen LJ: and when the courts of this country exercise this power, they are not depriving a man of a vested right. They are only exercising a control over their own procedure. No man, let alone a vexatious litigant, has a vested right to bring or continue proceedings which are an abuse of the process of the court."

97. Lord Phillips MR echoed this in *Bhamjee (No 2)* at §33:

> "... no litigant has any substantive right to trouble the court with litigation which represents an abuse of its process."

98. It is also noteworthy that in *Commonwealth Trading Bank v. Inglis* and *Stewart v. Auckland Transport Board*, cited above, the orders sought and held to fall beyond the court's inherent jurisdiction were blanket prohibitions against starting any fresh proceedings and not orders limited in the way that extended orders are limited. It is significant that in the *Inglis* case, Barwick CJ and McTiernan J pointed out that:

> "The application is not framed so as to limit such future proceedings to proceedings of the same kind as those that have been previously brought or to proceedings against the applicant or against other specified persons who have already been sued by the respondents. It refers to any legal proceedings against any person." (at p 313)

99. It is reasonable to suppose that the High Court of Australia might well have taken a different view if asked to consider an extended order containing the limitations referred to in the passage just cited. Indeed, this was precisely the assumption upon which French J based his decision in *Hunter v. Leahy* (1999) 91 FCR 214, in the Australian Federal Court. His Honour stated (at p 221):

> "I do not regard the decision in *Commonwealth Trading Bank v. Inglis* as so constraining the inherent jurisdiction or the implied incidental power of this Court or the application of s 23 [of the Federal Court of Australia Act 1976 (Cth)], that it can prevent this Court from restraining the institution of proceedings which, in effect, seek to relitigate the substance of matters already determined in proceedings which have been disposed of in the Court. As in the *Wentworth* case the touchstone of the Court's power must be substance rather than form. I think therefore that although on the authority of *Inglis*, Sheppard J's order was too widely cast, it can be recast to meet the difficulties posed by Mr Hunter's continued attempts to relitigate the issue on which he has thus far been unsuccessful."

100. The court's inherent jurisdiction to make extended orders is therefore now firmly established in England and Wales, as shown by *Ebert v. Venvil and Bhamjee (No 2)*. It also appears that a similar implied jurisdiction may be coming to be recognized in Australia. It has been recognized in Singapore: see *Chua Choon Lim Robert v. MN Swami* [2000] 4 SLR 494. It is, in my view, a soundly-based jurisdiction which is equally enjoyed by our courts. Accordingly, the subject order, which was intended to be an extended order, was made within jurisdiction and justified on the facts, although the appropriateness of its terms will require examination.

Other protective measures and statutory reform

101. The focus of this judgment has of course been on extended orders. It should not, however, be thought that the court's inherent jurisdiction to prevent abuse of its process is rigidly confined to the measures so far discussed. Abuse of process may come in a wide variety of forms and be of different degrees and, subject to the principles discussed above, the court's inherent jurisdiction enables it flexibly to develop such proportionate responses as may be appropriate.

(a) Ancillary directions

102. It is in this context that the courts have, for instance, developed ancillary directions aimed at increasing the effectiveness of *Grepe v. Loam* and extended orders. Examples of such directions were given by Lord Phillips MR in *Bhamjee (No 2)*:

> "The extended *Grepe v. Loam* order contained the novelty that the High Court was now able to restrict the litigant's activities in the county court (so long as they referred to the same matter). ... Other novelties were that all Mr Ebert's applications were reserved to one or other of two named judges in the Chancery Division (and, in due course, to only one), and that they might be disposed of on paper. It appears from Laws LJ's judgment in *Attorney-General v. Ebert* (unreported) 7 July 2000 (at para [33]) that two judges of that division later felt constrained to make a further order to the effect that Mr Ebert be not allowed to make applications under the *Grepe v. Loam* order more frequently than once every 2 months, unless he could demonstrate that a more urgent

application was called for." (at §29)

(b) Other types of constraint

103. As Lord Phillips MR further indicated, the court might also increase the range of its armoury, adding other types of constraint against persistent abuse:

"... we must not be taken to be excluding the possibility that other forms of order may be made if the situation seems to demand it. For instance, it may on occasion be thought appropriate to direct that permission to make an application or to institute an action will only be considered if an advocate with higher court rights of audience considers there is merit in it, or that the requisite applications in the High Court should be made to a Master in the first instance. The possibilities are unlimited. What is important is that the remedy should always be proportionate to the mischief that needs remedying." (*Bhamjee (No 2)* at §35)

(c)"General civil restraint orders"

104. In *Bhamjee (No 2)*, the English Court of Appeal developed the jurisdiction further by authorizing, on the basis of the inherent jurisdiction, imposition of what were called "*general* civil restraint orders" in cases where *Grepe v. Loam* orders (or "civil restraint orders") and extended orders ("extended civil restraint orders") were found insufficient. Lord Phillips MR stated that in such an event:

"At High Court level, a High Court judge may make an order generally restraining the litigant from instituting any action or making any application in the High Court without first obtaining the permission of an identified High Court judge in an all-paper proceeding. The purpose of such an order will be to protect the process of the High Court from abuse, so that the order may not be extended to include the county court. The order will identify the judge to whom any applications for the requisite permission should be made. A general civil restraint order should be made for a period not exceeding 2 years, unless subsequently extended."

105. Whether the Hong Kong courts have jurisdiction to make such an order does not arise for decision in the present appeal. Given the experience of the English courts, I would not wish to rule out such orders. But there may be jurisdictional difficulties. A general civil restraint order may be thought to come uncomfortably close to the blanket statutory orders presently obtainable under HCO, s 27. Introduction of general civil restraint orders would require serious consideration to be given to the statutory displacement argument in that context.

(d) Amending HCO, s 27

106. It would in any event be advisable to give urgent consideration to amending HCO, s 27 with a view to widening its scope. There is much force in the recommendation made in the Final Report (at §463) that the court should have power to make statutory orders upon the application of any person directly affected by the vexatious conduct without the intervention or consent of the Secretary for Justice. One could perhaps consider for adoption, legislation along the lines of the South African Vexatious Proceedings Act referred to in *Beinash v. Ernst & Young* [1999] 2 SA 116. Section 2(1)(b) of that Act materially provides:

"If on an application made by any person against whom legal proceedings have been instituted by any other person or who has reason to believe that the institution of legal proceedings against him is contemplated by any other person, the Court is satisfied that the said person has persistently and without any reasonable ground instituted legal proceedings in any Court ... whether against the same person or against different persons, ... the Court may [after the necessary procedures and being duly satisfied, make the statutory order]. "

(e) Injunctions and contempt of court

107. At the extreme end of the spectrum of responses to vexatious litigation, lies injunctive relief backed by the sanctions applicable to contempt of court.

108. This remedy was resorted to by the Attorney-General in *AG v. Ebert* [2002] 2 All ER 789, some 10 months after a statutory order had been made against Mr Ebert under s 42 of the Supreme Court Act 1981. The Attorney-General put his case for injunctive relief on the need "to stop [Mr Ebert's] interfering with the proper administration of justice"(at §23). Brooke LJ accepted that there was a distinction between "Mr Ebert's practice of making innumerable applications (which can be kept under control by other techniques)" and conduct involving "disturbances of the process of the court" (§39). The conduct in question (described at §§12–18) involved, for example, Mr Ebert repeatedly demanding that the court deal immediately with his applications, going so far as to interrupt, on several occasions, the designated judge's conduct of other proceedings to press for this; accusing the judge of corruption and other crimes; and physically seizing hold of a barrister who had appeared against him while purporting to make a citizen's arrest in respect of the barrister's alleged fraud.

109. Plainly, this was an extreme case and the relief sought– and obtained– by the Attorney–General was draconian. Brooke LJ summarised that relief in these terms:

"First, that Mr Ebert should be barred from entering the Royal Courts of Justice without express permission, except for the purposes of attending a hearing for which he has been granted permission. Secondly, that he should be barred from any form of communication with anyone at the court except for the purpose of making the formal applications mentioned in the draft order. Thirdly, that any application he makes must be made in writing in a particular form and determined in writing (unless the court directs an oral hearing). And finally, that any application of any kind which is not made in that form should stand dismissed without being heard." (at §24)

110. In my view, similar relief, on similar grounds, would in principle be available in this jurisdiction. The court's jurisdiction to grant injunctive relief to prevent anticipated interference with the administration of justice amounting to a contempt is well established: eg, *Attorney-General v. Times Newspapers Ltd* [1974] AC 273; *Raymond v. Honey* [1983] 1 AC 1 at 10. But it is only when the litigant's vexatious conduct passes into the realms of disrupting the administration of justice in a manner constituting a contempt that such powers should be invoked.

Formulating and implementing extended orders

111. This is an area of developing jurisprudence. As the case-law shows, the courts have been refining the form of extended orders and developing ancillary directions in aid thereof. Supporting arrangements also need to be put in place by the court system

to promote their effectiveness. Details concerning the terms of the orders, appropriate directions and the court system's operational arrangements will have to be progressively worked out in individual cases, in practice directions and perhaps in rules of court. This is [*sic*] applies also to cases where the court initiates consideration of *Grepe v. Loam* or extended orders of its own motion, as indicated by the Chief Justice. In the present judgment, it is necessary to refer to certain matters of principle regarding the contents and operation of extended orders which bear upon the viability of the subject order.

112. Where a *Grepe v. Loam* order or an extended order is made, it is important that the scope of the restraint is clear and that, supported by any desirable ancillary directions, it consciously aims to promote, in a workable manner, the objectives of preventing abuse at minimum cost to the vexed party and to the courts, in terms of time, effort and money.

(a) Grepe v. Loam orders

113. Simple *Grepe v. Loam* orders present few difficulties. The order restrains the making of all further applications in an existing case without leave of the judge. If such leave has not been obtained, everyone can simply ignore the application (including any purported application to the master) and it is deemed to have been dismissed. Operation of such an order requires no qualitative judgment as to when leave is required: it is always required. To improve its efficiency, directions can and should be given:

(a) for any application for leave to be made ex parte in writing to a designated judge or judges identified in the order, without notification to the proposed respondent and for the decision as to leave to be made without an oral hearing; and,

(b) where leave has been given, requiring the order giving leave to accompany service of the application on the respondent.

(b) Extended orders

114. The important difference between the extended order and the ordinary *Grepe v. Loam* order is that the former restrains the institution without leave of only certain classes of proceedings, usually defined by reference to the subject-matter of proceedings which have already been litigated. This means that extended orders *do* require a qualitative assessment of the new proceedings to see whether they fall within the class requiring leave.

115. One must therefore ask who makes that assessment. In my view, that task must fall to a judge. As a matter of course, all fresh proceedings issued by a party who is subject to an extended order have to be vetted for compliance with that order, ideally by the judge who made the extended order or, if not, by a designated judge who has some familiarity with the background. However, in principle, it should not be left to court staff who are not judges or judicial officers. Certainly the staff at the counter of the High Court Registry cannot be expected to undertake that task when deciding whether to seal a Writ or some other form of process.

116. There is no difficulty with putting the abovementioned decision-making process in train where the vexatious litigant duly applies to the court before issuing the fresh proceedings. But what if he chooses to issue proceedings without approaching the court? The Writ or other proceedings will be sealed and issued without any vetting and then served on the defendant. If this is allowed to go unchecked, it undermines the entire protective scheme.

117. Two measures ought to be put in place to deal with this situation. First, the court system, no doubt using its information technology resources, must have a means for detecting all fresh proceedings issued by persons subject to a valid extended order (bearing in mind that they may in some cases be of limited duration). Once detected, the system should ensure that the fresh proceedings are referred to a judge so that an appropriate decision can be taken: whether to dismiss the proceedings, to give leave to proceed or to direct that leave is not required, with the decision then notified to the named defendants.

118. Secondly, a rule or direction should be in place providing that if any fresh proceedings served on defendants protected by an extended order are unaccompanied by either a court order giving leave to proceed or a direction that leave is not required, such defendants are entitled to do nothing in response until such time as they are notified of the court's decision in relation to those fresh proceedings. Time for acknowledging service and defending the proceedings should automatically be deemed to be extended until such notice is received.

119. It is of course possible that, despite any monitoring system put in place in the High Court Registry, new proceedings commenced by a vexatious litigant who is subject to an extended order may slip through without being brought to the attention of the judge. In such cases, the second rule would still apply and no basis would exist for judgment to be entered in default of the defendant acknowledging service. If default judgment should nonetheless purport to be entered, the defendant should notify the court that he is protected by an extended order and the court should then set aside all steps taken since issue of the fresh proceedings and refer the matter to the designated judge for a decision as to whether it should be allowed to proceed in the light of the terms of the extended order, such curative measures all being taken without any oral hearing or further participation of the defendant.

120. A further consequence of the need for a qualitative assessment relates to the drawing up of the extended order. It is essential that there should be clarity in defining the class of proceedings where leave must be obtained.

(a) Plainly, an order may disallow any attempt to re-litigate without leave a cause of action disposed of as *res judicata* or a matter which comes within the principle explained in *Yat Tung Investment Co Ltd v. Dao Heng Bank Ltd* [1975] AC 581. However, experience shows that this may not give sufficient protection. The abuse may, for instance, involve the vexatious addition of defendants (such as witnesses who gave evidence for the other side, the lawyers, or even the judges, involved). Spurious new elements may be introduced into the case, perhaps hoping to disguise the fact that it is in reality no more than an attempt at re-litigating a lost cause. It is therefore legitimate for the order to be drawn so as to cover not merely the immediate subject-matter of the concluded proceedings but, for instance, also matters "involving or relating to or touching upon or leading to those proceedings" (as suggested by Lord Phillips MR in *Bhamjee (No 2)* at p 102). It is possible that non-abusive proceedings might be caught by some such wider formulation. However, in such cases the court could be expected to grant leave for the new proceedings to proceed.

(b) The order should also state whether the requirement only applies to cases in the High Court or whether it also extends to actions on the same subject-matter in the District Court. In my view, the latter option legitimately falls within the province of an extended order as a measure against the relevant abuse. The District Court equally has an inherent jurisdiction to protect its process against abuse and may make relevant orders applying the principles presently under consideration.

121. In construing the terms of a *Grepe v. Loam* order or an extended order and applying it to any fresh application or proceedings brought by the vexatious litigant, the court should look to the substance of what is sought to be done in the new matter and not to its form. Thus, it is not uncommon for some collateral attack to be launched by vexatious litigants in the course of proceedings, for instance, by making unfounded allegations of perjury in relation to an affidavit or trying to commit the other side's lawyers for contempt, and so forth. A judge would be justified in treating such unfounded collateral attacks as in substance applications within the same proceedings for the purposes of a *Grepe v. Loam* order, whatever their form. As already indicated, new proceedings, even if embellished with additional elements, may in substance be a vexatious attempt to re-litigate the concluded matter.

122. If the court itself is made the object of such a collateral attack, provided that the judge is satisfied that such attack is in substance no more than a vexatious attempt to re-litigate the exhausted matter, there ought generally to be no question of the judge having to disqualify himself from dealing with the matter. The test for disqualification is whether the circumstances are such as would lead a reasonable, fair-minded and well-informed observer to conclude that that there is a real possibility that the judge would be biased in dealing with the matter: see *Deacons v. White & Case Ltd Liability Partnership* (2003) 6 HKCFAR 322; and *Financial Secretary v. Wong* (2003) 6 HKCFAR 476 at 496-7, §48. In the situation postulated, it would be plain to such an observer that the attempt to disqualify the judge is itself part and parcel of the abuse and not such as to give rise to any apprehension of bias. For a judge to recuse himself in such circumstances would be to give in to the abuse.

The subject order

123. I have held that the subject order, which was intended to be an extended order, was made within jurisdiction and justified on the facts. However, in the terms in which it was drawn up (set out in paragraph 28 above), it is not workable. It adopts the wording of a simple *Grepe v. Loam* order but seeks to constrain entirely fresh proceedings which are "in respect of the same claim or subject matter" as the specified concluded proceedings. As discussed above, judicial consideration of whether the fresh proceedings fall within the order is required. However, the subject order directs that "such" fresh proceedings-meaning those caught by the prohibition-should be "dismissed without being heard" if leave has not been obtained. But in the absence of a judicial determination, one is not able to say that they are "such" fresh proceedings. And without anyone addressing that question, it is impossible to see how the new claim can be dismissed without being heard.

124. Accordingly, the subject order cannot stand without amendment. This was accepted by Mr Alan Leong SC. Certain suggested amendments were put forward at the hearing but it is evident that further thought is needed regarding the terms of the extended order in the present case. On the assumption that the respondents wish to submit for approval a draft amendment which takes into account the matters dealt with in the present decision, I would give the following directions, namely, that:

(a) All further proceedings with regard to the settling of the terms of any such amended order should be dealt with by a single Permanent Judge.

(b) The respondents should be at liberty, within 21 days after the date of the handing down of this judgment to submit to the Registrar of this Court, a draft amended order for approval by the Permanent Judge, serving a copy thereof on the appellant.

(c) Any representations, limited to comments on the terms of such draft amended order, which the appellant may wish to make for consideration by the Permanent Judge should be submitted in writing to the Registrar within 21 days thereafter, serving a copy thereof on the respondents.

(d) Any response which the respondents may wish to make should be submitted in writing to the Registrar within 14 days thereafter.

(e) Unless the Permanent Judge should direct otherwise, all of the aforesaid matters should be dealt with on the papers and without an oral hearing.

Vexatious appeals

125. As exemplified by this case, vexatious litigants characteristically engage in the lodging of appeals, however hopeless, whenever some vexatious application or proceeding encounters a reversal. This is part and parcel of the abuse which must be stopped. If, in cases justifying the making of a *Grepe v. Loam* order or an extended order, protective measures do not include prevention of abuse at the appellate level, one can expect the vexatious litigant to issue a stream of applications or fresh proceedings and, upon their rejection at first instance, appeal each such rejection to the next judicial tier. This would seriously undermine the effectiveness of the *Grepe v. Loam* jurisdiction. What is the proper judicial response in such cases?

126. The right of appeal is statutory. Section 14 of the High Court Ordinance provides that subject to certain exceptions set out in subsection (3) which do not concern vexatious litigants, "an appeal shall lie as of right to the Court of Appeal from every judgment or order of the Court of First Instance in any civil cause or matter." At present there is no statutory requirement for leave to appeal even in relation to interlocutory judgments, although the Final Report has recommended introducing such a requirement (Recommendation 110).

127. It is, however, important to construe HCO, s 14 in the light of its obvious purpose. We have seen that the right of access to the courts, recognized as a constitutional right at common law and guaranteed by the Basic Law, is not to be interpreted as giving any person a licence to abuse the court's process. Equally, the right of appeal granted by statute was not provided so that the appellate process can be abused by vexatious litigants. It is no less within the court's inherent jurisdiction to prevent abuse of its appellate process.

128. It is clear that the Court of Appeal may, in its inherent jurisdiction, strike out appeals which are frivolous, vexatious or an abuse of process: *Burgess v. Stafford Hotel Ltd* [1990] 1 WLR 1215; see Hong Kong Civil Procedure 59/3/6. Where a litigant has vexatiously abused the process of the court at first instance to a degree justifying a *Grepe v. Loam* order or an extended order,

and where he has also been shown to have abused the appellate process, the Court of Appeal has and should exercise the power to make a suitable form of order restricting future appeals by that litigant.

129. The fact that the right of appeal is given by statute does not mean that the court's inherent jurisdiction has in any way been displaced. HCO, s 14 does not seek to regulate vexatious conduct, unlike HCO, s 27. It defines the right of appeal and lays down exceptions, none of which concerns vexatious litigants. It is of the essence of the court's inherent jurisdiction that the court should have power to prevent the vexatious misuse of that statutory right.

130. Adopting this view, the English Court of Appeal in *Bhamjee (No 2)* held that it would be consistent with the United Kingdom's Human Rights protections to impose stringent restrictions on the right of appeal afforded to vexatious litigants:

> "... if a litigant subject to an extended civil restraint order or a general civil restraint order continues to make the requisite applications pursuant to the order which are customarily dismissed on the grounds that they are totally devoid of merit, a judge may, if he thinks fit, direct that if any further application is dismissed on the same grounds, the decision will be final. This type of order should only be made by a High Court judge or a designated civil judge (or his appointed deputy). Thereafter an appeal court will have no jurisdiction to grant permission to appeal against any subsequent refusal of permission any more than it has jurisdiction to grant permission to appeal against an order made by a judge exercising his statutory powers under s 42(4) of the 1981 Act. We consider that if a litigant persists in instituting proceedings or making applications which are totally devoid of merit despite all the earlier efforts the court has made to restrain his litigious activities and to protect its process from abuse, then this will be a legitimate reason why the court should eventually deprive him of the ordinary right to seek to appeal to a higher level of court. It will be sufficient if any subsequent applications are considered once only." (at §51)

131. The reference to s 42(4) is to the provision in the Supreme Court Act 1981 which provides that where a statutory order has been made against a vexatious litigant, a dismissal of a subsequent leave application is final. That was a provision upheld as valid in *Ebert v. Official Receiver* [2002] 1 WLR 320. No such provision currently exists in Hong Kong in relation to HCO, s 27 statutory orders.

132. In Hong Kong, the power to prevent abuse of the appellate process should, in my view, be exercised by the Court of Appeal. It should limit the right of appeal of vexatious litigants who have been made the subject of a *Grepe v. Loam* order or an extended order by the Court of First Instance and who are seen to have abused the appellate process, as follows:

(a) There should in every case remain an unmodified right of appeal to the Court of Appeal against the making of the *Grepe v. Loam* order or the extended order itself. Such an appeal would be heard *inter partes*, involving the party or parties seeking to uphold the extended order.

(b) If the original order is upheld or if it has not been challenged, there should, subject to the next sub-paragraph, remain an unmodified right of appeal against the judge's dismissal of an application for leave to issue a fresh application or fresh proceedings or dismissal of those proceedings themselves (where no application for leave had been made by the vexatious litigant). Such an appeal would again be dealt with on an *inter partes* basis.

(c) In relation to appeals of the type just described, the Court of Appeal should have a discretion, whether at the hearing of the first appeal or on a subsequent occasion, if satisfied that the appellate process has been abused, to order that the vexatious litigant should in future not be permitted to appeal to the Court of Appeal against any future refusals of leave or dismissals at first instance unless permission to bring an appeal is granted by the first instance judge.

(d) Such permission to appeal might be granted by the first instance judge, for example, in relation to extended orders, where the judge decides that the fresh proceedings are caught by the extended order and that no grounds exist for granting leave to proceed with them, but acknowledges that there may be reasonable grounds for challenging that decision so that an appeal would not be an abuse of the appellate process.

(e) Where the Court of Appeal makes an order restricting appeals, a subsequent decision by the first instance judge to refuse leave to proceed with, or to dismiss, further applications or fresh proceedings, coupled with a refusal of leave to appeal to the Court of Appeal, will be final. Neither the decision nor the refusal of leave to appeal to the Court of Appeal against the decision would be susceptible to appeal.

133. In my view, the foregoing restrictions on the right of appeal in the context of *Grepe v. Loam* orders and extended orders would be consistent with the protections provided under the Basic Law and the Bill of Rights.

134. In *The Belgian Linguistic Case (No 2)* (1968) 1 EHRR 252 at 283, the Strasbourg Court approached restrictions on appeal in the context of the analogous right of access under Art 6 of the European Convention on Human Rights as follows:

> "... Article 6 of the Convention does not compel States to institute a system of appeal courts. A State which does set up such courts consequently goes beyond its obligations under Article 6. However it would violate that Article, read in conjunction with Article 14 [which prohibits discrimination], were it to debar certain persons from these remedies without a legitimate reason while making them available to others in respect of the same type of actions."

135. Citing this decision, Buxton LJ in *Ebert v. Official Receiver* (at §12), considered it "trite law that Convention jurisprudence does not require a state to provide an appellate procedure, as opposed to access to a court of first instance." It does however appear that, taken in tandem with the Article 14 right against discrimination, where an appeal is in fact provided by statute, there must not be discrimination against any particular class of persons without a legitimate reason. Similar protection against discrimination exists under Article 1 of the Hong Kong Bill of Rights which may be read in conjunction with BOR 10.

136. In any event, the Strasbourg jurisprudence accepts that a restriction on the right of access to the courts imposed on

vexatious litigants–even a blanket restriction imposed by a statutory order–is in principle acceptable as a restriction on the access right subject to the criteria of legitimacy and proportionality already discussed. Since the right of access does not imply any right of appeal it must *a fortiori* be the case that the proposed restrictions on appeal, which represent a proportionate and judicially monitored measure against abuse of process at the appellate level is legitimate in the context of BL 35. On the same grounds, such restrictions are not inconsistent with the anti–discrimination provisions of the Bill of Rights.

137. In *[A] Solicitor v. Law Society of Hong Kong and Secretary for Justice* (2003) 6 HKCFAR 570, this Court examined the validity of statutory restrictions on appeals to itself (being the Court vested with the right of final appeal by the Basic Law). In that case, the limitation was contained in legislation making appeals from the Disciplinary Committee of the Law Society to the Court of Appeal final. It was, of course, not a case involving a restriction against a litigant with a history of vexatiously abusing the process, but a general restriction for all cases. This Court accepted that even such broad restrictions were constitutionally valid provided that the limitation pursues a legitimate purpose, with reasonable proportionality between the limitation and the purpose sought to be achieved: at p 584–5, §31. This reinforces my view that where the restriction on appeals is a response to sustained abuse of the court's process and a demonstrated tendency to extend such abuse to the appellate courts, that restriction is justified.

Conclusion and costs

138. I would accordingly dismiss the appeal subject to the respondents submitting a draft order which receives the Court's approval in accordance with the directions set out in paragraph 124 above.

139. This appeal has given the Court an opportunity to give general guidance in relation to a developing area of the law. While the respondents have succeeded in upholding the jurisdiction to make an extended order on the facts of the present case, it has been necessary for the subject order to be set aside as unworkable. In these circumstances, it is appropriate that there should be no order as to costs in relation to this appeal.

140. I would accordingly make an order *nisi* that each party should bear its own costs and direct that any submissions which the parties may wish to make regarding such order *nisi* should be made in writing, filed and served on the other side within 21 days from the date of the handing down of this judgment, with any written submissions in reply filed and served within 21 days thereafter; and that, in the event that no such submissions are filed within the time limited, the order for costs should become absolute without further order.

Lord Scott of Foscote NPJ:

141. I agree with the judgment of the Chief Justice and the judgment of Mr Justice Ribeiro PJ.

Chief Justice Li:

142. The Court unanimously dismisses the appeal subject to approval by a single Permanent Judge of the Court of a draft order to be submitted by the respondents, amending the extended order made below, in accordance with the directions set out in paragraph 124. The Court also makes the costs order *nisi* set out in the final paragraph of the judgment of Mr Justice Ribeiro PJ.

Chief Justice (Andrew Li)

Permanent Judge (Kemal Bokhary)

Permanent Judge (Patrick Chan)

Permanent Judge (R A V Ribeiro)

Non-Permanent Judge (Lord Scott of Foscote)

Appellant in person

Mr Alan Leong SC and Ms Alexandra Norton (instructed by Messrs Johnson Stokes & Master) for the respondents

Mr Bernard Man *Amicus Curiae*

Former Dealing Director Of Foreground Securities Co. Ltd. Yick Ming Kit v. Securities And Futures Commission

福廣証券有限公司前交易董事易明結對 證券及期貨事務監察委員會

HCA 2966/2004；CACV 252/2005

簡略案情

原告為福廣証券有限公司（下稱“福廣証券”）前交易董事。福廣証券成立於 1993 年 7 月，為香港證券交易所會員，從事證券經紀業務。福廣証券是《證券條例》（已於 2002 年被廢除）下的註冊交易商，而原告是福廣証券註冊的唯一認可交易員。1997 年 10 月 31 日，福廣証券接到香港證券交易所電話，稱其流動資金水平低於法定要求，令其在 15 分鐘內決定是否自行停業，否則將由香港證券交易所（下稱“港交所”）勒令停業。福廣証券選擇自行停業。1999 年 1 月 25 日，證券及期貨事務監察委員會（下稱“證監會”）以行為不當為由，撤銷了原告和福廣証券的交易註冊資格，但在他們向證券及期貨上訴委員會（下稱“上訴委員會”）申請上訴期屆滿前或在上訴裁決之前，該撤銷交易員註冊的決定暫不會執行。原告和福廣証券均進行了上訴。此外，1998 年 4 月 14 日，證監會根據《證券條例》第 40 條，向福廣証券發出了一份通知，限制福廣証券在沒徵得證監會的同意前不能處理公司的資產。最後，福廣証券於 1999 年 5 月 17 日因無法支付債務及員工薪酬被頒令清盤。

在福廣証券的清盤過程中，臨時清盤人認為繼續對上訴委員會進行上訴並不符合福廣証券的利益，而且原告已經無權再代表福廣証券，因此撤回了福廣証券的上訴。但原告個人的上訴程序繼續進行。2000 年 12 月，上訴委員會經過聆訊後維持了證監會的決定，駁回了原告的上訴。原告隨後企圖根據《證券條例》第 22 條的規定，要求上訴委員會向上訴庭呈述案件，尋求上訴庭的意見，但遭到拒絕。

原告對證監會的申索理由指稱，所有的問題源於福廣証券在 1997 年被不合法地暫停證券交易，其後又被撤銷交易商註冊，導致無法支付員工工資，繼而公司破產，名譽財產遭受重大損害。同時原告認為，他向法院申訴的權利被不合理地剝奪，違反了《基本法》第 35 條、第 38 條及第 105 條。

裁決摘要

法庭認為，原告以證監會違反《證券條例》為由請求賠償是沒有法律依據的。上訴庭引述英國案例 *X (Minors)* v. *Bedfordshire County Council* [1995] 2 AC 633 指出，除非立法機關以法條明確規定，對違反公法的行為，一般也沒有申索賠償的救助。而且，法庭在考慮了整體案情，認為原告沒有任何申索的理據。就原告基於《基本法》第 35 條、第 38 條及第 105 條提出的爭議，法庭認為原告尋求司法補救的權利並未被剝奪，而是由於沒有提出合理的訴由而被拒絕。如果允許原告這種訴訟繼續進行，將造成訴權的濫用。法庭援引 *Ng Yat Chi* v. *Max Share Limited & Another* [2005] 8 HKCFAR 1 一案，指出普通法和《基本法》第 35 條規定的提起訴訟的憲法性權利不應被濫用，否則將影響其他合理案件向法院申訴的權利。

CACV 252/2005

IN THE HIGH COURT OF THE
HONG KONG SPECIAL ADMINISTRATIVE REGION
COURT OF APPEAL

CIVIL APPEAL NO. 252 OF 2005
(ON APPEAL FROM HCA NO. 2966 OF 2004)

Between:

Former Dealing Director of Foreground Securities Company Limited
Yick Ming Kit
（福廣証券有限公司前交易董事）
（易明結） Plaintiffs

- and -

Securities and Futures Commission
（証券及期貨事務監察委員會） Defendant

Before: Hon Tang JA and Chu J in Court

Date of Hearing: 18 May 2006

Date of Judgment: 18 May 2006

Date of Reasons for Judgment: 29 May 2006

REASONS FOR JUDGMENT

Hon Tang JA (giving the reasons for judgment of the Court):

Introduction

1. The plaintiff's claim against the Securities and Futures Commission ("SFC"), was struck out by Deputy Judge To on the ground that it disclosed no reasonable cause of action.

2. The plaintiff appealed to us. At the conclusion of the hearing of the appeal, we dismissed the appeal with costs to be taxed if not agreed, but reserving our reasons, which we now provide.

Background

3. The plaintiff owned and controlled Foreground Securities Company Limited ("Foreground"), which was incorporated in July 1993. Foreground was a member of the Stock Exchange of Hong Kong Limited ("Stock Exchange"). It carried on business as stock brokers. Foreground was ordered to be wound up on 17 May 1999 for its inability to pay its debt.

4. Foreground was a registered dealer under the Securities Ordinance, Cap. 333 ("Securities Ordinance"). The plaintiff was registered as Foreground's sole accredited dealer.

5. The origin of the plaintiff's claim can be traced to the end of October 1997 when trading of Foreground was suspended.

6. The plaintiff's case is that the Stock Exchange wrongly presented Foreground with the stark choice of either having its trading suspended by the Stock Exchange, or a voluntary suspension. Foreground chose a voluntary suspension. It is the plaintiff's case that all the events which he complained of resulted from this wrongful act. It seems that the following is a correct summary of the plaintiff's complaint:

> "14. ... at 9am on 31 October 1997, Ms Mandy Lam of the SEHK informed Foreground by telephone that according to SEHK's computation, Foreground did not meet the liquid capital requirement. Foreground insisted that it met the requirement and asked for an opportunity to verify and identify the discrepancy. The SEHK refused and required Foreground to decide in 15 minutes whether voluntarily to suspend trading or be ordered to suspend. Foreground voluntarily suspended trading." See Decision of the Securities and Futures Appeals Panel dated 17 May 2001."

It is unnecessary for the purpose of this appeal for the court to determine whether there was any basis for the Stock Exchange's view that Foreground had inadequate liquid capital as at 29 October 1997.

7. The events which followed included the winding up of Foreground as well as the revocation of the registration of Foreground and the plaintiff as registered dealers by the SFC.

8. We deal with their revocation as dealers first.

9. On 1 September 1998, two letters of Mindedness were sent to Foreground and the plaintiff respectively informing them of the tentative conclusion that their dealers' registration would be revoked on the ground of misconduct. It is unnecessary to go into the grounds alleged in the letters.

10. Following representations by Foreground and the plaintiff on 25 January 1999, by two letters of the same date together with a statement of reasons under Section 56(4) of the Securities Ordinance, Foreground and the plaintiff were informed of the SFC's decision to revoke their registration as dealers under the Securities Ordinance. Each of these letters concluded by informing Foreground and the plaintiff respectively, that the decision would not come into effect until the time for the making of an appeal against the decision had expired or, when an appeal was made, the appeal was determined or withdrawn. Foreground and the plaintiff were entitled to appeal to the Securities and Futures Appeals Panel ("the Panel") under Section 19(1) and 21(3)(a) of the Securities and Futures Commission Ordinance, Cap. 24 ("SFC Ordinance"). If an appeal is lodged, the SFC's decision would not come into operation until the appeal is determined or withdrawn in Section 21(4) of the SFC Ordinance.

11. On 22 February 1999, both the plaintiff and Foreground duly appealed to the Panel.

12. On 14 April 1998, the SFC issued a notice under Section 40 of the SFC Ordinance restricting dealings of assets by Foreground. The notice is in the following terms:

> "THE COMMISSION HEREBY GIVES NOTICE THAT
>
> Foreground Securities Company Limited, a registered securities dealer and member of the Stock Exchange of Hong Kong Limited is, pursuant to section 40 of the SFC Ordinance, required until further notice, -
>
> (a) to obtain the prior written consent of the Commission before dealing, in any manner, with any asset held by it, whether as principal or agent. Such consent to be granted by the Executive Director of Intermediaries Division or Director of the Intermediaries Supervision Department.
>
> THE COMMISSION HEREBY CONSENTS AS FOLLOWS:

(b) Foreground Securities Company Ltd may, until further notice, take all actions necessary to settle securities transactions in the Central Clearing and Settlement System in Hong Kong, including, but not limited to, the related delivery or receipt of securities and funds and matters incidental thereto.

This Notice comes into effect on 14 April 1998.

Under sections 19, 21(3) and 44 of the SFC Ordinance, an appeal may be made to the Securities and Futures Appeals Panel against this Notice by any person on whom it is served, within thirty days commencing on the day on which this Notice is served on that person. An appeal will not affect the coming into force of this Notice.

By virtue of section 43 of the SFC Ordinance, a person on whom the Notice is served or who is affected by it may apply to the Commission for the Notice to be withdrawn, substituted or varied."

13. The Statement of Reasons required under Section 42(3)(a) of the SFC Ordinance are (where relevant) in the following terms:

"2. In the course of an inspection of Foreground Securities Company Limited by Commission staff, it was found that:

a) Foreground Securities Company Limited had pledged cash clients' securities to obtain banking facilities without obtaining proper authorization; and

b) Foreground Securities Company Limited and its related company, Foreground Finance Company Limited had liquidity and solvency problem.

3. Foreground Securities Company Limited voluntarily suspended its business on 31 October 1997 and had since been looking for a new buyer to purchase a majority stake in the company and to inject additional funding. On 24 March 1998, Foreground Securities Company Limited admitted there appeared to be no serious interested buyer.

4. On 25 March 1998, the Stock Exchange of Hong Kong Limited suspended the membership of Foreground Securities Company Limited. The Commission also suspended the registration of Foreground Securities Company Limited for breaches of the requirements of Financial Resources Rules under section 65c(2)(a) of the Securities Ordinance on the same day.

5. The Commission has therefore decided to exercise its powers under section 40 of the SFC Ordinance to restrict Foreground Securities Company Limited on its dealing with assets in the manner specified in the restriction notice issued on 14 April 1998, on the ground that the exercise of the powers is desirable in the interest of the investing public."

14. One of the plaintiff's complaints in relation to the winding up proceedings is that Foreground was unable to pay its employees' wages as a result of the Section 40 notice. In the reasons handed down by Le Pichon J (as she then was) on 31 May 1999, it was recorded that Foreground was indebted to the petitioner as well as to seven other employees for about $830,000. In relation to the plaintiff's complaint that Foreground was unable to pay because of the Section 40 notice, Le Pichon J said in para. 5 of her reasons:

"It is immediately obvious that there was nothing to prevent the Company from applying to the SFC for payment of an award made by the Labour Tribunal. Under the terms of the restriction notice, all that was required was prior consent from the SFC. Clearly, an application could and should have been made by the Company to the SFC to meet the award. It was not. In fact, nothing has been done by the Company to have the restriction notice (which has been in place for over a year) removed. Effectively, the Company has not been doing any business since its imposition."

15. Foreground had not appealed or applied to vary the Section 40 notice.

16. Following the appointment of the Official Receiver as the provisional liquidator of Foreground, the Section 40 notice was withdrawn on 21 June 1999.

17. On 3 April 2000, Messrs Joseph Lo kin-ching and Dermot Agnew, both of Deloitte Touche Tohmatsu, were appointed joint and several liquidators of Foreground on 3 April 2000.

18. By letter dated 10 May 2000, the liquidators informed the Panel that the liquidators did not consider that continuing the Foreground's appeal against its registration as a dealer would be beneficial to the winding up or the creditors, and that the plaintiff had no authority to represent Foreground in the appeal.

19. As a result, on 19 December 2000, the appeal by Foreground was dismissed on the ground that it had been abandoned by the liquidators of Foreground and that the plaintiff had no right to pursue the appeal on behalf of Foreground.

20. However, the plaintiff's own appeal proceeded and on 29 December 2000, after hearings on 19 and 21 December 2000, the Panel confirmed the decision of SFC to revoke the registration of the plaintiff as a dealing director of Foreground. In its reasons, the Panel said:

"43. The Tribunal is unanimously of the view that, in view of

(a) the Appellant's own admission before this Tribunal that he had been over aggressive in margin lending;

(b) Foreground's continuing breach of the Financial Resources Rules since 30 November 1997;

(c) the opinion of Foreground's liquidators that there was no prospect for Foreground to resume its business in the future;

(d) the Appellant as the sole dealing director of Foreground is responsible for Foreground's state of affairs, and

(e) a dealing director may carry on business only in relation to his corporation,

the Appellant is not a fit and proper person to be registered as a dealer. The decision of the Respondent is thus confirmed."

21. Subsequently, the plaintiff applied under Section 22 of the SFC Ordinance to the Panel to state a case for the consideration of the Court of Appeal. The application was made late and in any event, on 27 July 2001, the Panel refused to state the case because:

"We do not find that the applicant has raised or established any question of law which is fit for reference to the Court of Appeal relating to his appeal. Therefore, his application is refused."

Plaintiff's claim

22. We now turn to the statement of claim. The substance of the plaintiff's claim is that everything could be traced to the suspension of trading, thus he said:

"萬佛歸宗都是由於被暫停証券交易開始所致，上訴人的生計斷絕，精神受困擾，名譽財產遭受重大損害。這是在不公平、不公正原則下進行的上訴聆訊！因此，要求平反恢復上訴人交易商的註冊。並且要求名譽及財產重大損失的賠償。"

23. The learnt Deputy Judge in a carefully prepared and detailed judgment analyzed and dealt with each of the complaints which could be discerned from the plaintiff's statement of claim. We are in complete agreement with the learned Deputy Judge. That being the case, it is only necessary for us to state our reasons briefly.

Claim against SFC

24. Insofar as the plaintiff's claim against the SFC is based on the SFC's breaches of statutory duties under the SFC Ordinance, we agree with the judge that on the proper construction of the SFC Ordinance, no private law cause of action was created in favour of registered dealers such as the plaintiff. As Lord Browne-Wilkinson in *X (Minors) v. Bedfordshire County Council* [1995] 2 AC 633 at 730:

"... The breach of a public law right by itself gives rise to no claim for damages. A claim for damages must be based on a private law cause of action."

25. And at 731:

"The principles applicable in determining whether such statutory cause of action exists are now well established, although the application of those principles in any particular case remains difficult. The basic proposition is that in the ordinary case a breach of statutory duty does not, by itself, give rise to any private law cause of action. However, a private law cause of action will arise if it can be shown, as a matter of construction of the statute, that the statutory duty was imposed for the protection of a limited class of the public and that parliament intended to confer on members of that class a private right of action for breach of the duty."

26. In *Kaisilk Development Limited v. Urban Renewal Authority* [2004] 1 HKLRD 907, a decision of this court, the same approach was adopted by this court in relation to an attempt to bring a private law action against the Land Development Corporation under the Land Development Corporation Ordinance, Cap. 15, on the basis that the Land Development Corporation had failed to take reasonable steps to acquire property, prior to seeking resumption.

27. We believe it is clear that no private cause of action was created by the SFC Ordinance in favour of registered dealers such as Foreground or the plaintiff. If a registered dealer is aggrieved by the SFC's decision to revoke its registration, the redress provided by the SFC Ordinance is one of appeal to the Panel, followed possibly by a case stated on a point of law to the Court of Appeal.

28. It is not clear whether the plaintiff also complained of breaches of duties under the Securities Ordinance since the revocation of Foreground and his registration as dealers were made under the Securities Ordinance. For the sake of completion, we would state that no private cause of action was created under the Securities Ordinance.

29. As for the plaintiff's claim for damages. Insofar as the claim for damages is based on the suspension of trading of Foreground in October 1997, we agree with the judge that the proper claimant for such damages is Foreground and not the plaintiff. It would also seem that the proper defendant would be the Stock Exchange and not the SFC. Moreover, we also agree with the judge that in any event, any such claim has become statue barred prior to the commencement of the present action.

30. The plaintiff also relied on Articles 35, 38 and 105 of the Basic Law, and claimed that he has been denied access to the court. The plaintiff has not been denied access to the court. The plaintiff's claim has been struck out on the basis that it did not disclose a reasonable cause of action. It would have been an abuse of process to permit the claim to continue. As the Chief Justice has said in *Ng Yat Chi v. Max Share Limited and Another* [2005] 8 HKCFAR 1, at para. 5 in page 14:

"The right of access

5. The constitutional right of access to the courts is well established under the common law and is guaranteed by the Basic Law (art.35). But it would be absurd to suggest that the right of access involves a right to abuse the court's process. The pursuit of abusive proceedings would be an improper exercise of the right of access and may be regarded as adversely affecting the right of access of others with meritorious cases."

31. Lastly, the plaintiff submitted that the SFC Ordinance had been repealed by Securities and Futures Ordinance, Cap. 571 ("SFO"). The SFO came into effect on 1 April 2003 and that the SFC Ordinance has been repealed by it as from 1 April 2003. Since the events complained of by the plaintiff took place well before 1 April 2003. The repeal of the SFC Ordinance is irrelevant. Again, for the sake of completeness, we add that the repeal of the Securities Ordinance is also irrelevant.

32. The plaintiff also complained of alleged delay by the SFC regarding the hearing of his appeal to the Panel. We have seen no evidence of that. The three letters dated 26 March, 9 April and 11 May 1999 from SFC's counsel to the Panel referred to by the plaintiff, do not show the SFC to have delayed the hearing of the appeal. On the contrary, the third letter revealed that the plaintiff's own counsel had until then not responded to the Panel's request in March 1999 for an estimate of the length of the appeal hearing and indication of the available dates of counsel. But in any event, it cannot give rise to a private law cause of action and is therefore irrelevant.

Justice of Appeal (Robert Tang)

Judge of the Court of First Instance (Carlye Chu)

The Plaintiff (Appellant), in person, present.

Mr Jose-Antonie [*sic*] Maurellet, instructed by Messrs Clifford Chance, for the Defendant (Respondent).

CACV 252/2005

IN THE HIGH COURT OF THE

HONG KONG SPECIAL ADMINISTRATIVE REGION

COURT OF APPEAL

CIVIL APPEAL NO. 252 OF 2005
(ON APPEAL FROM HCA NO. 2966 OF 2004)

Between:

Former Dealing Director of Foreground Securities Company Limited Yick Ming Kit （福廣証券有限公司前交易董事）（易明結）	Plaintiffs
- and -	
Securities and Futures Commission （証券及期貨事務監察委員會）	Defendant

Before: Hon Yuen and Tang JJA in Court

Date of Hearing: 29 September 2006

Date of Judgment: 29 September 2006

JUDGMENT

Hon Tang JA (giving the judgment of the Court):

1. This is the plaintiff's application for leave to appeal to the Court of Final Appeal from the reasons for decision of this court (Tang JA and Chu J) which was handed down on 29 May 2006, which affirmed the judgment of Deputy Judge To, striking out the statement of claim on the ground that it disclosed no reasonable cause of action.

2. The sole issue on this application is whether leave should be granted under section 22(1)(b) of the Hong Kong Court of Final Appeal Ordinance, Cap. 484. No point is taken on the application being made out of time.

3. The written submissions supplied by the plaintiff, which we have considered, contain a litany of complaints against the Securities and Futures Commission. However, the issues involved in these proceedings had been identified in the judgment, and the most important for the present purpose is that the relevant legislation had not created a private cause of action. No question of great general or public importance is involved in this proposed appeal. In fact, the proposed appeal is completely devoid of merit.

4. So the application is dismissed with costs.

Justice of Appeal (Maria Yuen)

Justice of Appeal (Robert Tang)

The Plaintiff (Applicant), in person, present.

Mr Jose-Antonio Maurellet, instructed by Messrs Clifford Chance, for the Defendant (Respondent).

Lau Kwok Fai Bernard v. Commissioner Of Police Secretary For The Civil Service

Lau Kwok Fai Bernard 對 警務處長及公務員事務局局長

HCAL 95/2003；CACV 93/2005

簡略案情

申請人為一名警官，於 1983 年 1 月加入警隊成為督察，1988 年晉升為高級督察。2000 年 9 月，申請人因交通扣分制度被停牌 6 個月。同年 11 月，申請人被捕並被控超速、停牌期間駕駛及在沒有第三者保險的情況下駕駛。申請人承認上述指控並認罪，被判處罰款和停牌 16 個月。

由於此刑事罪行行為，警務處處長對申請人做出處罰決定（下稱“第一次處罰決定”），包括：1）由即日起停職且不發放薪金；2）申請人若要離開香港，須提前 24 小時通知警署，如果其離開香港將影響停職期間每日報到的責任，則需要預先取得警務處處長的許可；3）未經警務處處長允許，申請人不得從事任何有報酬的僱傭工作。

2001 年 10 月，申請人又被控非禮前下屬女警員，經審訊後被裁定罪名成立，申請人對該判罪的上訴均被駁回。2003 年 6 月，公務員事務局局長，對申請人做出處罰決定，即：1）因應非禮罪名，自 2003 年 6 月 13 日起被革職；2）因應超速、無牌駕駛、無保險駕駛等事由被嚴重譴責和沒收共兩個月薪金；3）被解僱後退休金和長俸等福利待遇亦予以沒收。

申請人就上述兩個處罰申請司法覆核。其依據的理由是：

1）第一次處罰決定中規定其離開香港需要提前 24 小時通知警署，如果影響其每日報到的責任則須預先取得許可，該決定侵犯了其遷徙自由權。《基本法》第 31 條規定，香港居民有在香港特別行政區境內遷徙的自由，有移居其他國家和地區的自由。香港居民有旅行和出入境的自由。有效旅行證件的持有人，除非受到法律制止，可自由離開香港特別行政區，無需特別批准。《香港人權法案》第 8 條亦規定，合法處在香港境內的人，在香港境內有遷徙往來之自由及擇居之自由；人人應有自由離開香港。根據《警隊條例》第 46 條規定而頒佈的《警察通例》第 6 章 6-06 條規定，可以對停職警官課以報到的責任，並且命令停職警官在準備離開香港前預先通知警務處處長。申請人認為上述規定和第一次處罰決定違反了《基本法》和《香港人權法案》規定的基本權利。

2）因第一次處罰決定後停止向其發放薪金，致使其在非禮罪的訴訟中無力聘請心儀的律師，違背了《基本法》第 35 條和《香港人權法案》第 11 條。《基本法》第 35 條規定，香港居民有權得到秘密法律諮詢、向法院提起訴訟、選擇律師及時保護自己的合法權益或在法庭上為其代理和獲得司法補救。

裁決摘要

對於第一個申請理由，原審法官認為，《警察通例》第 6 章 6-06 條並未禁止停職警員離開香港，而是要求其離開香港前需要提前 24 小時書面通知，問題在於該提前通知的限制是否不合比例，是否違反了遷徙自由權。答辯人認為，首先，停職警員可能需要面對刑事和紀律聆訊，令其離開香港前事先通知有利於保證該等程序不會因其缺席而無法進行；其次，上訴人的上司可能需要就個人或財務問題詢問上訴人，所以是項通知的要求也是基於行政管理的需要。原審法官同意答辯人的意見，並考慮到僅僅要求提前 24 小時通知且在某些特定情況下可以延遲或事後通知，而且申請人也有可能獲得豁免，認為《警察通例》第 6 章 6-06 條的限制是合乎比例的，未對遷徙自由權造成不適當的限制。

至於第二個上訴理由，原審法官援引 *Dr Ip Kay Lo v. Medical Council Of Hong Kong* [2003] 3 HKLRD 851 一案認為，《基本法》第 35 條規定的權利不是一項絕對的權利，它跟政府提供的免費法律服務沒有關係，也不意味著當事人有權在律師無法代理或者不願意代理的情形下堅持聘請某個律師。《基本法》第 35 條的基本要求是保證當事人有機會尋求法律代表並且獲得公正審訊。根據 *R v. Fu Yan* [1992] 2 HKPLR 109, and *R v. Mirchandani* [1992] 2 HKPLR 196 一案，《香港人權法案》第 11 條同樣不包含絕對的權利，不意味著必然的免費法律援助。申請人主張其未能以自身意願選擇的律師來進行上訴，這並無憲法性的保障，保證申請人的上訴由其選中的律師代表。因此申請人的理由不能成立。最後，法院拒絕了覆核的申請。申請人遂上訴至上訴庭。

關於《警察通例》第 6 章 6-06 條有否違反《基本法》的問題，上訴法庭對原審法官的意見有保留，認為《基本法》第 31 條和《香港人權法案》第 8 條規定的遷徙自由只能被法律規定所限制，僅憑《警隊條例》第 46 條或《警察通例》這樣的一般性條款對其進行限制是有疑問的。但是就本案而言，對申請人的處罰很久前就已作出，申請人沒有說明為何不更早提出覆核申請的理由，因此上訴庭拒絕他的上訴，維持原審法官的裁決。

CACV93/2005

IN THE HIGH COURT OF THE

HONG KONG SPECIAL ADMINISTRATIVE REGION

COURT OF APPEAL

CIVIL APPEAL NO. 93 OF 2005
(ON APPEAL FROM HCAL NO. 95 OF 2003)

BETWEEN:

LAU KWOK FAI BERNARD	Applicant
- and -	
COMMISSIONER OF POLICE	1st Respondent
SECRETARY FOR THE CIVIL SERVICE	2nd Respondent

Before: Hon Ma CJHC, Stock & Tang JJA in Court

Date of Hearing: 10 October 2006

Date of Judgment: 10 October 2006

Date of Handing Down Reasons for Judgment: 31 October 2006

REASONS FOR JUDGMENT

Hon Ma CJHC:

1. By a judgment handed down on 29 December 2004, Chu J dismissed the Applicant's application for judicial review in relation to two decisions: a decision of the Commissioner of Police ("the Commissioner") dated 1 June 2001 and the decision of the Secretary for the Civil Service ("the SCS") dated 10 June 2003. The Applicant appealed the dismissal of his application. On 10 October 2006, after hearing counsel (Mr Philip Dykes SC for the Applicant, Mr Anthony Ismail for the two Respondents), we dismissed the appeal with costs, with the Reasons for Judgment to be handed down.

2. The facts have been carefully set out in Chu J's judgment and I need only refer to them in summary:-

(1) The Applicant was a police officer, joining the Force in January 1983 and rising to become a Senior Inspector in 1988.

(2) On 18 September 2000, he was disqualified for driving for a period of 6 months, having accumulated sufficient demerit points to justify a disqualification. On 19 November 2000, he was arrested and later charged for speeding, driving while disqualified and driving without third party insurance. On 31 May 2001, he pleaded guilty to all charges (having initially contested them), and was fined and disqualified from driving all classes of vehicles for 16 months.

(3) Following these convictions, by a decision of the Commissioner made on 1 June 2001 ("the first Decision"), it was ordered that:-

(a) the Applicant be interdicted from duty with effect from 1 June 2001;

(b) no pay or allowance be payable to the Applicant with effect from that date;

(c) the Applicant be required to give to the Commissioner at least 24 hours advance notification in writing of any intention to leave Hong Kong, and to seek exemption from the Commissioner should he wish to leave Hong Kong for any period that would affect the daily reporting conditions associated with his interdiction; and

(d) the Applicant was not to take up any form of paid employment without the permission of the Commissioner.

(4) The Applicant was informed of the first Decision by a memorandum dated 1 June 2001. The memorandum also informed the Applicant that consideration was being given to recommending to the Chief Executive that a terminatory award be imposed on him under section 37(5) of the Police Force Ordinance, Cap.232. He was given a period of 14 days to make representations to the Commissioner and the Applicant did so on 15 June 2001.

(5) However, before the Commissioner could make any recommendation to the Chief Executive, the Applicant was charged with the indecent assault of a woman police officer who was a subordinate of the Applicant. The Commissioner thereupon decided to withhold making any recommendation until the Applicant's trial. On 22 October 2001, the Applicant was convicted of indecent assault and fined $3,000. His appeal to the Court of First Instance was dismissed on 12 July 2002 and his application to the Appeal Committee of the Court of Final Appeal for leave to appeal was likewise dismissed on 18 September 2002.

(6) After being invited by the Commissioner to make submissions as to why his service should not be terminated, the Applicant did so on 2 November 2002. On 16 December 2002, the Commissioner (through the Deputy Commissioner of Police (Management) by delegated power) made recommendations to the Chief Executive. The Applicant was permitted to make representations to the Chief Executive as well as comment on the recommendations made by the processing officers of the Civil Service Bureau.

(7) On 9 June 2003, the SCS, as the delegate of the Chief Executive, made the following award against the Applicant ("the second Decision"), namely that:-

(a) the Applicant be dismissed with effect from 13 June 2003 for his criminal conviction for indecent assault;

(b) he be severely reprimanded and that there be forfeiture of one month's pay with effect from 10 June 2003 in relation to the conviction for the offence of driving whilst disqualified;

(c) the Applicant be severely reprimanded and that there be forfeiture of one month's pay with effect from 10 June 2003 in relation to the conviction for the offence of driving without third party insurance;

(d) he be reprimanded with effect from 10 June 2003 in relation to the conviction for the offence of speeding; and

(e) upon dismissal, the Applicant would forfeit all claims to any pension, gratuity and any other benefits or advantages, as well as to the emoluments withheld during interdiction.

(8) The Applicant was informed of this award by a letter dated 10 June 2003.

3. On 15 September 2003, the Applicant applied for leave to issue judicial review proceedings in relation to the two Decisions. Leave was granted on 3 October 2003. In his application for judicial review, the Applicant relied on 8 grounds to challenge the Decisions. As stated above, Chu J dismissed the application.

4. The Notice of Appeal dated 9 March 2005 contained some 15 grounds of appeal, 6 in relation to the first Decision, 9 in relation to the second Decision. The hearing of the appeal was originally fixed to be heard on 19 October 2005 but the day before, the Applicant applied for legal aid. This necessitated an adjournment of the appeal by reason of section 15 of the Legal Aid Ordinance, Cap.91. The appeal was restored for hearing on 10 October 2006.

5. Mr Dykes was instructed late in the appeal before us. We are grateful to him for dealing with the appeal in these circumstances.

6. Notwithstanding the number of grounds contained in the Notice of Appeal, Mr Dykes essentially sought to raise only two arguments:

(1) The first related to the second Decision. The Applicant contended that the forfeiture of his pension, gratuity and other advantages and emoluments could not be ordered unless the Public Service Commission ("the PSC") had first been consulted. Reference was made to section 18 of the Public Service (Administration) Order. It was said that there may have been no proper consultation with the PSC and that what consultation there may have been, was only informal. This was an entirely new ground of challenge to the second Decision, hitherto not raised.

(2) The other ground of appeal related to the first Decision. Mr Dykes argued that the condition whereby the Applicant was required to give 24 hours notice in writing of his intention to leave Hong Kong and to seek prior exemption for leaving Hong Kong if this affected his daily reporting conditions, was an impermissible restriction of the Applicant's right to freedom of movement (guaranteed under Article 31 of the Basic Law and Article 8(3) of the Hong Kong Bill of Rights). Reliance was placed on the decision of Keith J in *The Association of Expatriate Civil Servants of Hong Kong v. The Chief Executive of HKSAR* [1998] 1 HKLRD 615 and of the Court of Final Appeal in *The Official Receiver and Trustee in bankruptcy of Chan Wing Hing v. Chan Wing Hing*, FACV7/2006, unreported, 20 July 2006.

7. Both points can be quite quickly disposed of in the circumstances of the present case.

8. As to the proposed ground of appeal relevant to the second Decision (relating to the loss of pension and other benefits), we refused leave to the Applicant to raise the point at this stage. Not only was it extremely late, the proper consideration of the point required the admission of new evidence. No evidence was placed before us in support of this new ground although it was hinted at in the Skeleton Arguments. There was no explanation given for only raising this point at a very late stage either.

9. In relation to the ground of appeal touching on the freedom of movement, this was raised in the Form 86A and dealt with by the judge. It is, with respect, certainly an arguable point. The requirements in Article 31 of the Basic Law and Article 8(3) of the Bill of Rights that any restriction on the right can only be by restraint or provision of law may not necessarily be satisfied merely by general provisions such as that contained in section 46 of the Police Force Ordinance (the power of the Commissioner to make Police General Orders). However, in the context of the present case, the point is entirely an academic one: the effects of the first Decision have long been overtaken by the second Decision. Besides, the first Decision was made as long ago as June 2001 and there was no reason why the alleged offending part of that decision could not have been challenged much sooner. There is of course jurisdiction in the court to deal with so called academic points (see *Chit Fai Motors Co Ltd v. Commissioner for Transport* [2004] 1 HKC 465 at paragraph 20; *Leung T C William Roy v. Secretary for Justice*, unreported, CACV317/2005, 20 September 2006), but there must be good reason to compel the court to do so. There is none in the present case.

10. The judge, however, dealt with the point in her judgment and concluded that section 46 of the Police Force Ordinance provided a sufficient legal basis to permit the existence of Police General Orders that could be used to restrict the freedom of movement of police officers. She also concluded that the relevant Police General Order satisfied the proportionality test. For the reasons above stated, we are of the view that argument before us on this point is not now justified. Although the judge's decision on the point can in a sense be said to remain (since we have upheld the decision on another ground), it should not be thought that the contrary view is not arguable: far from it, it does have some substance although admittedly we have not heard extensive argument on the point.

11. For the above reasons, the appeal was dismissed with costs.

Hon Stock JA:

12. I agree.

Hon Tang JA:

13. I agree.

Chief Judge, High Court (Geoffrey Ma)

Justice of Appeal (Frank Stock)

Justice of Appeal (Robert Tang)

Mr Philip Dykes SC, instructed by Messrs Henry Wan & Yeung for the Applicant/ Appellant

Mr Anthony Ismail, instructed by the Department of Justice for the 1st & 2nd Respondents/ Respondents

---

HCAL95/2003

IN THE HIGH COURT OF THE
HONG KONG SPECIAL ADMINISTRATIVE REGION
COURT OF FIRST INSTANCE

CONSTITUTIONAL AND ADMINISTRATIVE LAW LIST
(NO. 95 OF 2003)

BETWEEN:

LAU KWOK FAI BERNARD — Applicant

- and -

COMMISSIONER OF POLICE — 1st Respondent
SECRETARY FOR THE CIVIL SERVICE — 2nd Respondent

Before: Hon Chu J in Court

Date of Hearing: 17 & 28 May 2004

Date of Judgment: 29 December 2004

JUDGMENT

1. In these proceedings, the applicant applies to judicial review the following decisions:

(1) The decision of the Commissioner of Police ("the Commissioner") made on 1 June 2001 whereby the applicant was interdicted from duty with effect from 1 June 2001, in consequence thereof:

(a) no pay or allowance was paid to the applicant with effect from 1 June 2001,

(b) the applicant was required to give to the Commissioner at least 24 hours advance notification in writing of his intention to leave Hong Kong, and to seek exemption from the Commissioner should he wish to leave Hong Kong for any period that would affect the daily reporting condition associated with his interdiction; and

(c) the applicant might not take up any form of paid employment without the permission of the Commissioner.

(2) The decision of the Secretary for the Civil Service ("the Secretary") dated 10 June 2003, as delegate of the Chief Executive, imposing punishments as follows:

(a) dismissal with effect from 13 June 2003 for the conviction of indecent assault,

(b) severe reprimand and forfeiture of one month's pay for the conviction of driving whilst disqualified,

(c) severe reprimand and forfeiture of one month's pay for the conviction of driving without third party insurance, and

(d) reprimand for the conviction of speeding.

THE FACTUAL BACKGROUND

2. The applicant joined the Police Force as an inspector in January 1983. In 1988, he was promoted to be senior inspector.

3. On 18 September 2000, the applicant was disqualified from driving all classes of vehicles under the points demerit system for a period of six months. Two months into the disqualification period on 19 November 2000, the applicant was found driving a private car at a speed of 147.8 kmh when the speed limit at the location was 100 kmh. The applicant was arrested and charged with three offences of speeding, driving whilst disqualified and driving without third party insurance. He pleaded not guilty at the first court appearance. At the hearing on 31 May 2001, he changed his plea and admitted the brief facts. He was convicted of all charges, and was fined and disqualified from driving all classes of vehicles for 16 months. There was no review or appeal against the convictions and sentences.

4. As a result of the convictions, the Assistant Commissioner of Police (Personnel) in exercise of his delegated power, directed that the applicant be interdicted from duty with effect from 1 June 2001. The applicant was informed of the decision by a memo from the Commissioner dated 1 June 2001. By the same memo, the applicant was informed that under section 37(4) of the Police Force Ordinance ("PFO"), no pay or allowance was payable to him. The applicant was also reminded that he could not take up any form of paid employment without the permission of the Commissioner, and that he was required to notify the Commissioner in writing of his intention to leave Hong Kong at least 24 hours before departing and was also required to fulfil reporting condition associated with his interdiction in accordance with the Police General Order 6–06(1) ("GPO 6–01(1)"). The memo further informed the applicant that consideration was being given to recommending to the Chief Executive that a terminatory reward be imposed on him under section 37(5) of the PFO and the applicant was invited to show cause within 14 days why his service should not be terminated.

5. On 15 June 2001, the applicant made his representation to the Commissioner. Prior to that, the applicant was charged with an offence of indecent assault and was awaiting trial. The Commissioner therefore decided to withhold any recommendation to the Chief Executive for punishment in connection with the traffic offences pending the determination of the indecent assault case.

6. On 22 October 2001, the applicant was convicted after trial of the offence of indecent assault. The victim involved was a serving woman police constable who was an ex-subordinate of the applicant. The incident took place on 14 April 2001 after a dinner at a restaurant attended by the applicant and a group of his colleagues, including the victim. The applicant embraced the victim from behind, touched her breast and asked her to spend the night with him. The victim refused and struggled to get free. The applicant was fined $3000 for the conviction.

7. On 24 October 2001, the Commissioner informed the applicant that he would recommend to the Chief Executive that a terminatory punishment be imposed on him under section 37(5) of the PFO and invited the applicant to make representation as to why his service should not be terminated.

8. The applicant appealed against the conviction of indecent assault. By a memo dated 15 November 2001, the Commissioner informed the applicant that action under section 37(5) of the PFO would be suspended pending the determination of the appeal.

9. On 12 July 2002, the Court of First Instance dismissed the applicant's appeal. The applicant's application for leave

to appeal to the Court of Final Appeal was dismissed by the Appeal Committee on 18 September 2002. By a memo dated 16 October 2002, the Commissioner invited the applicant to make representations in mitigation of punishment. On 2 November 2002, the applicant submitted his written representations.

10. On 16 December 2002, the Deputy Commissioner of Police (Management) in exercise of his delegated power, made recommendation to the Chief Executive to impose the following punishments on the applicant under section 37(5) of the PFO:

(1) Speeding	Reprimand
(2) Driving whilst disqualified	Compulsory retirement with deferred benefit
(3) Driving without third party Insurance	Compulsory retirement with deferred benefit
(4) Indecent assault	Dismissal

11. By a memo of the same date, the applicant was served with a copy of the recommendation and was invited to make representations to the Chief Executive within 14 days on any awards that he may make under section 37(5) of the PFO.

12. On 3 January 2003, the applicant requested the Civil Service Bureau ("CSB") to provide him with a copy of the transcript of his trial on the indecent assault case, and further requested for the time to make representations be extended to after receipt of the court transcript. By a letter dated 10 January 2003, the CSB replied that it did not have the court transcript and the applicant was told to approach the relevant authority to obtain the same.

13. On 18 February and 14 March 2003, the applicant submitted his written representations to the Chief Executive.

14. Having considered the applicant's representations, the processing officers of the CSB agreed with the Commissioner on the recommendations relating to the convictions of indecent assault and speeding, but disagreed with the recommendations on the convictions of driving whilst disqualified and driving without third party insurance. In respect of each of the latter two convictions, the processing officers recommended severe reprimand and forfeiture of one month's pay as punishment.

15. On 10 May 2003, the processing officers' comments were forwarded to the applicant for his representations, if any, within 14 days. The applicant applied on 2 June 2003, after the 14 days' period, for an extension of time to make representations. A three days' extension was given. The letter notifying the applicant of the extension was handed to him personally on 3 June 2003.

16. The applicant did not make any representation within the extended period. On 9 June 2003, the Secretary, acting as the Chief Executive's delegate to award punishment under section 37(5) of the PFO decided to award the following punishments against the applicant:

(1) Speeding	Reprimand
(2) Driving whilst disqualified	Severe reprimand with forfeiture of one month's pay
(3) Driving without third party Insurance	Severe reprimand with forfeiture of one month's pay
(4) Indecent assault	Dismissal

17. By a letter dated 10 June 2003, the applicant was informed of the Secretary's decision. The dismissal took effect on 13 June 2003.

THE JUDICIAL REVIEW APPLICATION

18. On 15 September 2003, the applicant applied for leave to judicial review. Leave to judicial review was granted on 3 October 2004. On 17 October 2003, the applicant filed the Notice of Motion.

19. In his Form 86A, the applicant seeks the following relief:

(1) A declaration that the Commissioner's decision to interdict the applicant from duty is inconsistent with section 17(1) (a) of the PFO and is unlawful, irrational and unfair and of no effect.

(2) A declaration that the Commissioner's decision ordering that no pay or allowance be payable to the applicant is unlawful, irrational and unfair and of no effect.

(3) A declaration that the Commissioner's decision requiring the applicant to give prior written notice of his intention to leave Hong Kong and to seek exemption from the Commissioner should he wish to leave Hong Kong for any period that would affect the daily reporting condition associated with his interdiction, is in breach of Article 31 of the Basic Law ("BL") and Article 8 of the Hong Kong Bill of Rights Ordinance ("BORO"), cap. 383 and is unconstitutional, unlawful and of no effect.

(4) A declaration that the Commissioner's decision as a whole is in breach of Article 35 of the BL and is unconstitutional, unlawful and of no effect.

(5) A declaration that the Commissioner's decision as a whole is in breach of Article 11 of the BORO and is unconstitutional, unlawful and of no effect.

(6) Remedies for contravention of the BORO as stipulated in section 6, Part I of the BORO.

(7) A declaration that the Secretary's decision is unlawful, procedurally unfair, irrational and of no effect.

THE COMMISSIONER'S DECISION

20. The applicant challenges the Commissioner's decision on a total of eight grounds. I will deal with them in the sequence as they are set out in the Form 86A.

(1) Interdiction unlawful

21. The applicant's first ground of challenge is that the interdiction was unlawful in that section 17(1) (a) of the PFO did not extend to interdiction for conviction for criminal offence.

22. Section 17(1) (a) of the PFO provides that:

"(1) If the Commissioner considers that the public interest requires that a police officer other than a gazetted police officer should cease to exercise the powers and functions of his office forthwith, he may interdict the police officer from the exercise of such powers and functions where -

(a) disciplinary or criminal proceedings are being instituted or are about to be instituted against such officer; or ..."

23. The applicant contends that when the decision to interdict him was made on 1 June 2001, there was no criminal or disciplinary proceedings being or about to be instituted because the criminal proceedings relating to the three traffic offences were concluded on 31 May 2001 upon the pronouncement of his convictions and the passing of sentences, and the action under section 37(5) of the PFO was not disciplinary proceedings.

24. For the respondent, it is argued that the criminal proceedings did not cease to be instituted on 31 May 2001 in that the time for review or appeal remained operative for 14 days thereafter. It is further argued that disciplinary proceedings under section 37(5) of the PFO were being or about to be instituted against the applicant when the decision to interdict was made on 1 June 2001.

25. In my view, the applicant's contention is misconceived. While it may be said that the proceedings before the Magistrate relating to the three traffic offences came to an end when the applicant was convicted and sentenced on 31 May 2001, plainly on 1 June 2001 disciplinary proceedings against the applicant were being instituted or to be instituted. It is for this reason that he was invited by the same memo to make representation to the Chief Executive as to why a terminatory punishment should not be made. There is no merit in the applicant's argument that action under section 37(5) of the PFO does not entail disciplinary proceedings. Section 37(5) allows the Commissioner to initiate disciplinary sanctions against police officers who have been convicted of criminal offences. It is by any view part of a process of disciplinary proceedings.

26. Further, although as a matter of fact, there was no review or appeal against the applicant's conviction and sentence, it is evident from the provision in section 17(2) (a) dealing with the effect of interdiction on an officer's pay, that the statue envisages interdiction to take place or be continued after conviction and sentence.

(2) Interdiction irrational

27. The applicant's second ground of challenge is that the decision to interdict is irrational given that the offences in question are traffic offences and in view of the Secretary's disagreement with the Commissioner's recommendation of terminatory punishment for two of these offences.

28. To succeed in this challenge, the applicant must demonstrate that the decision to interdict is *Wednesbury* unreasonable and not merely a harsh or severe decision. The court will only intervene if the decision "is severe beyond any rational relationship to the seriousness of the offence and the situation of the offender": *Au Yeung Kwok Hing v. The Attorney General* (unreported) Civil Appeal No. 205 of 1994, per Bokhary JA (as he then was) at p.14 and per Nazareth VP at p.22.

29. In the memo to the applicant, the Commissioner explained the decision to interdict as follows:

> "[T]he offences for which you were convicted were very serious in nature. In particular, your criminal conviction for driving whilst under disqualification is a blatant disregard of the law and it is indicative of you having shown no respect to the court orders. Your misconduct has cast serious doubt upon your integrity and suitability for continued service as a police officer."

30. Plainly, the Commissioner took a serious view of the offences because they represented wilful disregard for the law and court orders. The Commissioner's view was shared by the applicant's own counsel who accepted in the course of mitigation that the offences were serious and objectively viewed, showed a flagrant disobedience of a court order. Indeed the magistrate in passing sentence also described the circumstances of the case as very serious, and indicated that the applicant should consider himself fortunate to have narrowly escaped an immediate custodial sentence on account of the mitigations that had been urged on his behalf.

31. The Commissioner's conclusions on the gravity of the offences and the case are amply justified. It cannot be said to be in any way so illogical or outrageous that no sensible person applying his mind to the matter could have come to the same conclusion: see the judgment of Hartmann J and of the Court of Appeal in *Wong Wai Tak v. the Secretary for Civil Service* (unreported) HCAL 2335 of 2000 at pp.14–15 and [2002] 3 HKC 1 at 16R–17D. This ground of challenge must fail.

(3) Interdiction unfair

32. The applicant's third complaint is that the Commissioner was prejudiced against him and that there was disparity in the treatment of him and other police officers. Among the cases cited by the applicant as comparables was an inspector, who was convicted of similar offences in January 2003, but was only interdicted in April 2003. There was also a police constable who was convicted of driving whilst disqualified but was not interdicted.

33. The Commissioner denies the allegation of bias and prejudice. It is also pointed out that each case was considered on its own merits and it was inappropriate to compare the applicant's case with other cases with different circumstances.

34. The authorities have long recognized that the responsibility for discipline in the police rests with the Commissioner, and the disciplinary officers' professional judgment is to be respected: see e.g. *Wong Wai Tak v. The Secretary for Civil Service, supra, Au Yeung Kwok Hing v. The Attorney General, supra, and Leung Fuk Wah Oil v. The commissioner for Police* (unreported) HCAL 317 of 2001. Disparity in punishments by itself is therefore not a ground for judicial review.

35. Likewise, difference in the treatment of different officers *per se* does not amount to unfairness. Neither does it in itself lead to inference of apparent bias or prejudice. The argument of disparity in treatment was considered at length in *Pang Chak Yum v. Secretary for the Civil Service* (unreported) HCMP 1349 of 1995. The late J Chan J held that disparity of treatment *per se* is not unfair and all would depend on the comparables used to demonstrate the unfairness of the situation. It was further held that the correctness of the other decisions used as the comparable must first be established before such decisions can be of any use in demonstrating the unfairness of the decision under challenge. In demonstrating the propriety of any comparable decision, its detail factual matrix, background and personal circumstances of the offender involved would have to be analysed. The judgment also pointed out that it is wrong to accept, in absolute term and without question, the propriety of the comparable decision simply because the decision had not been appealed. I respectfully agree with the judgment.

36. In the present case, the full circumstances of and the considerations involved in the comparable cases are unknown. The applicant has also not established the correctness or propriety of the comparable decisions. The argument that the decision to interdict is unfair by reference to other cases has no proper

foundation. This is particularly so when some of the cases used as comparables took place after the decision affecting the applicant.

37. As to the complaint of prejudice, in *Deacons v. White & Case Limited Liability Partnership & Ors* [2004] 1HKLRD 291 at 296–299, the Court of Final Appeal held that the test for apparent bias involves the court first ascertaining all the circumstances which have a bearing on the suggestion that the decision maker was biased and, secondly, enquiring whether those circumstances would lead a fair-minded and informed observer to conclude that there was a real possibility that the decision maker was biased.

38. In the present case, given that the full circumstances of the other police officers and, in particular, the inspector who was interdicted in April 2003, are not known, there is no factual basis for the contention that there had been disparity or inequality in the Commissioner's treatments of the applicant and the other inspector. There is nothing on which a fair-minded and informed observer could have concluded that there was a real possibility of the Commissioner being biased against the applicant in his decision made in 2001. The third ground therefore fails.

(4) No pay or allowance unlawful

39. The applicant's fourth complaint is that the Commissioner's decision that he shall receive no pay or allowance during interdiction is unlawful. The applicant refers to section 17(2)(a) of PFO, which provides that a police officer who had been interdicted shall be allowed to receive a proportion of his pay until he is convicted of an offence whereupon the matter falls to be determined by section 37(4) . He argues that as there is no power to interdict solely on account of criminal conviction and since section 37(4) does not empower the authority to withhold pay and allowance to an officer upon his conviction, the inference is that the legislature only intends to subject officers sentenced to immediate custodial sentence to the punishment of no pay or allowance.

40. Section 17(2) (a) of the PFO provides as follows:

> "(2) A police officer who has been interdicted under -
>
> (a) subsection (1) (a), shall be allowed to receive such proportion of his pay, not being less than one–half, as the Commissioner shall in every case direct, until such time as he may be convicted of an offence whereupon the matter shall be determined under section 37(4)".

41. Section 37(4) further provides:

> "(4) No pay or allowance shall be payable to any police officer following the date of the finding by a court in criminal proceedings that a charge against such officer in respect of a criminal offence has been proved against him, unless the approval of the Commissioner of such payment be given."

42. Irrespective of the provision in section 17(2) (a) for the payment of a proportion of the pay to an interdicted officer, upon the officer being convicted of an offence, as in the case of the applicant, his position falls to be governed by section 37(4) . Section 37(4) mandates no pay or allowance shall be payable to the officer except where the Commissioner had given approval for payment.

43. Properly analysed, the Commissioner did not make a separate decision to withhold payment of pay or allowance to the applicant. The non–payment of pay or allowance was by operation of law, which arose by reason of the decision to interdict and the convictions of the applicant. The argument that the Commissioner acted unlawfully in deciding that no pay or allowance be paid to the applicant has no proper basis.

44. The applicant relies on the opinion by Paul Goulding QC to the effect that any policy to withhold salary should, among other things, afford the individual an opportunity to make representations in respect of all relevant considerations. The applicant argues that he had throughout not been given an opportunity to make representations on the withholding of his pay. This argument is misplaced in that no government policy to withhold salary is engaged here. The basis for the non–payment of salary and allowance to the applicant is the legislation.

45. The applicant also refers to the decision in *Fung Yiu Bun v. Commissioner of Police* [2002] 4HKC 15 and contends that the Commissioner had acted unlawfully in unilaterally altering the terms of his employment contract. Quite apart from the fact that this is not a case of variation of contractual terms, the authority cited does not in fact assist the applicant. After holding that there was an employment relationship between a police officer and the government, Chung J went on in *Fung Yiu Bun's* case to hold further that complaints for breach of the applicant's employment contract is not a matter of public law, but falls to be dealt with under the private law. Accordingly, the application for judicial review was dismissed. Thus, even if the applicant is correct in saying that the terms of his employment contract had been unilaterally altered by the Commissioner's decision under challenge, it is not a matter for judicial review.

46. In the course of his oral submissions, the applicant submits that the Commissioner had failed to exercise his power under section 37(4) of the PFO to approve payment to the applicant. This argument is at variance with his Form 86A which puts the challenge on the basis that the Commissioner had by the 1 June 2001 memo decided to withhold payment of salary and allowance. That aside, the applicant's latest argument is without factual basis. It is not the applicant's case and there is no evidence that the applicant had ever asked the Commissioner to exercise his discretion under section 37(4) to approve payment of salary and allowance. The applicant says that he was not advised to apply and he was not aware of the existence of such procedure. This is irrelevant. The fact remains that the applicant never sought approval for payment of salary. That being the case, it is not open to the applicant to contend that the Commissioner had failed to exercise his power under section 37(4), let alone acted irrationally.

(5) No pay or allowance irrational

47. The applicant's fifth ground of challenge is that the Commissioner's decision to withhold pay or allowance is irrational. The applicant contends that the Commissioner failed to have any regard for his livelihood and further points to the fact that he had been without pay for over two years.

48. As with his fourth ground, the applicant is proceeding on the basis that the Commissioner had by the memo of 1 June 2001 made a separate decision to withhold payment of the applicant's pay or allowance. In truth, however, the Commissioner's only decision was to interdict the applicant. In consequence of the decision, section 37(4) applies and the applicant would not receive any pay. Similarly, the Commissioner did not, as the applicant contends, make a decision to prohibit him from taking up paid employment. Paragraph 6 of the memo dated 1 June 2001 is merely a reminder that the applicant required the Commissioner'

[*sic*] approval in taking up any paid employment. It was open to the applicant to apply to the Commissioner for approval of payment or for permission to take up paid employment. Further, the Commissioner had on 30 January 2003 written to the Director of Social Welfare requesting him to render assistance to the applicant. The applicant did not, however, draw on the Comprehensive Social Security Assistance.

49. In his reply submissions, the applicant says that during the period when he was interdicted, he had performed a number of duties, including carrying out the reporting conditions, attending interviews with his formation commander and acting as defence representative in disciplinary proceedings of other police officers. The applicant argues that as such, it would be perverse for the Commissioner not to grant approval for payment of his salary.

50. This is a new ground, on which no leave has been given to argue it at the judicial review application. It is also at variance with the case advanced in the Form 86A. Additionally, the argument presupposes that the Commissioner is under a positive duty to consider and make approval for payment of salary to the applicant. Such an assumption is not warranted by the terms of section 37(4) of the PFO. The power of the Commissioner under the section to approve payment is discretionary and not mandatory. The Commissioner cannot be regarded as acting irrationally for not exercising the discretion when the applicant had not sought the approval from him.

(6) No pay or allowance unfair

51. The sixth complaint of the applicant is that the Commissioner had arbitrarily invoked his authority of stopping the applicant's pay and allowance. The applicant refers again to the case of the inspector who was interdicted in April 2003 for similar offences and says he had been treated differently.

52. For the reasons discussed above, the Commissioner had not exercised any power of stopping pay and allowance to the applicant. Further, the argument of unfairness or prejudice by reference to the case of the other inspector has no merit. This ground of complaint must fail.

(7) Article 31 of the BL and Article 8 of the BORO

53. The applicant's seventh ground of complaint relates to the requirements to give prior notification of intention to leave Hong Kong and to seek prior approval for any absence from Hong Kong that will affect the reporting condition imposed on the applicant. These requirements stem from PGO 6–06, which provides that reporting conditions may be imposed on an interdicted officer. It also provides that an interdicted officer who wishes to leave Hong Kong is required to give prior notification to the Commissioner, and that late or post notification is permissible in exceptional circumstances. The applicant argues that these requirements violate the fundamental rights of freedom of movement guaranteed under Article 35 of the BL and Article 8 of the BORO.

54. Article 31 of the BL provides:

> "Hong Kong residents shall have freedom of movement within the Hong Kong Special Administration Region and freedom of emigration to other countries and regions. They shall have freedom to travel and to enter or leave the Region. Unless restrained by law, holders of valid travel documents shall be free to leave the Region without special authorization."

55. Article 8 of the BORO provides:

> "(1) Everyone lawfully within Hong Kong shall, within Hong Kong, have the right to liberty of movement and freedom to choose his residence.
>
> (2) Everyone shall be free to leave Hong Kong.
>
> (3) The above–mentioned rights shall not be subject to any restrictions except those which are provided by law, are necessary to protect national security, public order (ordre public), public health or morals or the rights and freedom of others, and are consistent with the other rights recognized in this Bill of Rights.
>
> (4) No one who has the right of abode in Hong Kong shall be arbitrarily deprived of the right to enter Hong Kong."

56. Article 39 of the BL further provides, *inter alia*, that the provisions of the ICCPR as applied to Hong Kong shall remain in force, and that the rights and freedoms enjoyed by Hong Kong residents shall not be restricted unless as prescribed by law.

57. Under section 46 of the PFO, the Commissioner may from time to time make such orders as he thinks expedient for, *inter alia*, the administration of the Police Force, the efficient discharge of the duties of the Police Force and for carrying out the objects and provisions of the PFO. The orders thus made are called Police General Orders, of which PGO 6–06 forms part. The imposition of reporting conditions and the requirement of giving prior notification of departure from Hong Kong under PGO 6–06 are therefore prescribed by law, and their contravention is a disciplinary offence under Regulation 3(2) (e) of the Police force (disciplinary) Regulations: *Fu Kin Chi Willy v. Secretary for Justice* (1997–98) 1HKCFAR 85 at 102D.

58. PGO 6–06 does not prohibit an interdicted officer from leaving Hong Kong. It only requires the officer to give 24 hours prior written notice of his intention to leave Hong Kong. The issue is whether the requirement of prior notice is so restrictive or so disproportionate as to violate the right of freedom of movement.

59. Two main reasons are put forward on behalf of the Commissioner to justify the requirement of prior notification and the imposition of reporting condition. Firstly, it is said that an interdicted officer is or will be subject to criminal or disciplinary proceedings. The reporting condition and the prior notice of departure from Hong Kong will ensure that any criminal or disciplinary proceedings will not be frustrated by the absence of the officer from Hong Kong and at the proceedings. Secondly, it is pointed out that the formation commander of the interdicted officer remains responsible for the welfare of the officer and may enquire into the personal and financial problems of the officer. The notification requirement is therefore conducive to good and efficient management and administration.

60. I accept these are proper justifications for the reporting condition and prior notification requirement under PGO 6–06. Considering that only 24 hours prior notice is required and that late or post notifications are accepted in exceptional circumstances, I am of the view that the requirements imposed by PGO 6–06 are proportionate and are not so restrictive as to cause an undue restriction of the freedom of movement. I agree with Mr Ismail's submission that it is an over–statement to say that the requirements make "any spontaneous trips or trips that are planned less than 24 hours ahead impossible". The evidence also shows that the reporting conditions were administered flexibly. There was occasion when the applicant was told he could report to

police station other than the designated one. It was also possible for him to seek exemption from reporting, if it should become necessary.

61. To the extent that the applicant seems at one stage to be arguing that he was not challenging the constitutionality of PGO 6–06, I am unable to understand the argument. Given that the Commissioner by the 1 June 2001 memo was reminding the applicant of the requirements under PGO 6–06, any challenge based on breach of the BL and the BORO must necessarily involves a challenge to PGO 6–06 itself. In short, the complaint that the Commissioner's decision infringes Article 31 of the BL and Article 8 of the BORO cannot stand.

(8) Article 35 of the BL and Article 11 of the BORO

62. The applicant's eighth and last ground of challenge to the Commissioner's decision complains that the prolonged period of no pay and allowance has deprived him of the prospect of timely engagement of counsel of his own choice to appeal against the conviction for indecent assault, to procure the notes of proceedings to enable him to prepare the appeal and the representations to the Chief Executive. The applicant argues that there is a breach of Article 35 of the BL and Article 11 of the BORO.

63. Article 35 of the BL provides:

> "Hong Kong residents shall have the right to confidential legal advice, access to courts, choice of lawyers for timely protection of their lawful rights and interests or for representations in the courts and to judicial remedies.
>
> Hong Kong residents shall have the right to institute legal proceedings in the courts against the acts of the executive authorities and their personnel."

64. Article 11(2) (d) of the BORO provides:

> "(2) In the determination of any criminal charge against him, everyone shall be entitled to the following minimum guarantees, in full equality:
>
> (d) ... to be tried in his presence, and to defend himself in person or through legal assistance of his own choosing; to be informed, if he does not have legal representation, of this right; and to have legal assistance assigned to him, in any case where the interests of justice so require, and without payment by him in any such case if he does not have sufficient means to pay for it."

65. In *Dr Ip Kay Lo v. Medical Council of Hong Kong* [2003] 3HKLRD 851 at 856, Cheung JA pointed out that the right under Article 35 of the BL is not absolute. The judgment stated that Article 35 is "not concerned with the provision of free legal service by the Government", and "does not enable the litigant to insist to have a particular lawyer, even though that lawyer may not be available to handle the case or is not willing to represent him". It is further said that the fundamental requirement for meeting the objective of Article 35 is to ensure that the litigant is given an opportunity to seek legal representation.

66. In the context of Article 11 of the BORO, it had been held that the Article did not confer an absolute right to free legal aid and to be provided with a full transcript at public expense: *R v. Fu Yan* [1992] 2 HKPLR 109, and *R v. Mirchandani* [1992] 2 HKPLR 196.

67. The essence of the applicant's complaint is that he did not have a counsel of his own choice to conduct his appeal. But as the authorities have laid down, there is no constitutionally guaranteed right to have an appeal conducted by a counsel of the applicant's own choice. The substance of the rights protected by Article 35 of the BL and Article 11 of the BORO is the right to have an opportunity to seek legal representation and in turn a fair trial. A fair trial, however, does not necessarily mean that the parties must be legally represented, let alone represented by a lawyer of his own choice: see *Dr Ip Kay Lo v. Medical Council of Hong Kong* at 859.

68. The applicant did have an opportunity to seek legal representation. He was represented by counsel at the trial in the Magistracy. He has no complaint against the counsel who was assigned by the Duty Lawyer Scheme to represent him and his conduct of the trial. In his own words, the counsel had demonstrated "superb professional competence" and "dedicated effort". The applicant, however, says that if he had been represented by a Senior Counsel, the result of his trial might have been different. This is a speculative argument given that there is no suggestion of incompetence or inadequacy of the assigned defence counsel. At the appeal in the Court of First Instance, the applicant had been granted three adjournments to seek legal representation before Beeson J refused to further adjourn the appeal at the hearing on 12 July 2002.

69. The applicant also had an opportunity to obtain the transcript of the trial before the appeal hearing, but he had not applied for it. He had no right or legitimate expectation to being provided with a transcript at public expense. The applicant argues that had he been provided with a copy of the trial transcript, his appeal would have a greater chance of success. The applicant also argues that if he were able to engage counsel in time, his prospect of appeal to the Court of Final Appeal would be better. These arguments are pure speculations. The thrust of the applicant's challenge on appeal was the Magistrate's findings of fact. The availability of the transcript will not lessen the difficulties that the applicant faced in launching an appeal against the Magistrate's factual findings. Further, appeal to Court of Final Appeal is only permissible where the case involves a point of great general public importance. There is nothing to show that the applicant is anywhere near the permissible limit.

70. The applicant therefore cannot complain that he did not stand to have a fair trial in the Magistracy or in the Court of First Instance on appeal. The complaint that there is a violation of Article 35 of the BL and Article 11 of he BORO has no merit.

THE CHALLENGE TO THE SECRETARY's DECISION

71. The applicant challenges the decision of the Secretary on three grounds.

(1) Delegation by the Chief Executive

72. The applicant's first ground of challenge to the Secretary's decision is that the power of the Chief Executive under section 37(5) (a) cannot be delegated to the Secretary.

73. Section 63(1) of the Interpretation and General Clauses Ordinance, cap. 1 provides:

> "Where any Ordinance confers powers or imposes duties upon the Chief Executive, he may delegate any person by name or the person holding any office delegated by him to exercise such powers or perform such duties on his behalf and whereupon, or from the date specified by the Chief Executive, the person so delegated shall have and

may exercise such powers and performs such duties."

74. By an Instrument of Delegation gazetted on 8 November 2002, the Chief Executive had delegated to the Secretary the exercise of the powers under section 37(5)(a) of the PFO. By the letter dated 23 June 2003, the applicant had been informed that the Secretary was exercising the power delegated to him by the Chief Executive. The applicant in his reply submissions lodged on 11 June 2004 accepted that the Secretary has been properly delegated and abandoned the argument.

75. The applicant however continues to argue that the Secretary had delegated his power to officers in the CSB and that such sub-delegation is unlawful. In answer to this complaint, paragraphs 28 and 29 of the affirmation of Wong Kwok Bun filed on behalf of the Secretary stated that two officers in the CSB had been involved in the applicant's case as processing officers. It further pointed out that the Secretary, being the head of the CSB, is entitled to rely on the collective knowledge, experience and expertise of the processing officers and other government officials serving directly or indirectly under the CSB, and that this was not sub-delegation of the Secretary's authority under section 37(5) of the PFO.

76. Clearly, the Secretary and the maker of the affirmation were having in their mind the judgment of Lord Diplock in *Bushell v. Secretary of State for the Environment* [1981] AC 75 at 95 which stated that:

> "Discretion in making administrative decisions is conferred upon a minister not as an individual but as the holder of an office in which he will have available to him in arriving at his decision the collective knowledge, experience and expertise of all those who serve the Crown in the department of which, for the time being, he is the political head. The collective knowledge, technical as well as factual, of the civil servants in the department and their collective expertise is to be treated as the minister's own knowledge, his own expertise."

77. The passage was considered by Hartmann J in *Ch' ng Poh v. The Chief Executive of the HKSAR* (unreported) HCAL 182 of 2002 at para.19, and was held to have equal application in Hong Kong, notwithstanding that at the time of the making of the application for judicial review that fell to be considered, Hong Kong did not have ministerial system as that system was understood in the United Kingdom. The view of Hartmann J was shared by Cheung J (as he then was) *in Kaisilk Development Ltd. v. Secretary for Planning, Environment and Lands* (unreported) HCAL 148 of 1999, when he stated that:

> "Hong Kong does not have the ministerial system of government. However, in my view the Secretary is clearly entitled to rely on the collective knowledge, experience and expertise of the government officials serving directly or indirectly under his Bureau."

78. I respectfully agree with these judgments. Indeed the authority to award punishment under section 37(5) of the PFO is delegated to the Secretary not as an individual but as a holder of the office of secretary for civil service. In that capacity, the Secretary must be entitled to avail himself of the knowledge, experience and expertise of the CSB as a whole in discharging his duties and arriving at a decision under the section. The collective knowledge experience and expertise of the processing officers as well as any other government officials serving under the CSB is to be treated as those of the Secretary personally. There is therefore no sub-delegation of authority from the Secretary to the processing officers.

79. The applicant argues that notwithstanding the introduction of the ministerial system to Hong Kong in July 2002, the Secretary, who was hitherto a civil servant, had retained his status as a civil servant, and that with his knowledge and expertise as a former civil servant, his reliance on the processing officers must be kept to the minimal. The applicant therefore says that there is no justification for the processing officers to have made what he called "pre-emptive decisions", including decision to refuse his request for transcript of the indecent assault case, without first conferring with the Secretary. This argument plainly cannot stand in the light of the observations of Hartmann J and Cheung J in the cases referred to in the preceding paragraphs, with which I agree entirely. Besides, the decision on the applicant's request to be provided with the transcript is not an exercise of the power under section 37(5) of the PFO. As to the comments the processing made on the applicant's representations, they were to assist the Secretary in the discharge of his duties. It is for the Secretary to consider them and to arrive at a decision under the section, in the course of which he may adopt or reject the processing officers' views and comments, whether in part or in whole: *Wong Wai Tak v. The Secretary for the Civil Service*, supra, per Hartmann J at p.20.

80. The applicant also points to the fact that Secretary made his decision on the same day the materials were placed before him for consideration as indicative of the Secretary having surrendered his independent judgment. The applicant in his reply submissions goes so far as suggesting that from his experience in the Police Force, the Secretary would have a busy schedule on a Monday, on which 9 June 2003 fell be one, and criticises the lack of evidence as to the exact time and the duration of the Secretary's deliberations on his case. These, in my view, are desperate submissions that in no way advance the applicant's challenge that the Secretary had unlawfully sub-delegated his authority. The fact that the Secretary completed his deliberations and made his decision within the same day the papers were placed before him for consideration cannot lead to any of the speculative conclusions suggested by the applicant. After all, the factual matrix and considerations involved in the applicant's case, objectively analysed, are not as complicated or complex as the applicant has endeavoured to depict.

81. This ground of unlawful delegation of authority therefore fails.

(2) Procedural unfairness

82. A number of matters were relied upon by the applicant under the challenge of procedural unfairness. Firstly, the applicant again points to the fact that Secretary made his decision on the same day the materials were placed before him for consideration as indicative of the Secretary having pre-determined the matter or was actuated by the motive of depriving him of the locus to pursue another judicial review application in connection with the government's decision to reduce the pay of the civil service. For reasons that have been canvassed in the preceding section of this judgment, the arguments are entirely speculative and have no objective basis.

83. Secondly, the applicant also asserts that he had sent by post an interim representation on 7 June 2003 and this had not been taken into account when the Secretary made the decision. The evidence filed on behalf of the Secretary denies that this interim representation had been sent or ever received by the CSB or the Secretary. In my view, there is no reason to disbelieve the evidence filed by the Secretary to the effect that this interim

representation was not received. Apart from this, as the applicant has pointed out, 7 June 2003 was a Saturday. The applicant has no reason to expect with any confidence that any interim representation sent on that day would have reached the Secretary before the expiration of the three days' extension granted on 3 June 2003. He could not complained [*sic*] of any procedural unfairness even if this court were to accept that the interim representation did arrive at the CSB but had not been considered by the Secretary, bearing also in mind that he had been given a total of three extensions of time to make representations.

84. Thirdly, the applicant also raises by way of submissions that the Secretary had given no reason for his decision. Section 37(5) of the PFO does not require reasons to be given for the decision. The common law does to recognize a general duty to give reasons. The court will imply a duty to give reasons only when it is necessary by way of procedural safeguard to ensure fairness, but the standard of fairness is not immutable. In the present case, it is obvious from that the Secretary was in agreement with the views of the CSB and had adopted its recommendations on the punishments to be made. There is also nothing exceptional in the decision made by the Secretary when one considers that the applicant was a senior inspector and the case involves four criminal convictions. In respect of the conviction that gives rise to the award of dismissal, it is a conviction after trial and upheld on appeal. There is no merit in the applicant's assertion that he has been left in the dark as to the reasons for his dismissal. The circumstances of the case and the mitigations advanced are within the applicant's personal knowledge. It mattes [*sic*] not that the applicant asserts that he is innocent and does not accept the factual basis for the conviction as found by the Magistrate. Additionally, it must be fairly obvious to him that a conviction of indecent assault committed on a junior police officer by a senior inspector is a very grave matter such that an award of dismissal is one that is open to the Secretary to impose.

85. Fourthly, the applicant refers to the "Procedural Manual on Discipline" ("PMD"), the Guidebook on Discipline ("the Guidebook") and the Public Service (Administrative) Order ("PS(A)O") annexed to the PMD as Annex 5.1, and contends that there had been non-compliance with the provisions in them. Specifically, the applicant relies upon paragraphs 4.3 and 4.4 of the Guidebook and contends it is unfair not to include the transcript of the indecent assault case in the papers placed before the Secretary. Paragraphs 4.3 and 4.4 of the Guidebook state:

> "4.3 Under section 11 of the PS(A)O, if an officer has been convicted of a criminal charge, the CE may, upon a consideration of the proceedings of the court on such charge, inflict such punishment upon the officer as may seem to him to be just. Accordingly, the department should, upon conclusion of the criminal proceedings, obtain a copy of the facts of the case (from the police or the ICAC) and the court transcript (through the Department of Justice) to examine the gravity of the offence and the circumstances surrounding the criminal conviction.
>
> 4.4 Having examined the case history and relevant court transcript, the department should promptly refer the case to the SCSD, with a recommendation on whether and if so what punishment should be imposed ..."

86. This argument is completely misconceived. The PMD and the PS(A)O have no application to officers who are subject to other disciplinary regulations: paragraph 1 of the PMD and paragraph 5.3 of the PS(A)O. The applicant as a police officer is subject to the PFO. Accordingly, the PMD and PS(A)O have no application to him. Further, the decision to award punishment was made under section 37(5) of the PFO and not under section 11 of the PS(A)O, so that paragraphs 4.3 and 4.4 of the Guidebook are not engaged. In any case, the applicant admittedly is not a gazetted officer covered by the Guidebook.

87. In addition, the purpose of the stipulations in the Guidebook on obtaining a transcript is to enable a view be taken of "the gravity of the offence and the circumstances surrounding the criminal conviction". Insofar as there are in existence other materials upon which the Secretary can properly exercise his power and make a decision, the failure to obtain a transcript is *per se* not procedurally unfair.

88. The applicant refers to the fact that the transcript of the traffic offences case had been obtained as supporting his argument that it was unfair not to obtain the transcript of the indecent assault case. The argument, however, ignores the fact that in the traffic offences case, there was no other material upon which a view can be taken of the gravity and the circumstances of the offences. In the case of indecent assault, there were the Statement of Findings and the Judgment on appeal. There were ample materials on which the Secretary could form a view of the matter.

89. Furthermore, the reasons put up by the applicant for his request for the court transcript are to enable him to make representations to the Chief Executive and to demonstrate what he perceived to be the shortcomings and errors in the Statement of Findings of the trial Magistrate. This is manifested by the applicant's second affirmation which introduces the witness statement of the sergeant who was present that evening. The use that the applicant seeks to put to the court transcript is plainly outside that envisaged by paragraphs 4.3 and 4.4. More fundamentally, it is not open to the applicant to seek to challenge the findings of the Magistrate that had been upheld on appeal. The applicant is bound by the findings of the court and any attempt to circumvent the court findings by the use of the transcript is an abuse. There is also no duty on the part of the Secretary to look beyond the court findings and the judge's reasons. No principle of fairness will impose upon a decision maker such an onerous duty. At any rate, it was open to the applicant, if he wished to labour the point, to include among his representations the witness statement of the sergeant, but for reasons unexplained, he had not seen fit to do so.

90. The applicant also argues that the Secretary was guilty of non-disclosure of documents and materials. The fact is that the CSB did not have in its possession the court transcript. The duty to disclosure cannot be extended to become a positive duty to call for documents that are not in the CSB's possession and which the CSB did not intend to relay upon and did not consider it necessary to obtain. In the same vein, the applicant's argument that the Secretary is under a duty to assist him and had failed in his duty in not providing the applicant with the court transcript is untenable.

(3) Decision to dismiss irrational

91. The third major ground advanced by the applicant to challenge the decision of the Secretary is that the decision to award a punishment of dismissal for the indecent assault conviction is irrational. As stated above, the court in judicial review proceedings only has a supervisory role and judicial review proceedings must not be used as a roundabout way to appeal against disciplinary award. The harshness or severity of an award

is not a ground for judicial review. To the extent that the applicant draws assistance from other disciplinary cases involving police officers, for reasons set out in the earlier part of this judgment, they do not afford the applicant with a valid ground for judicial review in that disparity in treatment *per se* is not irrational nor unfair.

92. In the present case, the applicant was a senior police officer holding a supervisory role. The victim involved was a junior officer. The evidence filed on behalf of the Secretary shows that the applicant's conduct was regarded as unacceptable and a breach of the trust placed on him by his superiors and subordinates as well as bringing the Police Force into disrepute. In my view, these are views that the Secretary is entitled to. In the circumstances, there is no room for challenging the Secretary's decision to award a dismissal when he concludes, as he is entitled to, that there are serious doubts on the applicant's integrity and suitability to remain in the Police Force. This ground therefore fails.

CONCLUSION

92. For the reasons set out above, the applicant's application for judicial review is dismissed. Applying the normal rule of costs follow event, I make an order nisi that the applicant pays the respondent the costs of this application, to be taxed if not agreed.

Judge of the Court of First Instance High Court (C Chu)

The applicants, unrepresented, appeared in person.

Mr Anthony Ismail instructed by the Department of Justice for the respondents.

葉德偉 對 香港警務處潘潔生警司

HCAL 27/2005

簡略案情

申請人在 1992 年加入香港警隊，任職警員。於 2004 年，警務處就 17 項違反《警察通例》及《總部通令》的控罪，通知申請人擬對他展開紀律聆訊。紀律聆訊安排在 2005 年 1 月 10 日首次召開，答辯人是聆訊主審官。在此之前，申請人在 2005 年 1 月 5 日向答辯人以書面提出下列要求：1） 准許他聘請執業律師作為辯護代表；2） 如上述要求不被批准，則由非警隊人員的公務員出任辯護代表；以及 3） 如上述兩項要求均不被批准，則准許一名當時正在停職的林達明督察出任辯護代表。在 2005 年 1 月 10 日聆訊中，答辯人向申請人解釋《警察（紀律）規例》中有關辯護代表的規定，並將聆訊押後至 2 月 14 日正式開審。在 2005 年 2 月 14 日當天，聆訊再次押後。基於答辯人其後已調職，申請人的紀律聆訊由另外一位警務人員出任主審官。紀律聆訊暫定在 2005 年 11 月 29 日重新召開。2005 年 2 月 22 日申請人向法庭提出司法覆核申請，認為答辯人不當拒絕其提出的人選擔任其辯護代表，並要求法庭頒令禁止繼續他的紀律聆訊，直至司法覆核有最終結果為止。申請人在司法覆核申請的其中一項理由是，《警察（紀律）規例》不容許申請人聘請律師作辯護代表，違反了《基本法》第 35 條的規定，即 “香港居民有權得到秘密法律咨詢、向法院提起訴訟、選擇律師及時保護自己的合法權益或在法庭上為其代理和獲得司法補救。” 在審訊過程中，答辯人同意在無需爭議的情況下，法庭可以認定警隊的紀律聆訊可被視為是《基本法》第 35 條中描述的 “法庭” 。

裁決摘要

法庭援引終審法院 *Financial Secretary* v. *Wong* [2003] 6 HKCFAR 476 一案，指出在司法覆核案件中法庭只具監督的作用。司法覆核機制的用意不在於管控從屬審裁處或行政決策者的一舉一動，故此除在絕無僅有的例外情況下，不應用以覆核純粹關於程序而非最終結果的裁決。而目前答辯人不准許申請人提出人選擔任辯護人僅為一個程序上的決定，紀律聆訊尚未就案件實質作出裁決，不能判斷結果是否對申請人有利，因此司法覆核不應在此階段介入。

關於申請人對《基本法》第 35 條的論據，法庭援引 *New World Development Co. Ltd.* v. *Stock*

Exchange Of Hong Kong Ltd. [2005] 2 HKLRD 612 一案的上訴庭判決認為，一般而言，除卻有強而有力的原因外，不應限制獲得《基本法》第 35 條的權利。但是《基本法》第 35 條不表示在研訊過程的每一個環節中，接受研訊者都必然有權以律師代表行事。在考慮所涉研訊是否有抵觸《基本法》第 35 條時，法庭必須衡量所涉審裁體的程序，從整體而言，有否充份反映第 35 條所賦予的保障。這又涉及一個"比例是否適當"（proportionally）的問題。法庭指出，《基本法》第 35 條的核心問題，是接受研訊者是否獲得公平審訊，而如同普通法的原則一樣，公平審訊須從多方面考慮。而申請人的紀律研訊尚未開審，目前不能判斷如果沒有律師出任辯護代表會否得不到公平審訊，和他在《基本法》第 35 條下的權利會否被削弱。基於此，申請人司法覆核的申請被駁回。

編者按：此案法官關於《基本法》第 35 條的附帶意見 (obiter dictum) 已經因為終審法院推翻了上訴庭於 New World Development Co. Ltd. v. Stock Exchange Of Hong Kong Ltd. [2005] 2 HKLRD 612的裁決而同時被否定。法院認定一般的紀律審裁組織並非《基本法》第 35 條所指的"法院"，所以，《基本法》第 35 條並不適用於這類案件。但是《香港人權法案條例》第 10 條和普通法的公平原則在此情況下適用。法庭進一步接受"比例是否適當"是考慮的標準。詳見終審法院 Lam Siu Po 一案（見書 P.493）。

HCAL27/2005

香港特別行政區
高等法院原訟法庭
憲法及行政訴訟 2005 年第 27 號

申請人　葉德偉
對
答辯人　香港警務處潘潔生警司

主審法官：高等法院原訟法庭法官朱芬齡

聆訊日期：2003 年 11 月 3 日

判決書日期：2003 年 11 月 21 日

判決書

1. 申請人要求批予許可，就答辯人在其紀律聆訊中所作的程序決定，提出司法覆核申請。

案件的事實背景

2. 申請人自 1992 年加入香港警隊，任職警員。

3. 2004 年 12 月 31 日，警務處就 17 項違反《警察通例》及《總部通令》的控罪，通知申請人擬對他展開紀律聆訊。

4. 紀律聆訊在 2005 年 1 月 10 日首次召開。答辯人是聆訊的適當審裁體（簡稱「主審官」）。在此之前，申請人在 2005 年 1 月 5 日向答辯人以書面提出下列要求：（1）准許他聘請執業律師作為辯護代表；（2）如上述要求不被批准，則由非警隊人員的公務員出任辯護代表；以及（3）如上述兩項要求均不被批准，則准許一名當時正在停職的林達明督察出任辯護代表（統稱「申請人有關辯護代表的要求」）。

5. 在2005年1月10日聆訊中，答辯人向申請人解釋《警察（紀律）規例》中有關辯護代表的規定，並將聆訊押後至 2 月 14 日正式開審。在 2005 年 2 月 14 日當天，聆訊再次押後。

6. 基於答辯人其後已調職，申請人的紀律聆訊現已由另外一位警務人員出任主審官。紀律聆訊現時暫定在 2005 年 11 月 29 日重新召開。

7. 2005 年 2 月 22 日申請人提出本申請，要求就下列事項申請司法覆核：

> 「於 2005 年 2 月 14 日，在香港警隊紀律聆訊中，主審官潘潔生警司不容許林達明督察、香港高等法院傳譯主任張國標先生或一名執業律師擔任本人的辯護代表。於同日，潘潔生警司亦不合理地拒絕本人申請押後聆訊。」

申請人同時要求頒令暫時禁止繼續進行他的紀律聆訊，直至司法覆核有最終結果為止。

8. 2005 年 2 月 22 日，本席指示以訴訟各方到庭形式，就許可申請和暫時禁制令的申請進行聆訊。由於申請人的法律援助申請問題，聆訊延至本年 11 月 3 日進行。

押後許可聆訊的申請

9. 申請人在 2005 年 10 月 24 日致函法院要求押後 11 月 3 日的聆訊。本席指示該申請在聆訊日作出。

10. 申請人要求押後聆訊主要是要待 *New World Development Co. Ltd v. Stock Exchange of Hong Kong Ltd* [2005] 2 HKLRD 612 一案在終審法院審結為止。申請人同時也稱需要更多時間回應答辯人代表大律師的書面陳詞和引用的歐洲人權法庭案例。

11. 經聆聽雙方陳詞後，本席拒絕押後許可聆訊。首先，*New World Development Co. Ltd* 在終審法院的裁決不影響申請人現時的申請，原因如下：

> (1) 申請人認為上訴法庭在 *New World Development Co. Ltd* 一案的判決對他有利，並因此要求修改其表格 86A 的申請理由。在終審法院未有推翻上訴法庭的判決前，該案中上訴法庭的判決對本庭有約束力。
>
> (2) 郭大律師陳詞時表示，為使本申請得以迅速和有效地進行，他願意假設警隊紀律聆訊的審裁體可被視為《基本法》第 35 條所述的「法庭」。

12. 至於郭大律師的陳詞，它只是以書面回應申請人在表格 86A 的申請理由和陳述。郭大律師是要待申請人按「實務指引」規定須存檔和送達書面陳詞大綱的期限過後，才送達他的書面陳詞大綱，這在程序安排上是無可厚非的。再者，郭大律師的書面陳詞相當簡短，並以中文撰寫。雖然他引用的案例，*Pellegrin v. France*（2001）E.H.H.R. 26 是以英文撰寫，但有關的法律原則和援引它的原因已在其陳詞第 11 和 12 段清楚說明。

13. 申請人親自進行訴訟，基於他沒有法律專業訓練，在處理和回應法律觀點出現困難在所難免。但法庭有責任對所有訴訟人一視同仁，不能單因為訴訟人沒有律師代表便給予特殊處理。此外，法庭不會期望沒有法律專業訓練的訴訟人對法律和案例進行研究或作出分析回應。法庭一般取態會較為主動，從多方面去考慮和衡量有關的法律和案例。因此，申請人在聆訊前一天收到答辯人的書面陳詞這點，不構成應押後聆訊的理由。

2005 年 2 月 14 日聆訊的錄音

14. 就 2005 年 2 月 14 日聆訊中，答辯人有否拒絕申請人有關辯護代表的要求，以及聆訊是在甚麼情況下押後，申請人表示有爭議。他在 2005 年 11 月 1 日存檔補充誓章，夾附了 11 卷紀律聆訊的錄音帶，要求在本申請聆訊中播放和引用。

15. 答辯人的說法是由於申請人單獨出席 1 月 10 日和 2 月 14 日的聆訊，沒有帶同任何辯護人，他未能就辯護人身份作出查證，所以並沒有就申請人有關辯護代表的要求作出決定。他是因為申請人表示身體不適，所以押後了 2 月 14 日的聆訊。

16. 申請人同意他沒有帶同辯護代表出席。他的說法是答辯人沒有正面拒絕他的要求，但在行為上卻拒絕了他有關辯護代表的要求。而且答辯人押後聆訊，並非是讓他安排辯護代表。

17. 綜上而言，本席不認為申請人與答辯人就 2 月 14 日的事實有重大或具影響性的分歧。再且，郭大律師的陳詞亦是在假設答辯人已拒絕了申請人有關辯護代表的要求，以及要求押後聆訊的申請的基礎上作出。在此情況下，沒有需要在本聆訊中參考 2 月 14 日紀律聆訊的錄音。

18. 本席同時也得指出，如果申請人有需要引用紀律聆訊的記錄，他應將相關的部份抄錄成謄本，夾附在誓章作證物，而非將全部紀律聆訊的錄音帶附於誓章存檔。在司法覆核申請的案件中，法庭只有在極例外的情況下才會聽取口頭證供，或在聆訊中播放錄音或錄像。

申請人的理據

19. 申請人在表格 86A 中提出下列理由，以支持其擬提的司法覆核申請：

（1）答辯人以林達明督察在停職中，拒絕讓他出任申請人的辯護代表是違法，並否定申請人選擇辯護代表的權利。

（2）《警察（紀律）規例》第 19（1）條的規定違反《香港人權法案條例》第 10 條中有關平等的規定。

（3）答辯人拒絕申請人有關辯護代表的要求，是違反《香港人權法案條例》第 10 條有關獨立無私的法定管轄法庭的規定。

（4）答辯人拒絕申請人的押後要求，違反了《警察（紀律）規例》第 9（8）條的規定。

20. 申請人在 2005 年 11 月 2 日存檔的誓章內要求修改表格 86A，增添一項新的申請理由，即 ：

（5）《警察（紀律）規例》不容許申請人聘請律師作辯護代表，違反了《基本法》第 35 條的規定。

答辯人不反對申請人加入這項修訂。因此本席在考慮許可申請時會把它一併考慮。

判決理由

（1）本申請是否適時？

21. 本席首要考慮的是申請人在現階段提出司法覆核申請是否得當。

22. 申請人提出本申請時，其紀律聆訊已押後，須另定日期繼續。直至目前，該紀律聆訊仍未完結。

23. 終審法院在 *Financial Secretary v. Wong* [2003] 6 HKCFAR 476，487C－488C 指出，法庭在司法覆核案件中只具監督的作用。司法覆核機制的用意不在於管控從屬審裁處或行政決策者的一舉一動，故此除在絕無僅有的例外情況下，不應用以覆核純粹關乎程序而非最終結果的裁決。

24. 申請人在本申請所挑戰的，是答辯人在 2005 年 2 月 14 日聆訊中的兩項決定。第一項是有關申請人辯護代表的安排。這明顯是一項純粹關乎程序的決定，不屬於實質的決定。

25. 就這方面而言，申請人的情況與*鄧強康對香港警務處潘潔生警司*（案件編號 HKAL3/2004）中的申請人並無兩樣。張法官在該案中裁定申請人在紀律聆訊未完成前，就辯護人代表問題提出司法覆核申請是過早。張法官指出若紀律聆訊最終結果是違紀控罪不成立，則司法覆核申請便是浪費時間和毫無意義：見第 3 段。本席同意張法官的分析。再者，有鑑於在司法覆核申請中，是否頒發濟助，屬法庭的酌情權力，因此當法庭考慮是否批予許可時，所涉司法覆核申請是否具有實質意義是一項重要的考慮因素。

26. 申請人在表格 86A 中表示他的情況有別於 *Financial Secretary v. Wong* 一案。他稱該案針對的是整個聆訊的過程，而他的申請是針對一個明確的「決定」，即答辯人錯誤詮釋《警察（紀律）規例》第 9（11）（a）條，以及他獲得公平審訊的權利。申請人更指一旦他在聆訊被入罪，屆時他可能為口奔馳無暇進行司法覆核。

27. 本席不同意 *Financial Secretary v. Wong* 案中，有關司法覆核機制的運用的法律原則，不適用於本案。雖然申請人挑戰的是答辯人據稱作出的「決定」，但在本性上該決定仍是一項程序上的裁定。至於申請人日後如控罪成立可能不會提出法律程序一點，這並非法庭在決定本申請是否得當應考慮的因素。

28. 至於申請人擬司法覆核的第二項決定，是答辯人拒絕押後聆訊讓他尋找辯護代表。然而不管怎樣，不爭的事實是紀律聆訊在 2 月 14 日並沒有繼續進行。申請人這項挑戰既沒有需要，也缺乏實質作用和意義。在此情況下，不應批予許可以啟動司法覆核的機制。

29. 基於上述分析，本席認為本申請是過早和不適時，亦不得當。單就這個原因，法庭便得拒絕批予司法覆核的許可。

30. 此外，本席亦已就申請人提出的申請理由加以考慮。適用的測試標準是這些理據經進一步考慮後，是否有潛在可爭辯的情況：*Ho Ming Sai v. Director of Immigration* [1994] HKLR 21。

（2）申請理由（1）：停職警務人員可否出任辯護代表？

31. 在關被停職警務人員可否在紀律聆訊出任辯護人一點，法庭的案例清楚顯示一名警務人員如遭警務處長按《警察條例》第 17 條停職，他不具資格代表違紀者在紀律聆訊中進行辯護：見上訴法庭在*何建民訴香港警務處陳健雄警司及其他人*（CACV145/2005）第 59 63 段的判決，和原訟法庭法官張舉能在鄧強康對香港警務處潘潔生警司 HCAL3/2004 第 8 13 段的判決。

32. 因此，即使答辯人已作出拒絕申請人要求由當時正停職的林督察出任辯護代表的決定，這亦沒有違法之處。而且也不構成否定申請人選擇辯護人的權利的情況。

（3）申請理由（2）：《警察（紀律）規則》第 19（1）（a）條

33. 申請人稱《警察（紀律）規則》第 19（1）（a）條限制了他選擇辯護代表的權利。事實上，該條文衹適用於督察級的警務人員，並不適用於申請人。有關初級警務人員的紀律聆訊的程序載於該規則的第 9 條。而第 9（11）條是關乎辯護代表的規定；它指明違紀者可由以下人士代表進行辯護 ：

（a）他所選定的督察或其他初級警級人員；或

（b）他所選定的任何具有大律師或律師資格的其他警務人員。

34. 申請人指警司職級的警務人員可由警隊以外的公務員出任辯護代表，而他卻因為是初級警務人員，故祇能在警隊裏挑選辯護代表。他因而認為這是違反《香港人權法案條例》第 10 條中「人人平等」的規定。

35. 警司級以下的警務人員與警司級或以上警務人員在紀律聆訊方面的安排是有所不同。警司級或以上的高級警務人的紀律研訊是按《公務人員（紀律）規則》進行。他們可選擇不具法律專業資格的公務人員作辯護代表。

36. 基於實際需要考慮，包括因為警司級或以上的警務人員人數有限和須考慮主審官、主控人員和辯護代表的職級，警司級或以上的紀律聆訊有必要在警隊外處理：見*陳國雄訴香港警務處處長曾蔭培*，HCAL86/2003 第 32 段。

37. 本席認為，不能單因為就辯護代表有不同的安排，便認定是存在不公平待遇的情況。首先，辯護代表只是整個紀律聆訊程序的一部份。如郭大律師指出，《警察（紀律）規例》第 9 條臚列了多項紀律聆訊程序的安排，對違紀者有清晰明確的程序保障。其次，警司級以下的警務人員與警司級或以上的警務人員的紀律聆訊是兩套不同的機制，除辯護代表的人選外，尚有其他不同之處。簡單而言，警司級以下警務人員的紀律研訊是在警隊內處理，主審官和主控人員都是由警務人員出任。在此情況下，違紀者的辯護代表由警務人員出任乃是合適，沒有不公平之處。另一方面，警司級或以上警務人員的紀律研訊，由於是在警隊外處理，因此有關的研訊人員、研訊委員會和協助人員都是由公務人員出任。是故，辯護代表由公務人員出任乃是合乎邏輯和適當的安排。

38. 此外，歐洲人權法庭在 *Pellegrin v. France*（2001）E.H.H.R. 26，第 65 67 段，裁定在一般情況下，《歐洲人權公約》第 6（1）條，不適用於獲授權行使公權的公務人員的行為和活動的爭議，其中以軍隊和警隊人員的情況最為明顯。公約第 6（1） 條與《香港人權法案條例》的內容相若。該案指出，這些行使公權的公務人員，實際上是分擔了國家的管治權力。他們肩負維護國家和公共機關整體利益的責任。在此情況下，國家的合理權益要求他們保持忠信的聯繫，而不須受制於第 6（1） 條的規定。

39. 基於上述理由，申請人指《警察（紀律）規則》第 9（1）條下有關辯護代表的規定，存在不公平和違反《香港人權法案條例》第 10 條的申請理由，沒有值得爭辯的地方。

（4）申請理由（3）：答辯人的決定違反《香港人權法案條例》第 10 條？

40. 申請人這項理由載於其表格 86A 的第 23 至 26 段。當中指出申請人有合理期望，其紀律聆訊會採用公平公正程序和刑事舉證標準。該部份進一步說答辯人不容許正停職的林督察、非警務人員的張國標先生或一名執業律師出任辯護代表，使申請人得不到公正審訊，所以要求法庭裁定答辯人的決定違反《香港人權法案條例》第 10 條。

41. 即使答辯人如申請人所說，作出了拒絕讓林督察、張先生或執業律師出任辯護代表的決定，答辯人也是按《警察（紀律）規則》第9（11）條的規定行事。這不能導致申請人得不到公平審訊的結論。

42. 申請人存檔的文件和口頭陳述都沒有具體說明，單就答辯人的決定而言，它如何使申請人得不到公平審訊，以致有違《香港人權法案條例》第 10 條下「獨立無私」的規定。再者，假若申請人所指稱的是答辯人並非「獨立無私」，不應由他出任主審官，則他是有權在正式聆訊前提出反對。按《警察（紀律）規則》第 6 條，申請人一旦提出反對，答辯人不得開始聆訊，而必須把反對的事情轉介一名高級警級人員，以便另外委派主審官。唯是申請人從沒有作出這樣的申請。

43. 申請人這項申請理由全然缺乏理據。

（5）申請理由（4）：答辯人拒絕押後聆訊的決定

44. 申請人指答辯人拒絕押後聆訊，以便他尋找合適的辯護代表。即使答辯人確實作出了這項決定，不爭的事實是聆訊在 2 月 14 日沒有開展，而是押後另訂日期。如前所述，就此進行司法覆核乃是沒有實際意義和徒然的。

（6）申請理由（5）：《基本法》第 35 條

45. 申請人新增的理據是，他在《警察（紀律）規則》下被剝奪聘請律師代表的權利，是抵觸了《基本法》第 35 條的規定。

46. 《基本法》第 35 條規定：

> 「香港居民有權得到秘密法律諮詢、向法院提起訴訟、選擇律師及時保護自己的合法權益或在法庭上為其代理和獲得司法補救。
>
> 香港居民有權對行政部門和行政人員的行為向法院提起訴訟。」

47. 郭大律師同意在處理本許可申請時，法庭可假設警隊紀律聆訊可被視為第 35 條下的「法庭」，因此本席無須就此作出裁決。

48. 在 *New World Development Co. Ltd* 一案中，上訴法庭確認尋求法律意見和獲得律師代表出席法律和法庭程序的重要性。一般而言，除卻有強而有力的原因外，不限制獲得《基本法》第 35 條的權利。上訴法庭同時指出《基本法》第 35 條不表示在研訊過程的每一個環節，接受研訊者都必然有權以律師代表行事。在考慮所涉研訊是否有抵觸《基本法》第 35 條時，法庭必須衡量所涉審裁體的程序，從整體而言，有否充份反映第 35 條所賦予的保障。這又涉及一個「比例是否適當」（proportionally）的問題，見判案書第 113 115 段。

49. 由此得見，法庭不能祇因為警隊的紀律聆訊，不容許違紀者由執業大律師代表辯護，便總論說這是抵觸了《基本法》第 35 條。誠如上訴法庭在 *New World Development Co. Ltd* 一案所強調，法庭必須衡量每宗個案的情況，不能一概而論。

50. 上訴法庭在該案同時指出，一如《香港人權法案條例》第 10 條一樣，《基本法》第 35 條的核心問題，是接受研訊者是否獲得公平審訊。就如在普通法下的原則一樣，衡量公平審訊須從多方面考慮，包括 ：

（1）控罪的嚴重性和可能引致的判罰；

（2）聆訊是否涉及法律觀點；

（3）涉案人士自我表述的能力；

（4）程序方面的困難處；

（5）合理迅速地作出裁決的需要；和

（6）在涉案各方之間取得平衡的需要。

51. 申請人的紀律研訊目前尚未開審。不能由律師作辯護代表，是否會對他做成損害，仍是言之過早。再者，申請人存檔的文件和所作的陳詞都沒有就其紀律研究可能涉及的議題和程序問題等加以說明。法庭無從評估申請人如果沒有律師出任辯護代表會否得不到公平審訊，和他在《基本法》第 35 條下的權利會否遭到削弱。

52. 另一方面，值得注意的是在警隊紀律研訊中，主審官和主控人員都並非專業律師。相反，違紀者卻可以選擇有法律訓練的警務人員出任辯護人。因此申請人指《警察（紀律）規則》否定違紀者委託辯護代表的權利的說法不確，而且違紀者縱使不能聘請執業律師代表辯護，這不等同他在聆訊中不能獲得法律方面的意見和協助，而且亦不等同必會對違紀者造成不公平之處。

53. 本席認為，以本申請的情況，這項申請理由沒有值得爭辯的情況。

總括

54. 基於上述原因和分析，本席認為不應酌情批予進行司法覆核申請的許可。本席因而拒絕申請人的許可申請。

55. 按一般訴訟常規，敗訴一方需付勝訴一方的訟費。在本申請中，申請人在表格 86A 除卻要求就其許可申請召開聆訊外，亦提出中期禁制令的申請。在此情況下，法庭不得不以訴訟各方到庭形式處理許可和禁制令的申請。在此情況下，申請人應付答辯人的訟費。本席因此頒下暫准訟費令，申請人須付答辯人本申請的訟費；如雙方不能就金額達成協議，可交法院評估。

高等法院原訟法庭法官（朱芬齡）

申請人：無律師代表，親自出庭。

答辯人：由律政司轉聘郭瑞熙大律師代表出庭。

第三十七條

香港居民的婚姻自由和自願生育的權利受法律保護。

案例

香港永久性居民的外國配偶是否必然享有逗留在香港的權利

P.583 | Marilyn G Aringo & Chaudhury Ispa 對 入境事務處處長

Marilyn G Aringo & Chaudhury Ispa v. Director of Immigration

Marilyn G Aringo & Chaudhury Ispa 對 入境事務處處長

HCAL96/2004

簡略案情

申請人為一對夫婦。妻子是菲律賓人並已經取得了在香港的居留權，而丈夫是打算在香港經商的孟加拉人。婚後不久，丈夫向入境處處長申請，希望根據當時的入境政策以作為其妻子的受供養人（dependant）身份延續其逗留香港的簽證。可是，入境處處長拒絕了他的申請和重新考慮他們請求的要求。申請人於是向原訟庭提出對入境處處長的決定進行司法覆核、並撤銷該項決定。申請人認為入境處處長的決定違反了《基本法》第 37 條即“香港居民的婚姻自由和自願生育的權利受法律保護”、以及《香港人權法案》第 19 條“關於結婚和家庭的權利”。

裁決摘要

申請人指出，因為丈夫是一名穆斯林教徒，而妻子卻信奉羅馬天主教，她不可能被當地的伊斯蘭社會所承認，所以他們兩人無法在孟加拉定居。另方面，妻子與前夫在香港辦理的離婚手續也不獲菲律賓法律的承認，因此，他們的婚姻在菲律賓是非法的，這意味著他們不可能在菲律賓合法地一起生活。據此，夫妻雙方唯一的希望就寄託在香港。

法庭認為，妻子擁有香港居留權，應該受到香港法律的保護，但這並不意味著夫妻雙方都能夠適用相關的香港法律，同時受到保護。先例中已經明確，《香港人權法案》並不影響任何關於入境事務的法律對無權進入或停留在香港的人士的適用。這些法律通常規定了進入、離開或在香港停留的事宜。既然無權進入或停留在香港的人士不能援引《香港人權法案》，當然也不可能通過由其家庭成員來援引《香港人權法案》和《基本法》中關於婚姻家庭權利的條款來為其提供保護。

法庭同時認為，申請人所申請的受供養關係無法成立。法庭指出，任何一對夫妻都必然有相互依賴的關係，但這種相互間的感性依賴並不等同於受供養關係。本案中丈夫有能力在香港開拓自己的事業，反之，妻子的經濟能力備受質疑，因此，入境處處長認為他們不受惠於當時的入境政策並非毫無根據，而且該決定亦在其法定權力範圍之內。最後，法庭駁回他們司法覆核的申請。

HCAL 96/2004

IN THE HIGH COURT OF THE

HONG KONG SPECIAL ADMINISTRATIVE REGION

COURT OF FIRST INSTANCE

CONSTITUTIONAL AND ADMINISTRATIVE LAW LIST
NO. 96 OF 2004

Between:

MARILYN G ARINGO	1st Applicant
CHAUDHURY ISPA	2nd Applicant
- and -	
Director of Immigration	Respondent

Before: Hon Hartmann J in Court

Date of Hearing: 5 September 2005

Date of Judgment: 5 September 2005

JUDGMENT

1. This is an application for judicial review. The applicants, who are husband and wife, seek to set aside a decision of the Director refusing to grant the husband what is commonly called a dependency visa. The visa, if granted, would allow the husband to live in Hong Kong as his wife's dependent.

2. The husband and wife were married on 29 June 2003 in Hong Kong. At the time of the marriage, the wife, a Filipino national, had right of abode in Hong Kong. The husband did not enjoy that right. He is a Bangladeshi national, having been born and raised in that country, and was at the time of the marriage a visitor only to Hong Kong.

3. A few days after the marriage, on 3 July 2003, the husband made an application to be allowed to remain in Hong Kong as a dependent of his wife. By letter dated 17 November 2003, the application was refused. The letter from the Director says:

> "I refer to your application for change of immigration status to take up residence in the Hong Kong Special Administrative Region as dependant of Ms Marilyn G. Aringo (the sponsor).
>
> Under existing immigration policy, a person may be allowed to come to the HKSAR to join his/her spouse or any resident here as his/her dependant if it is satisfied, amongst other things, that his/her intention is to come to HKSAR to join his/her spouse as his/her dependant, he/she is genuinely dependant on his/her spouse and his/her spouse is able to support his/her living in the HKSAR.
>
> After careful consideration of your application, I regret to inform you that your application is refused because we are not satisfied that:
>
> (a) your intention to come to the HKSAR to join the sponsor as her dependant;
>
> (b) the sponsor is financially capable to support your living in Hong Kong; and
>
> (c) you are genuinely dependant on the sponsor."

4. Requests were made to the Director to reconsider his decision. The Director refused to do so, those refusals being contained in letters of 22 March and 21 July 2004.

5. The applicants together now seek orders of *certiorari* to bring these decisions into this court and to quash them. It is the applicants' case that the decisions, read together and individually, were unreasonable in that they were decisions which could not have been made by any reasonable decision-maker.

6. The first ground of challenge, as I understand it, is that the husband is in fact a dependent of his wife and that it was unreasonable of the Director to conclude otherwise.

7. To determine this issue requires a brief consideration of the dependency policy itself. In *Christian Bulao Palmis v. Director of Immigration*, unreported, HCAL 2104/2001, I gave consideration to the meaning and extent of the policy. In paragraph 25, I said the following:

> "If dependency is the primary consideration, the starting point, in my view, must be the meaning of that word. It has a plain enough English meaning. It describes a state of reliance upon somebody. A dependant is somebody who must rely on another for maintenance, care and support, emotional and material, and is unable otherwise to manage. A person who can adequately support himself or herself by taking up employment or going into business and who does not require the care of a family member is therefore not dependent on another for that maintenance, care and support, not at least in material terms. It follows, in my view, that in accordance with the dependency scheme, if the primary purpose–or a principal purpose–of a person applying to reside in Hong Kong as a dependant of a family member is to work, then in the absence of special circumstances, that person is not a dependant."

I continued in the following paragraph by saying that mutual emotional dependency is not considered to be dependency for the purposes of the policy:

> "The facts will of course always determine the issue. If, for example, a wife seeks to accompany her husband to Hong Kong after he has obtained permission to work here, and while in Hong Kong has no intention to work herself but wishes only to occupy her natural place within the family setting, then even though she has private financial means, she may, it seems to me, whilst she is residing in Hong Kong, be her husband's dependant, looking to and needing his day-to-day care and support.
>
> *I say that, however, subject to the caveat that the mutual emotional dependency that is to be found in genuine family affection is not, of itself and viewed alone, a form of dependency which falls within the Director's policy. If it did, then all demonstrations of genuine family ties and the desire to be together would, on its own, fulfil the necessary criteria. That, in plain terms, would constitute a policy of family reunion, not a policy of dependency."* [my emphasis]

8. In the letter of 17 November 2003, it was said that the Director was not satisfied that the husband wished to remain in Hong Kong as a dependant of his wife; essentially, he was not satisfied

that a position of genuine dependency existed. That, in my view, cannot be criticised as being an irrational determination. The husband, a Bangladeshi, had first come to Hong Kong in early 2001 to conduct business here. Prior to his marriage, his essential connection to Hong Kong was as a visiting businessman.

9. Of more central relevance, when filling out his application form for a dependency visa, the husband filled out an information sheet. In that paper were two questions. The first question was: "My reasons for coming to the Hong Kong Special Administrative Region". In answer to that question, the husband wrote "To find business". The second question was: "My future plan in the Hong Kong Special Administrative Region". In answer, the husband wrote: "To make more business here in Hong Kong". With his own pen, therefore, the husband made it plain that he wished to settle with his wife in Hong Kong not only so that they could be together but so that he could carry on in business.

10. It has been suggested to me by Mr Beel, counsel for the husband and wife, that, as the first language of the husband is not English, the Director should not have taken these answers at face value. But the answers given by the husband are simple enough and their meaning is plain enough. In my view, if the meaning of answers is obvious, the Director is entitled to give them their plain and ordinary meaning.

11. It has been submitted by Mr Beel that the husband has not in fact worked in Hong Kong and has no intention of doing so. But if the husband is able to settle here and continues his business activities – as he has said he wishes to do – it would be rational, in my view, for the Director to hold that he would not be living here simply as a dependant of his wife but would be in the way of business here, even if that business, for example, concerned the despatch of goods to the Asian subcontinent, to India or Bangladesh.

12. It has been said that the husband intends to live in Hong Kong as a dependent in the sense that he wishes simply to be with his wife, as her dependent, as any married couple are dependent on each other. But as I have said when explaining the policy, mutual dependency by way of emotional ties in a marriage is not dependency for the purposes of the policy.

13. Accordingly, on the evidence, when the Director made the decisions under review I think it was well within his ambit of discretion to conclude that the husband was not intending to live in Hong Kong as his wife's dependent and was in truth seeking family union – an entirely laudible aim but not one that falls into the dependency policy.

14. On this issue alone, it seems to me, the application for judicial review must fail. The husband applied to remain in Hong Kong as a dependent; he did not apply on any other ground. The Director was not satisfied that he was a dependent. That determination, as I have said, was well within the discretion of the Director and it was the Director's decision to make.

15. In the event, however, that I am wrong in this regard, I move on to consider the further grounds of challenge advocated on behalf of the husband and wife.

16. The second ground of challenge is focused on the Director's finding that he was not satisfied that the wife had the financial capability to support the husband.

17. Mr Beel has submitted that there was no rational basis for the Director to conclude that the wife was not financially well enough off to act as her husband's sponsor. This was made evident, said Mr Beel, by the fact that, when the husband and wife sought legal aid to challenge the Director's decision, they were informed that the wife had too much money to qualify. In summary, the Director of Immigration said the wife did not have enough money while the Director of Legal Aid said she had too much. This conflict, said Mr Beel, is evidence that the Director must have reached a perverse decision.

18. I regret I do not see the logic in this. It is comparing apples with oranges. The Director of Immigration was looking to proof by the wife of sufficient financial substance to act as a sponsor for her husband, to be able to support him to a reasonable standard of living. It was his obligation to investigate the wife's finances and be assured of their substance. The Director of Legal Aid, however, had no need to investigate the wife's finances in the same manner. If she gave a financial statement which exceeded the margins allowed then that ended the matter: she was not entitled to legal aid. The two departments therefore were managing different policies at different times for different purposes.

19. In any event, on the evidence, it appears that the Director did have rational reason *for concern as to the wife's true* financial position. *Inter alia*, the Director's officers conducted an investigation into the financial affairs of the wife, including a visit to a shop which was meant to be managed by her, and including a visit to a place where she was meant to be working part-time. The shop was found to be shut. At the place where she was working part-time, it was discovered that she had not been working there for a while.

20. The third ground of challenge to the lawfulness of the Director's decisions is one which brings into focus the rights of the wife, as a permanent resident of Hong Kong, under art.19(1) of the Bill of Rights and art.37 of the Basic Law. The first article states that the family is the natural unit of society and is entitled to protection by the state. The second article guarantees freedom of marriage of Hong Kong residents and their right to raise a family. Mr Beel has said that the Director failed to take this into account in considering the application and, on this basis alone, the matter should be remitted for reconsideration.

21. This ground of challenge – an unusual one – is based on the fact that the husband is a Muslim while the wife is Roman Catholic. In Hong Kong, it is said, the fact that the couple have a 'mixed' marriage does not in any way impinge on their ability to live happily. However, if they are forced to live in Bangladesh or the Philippines their religious differences will attract such a high level of legal and social disapproval that it will jeopardise their marriage. In addition, certainly in the Philippines, their marriage will not even be recognised; this is because the wife is a divorcee.

22. This ground of challenge – which was not originally 'pleaded' and came before me almost informally – does not appear to be directly related to the Director's refusal to issue a dependency visa. It appears to be broader, going to the Director's discretion to permit a person to live in Hong Kong even though he or she may not qualify under any particular policy. In plain terms, the submission appears to be this. The husband and wife have only three places where they can live together: Bangladesh, the Philippines and Hong Kong. The first two places, however, offer real barriers. Only Hong Kong will allow them to live together in fulfilment of their marriage. The Director should therefore have considered the use of his discretion but either did not do so or did so arbitrarily.

23. In March 2004, the solicitors for the husband and wife wrote to the Philippines Consulate-General. The letter reads:

"We act for the captioned Philippine national, a HKSAR permanent resident. She has married and divorced two Filipino nationals in the HKSAR and has now married a Bangladeshi. She has applied to the HKSAR Director of Immigration for a dependant visa for her husband. Can you please confirm that, as a matter of Filipino domestic law, her divorces will not be recognised and, as such, her present marriage will not be recognised and her alien husband will therefore have no residency rights in the Philippines."

The Philippines Consulate replied in a letter of the same date, referring the solicitors to Article 26 of the Family Code of the Philippines:

"The only type of divorce recognised under Filipino law is one obtained between a Filipino and an alien spouse and not a divorce between two Filipino nationals. Thus, in a case where a Filipino spouse obtained a divorce from her Filipino husband in the United State of America, the Philippines Supreme Court declared the divorce as not recognisable under Philippines law, although it may be recognised in the United States."

24. Nothing is said in the letter concerning the husband's ability to stay in the Philippines with the wife if the couple wish to live in that country. There is therefore no evidence of the degree to which, if at all, the non-recognition of their marriage will affect rights of residence.

25. Nor is there evidence of the degree to which, if at all, on a day-to-day basis the husband and wife will be met by hostility in the Philippines. I am aware that, while the Philippines may be dominantly Christian, there is a large Muslim population.

26. A number of questions remain unanswered, a result perhaps of this challenge being created at the eleventh hour. Where, for example, if the husband and wife had to go to the Philippines, would they most likely have to live? In metropolitan Manila or out in the countryside? With respect, I do not see that the husband and wife can simply toss into the air a couple of balls marked 'possible difficulties' and then expect the Director to juggle with them.

27. The solicitors representing the husband and wife wrote to the Consulate-General of Bangladesh. They did not receive a reply. The solicitors then made inquiries in Bangladesh and received an opinion from an advocate in Bangladesh, Mr I Nurul Hoque. The opinion is to the following effect:

"Our country is Islamic State. Society and its culture pose Islam. Society and culture are to be observed as constitution of the State U/S 45(Ka) and 46(Kha). In respect of marriage between a son and a daughter, they are under compulsion to observe Islamic ideologies. One Muslim boy or girl may not be married to either Christian or Hindu, i.e. non-Muslim. If any girl/boy gets into marriage with any adverse religion, he/she might not be allowed in the society as per provision including in the State Constitution. He/she will not be allowed to live in a society as per law of Constitution or of community customs. He/she may not be allowed to live peacefully, violating provision of Constitution and sectarial custom. He/she becomes undeserving in his community, getting no mutual social prestige. So that if my Muslim boy/ girl gets married with Christian, he/she loses sectarial dignity in leading peaceful life. For that reason, that very person is isolated from the State and community."

28. I confess to having some difficulty understanding the full import of this opinion.

29. As to the existence of formal legal barriers, however, Mr Cooney, for the Director, has referred me to portions of the Constitution of Bangladesh. Fundamental rights are protected under Part 3 of the Constitution, art.28 saying the following :

"*Discrimination on grounds of religion*, etc.

(1) The State shall not discriminate against any citizen on grounds only of religion, race, caste, sex or place of birth.

(2) Women shall have equal rights with men in all spheres of the State and of public life.

(3) No citizen shall, on grounds only of religion, race, caste, sex or place of birth be subjected to any disability, liability, restriction or condition with regard to access to any place of public entertainment or resort, or admission to any educational institution."

In Part 3, art.41 reads :

"*Freedom of Religion*

(1) Subject to law, public order and morality–

(a) every citizen has the right to profess, practice or propagate any religion;

(b) every religious community or denomination has the right to establish, maintain and manage its religious institutions.

(2) No person attending any educational institution shall be required to receive religious instruction or to take part in or to attend any religious ceremony or worship, if that instruction, ceremony or worship relates to a religion other than his own."

30. The Constitution of Bangladesh, therefore, protects the fundamental right of persons who are resident in that country not to be discriminated against on the grounds of religion, race, caste, sex or place of birth.

31. In light of this and doing the best I can with the opinion from the Bangladeshi advocate, it seems to me that what is being said is the following. First, that Bangladesh is an Islamic State and that Islamic ideals, to a degree, will underline the meaning and intent of the Constitution. Second, that, in Islam, a marriage between an Islamic boy or girl and one who is not Islamic is forbidden. If there is to be a marriage, the spouse of the other religion must convert. Third, that if there is a marriage between a Muslim and a non-Muslim, that can lead to a loss of place in the community; that is, to being ostracised by the community.

32. However, nothing in the opinion that I have from the Bangladeshi advocate can be read as saying that a couple who have married elsewhere lawfully and who come to Bangladesh will not be recognised as a married couple simply because one of them is Muslim and one of them is not.

33. Social difficulties, of course, are a different matter. I recognise that in many societies, including Hong Kong, cross-cultural, cross-racial and cross-religious marriages may be faced with difficulties, the more so in traditional societies.

34. Mr Beel has submitted that the Director simply never considered the difficulties presented by the 'mixed' marriage of the husband and wife. But that is not correct. There is an affirmation from a senior officer in the Immigration Department, Ms Chan Suet-mui, who has said the following:

> "I did not think that the alleged ground relating to question on divorce in the Philippines and the religions in Bangladesh constituted a sufficient humanitarian ground for treating the 2nd Applicant's [husband's] application as an exception to the dependency policy."

35. Mr Beel's stronger point is this. He has submitted that the Director, being aware that the wife's fundamental rights as a married woman were in issue, and not having sufficient information before him to reach an informed decision, was obliged to carry out his own investigation. However, he failed to do so.

36. In this regard, Mr Beel has referred me to the decision of the Court of Final Appeal in *Secretary for Security v. Sakthevel Prabakar* [2004] 7 HKCFAR 187, in particular to headnote (5) which reads:

> "The following observations might be of assistance to the Secretary when considering individual cases. First, the difficulties of proof faced by persons in this situation should be appreciated. Second, it would not be appropriate for the Secretary to adopt an attitude of sitting back and putting the person concerned to strict proof of his claim; and it might be appropriate to draw attention to matters that obviously required clarification so that the person concerned could address them. Third, an understanding of country conditions at the time of the alleged torture in the past as well as the present time was usually relevant to the assessment of the claim."

37. In this case, however, the applicant, who had fled Sri Lanka, had claimed to be a victim of torture in that country and on that basis had resisted his return. The Hong Kong Government had given an undertaking to the United Nations to investigate all torture claims. As it was, however, it had delegated all responsibility to the United Nations High Commission for Refugees which had, without giving reasons, rejected the applicant's claim to be a victim of torture. The facts therefore were very different from the present case and the guidelines offered must be viewed in that context.

38. That being said, I accept, as a general principle, that there may be cases in which the Director will be under an obligation to institute investigations. But such cases will be rare. A person seeking to live in Hong Kong has the burden of demonstrating why he or she should be allowed to do so. The burden cannot simply be shifted to the Director.

39. Mr Cooney, for the Director, has pointed to the fact that there is nothing, on the evidence placed before the Director, to suggest that, if the husband and wife had to live in the Philippines, the husband would not be given right of residence there. He has also said there is nothing to suggest that, if the husband and wife were to live in Bangladesh, the wife would not be given residence there. Mr Cooney has said what I have said; namely, that the burden is always on a person seeking a visa to satisfy the Director that reasons exist for him to exercise his discretion favourably. The more so, he says, when the Director is being asked to exercise exceptional discretion. However, in the present case, other than the one letter from the Philippine Consulate-General and the somewhat opaque opinion from the advocate in Bangladesh, there was no material at all going either to legal handicaps or, just as important, to pressing social handicaps.

40. Mr Beel has replied by saying that at the very least the Director should have interviewed both the husband and the wife. Yes, that may have been desirable. But was a failure to do so, in all the circumstances, a failure that vitiated the Director's decisions? I do not believe so.

41. The applicants had plenty of opportunity – they were being legally represented, after all – to put forward fuller statements as to what the problems were. It was open to them to investigate matters with the respective immigration agencies, schools, local government and the like, but they did not do so. What is suggested instead is that the Director should, in cases of this kind – and therefore in all cases that throw up personal difficulties – institute his own extensive investigations. I do not see that the Director is under any such obligation. In the present case, for example, it would have been necessary not only to interview the applicants, but thereafter to check out the substance of their allegations. That itself, in respect of Bangladesh, could involve fairly extensive investigations on the part of the Director, and, in respect of the Philippines, to almost equally extensive investigations by him.

42. In any event, there is authority to the effect that the fact that the wife in the present case has protections under the Bill of Rights does not mean that *both* the applicants are covered by the Bill of Rights. In this regard I have been referred by Mr Cooney to the case of *Hai Ho Tak v. The Attorney-General* [1994] 2 HKLR 202. In this case, a 7-year-old boy sought leave to apply for judicial review to quash the decision of the Director to remove him from Hong Kong to the Mainland. His father and mother had the right of abode in Hong Kong and the boy would have had the right of abode too if he had been born here. The mother claimed that he had been born in Hong Kong. The Director said he had not. Central to the judgment was s.11 of the Bill of Rights which reads:

> "As regards persons not having the right to enter and remain in Hong Kong, this Ordinance does not affect any Immigration legislation governing entry into, stay in and departure from Hong Kong or the application of any such legislation."

In the judgment, Godfrey JA (as he then was) said the following (at 210):

> "In my opinion, the effect of section 11, on its true construction, is this.
>
> (1) The [Bill of Rights] Ordinance may not be invoked so as to effect [*sic*], as regards any person not having the right to enter and remain in Hong Kong, any immigration legislation governing his entry into, stay in or departure from Hong Kong, or the application of any such legislation.
>
> (2) This is so no matter who it is that invokes the Ordinance or on what ground he invokes it.
>
> (3) In particular (of course) *the Ordinance may not be invoked by the person not having the right to enter and remain in Hong Kong. That being so, it would be the height of absurdity if it could be invoked by someone else, e.g. another member of his family.* If the person not having the right to enter and remain in Hong Kong could not himself invoke the provisions of the Ordinance relating to his rights as a member

of the family, and it cannot make sense to allow other members of the family the right to invoke those provisions in relation to their rights as members of the same family. And section 11 should not be construed so as to attribute a non-sensical intention to the legislature." [my emphasis]

Applied in the present case – and I am bound by this judgment– what is being said, in plain terms, is that if the husband has no right to look to the Bill of Rights, then the matter cannot be approached via the back door, so to speak, by the wife doing so.

43. In the present case, the husband is a person who does not have the right to enter and remain in Hong Kong, save by permission of the Director of Immigration. In the circumstances, if the husband has no call upon the Bill of Rights or the provision concerning marriage in the Basic Law – and the matter essentially goes to him; it is, after all, his application for a dependency visa– then these provisions cannot be made applicable to him via the back door by looking to the wife's rights.

44. In the circumstances, for the reasons given, I am satisfied that this application for judicial review must be dismissed.

As to costs

45. Mr Cooney, for the Director, seeks costs. Mr Beel opposes the application. He does so on the basis that an important issue concerning the rights of the wife under the Bill of Rights has been raised.

46. The Bill of Rights issue, however, was not raised in the application for leave. Nor was it raised by way of an application to amend after leave had been granted. As I understand it, the issue only arose a few days ago. It first appeared in Mr Beel's skeleton argument and Mr Cooney did his best – over a weekend – to bring together some authorities to answer the challenge.

47. There should have been a formal application to amend. I only allowed the matter to be argued to ensure that the husband and wife should not be prejudiced.

48. Mr Beel has said that, in a broad sense, the constitutional issue was raised in the last paragraph of the application for judicial review which reads:

> "The Applicants say that both limbs of the decision are *Wednesbury* unreasonable and that the decision must be looked at in the round and rely on the comments of the Court of Appeal in the *Orizu* decision (copy enclosed) as to the treatment of the wife's income at the leave stage."

49. Mr Beel said that if the Director is obliged to act reasonably, he is obliged to consider the rights of relevant person under the Bill of Rights and/or the Basic Law. That may be correct but it does not thereby mean that when a legal challenge is made, the grounds of that challenge need not properly be identified. They must be adequately identified and that has not happened in the present case.

50. In applications of this kind, costs normally follow the event and, in my judgment, there is no reason why it should not do so in the present case. I therefore make an order in favour of the Director.

Judge of the Court of First Instance, High Court (M.J. Hartmann)

Mr Trevor Beel, instructed by Messrs Massie & Clement, for the Applicants

Mr Nicholas Cooney, instructed by the Department of Justice, for the Respondent

---

第三十九條

《公民權利和政治權利國際公約》、《經濟、社會與文化權利的國際公約》和國際勞工公約適用於香港的有關規定繼續有效，通過香港特別行政區的法律予以實施。

香港居民享有的權利和自由，除依法規定外不得限制，此種限制不得與本條第一款規定抵觸。

案例

具體的香港法律有無可能違反國際公約的規定？

Leung Kwok Hung, Fung Ka Keung, Christopher And Lo Wai Ming v. HKSAR

梁國雄、馮家強及盧偉明 對 香港特別行政區

HCMA 16/2003；FAMC 60 & 61/2004；FACC 1 & 2/2005

簡略案情

三名上訴人因其在組織遊行前拒絕依照《公安條例》第 13A 條的規定事前通知警務處處長（下稱“處長”），被起訴違反《公安條例》第 17 條舉行或協助舉行非法集會，在裁判署經審訊後被判有罪。上訴人遂向上訴庭提起上訴，認為《公安條例》的相關條款，尤其是其中第 13 條至第 15 條規定的通知要求，違反了《基本法》和《公民權利和政治權利國際公約》中有關“依法規定”和“必要性”的要求。

《基本法》第 27 條規定香港居民享有言論、集會、遊行等自由，第 39 條第一款規定《公民權利和政治權利國際公約》在香港繼續有效，通過香港的法律予以實施，即《香港人權法案》；第二款規定香港居民享有的權利和自由，除“依法規定”外不得限制，而此種限制不得與第一款規定抵觸。《公民權利和政治權利國際公約》第 21 條（即《香港人權法案》第 17 條）規定，除依法律之規定，且為民主社會維護國家安全或公共安全、公共秩序、維持公共衛生或風化、或保障他人權利自由所“必要”者外，不得限制行使和平集會之權利。

《公安條例》第 13 條至第 15 條賦予處長在其“合理地認為，為維護國家安全或公共安全、公共秩序或保障他人的權利和自由而有需要”時，反對公共遊行或對公共遊行施加條件的權力，上訴人指該權力用詞含糊，不合符“依法規定”的要求，可能被隨意主觀地行使甚至被濫用。上訴人認為尤其是“ordre public”的概念，因過於晦澀和含糊從而給予處長過大的酌情權，同時認為，在沒有充分指引的情況下，警員亦無法理解或應用該概念，引致執勤上的困難和不確定性。

裁決摘要

根據終審法院的判例，上訴庭確認對於《基本法》賦予的基本權利和自由應做目的性和廣泛性的解釋，以保證香港公民可充分享有該等權利和自由。但同時重申，基本的自由並非是絕對的，根據《基本法》第 39 條和《公民權利和政治權利國際公約》第 21 條，在下列情況下可對和平集會的權利施加限制：1）依法規定；2）為民主社會維護國家安全或公共安全、公共秩序、維持公共衛生或風化、或保障他人權利自由所必要。

從一般層面上來講，上訴庭認為《公民權利和政治權利國際公約》本身就定下了限制條件，因此，要求組織公共遊行人士須事先通知處長，並賦予其反對或對該遊行施加條件的權力（下稱“通知制度”）是有必要的，有關案例也確認了通知制度本身並無可非議之處，因此上訴庭認定在一般層面上通知制度是有必要性的，並未違憲。

對於“依法規定”的要求，上訴庭援引 *Shum Kwok Sher v. HKSAR* [2002] 5 HKCFAR 381，指出法律必須易於理解從而使人能夠將法律適用於自己的情形，且需足夠明確從而使人可預見後果並規範自己的行為，同時不應過於含糊而授予機構過多的權力。針對本案，上訴庭認為，通知制度符合“依法規定”的要求，理由包括：其中的限制直接來源於《公民權利和政治權利國際公約》，該公約被香港《基本法》認可，亦從未有法院認定公約中的規定由於不清晰而違憲；根據 *HKSAR v. Ng Kung Siu & Anr* [1999] 2 HKCFAR 442, 455，“ordre public”的概念雖然不精確，卻並非過於含糊而無法理解，只是更強化其固有的靈活性；而且，處長的決定是受到制衡的，受影響人士可向公共集會及遊行上訴委員會提起上訴甚至可向法院申請司法覆核。上訴庭強調涉及公共集會和遊行的法律從性質上來講就需要以概括性的措辭進行描述，否則會失去靈活性。上訴庭認為上述理由支持有關限制的“必要性”，並指出授予處長的權力與《基本法》和《公民權利和政治權利國際公約》中的有關限制是適度的，是合理且與其目的相稱的。因此上訴庭認定《公安條例》的有關規定並未違憲，從而駁回上訴人的請求。

作為該上訴的少數意見，有上訴庭法官認為答辯人未能證明《公安條例》授予員警限制集會和遊行的權力的必要性，而且，授予的權力亦過於廣泛從而影響其確定性。同時，《公安條例》亦未有向處長的權力限度提供任何指引，也未嘗試幫助可能受該權力影響的人士理解有關條款的含義。因此，認為《公安條例》的有關規定違反了《基本法》第 27 條和第 39 條，應撤銷上訴人的控罪。

上訴人不滿上訴庭的裁決，決定將案件上訴至終審法院，理由是處長以“public order（ordre public）”為理由而限制和平集會的酌情權因過於廣泛和不確定而違反了“依法規定”和“必要性”的要求。

終審法院認為“public order（ordre public）”包括法律和秩序層面的公共秩序，但不僅限於此，然而，其範圍無法被準確地界定。終審法院指出這個概念的明確性問題在憲法層面和法例層面的結論不一樣。憲法性規定往往以相對抽象的措辭表述，法例卻往往需要提供具體的指引。雖然《公安條例》只是照搬了《公民權利和政治權利國際公約》中的限制，終審法院認定《公民權利和政治權利國際公約》作為憲法性規定，其中“public order（ordre public）”的概念並無不妥，但《公安條例》中授權警務處處長以“public order（ordre public）”為理由而限制和平集會的酌情權則因缺乏具體指引而違反了“依法規定”的要求。不過，終審法院認為雖然“ordre public”含義不明確，但“public order”卻是一個清晰的概念，其僅包括法律和秩序層面的公共秩序。因此作為合理的補救，將“ordre public”從“public order（ordre public）”刪除即可，剩下的“public order”即符合“依法規定”的要求。

在判斷“必要性”要求時，終審法院則強調應適用“均衡比例”測試（Proportionality Test），即：1）有關限制必須與合法的目的（即《公民權利和政治權利國際公約》第 21 條中列明的目的）有關聯；2）限制和平集會權的手段不得超出為實現該合法目的所必須的限度。就本案而言，條件 1 顯然被滿足，而對於條件 2，終審法院考慮到以下幾個因素，認為亦被滿足：i）政府有積極的義務採取合理和恰當措施保障合法集會和平進行；ii）有關規定僅規範 30 人以上公共場所的公共遊行；iii）接到公共遊行的通知後，處長必須考慮各個方面的公共秩序，而其在決定反對公共遊行或限定條件時需要適用上述"均衡比例"測試；iv）處長必須在法定時限內表示反對公共遊行或要求限定條件；v）需要給出反對或者限定條件的適當理由；vi）針對處長的決定受影響人士可向公共集會及遊行上訴委員會提起上訴甚至可向法院申請司法覆核。因此，終審法院裁定雖然《公安條例》授予警務處處長為維持"public order（ordre public）"目的限制和平集會的酌情權因違反"依法規定"的要求而違憲，卻並不影響上訴人的定罪。同時，認為可通過將"ordre public"從"public order（ordre public）"中刪除，剩下的"public order"部份即同時符合"依法規定"和"必要性"的要求。終審法院因此駁回上訴人的請求。

在本案中終審法院同樣出現少數意見，有終審法院法官認為處長獲得事先通知的權力是合憲的，但可通過不那麼嚴苛的的方式，而不應以《公安條例》第 17 條規定的刑事制裁來強制執行。同時，其認為處長事先反對或限制公共遊行的權力是違憲的，因為該權力的界定不清晰，過於廣泛可能會危害到公民基本的自由和權利。因此認為應撤銷上訴人的控罪。

FACC Nos. 1 & 2 of 2005

IN THE HIGH COURT OF THE

HONG KONG SPECIAL ADMINISTRATIVE REGION

COURT OF APPEAL

FINAL APPEAL NOS. 1 & 2 OF 2005 (CRIMINAL)
(ON APPEAL FROM HCMA NO. 16 OF 2003)

Between:

LEUNG KWOK HUNG	1st Appellant
FUNG KA KEUNG , CHRISTOPHER	2nd Appellant
LO WAI MING	3rd Appellant
- and -	
HONG KONG SPECIAL ADMINISTRATIVE REGION	Respondent

Court: Chief Justice Li, Mr Justice Bokhary PJ, Mr Justice Chan PJ, Mr Justice Ribeiro PJ and Sir Anthony Mason NPJ

Dates of Hearing: 3, 5-6 & 10 May 2005

Date of Judgment: 8 July 2005

JUDGMENT

Chief Justice Li, Mr Justice Chan PJ, Mr Justice Ribeiro PJ and Sir Anthony Mason NPJ:

1. The freedom of peaceful assembly is a fundamental right. It is closely associated with the fundamental right of the freedom of speech. The freedom of speech and the freedom of peaceful assembly are precious and lie at the foundation of a democratic society.

2. These freedoms are of cardinal importance for the stability and progress of society for a number of inter-related reasons. The resolution of conflicts, tensions and problems through open dialogue and debate is of the essence of a democratic society. These freedoms enable such dialogue and debate to take place and ensure their vigour. A democratic society is one where the market place of ideas must thrive. These freedoms enable citizens to voice criticisms, air grievances and seek redress. This is relevant not only to institutions exercising powers of government but also to organizations outside the public sector which in modern times have tremendous influence over the lives of citizens. Minority views may be disagreeable, unpopular, distasteful or even offensive to others. But tolerance is a hallmark of a pluralistic society. Through the exercise of these freedoms minority views can be properly ventilated.

3. A peaceful assembly may consist of a procession, as it did in the present case. A procession is an effective means of communication because it involves an expression of the views of the participants as they move from one place to another. A procession has been aptly called an assembly in motion. The message the participants are seeking to communicate may have a wide exposure. A procession is a potent method of expression and is a common phenomenon in democratic societies including Hong Kong.

4. This appeal concerns a challenge to the constitutionality of the statutory scheme for the regulation of public processions contained in the Public Order Ordinance, Cap. 245 ("the Ordinance"). The focus of the challenge is on the contention that the statutory discretion conferred on the Commissioner of Police ("the Commissioner") to restrict the right of peaceful assembly for the purpose of "public order (ordre public)" is too wide and uncertain to satisfy the requirements of constitutionality.

The convictions

5. On 25 November 2002, the Chief Magistrate (Mr Patrick Li) convicted the 1st appellant of the offence of holding an unauthorized assembly and the 2nd and 3rd appellants of the offence of assisting the holding of such unauthorized assembly. These were offences under s. 17A(3)(b)(i) of the Ordinance. The offences were in respect of a public procession on 10 February 2002. Each appellant was bound over on his own recognizance for $500 for a period of three months.

The facts

6. The facts can be shortly stated. In the late morning of Sunday 10 February 2002, a number of persons gathered at Chater Garden for a procession to protest against the conviction of an activist for assault and obstruction of a public officer. The 2nd appellant, using a loudhailer, called on the participants to get ready. Police officers were at the scene since there was a demonstration concerning the right of abode at Chater Garden at that time. The 1st appellant, a well known activist, was the person in charge of the procession. A police officer invited him to go through the statutory notification procedure. He refused and was warned by the police officer of the consequences of his failure to comply before the procession started.

7. The procession comprising some 40 people then set off from Chater Garden in the direction of Police Headquarters at Arsenal Street proceeding along Queensway. Ignoring police advice to use the pedestrian pavement, they used the left traffic lane of the road. As the procession proceeded, others joined in so that the number swelled to about 96 persons.

8. On arrival outside Police Headquarters, again ignoring police advice not to use the North Gate where space was limited, the participants proceeded to that Gate. They stayed on the pavement there for about an hour when speeches were made. The procession was at all times peaceful.

Court of Appeal

9. The appellants appealed to the Court of First Instance which directed the appeal to be heard by the Court of Appeal. The Court of Appeal (Ma CJHC and Yeung JA, Stock JA dissenting) upheld the convictions: *HKSAR v. Leung Kwok Hung & Others* [2004] 3 HKLRD 729.

Leave to Appeal

10. The Appeal Committee granted leave to appeal, certifying the following question of law: Is the scheme which the Ordinance lays down for notification and control of public processions constitutional?

Representation

11. In considering this important appeal, the Court is indebted to Mr Martin Lee SC for the 2nd and 3rd appellants and Mr Gerard McCoy SC for the respondent, the Government, and their respective teams for their research and presentations which were of considerable assistance. The Court also wishes to thank the 1st appellant, who appeared in person, for his written submissions and his measured address.

The Basic Law

12. It is necessary, first, to set out the relevant constitutional provisions. Article 27 of the Basic Law in so far as relevant provides:

> "Hong Kong residents shall have freedom of speech...; freedom of association, of procession and of demonstration..."

As has been discussed, the freedom of assembly is closely associated with the freedom of speech. It is also closely related to and indeed overlaps with the freedoms of association, procession and demonstration. The freedom of assembly is of course a right to peaceful assembly. Obviously, the scope of the right does not extend to an assembly which is not peaceful.

13. Article 39 of the Basic Law in so far as relevant provides:

> "[1] The provisions of the International Covenant on Civil and Political Rights... as applied to Hong Kong shall remain in force and shall be implemented through the laws of the Hong Kong Special Administrative Region.
>
> [2] The rights and freedoms enjoyed by Hong Kong residents shall not be restricted unless as prescribed by law. Such restrictions shall not contravene the provisions of the preceding paragraph of this Article."

14. In accordance with Article 39, the Hong Kong Bill of Rights Ordinance Cap.383 ("BORO") incorporates the provisions of the International Covenant on Civil and Political Rights ("the ICCPR") as applied to Hong Kong. However, it should be noted that although Article 20 of the ICCPR has been applied to Hong Kong, it has not been incorporated into BORO. Article 20 provides:

> "1. Any propaganda for war shall be prohibited by law.
>
> 2. Any advocacy of national, racial or religious hatred that constitutes incitement to discrimination, hostility or violence shall be prohibited by law."

BORO

15. Article 17 of BORO which corresponds to Article 21 of the ICCPR guarantees the right of peaceful assembly as follows:

> "The right of peaceful assembly shall be recognized. No restrictions may be placed on the exercise of this right other than those imposed in conformity with the law and which are necessary in a democratic society in the interests of national security or public safety, public order (ordre public), the protection of public health or morals or the protection of the rights and freedoms of others."

The approach

16. As has been emphasized at the outset of this judgment, the freedom of peaceful assembly is a fundamental constitutional right. It is well established in our jurisprudence that the courts must give such a fundamental right a generous interpretation so as to give individuals its full measure. *Ng Ka Ling v. Director of Immigration* (1999) 2 HKCFAR 4 at 28–9. On the other hand, restrictions on such a fundamental right must be narrowly interpreted. *Gurung Kesh Bahadur v. Director of Immigration* (2002) 5 HKCFAR 480 at para.24. Plainly, the burden is on the Government to justify any restriction. This approach to constitutional review involving fundamental rights, which has been adopted by the Court, is consistent with that followed in many jurisdictions. Needless to say, in a society governed by the rule of law, the courts must be vigilant in the protection of fundamental rights and must rigorously examine any restriction that may be placed on them.

The constitutional requirements for restriction

17. The exercise of the right of peaceful assembly, whether under the Basic Law or under BORO, may be subject to restrictions provided two requirements are satisfied:

(1) The restriction must be prescribed by law ("the 'prescribed by law' requirement").

(2) The restriction must be necessary in a democratic society in the interests of national security or public safety, public order (ordre public), the protection of public health or morals or the protection of the rights and freedoms of others ("the necessity requirement"). It will be convenient to refer to the specified purposes as "the legitimate purposes".

It will be convenient to refer to these requirements as "the constitutional requirements for restriction".

18. As far as the right of peaceful assembly in BORO is concerned, the constitutional requirements for restriction are laid down in Article 17 itself. In relation to the first requirement, although Article 17 uses the expression of "in conformity with the law" rather than the expression of "as prescribed by law" found in Article 39(2) of the Basic Law, the principle involved is the same. See *Shum Kwok Sher v. HKSAR* (2002) 5 HKCFAR 381 at para.60 where the expression "according to law" in Article 11(1) of BORO, providing for the presumption of innocence in the trial for a criminal offence, was held to incorporate the same principle as that of "as prescribed by law" in Article 39(2).

19. As regards the right of peaceful assembly under the Basic Law, Article 39(2) provides that any restriction must not contravene Article 39(1), that is, the ICCPR as applied to Hong Kong, which has been implemented by BORO. In relation to the right of peaceful assembly, Article 39(2) provides that any restriction must comply with the two constitutional requirements for restriction in Article 21 of ICCPR, namely, (i) the requirement of "in conformity with the law" which is the same as the requirement of "as prescribed by law" in Article 39(2); and (ii) the necessity requirement.

20. There is no difference between the right of peaceful assembly guaranteed by the Basic Law and that provided for in BORO and no distinction will be made between them in this judgment except where necessary.

21. In the present case, the statutory scheme contained in the Ordinance provides for restrictions on the right of peaceful assembly. Having regard to the focus of the challenge, the crucial question which the Court must consider is whether the Commissioner's discretion to restrict the right of peaceful assembly for the purpose of "public order (ordre public)" satisfies the constitutional tests for restriction.

Positive duty on the Government

22. Before discussing the constitutional requirements for restriction, it must be pointed out that the right of peaceful assembly involves a positive duty on the part of the Government, that is the executive authorities, to take reasonable and appropriate measures to enable lawful assemblies to take place peacefully. However, this obligation is not absolute for

the Government cannot guarantee that lawful assemblies will proceed peacefully and it has a wide discretion in the choice of the measures to be used. What are reasonable and appropriate measures must depend on all the circumstances in the particular case.

23. The existence of this positive duty is acknowledged by the Government. In the "Second Report on the Hong Kong Special Administrative Region of the People's Republic [of] China in the light of the [ICCPR]" to the Human Rights Committee, the Government stated:

> "... essentially, the Police need advance notice of demonstrations so that, among other things, proper arrangements can be made to minimise any disruption to traffic and inconvenience caused to other members of the public. *The HKSAR has an obligation to assist and provide for the right of peaceful public assembly and demonstration* and cannot do so in Hong Kong's condition without prior notice of large peaceful processions and assemblies." (emphasis added)

See para.221 in the section dealing with the right of peaceful assembly. The reference to "Hong Kong's condition" in this passage presumably includes its density of population and its relatively narrow streets and roads in urban areas. Before this Court, Mr McCoy SC for the respondent, fully accepts and indeed relies on the fact that Government has this positive duty.

24. The recognition of this positive duty is consistent with the position under the European Convention for the Protection of Human Rights and Fundamental Freedoms ("the European Convention"). Article 11 of that Convention guarantees the right of peaceful assembly. In *Plattform 'Ärzte für das Leben' v. Austria* (1991) 13 EHRR 204, the European Court of Human Rights interpreted Article 11 to impose a duty on the state to take positive measures to enable lawful demonstrations to proceed. The case concerned anti-abortion demonstrations held by the applicant association and the allegedly insufficient protection given by the Austrian police against attempts at disruption by pro-abortion groups. The Court observed that a demonstration may give offence to those with opposing views and demonstrators must be able to proceed without fear of physical violence by opponents; such a fear would have a deterrent effect (para.32). It held that in a democracy, the right to counter-demonstrate cannot extend to inhibit the exercise of the right to demonstrate.

> "Genuine, effective freedom of peaceful assembly cannot, therefore, be reduced to a mere duty on the part of the State not to interfere: a purely negative conception would not be compatible with the object and purpose of Article 11. Like Article 8 [right to respect for private and family life], Article 11 sometimes requires positive measures to be taken, even in the sphere of relations between individuals, if need be." (para.32)

But the Court recognized that the obligation to take positive measures is not absolute.

> "While it is the duty of Contracting States to take reasonable and appropriate measures to enable lawful demonstrations to proceed peacefully, they cannot guarantee this absolutely and they have a wide discretion in the choice of the means to be used. In this area the obligation they enter into under Article 11 of the Convention is an obligation as to measures to be taken and not as to results to be achieved." (para.34)

The "prescribed by law" requirement

25. The "prescribed by law" requirement in Article 39(2) of the Basic Law was considered by this Court in *Shum Kwok Sher*. In that case, the Court held that the common law offence of misconduct in public office was sufficiently precise to satisfy the criteria of "prescribed by law".

26. In his judgment in *Shum Kwok Sher*, Sir Anthony Mason NPJ, taking into account a range of comparative materials, held that, consistently with international human rights jurisprudence, the expression "prescribed by law" in Article 39(2) mandates the principle of legal certainty (at para.60).

27. To satisfy this principle, certain requirements must be met. It must be adequately accessible to the citizen and must be formulated with sufficient precision to enable the citizen to regulate his conduct. As pointed out by Sir Anthony Mason NPJ (at para.63), the explanation of these requirements in the often quoted passage in the majority judgment of the European Court of Human Rights in *Sunday Times v. United Kingdom (No.1)* (1979–80) 2 EHRR 245 (at para.49, p.271), the "thalidomide" case, is of assistance:

> "First, the law must be adequately accessible: the citizen must be able to have an indication that is adequate in the circumstances of the legal rules applicable to a given case. Secondly, a norm cannot be regarded as a 'law' unless it is formulated with sufficient precision to enable the citizen to regulate his conduct: he must be able–if need be with appropriate advice–to foresee, to a degree that is reasonable in the circumstances, the consequences which a given action may entail. Those consequences need not be foreseeable with absolute certainty: experience shows this to be unattainable. Again, whilst certainty is highly desirable, it may bring in its train excessive rigidity and the law must be able to keep pace with changing circumstances. Accordingly, many laws are inevitably couched in terms which, to a greater or lesser extent, are vague and whose interpretation and application are questions of practice."

28. There is an inevitable tension between requiring a law to be formulated with sufficient precision and the desirability of avoiding excessive rigidity in the law. The appropriate level of precision must depend on the subject matter of the law in question. See *Shum Kwok Sher* at para.64.

29. A law which confers discretionary powers on public officials, the exercise of which may interfere with fundamental rights, must give an adequate indication of the scope of the discretion. The degree of precision required of the law in this connection will depend upon the particular subject matter of the discretion. *Malone v. United Kingdom* (1984) 7 EHRR 14 at para.68. See also *Silver v. United Kingdom* (1983) 5 EHRR 347 at para.88 and *Sunday Times v. United Kingdom* at para.49. In *Malone v. United Kingdom*, the police had tapped the applicant's telephone conversation in the course of a criminal investigation. The European Court of Human Rights held that this was an interference with his right to respect for his "private life" and "correspondence" under art. 8 of the European Convention (para.64). The issue was whether the interference was "in accordance with law" as required by art. 8(2), which mandates the principle of legal certainty. The Court held that English law did not indicate with reasonable clarity the scope and manner of exercise of the relevant discretion conferred on the public authorities in the field of interception of communications. Accordingly, the interferences with his right under art. 8 were not

"in accordance with law" (paras.79 and 80).

The necessity requirement

30. Turning to the constitutional requirement of necessity, any restriction on the right of peaceful assembly must be necessary in a democratic society in the interests of national security or public safety, public order (ordre public), the protection of public health or morals or the protection of the rights and freedoms of others.

31. As the Court has held, the word "necessary" in this requirement should be given its ordinary meaning and no assistance is to be gained by substituting for "necessary" a phrase such as "pressing social need". *HKSAR v. Ng Kung Siu* (1999) 2 HKCFAR 442 at 460 F–G; *Ming Pao Newspapers Limited v. Attorney-General* [1996] AC 907 at 919 G–H.

32. The Siracusa Principles on the limitation and derogation provisions in the ICCPR agreed to in 1984 by a group of experts ("the Siracusa Principles") state that, while there is no single model of a democratic society, a society which recognizes and respects the human rights set forth in the United Nations Charter and the Universal Declaration of Human Rights may be viewed as meeting the definition of a democratic society. This view is consistent with that of the European Court of Human Rights that the hallmarks of a democratic society include pluralism, tolerance and broadmindedness. *Handyside v. United Kingdom* (1976) 1 EHRR 737 at para.49; *Smith and Grady v. United Kingdom* (1999) 29 EHRR 493 at para.87.

The proportionality test

33. The Court has accepted that the constitutional requirement of necessity involves the application of a proportionality test. *Ng Kung Siu* at 461 A–B. See also *Ming Pao Newspapers Ltd v. Attorney-General* [1996] AC 907 at 917 D–E. In *Ng Kung Siu*, the Court considered the constitutionality of the statutory prohibition of desecration of the national and regional flags with criminal sanctions. The Court, applying the proportionality test, examined whether the limited restriction by such prohibition on the guaranteed right to freedom of expression is proportionate to the aims sought to be achieved thereby. The Court answered that question in the affirmative. *Ng Kung Siu* at 461.

34. The use of a proportionality principle in examining whether a restriction of a fundamental right is necessary in a democratic society is consistent with the approach to constitutional review in many jurisdictions. See for example: *Handyside v. United Kingdom* at para.49; *Sunday Times v. United Kingdom* at para.62; *Norris v. Ireland* (1991) 13 EHHR 186 at para.41 (the European Court of Human Rights); *R (Daly) v. Home Secretary* [2001] 2 AC 532 at para.27; *R v. Shayler* [2003] 1 AC 247 at paras.60 and 61 (United Kingdom); *R v. Oakes* (1986) 26 DLR (4th) 200 (Canada); *De Freitas v. Ministry of Agriculture* [1999] 1 AC 69 (Privy Council); *S. v. Makwanyane* 1995 (3) SA 391 (South Africa). See also Dr M Nowak: *UN Covenant on Civil and Political Rights: CCPR Commentary* (1993) ("*Nowak*") at 379. Although the terms in which the proportionality test is formulated for application may vary from one jurisdiction to another, having regard to matters such as the text of the constitutional instrument in question and the legal history and tradition informing constitutional interpretation in the jurisdiction concerned, the nature of the proportionality principle is essentially the same across the jurisdictions.

35. By applying a proportionality test for considering any restriction on the right of peaceful assembly, a proper balance is struck between the interests of society on the one hand and the individual's right of peaceful assembly on the other. In formulating the terms of the proportionality test in the Hong Kong context, it is of critical importance to bear in mind that the legitimate purposes for restriction of this right have been set out in the relevant constitutional text. It must be emphasised that the legitimate purposes specified in Article 21 of the ICCPR are the only legitimate purposes. This list is exhaustive. There cannot be a restriction for any other purpose. This is in contrast to constitutional instruments where the test for restriction is formulated only as a general formula, for example, by reference to what is necessary in a democratic society, without any specification of the purposes that may legitimately be pursued by a restriction.

36. As the legitimate purposes that may be pursued by any restriction on the right of peaceful assembly have been constitutionally specified in Hong Kong, the proportionality test should be formulated in these terms: (1) the restriction must be rationally connected with one or more of the legitimate purposes; and (2) the means used to impair the right of peaceful assembly must be no more than is necessary to accomplish the legitimate purpose in question.

37. In *De Freitas v. Ministry of Agriculture*, the Privy Council was concerned with the constitutionality of a statute restricting civil servants' freedom of speech in relation to any information or expressions of opinion on matters of political controversy. One of the requirements for restriction specified in the constitutional instrument in question was that it must be reasonably justifiable in a democratic society. See p.74 B and p.80 C. In relation to this requirement, the Privy Council adopted a three stage test which has been extensively cited in many jurisdictions:

> "whether: (i) the legislative objective is sufficiently important to justify limiting a fundamental right; (ii) the measures designed to meet the legislative objective are rationally connected to it; and (iii) the means used to impair the right or freedom are no more than is necessary to accomplish the objective." (at p.80 G)

38. Compared to the proportionality test formulated above for Hong Kong, the *De Freitas* test has incorporated an extra requirement, namely whether the legislative objective is sufficiently important to justify limiting a fundamental right. The Privy Council considered this extra requirement appropriate in *De Freitas* as the relevant constitutional instrument prescribed only the general formula of what is reasonably justifiable in a democratic society without specifying the permissible purposes for which a restriction could be imposed. In contrast, in the Hong Kong context, in relation to the right of peaceful assembly, the legitimate purposes for which a restriction may be imposed on the right are constitutionally set out in a comprehensive manner. That being so, the extra requirement, whatever its relevance may be in other situations, is unnecessary in the present context.

39. Having discussed the relevant constitutional provisions and the constitutional requirements for restriction, one can turn to the statutory scheme for the regulation of public processions contained in the Ordinance.

Background of the Ordinance

40. The Ordinance assumed its present form after enactment by the Provisional Legislative Council of the Public Order (Amendment) Ordinance (No. 119 of 1997), coming into effect on 1 July 1997.

41. The previous version of the Ordinance was the 1995 version after the amendments of that year. Under that version, the purposes for which the Commissioner could restrict the right of peaceful assembly were limited to public safety or public order. On 23 February 1997, the Standing Committee of the National People's Congress of the People's Republic of China adopted its Decision on treatment of the laws previously in force in Hong Kong in accordance with Article 160 of the Basic Law. By this Decision, the Standing Committee decided that major amendments to the Ordinance since 27 July 1995 were in contravention of the Basic Law and those provisions were not adopted as the laws of the Hong Kong Special Administrative Region.

42. It was to fill the lacuna resulting from the Standing Committee's Decision which would arise on 1 July 1997 that the Public Order (Amendment) Ordinance was enacted. This was done after a public consultation exercise with the issue of the Consultation Document on Civil Liberties and Social Order by the Chief Executive's Office in April 1997. As Mr McCoy for the respondent submits, the statute enacted in 1997 represented a sincere effort to comply with the ICCPR as applied to Hong Kong and there has been no suggestion that the law has in practice been abused, with countless public processions having taken place since it came into effect on 1 July 1997. However, the Court's duty is of course to adjudicate on the constitutionality of the scheme as a matter of law.

The statutory scheme

Limited scope

43. At the outset, it is important to appreciate the limited scope of the Ordinance in regulating public processions. The statute only regulates public processions consisting of more than 30 persons on a public highway or thoroughfare or in a public park. Section 13(2)(a) and (b). It will be convenient to refer to such a public procession as "a public procession subject to the statutory scheme". A public procession is defined as a procession in, to or from a public place organized as such for a common purpose and includes any meeting held in conjunction with such a procession. Public place is defined as any place to which the public or any section of the public are entitled or permitted to have access, whether on payment or otherwise. Section 2(1).

44. It follows that (i) a public procession consisting of not more than 30 persons, even though it is on a public highway, or thoroughfare or in a public park, or (ii) a public procession consisting of more than 30 persons, but not on a public highway or thoroughfare or in a public park, is not subject to the statute. A public procession of the kind in (i) or (ii) may freely take place without the need to observe the statutory requirements for a public procession subject to the statutory scheme.

45. A public procession subject to the statutory scheme may take place if and only if: (a) the Commissioner has been notified of the intention to hold the procession ("the notification requirement"); (b) the Commissioner has notified that he has no objection to the procession taking place or is taken to have issued a notice of no objection ("the no objection requirement"); and (c) the requirements under s. 15 of the Ordinance are complied with ("the s. 15 requirements"). Section 13.

(a) The notification requirement

46. The features of the notification requirement may be summarised as follows:

(1) Notice of the intention to hold the public procession must be given in writing to the Commissioner. Section 13A(1). The notice is usually given by the organizer.

(2) Notice must be given one week before the intended date for the procession. Section 13A(1)(b).

(3) The Commissioner has a discretion to accept shorter notice and must do so where he is reasonably satisfied that earlier notice could not have been given. Section 13A(2). If he decides not to accept shorter notice, he must inform the organizer in writing as soon as practicable and state the reasons why shorter notice is not acceptable. Section 13A(3).

(4) The written notice must be delivered to the officer in charge of a police station and must contain particulars of (a) the name, address and telephone number of (i) the organizer and any society or organization promoting or connected with the holding of the procession and (ii) a person able to act, if necessary, in place of the organizer for the purpose of s.15(1)(a) (which requires the organizer, or a person nominated by him to act in his place, to be present throughout the procession); (b) the purpose and subject matter of the procession; (c) its date, precise route, time of commencement and duration; (d) the location, time of commencement and duration of any meeting to be held in conjunction with the procession and (e) an estimate by the organizer of the number of people expected to attend the procession. The Commissioner must issue a written acknowledgement of receipt of the notice. Section 13A(4) and (5).

(b) The no objection requirement

47. Upon notification of the intention to hold a public procession, the statute confers on the Commissioner a discretion to object to the public procession being held

> "if he reasonably considers that the objection is necessary in the interests of national security or public safety, public order (ordre public) or the protection of the rights and freedom of others." Section 14(1).

It will be convenient to refer to the interests of national security or public safety, public order (ordre public) and the protection of the rights and freedoms of others collectively as "the statutory legitimate purposes". It should be noted that compared to the legitimate purposes set out in art. 21 of the ICCPR, the statutory legitimate purposes are more limited in that the purpose of "the protection of public health or morals" found in art. 21 has been omitted. Section 2(2) contains a direction as to how the statutory legitimate purposes should be interpreted. It relevantly provides:

> "In this Ordinance the expressions 'public safety', 'public order (ordre public)', ... and 'the protection of rights and freedoms of others' are interpreted in the same way as under [the ICCPR] as applied to Hong Kong. 'National security' means the safeguarding of the territorial integrity and the independence of the People's Republic of China."

48. If the Commissioner objects, he must do so as soon as practicable and in any event within the statutory time limits. His objection and the reasons must be notified in writing to the organizer. Section 14(2). The time limit varies depending on when notification is given: (a) where one week's notification is given, the time limit is not later than 48 hours before the notified commencement time of the procession; (b) where shorter notice of 72 hours or more has been accepted by the Commissioner, it

is not later than 24 hours before the notified commencement time; (c) where shorter notice of less than 72 hours has been accepted by the Commissioner, it is not later than the notified commencement time. Section 14(3).

49. If the Commissioner does not object, he must notify the organizer in writing as soon as practicable and in any event within the statutory time limit. In the absence of notification of objection within the time limit, the Commissioner is taken to have issued a notice of no objection. Section 14(4).

50. Under the statutory scheme, the Commissioner is obliged not to object if he reasonably considers that the relevant statutory legitimate purpose could be met by imposing conditions. Section 14(5). The test for the exercise of his discretion to impose conditions is in identical terms to that of his discretion to object, namely "where [the Commissioner] reasonably considers it necessary in the interests of national security or public safety, public order (ordre public) or the protection of the rights and freedoms of others", that is, for the statutory legitimate purposes. As has been noted, the statutory legitimate purposes of "public safety", "public order (ordre public)" and "the protection of the rights and freedoms of others" must be interpreted in the same way as under the ICCPR in accordance with the direction in s.2(2). Where the Commissioner decides to impose any condition, he must give written notice to the organizer and state the reasons why such condition is considered necessary. Section 15(2). The Commissioner may later amend any condition imposed. As with the imposition of the earlier condition, he must similarly give written notice and state the reasons. Section 15(3).

51. Although the statute does not specify the time limits within which the Commissioner must give notice of the conditions imposed, as a matter of statutory interpretation, he must do so within a reasonable time. What is a reasonable time in a particular case would depend on all the circumstances, including when the proposed procession was notified, when the proposed procession is to take place and the subject matter of the condition imposed. In this connection, the statutory time limits for objection may be considered as a useful reference point. Where the Commissioner imposes a condition, in order to avoid any misunderstanding, his notice to the organizer should clearly state the condition imposed and should distinguish it from other matters (not being conditions), such as advice on practical matters or reminders of statutory provisions, which he may consider it appropriate to put in the notice.

52. The Commissioner's discretion to object and his discretion to impose conditions are only delegable to police officers at a senior level, that is, of the rank of inspector or above. Section 52.

(c) The s.15 requirements

53. At every public procession subject to the statutory scheme:

(a) the organizer must be present throughout the procession or if he is not present, there must be a person nominated by him to act in his place;

(b) good order and public safety must throughout be maintained; and,

(c) the control of any amplification device that is used in such a manner that it causes noise that would not be tolerated by a reasonable person must be surrendered to a police officer, if so required, for the duration of the procession. Section 15(1).

The Commissioner's discretion to restrict

54. The Commissioner's discretion to object to a notified public procession and his discretion to impose conditions are expressed in identical terms and will simply be referred to collectively as "the discretion to restrict". The test for its exercise is if the Commissioner reasonably considers that the objection or the condition is necessary for the statutory legitimate purposes, including "public order (ordre public)" ("the statutory test of necessity"). The test imposed is an objective test.

55. The provenance of the statutory test of necessity is immediately recognizable. It incorporates the necessity requirement in art. 21 of the ICCPR (corresponding to art. 17 of BORO). And s.2(2) of the Ordinance directs that the statutory legitimate purposes of "public safety", "public order (ordre public)" and "the protection of the rights and freedoms of others" must be interpreted in the same way as under the ICCPR as applied to Hong Kong. This technique of incorporating the ICCPR into a statute is an unusual one.

56. Although the direction on interpretation in s.2(2) does not specifically cover the expression "necessary" and the statutory test of necessity does not refer to the expression "in a democratic society" found in art. 21 of the ICCPR, the clear legislative intent, evident from the incorporation of the ICCPR necessity requirement into the statute, is that the statutory necessity test should be interpreted and approached in the same way as the necessity requirement found in art. 21.

57. As the ICCPR necessity requirement involves the application of a proportionality test, it follows that that test must also be applied in relation to the statutory necessity test. The Commissioner has a discretion to restrict the right of peaceful assembly, by objecting to or by imposing conditions on a notified public procession. In deciding whether and if so what restriction to impose in the exercise of his discretion, the Commissioner must consider: (1) whether a potential restriction is rationally connected with one or more of the statutory legitimate purposes; and (2) whether the potential restriction is no more than is necessary to accomplish the legitimate purpose in question.

58. As discussed above, the conclusion that the proportionality test must be applied is based on the incorporation of the ICCPR necessity requirement into the Ordinance. As has been observed, this is an unusual technique. Even if this technique had not been used, although it is unnecessary to decide the point, the position would appear to be that, by virtue of art. 39(2) of the Basic Law, the proportionality test would in any event have to be applied in exercising a statutory discretion that may restrict the right of peaceful assembly. That Article provides that, in addition to the "prescribed by law" requirement, any restriction must not contravene the provisions of the ICCPR as applied to Hong Kong. As the ICCPR necessity requirement contained in art. 21 involves the application of a proportionality test, that test would have to be applied by virtue of art. 39(2).

Duty to give reasons

59. As has been stated, the Commissioner is under a statutory duty to give reasons where he decides not to accept shorter notice and where he objects to or imposes conditions on a notified procession. The duty is to give adequate reasons. Plainly, the bald assertion of a conclusion would not be sufficient. Where the Commissioner decides to object or to impose conditions, the reasons given must be sufficient to show that he has properly applied the proportionality test in making his decision.

Appeals

60. The statutory scheme provides for an appeal to an Appeal Board against a decision by the Commissioner to object to a public procession or to impose conditions. A person, society or organization (i) named in the notice of intention to hold a public procession; or (ii) to whom a notice of objection is given, who is aggrieved by such a decision, is entitled to appeal. Section 16(1).

61. The Chief Executive appoints a Chairman and a panel of 15 persons, including two Deputy Chairmen, for a term of not more than two years and they may be reappointed. The Chairman must be a retired Judge of the High Court or the District Court or a retired magistrate who has served for more than 10 years. Sections 43(2), 43(3) and 43(4). The Appeal Board for an appeal consists of four members; the Chairman (or a Deputy Chairman) and three persons selected in rotation in accordance with the alphabetical order of their surnames from the panel. Section 44(1). Decision is by majority, with the Chairman (or Deputy Chairman) having a casting vote in the case of an equality of votes. Section 44(2).

62. The Appeal Board must consider and determine an appeal "with the greatest expedition possible so as to ensure that the appeal is not frustrated" by reason of its decision being delayed until after the date on which the public procession is proposed to be held. Section 44A(6). It may receive and consider any material, whether or not admissible in a court of law. Section 44(3). The appeal is an appeal on the merits. The Appeal Board may confirm, reverse or vary the objection or condition appealed from. Section 44(4). Although not expressly stated in the statute, the Appeal Board is under a duty implied by law to give reasons.

Police powers and criminal offences

63. The Ordinance confers various powers on the police and provides for various criminal sanctions. See s.17 and s.17A. The powers of the police include preventing the holding of, stopping or dispersing any public procession which takes place in contravention of the notification, the no objection or the s.15 requirements or where any condition imposed by the Commissioner has been contravened. For present purposes, two criminal offences should be referred to. First, if a public procession subject to the statutory scheme takes place without complying with the notification or the no objection requirement, the public procession becomes an unauthorized assembly. Section 17A(2)(a). Every person who holds or assists in holding a public procession after the same has become an unauthorized assembly is guilty of an offence. The maximum penalty is five years' imprisonment on conviction on indictment or a fine of $5,000 and three years' imprisonment on summary conviction. Section 17A(3)(b)(i). The appellants were summarily convicted of this offence. In spite of the warning by the police, the notification requirement was not complied with and the public procession in question became an unauthorized assembly. Secondly, every organizer of a public procession (or any person acting in place of such person for the purpose of the requirement in s.15(1)(a) of having to be present throughout) must comply forthwith with a police officer's direction for ensuring compliance with or performance of the requirements in s.15(1) or any condition imposed by the Commissioner. Section 15(4). Any person who without reasonable excuse fails to comply with such a direction commits an offence. The maximum penalty is a fine of $5,000 and 12 months' imprisonment.

Judicial review

64. As has been noted, the Commissioner's decision to object to or to impose conditions on a notified public procession is subject to appeal to the Appeal Board. Assuming it is confirmed by the Appeal Board, the Commissioner's decision as so confirmed, is of course subject to judicial review. The Commissioner is bound to apply the proportionality test in the exercise of his discretion to restrict the right of peaceful assembly. On judicial review, the court will consider whether the Commissioner has properly applied this test.

Focus of challenge

65. It was not seriously argued that the mere statutory requirement for notification is unconstitutional. Plainly, such an argument would be untenable. Apart from anything else, notification is required to enable the Police to fulfil the positive duty resting on Government to take reasonable and appropriate measures to enable lawful demonstrations to take place peacefully. The statutory requirement for notification is constitutional. A legal requirement for notification is in fact widespread in jurisdictions around the world.

66. As has been noted, the focus of the constitutional challenge is on the contention that the Commissioner's discretion to restrict the right of peaceful assembly for the purpose of "public order (ordre public)" fails to satisfy the two constitutional requirements for restriction: (1) the "prescribed by law" requirement; and (2) the necessity requirement, on the ground that the concept of "public order (ordre public)" is too wide and uncertain.

(1) The constitutional requirement of "prescribed by law"

67. In considering whether the Commissioner's discretion in relation to "public order (ordre public)" satisfies the constitutional requirement of "prescribed by law", it is essential to distinguish between the use of the concept at the constitutional level on the one hand and its use at the statutory level on the other.

The constitutional level

68. The concept of "public order (ordre public)" operates at the constitutional level in Hong Kong. This is because art. 39(2) of the Basic Law requires any restriction of rights and freedoms to comply with the ICCPR as applied to Hong Kong, and the concept is specified in a number of ICCPR articles as a legitimate purpose for the restriction of rights, including the right of peaceful assembly.

69. There is no doubt that the concept of "public order (ordre public)" includes public order in the law and order sense, that is, the maintenance of public order and prevention of public disorder. But it is well recognised that it is not so limited and is much wider. See for example, *Ng Kung Siu* at 457 F–H, *Police v. Beggs* [1999] 3 NZLR 615 at 630; *Nowak* on art. 19 at p. 355–6 (para. 45), and on art. 21 at p. 380–1 (para. 24).

70. But the concept is an imprecise and elusive one. Its boundaries beyond public order in the law and order sense cannot be clearly defined. *Ng Kung Siu* at 459I–460A. "[It] is a concept that is not absolute or precise and cannot be reduced to a rigid formula but must remain a function of time, place and circumstances": Chapter 12 by Kiss on "Permissible Limitations on Rights" in Henkin (ed.): *The International Bill of Rights* (1981) 290 ("*Kiss*") at 302.

71. The Siracusa Principles state that it:

> "may be defined as the sum of rules which ensure the functioning of society or the set of fundamental principles on which society is founded. Respect for

human rights is part of public order (ordre public)." (para. 22)

The Principles also state that it must be interpreted in the context of the purpose of the particular human right which is limited on this ground (para. 23). The discussion by *Kiss* strikes the same chord in referring to what is necessary to the collectivity. He concludes his discussion in the following terms (at 302):

"In sum: [public order (ordre public)] may be understood as a basis for restricting some specified rights and freedoms in the interest of the adequate functioning of the public institutions necessary to the collectivity when other conditions, discussed below, are met. Examples of what a society may deem appropriate for the ordre public have been indicated: prescription for peace and good order; safety; public health; esthetic and moral considerations; and economic order (consumer protection, etc). It must be remembered, however, that in both civil law and common law systems, the use of this concept implies that courts are available and function correctly to monitor and resolve its tensions with a clear knowledge of the basic needs of the social organisation and a sense of its civilised values."

The other conditions referred to in this passage relate to the requirement of legal certainty (with expressions such as "provided by law", "prescribed by law", "in conformity with law" and "in accordance with law" found in the ICCPR) and the requirement of "necessary in a democratic society". *Nowak* is to similar effect in stating:

"... in addition to the prevention of disorder and crime, it is possible to include under the term *ordre public* all of those 'universally accepted fundamental principles, consistent with respect for human rights, on which a democratic society is based'." (at 356, para. 45; see also at 381 para. 24)

72. It may readily be appreciated that notions such as "the sum of rules which ensure the functioning of society or the set of fundamental principles on which society is founded", "in the interest of the adequate functioning of the public institutions necessary to the collectivity" and "universally accepted fundamental principles, consistent with respect for human rights, on which a democratic society is based" are notions which by their nature are somewhat vague.

73. A constitutional norm is usually and advisedly expressed in relatively abstract terms. There is no question of challenging a constitutional norm and the concept "public order (ordre public)" as a constitutional norm must be accepted.

74. Indeed, in Hong Kong, the courts have dealt with the concept at a constitutional level and have determined whether a particular matter falls within the concept. In *Ng Kung Siu*, the Court considered the concept in the context of a restriction on the freedom of speech under art. 19 of the ICCPR (corresponding to art. 16 of BORO). It held that the concept includes the legitimate interests in the protection of the national and regional flags. In *Secretary for Justice v. Oriental Press Group Ltd* [1998] 2 HKLRD 123, the Court of First Instance held that the contempt of court offences under the common law of scandalising the court and the interference with the administration of justice as a continuing process constitute permissible restrictions on the freedom of expression. The decision was upheld by the Court of Appeal [1999] 2 HKLRD 293. The Court of First Instance held that the due administration of justice is within the concept of "public order (ordre public)". This was conceded in the Court of Appeal (at 307I).

The statutory level

75. As has been observed, adopting an unusual technique, the concept of "public order (ordre public)" used in the ICCPR has been incorporated into the Ordinance in relation to the Commissioner's discretion. The question therefore arises whether the Commissioner's discretion to restrict the right of peaceful assembly for the purpose of "public order (ordre public)" satisfies the constitutional requirement of "prescribed by law".

76. In contrast to the use of the concept which is relatively abstract at the constitutional level, different considerations apply to its deployment at the statutory level. A statutory discretion conferred on a public official to restrict a fundamental right must satisfy the constitutional requirement of "prescribed by law". Such a discretion must give an adequate indication of the scope of the discretion with a degree of precision appropriate to the subject matter. The public official is part of the executive authorities which of course stand in a fundamentally different position from that of an independent Judiciary.

77. Here, the subject matter of the discretion is the regulation of public processions subject to the statutory scheme. As the situations that may arise for his consideration are of an infinite variety and would involve many different circumstances and considerations, it is important for the Commissioner to have a considerable degree of flexibility. But even taking this into account, the Commissioner's discretion to restrict the right of peaceful assembly for the statutory purpose of "public order (order public)" plainly does not give an adequate indication of the scope of that discretion. This is because of the inappropriateness of the concept taken from the ICCPR as the basis of the exercise of such a discretionary power vested in the executive authorities. That being so, the Commissioner's discretion to restrict the right for the purpose of "public order (ordre public)" falls foul of the constitutional requirement of "prescribed by law". Compare *Gurung Kesh Bahadur* at para.34. Accordingly, the Commissioner's discretion in relation to the purpose of "public order (ordre public)" in ss. 14(1), 14(5) and 15(2) of the Ordinance must be held to be unconstitutional.

78. It should be noted that apart from the provisions dealing with public processions subject to the statutory scheme, there are provisions in the Ordinance conferring on the Commissioner the discretion to restrict the right of peaceful assembly in other contexts where he reasonably considers it necessary in the interests of "public order (ordre public)"; for example in relation to public meetings subject to the scheme. Although the question does not arise in this appeal, having regard to the above conclusion, the validity of the discretion in relation to the purpose of "public order (ordre public)" in such contexts must be regarded as doubtful.

Remedy

79. Having regard to the above conclusion on the issue of constitutionality, the question as to the appropriate remedy must now be addressed.

80. Mr McCoy SC for the Government submits that "public order (ordre public)" should be read down to mean "serious disruption to the life of the community". This is an expression found in the *Public Order Act 1986* in England; see s.12(1). There is no basis for reading down in this way and this submission must be rejected.

81. Mr McCoy SC advances the alternative submission that "public order (ordre public)" should be read down to mean the matters covered by art. 20 of the ICCPR. As has been noted, this Article is part of the ICCPR as applied to Hong Kong, although it was not incorporated into BORO. Article 20 requires prohibition by law of any propaganda for war and any advocacy of national, racial or religious hatred that constitutes incitement to discrimination, hostility or violence. There is no basis for reading down "public order (ordre public)" in this way and this submission must also be rejected. It may well be argued that specific legislation providing for the restriction of the right of peaceful assembly for the purpose of enforcing the art. 20 prohibitions may be justified not only on the basis of the specific requirement of that Article, but also on the basis that society has legitimate interests in such prohibitions and that such interests may be regarded as within "public order (ordre public)" as a constitutional norm. Whether such an argument is correct does not need to be decided. But even if correct, it does not provide a basis for reading down "public order (ordre public)" as suggested.

Severance

82. As has been held, the Commissioner's discretion with "public order (ordre public)" as a purpose does not satisfy the "prescribed by law" requirement. But there is no doubt that it covers public order in the law and order sense, that is, the maintenance of public order and prevention of public disorder. Public order in this sense will simply be referred to as "public order" as distinguished from "public order (ordre public)".

83. As public order is sufficiently certain, the Commissioner's discretion to restrict the right of peaceful assembly for this purpose would give an adequate indication of its scope. It would satisfy the constitutional requirement of "prescribed by law" and would be constitutionally valid. That being so, the essential question is whether the appropriate remedy is to sever public order from "public order (ordre public)". With such severance, one would only be left with public order. The part which is constitutionally valid remains after the severance of the part which is constitutionally invalid.

84. In *Ming Pao Newspapers Ltd v. Attorney-General* at 921E, the Privy Council adopted the following approach on severance which had been stated in *Attorney-General for Alberta v. Attorney-General for Canada* [1947] AC 503 at 518:

> "The real question is whether what remains is so inextricably bound up with the part declared invalid that what remains cannot independently survive or, as it has sometimes been put, whether on a fair review of the whole matter it can be assumed that the legislature would have enacted what survives without enacting the part that is ultra vires at all."

Ng Ka Ling at 39D–F; *De Freitas v. Ministry of Agriculture* 79D–81B; *Independent Jamaica Council for Human Rights v. Marshall-Burnett* [2005] 2 WLR 923 at para. 22. See also *Vriend v. Alberta* (1998) 156 DLR (4th) 385 at para. 167; *Schachter v. Canada* (1992) 93 DLR (4th) 1 at 13–14.

85. Applying this approach, the constitutional part remaining after severance, namely public order, can independently survive. It can be said with confidence that had the Legislature appreciated the unconstitutionality of the rest of "public order (ordre public)" in the context of the Commissioner's discretion to restrict the right of peaceful assembly, it would nevertheless have enacted the statute only with public order. Accordingly, the proper remedy is to sever public order from "public order (ordre public)" in ss. 14(1), 14(5) and 15(2) of the Ordinance.

The protection of the rights and freedoms of others

86. Article 21 of the ICCPR (corresponding to art. 17 of BORO) provides that the protection of the rights and freedoms of others is a legitimate purpose for restricting the right of peaceful assembly. Using the unusual technique which has been referred to, the statute has incorporated it as a purpose in relation to the Commissioner's discretion to restrict the right and has directed in s.2(2) that it should be interpreted in the same way as under the ICCPR. As with "public order (ordre public)", it is important to distinguish its function as a constitutional norm in the ICCPR from its use at the statutory level.

87. As Mr Martin Lee SC for the 2nd and 3rd appellants fairly accepts, full arguments have not been addressed on the question whether the Commissioner's statutory discretion in relation to the purpose of the protection of the rights and freedoms of others complies with the constitutional requirement of "prescribed by law" and it would not be appropriate for any concluded view to be expressed on this question.

88. However, it must be pointed out that in the context of the ICCPR, the rights and freedoms of others are not limited to those found in the ICCPR. *Nowak*: Article 21 p.382 (para.28) and art. 19 p.354 (para.41). The scope of the additional rights and freedoms that are covered may be debatable. As the meaning of the expression in the ICCPR has been incorporated into the Ordinance by s.2(2), it can be seriously argued that in the context of the Commissioner's statutory discretion to restrict the right of peaceful assembly, a purpose based on a notion of such wide and imprecise import does not satisfy the constitutional requirement of "prescribed by law".

(2) The constitutional requirement of necessity

89. After severance, it would not be meaningful to deal with the question whether the Commissioner's statutory discretion in the state which it was before severance satisfies the constitutional requirement of necessity. It is the position after severance which should be considered.

The proportionality test

90. As has been discussed in relation to the constitutional requirement of necessity, the proportionality test has to be applied, that is: (a) whether the Commissioner's statutory discretion to restrict the right of peaceful assembly for the purpose of public order is rationally connected with the wider constitutional legitimate purpose of "public order (ordre public)"; and (b) whether such a statutory discretion is no more than is necessary to accomplish that constitutional purpose.

91. The first limb of the proportionality test is obviously satisfied. The constitutional purpose of public order within "public order (ordre public)" is incorporated into the statute and the statutory discretion is of course rationally connected with the legitimate purpose laid down at the constitutional level.

92. In considering the second limb, the following matters must be taken into account:

(1) The right of peaceful assembly involves a positive duty on the part of Government to take reasonable and appropriate measures to enable lawful assemblies to take place peacefully.

(2) The statutory scheme is limited to the regulation of public processions consisting of more than 30 persons on a public highway or thoroughfare or in a public park.

(3) Upon being notified of a public procession, the Commissioner would have to consider various facets of public order such as traffic conditions and crowd control. Depending on the case in question, factors that may be relevant include the date and time of the proposed procession, the topography of the route, the possible presence of rival groups and the reaction of members of the public. The Commissioner has to approach the matter in a flexible manner but his discretion to object or to impose condition is constrained: In considering its exercise, the Commissioner must apply the proportionality test: Whether the potential restriction (i) is rationally connected with the purpose of public order; and (ii) is no more than is necessary to accomplish that purpose.

(4) If the Commissioner objects to the proposed public procession, he must do so within the statutory time limits. And where he imposes conditions, he must do so within a reasonable time.

(5) If the Commissioner objects or imposes conditions, he is under a duty to give reasons which must be adequate.

(6) His decision is subject to appeal to the Appeal Board. And his decision, assuming it is upheld by the Appeal Board, is subject to judicial review.

93. Taking into account all these matters, the Commissioner's discretion to restrict the right in relation to public order should be held to be no more than is necessary to accomplish the constitutional legitimate purpose of "public order (ordre public)". It is limited to public processions consisting of more than 30 persons on a public highway or thoroughfare or in a public park. The discretion is of assistance in enabling Government to fulfil its positive duty. It is a limited discretion, constrained by the proportionality test. Adequate reasons have to be given for any objection or imposition of conditions. There is a right of appeal and a right of recourse to judicial review.

94. Accordingly, the Commissioner's statutory discretion to restrict the right of peaceful assembly for the purpose of public order must be held to satisfy the proportionality test and therefore the constitutional necessity requirement.

Summary

95. In summary, the conclusions reached on the question of constitutionality are:

(1) The Commissioner's statutory discretion to restrict the right of peaceful assembly for the purpose of "public order (ordre public)" provided for in ss. 14(1), 14(5) and 15(2) of the Ordinance does not satisfy the constitutional requirement of "prescribed by law" and is unconstitutional.

(2) The appropriate remedy is the severance of public order (in the law and order sense, that is, the maintenance of public order and prevention of public disorder) from "public order (ordre public)" in such provisions.

(3) After severance, the Commissioner's discretion in relation to public order satisfies the constitutional requirements of "prescribed by law" and necessity and is constitutional.

96. In relation to the exercise of his statutory discretion to restrict the right of peaceful assembly, it must be emphasised that the Commissioner must, as a matter of law, apply the proportionality test. He must consider whether a potential restriction is rationally connected with one or more of the statutory legitimate purposes and whether the potential restriction is no more than is necessary to accomplish the legitimate purpose in question. His discretion is thus not an arbitrary one but is a constrained one. The proportionality test is well recognized internationally as appropriate in relation to the protection of fundamental rights. The legal requirement to apply it in this context ensures the full protection of the fundamental right of peaceful assembly against any undue restriction.

Disposal of appeal

97. The offences for which the appellants were convicted did not relate to the statutory provisions conferring on the Commissioner the discretion to object or to impose conditions on a public procession where he considers it reasonably necessary in the interests of "public order (ordre public)". The offences arose out of the holding of a public procession without complying with the statutory notification requirement. The holding that "public order (ordre public)" in the relevant statutory provisions is unconstitutional and that public order should be severed from it does not affect the convictions. Accordingly, the appeal must be dismissed and the convictions upheld.

Costs

98. The parties should respectively provide in writing within 14 days any submissions as to the appropriate costs order.

Mr Justice Bokhary PJ:

99. This appeal arises out of a prosecution which the appellants deliberately brought upon themselves in order to advance the cause of free assembly by challenging the constitutionality of our statute law regulating public gatherings. Such law consists of two schemes. Each permits prior restraint backed by criminal sanctions. One entitles the Commissioner of Police to notification of public processions and empowers him to object to or control them. The other is a similar scheme for public meetings. In regard to public meetings the statute speaks in terms of prohibition. Objection and prohibition come to the same thing, namely a ban.

100. The processions challenge is direct in that the public gathering giving rise to the prosecution was a procession. But the meetings challenge is consequential. It is a consequence of the two schemes being so similar that a judgment striking down or reading down one scheme or part of it would similarly impact upon the other scheme.

Freedoms engaged

101. By its nature each of those schemes engages the freedoms of assembly, procession and demonstration. Article 27 of our constitution the Basic Law guarantees these freedoms for Hong Kong residents. And art. 41 extends the guarantee to persons in Hong Kong other than residents. Neither article specifies any restriction that can be placed on the freedoms which it guarantees. What these freedoms entail is a matter of interpretation. The courts always interpret fundamental rights and freedoms generously so as to ensure their enjoyment in full measure.

102. That interpretative approach is in no way diminished by the permissible restrictions specified in the Hong Kong Bill of Rights which is based essentially on the International Covenant on Civil

and Political Rights albeit with some modifications. To illustrate what I mean by modifications, I would point to art. 21 of the Bill of Rights and art. 25 of the International Covenant on Civil and Political Rights. They confer the same right to participate in public life. But the former confers that right on permanent residents in Hong Kong while the latter confers it on citizens in their country. In the indigenous villagers case of *Secretary for Justice v. Chan Wah* (2000) 3 HKCFAR 459 we applied the former. We could not have applied the latter. Previously the Bill of Rights was entrenched by the Letters Patent (which together with the Royal Instructions constituted Hong Kong's pre-handover constitutional instruments). The Bill of Rights is now, as we said in the arbitration appeal case of *Swire Properties Ltd v. Secretary for Justice* (2003) 6 HKCFAR 236 at p.258 I, entrenched by art. 39 of the Basic Law.

103. Taken word-for-word from art. 21 of the International Covenant on Civil and Political Rights, art. 17 of the Bill of Rights provides that:

> "The right of peaceful assembly shall be recognized. No restrictions may be placed on the exercise of this right other than those imposed in conformity with the law and which are necessary in a democratic society in the interests of national security or public safety, public order (ordre public), the protection of public health or morals or the protection of the rights and freedoms of others."

That is to be read side-by-side with arts 27 and 41 of the Basic Law. Article 27 provides that:

> "Hong Kong residents shall have freedom of speech, of the press and of publication; freedom of association, of assembly, of procession and of demonstration; and the right and freedom to form and join trade unions, and to strike."

And art. 41, which appears in the same chapter of the Basic Law, provides that:

> "Persons in the Hong Kong Special Administrative Region other than Hong Kong residents shall, in accordance with law, enjoy the rights and freedoms of Hong Kong residents prescribed in this Chapter."

104. Article 27's specific reference to demonstrations displays particular insight into the practical aspects of free assembly. It exemplifies the skill of the Basic Law framers of which Lord Cooke of Thorndon spoke in "The Judge in an Evolving Society" (1998) 28 HKLJ 145 at p.145. Traditional rights and freedoms are better understood when the constitutional text itself goes some way towards identifying their day-to-day uses. As an example of this, I would point to art. 31 of the Constitution of the Russian Federation. That article (as given in English in S E Finer, V Bogdanor and B Rudden: *Comparing Constitutions* (1995) at p.254) speaks of "the right to assemble peacefully without weapons and to hold meetings, rallies and demonstrations, processions and pickets".

105. The Basic Law speaks of *freedom* of assembly while the Bill of Rights speaks of the right of assembly. Rights connote benefits derived from duties owed by others while freedoms connote benefits derived from the absence of restraint upon oneself. Free assembly consists essentially of an absence of restraint but includes, as the European Court of Human Rights held in *Plattform Arzte für das Leben v. Austria* (1991) 13 EHRR 204, the right to positive protection by the state of one's exercise of this freedom.

Challenged schemes

106. Each of the challenged schemes is contained in the Public Order Ordinance, Cap. 245. This Ordinance is one of the two statutes containing post-handover amendments criticised by Prof. Yash Ghai in the rights chapter of his valuable book *Hong Kong's New Constitutional Order*, 2nd ed. (1999). At p.454 he said that "[t]here has been no serious restrictions on rights since [the handover] save for the amendments to the Public Order and Societies Ordinances". Reference was made in the Court of Appeal to what the United Nations Human Rights Committee said. In para. 19 of its *15 November 1999 Concluding Observations on Hong Kong*, CCPR/C/79/Add.117 the Committee expressed its concern that the Public Order Ordinance could be applied to "restrict unduly" enjoyment of freedom of assembly. This concern of the Committee's was noted in the United States Department of State's *2000 Country Reports on Human Rights Practices* at p.804. The State Department pointed out that this Court has not yet had the opportunity to rule on the matter. This appeal is the first such opportunity.

107. Save where otherwise indicated, all my references to statutory provisions will be to those of the Public Order Ordinance. Public gatherings are of two types: public meetings and public processions. The scheme for public meetings is contained essentially in sections 7, 8, 9, 10, 11 and 12. It applies to most public meetings of more than 500 persons in private premises or of more than 50 persons elsewhere. The scheme for public processions is contained essentially in sections 13, 13A, 14 and 15. It applies to most public processions of more than 30 persons. Sections 6, 17 and 17A cover both public meetings and public processions. Each provision of the Ordinance must of course be read in the context of the Ordinance as a whole. As we said in the restoration to the *medical register case of Medical Council v. Chow* (2000) 3 HKCFAR 144 at p.154 B–C, "it is necessary to read all of the relevant provisions together and in the context of the whole statute as a purposive unity in its appropriate legal and social setting."

108. Section 11 lays down certain requirements in regard to public meetings. These requirements concern: the presence of the organiser or his representative; the maintenance of good order and public safety; and the control of amplification devices. Section 15 lays down similar requirements in regard to public processions.

109. As for sections 7 and 8, their effect is that the Commissioner of Police is entitled to notification of most outdoor public meetings and that notifiable public meetings may take place only if he has been notified of them. Sections 13 and 13A have a similar effect in regard to most public processions.

110. Turning to the Commissioner of Police's powers under the challenged schemes, the position can be summarised as follows. His general powers under s.6 are, in such manner as he thinks fit, to control and direct the conduct of all public gatherings and specify the route by which, and the time at which, any public procession may pass. These general powers of his are followed by an elaborate set of specific powers conferred on him. Section 11 empowers him to impose conditions in respect of a public meeting. If he reasonably regards that as insufficient, s.9 empowers him to prohibit the meeting. Section 15 empowers him to impose conditions in respect of a public procession. If he reasonably regards that as insufficient, s.14 empowers him to

object to the procession.

111. Total prior restraint is involved in the Commissioner of Police's powers under the challenged schemes to

- prohibit a public meeting (under s.9) and
- object to a public procession (under s.14).

Partial prior restraint is involved in his powers under the challenged schemes to

- control and direct the conduct of a public gathering (under s.6),
- specify the route by which, and the time at which, a public procession may pass (under s.6),
- impose conditions in respect of a public meeting (under s.11) and
- impose conditions in respect of a public procession (under s.15).

Prior restraint is still prior restraint even if it is only partial.

Powers over meetings and processions under s.17

112. Section 17 empowers the police to: vary the place or route of public gatherings; prevent the holding of public gatherings; stop or disperse public gatherings; give or issue orders that they consider necessary or expedient for the exercise of such powers; and use reasonable force to exercise them. These powers are exercisable on the grounds of: non-notification; contravention of s.11 or s.15 requirements; contravention of conditions; or reasonable belief that a breach of the peace is likely. Also, reasonable belief that entry into a public place in contravention of s.7 or s.13 is likely empowers the police to bar access thereto, close it and use reasonable force to prevent entry or remaining.

Delegation

113. The references to what the Commissioner of Police is empowered to do have to be read together with his powers of delegation under s.52. Inspectors and above can be delegated the powers under sections 6(1), 6(3), 9, 11, 14 and 15. Chief Superintendents and above can be delegated the powers under s.6(2). Superintendents and above can be delegated the other powers under the Ordinance.

Appeal Board

114. By sections 43, 44 and 44A, the Ordinance creates, constitutes and lays down the procedure for an Appeal Board. And s.16 provides for an appeal to the Appeal Board against decisions of the Commissioner of Police to prohibit a public meeting, to object to a public procession or to impose conditions on the holding of a public meeting or procession.

Criminal offences created

115. Section 17A arms each challenged scheme with a formidable set of teeth capable of biting down with a maximum force of five years' imprisonment.

This procession, these charges and the court proceedings

116. The charges in the present case were laid under s.17A(3)(b)(i) (for which the maximum penalty is five years' imprisonment upon conviction on indictment or three years' imprisonment upon summary conviction). They were brought in respect of a public procession which took place on the morning of Sunday 10 February 2002. The procession consisted initially of about 40 persons and ultimately of about 96 persons. Starting at Chater Garden, it proceeded along Queensway and up to Police Headquarters in Arsenal Street. There the participants demonstrated for about an hour. The demonstration took the form of a protest against the conviction–for obstructing and assaulting a police officer in the due execution of his duty–of a person described in the judgment of the Chief Judge of the High Court as an "activist". No s.13A notification of the procession had been given to Commissioner of Police. The 1st appellant was charged with holding, while the 2nd and 3rd appellants were charged with assisting in the holding of, an unauthorized assembly. To these charges they pleaded not guilty.

117. Holding the meetings scheme constitutional, the Chief Magistrate (Patrick Li, Esq.) convicted the appellants, and bound them over in their own recognisance of $500 for three months. Their appeal to the High Court was referred by Pang J to the Court of Appeal. By a majority, the Court of Appeal (Ma CJHC and Yeung JA, Stock JA dissenting) upheld the constitutionality of that scheme and affirmed the appellants' convictions. By leave of the Appeal Committee, the appellants now appeal to us asking that their convictions be quashed on the ground that they were based on unconstitutional provisions. Mr Martin Lee SC and Mr Erik Shum appear for the 2nd and 3rd appellants. The 1st appellant, who appears in person, has, in addition to addressing us, handed us a note on the law prepared for him by Prof. Eric Cheung.

Free assembly: its nature and purpose

118. When deciding whether a scheme permitting restrictions on free assembly is or is not constitutional, one must bear in mind that this freedom is closely allied to freedom of expression and freedom of the media. If it falls, that could bring them down too. I adopt here what I recently said in the obstruction case of *Yeung May Wan v. HKSAR* [2005] 2 HKLRD 212, adding this.

119. Free assembly, as Lord Denning has noted judicially and extra-judicially, is a hard-earned freedom not to be taken for granted. In his book *Landmarks in the Law* (1984) at p.133 he wrote: "This freedom has only been won after much pain and anguish. It is bound up with the right to demonstrate ... History shows how much Governments have disliked these demonstrations." He spoke to similar effect in the English Court of Appeal case of *Hubbard v. Pitt* [1976] QB 142. Dissenting in favour of the picketing tenants, he said (at p.178 E-G) that "the right to demonstrate and the right to protest on matters of public concern... are rights which it is in the public interest that individuals should possess" and that "history is full of warnings against suppression of these rights".

120. As it happens, there is nothing new about Hong Kong residents gathering in public to discuss grievances and seek redress. We know that such a public gathering was held on 4 January 1849. It is referred to in James William Norton-Kyshe: *The History of the Laws and Courts of Hong Kong* (1898), vol. I at pp 217, 222, 224 and 257. That gathering seems to have been a somewhat elitist affair. But these things have become far more broadly based since then. In today's Hong Kong street demonstrations, both stationary and moving, form a significant and even potent element of public discourse. As long as they are peaceful, there is ample scope for such demonstrations under our constitutional arrangements. A peaceful demonstration is a sign of freedom and can have a legitimate effect on policy.

121. That is not to say that the law cannot regulate free assembly

in the public interest. The law can do so. And in doing so it can cater for the vulnerability of which Lord Radcliffe spoke in "*The Law and its Compass*" (1960) at p.75. He said that "modern societies are so vulnerable to disturbance, because they are so far from the security of bare earth and grass roots". But a sobering thought is raised in Richard Rudgley: *Lost Civilisations of the Stone Age* (1998) at p.7. There it is suggested that "the average Stone Age individual may have enjoyed greater freedom than ... the average citizen of a modern democratic state". Whenever the advantages of living in an organised society have to be paid for by a diminution of individual freedom or autonomy, it is the business of the judiciary to see that the price is not too high. Nor should it ever be thought that only individuals are protected when freedoms are preserved. The state itself, too, is protected. This was clearly explained by Hughes CJ when delivering the opinion of the United States Supreme Court in *De Jonge v. Oregon* 299 US 353 (1937). At p.365 he said:

> "The greater the importance of safeguarding the community from incitements to the overthrow of our institutions by force and violence, the more imperative is the need to preserve inviolate the constitutional rights of free speech, free press and free assembly in order to maintain the opportunity for free political discussion, to the end that government may be responsive to the will of the people and that changes, if desired, may be obtained by peaceful means."

Trigger for the challenged powers

122. The powers of prior restraint under the challenged schemes are exercisable when it is reasonably considered "necessary in the interests of national security or public safety, public order (*ordre public*) or the protection of the rights and freedoms of others" to exercise them.

123. Those words quoted from sections 6, 9, 11, 14 and 15 form the trigger for those powers of prior restraint. They are, with three omissions, lifted from the formula used in art. 17 of the Bill of Rights to specify the restrictions which it permits. Article 17 permits restrictions imposed "in conformity with the law and which are necessary in a democratic society in the interests of national security or public safety, public order (*ordre public*), the promotion of public health or morals or the protection of the rights and freedoms of others".

124. One of those omissions, namely the omission of the words "the promotion of public health or morals" is not a matter for complaint. It reduces the power to restrict freedom. But the other two omissions, namely of the words "in conformity with the law" and of the words "in a democratic society", have the opposite effect. If they were countenanced, these two omissions would weaken the brakes on the power to restrict freedom.

Conformity with law

125. Expressions like "in conformity with law" are used to underline the need for legal certainty as opposed to arbitrariness. What is one to think when such an expression is used in a constitutional guarantee of freedom but is omitted in a statutory provision that permits restrictions on the freedom concerned? It would be wise to examine such a statutory provision with particular care to see if it is sufficiently certain. I will deal with legal certainty in due course.

Necessity in a democratic society

126. First, I will say something in particular about the concept of necessity in a democratic society. One element of this concept is the inability of an official to do his public duty without imposing a restriction on freedom. This is illustrated by the *Irish case of O' Kelly v. Harvey* (1883) 14 LR Ir 105. Orangemen had threatened to attack a public meeting called by supporters of the Land League. To avoid that attack, a magistrate dispersed the meeting. Was he justified in doing so? The Irish Court of Appeal said (at p.112) that he would be justified in dispersing the meeting if he had reasonable grounds for his belief that there were "no other possible means" by which he could perform his duty of preserving the public peace. That is necessity.

127. Next, it has to be a freedom–friendly standard of necessity. Introducing the standard of a democratic society safeguards liberty. It means that even where a fundamental right or freedom is derogable, its exercise cannot be subjected to any limitation unless the limitation is necessary in a democratic society. A famous expression of this idea is found in art. 29 of the Universal Declaration of Human Rights 1948, its general limitation provision. The learned authors of Lockwood, Finn and Jubinsky, "Working Paper for the Committee of Experts on Limitation Provisions", Vol. 7, No. 1, Feb. 1985 *Human Rights Quarterly* 35 deal with the term "necessary in a democratic society". Citing the *travaux preparatoires* for the International Covenant on Civil and Political Rights, they say (at p.51) that "[t]he term was considered to be a guarantee against the risks of arbitrary treatment". We can look at the travaux for the Covenant. The House of Lords did so *R (Mullen) v. Home Secretary* [2005] 1 AC 1 when considering an English statutory expression drawn from that Covenant.

128. In *Rassemblement Jurassien and Unité Jurassienne v. Switzerland* (1980) 17 DR 93 at p.119 the European Commission of Human Rights stated its view of free assembly. It is, they said, "a fundamental right [in] a democratic society and, like the right to freedom of expression, is one of the foundations of such a society". This dovetails with what Lord Nicholls of Birkenhead spoke of in *Wilson v. First County Trust Ltd (No. 2)* [2004] 1 AC 816 at p.835E as "the proper role of courts in a democratic society."

129. Demonstrations are constitutionally protected whether they are held in majority causes or minority ones. If there is any difference between those two situations, it is that demonstrations are especially important to minority groups. This is because, as pointed out in Helen Fenwick, "The Right to Protest" (1999) 62 MLR 491 at p.493:

> "These methods may provide the only avenue available to such groups if they wish to participate in the democracy and it is of crucial importance that they should be able to take it since by its very nature the democratic process tends to exclude minorities with whom the majority may be out of sympathy."

I note with interest that in *Huntingdon Life Sciences Ltd v. Curtin* [1997] TLR 646 at p.647 Eady J referred to the rights of protest and public demonstration as part of a "democratic tradition". The expression "democracy's inherent requirements" is employed by Prof. Jeffrey Jowell QC in *Judicial Review and the Constitution* (ed. CF Forsyth) (2000) at p.335 when discussing the adjudication of constitutional claims. There may be some tension between human rights and what is merely majoritarian, but there is no tension between human rights and what is truly democratic.

130. That is so not only under a written constitution but also at common law. In his article "Law and Democracy" [1995] PL 72 at p.84 Sir John Laws explains:

"The democratic credentials of an elected government cannot justify its enjoyment of a right to abolish fundamental freedoms. If its power in the state is in the last resort absolute, such fundamental rights as free expression are only privileges; no less so if the absolute power rests in an elected body. The byword of every tyrant is 'My word is law'; a democratic assembly having sovereign power beyond the reach of curtailment or review may make just such an assertion, and its elective base cannot immunise it from playing the tyrant's role."

And in their article "Public Law" (1995) 48 Current Legal Problems 187 at p.188 J Jowell, R Austin, H Reece and S Hall cite the English Court of Appeal's decision in *R v. Home Secretary, ex p Leech (No. 2)* [1994] QB 198 to show that the common law "is prepared explicitly to recognise fundamental rights, deriving from [an] unwritten constitution". I mention these matters to show that Hong Kong's tradition of fundamental rights and freedoms took root long before the Bill of Rights was enacted and entrenched in 1991.

131. The 8th (2000) edition of HWR Wade and CF Forsyth: *Administrative Law* was written before the Human Rights Act 1998 came fully into force on 2 October 2000. In anticipation of that event, the learned authors raised the question (at p.184) of how the courts would "establish objective standards of democratic necessity." Now in the latest i.e. the 9th (2004) edition they discuss democratic necessity in connection with proportionality. These are areas of the law in which the courts'task can be as difficult as their responsibility is heavy. So be it. What matters is that people can be confident of enjoying their fundamental rights and freedoms in full measure. It would help if they received an assurance that those rights and freedoms cannot be restricted except in conformity with an objective standard of democratic necessity established and enforced through an independent judicial process.

Prior notification

132. Schemes involving prior notification of public gatherings are not the only means by which things like national security, public safety, public order (*ordre public*) and the rights and freedoms of others can be protected in public places. Let us not forget the other such means. For example, where public gatherings are not peaceable, there is room for arrest and prosecution for unlawful assembly or riot under sections 18 and 19 respectively. And to take the most extreme example, the advent of an emergency might even lead to the imposition of a curfew by the Chief Executive in the exercise of his powers under s.31.

133. As for crowd safety, the police regularly devise and implement crowd control measures in the interests of safety. In so doing they are able to act pursuant to s.10 of the Police Force Ordinance, Cap. 232, which provides that, their "duties shall be to take lawful measures for", among other things, "preserving the public peace" and "preventing injury to life and property". Such crowd control measures are often devised by estimating, rather than by receiving notification of, crowd size. That is what happens at festivals for example. One sees this from, for example, paras 4.7 and 4.8 of the *Final Report on the Lan Kwai Fong Disaster* dated 23 February 1993 which is included in the Brandeis Brief materials put in by the respondent.

134. That having been said, it should be made clear that notification requirements are not inherently inimical to the freedoms of assembly, procession and demonstration. In this connection I would mention the decision of the Supreme Court of Zambia in *Mulundika v. The People* [1996] 2 LRC 175. That case concerned a legislative provision under which a public assembly, meeting or procession required a police permit. Such a permit would be issued only if the police were satisfied that the assembly, meeting or procession is unlikely to cause or lead to a breach of peace. Not surprisingly, that provision was held to be inconsistent with freedom of assembly and struck down accordingly. At the same time Ngulube CJ saw (at p.190 a–f) nothing wrong with a requirement that the police be given prior notice of such an assembly, meeting or procession in order that they may issue directions and conditions for the purposes of preserving public peace and order.

135. In Hong Kong, as in many other places around the world, pavements are often crowded and vehicular traffic is often heavy. The vehicles liable to be affected by traffic congestion include ambulances and fire engines. As enjoyed peaceably and without causing intolerable interference with free passage along the highway or jeopardising crowd safety, the freedoms of assembly, procession and demonstration can be facilitated rather than hindered by reasonable arrangements made by the police. And the ability of the police to make such arrangements is of course greatly enhanced by receiving reasonable notification. Reasonableness is a two-way street. So the requirements have to be reasonable both from the point of view of those who have to give notification and from the point of view of those who are to receive it. Speaking of reasonableness, it may well be that many organisers of public gatherings would choose to notify the police of their plans even if there were no law requiring such notification.

136. Of course where prior notification is part of a scheme which permits prior restraint, then it is necessary to remember the point which Prof. AL Goodhart made in an article prompted by the decision of the Divisional Court of the King's Bench Division in *Thomas v. Sawkins* [1935] 2 KB 249. In this article, "Thomas v. Sawkins: a Constitutional Innovation" (1938) 6 CLJ 22, Prof. Goodhart said (at p.30) that "it is on [the] distinction between prevention and punishment that freedom of speech, freedom of public meeting, and freedom of the press are founded". Let us recall what was said in the Court of King's Bench in *The Dean of St Asaph's Case* (1784) 3 Term Rep 428 (note); 100 ER 657 at p.661. Lord Mansfield CJ regretted what he saw as excesses on the part of the press. But he did not regret–rather did he proclaim for the ages–the liberty of the press to print "without any previous licence".

137. In *Hashman v. United Kingdom* (2000) 30 EHRR 241 at p.256, para. 32 the European Court of Human Rights said that "prior restraint on freedom of expression must call for the most careful scrutiny". The same is true where any prior restraint on the freedoms of assembly, procession and demonstration is concerned. This makes certainty all the more important.

Certainty, necessity and proportionality

138. Some fundamental rights and freedoms are secure by virtue of being non-derogable. Others are derogable. To be secure they have to be kept free from any restriction that is repugnant to them or renders their due enjoyment uncertain. While extremely important, the freedoms of assembly, procession and demonstration are not non-derogable. So they can be restricted. But freedoms would be insecure indeed if they can be restricted to serve an elusive purpose. The concept of *ordre public* is, as the Chief Justice observed in the flag desecration case of *HKSAR v. Ng Kung Siu* (1999) 2 HKCFAR 442 at p.459I, "an imprecise and elusive one". What about the concepts of national security, public safety, public order and the protection of the rights and freedoms of

others? They are not elusive but are very wide.

139. Disputing the appellants' contention that the challenged schemes badly fail the test for constitutional certainty, Mr Gerard McCoy SC leading Mr Gavin Shiu and Mr David Leung for the respondent submits that a law permitting restrictions on fundamental rights and freedoms is sufficiently certain unless it is hopelessly vague. Dealing with this submission of the respondent's calls for a careful examination of the cases decided in a number of jurisdictions. I begin by looking at the restriction which the United States Supreme Court held constitutional in *Cox v. New Hampshire* 312 US 569 (1940). Under the state statutory scheme there in question, the holding of a procession required a licence from the municipal authorities. As can be seen at pp 575–576, the scheme was upheld by giving it an interpretation which limited the licensing conditions to "time, place and manner so as to conserve the public convenience [by] giving the public authorities notice in advance so as to afford opportunity for proper policing".

140. That statutory scheme is to be contrasted with the one which the General Division of the Supreme Court of Ciskei was concerned with in *African National Congress (Border Branch) v. Chairman, Council of State of Ciskei* 1992 (4) SA 434. Under the Ciskei scheme, most public gatherings of more than 20 persons required authorisation from a magistrate. And such authorisation could be refused if the magistrate "is satisfied that such refusal is necessary in the interests of national security or public safety or for the safeguarding of public health, the preservation of public morals, the prevention of crime or disorder or the protection of the rights of others". Noting (among other objections) the wide powers of prohibition under the scheme, the court held that the scheme was inconsistent with freedom of assembly as conferred by Ciskei's constitution.

141. Geoffrey Lane LJ (later Lord Lane CJ) had spoken to much the same effect in the English Court of Appeal case of *R v. Chief Immigration Officer, ex parte Salamat Bibi* [1976] 1 WLR 979. He did so when dealing with the argument that immigration officers had a discretion in the matter and that they had to have regard to art. 8 of the European Convention of Human Rights when exercising that discretion. Article 8 reads:

> "(1) Everyone has the right to respect for his private and family life, his home and his correspondence.
>
> (2) There shall be no interference by a public authority with the exercise of this right except such as is in accordance with the law and is necessary in a democratic society in the interests of national security, public safety or the economic well-being of the country, for the prevention of disorder or crime, for the protection of health or morals, or for the protection of the rights and freedoms of others."

At p.988 D–F Geoffrey Lane LJ said that even if (which he did not accept) immigration officers had a discretion, "[o]ne only has to read ... article 8(2), to realise that it would be an impossibility for any immigration officer to apply a discretion based on terms as wide and as vague as those in that sub-article".

142. I am aware that in *Nova Scotia Pharmaceutical Society v. R* (1992) 74 CCC (3d) 289 at p.313b Gonthier J of the Supreme Court of Canada issued a warning against insisting upon a degree of precision to which the subject-matter "does not lend itself". While respectfully agreeing with that, I do not think it amiss to add a counter-balancing caveat against failing to insist upon the degree of precision which the subject-matter requires.

143. In *Sabapathee v. The State* [1999] 1 WLR 1836 at p.1843E Lord Hope of Craighead who delivered the Privy Council's advice spoke of the law "as explained by its operation in practice through case law". Writing in *The Oxford Companion to the High Court of Australia* (eds Blackshield, Coper and Williams) (2001) Sir Gerard Brennan observed (at p.118, col. 1) that the common law "must conform with the Constitution, but is itself the legal matrix of the Constitution and informs its construction." The judicial process not only operates within the boundaries of the constitution but also plays a role in identifying them. After a statute has been passed, there is often much scope for its clarification by the courts. But where any statutory restriction on entrenched rights and freedoms is concerned, the restriction should be enacted along sufficiently circumscribed lines in the first place. As to this, I would cite a decision of Germany's federal constitutional court the Bundesverfassungsgericht. This is the *Mutlangen Military Depot Case 73* BVerfGE, 206 (1986). (I proceed on a translation into English provided by University College London's Institute of Global Law). At B II 1 the court said that "[w]hat is first and foremost relevant for the certainty of a penal provision is that the individual at whom the law is addressed be able to recognize and understand the *wording* of the statutory elements of the offence." (Emphasis supplied).

144. Judicial recognition of the constitutionality of a restriction on entrenched rights and freedoms should be witheld unless the restriction was enacted along sufficiently circumscribed lines in the first place. A body of case law informs the answer to the question of what "sufficiently" means in this context.

145. Delivering the opinion of the United States Supreme Court in *Shuttlesworth v. City of Birmingham* 394 US 147 (1968) Stewart J said (at pp 150–151) that "a law subjecting the exercise of First Amendment freedoms to the prior restraint of a license, without narrow, objective and definite standards to guide the licensing authority, is unconstitutional". The constitutional provision concerned there, namely the First Amendment to the United States Constitution, reads: "Congress shall make no law respecting an establishment of religion, or prohibiting the free exercise thereof; or abridging the freedom of speech, or of the press; or *the right of the people peaceably to assemble*, and to petition the Government for a redress of grievances." (Emphasis supplied).

146. *Shuttlesworth's* case concerned a city code which proscribed participation in any parade or procession on city streets or public ways without first obtaining a permit from the City Commission. The code empowered the commission to refuse a permit if its members believed that "the public welfare, peace, safety, health, decency, good order, morals or convenience" required its refusal. In 1963 Reverand Shuttlesworth led an orderly civil rights march without a permit. Prosecuted under the code for parading without a permit, he was convicted. His conviction was quashed by the Alabama Court of Appeals. But in 1967 it was reinstated by the Alabama Supreme Court which interpreted the code to authorise no more than the objective and even-handed regulation of traffic on the city's streets and public ways. Observing that only a clairvoyant would have known in 1963 how the code would eventually be read down in 1967, the United States Supreme Court allowed Reverand Shuttlesworth's appeal and quashed his conviction.

147. In the *Brokdorf Atomic Power Station Case* 69 BVerfGE, 315 (1985) the Bundesverfassungsgericht discussed the extent to which public gatherings can be regulated in conformity with

a constitutional freedom of assembly. This discussion is to be found at II 2(b). (I again proceed on a translation into English provided by University College London's Institute of Global Law). It was pointed out that even though the concepts of public order and public safety had been explained, those explanations were not enough on their own to guarantee that regulating public gatherings by reference to those concepts would conform with the constitution. This is how the court put it:

> "These explanations of the concepts on their own still admittedly do not guarantee an application of statute law which is in conformity with the Constitution. For the constitutional law assessment, two limitations are significant which are found in the statute itself and which have as a consequence that bans and dispersals can in essence only be considered for the protection of elemental legal interests. A mere endangering of the public order will not in general suffice."

148. As to the first limitation, the court said:

> "Bans and dispersals presuppose firstly as their ultima ratio that the less severe method of imposing conditions has been exhausted. That is based on the principle of proportionality. But this limits the discretion not only in the choice of methods, but also in actual decision by the competent authorities. The freedom of assembly protected by the basic right must only take second place when a balancing of interests which takes into consideration the importance of the freedoms shows that this is necessary for the protection of other legal interests of equal value. Accordingly, a limitation of this freedom will definitely not be justified by just any interest; inconveniences which inevitably arise from the large scale on which the basic right is exercised, and cannot be avoided without disadvantages for the purpose of the event, will generally have to be born by third parties. It will be just as inappropriate to consider banning of meetings on the basis of mere technical traffic grounds, since juxtaposition of the use of the highway by demonstrators and moving traffic is as a rule attainable by conditions."

149. And as to the second limitation, the court said:

> "Secondly, the power for authorities to intervene is limited by the fact that bans and dispersals are only permitted when there is a 'direct endangering' of public safety or order. The prerequisites for intervention are more severely restricted by the necessity for directness than in general police law. In each actual case a prognosis of the dangers is necessary. It is true that this will always contain a judgement about probability; but its basis can and must be shown. Accordingly the statute provides that it must be based on 'recognisable circumstances', and therefore on facts, situations, and other particulars; mere suspicion or assumptions cannot suffice. Taking into consideration the fundamental importance of freedom of assembly the authority may not, in particular when issuing a preventative ban set too low a standard for the prognosis of the dangers, especially as the possibility of a later dispersal still remains open to it when the situation has been incorrectly assessed. What standards are required in the individual case must be determined first of all by the specialist courts. They can hardly be prescribed independently of the actual circumstances because of the Constitution. They can however depend in relation for instance to large demonstrations on how far a preparedness by the organisers to make co-operative preparations exists and whether disturbances are feared only from third parties or from a small minority. § 15 of the Meetings Act as a whole is in any case reconcilable with Art 8 GG when it is interpreted and applied so that the guarantee remains that bans and dispersals will only take place for the protection of important community interests; and the principle of proportionality must be adhered to and there must be an endangering of these legal interests which is direct and capable of being deduced from recognisable circumstances."

By "Art 8 GG" is meant art. 8 of Germany's basic law the Grundgesetz. This is the article which confers freedom of assembly in that country.

150. In *Sunday Times v. United Kingdom* (1979) 2 EHRR 245 at p.271, para. 49 the European Court of Human Rights acknowledged that "many laws are inevitably couched in terms which, to a greater or lesser extent, are vague and whose interpretation and application are questions of practice". I do not read that as support for vagueness in regard to how fundamental rights and freedoms can be restricted. The Strasbourg jurisprudence on the need for certainty in that regard is to be found in the case of *Malone v. United Kingdom* (1984) 7 EHRR 14.

151. *Malone's* case concerned a system for the interception of postal and telephone communications on behalf of the police. Article 8 of the European Convention on Human Rights provides that there shall be no interference with a person's right to respect for his private life and correspondence save on certain specified conditions. One of these conditions is that the interference is necessary in a democratic society. The European Court of Human Rights said (at p.45, para. 81) that the interference could not satisfy the condition of democratic necessity unless it contained "adequate guarantees against abuse."

152. On the question of certainty in these matters, what was said in *Dawood, Shalabi and Thomas v. Minister of Home Affairs* 2000 (3) SA 936 is worthy of notice. In a judgment with which the other members of the Constitutional Court of South Africa agreed, O' Regan J said this (at p.969 D–E):

> "It is for the Legislature to ensure that, when necessary, guidance is provided as to when limitation of rights will be justifiable. It is therefore not ordinarily sufficient for the Legislature merely to say that discretionary powers that may be exercised in a manner that could limit rights should be read in a manner consistent with the Constitution in the light of the constitutional obligations placed on such officials to respect the Constitution."

It is succinctly put thus in ECS Wade, "Police Powers and Public Meetings" (1938) 6 CLJ 175 at p.179: "[t]he vagueness of a power increases the discretion of those to whom it is entrusted".

153. The principle of legal certainty has undergone considerable development recently. And I daresay there is still room for its further development. But insistence on certainty is in truth an integral part of a long constitutional tradition. Prof. AV Dicey made it the first of the three meanings which he famously attributed to the rule of law. One sees this in his lectures first published in 1885 and now to be found in AV Dicey: *The Law of the Constitution*, 10th ed. (1961) (ed. ECS Wade). He said (at p.202 of that edition) that the rule of law "means, in the first place, the

absolute supremacy or predominance of regular law as opposed to the influence of arbitrary power, and excludes the existence of arbitrariness, of prerogative, or even of wide discretionary authority on the part of the government." And long before that, Sir Edward Coke (in 4 *Inst.* 41) made the point in language as memorable as it is picturesque. He recommended it as "[a] good caveat to parliaments to leave all causes to be measured by the golden and straight metwand of the law, and not to the uncertain and crooked cord of discretion". This is not to be dismissed as an early common lawyer's mistrust of equity. There is much more to it than anything of that kind. After all, Coke also pointed out (in *Co. Litt.* 24b) that *"[b]onus judex secundum aequum et bonum judicat, et aequitatem stricto juri praefert"* (a good judge decides according to justice and right, and prefers equity to strict law).

154. Legal certainty is not hostile to purposive rather than literal statutory interpretation. It does not deprive the common law of its capacity for development. Nor is it hostile to the amelioration of the common law by equity. John Selden's 17th century jest or jibe about the Chancellor's foot (which the modern reader finds in *The Table Talk of John Selden* (1927, ed. Sir Frederick Pollock) at p.43) was answered by Lord Eldon LC in *Gee v. Pritchard* (1818) 2 Swans. 402; 36 ER 670. There the Lord Chancellor spoke (at p.414; p.674) of "laying down fixed principles, but taking care that they are to be applied according to the circumstances of each case." Legal certainty does not take away the flexibility needed to do justice under private and public law in the myriad circumstances of life. But it has its proper place. And in that place it is indispensable to the rule of law. Nowadays there are many things that the law properly leaves to discretion, but the maintenance of constitutional rights and freedoms is not among them.

155. It having been said that legal certainty is part of a long constitutional tradition, the same should be said of free assembly itself. It is a part of the common law, being that part of it which Lord Radcliffe discusses in *The Problem of Power* (1958) at pp 105–107. At the end of that discussion he refers to "the tradition that there are a citizen's rights standing between him and despotic power", saying

> "... certainly they exist, and exist by a very ancient tenure which brave men have had to vindicate in the past. Those rights are said to have this peculiarity, that they have been, in the main, won in the courts of law; they have been upheld by Judges as rights which exist by immemorial custom of the country under the common law and they have not been created by any deliberate act of constitution making."

156. The learned author of Francis Bennion: *Statutory Interpretation*, 4th ed. (2002) draws attention (at p.721) to Dicey's statement that the right of assembly is nothing more than a view taken by the courts of individual liberty. And he observes that Dicey might have added that it is also nothing less. Constitutions can create new rights and sometimes do so. But many old rights are, as Lord Cooke of Thorndon said in the House of Lords case of *R (Daly) v. Home Secretary* [2001] 2 AC 532 at p.548 F–G, "inherent and fundamental to democratic civilised society" so that constitutions "respond by recognising rather than creating them". Essentially fundamental rights are after all "the basic rights of individuals". That is how Lord Hoffmann described them in *R v. Home Secretary, ex parte Simms* [2000] 2 AC 115 at p.131 F. In that case the House of Lords was concerned with free speech as exercised by prisoners through the media.

157. The Basic Law's reach, as I said in the land resumption case of *Director of Lands v. Yin Shuen Enterprises Ltd* (2003) 6 HKCFAR 1 at p.8D, "extends beyond preserving old rights and includes conferring new ones". Article 27 of the Basic Law does the former while shading into the latter by referring in terms to processions and demonstrations. Those references underline the contemporary function and importance of the ancient right of free assembly. Of course the Basic Law's greatest contribution to human rights is to their enforcement rather than to their content. While much can be done by way of construction, the common law ultimately acquiesces in the majoritarian belief described by Prof. Dawn Oliver in the opening sentence of "Democracy, Parliament and constitutional watchdogs" [2000] Public Law 553. This is "the belief that a government with a majority ought to be able to push any measure through Parliament". Entrenched constitutions like the Basic Law do not subscribe to that belief. Basic Law rights and freedoms are beyond our legislature's power to undo.

158. Various expressions have been used in other cases to describe the extreme uncertainty of the provisions concerned in those cases. Among these are the expression "incomprehensible" used in the Supreme Court of Canada by L' Heureux–Dubé J in *Committee for Commonwealth of Canada v. Canada* at p.438a and the expression "uncontrolled" used in the Supreme Court of Zimbabwe by Gubbay CJ in *Re Munhumeso* [1994] 1 LRC 282 at p.294a. Of course the fact that a provision is condemned as extremely uncertain cannot be taken to mean that any lesser degree of uncertainty would necessarily be acceptable in a provision of that or any other kind. Adjectives can be convenient. But a proper appreciation of why certainty is necessary provides a better indication of the degree of certainty required than any adjective can provide.

159. As to why certainty is necessary, the decision of the United States Supreme Court in *Grayned v. City of Rockford* 408 US 104 (1971) is instructive. In a passage drawing on a number of their Honours' past decisions, Marshall J who delivered the opinion of the court said this (at pp 108–109):

> "It is a basic principle of due process that an enactment is void for vagueness if its prohibitions are not clearly defined. Vague laws offend several important values. First, because we assume that man is free to steer between lawful and unlawful conduct, we insist that laws give the person of ordinary intelligence a reasonable opportunity to know what is prohibited, so that he may act accordingly. Vague laws may trap the innocent by not providing fair warning. Second, if arbitrary and discriminatory enforcement is to be prevented, laws must provide explicit standards for those who apply them. A vague law impermissibly delegates basic policy matters to policemen, judges, and juries for resolution on an ad hoc and subjective basis, with the attendant dangers of arbitrary and discriminatory application. Third, but related, where a vague statute 'abut[s] upon sensitive areas of basic First Amendment freedoms,' it 'operates to inhibit the exercise of [those] freedoms.' 'Uncertain meanings inevitably lead citizens to ' 'steer far wider of the unlawful zone' ... than if the boundaries of the forbidden areas were clearly marked.'"

160. That is the point which I had in mind in the *noise control case of Noise Control Authority v. Step In Ltd* [2005] 1 HKLRD 702. Agreeing with the judgment of Sir Gerard Brennan NPJ, I added the following observations on legal certainty (at pp 706G–707A):

> *"Objection can be taken on constitutional grounds to any*

law, regulation or administrative action that creates a state of uncertainty in which persons are inhibited from enjoying their fundamental rights and freedoms in full measure. But playing loud music is not a fundamental right or freedom. And the law does not accord it precedence over the peace and quiet that people can reasonably expect to enjoy. This case is about low frequency noise transmitted through the structure of a building so as to disturb the sleep of occupants. The uncontradicted evidence is that such noise cannot be effectively controlled through a decibel-based noise limit. So the protection of occupants requires inaudibility at the nearest noise sensitive receiver. *To ensure that he complies with such a requirement, a noise-maker may have to steer well away from the line between legality and illegality. That is unfortunate. But it is unavoidable. And it is acceptable since no constitutional right or freedom is adversely affected in any way.*" (Emphasis supplied).

161. The proposition that vague laws inhibit the exercise of constitutional rights and freedoms goes to the core of what we have always acknowledged as our duty in respect of Basic Law rights and freedoms, namely to give them such application as ensures their enjoyment in full measure. Not everyone is prepared to risk being prosecuted on criminal or disciplinary charges. Nor does everyone relish having to bring a constitutional challenge in order to vindicate his or her beliefs. My express reference to disciplinary charges owes itself to *Ezelin v. France* (1992) 14 EHRR 362. That case involved a reprimand by the French Bar Council against a legal practitioner in relation to his participation in a public assembly. The European Court of Human Rights said (at pp 388-389) that necessity in a democratic society involved proportionality. And, the court continued, the balance had to be struck in such a way as to avoid discouraging persons from exercising their fundamental rights and freedoms.

162. Viewed in perspective, the loss of the Commissioner of Police's power to ban public meetings and processions could well prove to be a far smaller loss to him than might appear at first sight. This is, I think, well illustrated by the decision of France's Conseil d' Etat in *Benjamin's Case* CE 19 May 1933, Rec 541. There a right-wing speaker was due to address a public meeting. The mayor banned the meeting because some left-wing groups threatened public disorder if the proposed speaker addressed the meeting. That ban, the Conseil d' Etat held, was unjustified. As translated into English in Nicholas Emiliou: *The Principle of Proportionality in European Law* (1996) at p.98, the words used by the Conseil d' Etat include these:

> "The examination shows that the possibility of disturbances did not present such a degree of seriousness that he could not, without prohibiting the conference, have maintained order by issuing policing measures that it was [the mayor's] duty to take."

That was said in the context of one sort of situation, but it involves an idea of general application.

163. There is nothing to show that policing measures short of banning a public meeting or procession can never be effective. Being less drastic than a ban, such measures are inherently less vulnerable to a constitutional challenge.

164. Where the state acts to curtail a fundamental right or freedom, it bears the burden of justifying such curtailment. So if it asserts the existence of circumstances which it relies upon, it must prove the existence of those circumstances. As Acting President Steyn of the Court of Appeal of Lesotho put it in *Seeiso v. Minister of Home Affairs* 1998 (6) BCLR 765 (LesCA) at p.777 G-H, a "vigilant court" would not sustain such assertions unless they are supported by evidence which "can be evaluated" by the court.

165. That reference to judicial evaluation reminds me of Lord Atkin's insistence in *Liversidge v. Anderson* [1942] AC 206 at p.232 upon "a condition which, if necessary, can be examined by the courts". The other members of the House of Lords hearing that appeal saw it differently. But the move away from their view which the Privy Council began in *Nakkuda Ali v. Jayaratne* [1951] AC 66 can, I think, be regarded as having been completed by the House of Lords itself in *R v. IRC, ex parte Rossminster* [1980] AC 952. It was not until 1966 that the House of Lords announced its willingness to depart from its previous decisions. Otherwise I would be disposed to regard the move as having been completed in *Ridge v. Baldwin* [1964] AC 40. There Lord Reid, discussing the safeguard of an objective test the application of which the courts can examine, said at p.73: "I leave out of account the very peculiar decision of this House in *Liversidge v. Anderson*".

166. Even where the existence of the circumstances relied upon is proved, there still remains the question of proportionality. *R v. To Kwan-hang* [1995] 1 HKCLR 251 was a case decided by the Court of Appeal under the Bill of Rights. In that case there was a risk that, unless prevented from doing so by a police cordon, a large crowd of demonstrators would press right up against a building and that injury would result. At p.259 I said that the cordon which the police established was a "proportionate response" to that risk.

167. Proportionality was addressed by the Court of Justice of the European Communities in *X v. Commission of the European Communities* [1994] ECR I-4737. At 4790 the court said that "restrictions may be imposed on fundamental rights provided that they in fact correspond to objectives of general public interest and do not constitute, with regard to the objectives pursued, a disproportionate and intolerable interference which infringes upon the very substance of the right protected".

168. Lord Diplock put the point more shortly in the House of Lords when he said in *R v. Goldstein* [1983] 1 WLR 151 at p.155B that "[y] ou must not use a steam hammer to crack a nut, if a nutcracker would do." Especially, I would add, when what you are doing impacts upon fundamental rights and freedoms. This can be seen in two recent decisions of the House of Lords. One is *R v. A (No. 2)* [2002] 1 AC 45. The other is *R v. Shayler* [2003] 1 AC 247. *A's* case was about a legislative measure which impacted upon the guarantee of a fair trial. Lord Steyn said (p.65H) that the question was whether the measure "makes an excessive inroad into the guarantee". In *Shayler's* case Lord Bingham of Cornhill cited *Daly's* case on the difference between the approach laid down by the English Court of Appeal in *Associated Provincial Picture Houses Ltd v. Wednesbury Corporation* [1948] 1 KB 223 and the proportionality approach. And at p.272 E-F Lord Bingham said that "in any application for judicial review alleging an alleged violation of a Convention right the court will now conduct a much more rigorous and intrusive review than was once thought to be permissible".

169. Proportionality has perhaps been dormant but is not really new. *Magna Carta* (sealed in 1215 and put on the statute roll in 1297 as 25 Edw. I) had catered for it by providing that amercement be "after the manner of the fault". More recent are two valuable statements in the House of Lords by Lord Nicholls of Birkenhead.

In *Reynolds v. Times Newspapers Ltd* [2001] 2 AC 127 at p.200F he stated that the means employed to curtail freedom of expression "must be proportionate to the end sought to be achieved." And in *Polanski v. Condé Nash Publications Ltd* [2005] 1 WLR 637 at p.642B he noted the direction in which the relevant case law is moving, pointing out that "the courts increasingly recognise the need for proportionality".

170. Certainty, necessity and proportionality operate in unison. Like certainty, proportionality prevents arbitrariness. *Hentrich v. France* [1994] 18 EHRR 440 concerned an exercise of a right of pre-emption by the revenue. Did it breach the guarantee under Article 1 of Protocol No. 1 of the European Convention on Human Rights that "[n]o one shall be deprived of his possessions except in the public interest and subject to the conditions provided for by law and by general principles of international law"? Holding that it did, the European Court of Human Rights said (at p.470) that "[i]n order to assess the proportionality of the interference, the Court looks at the degree of protection from arbitrariness that is afforded." Then there is the House of Lords case of *Attorney General v. Guardian Newspapers (No. 2)* [1990] 1 AC 109. At pp 283H–284A Lord Goff of Chieveley said that necessity implies proportionality.

171. As to the ill effects of uncertainty, it is well to remember what Brennan J said when delivering the opinion of the United States Supreme Court in *National Association for the Advancement of Colored People v. Button* 371 US 415 (1963). He said (at p.433) that "[t]he threat of sanctions may deter [the exercise of freedoms] as potently as the actual application of sanctions." The passage in which he said that was cited by the Privy Council in *de Freitas v. Ministry of Agriculture* [1999] 1 AC 69 at p.79 A–C. Their Lordships were concerned with a restriction on free speech. And they cited Brennan J's statement for the principle on which they acted in condemning that restriction as too wide in its scope and possible application. I would mention that *de Freitas's* case was among those which informed our decision in the misconduct in public office case of *Shum Kwok Sher v. HKSAR* (2002) 5 HKCFAR 381. By that decision we saved the common law offence of misconduct in public office from unconstitutionality for uncertainty. We did that by demonstrating that the offence's full definition included elements of limitation not fully articulated in the past.

172. Another decision which we looked at in *Shum's* case is that of the Privy Council in *Ahnee v. Director of Public Prosecutions* [1999] 2 AC 294. No one would be able to repose suitable confidence in any constitutional right or freedom in the face of an uncertain law purporting to permit restriction of that right or freedom. Thus Lord Steyn who delivered the Privy Council's advice in *Ahnee's* case spoke (at p.306 H) of "the implied constitutional guarantee of certainty". This is the guarantee of all the other guarantees.

173. *Shum's* case is not the only one in which our decision was based on the principle of legal certainty. Our decision in the biding-over case of *Lau Wai Wo v. HKSAR* (2003) 6 HKCFAR 624 was also so based. At p.648 F–H Lord Scott of Foscote NPJ said:

> "Although the traditional form of bind-over order is an order requiring the person concerned to keep the peace and be of good behaviour, without any greater precision, we do not think that an order simply in that general form should any longer be regarded as satisfactory. Nor do we regard an implied limitation by reference to the facts that prompted the making of the order to be satisfactory. We think the principle of legal certainty requires that the order spell out with precision, in the same way as would be expected of an injunction, what it is that the person must not do."

174. The specified purpose of each of the challenged schemes is, as we have seen, to serve "the interests of national security or public safety, public order (*ordre public*) or the protection of the rights and freedoms of others". Subject to the problem that *ordre public* is imprecise and elusive, each of those concepts is a good one in itself. But that alone is not a sufficient safeguard. The mere fact that a concept is of value does not justify an undefined or ill-defined power to restrict a freedom in its name. Such a power would imperil the freedom and breed suspicion for the concept.

175. So it is not enough that a statute specifies the purposes to be served. The statute must also specify the means which it provides for serving those purposes. Presiding in the High Court of Australia, Mason CJ said in *Nationwide News Pty Ltd v. Wills* (1992) 177 CLR 1 at p.29 that "a reasonable proportionality must exist between the designated object or purpose and the means selected by the law for achieving that object or purpose".

176. Where a measure impacts upon a constitutional guarantee, the purposes which that measure is meant to serve has to be examined with anxious care. So will the means provided for achieving those purposes. To meet a constitutional challenge, the executive must "demonstrate, under rigorous scrutiny," that the means selected are necessary because nothing of less impact than means of that kind would be adequate. The words within quotation marks are borrowed from the opinion of the United States Supreme Court in *C & A Carbone, Inc. v. Clarkstown* 511 US 383 (1994) delivered by Kennedy J. He used them (at p.392) when explaining what a municipality has to do in order to justify discrimination against interstate commerce in favour of local business or investment. That approach of rigorous scrutiny is matched by the one taken in the House of Lords by Lord Nicholls of Birkenhead in *R (ProLife) v. BBC* [2004] 1 AC 185 concerning a restriction on a fundamental freedom, namely free speech. Such restrictions, Lord Nicholls said at p.224 C, "need to be examined rigorously by all concerned, not least the courts... as independent and impartial bodies ... charged with a vital supervisory role."

177. As Dixon CJ and Fullagar, Kitto and Taylor JJ of the High Court of Australia said in *Collier Garland Ltd v. Hotchkiss* (1957) 97 CLR 475 at p.486, "law and administrative practice must not be confused". No matter how piously such a power is expressed, the safety of fundamental rights and freedoms cannot be entrusted to a mere hope or expectation that a power to restrict their exercise would never be misused. In the limit of stay case of *Prem Singh v. Director of Immigration* (2003) 6 HKCFAR 26 the statutory provision under constitutional challenge purported to make a constitutional right subject to an administrative discretion. We struck down the challenged provision.

178. Whenever there is a power by which the exercise of a fundamental right or freedom is liable to be restricted, a constitution properly protective of human rights requires that such a power be clearly and carefully limited to avoid the danger of it being exercised arbitrarily or disproportionately. The rule of law so demands. It so demands for the purpose of preserving what Marshall CJ of the United States Supreme Court famously described in *Marbury v. Madison* 5 US 137 (1803) at p.163 as "a government of laws, and not of men". As explained in *Salmond on Jurisprudence*, 12th ed. (1966) at p.65, "a government of laws is preferable to one of men not simply by virtue of being less uncertain but by reason of releasing the citizen from the mercy of other human beings." In *Law Making, Law Finding and Law*

Shaping (ed. Basil S Markesinis) (1997) at p.161 President Limbach of the Bundesverfassungsgericht said that the Grundgesetz has "resolved the age-old tension between power and law in favour of the law". That offers, I think, a good way of describing what the rule of law has done and the courts must preserve. If a freedom is not an absolute one, then it may be governed. Even so, it will not be a freedom governed by men or women. It will be, as Lord Wright said (at p.627) when delivering the advice of the Privy Council in *James v. Commonwealth of Australia* [1936] AC 578, a "freedom governed by law".

179. The vital importance of the foregoing comes into particularly sharp focus in regard to free assembly. For this freedom, as I have pointed out earlier in this judgment, is typically resorted to for the purpose of advancing points of view opposed to the policies and practices of the executive. Free assembly must be put beyond–and be seen to lie beyond–the executive's temptation to suppress. Uncertainty's natural tendency would be to stimulate such temptation, its inevitable effect to facilitate such suppression. The Ghanaian case of *New Patriotic Party v. Inspector General of Police* [1996] 1 CHRLD 5 concerned a statutory scheme under which public meetings and processions required a permit. Holding that it did not subject the permit system to adequate guidelines or effective control and pointing to the danger of it being used to suppress fundamental rights, the Supreme Court of Ghana struck down the scheme.

180. All courts are aware of the difficulties that the police face. As to this, I refer to the case of *Redmond-Bate v. DPP* [2000] HRLR 249. In that case the Divisional Court of the Queen's Bench Division quashed a conviction for obstructing a police officer in the execution of his duty. The obstruction consisted of disobeying his order to stop preaching to a hostile crowd in front of a cathedral. At p.259 Sedley LJ said:

> "Police officers in a situation like this have difficult on-the-spot judgments to make. Because they are judgments which impinge directly on important civil liberties and human rights, the courts must in their t rutinise them with care."

181. A free society cannot avoid making heavy demands on the patience and other positive qualities of its police officers. Some difficult police decisions have to be made on-the-spot. Others can be made at comparative leisure. Some are made by a junior officer, perhaps a constable. Others are made by a senior officer, perhaps the Commissioner of Police himself. Legal certainty helps the police. I had that in mind in *To Kwan-hang's* case. At p.258 I said that "[w]hile police officers are required to exercise judgment, it is necessary that the powers within the ambit of which they are to exercise their judgment be carefully defined." Having to preserve freedom while maintaining order, the police would be in a very awkward position otherwise.

182. The opinion of the United States Supreme Court in *Smith v. Goguen* 415 US 566 (1974) is perhaps most remembered for the expression "standardless sweep" used by Powell J (at p.575). But for present purposes the passage which I would cite from that opinion is this one (at p.581):

> "There are areas of human conduct where, by the nature of the problems presented, legislatures simply cannot establish standards with great precision. Control of the broad range of disorderly conduct that may inhibit a policeman in the performance of his official duties may be one such area, requiring as it does an on-the-spot assessment of the need to keep order."

Great precision may not always be possible, but *some* precision is needed. And it should be backed by a freedom-friendly standard of reference.

183. What they aptly call a "problem of modern democracy" is identified by the learned authors of AW Bradley and KD Ewing: *Constitutional and Administrative Law*, 13th ed. (2003). This is, they say at p.456, the problem posed by "a need to ensure that the police have adequate measures to protect the public without at the same time conferring powers that undermine the very freedom which the police are employed to defend". It is not by vague laws that this objective can be attained. Its attainment requires laws that are fully and plainly stated so that they can be clearly understood. If a more graphic description of legal certainty is desired, one is to be found in the argument presented to the Court of Common Pleas in *Colthirst v. Bejushin* (1550) 1 Plowden 23 at p.25; 75 ER 36 at p.40 by Serjeant Pollard. He said that "certainty is the mother of repose, and incertainty the mother of contention, which our wise and provident law has ever guarded against and prevented all occasions thereof". Legal certainty is an integral part of the means by which freedom is preserved while order is maintained and harmony is sought. For this purpose, it is–as this Court said in the born in Hong Kong case of *Director of Immigration v. Chong Fung Yuen* (2001) 4 HKCFAR 211 at p.223 I-"important both that the law should be certain and that it should be ascertainable by the citizen." The citizen's entitlement to "an adequate indication" of the legal position was insisted upon by European Court of Human Rights in *Halford v. United Kingdom* (1997) 24 EHRR 523 at p.544.

184. In *SW v. United Kingdom* (1996) 21 EHRR 363 at p.399, para. 36/34 the European Court of Human Rights saw no objection to "the gradual clarification of the rules of criminal liability through judicial interpretation from case to case, provided that the resultant development is consistent with the essence of the offence and could reasonably be foreseen". The demand for certainty made by that proviso is directly in point since the schemes under challenge in the present case are backed by penal sanctions. Having said that, it is necessary to guard against giving the impression that certainty is unimportant in other areas of the law. In *Shaw v. Director of Public Prosecutions* [1962] AC 220 at p.282 Lord Reid concluded his dissent by strongly objecting to a criminal offence lacking "the certainty which we rightly prize in other branches of [the] law". This is not to deny that the need for certainty, and the degree of certainty needed, is greater in some situations than in others.

185. If there is one type of law more in need than any other of being clearly and carefully circumscribed, it is the type that places or permits restrictions on the exercise of fundamental rights and freedoms and criminalises exercising them beyond those restrictions. The laws containing the challenged schemes are of this type.

186. I had that type of law in mind when I said this in *Shum Kwok Sher's* case at p.390 A-D:

> "As Sir Anthony Mason NPJ points out, the degree of certainty required will depend on the context of the law in question. In agreeing that the offence of misconduct in public office is sufficiently certain, I am crucially influenced by the fact that it is not the type of offence which criminalises conduct in such a way as to limit the exercise of a fundamental freedom eg free speech. Where any offence of that type is concerned, I think that an

exceptionally high degree of certainty of definition would be required if, quite apart from any other objection, it is not to be open to objection as unconstitutional for uncertainty. For in the absence of such a degree of definitional certainty, the whole question of what is left of the fundamental freedom concerned would be thrown into doubt. It is not by countenancing such a state of affairs that the courts discharge their duty of protecting fundamental freedoms."

187. The materials placed before us include Headquarters Order No. 45 of 1997, Part One issued by the Commissioner of Police on 1 July 1997 and marked "For Police Use Only". It deals with the operation of the schemes now under challenge. Let us assume that it makes the position clearer to police officers for whose guidance it is issued and offers insights to prosecutors and judges to whom it is shown. But what about the rest of the population? The challenged schemes are backed by criminal sanctions. So it is well to remember the advisory opinion given by the Permanent Court of International Justice in the *Danzig Legislative Decrees Case* PCIJ, Ser. A/B, No. 65, 1935, p.41. At p.53 the court noted that under the decrees in question

"... a man may find himself placed on trial and punished for an act which the law did not enable him to know was an offence, because its criminality depends entirely upon the appreciation of the situation by the Public Prosecutor and by the judge. Accordingly, a system in which the criminal character of an act and the penalty attached to it will be known to the judge alone replaces a system in which this knowledge was equally open to both the judge and the accused."

"It must", the court said at p.57, "be possible for the individual to know, beforehand, whether his acts are lawful or liable to punishment."

188. As good a portrait of legal certainty as any is, I think, the one painted by Lord Mansfield CJ in the Court of King's Bench when speaking about outlawry in the forensic saga of *R v. Wilkes* (1763–70) 19 State Trials 1075. Giving judgment on 8 June 1768, he said (at p.1102, column 1) that "[t]he rules and method of proceeding are wisely calculated to prevent ignorance and surprise."

189. Mr Lee said that the question why cannot people do together what a person can do alone is what free assembly is all about. When that question is asked in respect of a restriction on free assembly, the answer must, in my view, be a wholly convincing one before the restriction can be upheld.

190. The idea that whatever is not hopelessly vague is therefore sufficiently certain finds its home in the law of contract, not in the law of the constitution. Once a court is satisfied that the parties intended to enter into a contract, it will strive to preserve their bargain. The books are full of the techniques by which that can be done. But where restrictions on fundamental rights and freedoms are concerned, the courts will protect the fundamental right or freedom concerned. The last thing the courts should do is to strive to uphold the restriction.

191. For the foregoing reasons I reject Mr McCoy's submission–which he ably argued but is far too bold–that a law permitting restrictions on fundamental rights and freedoms is sufficiently certain unless it is hopelessly vague. Greater certainty than that is needed.

To be sufficiently circumscribed so as to be constitutional

192. There is a large body of jurisprudence on the question of what restrictions can be placed on fundamental rights and freedoms. So much so that one must guard against drifting into a tendency to treat fundamental rights and freedoms as merely what is left after seemingly innocuous restrictions have been imposed. That would invert the priorities. The correct approach is to ascertain the nature of the fundamental right or freedom concerned and the purposes which it serves in a free society. And then to focus on keeping that right or freedom beyond any restriction that runs counter to its nature or stands in the way of it serving–and being seen to serve–its purposes in full measure. Powers to restrict fundamental rights or freedoms must therefore be clearly and carefully circumscribed.

193. In the course of the argument, I ventured an observation. The challenged schemes involve police powers of prior restraint, backed by criminal sanctions, on a fundamental freedom, namely free assembly, which is cognate to free speech and free press, which is important to the operation of democracy and which history shows has often been viewed with hostility by the executive. Is there any other category of power, I asked Mr McCoy, which it is more important to circumscribe with care? Mr McCoy is far too good a constitutional lawyer to have answered otherwise than he did, which was to say that the powers of prior restraint under challenge in the present case are "at the top of the range" in that regard. Indeed they are.

194. The case of *Mtikila v. Attorney General* [1996] 1 CHRLD 11 decided by the High Court of Tanzania illustrates the importance which courts around the world have attached to safeguarding free assembly. Not surprisingly the Bar Council cited that case in its 23 April 1997 Submission in response to the Office of the Chief Executive Designate's April 1997 Consultation Document on Civil Liberties and Social Order. That was the consultation document which ushered in what are now the challenged schemes. The Tanzanian statute contained a power to control assemblies. It also contained a safeguard, namely a provision that the power comes into play only when an assembly was "imminently likely" to cause a breach of the peace or to prejudice public safety or the maintenance of public order. In a constitutional challenge to that statutory power of prior restraint, the Tanzanian court applied the decision of the United States Supreme Court in *Saia v. New York* 334 US 558 (1948) and that of the Supreme Court of Pakistan in *Shariff v. President of Pakistan* PLD 1993 SC 473. Applying those decisions, it held that the power in question complied with the "clear and present danger" test under which, to be reasonably required in the interests of public order, the substantive evil must be extremely serious and the degree of imminence extremely high. In contrast s.17 treats reasonable belief that a breach of the peace is likely as sufficient to justify preventing the holding of, stopping or dispersing a public gathering. The contrast does not favour s.17.

195. I should mention the April 1997 consultation document refers to restrictions "which [the International Covenant on Civil and Political Rights] places on the rights under Articles 21 and 22". Stock JA rightly noted the inaccuracy there. Neither the Covenant nor the Bill of Rights places any restriction on free assembly. Rather do they limit the concepts for the protection of which free assembly may be restricted. That leaves the crucial question of what other safeguards must attend any restriction on free assembly for that restriction to be constitutional.

196. Statutory schemes for regulating the freedoms of assembly, procession and demonstration can take many different forms. So there is a limit to how prescriptive one can usefully be in regard

to the ways in which such schemes should be circumscribed. Nevertheless there are a number of points that can and should be made, including these:

(a) The purposes which the scheme is meant to serve should be specified. Such purposes must not be–and must be seen not to be–repugnant to free assembly. For example, the suppression of peaceable political opposition would be a repugnant purpose.

(b) When providing that scheme powers are triggered by necessity to act in the service of the specified purposes, the statute should also provide that it has to be necessity by a freedom–friendly standard of reference (such as, for example, that of a democratic society).

(c) Public meetings and processions are the lifeblood of free assembly. Powers to ban or control them involve prior restraint on free assembly which is a freedom of very great importance. So the circumstances in which such powers can be used should be limited to those in which prior restraint is a proportionate response. Suppose, for example, the Commissioner of Police reasonably suspects, for stated reasons which the courts can ascertain are good, that a meeting or procession would lead to an unreasonable obstruction or a serious threat to public safety. And suppose he reasonably fears, for stated reasons which the courts can ascertain are good, that the obstruction or threat would be more than ordinary policing could cope with adequately. In that scenario prior restraint would be proportionate. But in many other circumstances it would not.

(d) Where a scheme contains powers to impose conditions in respect of a public meeting or procession, the scheme should specify the sort of conditions that can be imposed rather than leaving them at large. The wider the concepts in the service of which conditions may be imposed, the more clearly and carefully must the scheme circumscribe the conditions that may be imposed.

(e) I would not rule out the possibility that a scheme can be devised so as constitutionally to empower the Commissioner of Police to ban a public meeting or procession. But judicial decision–making is attended by procedural safeguards absent from administrative decision–making. A possible arrangement is one under which the Commissioner of Police may apply to a court for a banning order. All other things being equal, the constitutionality of a banning power given to a court would be inherently easier to defend than the constitutionality of a banning power given to the Commissioner of Police himself.

Powers of prior restraint are unconstitutional

197. Having examined the challenged schemes and considered the relevant law, I will now give my answer to the question whether the Commissioner of Police's powers of prior restraint under those schemes are sufficiently circumscribed to be constitutional. Such is the similarity between the meetings scheme and the processions scheme that there is no distinction to be drawn between them on this question.

198. None of the púrposes which the Commissioner of Police's powers under the challenged schemes are meant to serve can be said to be repugnant to free assembly. Nor, apart from *ordre public*, can any of those purposes be condemned as elusive. But a concept may be wide even though it is not elusive. It is natural and appropriate to confer rights and freedoms in wide terms, but permitting wide restrictions on rights and freedoms endangers them. As Lord Devlin so neatly put it in his memoirs *Taken at the Flood* (1996) at p.64, concepts of this kind have a "potentiality as a suppressive of free speech". Similarly, I would add, of free assembly.

199. National security, public safety and public order are very wide concepts. The protection of the rights and freedoms of others is a particularly wide concept. For there are so many rights and freedoms that others have, and the challenged schemes do not say which of these may be protected by police powers restricting free assembly. This is a serious omission. After all, even some of the rights and freedoms under the Bill of Rights (eg. the right under art. 7 not to be imprisoned for breach of contract) are not obvious candidates for such an exercise.

200. Despite the width of the concepts concerned and the inclusion of banning powers, the challenged schemes omit to specify that the necessity to act in the service of those concepts must be necessity by a freedom–friendly standard. Nor is there any indication in the challenged schemes that the powers of prior restraint which it confers can only be used where ordinary policing cannot be relied upon to accomplish the necessary objective. Coming on top of all of that, the challenged schemes are open to this further objection. They contain powers to impose conditions in respect of public meetings and processions. But they do not specify the sort of conditions that can be imposed. Instead they leave them at large.

201. Striking down legislation is a course of last resort. The first thing for a court to do when faced with a vague statutory provision is as stated by Cooke J (now Lord Cooke of Thorndon) when delivering the judgment of the Court of Appeal in New Zealand in *Transport Ministry v. Alexander* [1978] 1 NZLR 306. This is, as he said at p.311, to try to solve the problem by interpretation. Sometimes the problem can be solved in that way. But sometimes, as in the *Transport Ministry* case itself, the provision cannot be saved by interpretation and has to be declared invalid.

202. Sometimes words can be read into a statute. We recognised that in the common law conspiracy case of *Chan Pun Chung v. HKSAR* (2000) 3 HKCFAR 392. But as Lord Camden CJ of the Court of Common Pleas so memorably put it in *Entick v. Carrington* (1765) 19 State Trials 1029 at p.1067, for the judges "to mould an unlawful power into a convenient authority, by new restrictions ... would be, not judgment, but legislation." It is for the judiciary to declare the constitutional limits within which derogable rights and freedoms can be restricted by statute. Within the limits so declared, it is for the legislature to decide what (if any) statutory restrictions should be enacted. So the Commissioner of Police's powers of prior restraint under the challenged schemes cannot be saved by supplying the necessary safeguards through interpretation.

203. Nor are those powers saved by the fact that their exercise is subject to an appeal to an appeal board. The availability of an appeal does not supply the missing certainty. At most it merely transfers the exercise of the uncertain powers from the Commissioner of Police or his delegate to the Appeal Board. In this connection, reference can usefully be made to the recent decision of the House of Lords concerning indefinite detention subject to an appeal to an appeals commission, *A v. Home Secretary* [2005] 2 WLR 87. Lord Nicholls of Birkenhead said this at p.132C:

> "Nor is the vice of indefinite detention cured by the provision made for independent review by the Special

Immigration Appeals Commission. The commission is well placed to check that the Secretary of State's powers are exercised properly. But what is in question on these appeals is the existence and width of the statutory powers, not the way they are being exercised."

204. Finally I come to judicial review. This, too, cannot save the Commissioner of Police's powers of prior restraint under the challenged schemes. The judiciary protects constitutional rights and freedoms by circumscribing powers to restrict them, not by transferring such powers to itself. For, as Lord Shaw of Dunfermline said in *Scott v. Scott* [1913] AC 417 at p.477, "[t]o remit the maintenance of constitutional right to the region of judicial discretion is to shift the foundations of freedom from the rock to the sand".

205. For the foregoing reasons, I regard the Commissioner of Police's powers of prior restraint under the challenged schemes as insufficiently circumscribed. So I would declare that those powers–being his powers to

(i) control and direct the conduct of a public gathering (under s.6,)

(ii) specify the route by which, and the time at which, a public procession may pass (under s.6),

(iii) prohibit a public meeting (under s.9),

(iv) impose conditions in respect of a public meeting (under s.11),

(v) object to a public procession (under s.14) and

(vi) impose conditions in respect of a public procession (under s.15) –

are unconstitutional. And I would strike them down accordingly.

206. Even in the absence of those powers, the Commissioner of Police can always offer advice to organisers of public meetings and processions. They may often think it wise to accept such advice. Among the things which accepting such advice could avert are: the risk of crowd disasters; circumstances in which strong police action is needed to prevent such disasters; and the commission of public place obstruction offences. These are just some examples. I should add that some of the "conditions" which we were shown look more like advice than anything else.

Amplified sound

207. No argument at all has been directed to the Commissioner of Police's power under s.6(2). This is his power in regard to the extent to which music may be played or to which music, human speech or any other sound may be amplified, broadcast, relayed or otherwise reproduced by artificial means. I say no more about s.6(2) than this. It may be appropriate to read it down to the sort of power which the Privy Council considered acceptable in *Francis v. Chief of Police* [1973] AC 761. By that I mean a power to protect unwilling listeners from what Lord Pearson terms (at p.773A) "aural aggression" reaching "unbearable intensity".

Entitlement to notification is constitutional

208. That still leaves the Commissioner of Police's entitlement to notification of public meetings and processions. Sections 8(4)(b) and 13A(4)(b) provide that the particulars to be delivered to the Commissioner of Police are to include the "purpose and subject–matter" of the public meeting or procession of which notification is being given. I have given this requirement anxious consideration. Does it mean that the demonstrators' message is to be vetted? Ultimately, I have come to the conclusion that the "purpose and subject–matter" requirement serves the purposes of proper policing. It helps the police to assess matters such as the number of interested onlookers that the public meeting or procession is likely to attract and whether it might provoke violent opposition with which they, the police, have to cope. On the basis that the purpose and subject–matter only have to be notified in general terms, this requirement is acceptable.

209. One problem remains. On one reading of the notification requirements for public meetings and processions, they operate to preclude spontaneous demonstrations. That would be incompatible with due enjoyment of free assembly. But this problem can be solved by reading those requirements–as I would read them–not to cover spontaneous demonstrations. If this is reading down, so be it. This problem having been solved, no problem with notification remains.

210. Notification of public meetings and processions enables the Commissioner of Police to make proper arrangements to police them. Proper policing is in the legitimate interests of organisers, participants and the general public. It keeps people safe in situations which could otherwise turn lethal. Even if I were capable of forgetting that fact, my memory of it would have been revived when Mr Shiu took us through the *Lan Kwai Fong Report*. The Commissioner of Police's entitlement to notification of public meetings and public processions is not unreasonable or otherwise objectionable. Accordingly sections 8 and 13A are constitutional. It follows that s.7 is constitutional in so far as it provides that a public meeting may take place only if the Commissioner of Police is notified under s.8 of the intention to hold the meeting. And it likewise follows that s.13 is constitutional in so far as it provides that a public procession may take place only if he is notified under s.13A of the intention to hold the procession.

211. Section 17 contain effective means by which the Commissioner of Police's entitlement to notification can be enforced. Those parts of s.17 which are tied to the Commissioner of Police's unconstitutional powers of prior restraint fall with them. But there are parts of s.17 which are sufficiently independent of those powers to remain on foot. And, in the various ways explained below, these independent parts of s.17 can play a role in the enforcement of the Commissioner of Police's entitlement to notification.

212. Having regard to the construction which I place on s.17, I am of the view that non–notified public meetings and processions contravene sections 7 and 13 respectively within the meaning of s.17. The construction which I place on s.17 is to read down the powers thereunder so that they arise only if non–notification renders proper policing of a public meeting or procession impracticable without resorting to s.17 powers. Where non–notification does that, s.17 has the following effect. First, it empowers the police to prevent the holding of, stop or disperse non–notified public meetings and processions. Secondly, it empowers them to give or issue necessary or expedient orders and use reasonable force to exercise those powers of prevention, stoppage and dispersal. Thirdly, it empowers them to bar access to and close public places in order to prevent non–notified public meetings or processions taking place there. And finally, it empowers them to use reasonable force to prevent any person from entering or remaining upon a public place thus closed to him. These are not powers of prior restraint. They arise when

non-spontaneous public meetings or processions are held without notification and non-notification renders proper policing otherwise impracticable. And they are constitutional as being compatible with free assembly.

213. Suppose notification of a public meeting or procession is given, and the police make arrangements for the meeting or procession to be policed properly in the legitimate interests of organisers, participants and the general public. Wilfully obstructing the implementation of those arrangements could amount to the offence of wilfully obstructing a police officer in the due execution of his duty, contrary to s.36(b) of the Offences against the Person Ordinance, Cap. 212. So could wilfully obstructing the police in their exercise of s.17 powers forced upon them by non-notification.

Section 17A (the criminal offence creating section) is unconstitutional

214. As explained above, there are constitutional means of enforcing the Commissioner of Police's entitlement to notification. But I would not include s.17A among them. Going by nothing more than linguistic considerations alone, there are parts of s.17A which might possibly be read as creating what are in effect non-notification offences independent of the Commissioner of Police's unconstitutional powers of prior restraint. But as the Privy Council said in *Attorney General for Alberta v. Attorney General for Canada* [1947] AC 503 at p.518:

> "The real question is whether what remains is so inextricably bound up with the part declared invalid that what remains cannot independently survive or, as it has sometimes been put, whether on a fair review of the whole matter it can be assumed that the legislature would have enacted what survives without enacting the part that is ultra vires at all."

Describing that as the "familiar test", the Privy Council recently applied it in *IJCHR v. Marshall-Burnett* [2005] 2 WLR 923 at pp 934H-935A. And at p.935B their Lordships cited a similar test articulated in the Supreme Court of Ireland by Fitzgerald CJ in *Maher v. Attorney General* [1973] IR 140 at p.147:

> "But if what remains is so inextricably bound up with the part held invalid that the remainder cannot survive independently, or if the remainder would not represent the legislative intent, the remaining part will not be severed and given constitutional validity."

215. In my view s.17A is too bound up with the Commissioner of Police's unconstitutional powers of prior restraint to have any life independent of those powers attributed to it. Putting it in the words used in the right of abode case of *Ng Ka Ling v. Director of Immigration* (1999) 2 HKCFAR 4 at p.37D, s.17A is not "distinct from" those powers. Quite apart from anything else, who can say that the legislature, realising that those powers are unconstitutional, would nevertheless enact the offences and penalties found in s.17A? In my view, s.17A falls together with the Commissioner of Police's unconstitutional powers of prior restraint. I would declare s.17A unconstitutional and strike it down.

Conclusion

216. I thank all concerned for the arguments which they have prepared and presented.

217. For the reasons which I have given, I hold as follows in regard to the challenged schemes. The Commissioner of Police's entitlement to prior notification of public meetings and processions is constitutional. This entitlement is enforceable in the various ways which I have indicated, but not by the criminal sanctions in s.17A. The Commissioner of Police's powers of prior restraint are unconstitutional. And the criminal sanctions follow the fate of those powers so as to be unconstitutional too. Accordingly I would allow this appeal so as to quash these convictions and set aside these binding-over orders on the ground that the penal provisions under which the appellants were convicted are unconstitutional. As to costs, I would order legal aid taxation of the 2nd and 3rd appellants' costs, and make an order nisi awarding all three appellants their costs here and in the courts below.

Chief Justice Li:

218. The Court (with Mr Justice Bokhary PJ dissenting) dismisses this appeal and upholds the convictions. The parties should respectively provide in writing within 14 days any submissions as to the appropriate costs order.

Chief Justice (Andrew Li)

Permanent Judge (Kemal Bokhary)

Permanent Judge (Patrick Chan)

Permanent Judge (R.A.V. Ribeiro)

Non-Permanent Judge (Sir Anthony Mason)

1st appellant in person

Mr Martin Lee SC and Mr Erik Shum (instructed by Messrs Ho, Tse, Wai & Partners and assigned by the Legal Aid Department) for the 2nd & 3rd appellants

Mr Gerard McCoy SC (instructed by the Department of Justice), Mr Gavin Shiu and Mr David Leung (of that Department) for the respondent

---

Shum Kwok Sher v. HKSAR

Shum Kwok Sher 對 香港特別行政區

CACC 3/2001；FAMC 1/2002；FACC 1/2002

簡略案情

上訴人曾擔任香港政府產業署總產業經理，被控身為公職人員行為失當，並被區域法院裁定有罪。上訴人遂向上訴庭提出上訴，其上訴理由包括：1）其被指控的罪名並不是香港普通法的一部份，在香港回歸中國後就已經不復存在；2）其被指控的罪名因為含糊，不確定，定義不清晰而違反了《公民權利和政治權利國際公約》第 9 條、第 14.2 條、第 15.1 條和第 26 條（分別對應於《香港人權法案》第 5（1）條，第 11（1）條，第 12 條和第 22 條）以及《基本法》第 28 條和第 39 條。

《公民權利和政治權利國際公約》的上述條款規定，任何人不受任意的逮捕或拘留，非按照法律規定的理由和程序，不得剝奪任何人的自由；被指控刑事犯罪的人在根據法律被認定有罪之前應推定無罪；不得基於任何理由，包括職位，歧視任何人。而《基本法》第 28 條則規定香港居民不受任意或非法逮捕、拘留、監禁。《基本法》第 39 條規定《公民權利和政治權利國際公約》在香港繼續有效並通過香港法律（即《人權法》）進行實施，同時規定香港居民享有的權利和自由，除依法規定外不得限制。

上訴人指出根據 *R v. Dytham* [1979] 1 QB 722 一案確立的普通法下，公職人員行為失當罪行必須具有罪責（culpability）的成份，行為上對公共利益損害必須達一定程度，才有必要進行定罪和懲處。上訴人認為該控罪至少要有兩個要素，即“公共利益”和“有定罪和懲處的必要”意思含糊，違反了《公民權利和政治權利國際公約》和《基本法》中有關法律確定性和保護公民不受歧視的規定。

裁決摘要

針對上訴人的第一個上訴理由，上訴庭認為《基本法》第 8 條和《香港回歸條例》第 7（1）條均規定，香港回歸中國之前的法律，包括普通法，除違反《基本法》者外，均在回歸後保持不變。上訴庭同意 *HKSAR v. Lui Chi Sum*, DCCC 709/1998 一案中區域法院法官認定公職人員行為失當的罪名，無論在香港回歸前後均是香港普通法的一部份，因此駁回上訴人認為香港不存在該罪名的上訴理由。

對法律明確性的爭議，上訴庭援引 *R* v. *Nova Scotia Pharmaceutical Society* [1992] 74 CCC (3d) 289 等案例，認同法律必須明確及易於理解，使人能夠依據法律因應自己的情況規範自己的行為。然而，法律的明確性要求會因涉及不同問題而不同。不應期望涉及公職人員的法律具有絕對的明確性，否則可能會過度僵化而無法適應變化。上訴庭同意答辯人的意見，即公職人員行為失當的罪名並未因過於廣泛和含糊而構成對公職人員不可接受的歧視，理由包括：該罪名在普通法中已被解釋和應用三百多年，從未發現因該罪名太過廣泛和含糊而違反了上訴人主張的普通法和憲法性權利。該罪名既要求有犯罪意圖又要求有犯罪行為，且僅適用於公職人員的公務履行或不履行行為。該罪名針對的是有不正當動機的行為，而非純粹的錯誤。同時，該罪名僅適用於需要進行定罪和懲處的非常嚴重行為。因此，上訴庭認定公職人員行為失當的罪名定義恰當，不存在上訴人主張的含糊或不明確的情況。據此，上訴庭駁回了該上訴，上訴人繼而向終審法院提起上訴。

終審法院同意《基本法》第 39 條以及《香港人權法案》第 11（1）條中的“依照法律”的規定，要求法律具有明確性。但是終審法院認為 *R* v. *Dytham* 中的描述，即“旨在侵害公共利益從而有必要進行定罪和懲處”並非是對公職人員行為失當罪行的定義，而只顯示該案的法官想說明不當行為必須有損公共利益且必須具有足夠的嚴重性，從而需要進行定罪和懲處。而且，也並無以前的案例明確說明必須證明“旨在侵害公共利益而有必要進行定罪和懲處”方可構成不當行為。因此，終審法院駁回了上訴人基於 *R* v. *Dytham* 中的描述而認為公職人員行為失當罪的定義不清的上訴理由。

終審法院根據一系列案例歸納出了公職人員行為失當罪的四個構成要件，即 1）身為公職人員；2）在履行其公職或與其公職相關；3）蓄意及故意地；4）從事有罪責的不當行為且該行為後果嚴重。基於此，終審法院認為普通法下公職人員行為失當的罪名並未因不清晰、不準確而違反了《基本法》第 39 條和《人權法》第 5（1）和 11（1）條的規定，也不存在《基本法》第 28 條所指的任意性。

終審法院重申上訴庭的意見，法律必須明確，易於理解，使人能夠依據法律因應自己的情況規範自己的行為，但是法律的明確性要求在不同的背景下會不同。為了涵蓋公職人員各種不當行為，普通法下公職人員行為失當的罪名需要用概括性的措辭表達，否則就可能失去靈活性，而不能覆蓋某些不當行為。另一方面，該罪名雖然用概括性的措辭表達，但是公職人員熟悉其職責和義務，應不難理解何謂故意不履行其職責及不誠實，或惡意行使其權力和裁量權，從而會構成有罪責的不當行為。終審法院認為在該案件中，有足夠證據證明上訴人的行為符合以上公職人員行為失當罪的構成要件，因此駁回上訴。

FACC No. 1 of 2002

IN THE COURT OF FINAL APPEAL OF THE HONG KONG SPECIAL ADMINISTRATIVE REGION FINAL APPEAL NO. 1 OF 2002 (CRIMINAL)

(ON APPEAL FROM CACC NO. 3 OF 2001)

Between:

SHUM KWOK SHER	Appellant
- and -	
HKSAR	Respondent

Court: Chief Justice Li, Mr Justice Bokhary PJ, Mr Justice Chan PJ, Mr Justice Ribeiro PJ and Sir Anthony Mason NPJ

Dates of Hearing: 7-10 May 2002

Date of Judgment: 10 July 2002

JUDGMENT

Chief Justice Li:

1. I agree with the judgment of Sir Anthony Mason NPJ.

Mr Justice Bokhary PJ:

2. In this important case the Court has had the benefit of two excellent arguments. In the course of one, Mr Michael Thomas SC for the prosecution made a powerful plea for the retention of every defensible means at the law's disposal for the maintenance of proper standards in the conduct of public affairs. And in the course of the other, Mr John Griffiths SC for the defendant made a no less powerful plea for insistence upon that measure of certainty in the criminal law without which measure of certainty the rule of law would be replaced by arbitrariness and there could be no freedom.

3. The prosecution submits that the elements of the common law offence of misconduct in public office are such that the offence is committed whenever (i) a public official (ii) in the course of or in relation to his public office; (iii) wilfully or intentionally (iv) culpably misconducts himself. If that alone formed its definition, I would regard this offence as unconstitutional for uncertainty. But I have had the advantage–the great advantage as always–of reading in draft the judgment prepared by Sir Anthony Mason NPJ. I have no doubt that the true definition of this offence is as he states it. This means, first, that the conduct must be both wilful *and* intentional rather than merely wilful *or* intentional. Secondly, it means that the conduct must be serious. Accordingly, the offence of misconduct in public office is committed when (i) a public official (ii) in the course of or in relation to his public office, (iii) wilfully and intentionally (iv) culpably misconducts himself and the misconduct is serious. I respectfully agree that, so defined, this offence is sufficiently certain to be constitutional.

4. As Sir Anthony Mason NPJ points out, the degree of certainty required will depend on the context of the law in question. In agreeing that the offence of misconduct in public office is sufficiently certain, I am crucially influenced by the fact that it is not the type of offence which criminalises conduct in such a way as to limit the exercise of a fundamental freedom eg. free speech. Where any offence of that type is concerned, I think that an exceptionally high degree of certainty of definition would be required if, quite apart from any other objection, it is not to be open to objection as unconstitutional for uncertainty. For in the absence of such a degree of definitional certainty, the whole question of what is left of the fundamental freedom concerned would be thrown into doubt. It is not by countenancing such a state of affairs that the courts discharge their duty of protecting fundamental freedoms.

5. For the reasons given by Sir Anthony Mason NPJ, I too would dismiss this appeal.

Mr Justice Chan PJ:

6. I agree with the judgment of Sir Anthony Mason NPJ.

Mr Justice Ribeiro PJ:

7. I agree with the judgment of Sir Anthony Mason NPJ.

Sir Anthony Mason NPJ:

8. This appeal from the Court of Appeal (Stuart–Moore VP, Mayo VP and Woo JA) comes to the Court by way of the Appeal Committee certifying that the decision of the Court of Appeal involved a point of law of great and general importance, namely, whether the common law offence of misconduct in public office is inconsistent with rights guaranteed by the Basic Law, and the grant of leave to appeal. By its decision, the Court of Appeal dismissed an appeal by the appellant against his conviction of 4 offences of misconduct in public office.

Offences charged

9. The appellant (the defendant) was tried before His Honour Judge Line in the District Court on 4 charges of misconduct in public office, contrary to Common Law. At all material times, the appellant was alleged to have held the office of Chief Property Manager of the Government Property Agency ("GPA") of the Hong Kong Government.

10. The particulars of Charge (1) were that between 1 August 1994 and 31 December 1994, without reasonable excuse or justification, the appellant did a series of acts calculated to injure the public interest, namely dishonestly causing and permitting Onclever Limited ("Onclever") to be wrongfully pre–qualified as a tenderer for government contracts for management of domestic accommodation by

- (i) failing to declare a conflict of interests arising from the appellant's family relationship with the directors and shareholders of Onclever, contrary to the Civil Service Branch Circular No. 19/1992 ("the Circular");
- (ii) failing to abstain from the decision making process in respect of the pre–qualification of Onclever; and
- (iii) acting partially in favour of Onclever in the said pre–qualification process, namely recommending Onclever to be pre–qualified despite knowledge of its lack of the necessary qualifications for pre–qualification.

11. The particulars of Charge (2) were that between 1 January 1997 and 31 December 1997, without reasonable excuse or justification, the appellant did a series of acts calculated to injure the public interest, namely dishonestly causing and permitting the wrongful award of a management contract with a contract sum of $56,147,076 in favour of Onclever by

- (i) failing to declare a conflict of interests arising from the appellant's family relationship with the directors and shareholders of Onclever, contrary to the Circular;

(ii) failing to abstain from the decision making process in respect of recommendations to the Central Tender Board ("CTB") of successful tenderers for the management contract of the Military Estate; and

(iii) acting partially in favour of Onclever, namely recommending Onclever to be awarded the said management contract despite knowledge of its lack of the necessary qualifications for the said management contract.

12. The particulars of Charge (3) were that between 1 January 1998 and 21 December 1998, without reasonable excuse or justification, the appellant did a series of acts calculated to injure the public interest, namely dishonestly causing and permitting the wrongful award of a management contract of the former Hong Kong International Airport at Kai Tak with an estimated contract value of $87,560,000 in favour of Onclever. Similar particulars as those enumerated under Charge (2) were repeated.

13. The particulars of Charge (4), as amended, were that between 1 February 1996 and 1 November 1999, without reasonable excuse and justification, the appellant did a series of acts calculated to injure the public interest, namely dishonestly acting partially in favour of Onclever, Southern Services Limited ("Southern Services") and their related company, AA Property Services Limited ("AA Property"), thereby causing and permitting the said companies to be awarded in excess of 90% of all short term contracts with a total contract sum in excess of $13,720,410.91 by

(i) failing to declare a conflict of interests arising from the appellant's family relationship with the directors and shareholders of Onclever and Southern Services, contrary to the Circular;

(ii) keeping all the quotation letters in his exclusive custody;

(iii) failing to abstain from the exercise of control of the quotation system in respect of the award of short-term contracts despite the conflict of interests aforesaid;

(iv) recommending the said companies to bid for the short term contracts, i.e. (a) Onclever on all such contracts from 1 April 1996 until the end of December 1998; (b) AA Property Services for all such contracts from 26 December 1996 until the end of August 1998; (c) Southern Services for all such contracts from 13 April 1998 and the end of September 1998.

The facts

14. The summary of the undisputed material, which follows, is taken from the judgment of Woo JA in the Court of Appeal. His Lordship's recital of the undisputed facts is based on two statements of admitted facts pursuant to s.65C of the Criminal Procedure Ordinance, Cap. 221.

15. Between 1 August 1994 and 21 December 1998, the appellant was posted to the GPA as the Chief Property Manager, and as such, he became responsible to the Government Property Administrator.

16. The Circular on conflict of interests was issued on 4 December 1992, which contains, inter alia, the following provisions:

"This circular sets out the common areas in which a conflict of interest may arise between an officer's official duties and his private interests...

2. The situations described in this circular are by no means exhaustive;...In case of doubt, officers should seek the advice of their superior officers or departmental secretaries.

3. All officers are strongly reminded that they should at all times make a conscious effort to avoid or declare, as appropriate, any conflict that may arise or has arisen. Failure to do so may render them liable to disciplinary action which may result in removal from the service.

4. A conflict of interest is likely to arise when an officer's loyalty to the Government conflicts with his loyalty to:–

(a) his family and other relations;

...

5. ...all civil servants should be honest and impartial in their dealings with members of the public and with their staff. A civil servant must not use his position in the Civil Service, nor any information made available to him in his capacity as a civil servant, to benefit himself or his family, financially or otherwise, or to favour his relations or friends or any other group of people with whom he has personal or social ties. He should also avoid putting himself in a position where he might arouse any suspicion of dishonesty, or of using his official position to benefit himself or favour his family and friends.

6. An officer should therefore:–

...

(d) report to his superior officer any private interest that might influence, or appear to influence, his judgment in the performance of his duties.

...

16. ..., the officer should declare his private interest to his superior officer, who will then advise him how to proceed."

17. The Discovery Bay Estate comprised around 6,000 residential units. Discovery Bay Services Management Limited ("DBSM") was responsible for management at the estate. DBSM had contracted out security services and cleaning services to other companies. Since 1989, up to 1999 and continuing, Onclever had been awarded the security services contract. Cleaning work had been contracted out to another company. There were about 90 security guards at the Discovery Bay Estate.

18. There are 3 methods by which government contracts are awarded to the private sector, namely,

(i) pre-qualify tendering, a method by which the government identifies, or shortlists, a number of suitable tenderers, with suitable qualifications to bid for particular types of government contracts. When the government intends to award a contract of the type in question, the pre-qualified tenderers will be invited to put in their tender documents and make a bid for the contract.

(ii) Open tendering, which is used where no initial screening of the qualifications and experience of bidders is necessary.

(iii) Quotation contracts, which are usually short term

contracts of a much lesser contract sum than those awarded under the two methods referred to above.

19. On 29 July 1994, by a memorandum dated that date, the Government Property Administrator sought approval from the Chairman of the CTB, who was the Secretary for the Treasury, for a pre-qualification exercise to shortlist a number of suitable tenderers with proven experience in residential property management. It was intended that a total of eight 3-year term management contracts would be awarded following the pre-qualification exercise. Such approval was given by the Chairman of the CTB on 11 August 1994.

20. At the assessment panel meeting on 19 October 1994, Onclever was not recommended to be pre-qualified for management contracts for non-domestic accommodation in accordance with the "Analysis of Documents" prepared by Winnie Chiu (PW1). It was recommended to be pre-qualified for management contracts for domestic accommodation.

21. LUN Kai-yeung (PW2) prepared a Revised Analysis of Documents to the effect that Onclever Limited had met all the pre-qualification requirements for domestic accommodation. The Revised Analysis of Documents was sent to the Assessment Panel members on 15 November 1994 for the record. On 25 November 1994, by a memo of that date, the CTB accepted the recommendation of the Government Property Administrator and approved the pre-qualification of Onclever and 7 other companies.

22. On 13 March 1997, by a memorandum signed by the appellant dated that date, approval was sought from the Secretary for the Treasury in respect of a Draft Tender Notice for the management of 10 military sites. The contract would be awarded through open tender. Paragraph 2 of the Draft Tender Notice read:

> "2. Tenders are invited from tenderers with the following qualifications and experience only –
>
> > 'Property managing agents in sound financial status with a minimum of five years of experience in estate management field and currently managing residential estates of not less than 1,000 units, one of which must comprise 300 or more units.'
> >
> > Documentary proof of the above qualification and experience must be submitted with the tender..."

23. On 1 May 1997, by a memorandum signed by the appellant and dated that date, approval was sought from the Secretary for the Treasury on a revised Draft Tender Notice in which para. 2 referred to above was deleted. It was stated in that memorandum:

> "In view of the nature of the properties managed i.e., they are all awaiting redevelopment or sale in the future and not intended for extensive use in their present condition, it is not expected that a first class management service is required. I am content that a tenderer who can meet the minimum tender specifications and offer the lowest cost will be competent to take on the job...Against this background, the 'Tender Notice' and 'Information on Tenderer's Qualification and Experience' have been revised and a copy of each is attached herewith for your reference please."

24. I n a memorandum signed by the appellant to the Secretary of the CTB dated 7 July 1997, it was stated:

> "The tender submitted by Onclever Ltd is the lowest ... Onclever Ltd was established in 1989 and has more than seven years in estate management field. It has more than 10,000 residential units under its management (with one estate at Discovery Bay with 6,064 units) and currently in sound financial status.... Onclever Ltd has previously been engaged in some minor service orders with this Agency and its performance has been good. I also confirm that Onclever Ltd is suitable to perform the contract. I therefore recommend that this contract with an estimated contract value at HK$56,147,076 be awarded to Onclever Ltd."

25. The CTB approved the award of the contract to Onclever at a total estimated cost of $56,147,076 for the 3-year management contract. The appellant executed the management agreement on behalf of the GPA. Patrick W Y Hui ("Patrick Hui") executed the agreement on behalf of Onclever in the presence of Paul W W Hui ("Paul Hui").

26. From April 1998, GPA intended to launch a tendering exercise to select a contractor for managing the Kai Tak site after decommissioning of the airport. The Tender Notice which was published in furtherance of this exercise specified that:

> "Tenders are invited from tenderers with the following qualifications and experience only –
>
> 'Property managing agents in sound financial status with a minimum of five years experience in estate management field and currently managing residential estates of not less than 2,000 units with one of which must comprise 1,000 or more units and non-domestic estates of substantial magnitude of not less than 100,000 square metre.' "

27. In a memorandum signed by the appellant to the Chairman of the CTB dated 17 July 1998, it was stated:

> "Apart from quoting the most competitive price, Onclever is also a reputable estate management company with good reference and track record in the business. It was incorporated in 1989 and has some eight years' experience in estate management ... The largest estate in the private sector under its management is Discovery Bay comprising 6,064 residential units and 2,310,000 square metre of non-domestic area. The Discovery Bay Services Management Ltd rated Onclever's performance as good and they had no hesitation in recommending Onclever's service....Onclever is also GPA's property management and leasing agent of all ten ex-military sites since 1 August 1997. The contract sum is HK$56 million. Its performance with GPA is of good standard."

28. The CTB approved the award of the contract to Onclever at a maximum amount of $87.56 million. As a result, Onclever was awarded this contract. The Chairperson of the CTB and the CTB would not have approved the award of this Kai Tak management contract to Onclever had she and it known that the representations as to Onclever's experience in the property management field set out in the appellant's memo dated 17 July 1998 were untrue.

29. On 20 September 1993, the appellant, Paul Hui and one NG Kit-ling passed through Hunghom Immigration Control Point at the same immigration terminal at 1431 hours, and departed from Hong Kong. On 21 September 1993, the appellant returned to Hong Kong at 2135 hours, Paul Hui at 2031 hours and NG Kit-ling

at 2135 hours.

30. The appellant had never declared any conflict of interest to his employers.

The prosecution case at trial

31. The case for the prosecution was that at all relevant times, the appellant, as the Chief Property Manager of the GPA, had misconducted himself in that public office in respect of his official dealing with Onclever and its associated companies.

32. The appellant had a younger brother, Eric Shum. Eric Shum married Stella Hui in December 1980. Stella Hui had two brothers, Paul Hui and Patrick Hui. Paul Hui was the managing director and majority shareholder of Onclever and a director of Southern Services. Patrick Hui was the president of Onclever and a director and shareholder of Southern Services.

33. In 1992, the appellant's wife and Stella Hui purchased a flat in Cheung Chau Island. The appellant gave Stella Hui money each month for the mortgage on the property. The appellant's wife and Stella Hui set up a computer company which worked for, and received income from, Onclever.

34. Before 1994, Eric Shum was employed by Paul Hui to fix Onclever's computers and maintain its computerised accounting system. When Onclever was pre-qualified for Government contracts in 1994 the appellant told Eric Shum to stop working for Paul Hui.

35. Onclever was a security company, providing security services to buildings. It did not have 5 years' experience in property management: this was one of the conditions of eligibility for pre-qualification to tender for large government contracts. Despite knowing this lack of experience on the part of Onclever, in 1994 the appellant pushed Onclever's cause and wrongly caused it to be qualified. Onclever and its associated companies were treated preferentially by the appellant by always being selected for government contracts.

36. In 1995, Mr Tanner (PW9) very soon after taking over from the appellant (who had moved to another post in the GPA) had doubts as to whether Onclever should have been pre-qualified due to their lack of experience. He successfully recommended to the CTB that they be removed for this reason. This was a unique event and it was common knowledge in the GPA where Mr Tanner's building management division and the military estates division, where the appellant then worked, had offices on the same floor.

37. In 1997, the appellant wrongfully caused Onclever to be awarded the $56 million management contract for government military sites despite its lack of the required qualification for having had 5 years' experience in property management. In 1998, the appellant did the same in relation to the $87 million Kai Tak contract.

38. The appellant could authorize short-term contracts. He favoured Onclever, Southern Services and AA Property in respect of such contracts by instructing a subordinate, Chan Ping-kwong (PW12), that they were always to be invited to tender for such contracts. These instructions were referred to at the trial as "the Chan instructions". The companies were awarded over 90% of these short-term contracts between April 1996 and December 1998 to a value in excess of $13 million. The appellant knew the family connection between himself and the Hui brothers ("the relationship") but never declared the relationship or any conflict of interest and never abstained from the decision making process in relation to these matters.

The judgment of the trial judge

39. The trial judge concluded that the defence case was not credible and rejected it. Material aspects of the appellant's case are dealt with below. He accepted the evidence given by the prosecution witnesses and rejected that of the appellant and his witnesses. The trial judge convicted the appellant on the 4 charges and sentenced him to concurrent terms of 9 months imprisonment (which sentence was increased to concurrent terms of 30 months imprisonment by the Court of Appeal upon an application for review by the Secretary for Justice).

40. The judge made the following findings. At latest since his visit to the Mainland with Paul Hui in September 1993, the appellant had known that Paul and Patrick Hui were brothers of Stella Hui, the wife of the appellant's younger brother, Eric Shum. Realising that the relationship posed a conflict of interests, the appellant failed to disclose the relationship to anyone in the GPA. Instead, he pushed Onclever to qualify in the pre-qualification exercise for Government tenderers though he knew perfectly well that Onclever did not have the required experience of 5 years in property management. He gave the Chan instructions in awarding contracts of less than $500,000, over which process he had control, and that resulted in over 90%, totalling in excess of $13 million, of such contracts in the relevant period being awarded to Onclever and its associated companies, Southern Services and AA Property. He also recommended Onclever to be awarded the management contract for the 10 military sites worth $56 million and that for the Kai Tak site worth $87 million, misrepresenting that it had the required experience. The Judge found that the reasons for the appellant's non-disclosure was "his desire to help and favour Onclever" and that in each case he was partial.

41. The judge said:

> "In relation to the assessment panel I was sure that his moving of it to recommend Onclever for pre-qualification was due in significant part to his hidden connection to Onclever and not just due to a desire for new blood and greater competition."

42. The judge went on to find that the appellant acted dishonestly, applying the test in *R v. Ghosh* [1982] QB 1053, by deliberately not disclosing a connection that itself prompted a public officer to favour a company in a significant way. The Judge further found that the appellant "must have ... realised" that what he did was dishonest.

43. He also found that the appellant's voice was the only voice raised in favour of the proposition that Onclever had met the criteria for pre-qualification, that he knew that Onclever did not meet the criteria, that he came to the meeting of the assessment panel knowing that Onclever did not do so but with the intention of having them pre-qualified if he could and that he successfully persuaded the panel to do so.

44. The judge found, in relation to the first three charges that Onclever was wrongfully pre-qualified and awarded the two contracts, that it was the appellant who caused the wrongful qualification and that, in relation to the fourth charge, that the appellant gave the Chan instructions.

45. The judge further found that the appellant's acts were calculated to injure the public interest in that the appellant, in each case, tilted in favour of Onclever what should have been a level playing-field.

The decision of the Court of Appeal

46. The Court of Appeal unanimously dismissed the appellant's appeal on the eleven grounds argued. Of these grounds, only the ground that the offence of public misconduct is so vague, uncertain and ill-defined that it is inconsistent with arts 9, 14.2, 14.3 and 26 of the International Covenant on Civil and Political Rights ("ICCPR") is material to the appeal to this Court. The Court of Appeal considered that the offence was not so vague, uncertain or ill-defined as to be inconsistent with the ICCPR.

Appellant's case in this Court

47. The appellant accepts that misconduct in public office was an offence at common law but contends that it is too vague, uncertain and ill-defined to comply with arts 8, 28 and 39 of the Basic Law and arts 9, 14.2, 15.1 and 26 of the ICCPR.

48. Central to the appellant's case are the remarks made by Lord Widgery CJ in *R v. Dytham* [1979] QB 722, which were quoted and applied in the courts below in this case. In that case, his Lordship said (at 727–728) with reference to the charge of misconduct in public office in that case:

> "This involves an element of culpability which is not restricted to corruption or dishonesty but which must be of such a degree that the misconduct impugned is calculated to injure the public interest so as to call for condemnation and punishment."

49. The appellant identifies various elements in this statement which are said to be uncertain. They relate both to the elements of the offence and its scope. Thus, the appellant argues that the elements of "culpability", "calculated to injure the public interest" and of conduct that calls for "condemnation and punishment" are uncertain, as is the requisite mens rea or culpable state of mind as well as the question whether it is one or more than one offence. The appellant also argues that, to the extent that dishonesty is an element in the offence, the *Reg v. Ghosh* test, applied by the trial judge, is uncertain and arbitrary. According to the argument, the process of reaching a conviction is therefore "arbitrary", contrary to art. 9 of the ICCPR. The appellant also argues that, in so far as it is necessary to embark upon research into constitutional and jurisprudential history in order to throw light on the elements of the offence, the law is insufficiently accessible and contravenes art. 39 of the Basic Law. Further, the appellant contends that the extension of the offence beyond its limits as described in the old authorities violates the principle against retrospective imposition of criminal liability contrary to art. 15 of the ICCPR.

Respondent's case in this Court

50. The respondent's case is that the characteristics of the common law offence of misconduct in public office are sufficiently certain to satisfy the standard of legal certainty. According to the respondent, the essential characteristics of the offence are:

(1) A public official;

(2) who in the course of or in relation to his public office;

(3) wilfully or intentionally;

(4) culpably misconducts himself in public office.

Articles 28 and 39 of the Basic Law and arts 9, 14, 15 and 26 of the ICCPR

51. Article 28 of the Basic Law provides:

> "The freedom of the person of Hong Kong residents shall be inviolable.
>
> No Hong Kong resident shall be subjected to arbitrary or unlawful arrest, detention or imprisonment..."

52. Article 39 of the Basic Law stipulates that the provisions of the ICCPR as applied in Hong Kong shall remain in force and shall be implemented through the laws of the HKSAR. The second paragraph of the article goes on to provide:

> "The rights and freedoms enjoyed by Hong Kong residents shall not be restricted unless as prescribed by law. Such restrictions shall not contravene the provisions of the preceding paragraph of this Article."

The Hong Kong Bill of Rights Ordinance (Cap. 383)

53. The Hong Kong Bill of Rights Ordinance provides for the incorporation into the laws of Hong Kong of the provisions of the ICCPR as applied to Hong Kong. The incorporated provisions are contained in the Hong Kong Bill of Rights ("the Bill") which is set out in Part II of the Ordinance. Articles 5(1), 11(1), 12 and 22 of the Bill incorporate the provisions of arts 9.1, 14.2, 15.1 and 26 of the ICCPR in the same terms. Accordingly, the provisions of the Bill are the embodiment of the ICCPR as applied to Hong Kong (*HKSAR v. Ng Kung Siu* (1999) 2 HKCFAR 442 at 455 BE, per Li CJ; 463 J, per Bokhary PJ).

54. Article 5(1) of the Bill provides:

> "Everyone has the right to liberty and security of person. No one shall be subjected to arbitrary arrest or detention. No one shall be deprived of his liberty except on such grounds and in accordance with such procedure as are established by law."

55. Article 11(1) of the Bill provides:

> "Everyone charged with a criminal offence shall have the right to be presumed innocent until proved guilty according to law."

56. Article 12(1) of the Bill provides:

> "No one shall be held guilty of any criminal offence on account of any act or omission which did not constitute a criminal offence, under Hong Kong or international law, at the time when it was committed..."

57. Article 22 of the Bill provides:

> "All persons are equal before the law and are entitled without any discrimination to the equal protection of the law. In this respect, the law shall prohibit any discrimination and guarantee to all persons equal and effective protection against discrimination on any ground such as race, colour, sex, language, religion, political or other opinion, national or social origin, property, birth or other status."

Mr Griffiths SC for the appellant did not advance oral argument in support of the case based on art. 22. Accordingly, I shall say no more about it.

The interpretation of the Basic Law and the Bill

58. It is established that art. 39, being part of Ch. III of the Basic Law which provides for the fundamental rights and duties of

the residents of the HKSAR, is to be given both a purposive and generous interpretation (*Ng Ka Ling v. Director of Immigration* (1999) 2 HKCFAR 4 at 28D–29A, per Li CJ). The same approach is to be adopted to the provisions of the Bill as the object of those provisions is to guarantee the fundamental rights and freedoms of the residents of the HKSAR.

59. In interpreting the provisions of Ch. III of the Basic Law and the provisions of the Bill, the Court may consider it appropriate to take account of the established principles of international jurisprudence as well as the decisions of international and national courts and tribunals on like or substantially similar provisions in the ICCPR, other international instruments and national constitutions. (See, for example, *Ahnee v. DPP* [1999] 2 AC 294 at 306, where the Privy Council, in construing s.10(4) of the Constitution of Mauritius which was in terms virtually identical with art. 12(1) of the Bill, applied to art. 10(4) the interpretation given by the European Court of Human Rights in *Sunday Times v. United Kingdom* (1979) 2 EHRR 245 to the expression "prescribed by law" in art. 10(2) of the European Convention on Human Rights.)

The principle of legal certainty and the requirement of accessibility

60. International human rights jurisprudence has developed to the point that it is now widely recognised that the expression "prescribed by law", when used in a context such as art. 39 of the Basic Law, mandates the principle of legal certainty. This principle is likewise incorporated in the expression "according to law" in art. 11(1) of the Bill.

61. As to art. 5(1), the expression "established by law" is used. However, there is a question as to the scope of art. 5(1), whether it is only concerned with laws relating to arrest or detention before trial or whether it extends to the substantive law for breach of which the person is charged. That question was not fully argued in this case. Since the appellant's case, based on art. 5(1) with the wider scope, does not add to his case based on art. 39 of the Basic Law or art. 11(1) of the Bill, it is unnecessary to consider the question of the scope of art. 5(1) in this case. Accordingly, I shall say nothing more on art. 5(1) .

62. The decisions of the European Court of Human Rights authoritatively establish that the expression "prescribed by law" in art. 10(2) of the European Convention on Human Rights and Fundamental Freedoms ("the European Convention") incorporate the requirements that the relevant law be certain and that it be adequately accessible (*Sunday Times v. United Kingdom* (1979) 2 EHRR 245 (the thalidomide case); *SW v. United Kingdom* (1995) 21 EHRR 363 at 398; *Hashman and Harrup v. United Kingdom* (1999) 30 EHRR 241). The Supreme Court of Canada has expressed the principle of legal certainty in like terms in the context of fundamental rights and freedoms guaranteed by the Canadian Charter of Rights and Freedoms (*R v. Nova Scotia Pharmaceutical Society* (1992) 74 CCC (3d) 289; *R v. Morales* (1992) 77 CCC (3d) 91), as indeed has the Privy Council in interpreting and applying the Constitution of Antigua (*De Freitas v. Ministry of Agriculture* [1999] 1 AC 69 at 78–79, per Lord Clyde).

63. In *Sunday Times v. United Kingdom*, the Court rejected an argument that the English law of contempt of court was so vague and uncertain and that the principles of contempt of court enunciated by the House of Lords in *Attorney-General v. Times Newspapers Ltd* [1974] AC 273 so novel that the restraint imposed upon freedom of expression by the law of contempt could not be considered as "prescribed by law" within the meaning of art. 10 of the Convention. The majority, with reference to that expression, said (at 271, para. 49):

> "First, the law must be adequately accessible: the citizen must be able to have an indication that is adequate in the circumstances of the legal rules applicable to a given case. Secondly, a norm cannot be regarded as a 'law' unless it is formulated with sufficient precision to enable the citizen to regulate his conduct: he must be able–if need be with appropriate advice–to foresee, to a degree that is reasonable in the circumstances, the consequences which a given action may entail. Those consequences need not be foreseeable with absolute certainty: experience shows this to be unattainable. Again, whilst certainty is highly desirable, it may bring in its train excessive rigidity and the law must be able to keep pace with changing circumstances. Accordingly, many laws are inevitably couched in terms which, to a greater or lesser extent, are vague and whose interpretation and application are questions of practice."

64. In *Hashman and Harrup v. United Kingdom* (1999) 30 EHRR 241, where conduct *contra bonos mores* was held to be too vague and imprecise to justify a restriction on the applicants' liberty of action in the form of an order binding them to keep the peace and be of good behaviour, the European Court of Human Rights pointed to the tension between requiring a law to be formulated with sufficient precision and the desirability of avoiding rigidity in the law. The Court said (at para. 31):

> "The Court recalls that one of the requirements flowing from the expression 'prescribed by law' is foreseeability. A norm cannot be regarded as a 'law' unless it is formulated with sufficient precision to enable the citizen to regulate his conduct. At the same time, whilst certainty in the law is highly desirable, it may bring in its train excessive rigidity and the law must be able to keep pace with changing circumstances. The level of precision required of domestic legislation–which cannot in any case provide for every eventuality–depends to a considerable degree on the content of the instrument in question, the field it is designed to cover and the number and status of those to whom it is addressed."

65. In conformity with this statement, in *SW v. United Kingdom* (1995) 21 EHRR 363, the Court rejected an argument that the offence of marital rape violated art. 7 of the European Convention (which is identical with art. 12(1) of the Bill) relating to retrospectivity. The argument was based on the recognition by the House of Lords that the old principle that a husband could not rape his wife no longer formed part of the law. The Court, accepting that art. 7 applied to a common law offence, stated (at para. 36):

> "There will always be a need for elucidation of doubtful points and for adaptation to changing circumstances. Indeed, in the United Kingdom, as in the other Convention States, the progressive development of the criminal law through judicial law-making is a well entrenched and necessary part of legal tradition. Article 7 of the Convention cannot be read as outlawing the gradual clarification of the rules of criminal liability through judicial interpretation from case to case, provided that the resultant development is consistent with the essence of the offence and could reasonably be foreseen."

See also *Reg v. Cotter* [2002] EWCA Crim 1033 at paras 35–36.

The offence of misconduct in public office

66. The offence of misconduct in public office has a long history, going back at least to 1704. In that year, in the case of *Anonymous* (1704) 6 Mod 96 (Case 136), the Court said:

> "If a man be made an officer by Act of Parliament, and misbehave himself in his office, he is indictable for it at common law, and any public officer is indictable for misbehaviour in his office."

A year later, in *R v. Wyat* (1705) 1 Salk 380 the offence was expressed again in very broad terms when the Court said:

> "Where an officer neglects a duty incumbent on him, either by common law or statute, he is for his default indictable."

67. Since then there have been many cases in which public officers have been convicted of the offence. It must be acknowledged, however, that over time the elements of the offence have been described in a variety of different ways. Thus, Stephen's Digest 9th Edn (1950), art. 142 stated

> "Every public officer commits a misdemeanour who, in the exercise or under colour of exercising the duties of his office, does any illegal act, or abuses any discretionary power with which he is invested by law from an improper motive ... But an illegal exercise of authority, caused by a mistake as to the law, made in good faith, is not a misdemeanour ..."

In *R v. Borron* (1820) 3 B & Ald 432, a case concerning the conduct of a magistrate, Abbott CJ stated (at 434) that the question was "from what motive had [the act] proceeded; whether from a dishonest, oppressive, or corrupt motive." And, in *R v. Marshall* (1855) 4 EL & BL 475, Lord Campbell CJ said that "a judge who maliciously obstructs the course of justice is guilty of a misdemeanour". Similar statements have been made in other cases. (See, for example, *R v. Young and Pitts* (1758) 1 Burr 556; *Commonwealth v. Steinberg* (1976) 362 A 2d 379). On the other hand, there are other authorities which state that a breach of duty on the part of a public official committed with wilful intent is all that is required to make out the offence. (See, for example, Bacon's Abridgement 1740 ed at 744; *R v. Halford* (Case 223) (1734) 7 Mod 193; *Question of Law Reserved (No. 2 of 1996)* 88 A Crim R 417 at 418, per Doyle CJ).

68. It is not surprising, therefore, that the comment has been made from time to time that the offence is not easy to define. It has been said that it is "not easy to lay down with precision the exact limits of the kind of misconduct or misbehaviour" (*R v. Llewellyn–Jones* (1967) 51 Cr App R 4 at 6); that "the offence is not easily capable of exhaustive definition" and "there is some uncertainty as to the precise content of the offence and even its correct title" (*Question of Law Reserved (No. 2 of 1996)* at 420, 438); that "the very notion of misfeasance in public office ... imports more nebulous issues [than murder] that are less easy to define" (*Ex parte Telegraph Group* [2001] 1 WLR 1983 at 1993); and that it is "obscure and often ill-defined" (PD Finn, "Official Misconduct" [1978] 2 Crim LJ 307 at 318). Nonetheless, it is clearly established that it is an offence at common law (*R v. Llewellyn–Jones*).

69. The difficulty which has been experienced in defining with precision the elements of the offence stem not so much from the various ways in which they have been expressed as from the range of misconduct by officials which may fall within the reach of the offence. This is because, to quote the words of PD Finn, "Public Officers: Some Personal Liabilities" (1977) 51 Australian Law Journal 313 at 315

> "The kernel of the offence is that an officer, having been entrusted with powers and duties for the public benefit, has in some way abused them, or has abused his official position."

It follows that what constitutes misconduct in a particular case will depend upon the nature of the relevant power or duty of the officer or of the office which is held and the nature of the conduct said to constitute the commission of the offence.

70. Lord Mansfield appears to have recognised this problem as early as 1783. In *R v. Bembridge* (1783) 22 ST 1, his Lordship spoke (at 155–156) of two principles, one governing the officeholder who accepts an office of trust and confidence concerning the public and acts "contrary to the duty of his office", the other governing "a breach of trust, a fraud, or an imposition in a subject concerning the public". Both principles were held to apply to Bembridge, an accountant in the office of the paymaster–general of the forces. It was his duty to see that amounts owing to the Crown were properly included in the account. Not only did he fail to perform his duty in this respect, he "corruptly" concealed from the auditors the existence of amounts owing.

71. It is not entirely clear whether Lord Mansfield's reference to two principles was intended to relate to the one offence or two different offences. Be this as it may, in the later cases, the offence has been regarded as a single offence.

72. It was only natural that, in the course of time, the description of the offence tended to focus on the nature of the misconduct charged, more particularly in those cases where the misconduct complained of was not a simple breach of a positive duty to which the officer was subject, but consisted of a failure to exercise, or amounted to a wrongful exercise of, a discretion or power, as, for example when an officer exercised a discretion or power attaching to his office for personal gain or advantage. There were other cases where the officer acted outside the scope of the powers of his office.

73. Most of the reported cases in the 18th and 19th centuries involved dishonest, corrupt or partial conduct on the part of officeholders who, in performing their functions or exercising their powers, did so for personal gain or personal advantage. In describing the relevant conduct, the courts referred to the defendant's motive as "dishonest", "corrupt", "partial" or used some other adjective to describe an improper motive. These descriptions appeared to reflect a view that, in some cases at least, a motive so described must be established before the defendant could be convicted of misconduct in public office.

R v. Dytham

74. It was in the light of the law as it had then developed that *R v. Dytham* was decided. In that case, the appellant, who was a uniformed constable, was present at and a witness to the criminal offence of violent assault on a man by others resulting in the man's death. The appellant failed to carry out his duty as a police constable by omitting to take any steps to preserve the Queen's peace or to protect the person of the man or to arrest or bring to justice his assailants. The appellant was convicted. The English Court of Appeal dismissed an appeal from the conviction.

75. Lord Widgery CJ, who delivered the judgment of the Court, in referring to the earlier cases, said (at 726C):

> "Indeed in some cases the conduct impugned cannot be shown to have been misconduct unless it was done with a corrupt or oblique motive. This was the position for example in *Rex v. Bembridge* (1783) 3 Doug KB 327; and also in the modern case of *Reg v. Llewellyn-Jones* [1968] 1 QB 429. There the registrar of a county court was charged in a count which alleged that he had made an order in relation to funds under his control 'in the expectation that he would gain a personal advantage from the making of such an order.' "

His Lordship went on to discuss the amended count in the indictment in the case before the Court. Speaking of neglect of duty, his Lordship observed (at 727G–728A):

> "The neglect must be wilful and not merely inadvertent; and it must be culpable in the sense that it is without reasonable excuse or justification.
>
> ... it was not suggested that the appellant could not have summoned or sought assistance to help the victim or to arrest his assailants ... The allegation made was not of mere non-feasance but of deliberate failure and wilful neglect.
>
> This involves an element of culpability which is not restricted to corruption or dishonesty but which must be of such a degree that the misconduct impugned is calculated to injure the public interest so as to call for condemnation and punishment. Whether such a situation is revealed by the evidence is a matter that a jury has to decide."

76. Two points need to be made about *R v. Dytham*. The first is that when Lord Widgery's remarks in the last paragraph just quoted are read in context, they are not to be understood as a definition of the offence of misconduct in public office or as a definition of the elements of the offence. The terms used by his Lordship "calculated to injure the public interest so as to call for condemnation and punishment" are not the language of definition. Read in context, the words suggest that his Lordship was endeavouring to convey the idea that the conduct complained must be injurious to the public interest and of a sufficiently serious nature to warrant conviction and punishment. The linkage his Lordship makes with the idea of culpability reinforces this view of his Lordship's purpose. In this respect, it is to be noted that Lord Widgery employs the concept of culpability to embrace two different matters, namely, first, the absence of reasonable excuse or justification and, secondly, that the conduct complained of may not involve corruption or dishonesty but must be of a sufficiently serious nature.

77. The second point is that there was no clear previous authority for the proposition that, in any category of case of misconduct in public office, the prosecution must prove to the satisfaction of a jury, as elements of the offence, that the conduct of the defendant was calculated to injure the public interest so as to call for condemnation and punishment.

78. For these reasons I do not accept the appellant's principal submission that the offence as defined in *R v. Dytham* is insufficiently precise to constitute "law" within the meaning of art. 11(1) of the Bill or to satisfy the requirements "prescribed by law" in art. 39 of the Basic Law and "established by law" in art. 5(1) of the Bill. This conclusion, however, by no means disposes of the appellant's case.

Question of Law Reserved (No. 2 of 1996)

79. It is necessary to identify the constituent elements of the offence. With that end in view I turn to *Question of Law Reserved (No. 2 of 1996)* 88 A Crim R 417. In that case, police officers and a private citizen were charged in a number of counts with "Abuse of Public Office (Common Law)". The prosecution case was that the three police officers gained access to confidential information in their official capacities and passed that information to the private citizen. The trial judge reserved questions of law for the consideration of the Court of Criminal Appeal. The Court held that there existed a generic indictable common law offence of misconduct in public office which covered misfeasance or nonfeasance in public office by a public officer.

80. Doyle CJ considered (at 418) that the object of the offence was correctly stated by PD Finn (as he then was) in his article "*Official Misconduct*" (1978) 2 Crim LJ 307 when he said (at 308):

> "Official misconduct is not concerned primarily with the abuse of official position for pecuniary gain, with corruption in the popular sense. Its object is simply to ensure that an official does not, by any wilful act or omission, act contrary to the duties of his office, does not abuse intentionally the trust reposed in him."

With Doyle CJ, I agree that this statement accurately states the object of the offence.

Identifying the elements of the offence, including its mental element

81. As I have already noted, in an earlier article, "*Public Officers: Some Personal Liabilities*" (1977) 51 Australian Law Journal 313, Dr Finn had correctly pointed out (at 315) that the essence of the offence is that an officer who has been entrusted with powers and duties for the public benefit has abused them or his official position. Abuse of such powers and duties may take various forms, ranging from fraudulent conduct, through nonfeasance of a duty, misfeasance in the performance of a duty or exercise of a power with a dishonest, corrupt or malicious motive, acting in excess of power or authority with a similar motive, to oppression. In all these instances the conduct complained of by the public officer takes place in or in relation to, or under colour of exercising, the office.

82. The critical question is: what is the mental element required to constitute commission of the offence? In the case of nonfeasance, non-performance of a duty arising by virtue of the office or the employment, all that is required is wilful intent, accompanied by absence of reasonable excuse or justification. Mere inadvertence is not enough. So much is established by the authorities, notably the more recent cases including *R v. Dytham and Question of Law Reserved (No. 2 of 1996)* at 418, per Doyle CJ.

83. In other cases, the question is more complex. That is because outside the area of non-performance of a duty, an additional element is generally, if not always required, to establish misconduct which is culpable for the purposes of the offence. In such cases, in the absence of breach of duty, the element of wilful intent will not be enough in itself to stamp the conduct as culpable misconduct. A dishonest or corrupt motive will be necessary as in situations where the officer is exercising a power or discretion with a view to conferring a benefit or advantage on himself, a relative or friend. A malicious motive will be necessary where the officer exercises a power or discretion with a view to harming another. And a corrupt, dishonest or malicious motive

will be required where, an officer acts in excess of power. The point about these cases is that, absent the relevant improper motive, be it dishonest, corrupt or malicious, the exercise of the power or discretion would not, or might not, amount to culpable misconduct. Although the examples constitute some only of the range of situations which fall within the reach of misconduct in public office, they are enough to illustrate the proposition that the existence of an improper motive, beyond the existence of a basic wilful intent, is necessary to stamp various categories of conduct by a public officer as culpable misconduct for the purposes of the offence.

84. In my view, the elements of the offence of misconduct in public office are:

(1) A public official;

(2) who in the course of or in relation to his public office;

(3) wilfully and intentionally;

(4) culpably misconducts himself.

A public official culpably misconducts himself if he wilfully and intentionally neglects or fails to perform a duty to which he is subject by virtue of his office or employment without reasonable excuse or justification. A public official also culpably misconducts himself if, with an improper motive, he wilfully and intentionally exercises a power or discretion which he has by virtue of his office or employment without reasonable excuse or justification. Subject to two qualifications, this statement of the elements of the offence accords with the respondent's submission.

85. The first qualification is that, although the respondent submits that the misconduct must be either "wilful" or "intentional", I consider that the misconduct must be "wilful" as well as "intentional". In *R v. Sheppard* [1981] AC 394, the House of Lords considered a statutory provision which made it an offence "wilfully" to neglect a child in a manner likely to cause him unnecessary suffering or injury to health. By majority it was held that a person "wilfully" fails to provide medical attention for a child if he (i) deliberately does so, knowing that the child's health may suffer unless he receives attention; or (ii) does so because he does not care whether the child may need medical attention or not. In other words, "wilfully" signifies knowledge or advertence to the consequences, as well as intent to do an act or refrain from doing an act. Wilfulness in this sense is the requisite mental element in the offence of misconduct in public office, most notably in cases of non–feasance. There is no reason why the same mental element should not be requisite in cases of misfeasance and other forms of misconduct in public office. For this reason "wilfully and "intentionally" are not employed disjunctively in the statement of the elements of the offence in the preceding paragraph.

86. The second qualification which I attach to the elements of the offence stated in the previous paragraph is that the misconduct complained of must be serious misconduct. Whether it is serious misconduct in this context is to be determined having regard to the responsibilities of the office and the officeholder, the importance of the public objects which they serve and the nature and extent of the departure from those responsibilities.

87. Although this qualification is not made in the earlier cases, it underlies the concluding observations of Lord Widgery CJ in *R v. Dytham*. The qualification is consistent with the concept of abuse of office and it is appropriate that the offence should be so qualified in the light of the creation of a range of disciplinary offences that now apply in the case of public sector employees. The qualification is not to be taken as a dividing line between the offence of misconduct in public office and disciplinary offences. There is no doubt a borderland in which the common law offence and disciplinary offences overlap.

The offence is not imprecise or vague or arbitrary

88. The common law offence as so explained is not so imprecise as to offend the requirement of Basic Law art. 39 or of arts 5(1) and 11(1) of the Bill. Nor is it arbitrary within the meaning of art. 28 of the Basic Law. The offence is unusual in that it applies to various forms of misconduct by a public officer with the result that what the prosecution needs to establish varies with the form of culpable misconduct alleged. That variation does not, however, lead to the existence at common law of more than one offence. Despite its variations, it has always been recognised as the one offence.

89. In expressing the view that there is no relevant imprecision, I bear in mind the passages in *Sunday Times v. United Kingdom, Sabapathee v. The State* [1999] 1 WLR 1836 and *R v. Nova Scotia Pharmaceutical Society* (1992) 74 CCC (3d) 289 to the effect that a law must be adequately accessible in the sense that it gives a person an adequate indication of the law relevant to his situation so that (if need be with advice) he can regulate his conduct. On the other hand, it is well settled that the degree of precision required will vary according to the context of the law. In *Sabapathee v. The State*, Lord Hope of Craighead, speaking for the Privy Council, said (at 1843):

> "But the precision which is needed to avoid [striking down as unconstitutional] will necessarily vary according to the subject matter. The fact that a law is expressed in broad terms does not mean that it must be held to have failed to reach the required standard. In an ideal world it ought to be possible to define a crime in terms which identified the precise dividing line between conduct which was, and that which was not, criminal. But some conduct which the law may quite properly wish to prescribe as criminal may best be described by reference to the nature of the activity rather than to particular methods of committing it. It may be impossible to predict all these methods with absolute certainty, or there may be good grounds for thinking that attempts to do so would lead to undesirable rigidity. In such situations a description of the nature of the activity which is to be penalised will provide sufficient notice to the individual that any conduct falling within that description is to be regarded as criminal. The application of that description to the various situations as they arise will then be a matter for the courts to decide in the light of experience."

90. To similar effect are the remarks of Gonthier J in *R v. Nova Scotia Pharmaceutical Society* in delivering the judgment of the Supreme Court of Canada. He noted (at 306c) that the threshold for a holding of vagueness is relatively high. He went on to say (at 310b–c):

> "an unintelligible provision gives insufficient guidance for legal debate and is therefore unconstitutionally vague."

He continued (at 311c–d):

> "... it is inherent [in] our legal system that some conduct will fall along the boundaries of the area of risk; no

definite prediction can then be made. Guidance, not direction, of conduct is a more realistic objective. The ECHR has repeatedly warned against a quest for certainty and adopted this 'area of risk' approach ..."

Gonthier J concluded his discussion of the point with comments which are particularly apposite to the case in hand. He said (at 312h–313c):

"... laws that are framed in general terms may be better suited to the achievement of their objectives, in as much as in fields governed by public policy circumstances may vary widely in time and from one case to the other. A very detailed enactment would not provide the required flexibility, and it might...obscure its purposes behind a veil of detailed provisions ... One must be wary of using the doctrine of vagueness to prevent or impede state action in furtherance of valid social objectives, by requiring the law to achieve a degree of precision to which the subject-matter does not lend itself."

91. The common law offence of misconduct in public office is necessarily cast in general terms because it is designed to cover many forms of misconduct on the part of public officers. An alternative way of dealing with misconduct by public officers would be to enact a statute formulating specific offences for particular categories of misconduct in public office. The adoption of that course would involve a loss of flexibility and run the risk that the net would fail to catch some forms of serious misconduct. To suggest that the offence requires further definition would be to pursue a degree of definition which is unattainable, having regard to the wide range of acts and omissions which are capable of amounting to misconduct by a public officer in or relating to his office. The offence serves an important purpose in providing a criminal sanction against misconduct by public officers.

92. The broad terms in which the offence is cast are sufficient to enable the public officer to regulate his conduct. The elements of the offence, quite apart from its title or description, alert the public officer to the risk that he runs by engaging in misconduct and that is all that art. 39 of the Basic Law and art. 11(1) of the Bill require. The offence targets misconduct as the relevant act or omission to be avoided, thereby providing the necessary "guidance", to use the term used by Gonthier J in the *Nova Scotia case*. A public officer, familiar with his powers and duties, should have no difficulty in appreciating that neglecting to perform his duty with wilful intent and dishonestly, corruptly and maliciously exercising his powers and discretions constitute misconduct which is criminally culpable as already explained.

93. Mr Griffiths SC mounted a separate attack on the *Reg v. Ghosh* test, invoking the criticism made of that test by the English Law Commission. In *Reg v. Ghosh* [1982] QB 1053, the question was whether the trial judge's direction correctly instructed the jury as to the word "dishonestly" in s.1 of the Theft Act, 1968. The Court of Appeal held that the word described the state of mind and not the conduct of the accused and, therefore, the test of dishonesty was subjective but the standard of honesty to be applied was the "ordinary standards of reasonable and honest people" (at 1064). In the result, the jury should have first considered whether the appellant had acted dishonestly by the standards of ordinary and honest people.

94. It was that test that the trial judge applied in the present case and it was the subject of the Law Commission's criticism in its Consultation Paper No. 155 "Legislating the Criminal Code–Fraud and Deception". In paras 5.11–5.18 of the Paper, the Commission criticised the *Ghosh* test on the ground that it required fact-finders to set a moral standard of honesty by making a semantic and moral inquiry in circumstances where there is no single community norm or standard of dishonesty. The standard in *Reg v. Ghosh* is an objective standard. A similar standard has been applied in other areas of the law without attracting adverse comment (see, for example, *Twinsectra Ltd v. Yardley* [2002] 2 WLR 802). Granted the difficulty of ascertaining what are the ordinary standards of reasonable and honest people, it is nonetheless a task which is not so imprecise or vague as to violate the relevant requirements of art. 39 of the Basic Law or of art. 11(1) in the Bill. Nor can it be characterized as an arbitrary standard. A further point to be made in relation to the Law Commission's criticism is that, in framing standards to be applied by tribunals of fact, the search for definition can be carried too far. A higher degree of definition of some standards– "reasonable" is in its various applications in both the civil and the criminal law an example–is often unattainable.

95. If, contrary to the conclusion I have reached, the offence were to be regarded as having been defined by Lord Widgery CJ in the terms which have been the target of Mr Griffiths' challenge, then the case of imprecision would have been stronger. Culpability of such a degree "that the misconduct impugned is calculated to injure the public interest so as to call for condemnation and punishment" might not provide an adequate "basis for legal debate and coherent judicial interpretation" and where judicial interpretation is not possible the law is constitutionally vague (*R v. Canadian Pacific Ltd* (1995) 99 CCC (3d) 97 at 140, per Gonthier J). That, however, is not the case on the conclusion I have reached.

96. This case is distinguishable from *Reg v. Withers* [1975] AC 842 where it was held that the law knew no such generalised offence as effecting a public mischief. There the House of Lords concluded, despite the existence of a considerable body of authority, that the so-called offence left too much to a jury because it lacked sufficient and judicial cogency and precision and because it was contrary to the spirit of the common law (see at 870 FG, per Lord Simon of Glaisdale). Their Lordships considered that, if they were to develop the law by creating a general offence of public mischief they would be creating a new offence, this being an undertaking that was impermissible (860 EF, per Viscount Dilhorne; 867 EF and 868 AB, per Lord Simon of Glaisdale; 877 GH, per Lord Kilbrandon, where their Lordships followed the authority of *Reg v. Knuller* [1973] AC 435).

97. *Hashman and Harrup v. United Kingdom* (1999) 30 EHRR 241 is to be distinguished from the present case for somewhat similar reasons. Conduct *contra bonos mores* lacked any sufficient precision to enable it to serve as a standard or guide by which people could regulate their conduct. It was, to use an expression employed by Lamer CJC in *R v. Morales* (1992) 77 CCC (3d) 91 at 101, no more than a "standardless sweep".

98. Mr Griffiths SC made the valid point that, in conformity with *Reg v. Withers* and *Reg v. Knuller*, it was not for this Court to create a new offence as an answer to a perceived problem of imprecise definition or accessibility. That said, it is well established that, by employing accepted and traditional judicial techniques, a court is entitled, indeed bound, to clarify the existing law where clarification is needed so long as, in doing so, the court does not extend the boundaries of criminal liability. To do so would create retrospective criminal liability and offend the provision of art. 12(1) of the Bill. The offence of misconduct in public office, as I have explained it, is consistent with the existing authorities. The explanation amounts at most to a clarification which, even if it

does not narrow the offence, does not expand it.

99. In this case, no issue was raised as to the meaning and scope of the expression "public office". The appellant clearly fell within the expression. Just how far it extends may perhaps be a question for the future. On the later authorities, the expression has been understood as having a wide application. See *Henly v. Lyme Corp* (1828) 5 Bing 91, 130 ER 995; *R v. Whitaker* [1914] 3 KB 1283; *R v. Bowden* [1995] 4 All ER 505.

Conclusion

100. The particulars given of the four charges and the facts found by the trial judge bring this case within the offence as it has been explained. The appellant was a public officer. The acts and omissions complained of took place in the course of that public office. His relevant duties and responsibilities, especially in relation to conflicts of interest and the obligation not to confer benefits on or favour relatives and friends were set out in the Circular. His departures from his duties and responsibilities were clearly established. In relation to these departures, the trial judge found that the appellant acted dishonestly, must have realised that what he was doing was dishonest and concluded that the reason for his non-disclosure of his connection with Onclever was "his desire to help and favour Onclever". Indeed, the trial judge found that his recommendation of Onclever for pre-qualification was "due to his hidden connection to Onclever". Accordingly, his conduct was wilful in that he was aware of his responsibilities, and realised that what he was doing was dishonest. And his conduct was culpable, being without reasonable excuse or justification and dishonest because his motive was to benefit and favour Onclever.

101. In the result the appeal should be dismissed.

Chief Justice Li:

102. The Court unanimously dismisses the appeal.

Chief Justice (Andrew Li)

Permanent Judge (Kemal Bokhary)

Permanent Judge (Patrick Chan)

Permanent Judge (R A V Ribeiro)

Non-Permanent Judge (Sir Anthony Mason)

Mr John Griffiths, SC and Mr Andrew Bullett (instructed by Messrs P C Woo & Co.) for the appellant

Mr Michael Thomas, SC (instructed by the Department of Justice), Mr Michael Blanchflower, SC, Mr Ian McWalters and Mr Gavin Shiu (of that Department) for the respondent

---

第四十條

"新界"原居民的合法傳統權益受香港特別行政區的保護。

案例

非原居民能否參選和選舉新界村代表

P.633 | 陳華 對 坑口鄉事委員會及其他；謝群生 對 八鄉鄉事委員會、律政司司長

Chan Wah v. Hang Hau Rural Committee & Another;
Tse Kwan Sang v. Pat Heung Rural Committee, Secretary for Justice

陳華 對 坑口鄉事委員會及其他；謝群生 對 八鄉鄉事委員會、律政司司長

HCAL 28/1999；HCAL 112/1998；CACV 279/1999；CACV 278/1999；CACV 139/1999；CACV 137/1999；FACV 11/2000

簡略案情

答辯人陳華為西貢坑口布袋澳村村民、謝群生為元朗八鄉石湖塘村村民，但二人不符合香港法例第 515 章《地租（評估及徵收）條例》對“原居村民”的定義，即非在 1898 年時是香港原有鄉村的居民或其父系後裔。因此，根據布袋澳村和石湖塘村於 1999 年就選舉村代表一職時各自作出的選舉安排，陳華被拒投票，而謝群生被拒參選。二人透過司法覆核程序質疑該選舉安排的法律效力，認為該等安排與《基本法》、香港法例第 383 章《香港人權法案條例》及香港法例第 480 章《性別歧視條例》均有抵觸。兩人在原訟法庭及上訴法庭均獲判勝訴。原居村民代表及政府遂向終審法院提出上訴，認為《鄉議局條例》第 3（3）條提及“以選舉或其他方式獲選為代表某鄉村的人”是指“代表原居村民”。

裁決摘要

終審法院認為過去曾有一段時期是所有村民皆屬原居人士，由於鄉村的人口主要是來自原居村民，因此村代表亦代表原居村民。然而，二十世紀末的數十年裏，新界經歷了急速的改變，在經濟及社會因素影響下，人口出現流動。村代表實際上已不再只代表原居村民，而是代表整個由原居村民和非原居村民所組成的鄉村。終審法院認為，即使假定《鄉議局條例》於 1959 年制定時，有關鄉村的人口只由原居村民組成，也沒有理據可指稱，立法者有意將該法例的涵義固定在制定之時間。終審法院強調《鄉議局條例》應具有前瞻性，認為應當按照詮釋其他條例的一般做法，把相關法例視為需要繼續施行的現行法例來進行闡釋。“代表某鄉村”應指代表整個鄉村，而非鄉村的一部份人士。因此，組成有關鄉村人口的原居村民及非原居村民均應該獲得代表。終審法院認為以非原居人士為由對答辯人的投票權及參選權加以限制，不應被視為合理的限制。至於《基本法》第 40 條規定的“新界原居民的合法傳統權益受香港特別行政區的保護”，終審法院認為該條所指的“合法傳統權益”並不能衍生出上訴人所辯稱原居民所擁有的政治權利。據此，上訴被駁回。

[中譯本 – 司法機構法庭語文組譯]

[Chinese Translation – Prepared by

Court Language Section, Judiciary]

FACV 11 及 13/2000

香港特別行政區
終審法院

終院民事上訴 2000 年第 11 及 13 號
（原本案件編號：高院民事上訴 1999 年第 137 及 139 號與高院民事上訴 1999 年第 278 及 279 號）

第一上訴人　律政司司長
第二上訴人　西貢民政事務處
第三上訴人　張錦泉
對
第一答辯人　陳華
第二答辯人　謝群生
第三答辯人　坑口鄉事委員會
第四答辯人　八鄉鄉事委員會

審理法官：終審法院首席法官李國能
終審法院常任法官包致金
終審法院常任法官李義
終審法院非常任法官邵祺
終審法院非常任法官苗禮治勳爵

聆訊日期：2000 年 11 月 20 至 23 日

判案書日期：2000 年 12 月 22 日

判案書

終審法院首席法官李國能：

儘管本港日趨都市化，以致鄉村數目減少，但目前新界仍有超過 600 個鄉村。年近古稀的陳華先生（"陳先生"）與年近五秩的謝群生先生（"謝先生"）均分別在其鄉村出生、成長，並一直居住至今。陳先生居於西貢坑口布袋澳村，而謝先生則住在元朗八鄉石湖塘村。事實上，兩人的父母均分別在其鄉村居住了一段時間。兩人皆已婚，育有子女。

原居村民

根據香港法例第 515 章《地租（評估及徵收）條例》，原居村民持有的某些物業獲豁免繳交地租的法律責任。該條例乃實施《基本法》第一百二十二條，而《基本法》第一百二十二條則源自聯合聲明附件三。該條例將"原居村民"界定為"在 1898 年時是香港原有鄉村的居民或其父系後裔"，而"原有鄉村"則界定為在 1898 年已在香港存在的，而地政署長亦已根據第 5 條信納在 1898 年已存在的鄉村。

本案涉及的鄉村，即布袋澳村及石湖塘村均為原有鄉村。（後者為另一在 1898 年已存在的鄉村的分支，但這點對本案並無影響。）就此等法律程序而言，"原居村民"一詞乃以該條例所述的意義使用，而"原居民"一詞於此使用時也與之意義相仿。這是雙方爭論中的共同基礎；儘管代表陳先生及謝先生的資深大律師戴啟思先生曾（就《基本法》第四十條中"原居民"一詞的意義）登錄知會備忘，但就本案而言這並非關鍵問題。

撇除特別長壽的人不說，在 1898 年時是新界鄉村居民的人士現在都已經離開人世。案中令人關注的是他們的男丁，即父系後裔。1898 年是意義重大的一年。中英兩國正是在該年簽訂北京條約，訂定了英方租借新界 99 年。當然，在 19 世紀末葉以至 20 世紀頗長的一段時間，新界屬於鄉郊之地，居民均住在鄉村。

顯然，若有人能證明其父系祖先於 1898 年時是某鄉村的居民，則他毋需居於該鄉村也可算是原居村民。事實上，該名人士甚至無須曾經在該鄉村居住。在經濟及社會因素影響下，人口出現流動，一些原居村民離開了鄉村，而一些非原居村民則成爲了鄉村的一份子。以陳先生畢生居住的布袋澳村為例，證據顯示，在約 800 至 900 名原居村民中，只有約 300 至 400 人仍然住在該處；而按照 1999 年村代表一職的選舉安排，約有 290 名非原居村民被拒投票。至於謝先生畢生居住的石湖塘村，證據顯示，在約 600 名村民中，470 人為非原居村民。

陳先生與謝先生既然分別在其鄉村居住了一輩子，故若乾脆把二人稱為其鄉村的村民也並無不妥。然而，由於他們不能證明其父系祖先於 1898 年是新界鄉村的居民，因此他們並非*原居*村民，也不可能是*原居*村民。在此等法律程序中，他們被稱為"非原居村民"。

根據案中兩村於 1999 年就選舉村代表一職時各自作出的選舉安排，陳先生被拒投票，而謝先生則被拒參選。陳先生的鄉村結果沒有進行選舉，而謝先生的鄉村則進行了選舉，選出了村代表。

透過司法覆核提出質疑

陳先生與謝先生透過司法覆核程序質疑上述選舉安排的法律效力。其所據理由為：該等安排與《基本法》、香港法例第 383 章《香港人權法案條例》（"人權法案條例"）及香港法例第 480 章《性別歧視條例》均有抵觸。兩人在原訟法庭獲判勝訴。參閱*陳華對坑口鄉事委員會及其他* [1999] 2 HKLRD 286（高等法院原訟法庭法官范達理）；亦可見於 [1999] 2 HKC 160。*謝群生對八鄉鄉事委員會及另一人* [1999] 3 HKLRD 267（高等法院原訟法庭法官張澤祐）；亦可見於 [1999] 3 HKC 457。他們在上訴法庭也同樣獲判勝訴；當時其上訴被綜合處理。參閱*陳華及另一人對坑口鄉事委員會及其他* [2000] 1 HKLRD 411（高等法院首席法官陳兆愷（當時官銜）、高等法院上訴法庭副庭長黎守律及高等法院上訴法庭法官梅賢玉（當時官銜））。

上訴

本上訴的上訴人爲：張錦泉先生（"張先生"）及政府，而後者以西貢民政事務處及律政司司長作爲當事人。上訴法庭給予他們上訴許可。張先生是布袋澳村的原居村民。陳先生與謝先生為答辯人，而有關鄉村所在地區的鄉事委員會也同樣是答辯人。兩個鄉事委員會均沒有派代表出席聆訊。平等機會委員會安排了大律師協助本院，作爲法庭之友，對本院幫助甚大。

本案的詳細事實已在原訟法庭及上訴法庭的判案書中臚列。就本上訴而言，無須再加瞥述。

村代表

由於雙方所爭議的是有關村代表一職的選舉安排的法律效力，因此了解該職位的性質甚為重要。

按照法例，"村代表"一職指的是"以選舉或其他方式獲選為代表某鄉村而又經民政事務局局長（"局長"）批准的人"。參閱《鄉議局條例》（"該局條例"）第 3（3）（a）條。

不管該片語的正確解釋為何，此處令人關注的是“以選舉……獲選……的人”及與之相對的“以其他方式……獲選……的人”。有三點應該提出。一，有關人士必須是獲選而又經局長批准才能出任村代表。在任命村代表的過程中，局長的批准是不可或缺的一環。然而局長可撤回批准。若有人對局長拒絕批准或撤回批准的決定不滿，可向行政長官會同行政會議提出上訴；行政長官會同行政會議的決定為最終決定。參閱第 3（d）（i）條。二，誠如該條文所言，村代表的職能是代表鄉村。此片語的正確釋義受到爭議，下文將有論述。三，該法例並沒有界定選舉的投票權，也沒有界定誰合資格參選。

鄉村

一份經全體大律師同意的文件將村代表的職能臚列如下：

“(1) 協助核證村民的原居身分，以便村民根據丁屋政策申請興建丁屋。

(2) 安排擁有原居身分的村民取得地租豁免或地租折減。

(3) 見證及安排山邊土葬。

(4) 見證村民根據《新界條例》申請繼承遺產。

(5) 核證由外國返港的原居民後裔的原居身分，並協助該等人士申請香港身分證。

(6) [就] 各種事項充當各個政府機構（特別是民政事務處和地政處）與村民之間的聯絡人，包括：

(a) 根據丁屋政策所提出的興建丁屋申請；

(b) 搬村、因發展而進行的清拆及收回土地；

(c) 把村民關心的問題及作出的投訴向政府機關反映；及

(d) 向村民宣布政府政策及政府通告。”

上述的村代表職能中，有部份只與原居村民有關。參閱第 1、2、3 及 6（a）段所述的職能。這些職能關乎原居村民的傳統權利及利益。村代表透過見證村民簽署文件和核證村民的原居身分，使他們在索請該等權利及利益時更爲便利。為方便起見，下文將把該等職能稱為“核證與便利職能”。此外，核證由外地返港的原居民後裔的原居身分，以便該等人士申請香港身分證這項職能，也只與原居村民有關（參閱第 5 段）。當然，享有身分證的權利須受法律規限，與原居村民的傳統權利及利益無關。然而，見證村民申請繼承遺產的這項職能，卻與原居及非原居村民均有關係（參閱第 4 段）。

至於村代表充當政府與村民之間的聯絡人這項職能，顯然不只是與原居村民有關而是與整個鄉村有關（參閱第6段和第（b）、（c）及（d）小段）。例如，某鄉村因排水系統不足，以致大雨成災，村代表在與政府機關就此問題進行聯絡時，顯然是代表整個鄉村而不只是代表村內的原居村民。

鄉村以外

村代表在鄉村以外也有一個角色。首先是鄉事委員會的層面。村代表會自動成爲有關鄉村所在地區的鄉事委員會委員，並會互相選出鄉事委員會正副主席。（現時共有 27 個鄉事委員會。）

其次是區議會的層面。由村代表選出的鄉事委員會主席是有關的區議會的當然議員。區議會對影響有關的地方行政區的種種事項有諮詢職能，同時也有行政職能，即在就有關目的獲得撥款的情況下，承擔有關的地方行政區內的改善事務及活動。參閱香港法例第 547 章《區議會條例》第 9 及第 61 條。

第三，就鄉議局（“該局”）的組合而言，村代表在該局也扮演了一個角色。該局是於 1926 年創立的社團。隨著《鄉議局條例》於 1959 年制定，該局成爲了一個法定團體。該條例的弁言肯定了該局過去的貢獻，指出該局是政府在新界區事務上的諮詢團體，並且為新界區意見領袖提供交換意見的場合；又指出當時認爲該局成爲一個法定諮詢團體乃屬合宜之事，而訂定其組織時，須確保該局盡可能真正代表新界區的明達而負責任的意見。

該局由一名主席及兩名副主席組成，他們須為執行委員會成員，並須由議員大會選出。參閱第 2（2）條。

執行委員會由以下人士組成：（a）當然委員，即（i）各鄉事委員會主席（他們如前所述是由村代表選出）；及（ii）新界太平紳士；及（b）普通委員（不得超逾 15 名），各普通委員須為議員大會的議員，並由議員大會選出。參閱第 4 條。

議員大會由下述三類議員組成。參閱第 3 條。從該等議員的組合可以清楚看見村代表所扮演的角色：

（1）當然議員。他們包括各鄉事委員會的正副主席（他們如前所述是由村代表選出）及新界太平紳士。

（2）特別議員（以 21 名為上限）。他們由當然議員從村代表（或從民政事務局局長所批准的其他人）之中選出。（組成新界的）大埔區、元朗區及南約區三區中以每區選出不超逾 7 名為限。

（3）增選議員（以 15 名為上限）。此類別是《鄉議局條例》於 1988 年進行修訂時增補的。鄉事委員會的委員並不符合資格被選，換句話說，由於村代表會自動成爲鄉事委員會會員，所以並不符合資格被選為增選議員。然而，候選人須由包括各鄉事委員會主席在內的鄉議局執行委員會提名（鄉事委員會主席由村代表選出），並須由議員大會確認。因此，村代表就透過當然議員與特別議員的組合而扮演一定的角色。此外，候選人須經民政事務局局長批准。

該局的法定宗旨為（參閱第 9 條）：

“(a) 促進和加深新界區的人之間的互相合作及了解；

(b) 促進和加深政府與新界區的人之間的合作及了解；

(c) 為新界區的人的福利及繁榮而就社會及經濟的發展向政府提供意見；

(d) 鼓勵遵守對新界區的人有益並有利於維持公衆道德的所有風俗及傳統習慣；及

(e) 執行行政長官所不時邀請執行的職能。”

雖然原居民顯然是（d）項宗旨描述的主要對象，但（a）、（b）及（c）項則與新界的人有關，而不只限於新界的原居民。

第四，該局由過去數年至今一直都是立法會的一個功能界別。該界別由該局正副主席及該局議員大會的當然議員、特別議員及增選議員組成。參閱香港法例第 542 章《立法會條例》第 20A 條。

爭論點

本上訴的爭論點如下：

（1）本案是否涉及《人權法案條例》；倘本案涉及該條例，則有關的選舉安排是否與該條例有抵觸。

（2）有關布袋澳村的選舉安排是否與《性別歧視條例》有抵觸。

（3）《基本法》第四十條是否保護了原居村民在村代表選舉中的投票權及參選權，而把其他人士排除於該等權利之外。

（4）現時透過司法覆核提出質疑是否言之過早；倘其並非過早，則有何妥善補救方法。

《人權法案條例》

《基本法》第三十九條所規定的事項中，其中一項是《公民權利和政治權利國際公約》（下稱"該公約"）適用於香港的有關規定繼續有效，通過香港特別行政區的法律予以實施。《人權法案條例》將該公約中適用於香港的規定收納入香港法律。《香港人權法案》於該條例（"人權法案"）的第 II 部予以列明。

《人權法案條例》第 7（1）條規定：該條例只對"（a）政府及所有公共主管當局；及（b）代表政府或公共主管當局行事的任何人"具有約束力。

由於《人權法案》條例只對政府、公共主管當局及代表此兩者其中一方行事的人士具約束力，故此，若要引用該條例，勢必涉及上述三方的其中一方。此可謂《人權法案》的關鍵所在。倘若有關團體不是政府或公共主管當局，亦非代表此兩者其中一方行事的人士，則該條例對有關團體並沒有約束力，根本不存在引用《人權法案》的問題。

政府牽涉於本案。根據該局條例第 3（3）（a）條，任何獲選為代表某鄉村的人，須經局長批准方可成為村代表。局長作為政府的一份子，顯然是受《人權法案條例》所約束。由於局長受《人權法案》約束，當他履行職責，決定是否給予批准時，必須考慮該名獲選為代表某鄉村的人，是否在合乎該法案的選舉安排下選出；倘若該等安排與《人權法案》有抵觸，他便不可給予批准。在這方面，便涉及《人權法案條例》。當決定選舉安排是否與有關條文有任何抵觸時，須把有關條文加以詮譯及應用。

第二十一條（甲）

《人權法案》第二十一條開列於該條例的第 II 部，內容如下所列。（本條與該公約第 25 條相符。）

"第二十一條

參與公眾生活的權利

凡屬永久性居民，無分人權法案第一（一）條所列之任何區別，不受無理限制，均應有權利及機會 —

（甲）直接或經由自由選擇之代表參與政事；

（乙）在真正、定期之選舉中投票及被選。選舉權必須普及而平等，選舉應以無記名投票法行之，以保證選民意志之自由表現；

（丙）以一般平等之條件，服香港之職。"

本上訴與第二十一條（甲）有關。第一條（一）所指的區別這點並非主要論點。（該條所指的區別包括：種族、膚色、性別、語言、宗教、政見或其他主張、民族本源或社會階級、財產、出生或其他身分等等。）有關方面所依據的是無理限制那點。

關鍵爭論點是：首先，由選舉產生，又經局長批准的村代表，是否有參與政事？第二，參與的權利及機會是否受到無理限制？

倘若這兩個問題的答案均屬肯定，本案的選舉安排便與第二十一條（甲）有抵觸。陳先生與謝先生是案中兩村的村民，屬永久性居民。直接參與的途徑是成為村代表，即是參選並於獲選後得到局長的批准。（間接參與）的途徑，便是在選舉時投票，經由自由選擇之代表（即獲選之村代表）參與。陳先生不獲准投票，令他經由自由選擇之代表參與的權利及機會遭剝奪。而謝先生不獲准參選，則令他直接參與的權利及機會遭剝奪。

探討關鍵的爭論點前，考慮村代表所代表的人士至為重要，因為兩個關鍵的爭論點均與此有關。

村代表所代表的人士

代表原居村民張先生的資深大律師郭兆銘先生呈述如下：正如其書面案由述要所言，原居村民是"近似私人會所的會員"，而取得會籍的唯一準則是有關人士必須為在 1898 年居於鄉村的居民之父系後裔。當該局條例第 3（3）（a）條提及"以選舉或其他方式獲選為代表某鄉村的人"時，其正確釋義是指"代表原居村民"。資深大律師郭兆銘先生辯稱：事實上，鄉議局主要是代表新界原居民的利益，而各村代表則主要是代表原居村民的利益。

實際上，過去必有一段時期是所有村民皆屬原居人士。根據有關定義，1898 年的情況便是如此。20 世紀頗長的一段時間，經濟及社會改變較為緩慢，人口流動可能因此亦相對地有限，故此，所有或大部份村民仍然是原居人士。在這情況下，鄉村幾乎等同組成其人口的原居村民。村代表掌管核證與便利職能，此等職能只與原居村民有關，因為那是涉及到他們的傳統權利及利益。此外，村代表還代表鄉村處理一些與政府聯絡之類的事務。由於鄉村的人口主要是來自原居村民，因此，村代表亦代表原居村民。

然而，在 20 世紀末的數十年裡，新界經歷了急速的改變，在經濟及社會因素影響下，人口出現流動。誠如前述，非原居村民在案中兩村的人口中，佔有相當比重。就石湖塘村而言，他們的人數其實比原居村民為多。由於兩村的人口成份發生了這樣的轉變，村代表在履行核證與便利以外的職能時，實際上已不再是只代表原居村民，而是代表整個由原居村民和非原居村民組成的鄉村。舉例來說，村代表履行與政府聯絡的職能時，便是代表整個鄉村。

鄉議局方面，其法定職能並非只囿於代表原居民的利益。不論以往的情況如何，現時鄉議局議員大會的組合中，非原居民佔有很大的比重（大約百分之二十五）（參閱高等法院原訟法庭法官張澤祐的判案書 [1999] 3 HKLRD at 281，[1999] 3 HKC at 472）。1988 年《鄉議局條例》的修訂，顯然是為了使非原居民的參與更為便利。

撇開實際情況不談，"…… 代表某鄉村 …… 的人"這片語的正確釋義應否闡釋為只代表原居村民？即使假定該局條例於 1959 年制定時，有關鄉村的人口只由原居村民組成，也沒有理據可指稱，立法者有意將該法例的涵意固定在制定之時。訂定鄉議局的設立及職能的《鄉議局條例》具前瞻性。正如詮釋其他法例的一般做法，本院應該根據把有關法例視為繼續施行的現行法律這需要來闡釋該局條例。參閱 Halsbury's Laws 第 44（1）冊，（第 4 版，再發行），第 1218 及 1473 段。如此闡釋，有關法例中，"代表某鄉村"這片語具其一般的涵義，即是代表整個鄉村。這片語不能解作只是代表鄉村的一部份。因此，組成有關鄉村人口的原居村民及非原居村民均獲代表。

政事

政事涉及公共行政的所有方面，其中包括鄉村的層面。村代表除了掌管關乎原居村民的傳統權利及利益的核證與便利職能外，還代表整個鄉村就一些影響及鄉村和村民福利的事宜跟主管當局聯絡。此等事宜涉及鄉村層面的公共行政。再者，村代表所扮演的角色不囿於鄉村的層面。一如以上之概述，這角色直接或間接地透過從村代表中選出的鄉事委員會的正副主席，伸展至公共層面的多個團體：即鄉事委員會、區議會、鄉議局，以及鄉議局最終在立法會內的功能界別中所佔的一席。鑑於村代表的職能及其在鄉村層面以外所扮演的角色，村代表應被視為如《人權法案》第二十一條（甲）所指般參與政事。這點可反映於獲選人士須先得一名政府官員，即局長批准方可成為村代表這項規定。

無理限制

村代表應被視為有參與政事的結論得出後，繼而出現的問題是：該等否定陳先生的投票權以及謝先生的參選權的限制是否屬無理限制。

本院當然不可能嘗試概括地為村代表選舉定出那些是合理的限制，那些是不合理的限制。本院只關注這兩宗訴訟所涉及的有關限制。值得注意的是，根據涉案的選舉安排，原居村民享有投票權及參選權，這點並沒有受到質疑。

本院必須以客觀的態度來考慮有關限制是否合理。考慮的事項必須包括：所參與的政事之性質、對參與的權利和機會所施加之限制的性質及限制之理由。限制被視為合理或不合理，可能因時代的變遷而截然不同。

陳先生和謝先生分別在其鄉村居住了一輩子，把他們視為其鄉村的村民顯然是恰當的。但他們卻由於本身並非原居人士，即其父系祖先並非於 1898 年居於新界鄉村的居民，而分別被拒投票及參選。須緊記的是，按照法例，村代表須，實際上亦然，代表整個鄉村（人口由原居村民及非原居村民組成）；更於鄉村層面外擔當了一個角色。以非原居人士為由而施加限制，這不可視為合理的限制。

因此，該等限制了陳先生的投票權和謝先生的參選權的選舉安排既不合理，亦與《人權法案》第二十一條（甲）有抵觸。

代表政府的資深大律師馮華健先生援引了《基本法》第六十八條（二）之規定，即立法會的產生是根據香港的實際情況和循序漸進的原則。但這只是關乎立法會，與本案無關。資深大律師馮華健先生亦以新界區有多個區議會，而當中有相當數目的成員是經選舉產生這事實作為依據，指出這是提供了參與政事的機會。雖然情況的確如此，但同樣與本案無關。本案兩村所進行的村代表選舉才是須考慮的問題。一如前文所得之結論，該等選舉安排與《人權法案》第二十一條（甲）有抵觸。

《性別歧視條例》

若村代表選舉的安排抵觸《性別歧視條例》，則局長不得認可獲選人士，這點雙方並無爭議。事實上，該條例第 IV 部第 35（5）（a）條明確規定：

> "即使《鄉議局條例》或其他條例有任何規定，凡任何人……是經由女性並未能與男性在平等的條款下以候選人、被提名人、投票人或其他有關身分參與的程序選舉……選出，民政事務局局長不得認可該人為村代表。"

該條例中關於針對女性性別歧視的有關條文（第 5 條及第 III 及 IV 部，其中包括第 35 條），按第 6（1）條適用於男性。該等條文

> "須理解為同樣地適用於男性所受的待遇；就此而言，該等條文經作出必要的變通後具有效力。"

上訴法庭維持原訟法庭的判決，裁定案中兩村的選舉安排在若干方面與《性別歧視條例》有抵觸。就謝先生的案件而言，他並沒有針對上訴法庭就歧視方面所作的判決提出上訴。本院現只須處理陳先生的案件中有關歧視的爭論點，因為原居村民張先生針對該爭論點提出了上訴。必須注意的是，政府並無針對任何有關歧視的爭論點向本院提出上訴。

就陳先生的案件而言，他所指稱的歧視包括以下各點。根據有關選舉安排，非原居*女性*與原居村民結婚後可享有*投票權*，但與原居村民結婚的非原居*男性*則*不能參與投票*。陳先生指稱這是針對男性的歧視。

《性別歧視條例》第 5（1）（a）條規定：

> "任何人如 —（a）基於一名女性的性別而給予她差於他給予或會給予男性的待遇，即屬在就本條例任何條文而言是有關的情況下，歧視該女性。"

第 35（3）（c）條規定：

> "任何人 —
>
> （c）在決定任何人於選舉有關團體的成員或有關職位的擔任者的投票資格方面，或參與揀選有關職位的擔任者的資格方面歧視另一人，即屬違法。"

有關職位包括《鄉議局條例》所指的村代表。參閱第 35（2）條。誠如前述，該等條文按第 6（1）條同樣適用於男性所受的待遇。

上訴法庭在考慮某項安排是否涉及性別歧視時，正確地採用了 *R v Birmingham City Council Ex parte Equal Opportunities Commission* [1989] 1 AC 1155 at 1194 A-C 一案中，Lord Goff 在考慮《1975 年性別歧視法令》時闡明的"若非"驗證標準：

> "如果基於性別而出現待遇較差的情況，在法例下即屬歧視，換言之，如果有關女生（或女生們）若非因為其性別，便會受到與男生們同等的待遇，此情況在法例下即屬歧視。被告人作出歧視行為的意圖或動機，儘管可能與補償有關，……卻並非要他承擔法律責任的必需條件；在某些情況下，雖然被告人沒有這個動機，但事實上卻基於性別而作出了歧視的行為，這是完全可以想像到的。"

Lord Bridge 在 *James v Eastleigh Borough Council* [1990] 2 AC 751 at 765D 一案中採用了這個驗證標準，並指出那是一個客觀的驗證標準。

引用這個驗證標準，本案顯然存在非法的歧視。（娶了原居村民的）非原居*男性*，若非因為其*性別*，便會獲得（嫁給原居村民的）非原居*女性*所得到的同等待遇，即享有投票權。

必須注意的是，論者亦依據另一點，指本案存在基於婚姻狀況的歧視，違反第 7（1）（a）條。即是說，把（嫁給原居村民的）非原居*已婚*女性與非原居*未婚*女性作比較。然而，由於此論點與陳先生的情況無關，本院毋需處理。

《基本法》第四十條

根據以上結論，涉案的選舉安排與《人權法案》及《性別歧視條例》有抵觸，局長不得認可在該等安排下獲選的人士。

然而，事情並未就此完結。代表原居村民張先生的資深大律師郭兆銘先生以《基本法》第四十條為依據，該條文規定：

"'新界'原居民的合法傳統權益受香港特別行政區的保護。"

他呈述如下：第四十條保護了原居民的合法傳統權益。為確保第四十條所指的原居民權益得到充分保護，應將之引申為：原居村民在村代表選舉中，可享有投票及參選的政治權利，而其他人士則沒有該等權利。他認同第四十條並沒有直接涵蓋這些政治權利。正如其書面案由述要所言："……我們並非辯稱原居村民擁有以投票方式選出村代表的明確傳統權利，一項直接受到第四十條保護的權利。"以上情況大抵同樣適用於參選權方面。所爭辯的是，該等政治權利屬派生權利性質。派生權利乃受憲法保護，即使與《人權法案》及《性別歧視條例》有抵觸，該等權利仍屬有效。因此，局長不應以抵觸有關法例為理由，拒絕認可獲選人士。

若資深大律師郭兆銘先生的陳詞正確，則所有對指稱的派生權利有不利影響的法例（包括所有法例改革），均與《基本法》第四十條有抵觸。

毫無疑問，原居民的合法傳統權益受到第四十條保護。我等現在所關注的，並非第四十條所指的"權益"的廣泛定義。該等權益包括多項財產權益，例如原居村民持有的某些物業可免繳地稅及差餉，以及與男性原居民根據所謂丁屋政策而獲批的土地有關的利益，這點並無爭議。問題的所在是，第四十條所指的原居民合法傳統權益是否可派生出原居民所辯稱擁有的政治權利。

此問題可以迅速解決。假設（但並非裁定）資深大律師郭兆銘先生的論點正確，即從《基本法》明文規定的權益可以合法地推斷出某些派生權益，則原居民所辯稱擁有的政治權利必須屬於第四十條明文保護的權益所必然隱含的權益，方可從第四十條派生出來。若然如此，本院便須斷定，原居民若沒有其辯稱擁有的政治權利，其傳統權益便得不到充分保護。本院認為，就本案而言，即使根據這項假定，該等權利也不能派生出來。

第四十條所指的原居民合法傳統權益受《基本法》保護。此外，其中部份權益也受本地法例明確保護。例如，《地租（評估及徵收）條例》及香港法例第 116 章《差餉條例》第 36 條分別述及有關免繳地稅及差餉事宜。（前者同時受《基本法》第一百二十二條的保護。）由於第四十條已提供憲法保護，因此，再要從第四十條所指的權益派生出原居民所辯稱擁有的政治權利，以確保該等權益獲得充分保護，便缺乏理據。

透過司法覆核提出質疑是否言之過早

以陳先生的案件而言，選舉並沒有進行。以謝先生的案件而言，雖然進行了選舉，但卻未向局長尋求認可獲選人士。代表政府的資深大律師馮華健先生呈述，鑑於局長在兩宗案件中均沒有作出認可村代表的決定，因此任何司法覆核均言之過早。

由於局長未有作出決定，當然也就不可以針對局長的決定透過司法覆核提出質疑。但凡雙方確實有爭議，法庭可就該項透過司法覆核提出的質疑作出權利宣告。

案中雙方明顯存在爭議。陳先生和謝先生辯稱，局長不得認可任何在案中選舉安排下獲選的人士，理由是有關安排與《人權法案》及／或《性別歧視條例》有抵觸。然而，代表原居村民張先生的資深大律師郭兆銘先生就此提出爭議。代表政府的資深大律師馮華健先生也不同意本案涉及《人權法案》或該法案適用於本案。

恰當的判令

基於上訴法庭的判決，多項宣告維持有效，而且就謝先生的案件而言，一項指示有關鄉事委員會讓他註冊成為候選人的履行義務令亦因此繼續生效。考慮到上述所得結論及其中的理由，本院認為作出下述宣告已經足夠，且屬恰當，該等宣告將替代所有下屬法庭曾頒發的判令，而有關判令亦隨之撤銷。

（1）就陳先生的案件而言：

> 本院宣告民政事務局局長不得認可在 1999 年選舉安排下獲選為布袋澳村村代表的人士，理由是該等安排與《香港人權法案條例》人權法案第二十一條（甲）及／或《性別歧視條例》第 35（3）條有抵觸。

（2）就謝先生的案件而言：

> 本院作出與上述第（1）項相同的宣告，惟"布袋澳村"一詞以"石湖塘村"代之。

本院作出以上宣告後，陳先生及謝先生實際上已在本上訴案中獲全面勝訴。

本判案書所關注的及唯一關注的，是案中兩村就選舉村代表一職時各自作出的選舉安排。上述法律結果乃由多方面的改變所引致。其中包括案中兩村人口成份的改變，現時村中住著相當數量的非原居村民。此外還有法律方面的改變，尤其是《人權法案條例》及《性別歧視條例》，兩者均對本案有重大影響。

有一點必須注意，應予撤銷的判令包括一項與陳先生有關的宣告，指選舉安排與《基本法》第二十六條有抵觸。本院並無聆聽過有關此點的辯論。明顯地，雙方沒有向下屬法庭就此點提出任何爭論。在此情況下，該宣告應予撤銷。若法庭在沒有聆聽詳盡辯論的情況下，便就此等憲法問題作出宣告，實難以令人滿意。

在本上訴案中，雙方促請本院參閱多份法律典據及有關新界的學術著作。本院認為毋需在本判案書引用該等資料。本院在此感謝各資深大律師及其領導的法律代表團的協助。

訟費

雙方就訟費事宜進行了全面的辯論。本院認為以下命令乃屬恰當：

（1）政府須支付陳先生及謝先生訟費的百分之八十五。

（2）張先生須支付陳先生及謝先生的訟費。

（3）所有有關訟費須按《法律援助規例》評定。

按照上述命令，政府及張先生須共同及各別負責支付陳先生及謝先生訟費的百分之八十五，而張先生則須獨自承擔餘下的百分之十五。

本院在第（1）項中命令政府須承擔訟費百分之八十五，理由是政府並無針對上訴法庭就歧視方面所作的判決提出反對。據估計，本院處理該等問題的時間約佔聆訊時間百分之十五。就第（2）項而言，由於張先生獲法律援助（無須繳付任何分擔費用），而陳先生及謝先生兩人雖然同樣獲法律援助，但卻須繳付分擔費用，因此，按照第（2）項命令，張先生便無須繳付任何費用，同時陳先生及謝先生亦可免去繳付費用之虞。

終審法院常任法官包致金：

本席同意終審法院首席法官李國能的判決。

終審法院常任法官李義：

本席同意終審法院首席法官李國能的判決。

終審法院非常任法官邵祺：

本席同意終審法院首席法官李國能的判決。

終審法院非常任法官苗禮治勳爵：

本席同意終審法院首席法官李國能的判決。

終審法院首席法官李國能：

本院一致作出本判案書內標題“*恰當的判令*”之下的兩項宣告，撤銷各下屬法庭頒發的所有判令，並頒發本判案書內標題“*訟費*”之下各項有關訟費的命令。

首席法官（李國能）

常任法官（包致金）

常任法官（李義）

非常任法官（邵祺）

非常任法官（苗禮治勳爵）

資深大律師馮華健先生及大律師莫樹聯先生（由律政司延聘）代表律政司及西貢民政事務處

資深大律師郭兆銘先生及大律師高禮治先生（由賈偉林、江令名律師行延聘並由法律援助署委派）代表張錦泉先生

資深大律師戴啟思先生及大律師任枝明先生（由袁家樂律師行延聘並由法律援助署委派）代表陳華先生及謝群生先生

資深大律師倫明高先生擔任法庭之友（由平等機會委員會安排出席聆訊）

坑口鄉事委員會，缺席聆訊

八鄉鄉事委員會，缺席聆訊

LAW418 FACV 11&13-2000

第四十一條

在香港特別行政區境內的香港居民以外的其他人，依法享有本章規定的香港居民的權利和自由。

案例

非香港居民是否同樣受到基本法的保護？

P.641 | Chu Woan Chyi 等 5 人及香港法輪大法協會 對 入境事務處處長

對正在港進行訴訟的外籍人士是否必須延長其居留期限

P.666 | Pasa Danaville Dizon 對 香港特別行政區

Chu Woan Chyi & Others v. Director Of Immigration

Chu Woan Chyi 等 5 人及香港法輪大法協會 對 入境事務處處長

HCAL 32/2003；CACV 119/2007；CACV 331/2003；FAMV 17/2004

簡略案情

首 4 名申請人均持有台灣身份證件，並持有香港入境處所簽發的多次入境簽證。他們於 2003 年 2 月 21 日從台灣飛抵香港國際機場，打算進入香港參加次日在香港舉行的法輪功信徒"經驗交流會"。然而，入境處職員卻發現上述申請人屬於監察名單中人士，基於安全理由拒絕 4 人入境、並遣返台灣。入境處人員在押送其中兩名申請人登機的過程中，遇到反抗而施行了一定程度的武力。

該 4 名申請人其後向高等法院原訴法庭提出覆核，認為入境處拒絕其入境是因為他們的法輪功信徒身份，因此違反了《基本法》保護他們宗教信仰自由的權利。同時第五申請人，（身為香港法輪大法協會的會長），以及第六申請人（香港法輪大法協會），後來也參與了訴訟。他們認為入境處職員的決定侵犯了他們依照《基本法》所享有的"與其他地方的宗教組織和教徒保持和發展關係"的權利。

裁決摘要

在考慮法輪功是否包含在《基本法》和《香港人權法案》中所稱的"宗教"時，法官引用了澳洲高等法院在 *Church Of The New Faith v. Commissioner Of Pay-Roll* [1982] 154 CLR 120 一案，認為法輪功信徒們承認一種超越肉體感知能力的精神世界的存在，應被視為宗教團體。法官同時否定了申請人的主張，即認為只要實質進入香港的土地，非香港居民也能根據《基本法》第 41 條，享有該法對權利和自由的保障，即時受《香港人權法案》的相關保護。法庭指出依據《基本法》第 4 條，它保護的只是"身處"特區內的人士，因此，認為第 41 條並沒有域外的效力。而且，《香港人權法案》第 11 條亦明確表示該條例並不影響控制入境的本地法律的適用性，所以，法官認為首 4 名申請人必須通過辦理入境手續進入香港後才能受到本地法律的保護。法庭進而確認持有多次入境簽證人士並不意味著必然可以順利入境，因為依據簽證發出的條款，他們仍須經過入境處的審核才能進入香港。

法官再指出，入境處處長有酌情權去考慮是否允許申請人進入香港，至於其決定是否正確並不在法庭考慮之列，但他在行使該酌情權時必須堅持合法和公平的原則，不能濫用，從而違背了法律賦予他行使該權力的原意。至於本案，法官在考慮了相關的事實背景後，接受入境處處長於本案的行為是遵守法律和指引的，並非如申請人所說僅僅是因為他們的信仰而拒絕他們入境。也因如此，第五和第六申請人認為入境處處長的行為違反了《基本法》第 141 條下所享有的"與其他地方的宗教組織和教徒保持和發展關係"的權利並不成立。據此，駁回了所有申請人的申請。申請人對該裁決不滿並上訴至上訴庭。

上訴庭認為該案的重點是入境處處長在該事情上有否盡了向法庭完全坦誠的義務，對原訟庭法官於《基本法》相關的分析並沒有深入探討。申請人的上訴最後被拒絕。

CACV 119/2007

IN THE HIGH COURT OF THE HONG KONG SPECIAL ADMINISTRATIVE REGION COURT OF APPEAL

CIVIL APPEAL NO. 119 OF 2007
(ON APPEAL FROM HCAL NO. 32 OF 2003)

BETWEEN:

CHU WOAN-CHYI

LIAO HSIAO-LAN

LU LIH CHING

CHANG JENN-YEU

KAN HUNG CHEUNG

HONG KONG ASSOCIATION OF FALUN DAFA — Applicants

- and -

DIRECTOR OF IMMIGRATION — Respondent

Before: Hon Ma CJHC, Stock VP & Barma J in Court

Date of Hearing: 10, 11, 12, 13 & 16 March 2009

Date of Handing Down Judgment: 4 September 2009

JUDGMENT

Hon Ma CJHC:

Introduction

1. The main issue in this appeal from the judgment dated 23 March 2007 of Hartmann J (now Hartmann JA) is one that is rarely encountered in the courts: the duty of candour that is incumbent on a decision-maker in judicial review proceedings (usually the Government or a branch of it) to discharge. Put simply, this is a duty to be full and frank to both the court and the other party or parties in public law litigation. In the present proceedings, the issue involves a determination of whether the Respondent, the Director of Immigration (but in reality the Government), has discharged this duty and if not, the consequences of this breach. There is another issue which will be identified in due course.

2. Given the unusual nature of the challenge, for reasons that will become apparent, it will be necessary to go into some detail as to the procedural history in the present judicial review proceedings, with a particular focus on the way the Respondent and his legal advisors have chosen to conduct the case.

3. We have, in this appeal, been considerably assisted by Mr Paul Shieh, SC who was the amicus curiae. The Applicants, though represented by leading counsel in the court below, acted in person in the appeal. Their submissions were made by the 1st Applicant, Ms Chu Woan Chyi, on behalf of all the Applicants. The Respondent was represented by Mr Daniel Fung, SC and Mr Johnny Mok, SC, who have acted for the Respondent at all material stages of the proceedings, including the hearing before Hartmann J.

4. The judicial review proceedings which have led to this appeal centre on the events of 21 and 22 February 2003. On 21 February 2003, the 1st to 4th Applicants, all residents of Taiwan and all in possession of valid multiple entry permits, sought to enter Hong Kong for the purposes of a Falun Gong event which was to take place the following day. This was a conference that was held at the Sheraton Hotel (the "Hong Kong Falun Gong Experience Sharing Conference").

5. The 1st to 4th Applicants (together with 76 Falun Gong practitioners from Taiwan) were stopped at the Immigration Counter at the airport and denied entry. All were told that this was for "security reasons". The 1st and 3rd Applicants had previously been permitted to enter Hong Kong when they were here for purposes unrelated to Falun Gong events.

6. The refusal of entry to the 4 Applicants and others led inevitably to their removal. Some physical force was applied to effect this. One of the original complaints made by the 3rd and 4th Applicants (no longer pursued in this appeal) was that excessive force was used in their removal.

7. On 3 April 2003, the 4 Applicants (together with the 5th Applicant) applied for leave to commence judicial review proceedings to challenge the Respondent's decision refusing them entry. A challenge was also mounted regarding the use of excessive force in the removal of the 3rd and 4th Applicants. The Relief sought included a declaration that the decision to deny the Applicants' entry was unlawful, that this decision should accordingly be quashed, and also another declaration to the effect that the use of excessive force was inappropriate or excessive.

8. For reasons unnecessary to go into, the 5th Applicant was eventually allowed by the Court of Appeal to be joined as an applicant in the proceedings (the court allowing an appeal on 29 June 2004 from Chu J who had refused leave to the 5th Applicant to commence judicial review proceedings). On the same day, the 6th Applicant was also given leave to join in the proceedings. The interests of the 5th and the 6th Applicants in the present judicial review proceedings stand or fall with those of the first 4 Applicants. It is not necessary to consider their interests separately.

The candour issue

9. In order to understand fully how the issue of the duty of candour arises in the present case and how this question was dealt with by Hartmann J in the court below, it is necessary of course to go into the evidence that was before the court justifying the decision refusing the 4 Applicants entry into Hong Kong on 21 February 2003. Before doing so and referring to the judgment of Hartmann J on this (and other) issues, I would deal with the law on this topic. There is, as I have indicated, another issue that arises for determination in this appeal. I will in due course identify and deal with this issue, but the crucial issue before us was the candour issue.

10. I ought, in this context, just summarize the parties' respective positions regarding this issue:–

(1) The Applicants' position was a simple one and one that was articulated time and time again before us by Ms Chu: at no stage has the Respondent frankly or openly vouchsafed, other than in terms couched in vagueness and ambiguity, the precise reason or reasons for denying the Applicants' entry to Hong Kong on 21 February 2003. Instead of being candid, the Respondent has chosen to obfuscate the issue, giving everyone including the court what can colloquially be described as the 'runaround'. This extended to the way the Respondent's legal advisors have conducted themselves in the whole

litigation. In particular, the Applicants point to the complete inability or refusal on the Respondent's part properly to reveal sources of knowledge and disclose relevant documents, even when specifically requested to do so. In summary, it was contended that the Respondent has been so lacking in candour that the court ought to find as a matter of fact that no or no proper reasons existed for the denial of entry. It has always been the Applicants' firm belief that they (and other Falun Gong followers) were denied entry solely by reason of their beliefs, and that the Mainland authorities must have exerted considerable pressure on the Hong Kong Government in this regard (the Falun Gong movement is an unlawful one in the Mainland). The Applicants were, however, content for the court to find merely that no proper cause existed to deny them entry. This was enough to render the decision unlawful. There was a related challenge to another decision (which came by way of amendment to the Form 86A–I shall deal with this later in my judgment) whereby the Applicants' names were put on the Immigration Department Watch List ("the Watch List"), which recorded the fact they were said to pose security risks.

(2) The Respondent's stance was equally simple. The reason for denying entry related to security concerns over the 4 Applicants. Details of these concerns could not be provided by reason of their sensitive nature; indeed the Respondent asserted that it was entirely up to the Government to determine the extent to which such concerns could be divulged. There is a straight denial that the Applicants were refused entry by reason of their being Falun Gong followers. It was also asserted that the Respondent (and hence the Government) has at all times fulfilled the duty of candour. In any event, it was argued that, at worst, insofar as there had been any failings on the Respondent's part (which failings were denied), these were somehow excused by the Applicants' own conduct (and this included the conduct of their own legal advisors) or, in any event, the consequence of any breach should not result in the court drawing any adverse inferences against the Respondent.

The duty of candour in judicial review proceedings: the law

11. In the context of the actual reasons for an impugned decision in judicial review proceedings, a discussion of the duty of candour rarely arises:–

(1) Where a decision, in the present case of the Government, is challenged in judicial review proceedings, it is in some cases unnecessary to go into any great (or indeed, any) detail as to the reasons underlying the decision. Sometimes, the fact that a decision was made is enough to enable an argument to be run along the lines that it was made contrary to law. For example, a decision that has been made without jurisdiction (say, made by the wrong person or body) will not require any evidence of the reasons for that decision. Or, where it is alleged there is procedural unfairness, it will be unnecessary to go into the reasons for the decision (although the duty of candour will require the decision maker to reveal all material facts relating to the aspect of procedural fairness). Constitutional challenges may not necessarily require going into the reasons for the relevant decision either.

(2) Sometimes though, it is necessary for the court to examine the reasons for a decision in order to test the legality of it (within of course the well-known limitations that exist in judicial review proceedings).

(3) However, even in those cases where it becomes necessary to go into the reasons for a decision, it is rare to have to refer to the duty of candour. This is because in the vast majority of judicial review proceedings, the reasons for a decision are readily apparent or are readily made available by the decision maker. As a consequence, the court need only examine the disclosed reasons to see whether or not the decision has been lawfully made.

12. The present case provides an exception to the usual position. As earlier stated, it has been submitted with considerable force by the Applicants and the amicus curiae that the Respondent has in the present case breached that duty. It is said that the reasons for the decision to deny the 4 Applicants entry into Hong Kong are neither readily apparent nor have they been fully or properly disclosed by the Respondent.

13. The duty of candour, from a practical point of view, is primarily relevant from an evidential point of view. Essentially, it is a duty placed on the decision maker (the respondent in judicial review proceedings) to be full and frank to *both* the court *and* the other side (the applicant) in disclosing all relevant facts and documents. The facts and documents may relate to the actual reasons for a decision (as in the present case) or to any other aspect that is relevant in the judicial review proceedings. A respondent is invariably in a position to be full and frank; afterall, he or she will be in possession of all the relevant facts going to a decision.

14. Thus stated, the duty appears at first blush to be simple enough. Indeed it is, but it is necessary also to highlight various facets and examine how the duty fits into the general scheme of judicial review proceedings, in order fully to comprehend the true nature and extent of the duty:-

(1) The duty arises once leave has been obtained by an applicant to commence judicial review proceedings. This is a recognition that an applicant must have proper grounds before commencing such proceedings and cannot simply rely on the existence of the duty of candour to 'fish' for a case. As Sir John Donaldson said in his judgment in *R v. Lancashire County Council, ex parte Huddleston* [1986] 2 All E R 941 at 945a-b:

"But in my judgment the position is quite different if and when the applicant can satisfy a judge of the public law court that the facts disclosed by her are sufficient to entitle her to apply for judicial review of the decision. Then it becomes the duty of the respondent to make full and fair disclosure."

(2) I emphasize again that the duty is one that is owed to both the court and the other party in judicial review proceedings. That the duty is one that is owed to the court reflects the public nature and public interest elements inherent in judicial review proceedings. It is an aspect of good governance, and proper and transparent administration. I recognize

of course that judicial review proceedings will not always necessarily involve the public interest, but in some cases, the public interest element may be substantial. This aspect provides, in my view, the justification for the existence of a separate duty of candour owed to the court, and not just to the other side. Although, admittedly, public law litigation does have similarities to private law litigation, some differences must nevertheless be recognized. Primary among such differences is the proper approach by a respondent in public law litigation:– "It is now clear that proceedings for judicial review should not be conducted in the same manner as hard-fought commercial litigation" (per Lord Walker of Gestingthorpe in his dissenting judgment in *Belize Alliance of Conservation Non-Governmental Organizations v. The Department of the Environment and Another* [2004] UKPC 6 (para.86); [2004] Env.L.R. 761, at 782 (an appeal to the Judicial Committee of the Privy Council from Belize)).

(3) One of the points emphasized by Mr Fung (for the Respondent) in his submissions regarding the duty of candour (which he effectively submitted was a narrow one), was the limited nature of discovery in judicial review proceedings. It is important to view this submission in context. In public law litigation (judicial review proceedings), in general, discovery is indeed much more limited than in normal private law litigation. Further, the necessity to call witnesses and have them examined or cross-examined is also much more limited. Rarely will the court entertain applications for discovery or order the cross-examination of deponents of affidavits. The reasons for this approach are easy to identify:–

(a) Although the issues in judicial review proceedings may be numerous, the *factual* issues in any given case are often limited.

(b) The facts are often irrelevant because the focus of any judicial review proceedings is usually on the legality of the decision that is impugned or, where no decision as such is involved, the court is again concerned with only questions of law (for example, where the only issue is the construction of a statute).

(c) Even where it is relevant to consider facts, the issue that will arise for consideration by the court will not usually be many. This is one of the reasons why discovery in judicial review proceedings will be limited.

(d) Perhaps the most compelling reason why discovery is so restricted in judicial review proceedings and why the court is unwilling in most cases to order discovery, is that the respondent in such proceedings is expected to, and usually does, discharge its duty of candour. As was stated by Lord Woolf MR in *R v. Secretary of State for the Home Department ex parte Fayed* [1998] 1 WLR 763, at 775C-D, there is usually no discovery in judicial review proceedings simply because it ought to be unnecessary, given the obligation on a respondent public body to be full and frank, particularly in relation to its decision making process. Parker LJ in *R v. Lancashire County Council ex parte Huddleston* at 947f, said in a well-known passage, that full and fair disclosure entailed "putting the cards face upwards on the table". Statements such as these reinforce the facet of the duty of candour I have already touched upon, namely, that in public law litigation a respondent (often, as I have said, the Government) must adopt a generous view of its role in such proceedings and not be too ready to indulge in tactical games, or to take unduly technical or legalistic points.

(4) The House of Lords and the Judicial Committee of the Privy Council have, in a number of recent decisions, reaffirmed this approach. In Tweed v. Parades Commission for Northern Ireland [2007] 1 AC 650, Lord Carswell referred to the obligation to make "candid" disclosure of the decision making process, laying before the court the real facts and the reasoning behind the decision under challenge: at 663H (paragraph 31). Reliance was here placed on the dissenting judgment of Lord Walker of Gestingthorpe in Belize Alliance of Conservation Non–Governmental Organizations v. The Department of the Environment and Another, where the duty was stated to be "to cooperate and to make candid disclosure by way of affidavit, of the relevant facts and (so far as they are not apparent from contemporaneous documents which have been disclosed) the reasoning behind the decision challenged in judicial review proceedings" (paragraph 86).

(5) As far as disclosure of documents is concerned, it is worthwhile being reminded that where the source of knowledge in an affidavit (by far the usual form of evidence in judicial review proceedings) is a document, that document ought itself to be exhibited unless sufficient reason exists to indicate the contrary: see *Tweed* at 665B (paragraph 33). As Lord Bingham of Cornhill observed earlier in the judgment, this is good practice not only because a document will contain the best evidence but any "summary, however conscientiously and skillfully made, may distort": at 655G (paragraph 4). Here, I should, as a comparison, also refer to RHC O.41, r.5(1) and (2), namely, the obligation to state sources and grounds in affidavits.

(6) The obligation to be full and frank in the discharge of the duty of candour is of course not an open-ended or imprecise concept. What in any given case may constitute the fulfilment of that duty is entirely dependent on the issue or issues that are before the court. The court will be astute in judicial review proceedings not to permit so called 'fishing' expeditions by applicants in the hope of unearthing material to enable a challenge to be mounted: see Tweed at 664A-B (paragraph 31). In my view, the court will, in most judicial review proceedings, not make a general order for discovery based on Peruvian Guano principles

because in most cases, there will simply be no necessity for such an order. This will explain why there is no automatic discovery in judicial review proceedings; if discovery is required, a separate application must be made: RHC O.53, r.8.

(7) However, once the critical issue is identified in judicial review proceedings and where the resolution of this issue requires that the court be provided with adequate material (by way of discovery or otherwise), I believe the court will in principle be more, not less, inclined to make the necessary orders. I know of no rule whereby in judicial review (or, indeed, any other) proceedings, the court will be reluctant to make wide-ranging orders to enable it fully and fairly to deal with the issue or issues before it. For example, in *Tweed*, the particular question before the House of Lords was essentially the court's approach in ordering discovery in cases involving the application of the European Convention for the Protection of Human Rights and Fundamental Freedoms (in particular cases involving Articles 9, 10 and 11: the European Convention equivalent of Articles 15 to 18 of the Hong Kong Bill of Rights guaranteeing the freedom of thought, conscience and religion, of opinion and expression, and of peaceful assembly and association): see 656F-G (paragraph 9). The House of Lords considered that in such cases and especially where questions of proportionality were involved, the court should be more inclined to order discovery.

(8) I have so far discussed the duty of candour in the context of discovery (which, of course, includes not only the discovery of documents, but also interrogatories). Much the same principles and approach will apply when the court considers whether or not to order the cross-examination of deponents of affirmations: in an appropriate case, the court will be more inclined to make such orders, although they are not by any means automatic.

15. The present case involves an examination of the Respondent's primary contention that the 4 Applicants were excluded by reason of security concerns. In the course of his arguments on the duty of candour, Mr Fung heavily relied on the decision of the European Court of Human Rights in *Nnyanzi v. United Kingdom*, Application No.21878 of 2006, as providing (in the present case) "the complete answer" (Mr Fung's words) to the Applicants' submissions on the duty of candour. *Nnyanzi* is authority for the proposition that each sovereign state has the right to control immigration, and the entry or removal of aliens. It was said that the denial of entry to the Applicants was therefore entirely an exercise of power consistent with this principle. It was then further submitted as a corollary of this general statement that an alien was accordingly not entitled to be provided with the reasons for his being excluded from entry, much less would a hearing be required. Hartmann J in his judgment recognized this, referring to Article 154(3) of the Basic Law and to a number of cases (among them, *Schmidt v. Secretary of State for Home Affairs* [1969] 2 Ch 149 and *Robert Flickinger v. Director of Immigration* [1988] 1 HKLR 81).

16. I accept these principles as far as they go, but in my view, they do not impact in the present case as far as the duty of candour is concerned. The right to control immigration and the various facets of this just referred to, does not mean that whenever there is a refusal to allow entry, no *proper* or *legitimate* reason need exist. In my judgment, there must always be a proper or legitimate reason whenever a decision is made to exclude entry. Put another way, a decision made on improper or illegitimate grounds will not be acceptable, and where as in this case, reasons are in fact given, they may be examined not least where it is suggested that they are so palpably false that the true reason must have been an impermissible one. The present case, involves not so much the right of the Respondent to control immigration but, instead, an examination of the supposed basis underlying the decision to deny entry to the Applicants, namely security reasons, in the context of the duty of candour. Accordingly, the following principles, I believe, are applicable:–

(1) It has of course to be instantly recognized that in immigration matters, and particularly when security concerns are involved, full recognition must be accorded to the views of the authorities; responsibility for these matters rests with them and not the court: see *R v. Secretary of State for Home Affairs ex parte Hosenball* [1977] 1 WLR 766; *Council of Civil Service Unions v. Minister for the Civil Service* [1985] 1 AC 374; *R v. Secretary of State for the Home Department ex parte Cheblak* [1991] 1 WLR 890.

(2) It follows from this that where security concerns are involved, a respondent (the Government) can legitimately restrict the amount of material which ought, in the public interest, be disclosed. Where the public interest lies in not revealing material, it cannot be said the respondent will have breached the duty of candour, *providing* the following conditions exist:–

(a) First, the respondent must have acted in good faith. Where there is any bad faith or abuse or any perversity in the relevant decision, the Government cannot hide behind the cloak of security concerns. This principle is entirely consistent with numerous authorities and was emphasized by Hartmann J in the court below.

(b) Secondly, where it is asserted by a respondent that security concerns require that relevant material should not be revealed, the burden is on the respondent to be full and frank as to the reasons justifying such a claim, provide explanations to obvious queries and where necessary, to make a claim for public interest immunity. Only then will the duty of candour be satisfied.

17. There are two further critical aspects of the duty of candour that merit discussion: the relevance of the conduct of the other party to the proceedings, and the consequences of a breach of the duty of candour.

18. It was submitted by Mr Fung that the duty of candour could be qualified by the conduct of the other party to the proceedings to the extent that such conduct could actually excuse a breach of the duty. I find this submission difficult to accept. As a matter of principle, where a decision-maker has failed to be candid, it is difficult to conceive of a situation where the conduct of the other party will lead a court to conclude there is no breach of the duty at all. Even where an applicant in judicial review proceedings appears to accept or does not challenge what is put forward by way of evidence by a respondent, where there is evidence that a

decision-maker (the respondent) has not been full and frank, he or she will have breached the duty of candour.

19. Where a breach of this duty occurs, the conduct of an applicant may, however, be of critical importance to the determination by a court of the consequences of the breach. Common examples of the type of conduct a court will take into account occur when procedural steps could have been, but were not, taken by an applicant to challenge a default on the part of the respondent. Where the evidence proffered by a respondent is deficient (a breach of the duty of candour), it is open to the applicant to make an application to court. Applications for discovery or for an order that deponents be cross-examined are common examples of the type of action an applicant may be expected to take. The failure to take all or any steps may, as I have earlier said, affect the conclusion reached by the court on the consequences of the breach of the duty of candour.

20. As I have earlier stated, by far the most significant impact of the duty of candour, from a practical point of view, is an evidential one. Normally, the failure to be full and frank on the evidence may well entitle a court to draw adverse inferences, but this will not *invariably* be the case. Whether or not an adverse inference is drawn depends on a number of facets. The conduct of the other side is one such factor.

21. Where, for whatever reason, a respondent's evidence is deficient, it may not always be appropriate for an adverse inference to be drawn when the other side has simply allowed the unsatisfactory state of the evidence to persist, rather than to make any necessary application to the court (for discovery, interrogatories or cross-examination). Of course, a party can just sit by, be content to do nothing and then submit that the respondent's evidence is so deficient that an adverse inference should be drawn, but I daresay in many cases, when the proceedings are essentially accusatorial in nature and particularly when steps *could have been* taken, this may not be an attractive position to adopt. Much will, of course, depend on the circumstances.

22. I now go into the evidence that was before Hartmann J dealing with the principal factual question before the court: why were the 4 Applicants refused entry into Hong Kong on 21 February 2003?

The evidence in the court below

23. As I have earlier indicated, the Applicants' basic contention was that the 4 Applicants were denied entry by reason of their Falun Gong affiliation. Each deposed to their good character. The Applicants relied on the fact that the 1st and 3rd Applicants had previously permitted to enter Hong Kong for non-Falun Gong activities in order to highlight, by way of contrast, the denial of entry on 21 February 2003 (which entry was for the purpose of participating in Falun Gong activities).

24. On arrival, the 4 Applicants (and others) were stopped at the Immigration Counter at the airport and interviewed. They were refused entry on the basis of "security reasons" and this was all they were told. Even after the Applicants demanded to know the evidence for this, this remained the position. They were then detained pending removal from Hong Kong.

25. I have mentioned earlier that the 4 Applicants each held valid multiple entry permits. An issue arose before Hartmann J (and this issue is a live one before us) to the effect that by possessing such multiple entry permits, the Applicants had a legitimate expectation that they would be accorded sufficient procedural fairness allowing them at least to be apprised of any objections to their being permitted entry into Hong Kong and if necessary, to have had an opportunity to make representations. The Applicants said that they had been denied this.

26. The reverse of the multiple entry permits contained conditions. Conditions 2 and 5 state as follows:–

> "2. The holder of this permit is subject to immigration control under the provisions of the Immigration Ordinance, Cap.115, Laws of Hong Kong."
>
> ...
>
> 5. The permit is the property of the Government of the Hong Kong Special Administrative Region. The Immigration Department, the Government of the Hong Kong Special Administrative Region may retrieve and cancel this permit at any time."

27. The Applicants' first point of contact with the Hong Kong authorities were the Senior Immigration Assistants at the Immigration Control Point in the airport. In the case of the 4 Applicants, before it was finally decided that they were to be denied entry, the matter was also handled by Immigration Officers (who interviewed them), Senior Immigration Officers and ultimately the Commander of the Airport Division of the Immigration Department.

28. Affirmations were provided by (at the relevant time) two Senior Immigration Officers (Lau Wing Yiu and Fung Pak Ho, William), the Commander of the Airport Division (Choy Tak Po) and the Acting Secretary for Security (Tong Hin Ming, Timothy). The Security Bureau was responsible overall for all security matters relating to Hong Kong; in particular, the obtaining of information and intelligence, and making assessments of all security matters.

29. The following facts emerge from the affirmations of Mr Lau (dated 8 February 2005), Mr Fung (dated 8 February 2005) and Mr Choy (dated 28 September 2004). I will separately deal with the affirmations of Mr Timothy Tong (dated 8 February 2005 and 22 September 2005) and the second affirmation of Mr Choy (dated 23 September 2005):–

(1) I have already made reference to the Watch List. The reasons for persons to be placed on the Watch List varied: known criminals would be on the List, persons subject to deportation orders or persons who were prohibited from leaving Hong Kong would also be on it (for example, wards of court). Persons said to pose security risks would also be named. The naming of a person on the Watch List did not mean that that person would automatically be denied entry into Hong Kong or prevented from departing. It was said to be essentially a starting point to enable further enquiries to be made and where necessary, interviews to be conducted.

(2) Where a person was named in the Watch List, only the general reason would be stated. As far as security risks were concerned, there would be no elaboration on the Watch List as to why the named person might pose a security risk. As might be expected, the details of any security concerns would be restricted to persons on a 'need to know' basis.

(3) All 4 Applicants were named in the Watch List on the basis that they posed "security risks to the HKSAR"

(this was the term used by Mr Choy Tak Po–others used terms such as "security grounds", "security risk concerns" but they mean the same thing).

(4) Following interviews with the Applicants, it was eventually determined by the Senior Immigration Officers that nothing that was said by them (or in the case of the 1st and 2nd Applicants, not said by them) overcame the security risks that they posed. In the case of the 1st and 2nd Applicants, it was said that they were uncooperative and refused to provide any details of their itinerary, or the nature of the meetings they said they intended to have in Hong Kong. As for the 3rd and 4th Applicants, they said they were in Hong Kong to meet the 5th Applicant.

(5) Accordingly, all 4 Applicants were denied entry into Hong Kong.

(6) It is worthwhile mentioning that Mr Choy emphasized the point that there was "no immigration policy of refusal of entry of persons merely by virtue of the fact that they are Falun Gong members or practitioners". He continued, "The refusal of entry of the 1st to 4th Applicants was, as aforesaid, on security grounds".

30. The affirmations of these persons just referred to are remarkable in that:

(1) Although all referred to security risks, no one provided any details whatsoever as to what these risks were, or even as to whether these risks were regarded as low or high or otherwise.

(2) No documents were exhibited to support the assertion that the Applicants posed security risks.

(3) No explanation was forthcoming as to why no details or documents were disclosed. For example, if no details or documents could be provided by reason of public interest immunity, one would have expected this to have been expressly stated.

(4) In summary then, all that was being said by these deponents in answer to the crucial question of why these Applicants were denied entry into Hong Kong, was no more than they posed security risks.

31. I now deal with the two affirmations of Mr Timothy Tong (then the Acting Secretary for Security).

32. The involvement of Mr Tong in these proceedings is important in that this seemed to indicate in clear terms an acceptance on the Respondent's part that the decision to exclude the Applicants was one that was not restricted to the Immigration Department alone. This is relevant when I come to consider the point made by Mr Fung in his submissions that, at least initially, the Respondent's legal advisors took the view that the judicial review proceedings only really concerned the Immigration Department and no other Government departments.

33. In Mr Tong's first affirmation (dated 8 February 2005), he deposes to the following facts:–

(1) As stated earlier, the Security Bureau had overall responsibility in security matters and to make assessments in relation to such matters. The information available to the Security Bureau came from a number of sources, both within the Bureau itself and from other Government departments.

(2) Insofar as security risks were concerned, it was the Bureau and other Government departments which would make the necessary assessment. It was as a result of this process that the Applicants came to be placed on the Watch List.

(3) Again, no details or relevant documents were provided by Mr Tong, and no explanation was given either as to why they were not provided.

34. It is only when Mr Tong provided the second affirmation (dated 22 September 2005, nearly 2½ years after the judicial review proceedings had been commenced) that there was even an attempt to touch upon what had up to them been unsatisfactory attempts by the Respondent to deal with the real issues in the case. As to Mr Tong's second affirmation:–

(1) This affirmation was provided only as a result of queries raised by Hartmann J (in the course of a discovery hearing) over the lack of details provided by the Respondent. I shall refer to this hearing when I come to deal with the procedural history.

(2) After describing the operation of the Watch List and how it was compiled, Mr Tong then focused on the reasons for the Applicants being denied entry in February 2003.

(3) Here, it is worthwhile setting out in full what was said by Mr Tong:–

"As stated in paragraph 3 of my first affirmation, the Security Bureau and related Government departments had, in the case of the 1st to 4th Applicants come to the view, based on information and intelligence obtained, that the entry into the HKSAR of a number of individuals including the 1st–4th Applicants would pose security risks to the HKSAR. The intelligence obtained included intelligence to the effect that, certain persons including the 1st–4th Applicants were involved with some other individuals engaged in organizing disruptive activities which pose threats to the public order in Hong Kong. In the view of the Security Bureau and related departments of the HKSARG, the admission into Hong Kong of said persons including the 1st–4th Applicants would, by reason of their involvement with the above-mentioned persons, be contrary to the public interest. Further confidential and sensitive details such as the identities of the individuals involved and the details of the disruptive activities concerned cannot be disclosed as fall within the ambit of public interest immunity and are therefore privileged from disclosure."

35. This quoted extract from Mr Tong's second affirmation represents the high watermark of the Respondent's case on the facts. It attempts to provide (for the first time in the proceedings) some details of what was meant by the security risks posed by the Applicants. The Acting Secretary for Security also makes the point that the disclosure of further details would fall within the ambit of public interest immunity. A number of observations can be made in relation to this affirmation:–

(1) Again, no documents were exhibited to support the factual assertions deposed to in the affirmation.

(2) It is not clear at all just what was the basis for the matters deposed to. Not only were documents not exhibited, Mr Tong did not even reveal his sources of knowledge.

(3) Although some details were given as to the meaning of security risks, it really could not be said that the nature or degree of such risks was properly spelt out. No indication was given as to whether such risks were low, high or otherwise. One would have thought that a simple statement of the nature of the risks could be given without this being so sensitive as to attract a claim for public interest immunity.

(4) The claim for public interest immunity that was made related only to "confidential and sensitive details such as the identities of the individuals involved and the details of the disruptive activities concerned". What is particularly remarkable here is not so much that a claim for public interest immunity was made but that this claim in relation to the most important factual aspect of the proceedings (that is, the crucial question of why the Applicants were denied entry) was only made in Mr Tong's second affirmation, which, as I have earlier observed, came some 2½ years after the present judicial review proceedings had commenced. There was no hint of this in the earlier affirmations served on behalf of the Respondent. As stated earlier, in these affirmations, the Respondent was content merely to refer to "security risks" without more.

36. I shall in due course refer again to Mr Tong's second affirmation (as well as Mr Choy's affirmation dated 23 September 2005, an affirmation that was also made for the purpose of a discovery application and which also referred to the Applicants posing security threats) to put these affirmations in proper context in the procedural history dealt with below. For the time being, I would just emphasize the point that the affirmation evidence provided by the Respondent, for the reasons articulated above, fell far short of what the court could have expected from the Respondent. In my judgment, the duty of candour was breached by the Respondent in this respect.

37. I arrive at this view notwithstanding the failure by the Applicants (who were at that time represented by a leading counsel) to make any application to cross-examine important deponents such as Mr Choy and Mr Tong (for it was they who arrived at the decision that the security risks posed by the Applicants were such that they should be denied entry into Hong Kong). An application to cross-examine was made but only in relation to a minor aspect, namely, the conduct of the interview of one of the Applicants. One would have thought that there were so many areas left vague or obscure by the deponents that might have been pursued in cross-examination. Nor was the claim for public interest immunity contained in Mr Tong's second affirmation (see paragraph 34 (3) above) challenged. This was, to say at the least, quite surprising. Instead, as we shall see, there was a public interest immunity challenge in relation to what turned out to be fairly irrelevant matters.

38. Mr Shieh submitted that, in the present case, the duty of candour incumbent on the Respondent was not excused or lessened in its impact by any failure on the part of the Applicants or their legal advisors. I have already touched upon this point in the analysis of the law (see paragraphs 18 to 21 above). I accept that the paucity of any meaningful material from the Respondent's affirmation evidence did not come about as a result of what the Applicants did or failed to do. However, this state of affairs was permitted to persist by reason of the inaction of the part of the Applicants. While, as we shall see, this does have important ramifications in the conclusion I eventually reach on the consequences, it did not in my view lessen or excuse, much less eliminate, the duty of candour that was incumbent on the Respondent.

39. Of course, it was not the case that the Applicants simply did nothing at all. There was considerable correspondence over a very important aspect of the case, namely, discovery, and applications were made in relation to this. It was in this area that the Respondent, clearly in my view, again breached the duty of candour. It is therefore necessary to go into the procedural history of the present proceedings to see how the aspect of discovery emerged and was dealt with.

The procedural history relevant to discovery

40. I have already mentioned the complete lack of relevant documents being exhibited to the affirmations filed on the Respondent's behalf. Hartmann J in his judgment said that the "issue of a lack of contemporaneous documents, even if protected by public interest immunity, was of concern to me".

41. The question that stood out starkly was this: what material supported the primary contention run by the Respondent that the Applicants posed security risks? Presumably, there must have been material in existence to support the position maintained by each of the deponents of the affirmations made on behalf of the Respondent. And, if security risks to Hong Kong were involved (it will be recalled that Mr Tong referred to activities which posed "threats to the public order of Hong Kong"), one would presume that such documents would still be in existence. Nothing in the affirmations evidence of the Respondent referred to above indicated otherwise.

42. The affirmations of Choy Tak Po, Lau Wing Yiu, Fung Pak Ho, William and the first affirmation of Mr Timothy Tong were all filed in late 2004 and early 2005. The date for the substantive hearing of the judicial review was fixed initially for 20 September 2005.

43. On 29 August 2005, the Applicants' solicitors, Messrs Ho, Tse, Wai & Partners ("HTW") wrote to the Department of Justice (for the Respondent) asking in straightforward terms for all documents material to the decision to refuse entry to the Applicants. A specific request was made for documents contained in or associated with the Watch List. This was admittedly a late request but a perfectly proper, legitimate and, above all, relevant one.

44. The response to the letter was in my view quite unacceptable. In its letter dated 8 September 2005, the Department of Justice simply said that it was trite that in judicial review proceedings there was no right to discovery and that no case had been made out for specific discovery. This was an unacceptable response for the following reasons:–

(1) The request for discovery was a proper one that merited a positive response.

(2) As a matter of law, the Respondent's approach was simply wrong; the documents that were requested, should obviously have been disclosed. They were clearly relevant.

(3) The inadequacy of this response was exacerbated

by the submissions of Mr Fung to this court. He informed the court that a narrow view on discovery was justified on the basis that the Applicants' original challenge in the judicial review proceedings was (according to him) a narrow one. Mr Fung submitted that since the challenge involved only a decision of the Director of Immigration, the focus of the proceedings was therefore restricted to the Respondent and did not involve any other Government department. The material which went into the reasons why the Applicants were considered security risks would have involved documents from other Government departments. It was said that the decision under scrutiny was the Respondent's decision refusing entry rather than the reasons for the Applicants to be placed on the Watch List. Mr Fung submitted that the issue of the Applicants being put on the Watch List in the first place did not become an issue until leave to amend was given by Hartmann J much later in the proceedings.

(4) This unacceptably narrow view taken by the Respondent (which was apparently on leading counsel's advice) cannot be justified at all. The point is really this: the documents that were requested in the letter went to the heart of the court's enquiry in the proceedings. There could not be any basis to believe that when the Director of Immigration was the named Respondent in proceedings such as the present, that all inquiries therefore ceased with the Immigration Department, and that other Government departments were not involved. This was all the more so in the context of security risks. I would reiterate the fact that Mr Timothy Tong made an affirmation for the purposes of the proceedings. He was of course at the time in the Security Bureau. For my part, I simply cannot accept this explanation made by Mr Fung to justify the stance taken by the Respondent.

45. What is, however, particularly pertinent in the context of this case and the history to which I shall come, is the fact that nowhere in this response from the Department of Justice was there any intimation of the non-existence of relevant documents. As will presently be seen, this eventually became the position adopted by the Respondent.

46. Not surprisingly, the somewhat unhelpful attitude of the Respondent (or rather, those advising him) led to the Applicants taking out a summons on 12 September 2005 applying for specific discovery of nine classes of documents. All nine classes were related to the critical question. I would draw attention to two of these classes of documents (paragraphs 1 and 8 of the Schedule to the summons):

"1. Documents which contain information relating to the First to Fourth Applicants being placed on a document maintained by the Respondent described as 'Immigration Watchlist' ('the Watch List') which was referred to in paragraphs 2-4 of the affirmation of Timothy Tong Hin Ming; paragraphs 6 and 11 of the affirmation of Lau Wing Yiu; and paragraphs 3-5 and 12-14 of the affirmation of Choy tak-Po, all affirmed on 8th February 2005;

...

8. Documents recording reasons why the names of the First to Fourth Applicants were placed on the Watch List."

47. As to these classes, I am of the view that clearly they were relevant to the question of why the Applicants were denied entry. Accordingly, subject to any claim for public interest immunity, I would have expected the Respondent readily agreeing to provide discovery of them. However, for reasons which are not at all readily apparent, the Applicants were eventually content to restrict the scope of discovery in relation to these two classes as follows:

"1. Documents *which were available to the decision makers Lau Wing Yiu and Choy Tak Po* which contain information relating to the First to Fourth Applicants being placed on a document maintained by the Respondent described as 'Immigration Watchlist' ('the Watch List') which was referred to in paragraphs 2-4 of the affirmation of Timothy Tong Hin Ming; paragraphs 6 and 11 of the affirmation of Lau Wing Yiu; and paragraphs 3-5 and 12-14 of the affirmation of Choy tak-Po, all affirmed on 8th February 2005;

...

8. Documents *which were available to the decision makers Lau Wing Yiu and Choy Tak Po* recording reasons why the names of the First to Fourth Applicants were placed on the Watch List." (emphasis added)

48. Restricted in this way, the Respondent consented to providing an affirmation stating whether documents in these classes existed. In the affirmation of Choy Tak Po dated 23 September 2005 (his second in these proceedings), he specifically accepted that discovery had to be made in relation to the documents referred to in these amended paragraphs in the summons. In this affirmation, Mr Choy also repeated the assertion made in Mr Timothy Tong's second affirmation that the Applicants were involved in disruptive activities and therefore posed security threats.

49. The amendments to these two classes of documents were significant. Instead of the Respondent being required to provide discovery essentially of why the Applicants were put on the Watch List (and therefore why they posed security risks), discovery was now only required of such documents *insofar as* they were actually available to Choy Tak Po and Lau Wing Yiu, the two decision makers. It may be that the Applicants regarded the existence of documents, though important as to the reasons why the Applicants were placed on the Watch List, as not being relevant if the actual decision makers did not have sight of them. However, in my view, they clearly were, irrespective of whether the decision makers saw them: afterall, they would explain exactly why the Applicants were considered security risks.

50. In this context, I ought to refer back to the second affirmation of Mr Timothy Tong (see paragraph above), filed for the purpose of the discovery application, in which he did indicate that certain matters could not be disclosed by reason of public interest immunity. It is noteworthy, however, that this reason was not used by the Respondent to resist the discovery sought in relation to the said two classes of documents; quite the contrary, the Respondent consented to provide an affirmation to comply with the discovery sought in relation thereto.

51. The hearing of the disputed items in the discovery summons

dated 12 September 2005 took place before Hartmann J on 20 September 2005 (for 4 days), taking over the dates originally scheduled for the substantive hearing of the judicial review.

52. Hartmann J's judgment on the discovery application was handed down on 4 November 2005. Although it is unnecessary to go into his actual decision on the contested items, it is nevertheless pertinent to highlight the fact that the judge fully recognized that the critical issue in the judicial review proceedings was the reason why the Applicants were denied entry. The orders for discovery made by him reflected this understanding.

53. By a letter dated 21 November 2005, the Department of Justice provided discovery in relation to the two categories of documents referred to in paragraph above. A List of Documents was provided. Extracts from a Confidential Register and Control Case Reports in relation to the 4 Applicants were also produced. These documents, however, provided no details of why the Applicants were denied entry, other than there were "security grounds".

54. What is of some significance was the reference in Schedule 2 of the List to:–

> "Paper files under Reference Nos 05795, 05923, 06001 and 05670 as recorded in the Confidential Register and computer records relating to the 1st to 4th Applicants."

The covering letter explained the status of these documents in the following way:–

> "The paper files and computer records enumerated in Schedule 2 are no longer in existence as they were destroyed in accordance with standard Immigration Department practice after the names of the persons in question were removed from the Watch list. Based on the entries under the 'Date of Destroy' column in the relevant pages of the Confidential Register, it can be seen that the destruction of the said files and records took place on 12th March 2003."

55. This statement is of some considerable importance. For the first time in the history of the proceedings (by this time the judicial review proceedings had been in existence for nearly 2 years 9 months), there was a reference to the destruction of relevant documents. Throughout the many affirmations that had been filed on behalf of the Respondent, there had been no hint given of the fact that important documents had, as long ago as 12 March 2003 (barely 3 weeks after the relevant decisions were made), been destroyed.

56. A dramatic revelation such as this required a proper explanation from the Respondent not only as part of the duty of candour he had to fulfil but also because the very act of destruction, without explanation, necessarily gave rise to questions of motive for the destruction and as to the bona fides of the decisions challenged. It also required elaboration. Furthermore, if important documents had been destroyed, what was the basis of knowledge for the belief of the various deponents for the Respondent; a question lent more force because the reasons for refusal was said to be time or event specific. And reference was made to "standard Immigration Department practice": what was this and what was the status of documents that was not in the possession of the Immigration Department but in other Government departments? Nothing was said about public interest immunity applying in any event to these decisions.

57. Neither an explanation nor elaboration was provided. This was to be a matter which Hartmann J eventually took up with Mr Fung at the substantive hearing in March 2007. Notwithstanding the fact that the Applicants did not take any action to compel the Respondent to provide an explanation or elaboration, I am of the view that the Respondent ought to have done so of his own volition as part of the overall duty of candour.

58. By a letter dated 23 January 2006, the Respondent produced another List of Documents, this time to deal with the other categories of documents ordered by Hartmann J to be discovered in his judgment of 4 November 2005.

59. There was another reference to destruction of the various documents itemized in Schedule 2 of the List:–

> "The paper files and computer records enumerated in Schedule 2 of the List are no longer in existence as they were destroyed in accordance with standard Immigration Department practice after the names of the persons in question were removed from the Watchlist or three years after the relevant files were downgraded to non-confidential files, whichever is applicable."

60. In many ways, this was an even more obscure statement than the one contained in the letter of 21 November 2005 (see paragraph 54 above). Apart from the reference to the so-called "Immigration Department practice", there was an additional reference to the destruction of documents "three years after the relevant files were downgraded to non-confidential files". A full explanation and further elaboration were most certainly called for. For example, the reference to the destruction of documents three years after files were downgraded would surely not apply in the present case: the relevant events took place on 20 and 21 February 2003, which was *less* than three years back from the date of this letter alone. Conceivably, there may have been material on the Applicants before 20 February 2003, but this was never explained by the Respondent. Neither the court nor the Applicants should be required to speculate on matters which were entirely within the Respondent's knowledge to disclose.

61. Unfortunately, this confusing state of affairs was never cleared up. The Respondent was quite content to leave everyone, including the court, in the dark.

62. In a contested hearing from 6 to 9 February 2006, (again these were dates originally intended for the refixed substantive hearing of the judicial review proper), Hartmann J dealt with two matters: an application by the Applicants to amend the Form 86A Notice to challenge the decision to put the Applicants on the Watch List on the basis they posed a security risk; and the disposal of various claims for public interest immunity.

63. The decision is again unimportant for present purposes but the following matters, which arise from the judgment of Hartmann J handed down on 8 May 2006, are of note:–

> (1) It will be remembered that before this court, Mr Fung sought to excuse the unduly narrow view taken by the Respondent and his legal advisors of the duty of candour by asserting that it was only after Hartmann J gave leave to amend in the way indicated above that the Respondent realized that the judicial review involved issues going to precisely why the Applicants were considered security risks and that this involved Government departments beyond the Immigration Department (see paragraphs 32 and 44(3) above).
>
> (2) This was an extremely surprising submission to

make and one that really has no merit to it at all. For my part, I am simply not prepared to accept this is a reason. From the original Form 86A Notice, it must have been clear beyond peradventure that the Applicants were challenging the very basis of their being denied entry. The issue of precisely why they were denied entry was at the heart of the proceedings. Also to suggest that only the Immigration Department was involved was bizarre to say the least, and even by the Respondent's own conduct of the proceedings was this suggestion a hollow one to make: as remarked earlier, the Respondent had seen fit to use affirmations made by Mr Timothy Tong who was the Acting Secretary for Security.

(3) Hartmann J referred in the judgment to the question (which he described as "fundamental" and "broad") of why the Applicants were refused permission to enter Hong Kong. This issue was also variously described by him as the "core of the dispute" and "the real dispute in issue". Most important, Hartmann J said that this issue had "always" been the basis of the judicial review proceedings. At paragraph 63, he said this:–

"*In my view, however, the Director, and those who represent him legally, must always have understood the real issue in dispute in these proceedings*. If the asserted reason for refusing the first four applicants permission to enter Hong Kong was based on the fact that they posed a security risk, they must have understood that such reason would itself inevitably be subject to challenge. Of course, the new challenges will result in some further delay but I do not see how it can be said that, in these circumstances, being forced to answer the challenges will be to the detriment of good administration. How the Director chooses to answer the challenges, of course, is a matter for him." (emphasis added)"

(4) Accordingly, Hartmann J allowed the amendments. On analysis, they simply reflected what had always been the main issue.

64. I should perhaps just briefly mention the public interest immunity aspect. Regarding the discovery that was ordered following the earlier hearing before Hartmann J in September 2005 (see paragraph 52 above), the Respondent produced a List of Documents (see paragraph 58 above), in which claims for public interest immunity were asserted. On 23 January 2006, the Respondent applied for an order that the documents for which public interest immunity was claimed, should not have to be produced for that reason. The hearing in February 2006 dealt with this summons. There were further hearings on 24 May 2006 and 2 June 2006 in relation to the public interest immunity claims as well. The outcome was that the judge was of the view that the claim was made out. What is of particular note, however, was that none of the documents, the subject matter of the public interest immunity claims, nor the Certificate provided by the Chief Secretary in support, really went to the critical issue of the reasons why the Applicants were refused entry. It will be recalled that the important second affirmation of Mr Timothy Tong made a reference to public interest immunity in relation to the facts going to the critical issue. Yet, quite surprisingly, no application was made by the Applicants to pursue this by way of a formal application for discovery or interrogatories. The discovery summons taken out on 12 September 2005 (see paragraph 46 above) did not really target this part of Mr Tong's affirmation at all.

65. The 2 June 2006 hearing is notable, however, in that counsel for the Applicants (Mr Paul Harris, SC) raised specifically the point that within the whole of Government, and not just the Immigration Department, there must have existed documents going to the core issue. Mr Harris further referred to the obligation on the part of the Respondent to put "all his cards face up on the table" (a reference to *Ex parte Huddleston*: see paragraph 14(3)(d) above).

66. In his judgment of 2 June 2006, Hartmann J said this:–

"That does not end the matter. Mr Harris said that, if one of the Director's senior officers was able in a recent affirmation to state that the first four applicants had been refused permission to enter Hong Kong on the basis that they posed a security threat, that information must, in all common sense, have been obtained from a written source of some sort. That source, however, has not been discovered by the Director. Mr Harris argues that, while that source material may not now be in the possession, control or power of the Director, it must surely be somewhere in the archives of Government. Mr Harris pointed to the fact that, although the Director is the cited respondent in these proceedings, he stands as a representative of the Hong Kong Government as a whole."

67. Leading counsel for the Applicants asked Hartmann J to request the Respondent to disclose the documents referred to. This was misconceived because the court was, at the June 2006 hearing, clearly dealing with the claim for public interest immunity only and in any event, it was not up to the court to make 'requests' as such. When eventually Mr Harris asked for an order that the Respondent should provide a further affirmation going to these documents, Mr Fung (who then, as now, represented the Respondent) indicated that the Respondent had already complied with all discovery orders. This is of course correct as far as compliance with actual orders of the court were concerned. However, I am far from satisfied, for the reasons already gone into, that the Respondent had at that stage complied fully with the duty of candour at all. Here again the Respondent was conducting himself as if these were ordinary adversarial proceedings, with no hint–as was later suggested–that there were in fact no documents elsewhere within Government.

68. Nevertheless, Hartmann J refused to order the Respondent to make another affirmation. He said this:–

"I am not prepared to make an order of the kind suggested by Mr Harris. Mr Fung, who has the assistance of Mr Mok, both being senior counsel, confirmed that the Director has acted at all times on legal advice. It seems to me that, if the applicants are of the view that there has been a lack of candour on the part of the Director or that further discovery should be made in respect of documents which perhaps do not lie in the possession, control or power of the Director himself but perhaps are in the possession of other departments of Government, then a formal application should be made going to these issues."

69. However, realizing the potential importance of such an application but also noting the fact that there had already been

substantial delays in the proceedings, Hartmann J indicated that the court would do its best to accommodate the Applicants in finding dates for the hearing of any application for discovery along the lines indicated.

70. Surprisingly, no application was made by the Applicants and this is a point that was seized upon by Mr Fung before us to support the argument that the Respondent had not breached the duty of candour. It will be necessary later in this judgment to deal with this.

71. On 6 June 2006, almost immediately following the hearing, HTW wrote to the Department of Justice requesting the discovery of documents within the whole of Government. The matter was put fairly and squarely to the Respondent:–

> "In the light of your continuing duty of candour and duty to provide full and fair disclosure of documents, and of the references in Mr. Choi's Affirmation and Affirmation of Mr. Tong, both dated 23rd September 2005, to information indicating that the 1st and 4th Applicants were involved with other individuals engaged in organising disruptive activities which pose threats to the public order of Hong Kong, we request that you please provide us with copies of all those documents which were the source of that information which are in your client's custody, control or power. Such documents would include but not be limited to all Reports, Memoranda, Minutes of meetings and records of decisions that were taken, which contain, reflect or record the assessments made by the Security Bureau and related Government departments and the information and intelligence upon which they based their assessments that the 1st to 4th Applicants were involved in organising disruptive activities which posed threats to public order in Hong Kong and that their admissions into Hong Kong would be contrary to the public interest."

72. The reply from the Department of Justice was, again, a surprising one. The expected response would have been to deal with the very inquiry that was made. The main point made by the Applicants was simply this. There had been numerous references in the affirmations filed on behalf of the Respondent to security risks. Yet, no underlying (or indeed any) documents had been disclosed or even referred to. The Applicants were anxious to obtain proper discovery of these documents. I cannot conceive that all this was anything other than self evident to the Respondent's legal advisers.

73. The reply from the Department of Justice was dated 20 June 2006. Essentially, the response was as follows:

(1) That discovery of the requested documents had already been provided. This was, in my view, an extremely dubious assertion to make. The Respondent had not previously indicated that the discovery covered also documents from Government departments other than the Immigration Department. For example, the letters dated 24 November 2005 and 23 January 2006 referred only to the Immigration Department (in the context of the destruction of documents). Further, the discovery that had up to then been provided did not reveal any documents from any department that provided any details of the security risks. It would, however, appear astonishing if no Government department, other than the Immigration Department, was in possession of relevant documents at some stage. What was to follow from the Respondent on this topic (as will be seen below) was even more astonishing.

(2) That the Respondent had fully complied with his discovery obligations. It was said therefore that there was no basis for the Applicants to make the request it did.

74. I would note also at this point that there was no mention in this letter of any missing documents, destruction of documents or non-existence of relevant documents. There was no claim for public interest immunity either.

75. By its letter dated 29 June 2006, not satisfied with the response from the Department of Justice, HTW repeated the request for documents. The Respondent was also asked to confirm that in the preparation of their affirmations, both Mr Choy and Mr Tong only relied on documents that had actually been disclosed and not on any other documents.

76. The reply from the Department of Justice dated 7 July 2006 repeated the assertion that full discovery had been made and that the Respondent did not have the documents requested in his possession, custody or power. There was a reference to some documents having been destroyed (these being the documents referred to earlier: see paragraphs and above). The letter ended:-

> "In these circumstances, it is plainly wrong for you to suggest that 'both Mr Choy and Mr Tong only relied on those documents which [we] have already provided to [you] and no other documents or materials that were in the possession of any Government department'."

77. This suggested that Mr Choy and Mr Tong did rely on other documents. Of course, what could have been meant was that these two gentlemen relied on documents that had since been destroyed but such a state of affairs would have been fairly bizarre.

78. The reply from HTW dated 24 July 2006 was, again, somewhat surprising. Having initiated an inquiry for relevant documents in the possession, custody or power of all Government departments, this letter appeared to narrow the request to just those documents that were *actually* relied on by Mr Choy and Mr Tong in preparing their affirmations. This was surprising in view of the fact that documents relevant as to why the Applicants were considered security risks, even if not actually relied on or seen by Mr Choy and Mr Tong, would certainly be discoverable. Such documents went to the main issue in the proceedings (and certainly to the issue of why the Applicants were placed on the Watch List), and this, whatever the Applicants or their legal advisors may have thought, must have been known to the Respondent and his legal advisors.

79. The Department of Justice replied in a letter dated 2 August 2006. It was yet another surprising response:–

(1) It started by reserving the position as to the correctness of the Applicants' contention that the court was entitled to have before it all documents relied on by Mr Choy and Mr Tong in their affirmations. This was a very revealing statement and indicative of the unduly narrow view taken by the Respondent of his discovery obligations, not to mention the duty of candour.

(2) The letter then continued by providing, without

prejudice to the argument referred to above and in order to avoid further hearings, a statement that Mr Choy and Mr Tong did not rely on any documents that had not already been made the subject of discovery. This was in fact quite the opposite of what had been said in the earlier letter dated 7 July 2006 (see paragraph 76 above). No explanation was offered as to this change of position.

80. No further discovery applications were made to the court. HTW, by their letter dated 19 August 2006, were content to apply for dates for the substantive hearing.

81. Before dealing with what took place before Hartmann J in the court below, I have to say that in spite of the numerous affirmations that had been placed before the court, the numerous interlocutory hearings that had taken place (this by itself is a rare occurrence in judicial review proceedings) and the extensive correspondence over discovery, the position by the time came to be heard by Hartmann J in March 2007 was this: no one was any the wiser as to why the Applicants were considered security risks. Further, in relation to the glaring question of what had happened to the documents relevant to the critical issue in the proceedings (which surely must have existed), no real answer had been provided by the Respondent. As will presently be seen, this was the very question that vexed Hartmann J at the substantive hearing.

The hearing and judgment in the court below

82. The substantive hearing of the judicial review before Hartmann J took place from 5 to 8 March 2007. Although I have so far in this judgment concentrated on by far the most important issue in this appeal (the duty of candour), other issues were raised for determination before Hartmann J. Before returning to the way in which the issue of the duty of candour (involving necessarily the issue of the Respondent's discovery) was dealt with by Hartmann J, I ought first to identify these other issues. Most of them are now irrelevant for determination in this appeal.

83. Hartmann J identified seven issues for determination. I quote from his judgment (which was handed down on 23 July 2007):–

"In light of this, it seems to me that the following issues arise in this application:

(i) In terms of the Basic Law and/or the Bill of Rights is the Falun Gong movement a religion?

(ii) Were the first four applicants, when they sought permission to enter Hong Kong, entitled to the protection of the fundamental freedoms, such as freedom of religion, enjoyed by Hong Kong residents under the Basic Law and/or the Bill of Rights?

(iii) If they were entitled to the protection of those freedoms, were they, in fact, denied permission to enter Hong Kong solely or substantially because of their religious or spiritual beliefs; that is, because of their Falun Gong following?

(iv) Were the decisions to place the first four applicants on the watchlist and to refuse them permission to enter Hong Kong *Wednesbury* unreasonable?

(v) If the first four applicants were denied permission to land solely or substantially because of their religious or spiritual affiliation, did that constitute a breach of the freedoms guaranteed to the fifth and sixth applicants under art.141(4) of the Basic Law?

(vi) By their possession of valid multiple entry permits, did the first four applicants have a legitimate expectation that, if denied entry, they would be accorded sufficient procedural fairness to enable them to know why that decision was made and to make representations? If so, were the first four applicants denied that procedural fairness?

(vii) Was the use of force employed to remove the third and fourth applicants from Hong Kong unlawful?"

84. It seems to me that the fundamental issue for determination by the court was whether the Respondent's decision to deny entry to the Applicants was a lawful one. In context, this meant in the present proceedings an examination of the reason given, namely, that the Applicants were considered security risks. It was in the end unnecessary to determine as a matter of fact whether the actual reason for their being denied entry was their Falun Gong affiliation. The Applicants did not have to go so far (as stated above): it was enough for the Applicants to point to an absence of any rational or proper basis for exclusion, or indeed to show that no reason really existed.

85. Other than the inquiry into the existence of reasons for the denial of entry and their lawfulness, ultimately it is, in my view, unnecessary for us to go into the first 5 issues as identified by Hartmann J. Whether or not fundamental freedoms guaranteed under the Basic Law or the Bill of Rights were engaged, are not critical issues to be determined. This can be tested in the following way. If the Applicants were right in their contention that the reason for their being denied entry into Hong Kong was no more than the mere fact of their Falun Gong association or that no proper reason existed, they were entitled to succeed in the judicial review proceedings. Even if fundamental freedoms under the Basic Law or Bill of Rights were not engaged, the decision of the Respondent would be liable to be impugned on the basis of irrationality or perverseness. Correspondingly, if the Respondent's case that the Applicants posed security risks was made out, then even if rights under the Basic Law or Bill of Rights were applicable, his decision to exclude would have been a legitimate one. It is therefore unnecessary for the purposes of the present appeal to deal with those five issues in the same way as Hartmann J did. Nor is it necessary to deal with the seventh issue relating to the use of force: this was not an issue that was pursued in the appeal.

86. Instead, the focus of this appeal was on the duty of candour, whether in the circumstances of the case there has been a breach of this duty and if so, the consequences of such breach. The significance of this issue goes to the very heart of the judicial review: the reason why the Applicants were denied entry. It is this aspect on which I have so far concentrated.

87. The sixth issue dealing with procedural fairness and the possession of valid multiple entry permits is admittedly a separate issue, and I will in due course deal with it. However, by far the more important issue for determination is the one I have already identified.

88. Hartmann J recognized the importance of the question of the lack of discovery on the Respondent's part. In paragraph 110 of his judgment, he said this:–

"110. The issue of a lack of substantive contemporary documents, even if protected by public interest immunity, was of concern to me. As I said during the course of the hearing, the reasonable man on the street would probably have difficulty accepting that Government would have destroyed all of its records going to why some 80 people were refused entry to Hong Kong, two of those people having to be placed under physical restraint."

89. In a nutshell, the quite extraordinary state of the Respondent's evidence was very much a concern to Hartmann J. In the course of Mr Fung's submissions on 8 March 2007 dealing with the compliance by the Respondent with the duty of candour (Mr Harris for the Applicants had submitted that the Respondent had breached this duty), it was submitted to the court that the Respondent had not only complied with his discovery obligations, but he had done so voluntarily. This was presumably a reference to the fact that *some* discovery had been provided voluntarily but, in view of the matters already gone into, it could hardly be said with any conviction that the Respondent had been at all forthcoming in discovery.

90. It was soon after leading counsel made this statement that the judge remarked that in fact there was really nothing before the court that went into the reasons for the denial of entry. Hartmann J posed the question "Is it credible that suddenly all the Government files and papers have been washed clean?" A reference was made to the duty of candour owed to both the other side and to the court. Hartmann J remarked twice about the possibility that there had been some sort of "hoovering" of Government papers.

91. The Respondent's counsel was then asked to take further instructions during the lunch break, although I find it somewhat surprising that the Respondent had not gone to court prepared to deal with this glaring admission in the evidence, and, furthermore, the Respondent ought really have been prepared to offer a full explanation without having been prompted by an inquiry from the court. The duty of candour in my view would have required that a proper explanation be placed before the court.

92. After the lunch break on 8 March 2007, when counsel had taken further instructions from (as Mr Fung puts it) "the highest level", the court was informed of the following facts:–

(1) All files relating to the entry of the four Applicants on the Watch List had been destroyed in accordance with standard procedures. The date of destruction took place about a month before the first time that the Respondent was informed that judicial review proceedings had been commenced (the Respondent was first informed of this by letter of 7 April 2003).

(2) Reference was made by Mr Fung to a column in the Confidential Register relating to the 4 Applicants (the Register had been disclosed in the List of Documents provided to the Applicants by the letter of 21 November 2005 (see paragraph 53 above). Indeed there is a column headed "Date of Destroy" and in the case of each Applicant, there has been inserted the date of 12 March 2003.

(3) Mr Fung then informed the court that this destruction was standard procedure. He reminded the court of the fact that there had been a reference to destruction "in accordance with standard Immigration Department practice" in the two said letters dated 24 November 2005 and 23 January 2006 (see paragraphs 54 and 59 above).

(4) Hartmann J was anxious to secure from counsel a clear answer to the question whether the reference to the destruction of the very documents that went to why the Applicants were considered security risks, was a reference, not just to the documents of the Immigration Department but whether this also applied to all such documents within any part of Government. Counsel confirmed this after assuring the court that this had been "checked and double-checked ... at the highest level responsible".

(5) Hartmann J then said that he had to accept what was said to him by counsel. For the reasons that shall in due course be articulated, in my judgment, Hartmann J erred in this approach.

(6) What followed was an important exchange between the court and leading counsel that made the position clear (it is a lengthy extract but one which I think should be set out in full):–

"COURT: All right. Then if you say to me that there simply is no material or there has been no material available in the archives of government which has any relevance to this matter, and which, in fairness, should have been shown to the court, even under public interest immunity ...

MR FUNG: Yes, yes. My Lord, we ...

COURT: ... in respect of 80 people being refused permission to enter Hong Kong, with proceedings taken within six weeks. Is that what you' re saying?

MR FUNG: My Lord, yes. Because I can only act on instructions ...

COURT: All right. No, if that's what you' re saying then that's ...

MR FUNG: ... MY Lord, because I not only ...

COURT: I don't reject it, your saying that to me.

MR FUNG: And we have checked and double-checked this point, including over the lunch hour, in direct response to your Lordship's question, at the very highest level of those responsible.

COURT: Well, I'll accept what you say. I have no reason not to.

MR FUNG: We've even brought the confidential register–the actual, the original register with us in order to satisfy your Lordship that there's been no tampering, if that is the suggestion. My Lord, that's the only ...

COURT: Mr Fung, don't–I did not suggest there was tampering.

MR FUNG: Well, if ...

COURT: What I actually said at the end was, you should go and take instructions so that, if for example there has been destruction of material in the ordinary course of events to protect individuals, you can explain that to me this afternoon. The point I made was that on the face of it, to receive discovery of documents which are protected by public interest immunity, and to have a situation in which those documents say nothing of anything, at its face, when you're aware that government as a whole here was being held liable not just the Director, seems strange. But if you say to me that all of the documentation concerning this matter in the archives of government was removed, destroyed or done away with insofar as it may have any relevance to these proceedings ...

MR FUNG: My Lord, absolutely not. Let me just illustrate that, just make that ...

COURT: When you say 'absolutely not' do you mean it was destroyed, removed ...

MR FUNG: It was destroyed but it wasn't destroyed because we didn't want to show it ...

COURT: No, I' m not suggesting it was, I'm just saying that as a matter of procedure ...

MR FUNG: Yes.

COURT: ... that's what happened.

MR FUNG: And indeed, can I just ...

COURT: So if somebody wanted to write a history of this in 25 years time under the Freedom of Information Act that we don't have here, that person would be told, sorry, everything's gone.

MR FUNG: Well, I mean, he can search all the files, both electronically and on paper, but can I just demonstrate why this is so–and that there's no withholding of information–would your Lordship go, please, to page 897. This refers to an earlier entry–does your Lordship have that?

COURT: I do, yes.

MR FUNG: An earlier entry of the 1st applicant's name on the Watchlist on 17 October 2002. Your Lordship sees that. Nothing to do with this case. Would your Lordship please note the date of destruction of the underlying file, 30 October 2002–nothing to do with this case. That destruction took place 13 days after the entry of the name on the Watchlist; a much shorter period.

COURT: I'm not disputing that or anything else. I have your answer now.

MR FUNG: I'm grateful. I'm grateful. And if I've misunderstood your Lordship then it's my fault. It's my fault that–I thought the matter was so important, since your Lordship has ventilated it, that it ...

COURT: Well, it is important, it's very important ...

MR FUNG: ... that it's worth ...

COURT: ... because Mr Harris, apart from anything else, says that the real reason for these people being refused entry was simply because of their beliefs. You say that's not the case ...

MR FUNG: That's not the case

COURT: ... Mr Harris says, well, his argument can be supported by lack of candour on the part of government and that lack of candour is shown in the fact that somehow or other there's not a document in existence which says anything about the reasons for the decisions.

MR FUNG: That is not the case.

COURT: And that's why I specifically referred to my ruling of 26 May when I said "as to the nature of the additional documents, it seem [*sic*]obvious to me they must contain the essential intelligence or a distillation of it' and then when I then said 'I was wrong in drawing that inference, they don't contain anything". But it may well be that I have–and Mr Harris–have to accept and do accept that this type of information does not have a shelf life, that in order to protect individuals it is done away with, and that's what you're saying to me, and that's where we stand with it.

MR FUNG: My Lord, yes. And it's not the same in every individual case either, because–let me give you another example, 899, my Lord ...

COURT: No, I've been through them, I can promise you.

MR FUNG: There is there, in the case of Liao Hsiao Lan, for an earlier entry into the Watchlist, a downgrading of the file; the file is not destroyed, so that file is still in existence. But that file has absolutely nothing to do with the present case.

COURT: No, of course.

MR FUNG: So it's not as if there is, as it were, a three-week magic period of shelf life only.

COURT: No, obviously not. If you've got files that are current you don't destroy them ...

MR FUNG: Less sensitive, yes.

COURT: ... or if they're especially sensitive you don't destroy them.

MR FUNG: And so on. Now there's no, as it were, corky cutter approach to these matters, so I understand, as to how the records or the underlying files are destroyed or not, as the case may be, and the Watchlist being this computer tool to protect Hong Kong's interests–not just security interests but all sorts of other interests–it's constantly being upgraded ...

COURT: Of course.

MR FUNG: ... and depending on the nature of the file, is either downgraded or destroyed and if it's downgraded, it's still in existence. My Lord, I was told that the reference your Lordship has made to your judgment of 26 May 2006 refers to documents which are not germane to the present hearing. But I'm just asking for those documents to be brought up so that we're not labouring under any sort of misapprehension.

COURT: No, no. I'm not suggesting that they necessarily are. You've given me your answer now and I have it. So the matter has been clearly stated from your point of view, which is, on instructions, that the Watchlist entries which I knew already–because my judgment was not concerned with the Watchlist entries–are deleted in order to protect individuals within a reasonably short period of time...

MR FUNG: Yes.

COURT: ... and that's why I mentioned it this morning, and that other documentation, either which was discovered under public interest immunity or otherwise, or which was not discovered, there are simply no documents of relevance to this case as to the reasons why these people were not allowed permission to enter Hong Kong in the archives of government.

MR FUNG: My Lord, we have taken steps directly in response to the various observations made by your Lordship at the highest level to give your Lordship, and confirm to your Lordship, that what we stated in the discovery process–and your Lordship sees that in the letter to which I've made reference and in the list of documents–that's page 888 of bundle D and 890, which is Schedule 2–is entirely accurate. The six dates I've given your Lordship are also entirely accurate. The interdepartmental memo, which is confidential, is a document which we would be prepared to share with your Lordship. It's not a matter for discovery but ...

COURT: I have your undertaking, on instructions, the government does not in its archives have any material that goes to why these 80-odd people were refused permission to enter Hong Kong.

MR FUNG: My Lord, that is correct. We have not just gone to the Immigration Department, may I make that point ...

COURT: And all I'm saying is and all I meant to say this morning, and if there was any misunderstanding, I apologise–is that the ordinary man on the street, he may say–leaving aside the Watchlist, which was never part of anything else–it is puzzling that there would be no documentary evidence of any kind in the archives of government anywhere going to an issue which was only six weeks old and involved the refusal to land of 80-odd persons and the carrying of two of them against their will back to their aircraft, in respect of an organisation which some would call notorious and others would say has about it considerable sensitivity. Now I don't know how government works. You've told me how it now works and I accept that absolutely and without reservation. I have no reason not to.

MR FUNG: I'm grateful, my Lord. We don't use any particular adjectives to describe the Falun Gong."

93. These exchanges between leading counsel for the Respondent and the court clearly demonstrate the unsatisfactory way with which the Respondent had approached the question of discovery. *If* (and I use this word quite deliberately in view of some of the statements made to the court in the course of leading counsel's submissions during this appeal and in the various hearings leading up to it) what was said was the true position, then it really was the *first time* in the whole proceedings that the Respondent had made clear his position in the following crucial respects:–

(1) That the documents underlying the reasons why the Applicants were considered security risks such as to be placed on the Watch List and such as to justify their being denied entry into Hong Kong on 20 and 21 February 2003, were all destroyed.

(2) This applied to all documents within the *whole* of Government, and not just the Immigration Department.

(3) The date of destruction of all these documents was 12 March 2003, less than a month after the relevant decisions were made.

94. Quite why these simple (albeit crucial) statements could not have been made by the Respondent right at the outset of the proceedings, frankly and fairly and consistent with the duty of candour, was never explained to the court. These were points that were not made in the many affirmations that were filed nor in the course of the lengthy correspondence exchange between the parties. Mr Fung was unable to assist us either in this respect. He referred to the narrow view that the Respondent's legal advisors took of the ambit of the judicial review. This was an obviously unsustainable argument. He relied heavily on the fact that the destruction of documents had been referred to in the

correspondence (see paragraphs 54 and 59 above). This is accurate only to the extent that there was a reference to destruction of documents in accordance with "standard Immigration Department practice". These references did not give the reader any idea that in fact *all* relevant documents within the *whole* of Government had been destroyed, or that the destroyed documents were in fact the crucial ones going to the critical issue.

95. Even with these revelations made by leading counsel, a number of obvious queries remained:–

(1) Nothing had been said to address the obvious contention that if these Applicants did pose (in the words of Mr Timothy Tong) "threats to the public order of Hong Kong", it was incredible that nowhere in the whole of Government would there be a written record of this.

(2) Even if all documents no longer existed, surely there would be persons within Government who would be able to provide details of what was in the destroyed documents going to the reasons why the Applicants were denied entry. The contents of the affirmations of Mr Choy and Mr Tong would suggest that they knew. Admittedly, in the second affirmation of Mr Tong, he does say that the disclosure of details would be within the ambit of public interest immunity, but with respect, this was not a point that was made by Mr Fung to Hartmann J at all. If this was a valid point, one would have expected leading counsel to have at least mentioned this.

(3) If all relevant documents had been destroyed since 12 March 2003, then on what basis did Mr Tong rely to depose to the facts contained in his second affirmation? It will be recalled he did not actually reveal the sources of his knowledge.

(4) Nevertheless, Hartmann J did accept the statements of fact made from the Bar table. The Applicants' leading counsel (Mr Harris) did respond but no application was made by the Applicants that the matters revealed to the court by Mr Fung should more properly be contained in an affidavit and, more important, no application was made for cross-examination of the main deponents of the Respondent (namely, Mr Choy and Mr Tong).

96. In the course of his judgment, Hartmann J did not feel able to reject the matters that he had been told by leading counsel. He came to the view that the duty of candour had not been breached and that the allegations of bad faith leveled against the Respondent, were not made out. This being the case, the judge was persuaded that the real reason for the Applicants' exclusion involved security concerns, which he regarded as a legitimate reason for the denial of entry into Hong Kong. The judge was not persuaded by the Applicants that they were denied entry by reason of their Falun Gong beliefs.

97. I shall return to Hartmann J's judgment when I set out the conclusions in this appeal (dealing with the issues of the duty of candour and of procedural fairness). Before doing that, I ought to mention briefly the history of this appeal, from the time the Applicants served their Notice of Appeal up to the hearing of the appeal itself.

The appeal

98. Following Hartmann J's judgment which was handed down on 23 March 2007, a Notice of Appeal was lodged by the Applicants on 23 April 2007. The appeal was eventually heard by this court on 16 March 2009. In between, however, there have been a number of hearings and numerous applications for the introduction of additional evidence for the appeal. It is largely unnecessary to go into much detail in respect of these hearings, but I shall in due course identify the various applications to adduce further evidence. This appeal was originally scheduled to be heard on 22 January 2008, but the matter was adjourned on the application of the Respondent to adduce further evidence (this following questions raised by this court over the state of the evidence). The application to adduce evidence by the Respondent was heard by this court on 23 September 2008 but this was adjourned. The adjourned hearing of the appeal was to be on 29 October 2008. On that day, however, the 6 Applicants appeared before us indicating their wish no longer to be legally represented in the appeal, choosing instead to act in person. Another adjournment was therefore granted. Following this hearing, the court appointed Mr Shieh as amicus curiae.

99. Before going into the details of the various applications made by both the Applicants and the Respondent relating to the introduction of further evidence on appeal, I ought to set out the context. At the hearing on 22 January 2008, considerable concerns were raised by this court over the question that has concerned this court in these proceedings at every stage: the lack of any details or documents going to the issue of why the Applicants were denied entry into Hong Kong. Despite what leading counsel had said to Hartmann J at the hearing on 8 March 2007 (see paragraph 92 above), it seemed quite remarkable that even at the appeal stage, no one was any the wiser on the reasons why the Applicants had been excluded. The queries set out in paragraphs 93 to 95 above were ones that seemed to us to call for a proper and full answer.

100. The concerns raised by the court led to a number of applications made by both parties in relation to these concerns. Other applications were made as well. The following applications made in the course of the appeal:–

(1) By a summons dated 28 December 2007, the Applicants applied to adduce new evidence by way of the introduction of 10 affirmations that had been filed by the Applicants in another set of judicial review proceedings (HCAL 74 of 2007) in which the decision of the Director of Immigration to deny entry to Falun Gong followers during another period (this time between 23 June 2007 and 1 July 2007), was challenged. This summons was not concerned with the question of the Respondent's discovery but was an attempt by the Applicants essentially to demonstrate that the real reason for their being denied entry into Hong Kong was their Falun Gong association.

(2) By a summons dated 5 February 2008, the Respondent applied to introduce an affirmation of Mr Lee Siu Kwong, Ambrose (the Secretary for Security) and Mr Li Kwok Kuen (a Chief Immigration Officer in the Immigration Department). These affirmations were an attempt to state on oath what leading counsel had told the court on 8 March 2007.

(3) By a Notice of Motion dated 4 December 2008, the Applicants applied, in the event the two set

affirmations were admitted under the Respondent's summons dated 5 February 2008, to cross-examine the two deponents.

(4) By a summons dated 11 February 2009, the Applicants applied to adduce an affirmation going to the perceived persecution of Falun Gong followers by the Central Government (the affirmation of one Terri Marsh) and also an affirmation (of the 5th Applicant) dealing with HCAL 74 of 2007. This latter affirmation was related to the summons dated 28 December 2007.

(5) In the course of the hearing of the appeal proper, the Respondent applied by a summons dated 11 March 2009 for leave to use a second affirmation made by Mr Ambrose Lee.

101. In the event, all these applications were dismissed by the court during the hearing, with reasons to be provided at a later stage.

102. I shall deal with the reasons for dismissing the summons dated 5 February 2008, the Notice of Motion dated 4 December 2008 and the summons dated 11 March 2009 when I set out my conclusions in relation to the issue of the duty of candour. The other two summonses do not really relate to this issue. I deal first with these.

103. As to the reasons for dismissing the summons dated 28 December 2007 (seeking leave to adduce the affirmation evidence in HCAL 74 of 2007):–

(1) The proceedings in HCAL 74 of 2007 never progressed beyond the leave stage. On 30 June 2007, Lunn J granted leave to commence judicial review proceedings. On the application of the Respondent to set aside leave on the ground of material non-disclosure, A Cheung J did so in a judgment handed down on 13 February 2008. Although a Notice of Appeal was served against this decision, eventually the appeal was abandoned by the Applicants. Accordingly, if the affirmations, all from the Applicants in those proceedings (since leave was set aside, the proceedings never reach the stage of the Respondent having to serve evidence), had been admitted as evidence in the present proceedings, a necessarily one-sided version of events would have been before this court. The spectre therefore loomed of the Respondent in the present proceedings being in turn given leave to file evidence to answer to these affirmations in HCAL 74 of 2007. There would also likely be cross-examination on all affidavit and affirmation evidence. Effectively, in such a scenario, HCAL 74 of 2007 would be litigated before this court when those proceedings had already terminated. This would have been absurd.

(2) Further, the only purposes for introducing the evidence in HCAL 74 of 2007 were originally stated to be only two (this was contained in a letter dated 22 January 2008 from HTW, then acting for the Applicants in the present proceedings, to the Department of Justice:–

(a) that the 1st Applicant in the present proceedings was denied entry into Hong Kong on two occasions in June 2007; and

(b) that she was one of 400 Falun Gong practitioners from Taiwan who were denied entry between 24 June 2007 and 1 July 2007.

(3) I have to say that these two facts were irrelevant to the issues that have to be determined in this appeal (indeed the Respondent had at one stage agreed to them). The 1st Applicant in her submissions eventually sought to widen the scope of the use of the affirmations in HCAL 74 of 2007 but it seems to me even then, the relevance of the affirmations was highly dubious to say the least.

104. As for the summons dated 11 February 2009, the reason for dismissing it was on the basis of lack of relevance:–

(1) The evidence of Terri Marsh (an Executive Director of a body known as the Human Rights Law Foundation) went to the perceived persecution of all Falun Gong followers by the Central People's Government. This is an irrelevant issue in the present proceedings. The focus in this appeal is really on whether the Respondent had any lawful basis to deny entry to the Applicants. It is irrelevant (at its highest, marginal) how Falun Gong followers perceived their treatment by the Chinese authorities. In any event, this type of evidence was open to the Applicants to adduce in the court below, but was not. The only new feature was the existence of newly discovered evidence going to the belief of this perceived persecution.

(2) As for the affirmation of the 5th Applicant, this was introduced to explain why the Applicants in HCAL 74 of 2007 abandoned the appeal from A Cheung J's decision setting aside the leave that had originally been granted. It was suggested that although the appeal was abandoned, A Cheung J's decision was wrong. In my view, it is irrelevant why the Applicants chose to abandon their appeal. None of this detracted from the cogent reasons for not otherwise admitting the evidence from those proceedings (see paragraph 103 above).

Conclusions on the duty of candour

105. As will already be apparent, the issue of whether the Respondent has complied with the duty of candour arises in the context of the court's examination of the lawfulness of the Respondent's decision to deny the Applicants entry into Hong Kong. The other decision that is impugned in these proceedings (the decision to place the Applicants on the Watch List) is merely a corollary of the decision to deny entry: it arises only to test the basis of the claim by the Respondent that the Applicants were denied entry by reason of security risks.

106. It will also be apparent that the focal point of the discussion into the duty of candour in the present case is very much the extent to which the Respondent has chosen to reveal, particularly in relation to the aspect of discovery, the true basis justifying the refusal of entry on security grounds.

107. I have already highlighted, when going through the affirmations and procedural history in the present proceedings, the extremely unsatisfactory way in which the deponents of affirmations filed on behalf of the Respondent have dealt with the matter, and also in which the discovery exercise has been

undertaken and dealt with in correspondence.

108. This was exacerbated by the way the matter was presented to Hartmann J. In my judgment, it was quite wrong for crucial statements of fact to be presented in the way it was to Hartmann J by leading counsel. At the very least, there ought to have been an affidavit verifying the matters that were stated to the court, together with an explanation as to why such matters were revealed so late in the proceedings.

109. It is fundamental that statements from the Bar table do not constitute evidence, unless agreed as such. On a matter as important as was the statement made by counsel for the Respondent, it was particularly inappropriate to accept the statement as evidence and particularly surprising that the judge's announced intention to do so was not met with objection by counsel for the Applicants.

110. In the light of the history of the case, the judge might have been forgiven in any event for testing the statement. I am bound to remark, in this regard, upon the inconsistent way in which Mr Fung addressed us during the appeal proper (and in previous hearings) on the issue of the material that existed to support the allegation that the Applicants posed security risks. It will be remembered that the impression clearly given to Hartmann J on 8 March 2007 hearing was that all relevant documents in any department of Government had been, as a matter of standard practice, destroyed. This obviously presupposed that relevant documents did exist at one stage within Government departments other than the Immigration Department. With documents having been destroyed on 12 March 2007, this raised a number of queries regarding the affirmations in particular made by Mr Choy Tak Po and Mr Timothy Tong. For example, in relation to those references made by them to security concerns and the threats to public order in Hong Kong posed by the Applicants, what were the sources of these statements of belief?; had the deponents read documents that had since 12 March 2007 been destroyed?; or were they deposing to matters within their own personal knowledge?; or did these matters originate from other unspecified sources?

111. These were precisely the sort of questions that arose in the appeal and it would not be an exaggeration to say that the court was anxiously looking to the Respondent's legal advisors for enlightenment. Unfortunately, this was not forthcoming, indeed far from it:–

(1) At the hearing which took place on 23 September 2008 (at the hearing of the Respondent's application to adduce further evidence), leading counsel for the Respondent indicated to the court that by reason of the destruction of documents, the various deponents of affirmations filed on behalf of the Respondent were relying "purely" on their own memory.

(2) At the hearing before us on 29 October 2008 (when the Applicants requested an adjournment after indicating they wished to appear in person: see paragraph 98 above), the following exchange took place between the court and leading counsel:–

"STOCK JA: What I can't remember, because the facts have become so complicated and the papers so voluminous, what I can't remember is whether it is the government's case that it knows of the detailed reasons though the papers have been destroyed, on the one hand, or, on the other hand, whether because the papers have been destroyed, the precise reasons, in other words, precise as opposed to security reasons, are now forgotten.

MR FUNG: It's really the latter.

STOCK JA: It's the latter."

(3) The court was thus told in no uncertain terms that the detailed reasons going to the security concerns posed by the Applicants, could no longer be recollected by anyone.

(4) It will be noted at once that not only did this emerge *for the first time* in this litigation, but this seemed to contradict the previous position. For example, in Mr Timothy Tong's second affirmation (see paragraph 34(3) above), he was stating that the detailed reasons going to security concerns could not be disclosed by reason of sensitivity, and that they would be covered by public interest immunity. These statements made by Mr Fung were also contradictory to what the court had been informed on 23 September 2008 when all that was said was that the deponents would have relied on their own memory. Nothing was said about their inability to remember details.

(5) On the second day of the hearing of the appeal (11 March 2009), leading counsel then informed the court that in fact no Government department other than the Immigration Department had ever possessed any relevant documents. This statement again directly contradicted much of what had previously been said on behalf of the Respondent. It will be recalled that the crucial exchange on 8 March 2007, leading counsel assured the court that all documents *within the whole of Government* had been destroyed as a result of standard procedure. This implied the existence of documents possessed by Government departments other than the Immigration Department. Moreover, nowhere had this position even been hinted at in the course of the proceedings, certainly not mentioned in the affirmations filed by the Respondent nor in the correspondence exchanged between the parties. Nor had this point been mentioned in any previous court hearings.

(6) Eventually, on the third day of the appeal (12 March 2008), leading counsel indicated to the court that what had been said the previous day may have been erroneous. The position that day appeared to be that the detailed reasons for considering the Applicants as security risks were known but if pressed, a claim for public interest immunity would be made (cf the position in the second affirmation of Mr Timothy Tong: see paragraph 34(3) above).

112. I have already made reference to the Respondent's application to adduce further evidence. This was the summons dated 5 February 2008 which was countered by the Applicants'summons dated 4 December 2008 seeking leave to cross-examine: see paragraphs 100 (2) and (3) above.

113. One of the affirmations sought to be introduced was that of the Secretary for Security, Mr Ambrose Lee. In it, he says this:–

"In the case relating to the refusal of entry to Hong Kong of he [*sic*] 1st–4th Applicants on 21st–22nd February 2003, based on my understanding and a full search conducted by serving officers in the SB, I can confirm that at the time of the Applicants' application for leave for judicial review in HCAL 32 of 2003 on 3rd April 2003, neither the SB nor related Government Departments were in possession of any records relevant to the reasons why the 1st–4th Applicants were considered a security risk or why they were recommended to be put on the Watch List. The SB and related Government Departments did not keep or retain such records. At the material time, the Applicants did not pose ongoing security risks to warrant the retention of such information. However, operational records in respect of the actions of refusal of entry, including the interview records as contained in the Control Case Reports as well as the Confidential Register, were retained by the ImmD in accordance with the Department's normal procedure and practice which, as I understand it, have already been disclosed by the Director of Immigration in HCAL 32 of 2003."

114. This was an attempt to put in affidavit form what Hartmann J had been informed by counsel on 8 March 2007. The other affirmation sought to be introduced (that of Li Kwok Kuen) added little.

115. In the end, the court decided to refuse the Respondent's application to adduce further evidence. As will already have been seen, the conduct of the Respondent and his legal advisors throughout the proceedings had been far from satisfactory, indeed contradictory. In these circumstances, it would simply have been wrong to allow such further evidence be used in this appeal. In any event, on any view, this evidence ought to have been placed before the court below rather than at the appeal stage. With this application dismissed, the Applicants' Notice of Motion for cross-examination also fell away.

116. For completeness' sake, I ought also to deal with the Respondent's application (made during the course of the appeal on 11 March 2009), seeking leave to adduce yet another affidavit of Mr Ambrose Lee. In it, Mr Lee sought to make the point that no other Government department possessed any relevant documents: all had been passed to the Immigration Department "on or around 14 February 2003". This point had never been made before and represented yet another factual twist. For the same reasons dismissing the 5 February 2008 summons, this summons was also dismissed. This summons was yet another late attempt to deal once more–only when forced to–with the key issue in this appeal: the duty of candour. But that was not the end of it. On 13 March 2009, without any prior intimation, a letter was provided to the court by the Department of Justice (just before the hearing commenced that day) in which, at this late stage (Day 4 of the appeal), it was indicated that all key deponents of the Respondent (the Secretary for Security, Mr Timothy Tong, Mr Choy Tak Po and Mr Lee Kwok Kuen) were ready to present themselves for cross-examination. This came without any real explanation as to why, when the Applicants' application for cross-examination was resisted all along and in view of the quite uncooperative way in which the litigation had been conducted by the Respondent, this offer was made at all. Despite Mr Fung's submissions to the contrary, for my part, I see no reason other than this offer having been made purely for tactical purposes.

117. And so I come to my conclusions on the duty of candour. Without the additional material that was put before Hartmann J on 8 March 2007 by way of submissions from the Bar table and the material which was sought to be put before us by way of additional evidence, the court is left to deal with this issue on the basis of the other facts and matters that were before Hartmann J.

118. Regretfully (and I use this expression deliberately since, in most cases, the issue simply does not arise because the duty is almost invariably observed by the Government), the duty of candour has been breached in the present case by the Respondent. In the course of this judgment, I have tried to highlight those areas in which the Respondent has failed to discharge the duty of candour. Ms Chu (the 1st Applicant) submitted forcefully that all the Applicants wanted to know was why they were denied entry. If the Respondent's position was that this was not by reason of their Falun Gong association alone, then just what were the reasons? The most that was said was that there were security concerns. The furthest that this aspect was ever developed was that the 4 Applicants were "involved with some other individuals engaged in organizing disruptive activities which pose threats to the public order in Hong Kong". Even to this day, over six years since the date the 4 Applicants were denied entry, it is still unclear just what was the basis for this statement, nor is it clear as to whether any documents exist to support it. It is a most extraordinary state of affairs.

119. The particular coyness by which the Respondent approached discovery and the inconsistent versions given as to the existence (or non-existence) of relevant documents, coupled with the way the court has been addressed on various occasions by counsel, substantially exacerbated what was already a highly unsatisfactory situation.

120. Normally, where the duty of candour has been breached in such a way in relation to the disclosure and presentation of relevant facts, the consequence in judicial review proceedings (as in other proceedings) is that the court is entitled to draw adverse inferences.

121. In the present case, the inference which the Applicants invited the court to draw was that the Respondent did not have any valid or justifiable reasons to deny the 4 Applicants entry into Hong Kong on 21 and 22 February 2003 (nor to put their names on the Watch List). As stated before, it was not necessary for the Applicants to show that the real reason was their Falun Gong association.

122. But is this the correct or fair conclusion to reach?

123. In my judgment, I am unable in the circumstances of the present case to draw this adverse inference. I am particularly mindful of the fact that the Respondent's case remains that the Applicants were excluded from entering Hong Kong by reason of security concerns. Even taking into account every unsatisfactory aspect of the way the Respondent has conducted this case, he has at least been consistent in this being the reason for the denial of entry into Hong Kong.

124. By itself, the reason that was provided (namely security concerns) is not one that can be rejected out of hand as being inherently implausible. In addition, when Mr Tong (in his second affirmation) states that the detailed reasons are sensitive matters that ought not to be in the public domain, and which might attract a claim for public interest immunity, this is not a statement that can be rejected out of hand either.

125. What is really being suggested by the Applicants is that Mr Tong (and others who have provided a similar version such as Mr

Choy) should not, in circumstances where the duty of candour has not been observed, be believed. It is this position that I have the greatest difficulty in accepting in the present case:–

(1) There has been no cross-examination sought of either Mr Tong or Mr Choy. It is of course possible for the court to reject affidavit evidence given on oath even where there has been no cross-examination, but the circumstances will be rare. Inherent improbability, implausibility or contradiction may provide adequate reasons. So might a failure to observe the duty of candour, but it is necessary for the circumstances to be critically examined.

(2) It therefore becomes relevant to look at the conduct of the Applicants themselves. It will be remembered that in the court below and for a part of the appeal proceedings, the Applicants were legally represented. Leading counsel was retained on their behalf. Account must be taken of the fact that the Applicants and their legal advisors may well have had their own reasons not to make the various applications I have mentioned.

(3) It could not really be said that the possibility of applying for cross-examination of deponents of affirmations was lost on the Applicants. In fact, in the court below, an application was made (and granted) to cross-examine Mr Lau Wing Yiu on his affirmation (in relation to the answering of questions by the 4 Applicants on their arrival in Hong Kong on 20 February 2003). It was never made clear to us just why the Applicants did not seek to cross-examine anyone else.

(4) No application was made either to seek further discovery from the Respondent in relation to critical documents. It will be remembered that during the hearing before Hartmann J on 2 June 2006 when leading counsel for the Applicants sought an order for discovery in respect of relevant documents within the whole of Government, the judge indicated that this matter was not before the court at that time but that he would do his best to accommodate the parties if a formal application was made: see paragraph 69 above. The Applicants never did, choosing instead to take a somewhat narrow view of discovery in the correspondence: see paragraph 78 above.

(5) It was also surprising that the Applicants did not challenge the public interest immunity assertion made by Mr Tong in his second affirmation (see paragraph 34(3) above). Instead, public interest immunity challenges were made in relation to other (as it turned out) irrelevant aspects (see paragraph 64 above).

(6) I have already commented (in paragraphs 95(4) and 109 above) on the failure, surprising in my view, to insist that the matters asserted by Mr Fung at the substantive hearing before Hartmann J be placed before the court in proper form. Had this been done, it would of course have been open to the Applicants to seek to cross examine any relevant dependent.

(7) It was at no stage suggested by the Applicants before us (in the course of Ms Chu's submissions) that their previous legal advisors were in any way at fault; indeed quite the contrary was submitted.

(8) While the conduct of the Applicants did not in my view excuse the Respondent from complying with the duty of candour (for the reasons already discussed above), it is nevertheless relevant in the consideration of whether adverse inferences should, as a matter of fairness, be drawn.

126. The end result becomes then that the only evidence going to the reason why the 4 Applicants were refused entry into Hong Kong on 21 and 22 February 2003 were the security concerns referred to by the Respondent. In particular, as Mr Tong deposed in his second affirmation, they posed "threats to the public order of Hong Kong". The detailed reasons could not be provided by reason, according to Mr Tong, of sensitivity. Given these facts which, for the reasons I have given, cannot properly be dismissed, despite the Respondent's conduct and breach of the duty of candour, I reach the same conclusion as Hartmann J did that it has not been shown by the Applicants that either of the relevant decisions can be impugned in these proceedings.

Procedural fairness and the possession of valid multiple entry permits

127. I have already identified this issue as one that requires to be determined in this appeal: paragraphs 83 and 87 above. The terms of the entry permits have already been set out: see paragraph 26 above.

128. I can dispose of this issue shortly. In his judgment, Hartmann J highlighted the relevant principle to be that aliens had no right to be afforded a hearing to determine whether or not they should be permitted to enter. As long as the Respondent did not act arbitrarily or without proper reasons, there was no legitimate expectation either to be admitted into Hong Kong or to be entitled to a hearing to determine this. This is notwithstanding the possession of a valid multiple entry permit. Hartmann J emphasized as well the fact that the permit expressly stated on their face that the holder would be subject to immigration control. This was enough to subject the Applicants to the provisions of the Immigration Ordinance, Cap. 115 giving the Respondent the widest power to control entry into Hong Kong.

129. I am entirely in agreement with the conclusion reached by Hartmann J on this aspect and the reasons he articulated in his judgment. The Applicants, accordingly, failed on this ground as well.

Conclusion

130. For the above reasons, I would dismiss this appeal.

131. I conclude this judgment by saying that the Respondent can consider himself extremely fortunate in these proceedings. If the Applicants had conducted themselves differently by, for example, making the necessary discovery applications or applying for cross-examination of various deponents, these judicial proceedings would have taken a much different course and, depending on what evidence emerged, the court may have been driven to arrive at a quite different result. However, this is not in any way to lessen what I have determined to have been a breach of the duty of candour on the Respondent's part. It is not something of which the court would want to see a repetition in future.

132. For this reason, I would also make a costs order nisi that

notwithstanding the dismissal of the appeal, there should be no order for costs in this appeal and this would include the costs in relation to the various interlocutory applications before this court where costs had been reserved. I understand that as far as the costs below (including the costs of various interlocutory applications) are concerned, the determination of such costs have been adjourned pending the determination of this appeal.

Hon Stock VP:

133. This is a case in which a reason for refusal of entry into Hong Kong was in fact given. The reason is said to be demonstrably false thereby illustrating (it is argued) that the decision to refuse entry was exercised on illegitimate grounds. In this way the reason became the issue in the application for judicial review.

134. The reason given was security threat. In September 2005, a few weeks before the substantive judicial review was due to be heard, the Respondent filed affirmations in the course of which the contention was made that the first four Applicants "were involved with some other individuals engaged in organising disruptive activities which pose threats to public order in Hong Kong." That was said to be the security threat in the case. The nature of those disruptive activities were not then disclosed. They have not been disclosed since.

135. The Applicants say that even if the source of the information cannot be disclosed, it is puzzling to understand why no one is prepared to say what the suggested planned disruptive activities were. There was a hint by counsel for the Respondent in the course of oral submissions before us, that the feared disruption had to do with the forthcoming conference or demonstration. If so, one might ponder, what was the problem with stating that in terms in an affirmation? There is no suggestion that such disruption was feared from the Falun Gong adherents resident in Hong Kong either then or on previous or subsequent occasions. The Applicants assert that the history of Falun Gong demonstrations is one of peaceful activity; that the individual Applicants cannot have been thought generally to be conducting secret subversive plotting in Hong Kong, else they would have been refused entry, before and since, on all attempted visits to the Region. They point too to the (uncontested) fact that they were not singled out as four individuals for refusal of entry. Instead, they say, no fewer than 80 Falun Gong practitioners not resident in Hong Kong were turned back that day, a fact they contend that sits more obviously with a blanket refusal policy than with one tied to individual risk; and that if one puts these facts together with:

(1) the failure of the Respondent to specify the nature of the feared disruptive activities;

(2) the Respondent's contention that all documentation that revealed the underlying reasons has been destroyed; and

(3) the Respondent's coy, 'tight', adversarial and legalistic conduct of these proceedings amounting, they say, to a lack of candour;

the only reasonable inference to be drawn is that the reason provided by the Respondent for refusal of entry is not the true reason.

136. The Applicants do not doubt that the front line immigration officers were told that the Applicants were a security risk, and acted accordingly, but the case is that their decision to refuse them entry was tainted by the feeding of a bogus reason. In this case, the immigration authorities chose to provide a reason for refusal of entry. If a bogus reason has been put forward that can only mean, say the Applicants, that the true reason is one that is outwith the policy and objects of the immigration legislation with which we are concerned.

137. The issue that evidently caused Hartmann J much concern is the one that has been the centre of this appeal. The Applicants contended, both in correspondence and before him, that the Respondent was playing matters close to the chest in a way that was inappropriate in judicial review proceedings and that this was but part of the picture which, when viewed as a whole, illustrated that the truth of the matter was being hidden. This suggested lack of candour was most obviously evidenced by the Respondent's attitude to discovery and by the apparent absence–going back to March 2003–of any documents whatsoever in the hands of the Director, as well as in the hands of the Government at large, supporting the Respondent's case, save for some entries in a confidential register that went no further than the fact that the Director had been told by the Security Branch that these people were a threat to security.

138. The Respondent's answer to this concern was then, and remains, that, save in respect of those who pose a continuing risk, watchlist records are and were at the material time kept no longer than was relevant to an event–specific threat; so that is why there exist no records throughout the whole of Government which reveal any detail of the security threat posed. Insofar as criticism has been levelled at the legalistic approach taken by the Respondent to discovery, the contention was, and remains, that, first, the Respondent was until May 2006 meeting a limited challenge, namely, the legality of the decision to refuse entry, rather than the legality of the decision to place the names of the Applicants on the watchlist; and, secondly, that the duty of candour is directed at the narrative part of a respondent's case rather than at discovery. It is suggested that the Respondent has at all times been open about the reason for the refusal of entry and that that fact is not altered by a legalistic approach to discovery.

139. In my judgment, the point is not that simple. Hartmann J did not think it that simple and correctly so. He took the view that the absence of documents was "a very important point in this case. In fact, it goes to the heart of the Applicants' case ... this was 80 people being refused entry to Hong Kong, a number of whom, according to the Director, protested by adopting an uncooperative attitude as a means of protest, two of whom had to be carried to the aircraft. So nobody can pretend this was not an incident of some moment, and yet it appears that all evidence of anything going to issues of merit or otherwise was deleted."

140. I do not in any event think that the attitude to discovery is one that is realistically susceptible to compartmentalization or isolation. The Applicants' case, as I have explained above, is that it is but part of a telling picture.

141. The analysis of the candour issue in this case requires to be infused with sensitivity to the fact that the court's role in judicial review is not merits–based; in other words, it is not for the courts to second–guess the merits of a decision unless it be demonstrably irrational. More particularly it is not for the courts to second–guess security decisions. The court is neither entrusted nor equipped to do so. Security analyses and determinations are necessarily reserved for those responsible for the security of the Region.

142. On the other hand, the court is entrusted to determine issues of legality of administrative decisions challenged by persons with standing to do so and it has for long been recognized that the

court's function is hampered if there is lack of cooperation and candour by the executive and that the expectation of candour is not inconsistent with the respective responsibilities of the executive and the courts. In carrying out its function where the executive prays in aid sensitive security matters, there are established rules by which that sensitivity can, in proper cases, be protected. In this particular case there have been periodic claims that certain information is protected by public interest privilege and determinations have been made in that regard. But the issue joined between the parties in this case is not whether the security grounds alleged were sufficient to warrant the action taken against the Applicants. The issue rather has always been whether there were in truth ever any security grounds at all.

143. Nor is the court's role punitive; by which I mean that the court must take care not to confuse the line between, on the one hand, disquiet over lack of openness, where that is established, and, on the other, concluding that the essential truth has not been told. That is to say that curial irritation–and much irritation has been expressed in this Court as in the court below–must not blur a proper adjudicative assessment of the evidence.

144. The courts in this jurisdiction have the same expectation of candour in the conduct of judicial review as have the courts in other jurisdictions and the type of concern that has so exposed itself in this case is, happily, rare. The principles which emerge from the citations that follow are well–established.

145. In *R v. Lancashire County Council ex parte Huddleston*[1], the Master of the Rolls, Sir John Donaldson, remarked that once an applicant had crossed the threshold of persuading a judge that there was enough to warrant the granting of leave to apply for judicial review the position, in terms of what was required of the decision–maker, changed. From that stage on it was the duty of the decision–maker to make to the court full and fair disclosure. The court, in exercising its function of review of administrative decisions was a public law court and the evolution of this branch of the law in the second half of the twentieth century 'created a new relationship between the courts and those who derive their authority from the public law, one of partnership based on a common aim, namely the maintenance of the highest standards of public administration.' [2] He described as discreditable a reluctance by an authority to explain fully what has occurred and why. He referred to a suggestion by counsel on behalf of the local authority that it was for the applicant to make out his case and not for the respondent authority to do it for him as to which the Master of the Rolls said:

> "This, in my judgment, is only partially correct. Certainly it is for the applicant to satisfy the court of his entitlement to judicial review and it is for the respondent to resist his application, if it considers it to be unjustified. But it is a process which falls to be conducted with all the cards face upwards on the table and the vast majority of the cards will start in the authority's hands." [3]

146. Whereas 'it is...clear,' (*Belize Alliance of Conservation Non–Governmental Organizations v. The Department of the Environment and another*[4]) 'that proceedings for judicial review should not be conducted in the same manner as hard–fought commercial litigation', there was much in the instant case which disclosed a highly legalistic approach adopted by the Respondent, an emphasis on not revealing an iota more than was demanded by the specific words of the notice of motion, as originally drawn, and by correspondence. As the Chief Judge has explained, the suggestion from the Respondent was that more was not required in terms of the original notice of motion, as if the Respondent did not all along appreciate that the Applicants' grievance was directed at the root cause of their expulsion, a notion that was rejected by Hartmann J. In this regard Lord Denning commented in *R v. Barnsley Council ex parte Hook*[5] that:

> "It must be remembered that, in applications for certiorari, the applicant knows very little of what has happened behind the scenes. He only knows that a decision has been taken which is adverse to him, and he complains of it. His statement of grounds ... should not be treated as rigidly as a pleading in an ordinary civil action. If the Divisional Court gives leave (as it did here) the practice is for the respondent to put on affidavits the full facts as known to them. The matter is then considered at large upon the affidavits. If there then appear to be other grounds on which certiorari may be granted, the court can inquire into them without being bound by the grounds stated in the original statement. The Divisional Court will always look into the substance of the matter."

147. As we have seen from the judgment of the Chief Judge, facts emerged from the Respondent in this case only in response to pressure from the first instance judge; interlocutory applications of all kinds resisted at each turn, and reasonable requests by letter for discovery turned down. As in *Secretary of State for Foreign and Commonwealth Affairs v. Quark Fishing Limited*, the business of uncovering what happened, certainly in relation to what reasons were ever reduced to writing and what happened to documents has been 'tortuous and problematic.' [6] In that case, Laws LJ commented that although there was in judicial review proceedings no general duty of disclosure, there was:

> "... a very high duty on public authority respondents, not least central government, to assist the court with full and accurate explanations of all the facts relevant to the issue the court must decide. The real question here is whether in the evidence put forward on his behalf the Secretary of State has given a true and comprehensive account of the way the relevant decisions in the case were arrived at. If the court has not been given a true and comprehensive account, but has had to tease the truth out of late discovery, it may be appropriate to draw inferences against the Secretary of State upon points which remain obscure."[7]

148. The Chief Judge has referred to some of the interchange between Bench and Bar at first instance. The transcript of that particular hearing makes instructive reading, not least for those who might think that frustration at the advocacy for the Respondent was limited to this Court. It reveals that Hartmann J frequently expressed fundamental incredulity at the Respondent's case in relation to documents, deep frustration at the piecemeal manner in which facts were put before him and concern that the Respondent was not demonstrating candour. After a lengthy exchange in which these views were repeatedly expressed, there was an adjournment during which counsel for the Respondent took instructions and then said that files in the possession of the Director were destroyed on 12 March 2003 in the course of a routine and standard document destruction procedure for those placed on the watchlist in relation to event–specific occurrences. Hardly surprisingly, the judge asked: 'Why did we have to go through all of this in the first place then? Why not simply have said: all of this material–the watchlist works on the basis that it's

destroyed within X number of days this is what happened. It's standard procedure ... ?'

149. That, I regret to say has been the history of much of the conduct of the case on behalf on the Respondent: a marked and regular reluctance to say what had happened; or so it has been made to seem.

150. Take another example of the confusion into which the advocacy in this case threw the Court. The Chief Judge has referred to it at paragraph above where Mr Fung said in answer to a question I posed that precise reasons for refusal of entry (as opposed to the broad reason 'security reasons') were forgotten. I found the answer inherently incredible and because I was disturbed by the answer I went back to it in the course of the same hearing. I told Mr Fung that what he had said was "troubling me a little". But Mr Fung confirmed my understanding of what he had said and went on to suggest that the contention that the precise reasons had been forgotten emerged from affidavits before us. The effect of the exchange that then followed, as I read it, was that, according to Mr Fung, what was remembered was that the Applicants posed a risk to public order but why they posed such a risk, on what basis the assertion was made, could not be remembered. Apart from the stark fact that counsel's statement did not sit at all with the evidence of Mr Tong who said that the details could not be divulged because they were covered by public interest immunity, the statement did not sit with common sense. I simply do not believe that no official is in a position, subject to the question of privilege, to say what the detailed reasons were–and indeed that is not what the officials were saying on oath. So either Mr Fung misunderstood what his client's position was or was not expressing himself felicitously.

151. The question however, at the end of the day, is whether *in the face of untested evidence on oath or affirmation* that there were sound security reasons for refusing the first four Applicants entry the Court is entitled, because of the way the Respondent has chosen to run his case, to draw an inference that what has been said on oath or affirmation is untrue. It is not in my judgment a question of balancing the conduct of a respondent who has not put cards on the table against the conduct of an applicant who ought but did not seek cross-examination or further discovery and it is not a question of penalizing an applicant for not taking steps which he or she might have taken but did not. It is a question of examining what evidence there is, absent such steps and what inferences, if any, one is entitled to draw from that evidence. If an inference adverse to a respondent may properly be drawn from a lack of candour as demonstrated by the evidence and history of proceedings, then it must be drawn and, in such circumstances, the conduct of the applicant is irrelevant.

152. I fail to see how in this case this Court can properly conclude that what has been said on behalf of the Respondent on oath and affirmation, untested by cross-examination, is untrue. Untruth may in such a case be one reason for lack of openness. Yet in this case I can readily think of other reasons why the Respondent has played matters so close to his chest. One reason may be that he has–perhaps on advice, I know not–thought it permissible to conduct these proceedings as if they were normal adversarial proceedings, an attitude encouraged by political or security sensitivities. By saying this, I am not for one moment approving the approach adopted. Nor am I saying that the absence of cross–examination will always save a respondent. I am addressing the essential question which is whether in this particular case the court is entitled to draw the single inference against the Respondent which the Applicants would have this Court draw. To conclude in the absence of cross–examination that a person–let alone a senior official–has been deliberately untruthful on oath or affirmation on a material matter is a serious step indeed and, in my judgment, would be warranted only if the nature of the testimony itself or the surrounding circumstances as a whole forced the Court to say that that was an irresistible conclusion.

153. The key fact is that there has in this case be no cross–examination and I confess to some puzzlement at the absence of an application for it. Counsel previously acting for the Applicants explained that course by suggesting that he had read the judge below as expressing such incredulity as to render cross–examination unnecessary. I can readily understand why at one stage counsel thought so. But once the judge who had so firmly expressed incredulity, then fully accepted important assertions of fact from the Bar table–a departure, in my respectful view, from established practice and principle save where the assertion is agreed–the correct approach would have been for counsel to call for evidence in support of what had come from the Bar table and in any event to seek cross–examination of the deponents. Absent that cross–examination, what we are left with is considerable frustration at the way the case has been conducted by or on behalf of the Respondent, but in this instance that does not suffice of itself as a basis to draw an adverse inference on the substance of the case.

154. It will be obvious that, regretfully, the hearing of the appeal was not an attractive experience and the voicing of the Court's frustration resulted in much to–ing and fro–ing by counsel, taking of instructions, piecemeal revelations, some of them contradictory, culminating in an offer to present officials for cross–examination; an offer accompanied by assurances that it was non–tactical, assurances then undermined by counsel's submission that it would be unfortunate if the court were to make an adverse inference against the Respondent given that officials had been offered for cross–examination. It may be of course that the offer was born of a sense of frustration by the Respondent at reports of the Court's irritation and a desire to show that there was nothing to hide. I cannot say, and it is not necessary for me to decide. The only point I wish to make is that had this case been conducted for the Respondent from the outset in the way in which governmental respondents in this jurisdiction normally conduct their side of things in judicial review applications, the unfortunate air that permeated these proceedings would have been avoided.

155. For the reason I have provided I am not in a position to draw the adverse inference which the Applicants would have the court draw from the manner in which the case has been conducted on behalf of the Respondent.

156. For the reasons given by the Chief Judge the Applicants fail on the other limbs of their appeal and I agree with the orders he proposes.

157. No challenge has been raised in these proceedings to the (suggested) practice of destruction of documents. If such a practice existed and if it persists, the result is that, whatever the motive for destruction, documentation that evidences the decision–making process is destroyed before expiry of the time for seeking leave to apply for judicial review. There would have to be compelling reasons to justify such a policy or practice, absent which the question is begged whether the policy or practice itself is lawful.

Hon Barma J:

158. I agree with the judgments of Ma CJHC and Stock VP.

Chief Judge, High Court (Geoffrey Ma)

Justice of Appeal (Frank Stock)

Judge of the Court of First Instance (Aarif Barma)

1st Applicant Chu Woan Chyi acting in person

2nd Applicant Liao Hsiao Lan acting in person

3rd Applicant Lu Lih Ching acting in person

4th Applicant Chang Jenn Yeu acting in person

5th Applicant Kan Hung Cheung acting in person

6th Applicant Hong Kong Association of Falun Dafa acting in person represented by Mr Kan Hung Cheung

Mr Daniel R Fung, SC & Mr Johnny Mok, SC, instructed by Department of Justice for the Respondent

Mr Paul Shieh, SC as amicus curiae

Footnotes:

1. [1986] 2 All E R 941 at 945

2 at 945c.

3 at 945g.

4 [2004] UKPC 6 para 86.

5 [1976] 1 WLR 1052 at 1058.

6 [2002] EWCA Civ 1409 para 22.

7 at para 50

Applicant Pasa Danaville Dizon

Pasa Danaville Dizon 對 香港特別行政區

HCAL 97/2009

簡略案情

申請人為 26 歲的菲律賓籍女士，在 2006 年和 2008 年期間曾多次以訪客身份進入香港。2008 年 7 月 13 日她再度以此身份進入香港並獲准逗留 14 天。在 7 月 28 日申請人準備與朋友離開香港去澳門時，不滿被入境處職員扣留查詢，她其後對特區政府提起索償。雖然她的非法禁錮指控在小額錢債審裁處被拒絕，但她繼續向法律援助處申請援助，企圖對該判決作出上訴，期間入境處一直允許延長她的居留期限。

然而，在她的法援申請被拒絕後，申請人亦對該決定提出上訴。可是入境處並不同意繼續延長她的居留期限，於是她便向原訟庭申請司法覆核許可，要求推翻入境處的決定。申請人指出，如果強迫她離開香港，她將沒有經濟能力回香港繼續進行她對法律援助處決定所提出的上訴，因此違反了《基本法》第 35 條，保障她向法院提起訴訟的權利。

裁決摘要

雖然對於申請人非香港居民的身份，原訟庭法官認為《基本法》第 35 條並不適用，可是，《基本法》第 41 條對作為身在香港境內的申請人，賦予其根據香港法律享有第 35 條的權利和自由。而香港法律必然包括《入境條例》，其中關於條例中所牽涉的問題，應該留待入境處處長處理，在公共法律的層面上，法院行使的主要是監察角色，應該儘量避免干預入境處處長的決定。

對於申請人聲稱她缺乏經濟能力重回香港繼續她的訴訟，原訟庭法官並不接納。法庭觀察到申請人這起案件極不尋常，事源僅僅因為一件發生於 2008 年對入境處的輕微指控，申請人便成功多次延長其居留期限，期間申請人亦曾多次離開香港，看不出她有任何經濟困難。因此，法院最後拒絕了申請人覆核許可的申請。

HCAL 97/2009

IN THE HIGH COURT OF THE

HONG KONG SPECIAL ADMINISTRATIVE REGION

COURT OF FIRST INSTANCE
CONSTITUTIONAL AND ADMINISTRATIVE LAW LIST
NO 97 OF 2009

PASA DANAVILLE DIZON — Applicant

Before: Hon Andrew Cheung J in Chambers (Not open to the public)

Dates of Hearing: 11 September 2009

Date of Judgment: 11 September 2009

JUDGMENT

[Permission to publish this judgment has been given]

1. The test for granting leave is whether the applicant has shown a reasonably arguable case. Interim relief is normally granted after the obtaining of such leave as per the Practice Direction, but in exceptional cases, interim relief such as the type of relief sought by the applicant in this afternoon's hearing may be granted even before leave to apply for judicial review is obtained.

2. Having had the benefit of argument from the applicant as well as from the putative respondent, I am in a position to decide not only the application for interim relief but the application for leave to apply for judicial review as well.

3. I find the fact that the applicant would go to the extent of suing the Government for the alleged one hour's false imprisonment in the circumstances of the present case rather surprising. I also find the argument that the applicant was not an overstayer for one day by reason of section 71 of the Interpretation and General Clauses Ordinance, Cap 1, which applies generally, not only to Ordinances but also to "instruments" as per section 2(1) of that Ordinance, in the context of a limit of stay granted by an immigration officer to a visitor to Hong Kong, equally surprising.

4. Even if one were to proceed on the basis that she did have an arguable case on her reading of the law, it would not, under normal circumstances, render the questioning of her by the immigration officer on 28 July 2008, when she and her companion sought to depart Hong Kong for Macau, unlawful. Section 4(1) of the Immigration Ordinance, Cap 115, clearly provides an immigration officer with the power to examine a person prior to his departure from Hong Kong if he has reasonable cause for believing that such a person is contravening, or has contravened, a condition of stay, including a limit of stay, in respect of him. Such a person may be required by the immigration officer to submit to further examination. In other words, I am not surprised at all that the applicant's claim against the Government in the Small Claims Tribunal was dismissed.

5. The applicant then applied for legal aid in respect of her intended application for leave to appeal against the dismissal of her claim in the Small Claims Tribunal. Again, I am not surprised to find that her application has been refused. Apart from what I have observed regarding the merits of her claim against the Government, I also have doubt whether legal aid is available to such an application for leave, by reason of paragraphs 8 and 9 in Part II in Schedule 2 to the Legal Aid Ordinance, Cap 91, but I need not express any definite view in this regard.

6. The applicant now says that she should be given a further extension of stay to remain in Hong Kong to pursue her legal aid appeal, which will come on for hearing in early October. By reason of her proceedings in the Small Claims Tribunal, she has already been allowed to remain in Hong Kong since January this year. She claims that if she were forced to leave Hong Kong, she would have no financial means to return to Hong Kong to prosecute her legal aid appeal. That would be, in effect, denying her access to the courts in breach of her rights guaranteed under article 35 of the Basic Law.

7. Pausing here, it is plain beyond argument that article 35, which applies to Hong Kong residents, does not apply to the applicant directly because she is neither a permanent resident nor a non-permanent resident in Hong Kong. The definition of a 'non-permanent resident' is defined in article 24(4) of the Basic Law as a person who is qualified to obtain a Hong Kong identity card in accordance with the laws of the Region, but has no right of abode.

8. That said, I believe the applicant still falls within article 41 of the Basic Law which applies to persons in Hong Kong, other than Hong Kong residents. These persons also enjoy the rights and freedoms of Hong Kong residents prescribed in Chapter III of the Basic Law "in accordance with law". In this regard, I would say that "law" must include, amongst other things, the Immigration Ordinance.

9. It is trite that the legislature has left immigration matters in the hands of the Director of Immigration, rather than the courts. The court, sitting in its public law function, only plays a supervisory role in these matters and the decisions of the Director of Immigration are entitled to great respect. The court does not lightly interfere with his decisions.

10. The alleged lack of means to return to Hong Kong and thus the alleged claim of denial of access to the courts is contradicted by the movement records of the applicant, which the applicant has failed to place before the Court. The records supplied by the putative respondent show that between 2006 and this year, there have been many trips to and from Hong Kong by this particular applicant. The records cast serious doubts on the claim by the applicant – and I would emphasise that it is a bare claim – that she will not have the financial means to return to Hong Kong to prosecute the legal aid appeal if she is not allowed to stay.

11. When confronted with the records, the applicant, through counsel appearing for her, via the good services of the Bar Free Legal Service Scheme, maintains that many of her previous trips were financed by her former boyfriend.

12. I have borne in mind the facts in the present case which are by no means ordinary; rather, I would describe them as peculiar and extraordinary. Because of an alleged hour's false imprisonment in July last year, the applicant has managed to stay and remain in Hong Kong since then, until now, with the interruption of several short trips that she now says were financed by her former boyfriend.

13. Having borne in mind everything that I have said, including the fact that whatever protection under the Basic Law the applicant may have is to be in accordance with law, including the Immigration Ordinance which leaves immigration matters generally in the hands of the Director of Immigration, I am not

satisfied that the applicant has shown a reasonably arguable case to apply for judicial review against the Director's refusal to further extend her stay in Hong Kong.

14. For those reasons, the application for leave is refused and it must follow from that, that the application for interim relief is also refused.

15. No order as to costs.

Judge of the Court of First Instance, High Court (Andrew Cheung)

Mr Philip Ross, instructed by Hong Kong Bar Association's Bar Free Legal Service Scheme, for the applicant

Mr Clifford Tavares, SGC, of the Department of Justice, for the Director of Immigration

---

責任編輯 | 莊櫻妮

全書審訂 | 李安

協力 | 李浩銘

書籍設計 | 陳曦成

製作 | 郭思敏、陳務華、陳鈺、李國明

書名 | 香港基本法案例彙編（1997-2010）（第一條至第四十二條）

編著 | 李浩然、尹國華

清華大學法學院研究團隊 | 丁如、李陶、魏晶、沈偉、莊葉群、郭文成、匙文宇、徐樹、陳慧怡、陳倩、張丹桐、趙力鎣、鄭涵文、石亞淙

出版 | 三聯書店（香港）有限公司
香港北角英皇道 499 號北角工業大廈 20 樓
Joint Publishing (H.K.) Co., Ltd.
20/F., North Point Industrial Building,
499 King's Road, North Point, Hong Kong

發行 | 香港聯合書刊物流有限公司
香港新界大埔汀麗路 36 號 3 字樓

印刷 | 中華商務彩色印刷有限公司
香港新界大埔汀麗路 36 號 14 字樓

印次 | 2012 年 12 月香港第一版第一次印刷

規格 | 大 16 開（190mm× 245mm）680 面

國際書號 | ISBN 978-962-04-3158-6

本書所有判案書內容取材自香港司法機構網站，以該網站版本為準。

網址 | http://www.judiciary.gov.hk/tc/legal_ref/judgments.htm